Official BASEBALL GUIDE

1984 EDITION

Editor/Baseball Guide
JOE HOPPEL

Associate Editor/Baseball Guide
DAVE SLOAN

Contributing Editors/Baseball Guide
CRAIG CARTER
CARL CLARK
LARRY WIGGE

President-Chief Executive Officer
RICHARD WATERS

Editor
DICK KAEGEL

Director of Books and Periodicals
RON SMITH

Published by

The Sporting News

1212 North Lindbergh Boulevard
P.O. Box 56 — St. Louis, Mo. 63166

ISBN 0-89204-149-8 ISSN 0078-3838

TABLE OF CONTENTS

For Index to Contents See Page 477

(Index to Minor League Cities on Page 478)

ON THE COVER: American League Most Valuable Player Cal Ripken of the Baltimore Orioles belted 27 homers, had 102 runs batted in and hit .318 to lead his club to its first world title since 1970.

—Photo by Richard Pilling

Drug Problem Throws Cloud Over Bright Baseball Picture

By CLIFFORD KACHLINE

Commissioner Bowie Kuhn agreed to remain in control of the sport until March 1, 1984.

Baseball seldom has witnessed as many positive achievements as 1983 produced. Unparalleled attendance, the most lucrative television deal ever and record-shattering performances combined to provide fans, players and management alike with many pleasant moments. Nevertheless, the sport found itself entering 1984 with some familiar problems and a few new ones.

The failure to find a new commissioner after a 14-month search and a troublesome drug situation left a cloud over an otherwise bright picture. A sudden upheaval late in the year in the leadership of the Major League Players Association also tempered some of the optimism.

Still, the positive factors far outweighed the negative. On the field, at the box office and on television the game enjoyed what surely will rank as one of its finest years. The major league races lacked the down-to-the-wire dramatics of recent campaigns, but the spectacular early showing of two perennial doormats and numerous historic individual accomplishments were responsible for more fans catching "baseball fever" than ever before.

For the 10th time in 15 years, the majors established a regular-season attendance record, drawing 45,540,338 customers. The figure was even more impressive considering the unusually poor spring weather, which caused 33 postponements in the season's first five weeks. Spring exhibition games also drew a record total, 1,463,345, despite numerous rainouts. Counting all exhibitions, the All-Star Game, League Championship Series and World Series, the big leagues attracted 48,064,553, another all-time high.

National Association attendance continued to climb. With the Louisville Redbirds drawing 1,052,438—the first time a minor league team had reached the million mark—the minor league system reported a gate of 18,560,690 for the regular season. Another 363,289 attended minor league all-star games and postseason playoffs.

A record 10 major league clubs topped the two-million mark in home attendance, shattering the record of eight set in 1979 and equalled in 1980. The Baltimore Orioles and the Chicago White Sox, American League division champions, drew two million for the first time, as did the Milwaukee Brewers and the Atlanta Braves (both of whom failed in bids to repeat as division winners). Also establishing single-season club attendance records were the St. Louis Cardinals, Montreal Expos and Toronto Blue Jays.

The Los Angeles Dodgers led all clubs for the seventh consecutive year, drawing 3,510,313. The figure was about 98,500 short of the all-time high of 3,608,881, which the Dodgers set in 1982. It marked the fourth time the Dodgers exceeded three million. Rounding out the teams with at least two million in home attendance were the Expos, Cardinals, California Angels, New York Yankees and Philadelphia Phillies.

At the other extreme were the Minnesota Twins, Seattle Mariners and Cleveland Indians. All finished below 900,000, with the Indians bringing up the rear at 768,971. Nevertheless, the American League overall attracted 23,988,661, a record for any professional sports league.

A new six-year television contract promises better days for all clubs, even those languishing at the gate. Broadcasting sources estimated the escalating package, which runs from 1984 through 1989, will be worth $1.125 billion to the clubs.

The television deal was wrapped up on April 7 when ABC agreed to terms. NBC previously had approved its half of the contract. ABC reportedly will pay $575 million for the right to continue its prime-time coverage and to beam some Sunday afternoon games, while NBC will pay $550 million for an expanded Saturday schedule of 30 games and additional prime-time telecasts each year. The bigger fee being paid by ABC reflects the higher ratings of its Monday night telecasts. The two networks will continue to alternate coverage of the All-Star Game, League Championship Series and World Series, with ABC televising the All-Star and Championship Series games and NBC the World Series in 1984.

The new contract was regarded as a bonanza for baseball. In 1983, NBC paid $23 million and ABC paid $25 million under the expiring four-year agreement. This gave each team $1.9 million a year. The new pact could earn each club an average of more than $7 million per year, starting with $4.5 million in 1984 (the first year) and reaching $10 million in 1989 (the final year). The figures, of course, could be reduced by a players-union claim to a legal right to share in the TV revenues.

The lucrative television deal was engineered by an owners' committee chaired by Commissioner Bowie Kuhn. Other committee members were Eddie Einhorn of the White Sox and Bill Giles of the Phillies.

Early in the negotiations, the committee wanted to involve CBS. At one point, CBS showed interest in a plan that would include three interleague games each Thursday night. The proposal would have led to limited interleague play on that night only, pitting American League East vs. National League East and A.L. West vs. N.L. West. Later, CBS reportedly switched its attention to Sunday afternoons before eventually dropping out of the discussions.

The club owners, meeting in separate league sessions, approved plans for the clubs to share pay-television revenues. In the A.L., a percentage of revenue received from each telecast goes to a fund which is later divided equally among the 14 A.L. clubs. In the N.L., clubs which put games on pay TV pay a percentage of the revenue received directly to their opponents.

Late in the year, the majors also signed a new five-year national contract with CBS Radio. The agreement, which extends from 1985 through 1989, was described as "record-breaking," financially.

The breakthrough in network television money stirred speculation that Kuhn, the lame-duck commissioner, might be retained after all. Orioles Owner Edward Bennett Williams was among those who thought Kuhn's chances had been boosted by the TV deal.

"I think a lot of people were impressed with the way Kuhn, after he'd been kicked out of his job, still worked 16 hours a day to help put together the TV contract," Williams told Tom Boswell of the Washington Post. "It's safe to assume that $1 billion buys a lot of good will."

Kuhn's chances of winning a new term were squelched, however, by subsequent developments. In addition, with the Basic Agreement between management and the players' union coming up for renewal after the 1984 season, there was conjecture that the players would continue their demands for a slice of the television bonanza.

As 1983 drew to a close, there was no indication that the owners' Search Committee had found a candidate to recommend for commissioner. As a result, Kuhn was asked to remain on the job until March 1, 1984, to give the committee additional time.

Brewers President Bud Selig headed the eight-man Search Committee and, late in the year, he conceded his chairmanship duties were far more time-consuming than he anticipated. "It's a lot more work than I expected," he declared. "It has become a full-time job. I'm shocked and I'm tired."

Other committee members were Baltimore's Williams, Bob Lurie of the San Francisco Giants, Dan Galbreath of the Pittsburgh Pirates, Charles Bronfman of the Montreal Expos, Peter Hardy of the Toronto Blue Jays, George Argyros of the Seattle Mariners and John McMullen of the Houston Astros.

One of the first persons suggested for the commissioner's job was Tal Smith, president and general manager of the Houston Astros before he was fired late in 1980. Smith, who headed a consulting firm and represented baseball management in salary arbitration cases, announced he had no interest in being commissioner.

Late in spring training, Hank Aaron, the Braves' vice president in charge of player development, sent letters to all 26 club owners expressing a desire to become commissioner. The homer king continued his campaign throughout the season and in September was interviewed by several members of the Search Committee.

Two others who declared for the job were Silvio Conte, a U.S. representative from Massachusetts, and Frank Mankiewicz, who served as press secretary to Sen. Robert F. Kennedy.

In May, two nationally prominent businessmen revealed they had been contacted about the position, although Selig said no offer was ever made. Jack Valenti, president of the Motion Picture Association of America, informed Selig on May 12 that he was not interested. Two weeks later, William Simon, president of the U.S. Olympic Committee and former Secretary of the Treasury, became the second candidate to withdraw from possible consideration. Simon originally was scheduled to meet with Selig on May 19, but postponed the session to spend the weekend deliberating on the matter. He later disclosed he had canceled a May 27 date with Selig after deciding he wasn't the man for the job, anyway.

"My No. 1 responsibility is being president of the USOC," Simon said. "I will devote almost all of my time to that job until my term expires December 31, 1984."

Commenting on a discussion with Selig about not filling the commissioner's post until the expiration of his USOC term, Simon said: "To wait a year and a half is not in the best interest of baseball. I think the owners ought to move quickly to pick someone."

Other names mentioned during the summer for the position included Lee Iacocca, president of Chrysler Corp.; Peter Ueberroth, president of the Los Angeles Olympic Organizing Committee; Dr. A. Bartlett Giamatti, president of Yale University; William Resch, president of U.S. Steel; Arthur Watson, president of NBC Sports; Neil Pilson, president of CBS Sports; Brendan T. Byrne, former governor of New Jersey; Francis Dale, newspaper magnate and former majority stockholder of the Cincinnati Reds, and Sargent Shriver, former head of the Peace Corps.

In September, Selig said the number of candidates was "under 10." He declined to mention names.

Frustration mounted as the search continued. According to Peter Gammons of the Boston Globe, owners increasingly expressed the feeling that someone from within baseball should be chosen. "It would take too long to learn the business," Gammons quoted one unidentified owner as saying. "But no one inside the game—not even Selig—will take the job."

Kuhn disputed the claim that no baseball executive would accept the commissioner's position.

"I think he (a baseball man) is there and can be cajoled, persuaded and entreated to this glorious agony," Kuhn said. "The problem with an outsider is that he will have to pick his way through a time-consuming period of wheel spinning where he develops the needed feel for this unique institution. While I would prefer a baseball man, there is no question that baseball can lure high-quality outsiders who have the necessary arsenal of talents."

In addition to Selig, baseball men apparently considered for the commissioner's job included Lee MacPhail, who was winding up his tenure as American League president; John McHale, president of the Expos; Hank Peters, general manager of the Orioles; Frank Cashen, general manager of the New York Mets, and Peter Bavasi, former president of the Blue Jays.

Meanwhile, several Kuhn supporters continued their efforts to induce anti-Kuhn factions to switch sides. At the owners' November 1, 1982, meeting in Chicago, negative votes by five National League teams—Atlanta, Cincinnati, Houston, New York and St. Louis—defeated a plan to re-elect Kuhn for a three-year term.

The Cardinals reportedly were the chief target of the commissioner's boosters, and an 11th-hour attempt was made to romance Louis Susman, attorney for Cardinals President August A. Busch Jr. When the move proved unsuccessful, some owners considered another form of persuasion, according to Jerome Holtzman of the Chicago Tribune.

"Some individual owners are threatening to not renew their contracts with the giant beer manufacturer (Anheuser-Busch) unless the Cardinals relax their position against Kuhn's re-election," Holtzman wrote. Anheuser-Busch was a primary or partial sponsor of the broadcasts or telecasts of all major league clubs except Milwaukee, Toronto and Montreal. Late in '83, the Dodgers confirmed they were dropping Anheuser-Busch as a sponsor, but didn't say why.

Shortly before the owners' August 3-4 meeting in Boston, Dave Nightingale of The Sporting News reported that the Executive Council was considering a plan to keep Kuhn in office after expiration of his contract on August 12. As described by Nightingale, the scenario provided that if another bid to re-elect Kuhn failed and no successor was chosen by August 13, control of the sport would revert to the 10-man Executive Council, and that body then would designate Kuhn to continue as administrator.

After battling 20 months to retain his position, Kuhn suddenly did an about-face. At an August 2 meeting with members of the Executive Council, he revealed that he had decided to quit. Kuhn requested a 17-hour vow of silence until he could address the full ownership body. When the magnates gathered the next morning, he formally announced his resignation.

"This decision is final, irrevocable and emphatic," Kuhn told the owners.

With the Search Committee needing more time to find a suitable candidate, Selig immediately proposed that Kuhn's term be extended to the end of the year or until a successor was named, whichever came first. The resolution passed unanimously.

The realization that some members of the Executive Council couldn't stomach a continuation of the battle led to his decision, Kuhn explained.

"I felt it was beneath the dignity of me and the office to keep fighting under the circumstances," Kuhn declared.

"That could have undermined the respect of the public (for baseball). I decided I really didn't want a watered-down position or stewardship where I felt the game would be exposed to criticism. And I felt that if I remained, the acrimony would continue, that it would widen the breach rather than heal it."

Kuhn also told reporters that he hoped the next commissioner "will have more power, and I suspect he will," adding: "The character of this office will depend on the new man. A lot hangs on his personality because he will be in a position to structure his own office. I recommend that he be tough and fearless; that he have a thick skin; that he be a diplomat, and that he have an understanding and a feel for the dynamics of baseball. Those are tough qualifications."

Several months later, Dick Young of the New York Post reported the owners had agreed to give Kuhn $1.3 million in severance pay. The settlement, Young wrote, was spearheaded by Dodgers President Peter O'Malley, who pointed out that Kuhn's firing—or the owners' failure to rehire him—had hurt his reputation.

The name of another candidate surfaced during baseball's winter meetings in Nashville, Tenn., during the first week in December. He was James A. Baker III, the White House chief of staff. Like Kuhn, Baker, 53, is a graduate of Princeton University. He earned his law degree at the University of Texas. When asked about reports that Baker would switch jobs, President Ronald Reagan commented: "I was as surprised as anyone to read that." Presidential spokesman Larry Speakes cracked, "The truth is there's been a mixup. He (Baker) is going to replace Billy Martin as manager of the Yankees. The main reason is he wants to be in the television commercials."

Eddie Chiles, owner of the Texas Rangers and a friend of Baker's, expressed surprise over the story. "I've never heard Jim's name mentioned in connection with baseball," Chiles said. "With the state of affairs in the country right now, I think we need him more in the White House than in baseball."

Another person with contacts in baseball and in Washington, who asked not to be identified, told the Associated Press: "Apparently he (Baker) was the fifth or sixth choice (of the Search Committee). It looks like that's how far down they have gone." The same source said MacPhail was "everyone's first choice," adding that not only did MacPhail decline but some owners thought he would be more important in his new role of labor chief.

On December 8, the day after the Baker story broke, Selig made a report to a joint meeting of major league owners on his committee's efforts and, at the same session, the magnates extended Kuhn's contract for the second time. The new extension was to March 1, 1984, and the vote again was unanimous. At a subsequent press briefing, Selig told the media: "No one has withdrawn (from consideration for the position) because no one has been offered the job . . . We are nowhere near making any offer to anybody," but he added: "I believe (we) will be very shortly."

On balance, most observers thought Kuhn, who assumed the commissioner's job on February 4, 1969, was as good a commissioner as possible under the restrictions imposed by the owners. The severest criticism leveled at him concerned his decision to keep Willie Mays and

Kansas City outfielder Willie Wilson was one of four major league players suspended by Kuhn for involvement with drugs.

Mickey Mantle out of baseball after they took jobs with gambling casinos, the voiding in 1976 of Charlie Finley's sale of three Oakland players for $3.5 million and his failure to make an impact on the 1981 player strike.

Kuhn's perception of himself as "guardian of baseball" may have cost him his job, in the opinion of Marvin Miller.

"There's been a mythology for a long time that the commissioner is some kind of a neutral authority on high, representing the public and so on," commented Miller, who earlier in the year retired as executive director of the players' association. "That's absurd. The commissioner is in a management position, and there's nothing wrong with that. He is selected, hired, paid and occasionally fired by the owners."

The squabble over his job aside, Kuhn found 1983 one of his most taxing years. The Mantle situation, a series of outbursts by Yankees Owner George Steinbrenner, indiscretions by several other owners and a serious drug problem involving several players necessitated weighty decisions.

The most stunning and severe decision came on December 15 when Kuhn meted out one-year suspensions for drug involvement to first baseman Willie Aikens and outfielders Willie Wilson and Jerry Martin, all of whom were with the Kansas City Royals in 1983, and Los Angeles Dodgers relief pitcher Steve Howe.

The penalties were the stiffest assessed by Kuhn against any athletes during his 15-year tenure. Possible action by the commissioner against former Royals pitcher Vida Blue was delayed because disposition of Blue's case by the courts came a month after rulings were reached on Aikens, Wilson and Martin.

Kuhn said Howe's case would be reviewed in one year and that the ban could be extended at that time unless the pitcher overcame his drug habit. The suspensions of Aikens, Wilson and Martin were to be reviewed on May 15, 1984, at which time the players could be reinstated. The commissioner pointed out that Howe had undergone repeated treatment for cocaine use over a 13-month period and had failed a drug test as recently as November. In the case of the Kansas City trio, he cited prison sentences (three-month terms, which Blue also received) and the players' public apologies as mitigating circumstances.

Howe's addiction became public knowledge on March 4 when he told about it at a press conference at Dodgertown in Vero Beach, Fla. In a startling disclosure, Howe admitted that he had become dependent daily on alcohol and cocaine during the final month of the 1982 season.

"Last year I spent about $10,000 on cocaine," Howe told the media. He said the problem reached its peak some six weeks after the '82 season ended and on November 21, with help from the Dodger organization, he entered The Meadows drug rehabilitation center in Wickenburg, Ariz., for five weeks of treatment.

It also was revealed that another Dodger, outfielder Ken Landreaux, likewise spent part of the winter in a drug clinic. While there were no indications of a relapse on Landreaux's part, Howe wound up being suspended three times during the '83 season by the Dodgers, twice for drug-related incidents.

The first occurred on May 28 when the 25-year-old lefthander failed to report to Dodger Stadium for a game. He was suspended the next day and admitted to the CareUnit in Orange, Calif., another drug rehabilitation center. Upon reinstating him on June 29, O'Malley announced that Howe had been fined one month's salary—approximately $54,000. In addition, the pitcher was placed on three-year probation because it was his second involvement with cocaine in six months. Part of Howe's probation called for him to submit to periodic testing.

While O'Malley announced the suspension and fine, Kuhn noted that the Dodgers' action had been taken in coordination and after consultation with the commissioner's office.

The stiff penalty brought repercussions from the Major League Players Association. Ken Moffett, executive director of the players' union, suggested the fine—the largest ever levied against a baseball player—was politically motivated and linked to Kuhn's impending departure from office. The association filed a grievance appealing the fine and parts of the probation terms.

"This decision (in Howe's case) is entirely consistent with baseball policy granting amnesty . . . on the first occasion," Kuhn commented in response to Moffett's contention. "It does not guarantee amnesty for renewed drug usage or failure to follow a rehabilitation program."

Kuhn disputed the thought that Howe should not have been punished because he voluntarily submitted to treatment, saying the pitcher sought help "only after a series of absences alerted the Dodgers to his current problems."

The Dodgers suspended Howe again on July 16 after he reported to Dodger Stadium three hours late the previous afternoon and declined to submit to a drug test. However, the suspension was lifted after one day when blood and urine tests conducted by CareUnit failed to show the presence of any prohibited substances and Howe's explanation for his tardiness satisfied club officials. Howe nevertheless was docked one day's pay—approximately $1,900.

Howe's third suspension came when he missed the team's charter to Atlanta on September 22. Upon arriving later that night, Howe refused to undergo urinalysis. When Howe returned to Los Angeles the next day, the Dodgers immediately placed him under indefinite suspension. Four days later, Howe's physician, Dr. Michael Stone, notified the Dodgers that the reliever "will be undergoing treatment and is not able to play for the remainder of the season." Tony Attanasio, the pitcher's agent, said Howe's latest woes involved stress and psychological problems, not drugs, but Howe remained under treatment in the CareUnit until late October.

Rumors that several Kansas City players might be involved in drugs first circulated in midseason. Early in August, Jim J. Marquez, U.S. attorney for the state of Kansas, confirmed that the Federal Bureau of Investigation had conducted a three-month investigation and that several Royals were implicated. He said the probe centered on illegal drug traffic rooted in Dodge City, Kan., and spreading to Johnson County, Kan., on the southwestern edge of Kansas City.

On August 9, four days after the Royals asked waivers on Blue for the purpose of releasing him, it was revealed that the 34-year-old veteran was one of the Kansas City players named in documents relating to the investigation of "possible use, distribution and sale of cocaine." Sources close to the probe indicated that Wilson (the American League's 1982 batting champion), Aikens and Martin also were named. Royals General Manager John Schuerholz was quick to point out that the release of Blue was not tied to the investigation, but rather the result of poor performance. A former Cy Young Award winner who had nearly a year and a half remaining on a guaranteed contract, Blue was 0-5 with a 6.01 earned-run average when he was dropped.

A few weeks later, on the Royals' final visit of the season to Chicago, a group of fans took note of the situation by hanging a sign from the upper deck in Comiskey Park. "Hey, K.C., don't snort the foul lines," read the sign, which was removed in the second inning.

Shortly after the 1983 season concluded, the four Kansas City-associated players appeared in U.S. District Court in Kansas City, Kan. On October 13-14, Wilson, Aikens and Martin pleaded guilty to one count each of attempted possession of cocaine. In plea-bargaining arrangements, the three players agreed to accept misdemeanor charges—rather than face felony counts—in exchange for their cooperation in the continuing statewide investigation. Blue appeared in court on October 17 and pleaded guilty to possession of three grams of cocaine, a federal misdemeanor.

Twelve other persons, none connected with the Royals or professional sports, were indicted by a federal grand jury that heard evidence turned up in the investigation. Their trials were to begin early in 1984.

FBI wiretaps revealed that Wilson, Aikens and Martin had made one phone call each in June to a home in suburban Johnson County in an effort to purchase cocaine. Wilson claimed he was attempting to get the drug for a former teammate.

Even before his court appearance, Martin had been notified by the Royals that they would not exercise their option to renew his contract. Later, club officials announced that Aikens, despite a .302 average and 23 homers in 1983, also would not be back with the team. Apparently in Manager Dick Howser's doghouse, Aikens was traded from Kansas City to Toronto on December 19.

Royals Owner Ewing Kauffman apolo-

Los Angeles relief pitcher Steve Howe was suspended three times during the season by Dodgers President Peter O'Malley (below) and for one full year by Kuhn after the '83 season.

gized to Kansas City's baseball fans for the situation.

Sentencing of Wilson, Aikens and Martin was set for November 17, while Blue was granted a delay until December 19. After listening to pleas of the players and their lawyers, U.S. District Magistrate J. Milton Sullivant gave Wilson and Aikens the maximum sentence for the charge—one year in federal prison (with the last nine months of the terms suspended), a $5,000 fine and two years' probation. Martin also was ordered to serve three months in a federal institution with two years' probation, but was fined only $2,500. The sentences marked the first time any major league baseball players had been ordered to jail for drug offenses.

Wilson's attorney, David W. Russell, contended the judge's imposition of jail terms "gave you (the media) what you wanted." Russell maintained that Wilson "doesn't need rehabilitation in jail or a supervised program. He is paying back to the community by setting up the community program to educate others (a reference to Wilson's public apology and $50,000 donation on November 11 to help fund a drug and alcohol program in Kansas City)."

Sullivant agreed with Russell about the publicity factor but, noting a pro athlete's "special place in society," declared there is a necessary double standard to the law. Sullivant said that because of the unusual publicity surrounding the case, his decision on jail terms could serve as an example to others.

Wilson, 28, and Martin, 34, started serving time on December 5. Aikens, 29, asked for and received a delay in the start of his jail sentence until January 3 to allow him to complete a private drug rehabilitation program in Baltimore. Aikens' attorney, James E. Kelley Jr., also filed a motion to have the sentence reduced from three to two months, but Sullivant rejected the request.

Like his three former teammates, Blue drew a one-year sentence, with the last nine months suspended, when he appeared before Sullivant on December 19. The judge told Blue, who also was fined $5,000, that had he not cooperated with the government in the case, his sentence would have been much more severe.

Besides Howe, one other player missed part of the season specifically because of drug dependency. Prior to a game in Philadelphia on June 9, Cardinals outfielder Lonnie Smith informed Manager Whitey Herzog of his addiction. Two days later, Smith left the club to enter Hyland Center at St. Anthony's Hospital in St. Louis for treatment of drug and alcohol abuse. While Smith was hitting .311 at the time, Herzog later acknowledged that Lonnie's lack of aggressiveness on the bases had raised his suspicions. Smith rejoined the Cardinals on July 10 and finished the season with a .321 average, two points off the N.L.-leading figure posted by Pittsburgh's Bill Madlock.

A former major league pitcher who became a medical doctor also experienced a recurrence of a drug habit that dogged his baseball career. George (Doc) Medich, 34, was charged on November 14 with seven counts of writing prescriptions for nonexistent patients and others who never received drugs. Medich, a resident in orthopedic surgery at Children's Hospital in Pittsburgh, was ordered to undergo treatment. Dr. Albert Ferguson, head of the orthopedic surgery program, explained that Medich had become dependent on addictive pain killers and muscle relaxants, the same drugs he was charged with improperly prescribing.

Another prominent ex-major leaguer, Maury Wills, was arrested in Los Angeles on December 29 and charged with possession of cocaine. The incident brought to light the fact that the former Dodger base-stealing star had undergone treatment during the summer for drug dependency.

Chronic alcoholism proved troublesome for pitchers Dickie Noles of the Chicago Cubs and Sammy Stewart of the Baltimore Orioles and Minnesota Twins coach Johnny Podres.

Noles was arrested in Cincinnati on April 9 following a tavern brawl. He was charged with assault, resisting arrest and disorderly conduct. Besides being fined by the Cubs, Noles was named in a $500,000 civil suit by one of the arresting police officers and a $300,000 suit by the doorman at the bar. When the pitcher appeared before Judge David Albanese in Hamilton County (O.) Municipal Court on July 6, he entered a plea of no contest. The judge sentenced Noles to 180 days in jail, but suspended 150 days. He also credited him with the 14 days he spent in confinement at Chicago's Northwestern Memorial Hospital, where he had undergone treatment the previous year at the club's insistence.

Noles spent one night in jail, but was freed the next day pending an appeal. Shortly after the season ended, he dropped the appeal and began serving the remainder of the 16-day sentence. At the same time, Noles donated $1,000 to the Greater

Cincinnati Knothole Baseball League.

Podres and Stewart both encountered problems in midseason. Podres left the Twins to enter a rehabilitation center for treatment of alcoholism. Arrested on July 8 on charges of driving while intoxicated, Stewart began treatment and was placed on 18 months of unsupervised probation.

Former major league outfielder Ron LeFlore was found not guilty in Chicago of drug and weapons charges brought against him late in the 1982 season. However, the Chicago White Sox, who released LeFlore in April of '83 even though he had one year remaining on his contract, refused to pay him the $735,000 due under the pact. The players' union took the case to arbitration.

In a continuing effort to meet the drug problem, the game's officials took several steps. Early in the season, the security division of the commissioner's office added investigators to watch for drug trafficking. In September, the club owners and the players' union joined forces to organize a study committee to examine the situation. Management named MacPhail, Montreal's McHale and Roy Eisenhardt of the Oakland A's to the committee, while the players' union was represented by Moffett, legal counsel Don Fehr and Mark Belanger, a union official and former player.

Dr. Donald J. Ottenburg was appointed a consultant on drugs and alcohol by the committee. A specialist in this field, Ottenburg recently had retired as executive director of the Eagleville (Pa.) Hospital and Rehabilitation Center.

The Dodgers sought to counter the problem by hiring Dr. Forest S. Tennant as a consultant to the entire Los Angeles organization in drug abuse. Tennant was executive director of Community Health Projects Inc. in West Covina, Calif., and also an associate professor at the UCLA School of Public Health.

Professional baseball, of course, wasn't the only sport beset by drug problems. Several National Football League players were dealt suspensions during the summer by Commissioner Pete Rozelle, while the National Basketball Association adopted the toughest policy yet.

Shortly before the basketball season was to begin, it was announced that a joint NBA player-management committee had approved a policy providing that any player with a chemical-abuse habit could step forward and get help without punishment until December 31, but any drug involvement thereafter would bring permanent banishment from the league.

Although of considerably less consequence than the drug cases, Steinbrenner's run-ins with the commissioner caused concern among his fellow owners. In each instance, foot-in-the-mouth comments got the Yankee owner in hot water.

Kuhn fined Steinbrenner $5,000 and tagged Chicago White Sox co-owners Jerry Reinsdorf and Einhorn with $2,500 penalties early in January for a name-calling episode. It began when Reinsdorf termed the Yankee boss "irresponsible" several weeks earlier for signing free agent Steve Kemp to a five-year, $5.5 million contract. Steinbrenner countered by calling the White Sox duo "the Abbott and Costello of baseball." Orioles Owner Williams, who also criticized Steinbrenner, received a letter of admonition from the commissioner for his comments.

Steinbrenner, displeased by the fine, declared: "Those other guys started the whole thing . . . it's a shame that one of the last official acts of the commissioner had to be fining owners. But his record's intact. During his term there have been 12 disputes involving the Yankees and he has ruled against us 12 times." As it turned out, there was more to come.

An umpire's decision in a spring-training game prompted another incident. While watching a Yankee-Montreal exhibition at Fort Lauderdale, Fla., on March 25, Steinbrenner exploded at National League umpire Lee Weyer when a call on a close play at first base went against the Yankees.

Shouting at the arbiter, the Yankee owner called him a "National League homer"—among other things. With several reporters standing nearby, he added: "That's the way (National League President Chub) Feeney tells them to do it. If it's close, give it to the National League."

As might be expected, the outburst was played up big, and the Umpires Association immediately filed a protest with the commissioner. Several weeks later, Kuhn slapped Steinbrenner with a $50,000 fine. At that point, the fine was believed to be the second heaviest ever levied by Kuhn, ranking only behind the $100,000 assessment in 1979 against San Diego Padres Owner Ray Kroc for tampering with potential free agents Graig Nettles and Joe Morgan. Despite the hefty figure, the Yankee owner never contested the fine, presumably thinking it was better than the alternative (a possible suspension).

The third Steinbrenner-Kuhn confrontation was an upshot of The Great Pine Tar Case. Angered by MacPhail's decision upholding a Kansas City protest, Steinbrenner issued derogatory and inflammatory remarks about the American League president. An attempt to block completion of the protested game also became part of the issue.

The original dispute developed in the ninth inning of a game at Yankee Stadium on July 24. With two out and Kansas City trailing, 4-3, U. L. Washington singled off Dale Murray. Yankees Manager Martin then summoned relief ace Goose Gossage to face Royals slugger George Brett, who promptly drilled the ball into the right-field stands for an apparent two-run homer and a 5-4 Kansas City lead. As Brett headed for the dugout after circling the bases, Martin, at coach Don Zimmer's behest, asked the umpires to check Brett's bat. Plate umpire Tim McClelland, after examining the bat, consulted his three associates and crew chief Joe Brinkman finally took over.

Like many players, Brett applied pine tar to the bat handle to improve his grip and prevent blisters. When Brinkman measured the pine tar against the front of home plate, he found the substance on Brett's bat extended an inch or two beyond the 18-inch limit stipulated in Rule 1.10 (b). Thereupon the umpires signaled Brett out, nullifying the homer. This represented the third out and presumably gave the Yankees a 4-3 victory. Martin later claimed he had known for two weeks that Brett's bat was technically illegal and had been waiting for the right time to protest.

Enraged by the umpires' ruling, Brett raced onto the field and had to be physically restrained by Brinkman. While Howser pursued the argument, Royals pitcher Gaylord Perry sneaked behind the home-plate mob scene and grabbed the bat. A few moments later, a uniformed guard intercepted it and took it to the umpires' dressing room. The Royals wound up filing an official protest with MacPhail.

Four days after the incident, the American League president upheld the Kansas City protest. It marked the first time in his 10 years as league head that MacPhail had overturned a decision by one of his umpires; rather than blaming the umpires, though, MacPhail criticized the official playing rules, saying they "should be rewritten and clarified."

MacPhail maintained it was the intent of the rules-makers to distinguish between a bat carrying excessive pine tar and a "doctored" bat—one that has been altered "to improve the distance factor or cause an unusual reaction on the baseball." In the former instance, he noted, the intent was merely to remove the bat from the game rather than to penalize the player. In backing the protest, MacPhail ruled the game must be completed from the point of Brett's home run.

Predictably, the decision outraged the Yankees, especially Steinbrenner.

"It sure tests our faith in our leadership," Steinbrenner said of the ruling. "If the Yankees lose the division by one game, I wouldn't want to be Lee MacPhail living in New York. Maybe he should go house-hunting in Kansas City."

To MacPhail's suggestion that the game be completed on August 18, an open date for both clubs, Steinbrenner responded: "Hell, no, I'd rather forfeit than play it the 18th. Lee has made enough of a mess out of this. I'm not letting him take my players' off-day away."

The game, of course, was completed on August 18, but not before there were further ramificiations. Kansas City players, scheduled to open a series in Baltimore the next night, voted 15-10 in favor of the date. The Yankee players, for whom it would have been the only off-day in a 31-game stretch, voted against playing. However, when MacPhail notified them the game would be forfeited if they didn't play, the Yankees took another vote and approved the date.

Steinbrenner then planned for a 2 p.m. starting time, saying he was arranging to bring in thousands of kids from day camps as guests. He set a $2.50 admission price for others, with the money to go to charity. However, because the Royals were due to play in Kansas City the previous night, MacPhail declared that play could not start until 6 p.m. in keeping with the agreement with the players' union. He also announced that Brett, Howser, Perry and coach Rocky Colavito of the Royals had been fined for their roles in the pine-tar episode and would not be permitted to participate in the game.

The confusion and intrigue continued to mount. At 10 a.m. on the day of the game, Justice Orest V. Maresca of the Bronx Supreme Court granted a preliminary injunction barring the game. He said more time was needed to hear the merits of two lawsuits from fans who were protesting the $2.50 admission charge. As a result, it wasn't until 3:34 p.m.—when Justice Joseph P. Sullivan of the New York State Supreme Court Appellate Division stayed the ruling—that the way was paved to complete the game.

When play eventually was resumed at 6:05, the Yankees had pitcher Ron Guidry

The Royals' George Brett had to be restrained by umpire Joe Brinkman after his apparent two-run homer in the ninth inning against the Yankees on July 24 was disallowed because of too much pine tar on his bat. A.L. President Lee MacPhail later overruled the umpires' decision.

in center field and first baseman-outfielder Don Mattingly, a lefthanded thrower, at second base. Before George Frazier delivered the first pitch to the Royals' Hal McRae, the Yankees tried appeal plays at first and second bases. When the umpires gave the safe sign, Martin marched onto the field and filed a protest with umpire crew chief Dave Phillips. The umpire, though, whipped out a notarized letter signed by the four umpires in the original game. It stated that Brett and Washington had touched all bases.

Play finally proceeded and, after McRae struck out, the skimpy turnout of 1,245 fans saw Royals relief ace Dan Quisenberry retire three Yankees in order to nail down the 5-4 Kansas City victory.

While it took only 12 minutes and 16 pitches to wrap up the game and close out a 25-day period of intrigue, the controversy wasn't ended. On August 30, the commissioner notified Steinbrenner that he intended to hold a hearing into the Yankee owner's behavior and comments about MacPhail. There also was some question as to what role, if any, the Yankees might have played in the legal efforts by two fans to block resumption of the game.

Steinbrenner, fearing the possibility of a heavy fine and suspension, reportedly made repeated efforts to reach a settlement with Kuhn but without success. A hearing finally was set for November 7, but four days earlier the Yankee owner obtained a temporary restraining order against the hearing from the New York State Supreme Court.

Fourteen lawyers—six for Steinbrenner, eight for the commissioner—then appeared before New York State Supreme Justice Irwin Silbowitz to argue Steinbrenner's request for an injunction. However, Steinbrenner soon decided to abandon his legal effort to bar Kuhn from conducting a hearing.

The next step was Kuhn's.

On December 23, the Yankees announced they had been fined $250,000 by Kuhn for, in part, "certain public statements" made by Steinbrenner in connection with the pine-tar game.

The fine, the largest ever assessed by Kuhn, also resulted from "positions espoused by other representatives of the New York Yankees," the club said, in connection with lawsuits brought by two fans. The team did not elaborate.

"While we feel the penalty to be excessive, we will abide by the commissioner's decision," said Steinbrenner. "We certainly do not wish to cause him any problems in his last days as commissioner."

When Kuhn officially announced his decision three days later, he also ordered reimbursement to the commissioner's office of $50,000 "for legal fees incurred in connection with the litigation brought by you (Steinbrenner) and the Yankees to enjoin me from conducting the aforesaid hearing" (on the pine-tar case).

Kuhn slapped Reinsdorf with a second fine early in August. A remark that the White Sox board chairman made about Steinbrenner during the All-Star Game party cost him $5,000. "I know how to tell when George Steinbrenner is lying. His lips move," Reinsdorf commented.

Several weeks later, Atlanta Braves Owner Ted Turner was docked $25,000 by the commissioner for, of all things, leveling with a player. In this case, though, Turner's honesty violated a rule.

It all began on August 28 when the Braves acquired pitcher Len Barker from the Cleveland Indians for "three players to be named later." Newspapers in both cities reported the next day that the three were Brett Butler, Atlanta's regular left fielder, and two farmhands at Richmond of the International League—pitcher Rick Behenna and infielder Brook Jacoby.

A few days later, with the International League's regular season completed, Jacoby joined Atlanta but Behenna was ordered to report to Cleveland. Concerned about his status, Butler on September 19 sought out Turner, who admitted that Butler, Behenna and Jacoby were the "players to be named later."

While fining the Atlanta owner, Kuhn allowed the Braves to keep Butler for the remainder of the season "in fairness to the player and his teammates, who remain in the National League West race."

The situation left Butler confused. "How can a lame-duck commissioner make a judgment on a lame-duck player?" he asked one newspaperman.

Kuhn was kept busy on other fronts, too.

Three years after Mays took a job with a gambling casino and was prohibited from baseball employment for the duration of his casino ties, Mantle did the same thing and met a similar fate. In a decision announced February 8, Kuhn ruled that the former Yankee star could not take a baseball job after being named director of sports promotion for the Claridge Hotel and Casino of Atlantic City, N.J. Mantle's annual salary in the new role was said to be $100,000.

"Baseball and casino employment are incompatible," Kuhn declared. "I would much prefer that Mickey and Willie were in baseball, and I hope in time it can be worked out." He added that his decree "follows the pattern I set in 1969 when I said club owners could not be involved in Las Vegas casinos."

Since his retirement, Mantle had served as a spring-training batting instructor and good-will ambassador for the Yankees.

Like the commissioner, MacPhail took punitive action against Steinbrenner in 1983. He slapped him with a one-week suspension and also banished the Yankees' Martin on two occasions. In each instance, criticism of the umpires was the cause.

Ironically, Steinbrenner didn't even attend the game that got him in trouble. Instead, he watched it on television in Tampa. During the Yankees-Oakland game at Yankee Stadium on May 27, New York's Dave Winfield reacted to a brushback pitch thrown by Mike Norris by mixing with catcher Mike Heath. This brought players rushing from both dugouts. When order was restored, the umpires ejected Winfield.

Steinbrenner, undeterred by the $50,000 fine levied earlier by Kuhn, lashed out at umpire Derryl Cousins because he banished only Winfield and not Heath. He noted that Cousins and partner John Shulock were promoted from the minors during the 1979 umpire strike and said their umpiring was "a disgrace."

MacPhail responded with a statement that "Steinbrenner's intemperate blast is completely unacceptable and will result in disciplinary action." That prompted Steinbrenner to comment: "We are all free to express our opinion unless Lee MacPhail has authored a new Constitution or Bill of Rights for the U.S."

Citing "repeated problems" with Steinbrenner's approach to umpires, the American League president imposed a one-week suspension effective June 3. He ruled the Yankee owner could not attend games or be in his office at Yankee Stadium during that period. It was Steinbrenner's second suspension since he bought the club in 1973. Kuhn barred him in November of 1974 after he pleaded guilty to charges of making illegal contributions to Richard Nixon's 1972 presidential campaign.

Martin's clashes with the men in blue began in the season opener at Seattle when he criticized Dan Morrison. Ten days later, Martin was ejected at Yankee Stadium for arguing with Vic Voltaggio. The two episodes prompted MacPhail to fine Martin $5,000 on April 21. Accompanying the penalty was a warning that Martin would be suspended unless his general behavior toward umpires improved.

Just eight days later, Martin became embroiled in three arguments in a game in Texas and, after being ejected, kicked dirt at plate umpire Drew Coble. The result was a three-game suspension, the fourth of Martin's 14-year managerial career. He appealed the ruling, but on May 10 MacPhail rejected the appeal. Zimmer managed the club for the next three games.

Martin drew his second suspension of the season—this one for two games—on August 5. It resulted from his alleged references to umpire Dale Ford as "a stone liar" following a dispute in a July 31 game at Chicago. Martin's appeal again was turned down by MacPhail, and the Yankees' pilot served the penalty on September 2-3. To add to Martin's problems, Ford filed suit against him in U.S. District Court in Philadelphia late in September. The umpire contended he "suffered serious injury in name and reputation" when the media reported the "stone liar" remark.

Except for his difficulties with the Yankee duo, MacPhail found the final year of his 10-year tenure as league president to be enjoyable. Not only did the American League finally win an All-Star Game after 11 consecutive defeats, but it also produced the World Series winner in the Baltimore Orioles. MacPhail had notified A.L. owners the previous winter that he planned to retire at year's end.

Instead of retiring, MacPhail wound up accepting a new position even before his term ended on December 31, thus assuring his continued association with baseball. In June, he agreed to become president of the Player Relations Committee after being endorsed unanimously by owners of the 26 clubs. He succeeded Ray Grebey, who resigned on April 7 at the request of the PRC's board of directors.

Grebey, who had served as management's labor representative and chief negotiator for five years, remained as a consultant until MacPhail's appointment. Barry Rona, counsel to the PRC, functioned as acting director during the interim.

MacPhail's appointment to the Player Relations post, coming just six months after Moffett succeeded Miller as executive director of the players' union, prompted the feeling that the sport was about to enter a new era in which players and owners could agree on what each side needed. MacPhail had been instrumental in bringing about a settlement of the 1981 player strike, while Moffett, then with the

Federal Mediation and Conciliation Service, served as mediator during that settlement.

However, the picture changed on November 22 when the union's Executive Board abruptly dismissed Moffett. A few days earlier, Moffett had left midway through an important hearing on a grievance filed by the players. The grievance was over a rule adopted by the owners early in the year that requires each club to show at least a 60-40 assets-to-liabilities ratio. The players viewed this as an attempt to curtail the amount of money the clubs could give the athletes. With the current Basic Agreement due to expire on December 31, 1984, the players reportedly had begun to feel that Moffett could be a weak link in negotiations for a new labor agreement.

Moffett had assumed the job effective January 1 under a three-year contract. It was said to provide for a $125,000 salary in '83 and a total of approximately $285,000 over the next two years. When the players proposed a negotiated settlement on the final two years, Moffett announced he was retaining a law firm to obtain the money due him. "It's ironic," he said later, "that one thing the players look for is a guaranteed contract. But that's not the case when you work for the association."

To replace Moffett, the players brought back Miller temporarily. This triggered charges by Moffett that Miller had orchestrated his ouster. "He never retired," Moffett said. "He didn't want anyone messing with his monument."

Miller held the position until December 8 when, in the final day of a three-day meeting in Hawaii, the union board elected Fehr as acting executive director. Fehr, 35, had been general counsel of the union for the last six years. At the same time, Miller, who served as executive director for 16½ years before retiring, was named a consultant to the board. Among other duties, he was to serve as a member of the union's negotiating team.

The American League also came up with a new leader during the annual major-minor league winter meetings in Nashville. Numerous prominent baseball officials apparently were approached earlier about the A.L. presidency but turned it down. The list included Montreal's McHale, Baltimore's Peters, Harry Dalton of the Milwaukee Brewers, Al Rosen of the Houston Astros, John Harrington of the Boston Red Sox and Johnny Johnson, president of the National Assocation. Peter Bavasi also was mentioned.

The post finally was filled on December 8 by Dr. Bobby Brown, widely known Texas cardiologist and former New York Yankee infielder. Brown, who reportedly received a three-year contract worth $170,000 annually, revealed that his appointment came about after he had been interviewed earlier for the commissioner's job.

Brown was due to take the A.L. reins on January 1, but conceded he might not be a full-time executive until midsummer because of the need to find other doctors for his cardiology patients.

While electing Brown, American League owners also elevated Bob Fishel, MacPhail's longtime assistant, to executive vice president. Phyllis Merhige was promoted to director of public relations.

A step in consolidating baseball's offices under one roof took place in September. In keeping with a recommendation of the Committee on Restructuring, the commissioner and his staff, the American League, the National League and the Player Relations Committee all moved to new headquarters on the 17th and 18th floors at 350 Park Avenue in New York City.

Although none of the 1983 division races went down to the wire, the regular season produced its share of excitement. The remarkable first-half showings of usual also-rans Toronto and Texas enlivened the American League scene. They occupied first place in their respective divisions at the All-Star Game break, but both later faded from the pennant picture.

Following a poor early performance that almost cost Manager Tony LaRussa his job, the Chicago White Sox became the only club to break away from the field. In their last 100 games, the scrappy White Sox (for whom the phrase "Winning Ugly" became a rallying cry) played at a .700 clip and posted the year's best record (99-63). In the process, they set an American League record by finishing 20 games ahead of West Division runner-up Kansas City. In the A.L. East, the Baltimore Orioles chalked up a 98-64 record to outdistance second-place Detroit by six games.

In the National League East, the four contenders entered September with a combined 266-256 record. Just when it appeared that no team wanted the title, the Philadelphia Phillies (known as the "Wheeze Kids" because of their many veterans) reeled off 14 victories in their last 16 games and wound up six lengths in front of second-place Pittsburgh.

As happened a year earlier, the Atlanta Braves built a comfortable lead in the West only to have the Los Angeles

Dodgers overtake them. This time, Los Angeles managed to hold on after seizing the lead and edged the Braves by three games. Ironically, the Atlanta skid began as it had in '82—when Turner ordered the removal of Chief Noc-a-Homa's tepee from the left-field bleachers to accommodate big crowds. At the time (preceding an August 12-14 series with the Dodgers), the Braves had a 6½-game advantage.

After losing 11 of 12 decisions to the Dodgers in the regular season, the Phillies turned the tables in the League Championship Series, winning three games to one. Meanwhile, the Orioles rebounded from a loss in their LCS opener and ousted the White Sox in four games. The Orioles then dropped Game 1 of the World Series before winning four straight to give Joe Altobelli a world championship in his first year as successor to Earl Weaver as Baltimore manager.

The campaign was marked by numerous milestone performances and the farewells of several superstars.

Nolan Ryan, Houston fireballer, shattered one of the game's oldest records—Walter Johnson's 56-year-old strikeout mark of 3,508—when he fanned pinch-hitter Brad Mills in the eighth inning of a 4-2 victory at Montreal on April 27. In his next outing, the 36-year-old Astro suffered a pulled hamstring that sidelined him for more than a month.

During Ryan's absence, lefthander Steve Carlton overtook the righthander, seizing the strikeout lead during a 2-1 loss to the Cardinals in Philadelphia on June 7. The Phillies' 38-year-old ace finished the season with 3,709 career strikeouts, 32 ahead of Ryan.

Carlton achieved an even more memorable goal on September 23 when he beat the Cardinals, 6-2, in St. Louis to become only the 16th pitcher in major league history to attain the 300-victory plateau. After agreeing a few days earlier to a radio-TV interview that was to be piped to the press box after the triumph, Carlton had second thoughts and turned down the idea. It kept intact his record of not granting an interview to a newspaper reporter since 1979.

Several other veterans also achieved notable milestones. Carl Yastrzemski of the Boston Red Sox equalled a major league record by playing his 23rd season with the same club and also became the all-time leader in games played with 3,308, passing Aaron's 3,298. Despite a .245 batting average, Pete Rose of the Phillies pulled within 10 hits of the 4,000 figure in his bid to catch Ty Cobb, the only player to reach that

It took 56 years, but Walter Johnson's (above) all-time strikeout mark fell to Houston's Nolan Ryan on April 27. Philadelphia's Steve Carlton later surpassed them both.

level (Cobb's total is 4,191).

Steve Garvey, signed as a free agent by San Diego, broke Billy Williams' National League record for consecutive games played when he appeared in No. 1,118 on April 16 and then ran his string to 1,207 before a thumb injury suffered on July 29 sidelined him for the remainder of the season. And lefthander Jim Kaat extended his own record for most years as a pitcher in the majors to 25 before drawing his release from the St. Louis Cardinals during the All-Star break.

After going without a no-hitter the previous year, the majors witnessed three in 1983 while another pitcher came within one out of a perfect game. Milt Wilcox, Detroit righthander, missed immortality on April 15 when he retired the first 26 White Sox in order before pinch-hitter Jerry Hairston singled as the Tigers won, 6-0, in a night game at Chicago. Chuck Rainey of the Chicago Cubs missed a no-hitter with two out in the ninth on August 24 when Eddie Milner singled as the Cubs downed Cincinnati, 3-0, at Wrigley Field. Rainey issued two walks.

Lefthander Dave Righetti notched the season's initial no-hitter—and the first by a Yankee since Don Larsen's perfect game in the 1956 World Series—when he stopped the Boston Red Sox, 4-0, at Yankee Stadium on July 4. Bob Forsch registered the second no-hit performance of his career with a 3-0 conquest of Montreal at St. Louis on September 26. Three nights later in Oakland, rookie Mike Warren stopped the White Sox without a hit, 3-0.

Red Sox third baseman Wade Boggs was the majors' top hitter, leading the American League with a .361 average in only his second season in the big leagues. Another third baseman, Bill Madlock of Pittsburgh, captured the National League title at .323 and became only the 11th player to win at least four batting championships in the majors.

Boston's Jim Rice topped the American League in home runs (39) and total bases (344) and shared runs-batted-in honors with Cecil Cooper of Milwaukee at 126. Cal Ripken of Baltimore led in hits (211), runs (121) and doubles (47), while Kansas City's Brett compiled the best slugging percentage with .563. Rickey Henderson of Oakland, who set a major league record a year earlier with 130 stolen bases, led in thefts again with 108 to become the first major leaguer to steal 100 bases in three seasons. He also paced American League batters in walks with 103.

In the National League, Dale Murphy of Atlanta had the most RBIs (121) and best slugging mark (.540). Mike Schmidt of Philadelphia won the homer title with 40 and also led in walks with 128. Montreal's Tim Raines not only was No. 1 in runs scored (133) and stolen bases (90), but became the first National Leaguer ever to attain 70 thefts and 70 RBIs in the same season.

A pitcher who spent the last six weeks of the season in the National League topped the American League in earned-run average, and a pitcher who didn't win after July 10 captured the senior circuit's ERA title. Lefthander Rick Honeycutt, traded by Texas to the Dodgers in an August 19 waiver deal, paced the American League with a 2.42 ERA, while lefthander Atlee Hammaker of San Francisco topped the National League at 2.25 despite going 0-6 in the season's final 12 weeks.

The American League came up with four 20-game winners, but the National League had none. LaMarr Hoyt of the White Sox posted 24 victories and teammate Richard Dotson added 22. Ron Guidry won 21 games for the Yankees and Jack Morris notched 20 for Detroit. The National League's biggest winner was John Denny, who chalked up 19 victories for the Phillies.

Kansas City's Quisenberry set a major league record with 45 saves and paced American League pitchers with 69 appearances.

Kaat's midseason release by the Cardinals probably ended his major league career, while another veteran hung up his spikes a few weeks earlier and became a television broadcaster. And three other longtime stars formally announced their retirements.

The Yankees disclosed on June 20 that they had asked outfielder Bobby Murcer, 37, to retire, and the next day he joined the club's TV crew as a color commentator.

Perry, who joined Kansas City following his release by Seattle, bade farewell to baseball on September 23 and headed for his North Carolina peanut farm. The 45-year-old righthander compiled a 7-14 record in his final season and closed out his 22-year big-league career with 314 victories.

Although only 35, Johnny Bench informed the media on June 10 that he had decided to retire at season's close after 16-plus years with the Cincinnati Reds. Bench, who thus passed up the last two seasons of a three-year, $3 million contract, was honored with a night on September 17, and he thrilled a sellout crowd of 53,790 at Riverfront Stadium by smashing a game-tying, two-run homer in the third inning. Houston went on to win, 4-3. As part of the festivities, the Reds set up a Johnny Bench Scholarship Fund and contributed $25,000 toward it.

Yastrzemski announced prior to the season that 1983 would be his last year. American League clubs sought to honor the 44-year-old Boston Red Sox great on his final swing around the league, but he refused all such attempts. On October 1, a one-hour Yaz Day celebration was held at Fenway Park preceding the next-to-last game of the season. With 33,491 fans on hand, Yastrzemski was given a car, boat, pickup truck and several checks. He said he was turning the checks over to Merrimack College in North Andover, Mass., to set up a baseball program. Mrs. Tom Yawkey, one of the Red Sox owners, also provided funds for a "Yaz Room" at Dana-Farber Cancer Institute in Boston.

Several other veterans received their releases at season's end but had no intention of retiring. Phil Niekro's 25-year stay in the Braves' organization came to a close on October 7 when the 44-year-old knuckleballer was cut loose. Unwilling to guarantee Rose that he would play regularly in 1984, the Phillies released the 42-year-old first baseman on October 19. By declining to renew his $1 million contract, the Phils obligated themselves to pay Rose $300,000 in severance money.

The Phillies also said goodbye to two other "Wheeze Kids," second baseman Morgan, 40, and first baseman-pinch-hitter Tony Perez, 41. The buyout of Morgan's contract cost the club another $200,000.

Later in the off-season, Niekro signed with the Yankees, Morgan joined the A's and Perez returned to his old club, Cincinnati, via a trade.

Minnesota outfielder Jim Eisenreich quit the Twins after the first two games of the '83 season and announced he was retiring. As a rookie in 1982, he sat out the last 3½ months of the year because of a nervous disorder. Eisenreich, 24, returned to college and later played for an amateur team in his hometown of St. Cloud, Minn. Late in the year, he indicated he would try a comeback in '84.

Rick Reuschel, former Chicago Cub pitching ace, made a remarkable comeback in 1983, while first baseman Bruce Bochte announced he was ready to return to baseball after sitting out all of '83.

Reuschel, 34, missed the entire 1982 season because of a rotator-cuff tear. Released by the Yankees, he joined the Cubs' Class A Quad City (Midwest) farm team and in September was brought up by the Cubs. Bochte, a .286 hitter over 8½ big-league seasons, signed as a free agent with Oakland on November 14 after a one-year retirement. He had spent his previous five seasons in the majors with Seattle before opting for free agency in November of 1982.

The numerous oldsters in uniform in 1983 prompted The Sporting News to conduct a study on the subject. It revealed that major league rosters (as of May 30) listed 75 players who were 35 or older, with 48 in the 35-37 age bracket, 16 in 38-39 category and 11 who were 40 or more. The Phillies had seven players in the over-35 club and an average age of 32.8 years for their 25-man roster. The 75 veterans represented 11.5 percent of the majors' 650 active players.

Perry was the eldest of the group, followed in order by Kaat, Niekro, Yastrzemski, Woodie Fryman, Ron Reed, Rose, Bert Campaneris, Perez, Jerry Koosman and Tommy John. Five others turned 40 before the year ended.

By contrast, The Sporting News' Nightingale pointed out, the majors had only one 40-year-old (Willie Mays) in 1973, five in 1963 and four in 1953. Nightingale attributed the dramatic increase in elder statesmen to sharply higher salaries resulting from free agency, multi-year guaranteed contracts, expansion and the American League's use of the designated hitter.

Six American League teams and one in the National began the '83 season with new managers. Three were making their debuts as major league pilots—Mike Ferraro of Cleveland, Steve Boros of Oakland and Doug Rader of Texas. Other managerial shifts sent John McNamara to California, Bill Virdon to Montreal, Altobelli to Baltimore and Martin back to New York for his third hitch with the Yankees.

Five managers failed to survive the campaign. First to depart was George Bamberger of the New York Mets. When Bamberger resigned on June 3, the Mets had the worst record (16-30) in either league. Coach Frank Howard served as interim pilot for the remainder of the season.

Rene Lachemann, the majors' youngest skipper at 38, was fired on June 25 by the Seattle Mariners, who had lost eight straight games and skidded to 26-47. The Mariners, beset by dissension, dropped Perry and infielder Todd Cruz the same day. Del Crandall, who had been managing the Dodgers' Albuquerque (Pacific Coast) farm team, succeeded Lachemann and was given a contract through 1986.

Yogi Berra returned to manage the Yankees for the second time after Owner George Steinbrenner (right) fired Billy Martin for the third time.

Firing a manager when a team occupies the cellar is common practice, but the Phillies axed Pat Corrales on July 18 with the club in first place. Although in the lead, the Phils were barely over .500 at 43-42. Phillies President Giles contended that Corrales had failed to motivate the players. General Manager Paul Owens took over as field manager and, despite some trying times, guided the Phillies to the N.L. pennant.

Corrales was out of a job only 13 days. On July 31, with Cleveland in last place in the A.L. East and sporting a 40-60 record, the Indians surprised everyone by ousting Ferraro and hiring Corrales.

"I feel like I was shot in the back," said Ferraro, who had undergone surgery for removal of a cancerous kidney in February but recovered in time to go to spring training.

Lee Elia became the season's fifth managerial casualty when the Chicago Cubs, 54-69 at the time, canned him on August 22. Charlie Fox, special assistant to General Manager Dallas Green, stepped in as manager. Elia came close to losing his job earlier in the season following a tirade against Cub fans on April 29. A month later, he was involved in a shoving match with a TV cameraman.

Four clubs announced managerial changes within a 48-hour period at the end of the season. Howard of the Mets and Harvey Kuenn of the Brewers, who led Milwaukee to the 1982 A.L. pennant, were notified on closing day that they would be replaced. Fox disclosed he would not return as the Cubs' skipper, and the Cincinnati Reds announced that Russ Nixon was finished.

The Brewers introduced Lachemann as their new manager on October 3. The following day, Vern Rapp, a coach at Montreal for the last five seasons, was named manager of the Reds, and two days later the Cubs hired Jim Frey, a coach with the Mets, as their skipper. Ironically, Nixon succeeded Rapp as a coach with the Expos.

The Mets filled their managerial vacancy on October 13 with the appointment of Dave Johnson, 40-year-old former major league infielder who led their Tidewater (International) team to the Triple-A World Series title in '83. Johnson, Rapp and Frey received two-year contracts.

The year's final managerial switch came on December 16. Confirming a long-rumored change, Steinbrenner announced that Yogi Berra would succeed Martin at the Yankee helm. Berra, a longtime coach and Yankee legend who managed the club in 1964, received a two-year contract. Steinbrenner said Martin would serve as his "top adviser."

The Berra-for-Martin move marked the 11th time in his 11 years as the Yankees' principal owner that Steinbrenner had changed managers—and it was the ninth switch in less than six years.

Martin's third term as Yankee manager, like his second, lasted less than a year. His return had become official on January 11 when Steinbrenner disclosed he had signed Martin to a five-year contract. The pact was believed worth $1.5 million, making Martin the highest-paid manager in baseball history. It was reported that about $300,000 of the total would be paid as a settlement by the Oakland A's, who fired Martin the previous October with three years remaining on a contract that paid $250,000 annually.

The Yankees hoped to capitalize on Martin's mystique and the New York fans' love affair with him. However, his frequent tirades against umpires, several run-ins with members of the press, a cocktail lounge incident and constant tinkering with the lineup led to numerous problems.

Steinbrenner admitted on June 14 that he was troubled by reports that Martin had missed workouts and team flights and was being distracted by a female companion. A meeting seemingly resolved the matter, but on June 17 Martin became involved in another job-threatening incident. He was accused of making obscene remarks while ordering Deborah Henschel, a female researcher for the New York Times, out of the Yankees' clubhouse. Following an investigation, A.L. President MacPhail and Steinbrenner decided there was no cause for disciplinary action.

Shortly after the season ended, Steinbrenner tried to lure Dodgers Manager Tommy Lasorda to the Yankees as manager-general manager, according to the New York Post. The newspaper reported the Yankee owner was prepared to offer Lasorda a five-year contract at $450,000 annually. The Dodgers scuttled all speculation on October 20 when O'Malley announced that Lasorda had accepted a three-year contract worth a reported $1 million. The multi-year pact was a sharp break in tradition for the Dodgers, who previously gave their managers only one-year contracts.

Three other managers received long-term contract extensions. In June, the Pittsburgh Pirates announced that Chuck Tanner, whose contract had another year to go, has signed a new document running through 1987. At the close of the season, the Detroit Tigers gave Sparky Anderson an extension through 1986, and in November the St. Louis Cardinals handed Herzog, who had one year remaining, a new three-year contract through 1986.

The Yankees were the focus of controversy from the outset in '83. Repair work at Yankee Stadium led to the initial hassle. Concerned that the stadium might not be ready by opening day, Steinbrenner made arrangements to play the club's first home series (April 12-14 against Detroit) in Denver. Acting on a suit brought by outraged fans, Judge Richard Lane ruled on January 10 that the Yankees had to play the series in New York.

A hassle over rent at Olympic Stadium almost forced the Montreal Expos to find another home. In 1982, the final year of a three-year agreement, the Expos paid about $2.6 million, third highest rental in the majors, according to McHale. When the provincial government's Olympic Installation Board sought an increase and the Expos rejected the proposal, the board threatened to lock the team out of the facility.

The National League immediately granted the Expos permission to seek an alternate site, but shortly before the season was to open the two sides reached a truce. In August, the Expos signed a five-year lease extending through 1987 with an option for an additional five years.

The California Angels and the Cleveland Indians also became embroiled in stadium controversies. Owner Gene Autry threatened to move the Angels from Anaheim Stadium unless the city dropped plans for a high-rise development that would take up more than half of the stadium's existing 16,000 parking spaces. The Indians were in the final season of a 10-year lease, and their dispute centered around negotiations for a new lease and improvements on deteriorating, 52-year-old Cleveland Stadium.

The Texas Rangers, meantime, finalized a lease-purchase agreement with the city of Arlington to take over Arlington Stadium on November 1, while in San Francisco city officials were considering the possibility of putting a dome on Candlestick Park at a projected cost of $70 million or building a new stadium at an estimated cost of $135 million, excluding land and financing costs.

A suggestion by Cubs General Manager Green that lights be installed at Wrigley Field created a furor in Chicago. He contended the Cubs never can be a contender while playing all home games in the daytime. His proposal drew opposition from several Chicago groups, including Citizens United for Baseball in Sunshine (CUBS). Late in the year, the state legislature passed a bill prohibiting night games at Wrigley Field.

Significant changes in club ownership occurred during the year, although only one deal involved the sale of controlling interest.

On October 10, John Fetzer announced he was selling the Detroit Tigers to Thomas S. Monaghan, an Ann Arbor, Mich., businessman, for an estimated $43 million. Under terms of the transaction, Fetzer, 82, will retain control of the club for two to five years while training the new owner.

Monaghan, 46, built his financial empire as chairman and president of the Domino's Pizza chain of more than 1,100 restaurants. Monaghan will serve as vice chairman of a three-man Tiger board of directors—Fetzer and club President Jim Campbell are the other directors—for at least two years.

In May, Royals Owner Kauffman sold 49 percent interest in the A.L. club to Avron Fogelman, 43, of Memphis, Tenn. Fogelman, a real estate developer and owner of the Memphis (Southern) club, paid $10 million for the 49 percent share, plus another $1 million for an option to purchase Kauffman's 51 percent holdings for an additional $11 million. The arrangement allows Kauffman to retain control until 1991 unless he chooses to sell sooner.

Warner Communications, one of the giants of the communications industry, acquired a 48 percent interest in the Pittsburgh Pirates in January for a reported $10 million. John Galbreath and his son Dan retained 51 percent of the club's stock, with the remaining 1 percent scattered among several investors. Several weeks earlier, the Pirates closed a deal with Warner Amex, a Warner Communications subsidiary, to carry 60 Pirate games per year on pay TV for a five-year period. The cable company also agreed to purchase 100,000 tickets for distribution to subscribers.

The death of F. J. (Steve) O'Neill, Cleveland Indians board chairman and majority owner since 1978, in late August placed the future of the Tribe in doubt. O'Neill, 83, owned more than 60 percent of the club's stock. A nephew, Patrick O'Neill, succeeded him as board chairman and on September 15 revealed the team was for sale. He estimated the club's worth at $20 million-$24 million.

Indians President Gabe Paul, who had a 5 percent equity in the club, was in charge of screening prospective buyers. Two groups of potential purchasers were led by David LeFevre, grandson of the late millionaire industrialist Cyrus Eaton and the second largest stockholder in the Houston Astros, and former major league pitcher Ken McBride, head of a Cleveland structural steel and heavy machinery firm.

Argyros gained full control of the Seattle Mariners early in the year when he purchased the 8 percent holdings of Danny Kaye, Lester Smith, Walter Schoenfeld and Stan Golub, four of the club's original owners. On May 4, brothers William and James Williams, majority owners of the Cincinnati Reds, disclosed that a limited partnership in the club had been sold to Multimedia Inc., which operates approximately 150 television and radio stations, cable franchises and newspapers.

Serious internal ownership problems and an attempted takeover by a minority group left the Boston Red Sox in year-long confusion. The squabble reached a climax when Edward (Buddy) LeRoux tried to unseat the two other general partners, General Manager Haywood Sullivan and Mrs. Yawkey, club president and widow of the club's former owner.

Claiming he found a loophole in their 1978 partnership agreement, LeRoux attempted his takeover on June 6. That also was the date of Tony Conigliaro Night, when members of Boston's 1967 Impossible Dream Team returned to Fenway Park to honor the stricken former Red Sox player.

Dick O'Connell, fired as general manager by Mrs. Yawkey in 1977, was brought in by LeRoux to replace Sullivan as G.M.

For two days, the club had two sets of owners and two general managers, but on June 8 the court granted a restraining order against the LeRoux group.

Chief Justice James P. Lynch Jr. of the Massachusetts Superior Court heard seven days of testimony in July, and three weeks later issued a 113-page ruling. It held the LeRoux takeover was illegal, barred LeRoux and his limited-partner associates (Kentucky coal magnate Rogers Badgett and attorney Albert Curran) from further such attempts and declared that the Yawkey-Sullivan team could not force LeRoux to sell his share of the club.

LeRoux, Badgett and Curran controlled 16 of the 30 limited-partner shares (in addition to LeRoux's general partnership) and owned about 42 percent of the team. At the annual partners meeting on October 28, the LeRoux group offered to sell, and a four-man committee was named to work out an appropriate purchase price.

Confusion also reigned in Minnesota. Poor attendance, an escape clause in the Twins' lease with the Hubert H. Humphrey Metrodome, a continuing rift between President Calvin Griffith and his son Clark and bids by numerous cities for the franchise caused great uncertainty.

With a gate of only 858,939, Calvin Griffith informed club directors in December that the Twins lost $1.7 million for the year, the biggest deficit in the team's history. Terms of the club's 30-year Metrodome lease permit the Twins to void the contract with one year's notice if attendance fails to average 1.4 million over a three-season span.

Late in August, the elder Griffith admitted receiving an offer of "substantially more" than $24 million from a Tampa group. The offer also reportedly included five-year contracts for Griffith family members after the move. Meanwhile, Minneapolis Chamber of Commerce officials were shaping plans aimed at selling the 2,419,000 tickets needed in 1984 to meet the three-year average of 1.4 million.

Six clubs wound up naming a new president or general manager in '83. As a successor to Lou Saban, who resigned late in 1982, the Yankees promoted Gene McHale to president in January and also gave treasurer Dave Weidler the added title of administrative vice president. The Cincinnati Reds fired Dick Wagner as president and chief executive officer on July 11 and brought back his predecessor, Bob Howsam, who had stepped down preceding the 1978 season. Jim Finks, former general manager of the Chicago Bears football team, was appointed president of the Chicago Cubs in September, succeeding Andrew McKenna, who continued as the club's chief operating officer.

The Seattle Mariners dismissed Dan O'Brien as president and general manager on October 7. Hal Keller moved up to G.M. and vice president of baseball operations, while Chuck Armstrong, who headed Argyros' real estate investment firm, became president and chief operating officer. After 24 years as Detroit's general manager, Campbell handed the G.M. duties to Bill Lajoie in September but remained as president and chief executive officer.

And on November 18, Texas Rangers Owner Chiles turned the club presidency over to Mike Stone, an executive with Chiles' Western Co. and a Ranger consultant for the last year.

Early in the year, Samuel Meason, former Mattel president, departed as executive vice president of the Rangers and was replaced by Larry Schmittou, former president of the Nashville (Southern) club. Other front-office changes prior to the season saw Tom Ferguson resign as vice president/traveling secretary of the Milwaukee Brewers: former Ohio con-

Twins Owner Calvin Griffith was plagued by a bad team and poor attendance in 1983.

gressman Ron Mottl join the Indians as special assistant to Paul; Elliott Wahle quit as Toronto Blue Jays' farm director to enter private business; Murray Cook resign as director of scouting at Pittsburgh to join the Yankees in a similar capacity; Fox give up his Montreal scouting supervisor role to become special assistant to the Cubs' Green; Willie Stargell return to the Pirates as special assistant to General Manager Harding Peterson; Leo Breen, longtime treasurer of the White Sox, join the Cubs; and Jeff Odenwald take over as vice president of marketing/advertising for the Cubs following the resignations of the husband-wife team of Bing Hampton and Patty Cox Hampton. The Hamptons returned to duties with the Oklahoma City (American Association) team they owned.

Cook was elevated to vice president and general manager of the Yankees on July 1. Four days later, Bryan Burns, director of broadcasting and marketing for the Kansas City Royals, was named director of broadcasting for the major leagues by

Kuhn. Dennis Cryder, formerly of the NCAA staff, succeeded Burns in the Kansas City job.

In August, the Oakland A's promoted Sandy Alderson to vice president of baseball operations and Clark Griffith, one of the Twins' seven vice presidents, disclosed he was taking leave from the club to enter law school in St. Paul.

Later in the summer, Karl Kuehl was appointed farm director of the Oakland A's; the Cincinnati Reds announced that Bob Howsam Jr., former New York advertising executive, would take over as vice president of marketing from Roger Ruhl, who planned to leave at the end of the season; and Gene Mauch, who quit as California manager 11 months earlier, returned to the Angels on September 17 as director of player personnel.

After the season ended, former pilot Weaver resigned as special consultant to the Orioles to sign a new contract with ABC and serve as a commentator during World Series telecasts; Dave Hersh, former general manager and part owner of Portland (Pacific Coast), was named director of minor league operations by the Yankees; Cedric Tallis resigned as executive vice president of the Yankees to become managing director of the Tampa Baseball Group (formed to seek a major league franchise); Bill Stoneman, who pitched two no-hitters for Montreal before going on to a successful banking career, returned to the Expos as an assistant to John McHale; Jim Nagourney quit as vice president/administration of the New York Mets to join the New York Islanders hockey team and was succeeded by Bob Mandt, longtime Mets ticket director and recently manager of stadium operations; and Mike Storen, former commissioner of the American Basketball Association and onetime president of the Atlanta Hawks, was named vice president of marketing and sales for the Houston Sports Association, parent company of the Astros.

The continuing escalation of player salaries and increasing losses experienced by several clubs raised concern among baseball officials in 1983. Giles, president of the Phillies, claimed collective big-league club losses of $100 million in '82, but there was anticipation, of course, that rising television revenues would reverse the trend and offset soaring player compensation.

According to figures compiled by the players' union, the Yankees had the highest average salary, $463,687, in 1983. The Phillies ranked second at $442,165, while the Angels, who had replaced the Yankees at the top of the salary structure in 1982, came in third at $389,833.

San Diego, whose payroll bulged after the signing of free agent Garvey, showed an 89.8 percent boost in average salary over 1982. The Padres' figure of $261,820 nevertheless ranked only 18th among the majors' 26 clubs.

Minnesota brought up the rear, with the Twins averaging only $97,980 per man. Overall, the average salary per major league player in 1983 was $289,194.

California's figure was expected to jump markedly in 1984 as a result of new three-year contracts given after the '83 season to three players who were eligible for free agency. The contracts will earn Bob Boone $2.75 million, Doug DeCinces $2.7 million and Brian Downing $2.025 million. The Angels paid out more than $1 million in '83 to four players who had been released—Dave Goltz, Bill Travers, Joe Ferguson and John D'Aquisto.

The Phillies' Carlton became the highest-paid pitcher in history when he signed a four-year guaranteed contract worth $4.15 million in March. The new document, replacing one that still had a year remaining, provided for a minimum $1.15 million in 1983 and $1 million in each of the next three seasons. Carlton thus joined two other Phils—Schmidt and Rose—in the million-dollar class. The Yankees also had a trio earning a million each in Kemp, Winfield and Ken Griffey.

At least 60 players had contracts calling for $750,000 or more per season. Special stipulations and covenants caused contracts to run as long as the 75-page pact written for Toronto pitcher Jim Clancy. Clancy agreed to a four-year contract worth an estimated $3 million.

In addition to the Angels' trio, seven other players who could have become free agents following the 1983 season chose to sign with their current teams after being offered contracts approaching or exceeding $2 million. Figures obtained by Murray Chass of the New York Times revealed that pitcher Honeycutt received a five-year pact totaling $3,750,000 after the Dodgers obtained him from Texas; pitcher Jerry Reuss accepted a four-year, $4.4 million deal with the Dodgers; third baseman Nettles and pitcher John Montefusco signed respective two-year, $1.8 million and three-year, $2.3 million contracts with the Yankees; pitcher Barker got a five-year, $4.5 million deal upon joining Atlanta from the Indians; pitcher Moose Haas re-signed with Milwaukee for three years and $2,062,500; and third baseman Carney Lansford signed a five-year, $5.4

million pact with Oakland. Lansford's agreement contains a controversial escape clause which allows him to seek renegotiation or become a free agent after the 1984 season.

Although not eligible for free agency, shortstop Robin Yount was signed to a lucrative and equally controversial contract by Milwaukee. The six-year, $5.55 million package includes an interest-free loan of $600,000, a $100,000 loan at a low rate, a $3 million bank loan on which the Brewers must pay any interest in excess of 16 percent, use of a car and salaries of $850,000 annually in 1984-85-86 and, if Yount chooses to exercise his option, salaries of $1 million a year in 1987-88-89.

A bench mark was established in salary arbitration in 1983. Fernando Valenzuela, the Dodgers' sensational 22-year-old left-hander, made history when he was awarded a $1 million salary by arbitrator Tom Roberts.

Altogether, 30 players submitted to salary arbitration, with the clubs winning 17 cases and the players 13. The 17 players who lost still gained a collective increase of 54 percent over their 1982 salaries. Another 57 players who filed for arbitration reached contract agreements before the process began, including infielder Paul Molitor of Milwaukee, who emerged with a five-year package worth $5.1 million.

The salaries awarded the 13 players who won their cases, according to data obtained by Chass, were as follows (club's offer in parentheses): Valenzuela, $1,000,000 ($750,000); Mario Soto, Cincinnati, $625,000 ($450,000); Ron Davis, Minnesota, $475,000 ($360,000); Doug Bair, St. Louis, $450,000 ($325,000); Damaso Garcia, Toronto, $400,000 ($300,000); Dan Petry, Detroit, $390,000 ($350,000); Tony Pena, Pittsburgh, $365,000 ($260,000); Mookie Wilson, New York Mets, $325,000 ($215,000); Tim Lollar, San Diego, $300,000 ($200,000); Jim Barr, San Francisco, $280,000 ($165,000); Rudy Law, Chicago White Sox, $220,000 ($130,000); Joe Price, Cincinnati, $210,000 ($130,000); Bobby Clark, California, $145,000 ($105,000).

The 17 who had to settle for the club's offer, with the player's requested amount in parentheses, were: Broderick Perkins, Cleveland, $125,000 ($185,000); Bruce Berenyi, Cincinnati, $150,000 ($229,000); Mike Scioscia, Los Angeles, $150,000 ($215,000); Goltz, California, $150,000 ($320,000); Roy Lee Jackson, Toronto, $155,000 ($225,000); Bobby Castillo, Minnesota, $185,000 ($350,000); Billy Sample, Texas, $215,000 ($300,000); Kirk Gibson, Detroit, $220,000 ($275,000); Aurelio Lopez, Detroit, $250,000 ($315,000); Tony Bernazard, Chicago White Sox, $252,000 ($400,000); Bill Gullickson, Montreal, $275,000 ($365,000); Dennis Lamp, Chicago White Sox, $312,500 ($750,000); Howe, Los Angeles, $325,000 ($450,000); Julio Cruz, Seattle, $425,000 ($550,000); Barker, Cleveland, $475,000 ($805,000); Lonnie Smith, St. Louis, $500,000 ($580,000); Pedro Guerrero, Los Angeles, $600,000 ($750,000).

Forty-five players opted for free agency and became eligible for the eighth annual re-entry draft. Leading choices in the selection process, conducted on November 7 at the New York Sheraton, were first baseman Darrell Evans of San Francisco and relief aces Kent Tekulve of Pittsburgh and Gossage of the Yankees. Evans was selected by 17 teams (plus his own club), the most ever for a non-pitcher, while 12 clubs picked Tekulve and 11 chose Gossage. Rights to Tekulve and Gossage also were retained by their former clubs.

Conversely, 14 players, including seven-time batting champion Rod Carew, were not selected by any of the 26 teams. Another 15 were chosen by fewer than four clubs (excluding their former teams) and thus also were free to negotiate with any team.

Some observers said the slackening interest signaled a change in management's approach to free agency and the annual bidding war. They attributed the light activity to a paucity of talent (largely the result of clubs signing their big stars to multi-year contracts to keep them from free agency) and the decision by many organizations to rely more heavily on their farm systems.

The Texas Rangers made the most selections, 13, followed by the Seattle Mariners with 12. Only the Minnesota Twins and New York Mets failed to choose anyone. With two exceptions—Derrel Thomas of Los Angeles and Gene Richards of San Diego—current clubs retained negotiating rights to their free-agent players, either through declaring their desire to keep the rights or by the fact the players were drafted by fewer than four clubs excluding their own.

Of the 45 free agents, five were rated Type A—Tekulve, Wilcox, Doug Bair, Dennis Lamp and Tom Underwood, all pitchers. Two qualified as Type B—second baseman Manny Trillo and outfielder Ruppert Jones. A team losing a Type A free agent receives compensation in the form of a professional player chosen from

After negotiating with several clubs, free-agent reliever Rich Gossage finally decided to cast his lot with the San Diego Padres.

a special pool as well as an amateur draft choice. Compensation for the loss of a Type B player consists of two amateur draft picks.

The 45 players involved in the re-entry process, with the number of teams selecting them shown in parentheses and an asterisk indicating whether the player was picked by his own team, follow:

AMERICAN LEAGUE

Baltimore—Dan Ford (6*); Boston—Doug Bird (0); California—Rod Carew (0); Chicago—Julio Cruz (7*), Jerry Koosman (8*), Dennis Lamp (6*), Aurelio Rodriguez (0); Cleveland—Bake McBride (1), Lary Sorensen (8*); Detroit—Doug Bair (2), Enos Cabell (6*), Milt Wilcox (8*); Kansas City—Don Hood (0), Jerry Martin (0), Amos Otis (1); Milwaukee—Jamie Easterly (0), Rob Picciolo (1), Ted Simmons (2); Minnesota—None; New York—Bert Campaneris (0), Oscar Gamble (8*), Goose Gossage (12*), Dale Murray (2); Oakland—Tom Underwood (1); Seattle—Steve Henderson (2); Texas—Mark Wagner (0); Toronto—Randy Moffitt (0).

NATIONAL LEAGUE

Atlanta—None; Chicago—None; Cincinnati—None; Houston—Art Howe (0), Frank LaCorte (8*), J.R. Richard (0), Denny Walling (9*); Los Angeles—Derrel Thomas (7); Montreal—Warren Cromartie (3), Dan Schatzeder (9*), Manny Trillo (1), Jerry White (0); New York—None; Philadelphia—None; Pittsburgh—Jim Bibby (1), Miguel Dilone (0), Richie Hebner (1), Dave Parker (2), Kent Tekulve (13*), Dave Tomlin (0); St. Louis—None; San Diego—Ruppert Jones (3), Gene Richards (4), Elias Sosa (1); San Francisco—Darrell Evans (18*).

The election of Brown as American League president and the agreement keeping Kuhn as commissioner through the first two months of 1984 produced the biggest headlines from the annual winter meetings, held December 5-9 in Nashville. However, a potentially more significant development was a decision by major league magnates that could lead to a pair of 16-team leagues, with the owners instructing their Long-Range Planning Committee to undertake a feasibility study on expansion.

The move brightened hopes of groups from Tampa, Indianapolis, Denver, Phoenix, Vancouver, Buffalo and St. Petersburg, Fla., all of which had representatives at the meetings. Vancouver and Indianapolis opened new domed stadiums during the summer, while Tampa, St. Petersburg and Buffalo were considering building new stadiums. The debut earlier in the year of the United States Football League and the possibility that a similar new baseball league might be formed may have spurred major league owners to act.

Members of the Long-Range Planning Committee are Buzzie Bavasi of the Angels, Sullivan of the Red Sox, Reinsdorf of the White Sox, McKenna of the Cubs, O'Malley of the Dodgers, Bronfman of the Expos and the two league presidents. The committee is chaired by the commissioner.

In other action at the winter meetings, the owners rejected a proposal that would have meant using the designated hitter in the World Series each year but only in games played in American League parks, established a committee to study the future of the designated-hitter rule during the regular season, approved a plan by which teams can share game telecasts for local pay-TV operations, okayed a motion that all clubs participate in the Major League Scouting Bureau starting in 1984 and expanded the 15-day supplementary disabled list from one player to two with one allowed to be a pitcher.

The owners also adopted an improved pension plan for non-playing club personnel, rejected a proposal for an additional waiver period starting August 1 that would have mitigated against the easy transfer of players during the stretch drive, rejected a proposal that all minor league postseason play be subject to approval by the Professional Baseball Executive Committee and elected Nelson Doubleday of the New York Mets and Eisenhardt of the Oakland A's to the majors' Executive Council, replacing San Francisco's Lurie and Boston's Sullivan.

The Official Playing Rules Committee also clarified the so-called "pine tar rule" to provide that violation shall call for ejection of the bat but not nullification of any play that results.

Ripken, 23-year-old Baltimore shortstop, emerged as the year's most honored player. Named American League Rookie of the Year in 1982, Ripken was voted the circuit's Most Valuable Player of '83 by the Baseball Writers' Association of America and also was selected the A.L. and Major League Player of the Year by The Sporting News. Kuhn was designated Man of the Year in sports by The Sporting News, while the publication bestowed other No. 1 Man of the Year designations in the majors on LaRussa of the White Sox as top manager and Peters of the Orioles as the leading executive.

With two writers from each city participating, Ripken won the BBWAA's American League MVP poll over teammate Eddie Murray. Ripken received 15 first-place votes and a total of 322 points, compared with 10 first-place votes and 290 points for runner-up Murray. In National League balloting, Atlanta's Murphy was a landslide winner over Andre Dawson of Montreal as he earned his second consecutive Most Valuable Player award and also

Atlanta outfielder Dale Murphy easily outdistanced the competition in winning his second straight MVP award in the National League.

repeated as The Sporting News' National League Player of the Year. Murphy was listed first on 21 of 24 MVP ballots to finish with 318 points, 105 more than Dawson.

Results of the MVP voting in the two leagues, based on 14 points for first place, nine for second and on down to one point for 10th place, follow:

National League

Player—Club	1	2	3	4	5	6	7	8	9	10	Pts.
Dale Murphy, Atlanta	21	2	—	—	1	—	—	—	—	—	318
Andre Dawson, Montreal	1	16	6	1	—	—	—	—	—	—	213
Mike Schmidt, Philadelphia	1	5	9	7	1	1	—	—	—	—	191
Pedro Guerrero, Los Angeles	1	1	9	9	4	—	—	—	—	—	182
Tim Raines, Montreal	—	—	—	4	4	4	1	1	2	—	83
Jose Cruz, Houston	—	—	—	1	3	5	1	5	2	3	76
Dickie Thon, Houston	—	—	—	—	6	3	2	—	3	2	67
Bill Madlock, Pittsburgh	—	—	—	—	2	1	3	3	3	1	45
Al Holland, Philadelphia	—	—	—	1	—	1	5	2	2	—	42
Terry Kennedy, San Diego	—	—	—	—	1	1	3	2	3	2	37
George Hendrick, St. Louis	—	—	—	—	—	2	3	2	2	1	33
Tony Pena, Pittsburgh	—	—	—	1	1	1	1	1	—	—	25
John Denny, Philadelphia	—	—	—	—	1	2	1	—	1	2	24
Mario Soto, Cincinnati	—	—	—	—	—	—	3	1	—	1	16
Darrell Evans, San Francisco	—	—	—	—	—	1	—	2	2	1	16
Rafael Ramirez, Atlanta	—	—	—	—	—	1	1	1	1	1	15
Jesse Orosco, New York	—	—	—	—	—	—	—	3	1	3	14
Lee Smith, Chicago	—	—	—	—	—	1	—	—	1	1½	8½
Al Oliver, Montreal	—	—	—	—	—	—	—	1	—	—	3
Jeff Leonard, Houston	—	—	—	—	—	—	—	—	1	—	2
Lonnie Smith, St. Louis	—	—	—	—	—	—	—	—	—	1½	1½
Jody Davis, Chicago	—	—	—	—	—	—	—	—	—	1	1
Keith Hernandez, St.L.-N.Y.	—	—	—	—	—	—	—	—	—	1	1
Bob Horner, Atlanta	—	—	—	—	—	—	—	—	—	1	1
Ozzie Smith, St. Louis	—	—	—	—	—	—	—	—	—	1	1

American League

Player—Club	1	2	3	4	5	6	7	8	9	10	Pts.
Cal Ripken, Baltimore	15	9	3	1	—	—	—	—	—	—	322
Eddie Murray, Baltimore	10	11	5	1	—	—	1	—	—	—	290
Carlton Fisk, Chicago	3	4	9	4	3	2	—	1	—	—	209
Jim Rice, Boston	—	2	3	9	4	2	—	2	2	1	150
Cecil Cooper, Milwaukee	—	1	3	2	3	5	4	5	1	—	123
Dan Quisenberry, Kansas City	—	—	2	2	5	4	4	3	1	½	107½
Dave Winfield, New York	—	—	—	—	4	3	6	4	4	2	85
Lou Whitaker, Detroit	—	—	1	3	2	5	2	2	1	2	84
Lance Parrish, Detroit	—	—	1	3	1	2	1	3	2	4	66
Harold Baines, Chicago	—	1	—	1	3	—	2	1	1	2	49
Willie Upshaw, Toronto	—	—	—	—	2	1	1	1	5	7½	41½
Wade Boggs, Boston	—	—	—	1	—	1	—	2	3	1	25
LaMarr Hoyt, Chicago	—	—	—	1	—	—	2½	2	—	—	23
Lloyd Moseby, Toronto	—	—	—	—	1	1	—	1	3	1	21
Bob Stanley, Boston	—	—	1	—	—	—	—	—	1	1½	11½
Alan Trammell, Detroit	—	—	—	—	—	1	1	—	1	—	11
Greg Luzinski, Chicago	—	—	—	—	—	1	1	—	—	—	9
Robin Yount, Milwaukee	—	—	—	—	—	—	1	—	1	—	6
Richard Dotson, Chicago	—	—	—	—	—	—	½	1	—	—	5
Ted Simmons, Milwaukee	—	—	—	—	—	—	1	—	—	—	4
Rudy Law, Chicago	—	—	—	—	—	—	—	—	—	2	2
Ron Guidry, New York	—	—	—	—	—	—	—	—	1	—	2
Jack Morris, Detroit	—	—	—	—	—	—	—	—	1	—	2
Julio Cruz, Chicago	—	—	—	—	—	—	—	—	—	1	1
Rickey Henderson, Oakland	—	—	—	—	—	—	—	—	—	1	1
George Wright, Texas	—	—	—	—	—	—	—	—	—	1	1
Tippy Martinez, Baltimore	—	—	—	—	—	—	—	—	—	½	½

Hoyt of the White Sox and Denny of the Phillies captured the Cy Young Awards and The Sporting News' Pitcher of the Year honors. Hoyt was the only pitcher named on every ballot in capturing the A.L.'s Cy Young prize by a 116-81 point margin over Kansas City's Quisenberry. Denny won even more overwhelmingly in the National League, finishing with 103 Cy Young points compared with 61 for runner-up Mario Soto of Cincinnati.

A breakdown of the Cy Young voting in each league, based on a 5-3-1 point system, follows:

American League

	1	2	3	Pts.
Hoyt, Chicago	17	10	1	116
Quisenberry, Kan. City	9	11	3	81
Morris, Detroit	2	5	13	38
Dotson, Chicago	-	2	3	9
Guidry, New York	-	-	5	5
McGregor, Baltimore	-	-	3	3

Five points for first-place vote, three points for second, one point for third.

National League

	1	2	3	Pts.
Denny, Philadelphia	20	1	-	103
Soto, Cincinnati	2	15	6	61
Orosco, New York	1	3	5	19
Rogers, Montreal	1	1	7	15
McWilliams, Pittsburgh	-	2	1	7
Holland, Philadelphia	-	1	1	4
McMurtry, Atlanta	-	1	-	3
Welch, Los Angeles	-	-	2	2
Ryan, Houston	-	-	1	1
Smith, Chicago	-	-	1	1

The majors' Relief Man of the Year awards went to Quisenberry and Al Holland of Philadelphia. With two points credited for each relief victory and save and one point deducted for each relief loss, Quisenberry defeated Bob Stanley of Boston, 97-72, in the American League and Holland topped Lee Smith of the Cubs, 62-56, in the National League. Meantime, The Sporting News' Fireman of the Year competition, based on one point for each relief triumph and save, found Quisenberry besting Stanley, 50-41, while Holland and Smith tied in the National League at 33.

Other award winners named by The Sporting News: A.L. Rookie Player and Pitcher of the Year—Ron Kittle of the Chicago White Sox and Mike Boddicker of Baltimore; N.L. Rookie Player and Pitcher of the Year—Darryl Strawberry of the New York Mets and Craig McMurtry of Atlanta; Comeback Player of the Year—Alan Trammell of Detroit in the A.L. and Denny in the N.L.

A.L. Cy Young Award winner LaMarr Hoyt not only led the majors with 24 victories, he led the White Sox to the A.L. West Division crown.

The All-Star Teams selected by The Sporting News for the two leagues consisted of:

American League: 1B—Eddie Murray, Baltimore; 2B—Lou Whitaker, Detroit; SS—Cal Ripken, Baltimore; 3B—Wade Boggs, Boston; OF—Jim Rice, Boston; Dave Winfield, New York, and Lloyd Moseby, Toronto; C—Carlton Fisk, Chicago; RHP—LaMarr Hoyt, Chicago; LHP—Ron Guidry, New York; DH—Greg Luzinski, Chicago.

National League: 1B—George Hendrick, St. Louis; 2B—Glenn Hubbard, Atlanta; SS—Dickie Thon, Houston; 3B—Mike Schmidt, Philadelphia; OF—Dale Murphy, Atlanta; Andre Dawson, Montreal, and Tim Raines, Montreal; C—Tony Pena, Pittsburgh; RHP—John Denny, Philadelphia; LHP—Larry McWilliams, Pittsburgh.

The Hillerich & Bradsby Silver Slugger teams consisted of:

1B—Murray, Baltimore, in the American League and Hendrick, St. Louis, in the National; 2B—Whitaker, Detroit, and Johnny Ray, Pittsburgh; SS—Ripken, Baltimore, and Thon, Houston; 3B—Boggs, Boston, and Schmidt, Philadelphia; OF—Rice, Boston; Winfield, New York, and Moseby, Toronto, in the American and Dawson, Montreal; Murphy, Atlanta, and Jose Cruz, Houston, in the National; C-Lance Parrish, Detroit, and Terry Kennedy, San Diego; P—Fernando Valenzuela, Los Angeles, and DH—Don Baylor, New York Yankees.

The Rawlings Gold Glove winners for fielding excellence, as selected by the managers and coaches, were:

1B—Murray, Baltimore, in the American League and Keith Hernandez, New York, in the National League; 2B—Whitaker, Detroit, and Ryne Sandberg, Chicago; SS—Alan Trammell, Detroit, and Ozzie Smith, St. Louis; 3B—Buddy Bell, Texas, and Schmidt, Philadelphia; OF—Winfield, New York; Dwight Evans, Boston, and Dwayne Murphy, Oakland, in the American and Dawson, Montreal; Murphy, Atlanta, and Willie McGee, St. Louis, in the National; C—Parrish, Detroit, and Pena, Pittsburgh; P—Guidry, New York, and Phil Niekro, Atlanta.

Louisville's remarkable feat of topping the million mark at the gate claimed the spotlight in the minor leagues, but Vancouver served notice that it will contend for future honors. In the first baseball game ever played in the new domed stadium in downtown Vancouver on August 12, the Canadians established a single-game Pacific Coast League attendance record of 41,875.

The Pacific Coast League also became the first Triple-A circuit to employ a woman umpire. She was Pam Postema, who had worked the two previous seasons in the Texas League. Two minor league players claimed the limelight by exceeding the record 130 stolen bases registered by Oakland's Rickey Henderson in 1982. Outfielder Vince Coleman swiped 145 bases for Macon (South Atlantic), while third baseman Donell Nixon accounted for 144 thefts for Bakersfield (California).

Kevin McReynolds blasted 32 homers and drove in 116 runs for Las Vegas of the PCL and was named TSN's Minor League Player of the Year.

Kevin McReynolds, outfielder with Las Vegas (Pacific Coast), was named winner of the Topps/National Association Player of the Year Award, while The Sporting News designated Bill Dancy of Reading (Eastern) as the minors' Manager of the Year and chose the following as Executives of the Year: Class AAA—A. Ray Smith, Louisville (American Association); Class AA—Ed Kenney, New Britain (Eastern), and Class A—Terry Reynolds, Vero Beach (Florida State).

AMERICAN LEAGUE

Including

Team Reviews of 1983 Season

Team Day-by-Day Scores

1983 Standings, Home-Away Records

1983 Official A.L. Batting Averages

1983 Official A.L. Fielding Averages

1983 Official A.L. Pitching Averages

1983 Pitching Against Each Club

Eddie Murray's big bat pounded out 33 home runs and 111 RBIs.

Weaver-less Orioles Fly High

By JIM HENNEMAN

It was supposed to be the toughest act in baseball, but Joe Altobelli and the Baltimore Orioles turned the 1983 season into a joy ride that encountered only mild bumps.

Altobelli had replaced longtime Manager Earl Weaver at the Baltimore helm, and many so-called experts expected Altobelli and the Orioles to encounter some troubled times in '83. However, the only noticeable difference in the transition was the handwriting on the lineup cards. The Orioles continued to function as a cohesive unit—a team that proved the whole can sometimes be better than the sum of its parts.

All the Orioles did during Altobelli's first year as manager was cruise to a 98-64 record to win the American League's East Division title by six games, then defeat the Chicago White Sox and Philadelphia Phillies in postseason play to give Baltimore its first world championship since 1970. In Weaver's farewell, the Orioles had lost out in the '82 A.L. East race on the final day.

There were remarkable individual performances in '83, most notably by first baseman Eddie Murray, shortstop Cal Ripken and pitchers Scott McGregor, rookie Mike Boddicker and Tippy Martinez. Still, the Orioles continued to be a team dominated by role players.

After struggling through much of the first half of the season, the Baltimore pitching staff, despite injuries to Mike Flanagan and Jim Palmer and a prolonged slump by Dennis Martinez, posted the A.L.'s second-lowest earned-run average (3.63) and led the league with 15 shutouts (five by Boddicker).

The Orioles had five players on the disabled list at one time and suffered two seven-game losing streaks (falling out of first place both times), but someone always stepped in and did a clutch job. The Birds topped the division or shared the lead for 115 of the season's 181 days, never trailed by more than three games and took the lead for good on August 26 (building an advantage that once reached 8½ games).

Altobelli, a Yankee coach in 1981 and 1982 and a longtime manager in the Orioles' minor league system, proved a masterful leader as the successor to Weaver, who had guided Baltimore since mid-1968.

The first key point of the season for Altobelli's club came May 17 when Flana-

Mike Boddicker (above) came out of nowhere to plug a hole in the Oriole pitching staff and Tippy Martinez continued his bullpen mastery.

SCORES OF BALTIMORE ORIOLES' 1983 GAMES

APRIL			Winner	Loser
4—Kan. City	L	2-7	Gura	D. Martinez
6—Kan. City	W	11-1	Flanagan	Leonard
9—At Cleve.	L	4-8	Sutcliffe	Stewart
10—At Cleve.	W	13-2	D. Martinez	Sorensen
12—At Chicago	W	10-8	Stewart	Lamp
14—At Chicago	L	11-12	Barojas	Welchel
16—Cleveland	W	2-0	Palmer	Sorensen
16—Cleveland	L	4-7	Heaton	D. Martinez
17—Cleveland	W	6-1	Flanagan	Blyleven
18—Cleveland	W	4-1	McGregor	Barker
19—Texas	W	4-2	Stewart	Hough
20—Texas	L	2-11	Smithson	D. Martinez
21—Texas	W	3-2x	Stoddard	Jones
22—At Calif.	L	5-6‡	Sanchez	Welchel
23—At Calif.	W	3-1	McGregor	John
24—At Calif.	L	3-7	Witt	D. Martinez
26—At Oak.	L	3-4	Codiroli	Palmer
27—At Oak.	W	6-0	Flanagan	Krueger
29—At Seattle	W	9-1	McGregor	Beattie
30—At Seattle	L	2-6	Stoddard	D. Martinez

Won 11, Lost 9

MAY				
1—At Seattle	W	8-2	Davis	Perry
3—California	W	4-2	Flanagan	Zahn
4—California	L	8-16	Sanchez	McGregor
6—Oakland	W	9-2	D. Martinez	Norris
7—Oakland	W	8-6	Flanagan	Codiroli
8—Oakland	L	0-1	Krueger	T. Martinez
9—Seattle	L	4-6	Beattie	McGregor
10—Seattle	W	13-2	D. Martinez	Nunez
11—Seattle	W	1-0	Flanagan	Perry
13—At Texas	W	8-1	Davis	Hough
14—At Texas	W	14-11‡	T. Martinez	Tobik
15—At Texas	L	1-2	Darwin	D. Martinez
17—Chicago	W	7-2	Stoddard	Hoyt
17—Chicago	W	5-0	Boddicker	Lamp
18—Chicago	W	1-0	T. Martinez	Dotson
19—At Toronto	W	2-1	McGregor	Morgan
20—At Toronto	L	5-7	Gott	D. Martinez
21—At Toronto	L	0-6	Stieb	Stewart
22—At Toronto	L	0-5	Clancy	Boddicker
23—Minnesota	L	4-12	Viola	Davis
24—Minnesota	L	1-6	Castillo	McGregor
25—Minnesota	L	4-7	Schrom	D. Martinez
26—At Kan. C.	L	2-8	Renko	Boddicker
27—At Kan. C.	W	7-4	Davis	Gura
28—At Kan. C.	W	1-0	McGregor	Armstrong
29—At Kan. C.	L	0-4	Splittorff	D. Martinez
30—At Minn.	W	6-1	Boddicker	Castillo
31—At Minn.	L	3-10	Schrom	Davis

Won 15, Lost 13

JUNE				
1—At Minn.	W	6-3	McGregor	Lysander
3—Toronto	W	3-2	T. Martinez	McLaughlin
4—Toronto	W	6-4	Boddicker	Stieb
5—Toronto	L	2-5	Clancy	Davis
6—Toronto	W	8-1*	McGregor	Leal
7—Milwaukee	W	6-4	D. Martinez	Caldwell
8—Milwaukee	W	7-3	Stoddard	Tellmann
9—Milwaukee	W	10-7	Boddicker	Augustine
10—At Boston	W	3-0	Davis	Hurst
11—At Boston	W	10-6	McGregor	Ojeda
12—At Boston	L	6-7	Stanley	T. Martinez
13—At Milw.	W	3-2	Ramirez	Sutton
15—At Milw.	W	11-8†	T. Martinez	Gibson
16—At Milw.	L	1-2‡	Slaton	Stoddard
17—Boston	L	3-5	Ojeda	D. Martinez
18—Boston	L	2-3	Tudor	T. Martinez
19—Boston	W	6-3	Palmer	Brown
21—New York	W	5-2	T. Martinez	Rawley
22—New York	L	2-5	Guidry	McGregor
24—Detroit	L	0-9	Petry	D. Martinez
25—Detroit	L	3-9	Bair	Palmer
26—Detroit	W	3-1	Davis	Morris
27—At N.Y.	L	3-4‡	Gossage	Stoddard
29—At N.Y.	L	0-7	Righetti	Boddicker
30—At N.Y.	L	3-4§	Gossage	Stoddard

Won 14, Lost 11

JULY			Winner	Loser
1—At Detroit	W	9-5	Davis	Wilcox
2—At Detroit	W	7-2	McGregor	Petry
3—At Detroit	L	1-10	Berenguer	Boddicker
8—Seattle	L	0-3	Beattie	Davis
9—Seattle	L	2-3†	Caudill	Stewart
10—Seattle	W	2-0	Boddicker	Young
11—Oakland	W	7-6	D. Martinez	Baker
12—Oakland	W	3-1	Ramirez	Heimueller
13—Oakland	W	6-2	Davis	Conroy
14—California	W	5-1	McGregor	Forsch
15—California	W	10-4	Boddicker	John
16—California	L	5-8	Zahn	D. Martinez
17—California	W	11-1	Ramirez	McLaughlin
18—At Seattle	W	9-4	Davis	Beattie
19—At Seattle	W	8-1	McGregor	Abbott
20—At Seattle	W	4-2	Stewart	Young
21—At Oak.	L	7-9	Beard	Morogiello
22—At Oak.	L	3-4	Burgmeier	Ramirez
23—At Oak.	W	7-3	Davis	Conroy
24—At Oak.	W	4-3	McGregor	McCatty
25—At Calif.	L	2-5	John	Boddicker
26—At Calif.	W	5-4	D. Martinez	Zahn
27—At Calif.	W	10-4	Ramirez	Witt
29—Texas	W	8-6	Stewart	Schmidt
30—Texas	W	7-4	McGregor	Smithson
31—Texas	W	6-0	Boddicker	Tanana

Won 19, Lost 7

AUGUST				
2—At Cleve.	L	1-3	Blyleven	D. Martinez
2—At Cleve.	L	3-4	Brennan	Ramirez
3—At Cleve.	W	8-2	Davis	Sutcliffe
4—At Cleve.	W	4-3†	McGregor	Anderson
5—Chicago	W	5-4	Boddicker	Lamp
6—Chicago	L	4-6	Bannister	D. Martinez
7—Chicago	L	3-4	Hoyt	Flanagan
8—Cleveland	L	4-9	Sutcliffe	Davis
9—Cleveland	L	3-4	Heaton	McGregor
10—Cleveland	L	3-4	Sorensen	Boddicker
11—At Chicago	L	3-9	Bannister	Ramirez
12—At Chicago	L	1-2	Hoyt	Flanagan
13—At Chicago	W	5-2	Stewart	Koosman
14—At Chicago	W	2-1	McGregor	Dotson
15—At Texas	W	6-4	Boddicker	Smithson
16—At Texas	L	0-2	Butcher	Ramirez
17—At Texas	W	4-2†	Flanagan	Jones
19—Kan. City	W	5-4	Stewart	Quisenberry
19—Kan. City	W	3-1	T. Martinez	Rasmussen
20—Kan. City	W	6-1	Boddicker	Gura
21—Kan. City	L	3-8	Black	Palmer
23—Toronto	L	3-9	Leal	Flanagan
24—Toronto	W	7-4†	T. Martinez	McLaughlin
25—Toronto	W	2-1†	T. Martinez	Jackson
26—Minnesota	W	9-0	Boddicker	Schrom
27—Minnesota	W	5-3	Palmer	Williams
28—Minnesota	W	11-4	Flanagan	Castillo
29—At Kan. C.	W	9-2	McGregor	Perry
30—At Kan. C.	W	12-4	Davis	Rasmussen
31—At Toronto	W	10-2	Boddicker	Gott

Won 18, Lost 12

SEPTEMBER				
1—At Toronto	L	3-5	Alexander	Palmer
2—At Minn.	W	1-0	Flanagan	Viola
3—At Minn.	W	13-0	McGregor	Schrom
4—At Minn.	W	9-6	S. Davis	R. Davis
5—Boston	L	0-2	Ojeda	Boddicker
6—Boston	W	8-1	Palmer	Eckersley
7—Boston	W	5-2	Flanagan	Boyd
9—At N.Y.	L	3-5	Guidry	McGregor
10—At N.Y.	W	8-4	Stewart	Rawley
10—At N.Y.	W	3-1	Boddicker	May
11—At N.Y.	W	5-3	Flanagan	Righetti
13—At Boston	W	7-4§	Stewart	Stanley
13—At Boston	W	7-1	Swaggerty	Nipper
14—At Boston	W	5-0	D. Martinez	Tudor
15—At Boston	L	1-7	Hurst	Davis
16—Milwaukee	W	8-1	Boddicker	Candiotti
17—Milwaukee	W	5-4	Flanagan	Gibson
18—Milwaukee	W	10-9	T. Martinez	Ladd
19—Milwaukee	W	8-7‡	Stoddard	Tellmann
20—At Detroit	L	1-14*	Petry	D. Martinez
21—At Detroit	W	6-0	Boddicker	Morris
21—At Detroit	W	7-3	Stewart	Gumpert
22—At Detroit	L	4-5†	Bair	Stewart
23—At Milw.	W	4-2	McGregor	Gibson
24—At Milw.	L	2-5	Cocanower	D. Martinez
25—At Milw.	W	5-1	Davis	Porter
27—Detroit	L	2-9	Morris	McGregor
28—Detroit	L	5-9	Petry	Boddicker
29—Detroit	L	4-9	Wilcox	Flanagan
30—New York	L	4-6	Montefusco	Davis
30—New York	W	3-2	Palmer	Howell

Won 20, Lost 11

OCTOBER				
1—New York	L	4-5§	Gossage	Swaggerty
2—New York	W	2-0	Boddicker	Rawley

Won 1, Lost 1

*5 innings. †10 innings. ‡11 innings. §12 innings. x14 innings.

gan, off to a 6-0 start, went down with a knee injury in the first game of a doubleheader against the White Sox. But Boddicker, making his first start after being summoned from the minors as a roster replacement for Palmer (sidelined because of stiffness in his neck, back and side), gave an indication of things to come by shutting out Chicago in the nightcap as the Orioles swept the twin bill.

Ten days later, after Baltimore had dropped to fourth place following a two-game A.L. East lead, Storm Davis ended the Orioles' first seven-game losing streak with a strong effort in Kansas City and McGregor followed with a two-hitter the next night against the Royals.

The Orioles had another two-game divisional lead preceding their second seven-game skid, which came in August and again dropped them to fourth place. Bill Swaggerty, making his first major league appearance, held the White Sox to two runs in six innings on August 13 and Ripken's two-run homer in the eighth inning was the big blow as the losing streak ended in a 5-2 victory.

Beginning with that triumph in Chicago and culminating with their A.L. East-clinching victory in Milwaukee on September 25, the Orioles won 34 of 44 games, a .773 stretch that began with a 26-of-32 victory surge. Included were two straight 10-inning victories at home against the still-contending Toronto Blue Jays—and they were wins that typified the Orioles' season.

The first came on August 24 when the Orioles scored twice with two out in the ninth to tie the game. In the 10th, with Baltimore infielder Lenn Sakata pressed into duty as a catcher, the Blue Jays took a 4-3 lead before Tippy Martinez came in and picked three straight Jays off first base. Sakata then won the game with a three-run homer in the bottom of the 10th.

The next night, the last evening the Orioles would spend out of first place, Dan Ford's two-run double with one out in the 10th gave Baltimore a 2-1 win.

Last-chance victories were common during the Orioles' title drive. The Birds needed five straight singles with two out in the ninth to beat the White Sox, 5-4, on August 5. They scored six runs in the ninth to beat the Yankees, 8-4, in the first game of a doubleheader sweep on September 10. And on September 18-19, John Stefero, a catcher recalled for the stretch drive, singled in the ninth and 11th innings to beat the Brewers in successive games.

Murray and Ripken were phenomenal down the stretch. Murray, who finished with 33 home runs, 111 runs batted in and a .306 average, hit nine home runs, drove in 32 runs and scored 32 in his last 37 games.

Ripken, who played every inning at shortstop, hit .394 with 10 homers, 30 RBIs and 42 runs scored in his last 43 games. He wound up leading the league in runs (121), hits (211) and doubles (47) while batting .318.

The Orioles socked a major league-leading 168 homers and had eight grand slams (all after July 12).

The Orioles' outfield platoon system again played a major role in the club's success as John Lowenstein and Gary Roenicke combined for 34 home runs and 124 RBIs as the left fielders, and Al Bumbry and John Shelby teamed for 27 stolen bases and 115 runs scored while sharing center field. Right fielder Ford batted .280 and his backup, Jim Dwyer, hit .286.

Perhaps the most unsung Oriole was designated hitter Ken Singleton, who bounced back from a poor 1982 performance and drove in 84 runs, hit 18 homers, batted .276 and drew 99 walks.

Neither second baseman Rich Dauer, third baseman Todd Cruz (who joined the club at midseason) nor catcher Rick Dempsey had big offensive numbers, but all three were vital defensively. Joe Nolan (.277) boosted the bottom of the order as an occasional replacement for Dempsey.

McGregor (18-7 record, 3.18 ERA) and Boddicker (16-8, 2.77) were the standouts among the starting pitchers. During Flanagan's absence, McGregor won 11 of 13 decisions. Davis finished with a 13-7 mark, and Flanagan won six of 10 decisions after his return for a 12-4 record.

In the bullpen, Tippy Martinez was the unquestioned leader despite missing three weeks because of an appendectomy. The lefthander, who worked in 65 games, finished with a career-high 21 saves. He was nearly invincible in his last 37 appearances, compiling a 5-0 record, 12 saves and a 1.34 ERA. Sammy Stewart struggled through the first half, but finished strong with seven straight victories in one stretch and season totals of nine wins and seven saves.

It all added up to a team that produced more than 90 victories for the 13th time in the last 16 seasons; won its seventh divisional title, sixth A.L. pennant and third World Series crown, and drew a Baltimore record season attendance of 2,041,349.

Not a bad haul, especially considering it was supposed to be a season of adjustment.

Jack Morris hurdled a mental barrier by posting the first 20-victory season of his career.

Tigers Shed 'Mediocre' Label

By TOM GAGE

Try as he might, Sparky Anderson could not come up with many complaints about the 1983 Detroit Tigers.

He called them a bad baserunning team, the worst he has ever had. Terrible bunters, too.

Then Anderson sat back, smiled and savored everything that went right in the Tigers' best season since 1972 (the year in which Detroit won its only American League divisional championship).

No longer was Detroit a fourth-place team whose mediocrity matched its anonymity. The Tigers finally were heard from.

For one thing, they finished second in the A.L. East, breaking a string of fourth- and fifth-place finishes that dated to 1976 (excluding a tie for second in the second half of 1981's split season). In 1974 and 1975, the Tigers were a sixth-place team.

The Tigers won 92 games in '83, their highest total in 15 years. But they still finished six games behind the Baltimore Orioles.

"If anybody had told me at the start of the season we would win 92 games and still end up six games out, I wouldn't have believed them," Anderson said. "I thought you would win with a record like that. Shows you how smart I am."

The Tigers thought Anderson was bright enough, however. They gave him an extension of his contract through 1986 as soon as the season was over, which was one week after the front office underwent a major change.

Jim Campbell, general manager for the last 21 years, took over as chief executive officer while retaining the position of president, and Bill Lajoie became general manager.

"I'm not retiring," said Campbell, who had open heart surgery in 1982, "but doctors have suggested that I slow down."

On the field, the Tigers treated May 25 like opening day. In a sense, they didn't start playing until then. Detroit was in last place at the time with a 17-22 record, then went 75-48.

"If we hadn't spent so much time getting started," said Enos Cabell, "it might have been a different ending. I'd say it was a learning year."

Three Tigers—Lou Whitaker, Larry Herndon and Cabell—learned how to hit .300, and Alan Trammell reached that figure for the second time in his career. Lance Parrish attained 100 runs batted in for the first time (finishing with 114), and another Tiger discovered how to win 20 games.

Lou Whitaker joined the American League elite with his .320 average and 206 hits.

Whitaker led the Tigers with a .320 average, becoming the first lefthanded hitter to have 200 hits for Detroit since Dick Wakefield in 1943. Whitaker also drove in 72 runs from his leadoff position.

"That's the thing which astounds me the most," said Anderson. "Seventy-two RBIs from your leadoff hitter is like 100 anywhere else."

Trammell enjoyed his finest season at the plate, hitting .319, and he became the first Tiger shortstop to steal 30 bases since Donie Bush swiped 34 in 1917.

Cabell hit .311 and provided leadership, while Herndon checked in at .302 as he completed his second straight productive year for Detroit with 20 home runs and 92 RBIs.

Parrish didn't bat .300, but he slugged 27 home runs and compiled the second-highest RBI total for a Detroit player since 1961.

Among the pitching exploits was Jack Morris' 20-13 record. Morris entered September at 17-8 after winning Pitcher of the Month honors for August when he won

SCORES OF DETROIT TIGERS' 1983 GAMES

APRIL

			Winner	Loser
5—At Minn.	W	11-3	Morris	Havens
6—At Minn.	W	9-5	Petry	Lysander
7—At Minn.	L	4-5	Williams	Ujdur
8—Chicago	L	3-6	Lamp	Wilcox
10—Chicago	L	5-7	Hoyt	Morris
12—At N.Y.	W	13-2	Petry	Guidry
13—At N.Y.	W	7-5	Bailey	Frazier
14—At N.Y.	L	3-6	Righetti	Morris
15—At Chicago	W	6-0	Wilcox	Hoyt
16—At Chicago	L	1-3	Bannister	Bailey
17—At Chicago	L	1-6	Lamp	Ujdur
20—Kan. City	L	7-8	Quisenberry	Bailey
22—Seattle	W	4-0	Wilcox	Stoddard
23—Seattle	W	4-0	Petry	Moore
24—Seattle	W	4-2	Morris	Nunez
27—At Calif.	L	3-13	Zahn	Wilcox
29—At Oak.	L	4-5	Baker	Morris

Won 8, Lost 9

MAY

1—At Oak.	L	3-8	Codiroli	Ujdur
1—At Oak.	L	0-2	Norris	Wilcox
3—At Seattle	W	2-1‡	Lopez	Caudill
4—At Seattle	L	1-5	Beattie	Morris
6—California	L	2-4	Kison	Wilcox
7—California	L	5-6§	Sanchez	Lopez
8—California	W	5-1	Morris	Forsch
10—Oakland	W	4-3	Rucker	Langford
11—Oakland	W	5-2	Wilcox	Norris
12—Oakland	L	4-11	Burgmeier	Petry
13—At Kan. C.	L	2-5	Leonard	Morris
14—At Kan. C.	W	11-10	Rozema	Hood
15—At Kan. C.	W	6-4‡	Lopez	Renko
16—New York	L	0-7	Guidry	Petry
17—New York	L	5-7‡	Gossage	Lopez
18—New York	L	4-6	Righetti	Rucker
19—Texas	W	2-1†	Wilcox	Smithson
20—Texas	L	0-4	Darwin	Ujdur
21—Texas	W	5-3	Petry	Honeycutt
22—Texas	W	12-5	Berenguer	Butcher
23—At Toronto	L	0-4	Leal	Wilcox
24—At Toronto	L	6-7	Jackson	Rucker
25—At Toronto	W	6-2	Petry	Gott
27—Minnesota	W	7-4	Pashnick	Lysander
27—Minnesota	W	2-1§	Bailey	Lysander
28—Minnesota	W	6-1	Wilcox	Williams
29—Minnesota	W	7-6	Lopez	Lysander
30—Toronto	L	4-6†	McLaughlin	Gumpert

Won 14, Lost 14

JUNE

1—Toronto	W	3-1	Rozema	Clancy
2—Toronto	L	1-6	Leal	Wilcox
3—At Texas	W	12-1	Morris	Smithson
4—At Texas	L	2-5	Hough	Petry
5—At Texas	W	5-4†	Lopez	Butcher
6—At Boston	W	11-6	Berenguer	Stanley
7—At Boston	W	4-2	Wilcox	Tudor
8—At Boston	W	6-3	Morris	Boyd
9—At Boston	W	8-2	Petry	Eckersley
10—Cleveland	W	7-1	Rozema	Sorensen
11—Cleveland	L	1-9	Eichelberger	Pashnick
12—Cleveland	W	4-1	Wilcox	Blyleven
12—Cleveland	W	3-1	Morris	Barker
14—Boston	L	2-6	Brown	Petry
15—Boston	W	4-2	Rozema	Eckersley
16—Boston	W	10-2	Berenguer	Hurst
17—At Cleve.	W	11-4	Morris	Barker
18—At Cleve.	L	8-12	Sutcliffe	Wilcox
19—At Cleve.	L	2-7	Sorensen	Petry
20—Milwaukee	W	4-1	Rozema	Porter
21—Milwaukee	L	3-10	Haas	Berenguer
22—Milwaukee	W	6-2	Morris	Caldwell
24—At Balt.	W	9-0	Petry	D. Martinez
25—At Balt.	W	9-3	Bair	Palmer
26—At Balt.	L	1-3	Davis	Morris
28—At Milw.	W	5-4	Lopez	Slaton
29—At Milw.	L	3-4	Ladd	Lopez
30—At Milw.	L	1-4	McClure	Morris

Won 18, Lost 10

JULY

			Winner	Loser
1—Baltimore	L	5-9	Davis	Wilcox
2—Baltimore	L	2-7	McGregor	Petry
3—Baltimore	W	10-1	Berenguer	Boddicker
8—Oakland	W	3-2	Bair	Baker
9—Oakland	L	1-3	McCatty	Morris
10—Oakland	W	5-3	Bailey	Beard
11—California	W	12-6	Rozema	Zahn
12—California	W	5-4x	Bailey	Witt
13—California	W	7-1	Petry	Kison
14—At Seattle	W	4-2	Morris	Abbott
15—At Seattle	L	2-7	Young	Berenguer
16—At Seattle	L	0-1	Moore	Lopez
17—At Seattle	W	8-1†	Bair	Caudill
18—At Oak.	W	4-2	Petry	Conroy
19—At Oak.	W	4-3	Morris	Beard
20—At Oak.	L	2-9	Codiroli	Bair
21—At Calif.	W	5-1	Bailey	Witt
21—At Calif.	L	2-3	Zahn	Rozema
22—At Calif.	W	13-11	Wilcox	McLaughlin
23—At Calif.	W	7-2	Petry	Kison
24—At Calif.	W	4-3§	Lopez	Sanchez
26—Seattle	W	8-3	Rozema	Young
27—Seattle	L	3-5	Moore	Bair
28—Seattle	W	6-1	Petry	Clark
29—Kan. City	W	10-1y	Morris	Gura
30—Kan. City	W	4-1	Berenguer	Black
31—Kan. City	W	8-6	Rozema	Splittorff
31—Kan. City	L	5-7	Armstrong	Bailey

Won 19, Lost 9

AUGUST

1—Kan. City	W	3-2	Lopez	Hood
2—At Chicago	L	5-7	Hoyt	Petry
3—At Chicago	W	6-3	Morris	Koosman
4—At Chicago	L	2-4	Dotson	Bair
5—At N.Y.	L	3-12	Righetti	Rozema
6—At N.Y.	L	3-13	Fontenot	Bailey
7—At N.Y.	W	8-5	Petry	Keough
8—Chicago	L	4-5	Burris	Berenguer
8—Chicago	W	7-2	Morris	Koosman
9—Chicago	L	5-6	Lamp	Lopez
11—New York	L	5-6†	Gossage	Bailey
12—New York	W	7-6†	Bair	Murray
13—New York	W	6-3	Morris	Guidry
14—New York	L	1-4	Rawley	Berenguer
15—At Kan. C.	L	4-6	Gura	Pashnick
16—At Kan. C.	L	7-18	Huismann	Rozema
17—At Kan. C.	W	10-4	Petry	Huismann
19—At Minn.	W	5-1	Morris	Castillo
20—At Minn.	W	9-1	Berenguer	Viola
21—At Minn.	L	3-4	Schrom	Pashnick
22—At Texas	L	1-3	Tanana	Petry
23—At Texas	W	2-0	Bair	Hough
24—At Texas	W	5-2	Morris	Cruz
25—Chicago	W	10-1	Berenguer	Burns
26—Toronto	W	4-3†	Lopez	Gott
27—Toronto	L	4-7	Alexander	Lopez
28—Toronto	W	4-2	Morris	McLaughlin
29—Minnesota	L	4-5‡	Lysander	Lopez
30—Minnesota	W	4-3	Petry	Schrom
31—Texas	L	1-5	Butcher	Abbott

Won 15, Lost 15

SEPTEMBER

1—Texas	W	5-0	Morris	Tanana
2—At Toronto	W	9-8†	Lopez	Gott
2—At Toronto	L	7-8	Acker	Wilcox
3—At Toronto	W	7-4	Petry	Clancy
4—At Toronto	L	3-6†	Stieb	Lopez
5—At Cleve.	L	2-3	Anderson	Morris
7—At Cleve.	L	1-7	Sorensen	Wilcox
7—At Cleve.	W	7-3	Petry	Camacho
9—At Milw.	L	1-2	Haas	Morris
9—At Milw.	W	2-1	Abbott	Slaton
10—At Milw.	W	4-0	Berenguer	Candiotti
11—At Milw.	W	6-4	Petry	Vuckovich
12—Cleveland	W	5-1	Wilcox	Blyleven
13—Cleveland	W	3-2	Morris	Behenna
14—Cleveland	W	5-0	Abbott	Sutcliffe
16—At Boston	L	1-6	Ojeda	Petry
17—At Boston	L	2-3	Eckersley	Morris
18—At Boston	W	9-6	Wilcox	Boyd
20—Baltimore	W	14-1*	Petry	D. Martinez
21—Baltimore	L	0-6	Boddicker	Morris
21—Baltimore	L	3-7	Stewart	Gumpert
22—Baltimore	W	5-4†	Bair	Stewart
23—Boston	W	7-0	Berenguer	Eckersley
24—Boston	L	3-5	Tudor	Petry
25—Boston	W	3-2	Bair	Boyd
27—At Balt.	W	9-2	Morris	McGregor
28—At Balt.	W	9-5	Petry	Boddicker
29—At Balt.	W	9-4	Wilcox	Flanagan
30—Milwaukee	L	2-6	Gibson	Berenguer

Won 18, Lost 11

OCTOBER

1—Milwaukee	L	1-10	Cocanower	Morris
2—Milwaukee	L	4-7	Porter	Petry

Won 0, Lost 2

*5 innings. †10 innings. ‡11 innings. §12 innings. x14 innings. ySuspended game, completed July 30.

Alan Trammell returned to the ranks of .300 hitters and emerged as a dangerous baserunner.

six games without a loss. But his final month mirrored the frustration the Tigers encountered.

After posting his 18th victory on September 1, Morris won only two of his last seven starts, losing three one-run games in the process.

"The best thing about winning 20," Morris said, "is that I can now forget about it. The mental part is over. It's out of my mind.

"I always thought I was capable of it. But I had to prove it."

Dan Petry had a chance to join Morris as a 20-game winner on the final day of the season, but lost, 7-4, to the Milwaukee Brewers.

Battle as they did in September, the Tigers could not close the gap between first and second place. Seven of their last 13 games were against Baltimore, however, so they retained hope as long as possible.

"Nobody has to tell us the consequences of losing a game," Anderson said at the time. "We have to win all seven." Instead, the Tigers went 5-2 against the Orioles and lost four of their other six games in the season's final two weeks.

Detroit's last hurrah was an 11-run first inning against the Orioles in the first of the seven head-to-head games. The outburst included 10 consecutive hits, interrupted only by a walk.

"Did you ever feel your hands were tied behind your back and there was a fly on your nose?" asked Baltimore Manager Joe Altobelli. "That's how that inning felt."

The next night (September 21), however, the Birds swept a doubleheader and the Tigers—8½ games behind as a result—looked to second place as a consolation.

There was other solace in the season.

Milt Wilcox pitched the game of his career on April 15, coming within an out of a perfect game against the Chicago White Sox in Comiskey Park. Pinch-hitter Jerry Hairston singled to center field, though, making Wilcox settle for a one-hitter.

Juan Berenguer came off the scrapheap—he entered the season with a 3-17 major league record—to establish himself as one of the Tigers' returning starters for 1984. Berenguer was 9-5 with a 3.14 ERA and struck out 129 batters in 157⅔ innings. Morris led the league with 232 strikeouts.

Chet Lemon starred in the Tigers' two most dramatic games of the season. He stole a game-winning home run away from Rod Carew on a sensational catch with two out in the ninth at Anaheim on July 24, then beat Toronto, 4-2, with a three-run homer on August 28, also with two out in the ninth.

Aurelio Lopez was one of the league's more dominant relief pitchers with 16 saves and seven victories through August 1 before slumping in the final two months.

And Dave Rozema bounced back from a career-threatening knee injury to post an 8-3 record.

"Overall, I was very pleased," said Anderson. "Anytime you win 90 games or more there can't be much wrong. But we have to pick up six games somewhere."

In other words, second place was nice—but not nice enough.

Ace lefthander Ron Guidry posted the second 20-victory season of his Yankee career.

Wild, Wild Yankees Fall Short

By MOSS KLEIN

The New York Yankees added numerous episodes to their book of controversies during the 1983 season—but failed to add to their winning tradition.

The season was filled with Yankee-style commotion: Owner George Steinbrenner was fined $50,000 by Commissioner Bowie Kuhn and suspended for one week by American League President Lee MacPhail for incidents involving umpires; Manager Billy Martin was suspended twice for a total of five games by MacPhail, also for run-ins with umpires; several star players were critical of Steinbrenner and Martin and expressed desires to become former Yankees; and rumors circulated periodically that Martin, who had returned for his third reign as Yankees manager, was on the verge of being fired.

Add to that the historic Pine Tar Game, which dragged on for nearly a month, and the Sea Gull Episode, in which Dave Winfield stirred up an international incident when he accidentally killed a sea gull at Toronto's Exhibition Stadium in August, and it becomes apparent this was another vintage season in the Bronx Zoo.

Along the way, the Yankees managed to show improvement from 1982, when they had finished fifth in the A.L. East with a 79-83 record, the lowest finish by a Yankee team since 1969 and the club's worst record since 1967. With Martin back in control and Winfield, Don Baylor, Graig Nettles, Ken Griffey and pitchers Ron Guidry and Dave Righetti enjoying outstanding seasons, the Yankees posted a 91-71 record and finished third.

The excitement reached a fever pitch on September 10 when a crowd of 55,605—a regular-season record since Yankee Stadium was reopened in 1976 after two years of renovation—attended a doubleheader against the first-place Baltimore Orioles. The Yankees had won the opener of the four-game series the previous night and a doubleheader sweep would have reduced Baltimore's lead over New York to two games. But Baltimore won both games and took the series finale the next day, knocking the Yankees seven games back.

The season was viewed by Steinbrenner as a disappointment, even though the Yankees' attendance climbed to 2,256,663, an increase of more than 215,000 over 1982. "I'm never satisfied unless we win the World Series," said Steinbrenner. "I think we had the best material. We had injuries, but the Orioles had injuries, too."

The Yankees started slowly and had a 29-30 record on June 14 when rumors of Martin's firing began. But Martin and attorney Eddie Sapir held a midnight meeting with Steinbrenner at a Cleveland restaurant and settled their problems, although Steinbrenner insisted on firing pitching coach Art Fowler, Martin's longtime coach and friend. The Yankees won 12 of their next 17 games, with Righetti pitching a no-hitter July 4 against the Boston Red Sox to bring the team to a high note before the All-Star break.

But despite fine individual efforts, the Yankees couldn't catch Baltimore. Winfield batted .283 with 32 homers and 116 runs batted in—the highest RBI total by a Yankee since 1961 when Roger Maris had 142 and Mickey Mantle 128. Baylor, in his first Yankee season after receiving a four-year, $3.675 million free-agent contract, batted .303 with 21 homers and 85 RBIs. Third baseman Nettles, whom Martin kept in the lineup against Steinbrenner's wishes early in the season, had his best year since 1978, batting .266 with 20 homers and 75 RBIs.

Guidry posted the second 20-victory season of his career, going 21-9. Righetti, a victim of minimal run support in the second half, finished at 14-8. Shane Rawley was an effective third starter with a 14-14 record, and rookie Ray Fontenot, the fourth lefthander in the rotation, contributed an 8-2 mark after coming up from Columbus (International) in June. Righthander John Montefusco, a late-season addition, made six starts and compiled a 5-0 record.

Rich Gossage, not quite as formidable as in years past, managed a 13-5 record and 22 saves despite blowing 13 save opportunities. But except for George Frazier (eight saves), Gossage had little help in the bullpen.

Martin blamed the failure to win the East on a series of injuries. First baseman Griffey, who adjusted surprisingly well to his new position and batted .306, was sidelined nearly six weeks because of a hamstring pull, and second baseman Willie Randolph was out five weeks with knee and hamstring injuries. Guidry missed three weeks with back spasms, reliever Rudy May was out 10 weeks with a back injury and veteran outfielder Lou Piniella missed most of the last two months because of dizzy spells.

SCORES OF NEW YORK YANKEES' 1983 GAMES

APRIL

			Winner	Loser
5—At Seattle	L	4-5	Clark	Erickson
6—At Seattle	L	2-6	Young	Shirley
7—At Seattle	W	8-1	Righetti	Stoddard
9—At Toronto	L	4-7	Jackson	Gossage
10—At Toronto	W	3-0	Rawley	Stieb
12—Detroit	L	2-13	Petry	Guidry
13—Detroit	L	5-7	Bailey	Frazier
14—Detroit	W	6-3	Righetti	Morris
15—Toronto	L	5-6	Stieb	May
17—Toronto	W	7-5	Rawley	Clancy
18—Toronto	W	3-0	Guidry	Leal
19—At Chicago	L	3-13	Dotson	Howell
20—At Chicago	W	6-4	Righetti	Hoyt
22—Minnesota	L	3-5	Havens	Alexander
23—Minnesota	W	7-4	Rawley	O'Connor
25—Minnesota	W	2-1	Guidry	Viola
26—Kan. City	L	4-10	Gura	Righetti
27—Kan. City	W	6-0	Shirley	Leonard
29—At Texas	L	3-8	Honeycutt	Rawley
30—At Texas	L	3-6	Hough	Guidry

Won 9, Lost 11

MAY

1—At Texas	W	8-4	Righetti	Smithson
2—At Kan. C.	L	1-4	Leonard	Shirley
3—At Kan. C.	L	2-5	Splittorff	Alexander
4—At Kan. C.	W	8-1	Rawley	Blue
6—At Minn.	W	8-4	Guidry	O'Connor
7—At Minn.	W	8-7	Frazier	Williams
8—At Minn.	L	5-6	Whitehouse	Murray
10—Texas	L	2-4	Tanana	Rawley
11—Texas	L	1-3	Honeycutt	Guidry
13—Chicago	W	3-1	Righetti	Dotson
14—Chicago	W	8-5	Shirley	Burns
15—Chicago	L	3-7	Bannister	Rawley
16—At Detroit	W	7-0	Guidry	Petry
17—At Detroit	W	7-5†	Gossage	Lopez
18—At Detroit	W	6-4	Righetti	Rucker
20—At Oak.	L	4-8	Underwood	Shirley
21—At Oak.	W	1-0	Rawley	Norris
22—At Oak.	W	4-2	Guidry	Burgmeier
23—At Calif.	L	0-3	Zahn	Righetti
24—At Calif.	L	6-7*	Witt	May
25—At Calif.	L	1-7	John	Rawley
27—Oakland	W	4-2	Guidry	Norris
28—Oakland	W	5-2	Righetti	Codiroli
29—Oakland	W	5-0	May	Krueger
30—Oakland	W	10-5	Gossage	Burgmeier
31—California	W	5-3	Murray	Witt

Won 16, Lost 10

JUNE

1—California	W	3-0	Guidry	Goltz
2—California	L	8-9	Sanchez	May
3—Seattle	L	0-5	Young	Howell
4—Seattle	L	4-5	Beattie	Shirley
5—Seattle	L	7-8	Clark	Rawley
6—Seattle	W	6-2	Guidry	Vande Berg
7—Cleveland	L	1-2*	Heaton	Gossage
8—Cleveland	W	6-5	Gossage	Spillner
10—At Milw.	W	7-1	Rawley	Haas
11—At Milw.	L	2-6	McClure	Guidry
12—At Milw.	L	5-6‡	Tellmann	May
13—At Cleve.	L	0-9	Sutcliffe	Howell
14—At Cleve.	L	6-9	Sorensen	Shirley
15—At Cleve.	W	8-5	Rawley	Eichelberger
16—At Cleve.	W	8-1	Guidry	Blyleven
17—Milwaukee	W	7-2	Righetti	Caldwell
18—Milwaukee	W	5-4	Frazier	Gibson
19—Milwaukee	W	8-3	Keough	Waits
21—At Balt.	L	2-5	T. Martinez	Rawley
22—At Balt.	W	5-2	Guidry	McGregor
24—At Boston	L	4-5	Tudor	Righetti
25—At Boston	W	4-1	Howell	Eckersley
26—At Boston	L	5-12	Hurst	Keough
27—Baltimore	W	4-3†	Gossage	Stoddard
29—Baltimore	W	7-0	Righetti	Boddicker
30—Baltimore	W	4-3‡	Gossage	Stoddard

Won 14, Lost 12

JULY

			Winner	Loser
1—Boston	W	12-8	Shirley	Johnson
2—Boston	L	4-10	Hurst	Keough
3—Boston	L	3-7	Ojeda	Rawley
4—Boston	W	4-0	Righetti	Tudor
8—At Kan. C.	W	9-2	Rawley	Gura
9—At Kan. C.	L	2-3†	Quisenberry	Gossage
10—At Kan. C.	W	6-4	Fontenot	Splittorff
11—At Minn.	L	2-4	Castillo	Howell
12—At Minn.	W	4-3	Frazier	Lysander
13—At Minn.	L	1-6	Schrom	Guidry
14—Texas	L	2-11	Hough	Rawley
15—Texas	W	7-5	Righetti	Honeycutt
16—Texas	W	3-1	Fontenot	Smithson
17—Texas	W	8-6	Murray	Jones
18—Minnesota	W	4-2	Guidry	Williams
19—Minnesota	W	4-0	Rawley	Castillo
20—Minnesota	W	6-4*	Gossage	Davis
22—Kan. City	W	7-6	Gossage	Armstrong
22—Kan. City	L	2-3‡	Quisenberry	Frazier
23—Kan. City	W	5-1	Guidry	Gura
24—Kan. City	L	4-5y	Armstrong	Gossage
25—At Texas	W	6-5	Gossage	Butcher
26—At Texas	W	5-0	Fontenot	Tanana
27—At Texas	W	4-3	Keough	Hough
29—At Chicago	L	2-7	Koosman	Guidry
30—At Chicago	L	1-5	Dotson	Rawley
31—At Chicago	W	12-6†	Gossage	Lamp

Won 17, Lost 10

AUGUST

1—At Chicago	L	1-4	Bannister	Fontenot
2—At Toronto	L	9-10*	Jackson	Murray
2—At Toronto	L	6-13	Williams	Shirley
3—At Toronto	L	2-6	Clancy	Guidry
4—At Toronto	W	3-1	Rawley	Stieb
5—Detroit	W	12-3	Righetti	Rozema
6—Detroit	W	13-3	Fontenot	Bailey
7—Detroit	L	5-8	Petry	Keough
8—Toronto	W	8-3	Guidry	Clancy
8—Toronto	W	11-3	Shirley	Williams
9—Toronto	L	0-8	Stieb	Rawley
10—Toronto	W	8-3	Righetti	Gott
11—At Detroit	W	6-5*	Gossage	Bailey
12—At Detroit	L	6-7*	Bair	Murray
13—At Detroit	L	3-6	Morris	Guidry
14—At Detroit	W	4-1	Rawley	Berenguer
15—Chicago	L	0-1	Burns	Righetti
16—Chicago	L	3-5	Bannister	Fontenot
17—Chicago	L	5-7§	Barojas	Murray
19—California	W	11-6	Guidry	Forsch
20—California	W	6-2	Rawley	John
21—California	W	2-1	Gossage	Zahn
22—Oakland	L	2-3x	Beard	Frazier
23—Oakland	L	3-9	Warren	Keough
24—Seattle	W	6-3	Guidry	Clark
25—Seattle	W	7-4	Rawley	Beattie
26—At Calif.	W	3-2	Righetti	Zahn
27—At Calif.	L	6-7	S. Brown	Gossage
28—At Calif.	W	7-3	Montefusco	Forsch
30—At Oak.	W	8-5	Guidry	Beard
31—At Oak.	W	6-4	Rawley	Conroy

Won 17, Lost 14

SEPTEMBER

1—At Oak.	L	0-2	Codiroli	Righetti
2—At Seattle	W	5-4	Fontenot	Young
3—At Seattle	W	5-3	Montefusco	Moore
4—At Seattle	W	4-3	Guidry	Clark
5—At Milw.	L	1-3	Candiotti	Rawley
6—At Milw.	L	3-6	Slaton	Righetti
7—At Milw.	W	11-5	Fontenot	Porter
8—At Milw.	W	6-5	Shirley	Caldwell
9—Baltimore	W	5-3	Guidry	McGregor
10—Baltimore	L	4-8	Stewart	Rawley
10—Baltimore	L	1-3	Boddicker	May
11—Baltimore	L	3-5	Flanagan	Righetti
12—Milwaukee	W	1-0	Fontenot	Porter
13—Milwaukee	W	2-1	Gossage	Caldwell
14—Milwaukee	W	4-1	Guidry	Sutton
17—At Cleve.	L	6-7	Easterly	Frazier
18—At Cleve.	L	6-10	Jeffcoat	Righetti
18—At Cleve.	W	13-8	Fontenot	Behenna
19—At Boston	L	3-5	Tudor	Guidry
20—At Boston	W	3-2	Montefusco	Hurst
21—At Boston	L	1-3	Ojeda	Shirley
23—Cleveland	W	7-4	Frazier	Easterly
24—Cleveland	W	9-1	Guidry	Sutcliffe
25—Cleveland	W	6-4	Montefusco	Barnes
26—Cleveland	L	0-7	Heaton	Shirley
27—Boston	W	7-2	Keough	Hurst
28—Boston	L	2-3	Ojeda	Rawley
29—Boston	W	4-3	Guidry	Tudor
30—At Balt.	W	6-4	Montefusco	Davis
30—At Balt.	L	2-3	Palmer	Howell

Won 17, Lost 13

OCTOBER

1—At Balt.	W	5-4‡	Gossage	Swaggerty
2—At Balt.	L	0-2	Boddicker	Rawley

Won 1, Lost 1

*10 innings. †11 innings. ‡12 innings. §13 innings. x14 innings. ySuspended game, completed August 18.

The big bats of Dave Winfield (above) and Don Baylor gave the Yankees plenty of punch.

Steve Kemp, who had received a five-year, $5.45 million free-agent contract, had several minor injuries, eventually lost his right-field job to rookie Don Mattingly and was sidelined for the season with a fractured left cheekbone after being struck by a line drive hit by teammate Omar Moreno during batting practice on September 8. Kemp, whose three previous full seasons (excluding strike-shortened 1981) had produced a .298 batting mark and an average of 22 homers and 101 RBIs per year, slumped to .241 with 12 homers and 49 RBIs.

The injury that hurt the Yankees the most occurred in the early morning hours of August 18 when shortstop Andre Robertson was involved in an auto wreck on New York's West Side Highway. Robertson suffered a fractured neck, a dislocated left shoulder, a broken rib and severe contusions and lacerations. The slick defensive player had won the shortstop job from veteran Roy Smalley early in the season and became the key to the infield.

After Robertson's accident, Smalley returned to shortstop and played effectively most of the time (contributing 18 homers and 62 RBIs). Still, Smalley's defense was lacking.

Ironically, Robertson's accident occurred 12 hours before the completion of the Pine Tar Game, the Yankees' biggest headache of the season. On July 24, Kansas City's George Brett hit a two-run homer off Gossage with two out in the ninth inning at Yankee Stadium, giving the Royals a 5-4 lead. But Martin, prodded by the alert Nettles, showed the umpires that Brett's bat had pine tar beyond the legal limit of 18 inches up the handle. While the fans and players waited breathlessly, the umpires discussed the situation and then umpire Tim McClelland called Brett out, ending the game.

But the incident had only just begun. Kansas City protested and MacPhail, citing the "spirit of the rules," overturned the umpires' decision and said the game must be completed from the point of the homer. Steinbrenner and Martin protested loudly and the case wound up in two New York courts before the game was finally completed on August 18 before a gathering of 1,200 fans at Yankee Stadium. The Yankees went down in order in the ninth inning against Dan Quisenberry, and the Pine Tar Game became history.

The Yankees, without Robertson, then won 14 of their next 20 games before the showdown against Baltimore. Guidry won the series opener, 5-3, as Nettles hit a tie-breaking homer in the eighth inning, moving the Yankees within four games of first place. But that turned out to be the last hurrah in another Yankee season filled with sound and fury.

First baseman Willie Upshaw hit .306 and became the first Blue Jay ever to drive in 100 runs.

Blue Jays Finally Grow Up

By NEIL MacCARL

Season No. 7 was a fun year not only for the Blue Jays but for Blue Jay watchers, who turned out in greater numbers than ever before.

Toronto fans were ready with the chant "We're No. 1" when the Blue Jays soared to the top of the American League East in late May. And when the weather turned nice in June, the spectators turned their excitement into a season-long celebration.

Sure, everyone was disappointed when a leak in the bullpen let the air out of the balloon at the end of August, but all was forgiven. The fans proved the point when 40,692 attended the meaningless season finale against the Minnesota Twins.

The fans set Toronto records for season attendance (1,930,292, an average of 25,069 per date) and best single date (with 45,102 swelling Exhibition Stadium for an August 2 doubleheader sweep over the New York Yankees).

"I really enjoyed this year," Manager Bobby Cox said of the 1983 season. "We led for almost six weeks, and that's something. It was a lot of fun to be on top. We had a good year except for a bad week when we just got beat in the late innings."

Toronto posted its first winning A.L. season (89-73) and highest finish (fourth place). Cox's team finished only three games out of second place.

The Blue Jays hit better than ever before. Their .277 team average tied for the major league lead. They also demonstrated surprising power by hitting 167 home runs, just one fewer than the Baltimore Orioles (who led the majors).

Exhibition Stadium was the launching pad for more home runs, 185, than any park in the big leagues. The Jays, who hit only 106 homers overall in 1982, accounted for 101 in their home park in 1983, with outfielder Jesse Barfield hitting 22 of his 27 at Exhibition Stadium.

Willie Upshaw shared the team homer lead with Barfield. Designated hitter Cliff Johnson contributed 22 homers, Lloyd Moseby 18 and Ernie Whitt 17.

Upshaw batted .306 and set a team record with 104 runs batted in.

"I guess that puts me in a class with the big boys," said Upshaw after becoming the first Jay in history to knock in 100.

Moseby blossomed as a hitter. Although he started the season being platooned, the lefthanded batter soon became a regular and established a team record with a .315 average, hitting better than .300 against lefthanders and righthanders. Moseby also became the first Jay to score 100 runs (finishing with 104) and stole 27 bases.

Lloyd Moseby blossomed into a star, hitting .315 and becoming the first Blue Jay ever to score 100 runs.

Barry Bonnell, who played all three outfield positions without being a regular, finished with Toronto's top average, .318, but batted officially only 377 times. Second baseman Damaso Garcia, who hit .310 in 1982, came back with a .307 season, although a sore knee hurt his stolen base production (it dropped from 54 to 31).

Before the season started, Cox anticipated a total of 100 steals from Garcia and newcomer Dave Collins (who also finished with 31); however, both players were hob-

SCORES OF TORONTO BLUE JAYS' 1983 GAMES

APRIL

			Winner	Loser
5—At Boston	W	7-1	Stieb	Eckersley
7—At Boston	L	4-7	Stanley	Leal
9—New York	W	7-4	Jackson	Gossage
10—New York	L	0-3	Rawley	Stieb
12—Milwaukee	L	5-6	Sutton	Morgan
13—Milwaukee	W	7-2	Clancy	Caldwell
14—Milwaukee	L	4-5	Slaton	McLaughlin
15—At N.Y.	W	6-5	Stieb	May
17—At N.Y.	L	5-7	Rawley	Clancy
18—At N.Y.	L	0-3	Guidry	Leal
19—Cleveland	W	9-7	Moffitt	Spillner
20—Cleveland	W	4-1	Stieb	Sorensen
22—At Kan. C.	L	5-6	Leonard	Jackson
23—At Kan. C.	W	5-4	Moffitt	Quisenberry
24—At Kan. C.	L	1-7	Renko	Gott
26—At Texas	L	1-2	Smithson	Stieb
27—At Texas	W	3-2	Moffitt	Darwin
29—Chicago	L	3-9	Dotson	Leal

Won 8, Lost 10

MAY

			Winner	Loser
1—Chicago	W	8-0	Stieb	Bannister
2—Texas	W	6-5	Clancy	Darwin
3—Texas	L	2-7	Matlack	Gott
4—Texas	W	7-1	Leal	Honeycutt
6—Kan. City	W	6-1	Stieb	Gura
7—Kan. City	W	7-4	Jackson	Leonard
8—Kan. City	L	1-6	Renko	Gott
9—At Chicago	W	6-1	Leal	Burns
11—At Chicago	W	3-1‡	Stieb	Hoyt
12—At Cleve.	W	6-3	Clancy	Sorensen
13—At Cleve.	L	1-5	Eichelberger	Morgan
14—At Cleve.	W	8-1	Leal	Blyleven
16—At Milw.	W	2-1§	Stieb	McClure
17—At Milw.	L	6-9	Caldwell	Clancy
18—At Milw.	L	6-7	Slaton	Geisel
19—Baltimore	L	1-2	McGregor	Morgan
20—Baltimore	W	7-5	Gott	D. Martinez
21—Baltimore	W	6-0	Stieb	Stewart
22—Baltimore	W	5-0	Clancy	Boddicker
23—Detroit	W	4-0	Leal	Wilcox
24—Detroit	W	7-6	Jackson	Rucker
25—Detroit	L	2-6	Petry	Gott
26—Boston	L	2-7	Stanley	Stieb
27—Boston	L	0-2	Tudor	Clancy
28—Boston	W	9-5	Jackson	Aponte
29—Boston	W	6-1†	Gott	Eckersley
30—At Detroit	W	6-4‡	McLaughlin	Gumpert

Won 18, Lost 9

JUNE

			Winner	Loser
1—At Detroit	L	1-3	Rozema	Clancy
2—At Detroit	W	6-1	Leal	Wilcox
3—At Balt.	L	2-3	T. Martinez	McLaughlin
4—At Balt.	L	4-6	Boddicker	Stieb
5—At Balt.	W	5-2	Clancy	Davis
6—At Balt.	L	1-8*	McGregor	Leal
7—At Oak.	L	3-5	Conroy	Gott
8—At Oak.	W	5-2	Stieb	Codiroli
9—At Oak.	L	1-3	Underwood	Clancy
10—At Calif.	L	3-5	C. Brown	Leal
11—At Calif.	W	3-2	Gott	Goltz
12—At Calif.	W	6-5z	Clarke	C. Brown
14—Oakland	W	13-7	Jackson	Underwood
15—Oakland	L	1-10	Krueger	Leal
16—Oakland	W	9-1	Gott	McCatty
17—California	W	6-3	Stieb	Travers
18—California	L	6-7	Sanchez	Clarke
19—California	W	6-1	Leal	Goltz
20—Minnesota	W	2-1	Gott	Davis
21—Minnesota	W	8-3	Acker	Oelkers
22—Minnesota	L	3-4	Schrom	Stieb
23—At Seattle	W	5-4	Clancy	Stanton
24—At Seattle	W	4-2	Leal	Young
25—At Seattle	L	2-5	Beattie	Gott
26—At Seattle	W	19-7	Acker	Stoddard
28—At Minn.	L	2-5	Schrom	Stieb
29—At Minn.	W	4-2	Clancy	Castillo
30—At Minn.	W	11-3	Leal	Williams

Won 16, Lost 12

JULY

			Winner	Loser
1—Seattle	L	2-11	Beattie	Gott
2—Seattle	W	7-6	Jackson	Caudill
3—Seattle	L	1-4	Abbott	Stieb
8—Texas	W	8-5	Clancy	Darwin
9—Texas	W	5-1	Leal	Hough
10—Texas	W	6-4	Stieb	Honeycutt
11—At Kan. C.	W	7-4§	Moffitt	Creel
12—At Kan. C.	W	9-6	Jackson	Renko
13—At Kan. C.	L	4-5	Gura	Clancy
14—At Chicago	W	8-0	Leal	Koosman
15—At Chicago	W	3-2	McLaughlin	Dotson
16—At Chicago	W	7-5	McLaughlin	Agosto
17—At Chicago	L	2-3	Bannister	Alexander
18—Kan. City	W	8-2	Clancy	Gura
19—Kan. City	L	2-6	Black	Leal
20—Kan. City	L	8-14	Splittorff	Stieb
21—At Texas	L	2-3	Tanana	Gott
22—At Texas	W	10-5§	Moffitt	Schmidt
23—At Texas	W	3-2	Clancy	Darwin
24—At Texas	L	0-3	Honeycutt	Leal
25—Chicago	L	4-7	Dotson	Stieb
26—Chicago	W	6-4	Gott	Burns
26—Chicago	L	3-4	Bannister	Alexander
27—Chicago	L	3-11	Hoyt	Leal
29—Cleveland	W	4-2	Clancy	Sutcliffe
30—Cleveland	W	6-5y	McLaughlin	Anderson
31—Cleveland	L	11-16	Eichelberger	Acker

Won 15, Lost 12

AUGUST

			Winner	Loser
1—Cleveland	L	0-6	Barker	Alexander
2—New York	W	10-9‡	Jackson	Murray
2—New York	W	13-6	Williams	Shirley
3—New York	W	6-2	Clancy	Guidry
4—New York	L	1-3	Rawley	Stieb
5—At Milw.	L	0-7	Haas	Gott
6—At Milw.	L	0-3	Porter	Alexander
7—At Milw.	L	6-9	Caldwell	Leal
8—At N.Y.	L	3-8	Guidry	Clancy
8—At N.Y.	L	3-11	Shirley	Williams
9—At N.Y.	W	8-0	Stieb	Rawley
10—At N.Y.	L	3-8	Righetti	Gott
11—Milwaukee	L	4-6	Porter	Alexander
12—Milwaukee	W	5-4	McLaughlin	Slaton
13—Milwaukee	W	3-1	Clancy	McClure
14—Milwaukee	W	4-3	Stieb	Ladd
15—At Cleve.	W	3-2	Moffitt	Spillner
16—At Cleve.	L	2-3	Easterly	Moffitt
16—At Cleve.	W	9-6	McLaughlin	Anderson
17—At Cleve.	W	6-5‡	McLaughlin	Sutcliffe
19—At Boston	W	8-7	Acker	Clear
20—At Boston	L	2-5	Eckersley	Stieb
21—At Boston	W	7-3	Gott	Hurst
22—At Boston	L	2-4	Ojeda	Alexander
23—At Balt.	W	9-3	Leal	Flanagan
24—At Balt.	L	4-7‡	T. Martinez	McLaughlin
25—At Balt.	L	1-2‡	T. Martinez	Jackson
26—At Detroit	L	3-4‡	Lopez	Gott
27—At Detroit	W	7-4	Alexander	Lopez
28—At Detroit	L	2-4	Morris	McLaughlin
29—Boston	W	5-1	Clancy	Tudor
29—Boston	L	7-8	Clear	Moffitt
30—Boston	L	4-5x	Johnson	Jackson
31—Baltimore	L	2-10	Boddicker	Gott

Won 15, Lost 19

SEPTEMBER

			Winner	Loser
1—Baltimore	W	5-3	Alexander	Palmer
2—Detroit	L	8-9‡	Lopez	Gott
2—Detroit	W	8-7	Acker	Wilcox
3—Detroit	L	4-7	Petry	Clancy
4—Detroit	W	6-3‡	Stieb	Lopez
5—California	W	7-0	Gott	Zahn
6—California	W	6-4	Alexander	Curtis
7—California	L	6-9	Sanchez	Geisel
9—Oakland	L	5-7	McCatty	Clancy
10—Oakland	W	7-5	Stieb	Underwood
11—Oakland	W	16-6	Gott	Codiroli
13—At Seattle	W	6-4	Leal	Stoddard
14—At Seattle	W	4-3	Alexander	Thomas
15—At Minn.	L	2-6	Schrom	Stieb
16—At Minn.	L	4-11	Lysander	Gott
17—At Minn.	W	13-3	Leal	Pettibone
19—Seattle	L	6-9	Young	Geisel
20—Seattle	W	7-3	Stieb	Moore
21—Seattle	W	4-3	Alexander	Clark
23—At Oak.	L	0-2	Conroy	Leal
24—At Oak.	L	1-2‡	Warren	Clancy
25—At Oak.	W	8-6	Acker	Atherton
26—At Calif.	W	3-2‡	Alexander	Lacey
27—At Calif.	L	1-7	McLaughlin	Leal
28—At Calif.	W	5-3	Clancy	Witt
30—Minnesota	W	8-0	Stieb	Viola

Won 16, Lost 10

OCTOBER

			Winner	Loser
1—Minnesota	W	4-3	Alexander	Pettibone
2—Minnesota	L	3-9	Williams	Clancy

Won 1, Lost 1

*5 innings. †6 innings. ‡10 innings. §11 innings. x12 innings. y13 innings. z15 innings.

Ace Dave Stieb ran into late-season problems, but still won 17 games.

bled by injuries, especially in the first half of the season. But the Jays turned on the power, and Cox was not forced to rely on a running game.

Toronto's greatest improvement was the run production from its designated hitters. The Jays jumped from worst to first, with veterans Johnson and Jorge Orta totaling 32 home runs and 114 RBIs. In 1982, the Jays' DH platoon hit eight home runs and drove in 56 runs.

Cox continued to platoon at third base and behind the plate, and the results were positive.

Third basemen Rance Mulliniks and Garth Iorg accounted for 56 doubles, eight triples and a dozen homers (10 by Mulliniks). Both batted .275 and they drove in 88 runs.

Catchers Whitt and Buck Martinez had 29 doubles, 27 homers and drove in 89 runs.

Tony Fernandez, the heralded switch-hitting shortstop from the Dominican Republic, finally arrived in September after hitting .300 for two seasons in Triple-A. But Alfredo Griffin, the Jays' shortstop since 1979, played in every game for the second straight year.

The Jays thought they had better pitching depth than ever after acquiring Mike Morgan from the New York Yankees to go with holdovers Dave Stieb, Jim Clancy, Luis Leal and Jim Gott. But Morgan failed to win a game. He had tenderness in his shoulder and pitched only 45⅓ innings.

Stieb won eight of his first 10 decisions. In July, though, a blister on the middle finger of his pitching hand restricted the use of his best pitch, a slider. Stieb still led the team in victories (17), shutouts (four), complete games (14) and earned-run average (3.04).

Clancy won 15 games. Leal couldn't win in April, but was unbeatable in May; he collected 13 victories in his up-and-down year. Gott was the Jays' best pitcher in spring training, so plans to make him a short reliever were shelved. However, Gott's 9-14 record did not show the improvement expected.

The big surprise was veteran Doyle Alexander, a castoff from the New York Yankees. Alexander lost his first six decisions for the Jays after going 0-2 for the Yankees, but Cox kept giving him the ball. The righthander justified the confidence, winning his last seven decisions.

The bullpen was suspect because of concern over Joey McLaughlin's shoulder problem in 1982 and the loss of Dale Murray in a trade. But National League castoff Randy Moffitt quickly took over Murray's spot, McLaughlin showed no indication of arm trouble and Roy Lee Jackson was effective overall.

The Jays were seldom out of a game because of good starting pitching and an offense that was capable of playing catch-up, and they won their first nine extra-inning games.

The week that wrecked everything started in Baltimore on August 24 when Clancy had a 3-1 lead entering the ninth. The Orioles tied the score, but Johnson homered for the Jays in the 10th. Toronto got three more runners (Bonnell, Collins and Upshaw) on base in that inning and each was eager to run on Baltimore's Lenn Sakata, an infielder who had been pressed into catching duty. However, Orioles reliever Tippy Martinez picked off all three runners and Baltimore went on to hand Toronto its first extra-inning defeat of the season when Cal Ripken homered off McLaughlin and Sakata connected against Moffitt in the bottom of the 10th.

In the next six days, the Jays lost three more times in extra innings and twice in the ninth.

One horrendous week aside, though, 1983 was clearly a year in which the Blue Jays learned how to win.

Power Dropoff Kills Brewers

By TOM FLAHERTY

In the not too distant past, the Milwaukee Brewers would have considered an 87-75 season a huge success, prompting celebrations in the offices at County Stadium.

But that was in the pre-1978 years, when the Brewers were still a struggling expansion club. After winning the American League pennant in 1982, the fall to fifth place in the A.L. East in 1983 was a disaster for Milwaukee.

There was a major casualty. Harvey Kuenn, the toast of the town the year before when he took over a struggling team and led it to the World Series, was fired at the end of the season. He was replaced by Rene Lachemann, who had been fired earlier in 1983 by the Seattle Mariners.

The '83 Brewers were faced with two major problems at the start when they lost pitchers Rollie Fingers and Pete Vuckovich, the 1981 and 1982 Cy Young Award winners.

When spring training opened, the big question was, "How's Rollie?" Fingers, who had missed the final month of the 1982 season with a torn muscle in his right forearm, appeared to be recovered from the injury and hopes were high. However, a new injury was soon discovered—a bone spur in his right elbow—and Fingers underwent surgery and didn't pitch all season.

Shortly after opening camp, the Brewers discovered that Vuckovich had a severe rotator-cuff tear. He missed most of the season, making just three starts and finishing with a 0-2 record.

Despite the loss of two star pitchers, Milwaukee's biggest problem turned out to be hitting. After slugging 216 home runs in 1982 and becoming known as Harvey's Wallbangers, the Brewers hit only 132 in '83 and a lack of run production wasted some good pitching down the stretch.

Gorman Thomas, who had shared the league lead in home runs in '82, was traded to Cleveland in early June for outfield defensive specialist Rick Manning. With Thomas' big bat missing from the lineup, Cecil Cooper and Ted Simmons proved the only consistent run producers for the Brewers.

Cooper shared the A.L. lead with 126 runs batted in and hit 30 home runs while batting .307, the seventh straight year he had reached .300. Simmons had his best season as a Brewer, hitting .308 and driving in 108 runs.

Robin Yount also batted .308, but he was hampered by a bad back during the last half of the season and didn't drive the ball the way he had in '82 and the first half of '83. Paul Molitor, who was batting around .300 in late August, went into a tailspin and finished at .269. Ben Oglivie, slowed by a rash of injuries all season, batted .280 but hit only 13 home runs and drove in only 66 runs.

Despite all their problems, the Brewers survived a shaky start and made a bid to repeat as division titlists. After falling into last place on June 22, they started to resemble the champions of the year before when they raced through July with a 20-8 record.

Cooper, who hit .366 with 10 home runs and 39 RBIs during July, led the charge. Pete Ladd, who had spent a month with the Brewers' Triple-A Vancouver farm club after a bad start, developed into the stopper the Brewers had been looking for in the bullpen. Ladd saved seven games and won two in July and finished the season with 25 saves—23 after his recall on June 21.

The Brewers went on to win nine of their first 13 games in August, shooting to the top of the glove-tight East Division. And Milwaukee was in first place by a half-game on August 25 before the team went into a three-week batting slump and won only six of its next 24 games, finishing the dive with 10 consecutive losses.

The final defeat in the losing streak officially eliminated the Brewers from the pennant race.

The Brewers had more pitching problems at the end of the season. Moose Haas, who finished with a 13-3 record and a 3.27 earned-run average, missed most of the last month with a sore arm. Bob McClure, who had a disappointing 9-9 mark after the Brewers re-signed him as a free agent, pulled a muscle in his side on August 20 and was out for the rest of the season.

Jim Slaton, who won his first five decisions, led the club in victories with 14. Another effective pitcher was reliever Tom Tellmann, who had a 9-4 record, eight saves and a 2.80 ERA.

Veteran Don Sutton, victimized by little batting support, pitched better than his record (8-13, 4.08 ERA) indicated.

For almost everybody, though, 1983 was a major disappointment. One high note was the Brewers' record attendance of 2,397,131, which even surpassed the totals of the Braves' glory years in Milwaukee.

Cecil Cooper continued his devastating consistency, hitting .307 with 30 home runs and 126 RBIs.

SCORES OF MILWAUKEE BREWERS' 1983 GAMES

APRIL

5—At Calif.	L	2-3	Kison	Sutton
6—At Calif.	L	3-4	John	Caldwell
7—At Calif.	W	5-3	Augustine	Witt
9—At Kan. C.	L	2-5	Gura	McClure
10—At Kan. C.	W	9-5	Tellmann	Armstrong
12—At Toronto	W	6-5	Sutton	Morgan
13—At Toronto	L	2-7	Clancy	Caldwell
14—At Toronto	W	5-4	Slaton	McLaughlin
15—Kan. City	L	3-4	Gura	McClure
17—Kan. City	W	6-3	Caldwell	Renko
18—At Boston	W	14-0	Sutton	Brown
20—At Boston	L	4-5	Clear	Ladd
22—At Texas	L	2-3	Darwin	McClure
23—At Texas	W	3-0	Caldwell	Honeycutt
24—At Texas	W	3-1	Sutton	Hough
26—Chicago	W	4-3	Slaton	Hickey
27—Chicago	W	6-2	Tellmann	Bannister
29—At Minn.	L	4-7	Havens	McClure
30—At Minn.	L	7-9	Davis	Ladd

Won 10, Lost 9

MAY

1—At Minn.	W	8-4	Sutton	Williams
2—At Chicago	W	8-4	Slaton	Hoyt
3—At Chicago	L	6-7	Dotson	Porter
4—At Chicago	L	2-3	Lamp	McClure
6—Texas	L	4-9	Butcher	Caldwell
8—Texas	W	6-3	Slaton	Jones
10—Minnesota	W	4-1	Haas	Havens
11—Minnesota	W	4-1	McClure	Williams
12—Boston	L	3-5	Brown	Caldwell
14—Boston	W	8-7*	Gibson	Clear
15—Boston	L	1-6	Ojeda	Haas
16—Toronto	L	1-2†	Stieb	McClure
17—Toronto	W	9-6	Caldwell	Clancy
18—Toronto	W	7-6	Slaton	Geisel
20—At Seattle	W	4-3	Tellmann	Clark
21—At Seattle	L	4-5	Clark	McClure
22—At Seattle	W	6-0	Caldwell	Perry
23—At Oak.	L	4-5y	Baker	Slaton
24—At Oak.	L	7-8	Keough	Easterly
25—At Oak.	W	7-6	Haas	Underwood
27—Seattle	L	5-7	Perry	Tellmann
28—Seattle	L	3-4	Vande Berg	Slaton
29—Seattle	L	4-6	Young	Sutton
30—Seattle	W	6-3	Augustine	Beattie
31—Oakland	W	5-2	Haas	Conroy

Won 13, Lost 12

JUNE

1—Oakland	L	5-7	Burgmeier	Porter
2—Oakland	W	6-1	Caldwell	Codiroli
3—California	L	0-3	Forsch	Sutton
4—California	L	3-8	John	Augustine
5—California	W	5-4	Haas	Hassler
6—California	W	9-7	McClure	Goltz
7—At Balt.	L	4-6	D. Martinez	Caldwell
8—At Balt.	L	3-7	Stoddard	Tellmann
9—At Balt.	L	7-10	Boddicker	Augustine
10—New York	L	1-7	Rawley	Haas
11—New York	W	6-2	McClure	Guidry
12—New York	W	6-5‡	Tellmann	May
13—Baltimore	L	2-3	Ramirez	Sutton
15—Baltimore	L	8-11*	T. Martinez	Gibson
16—Baltimore	W	2-1†	Slaton	Stoddard
17—At N.Y.	L	2-7	Righetti	Caldwell
18—At N.Y.	L	4-5	Frazier	Gibson
19—At N.Y.	L	3-8	Keough	Waits
20—At Detroit	L	1-4	Rozema	Porter
21—At Detroit	W	10-3	Haas	Berenguer
22—At Detroit	L	2-6	Morris	Caldwell
24—Cleveland	W	6-2	Sutton	Sorensen
25—Cleveland	W	7-2	Slaton	Eichelberger
26—Cleveland	W	4-3	Tellmann	Blyleven
28—Detroit	L	4-5	Lopez	Slaton
29—Detroit	W	4-3	Ladd	Lopez
30—Detroit	W	4-1	McClure	Morris

Won 12, Lost 15

JULY

			Winner	Loser
1—At Cleve.	W	11-10	Caldwell	Eichelberger
2—At Cleve.	W	6-5	Haas	Blyleven
3—At Cleve.	L	2-5	Sutcliffe	Porter
4—At Cleve.	W	8-3	Sutton	Barker
8—At Chicago	W	4-3	McClure	Hoyt
9—At Chicago	L	3-8	Koosman	Sutton
10—At Chicago	W	12-9	Slaton	Barojas
11—At Texas	L	4-5x	Tobik	Augustine
12—At Texas	W	9-2	Porter	Tanana
13—At Texas	W	6-2	McClure	Darwin
14—Minnesota	W	5-1	Sutton	Williams
15—Minnesota	W	6-3	Caldwell	Castillo
16—Minnesota	W	5-0	Haas	Viola
17—Minnesota	W	10-6	Porter	Schrom
18—Texas	W	4-3	Augustine	Darwin
18—Texas	W	5-4	Tellmann	Hough
19—Texas	L	1-3	Honeycutt	Sutton
20—Texas	W	4-3	Tellmann	Smithson
21—Chicago	W	7-6	Ladd	Agosto
22—Chicago	L	1-2	Bannister	Porter
23—Chicago	W	8-7	McClure	Hoyt
24—Chicago	W	8-7	Ladd	Tidrow
25—At Minn.	L	3-17	Viola	Caldwell
26—At Minn.	L	5-6	Whitehouse	Tellmann
27—At Minn.	W	13-9	Slaton	Havens
29—At Boston	W	11-5	McClure	Eckersley
30—At Boston	L	5-10	Tudor	Sutton
31—At Boston	W	7-5	Haas	Stanley

Won 20, Lost 8

AUGUST

1—At Boston	W	6-2	Porter	Ojeda
2—Kan. City	W	5-1	Gibson	Perry
2—Kan. City	W	3-2	Caldwell	Gura
3—Kan. City	L	5-8	Creel	McClure
4—Kan. City	L	2-6	Black	Sutton
5—Toronto	W	7-0	Haas	Gott
6—Toronto	W	3-0	Porter	Alexander
7—Toronto	W	9-6	Caldwell	Leal
8—At Kan. C.	L	4-5	Gura	Slaton
8—At Kan. C.	W	8-5	McClure	Renko
9—At Kan. C.	L	2-8	Black	Sutton
10—At Kan. C.	W	4-0	Haas	Splittorff
11—At Toronto	W	6-4	Porter	Alexander
12—At Toronto	L	4-5	McLaughlin	Slaton
13—At Toronto	L	1-3	Clancy	McClure
14—At Toronto	L	3-4	Stieb	Ladd
15—Boston	W	2-0	Haas	Hurst
16—Boston	W	4-3§	Slaton	Clear
17—Boston	W	4-3*	Tellmann	Ojeda
17—Boston	W	5-1	Candiotti	Johnson
19—Oakland	L	1-9	Conroy	Sutton
20—Oakland	W	3-1	Tellmann	McCatty
21—Oakland	W	7-1	Haas	Codiroli
22—Seattle	W	3-2*	Porter	Stoddard
23—Seattle	L	0-5	Moore	Caldwell
24—California	W	1-0§	Slaton	Hassler
25—California	W	7-0	Candiotti	John
26—At Oak.	L	3-4	Codiroli	Haas
27—At Oak.	L	2-5	Heimueller	Porter
28—At Oak.	W	4-2	Caldwell	Warren
29—At Seattle	L	1-2	Clark	Sutton
30—At Seattle	W	3-2	Candiotti	Beattie
31—At Seattle	L	1-4	Stoddard	Vuckovich

Won 20, Lost 13

SEPTEMBER

2—At Calif.	L	5-6	Steirer	Waits
3—At Calif.	W	4-3	Caldwell	Witt
4—At Calif.	L	3-5	John	Sutton
5—New York	W	3-1	Candiotti	Rawley
6—New York	W	6-3	Slaton	Righetti
7—New York	L	5-11	Fontenot	Porter
8—New York	L	5-6	Shirley	Caldwell
9—Detroit	W	2-1	Haas	Morris
9—Detroit	L	1-2	Abbott	Slaton
10—Detroit	L	0-4	Berenguer	Candiotti
11—Detroit	L	4-6	Petry	Vuckovich
12—At N.Y.	L	0-1	Fontenot	Porter
13—At N.Y.	L	1-2	Gossage	Caldwell
14—At N.Y.	L	1-4	Guidry	Sutton
16—At Balt.	L	1-8	Boddicker	Candiotti
17—At Balt.	L	4-5	Flanagan	Gibson
18—At Balt.	L	9-10	T. Martinez	Ladd
19—At Balt.	L	7-8†	Stoddard	Tellmann
20—At Cleve.	W	11-7	Slaton	Anderson
21—At Cleve.	W	10-7	Sutton	Heaton
22—At Cleve.	L	5-9	Sorensen	Candiotti
23—Baltimore	L	2-4	McGregor	Gibson
24—Baltimore	W	5-2	Cocanower	D. Martinez
25—Baltimore	L	1-5	Davis	Porter
27—Cleveland	W	8-4	Caldwell	Sorensen
28—Cleveland	W	6-4	Slaton	Easterly
29—Cleveland	L	2-4	Sutcliffe	Candiotti
30—At Detroit	W	6-2	Gibson	Berenguer

Won 10, Lost 18

OCTOBER

1—At Detroit	W	10-1	Cocanower	Morris
2—At Detroit	W	7-4	Porter	Petry

Won 2, Lost 0

*10 innings. †11 innings. ‡12 innings. §14 innings. x15 innings. y17 innings.

Pitching Pulls Down Red Sox

By JOE GIULIOTTI

The 1983 Red Sox had the leading hitter in the major leagues and the American League's home run champion. They had the majors' co-leader in runs batted in (plus a second player with more than 100 RBIs) and a relief pitcher with 33 saves.

But they also had a team earned-run average of 4.34 (third worst in the league), only 19 home runs from lefthanded batters (10 from 44-year-old Carl Yastrzemski), no pitcher with more than 13 victories, a losing record at home (38-43) and a one-man bullpen.

The negatives far outweighed the positives and the team ended with its first losing record in 17 years (Boston had the longest active plus-.500 stretch in the majors). The Red Sox, 78-84, finished in sixth place, 20 games behind the East Division-winning Baltimore Orioles.

Boston also had its share of injuries to key personnel, the most damaging being to rookie righthander Mike Brown, who suffered a groin pull in May when he was leading the staff in victories and complete games. He was never the same pitcher afterward.

Wade Boggs, a .349 hitter in 338 at-bats during his rookie season of 1982, batted .361 to become the third Red Sox player to win the A.L. batting title in five years. He also knocked in 74 runs.

Jim Rice slugged an A.L.-leading 39 homers and tied Milwaukee's Cecil Cooper for the majors' RBI crown with 126. Not far behind was Tony Armas, who had 36 homers and 107 RBIs. And Bob Stanley was the workhorse out of the overworked bullpen, accounting for all but nine of Boston's 42 saves and recording a 2.85 ERA in 64 appearances.

But their contributions weren't close to being enough. The Red Sox managed to hang in contention in the first half only because no other A.L. East club took charge.

Dennis Eckersley, counted on as the ace of the pitching staff, went 9-13 and managed just two complete games in 28 starts.

Reliever Mark Clear had one of his worst seasons. He never had his control and finished with just four saves and an ERA of 6.28.

John Tudor, one of three lefthanders in Manager Ralph Houk's starting rotation, had a 13-12 record but served up 32 home runs. The other lefthanders, Bruce Hurst and Bob Ojeda, went 12-12 and 12-7, respectively. Hurst was the Red Sox's hard-luck pitcher, losing many games in which he pitched well. Ojeda finished fast, winning his last six decisions and seven of his last eight.

Luis Aponte and Doug Bird were big disappointments out of the bullpen, while lefthanded reliever John Henry Johnson did a creditable job (but he wasn't used with a game on the line until mid-June).

Dwight Evans, the team's Most Valuable Player the previous two years, hit 22 home runs but never really found the groove at the plate. He batted .238 and didn't play in the field after August 6 because of a torn groin muscle.

The Red Sox grounded into 171 double plays in '83, matching the major league record they had set in '82.

While Armas was long on power, his batting average was .218. The outfielder termed the figure "an embarrassment."

First baseman Dave Stapleton struggled all season at the plate, as did catchers Gary Allenson and Jeff Newman. Rich Gedman started the season as the regular catcher, but lost the job to Allenson because of his poor defense.

Jerry Remy, who missed most of spring training because of a back problem, was hitting only .245 at the All-Star break. However, the second baseman bounced back and finished at .275.

The '83 season marked the end of an era when Yastrzemski called it quits after 23 seasons with Boston. After batting .323 through July 4, Yastrzemski slipped to .266 by season's end—the same average he had in his rookie season of 1961. Careerwise, Yaz finished at .285.

Not only did things falter on the field for the Red Sox, there were problems in the front office as well. On June 6, which had been designated Tony Conigliaro Night (Boston's '67 pennant team was brought back and proceeds from that evening's game went toward medical expenses for the ailing Red Sox standout of the past), Co-Owner Edward (Buddy) LeRoux staged an attempted takeover of the team.

LeRoux set himself up as the sole authority, fired Haywood Sullivan as general manager and replaced him with Dick O'Connell (the club's former general manager).

A court battle followed and when it was over, the presiding judge ruled the takeover illegal and ordered the partnership to function as set down in the original agreement between LeRoux, Sullivan and Mrs. Jean Yawkey.

SCORES OF BOSTON RED SOX' 1983 GAMES

APRIL			Winner	Loser
5—Toronto	L	1-7	Stieb	Eckersley
7—Toronto	W	7-4	Stanley	Leal
8—At Texas	W	8-5	Aponte	Mason
9—At Texas	L	3-10	Smithson	Ojeda
10—At Texas	L	7-9	Hough	Stanley
11—At Kan. C.	L	2-6	Leonard	Hurst
12—At Kan. C.	L	1-5	Armstrong	Tudor
13—At Kan. C.	W	18-4	Brown	Splittorff
15—Texas	W	4-1	Eckersley	Matlack
16—Texas	W	2-1	Hurst	Darwin
17—Texas	L	0-1y	Jones	Stanley
18—Milwaukee	L	0-14	Sutton	Brown
20—Milwaukee	W	5-4	Clear	Ladd
22—At Oak.	W	3-1	Hurst	Krueger
24—At Oak.	W	4-2	Tudor	Norris
26—At Seattle	L	6-7	Perry	Brown
27—At Seattle	W	2-1	Eckersley	Young
29—At Calif.	W	6-5	Aponte	Sanchez
30—At Calif.	L	1-4‡	Corbett	Clear

Won 10, Lost 9

MAY			Winner	Loser
1—At Calif.	W	10-9	Stanley	Hassler
3—Oakland	W	3-1	Eckersley	Krueger
4—Oakland	W	7-1	Hurst	Langford
6—Seattle	W	6-4	Aponte	Vande Berg
7—Seattle	W	8-0	Brown	Stoddard
8—Seattle	L	2-4	Young	Bird
9—California	W	8-2	Stanley	John
10—California	L	5-6	Sanchez	Aponte
11—California	L	1-3	Kison	Tudor
12—At Milw.	W	5-3	Brown	Caldwell
14—At Milw.	L	7-8†	Gibson	Clear
15—At Milw.	W	6-1	Ojeda	Haas
17—Kan. City	W	4-1	Tudor	Gura
18—Kan. City	L	1-2	Leonard	Brown
19—Minnesota	W	4-1	Bird	Castillo
20—Minnesota	L	4-10	Schrom	Hurst
21—Minnesota	W	11-4	Ojeda	Havens
22—Minnesota	L	3-4x	Davis	Aponte
23—At Chicago	W	6-4	Brown	Dotson
24—At Chicago	L	4-12	Koosman	Bird
25—At Chicago	W	2-0	Hurst	Lamp
26—At Toronto	W	7-2	Stanley	Stieb
27—At Toronto	W	2-0	Tudor	Clancy
28—At Toronto	L	5-9	Jackson	Aponte
29—At Toronto	L	1-6*	Gott	Eckersley
30—Chicago	L	4-6	Burns	Hurst
31—Chicago	W	2-1	Ojeda	Bannister

Won 16, Lost 11

JUNE			Winner	Loser
1—Chicago	L	3-8	Hoyt	Tudor
3—At Minn.	W	6-3	Boyd	Williams
4—At Minn.	W	8-6	Eckersley	Viola
5—At Minn.	L	4-10	Havens	Hurst
6—Detroit	L	6-11	Berenguer	Stanley
7—Detroit	L	2-4	Wilcox	Tudor
8—Detroit	L	3-6	Morris	Boyd
9—Detroit	L	2-8	Petry	Eckersley
10—Baltimore	L	0-3	Davis	Hurst
11—Baltimore	L	6-10	McGregor	Ojeda
12—Baltimore	W	7-6	Stanley	T. Martinez
14—At Detroit	W	6-2	Brown	Petry
15—At Detroit	L	2-4	Rozema	Eckersley
16—At Detroit	L	2-10	Berenguer	Hurst
17—At Balt.	W	5-3	Ojeda	D. Martinez
18—At Balt.	W	3-2	Tudor	T. Martinez
19—At Balt.	L	3-6	Palmer	Brown
20—Cleveland	W	6-3	Eckersley	Eichelberger
21—Cleveland	L	1-3	Blyleven	Hurst
22—Cleveland	L	4-9	Barker	Ojeda
23—Cleveland	L	4-5	Sutcliffe	Bird
24—New York	W	5-4	Tudor	Righetti
25—New York	L	1-4	Howell	Eckersley
26—New York	W	12-5	Hurst	Keough
28—At Cleve.	W	11-3	Clear	Sutcliffe
29—At Cleve.	L	3-5	Barker	Stanley
29—At Cleve.	W	11-10‡	Johnson	Anderson

Won 11, Lost 16

JULY			Winner	Loser
1—At N.Y.	L	8-12	Shirley	Johnson
2—At N.Y.	W	10-4	Hurst	Keough
3—At N.Y.	W	7-3	Ojeda	Rawley
4—At N.Y.	L	0-4	Righetti	Tudor
8—California	L	3-9	Kison	Eckersley
9—California	W	10-3	Tudor	Forsch
10—California	L	3-5	John	Hurst
11—Seattle	W	6-5†	Aponte	Stanton
12—Seattle	L	2-3	Clark	Brown
13—Seattle	L	4-6	Beattie	Eckersley
14—Oakland	W	9-4	Tudor	McCatty
15—Oakland	W	10-7	Clear	Burgmeier
16—Oakland	L	5-12	Atherton	Stanley
17—Oakland	L	9-13	Codiroli	Clear
18—At Calif.	W	7-2	Eckersley	Kison
19—At Calif.	L	1-6	Forsch	Tudor
20—At Calif.	W	6-4	Stanley	John
21—At Seattle	W	14-13†	Johnson	Vande Berg
22—At Seattle	W	5-4	Brown	Vande Berg
23—At Seattle	L	0-5	Stoddard	Eckersley
24—At Seattle	W	6-0	Tudor	Abbott
25—At Oak.	W	3-0	Hurst	Codiroli
26—At Oak.	L	2-9	Underwood	Stanley
26—At Oak.	W	5-3	Stanley	Burgmeier
27—At Oak.	L	6-7	Krueger	Brown
29—Milwaukee	L	5-11	McClure	Eckersley
30—Milwaukee	W	10-5	Tudor	Sutton
31—Milwaukee	L	5-7	Haas	Stanley

Won 14, Lost 14

AUGUST			Winner	Loser
1—Milwaukee	L	2-6	Porter	Ojeda
2—At Texas	W	6-5	Boyd	Hough
3—At Texas	W	5-4†	Aponte	Cruz
4—At Texas	L	1-6	Honeycutt	Tudor
5—At Kan. C.	W	5-4	Hurst	Armstrong
6—At Kan. C.	L	0-4	Rasmussen	Ojeda
7—At Kan. C.	L	0-1	Perry	Boyd
8—Texas	L	7-12	Butcher	Stanley
9—Texas	W	6-4	Tudor	Honeycutt
10—Texas	W	4-2	Hurst	Smithson
13—Kan. City	L	4-5	Perry	Aponte
13—Kan. City	W	12-3	Boyd	Rasmussen
14—Kan. City	W	4-3	Stanley	Renko
14—Kan. City	L	3-6	Creel	Tudor
15—At Milw.	L	0-2	Haas	Hurst
16—At Milw.	L	3-4y	Slaton	Clear
17—At Milw.	L	3-4†	Tellmann	Ojeda
17—At Milw.	L	1-5	Candiotti	Johnson
19—Toronto	L	7-8	Acker	Clear
20—Toronto	W	5-2	Eckersley	Stieb
21—Toronto	L	3-7	Gott	Hurst
22—Toronto	W	4-2	Ojeda	Alexander
23—At Minn.	L	2-3	Williams	Boyd
24—At Minn.	L	7-8	Whitehouse	Stanley
25—At Minn.	L	2-5	Viola	Eckersley
26—At Chicago	W	3-1	Hurst	Bannister
27—At Chicago	L	1-2	Hoyt	Ojeda
28—At Chicago	L	2-6	Koosman	Boyd
29—At Toronto	L	1-5	Clancy	Tudor
29—At Toronto	W	8-7	Clear	Moffitt
30—At Toronto	W	5-4§	Johnson	Jackson

Won 12, Lost 19

SEPTEMBER			Winner	Loser
1—Minnesota	L	0-11	Williams	Eckersley
1—Minnesota	W	9-3	Ojeda	Lysander
2—Chicago	W	5-1	Boyd	Koosman
3—Chicago	L	6-9	Dotson	Tudor
4—Chicago	W	6-2	Hurst	Burns
5—At Balt.	W	2-0	Ojeda	Boddicker
6—At Balt.	L	1-8	Palmer	Eckersley
7—At Balt.	L	2-5	Flanagan	Boyd
9—At Cleve.	W	6-4	Tudor	Heaton
10—At Cleve.	L	6-8	Barnes	Bird
11—At Cleve.	W	4-1	Ojeda	Sorensen
13—Baltimore	L	4-7§	Stewart	Stanley
13—Baltimore	L	1-7	Swaggerty	Nipper
14—Baltimore	L	0-5	D. Martinez	Tudor
15—Baltimore	W	7-1	Hurst	Davis
16—Detroit	W	6-1	Ojeda	Petry
17—Detroit	W	3-2	Eckersley	Morris
18—Detroit	L	6-9	Wilcox	Boyd
19—New York	W	5-3	Tudor	Guidry
20—New York	L	2-3	Montefusco	Hurst
21—New York	W	3-1	Ojeda	Shirley
23—At Detroit	L	0-7	Berenguer	Eckersley
24—At Detroit	W	5-3	Tudor	Petry
25—At Detroit	L	2-3	Bair	Boyd
27—At N.Y.	L	2-7	Keough	Hurst
28—At N.Y.	W	3-2	Ojeda	Rawley
29—At N.Y.	L	3-4	Guidry	Tudor
30—Cleveland	W	10-0	Eckersley	Heaton

Won 14, Lost 14

OCTOBER			Winner	Loser
1—Cleveland	L	1-3	Sorensen	Boyd
2—Cleveland	W	3-1	Nipper	Anderson

Won 1, Lost 1

*6 innings. †10 innings. ‡11 innings. §12 innings. x13 innings. y14 innings.

Wade Boggs proved his rookie season was no fluke by winning the A.L. batting title with a .361 average.

The strong right arm of Rick Sutcliffe accounted for 17 of the Indians' 70 victories.

Indians Continue Losing Ways

By SHELDON OCKER

To begin with, the Cleveland Indians' expectations for 1983 had been modest.

The ace of Cleveland's pitching staff, Bert Blyleven, was returning after missing almost an entire season because of elbow surgery. Little had been done to improve an offense that had relied on Andre Thornton and Toby Harrah, and the Tribe failed to acquire a tested reliever for a bullpen that had banked too heavily on Dan Spillner.

Nevertheless, Manager Mike Ferraro already had overcome his most serious obstacle, removal of a cancerous kidney over the winter. Ferraro was so eager to begin his new job that he was in Tucson for spring training barely two weeks after his operation, trying to minimize his fatigue by riding a golf cart.

Becoming an effective manager was a more elusive challenge for Ferraro. On July 31, Cleveland was mired in last place with a 40-60 record and Ferraro was replaced by Pat Corrales, who had been dismissed as manager of the Philadelphia Phillies only two weeks earlier.

Corrales seemed to have a positive impact on the Tribe. Under him, Cleveland won 30 of 62 games. Corrales missed a .500 record on the final day of the season when the Indians lost to Boston.

As the 1983 American League race began, Cleveland's most obvious asset seemed to be deep and talented starting pitching. Rick Sutcliffe, Lary Sorensen, Len Barker, rookie Neal Heaton, Rick Waits and off-season acquisition Juan Eichelberger were primed.

In addition, rookie shortstop Julio Franco appeared every bit as good as his press clippings. He went on to lead the club in runs batted in with 80 and in stolen bases with 32, batted .273 and routinely made acrobatic plays in the field.

Rookie Julio Franco emerged as one of the top shortstops in baseball.

Another cause for optimism was the trade of shortstop Jerry Dybzinski to the Chicago White Sox for Pat Tabler. Though Tabler was sent to Charleston, the Tribe's Class AAA affiliate, he soon was summoned to Cleveland after third baseman Harrah broke a bone in his left hand.

When Harrah returned a month later, Tabler was moved to left field, where a sometimes-painful learning process began. But his work at the plate was consistently good. Tabler finished with a .293 average and 65 RBIs in 430 at-bats.

Harrah's injury was the first breakdown. Others followed quickly as the Indians headed for a last-place finish in the A.L. East.

Barker never was able to win consistently. Having compiled an 8-13 record, he was traded to the Atlanta Braves in late August for three players. Indians President Gabe Paul said Barker was dealt because there was little chance he would resign with Cleveland when he became a free agent at the end of the season.

Most observers blamed Barker's problems in 1983 on the effects of a bone spur

SCORES OF CLEVELAND INDIANS' 1983 GAMES

APRIL

			Winner	Loser
4—At Oak.	W	8-5	Sutcliffe	Langford
6—At Oak.	L	3-5	Norris	Blyleven
7—At Oak.	W	9-1	Barker	Underwood
9—Baltimore	W	8-4	Sutcliffe	Stewart
10—Baltimore	L	2-13	D. Martinez	Sorensen
12—Texas	L	1-2	Honeycutt	Blyleven
13—Texas	W	4-3	Barker	Mason
16—At Balt.	L	0-2	Palmer	Sorensen
16—At Balt.	W	7-4	Heaton	D. Martinez
17—At Balt.	L	1-6	Flanagan	Blyleven
18—At Balt.	L	1-4	McGregor	Barker
19—At Toronto	L	7-9	Moffitt	Spillner
20—At Toronto	L	1-4	Stieb	Sorensen
22—Chicago	W	5-1	Blyleven	Bannister
23—Chicago	W	6-3	Barker	Lamp
24—Chicago	L	3-9	Dotson	Sutcliffe
26—Minnesota	W	7-1	Sorensen	Castillo
27—Minnesota	L	3-5	Williams	Glynn
29—At Kan. C.	L	5-6†	Armstrong	Spillner
30—At Kan. C.	W	5-1	Sutcliffe	Renko

Won 9, Lost 11

MAY

1—At Kan. C.	W	2-1	Sorensen	Gura
3—At Minn.	W	3-1	Blyleven	Castillo
4—At Minn.	W	11-7	Spillner	Davis
5—At Minn.	W	7-5	Sutcliffe	Havens
6—At Chicago	L	3-8	Koosman	Sorensen
7—At Chicago	L	3-4	Hoyt	Eichelberger
8—At Chicago	W	13-6	Blyleven	Dotson
10—Kan. City	W	4-1	Barker	Blue
11—Kan. City	W	2-0	Sutcliffe	Gura
12—Toronto	L	3-6	Clancy	Sorensen
13—Toronto	W	5-1	Eichelberger	Morgan
14—Toronto	L	1-8	Leal	Blyleven
16—At Texas	L	1-3	Honeycutt	Barker
17—At Texas	L	5-6‡	Schmidt	Glynn
18—At Texas	L	2-3x	Tobik	Heaton
20—At Calif.	L	4-5	John	Eichelberger
21—At Calif.	W	9-3	Blyleven	Travers
22—At Calif.	L	0-9	Kison	Barker
23—At Seattle	L	2-3	Stoddard	Sutcliffe
24—At Seattle	W	6-4	Heaton	Caudill
25—At Seattle	L	1-2	Beattie	Eichelberger
27—California	L	4-5‡	Sanchez	Spillner
28—California	L	4-7	Zahn	Barker
29—California	L	4-6	Witt	Spillner
30—California	W	6-5	Heaton	Sanchez
31—Seattle	W	5-2	Eichelberger	Nelson

Won 12, Lost 14

JUNE

1—Seattle	W	5-2	Heaton	Perry
2—Seattle	W	3-1	Sutcliffe	Stoddard
4—Oakland	L	3-6	Burgmeier	Waits
5—Oakland	L	3-8	Keough	Heaton
5—Oakland	L	2-9	McCatty	Barker
7—At N.Y.	W	2-1*	Heaton	Gossage
8—At N.Y.	L	5-6	Gossage	Spillner
10—At Detroit	L	1-7	Rozema	Sorensen
11—At Detroit	W	9-1	Eichelberger	Pashnick
12—At Detroit	L	1-4	Wilcox	Blyleven
12—At Detroit	L	1-3	Morris	Barker
13—New York	W	9-0	Sutcliffe	Howell
14—New York	W	9-6	Sorensen	Shirley
15—New York	L	5-8	Rawley	Eichelberger
16—New York	L	1-8	Guidry	Blyleven
17—Detroit	L	4-11	Morris	Barker
18—Detroit	W	12-8	Sutcliffe	Wilcox
19—Detroit	W	7-2	Sorensen	Petry
20—At Boston	L	3-6	Eckersley	Eichelberger
21—At Boston	W	3-1	Blyleven	Hurst
22—At Boston	W	9-4	Barker	Ojeda
23—At Boston	W	5-4	Sutcliffe	Bird
24—At Milw.	L	2-6	Sutton	Sorensen
25—At Milw.	L	2-7	Slaton	Eichelberger
26—At Milw.	L	3-4	Tellmann	Blyleven
28—Boston	L	3-11	Clear	Sutcliffe
29—Boston	W	5-3	Barker	Stanley
29—Boston	L	10-11†	Johnson	Anderson

Won 12, Lost 16

JULY

			Winner	Loser
1—Milwaukee	L	10-11	Caldwell	Eichelberger
2—Milwaukee	L	5-6	Haas	Blyleven
3—Milwaukee	W	5-2	Sutcliffe	Porter
4—Milwaukee	L	3-8	Sutton	Barker
8—At Minn.	W	10-4	Blyleven	Viola
9—At Minn.	L	2-3	Schrom	Sutcliffe
10—At Minn.	L	4-6	Williams	Eichelberger
11—At Chicago	L	2-9	Burns	Barker
12—At Chicago	L	0-8	Bannister	Sorensen
13—At Chicago	L	1-5	Hoyt	Blyleven
14—Kan. City	W	4-3*	Sutcliffe	Armstrong
15—Kan. City	L	0-10	Splittorff	Eichelberger
16—Kan. City	W	17-3	Barker	Perry
17—Kan. City	L	2-7	Hood	Spillner
18—Chicago	L	3-5	Hoyt	Eichelberger
19—Chicago	W	5-4	Sutcliffe	Tidrow
20—Chicago	L	2-8	Dotson	Heaton
22—Minnesota	W	8-5	Easterly	Lysander
23—Minnesota	L	2-5	Williams	Barker
24—Minnesota	L	5-7	Castillo	Sutcliffe
24—Minnesota	L	4-5	Havens	Brennan
25—At Kan. C.	L	1-6	Splittorff	Heaton
26—At Kan. C.	W	2-0	Sorensen	Renko
27—At Kan. C.	L	4-5	Perry	Barker
29—At Toronto	L	2-4	Clancy	Sutcliffe
30—At Toronto	L	5-6§	McLaughlin	Anderson
31—At Toronto	W	16-11	Eichelberger	Acker

Won 8, Lost 19

AUGUST

1—At Toronto	W	6-0	Barker	Alexander
2—Baltimore	W	3-1	Blyleven	D. Martinez
2—Baltimore	W	4-3	Brennan	Ramirez
3—Baltimore	L	2-8	Davis	Sutcliffe
4—Baltimore	L	3-4*	McGregor	Anderson
5—Texas	L	0-2	Smithson	Sorensen
6—Texas	L	1-6	Tanana	Barker
7—Texas	L	3-4	Hough	Spillner
7—Texas	W	7-0	Brennan	Matlack
8—At Balt.	W	9-4	Sutcliffe	Davis
9—At Balt.	W	4-3	Heaton	McGregor
10—At Balt.	W	4-3	Sorensen	Boddicker
12—At Texas	L	2-6	Tanana	Brennan
13—At Texas	L	3-4	Hough	Sutcliffe
14—At Texas	W	3-0	Heaton	Honeycutt
15—Toronto	L	2-3	Moffitt	Spillner
16—Toronto	W	3-2	Easterly	Moffitt
16—Toronto	L	6-9	McLaughlin	Anderson
17—Toronto	L	5-6*	McLaughlin	Sutcliffe
19—Seattle	W	6-5	Heaton	Best
20—Seattle	W	3-2	Easterly	Beattie
21—Seattle	L	2-7	Abbott	Jeffcoat
22—California	L	3-7§	Kison	Spillner
23—California	L	2-5	Witt	Barker
24—Oakland	W	1-0	Heaton	Conroy
24—Oakland	W	4-2	Sorensen	Atherton
25—Oakland	L	0-6	McCatty	Jeffcoat
26—At Seattle	W	4-1	Sutcliffe	Stoddard
27—At Seattle	L	3-6	Young	Eichelberger
28—At Seattle	W	5-2	Sorensen	Moore
29—At Calif.	W	6-4	Heaton	Witt
30—At Calif.	L	6-10	Steirer	Jeffcoat
31—At Calif.	W	7-5*	Sutcliffe	Sanchez

Won 17, Lost 16

SEPTEMBER

2—At Oak.	W	4-2	Sorensen	Heimueller
3—At Oak.	W	13-6	Spillner	Beard
4—At Oak.	W	9-2	Sutcliffe	McCatty
5—Detroit	W	3-2	Anderson	Morris
7—Detroit	W	7-1	Sorensen	Wilcox
7—Detroit	L	3-7	Petry	Camacho
9—Boston	L	4-6	Tudor	Heaton
10—Boston	W	8-6	Barnes	Bird
11—Boston	L	1-4	Ojeda	Sorensen
12—At Detroit	L	1-5	Wilcox	Blyleven
13—At Detroit	L	2-3	Morris	Behenna
14—At Detroit	L	0-5	Abbott	Sutcliffe
17—New York	W	7-6	Easterly	Frazier
18—New York	W	10-6	Jeffcoat	Righetti
18—New York	L	8-13	Fontenot	Behenna
20—Milwaukee	L	7-11	Slaton	Anderson
21—Milwaukee	L	7-10	Sutton	Heaton
22—Milwaukee	W	9-5	Sorensen	Candiotti
23—At N.Y.	L	4-7	Frazier	Easterly
24—At N.Y.	L	1-9	Guidry	Sutcliffe
25—At N.Y.	L	4-6	Montefusco	Barnes
26—At N.Y.	W	7-0	Heaton	Shirley
27—At Milw.	L	4-8	Caldwell	Sorensen
28—At Milw.	L	4-6	Slaton	Easterly
29—At Milw.	W	4-2	Sutcliffe	Candiotti
30—At Boston	L	0-10	Eckersley	Heaton

Won 11, Lost 15

OCTOBER

1—At Boston	W	3-1	Sorensen	Boyd
2—At Boston	L	1-3	Nipper	Anderson

Won 1, Lost 1

*10 innings. †11 innings. ‡12 innings. §13 innings. x14 innings.

Though unsteady at times defensively, Pat Tabler impressed Indian fans with his consistent bat.

on his right elbow. Though he had pitched with the injury since high school, the pain had increased in the last two seasons.

Second baseman Manny Trillo was another disappointment to the Indians. Trillo was acquired by Cleveland from Philadelphia along with Franco, George Vukovich and two minor leaguers for Von Hayes.

Free agency also awaited Trillo at the end of the season. From the moment the deal with the Phillies was struck, Trillo said he didn't want to play for the Indians and would leave via the re-entry draft. But in August, Trillo was traded to Montreal for minor league outfielder Don Carter, who was assigned to Class AA Buffalo.

Blyleven seemed recovered from his surgery, but he posted only a 7-10 record with a 3.91 earned-run average. He made only 24 starts because of a sore shoulder that limited his activity in the second half of the season.

Spillner was not able to build on 1982, a season in which he tied a club record with 21 saves and posted a 12-10 mark with a 2.49 ERA.

His troubles began with a game at Toronto in April. The temperature was 32 degrees, with a wind-chill factor of 13. Spillner was called on in the eighth inning to protect a 7-5 lead, but he allowed two, two-run homers in the ninth. After that, he was never the same, finishing the season with a 2-9 record, eight saves and a 5.07 ERA.

The Indians attempted to boost their power output in June when they traded center fielder Rick Manning and Waits to the Milwaukee Brewers for center fielder Gorman Thomas and lefthanded reliever Jamie Easterly.

Thomas was hitting only .183 with five homers and 18 RBIs when the deal was made. He improved his output for the Indians, finishing the season with 22 homers, 69 RBIs and a .209 batting average. Thornton had 17 homers and 77 RBIs.

Sutcliffe was the Indians' winningest pitcher with a 17-11 record. In his two years with Cleveland since being obtained from the Los Angeles Dodgers, the righthander has posted a 31-19 record. Heaton showed great promise, compiling an 11-7 mark with seven saves and a 4.16 ERA. Sorensen won 12 games, but Eichelberger struggled to a 4-11 record.

In all, it was another long season for the Indians, who haven't finished higher than fourth since divisional play was introduced in the big leagues in 1969. And Cleveland fans responded in turn, with only 768,971 spectators (the majors' low for 1983) being attracted to Municipal Stadium.

Rookie Ron Kittle took the American League by storm, hitting 35 home runs and driving in 100 runs.

White Sox 'Win Ugly,' Win Big

By JOE GODDARD

The White Sox started like a tin lizzie in 1983, jerking along in spurts and sputters. But they went into gear for Manager Tony LaRussa in the middle of the season, moved into power glide for the last two months (winning 46 of their final 61 games) and raised the first flag over Comiskey Park in 24 years.

In winning the West Division by 20 games over Kansas City, the White Sox broke a 47-year-old record for largest margin in an American League race (pennant or divisional chase).

Chicago's 99-63 record topped the major leagues, and the club's home attendance of 2,131,530 was more than 450,000 above the city record set by the '69 Cubs.

The White Sox did it "winning ugly."

Thank you, Doug Rader.

Before a mid-August series at Arlington, Tex., the White Sox read a quote by Rangers Manager Rader saying they were winning ugly "because they don't win in the classic sense. They get six hits and score six runs."

Rader later amended his remark, saying there was nothing wrong with winning that way. By then, the White Sox had adopted the theme. They went 22-9 in August, 22-6 in September and 2-0 in October.

The winning-ugly White Sox, who got off to a 16-24 start, led the majors in runs (800) and were the only big-league team with two 20-game winners (LaMarr Hoyt, 24-10, and Richard Dotson, 22-7).

Although most regulars posted impressive numbers, LaRussa made good use of everyone. As leading hitting Tom Paciorek (.307) put it, "Individually, we were not that good, but collectively, we were great."

"There was no single game or player who turned our season around," said LaRussa, who was the target of heavy criticism when the club struggled early in the season. "Fit the pieces and you'll see why."

The pieces fell together like this:

• Harold Baines led the majors with 22 game-winning runs batted in and had 99 RBIs overall. He batted .280.

• Greg Luzinski set a designated-hitter record for home runs with 32 and knocked in 95 runs.

• Rookie Ron Kittle, who had totaled 247 RBIs and 90 homers in the minors in 1981 and 1982, drove in 100 runs and slugged 35 homers (two short of Dick Allen's club

Cy Young winner LaMarr Hoyt (above) and teammate Richard Dotson combined for 46 White Sox victories.

SCORES OF CHICAGO WHITE SOX' 1983 GAMES

APRIL			Winner	Loser
4—At Texas	L	3-5	Butcher	Hoyt
5—At Texas	L	1-4	Matlack	Bannister
6—At Texas	L	1-4	Honeycutt	Dotson
8—At Detroit	W	6-3	Lamp	Wilcox
10—At Detroit	W	7-5	Hoyt	Morris
12—Baltimore	L	8-10	Stewart	Lamp
14—Baltimore	W	12-11	Barojas	Welchel
15—Detroit	L	0-6	Wilcox	Hoyt
16—Detroit	W	3-1	Bannister	Bailey
17—Detroit	W	6-1	Lamp	Ujdur
19—New York	W	13-3	Dotson	Howell
20—New York	L	4-6	Righetti	Hoyt
22—At Cleve.	L	1-5	Blyleven	Bannister
23—At Cleve.	L	3-6	Barker	Lamp
24—At Cleve.	W	9-3	Dotson	Sutcliffe
26—At Milw.	L	3-4	Slaton	Hickey
27—At Milw.	L	2-6	Tellmann	Bannister
29—At Toronto	W	9-3	Dotson	Leal

Won 8, Lost 10

MAY				
1—At Toronto	L	0-8	Stieb	Bannister
2—Milwaukee	L	4-8	Slaton	Hoyt
3—Milwaukee	W	7-6	Dotson	Porter
4—Milwaukee	W	3-2	Lamp	McClure
6—Cleveland	W	8-3	Koosman	Sorensen
7—Cleveland	W	4-3	Hoyt	Eichelberger
8—Cleveland	L	6-13	Blyleven	Dotson
9—Toronto	L	1-6	Leal	Burns
11—Toronto	L	1-3†	Stieb	Hoyt
13—At N.Y.	L	1-3	Righetti	Dotson
14—At N.Y.	L	5-8	Shirley	Burns
15—At N.Y.	W	7-3	Bannister	Rawley
17—At Balt.	L	2-7	Stoddard	Hoyt
17—At Balt.	L	0-5	Boddicker	Lamp
18—At Balt.	L	0-1	T. Martinez	Dotson
20—At Kan. C.	W	9-6	Burns	Blue
21—At Kan. C.	L	4-8	Renko	Bannister
22—At Kan. C.	W	11-3	Hoyt	Gura
23—Boston	L	4-6	Brown	Dotson
24—Boston	W	12-4	Koosman	Bird
25—Boston	L	0-2	Hurst	Lamp
26—Texas	L	1-3	Honeycutt	Bannister
27—Texas	W	3-2	Hoyt	Tanana
28—Texas	W	8-3	Dotson	Hough
29—Texas	W	8-3	Koosman	Smithson
30—At Boston	W	6-4	Burns	Hurst
31—At Boston	L	1-2	Ojeda	Bannister

Won 12, Lost 15

JUNE				
1—At Boston	W	8-3	Hoyt	Tudor
2—Kan. City	W	6-3	Agosto	Gura
3—Kan. City	W	2-0	Koosman	Creel
4—Kan. City	L	1-7	Splittorff	Burns
5—Kan. City	L	5-7	Quisenberry	Hickey
5—Kan. City	W	5-2	Hoyt	Armstrong
7—At Calif.	W	12-11†	Tidrow	Hassler
8—At Calif.	L	4-7	Forsch	Koosman
9—At Calif.	L	2-3	John	Lamp
10—At Oak.	L	1-2y	Burgmeier	Tidrow
11—At Oak.	L	4-5	Conroy	Hoyt
12—At Oak.	W	12-10‡	Tidrow	Warren
12—At Oak.	W	8-1	Koosman	Codiroli
13—California	L	4-7	Forsch	Burns
15—California	W	5-2	Hoyt	John
17—Oakland	W	6-3	Hickey	Burgmeier
18—Oakland	L	1-3	Codiroli	Bannister
19—Oakland	W	1-0	Burns	Underwood
20—Seattle	W	7-3	Hoyt	Beattie
21—Seattle	W	4-2	Dotson	Stoddard
22—Seattle	W	6-3	Koosman	Perry
23—Minnesota	W	8-6	Bannister	Castillo
24—Minnesota	L	1-5	Williams	Burns
25—Minnesota	W	8-3	Hoyt	Viola
26—Minnesota	W	9-7	Dotson	Oelkers
27—At Seattle	W	7-4	Lamp	Clark
28—At Seattle	L	2-6	Abbott	Bannister
29—At Seattle	W	5-3	Burns	Young

Won 18, Lost 10

JULY			Winner	Loser
1—At Minn.	L	3-6	Viola	Hoyt
2—At Minn.	W	4-2	Dotson	Schrom
3—At Minn.	L	3-4	Davis	Barojas
4—At Minn.	W	12-6	Lamp	Lysander
8—Milwaukee	L	3-4	McClure	Hoyt
9—Milwaukee	W	8-3	Koosman	Sutton
10—Milwaukee	L	9-12	Slaton	Barojas
11—Cleveland	W	9-2	Burns	Barker
12—Cleveland	W	8-0	Bannister	Sorensen
13—Cleveland	W	5-1	Hoyt	Blyleven
14—Toronto	L	0-8	Leal	Koosman
15—Toronto	L	2-3	McLaughlin	Dotson
16—Toronto	L	5-7	McLaughlin	Agosto
17—Toronto	W	3-2	Bannister	Alexander
18—At Cleve.	W	5-3	Hoyt	Eichelberger
19—At Cleve.	L	4-5	Sutcliffe	Tidrow
20—At Cleve.	W	8-2	Dotson	Heaton
21—At Milw.	L	6-7	Ladd	Agosto
22—At Milw.	W	2-1	Bannister	Porter
23—At Milw.	L	7-8	McClure	Hoyt
24—At Milw.	L	7-8	Ladd	Tidrow
25—At Toronto	W	7-4	Dotson	Stieb
26—At Toronto	L	4-6	Gott	Burns
26—At Toronto	W	4-3	Bannister	Alexander
27—At Toronto	W	11-3	Hoyt	Leal
29—New York	W	7-2	Koosman	Guidry
30—New York	W	5-1	Dotson	Rawley
31—New York	L	6-12‡	Gossage	Lamp

Won 15, Lost 13

AUGUST				
1—New York	W	4-1	Bannister	Fontenot
2—Detroit	W	7-5	Hoyt	Petry
3—Detroit	L	3-6	Morris	Koosman
4—Detroit	W	4-2	Dotson	Bair
5—At Balt.	L	4-5	Boddicker	Lamp
6—At Balt.	W	6-4	Bannister	D. Martinez
7—At Balt.	W	4-3	Hoyt	Flanagan
8—At Detroit	W	5-4	Burns	Berenguer
8—At Detroit	L	2-7	Morris	Koosman
9—At Detroit	W	6-5	Lamp	Lopez
11—Baltimore	W	9-3	Bannister	Ramirez
12—Baltimore	W	2-1	Hoyt	Flanagan
13—Baltimore	L	2-5	Stewart	Koosman
14—Baltimore	L	1-2	McGregor	Dotson
15—At N.Y.	W	1-0	Burns	Righetti
16—At N.Y.	W	5-3	Bannister	Fontenot
17—At N.Y.	W	7-5x	Barojas	Murray
19—At Texas	W	3-2†	Dotson	Cruz
19—At Texas	W	6-1	Koosman	Hough
20—At Texas	L	1-6	Stewart	Burns
21—At Texas	W	3-1	Bannister	Butcher
22—At Kan. C.	W	3-1	Hoyt	Splittorff
23—At Kan. C.	L	2-10	Renko	Koosman
24—At Kan. C.	W	4-3†	Dotson	Quisenberry
25—At Detroit	L	1-10	Berenguer	Burns
26—Boston	L	1-3	Hurst	Bannister
27—Boston	W	2-1	Hoyt	Ojeda
28—Boston	W	6-2	Koosman	Boyd
29—Texas	W	2-1	Dotson	Smithson
30—Texas	W	5-0	Burns	Stewart
31—Kan. City	W	7-3	Bannister	Gura

Won 22, Lost 9

SEPTEMBER				
1—Kan. City	W	12-0	Hoyt	Black
2—At Boston	L	1-5	Boyd	Koosman
3—At Boston	W	9-6	Dotson	Tudor
4—At Boston	L	2-6	Hurst	Burns
5—Oakland	W	11-1	Bannister	Conroy
6—Oakland	W	7-6	Hoyt	Codiroli
7—Oakland	W	8-7†	Agosto	Atherton
8—California	W	8-5	Dotson	Witt
9—California	W	11-0	Burns	John
10—California	W	7-6§	Barojas	S. Brown
11—California	W	5-4†	Hoyt	Forsch
13—At Minn.	W	5-1	Dotson	Viola
14—At Minn.	L	0-1	Davis	Burns
15—Seattle	W	12-0*	Hoyt	Moore
16—Seattle	W	7-0	Bannister	Clark
17—Seattle	W	4-3	Lamp	Caudill
18—Seattle	W	6-0	Dotson	Stoddard
19—Minnesota	L	5-7	Walters	Barojas
21—Minnesota	W	2-1	Hoyt	Schrom
21—Minnesota	W	7-6	Hoffman	Davis
22—At Calif.	W	3-2	Koosman	Forsch
23—At Calif.	W	2-1	Dotson	Witt
24—At Calif.	W	2-0	Burns	S. Brown
25—At Calif.	W	8-5	Hoyt	John
27—At Oak.	L	4-5	Underwood	Tidrow
28—At Oak.	W	5-3	Dotson	Conroy
29—At Oak.	L	0-3	Warren	Burns
30—At Seattle	W	9-4	Hoyt	Stoddard

Won 22, Lost 6

OCTOBER				
1—At Seattle	W	9-3	Bannister	Young
2—At Seattle	W	3-0	Dotson	Beattie

Won 2, Lost 0

*6½ innings. †10 innings. ‡11 innings. §12 innings. x13 innings. y16 innings.

Free-agent signee Floyd Bannister recovered from a rocky first half and won 13 of 14 decisions after the All-Star break.

record).

• For the first time in White Sox history, four players had 20 or more homers. Besides Kittle and Luzinski, Carlton Fisk (26) and Baines (20) reached that figure.

• Five pitchers were double-figure winners—Hoyt, Dotson, Floyd Bannister (16-10), Jerry Koosman (11-7) and Britt Burns (10-11).

• Hoyt won his last 13 decisions and stretched his two-year victory total to a major league high of 43. Dotson captured his last 10 decisions.

• Bannister, signed to a five-year, $4.5 million contract as a free agent over the winter, was 13-1 after the All-Star break and finished second in A.L. strikeouts with 193.

• Burns tied for second in the league in shutouts (four).

• Led by Dennis Lamp with 15 saves and Salome Barojas with 12, the bullpen was second in the A.L. with 48 saves. Barojas posted a team-low 2.47 earned-run average.

• Rudy Law was the league runner-up in stolen bases with 77 and scored a team-high 95 runs. Second baseman Julio Cruz, who started the season with Seattle, had 57 steals overall.

• Hitting .197 on June 16 with only five homers and 18 RBIs, and criticized and benched for his pitch-calling, Fisk was moved to the No. 2 spot in the batting order (up from sixth and seventh). He responded immediately, hitting .330 the rest of the way for a season figure of .289 to go with 26 homers and 86 RBIs.

• The left side of the infield—Vance Law at third base and Scott Fletcher and Jerry Dybzinski at shortstop—gained considerable praise for shoring up the defense, which was suspect early in the season. Overall, the White Sox made 119 errors, a decline of 35 from '82.

"Cruz was the last cement," Dotson said of the acrobatic second baseman who was obtained by General Manager Roland Hemond on the June 15 trading deadline for Tony Bernazard.

The West Division title came in the third season after Jerry Reinsdorf and Eddie Einhorn had purchased the club from Bill Veeck.

"If you had to pick a perfect year, this was it," Einhorn said.

Not even the failure to win (ugly or otherwise) the A.L. Championship Series could detract from what the White Sox achieved in 1983.

Bullpen ace Dan Quisenberry enjoyed phenomenal success in the Royals' otherwise dismal season.

Royal Armor Shows Rust

By MIKE McKENZIE

When the curtain dropped on the Royals' 1983 season, "bravos" rang out for Dan Quisenberry. Otherwise, the cheering was muted.

Oh, polite hurrahs poured forth for Frank White and some applause, perhaps, was heard for George Brett and Hal McRae. And there was appreciation for a few aspiring Royals—like Pat Sheridan, Don Slaught, Bud Black and Butch Davis—whose performances indicated they will be on the scene to stay.

But on the whole, memories of the '83 season will focus more on the cast on Dennis Leonard's knee, the tar on Brett's bat, the deterioration of Vida Blue's arm, the breakup of a long-revered lineup, the nastiness of a drug investigation and, above all, the humbling distance between the second-place Royals and the American League West champion Chicago White Sox.

Falling out of first place to stay as early as May 4, the Royals went on to their worst record, 79-83, since 1974. In doing so, they left large question marks about their future.

Winter activity probably will determine if the Royals can recover. They have plenty to recover from.

Quisenberry broke John Hiller's major league record of 38 saves, finishing with an astounding 45 for his third Fireman of the Year award in four years. He had a 5-3 won-lost record and a 1.94 earned-run average.

White turned in his most consistent overall season. Again, he sparkled afield, committing just nine errors on a team that led the league in that department with 165. Additionally, White set a club record for runs batted in by a second baseman, 77, tops in the majors at his position in '83, and matched his personal best in home runs, 11.

Aside from Quisenberry and White, Manager Dick Howser's Royals had to strain for star material. Brett started the season ablaze at bat. He had hits in the first 19 games, finished April at .460 and furthered talk of a season-long race with California's Rod Carew for A.L. batting honors.

But as Boston's Wade Boggs moved to the fore, Brett struggled through two injuries (one a stubbed, broken toe) and the infamous pine-tar incident in New York. Brett still finished with a personal-high 25 home runs, plus 93 RBIs and a .310 average, none of which satisfied him. "I got too home run happy," he said.

Brett was the central figure in one of the season's wackiest stories. On July 24 at Yankee Stadium, Brett hit a two-run homer off New York's Goose Gossage in the ninth inning. The drive gave Kansas City a 5-4 lead, but the homer was then disallowed when pine tar was discovered beyond the legal limit of 18 inches up the bat handle. The Royals filed a protest.

Although the homer off Gossage was restored and the Royals eventually won the suspended Pine Tar Game that inspired everything from a song by C.W. McCall to T-shirts by teammate Gaylord Perry, Brett batted only .254 over the remainder of the season (with five homers and 29 RBIs).

McRae proved he was still a skilled designated hitter with a .311 average, but his homer and RBI totals dropped from 27 and 133 in '82 to 12 and 82 for '83.

Willie Wilson shared the Royals' gloom as much as anyone, plummeting from league batting champion (.332 in '82) to a .276 hitter. He suffered a broken knuckle on the field and a broken spirit off the field.

Wilson began the season not speaking to the press, but eventually made headlines because of a hotel fracas in Milwaukee and a courtroom appearance in Kansas City, Kan.

Wilson was one of four ballplayers who pleaded guilty on charges reduced to misdemeanor status in a cocaine bust. Teammate Willie Aikens was another. By the time Jerry Martin and Blue had entered their pleas, they were former Royals.

Blue was released August 5, winless, and he entered a drug abuse rehabilitation program. Martin joined Amos Otis on the discharged list, their options passed over by the Royals.

Martin had begun the year strong, but his season ended April 25 with a hand injury. Leonard's ended about a month later when a tendon in the pitcher's knee snapped while he delivered a pitch.

A telltale mark about the '83 Royals: Leonard pitched just two months, yet he tied Steve Renko for the most victories, six, by a righthanded starter on the staff.

By the time Leonard went down, Larry Gura had gone sour. Gura started the season 4-0, but encountered a seven-game losing streak and went from 18 wins in '82 to 18 losses in '83.

The threesome that headed the starting

SCORES OF KANSAS CITY ROYALS' 1983 GAMES

APRIL

			Winner	Loser
4—At Balt.	W	7-2	Gura	D. Martinez
6—At Balt.	L	1-11	Flanagan	Leonard
9—Milwaukee	W	5-2	Gura	McClure
10—Milwaukee	L	5-9	Tellman	Armstrong
11—Boston	W	6-2	Leonard	Hurst
12—Boston	W	5-1	Armstrong	Tudor
13—Boston	L	4-18	Brown	Splittorff
15—At Milw.	W	4-3	Gura	McClure
17—At Milw.	L	3-6	Caldwell	Renko
20—At Detroit	W	8-7	Quisenberry	Bailey
22—Toronto	W	6-5	Leonard	Jackson
23—Toronto	L	4-5	Moffitt	Quisenberry
24—Toronto	W	7-1	Renko	Gott
26—At N.Y.	W	10-4	Gura	Righetti
27—At N.Y.	L	0-6	Shirley	Leonard
29—Cleveland	W	6-5§	Armstrong	Spillner
30—Cleveland	L	1-5	Sutcliffe	Renko

Won 10, Lost 7

MAY

1—Cleveland	L	1-2	Sorensen	Gura
2—New York	W	4-1	Leonard	Shirley
3—New York	W	5-2	Splittorff	Alexander
4—New York	L	1-8	Rawley	Blue
6—At Toronto	L	1-6	Stieb	Gura
7—At Toronto	L	4-7	Jackson	Leonard
8—At Toronto	W	6-1	Renko	Gott
10—At Cleve.	L	1-4	Barker	Blue
11—At Cleve.	L	0-2	Sutcliffe	Gura
13—Detroit	W	5-2	Leonard	Morris
14—Detroit	L	10-11	Rozema	Hood
15—Detroit	L	4-6§	Lopez	Renko
17—At Boston	L	1-4	Tudor	Gura
18—At Boston	W	2-1	Leonard	Brown
20—Chicago	L	6-9	Burns	Blue
21—Chicago	W	8-4	Renko	Bannister
22—Chicago	L	3-11	Hoyt	Gura
23—Texas	W	5-2	Leonard	Hough
24—Texas	T	2-2*	....	....
25—Texas	W	5-2	Black	Darwin
26—Baltimore	W	8-2	Renko	Boddicker
27—Baltimore	L	4-7	Davis	Gura
28—Baltimore	L	0-1	McGregor	Armstrong
29—Baltimore	W	4-0	Splittorff	D. Martinez
31—At Texas	W	6-5	Black	Darwin

Won 11, Lost 13

JUNE

1—At Texas	L	4-7	Honeycutt	Renko
2—At Chicago	L	3-6	Agosto	Gura
3—At Chicago	L	0-2	Koosman	Creel
4—At Chicago	W	7-1	Splittorff	Burns
5—At Chicago	W	7-5	Quisenberry	Hickey
5—At Chicago	L	2-5	Hoyt	Armstrong
7—Minnesota	W	9-4	Gura	Schrom
8—Minnesota	W	9-2	Renko	Filson
9—Minnesota	W	6-5	Castro	Lysander
10—At Seattle	W	2-0	Splittorff	Stoddard
11—At Seattle	W	4-1	Black	Perry
12—At Seattle	L	1-8	Abbott	Gura
13—At Minn.	L	4-9	Castillo	Renko
14—At Minn.	L	1-8	Williams	Creel
15—At Minn.	L	2-6	Viola	Splittorff
17—Seattle	W	3-1	Gura	Perry
18—Seattle	W	6-5	Quisenberry	Caudill
19—Seattle	W	4-2	Castro	Young
20—Oakland	L	2-7	Krueger	Blue
21—Oakland	W	4-2	Splittorff	McCatty
22—Oakland	W	7-6x	Armstrong	Callahan
23—California	L	2-7	Forsch	Black
24—California	W	11-3	Armstrong	John
25—California	L	2-9	Witt	Creel
27—At Oak.	L	1-7	Callahan	Gura
28—At Oak.	L	3-4	Underwood	Black
29—At Oak.	L	6-11	Jones	Renko
30—At Oak.	W	7-4	Hood	Burgmeier

Won 14, Lost 14

JULY

			Winner	Loser
1—At Calif.	L	6-7	McLaughlin	Blue
2—At Calif.	W	5-3	Gura	Kison
3—At Calif.	L	2-5	Forsch	Black
4—At Calif.	W	5-1	Splittorff	John
8—New York	L	2-9	Rawley	Gura
9—New York	W	3-2x	Quisenberry	Gossage
10—New York	L	4-6	Fontenot	Splittorff
11—Toronto	L	4-7§	Moffitt	Creel
12—Toronto	L	6-9	Jackson	Renko
13—Toronto	W	5-4	Gura	Clancy
14—At Cleve.	L	3-4‡	Sutcliffe	Armstrong
15—At Cleve.	W	10-0	Splittorff	Eichelberger
16—At Cleve.	L	3-17	Barker	Perry
17—At Cleve.	W	7-2	Hood	Spillner
18—At Toronto	L	2-8	Clancy	Gura
19—At Toronto	W	6-2	Black	Leal
20—At Toronto	W	14-8	Splittorff	Stieb
22—At N.Y.	L	6-7	Gossage	Armstrong
22—At N.Y.	W	3-2x	Quisenberry	Frazier
23—At N.Y.	L	1-5	Guidry	Gura
24—At N.Y.	W	5-4a	Armstrong	Gossage
25—Cleveland	W	6-1	Splittorff	Heaton
26—Cleveland	L	0-2	Sorensen	Renko
27—Cleveland	W	5-4	Perry	Barker
29—At Detroit	L	1-10z	Morris	Gura
30—At Detroit	L	1-4	Berenguer	Black
31—At Detroit	L	6-8	Rozema	Splittorff
31—At Detroit	W	7-5	Armstrong	Bailey

Won 13, Lost 15

AUGUST

1—At Detroit	L	2-3	Lopez	Hood
2—At Milw.	L	1-5	Gibson	Perry
2—At Milw.	L	2-3	Caldwell	Gura
3—At Milw.	W	8-5	Creel	McClure
4—At Milw.	W	6-2	Black	Sutton
5—Boston	L	4-5	Hurst	Armstrong
6—Boston	W	4-0	Rasmussen	Ojeda
7—Boston	W	1-0	Perry	Boyd
8—Milwaukee	W	5-4	Gura	Slaton
8—Milwaukee	L	5-8	McClure	Renko
9—Milwaukee	W	8-2	Black	Sutton
10—Milwaukee	L	0-4	Haas	Splittorff
13—At Boston	W	5-4	Perry	Aponte
13—At Boston	L	3-12	Boyd	Rasmussen
14—At Boston	L	3-4	Stanley	Renko
14—At Boston	W	6-3	Creel	Tudor
15—Detroit	W	6-4	Gura	Pashnick
16—Detroit	W	18-7	Huismann	Rozema
17—Detroit	L	4-10	Petry	Huismann
19—At Balt.	L	4-5	Stewart	Quisenberry
19—At Balt.	L	1-3	T. Martinez	Rasmussen
20—At Balt.	L	1-6	Boddicker	Gura
21—At Balt.	W	8-3	Black	Palmer
22—Chicago	L	1-3	Hoyt	Splittorff
23—Chicago	W	10-2	Renko	Koosman
24—Chicago	L	3-4‡	Dotson	Quisenberry
25—Texas	W	3-1	Rasmussen	Matlack
25—Texas	W	5-4	Armstrong	Schmidt
26—Texas	W	8-3	Black	Butcher
27—Texas	W	2-0	Splittorff	Tanana
28—Texas	L	0-1	Hough	Renko
29—Baltimore	L	2-9	McGregor	Perry
30—Baltimore	L	4-12	Davis	Rasmussen
31—At Chicago	L	3-7	Bannister	Gura

Won 16, Lost 18

SEPTEMBER

1—At Chicago	L	0-12	Hoyt	Black
2—At Texas	L	0-7	Hough	Splittorff
3—At Texas	W	5-0	Perry	Darwin
3—At Texas	L	1-8	Smithson	Creel
4—At Texas	L	2-3	Stewart	Rasmussen
5—Seattle	L	6-13	Beattie	Gura
6—Seattle	L	1-3	Stoddard	Black
7—Seattle	W	3-2	Splittorff	Young
9—At Minn.	L	6-7‡	O'Connor	Armstrong
10—At Minn.	L	3-6	Filson	Rasmussen
11—At Minn.	W	3-1	Jackson	Pettibone
13—At Calif.	W	4-3	Black	Sanchez
14—At Calif.	W	1-0y	Armstrong	Steirer
16—Oakland	W	6-5	Gura	Atherton
17—Oakland	W	10-1	Rasmussen	Heimueller
18—Oakland	L	2-6	Warren	Wills
19—California	W	8-4	Armstrong	Hassler
19—California	W	7-6	Huismann	McLaughlin
20—California	L	4-6	John	Splittorff
21—California	L	0-3	Zahn	Perry
22—Minnesota	L	1-2	Filson	Rasmussen
23—Minnesota	W	3-2	Wills	Pettibone
24—Minnesota	W	12-4†	Black	Viola
25—Minnesota	L	1-7	Schrom	Jackson
26—At Seattle	W	6-2	Splittorff	Clark
27—At Seattle	L	0-4	Beattie	Gura
28—At Seattle	W	11-8	Wills	Nelson
29—At Seattle	L	4-5	Stanton	Black

Won 13, Lost 15

OCTOBER

1—At Oak.	W	4-1	Splittorff	McCatty
1—At Oak.	W	7-3	Armstrong	Jones
2—At Oak.	L	4-8	Smith	Hood

Won 2, Lost 1

*5 innings. †5½ innings. ‡10 innings. §11 innings. x12 innings. y14 innings. zSuspended game, completed July 30. aSuspended game, completed August 18.

After the pine-tar controversy, George Brett's bat went silent and the Royals slipped out of contention.

rotation out of spring training—Leonard, Gura and Blue—finished 17-26.

The bright spots on a dismal pitching scene, besides Quisenberry, were Paul Splittorff's consistency (he led the club with 13 victories) and the emergence of Black (10-7) as a winner. Reliever Mike Armstrong also was 10-7.

Kansas City entered August 3½ games from the top, but by September 1 the deficit was an 11½-game gap that eventually expanded to 20. Clearly, the Royals faced prospects of a major revamping.

Brett might change positions, moving from third base to either left field or first base. John Wathan already has yielded catching duties to Slaught (who batted .312 in 276 at-bats), and first baseman Aikens lacked security despite his .302 average and 23 homers. And U.L. Washington's future at shortstop was jeopardized, in large part, by his 36 errors.

Otis, although he reached the 2,000-hit plateau, was blunted by injuries and turned out to the free-agent pasture after 14 years with the Royals. Sheridan (.270 and a defensive standout) and Davis (.344 with 18 RBIs in a 33-game stint) proved their mettle.

Though the year began on a bright, sunny day of victory in Baltimore, it turned quickly to mush—literally and figuratively.

The Royals had the smallest opening-night crowd in their history, 17,078, because of poor weather and eventually played 12 doubleheaders because of snow, cold and rain postponements.

All in all, '83 was not the warmest of greeting cards for a new partner in ownership, Avron Fogelman of Memphis, to whom Ewing Kauffman sold 49 percent of the club in May with plans for eventually turning it all over.

"A lot of factors combined to sap the spirit and energy of our club," said General Manager John Schuerholz.

"This club always has epitomized strong emotional qualities, and no one thing can be pointed to that broke that down. Injury to our No. 1 pitcher, the inability of Vida Blue to win, Larry Gura's struggle, a wide assortment of nagging injuries, disappointing performances by key people and the distraction of the announcement of a federal investigation—the whole was far more dynamic than the simple parts in bringing us down."

Larry Parrish was the most productive Ranger with 26 home runs, 88 runs batted in and 17 game-winning RBIs.

Rangers Half Good, Half Bad

By JIM REEVES

The best part of 1983 for the Texas Rangers was their giant Fourth of July celebration. For a change, the Rangers and their fans had something besides the holiday to shout about.

When baseball took its All-Star Game break after the July 4 schedule, a strange phenomenon was observed in newspapers across the country—the Rangers were in first place in the American League West standings.

Now everyone knows that's not how the West was won. When the Rangers took a vacation later in July (as they seemingly always do), the White Sox caught fire. And while Texas was losing 22 games over a four-week span, Chicago was beginning to pull away from the rest of the division.

It was a season in which the Rangers made a half-dozen giant strides forward, then took three steps back. Yet, there was no repeat of the dismal performance of 1982 when the Rangers slipped to 98 losses and sixth place in the West.

In 1983, under rookie Manager Doug Rader, the Rangers finished 77-85, good enough for third place but still 22 games behind the White Sox.

"It's a start," Rader said. "Our goal was to finish at .500 and we didn't quite make it. But we made progress. If we can make as much next season, we're going to be getting close to where we want to be."

The Rangers learned some things about themselves in '83. They learned they could pitch (Texas led the league with a 3.31 earned-run average) and field (Rader's team had the fewest errors, 113, in the majors). They even learned they could run a little. Billy Sample set a career high with 44 stolen bases and Wayne Tolleson added 33.

What the Rangers didn't do particularly well was hit, as their .255 team batting average (next to last in the A.L.) attests.

"We're still one or two bats short," Rader said repeatedly as the Rangers suffered 28 one-run losses. "If one or two guys shut down, the whole offense shuts down."

There were some bright spots offensively, however. Larry Parrish put together a consistent season, avoiding the cold-hot flashes he had in 1982 and hitting .272 with a team-leading 26 home runs, 88 runs batted in and 17 game-winning RBIs.

Third baseman Buddy Bell led the club in hitting with a .277 mark. One of the most impressive performances of the season, though, was turned in by center fielder George Wright, who followed up a good rookie season by hitting .276 with 18 homers and 80 RBIs. Wright also was outstanding defensively.

Center fielder George Wright was a bright spot, both offensively and defensively.

When second baseman Mike Richardt suffered a knee injury in Baltimore on April 21, the Rangers discovered Tolleson. A utility player previously, Tolleson stepped in and did a creditable job defensively and batted .260. The position is now Tolleson's until someone beats him out.

Bucky Dent played superb defense at

SCORES OF TEXAS RANGERS' 1983 GAMES

APRIL

Game		Score	Winner	Loser
4—Chicago	W	5-3	Butcher	Hoyt
5—Chicago	W	4-1	Matlack	Bannister
6—Chicago	W	4-1	Honeycutt	Dotson
8—Boston	L	5-8	Aponte	Mason
9—Boston	W	10-3	Smithson	Ojeda
10—Boston	W	9-7	Hough	Stanley
12—At Cleve.	W	2-1	Honeycutt	Blyleven
13—At Cleve.	L	3-4	Barker	Mason
15—At Boston	L	1-4	Eckersley	Matlack
16—At Boston	L	1-2	Hurst	Darwin
17—At Boston	W	1-0z	Jones	Stanley
19—At Balt.	L	2-4	Stewart	Hough
20—At Balt.	W	11-2	Smithson	D. Martinez
21—At Balt.	L	2-3z	Stoddard	Jones
22—Milwaukee	W	3-2	Darwin	McClure
23—Milwaukee	L	0-3	Caldwell	Honeycutt
24—Milwaukee	L	1-3	Sutton	Hough
26—Toronto	W	2-1	Smithson	Stieb
27—Toronto	L	2-3	Moffitt	Darwin
29—New York	W	8-3	Honeycutt	Rawley
30—New York	W	6-3	Hough	Guidry

Won 12, Lost 9

MAY

Game		Score	Winner	Loser
1—New York	L	4-8	Righetti	Smithson
2—At Toronto	L	5-6	Clancy	Darwin
3—At Toronto	W	7-2	Matlack	Gott
4—At Toronto	L	1-7	Leal	Honeycutt
6—At Milw.	W	9-4	Butcher	Caldwell
8—At Milw.	L	3-6	Slaton	Jones
10—At N.Y.	W	4-2	Tanana	Rawley
11—At N.Y.	W	3-1	Honeycutt	Guidry
13—Baltimore	L	1-8	Davis	Hough
14—Baltimore	L	11-14§	T. Martinez	Tobik
15—Baltimore	W	2-1	Darwin	D. Martinez
16—Cleveland	W	3-1	Honeycutt	Barker
17—Cleveland	W	6-5x	Schmidt	Glynn
18—Cleveland	W	3-2z	Tobik	Heaton
19—At Detroit	L	1-2‡	Wilcox	Smithson
20—At Detroit	W	4-0	Darwin	Ujdur
21—At Detroit	L	3-5	Petry	Honeycutt
22—At Detroit	L	5-12	Berenguer	Butcher
23—At Kan. C.	L	2-5	Leonard	Hough
24—At Kan. C.	T	2-2*	.....	.....
25—At Kan. C.	L	2-5	Black	Darwin
26—At Chicago	W	3-1	Honeycutt	Bannister
27—At Chicago	L	2-3	Hoyt	Tanana
28—At Chicago	L	3-8	Dotson	Hough
29—At Chicago	L	3-8	Koosman	Smithson
31—Kan. City	L	5-6	Black	Darwin

Won 10, Lost 15

JUNE

Game		Score	Winner	Loser
1—Kan. City	W	7-4	Honeycutt	Renko
3—Detroit	L	1-12	Morris	Smithson
4—Detroit	W	5-2	Hough	Petry
5—Detroit	L	4-5‡	Lopez	Butcher
7—At Seattle	W	10-0	Honeycutt	Stoddard
8—At Seattle	W	1-0	Smithson	Young
9—At Seattle	L	2-3§	Caudill	Hough
10—At Minn.	W	4-2	Tanana	Viola
11—At Minn.	W	11-0	Darwin	Havens
12—At Minn.	W	4-3§	Jones	Davis
13—Seattle	W	5-2	Smithson	Young
14—Seattle	W	7-1	Hough	Beattie
15—Seattle	L	4-6	Vande Berg	Jones
16—Minnesota	L	3-4	Lysander	Darwin
17—Minnesota	W	10-1	Honeycutt	Schrom
18—Minnesota	L	4-8	Castillo	Smithson
19—Minnesota	W	4-1	Hough	Williams
20—California	L	9-10y	Curtis	Matlack
21—California	W	3-2	Darwin	McLaughlin
22—California	W	9-1	Honeycutt	Travers
24—Oakland	W	6-5	Smithson	Baker
24—Oakland	W	6-2	Hough	Young
25—Oakland	W	8-3	Tanana	Krueger
26—Oakland	W	4-1†	Darwin	McCatty
27—At Calif.	L	0-8	Kison	Honeycutt
28—At Calif.	W	3-1	Hough	Forsch
29—At Calif.	L	1-2	Sanchez	Smithson
30—At Calif.	W	4-2‡	Schmidt	Sanchez

Won 19, Lost 9

JULY

Game		Score	Winner	Loser
1—At Oak.	W	8-5	Darwin	Callahan
2—At Oak.	W	13-3	Honeycutt	Underwood
3—At Oak.	W	16-4a	Jones	Beard
4—At Oak.	L	3-4	McCatty	Smithson
8—At Toronto	L	5-8	Clancy	Darwin
9—At Toronto	L	1-5	Leal	Hough
10—At Toronto	L	4-6	Stieb	Honeycutt
11—Milwaukee	W	5-4a	Tobik	Augustine
12—Milwaukee	L	2-9	Porter	Tanana
13—Milwaukee	L	2-6	McClure	Darwin
14—At N.Y.	W	11-2	Hough	Rawley
15—At N.Y.	L	5-7	Righetti	Honeycutt
16—At N.Y.	L	1-3	Fontenot	Smithson
17—At N.Y.	L	6-8	Murray	Jones
18—At Milw.	L	3-4	Augustine	Darwin
18—At Milw.	L	4-5	Tellmann	Hough
19—At Milw.	W	3-1	Honeycutt	Sutton
20—At Milw.	L	3-4	Tellmann	Smithson
21—Toronto	W	3-2	Tanana	Gott
22—Toronto	L	5-10§	Moffitt	Schmidt
23—Toronto	L	2-3	Clancy	Darwin
24—Toronto	W	3-0	Honeycutt	Leal
25—New York	L	5-6	Gossage	Butcher
26—New York	L	0-5	Fontenot	Tanana
27—New York	L	3-4	Keough	Hough
29—At Balt.	L	6-8	Stewart	Schmidt
30—At Balt.	L	4-7	McGregor	Smithson
31—At Balt.	L	0-6	Boddicker	Tanana

Won 8, Lost 20

AUGUST

Game		Score	Winner	Loser
2—Boston	L	5-6	Boyd	Hough
3—Boston	L	4-5‡	Aponte	Cruz
4—Boston	W	6-1	Honeycutt	Tudor
5—At Cleve.	W	2-0	Smithson	Sorensen
6—At Cleve.	W	6-1	Tanana	Barker
7—At Cleve.	W	4-3	Hough	Spillner
7—At Cleve.	L	0-7	Brennan	Matlack
8—At Boston	W	12-7	Butcher	Stanley
9—At Boston	L	4-6	Tudor	Honeycutt
10—At Boston	L	2-4	Hurst	Smithson
12—Cleveland	W	6-2	Tanana	Brennan
13—Cleveland	W	4-3	Hough	Sutcliffe
14—Cleveland	L	0-3	Heaton	Honeycutt
15—Baltimore	L	4-6	Boddicker	Smithson
16—Baltimore	W	2-0	Butcher	Ramirez
17—Baltimore	L	2-4‡	Flanagan	Jones
19—Chicago	L	2-3‡	Dotson	Cruz
19—Chicago	L	1-6	Koosman	Hough
20—Chicago	W	6-1	Stewart	Burns
21—Chicago	L	1-3	Bannister	Butcher
22—Detroit	W	3-1	Tanana	Petry
23—Detroit	L	0-2	Bair	Hough
24—Detroit	L	2-5	Morris	Cruz
25—At Kan. C.	L	1-3	Rasmussen	Matlack
25—At Kan. C.	L	4-5	Armstrong	Schmidt
26—At Kan. C.	L	3-8	Black	Butcher
27—At Kan. C.	L	0-2	Splittorff	Tanana
28—At Kan. C.	W	1-0	Hough	Renko
29—At Chicago	L	1-2	Dotson	Smithson
30—At Chicago	L	0-5	Burns	Stewart
31—At Detroit	W	5-1	Butcher	Abbott

Won 12, Lost 19

SEPTEMBER

Game		Score	Winner	Loser
1—At Detroit	L	0-5	Morris	Tanana
2—Kan. City	W	7-0	Hough	Splittorff
3—Kan. City	L	0-5	Perry	Darwin
3—Kan. City	W	8-1	Smithson	Creel
4—Kan. City	W	3-2	Stewart	Rasmussen
5—Minnesota	W	7-3	Butcher	Lysander
6—Minnesota	L	3-5‡	Davis	Tanana
7—Minnesota	W	3-0	Hough	Williams
9—At Seattle	L	4-6	Moore	Smithson
10—At Seattle	L	2-4	Clark	Darwin
11—At Seattle	W	2-1	Stewart	Beattie
13—At Oak.	L	5-6	Warren	Tanana
14—At Oak.	W	4-2	Hough	McCatty
15—At Oak.	W	6-5	Schmidt	Conroy
16—At Calif.	L	6-8	Sanchez	Butcher
17—At Calif.	W	5-2	Stewart	Forsch
18—At Calif.	W	7-6	Cruz	Lacey
20—Oakland	W	3-2	Hough	Atherton
21—Oakland	W	4-2	Smithson	Codiroli
22—Seattle	W	5-2	Darwin	Beattie
23—Seattle	W	2-1	Stewart	Nelson
24—Seattle	L	0-2	Moore	Tanana
25—Seattle	L	1-2	Stoddard	Hough
27—At Minn.	W	6-1	Smithson	Williams
28—At Minn.	L	0-3	Filson	Darwin
29—At Minn.	L	0-2	Schrom	Stewart
30—California	W	4-3‡	Henke	Corbett

Won 16, Lost 11

OCTOBER

Game		Score	Winner	Loser
1—California	L	5-6	Lacey	Jones
2—California	L	0-2	S. Brown	Lachowicz

Won 0, Lost 2

*5 innings. †7 innings. ‡10 innings. §11 innings. x12 innings. y13 innings. z14 innings. a15 innings.

Knuckleballer Charlie Hough (above) enjoyed another productive season while Dave Tobik came on late to save nine games.

shortstop, left fielder Sample put in his first season of full-time play and batted .274 with 12 homers and 57 RBIs and veteran Mickey Rivers gained Rader's respect by filling in admirably at designated hitter and in the outfield.

But there were disappointments, too. Catcher Jim Sundberg slipped to .201, 57 points under his lifetime average. Reserve catcher Bobby Johnson failed to take up the slack, hitting just .210. The two catchers combined for only seven homers and 44 RBIs.

Designated hitter Dave Hostetler was another bust. He couldn't seem to get rolling and finished the season as a platoon player, batting just .220 with 11 homers and 46 RBIs. Rookie first baseman Pete O'Brien, gifted defensively, hit only .237 with eight homers and 53 RBIs.

Pitching was the highlight of the season, even after Rick Honeycutt—the A.L. leader in ERA at 2.42—was traded to Los Angeles in August. Dave Stewart was obtained in the deal for Honeycutt (who was 14-8 for the Rangers), and he registered a 5-2 record and a 2.14 ERA in eight starts.

Veteran Charlie Hough, another Dodger castoff, nearly matched his 16-13 record of 1982 (he went 15-13) and recorded a 3.18 ERA.

Rookie Mike Smithson was 10-14 and showed signs of potential stardom. Veteran Frank Tanana replaced Jon Matlack in the rotation in late May and went 7-9 with a 3.16 ERA, and Danny Darwin, fighting an assortment of illnesses and injuries, was 8-13 with a 3.49 ERA.

Rader's No. 1 concern in spring training was the bullpen, but Texas' relievers—except for a six-week period after the All-Star break—were surprisingly effective. Odell Jones carried the bullpen for the first half of the year—he had eight saves at the break—and finished 3-6 with 10 saves and a 3.09 ERA. The man who came to the fore late was Dave Tobik, who spent six weeks in Oklahoma City. Tobik was 2-1 with nine saves overall.

Victor Cruz picked up five saves and John Butcher, who tossed a one-hitter against Baltimore in a spot start, was 6-6 with five saves.

"I'm convinced," said General Manager Joe Klein, "that the way Rader handled the bullpen can be done successfully. Except for that one six-week period, we had excellent relief."

"What we need most is more runs," Rader emphasized. "It's pretty obvious we could have had a much better season if we'd scored more runs."

Or if the season had ended on July 4.

Rickey Henderson had an up-and-down season, but still managed to steal a major league-leading 108 bases.

Wounded A's Make Progress

By KIT STIER

The American Medical Association could make the 1983 A's the major topic of its annual convention.

The A's seemingly made more visits to orthopedic surgeons, neurologists and other medical types than they did to the victory column.

It is almost a miracle that rookie Manager Steve Boros guided the club to a 74-88 record and a fourth-place finish in the American League West, six victories and a notch higher than the team finished under Billy Martin a year earlier.

Boros left spring training with the idea of using the same nine everyday players from green flag to checkered flag, resting them only occasionally. He set his pitching staff and lined up his bullpen.

So much for Boros' carefully constructed plans.

By season's end, 21 pitchers and infielder Wayne Gross had worked the mound for the A's. Ten of those pitchers were rookies, and 18 rookies in all wore the green, white and gold in '83.

Rookie pitchers accounted for 38 of the club's victories and 44 of its losses. There were 22 complete games, 17 by rookies.

"It's been a frustrating year," Boros said at the finish. "That's the best word I can use. I can't be disappointed. Frustrated, frustrated.

"I don't feel young players will play the part next year that they did this year. From the middle of the summer on we had seven to 10 first-year players on the roster at one time and I feel that's really too many."

The rookies had their moments, though.

In the final week of the season, Mike Warren pitched a no-hitter against the Chicago White Sox, facing only 29 batters. The 22-year-old righthander was the first rookie in 10 years to throw a no-hitter, and the gem was his fourth straight victory.

Rookie Chris Codiroli was the A's leading winner with a 12-12 record and had a stretch of 25 straight scoreless innings. The A's staff produced 37 consecutive scoreless innings in mid-August, an A's record. The streak included one shutout against Minnesota and two against California.

Left fielder Rickey Henderson had an up-and-down season, but still stole 100 bases for the third time. He finished with 108 steals to lead the league for the fourth straight year. Henderson also drew 103

Rookie Chris Codiroli (above) led the A's with 12 victories while Mike Warren entered the record books with a late-season no-hitter.

SCORES OF OAKLAND ATHLETICS' 1983 GAMES

APRIL

			Winner	Loser
4—Cleveland	L	5-8	Sutcliffe	Langford
6—Cleveland	W	5-3	Norris	Blyleven
7—Cleveland	L	1-9	Barker	Underwood
8—California	W	5-3	Beard	Zahn
9—California	L	2-10	Forsch	Keough
10—California	W	11-4	Krueger	Kison
12—Minnesota	W	4-3y	Beard	Whitehouse
13—Minnesota	W	5-4	Baker	Williams
14—At Seattle	W	5-3	Codiroli	Nunez
15—At Seattle	L	1-5	Perry	Keough
16—At Seattle	W	5-2	Krueger	Young
17—At Seattle	W	7-4	Norris	Stoddard
18—At Calif.	W	5-3	Underwood	Witt
21—At Calif.	L	2-6	Zahn	Codiroli
21—At Calif.	L	5-6	Forsch	Keough
22—Boston	L	1-3	Hurst	Krueger
24—Boston	L	2-4	Tudor	Norris
26—Baltimore	W	4-3	Codiroli	Palmer
27—Baltimore	L	0-6	Flanagan	Krueger
29—Detroit	W	5-4	Baker	Morris

Won 11, Lost 9

MAY

1—Detroit	W	8-3	Codiroli	Ujdur
1—Detroit	W	2-0	Norris	Wilcox
3—At Boston	L	1-3	Eckersley	Krueger
4—At Boston	L	1-7	Hurst	Langford
6—At Balt.	L	2-9	D. Martinez	Norris
7—At Balt.	L	6-8	Flanagan	Codiroli
8—At Balt.	W	1-0	Krueger	T. Martinez
10—At Detroit	L	3-4	Rucker	Langford
11—At Detroit	L	2-5	Wilcox	Norris
12—At Detroit	W	11-4	Burgmeier	Petry
13—Seattle	W	9-2	Krueger	Stoddard
14—Seattle	L	1-4	Young	Langford
15—Seattle	W	3-0	Underwood	Beattie
16—At Minn.	W	7-6	Norris	Havens
17—At Minn.	W	7-6	Codiroli	Williams
18—At Minn.	L	5-16	Viola	Krueger
20—New York	W	8-4	Underwood	Shirley
21—New York	L	0-1	Rawley	Norris
22—New York	L	2-4	Guidry	Burgmeier
23—Milwaukee	W	5-4b	Baker	Slaton
24—Milwaukee	W	8-7	Keough	Easterly
25—Milwaukee	L	6-7	Haas	Underwood
27—At N.Y.	L	2-4	Guidry	Norris
28—At N.Y.	L	2-5	Righetti	Codiroli
29—At N.Y.	L	0-5	May	Krueger
30—At N.Y.	L	5-10	Gossage	Burgmeier
31—At Milw.	L	2-5	Haas	Conroy

Won 11, Lost 16

JUNE

1—At Milw.	W	7-5	Burgmeier	Porter
2—At Milw.	L	1-6	Caldwell	Codiroli
4—At Cleve.	W	6-3	Burgmeier	Waits
5—At Cleve.	W	8-3	Keough	Heaton
5—At Cleve.	W	9-2	McCatty	Barker
7—Toronto	W	5-3	Conroy	Gott
8—Toronto	L	2-5	Stieb	Codiroli
9—Toronto	W	3-1	Underwood	Clancy
10—Chicago	W	2-1a	Burgmeier	Tidrow
11—Chicago	W	5-4	Conroy	Hoyt
12—Chicago	L	10-12‡	Tidrow	Warren
12—Chicago	L	1-8	Koosman	Codiroli
14—At Toronto	L	7-13	Jackson	Underwood
15—At Toronto	W	10-1	Krueger	Leal
16—At Toronto	L	1-9	Gott	McCatty
17—At Chicago	L	3-6	Hickey	Burgmeier
18—At Chicago	W	3-1	Codiroli	Bannister
19—At Chicago	L	0-1	Burns	Underwood
20—At Kan. C.	W	7-2	Krueger	Blue
21—At Kan. C.	L	2-4	Splittorff	McCatty
22—At Kan. C.	L	6-7§	Armstrong	Callahan
24—At Texas	L	5-6	Smithson	Baker
24—At Texas	L	2-6	Hough	Young
25—At Texas	L	3-8	Tanana	Krueger
26—At Texas	L	1-4*	Darwin	McCatty
27—Kan. City	W	7-1	Callahan	Gura
28—Kan. City	W	4-3	Underwood	Black
29—Kan. City	W	11-6	Jones	Renko
30—Kan. City	L	4-7	Hood	Burgmeier

Won 14, Lost 15

JULY

			Winner	Loser
1—Texas	L	5-8	Darwin	Callahan
2—Texas	L	3-13	Honeycutt	Underwood
3—Texas	L	4-16z	Jones	Beard
4—Texas	W	4-3	McCatty	Smithson
8—At Detroit	L	2-3	Bair	Baker
9—At Detroit	W	3-1	McCatty	Morris
10—At Detroit	L	3-5	Bailey	Beard
11—At Balt.	L	6-7	D. Martinez	Baker
12—At Balt.	L	1-3	Ramirez	Heimueller
13—At Balt.	L	2-6	Davis	Conroy
14—At Boston	L	4-9	Tudor	McCatty
15—At Boston	L	7-10	Clear	Burgmeier
16—At Boston	W	12-5	Atherton	Stanley
17—At Boston	W	13-9	Codiroli	Clear
18—Detroit	L	2-4	Petry	Conroy
19—Detroit	L	3-4	Morris	Beard
20—Detroit	W	9-2	Codiroli	Bair
21—Baltimore	W	9-7	Beard	Morogiello
22—Baltimore	W	4-3	Burgmeier	Ramirez
23—Baltimore	L	3-7	Davis	Conroy
24—Baltimore	L	3-4	McGregor	McCatty
25—Boston	L	0-3	Hurst	Codiroli
26—Boston	W	9-2	Underwood	Stanley
26—Boston	L	3-5	Stanley	Burgmeier
27—Boston	W	7-6	Krueger	Brown
29—At Calif.	W	5-2	Conroy	Forsch
30—At Calif.	W	13-8	Burgmeier	Sanchez
30—At Calif.	W	2-1§	Beard	John
31—At Calif.	L	0-4	Zahn	Heimueller

Won 12, Lost 17

AUGUST

1—At Seattle	W	4-3	Underwood	Stanton
2—At Seattle	L	12-15	Thomas	Codiroli
3—At Seattle	W	6-1	Conroy	Beattie
4—At Minn.	L	3-4	Whitehouse	Burgmeier
5—At Minn.	W	3-2	Heimueller	O'Connor
6—At Minn.	W	6-4x	Atherton	Davis
7—At Minn.	W	6-0	Codiroli	Viola
8—Seattle	W	2-1	Conroy	Beattie
9—Seattle	W	7-6	Underwood	Stoddard
10—Seattle	L	5-7	Young	Heimueller
11—Minnesota	W	6-0	Codiroli	Viola
12—Minnesota	L	3-5	Schrom	Underwood
13—Minnesota	L	3-7	Williams	Conroy
14—Minnesota	W	6-0	McCatty	Castillo
15—California	W	5-0	Heimueller	Zahn
16—California	W	4-0	Codiroli	Steirer
17—California	L	5-6	Witt	Warren
19—At Milw.	W	9-1	Conroy	Sutton
20—At Milw.	L	1-3	Tellmann	McCatty
21—At Milw.	L	1-7	Haas	Codiroli
22—At N.Y.	W	3-2y	Beard	Frazier
23—At N.Y.	W	9-3	Warren	Keough
24—At Cleve.	L	0-1	Heaton	Conroy
24—At Cleve.	L	2-4	Sorensen	Atherton
25—At Cleve.	W	6-0	McCatty	Jeffcoat
26—Milwaukee	W	4-3	Codiroli	Haas
27—Milwaukee	W	5-2	Heimueller	Porter
28—Milwaukee	L	2-4	Caldwell	Warren
30—New York	L	5-8	Guidry	Beard
31—New York	L	4-6	Rawley	Conroy

Won 17, Lost 13

SEPTEMBER

1—New York	W	2-0	Codiroli	Righetti
2—Cleveland	L	2-4	Sorensen	Heimueller
3—Cleveland	L	6-13	Spillner	Beard
4—Cleveland	L	2-9	Sutcliffe	McCatty
5—At Chicago	L	1-11	Bannister	Conroy
6—At Chicago	L	6-7	Hoyt	Codiroli
7—At Chicago	L	7-8†	Agosto	Atherton
9—At Toronto	W	7-5	McCatty	Clancy
10—At Toronto	L	5-7	Stieb	Underwood
11—At Toronto	L	6-16	Gott	Codiroli
13—Texas	W	6-5	Warren	Tanana
14—Texas	L	2-4	Hough	McCatty
15—Texas	L	5-6	Schmidt	Conroy
16—At Kan. C.	L	5-6	Gura	Atherton
17—At Kan. C.	L	1-10	Rasmussen	Heimueller
18—At Kan. C.	W	6-2	Warren	Wills
20—At Texas	L	2-3	Hough	Atherton
21—At Texas	L	2-4	Smithson	Codiroli
23—Toronto	W	2-0	Conroy	Leal
24—Toronto	W	2-1†	Warren	Clancy
25—Toronto	L	6-8	Acker	Atherton
27—Chicago	W	5-4	Underwood	Tidrow
28—Chicago	L	3-5	Dotson	Conroy
29—Chicago	W	3-0	Warren	Burns

Won 8, Lost 16

OCTOBER

1—Kan. City	L	1-4	Splittorff	McCatty
1—Kan. City	L	3-7	Armstrong	Jones
2—Kan. City	W	8-4	Smith	Hood

Won 1, Lost 2

*7 innings. †10 innings. ‡11 innings. §12 innings. x13 innings. y14 innings. z15 innings. a16 innings. b17 innings.

Mike Davis impressed fans with his solid right-field play and .275 batting average.

walks, pacing the A.L. in that category for the second consecutive season.

But the good times came infrequently as the A's suffered four six-game losing streaks. Their longest winning spell was five games.

Oakland was at .500 for the last time on June 20, then dropped to 12 games under on four occasions before climbing back to two under (65-67) on August 27. Then the roof caved in as the A's lost 21 of their final 30 games.

It is easy to see why the A's struggled. By September 1, 40 players had been in uniform. Thirteen had been on the disabled list, including pitchers Rick Langford and Mike Norris (twice each) and third baseman Carney Lansford.

Other key players who missed time included center fielder Dwayne Murphy, catcher Mike Heath, right fielder Mike Davis, reliever Dave Beard and starting pitcher Bill Krueger.

Lansford, whom the A's had counted on to anchor the infield, played in just 80 games and in only two (as a pinch-hitter) after August 24. His 2-year-old son, Nicholas, died of kidney disease in April. Later, Lansford was disabled with a sprained left wrist and then had to have bone chips removed from his left ankle.

Heath, named Oakland's No. 1 catcher in the spring, appeared in only 96 games and saw duty as an outfielder. A bad back and sore toe cut into his playing time.

Starters Norris and Langford were never right. Langford was 0-4 with a 12.15 earned-run average in seven starts and had numerous problems with his right arm. Norris, who had an injured right shoulder, was 4-5 in 16 starts.

Many blamed the troubles of Norris, Langford, Steve McCatty (who began the season on a rehabilitation program and finished with a 6-9 record) and Matt Keough (traded to the Yankees on June 15) on Billy Burnout. Those four and Brian Kingman (traded away before the '83 season) had pitched 93 of the 94 complete games turned in by Billy Martin's staff in 1980. In 1983, McCatty had three complete games, Norris two, Keough and Langford none.

In all, 16 pitchers started games for the A's.

Another key setback for the pitching staff was the loss of veteran reliever Tom Burgmeier. A sore left rotator cuff sidelined the veteran lefthander, who didn't pitch after making his 49th appearance on August 23.

Beard led the team in saves with 10, but had none after August 26. In a 24-game stretch beginning August 28, the bullpen produced only two saves as Oakland went 6-18.

One of Boros' goals was to have the pitching staff (which yielded 648 walks in 1982, an average of four per game) average fewer than three walks an outing in '83. But A's pitchers still struggled, issuing 626 walks, a 3.86 average.

On offense, there was a severe power shortage. The club hit 121 homers, ranking 10th in the league, with Murphy and Davey Lopes leading the way with 17 each.

However, the A's managed to hit .262 as a team, two points higher than any Oakland team had ever hit.

Also on the bright side, Davis played solidly in right field in his first full season in the majors and batted .275. And rookie Donnie Hill emerged as the A's shortstop of the future.

"All I can hope for is that all the young players will learn something from this season and be better for it next year," Boros said.

Good health wouldn't hurt, either.

Ken Schrom started the 1983 season in Toledo, but ended up leading the Twins with 15 victories.

Twins Escape Cellar, but . . .

By PATRICK REUSSE

The Minnesota Twins escaped last place in the American League West in 1983 and improved on their '82 victory total by 10 games. Still, the Twins compiled the second-worst full-season winning percentage in the 23-year history of the franchise.

Excluding the strike-shortened 1981 season, the Twins' 1983 percentage of .432 (70-92) ranked ahead of only the .370 figure of '82 (when Minnesota had the worst record in the major leagues, 60-102). The improvement in games won, though, enabled the Twins to tie '82 West champion California for fifth place, ahead of the Seattle Mariners.

The improvement could have been more dramatic if Minnesota's starting pitching—one of the team's hoped-for strengths entering the season—had delivered. The team's best starter turned out to be Ken Schrom, a longtime minor leaguer who wasn't on the roster when the season began.

Schrom had only two major league decisions in seven professional seasons before 1983. He was called up from the Triple-A Toledo Mud Hens in early May and, after one victory out of the bullpen, was moved into the starting rotation on May 20. He won 14 games as a starter and finished 15-8 with an earned-run average of 3.71.

Troubles hounded the rest of the Twins' starters. For the last two months of the 1982 season, the rotation of Bobby Castillo, Al Williams, Brad Havens, Jack O'Connor and Frank Viola had been solid for the Twins. It was a different story in '83.

Castillo, 13-11 with a 3.66 ERA in '82, dropped to 8-12 and 4.77 and his season ended in late August when a rotator-cuff problem developed. Williams was bothered most of the season with a sore elbow and finished 11-14 with a 4.14 ERA.

Havens, the Twins' opening-night pitcher, went sour early, spent much of the year in Toledo and had an 8.18 ERA to go with a 5-8 record. O'Connor also was shipped to the minor leagues, and Viola showed little improvement over his rookie season as he posted a 7-15 record and a 5.49 ERA. Viola surrendered 34 home runs, second most in the A.L.

The Twins' search for starters included two stretches of duty for rookie Bryan Oelkers, the club's No. 1 draftee from June of '82. The Twins projected Oelkers as a starter after a strong spring showing, but he wound up 0-5 overall with an 8.65 ERA.

In 1982, Minnesota's staff ERA was 4.72; in 1983, it improved only slightly, to 4.66, despite a much better performance by the bullpen.

Despite a meager .227 average, Tom Brunansky led the Twins with 28 home runs.

Ron Davis, the late-inning stopper, earned a $175,000 raise to $475,000 with a preseason victory in arbitration, then upgraded his statistics considerably. In 1982, Davis was 3-9 with 22 saves and a 4.42 ERA. In 1983, Davis increased his save total to 30 and was 5-8 with a 3.34 ERA.

Davis was the major ingredient of an improved bullpen, a unit whose new middle-relief corps was a vast improvement over the '82 group. Righthanders Rick Lysander and Mike Walters and lefthanders Len Whitehouse and Pete Filson worked well as the link between the struggling starters and the reliable Davis.

"If our starting pitching had been what we expected it to be, we could have fin-

SCORES OF MINNESOTA TWINS' 1983 GAMES

APRIL

			Winner	Loser
5—Detroit	L	3-11	Morris	Havens
6—Detroit	L	5-9	Petry	Lysander
7—Detroit	W	5-4	Williams	Ujdur
8—At Seattle	W	5-4‡	Lysander	Caudill
9—At Seattle	L	2-3	Thomas	Oelkers
10—At Seattle	W	6-3	Havens	Perry
12—At Oak.	L	3-4y	Beard	Whitehouse
13—At Oak.	L	4-5	Baker	Williams
15—California	L	2-8	Forsch	Viola
16—California	L	5-9	Kison	Oelkers
17—California	W	11-8	Whitehouse	Goltz
18—Seattle	W	8-5	O'Connor	Moore
19—Seattle	W	6-2	Whitehouse	Nunez
20—Seattle	W	11-2	Castillo	Perry
21—Seattle	L	0-2	Young	Oelkers
22—At N.Y.	W	5-3	Havens	Alexander
23—At N.Y.	L	4-7	Rawley	O'Connor
25—At N.Y.	L	1-2	Guidry	Viola
26—At Cleve.	L	1-7	Sorensen	Castillo
27—At Cleve.	W	5-3	Williams	Glynn
29—Milwaukee	W	7-4	Havens	McClure
30—Milwaukee	W	9-7	Davis	Ladd

Won 11, Lost 11

MAY

			Winner	Loser
1—Milwaukee	L	4-8	Sutton	Williams
3—Cleveland	L	1-3	Blyleven	Castillo
4—Cleveland	L	7-11	Spillner	Davis
5—Cleveland	L	5-7	Sutcliffe	Havens
6—New York	L	4-8	Guidry	O'Connor
7—New York	L	7-8	Frazier	Williams
8—New York	W	6-5	Whitehouse	Murray
10—At Milw.	L	1-4	Haas	Havens
11—At Milw.	L	1-4	McClure	Williams
13—At Calif.	W	5-4‡	Whitehouse	Witt
14—At Calif.	W	2-1	Schrom	Forsch
15—At Calif.	W	8-6	Filson	Goltz
16—Oakland	L	6-7	Norris	Havens
17—Oakland	L	6-7	Codiroli	Williams
18—Oakland	W	16-5	Viola	Krueger
19—At Boston	L	1-4	Bird	Castillo
20—At Boston	W	10-4	Schrom	Hurst
21—At Boston	L	4-11	Ojeda	Havens
22—At Boston	W	4-3x	Davis	Aponte
23—At Balt.	W	12-4	Viola	Davis
24—At Balt.	W	6-1	Castillo	McGregor
25—At Balt.	W	7-4	Schrom	D. Martinez
27—At Detroit	L	4-7	Pashnick	Lysander
27—At Detroit	L	1-2§	Bailey	Lysander
28—At Detroit	L	1-6	Wilcox	Williams
29—At Detroit	L	6-7	Lopez	Lysander
30—Baltimore	L	1-6	Boddicker	Castillo
31—Baltimore	W	10-3	Schrom	Davis

Won 11, Lost 17

JUNE

			Winner	Loser
1—Baltimore	L	3-6	McGregor	Lysander
3—Boston	L	3-6	Boyd	Williams
4—Boston	L	6-8	Eckersley	Viola
5—Boston	W	10-4	Havens	Hurst
7—At Kan. C.	L	4-9	Gura	Schrom
8—At Kan. C.	L	2-9	Renko	Filson
9—At Kan. C.	L	5-6	Castro	Lysander
10—Texas	L	2-4	Tanana	Viola
11—Texas	L	0-11	Darwin	Havens
12—Texas	L	3-4‡	Jones	Davis
13—Kan. City	W	9-4	Castillo	Renko
14—Kan. City	W	8-1	Williams	Creel
15—Kan. City	W	6-2	Viola	Splittorff
16—At Texas	W	4-3	Lysander	Darwin
17—At Texas	L	1-10	Honeycutt	Schrom
18—At Texas	W	8-4	Castillo	Smithson
19—At Texas	L	1-4	Hough	Williams
20—At Toronto	L	1-2	Gott	Davis
21—At Toronto	L	3-8	Acker	Oelkers
22—At Toronto	W	4-3	Schrom	Stieb
23—At Chicago	L	6-8	Bannister	Castillo
24—At Chicago	W	5-1	Williams	Burns
25—At Chicago	L	3-8	Hoyt	Viola
26—At Chicago	L	7-9	Dotson	Oelkers
28—Toronto	W	5-2	Schrom	Stieb
29—Toronto	L	2-4	Clancy	Castillo
30—Toronto	L	3-11	Leal	Williams

Won 9, Lost 18

JULY

			Winner	Loser
1—Chicago	W	6-3	Viola	Hoyt
2—Chicago	L	2-4	Dotson	Schrom
3—Chicago	W	4-3	Davis	Barojas
4—Chicago	L	6-12	Lamp	Lysander
8—Cleveland	L	4-10	Blyleven	Viola
9—Cleveland	W	3-2	Schrom	Sutcliffe
10—Cleveland	W	6-4	Williams	Eichelberger
11—New York	W	4-2	Castillo	Howell
12—New York	L	3-4	Frazier	Lysander
13—New York	W	6-1	Schrom	Guidry
14—At Milw.	L	1-5	Sutton	Williams
15—At Milw.	L	3-6	Caldwell	Castillo
16—At Milw.	L	0-5	Haas	Viola
17—At Milw.	L	6-10	Porter	Schrom
18—At N.Y.	L	2-4	Guidry	Williams
19—At N.Y.	L	0-4	Rawley	Castillo
20—At N.Y.	L	4-6†	Gossage	Davis
22—At Cleve.	L	5-8	Easterly	Lysander
23—At Cleve.	W	5-2	Williams	Barker
24—At Cleve.	W	7-5	Castillo	Sutcliffe
24—At Cleve.	W	5-4	Havens	Brennan
25—Milwaukee	W	17-3	Viola	Caldwell
26—Milwaukee	W	6-5	Whitehouse	Tellmann
27—Milwaukee	L	9-13	Slaton	Havens
29—Seattle	W	4-3	Castillo	Caudill
30—Seattle	L	3-7	Abbott	Viola
31—Seattle	L	2-3	Thomas	Davis

Won 12, Lost 15

AUGUST

			Winner	Loser
1—California	L	6-12	Witt	Havens
1—California	W	7-0	Lysander	S. Brown
2—California	L	1-2	Kison	Castillo
3—California	L	5-7†	Kison	Walters
4—Oakland	W	4-3	Whitehouse	Burgmeier
5—Oakland	L	2-3	Heimueller	O'Connor
6—Oakland	L	4-6x	Atherton	Davis
7—Oakland	L	0-6	Codiroli	Viola
8—At Calif.	W	4-2	Schrom	John
9—At Calif.	L	2-8	Steirer	Lysander
10—At Calif.	W	4-1	Castillo	Zahn
11—At Oak.	L	0-6	Codiroli	Viola
12—At Oak.	W	5-3	Schrom	Underwood
13—At Oak.	W	7-3	Williams	Conroy
14—At Oak.	L	0-6	McCatty	Castillo
15—At Seattle	W	7-4	Viola	Clark
16—At Seattle	W	5-1	Schrom	Young
17—At Seattle	W	7-4	Williams	Moore
19—Detroit	L	1-5	Morris	Castillo
20—Detroit	L	1-9	Berenguer	Viola
21—Detroit	W	4-3	Schrom	Pashnick
23—Boston	W	3-2	Williams	Boyd
24—Boston	W	8-7	Whitehouse	Stanley
25—Boston	W	5-2	Viola	Eckersley
26—At Balt.	L	0-9	Boddicker	Schrom
27—At Balt.	L	3-5	Palmer	Williams
28—At Balt.	L	4-11	Flanagan	Castillo
29—At Detroit	W	5-4‡	Lysander	Lopez
30—At Detroit	L	3-4	Petry	Schrom

Won 14, Lost 15

SEPTEMBER

			Winner	Loser
1—At Boston	W	11-0	Williams	Eckersley
1—At Boston	L	3-9	Ojeda	Lysander
2—Baltimore	L	0-1	Flanagan	Viola
3—Baltimore	L	0-13	McGregor	Schrom
4—Baltimore	L	6-9	S. Davis	R. Davis
5—At Texas	L	3-7	Butcher	Lysander
6—At Texas	W	5-3†	Davis	Tanana
7—At Texas	L	0-3	Hough	Williams
9—Kan. City	W	7-6†	O'Connor	Armstrong
10—Kan. City	W	6-3	Filson	Rasmussen
11—Kan. City	L	1-3	Jackson	Pettibone
13—Chicago	L	1-5	Dotson	Viola
14—Chicago	W	1-0	Davis	Burns
15—Toronto	W	6-2	Schrom	Stieb
16—Toronto	W	11-4	Lysander	Gott
17—Toronto	L	3-13	Leal	Pettibone
19—At Chicago	W	7-5	Walters	Barojas
21—At Chicago	L	1-2	Hoyt	Schrom
21—At Chicago	L	6-7	Hoffman	Davis
22—At Kan. C.	W	2-1	Filson	Rasmussen
23—At Kan. C.	L	2-3	Wills	Pettibone
24—At Kan. C.	L	4-12*	Black	Viola
25—At Kan. C.	W	7-1	Schrom	Jackson
27—Texas	L	1-6	Smithson	Williams
28—Texas	W	3-0	Filson	Darwin
29—Texas	W	2-0	Schrom	Stewart
30—At Toronto	L	0-8	Stieb	Viola

Won 12, Lost 15

OCTOBER

			Winner	Loser
1—At Toronto	L	3-4	Alexander	Pettibone
2—At Toronto	W	9-3	Williams	Clancy

Won 1, Lost 1

*5½ innings. †10 innings. ‡11 innings. §12 innings. x13 innings. y14 innings.

Mickey Hatcher hit .317 for Minnesota after the Twins almost released him last spring.

ished around .500," Manager Billy Gardner said.

On offense, outfielder Gary Ward and first baseman Kent Hrbek didn't match their impressive '82 statistics, but Minnesota found enough hitting to increase its run production from 657 to 709.

Ward, named to the A.L. All-Star team as a reserve, did not hit a home run after August 12 and finished with 19 homers and 88 runs batted in (compared with '82 totals of 28 and 91). He had 15 homers at the All-Star break.

Hrbek saw his home run production fall from 23 as a rookie in '82 to 16 and his RBIs decline from 92 to 84. Hrbek's .297 average was just four points below his first-year mark.

For Tom Brunansky, it was a different kind of year. His average was below .200 for nearly half of the season and his final mark of .227 was 45 points off his rookie figure. Yet, Brunansky had a much more productive second season as his home runs went from 20 to a club-leading 28 and his RBIs jumped from 46 to 82 (and included 15 game-winners).

The Twins tried to trade outfielder Mickey Hatcher in spring training, but found no takers. They considered giving him his release, but Gardner urged he be kept as a reserve. It took more than a month of the season for Hatcher to find a place in the lineup and he had two stretches on the disabled list. Nevertheless, Hatcher batted .317 in 375 at-bats.

Dave Engle, who became a regular by converting from the outfield to catcher during the off-season, hit .305 in 374 at-bats. He struggled defensively in the early going, but his strong hitting kept him in the lineup and his catching improved.

Second baseman John Castino demonstrated his usual consistency in the field and improved dramatically at the plate. Castino had batted .241 with 37 RBIs in 1982 while coming off spinal-fusion surgery. With his back stronger in 1983, Castino hit .277 and had 57 RBIs.

Castino also spent time at his original major league position, third base, when second baseman Tim Teufel was summoned from Toledo in September. Teufel batted .308 in 21 games. By the end of the year, Gardner was attempting to work a three-man rotation between second and third involving Castino, Teufel and regular third baseman Gary Gaetti (21 home runs, 78 RBIs, .245).

There would be room for all three players in the infield if any was a shortstop. That position was a season-long problem for the Twins, who tried four men at the spot—Lenny Faedo, Ron Washington, Houston Jimenez and Greg Gagne—and still were looking for the answer.

There was similar uncertainty in center field. Jim Eisenreich's comeback lasted only two games into the regular season. After batting .400 in spring training, Eisenreich suffered a recurrence of the nervous disorder that kept him out most of 1982 and he went on the retired list (although he hopes to try again in '84).

Darrell Brown, Bobby Mitchell and Rusty Kuntz had stretches in center field, but the best temporary solution Gardner could find was moving Brunansky over from his regular right-field position.

Gardner's goals for '84: Find long-term solutions to his shortstop, center-field and starting-pitching problems.

Second baseman Bobby Grich was solid both offensively and defensively until his season ended in late August.

Angels Fall From Lofty Perch

By JOHN STREGE

In 1961, the Angels' first year of existence, they lost 91 games. In 1983, they lost 92.

They haven't made much progress, have they? In 23 seasons, the Angels still are seeking their first American League pennant.

Just once have the Angels had consecutive winning seasons, in 1978-1979. In 1982, they won the A.L. West title and, in many circles, were predicted to repeat.

Alas, they unraveled in the second half of the '83 season, collapsing to a 70-92 finish and a tie for fifth place with Minnesota in the West Division.

As late as July 10, the Angels were tied for first place. Then they lost five straight, seven of eight, and were in the throes of a second-half nightmare in which they won just 26 and lost 55.

The primary reason for the Angels' demise was a wave of injuries. Thirteen California players served time on the disabled list in '83 and one—shortstop Rick Burleson—was on the list twice.

Pitcher Don Aase and catcher Ed Ott missed the entire year, while Burleson, Doug DeCinces, Brian Downing, Geoff Zahn, Bruce Kison, Bill Travers, Joe Ferguson, Juan Beniquez, Bobby Clark, Ellis Valentine and Bobby Grich missed parts of the season due to injuries.

Further muddling the situation was the fact Rod Carew played in just 129 games and Fred Lynn in 117, though neither was on the disabled list.

Catcher Bob Boone, in fact, led the team in games played with 142. He also was awarded the Owner's Trophy symbolizing the most valuable member of the team. Boone batted .256 with nine home runs and 52 runs batted in.

The starting lineup projected by new Manager John McNamara in spring training was not used once during the regular season.

"This has been my most frustrating season ever," said McNamara. "We had a lot of injuries in Cincinnati in 1979, but I've never seen anything like this."

Then there were those players who performed below expectations, most notably Reggie Jackson, who had hit 39 homers and driven in 101 runs the season before.

Jackson, who started slowly and then severely bruised his ribs, never got untracked and experienced the worst season of his storied career. He batted just .194 with 14 home runs and 49 RBIs—and he struck out 140 times in 397 at-bats.

Reggie Jackson struggled to the worst season of his storied career.

The pitching lived down to expectations, with the staff earned-run average of 4.31 tying for 22nd place among the majors' 26 clubs. Among the disappointments were Tommy John (11-13 record, 4.33 ERA), Mike Witt (7-14, 4.91) and Ken Forsch (11-12, 4.06). Dave Goltz was 0-6 before getting released and Andy Hassler posted a 0-5 mark.

Of the pitchers with the Angels all season, just three finished with ERAs under 4.00—Zahn (3.33 in 203 innings), Luis Sanchez (3.66 in 98⅓ innings) and John Curtis (3.80 in 90 innings).

All was not gloomy in Anaheim, though. For about three months, Carew single-handedly provided excitement.

At age 37, Carew got off to the fastest start of his notable career. In early May, he was batting .500 with 48 hits in 96 at-bats. He was still hitting .402 at the All-

SCORES OF CALIFORNIA ANGELS' 1983 GAMES

APRIL

			Winner	Loser
5—Milwaukee	W	3-2	Kison	Sutton
6—Milwaukee	W	4-3	John	Caldwell
7—Milwaukee	L	3-5	Augustine	Witt
8—At Oak.	L	3-5	Beard	Zahn
9—At Oak.	W	10-2	Forsch	Keough
10—At Oak.	L	4-11	Krueger	Kison
11—Seattle	W	6-1	John	Young
12—Seattle	L	1-8	Stoddard	Witt
13—Seattle	W	6-1	Zahn	Moore
15—At Minn.	W	8-2	Forsch	Viola
16—At Minn.	W	9-5	Kison	Oelkers
17—At Minn.	L	8-11	Whitehouse	Goltz
18—Oakland	L	3-5	Underwood	Witt
21—Oakland	W	6-2	Zahn	Codiroli
21—Oakland	W	6-5	Forsch	Keough
22—Baltimore	W	6-5†	Sanchez	Welchel
23—Baltimore	L	1-3	McGregor	John
24—Baltimore	W	7-3	Witt	D. Martinez
27—Detroit	W	13-3	Zahn	Wilcox
29—Boston	L	5-6	Aponte	Sanchez
30—Boston	W	4-1†	Corbett	Clear

Won 13, Lost 8

MAY

			Winner	Loser
1—Boston	L	9-10	Stanley	Hassler
3—At Balt.	L	2-4	Flanagan	Zahn
4—At Balt.	W	16-8	Sanchez	McGregor
6—At Detroit	W	4-2	Kison	Wilcox
7—At Detroit	W	6-5‡	Sanchez	Lopez
8—At Detroit	L	1-5	Morris	Forsch
9—At Boston	L	2-8	Stanley	John
10—At Boston	W	6-5	Sanchez	Aponte
11—At Boston	W	3-1	Kison	Tudor
13—Minnesota	L	4-5†	Whitehouse	Witt
14—Minnesota	L	1-2	Schrom	Forsch
15—Minnesota	L	6-8	Filson	Goltz
17—At Seattle	W	3-1	Kison	Perry
18—At Seattle	L	1-2	Stoddard	Zahn
19—At Seattle	L	0-1	Young	Forsch
20—Cleveland	W	5-4	John	Eichelberger
21—Cleveland	L	3-9	Blyleven	Travers
22—Cleveland	W	9-0	Kison	Barker
23—New York	W	3-0	Zahn	Righetti
24—New York	W	7-6*	Witt	May
25—New York	W	7-1	John	Rawley
27—At Cleve.	W	5-4‡	Sanchez	Spillner
28—At Cleve.	W	7-4	Zahn	Barker
29—At Cleve.	W	6-4	Witt	Spillner
30—At Cleve.	L	5-6	Heaton	Sanchez
31—At N.Y.	L	3-5	Murray	Witt

Won 14, Lost 12

JUNE

			Winner	Loser
1—At N.Y.	L	0-3	Guidry	Goltz
2—At N.Y.	W	9-8	Sanchez	May
3—At Milw.	W	3-0	Forsch	Sutton
4—At Milw.	W	8-3	John	Augustine
5—At Milw.	L	4-5	Haas	Hassler
6—At Milw.	L	7-9	McClure	Goltz
7—Chicago	L	11-12*	Tidrow	Hassler
8—Chicago	W	7-4	Forsch	Koosman
9—Chicago	W	3-2	John	Lamp
10—Toronto	W	5-3	C. Brown	Leal
11—Toronto	L	2-3	Gott	Goltz
12—Toronto	L	5-6y	Clarke	C. Brown
13—At Chicago	W	7-4	Forsch	Burns
15—At Chicago	L	2-5	Hoyt	John
17—At Toronto	L	3-6	Stieb	Travers
18—At Toronto	W	7-6	Sanchez	Clarke
19—At Toronto	L	1-6	Leal	Goltz
20—At Texas	W	10-9§	Curtis	Matlack
21—At Texas	L	2-3	Darwin	McLaughlin
22—At Texas	L	1-9	Honeycutt	Travers
23—At Kan. C.	W	7-2	Forsch	Black
24—At Kan. C.	L	3-11	Armstrong	John
25—At Kan. C.	W	9-2	Witt	Creel
27—Texas	W	8-0	Kison	Honeycutt
28—Texas	L	1-3	Hough	Forsch
29—Texas	W	2-1	Sanchez	Smithson
30—Texas	L	2-4*	Schmidt	Sanchez

Won 13, Lost 14

JULY

			Winner	Loser
1—Kan. City	W	7-6	McLaughlin	Blue
2—Kan. City	L	3-5	Gura	Kison
3—Kan. City	W	5-2	Forsch	Black
4—Kan. City	L	1-5	Splittorff	John
8—At Boston	W	9-3	Kison	Eckersley
9—At Boston	L	3-10	Tudor	Forsch
10—At Boston	W	5-3	John	Hurst
11—At Detroit	L	6-12	Rozema	Zahn
12—At Detroit	L	4-5x	Bailey	Witt
13—At Detroit	L	1-7	Petry	Kison
14—At Balt.	L	1-5	McGregor	Forsch
15—At Balt.	L	4-10	Boddicker	John
16—At Balt.	W	8-5	Zahn	D. Martinez
17—At Balt.	L	1-11	Ramirez	McLaughlin
18—Boston	L	2-7	Eckersley	Kison
19—Boston	W	6-1	Forsch	Tudor
20—Boston	L	4-6	Stanley	John
21—Detroit	L	1-5	Bailey	Witt
21—Detroit	W	3-2	Zahn	Rozema
22—Detroit	L	11-13	Wilcox	McLaughlin
23—Detroit	L	2-7	Petry	Kison
24—Detroit	L	3-4‡	Lopez	Sanchez
25—Baltimore	W	5-2	John	Boddicker
26—Baltimore	L	4-5	D. Martinez	Zahn
27—Baltimore	L	4-10	Ramirez	Witt
29—Oakland	L	2-5	Conroy	Forsch
30—Oakland	L	8-13	Burgmeier	Sanchez
30—Oakland	L	1-2‡	Beard	John
31—Oakland	W	4-0	Zahn	Heimueller

Won 9, Lost 20

AUGUST

			Winner	Loser
1—At Minn.	W	12-6	Witt	Havens
1—At Minn.	L	0-7	Lysander	S. Brown
2—At Minn.	W	2-1	Kison	Castillo
3—At Minn.	W	7-5*	Kison	Walters
4—At Seattle	L	5-11	Clark	Curtis
5—At Seattle	L	1-3	Stoddard	Zahn
6—At Seattle	L	1-2	Moore	Witt
7—At Seattle	W	4-3	Forsch	Clark
8—Minnesota	L	2-4	Schrom	John
9—Minnesota	W	8-2	Steirer	Lysander
10—Minnesota	L	1-4	Castillo	Zahn
12—Seattle	L	6-7	Stanton	Sanchez
13—Seattle	W	10-5	Forsch	Stoddard
14—Seattle	W	7-2	John	Beattie
15—At Oak.	L	0-5	Heimueller	Zahn
16—At Oak.	L	0-4	Codiroli	Steirer
17—At Oak.	W	6-5	Witt	Warren
19—At N.Y.	L	6-11	Guidry	Forsch
20—At N.Y.	L	2-6	Rawley	John
21—At N.Y.	L	1-2	Gossage	Zahn
22—At Cleve.	W	7-3§	Kison	Spillner
23—At Cleve.	W	5-2	Witt	Barker
24—At Milw.	L	0-1x	Slaton	Hassler
25—At Milw.	L	0-7	Candiotti	John
26—New York	L	2-3	Righetti	Zahn
27—New York	W	7-6	S. Brown	Gossage
28—New York	L	3-7	Montefusco	Forsch
29—Cleveland	L	4-6	Heaton	Witt
30—Cleveland	W	10-6	Steirer	Jeffcoat
31—Cleveland	L	5-7*	Sutcliffe	Sanchez

Won 12, Lost 18

SEPTEMBER

			Winner	Loser
2—Milwaukee	W	6-5	Steirer	Waits
3—Milwaukee	L	3-4	Caldwell	Witt
4—Milwaukee	W	5-3	John	Sutton
5—At Toronto	L	0-7	Gott	Zahn
6—At Toronto	L	4-6	Alexander	Curtis
7—At Toronto	W	9-6	Sanchez	Geisel
8—At Chicago	L	5-8	Dotson	Witt
9—At Chicago	L	0-11	Burns	John
10—At Chicago	L	6-7‡	Barojas	S. Brown
11—At Chicago	L	4-5*	Hoyt	Forsch
13—Kan. City	L	3-4	Black	Sanchez
14—Kan. City	L	0-1x	Armstrong	Steirer
16—Texas	W	8-6	Sanchez	Butcher
17—Texas	L	2-5	Stewart	Forsch
18—Texas	L	6-7	Cruz	Lacey
19—At Kan. C.	L	4-8	Armstrong	Hassler
19—At Kan. C.	L	6-7	Huismann	McLaughlin
20—At Kan. C.	W	6-4	John	Splittorff
21—At Kan. C.	W	3-0	Zahn	Perry
22—Chicago	L	2-3	Koosman	Forsch
23—Chicago	L	1-2	Dotson	Witt
24—Chicago	L	0-2	Burns	S. Brown
25—Chicago	L	5-8	Hoyt	John
26—Toronto	L	2-3*	Alexander	Lacey
27—Toronto	W	7-1	McLaughlin	Leal
28—Toronto	L	3-5	Clancy	Witt
30—At Texas	L	3-4*	Henke	Corbett

Won 7, Lost 20

OCTOBER

			Winner	Loser
1—At Texas	W	6-5	Lacey	Jones
2—At Texas	W	2-0	S. Brown	Lachowicz

Won 2, Lost 0

*10 innings. †11 innings. ‡12 innings. §13 innings. x14 innings. y15 innings.

Bob Boone (above) stayed healthy and produced a solid season while Fred Lynn fought off injuries to hit a team-leading 22 home runs.

Star Game break.

However, following those first 96 at-bats, Carew batted just .298 the rest of the season to finish with a .339 average, the top mark in club history.

Four Angels played in the All-Star Game in Chicago. Lynn, Jackson and Carew were voted as A.L. starters, but Jackson did not attend because of his sore ribs. DeCinces and Boone competed as reserves.

Lynn led California with 22 home runs and 74 RBIs. DeCinces had 15 homers and 46 RBIs at the break, but injuries limited him to 34 games in the second half and he finished with 18 homers and 65 RBIs.

Grich had been one of the Angels' most productive players until his season ended in late August after he suffered a broken hand when hit by a pitch. Grich finished with a .292 average, 16 homers and 62 RBIs.

Kison compiled an 11-5 record for California, and Sanchez went 10-8 with seven saves. Zahn was 9-11.

The Angels enjoyed their most success of '83 at the gate. They led the league in attendance for the second straight season, drawing 2,555,016 fans.

Matt Young replaced Floyd Bannister in the Mariners' rotation and led the team with 11 victories.

Mariners Return to Old Ways

By SCOTT BARRY

So many hopes; so much heartache.

So went the Seattle Mariners in 1983.

A season that began with such promise—the Mariners were coming off a club-record 76 victories and a fourth-place finish in 1982—ended with some observers calling Seattle the best minor league team in baseball.

From A to Z, Owner George Argyros to designated hitter Richie Zisk, and all the alphabet in between, the Mariners of 1983 were at best a disappointment, at worst a joke.

The optimism for 1983 surely should have been tempered, anyway. After all, Seattle entered the season minus Floyd Bannister (the club's best pitcher) and first baseman-outfielder Bruce Bochte (three times a .300 hitter in the majors). Bannister was lost to free agency, and Bochte quit baseball.

The '83 Mariners failed in the standings with a 60-102 record that was the worst in the big leagues and buried them deep in the American League West cellar. They failed statistically, finishing last in the A.L. in most offensive categories. Their .240 team batting average surpassed only Cincinnati's in the majors—and the National League Reds, of course, had no DH in their lineup. And the Mariners failed at the gate, where a club record-low (excluding strike-shortened 1981) 814,637 fans paid to see them play. The season's biggest crowd, 37,807, probably came—in large part, anyway—to see a postgame Beach Boys concert.

On April 12, Seattle was 4-4. The Mariners never saw .500 again. Twenty-one games later, they were 9-20. The slide had begun.

For the second straight year, outfielder Al Cowens started the season in a batting slump. Whereas it lasted only a month in 1982, it never really ended in 1983. The veteran Zisk went to spring training feeling better physically than he had in years. Despite that, his legs finally felt the effects of six knee operations and failed him. Toward the end of his 11th major league summer, Zisk acknowledged that as an everyday player, he probably had reached the end.

In 1982, Zisk and Cowens had combined for a .280 average, 298 hits, 67 doubles, 41 home runs and 140 runs batted in. In 1983, they combined for a .222 average, 142 hits, 31 doubles, 19 homers and 71 RBIs. In other words, it took two of them to accomplish in 1983 what one had done the year before.

With Bill Caudill having been traded away, even more responsibility will fall to Ed Vande Berg, Seattle's left-handed reliever.

Pat Putnam topped Seattle with 19 homers and 67 RBIs, and Steve Henderson batted .294 with 10 homers. Overall, though, the Mariners were a study in futility at the plate.

But 1983 was much more than a simple vanishing act by the Mariner offense (which suffered greatly from the lack of Bochte's clutch, run-producing bat). It also was a time of transition for the franchise.

SCORES OF SEATTLE MARINERS' 1983 GAMES

APRIL

5—New York	W	5-4	Clark	Erickson
6—New York	W	6-2	Young	Shirley
7—New York	L	1-8	Righetti	Stoddard
8—Minnesota	L	4-5‡	Lysander	Caudill
9—Minnesota	W	3-2	Thomas	Oelkers
10—Minnesota	L	3-6	Havens	Perry
11—At Calif.	L	1-6	John	Young
12—At Calif.	W	8-1	Stoddard	Witt
13—At Calif.	L	1-6	Zahn	Moore
14—Oakland	L	3-5	Codiroli	Nunez
15—Oakland	W	5-1	Perry	Keough
16—Oakland	L	2-5	Krueger	Young
17—Oakland	L	4-7	Norris	Stoddard
18—At Minn.	L	5-8	O'Connor	Moore
19—At Minn.	L	2-6	Whitehouse	Nunez
20—At Minn.	L	2-11	Castillo	Perry
21—At Minn.	W	2-0	Young	Oelkers
22—At Detroit	L	0-4	Wilcox	Stoddard
23—At Detroit	L	0-4	Petry	Moore
24—At Detroit	L	2-4	Morris	Nunez
26—Boston	W	7-6	Perry	Brown
27—Boston	L	1-2	Eckersley	Young
29—Baltimore	L	1-9	McGregor	Beattie
30—Baltimore	W	6-2	Stoddard	D. Martinez

Won 8, Lost 16

MAY

1—Baltimore	L	2-8	Davis	Perry
3—Detroit	L	1-2‡	Lopez	Caudill
4—Detroit	W	5-1	Beattie	Morris
6—At Boston	L	4-6	Aponte	Vande Berg
7—At Boston	L	0-8	Brown	Stoddard
8—At Boston	W	4-2	Young	Bird
9—At Balt.	W	6-4	Beattie	McGregor
10—At Balt.	L	2-13	D. Martinez	Nunez
11—At Balt.	L	0-1	Flanagan	Perry
13—At Oak.	L	2-9	Krueger	Stoddard
14—At Oak.	W	4-1	Young	Langford
15—At Oak.	L	0-3	Underwood	Beattie
17—California	L	1-3	Kison	Perry
18—California	W	2-1	Stoddard	Zahn
19—California	W	1-0	Young	Forsch
20—Milwaukee	L	3-4	Tellmann	Clark
21—Milwaukee	W	5-4	Clark	McClure
22—Milwaukee	L	0-6	Caldwell	Perry
23—Cleveland	W	3-2	Stoddard	Sutcliffe
24—Cleveland	L	4-6	Heaton	Caudill
25—Cleveland	W	2-1	Beattie	Eichelberger
27—At Milw.	W	7-5	Perry	Tellmann
28—At Milw.	W	4-3	Vande Berg	Slaton
29—At Milw.	W	6-4	Young	Sutton
30—At Milw.	L	3-6	Augustine	Beattie
31—At Cleve.	L	2-5	Eichelberger	Nelson

Won 12, Lost 14

JUNE

1—At Cleve.	L	2-5	Heaton	Perry
2—At Cleve.	L	1-3	Sutcliffe	Stoddard
3—At N.Y.	W	5-0	Young	Howell
4—At N.Y.	W	5-4	Beattie	Shirley
5—At N.Y.	W	8-7	Clark	Rawley
6—At N.Y.	L	2-6	Guidry	Vande Berg
7—Texas	L	0-10	Honeycutt	Stoddard
8—Texas	L	0-1	Smithson	Young
9—Texas	W	3-2‡	Caudill	Hough
10—Kan. City	L	0-2	Splittorff	Stoddard
11—Kan. City	L	1-4	Black	Perry
12—Kan. City	W	8-1	Abbott	Gura
13—At Texas	L	2-5	Smithson	Young
14—At Texas	L	1-7	Hough	Beattie
15—At Texas	W	6-4	Vande Berg	Jones
17—At Kan. C.	L	1-3	Gura	Perry
18—At Kan. C.	L	5-6	Quisenberry	Caudill
19—At Kan. C.	L	2-4	Castro	Young
20—At Chicago	L	3-7	Hoyt	Beattie
21—At Chicago	L	2-4	Dotson	Stoddard
22—At Chicago	L	3-6	Koosman	Perry
23—Toronto	L	4-5	Clancy	Stanton
24—Toronto	L	2-4	Leal	Young
25—Toronto	W	5-2	Beattie	Gott
26—Toronto	L	7-19	Acker	Stoddard
27—Chicago	L	4-7	Lamp	Clark
28—Chicago	W	6-2	Abbott	Bannister
29—Chicago	L	3-5	Burns	Young

Won 8, Lost 20

JULY

			Winner	Loser
1—At Toronto	W	11-2	Beattie	Gott
2—At Toronto	L	6-7	Jackson	Caudill
3—At Toronto	W	4-1	Abbott	Stieb
8—At Balt.	W	3-0	Beattie	Davis
9—At Balt.	W	3-2†	Caudill	Stewart
10—At Balt.	L	0-2	Boddicker	Young
11—At Boston	L	5-6†	Aponte	Stanton
12—At Boston	W	3-2	Clark	Brown
13—At Boston	W	6-4	Beattie	Eckersley
14—Detroit	L	2-4	Morris	Abbott
15—Detroit	W	7-2	Young	Berenguer
16—Detroit	W	1-0	Moore	Lopez
17—Detroit	L	1-8†	Bair	Caudill
18—Baltimore	L	4-9	Davis	Beattie
19—Baltimore	L	1-8	McGregor	Abbott
20—Baltimore	L	2-4	Stewart	Young
21—Boston	L	13-14†	Johnson	Vande Berg
22—Boston	L	4-5	Brown	Vande Berg
23—Boston	W	5-0	Stoddard	Eckersley
24—Boston	L	0-6	Tudor	Abbott
26—At Detroit	L	3-8	Rozema	Young
27—At Detroit	W	5-3	Moore	Bair
28—At Detroit	L	1-6	Petry	Clark
29—At Minn.	L	3-4	Castillo	Caudill
30—At Minn.	W	7-3	Abbott	Viola
31—At Minn.	W	3-2	Thomas	Davis

Won 12, Lost 14

AUGUST

1—Oakland	L	3-4	Underwood	Stanton
2—Oakland	W	15-12	Thomas	Codiroli
3—Oakland	L	1-6	Conroy	Beattie
4—California	W	11-5	Clark	Curtis
5—California	W	3-1	Stoddard	Zahn
6—California	W	2-1	Moore	Witt
7—California	L	3-4	Forsch	Clark
8—At Oak.	L	1-2	Conroy	Beattie
9—At Oak.	L	6-7	Underwood	Stoddard
10—At Oak.	W	7-5	Young	Heimueller
12—At Calif.	W	7-6	Stanton	Sanchez
13—At Calif.	L	5-10	Forsch	Stoddard
14—At Calif.	L	2-7	John	Beattie
15—Minnesota	L	4-7	Viola	Clark
16—Minnesota	L	1-5	Schrom	Young
17—Minnesota	L	4-7	Williams	Moore
19—At Cleve.	L	5-6	Heaton	Best
20—At Cleve.	L	2-3	Easterly	Beattie
21—At Cleve.	W	7-2	Abbott	Jeffcoat
22—At Milw.	L	2-3†	Porter	Stoddard
23—At Milw.	W	5-0	Moore	Caldwell
24—At N.Y.	L	3-6	Guidry	Clark
25—At N.Y.	L	4-7	Rawley	Beattie
26—Cleveland	L	1-4	Sutcliffe	Stoddard
27—Cleveland	W	6-3	Young	Eichelberger
28—Cleveland	L	2-5	Sorensen	Moore
29—Milwaukee	W	2-1	Clark	Sutton
30—Milwaukee	L	2-3	Candiotti	Beattie
31—Milwaukee	W	4-1	Stoddard	Vuckovich

Won 11, Lost 18

SEPTEMBER

2—New York	L	4-5	Fontenot	Young
3—New York	L	3-5	Montefusco	Moore
4—New York	L	3-4	Guidry	Clark
5—At Kan. C.	W	13-6	Beattie	Gura
6—At Kan. C.	W	3-1	Stoddard	Black
7—At Kan. C.	L	2-3	Splittorff	Young
9—Texas	W	6-4	Moore	Smithson
10—Texas	W	4-2	Clark	Darwin
11—Texas	L	1-2	Stewart	Beattie
13—Toronto	L	4-6	Leal	Stoddard
14—Toronto	L	3-4	Alexander	Thomas
15—At Chicago	L	0-12*	Hoyt	Moore
16—At Chicago	L	0-7	Bannister	Clark
17—At Chicago	L	3-4	Lamp	Caudill
18—At Chicago	L	0-6	Dotson	Stoddard
19—At Toronto	W	9-6	Young	Geisel
20—At Toronto	L	3-7	Stieb	Moore
21—At Toronto	L	3-4	Alexander	Clark
22—At Texas	L	2-5	Darwin	Beattie
23—At Texas	L	1-2	Stewart	Nelson
24—At Texas	W	2-0	Moore	Tanana
25—At Texas	W	2-1	Stoddard	Hough
26—Kan. City	L	2-6	Splittorff	Clark
27—Kan. City	W	4-0	Beattie	Gura
28—Kan. City	L	8-11	Wills	Nelson
29—Kan. City	W	5-4	Stanton	Black
30—Chicago	L	4-9	Hoyt	Stoddard

Won 9, Lost 18

OCTOBER

1—Chicago	L	3-9	Bannister	Young
2—Chicago	L	0-3	Dotson	Beattie

Won 0, Lost 2

*6½ innings. †10 innings. ‡11 innings.

On June 25, Argyros and Mariners President Dan O'Brien fired Rene Lachemann, the most popular manager the Mariners ever had. They also released Gaylord Perry, the only future Hall of Fame pitcher the club ever had, and shortstop Todd Cruz, who had combined with Julio Cruz to form a talented middle-infield combination.

Del Crandall, who had been managing the Dodgers' Triple-A affiliate in Albuquerque, replaced Lachemann, and the club announced it would make a determined effort to go with youth the rest of the season.

Ten days earlier, Julio Cruz, who many times had said he planned to become a free agent at the end of 1983, had been traded to Chicago for another second baseman, Tony Bernazard. In August, pitcher Glenn Abbott, the lone remaining member of the original 1977 Mariners, was waived.

While the veterans were leaving, the rookies were arriving. Seattle, in fact, had as many as eight on the field at one time. Of the 33 players on the roster as the season ended, only 11 were holdovers from 1982 and 17 of the others were rookies.

First-year lefthander Matt Young replaced Bannister in the rotation and led the Mariners in victories (11) and earned-run average (3.27). Righthander Jim Beattie won a career-high 10 games and posted the first one-hitter in club history. Reliever Bill Caudill saved 26 games for the second consecutive year and got some help from Mike Stanton, who collected a career-high seven saves and had a 3.32 ERA. Lefthander Ed Vande Berg had a 3.36 ERA, five saves and pitched in 68 games, giving him a league-high 146 appearances over the last two years.

As good as the pitching was, it couldn't carry the offense.

"We have to feel very good about the pitching. It was very consistent," said Crandall, "but so was our inability to score runs. It made for some close ballgames, but we just didn't have the firepower to overcome some of the mistakes we made."

"It's very frustrating knowing that if you give up a run or two, you've got a good chance of losing," said Beattie, who during one 10-game stretch was supported with only 15 runs. He lost nine of the 10 games.

Seattle's transition wasn't confined to the playing field during 1983. Five days after the season ended, Argyros fired O'Brien, who, in effect, has served as the club's general manager, and replaced him with Hal Keller, who had been the Mariners' director of player development.

Pat Putnam (above) and Steve Henderson were Seattle's main offensive forces.

American League Averages for 1983

CHAMPIONSHIP WINNERS IN PREVIOUS YEARS

1900—Chicago* .607
1901—Chicago .610
1902—Philadelphia .610
1903—Boston .659
1904—Boston .617
1905—Philadelphia .622
1906—Chicago .616
1907—Detroit .613
1908—Detroit .588
1909—Detroit .645
1910—Philadelphia .680
1911—Philadelphia .669
1912—Boston .691
1913—Philadelphia .627
1914—Philadelphia .651
1915—Boston .669
1916—Boston .591
1917—Chicago .649
1918—Boston .595
1919—Chicago .629
1920—Cleveland .636
1921—New York .641
1922—New York .610
1923—New York .645
1924—Washington .597
1925—Washington .636
1926—New York .591
1927—New York .714
1928—New York .656
1929—Philadelphia .693
1930—Philadelphia .662
1931—Philadelphia .704
1932—New York .695
1933—Washington .651
1934—Detroit .656
1935—Detroit .616
1936—New York .667
1937—New York .662
1938—New York .651
1939—New York .702
1940—Detroit .584
1941—New York .656
1942—New York .669
1943—New York .636
1944—St. Louis .578
1945—Detroit .575
1946—Boston .675
1947—New York .630
1948—Cleveland† .626
1949—New York .630
1950—New York .636
1951—New York .636
1952—New York .617
1953—New York .656
1954—Cleveland .721
1955—New York .623
1956—New York .630
1957—New York .636
1958—New York .597
1959—Chicago .610
1960—New York .630
1961—New York .673
1962—New York .593
1963—New York .646
1964—New York .611
1965—Minnesota .630
1966—Baltimore .606
1967—Boston .568
1968—Detroit .636
1969—Baltimore (East)‡ .673
1970—Baltimore (East)‡ .667
1971—Baltimore (East)§ .639
1972—Oakland (West)a .600
1973—Oakland (West)b .580
1974—Oakland (West)b .556
1975—Boston (East)c .594
1976—New York (East)d .610
1977—New York (East)d .617
1978—New York (East)d .613
1979—Baltimore (East)e .642
1980—Kansas City (West)f .599
1981—New York (East)c .551
1982—Milwaukee (East)e .586

*Not recognized as major league in 1900. †Defeated Boston in one-game playoff for pennant. ‡Defeated Minnesota (West) in Championship Series. §Defeated Oakland (West) in Championship Series. aDefeated Detroit (East) in Championship Series. bDefeated Baltimore (East) in Championship Series. cDefeated Oakland (West) in Championship Series. dDefeated Kansas City (West) in Championship Series. eDefeated California (West) in Championship Series. fDefeated New York (East) in Championship Series.

STANDING OF CLUBS AT CLOSE OF SEASON

EAST DIVISION

Club	Balt.	Det.	N.Y.	Tor.	Mil.	Bos.	Clev.	Cal.	Chi.	K.C.	Min.	Oak.	Sea.	Tex.	W.	L.	Pct.	G.B.
Baltimore	..	5	6	7	11	8	6	7	7	8	8	8	8	9	98	64	.605	....
Detroit	8	..	5	6	6	9	8	8	4	7	9	6	8	8	92	70	.568	6
New York	7	8	..	7	9	6	7	7	4	6	8	8	7	7	91	71	.562	7
Toronto	6	7	6	..	5	6	9	8	7	6	7	6	8	8	89	73	.549	9
Milwaukee	2	7	4	8	..	9	10	6	8	6	8	6	5	8	87	75	.537	11
Boston	5	4	7	7	4	..	7	6	6	5	5	8	7	7	78	84	.481	20
Cleveland	7	5	6	4	3	6	..	4	4	7	6	7	8	3	70	92	.432	28

WEST DIVISION

Club	Chi.	K.C.	Tex.	Oak.	Cal.	Min.	Sea.	Balt.	Bos.	Clev.	Det.	Mil.	N.Y.	Tor.	W.	L.	Pct.	G.B.
Chicago	..	9	8	8	10	8	12	5	6	8	8	4	8	5	99	63	.611	....
Kansas City	4	..	8	7	7	6	8	4	7	5	5	6	6	6	79	83	.488	20
Texas	5	5	..	11	7	8	7	3	5	9	4	4	5	4	77	85	.475	22
Oakland	5	6	2	..	8	9	9	4	4	5	6	6	4	6	74	88	.457	25
California	3	6	6	5	..	6	6	5	6	8	4	6	5	4	70	92	.432	29
Minnesota	5	7	5	4	7	..	9	4	7	6	3	4	4	5	70	92	.432	29
Seattle	1	5	6	4	7	4	..	4	5	4	4	7	5	4	60	102	.370	39

Tie Game—Texas vs. Kansas City.
Championship Series—Baltimore defeated Chicago, three games to one.

RECORD AT HOME

EAST DIVISION

Club	Mil.	N.Y.	Balt.	Det.	Tor.	Bos.	Clv.	Chi.	K.C.	Tex.	Oak.	Min.	Cal.	Sea.	W.	L.	Pct.
Milwaukee	......	4-3	2-4	3-4	5-1	5-2	5-1	5-1	3-3	4-2	4-2	6-0	4-2	2-4	52	29	.642
New York	6-0	......	4-3	3-3	5-2	4-3	4-2	2-4	3-3	3-3	4-2	5-1	5-1	3-3	51	30	.630
Baltimore	7-0	3-3	......	1-5	5-2	3-3	3-4	4-2	4-2	5-1	5-1	3-3	4-2	3-3	50	31	.617
Detroit	2-4	2-5	3-4	......	3-3	4-2	6-1	2-4	4-2	4-2	4-2	5-1	4-2	5-1	48	33	.593
Toronto	4-3	4-2	4-2	4-3	......	3-4	4-2	2-4	3-3	5-1	4-2	4-2	4-2	3-3	48	33	.593
Boston	2-4	4-2	2-5	2-5	3-3	......	3-4	3-3	3-3	4-2	4-2	3-3	2-4	3-3	38	43	.469
Cleveland	2-5	4-3	3-3	4-2	2-5	2-4	......	3-3	4-2	2-4	2-4	2-4	1-5	5-1	36	45	.444

WEST DIVISION

Club	Chi.	K.C.	Tex.	Oak.	Min.	Cal.	Sea.	Mil.	N.Y.	Balt.	Det.	Tor.	Bos.	Clv.	W.	L.	Pct.
Chicago	......	5-2	5-1	5-1	5-2	5-1	7-0	3-3	4-2	3-3	4-2	1-5	3-3	5-1	55	26	.679
Kansas City	2-4	......	6-1	4-2	5-2	3-4	4-2	3-3	3-3	2-4	3-3	3-3	4-2	3-3	45	36	.556
Texas	4-3	4-2	......	6-0	4-3	3-3	4-3	2-4	2-4	2-4	2-4	3-3	3-3	5-1	44	37	.543
Oakland	4-3	4-3	2-5	......	4-2	4-2	4-2	4-2	2-4	3-3	4-2	4-2	2-4	1-5	42	39	.519
Minnesota	3-3	5-1	2-4	2-5	......	2-5	4-3	4-2	3-3	1-5	2-4	3-3	4-2	2-4	37	44	.457
California	2-5	2-4	3-4	3-4	1-5	......	4-2	4-2	4-2	3-3	2-4	2-4	2-4	3-3	35	46	.432
Seattle	1-5	3-4	3-3	2-5	1-5	5-2	......	3-3	2-4	1-5	3-3	1-5	2-4	3-3	30	51	.370

RECORD ABROAD

EAST DIVISION

Club	Balt.	Det.	Tor.	Bos.	N.Y.	Mil.	Clv.	Chi.	Cal.	K.C.	Min.	Tex.	Oak.	Sea.	W.	L.	Pct.
Baltimore	......	4-3	2-4	5-2	3-4	4-2	3-3	3-3	3-3	4-2	5-1	4-2	3-3	5-1	48	33	.593
Detroit	5-1	......	3-4	5-2	3-3	4-3	2-4	2-4	4-2	3-3	4-2	4-2	2-4	3-3	44	37	.543
Toronto	2-5	3-3	......	3-3	2-5	1-5	5-2	5-1	4-2	3-3	3-3	3-3	2-4	5-1	41	40	.506
Boston	3-3	2-4	4-3	......	3-4	2-5	4-2	3-3	4-2	2-4	2-4	3-3	4-2	4-2	40	41	.494
New York	3-3	5-2	2-4	2-4	......	3-4	3-4	2-4	2-4	3-3	3-3	4-2	4-2	4-2	40	41	.494
Milwaukee	0-7	4-2	3-4	4-2	0-6	......	5-2	3-3	2-4	3-3	2-4	4-2	2-4	3-3	35	46	.432
Cleveland	4-3	1-6	2-4	4-3	2-4	1-5	......	1-5	3-3	3-3	4-2	1-5	5-1	3-3	34	47	.420

WEST DIVISION

Club	Chi.	Cal.	K.C.	Min.	Tex.	Oak.	Sea.	Balt.	Det.	Tor.	Bos.	N.Y.	Mil.	Clv.	W.	L.	Pct.
Chicago	......	5-2	4-2	3-3	3-4	3-4	5-1	2-4	4-2	4-2	3-3	4-2	1-5	3-3	44	37	.543
California	1-5	......	4-3	5-2	3-3	2-4	2-5	2-4	2-4	2-4	4-2	1-5	2-4	5-1	35	46	.432
Kansas City	2-5	4-2	......	1-5	2-4	3-4	4-3	2-4	2-4	3-3	3-3	3-3	3-3	2-4	34	47	.420
Minnesota	2-5	5-1	2-5	......	3-4	2-4	5-1	3-3	1-5	2-4	3-3	1-5	0-6	4-2	33	48	.407
Texas	1-5	4-3	1-6	4-2	......	5-2	3-3	1-5	2-4	1-5	2-4	3-3	2-4	4-2	33	48	.407
Oakland	1-5	4-3	2-4	5-2	0-6	......	5-2	1-5	2-4	2-4	2-4	2-4	2-4	4-2	32	49	.395
Seattle	0-7	2-4	2-4	3-4	3-4	2-4	......	3-3	1-5	3-3	3-3	3-3	4-2	1-5	30	51	.370

SHUTOUT GAMES

Club	Mil.	Oak.	Balt.	Chi.	N.Y.	Det.	Clv.	Tor.	Tex.	K.C.	Bos.	Cal.	Sea.	Min.	W.	L.	Pct.
Milwaukee	..	0	0	0	0	0	0	2	1	1	2	2	1	1	10	4	.714
Oakland	0	..	1	1	1	1	1	1	0	0	0	2	1	3	12	7	.632
Baltimore	0	1	..	2	1	1	1	0	1	1	2	0	2	3	15	9	.625
Chicago	0	1	0	..	1	0	1	0	1	2	0	2	4	0	12	8	.600
New York	1	2	1	0	..	1	0	2	1	1	1	1	0	1	12	8	.600
Detroit	1	0	1	1	0	..	1	0	2	0	1	0	2	0	9	6	.600
Cleveland	0	1	0	0	2	0	..	1	2	2	0	0	0	0	8	8	.500
Toronto	0	0	2	2	1	1	0	..	0	0	0	1	0	1	8	8	.500
Texas	0	0	1	0	0	1	1	1	..	2	1	0	2	2	11	15	.423
Kansas City	0	0	1	0	0	0	1	0	2	..	2	1	1	0	8	11	.421
Boston	0	1	1	1	0	0	1	1	0	0	..	0	2	0	7	11	.389
California	1	1	0	0	1	0	1	0	2	1	0	..	0	0	7	11	.389
Seattle	1	0	1	0	1	1	0	0	1	1	1	1	..	1	9	15	.375
Minnesota	0	0	0	1	0	0	0	0	2	0	1	1	0	..	5	12	.294

OFFICIAL AMERICAN LEAGUE BATTING AVERAGES

Compiled by Sports Information Center

CLUB BATTING

Club	Pct.	G.	AB.	R.	OR.	H.	TB.	2B.	3B.	HR.	RBI.	SH.	SF.	SB.	CS.	LOB.
Toronto	.277	162	5581	795	726	1546	2431	268	58	167	748	36	54	131	72	1106
Milw.	.277	162	5620	764	708	1556	2347	281	57	132	732	61	57	101	49	1132
Detroit	.274	162	5592	789	679	1530	2387	283	53	156	749	48	59	93	53	1128
N. York	.273	162	5631	770	703	1535	2343	269	40	153	728	37	41	84	42	1168
Kan. City	.271	163	5598	696	767	1515	2223	273	54	109	653	32	33	182	47	1063
Boston	.270	162	5590	724	775	1512	2289	287	32	142	691	49	48	30	26	1183
Balt.	.269	162	5546	799	652	1492	2333	283	27	168	761	46	56	61	33	1165
Cleve.	.265	162	5476	704	785	1451	2020	249	31	86	659	48	64	109	71	1165
Chicago	.262	162	5484	800	650	1439	2264	270	42	157	762	53	56	165	50	1081
Oakland	.262	162	5516	708	782	1447	2103	237	28	121	662	55	62	235	98	1094
Minn.	.261	162	5601	709	822	1463	2248	280	41	141	671	29	45	44	29	1118
Calif.	.260	162	5640	722	779	1467	2214	241	22	154	682	68	46	41	39	1122
Texas	.255	163	5610	639	609	1429	2055	242	33	106	587	38	42	119	60	1114
Seattle	.240	162	5336	558	740	1280	1922	247	31	111	536	40	45	144	80	1034
Totals	.266	1135	77821	10177	10177	20662	31179	3710	549	1903	9621	640	708	1539	749	15673

INDIVIDUAL BATTING

(Top Fifteen Qualifiers for Batting Championship—502 or More Plate Appearances)

*Bats lefthanded. †Switch-hitter.

Player and Club	Pct.	G.	AB.	R.	H.	TB.	2B.	3B.	HR.	RBI.	GW.	SH.	SF.	SB.	CS.
Boggs, Wade, Boston*	.361	153	582	100	210	283	44	7	5	74	8	3	7	3	3
Carew, Rodney, California*	.339	129	472	66	160	194	24	2	2	44	5	3	3	6	7
Whitaker, Louis, Detroit*	.320	161	643	94	206	294	40	6	12	72	8	2	8	17	10
Trammell, Alan, Detroit	.319	142	505	83	161	238	31	2	14	66	8	15	4	30	10
Ripken, Calvin, Baltimore	.318	162	663	121	211	343	47	2	27	102	17	0	5	0	4
Moseby, Lloyd, Toronto*	.315	151	539	104	170	269	31	7	18	81	11	3	6	27	8
McRae, Harold, Kansas City	.311	157	589	84	183	272	41	6	12	82	9	0	5	2	3
Brett, George, Kansas City*	.310	123	464	90	144	261	38	2	25	93	12	0	3	0	1
Simmons, Ted, Milwaukee†	.308	153	600	76	185	269	39	3	13	108	17	0	7	4	2
Yount, Robin, Milwaukee	.308	149	578	102	178	291	42	10	17	80	10	1	8	12	5
Cooper, Cecil, Milwaukee*	.307	160	661	106	203	336	37	3	30	126	17	3	8	2	1
Garcia, Damaso, Toronto	.307	131	525	84	161	205	23	6	3	38	2	5	5	31	17
Murray, Eddie, Baltimore†	.306	156	582	115	178	313	30	3	33	111	17	0	9	5	1
Upshaw, Willie, Toronto*	.306	160	579	99	177	298	26	7	27	104	16	3	7	10	7
Rice, James, Boston	.305	155	626	90	191	344	34	1	39	126	14	0	5	0	2

DEPARTMENTAL LEADERS: G—Griffin, Ripken, 162; AB—Ripken, 663; R—Ripken, 121; H—Ripken, 211; TB—Rice, 344; 2B—Ripken, 47; 3B—Yount, 10; HR—Rice, 39; RBI—Cooper, Rice, 126; GW—Baines, 22; SH—Trammell, 15; SF—Lan. Parrish, 13; SB—R. Henderson, 108; CS—R. Henderson, 19.

(All Players—Listed Alphabetically)

Player and Club	Pct.	G.	AB.	R.	H.	TB.	2B.	3B.	HR.	RBI.	GW.	SH.	SF.	SB.	CS.
Adams, Ricky California	.250	58	112	22	28	36	2	0	2	6	0	3	0	1	1
Aikens, Willie, Kansas City*	.302	125	410	49	124	221	26	1	23	72	4	0	1	0	0
Allen, James, Seattle	.223	86	273	23	61	83	10	0	4	21	2	6	0	6	5
Allen, Roderick, Seattle	.167	11	12	1	2	2	0	0	0	0	0	0	0	0	0
Allenson, Gary, Boston	.230	84	230	19	53	73	11	0	3	30	1	5	5	0	1
Almon, William, Oakland	.266	143	451	45	120	163	29	1	4	63	5	5	11	26	8
Anderson, James, Texas	.216	50	102	8	22	25	1	1	0	6	0	4	0	1	2
Armas, Antonio, Boston	.218	145	574	77	125	260	23	2	36	107	10	0	8	0	1
Atherton, Keith, Oakland	.000	29	1	0	0	0	0	0	0	0	0	0	0	0	0
Ayala, Benigno, Baltimore	.221	47	104	12	23	42	7	0	4	13	2	0	2	0	0
Baines, Harold, Chicago*	.280	156	596	76	167	264	33	2	20	99	22	3	6	7	5
Balboni, Stephen, New York	.233	32	86	8	20	37	2	0	5	17	2	0	1	0	0
Bando, Christopher, Cleveland†	.256	48	121	15	31	46	3	0	4	15	1	1	1	0	1
Bannister, Alan, Cleveland	.265	117	377	51	100	148	25	4	5	45	2	7	4	6	6
Barfield, Jesse, Toronto	.253	128	388	58	98	198	13	3	27	68	9	1	5	2	5
Barrett, Martin, Boston	.227	33	44	7	10	13	1	1	0	2	0	0	1	0	0
Baylor, Donald, New York	.303	144	534	82	162	264	33	3	21	85	8	2	8	17	7
Bell, David, Texas	.277	156	618	75	171	254	35	3	14	66	7	0	6	3	5
Bell, George, Toronto	.268	39	112	5	30	49	5	4	2	17	1	0	0	1	1
Beniquez, Juan, California	.305	92	315	44	96	120	15	0	3	34	5	6	1	4	2
Bernazard, Antonio, Chi-Sea†	.265	139	533	65	141	205	34	3	8	56	4	9	7	23	9
Biancalana, Roland, Kansas City†	.200	6	15	2	3	3	0	0	0	0	0	0	0	1	0
Biittner, Lawrence, Texas*	.276	66	116	5	32	39	5	1	0	18	0	0	2	0	0
Boggs, Wade, Boston*	.361	153	582	100	210	283	44	7	5	74	8	3	7	3	3
Bonnell, R. Barry, Toronto	.318	121	377	49	120	177	21	3	10	54	4	2	5	10	7
Bonner, Robert, Baltimore	.000	6	0	0	0	0	0	0	0	0	0	0	0	0	0
Boone, Robert, California	.256	142	468	46	120	165	18	0	9	52	5	10	7	4	3
Bradley, Philip, Seattle	.269	23	67	8	18	20	2	0	0	5	0	1	1	3	1
Brant, Marshall, Oakland	.143	5	14	2	2	2	0	0	0	2	0	0	0	0	0
Brett, George, Kansas City*	.310	123	464	90	144	261	38	2	25	93	12	0	3	0	1
Brookens, Thomas, Detroit	.214	138	332	50	71	108	13	3	6	32	2	5	6	10	4
Brouhard, Mark, Milwaukee	.276	56	185	25	51	84	10	1	7	23	3	1	1	0	4
Brown, Darrell, Minnesota†	.272	91	309	40	84	94	6	2	0	22	2	3	0	3	3
Brown, Michael, California	.231	31	104	12	24	40	5	1	3	9	1	0	0	1	0
Brunansky, Thomas, Minnesota	.227	151	542	70	123	241	24	5	28	82	15	1	3	2	5
Bulling, Terry, Seattle	.000	5	5	0	0	0	0	0	0	0	0	0	0	0	0
Bumbry, Alonza, Baltimore*	.275	124	378	63	104	135	14	4	3	31	2	4	3	12	5
Burgmeier, Thomas, Oakland*	.000	51	0	1	0	0	0	0	0	0	0	0	0	0	0
Burleson, Richard, California	.286	33	119	22	34	41	7	0	0	11	2	2	1	0	2
Burroughs, Jeffrey, Oakland	.269	121	401	43	108	155	15	1	10	56	6	0	7	0	2
Bush, R. Randall, Minnesota*	.249	124	373	43	93	156	24	3	11	56	4	0	1	0	1
Butera, Salvatore, Detroit	.200	4	5	1	1	1	0	0	0	0	0	0	0	0	0
Cabell, Enos, Detroit	.311	121	392	62	122	170	23	5	5	46	6	5	6	4	8
Campaneris, Dagoberto, New York	.322	60	143	19	46	51	5	0	0	11	1	3	1	6	7
Capra, Nick, Texas	.000	8	2	2	0	0	0	0	0	0	0	0	0	0	0
Carew, Rodney, California*	.339	129	472	66	160	194	24	2	2	44	5	3	3	6	7
Castillo, E. Manuel, Seattle†	.207	91	203	13	42	54	6	3	0	24	4	1	4	1	1
Castillo, Martin, Detroit	.193	67	119	10	23	33	4	0	2	10	1	6	0	2	0
Castillo, M. Carmelo, Cleveland	.278	23	36	9	10	17	2	1	1	3	0	0	0	1	1
Castino, John, Minnesota	.277	142	563	83	156	227	30	4	11	57	8	10	4	4	2
Cerone, Richard, New York	.220	80	246	18	54	67	7	0	2	22	4	4	0	0	0
Chambers, Albert, Seattle*	.209	31	67	11	14	20	3	0	1	7	1	0	0	0	1
Cias, Darryl, Oakland	.333	20	18	1	6	7	1	0	0	1	0	0	0	1	0

Player and Club	Pct.	G.	AB.	R.	H.	TB.	2B.	3B.	HR.	RBI.	GW.	SH.	SF.	SB.	CS.
Clark, Robert, California	.231	76	212	17	49	75	9	1	5	21	3	3	1	0	0
Coles, Darnell, Seattle	.283	27	92	9	26	36	7	0	1	6	1	1	0	0	3
Collins, David, Toronto†	.271	118	402	55	109	132	12	4	1	34	5	2	2	31	7
Concepcion, Onix, Kansas City	.242	80	219	22	53	70	11	3	0	20	0	6	2	10	3
Cooper, Cecil, Milwaukee*	.307	160	661	106	203	336	37	3	30	126	17	3	8	2	1
Cowens, Alfred, Seattle	.205	110	356	39	73	117	19	2	7	35	3	0	3	10	2
Cruz, Julio, Seattle-Chicago†	.252	160	515	71	130	168	19	5	3	52	8	5	7	57	12
Cruz, Todd, Seattle-Baltimore	.199	146	437	37	87	136	13	3	10	48	7	10	3	4	7
Culmer, Wilfred, Cleveland	.105	7	19	0	2	2	0	0	0	1	0	0	1	0	1
Dauer, Richard, Baltimore	.235	140	459	49	108	142	19	0	5	41	5	7	5	1	1
Davis, Michael, Oakland*	.275	128	443	61	122	178	24	4	8	62	3	5	4	32	15
Davis, Wallace, Kansas City	.344	33	122	13	42	62	2	6	2	18	2	2	2	4	3
Dayett, Brian, New York	.207	11	29	3	6	8	0	1	0	5	1	1	0	0	0
DeCinces, Douglas, California	.281	95	370	49	104	183	19	3	18	65	6	1	8	2	0
Dempsey, J. Rikard, Baltimore	.231	128	347	33	80	112	16	2	4	32	1	5	5	1	1
Dent, Russell, Texas	.237	131	417	36	99	124	15	2	2	34	1	7	2	3	7
Dilone, Miguel, Cleveland-Chicago†	.183	36	71	16	13	18	3	1	0	7	0	0	0	6	1
Downing, Brian, California	.246	113	403	68	99	173	15	1	19	53	5	1	2	1	2
Dunbar, Thomas, Texas*	.250	12	24	3	6	6	0	0	0	3	0	0	0	3	1
Dwyer, James, Baltimore*	.286	100	196	37	56	99	17	1	8	38	6	1	1	1	1
Dybzinski, Jerome, Chicago	.230	127	256	30	59	74	10	1	1	32	3	11	3	11	4
Easterly, James, Milw.-Cleveland*	.000	54	1	0	0	0	0	0	0	0	0	1	0	0	0
Edler, David, Seattle	.190	29	63	2	12	18	1	1	1	4	1	2	1	3	3
Edwards, Marshall, Milwaukee*	.297	51	74	14	22	25	1	1	0	5	0	3	1	5	5
Eisenreich, James, Minnesota*	.286	2	7	1	2	3	1	0	0	0	0	0	0	0	0
Engle, R. David, Minnesota	.305	120	374	46	114	168	22	4	8	43	4	0	5	2	1
Espino, Juan, New York	.261	10	23	1	6	9	0	0	1	3	0	0	1	0	0
Essian, James, Cleveland	.204	48	93	11	19	29	4	0	2	11	0	1	2	0	1
Evans, Dwight, Boston	.238	126	470	74	112	205	19	4	22	58	8	0	2	3	0
Faedo, Leonard, Minnesota	.277	51	173	16	48	58	7	0	1	18	2	3	2	0	0
Fahey, William, Detroit*	.273	19	22	4	6	7	1	0	0	2	0	0	0	0	0
Ferguson, Joseph, California	.074	12	27	3	2	2	0	0	0	2	0	1	0	0	0
Fernandez, Octavio, Toronto†	.265	15	34	5	9	12	1	1	0	2	0	1	0	0	1
Fischlin, Michael, Cleveland	.209	95	225	31	47	62	5	2	2	23	2	11	2	9	2
Fisk, Carlton, Chicago	.289	138	488	85	141	253	26	4	26	86	9	2	3	9	6
Fletcher, Scott, Chicago	.237	114	262	42	62	97	16	5	3	31	5	7	2	5	1
Foli, Timothy, California	.252	88	330	29	83	99	10	0	2	29	3	11	2	2	3
Ford, Darnell, Baltimore	.280	103	407	63	114	179	30	4	9	55	10	3	6	9	2
Franco, Julio, Cleveland	.273	149	560	68	153	217	24	8	8	80	9	3	6	32	12
Gaetti, Gary, Minnesota	.245	157	584	81	143	242	30	3	21	78	2	0	8	7	1
Gagne, Gregory, Minnesota	.111	10	27	2	3	4	1	0	0	3	0	0	2	0	0
Gamble, Oscar, New York*	.261	74	180	26	47	82	10	2	7	26	5	0	0	0	0
Gantner, James, Milwaukee*	.282	161	603	85	170	242	23	8	11	74	8	11	4	5	6
Garcia, Damaso, Toronto	.307	131	525	84	161	205	23	6	3	38	2	5	5	31	17
Gedman, Richard, Boston*	.294	81	204	21	60	84	16	1	2	18	2	3	0	0	1
Geronimo, Cesar, Kansas City*	.207	38	87	2	18	22	4	0	0	4	2	0	0	0	1
Gibson, Kirk, Detroit*	.227	128	401	60	91	166	12	9	15	51	6	5	4	14	3
Gonzalez, Julio, Detroit	.143	12	21	0	3	4	1	0	0	2	0	1	0	0	0
Graham, Lee, Boston*	.000	5	6	2	0	0	0	0	0	1	0	0	1	0	1
Gray, Lorenzo, Chicago	.179	41	78	18	14	20	3	0	1	4	0	1	0	1	0
Grich, Robert, California	.292	120	387	65	113	178	17	0	16	62	3	4	3	2	4
Griffey, G. Kenneth, New York*	.306	118	458	60	140	200	21	3	11	46	7	3	2	6	1
Griffin, Alfredo, Toronto†	.250	162	528	62	132	184	22	9	4	47	2	11	3	8	11
Gross, Wayne, Oakland*	.233	137	339	34	79	133	18	0	12	44	6	4	2	3	5
Grubb, John, Detroit*	.254	57	134	20	34	55	5	2	4	22	5	0	1	0	0
Gulliver, Glenn, Baltimore*	.213	23	47	5	10	13	3	0	0	2	1	0	1	0	1
Gutierrez, Joaquin, Boston	.300	5	10	2	3	3	0	0	0	0	0	0	0	0	1
Hairston, Jerry, Chicago†	.294	101	126	17	37	63	9	1	5	22	0	0	2	0	1
Hancock, R. Garry, Oakland*	.273	101	256	29	70	107	7	3	8	30	3	3	1	2	0
Hargrove, D. Michael, Cleveland*	.286	134	469	57	134	172	21	4	3	57	8	7	7	0	6
Harrah, Colbert, Cleveland	.266	138	526	81	140	192	23	1	9	53	5	4	3	16	10
Hassey, Ronald, Cleveland*	.270	117	341	48	92	131	21	0	6	42	3	2	5	2	2
Hatcher, Michael, Minnesota	.317	106	375	50	119	167	15	3	9	47	3	3	2	2	0
Heath, Michael, Oakland	.281	96	345	45	97	132	17	0	6	33	4	1	1	3	4
Henderson, David, Seattle	.269	137	484	50	130	215	24	5	17	55	4	2	6	9	3
Henderson, Rickey, Oakland	.292	145	513	105	150	216	25	7	9	48	6	1	1	108	19
Henderson, Stephen, Seattle	.294	121	436	50	128	196	32	3	10	54	6	1	3	10	14
Hernandez, Leonard, Baltimore	.246	64	203	21	50	76	6	1	6	26	3	0	1	1	0
Herndon, Larry, Detroit	.302	153	603	88	182	288	28	9	20	92	9	0	6	9	3
Hill, Donald, Oakland†	.266	53	158	20	42	55	7	0	2	15	0	5	2	1	1
Hill, Marc, Chicago	.226	58	133	11	30	39	6	0	1	11	1	4	0	0	1
Hoffman, Glenn, Boston	.260	143	473	56	123	161	24	1	4	41	8	11	2	1	1
Hostetler, David, Texas	.220	94	304	31	67	113	9	2	11	46	5	0	2	0	2
Howell, Roy, Milwaukee*	.278	69	194	23	54	87	9	6	4	25	0	2	0	1	3
Hrbek, Kent, Minnesota*	.297	141	515	75	153	252	41	5	16	84	8	0	7	4	6
Hudgens, David, Oakland*	.143	6	7	0	1	1	0	0	0	0	0	0	0	0	0
Hulett, Timothy, Chicago	.200	6	5	0	1	1	0	0	0	0	0	0	0	1	0
Huppert, David, Baltimore	.000	2	0	0	0	0	0	0	0	0	0	0	0	0	0
Iorg, Garth, Toronto	.275	122	375	40	103	141	22	5	2	39	5	2	3	7	0
Ivie, Michael, Detroit	.214	12	42	4	9	13	4	0	0	7	2	0	1	0	0

Player and Club	Pct.	G.	AB.	R.	H.	TB.	2B.	3B.	HR.	RBI.	GW.	SH.	SF.	SB.	CS.
Jackson, Reginald, California*	.194	116	397	43	77	135	14	1	14	49	3	0	5	0	2
Jackson, Ronnie, California	.230	102	348	41	80	122	16	1	8	39	5	1	0	2	2
James, Dion, Milwaukee*	.100	11	20	1	2	2	0	0	0	1	0	0	0	1	0
Jimenez, Alfonso, Minnesota	.174	36	86	5	15	22	5	1	0	9	1	0	2	0	1
Johnson, Bobby, Texas	.211	72	175	18	37	60	6	1	5	16	2	0	1	3	0
Johnson, Clifford, Toronto	.265	142	407	59	108	199	23	1	22	76	9	1	4	0	1
Johnson, Howard, Detroit†	.212	27	66	11	14	23	0	0	3	5	0	0	0	0	0
Johnson, Ronald, Kansas City	.259	9	27	2	7	7	0	0	0	1	0	0	0	0	0
Jones, Lynn, Detroit	.266	49	64	9	17	22	1	2	0	6	0	3	0	1	0
Jones, Robert, Texas*	.222	41	72	5	16	23	4	0	1	11	2	0	2	0	2
Jurak, Edward, Boston	.277	75	159	19	44	60	8	4	0	18	0	3	2	1	2
Kearney, Robert, Oakland	.255	108	298	33	76	111	11	0	8	32	6	4	1	1	4
Kemp, Steven, New York*	.241	109	373	53	90	149	17	3	12	49	9	1	2	1	0
Kittle, Ronald, Chicago	.254	145	520	75	132	262	19	3	35	100	9	0	3	8	3
Klutts, Gene, Toronto	.256	22	43	3	11	20	0	0	3	5	0	0	0	0	1
Krenchicki, Wayne, Detroit*	.278	59	133	18	37	47	7	0	1	16	1	2	2	0	0
Kuntz, Russell, Chicago-Minnesota	.211	59	142	19	30	43	4	0	3	6	1	0	1	1	0
Laga, Michael, Detroit*	.190	12	21	2	4	4	0	0	0	2	0	0	0	0	0
Landrum, Terry, Baltimore	.310	26	42	8	13	18	2	0	1	4	0	0	1	0	2
Lansford, Carney, Oakland	.308	80	299	43	92	142	16	2	10	45	6	0	4	3	8
Laudner, Timothy, Minnesota	.185	62	168	20	31	58	9	0	6	18	2	0	1	0	0
Law, Rudy, Chicago*	.283	141	501	95	142	185	20	7	3	34	3	4	2	77	12
Law, Vance, Chicago	.243	145	408	55	99	142	21	5	4	42	4	6	5	3	1
Leach, Richard, Detroit*	.248	99	242	22	60	86	17	0	3	26	3	0	0	2	2
Lemon, Chester, Detroit	.255	145	491	78	125	228	21	5	24	69	11	4	4	0	7
Lopes, David, Oakland	.277	147	494	64	137	209	13	4	17	67	7	4	10	22	4
Lowenstein, John, Baltimore*	.281	122	310	52	87	149	13	2	15	60	9	0	6	2	1
Lubratich, Steven, California	.218	57	156	12	34	43	9	0	0	7	0	13	1	0	1
Luzinski, Gregory, Chicago	.255	144	502	73	128	252	26	1	32	95	10	0	10	2	1
Lynn, Fredric, California*	.272	117	437	56	119	211	20	3	22	74	11	0	6	2	2
Maler, James, Seattle	.182	26	66	5	12	16	1	0	1	3	0	0	0	0	3
Manning, Richard, Clev.-Milwaukee*	.246	158	569	60	140	180	20	4	4	43	4	3	4	18	5
Martin, Jerry, Kansas City	.318	13	44	4	14	22	2	0	2	13	2	0	3	1	0
Martinez, John, Toronto	.253	88	221	27	56	100	14	0	10	33	4	1	2	0	1
Mattingly, Donald, New York*	.283	91	279	34	79	114	15	4	4	32	3	2	2	0	0
McBride, Arnold, Cleveland*	.291	70	230	21	67	80	8	1	1	18	3	1	2	8	2
McNealy, Robert, Oakland*	.000	15	4	5	0	0	0	0	0	0	0	0	0	0	1
McRae, Harold, Kansas City	.311	157	589	84	183	272	41	6	12	82	9	0	5	2	3
Meacham, Robert, New York†	.235	22	51	5	12	14	2	0	0	4	0	0	0	8	0
Mercado, Orlando, Seattle	.197	66	178	10	35	53	11	2	1	16	3	2	2	2	2
Meyer, Daniel, Oakland*	.189	69	169	15	32	44	9	0	1	13	0	1	2	0	0
Milbourne, Lawrence, New York†	.200	31	70	5	14	18	4	0	0	2	0	0	0	1	1
Miller, Richard, Boston*	.286	104	262	41	75	95	10	2	2	21	2	1	1	3	3
Mitchell, Robert, Minnesota*	.230	59	152	26	35	46	4	2	1	15	2	0	0	1	1
Molinaro, Robert, Detroit*	.000	8	2	3	0	0	0	0	0	0	0	0	0	1	1
Molitor, Paul, Milwaukee	.270	152	608	95	164	249	28	6	15	47	7	7	6	41	8
Money, Donald, Milwaukee	.149	43	114	5	17	25	5	0	1	8	1	1	2	0	0
Moore, Charles, Milwaukee	.284	151	529	65	150	195	27	6	2	49	4	14	3	11	4
Moore, Kelvin, Oakland	.210	41	124	12	26	45	4	0	5	16	0	0	1	2	4
Moreno, Omar, New York*	.250	48	152	17	38	52	9	1	1	17	1	3	0	7	3
Morris, John, Detroit	.000	44	0	3	0	0	0	0	0	0	0	0	0	0	0
Moseby, Lloyd, Toronto*	.315	151	539	104	170	269	31	7	18	81	11	3	6	27	8
Moses, John, Seattle†	.208	93	130	19	27	33	4	1	0	6	0	0	0	11	5
Motley, Darryl, Kansas City	.235	19	68	9	16	30	1	2	3	11	1	0	1	2	1
Mulliniks, S. Rance, Toronto*	.275	129	364	54	100	170	34	3	10	49	4	3	2	0	2
Mumphrey, Jerry, New York†	.262	83	267	41	70	110	11	4	7	36	5	2	5	2	3
Murcer, Bobby, New York*	.182	9	22	2	4	9	2	0	1	1	1	0	0	0	0
Murphy, Dwayne, Oakland*	.227	130	471	55	107	179	17	2	17	75	8	7	6	7	5
Murray, Eddie, Baltimore†	.306	156	582	115	178	313	30	3	33	111	17	0	9	5	1
Nahorodny, William, Detroit	.000	2	1	0	0	0	0	0	0	0	0	0	0	0	0
Narron, Jerry, California*	.136	10	22	1	3	6	0	0	1	4	1	0	0	0	0
Nelson, James, Seattle	.219	40	96	9	21	27	3	0	1	5	0	1	1	4	2
Nelson, Ricky, Seattle*	.254	98	291	32	74	108	13	3	5	36	6	2	1	7	4
Nettles, Graig, New York*	.266	129	462	56	123	206	17	3	20	75	5	0	3	0	1
Newman, Jeffrey, Boston	.189	59	132	11	25	38	4	0	3	7	0	2	1	0	1
Nichols, T. Reid, Boston	.285	100	274	35	78	120	22	1	6	22	3	3	1	7	5
Nixon, Otis, New York†	.143	13	14	2	2	2	0	0	0	0	0	0	0	2	0
Nolan, Joseph, Baltimore*	.277	73	184	25	51	79	11	1	5	24	2	0	0	0	0
Nyman, Christopher, Chicago	.286	21	28	12	8	14	0	0	2	4	0	0	0	2	2
O'Berry, P. Michael, California	.167	26	60	7	10	14	1	0	1	5	0	2	0	0	0
O'Brien, Peter, Texas*	.237	154	524	53	124	182	24	5	8	53	7	3	2	5	4
Office, Rowland, New York*	.000	2	2	0	0	0	0	0	0	1	0	0	1	0	0
Oglivie, Benjamin, Milwaukee*	.280	125	411	49	115	179	19	3	13	66	10	0	8	4	6
Orta, Jorge, Toronto*	.237	103	245	30	58	100	6	3	10	38	1	0	4	1	2
Otis, Amos, Kansas City	.261	98	356	35	93	127	16	3	4	41	7	0	1	5	2
Owen, Spike, Seattle	.196	80	306	36	60	83	11	3	2	21	3	5	3	10	6
Paciorek, Thomas, Chicago	.307	115	420	65	129	194	32	3	9	63	8	4	4	6	1
Page, Mitchell, Oakland*	.241	57	79	16	19	22	3	0	0	1	0	1	0	3	3
Pagel, Karl, Cleveland*	.300	8	20	1	6	6	0	0	0	1	1	0	0	0	0
Parrish, Lance, Detroit	.269	155	605	80	163	292	42	3	27	114	14	0	13	1	3

Player and Club	Pct.	G.	AB.	R.	H.	TB.	2B.	3B.	HR.	RBI.	GW.	SH.	SF.	SB.	CS.
Parrish, Larry, Texas	.272	145	555	76	151	263	26	4	26	88	17	0	9	0	0
Parsons, Casey, Chicago*	.200	8	5	1	1	1	0	0	0	0	0	0	0	0	0
Pastornicky, Clifford, Kansas City	.125	9	32	4	4	10	0	0	2	5	2	0	0	0	0
Perconte, John, Cleveland	.269	14	26	1	7	8	1	0	0	0	0	0	0	3	1
Perkins, Broderick, Cleveland*	.272	79	184	23	50	60	10	0	0	24	2	0	4	1	5
Peters, Richard, Oakland†	.287	55	178	20	51	58	7	0	0	20	3	2	5	4	9
Petralli, Eugene, Toronto†	.000	6	4	0	0	0	0	0	0	0	0	0	0	0	0
Pettis, Gary, California†	.294	22	85	19	25	42	2	3	3	6	0	1	0	8	3
Phelps, Kenneth, Seattle*	.236	50	127	10	30	57	4	1	7	16	1	1	3	0	0
Phillips, K. Anthony, Oakland†	.248	148	412	54	102	132	12	3	4	35	3	11	3	16	5
Picciolo, Robert, Milwaukee	.222	14	27	2	6	9	3	0	0	1	0	1	1	0	0
Piniella, Louis, New York	.291	53	148	19	43	60	9	1	2	16	2	0	0	1	1
Powell, Hosken, Toronto*	.169	40	83	6	14	17	0	0	1	7	1	0	1	2	0
Pryor, Gregory, Kansas City	.217	68	115	9	25	32	4	0	1	14	1	2	1	0	0
Putnam, Patrick, Seattle*	.269	144	469	58	126	210	23	2	19	67	8	1	5	2	1
Quinones, Luis, Oakland†	.190	19	42	5	8	12	2	1	0	4	1	1	1	1	1
Ramos, Domingo, Seattle	.283	53	127	14	36	46	4	0	2	10	0	1	0	3	1
Randolph, William, New York	.279	104	420	73	117	146	21	1	2	38	1	3	0	12	4
Ready, Randy, Milwaukee	.405	12	37	8	15	25	3	2	1	6	0	0	0	0	1
Remy, Gerald, Boston*	.275	146	592	73	163	189	16	5	0	43	7	12	3	11	3
Reynolds, Harold, Seattle†	.203	20	59	8	12	18	4	1	0	1	0	1	1	0	2
Rhomberg, Kevin, Cleveland	.476	12	21	2	10	10	0	0	0	2	0	0	1	1	1
Rice, James, Boston	.305	155	626	90	191	344	34	1	39	126	14	0	5	0	2
Richardt, Michael, Texas	.157	22	83	9	13	20	2	1	1	7	0	0	1	2	1
Ripken, Calvin, Baltimore	.318	162	663	121	211	343	47	2	27	102	17	0	5	0	4
Rivers, John, Texas*	.285	96	309	37	88	108	17	0	1	20	3	5	3	9	4
Roberts, Leon, Kansas City	.258	84	213	24	55	86	7	0	8	24	1	1	2	1	1
Robertson, Andre, New York	.248	98	322	37	80	105	16	3	1	22	1	7	3	2	4
Rodriguez, Aurelio, Balt-Chicago	.138	67	87	1	12	16	1	0	1	3	0	2	1	0	0
Roenicke, Gary, Baltimore	.260	115	323	45	84	154	13	0	19	64	6	4	5	2	2
Roenicke, Ronald, Seattle†	.253	59	198	23	50	74	12	0	4	23	0	2	2	6	2
Romero, Edgardo, Milwaukee	.317	59	145	17	46	56	7	0	1	18	1	3	2	1	0
Sakata, Lenn, Baltimore	.254	66	134	23	34	50	7	0	3	12	3	1	0	8	4
Sample, William, Texas	.274	147	554	80	152	222	28	3	12	57	4	4	4	44	8
Schofield, Richard, California	.204	21	54	4	11	22	2	0	3	4	0	1	0	0	0
Schroeder, A. William, Milwaukee	.178	23	73	7	13	26	2	1	3	7	0	2	0	0	1
Sconiers, Daryl, California*	.274	106	314	49	86	135	19	3	8	46	4	2	1	4	2
Scott, Donald, Texas†	.000	2	4	0	0	0	0	0	0	0	0	0	0	0	0
Shelby, John, Baltimore†	.258	126	325	52	84	118	15	2	5	27	2	6	0	15	2
Sheridan, Patrick, Kansas City*	.270	109	333	43	90	127	12	2	7	36	7	4	0	12	3
Simmons, Ted, Milwaukee†	.308	153	600	76	185	269	39	3	13	108	17	0	7	4	2
Simpson, Joe, Kansas City*	.168	91	119	16	20	26	2	2	0	8	0	2	1	1	1
Singleton, Kenneth, Baltimore†	.276	151	507	52	140	221	21	3	18	84	2	2	3	0	2
Skinner, Joel, Chicago	.273	6	11	2	3	3	0	0	0	1	0	0	0	0	0
Skube, Robert, Milwaukee*	.200	12	25	2	5	8	1	1	0	9	0	0	0	0	0
Slaught, Donald, Kansas City	.312	83	276	21	86	107	13	4	0	28	6	1	2	3	1
Smalley, Roy, New York†	.275	130	451	70	124	204	24	1	18	62	5	5	4	3	3
Smith, Raymond, Minnesota	.224	59	152	11	34	39	5	0	0	8	1	3	1	1	0
Squires, Michael, Chicago*	.222	143	153	21	34	43	4	1	1	11	1	2	1	3	3
Stapleton, David, Boston	.247	151	542	54	134	197	31	1	10	66	7	6	8	1	1
Stefero, John, Baltimore*	.455	9	11	2	5	6	1	0	0	4	2	0	0	0	0
Stegman, David, Chicago	.170	30	53	5	9	11	2	0	0	4	0	0	2	0	1
Stein, William, Texas	.310	78	232	21	72	95	15	1	2	33	4	0	2	2	3
Sundberg, James, Texas	.201	131	378	30	76	96	14	0	2	28	4	7	1	0	4
Sweet, Richard, Seattle†	.221	93	249	18	55	67	9	0	1	22	4	2	1	2	2
Tabler, Patrick, Cleveland	.291	124	430	56	125	176	23	5	6	65	5	0	5	2	4
Teufel, Timothy, Minnesota	.308	21	78	11	24	42	7	1	3	6	3	2	0	0	0
Thomas, J. Gorman, Milw-Clev	.209	152	535	72	112	203	23	1	22	69	4	4	8	10	4
Thornton, Andre, Cleveland	.281	141	508	78	143	223	27	1	17	77	12	0	8	4	2
Tolleson, J. Wayne, Texas†	.260	134	470	64	122	148	13	2	3	20	2	7	2	33	10
Trammell, Alan, Detroit	.319	142	505	83	161	238	31	2	14	66	8	15	4	30	10
Trillo, J. Manuel, Cleveland	.272	88	320	33	87	105	13	1	1	29	2	4	2	1	3
Ullger, Scott, Minnesota	.190	35	79	8	15	19	4	0	0	5	1	0	0	0	2
Upshaw, Willie, Toronto*	.306	160	579	99	177	298	26	7	27	104	16	3	7	10	7
Valdez, Julio, Boston†	.120	12	25	3	3	3	0	0	0	0	0	0	0	0	0
Valentine, Ellis, California	.240	86	271	30	65	118	10	2	13	43	2	1	4	2	1
Velez, Otoniel, Cleveland	.080	10	25	1	2	2	0	0	0	1	0	0	0	0	0
Vukovich, George, Cleveland*	.247	124	312	31	77	103	13	2	3	44	1	3	4	3	4
Wagner, Mark, Texas	.000	2	2	0	0	0	0	0	0	0	0	0	0	0	0
Walker, Cleotha, Boston†	.400	4	5	2	2	6	0	2	0	1	0	0	0	0	0
Walker, Gregory, Chicago*	.270	118	307	32	83	135	16	3	10	55	9	0	3	2	1
Ward, Gary, Minnesota	.278	157	623	76	173	274	34	5	19	88	4	1	5	8	1
Washington, Ronald, Minnesota	.246	99	317	28	78	103	7	3	4	26	5	3	1	10	5
Washington, U.L., Kansas City†	.236	144	547	76	129	175	19	6	5	41	7	7	1	40	7
Wathan, John, Kansas City	.245	128	437	49	107	137	18	3	2	32	4	2	2	28	7
Webster, Mitchell, Toronto†	.182	11	11	2	2	2	0	0	0	0	0	0	0	0	0
Whitaker, Louis, Detroit*	.320	161	643	94	206	294	40	6	12	72	8	2	8	17	10
White, Frank, Kansas City	.260	146	549	52	143	223	35	6	11	77	10	4	6	13	5
Whitt, L. Ernest, Toronto*	.256	123	344	53	88	158	15	2	17	56	11	1	5	1	1
Wilfong, Robert, California*	.254	65	177	17	45	60	7	1	2	17	3	2	1	0	2

Player and Club	Pct.	G.	AB.	R.	H.	TB.	2B.	3B.	HR.	RBI.	GW.	SH.	SF.	SB.	CS.
Wilkerson, Curtis, Texas†	.171	16	35	7	6	8	0	1	0	1	0	0	0	3	0
Wilson, Glenn, Detroit	.268	144	503	55	135	205	25	6	11	65	6	0	2	1	1
Wilson, Michael, Minnesota	.250	5	4	4	1	2	1	0	0	1	0	0	0	0	0
Wilson, Willie, Kansas City†	.276	137	576	90	159	203	22	8	2	33	1	1	0	59	8
Winfield, David, New York	.283	152	598	99	169	307	26	8	32	116	21	0	6	15	6
Wockenfuss, Johnny, Detroit	.269	92	245	32	66	103	8	1	9	44	7	0	2	1	1
Wright, George, Texas†	.276	162	634	79	175	269	28	6	18	80	12	1	3	8	7
Wynegar, Harold, New York†	.296	94	301	40	89	129	18	2	6	42	3	1	2	1	1
Yastrzemski, Carl, Boston*	.266	119	380	38	101	155	24	0	10	56	5	0	1	0	0
Yost, Edgar, Milwaukee	.224	61	196	21	44	69	5	1	6	28	1	8	1	1	0
Young, Michael, Baltimore†	.167	25	36	5	6	10	2	1	0	2	1	4	0	1	0
Yount, Robin, Milwaukee	.308	149	578	102	178	291	42	10	17	80	10	1	8	12	5
Zisk, Richard, Seattle	.242	90	285	30	69	117	12	0	12	36	4	0	3	0	0

The following pitchers neither had a plate appearance nor scored a run, but made appearances in addition to their games pitched as indicated: Michael Armstrong, Kansas City—one game postponed before he made his first delivery; Ronald Guidry, New York—one game as an outfielder but did not pitch; Lawrence Gura, Kansas City—one game as a pinch-runner; Bryan Haas, Milwaukee—one game as a pinch-runner; Steven McCatty, Oakland—one game as a pinch-runner; Kenneth Schrom, Minnesota—one game as a pinch-runner; Samuel Stewart, Baltimore—one game as a pinch-runner.

AWARDED FIRST BASE ON INTERFERENCE—Sweet, Sea. 2 (Smith, Heath); Rodriguez, Balt. (Engle); Parrish, Tex. (Hill); J. Cruz, Chi. (Allenson).

PLAYERS WITH TWO OR MORE CLUBS

(Alphabetically Arranged With Player's First Club on Top)

Player and Club	Pct.	G.	AB.	R.	H.	TB.	2B.	3B.	HR.	RBI.	GW.	SH.	SF.	Tot. BB.	Int. BB.	HP.	SO.	SB.	CS.	GI. DP.
Bernazard, Chi.	.262	59	233	30	61	87	16	2	2	26	3	4	5	17	0	0	45	2	1	5
Bernazard, Sea.	.267	80	300	35	80	118	18	1	6	30	1	5	2	38	3	2	52	21	8	4
J. Cruz, Sea.	.254	61	181	24	46	64	10	1	2	12	1	1	2	20	1	2	22	33	6	3
J. Cruz, Chi.	.251	99	334	47	84	104	9	4	1	40	7	4	5	29	0	2	44	24	6	9
T. Cruz, Sea.	.190	65	216	21	41	70	4	2	7	21	3	2	1	7	2	2	56	1	3	2
T. Cruz, Balt.	.208	81	221	16	46	66	9	1	3	27	4	8	2	15	0	1	52	3	4	12
Dilone, Cleve.	.191	32	68	15	13	18	3	1	0	7	0	0	0	10	0	0	5	5	1	1
Dilone, Chi.	.000	4	3	1	0	0	0	0	0	0	0	0	0	0	0	0	0	1	0	0
Easterly, Milw.	.000	13	1	0	0	0	0	0	0	0	0	1	0	0	0	0	0	0	0	0
Kuntz, Chi.	.262	28	42	6	11	12	1	0	0	1	1	0	0	6	0	0	13	1	0	1
Kuntz, Minn.	.190	31	100	13	19	31	3	0	3	5	0	0	1	12	0	0	28	0	0	4
Manning, Clev.	.278	50	194	20	54	63	6	0	1	10	0	2	1	12	1	0	22	7	3	5
Manning, Milw.	.229	108	375	40	86	117	14	4	3	33	4	1	3	26	4	1	40	11	2	8
Rodriguez, Balt.	.119	45	67	0	8	8	0	0	0	2	0	1	1	0	0	1	13	0	0	0
Rodriguez, Chi.	200	22	20	1	4	8	1	0	1	1	0	1	0	0	0	0	3	0	0	1
Thomas, Milw.	.183	46	164	21	30	53	6	1	5	18	0	2	2	23	0	1	50	2	1	6
Thomas, Clev.	.221	106	371	51	82	150	17	0	17	51	4	2	6	57	2	1	98	8	3	7

OFFICIAL MISCELLANEOUS AMERICAN LEAGUE BATTING RECORDS

CLUB MISCELLANEOUS BATTING RECORDS

Club	Slg. Pct.	G.	Tot. BB.	Int. BB.	HP.	SO.	GIDP.	ShO.
Toronto	.436	162	510	44	32	810	117	8
Detroit	.427	162	508	37	39	831	123	6
Baltimore	.421	162	601	48	23	800	144	9
Milwaukee	.418	162	475	51	27	665	135	4
New York	.416	162	533	36	37	686	148	8
Chicago	.413	162	527	50	43	888	111	8
Boston	.409	162	536	44	28	758	171	11
Minnesota	.401	162	467	27	29	802	150	12
Kansas City	.397	163	397	41	23	722	123	11
California	.393	162	509	39	31	835	147	11
Oakland	.381	162	524	47	31	872	128	7
Cleveland	.369	162	605	38	29	691	146	8
Texas	.366	163	442	33	29	767	123	15
Seattle	.360	162	460	31	24	840	113	15
Totals	.401	1135	7094	566	425	10967	1879	133

INDIVIDUAL MISCELLANEOUS BATTING RECORDS

(Top Ten Qualifiers for Slugging Championship)

Player—Club	Slg. Pct.	Tot. BB.	Int. BB.	HP.	SO.	GI DP.
Brett, K.C.	.563	57	13	1	39	9
Rice, Bos.	.550	52	10	6	102	31
Murray, Balt.	.538	86	13	3	90	13
Fisk, Chi.	.518	46	3	6	88	8
Ripken, Balt.	.517	58	0	0	97	24
Upshaw, Tor.	.515	61	8	5	98	8
Winfield, N.Y.	.513	58	2	2	77	30
Cooper, Milw.	.508	37	7	1	63	17
Kittle, Chi.	.504	39	8	8	150	10
Yount, Milw.	.503	72	6	3	58	11

DEPARTMENTAL LEADERS: Tot. BB—R. Henderson, 103; Int. BB—Singleton, 19; HP—Lemon, 20; SO—Kittle, 150; GIDP—Armas, 31.

(All Players—Listed Alphabetically)

Player—Club	Slg. Pct.	Tot. BB.	Int. BB.	HP.	SO.	GI DP.
Adams, Calif.	.321	5	0	3	12	2
Aikens, K.C.	.539	45	9	2	75	16
J. Allen, Sea.	.304	33	0	1	52	8
R. Allen, Sea.	.167	0	0	0	1	0
Allenson, Bos.	.317	27	0	2	43	8
Almon, Oak	.361	26	3	2	67	8
Anderson, Tex.	.245	5	0	0	8	3
Armas, Bos.	.453	29	0	2	131	31
Atherton, Oak	.000	0	0	0	1	0
Ayala, Balt.	.404	9	0	0	18	2
Baines, Chi.	.443	49	13	1	85	15
Balboni, N.Y.	.430	8	0	0	23	2
Bando, Clev.	.380	15	0	0	19	5
Bannister, Clev.	.393	31	0	3	43	7
Barfield, Tor.	.510	22	0	4	110	8
Barrett, Bos.	.295	3	0	0	1	1
Baylor, N.Y.	.494	40	11	13	53	10
Bell, Tex.	.411	50	5	4	48	24
Bell, Tor.	.438	4	1	2	17	4
Beniquez, Calif.	.381	15	0	4	29	10
Bernazard, Chi.-Sea.	.385	55	3	2	97	9
Biancalana, K.C.	.200	0	0	0	7	0
Biittner, Tex.	.336	9	5	0	16	0
Boggs, Bos.	.486	92	2	1	36	15
Bonnell, Tor.	.469	33	5	0	52	8
Bonner, Balt.	.000	0	0	0	0	0
Boone, Calif.	.353	24	1	0	42	19
Bradley, Sea.	.299	8	0	0	5	0
Brant, Oak.	.143	0	0	0	3	0
Brett, K.C.	.563	57	13	1	39	9
Brookens, Det.	.325	29	2	2	46	3
Brouhard, Milw.	.454	9	0	2	39	7
Brown, Minn.	.304	10	0	1	28	9
Brown, Calif.	.385	7	0	0	20	3
Brunansky, Minn.	.445	61	4	4	95	13
Bulling, Sea.	.000	0	0	0	0	0
Bumbry, Balt.	.357	31	2	0	33	1
Burleson, Calif.	.345	12	0	0	12	5
Burroughs, Oak.	.387	47	4	0	79	16
Bush, Minn.	.418	34	8	7	51	7
Butera, Det.	.200	0	0	0	0	0
Cabell, Det.	.434	16	2	1	41	14
Campaneris, N.Y.	.357	8	0	0	9	4
Capra, Tex.	.000	0	0	0	0	0
Carew, Calif.	.411	57	9	1	48	15
Castillo, Sea.	.266	7	2	1	20	4
Castillo, Det.	.277	7	0	0	22	4
Castillo, Clev.	.472	4	0	1	6	0
Castino, Minn.	.403	62	1	1	54	11
Cerone, N.Y.	.272	15	1	1	29	5
Chambers, Sea.	.299	18	1	0	20	1
Cias, Oak.	.389	2	0	0	4	0
Clark, Calif.	.354	9	0	0	45	7
Coles, Sea.	.391	7	0	0	12	8
Collins, Tor.	.328	43	1	2	67	7
Concepcion, K.C.	.320	12	0	1	12	4
Cooper, Milw.	.508	37	7	1	63	17
Cowens, Sea.	.329	23	0	2	38	13
J. Cruz, Sea.-Chi.	.326	49	1	4	66	12
T. Cruz, Sea.-Balt.	.311	22	2	3	108	14
Culmer, Clev.	.105	0	0	0	4	1
Dauer, Balt.	.309	47	2	2	29	20
Davis, Oak.	.402	27	1	5	74	9
Davis, K.C.	.508	4	0	0	19	3
Dayett, N.Y.	.276	2	0	0	4	0
DeCinces, Calif.	.495	32	2	0	56	13
Dempsey, Balt.	.323	40	1	3	54	9
Dent, Tex.	.297	23	0	1	31	3
Dilone, Clev.-Chi.	.254	10	0	0	5	1
Downing, Calif.	.429	62	4	5	59	8
Dunbar, Tex.	.250	5	0	0	7	1
Dwyer, Balt.	.505	31	3	0	29	3
Dybzinski, Chi.	.289	18	0	2	29	8
Easterly, Milw.-Clev.	.000	0	0	0	0	0
Edler, Sea.	.286	5	0	1	11	2
Edwards, Milw.	.338	1	0	0	9	1
Eisenreich, Minn.	.429	1	0	0	1	0
Engle, Minn.	.449	28	1	1	39	13
Espino, N.Y.	.391	1	0	0	5	0
Essian, Clev.	.312	16	0	0	8	1
Evans, Bos.	.436	70	5	2	97	12
Faedo, Minn.	.335	4	1	0	19	4
Fahey, Det.	.318	5	1	0	3	0
Ferguson, Calif.	.074	5	0	0	8	3
Fernandez, Tor.	.353	2	0	1	2	1
Fischlin, Clev.	.276	26	0	2	32	2
Fisk, Chi.	.518	46	3	6	88	8
Fletcher, Chi.	.370	29	0	2	22	8
Foli, Calif.	.300	5	1	1	18	5
Ford, Balt.	.440	29	1	3	55	9
Franco, Clev.	.388	27	1	2	50	21
Gaetti, Minn.	.414	54	2	4	121	18
Gagne, Minn.	.148	0	0	0	6	0
Gamble, N.Y.	.456	25	1	3	23	3
Gantner, Milw.	.401	38	5	6	46	10
Garcia, Tor.	.390	24	3	2	34	10
Gedman, Bos.	.412	15	6	1	37	4
Geronimo, K.C.	.253	2	0	2	13	1
Gibson, Det.	.414	53	3	4	96	2
Gonzalez, Det.	.190	1	0	0	7	1
Graham, Bos.	.000	0	0	0	0	0
Gray, Chi.	.256	8	0	0	16	3
Grich, Calif.	.460	76	2	7	62	11
Griffey, N.Y.	.437	34	3	2	45	3
Griffin, Tor.	.348	27	0	3	44	5
Gross, Oak.	.392	36	4	3	52	5
Grubb, Det.	.410	28	1	2	17	5
Gulliver, Balt.	.277	9	0	0	5	1
Gutierrez, Bos.	.300	1	0	0	1	1
Hairston, Chi.	.500	23	4	0	16	1
Hancock, Oak.	.418	5	4	1	13	3
Hargrove, Clev.	.367	78	5	5	40	11
Harrah, Clev.	.365	75	1	7	49	13
Hassey, Clev.	.384	38	2	2	35	11
Hatcher, Minn.	.445	14	0	1	19	12
Heath, Oak.	.383	18	4	1	59	9
D. Henderson, Sea.	.444	28	3	1	93	5
Henderson, Oak.	.421	103	8	4	80	11
S. Henderson, Sea.	.450	44	2	0	82	9
Hernandez, Balt.	.374	12	1	0	19	4
Herndon, Det.	.478	46	6	3	95	20
Hill, Oak.	.348	4	0	0	21	3
Hill, Chi.	.293	9	2	0	24	4
Hoffman, Bos.	.340	30	1	2	76	5
Hostetler, Tex.	.372	42	1	5	103	10
Howell, Milw.	.448	15	0	0	29	4
Hrbek, Minn.	.489	57	5	3	71	12
Hudgens, Oak.	.143	0	0	0	3	0
Hulett, Chi.	.200	0	0	0	0	0
Huppert, Balt.	.000	0	0	0	0	0
Iorg, Tor.	.376	13	3	1	45	10
Ivie, Det.	.310	2	1	0	4	2
Re. Jackson, Calif.	.340	52	5	4	140	5
Ro. Jackson, Calif.	.351	27	2	3	33	10
James, Milw.	.100	2	0	0	2	0
Jimenez, Minn.	.256	4	0	0	11	0
Johnson, Tex.	.343	16	0	1	55	7
Johnson, Tor.	.489	67	8	5	69	10
Johnson, Det.	.348	7	0	1	10	1
Johnson, K.C.	.259	3	0	0	1	0
Jones, Det.	.344	3	0	0	6	1
R. Jones, Tex.	.319	5	1	2	17	2
Jurak, Bos.	.377	18	1	1	25	4
Kearney, Oak.	.372	21	1	4	50	11
Kemp, N.Y.	.399	41	3	2	37	17
Kittle, Chi.	.504	39	8	8	150	10
Klutts, Tor.	.465	1	1	1	11	0
Krenchicki, Det.	.353	11	0	1	27	1
Kuntz, Chi.-Minn.	.303	18	0	0	41	5
Laga, Det.	.190	1	0	0	9	1
Landrum, Balt.	.429	1	0	0	11	1
Lansford, Oak.	.475	22	4	3	33	8
Laudner, Minn.	.345	15	0	0	49	2
R. Law, Chi.	.369	42	2	2	36	4
V. Law, Chi.	.348	51	1	1	56	7
Leach, Det.	.355	19	1	1	21	6
Lemon, Det.	.464	54	1	20	70	11

Player—Club	Slg. Pct.	Tot. BB.	Int. BB.	HP.	SO.	GI DP.
Lopes, Oak.	.423	51	7	2	61	9
Lowenstein, Balt.	.481	49	1	1	55	2
Lubratich, Calif.	.276	4	0	0	17	3
Luzinski, Chi.	.502	70	6	11	117	10
Lynn, Calif.	.483	55	10	2	83	7
Maler, Sea.	.242	5	0	2	11	3
Manning, Clev.-Milw.	.316	38	5	1	62	13
Martin, K.C.	.500	1	0	0	7	0
Martinez, Tor.	.452	29	0	0	39	7
Mattingly, N.Y.	.409	21	5	1	31	8
McBride, Clev.	.348	9	2	1	26	9
McNealy, Oak.	.000	0	0	0	0	0
McRae, K.C.	.462	50	7	10	68	18
Meacham, N.Y.	.275	4	0	1	10	0
Mercado, Sea.	.298	14	0	1	27	3
Meyer, Oak.	.260	19	2	0	11	8
Milbourne, N.Y.	.257	5	0	1	10	0
Miller, Bos.	.363	28	1	1	30	6
Mitchell, Minn.	.303	28	2	1	21	3
Molinaro, Det.	.000	1	0	0	1	0
Molitor, Milw.	.410	59	4	2	74	12
Money, Milw.	.219	11	1	0	17	3
Moore, Milw.	.369	55	5	4	42	14
Moore, Oak.	.363	10	0	1	39	3
Moreno, N.Y.	.342	8	0	0	31	4
Moseby, Tor.	.499	51	4	5	85	10
Moses, Sea.	.254	12	0	1	20	4
Motley, K.C.	.441	2	0	1	8	3
Mulliniks, Tor.	.467	57	5	1	43	13
Mumphrey, N.Y.	.412	28	2	0	33	11
Murcer, N.Y.	.409	1	0	0	1	3
Murphy, Oak.	.380	62	4	0	105	16
Murray, Balt.	.538	86	13	3	90	13
Nahorodny, Det.	.000	1	0	0	0	0
Narron, Calif.	.273	1	0	0	3	0
J. Nelson, Sea.	.281	13	1	0	12	2
R. Nelson, Sea.	.371	17	3	0	50	4
Nettles, N.Y.	.446	51	2	3	65	9
Newman, Bos.	.288	10	1	2	31	4
Nichols, Bos.	.438	26	2	3	36	5
Nixon, N.Y.	.143	1	0	0	5	0
Nolan, Balt.	.429	16	1	2	31	5
Nyman, Chi.	.500	4	0	1	7	0
O'Berry, Calif.	.233	3	0	0	11	1
O'Brien, Tex.	.347	58	2	1	62	12
Office, N.Y.	.000	0	0	0	0	0
Oglivie, Milw.	.436	60	12	4	64	9
Orta, Tor.	.408	19	0	0	29	6
Otis, K.C.	.357	27	3	0	63	7
Owen, Sea.	.271	24	0	2	44	2
Paciorek, Chi.	.462	25	4	3	58	9
Page, Oak.	.278	10	0	2	22	2
Pagel, Clev.	.300	0	0	0	5	0
Parrish, Det.	.483	44	7	1	106	21
Parrish, Tex.	.474	46	8	3	91	20
Parsons, Chi.	.200	2	1	0	1	0
Pastornicky, K.C.	.313	0	0	0	3	4
Perconte, Clev.	.308	5	0	0	2	0
Perkins, Clev.	.326	9	3	0	19	3
Peters, Oak.	.326	12	0	1	21	2
Petralli, Tor.	.000	1	0	0	1	0
Pettis, Calif.	.494	7	0	0	15	1
Phelps, Sea.	.449	13	0	0	25	0
Phillips, Oak.	.320	48	1	2	70	5
Picciolo, Milw.	.333	0	0	0	4	0
Piniella, N.Y.	.405	11	3	1	12	4
Powell, Tor.	.205	5	0	0	8	1
Pryor, K.C.	.278	7	0	0	8	3
Putnam, Sea.	.448	39	8	3	57	12
Quinones, Oak.	.286	1	0	0	4	0
Ramos, Sea.	.362	7	0	1	12	4
Randolph, N.Y.	.348	53	0	1	32	11
Ready, Milw.	.676	6	1	0	3	0
Remy, Bos.	.319	40	2	0	35	12
Reynolds, Sea.	.305	2	0	0	9	1
Rhomberg, Clev.	.476	2	0	0	4	0
Rice, Bos.	.550	52	10	6	102	31
Richardt, Tex.	.241	2	0	0	11	2
Ripken, Balt.	.517	58	0	0	97	24
Rivers, Tex.	.350	11	0	1	21	1
Roberts, K.C.	.404	17	1	1	27	7
Robertson, N.Y.	.326	8	0	3	54	8
Rodriguez, Balt.-Chi.	.184	0	0	1	16	1
Roenicke, Balt.	.477	30	2	4	35	9
Roenicke, Sea.	.374	33	1	2	22	2
Romero, Milw.	.386	8	0	0	8	2
Sakata, Balt.	.373	16	0	1	17	4
Sample, Tex.	.401	44	2	5	46	8
Schofield, Calif.	.407	6	0	1	8	2
Schroeder, Milw.	.356	3	0	1	23	0
Sconiers, Calif.	.430	17	2	0	41	9
Scott, Tex.	.000	0	0	0	0	0
Shelby, Balt.	.363	18	2	0	64	2
Sheridan, K.C.	.381	20	0	0	64	3
Simmons, Milw.	.448	41	6	2	51	23
Simpson, K.C.	.218	11	2	2	21	1
Singleton, Balt.	.436	99	19	1	83	22
Skinner, Chi.	.273	0	0	0	1	2
Skube, Milw.	.320	4	0	0	7	2
Slaught, K.C.	.388	11	0	0	27	8
Smalley, N.Y.	.452	58	2	2	68	9
Smith, Minn.	.257	10	0	1	12	4
Squires, Chi.	.281	22	3	2	11	2
Stapleton, Bos.	.363	40	2	2	44	19
Stefero, Balt.	.545	3	0	0	2	0
Stegman, Chi.	.208	10	0	0	9	1
Stein, Tex.	.409	8	0	0	31	5
Sundberg, Tex.	.254	35	0	2	64	8
Sweet, Sea.	.269	13	1	0	26	11
Tabler, Clev.	.409	56	1	1	63	18
Teufel, Minn.	.538	2	0	0	8	1
Thomas, Milw.-Clev.	.379	80	2	2	148	13
Thornton, Clev.	.439	87	14	2	72	10
Tolleson, Tex.	.315	40	0	2	68	8
Trammell, Det.	.471	57	2	0	64	7
Trillo, Clev.	.328	21	2	0	46	13
Ullger, Minn.	.241	5	0	1	21	6
Upshaw, Tor.	.515	61	8	5	98	8
Valdez, Bos.	.120	1	0	1	4	0
Valentine, Calif.	.435	18	0	0	48	6
Velez, Clev.	.080	3	0	0	6	0
Vukovich, Clev.	.330	24	4	2	37	8
Wagner, Tex.	.000	0	0	0	1	0
Walker, Bos.	1.200	0	0	0	0	0
Walker, Chi.	.440	28	3	2	57	3
Ward, Minn.	.440	44	2	3	98	24
Washington, Minn.	.325	22	1	1	50	7
Washington, K.C.	.320	48	0	1	78	3
Wathan, K.C.	.314	27	0	1	56	11
Webster, Tor.	.182	1	0	0	1	0
Whitaker, Det.	.457	67	8	0	70	9
White, K.C.	.406	20	4	0	51	18
Whitt, Tor.	.459	50	5	0	55	9
Wilfong, Calif.	.339	10	1	0	25	2
Wilkerson, Tex.	.229	2	0	0	5	0
Wilson, Det.	.408	25	1	3	79	9
Wilson, Minn.	.500	0	0	0	0	0
Wilson, K.C.	.352	33	2	1	75	4
Winfield, N.Y.	.513	58	2	2	77	30
Wockenfuss, Det.	.420	31	1	0	37	5
G. Wright, Tex.	.424	41	9	2	82	9
Wynegar, N.Y.	.429	52	1	1	29	7
Yastrzemski, Bos.	.408	54	11	2	29	13
Yost, Milw.	.352	5	0	0	36	6
Young, Balt.	.278	2	0	1	8	1
Yount, Milw.	.503	72	6	3	58	11
Zisk, Sea.	.411	30	3	0	61	6

OFFICIAL AMERICAN LEAGUE DESIGNATED HITTING

CLUB DESIGNATED HITTING

Club	Pct.	AB.	R.	H.	TB.	2B.	3B.	HR.	RBI.	SH.	SF.	BB.	HP.	SO.	SB.	CS.	GI DP.
Kansas City	.313	620	89	194	287	42	6	13	88	0	5	52	10	75	2	3	19
Milwaukee	.290	620	78	180	275	39	10	12	96	6	4	55	3	79	4	5	18
New York	.288	628	93	181	299	38	4	24	96	2	8	52	14	68	16	7	14
Cleveland	.281	604	90	170	255	35	1	16	81	0	7	87	1	79	5	4	11
Baltimore	.269	573	68	154	249	26	3	21	90	3	3	109	1	96	2	4	23
Minnesota	.268	613	80	164	264	37	6	17	83	0	3	47	9	62	0	1	17
Chicago	.259	595	99	154	298	34	1	36	105	0	9	81	11	132	6	2	13
Detroit	.258	619	92	160	251	28	6	17	96	4	6	76	1	123	9	6	15
California	.257	635	84	163	247	21	0	21	82	2	5	76	3	138	2	6	6
Boston	.256	624	75	160	264	33	1	23	96	0	3	66	2	76	1	2	22
Oakland	.253	613	78	155	216	24	2	11	73	2	9	66	3	121	6	6	20
Toronto	.250	604	86	151	288	29	3	34	113	1	6	81	5	101	0	2	15
Texas	.248	618	68	153	231	27	3	15	78	5	5	63	8	134	5	8	13
Seattle	.235	586	72	138	227	29	0	20	74	1	7	67	2	113	5	5	14
Totals	.266	8552	1152	2277	3651	442	46	280	1251	26	80	978	73	1397	63	61	220

INDIVIDUAL DESIGNATED HITTING

(Listed Alphabetically)

Player and Club	Pct.	G.	AB.	R.	H.	TB.	2B.	3B.	HR.	RBI.	SH.	SF.	BB.	HP.	SO.	SB.	CS.	GI DP.
Aikens, K.C.	.409	6	22	2	9	12	0	0	1	6	0	0	2	0	5	0	0	1
J. Allen, Sea	1.000	2	1	0	1	1	0	0	0	1	0	0	0	0	0	0	1	0
R. Allen, Sea.	.000	3	0	0	0	0	0	0	0	0	0	0	0	0	0	0	0	0
Almon, Oak	.111	4	9	0	1	2	1	0	0	0	0	0	0	0	1	0	0	0
Anderson, Tex.	.200	2	5	0	1	1	0	0	0	1	0	0	0	0	1	0	1	0
Armas, Bos.	.250	27	108	16	27	56	6	1	7	24	0	1	5	0	23	0	1	5
Ayala, Balt.	.192	11	26	3	5	11	3	0	1	1	0	0	3	0	3	0	0	1
Balboni, N.Y.	.200	4	15	0	3	3	0	0	0	0	0	0	1	0	4	0	0	0
Bannister, Clev	.273	3	11	2	3	4	1	0	0	0	0	0	1	0	3	0	0	0
Barfield, Tor.	.143	5	14	1	2	5	0	0	1	2	0	0	0	0	3	0	0	0
Barrett, Bos.	.000	5	0	0	0	0	0	0	0	0	0	0	0	0	0	0	0	0
Baylor, N.Y.	.303	136	508	82	154	254	31	3	21	83	2	8	40	12	52	16	7	10
Bell, Tor.	.500	2	6	1	3	8	2	0	1	3	0	0	0	0	0	0	0	0
Beniquez, Cal.	.300	6	20	6	6	6	0	0	0	2	2	0	0	0	3	0	0	1
Biittner, Tex.	.174	9	23	0	4	4	0	0	0	2	0	1	1	0	4	0	0	0
Bonnell, Tor.	.000	1	3	0	0	0	0	0	0	0	0	0	0	0	2	0	0	0
Bonner, Balt	.000	1	0	0	0	0	0	0	0	0	0	0	0	0	0	0	0	0
Bradley, Sea.	.000	1	1	0	0	0	0	0	0	0	0	0	0	0	1	0	0	0
Brant, Oak.	.000	1	2	0	0	0	0	0	0	0	0	0	0	0	2	0	0	0
Brett, K.C.	.000	1	3	0	0	0	0	0	0	0	0	0	0	0	1	0	0	0
Brookens, Det	.000	1	0	1	0	0	0	0	0	0	0	0	0	0	0	0	0	0
Brouhard, Milw.	.179	11	28	2	5	5	0	0	0	2	1	0	3	0	9	0	2	1
Brown, Minn.	.000	3	1	0	0	0	0	0	0	0	0	0	0	0	0	0	0	0
Brunansky, Minn.	.182	4	11	1	2	3	1	0	0	0	0	0	2	0	1	0	0	1
Bumbry, Balt	.167	11	6	5	1	1	0	0	0	0	1	0	2	0	1	1	1	0
Burgmeier, Oak	.000	2	0	1	0	0	0	0	0	0	0	0	0	0	0	0	0	0
Burroughs, Oak.	.271	114	395	43	107	154	15	1	10	56	0	7	46	0	78	0	2	16
Bush, Minn.	.248	103	347	39	86	143	23	2	10	49	0	1	32	7	48	0	1	6
Cabell, Det.	.286	8	28	4	8	13	2	0	1	6	1	0	1	0	1	0	0	3
Carew, Cal	.370	24	100	10	37	42	2	0	1	12	0	1	14	0	11	1	3	1
Castillo, Sea.	.400	6	5	2	2	2	0	0	0	2	0	0	1	0	1	0	0	0
Castillo, Clev.	.000	1	0	0	0	0	0	0	0	0	0	0	0	0	0	0	1	0
Castino, Minn.	.000	1	1	0	0	0	0	0	0	0	0	0	0	0	0	0	0	0
Chambers, Sea.	.240	22	50	10	12	15	3	0	0	5	0	0	18	0	13	0	1	1
Clark, Cal.	.333	2	6	1	2	5	0	0	1	2	0	0	1	0	1	0	0	0
Collins, Tor.	.000	1	1	0	0	0	0	0	0	0	0	0	0	0	1	0	0	0
Concepcion, K.C.	.000	1	0	1	0	0	0	0	0	0	0	0	0	0	0	0	0	0
Cooper, Milw.	.700	2	10	5	7	10	0	0	1	4	0	0	0	0	0	0	0	0
Cowens, Sea.	.246	34	118	17	29	52	8	0	5	14	0	0	4	1	15	2	1	4
J. Cruz, Sea.	.000	1	1	1	0	0	0	0	0	0	0	0	0	0	0	1	0	0
Culmer, Clev.	.286	2	7	0	2	2	0	0	0	0	0	0	0	0	1	0	1	0
Davis, Oak.	.000	3	1	0	0	0	0	0	0	0	0	0	0	0	0	0	0	0
DeCinces, Cal.	.225	10	40	1	9	9	0	0	0	1	0	0	2	0	4	0	0	1
Dent, Tex.	.000	1	0	1	0	0	0	0	0	0	0	0	0	0	0	0	0	0
Dilone, Chi.	.000	2	0	1	0	0	0	0	0	0	0	0	0	0	0	1	0	0
Downing, Cal.	.255	26	98	18	25	42	2	0	5	10	0	1	14	1	11	0	1	1
Dunbar, Tex.	1.000	1	2	1	2	2	0	0	0	1	0	0	1	0	0	0	0	0
Dwyer, Balt.	.294	10	17	4	5	9	1	0	1	4	0	0	3	0	2	0	1	0
Easterly, Milw.	.000	1	1	0	0	0	0	0	0	0	1	0	0	0	0	0	0	0
Edler, Sea.	.000	6	5	0	0	0	0	0	0	1	0	1	0	1	0	0	0	0
Edwards, Milw.	.000	4	0	2	0	0	0	0	0	0	1	0	0	0	0	0	0	0
Engle, Minn.	.278	29	97	14	27	47	4	2	4	10	0	1	7	1	6	0	0	3
Evans, Bos.	.200	21	85	9	17	30	1	0	4	9	0	1	6	0	16	1	0	0
Fernandez, Tor.	.000	1	1	1	0	0	0	0	0	0	0	0	0	0	0	0	0	0
Fischlin, Clev.	.000	1	0	0	0	0	0	0	0	0	0	0	0	0	0	0	0	0

Player and Club	Pct.	G.	AB.	R.	H.	TB.	2B.	3B.	HR.	RBI.	SH.	SF.	BB.	HP.	SO.	SB.	CS.	GI DP.
Fisk, Chi.	.333	2	3	1	1	4	0	0	1	1	0	0	1	0	0	0	0	0
Fletcher, Chi.	.000	1	0	0	0	0	0	0	0	0	0	0	0	0	0	0	0	0
Gaetti, Minn.	.750	1	4	2	3	4	1	0	0	0	0	0	0	0	0	0	0	0
Gamble, N.Y.	.219	21	64	8	14	25	3	1	2	10	0	0	8	2	9	0	0	0
Gibson, Det.	.252	66	210	33	53	91	7	5	7	28	3	2	34	1	47	7	3	2
Gray, Chi.	.000	7	1	4	0	0	0	0	0	0	0	0	1	0	1	0	0	0
Griffey, N.Y.	.222	2	9	0	2	2	0	0	0	1	0	0	0	0	1	0	0	0
Griffin, Tor.	.000	1	0	1	0	0	0	0	0	0	0	0	0	0	0	0	0	0
Gross, Oak.	1.000	1	1	1	1	1	0	0	0	0	0	0	0	0	0	0	0	0
Grubb, Det.	.298	18	57	9	17	23	4	1	0	9	0	1	8	0	8	0	0	2
Hairston, Chi.	.100	4	10	0	1	2	1	0	0	1	0	0	1	0	3	0	0	1
Hancock, Oak.	.300	9	20	1	6	8	0	1	0	3	1	0	0	0	1	0	0	1
Hargrove, Clev.	1.000	1	1	0	1	1	0	0	0	0	0	0	0	0	0	0	0	0
Harrah, Clev.	.000	1	4	0	0	0	0	0	0	0	0	0	0	0	0	0	0	0
Hassey, Clev.	.333	1	3	0	1	2	1	0	0	1	0	1	0	0	0	0	0	0
Hatcher, Minn.	.304	39	135	18	41	60	6	2	3	22	0	0	5	0	5	0	0	6
Heath, Oak.	.000	2	5	0	0	0	0	0	0	0	0	0	0	0	2	0	0	0
Henderson, Oak.	.000	1	5	0	0	0	0	0	0	0	0	0	0	0	3	0	0	0
D. Henderson, Sea.	.500	3	4	1	2	2	0	0	0	1	0	0	0	0	1	0	0	0
S. Henderson, Sea.	.211	6	19	2	4	8	1	0	1	3	0	0	2	0	2	0	1	0
Herndon, Det.	.230	19	74	12	17	28	2	0	3	11	0	0	7	0	15	1	1	1
Hill, Chi.	.250	2	4	0	1	2	1	0	0	2	0	0	1	0	1	0	0	0
Hostetler, Tex.	.218	88	293	28	64	110	9	2	11	46	0	2	41	5	98	0	2	9
Howell, Milw.	.262	54	172	19	45	67	9	5	1	12	2	0	15	0	25	1	2	4
Hrbek, Minn.	.400	2	5	2	2	3	1	0	0	1	0	1	1	1	1	0	0	1
Hudgens, Oak.	.333	1	3	0	1	1	0	0	0	0	0	0	0	0	0	0	0	0
Re. Jackson, Cal.	.176	62	227	23	40	64	9	0	5	23	0	3	34	2	85	0	1	1
Ro. Jackson, Cal.	.289	16	38	6	11	21	1	0	3	11	0	0	5	0	8	0	0	0
James, Milw.	.000	2	1	0	0	0	0	0	0	0	0	0	0	0	0	0	0	0
Johnson, Tor.	.271	130	380	56	103	192	21	1	22	74	1	4	64	5	68	0	1	10
Johnson, Det.	.250	2	4	2	1	1	0	0	0	0	0	0	1	0	0	0	0	0
Jones, Det.	.200	6	15	0	3	3	0	0	0	1	0	0	0	0	1	0	0	0
B. Jones, Tex.	.136	11	22	0	3	3	0	0	0	0	0	0	3	2	6	0	0	1
Jurak, Bos.	.000	5	1	1	0	0	0	0	0	0	0	0	0	0	0	0	0	0
Kearney, Oak.	.000	3	3	0	0	0	0	0	0	0	0	0	1	0	1	0	0	0
Kemp, N.Y.	.250	2	8	1	2	3	1	0	0	0	0	0	1	0	1	0	0	1
Kittle, Chi.	.250	2	4	0	1	1	0	0	0	2	0	0	0	0	0	0	0	0
Klutts, Tor.	.000	2	2	0	0	0	0	0	0	0	0	0	1	0	0	0	0	0
Kuntz, Chi.	.000	1	0	0	0	0	0	0	0	0	0	0	0	0	0	0	0	0
Laga, Det.	.067	6	15	1	1	1	0	0	0	1	0	0	1	0	6	0	0	1
Laudner, Minn.	.500	4	4	1	2	3	1	0	0	1	0	0	0	0	0	0	0	0
R. Law, Chi.	1.000	3	1	0	1	1	0	0	0	1	0	0	1	0	0	1	0	0
V. Law, Chi.	.000	1	0	0	0	0	0	0	0	0	0	0	0	0	0	0	0	0
Leach, Det.	.333	3	9	0	3	4	1	0	0	1	0	0	2	0	4	0	0	0
Lopes, Oak.	.244	12	41	3	10	11	1	0	0	3	0	0	5	1	5	4	0	0
Lowenstein, Balt.	.250	1	4	1	1	2	1	0	0	0	0	0	0	0	2	0	0	0
Luzinski, Chi.	.253	139	495	73	125	248	25	1	32	92	0	9	68	11	115	2	1	10
Lynn, Cal.	.375	2	8	2	3	9	0	0	2	2	0	0	1	0	2	0	0	0
Maler, Sea.	.063	5	16	0	1	1	0	0	0	0	0	0	1	0	2	0	0	2
McBride, Clev.	.259	15	54	8	14	19	2	0	1	2	0	0	4	0	5	1	0	2
McNealy, Oak.	.000	7	1	5	0	0	0	0	0	0	0	0	0	0	0	0	0	0
McRae, K.C.	.311	156	588	84	183	272	41	6	12	82	0	5	50	10	68	2	3	18
Meyer, Oak.	.172	12	29	2	5	7	2	0	0	3	0	1	2	0	2	0	0	0
Miller, Bos.	.000	2	6	0	0	0	0	0	0	0	0	0	0	0	1	0	0	1
Molinaro, Det.	.000	1	0	1	0	0	0	0	0	0	0	0	0	0	0	1	0	0
Molitor, Milw.	.000	2	2	1	0	0	0	0	0	0	0	0	1	0	0	0	0	0
Money, Milw.	.164	28	67	2	11	15	4	0	0	3	1	0	9	0	10	0	0	1
Moore, Milw.	.000	1	4	0	0	0	0	0	0	0	0	0	0	0	0	0	0	0
Morris, Det.	.000	2	0	2	0	0	0	0	0	0	0	0	0	0	0	0	0	0
Moses, Sea.	.333	10	3	1	1	1	0	0	0	1	0	0	0	0	0	2	0	0
Motley, K.C.	.000	1	1	1	0	0	0	0	0	0	0	0	0	0	0	0	0	0
Murcer, N.Y.	.222	5	18	2	4	9	2	0	1	1	0	0	1	0	1	0	0	3
Murphy, Oak.	.080	7	25	4	2	6	1	0	1	3	0	0	4	0	9	0	0	1
Murray, Balt.	.333	2	6	1	2	5	0	0	1	2	0	0	0	0	2	0	0	0
Narron, Cal.	.250	1	4	0	1	1	0	0	0	2	0	0	0	0	0	0	0	0
R. Nelson, Sea.	.000	1	0	1	0	0	0	0	0	0	0	0	0	0	0	0	0	0
Nettles, N.Y.	.000	1	4	0	0	0	0	0	0	0	0	0	0	0	0	0	0	0
Newman, Bos.	.059	6	17	0	1	1	0	0	0	0	0	0	2	0	5	0	0	0
Nichols, Bos.	.423	18	26	7	11	14	3	0	0	2	0	0	3	0	1	0	1	1
Nyman, Chi.	.000	10	0	6	0	0	0	0	0	0	0	0	0	0	0	2	1	0
O'Brien, Tex.	1.000	1	1	1	1	3	0	1	0	0	0	0	0	0	0	0	0	0
Oglivie, Milw.	.389	8	18	1	7	11	1	0	1	7	0	0	2	1	3	1	0	2
Orta, Tor.	.219	69	192	26	42	82	6	2	10	33	0	2	16	0	26	0	1	5
Otis, K.C.	.000	1	1	0	0	0	0	0	0	0	0	0	0	0	0	0	0	0
Paciorek, Chi.	.500	2	2	0	1	1	0	0	0	0	0	0	0	0	1	0	0	0
Page, Oak.	.291	34	55	11	16	19	3	0	0	1	1	0	7	2	15	2	3	2
Pagel, Clev.	.333	5	18	1	6	6	0	0	0	1	0	0	0	0	5	0	0	0
Parrish, Det.	.276	27	105	15	29	49	8	0	4	22	0	2	7	0	19	0	1	4
Parrish, Tex.	.244	13	45	7	11	20	3	0	2	8	0	1	6	0	11	0	0	2

Player and Club	Pct.	G.	AB.	R.	H.	TB.	2B.	3B.	HR.	RBI.	SH.	SF.	BB.	HP.	SO.	SB.	CS.	GIDP.
Parsons, Chi.	.000	2	1	0	0	0	0	0	0	0	0	0	0	0	1	0	0	0
Perkins, Clev.	.320	16	50	8	16	20	4	0	0	8	0	0	3	0	3	1	1	0
Peters, Oak.	.273	8	11	2	3	3	0	0	0	2	0	0	1	0	2	0	1	0
Petralli, Tor.	.000	1	1	0	0	0	0	0	0	0	0	0	0	0	1	0	0	0
Phelps, Sea.	.191	19	47	2	9	13	1	0	1	4	0	2	6	0	14	0	0	0
Phillips, Oak	.000	1	1	1	0	0	0	0	0	0	0	0	0	0	0	0	0	0
Picciolo, Milw.	.000	1	1	0	0	0	0	0	0	0	0	0	0	0	0	0	0	0
Piniella, N.Y.	1.000	1	2	0	2	3	1	0	0	1	0	0	1	0	0	0	0	0
Powell, Tor.	.333	1	3	0	1	1	0	0	0	1	0	0	0	0	0	0	0	0
Putnam, Sea.	.273	11	33	5	9	15	3	0	1	5	0	1	6	0	4	0	1	1
Quinones, Oak.	.500	4	6	4	3	4	1	0	0	2	0	1	0	0	0	0	0	0
Ramos, Sea.	.000	2	0	0	0	0	0	0	0	0	0	0	0	0	0	0	0	0
Ready, Milw.	.333	6	21	3	7	10	1	1	0	4	0	0	3	0	3	0	0	0
Rhomberg, Clev.	.000	1	0	1	0	0	0	0	0	0	0	0	0	0	0	0	0	0
Rice, Bos.	.316	4	19	3	6	13	1	0	2	7	0	0	0	0	3	0	0	2
Rivers, Tex.	.290	53	210	27	61	78	14	0	1	16	5	1	9	1	13	4	4	0
Roberts, K.C.	.000	1	1	0	0	0	0	0	0	0	0	0	0	0	1	0	0	0
Roenicke, Balt.	.000	2	4	0	0	0	0	0	0	0	0	0	1	0	2	0	0	0
Roenicke, Sea.	.500	1	2	0	1	2	1	0	0	1	1	0	1	0	0	0	0	0
Romero, Milw.	.286	5	7	1	2	5	0	0	1	2	0	0	0	0	0	0	0	0
Sakata, Balt.	.000	1	0	0	0	0	0	0	0	0	0	0	0	0	0	0	0	0
Sconiers, Cal.	.309	27	94	17	29	48	7	0	4	17	0	0	5	0	13	1	1	1
Shelby, Balt.	1.000	1	1	2	1	1	0	0	0	0	0	0	1	0	0	0	0	0
Simmons, Milw.	.329	66	258	37	85	134	21	2	8	56	0	3	16	2	24	2	1	9
Simpson, K.C.	.000	1	0	0	0	0	0	0	0	0	0	0	0	0	0	0	0	0
Singleton, Balt.	.275	150	506	52	139	220	21	3	18	83	2	3	99	1	83	0	2	22
Skube, Milw.	.000	2	2	1	0	0	0	0	0	1	0	0	1	0	0	0	0	1
Slaught, K.C.	.500	1	4	1	2	3	1	0	0	0	0	0	0	0	0	0	0	0
Squires, Chi.	.000	5	0	3	0	0	0	0	0	0	0	0	1	0	0	0	0	0
Stein, Tex.	.353	6	17	3	6	10	1	0	1	4	0	0	2	0	1	1	0	1
Stewart, Balt.	.000	1	0	0	0	0	0	0	0	0	0	0	0	0	0	0	0	0
Tabler, Clev.	.300	6	20	3	6	11	3	1	0	3	0	0	1	0	3	0	0	1
Teufel, Minn.	.000	1	1	0	0	0	0	0	0	0	0	0	0	0	0	0	0	0
Thornton, Clev.	.288	114	413	66	119	188	24	0	15	65	0	6	75	1	54	3	1	8
Tolleson, Tex.	.000	1	0	0	0	0	0	0	0	0	0	0	0	0	0	0	1	0
Ullger, Minn.	.000	1	2	1	0	0	0	0	0	0	0	0	0	0	0	0	0	0
Upshaw, Tor.	.000	1	1	0	0	0	0	0	0	0	0	0	0	0	0	0	0	0
Valdez, Bos.	.000	1	0	1	0	0	0	0	0	0	0	0	0	0	0	0	0	0
Velez, Clev.	.087	8	23	1	2	2	0	0	0	1	0	0	3	0	5	0	0	0
Walker, Chi.	.311	21	74	11	23	39	7	0	3	6	0	0	7	0	10	0	0	2
Ward, Minn.	.200	2	5	0	1	1	0	0	0	0	0	0	0	0	1	0	0	0
Washington, Minn.	.000	1	0	1	0	0	0	0	0	0	0	0	0	0	0	0	0	0
Washington, K.C.	.000	1	0	0	0	0	0	0	0	0	0	0	0	0	0	0	0	0
Webster, Tor.	.000	2	0	0	0	0	0	0	0	0	0	0	0	0	0	0	0	0
Wilfong, Cal.	.000	1	0	0	0	0	0	0	0	0	0	0	0	0	0	0	0	0
Wilson, Minn.	.000	2	0	1	0	0	0	0	0	0	0	0	0	0	0	0	0	0
Wockenfuss, Det.	.275	39	102	12	28	38	4	0	2	17	0	1	15	0	22	0	1	2
Yastrzemski, Bos.	.271	107	362	38	98	150	22	0	10	54	0	1	50	2	27	0	0	13
Young, Balt.	.000	3	3	0	0	0	0	0	0	0	0	0	0	0	1	1	0	0
Yount, Milw.	.393	8	28	4	11	18	3	2	0	5	0	1	5	0	5	0	0	0
Zisk, Sea.	.238	84	281	30	67	115	12	0	12	36	0	3	28	0	60	0	0	6

Game-winning RBIs by designated hitters, listed alphabetically by club, follow: Baltimore (4)—Dwyer 1, Murray 1, Singleton 2. Boston (9)—Armas 2, Evans 2, Rice 1, Yastrzemski 4. California (8)—Beniquez 1, Carew 1, Downing 1, Re. Jackson 1, Ro. Jackson 1, Lynn 1, Sconiers 2. Chicago (12)—Kittle 1, Luzinski 10, Walker 1. Cleveland (12)—Hassey 1, Pagel 1, Thornton 10. Detroit (12)—Cabell 1, Gibson 3, Grubb 3, Herndon 1, Parrish 3, Wockenfuss 1. Kansas City (9)—McRae 9. Milwaukee (9)—Cooper 1, Money 1, Oglivie 1, Simmons 6. Minnesota (7)—Bush 4, Engle 1, Hatcher 2. New York (13)—Baylor 8, Gamble 4, Murcer 1. Oakland (8)—Burroughs 6, Lopes 1, Quinones 1. Seattle (6)—Chambers 1, Cowens 1, Zisk 4. Texas (11)—Hostetler 5, Parrish 2, Rivers 3, Stein 1. Toronto (9)—Johnson 8, Orta 1.

OFFICIAL AMERICAN LEAGUE FIELDING AVERAGES

CLUB FIELDING

Club	Pct.	G.	PO.	A.	E.	TC.	DP.	TP.	PB.
Texas	.982	163	4400	1899	113	6412	151	0	14
Milwaukee	.982	162	4362	1771	113	6246	162	0	8
Toronto	.981	162	4336	1637	115	6088	148	0	7
Chicago	.981	162	4336	1853	120	6309	158	0	12
Baltimore	.981	162	4357	1784	121	6262	159	0	5
Cleveland	.980	162	4325	1786	122	6233	174	0	17
Minnesota	.980	162	4312	1700	121	6133	170	1	10
Detroit	.980	162	4353	1703	125	6181	142	0	12
Boston	.979	162	4339	1719	130	6188	168	0	8
Seattle	.978	162	4255	1858	136	6249	159	0	16
New York	.978	162	4370	1733	139	6242	157	0	6
California	.977	162	4422	2077	154	6653	190	0	6
Oakland	.974	162	4363	1602	157	6122	157	1	14
Kansas City	.974	163	4313	1816	165	6294	178	0	4
Totals	.979	1135	60843	24938	1831	87612	2273	2	139

INDIVIDUAL FIELDING

*Throws lefthanded.

FIRST BASEMEN

Leader—Club	Pct.	G.	PO.	A.	E.	DP.
SQUIRES, Chi.*	.996	124	515	40	2	55

Player—Club	Pct.	G.	PO.	A.	E.	DP.
Aikens, K.C.	.989	112	884	64	11	101
Almon, Oak	.996	38	208	21	1	14
Balboni, N.Y.	.984	23	178	9	3	19
Biittner, Tex.*	.987	22	136	15	2	13
Brett, K.C.	.991	14	104	3	1	9
Cabell, Det.	.997	106	830	79	3	76
Carew, Cal.	.994	89	890	42	6	94
Castillo, Sea.	.976	11	37	3	1	4
Cooper, Milw.*	.993	158	1452	87	11	144
Griffey, N.Y.*	.992	101	830	57	7	82
Gross, Oak	.996	74	426	21	2	41
Hancock, Oak.*	.987	27	149	6	2	14
Hargrove, Clev.*	.994	131	1098	115	7	131
Hrbek, Minn.	.990	137	1151	89	13	125
Ivie, Det.	1.000	12	86	6	0	6
Ro. Jackson, Cal.	.992	35	334	21	3	34
B. Johnson, Tex.	.980	10	94	4	2	11
Jurak, Bos.	.984	19	160	21	3	19
Leach, Det.*	.994	73	447	45	3	37
Maler, Sea.	1.000	19	152	9	0	8
Mattingly, N.Y.*	.997	42	278	12	1	30
Meyer, Oak.	.987	41	293	16	4	28
Moore, Oak.*	.994	40	293	16	2	38
Murray, Balt.	.993	153	1393	114	10	136
Nyman, Chi.	1.000	10	87	5	0	8
O'Brien, Tex.*	.993	133	1144	120	9	104
Paciorek, Chi.	1.000	67	555	36	0	42
Perkins, Clev.*	.991	19	112	3	1	12
Phelps, Sea.*	1.000	22	164	16	0	11
Putnam, Sea.	.994	125	1067	85	7	105
Sconiers, Cal.*	.986	57	473	23	7	46
Simpson, K.C.*	.995	54	167	14	1	18
Smalley, N.Y.	.994	22	153	8	1	11
Squires, Chi.*	.996	124	515	40	2	55
Stapleton, Bos.	.993	145	1242	95	9	129
Stein, Tex.	1.000	23	161	13	0	17
Thornton, Clev.	.991	27	201	21	2	20
Ullger, Minn.	.990	30	185	8	2	14
Upshaw, Tor.*	.985	159	1294	117	21	131
Walker, Chi.	.985	59	426	19	7	40
Wathan, K.C.	.989	37	244	26	3	24
Wockenfuss, Det.	.979	13	84	10	2	8

TRIPLE PLAYS: Gross, Oak.; Hrbek, Minn.

(Fewer Than Ten Games)

Player—Club	Pct.	G.	PO.	A.	E.	DP.
Bannister, Clev.	1.000	3	3	0	0	0
Baylor, N.Y.	.938	1	13	2	1	0
Brant, Oak.	.905	3	19	0	2	4
Bush, Minn.*	1.000	3	21	3	0	1
Collins, Tor.*	1.000	5	19	1	0	2
Dwyer, Balt.*	.975	4	38	1	1	3
Edler, Sea.	.968	5	26	4	1	5
Hatcher, Minn.	1.000	7	62	4	0	6
Hill, Chi.	1.000	1	1	0	0	0
Hostetler, Tex.	1.000	2	11	0	0	0
Howell, Milw.	.960	2	20	4	1	4
Hudgens, Oak.*	1.000	3	4	0	0	0
Johnson, Tor.	1.000	6	47	4	0	5
Johnson, K.C.	.971	7	63	3	2	9
B. Jones, Tex.*	.000	1	0	0	0	0
Krenchicki, Det.	1.000	3	7	1	0	0
Laga, Det.*	1.000	5	9	1	0	2
Luzinski, Chi.	1.000	2	6	1	0	1
Miller, Bos.*	1.000	2	10	1	0	1
Money, Milw.	1.000	2	10	0	0	2
Picciolo, Milw.	.923	1	10	2	1	1
Powell, Tor.*	1.000	1	0	1	0	1
Pryor, K.C.	1.000	6	13	0	0	0
Roenicke, Balt.	1.000	7	60	2	0	5
Roenicke, Sea.	.978	8	44	1	1	4
Skube, Milw.*	1.000	1	5	0	0	0
Yastrzemski, Bos.	1.000	2	22	1	0	1

SECOND BASEMEN

Leader—Club	Pct.	G.	PO.	A.	E.	DP.
WHITE, K.C.	.990	145	390	442	8	123

Player—Club	Pct.	G.	PO.	A.	E.	DP.
Anderson, Tex.	.971	17	26	41	2	6
Bannister, Clev.	.979	27	35	59	2	12
Barrett, Bos.	.984	23	32	28	1	8
Bernazard, Chi.-Sea.	.973	138	262	422	19	89
Bookens, Det.	.973	10	8	28	1	4
Campaneris, N.Y.	.964	32	40	67	4	18
Castino, Minn.	.990	132	301	406	7	94
Concepcion, K.C.	.962	28	33	69	4	16
J. Cruz, Sea.-Chi.	.983	157	344	471	14	112
Dauer, Balt.	.988	131	273	322	7	78
Fischlin, Clev.	.965	71	151	179	12	46
Fletcher, Chi.	.978	12	18	26	1	12
Gantner, Milw.	.984	158	374	512	14	128
Garcia, Tor.	.981	130	266	360	12	75
Grich, Cal.	.969	118	270	415	22	94
Iorg, Tor.	.971	39	69	96	5	22
Lopes, Oak.	.983	123	254	278	9	81
Lubratich, Cal.	.988	14	44	39	1	13
Milbourne, N.Y.	1.000	19	40	44	0	9
Perconte, Clev.	.950	13	20	37	3	12
Phillips, Oak.	.970	63	103	124	7	26
Randolph, N.Y.	.979	104	265	298	12	77
Remy, Bos.	.990	144	295	376	7	104
Reynolds, Sea.	.975	18	30	48	2	14
Richardt, Tex.	.992	20	56	61	1	16
Robertson, N.Y.	.992	29	72	60	1	15
Sakata, Balt.	.990	60	84	117	2	36
Stein, Tex.	.975	32	56	62	3	20
Teufel, Minn.	.990	18	46	55	1	14
Tolleson, Tex.	.972	112	246	315	16	69
Trillo, Clev.	.989	87	172	269	5	58
Washington, Minn.	.967	14	19	39	2	5
Whitaker, Det.	.983	160	299	447	13	92
White, K.C.	.990	145	390	442	8	123
Wilfong, Cal.	.995	39	92	110	1	26

TRIPLE PLAYS: Castino, Minn.; Phillips, Oak.

(Fewer Than Ten Games)

Player—Club	Pct.	G.	PO.	A.	E.	DP.
Adams, Cal.	1.000	4	8	18	0	5
Almon, Oak	1.000	5	1	4	0	0
Bonner, Balt	1.000	5	1	0	0	0
Carew, Cal.	1.000	2	1	0	0	0
Castillo, Sea.	.952	5	6	14	1	4
T. Cruz, Balt.	.000	2	0	0	0	0
Gonzalez, Det.	.923	5	5	7	1	2
Griffin, Tor.	1.000	5	7	9	0	2
Harrah, Clev.	.000	1	0	0	0	0
Hulett, Chi.	.875	6	8	6	2	1
Jurak, Bos.	.000	1	0	0	0	0
Krenchicki, Det.	.938	6	5	10	1	2
V. Law, Chi.	1.000	3	3	2	0	0
Lowenstein, Balt.	.000	1	0	0	0	0
Mattingly, N.Y.*	.000	1	0	0	0	0
Mulliniks, Tor.	1.000	2	0	1	0	0
Picciolo, Milw.	1.000	2	6	2	0	0
Pryor, K.C.	1.000	3	2	9	0	2
Quinones, Oak.	1.000	6	11	15	0	3
Ramos, Sea.	1.000	8	9	21	0	2
Romero, Milw.	1.000	3	4	6	0	1
Stapleton, Bos.	.944	5	7	10	1	3
Tabler, Clev.	.000	2	0	0	0	0
Valdez, Bos.	.939	9	16	15	2	3
Wilkerson, Tex.	1.000	2	7	6	0	2

SECOND BASEMAN WITH TWO OR MORE CLUBS

Player—Club	Pct.	G.	PO.	A.	E.	DP.
Bernazard, Chi.	.976	59	96	189	7	38
Bernazard, Sea.	.971	79	166	233	12	51
J. Cruz, Sea.	.984	60	131	173	5	41
J. Cruz, Chi.	.983	97	213	298	9	71

THIRD BASEMEN

Leader—Club	Pct.	G.	PO.	A.	E.	DP.
HARRAH, Clev.	.971	137	101	273	11	32

(Listed Alphabetically)

Player—Club	Pct.	G.	PO.	A.	E.	DP.
Adams, Cal.	.933	16	3	25	2	2
J. Allen, Sea.	.959	82	55	155	9	16
Almon, Oak.	.911	40	34	58	9	5
Bell, Tex.	.967	154	123	383	17	29
Boggs, Bos.	.947	153	118	368	27	40
Brett, K.C.	.919	102	85	188	24	25
Brookens, Det.	.928	103	54	164	17	21
Campaneris, N.Y.	.932	24	12	29	3	1
Castillo, Sea.	.971	55	35	101	4	9
Castillo, Det.	.990	58	35	68	1	6
Coles, Sea.	.941	26	17	47	4	8
Concepcion, K.C.	.913	31	19	54	7	8
T. Cruz, Balt.	.942	79	49	162	13	19
Dauer, Balt.	.947	17	7	11	1	1
DeCinces, Cal.	.955	84	79	216	14	26
Edler, Sea.	.875	13	3	18	3	1
Foli, Cal.	.930	13	16	24	3	3
Gaetti, Minn.	.967	154	131	360	17	46
Gray, Chi.	.940	31	17	46	4	3
Gross, Oak.	.952	67	47	92	7	10
Gulliver, Balt.	1.000	21	14	31	0	3
Harrah, Clev.	.971	137	101	273	11	32
Hernandez, Balt.	.922	64	44	109	13	3
Iorg, Tor.	.976	85	36	127	4	9
Ro. Jackson, Cal.	.957	38	41	92	6	9
Johnson, Det.	.851	21	10	30	7	2
Jurak, Bos.	.944	12	5	29	2	2
Klutts, Tor.	1.000	17	4	11	0	2
Krenchicki, Det.	.934	48	29	56	6	8
Lansford, Oak.	.957	78	60	163	10	19
V. Law, Chi.	.966	139	91	309	14	28
Lubratich, Cal.	.984	22	14	49	1	5
Molitor, Milw.	.966	146	105	343	16	37
Money, Milw.	.980	11	15	33	1	0
Mulliniks, Tor.	.971	116	70	161	7	12
Nettles, N.Y.	.956	126	78	273	16	18
Pastornicky, K.C.	.929	10	5	21	2	0
Pryor, K.C.	.958	60	23	91	5	8
Rodriguez, Balt.-Chi.	.978	67	22	67	2	7
Smalley, N.Y.	.932	26	11	57	5	7
Stein, Tex.	.943	10	5	28	2	3
Tabler, Clev.	.986	25	17	51	1	6
Wilfong, Cal.	.978	13	11	33	1	6

TRIPLE PLAY: Gaetti, Minn.

(Fewer Than Ten Games)

Player—Club	Pct.	G.	PO.	A.	E.	DP.
Anderson, Tex.	1.000	3	0	1	0	0
Bonnell, Tor.	1.000	4	1	6	0	1
Cabell, Det.	.000	4	0	0	0	0
Castino, Minn.	.975	8	15	24	1	1
Cerone, N.Y.	.000	1	0	0	0	0
Clark, Cal.	.000	1	0	0	0	0
Dybzinski, Chi.	1.000	9	1	6	0	0
Essian, Clev.	.000	1	0	0	0	0
Fischlin, Clev.	.889	4	2	6	1	1
Fletcher, Chi.	.889	7	1	7	1	0
Gonzalez, Det.	.000	1	0	0	0	0
Hatcher, Minn.	1.000	1	0	3	0	2
Heath, Oak.	1.000	2	1	0	0	0
Lopes, Oak.	1.000	5	5	9	0	2
Meacham, N.Y.	.938	4	3	12	1	1
Meyer, Oak.	.000	1	0	0	0	0
Milbourne, N.Y.	1.000	4	1	2	0	1
Phillips, Oak.	1.000	4	3	2	0	0
Picciolo, Milw.	1.000	2	0	2	0	0
Quinones, Oak.	1.000	4	0	2	0	0
Ramos, Sea.	.909	8	7	13	2	1
Ready, Milw.	1.000	4	5	8	0	1
Roenicke, Balt.	.000	2	0	0	0	0
Romero, Milw.	.909	5	6	4	1	0
Squires, Chi.*	.000	1	0	0	0	0
Ullger, Minn.	1.000	3	1	3	0	0
Washington, Minn.	.750	1	0	3	1	0
Wilkerson, Tex.	.000	2	0	0	1	0
Wockenfuss, Det.	.000	1	0	0	0	0

THIRD BASEMAN WITH TWO OR MORE CLUBS

Player—Club	Pct.	G.	PO.	A.	E.	DP.
Rodriguez, Balt.	.969	45	18	45	2	2
Rodriguez, Chi.	1.000	22	4	22	0	5

SHORTSTOPS

Leader—Club	Pct.	G.	PO.	A.	E.	DP.
DENT, Tex.	.979	129	150	369	11	71

(Listed Alphabetically)

Player—Club	Pct.	G.	PO.	A.	E.	DP.
Adams, Cal.	.960	38	47	98	6	22
Almon, Oak.	.941	52	51	93	9	14
Anderson, Tex.	.963	27	17	60	3	7
Brookens, Det.	.960	30	35	62	4	9
Burleson, Cal.	.969	31	54	102	5	16
Concepcion, K.C.	.958	21	40	52	4	11
T. Cruz, Sea.	.964	63	97	224	12	42
Dent, Tex.	.979	129	150	369	11	71
Dybzinski, Chi.	.966	118	140	252	14	47
Faedo, Minn.	.954	51	53	133	9	22
Fernandez, Tor.	1.000	13	16	17	0	6
Fischlin, Clev.	.983	15	16	41	1	12
Fletcher, Chi.	.965	100	107	275	14	52
Foli, Cal.	.975	74	115	274	10	51
Franco, Clev.	.961	149	247	438	28	92
Gagne, Minn.	.923	10	10	14	2	2
Griffin, Tor.	.965	157	280	413	25	84
Hill, Oak.	.961	53	87	136	9	24
Hoffman, Bos.	.962	143	240	417	26	82
Jimenez, Minn.	.969	36	43	83	4	20
Jurak, Bos.	.943	38	32	67	6	13
Lubratich, Cal.	.949	23	33	61	5	16
Meacham, N.Y.	.929	18	13	52	5	8
Mulliniks, Tor.	1.000	15	7	23	0	7
Owen, Sea.	.970	80	122	233	11	45
Phillips, Oak.	.941	101	112	257	23	59
Ramos, Sea.	.948	28	35	75	6	19
Ripken, Balt.	.970	162	272	534	25	113
Robertson, N.Y.	.960	78	91	242	14	49
Romero, Milw.	.962	22	30	46	3	13
Schofield, Cal.	.929	21	24	67	7	10
Smalley, N.Y.	.959	91	125	230	15	40
Tolleson, Tex.	.988	26	22	57	1	12
Trammell, Det.	.979	140	236	367	13	71
Washington, Minn.	.962	81	121	204	13	49
Washington, K.C.	.947	140	201	448	36	91
Yount, Milw.	.973	139	256	420	19	86

TRIPLE PLAY: Almon, Oak.

(Fewer Than Ten Games)

Player—Club	Pct.	G.	PO.	A.	E.	DP.
Biancalana, K.C.	.914	6	11	21	3	3
Cabell, Det.	.000	1	0	0	0	0
Gaetti, Minn.	1.000	3	0	1	0	0
Gonzalez, Det.	.889	6	5	19	3	1
Grich, Cal.	1.000	1	1	0	0	0
Gutierrez, Bos.	.938	4	9	6	1	1
Iorg, Tor.	1.000	1	1	0	0	0
Krenchicki, Det.	.909	6	2	8	1	1
Lansford, Oak.	.000	1	0	0	0	0
V. Law, Chi.	.000	2	0	0	0	0
Milbourne, N.Y.	.941	6	5	11	1	3
Nichols, Bos.	1.000	1	0	1	0	0
Picciolo, Milw.	1.000	7	11	14	0	6
Quinones, Oak.	.933	3	7	7	1	4
Teufel, Minn.	1.000	1	1	3	0	0
Valdez, Bos.	1.000	2	0	1	0	0
Wagner, Tex.	1.000	2	2	4	0	0
Wilfong, Cal.	1.000	6	4	1	0	1
Wilkerson, Tex.	1.000	9	11	25	0	3

OUTFIELDERS

Leader—Club	Pct.	G.	PO.	A.	E.	DP.
R. LAW, Chi.*	.994	132	302	5	2	2

(Listed Alphabetically)

Player—Club	Pct.	G.	PO.	A.	E.	DP.
Almon, Oak	.971	23	33	0	1	0
Armas, Bos.	.985	116	326	5	5	0
Ayala, Balt.	.953	24	41	0	2	0
Baines, Chi.*	.973	155	312	10	9	3
Bannister, Clev.	.969	91	148	7	5	2
Barfield, Tor.	.966	120	213	16	8	4
Bell, Tor.	.954	34	61	1	3	0
Beniquez, Calif.	.968	84	174	8	6	1
Bonnell, Tor.	.986	117	212	7	3	0
Bradley, Sea.	.974	21	36	1	1	0
Brett, K.C.	1.000	13	21	1	0	0
Brouhard, Milw.	.991	42	112	1	1	0
Brown, Minn.	.995	81	188	2	1	0
M. Brown, Calif.	.949	31	52	4	3	1
Brunansky, Minn.	.985	146	375	16	6	8
Bumbry, Balt.	.988	104	235	3	3	1
Castillo, Clev.	.929	19	23	3	2	1
Clark, Calif.	1.000	72	122	0	0	0
Collins, Tor.*	.989	112	251	8	3	1
Cowens, Sea.	.985	70	124	7	2	1
Davis, Oak.*	.974	121	278	16	8	4
Davis, K.C.	.977	33	83	1	2	0
Dilone, Cleve.-Chi	1.000	21	47	0	0	0
Downing, Calif.	.994	84	160	9	1	0
Dwyer, Balt.*	.966	56	85	1	3	1
Edwards, Milw.*	1.000	35	57	4	0	1
Evans, Bos.	.987	99	222	6	3	1
Ford, Balt.	.987	103	218	2	3	0
Gamble, N.Y.	.942	32	64	1	4	1
Geronimo, K.C.*	.986	35	69	2	1	0
Gibson, Det.*	.975	54	116	2	3	0
Griffey, N.Y.*	.976	14	40	0	1	0
Grubb, Det.	1.000	26	34	1	0	0
Hairston, Chi.	.968	32	29	1	1	0
Hancock, Oak.*	.981	67	100	4	2	3
Hatcher, Minn.	.979	56	137	4	3	1
Heath, Oak.	.978	24	45	0	1	0
Henderson, Oak.*	.992	142	349	9	3	1
D. Henderson, Sea.	.982	133	304	17	6	4
S. Henderson, Sea.	.970	112	182	15	6	2
Herndon, Det.	.951	133	283	6	15	1
Re. Jackson, Calif.*	.986	47	66	4	1	1
Ro. Jackson, Calif.	.875	15	27	1	4	0
Jones, Det.	.968	31	28	2	1	0
B. Jones, Tex.*	1.000	11	24	0	0	0
Kemp, N.Y.*	.987	101	215	5	3	3
Kittle, Chi.	.964	139	234	7	9	0
Kuntz, Chi.-Minn.	.982	57	106	3	2	1
Landrum, Balt.	1.000	26	39	0	0	0
R. Law, Chi.*	.994	132	302	5	2	2
Leach, Det.*	.947	13	18	0	1	0
Lemon, Det.	.988	145	406	6	5	3
Lowenstein, Balt.	.982	107	155	8	3	1
Lynn, Calif.*	.993	113	274	8	2	4
Manning, Clev.-Milw.	.990	158	471	2	5	0
Martin, K.C.	.957	13	22	0	1	0
Mattingly, N.Y.*	.974	48	72	3	2	1
McBride, Clev.	.977	46	81	4	2	1
Meyer, Oak.	1.000	11	12	0	0	0
Miller, Bos.*	.993	66	141	4	1	1
Mitchell, Minn.*	.990	44	94	2	1	1
Moore, Milw.	.978	150	301	9	7	1
Moreno, N.Y.*	.992	48	120	1	1	1
Moseby, Tor.	.983	147	399	10	7	1
Moses, Sea.*	.979	71	87	8	2	1
Motley, K.C.	.978	18	42	2	1	0
Mumphrey, N.Y.	.983	83	227	7	4	1
Murphy, Oak.	.979	124	365	7	8	0
R. Nelson, Sea.	.971	91	122	10	4	1
Nichols, Bos.	.994	72	168	4	1	1
O'Brien, Tex.*	.960	27	47	1	2	1
Oglivie, Milw.*	.985	113	259	8	4	1
Orta, Tor.	1.000	17	16	1	0	1
Otis, K.C.	.996	96	233	6	1	1
Paciorek, Chi.	.987	55	74	2	1	0
Page, Oak.*	1.000	10	12	0	0	0
Parrish, Tex.	.962	132	215	11	9	1
Perkins, Clev.*	.975	17	36	3	1	0
Peters, Oak.	.986	47	141	3	2	1
Pettis, Calif.	.982	21	49	5	1	2
Piniella, N.Y.	.959	43	67	4	3	2
Powell, Tor.*	.981	33	52	0	1	0
Rice, Bos.	.984	151	339	21	6	5
Rivers, Tex.*	.980	23	48	1	1	0
Roberts, K.C.	.979	76	139	3	3	0
Roenicke, Balt.	.982	100	159	7	3	0
Roenicke, Sea.	.993	54	124	12	1	3
Romero, Milw.	.955	15	19	2	1	0
Sample, Tex.	.988	146	329	8	4	0
Shelby, Balt.	.981	115	200	9	4	3
Sheridan, K.C.	.988	100	237	6	3	2
Simpson, K.C.*	.988	38	75	4	1	2
Stegman, Chi.	1.000	29	31	1	0	0
Tabler, Clev.	.948	88	180	4	10	0
Thomas, Milw.-Clev.	.985	152	439	7	7	2
Valentine, Calif.	.963	85	152	5	6	1
Vukovich, Clev.	.986	122	203	3	3	0
Ward, Minn.	.978	152	374	24	9	6
Wilson, Det.	.988	143	225	12	3	2
Wilson, K.C.	.975	136	354	3	9	0
Winfield, N.Y.	.978	151	313	5	7	2
G. Wright, Tex.	.985	161	460	6	7	1
Young, Balt.	.929	22	25	1	2	0

TRIPLE PLAY: Peters, Oak.

(Fewer Than Ten Games)

Player—Club	Pct.	G.	PO.	A.	E.	DP.
R. Allen, Sea.	1.000	2	5	0	0	0
Anderson, Tex.	1.000	3	2	0	0	0
Baylor, N.Y.	1.000	5	10	0	0	0
Biittner, Tex.*	1.000	2	4	0	0	0
Capra, Tex.	.000	4	0	0	0	0
Chambers, Sea.*	1.000	3	3	0	0	0
Culmer, Clev.	1.000	4	2	0	0	0
Dayett, N.Y.	1.000	9	22	1	0	0
Dunbar, Tex.*	.875	9	7	0	1	0
Edler, Sea.	.000	1	0	0	0	0
Eisenreich, Minn.*	1.000	2	6	1	0	0
Engle, Minn.	1.000	4	7	0	0	0
Ferguson, Calif.	1.000	3	4	0	0	0
Graham, Bos.*	1.000	3	6	1	0	0
Guidry, N.Y.*	.000	1	0	0	0	0
James, Milw.*	1.000	9	12	1	0	0
V. Law, Chi.	.000	1	0	0	0	0
Lopes, Oak.	1.000	7	8	0	0	0
McNealy, Oak.*	1.000	5	6	0	0	0
Nixon, N.Y.	.938	9	14	1	1	0
Office, N.Y.*	1.000	2	2	0	0	0
Pagel, Clev.*	.000	1	0	0	1	0
Parsons, Chi.*	1.000	3	3	0	0	0
Quinones, Oak.	1.000	4	4	0	0	0
Rhomberg, Clev.	1.000	9	10	0	0	0
Sconiers, Calif.*	.000	1	0	0	1	0
Skube, Milw.	1.000	8	17	0	0	0
Walker, Bos.	1.000	3	4	1	0	0
Wathan, K.C.	1.000	9	11	0	0	0
Webster, Tor.*	1.000	7	5	0	0	0
Wilson, Minn.	1.000	1	1	0	0	0
Wockenfuss, Det.	.000	1	0	0	0	0
Yastrzemski, Bos.	.000	1	0	0	0	0

OUTFIELDERS WITH TWO OR MORE CLUBS

Player—Club	Pct.	G.	PO.	A.	E.	DP.
Dilone, Clev.	1.000	19	46	0	0	0
Dilone, Chi.	1.000	2	1	0	0	0
Kuntz, Chi.	.976	27	40	0	1	0
Kuntz, Minn.	.986	30	66	3	1	1
Manning, Clev.	.987	50	146	1	2	0
Manning, Milw.	.991	108	325	1	3	0
Thomas, Milw.	.992	46	126	0	1	0
Thomas, Clev.	.982	106	313	7	6	2

CATCHERS

Leader—Club	Pct.	G.	PO.	A.	E.	DP.	PB.
DEMPSEY, Balt.	.997	128	591	65	2	7	1

(Listed Alphabetically)

Player—Club	Pct.	G.	PO.	A.	E.	DP.	PB.
Allenson, Bos.	.984	84	393	29	7	6	3
Bando, Clev.	.995	43	170	19	1	2	7
Boone, Cal.	.980	142	606	83	14	12	5
Castillo, Det.	1.000	10	38	1	0	0	1
Cerone, N.Y.	.991	78	412	18	4	2	1
Cias, Oak.	.967	19	27	2	1	1	1
Dempsey, Balt.	.997	128	591	65	2	7	1
Engle, Minn.	.973	73	299	26	9	3	7
Espino, N.Y.	1.000	10	38	1	0	0	0
Essian, Clev.	.989	47	170	14	2	3	5
Fahey, Det.	1.000	18	39	2	0	0	1
Fisk, Chi.	.991	133	709	46	7	5	11
Gedman, Bos.	.980	89	274	26	6	5	5
Hassey, Clev.	.995	113	514	43	3	4	5
Heath, Oak.	.973	80	316	47	10	6	5
Hill, Chi.	.991	55	214	12	2	1	1
B. Johnson, Tex.	1.000	62	252	15	0	4	4
Kearney, Oak.	.982	101	437	41	9	5	8
Laudner, Minn.	.986	57	259	22	4	5	2
Martinez, Tor.	.989	85	331	25	4	3	1
Mercado, Sea.	.995	65	342	27	2	2	1
J. Nelson, Sea.	.978	39	202	16	5	2	10
Newman, Bos.	.990	51	171	19	2	3	0
Nolan, Balt.	.980	65	223	16	5	2	3
O'Berry, Cal.	1.000	26	77	8	0	0	1
Parrish, Det.	.995	131	695	73	4	8	10
Schroeder, Milw.	.980	23	92	5	2	1	1
Simmons, Milw.	.975	86	395	41	11	4	2
Slaught, K.C.	.964	79	299	18	12	7	2
Smith, Minn.	.984	59	272	27	5	3	1
Sundberg, Tex.	.993	131	618	56	5	2	10
Sweet, Sea.	.987	85	413	34	6	6	4
Wathan, K.C.	.985	92	360	32	6	5	2
Whitt, Tor.	.992	119	554	50	5	4	6
Wockenfuss, Det.	1.000	29	141	11	0	2	0
Wynegar, N.Y.	.985	93	480	29	8	4	5
Yost, Milw.	.971	61	252	16	8	2	5

(Fewer Than Ten Games)

Player—Club	Pct.	G.	PO.	A.	E.	DP.	PB.
Anderson, Tex.	1.000	1	1	0	0	0	0
Bulling, Sea.	1.000	5	17	0	0	0	1
Butera, Det.	.929	4	12	1	1	0	0
Ferguson, Cal.	.968	9	27	3	1	0	0
Huppert, Balt.	1.000	2	3	0	0	0	0
Johnson, K.C.	1.000	2	3	0	0	0	0
Moore, Milw.	1.000	7	8	1	0	0	0
Narron, Cal.	.895	6	14	3	2	0	0
Petralli, Tor.	1.000	5	7	0	0	0	0
Sakata, Balt.	.000	1	0	0	0	0	0
Scott, Tex.	1.000	2	8	2	0	0	0
Skinner, Chi.	.960	6	20	4	1	1	0
Stefero, Balt.	.920	9	20	3	2	0	1

PITCHERS

Leader—Club	Pct.	G.	PO.	A.	E.	DP.
SUTCLIFFE, Clev.	1.000	36	36	29	0	1

(Listed Alphabetically)

Player—Club	Pct.	G.	PO.	A.	E.	DP.
Abbott, Sea.-Det.	.897	21	17	9	3	2
Acker, Tor.	1.000	38	12	15	0	4
Agosto, Chi.*	.833	39	2	8	2	1
Alexander, N.Y.-Tor.	.970	25	13	19	1	1
Anderson, Clev.	.818	39	3	6	2	0
Aponte, Bos.	1.000	34	10	8	0	1
Armstrong, K.C.	1.000	58	8	12	0	1
Atherton, Oak.	1.000	29	1	7	0	0
Augustine, Milw.*	1.000	34	4	7	0	0
Bailey, Det.*	.864	33	9	10	3	1
Bair, Det.	.889	27	1	7	1	0
Baker, Oak.	1.000	35	3	4	0	0
Bannister, Chi.*	.939	34	8	23	2	0
Barker, Clev.	.955	24	5	16	1	3
Barojas, Chi.	1.000	52	2	14	0	1
Beard, Oak.	1.000	43	1	3	0	0
Beattie, Sea.	.965	30	18	37	2	5
Berenguer, Det.	.875	37	10	11	3	1
Bird, Bos.	1.000	22	7	7	0	1
Black, K.C.*	.975	24	7	32	1	5
Blue, K.C.*	1.000	19	3	10	0	1
Blyleven, Clev.	.971	24	7	26	1	3
Boddicker, Balt.	.949	27	24	32	3	4
Boyd, Bos.	.938	15	5	10	1	1
Brennan, Clev.	.889	11	4	4	1	0
Brown, Bos.	.917	19	11	11	2	0
C. Brown, Cal.	1.000	10	1	1	0	0
S. Brown, Cal.	1.000	12	4	5	0	1
Burgmeier, Oak.*	.909	49	7	23	3	2
Burns, Chi.*	.941	29	1	15	1	1
Butcher, Tex.	1.000	38	11	17	0	0
Caldwell, Milw.*	.955	32	4	38	2	4
Candiotti, Milw.	1.000	10	4	5	0	1
Castillo, Minn.	.972	27	13	22	1	1
Castro, K.C.	.800	18	5	7	3	0
Caudill, Sea.	.778	63	2	5	2	0
Clancy, Tor.	.976	34	23	17	1	1
Clark, Sea.*	.939	41	8	38	3	4
Clarke, Tor.*	1.000	10	0	2	0	0
Clear, Bos.	.929	48	8	5	1	0
Codiroli, Oak.	.897	37	14	21	4	1
Conroy, Oak.*	.900	39	7	11	2	0
Corbett, Cal.	1.000	11	0	1	0	0
Creel, K.C.	1.000	25	6	8	0	0
Cruz, Tex.	.750	17	1	2	1	0
Curtis, Cal.*	.917	37	1	10	1	1
Darwin, Tex.	.927	28	20	18	3	1
Davis, Balt.	.917	34	14	19	3	1
Davis, Minn.	.800	66	0	4	1	0
Dotson, Chi.	.986	35	20	48	1	8
Easterly, Milw.-Clev.*	1.000	53	5	10	0	0
Eckersley, Bos.	.974	28	19	18	1	0
Eichelberger, Clev.	1.000	28	9	14	0	3
Filson, Minn.*	.889	26	2	6	1	0
Flanagan, Balt.*	.913	20	6	15	2	1
Fontenot, N.Y.*	.957	15	3	19	1	1
Forsch, Cal.	.930	31	9	31	3	2
Frazier, N.Y.	.917	61	5	17	2	0
Geisel, Tor.*	1.000	47	0	4	0	0
Gibson, Milw.	.875	27	6	8	2	0
Glynn, Clev.*	.500	11	0	1	1	0
Goltz, Cal.	.923	15	4	8	1	1
Gossage, N.Y.	.833	57	2	3	1	0
Gott, Tor.	.967	34	9	20	1	2
Guidry, N.Y.*	1.000	31	9	33	0	2
Gumpert, Det.	1.000	26	2	3	0	0
Gura, K.C.*	1.000	34	12	42	0	5
Haas, Milw.	1.000	25	12	22	0	1
Hassler, Cal.*	.917	42	3	8	1	2
Havens, Minn.*	1.000	16	0	2	0	0
Heaton, Clev.*	1.000	39	7	14	0	0
Heimueller, Oak.*	1.000	16	7	23	0	1
Hickey, Chi.*	1.000	23	1	3	0	0
Hoffman, Chi.*	1.000	11	1	0	0	0
Honeycutt, Tex.*	.980	25	11	39	1	5
Hood, K.C.*	.850	27	3	14	3	3
Hough, Tex.	.973	34	25	46	2	4
Howell, N.Y.	.944	19	7	10	1	0
Hoyt, Chi.	.975	36	21	56	2	4
Huismann, K.C.	1.000	13	1	2	0	0
Hurst, Bos.*	.958	33	12	34	2	2
Jackson, Tor.	1.000	49	6	14	0	1

PITCHERS—Continued

Player—Club	Pct.	G.	PO.	A.	E.	DP.
Jeffcoat, Clev.*	1.000	11	2	4	0	0
John, Cal.*	1.000	34	16	39	0	4
Johnson, Bos.*	.875	34	2	5	1	0
Jones, Oak.	1.000	13	1	4	0	0
O. Jones, Tex.	1.000	42	3	5	0	0
Keough, Oak.-N.Y.	.938	26	6	9	1	1
Kison, Cal.	1.000	26	5	22	0	2
Koosman, Chi.*	.939	37	5	26	2	2
Krueger, Oak.*	.909	17	3	7	1	0
Ladd, Milw.	1.000	44	1	5	0	0
Lamp, Chi.	1.000	49	9	16	0	2
Leal, Tor.	.977	35	20	23	1	2
Leonard, K.C.	.867	10	2	11	2	2
Lopez, Det.	.938	57	2	13	1	0
Lysander, Minn.	.971	61	19	14	1	2
Martin, Det.*	1.000	15	0	2	0	0
F. Martinez, Balt.*	1.000	65	5	23	0	1
J. D. Martinez, Balt.	.983	32	16	42	1	8
Matlack, Tex.*	.941	25	2	14	1	3
May, N.Y.*	1.000	15	0	3	0	0
McCatty, Oak.	.958	38	7	16	1	1
McClure, Milw.*	.958	24	4	19	1	1
McGregor, Balt.*	.964	36	19	35	2	2
McLaughlin, Tor.	1.000	50	6	6	0	1
McLaughlin, Cal.	1.000	16	0	8	0	0
Moffitt, Tor.	1.000	45	1	8	0	1
Moore, Sea.	.969	22	7	24	1	0
Morgan, Tor.	.923	16	2	10	1	0
Morogiello, Balt.*	.750	22	0	3	1	0
Morris, Det.	.965	37	29	26	2	2
Murray, N.Y.	.909	40	5	15	2	1
G. Nelson, Sea.	.917	10	5	6	1	0
Norris, Oak.	.875	16	3	4	1	1
Nunez, Sea.	1.000	14	0	6	0	1
O'Connor, Minn.*	1.000	27	2	6	0	0
Oelkers, Minn.*	1.000	10	1	1	0	0
Ojeda, Bos.*	.971	29	11	23	1	2
Palmer, Balt.	.929	14	5	8	1	0
Pashnick, Det.	1.000	12	6	6	0	0
Perry, Sea.-K.C.	.976	30	10	30	1	1
Petry, Det.	.973	38	30	43	2	10
Porter, Milw.	1.000	25	11	18	0	2
Quisenberry, K.C.	.927	69	8	30	3	1
Ramirez, Balt.	1.000	11	6	9	0	0
Rasmussen, K.C.	1.000	11	2	7	0	1
Rawley, N.Y.*	.959	34	14	33	2	3
Renko, K.C.	1.000	25	8	13	0	1
Righetti, N.Y.*	.964	31	3	24	1	2
Rozema, Det.	.935	29	12	17	2	1
Sanchez, Cal.	1.000	56	1	24	0	2
Schmidt, Tex.	1.000	31	6	4	0	1
Schrom, Minn.	.920	33	8	15	2	1
Shirley, N.Y.*	1.000	25	5	20	0	1
Slaton, Milw.	1.000	46	4	16	0	1
Smithson, Tex.	.963	33	19	33	2	3
Sorensen, Clev.	.967	36	20	39	2	1
Spillner, Clev.	.923	60	4	8	1	0
Splittorff, K.C.*	.970	27	9	23	1	2
Stanley, Bos.	.900	64	9	18	3	3
Stanton, Sea.	1.000	50	1	7	0	1
Steirer, Cal.	.941	19	5	11	1	1
Stewart, Balt.	1.000	58	6	17	0	1
Stieb, Tor.	.968	36	28	33	2	1
Stoddard, Balt.	1.000	47	3	7	0	1
Stoddard, Sea.	.962	35	15	36	2	2
Sutcliffe, Clev.	1.000	36	36	29	0	1
Sutton, Milw.	.973	31	13	23	1	1
Tanana, Tex.*	.958	29	9	37	2	0
Tellmann, Milw.	1.000	44	9	26	0	0
Thomas, Sea.	1.000	43	7	8	0	0
Tidrow, Chi.	.958	50	7	16	1	0
Tobik, Tex.	1.000	27	6	4	0	0
Travers, Cal.*	.889	10	0	8	1	1
Tudor, Bos.*	.950	34	12	26	2	4
Ujdur, Det.	.800	11	3	1	1	0
Underwood, Oak.*	.875	51	3	11	2	2
Vande Berg, Sea.*	.857	68	3	9	2	0
Viola, Minn.*	.968	35	7	23	1	2
Waits, Clev.-Milw.*	.875	18	0	7	1	0
Walters, Minn.	1.000	23	3	10	0	1
Warren, Oak.	.900	12	2	7	1	1
Welchel, Balt.	.833	11	2	3	1	0
Whitehouse, Minn.*	1.000	60	3	6	0	0
Wilcox, Det.	.981	26	19	34	1	3
Williams, Minn.	.917	36	11	22	3	1
Witt, Cal.	.968	43	6	24	1	2
Young, Sea.*	.941	33	9	39	3	0
Zahn, Cal.*	.919	29	9	25	3	2

(Fewer Than Ten Games)

Player—Club	Pct.	G.	PO.	A.	E.	DP.
Barnes, Clev.*	1.000	4	1	1	0	1
Beene, Milw.	.000	1	0	0	0	0
Behenna, Clev.	1.000	5	3	4	0	1
Best, Sea.	.000	4	0	0	0	0
Bradley, Oak.	1.000	6	0	3	0	2
Callahan, Oak.	1.000	4	0	3	0	0
Camacho, Clev.	.000	4	0	0	0	0
Castillo, Sea.	.000	1	0	0	0	0
Cocanower, Milw.	.909	5	4	6	1	0
Cooper, Tor.	.000	4	0	0	0	0
Erickson, N.Y.	1.000	5	4	2	0	0
Farmer, Oak.	1.000	5	1	0	0	0
Gross, Oak.	.000	1	0	0	0	0
Henke, Tex.	.750	8	0	3	1	0
Jackson, K.C.*	1.000	4	2	3	0	0
James, Det.	.000	4	0	0	0	0
Jones, Chi.	.000	2	0	0	0	0
Kaufman, N.Y.	1.000	4	0	1	0	0
Kern, Chi.	.000	1	0	0	0	0
Lacey, Cal.*	1.000	8	0	1	0	0
Lachowicz, Tex.	1.000	2	1	1	0	0
Langford, Oak.	1.000	7	1	2	0	0
LaRoche, N.Y.*	1.000	1	0	1	0	0
Lewis, Minn.	1.000	6	1	3	0	0
Martz, Chi.	1.000	1	1	0	0	0
Mason, Tex.*	1.000	5	1	2	0	0
Mirabella, Balt.*	.500	3	0	1	1	0
Montefusco, N.Y.	1.000	6	2	3	0	0
Mura, Chi.	.500	6	0	1	1	0
Nipper, Bos.	1.000	3	1	2	0	0
Pettibone, Minn.	1.000	4	4	4	0	0
Reed, Clev.	.917	7	3	8	1	0
Rucker, Det.*	1.000	4	1	3	0	0
Simpson, K.C.*	.000	2	0	0	0	0
Smith, Oak.	1.000	8	0	1	0	0
Stewart, Tex.	1.000	8	3	10	0	0
Swaggerty, Balt.	1.000	7	4	7	0	0
Tufts, K.C.*	1.000	6	0	2	0	0
Underwood, Det.*	1.000	4	1	0	0	0
Vuckovich, Milw.	1.000	3	1	1	0	0
Williams, Tor.	1.000	4	0	3	0	0
Wills, K.C.	.800	6	1	3	1	1
Wortham, Oak.*	.000	1	0	0	0	0
R. Wright, Tex.*	.000	1	0	0	1	0
Young, Oak.*	.000	8	0	0	0	0

PITCHERS WITH TWO OR MORE CLUBS

Player—Club	Pct.	G.	PO.	A.	E.	DP.
Abbott, Sea.	.850	14	10	7	3	1
Abbott, Det.	1.000	7	7	2	0	1
Alexander, N.Y.	1.000	8	2	2	0	0
Alexander, Tor.	.966	17	11	17	1	1
Easterly, Milw.	1.000	12	1	1	0	0
Easterly, Clev.	1.000	41	4	9	0	0
Keough, Oak.	1.000	14	1	3	0	0
Keough, N.Y.	.917	12	5	6	1	1
Perry, Sea.	.957	16	6	16	1	0
Perry, K.C.	1.000	14	4	14	0	1
Waits, Clev.	1.000	8	0	3	0	0
Waits, Milw.	.800	10	0	4	1	0

OFFICIAL AMERICAN LEAGUE PITCHING AVERAGES

CLUB PITCHING

Club	ERA.	G.	CG.	ShO.	Sv.	IP.	H.	BFP.	R.	ER.	HR.	SH.	SF.	HB.	Tot. BB.	Int. BB.	SO.	WP.	Bk.
Texas	3.31	163	43	11	32	1466.2	1392	6127	609	540	97	48	43	38	471	25	826	36	6
Baltimore	3.63	162	36	15	38	1452.1	1451	6105	652	585	130	46	46	10	452	25	774	36	4
Chicago	3.67	162	35	12	48	1445.1	1355	6019	650	589	128	37	39	33	447	32	877	38	2
Detroit	3.80	162	42	9	28	1451.0	1318	6071	679	613	170	32	39	29	522	48	875	59	7
New York	3.86	162	47	12	32	1456.2	1449	6165	703	624	116	54	59	20	455	24	892	36	7
Milwaukee	4.02	162	35	10	43	1454.0	1513	6224	708	650	133	48	57	28	491	32	689	29	9
Seattle	4.12	162	25	9	39	1418.1	1455	6094	740	649	145	45	40	40	544	46	910	48	16
Toronto	4.12	162	43	8	32	1445.1	1434	6174	726	662	145	34	50	42	517	38	835	25	5
Kansas City	4.25	163	19	8	49	1437.2	1535	6210	767	679	133	46	62	27	471	23	593	40	3
California	4.31	162	39	7	23	1474.0	1636	6393	779	706	130	57	50	30	496	71	668	51	1
Boston	4.34	162	29	7	42	1446.1	1572	6255	775	697	158	40	57	31	493	43	767	28	9
Oakland	4.34	162	22	12	33	1454.1	1462	6340	782	702	135	55	59	31	626	44	719	43	9
Cleveland	4.43	162	34	8	25	1441.2	1531	6219	785	710	120	43	54	31	529	61	794	54	6
Minnesota	4.66	162	20	5	39	1437.1	1559	6297	822	745	163	55	53	35	580	54	748	41	13
Totals	4.06	1135	469	133	503	20281.0	20662	86693	10177	9151	1903	640	708	425	7094	566	10967	564	97

NOTE—Totals for earned runs for several clubs do not agree wiith the composite totals for all pitchers of each respective club due to instances in which provisions of Section 10.18 (i) of the Scoring Rules were applied. The following differences are to be noted: Baltimore pitchers add to 655; Boston, 698; California, 708; Chicago, 593; Detroit, 616; Kansas City, 681; Minnesota, 746; New York, 630; Oakland, 703; Seattle, 661.

PITCHERS' RECORDS

(Top Fifteen Qualifiers for Earned-Run Leadership—162 or More Innings)

*Throws lefthanded.

Pitcher and Club	W.	L.	Pct.	ERA.	G.	GS.	CG.	ShO.	GF.	Sv.	IP.	H.	BFP.	R.	ER.	HR.	SH.	SF.	HB.	Tot. BB.	Int. BB.	SO.	WP.	Bk.
Honeycutt, Frederick, Texas*	14	8	.636	2.42	25	25	5	2	0	0	174.2	168	693	59	47	9	3	6	6	37	2	56	1	2
Boddicker, Michael, Baltimore	16	8	.667	2.77	27	26	10	5	1	0	179.0	141	711	65	55	13	4	3	0	52	1	120	5	0
Stieb, David, Toronto	17	12	.586	3.04	36	36	14	4	0	0	278.0	223	1141	105	94	21	6	9	14	93	6	187	5	1
Hough, Charles, Texas	15	13	.536	3.18	34	33	11	3	1	0	252.0	219	1030	96	89	22	5	5	3	95	0	152	6	1
McGregor, Scott, Baltimore*	18	7	.720	3.18	36	36	12	2	0	0	260.0	271	1072	101	92	24	8	10	1	45	2	86	0	0
Dotson, Richard, Chicago	22	7	.759	3.23	35	35	8	1	0	0	240.0	209	997	92	86	19	4	7	8	106	1	137	7	0
Haas, Bryan, Milwaukee	13	3	.813	3.27	25	25	7	3	0	0	179.0	170	729	66	65	12	4	6	1	42	5	75	2	0
Young, Matthew, Seattle*	11	15	.423	3.27	33	32	5	2	0	0	203.2	178	851	86	74	17	4	8	7	79	2	130	4	2
Zahn, Geoffrey, California*	9	11	.450	3.33	29	28	11	3	1	0	203.0	212	852	90	75	22	6	8	0	51	2	81	4	0
Morris, John, Detroit	20	13	.606	3.34	37	37	20	1	0	0	293.2	257	1204	117	109	30	8	9	3	83	5	232	18	0
Bannister, Floyd, Chicago*	16	10	.615	3.35	34	34	5	2	0	0	217.1	191	902	88	81	19	4	4	2	71	3	193	8	1
Guidry, Ronald, New York*	21	9	.700	3.42	31	31	21	3	0	0	250.1	232	1024	99	95	26	4	9	2	60	3	156	4	2
Righetti, David, New York*	14	8	.636	3.44	31	31	7	2	0	0	217.0	194	900	96	83	2	10	4	2	67	2	169	10	1
Darwin, Danny, Texas	8	13	.381	3.49	28	26	9	2	0	0	183.0	175	780	86	71	9	7	7	3	62	3	92	2	0
Burns, R. Britt, Chicago*	10	11	.476	3.58	29	26	8	4	0	0	173.2	165	732	79	69	14	6	3	5	55	2	115	6	0

DEPARTMENTAL LEADERS: W—Hoyt, 24; L—Gura, 18; Pct.—Dotson, .759; G—Quisenberry, 69; GS—Petry, 38; CG—Guidry, 21; ShO—Boddicker, 5; GF—Quisenberry, 62; Sv—Quisenberry, 45; IP—Morris, 293.2; H—John, 287; BFP—Morris, 1,204; R—Viola, 141; ER—Viola, 128; HR—Petry, 37; SH—Perry, Stanley, 11; SF—Gura, 17; HB—Stieb, 14; Tot. BB—Dotson, 106; Int. BB—Sanchez, 14; SO—Morris, 232; WP—Morris, 18; Bk—McClure, 6.

(All Pitchers—Listed Alphabetically)

Pitcher and Club	W.	L.	Pct.	ERA.	G.	GS.	CG.	ShO.	GF.	Sv.	IP.	H.	BFP.	R.	ER.	HR.	SH.	SF.	HB.	Tot. BB.	Int. BB.	SO.	WP.	Bk.
Abbott, W. Glenn, Seattle-Detroit	7	4	.636	3.63	21	21	3	1	0	0	129.0	146	541	58	52	14	5	3	4	22	3	49	2	2
Acker, James, Toronto	5	1	.833	4.33	38	5	0	0	8	1	97.2	103	426	52	47	7	1	2	8	38	1	44	1	0
Agosto, Juan, Chicago*	2	2	.500	4.10	39	0	0	0	13	7	41.2	41	166	20	19	2	5	4	1	11	1	29	2	0
Alexander, Doyle, New York-Toronto	7	8	.467	4.41	25	20	5	0	3	0	145.0	157	603	76	71	20	1	4	1	33	1	63	4	0
Anderson, Karl, Cleveland	1	6	.143	4.08	39	1	0	0	27	7	68.1	64	290	34	31	8	5	2	0	32	6	32	4	0
Aponte, Luis, Boston	5	4	.556	3.63	34	0	0	0	18	3	62.0	74	276	28	25	7	4	1	2	23	3	32	1	0
Armstrong, Michael, Kansas City	10	7	.588	3.86	58	0	0	0	33	3	102.2	86	432	53	44	11	3	4	3	45	3	52	5	0
Atherton, Keith, Oakland	2	5	.286	2.77	29	0	0	0	21	4	68.1	53	277	22	21	7	2	5	1	23	4	40	1	1
Augustine, Gerald, Milwaukee*	3	3	.500	5.74	34	7	1	0	9	2	64.1	89	304	45	41	11	4	3	1	25	4	40	1	0
Bailey, Howard, Detroit*	5	5	.500	4.88	33	3	0	0	15	0	72.0	69	302	45	39	11	3	1	2	25	3	21	1	0
Bair, C. Douglas, Detroit	7	3	.700	3.88	27	1	0	0	10	4	55.2	51	233	27	24	8	2	0	1	19	4	39	0	0
Baker, Steven, Oakland	3	3	.500	4.33	35	1	0	0	18	5	54.0	59	244	32	26	4	4	3	2	26	4	23	3	0
Bannister, Floyd, Chicago*	16	10	.615	3.35	34	34	5	2	0	0	217.1	191	902	88	81	19	4	4	2	71	3	193	8	1
Barker, Leonard, Cleveland	8	13	.381	5.11	24	24	4	1	0	0	149.2	150	633	92	85	16	10	5	2	52	3	105	6	0
Barnes, Richard, Cleveland*	1	1	.500	6.94	4	2	0	0	1	0	11.2	18	59	10	9	0	0	1	0	10	2	2	1	0
Barojas, Salome, Chicago	3	3	.500	2.47	52	0	0	0	29	12	87.1	70	355	24	24	2	3	2	5	32	2	38	1	0
Beard, David, Oakland	5	5	.500	5.61	43	0	0	0	26	10	61.0	55	268	39	38	8	3	3	2	36	4	40	3	0
Beattie, James, Seattle	10	15	.400	3.84	30	29	8	2	0	0	196.2	197	834	89	84	12	3	2	3	66	6	132	6	1
Beene, R. Andrew, Milwaukee	0	0	.000	4.50	1	0	0	0	1	0	2.0	3	10	3	1	0	0	0	0	1	1	0	1	0
Behenna, Richard, Cleveland	0	2	.000	4.15	5	4	0	0	0	0	26.0	22	111	13	12	0	1	0	1	14	1	9	1	0
Berenguer, Juan, Detroit	9	5	.643	3.14	37	19	2	1	7	1	157.2	110	650	58	55	19	1	2	6	71	3	129	3	1
Best, Karl, Seattle	0	1	.000	13.50	4	0	0	0	0	0	5.1	14	36	9	8	2	0	0	2	5	0	3	1	0
Bird, J. Douglas, Boston	1	4	.200	6.65	22	6	0	0	7	1	67.2	91	303	52	50	14	0	4	2	16	4	33	1	0
Black, Harry, Kansas City*	10	7	.588	3.79	24	24	3	0	0	0	161.1	159	672	75	68	19	4	5	2	43	1	58	4	0
Blue, Vida, Kansas City*	0	5	.000	6.01	19	14	1	0	4	0	85.1	96	382	62	57	12	4	5	2	35	0	53	6	2
Blyleven, Rikalbert, Cleveland	7	10	.412	3.91	24	24	5	0	0	0	156.1	160	660	74	68	8	2	5	10	44	4	123	5	1
Boddicker, Michael, Baltimore	16	8	.667	2.77	27	26	10	5	1	0	179.0	141	711	65	55	13	4	3	0	52	1	120	5	0
Boyd, Dennis, Boston	4	8	.333	3.28	15	13	5	0	2	0	98.2	103	413	46	36	9	1	5	1	23	0	43	3	1
Bradley, S. Bert, Oakland	0	0	.000	6.48	6	0	0	0	2	0	8.1	14	40	7	6	1	0	1	0	4	1	3	1	0
Brennan, Thomas, Cleveland	2	2	.500	3.86	11	5	1	1	2	0	39.2	45	167	22	17	3	0	2	1	8	1	21	0	0
Brown, Curtis, California	1	1	.500	7.31	10	0	0	0	7	0	16.0	25	73	13	13	1	0	1	0	4	1	7	1	0
Brown, Michael G., Boston	6	6	.500	4.67	19	18	3	1	0	0	104.0	110	454	62	54	12	5	6	2	43	1	35	4	4
Brown, Steven, California	2	3	.400	3.52	12	4	2	1	4	0	46.0	45	195	19	18	4	1	2	0	16	1	23	0	0
Burgmeier, Thomas, Oakland*	6	7	.462	2.81	49	0	0	0	22	4	96.0	89	409	33	30	2	10	2	0	32	8	39	2	2
Burns, R. Britt, Chicago*	10	11	.476	3.58	29	26	8	4	0	0	173.2	165	732	79	69	14	6	3	5	55	2	115	6	0
Butcher, John, Texas	6	6	.500	3.51	38	6	1	1	14	5	123.0	128	522	50	48	8	4	2	1	41	4	58	4	0
Caldwell, R. Michael, Milwaukee*	12	11	.522	4.53	32	32	10	2	0	0	228.1	269	970	125	115	35	4	4	1	51	1	58	3	1
Callahan, Benjamin, Oakland	1	2	.333	12.54	4	2	0	0	1	0	9.1	18	52	16	13	0	1	1	0	5	1	2	0	0
Camacho, Ernie, Cleveland	0	1	.000	5.06	4	0	0	0	1	0	5.1	5	23	3	3	1	0	0	1	2	0	2	0	0
Candiotti, Thomas, Milwaukee	4	4	.500	3.23	10	8	2	1	1	0	55.2	62	233	21	20	4	0	2	2	16	0	21	0	0
Castillo, E. Manuel, Seattle	0	0	.000	23.63	1	0	0	0	0	0	2.2	8	19	7	7	3	0	0	1	3	0	2	1	0
Castillo, Robert, Minnesota	8	12	.400	4.77	27	25	3	0	0	0	158.1	170	686	91	84	17	6	2	1	65	4	90	3	1
Castro, William, Kansas City	2	0	1.000	6.64	18	0	0	0	6	0	40.2	51	190	34	30	4	0	3	5	12	1	17	1	0
Caudill, William, Seattle	2	8	.200	4.71	63	0	0	0	54	26	72.2	70	317	39	38	10	1	4	2	38	6	73	4	1
Clancy, James, Toronto	15	11	.577	3.91	34	34	11	1	0	0	223.0	238	955	115	97	23	4	12	1	61	0	99	3	0
Clark, Bryan, Seattle*	7	10	.412	3.94	41	17	2	0	7	0	162.1	160	697	82	71	14	6	3	3	72	6	76	10	0
Clarke, Stanley, Toronto*	1	1	.500	3.27	10	0	0	0	5	0	11.0	10	46	4	4	2	1	1	0	5	0	7	0	1
Clear, Mark, Boston	4	5	.444	6.28	48	0	0	0	33	4	96.0	101	448	71	67	10	1	6	3	68	5	81	2	0
Cocanower, James, Milwaukee	2	0	1.000	1.80	5	3	1	0	0	0	30.0	21	118	8	6	1	0	0	1	12	0	8	1	0

Pitcher and Club	W.	L.	Pct.	ERA.	G.	GS.	CG.	ShO.	GF.	Sv.	IP.	H.	BFP.	R.	ER.	HR.	SH.	SF.	HB.	Tot. BB.	Int. BB.	SO.	WP.	Bk.
Codiroli, Christopher, Oakland	12	12	.500	4.46	37	31	7	2	3	1	205.2	208	884	115	102	17	10	6	7	72	4	85	2	2
Conroy, Timothy, Oakland*	7	10	.412	3.94	39	18	3	1	6	0	162.1	141	715	89	71	17	3	4	2	98	2	112	8	1
Cooper, Donald, Toronto	0	0	.000	6.75	4	0	0	0	1	0	5.1	8	23	4	4	3	0	0	0	0	0	5	0	0
Corbett, Douglas, California	1	1	.500	3.63	11	0	0	0	7	0	17.1	26	80	10	7	1	1	0	1	4	2	18	0	0
Creel, S. Keith, Kansas City	2	5	.286	6.35	25	10	1	0	9	0	89.1	116	404	66	63	17	1	3	2	35	0	31	1	0
Cruz, Victor, Texas	1	3	.250	1.44	17	0	0	0	13	5	25.0	16	103	7	4	2	3	2	1	10	3	18	0	0
Curtis, John, California*	1	2	.333	3.80	37	3	0	0	14	5	90.0	89	394	44	38	5	2	5	2	40	11	36	8	0
Darwin, Danny, Texas	8	13	.381	3.49	28	26	9	2	0	0	183.0	175	780	86	71	9	7	7	3	62	3	92	2	0
Davis, George, Baltimore	13	7	.650	3.59	34	29	6	1	0	0	200.1	180	831	90	80	14	5	4	2	64	4	125	7	2
Davis, Ronald, Minnesota	5	8	.385	3.34	66	0	0	0	61	30	89.0	89	382	34	33	6	6	6	3	33	3	84	4	1
Dotson, Richard, Chicago	22	7	.759	3.23	35	35	8	1	0	0	240.0	209	997	92	86	19	4	7	8	106	1	137	7	0
Easterly, James, Milw.-Cleveland*	4	3	.571	3.67	53	0	0	0	25	4	68.2	83	306	32	28	4	5	2	4	32	5	45	1	0
Eckersley, Dennis, Boston	9	13	.409	5.61	28	28	2	0	0	0	176.1	223	787	119	110	27	1	5	6	39	4	77	1	0
Eichelberger, Juan, Cleveland	4	11	.267	4.90	28	15	2	0	5	0	134.0	132	577	80	73	10	2	4	2	59	3	56	9	0
Erickson, Roger, New York	0	1	.000	4.32	5	0	0	0	2	0	16.2	13	69	8	8	1	0	0	0	8	1	7	2	0
Farmer, Edward, Oakland	0	0	.000	3.48	5	1	0	0	1	0	10.1	15	42	4	4	1	0	1	0	0	0	7	0	0
Filson, W. Peter, Minnesota*	4	1	.800	3.40	26	8	0	0	10	1	90.0	87	378	34	34	9	1	2	1	29	0	49	1	2
Flanagan, Michael, Baltimore*	12	4	.750	3.30	20	20	3	1	0	0	125.1	135	528	53	46	10	4	6	2	31	2	50	1	0
Fontenot, S. Ray, New York*	8	2	.800	3.33	15	15	3	1	0	0	97.1	101	408	41	36	3	2	1	1	25	0	27	0	0
Forsch, Kenneth, California	11	12	.478	4.06	31	31	11	1	0	0	219.1	226	921	107	99	21	4	3	4	61	6	81	6	0
Frazier, George, New York	4	4	.500	3.43	61	0	0	0	30	8	115.1	94	479	44	44	5	6	10	3	45	4	78	5	0
Geisel, J. David, Toronto*	0	3	.000	4.64	47	0	0	0	16	5	52.1	47	230	28	27	4	1	0	2	31	5	50	2	1
Gibson, Robert, Milwaukee	3	4	.429	3.90	27	7	0	0	16	2	80.2	71	357	40	35	6	4	6	1	46	2	46	5	1
Glynn, Edward, Cleveland*	0	2	.000	5.84	11	0	0	0	5	0	12.1	22	66	11	8	2	0	1	0	6	0	13	4	0
Goltz, David, California	0	6	.000	6.22	15	6	0	0	2	0	63.2	81	301	48	44	10	3	3	1	37	2	27	1	1
Gossage, Richard, New York	13	5	.722	2.27	57	0	0	0	47	22	87.1	82	367	27	22	5	5	6	1	25	5	90	0	0
Gott, James, Toronto	9	14	.391	4.74	34	30	6	1	2	0	176.2	195	776	103	93	15	4	3	5	68	5	121	2	0
Gross, Wayne, Oakland	0	0	.000	0.00	1	0	0	0	1	0	2.1	2	11	0	0	0	0	0	1	1	0	0	0	0
Guidry, Ronald, New York*	21	9	.700	3.42	31	31	21	3	0	0	250.1	232	1024	99	95	26	4	9	2	60	3	156	4	2
Gumpert, David, Detroit	0	2	.000	2.64	26	0	0	0	17	2	44.1	43	179	16	13	1	1	4	0	7	3	14	2	0
Gura, Lawrence, Kansas City*	11	18	.379	4.90	34	31	5	0	1	0	200.1	220	881	119	109	23	5	17	8	76	6	57	0	0
Haas, Bryan, Milwaukee	13	3	.813	3.27	25	25	7	3	0	0	179.0	170	729	66	65	12	4	6	1	42	5	75	2	0
Hassler, Andrew, California*	0	5	.000	5.45	42	0	0	0	19	4	36.1	42	160	22	22	2	4	0	0	17	8	20	5	0
Havens, Bradley, Minnesota*	5	8	.385	8.18	16	14	1	0	0	0	80.1	110	378	75	73	11	1	9	0	38	3	40	6	0
Heaton, Neal, Cleveland*	11	7	.611	4.16	39	16	4	3	19	7	149.1	157	637	79	69	11	3	5	1	44	10	75	1	0
Heimueller, Gorman, Oakland*	3	5	.375	4.41	16	14	2	1	2	0	83.2	93	362	43	41	8	6	1	1	29	2	31	3	0
Henke, Thomas, Texas	1	0	1.000	3.38	8	0	0	0	5	1	16.0	16	65	6	6	1	0	0	0	4	0	17	0	0
Hickey, Kevin, Chicago*	1	2	.333	5.23	23	0	0	0	13	5	20.2	23	98	14	12	5	0	0	0	11	2	8	1	0
Hoffman, Guy, Chicago*	1	0	1.000	7.50	11	0	0	0	4	0	6.0	14	32	5	5	1	0	1	0	2	0	2	0	0
Honeycutt, Frederick, Texas*	14	8	.636	2.42	25	25	5	2	0	0	174.2	168	693	59	47	9	3	6	6	37	2	56	1	2
Hood, Donald, Kansas City*	2	3	.400	2.27	27	0	0	0	15	0	47.2	48	199	20	12	5	4	3	2	14	2	17	3	0
Hough, Charles, Texas	15	13	.536	3.18	34	33	11	3	1	0	252.0	219	1030	96	89	22	5	5	3	95	0	152	6	1
Howell, Jay, New York	1	5	.167	5.38	19	12	2	0	3	0	82.0	89	368	53	49	7	1	5	3	35	0	61	2	1
Hoyt, D. LaMarr, Chicago	24	10	.706	3.66	36	36	11	1	0	0	260.2	236	1034	115	106	27	4	8	1	31	4	148	1	1
Huismann, Mark, Kansas City	2	1	.667	5.58	13	0	0	0	5	0	30.2	29	135	20	19	1	1	1	0	17	3	20	4	1
Hurst, Bruce, Boston*	12	12	.500	4.09	33	32	6	2	0	0	211.1	241	903	102	96	22	3	4	3	62	5	115	1	2
Jackson, Danny, Kansas City*	1	1	.500	5.21	4	3	0	0	0	0	19.0	26	87	12	11	1	1	0	0	6	0	9	0	0
Jackson, Roy Lee, Toronto	8	3	.727	4.50	49	0	0	0	19	7	92.0	92	402	48	46	6	7	7	3	41	2	48	0	0
James, Robert, Detroit	0	0	.000	11.25	4	0	0	0	3	0	4.0	5	19	5	5	2	0	0	0	3	0	4	0	0
Jeffcoat, J. Michael, Cleveland*	1	3	.250	3.31	11	2	0	0	1	0	32.2	32	140	13	12	1	1	0	1	13	1	9	1	1

Pitcher and Club	W.	L.	Pct.	ERA.	G.	GS.	CG.	ShO.	GF.	Sv.	IP.	H.	BFP.	R.	ER.	HR.	SH.	SF.	HB.	Tot. BB.	Int. BB.	SO.	WP.	Bk.
John, Thomas, California*	11	13	.458	4.33	34	34	9	0	0	0	234.2	287	1010	126	113	20	8	7	2	49	5	65	11	0
Johnson, John Henry, Boston*	3	2	.600	3.71	34	1	0	0	19	1	53.1	58	234	28	22	3	3	5	1	20	4	51	1	0
Jones, Alfornia, Chicago	0	0	.000	3.86	2	0	0	0	1	0	2.1	3	10	1	1	0	0	0	0	2	0	2	0	0
Jones, Jeffrey, Oakland	1	1	.500	5.76	13	1	0	0	5	0	29.2	43	138	19	19	7	1	0	2	8	1	14	0	0
Jones, Odell, Texas	3	6	.333	3.09	42	0	0	0	33	10	67.0	56	281	28	23	4	4	2	2	22	1	50	1	0
Kaufman, Curt, New York	0	0	.000	3.12	4	0	0	0	1	0	8.2	10	39	3	3	0	0	2	0	4	0	8	0	0
Keough, Matthew, Oakland-New York	5	7	.417	5.33	26	16	0	0	3	0	99.2	109	456	71	59	19	2	3	2	51	1	54	3	1
Kern, James, Chicago	0	0	.000	0.00	1	0	0	0	0	0	0.2	1	3	1	0	0	0	0	0	0	0	0	1	0
Kison, Bruce, California	11	5	.688	4.05	26	17	4	1	5	2	126.2	128	540	59	57	13	7	2	4	43	4	83	0	0
Koosman, Jerry, Chicago*	11	7	.611	4.77	37	24	2	1	6	2	169.2	176	730	96	90	19	5	5	6	53	2	90	5	0
Krueger, William, Oakland*	7	6	.538	3.61	17	16	2	0	0	0	109.2	104	473	54	44	7	0	5	2	53	1	58	1	1
Lacey, Robert, California*	1	2	.333	5.19	8	0	0	0	4	0	8.2	12	35	5	5	1	0	0	0	0	0	7	0	0
Lachowicz, Allen, Texas	0	1	.000	2.25	2	1	0	0	0	0	8.0	9	34	2	2	0	0	0	0	2	0	8	1	0
Ladd, Peter, Milwaukee	3	4	.429	2.55	44	0	0	0	40	25	49.1	30	194	17	14	3	0	3	1	16	2	41	3	0
Lamp, Dennis, Chicago	7	7	.500	3.71	49	5	1	0	31	15	116.1	123	483	52	48	6	2	1	4	29	7	44	0	0
Langford, J. Rick, Oakland	0	4	.000	12.15	7	7	0	0	0	0	20.0	43	112	28	27	4	1	3	2	10	1	2	0	0
LaRoche, David, New York*	0	0	.000	18.00	1	0	0	0	1	0	1.0	2	5	2	2	1	0	0	0	0	0	0	0	0
Leal, Luis, Toronto	13	12	.520	4.31	35	35	7	1	0	0	217.1	216	918	113	104	23	3	5	6	65	5	116	2	2
Leonard, Dennis, Kansas City	6	3	.667	3.71	10	10	1	0	0	0	63.0	69	270	29	26	3	0	2	0	19	1	31	1	0
Lewis, James, Minnesota	0	0	.000	6.50	6	0	0	0	0	0	18.0	24	82	13	13	5	0	0	1	7	0	8	0	0
Lopez, Aurelio, Detroit	9	8	.529	2.81	57	0	0	0	46	18	115.1	87	473	36	36	12	4	5	1	49	7	90	7	1
Lysander, Richard, Minnesota	5	12	.294	3.38	61	4	1	1	19	3	125.0	132	543	63	47	8	10	8	2	43	12	58	6	1
Martin, John R., Detroit*	0	0	.000	7.43	15	0	0	0	5	1	13.1	15	56	11	11	2	0	1	0	4	1	11	0	0
Martinez, Felix, Baltimore*	9	3	.750	2.35	65	0	0	0	51	21	103.1	76	406	30	27	10	3	5	0	37	3	81	6	0
Martinez, J. Dennis, Baltimore	7	16	.304	5.53	32	25	4	0	3	0	153.0	209	688	108	94	21	3	5	2	45	0	71	2	0
Martz, Randy, Chicago	0	0	.000	3.60	1	1	0	0	0	0	5.0	4	23	2	2	0	0	0	0	4	0	1	0	0
Mason, Michael, Texas*	0	2	.000	5.91	5	0	0	0	2	0	10.2	10	50	7	7	0	2	0	1	6	0	9	0	0
Matlack, Jonathan, Texas*	2	4	.333	4.66	25	9	2	0	7	0	73.1	90	330	43	38	7	2	5	3	27	1	38	4	0
May, Rudolph, New York*	1	5	.167	6.87	15	0	0	0	4	0	18.1	22	90	15	14	1	2	0	1	12	1	16	2	0
McCatty, Steven, Oakland	6	9	.400	3.99	38	24	3	2	11	5	167.0	156	725	79	74	16	4	6	1	82	4	65	5	0
McClure, Robert, Milwaukee*	9	9	.500	4.50	24	23	4	0	0	0	142.0	152	625	75	71	11	0	4	5	68	1	68	4	6
McGregor, Scott, Baltimore*	18	7	.720	3.18	36	36	12	2	0	0	260.0	271	1072	101	92	24	8	10	1	45	2	86	0	0
McLaughlin, Byron, California	2	4	.333	5.17	16	7	0	0	2	0	55.2	63	250	32	32	3	2	4	2	22	3	45	0	0
McLaughlin, Joey, Toronto	7	4	.636	4.45	50	0	0	0	31	9	64.2	63	285	33	32	11	2	3	0	37	7	47	3	0
Mirabella, Paul, Baltimore*	0	0	.000	5.59	3	2	0	0	1	0	9.2	9	45	6	6	1	1	0	0	7	0	4	0	0
Moffitt, Randall, Toronto	6	2	.750	3.77	45	0	0	0	33	10	57.1	52	247	27	24	5	5	3	1	24	6	38	0	0
Montefusco, John, New York	5	0	1.000	3.32	6	6	0	0	0	0	38.0	39	157	14	14	3	0	2	1	10	0	15	0	0
Moore, Michael, Seattle	6	8	.429	4.71	22	21	3	2	1	0	128.0	130	556	75	67	10	1	6	3	60	4	108	7	0
Morgan, Michael, Toronto	0	3	.000	5.16	16	4	0	0	2	0	45.1	48	198	26	26	6	0	1	0	21	0	22	3	0
Morogiello, Daniel, Baltimore*	0	1	.000	2.39	22	0	0	0	8	1	37.2	39	160	10	10	1	1	1	1	10	3	15	1	0
Morris, John, Detroit	20	13	.606	3.34	37	37	20	1	0	0	293.2	257	1204	117	109	30	8	9	3	83	5	232	18	0
Mura, Stephen, Chicago	0	0	.000	4.38	6	0	0	0	3	0	12.1	13	57	11	6	1	0	1	0	6	0	4	5	0
Murray, Dale, New York	2	4	.333	4.48	40	0	0	0	21	1	94.1	113	415	56	47	5	6	6	1	22	4	45	4	1
Nelson, W. Eugene, Seattle	0	3	.000	7.88	10	5	1	0	2	0	32.0	38	153	29	28	6	2	0	1	21	2	11	1	0
Nipper, Albert, Boston	1	1	.500	2.25	3	2	1	0	1	0	16.0	17	67	4	4	0	0	1	1	7	0	5	0	0
Norris, Michael, Oakland	4	5	.444	3.76	16	16	2	0	0	0	88.2	68	365	42	37	11	5	2	3	36	0	63	1	1
Nunez, Edwin, Seattle	0	4	.000	4.38	14	5	0	0	4	0	37.0	40	170	21	18	3	1	0	3	22	1	35	0	2
O'Connor, Jack, Minnesota*	2	3	.400	5.86	27	8	0	0	9	0	83.0	107	383	59	54	13	3	4	0	36	1	56	3	0
Oelkers, Bryan, Minnesota*	0	5	.000	8.65	10	8	0	0	1	0	34.1	56	167	34	33	7	0	1	0	17	0	13	0	0
Ojeda, Robert, Boston*	12	7	.632	4.04	29	28	5	0	0	0	173.2	173	746	85	78	15	6	11	3	73	2	94	2	0

Pitcher and Club	W.	L.	Pct.	ERA.	G.	GS.	CG.	ShO.	GF.	Sv.	IP.	H.	BFP.	R.	ER.	HR.	SH.	SF.	HB.	Tot. BB.	Int. BB.	SO.	WP.	Bk.
Palmer, James, Baltimore	5	4	.556	4.23	14	11	0	0	1	0	76.2	86	330	42	36	11	4	3	0	19	0	34	1	1
Pashnick, Larry, Detroit	1	3	.250	5.26	12	6	0	0	4	0	37.2	48	181	27	22	5	1	3	3	18	1	17	0	0
Perry, Gaylord, Seattle-Kansas City	7	14	.333	4.64	30	30	3	1	0	0	186.1	214	811	108	96	24	11	6	4	49	4	82	5	0
Petry, Daniel, Detroit	19	11	.633	3.92	38	38	9	2	0	0	266.1	256	1115	126	116	37	5	5	6	99	7	122	12	0
Pettibone, H. Jonathan, Minnesota	0	4	.000	5.33	4	4	1	0	0	0	27.0	28	111	16	16	8	1	0	2	8	0	10	0	1
Porter, Charles, Milwaukee	7	9	.438	4.50	25	21	6	1	1	0	134.0	162	595	72	67	9	4	7	2	38	2	76	0	0
Quisenberry, Daniel, Kansas City	5	3	.625	1.94	69	0	0	0	62	45	139.0	118	536	35	30	6	6	4	0	11	2	48	0	0
Ramirez, D. Allan, Baltimore	4	4	.500	3.47	11	10	1	0	0	0	57.0	46	233	22	22	6	1	1	0	30	1	20	1	0
Rasmussen, Eric, Kansas City	3	6	.333	4.78	11	9	2	1	1	0	52.2	61	236	28	28	4	2	1	0	22	0	18	0	0
Rawley, Shane, New York*	14	14	.500	3.78	34	33	13	2	1	1	238.1	246	1010	111	100	19	7	6	3	79	1	124	5	1
Reed, Jerry, Cleveland	0	0	.000	7.17	7	0	0	0	1	0	21.1	26	95	19	17	4	1	1	0	9	1	11	0	0
Renko, Steven, Kansas City	6	11	.353	4.30	25	17	1	0	2	0	121.1	144	536	63	58	9	4	4	0	36	1	54	4	0
Righetti, David, New York*	14	8	.636	3.44	31	31	7	2	0	0	217.0	194	900	96	83	12	10	4	2	67	2	169	10	1
Rozema, David, Detroit	8	3	.727	3.43	29	16	1	0	7	2	105.0	100	441	50	40	10	3	5	1	29	6	63	1	3
Rucker, David, Detroit*	1	2	.333	17.00	4	3	0	0	0	0	9.0	18	52	17	17	2	0	0	1	8	0	6	0	0
Sanchez, Luis, California	10	8	.556	3.66	56	1	0	0	34	7	98.1	92	416	42	40	6	9	2	3	40	14	49	2	0
Schmidt, David, Texas	3	3	.500	3.88	31	0	0	0	20	2	46.1	42	191	20	20	3	1	1	1	14	1	29	2	0
Schrom, Kenneth, Minnesota	15	8	.652	3.71	33	28	6	1	2	0	196.1	196	843	92	81	14	7	9	9	80	3	80	2	1
Shirley, Robert, New York*	5	8	.385	5.08	25	17	1	1	3	0	108.0	122	467	71	61	10	9	6	0	36	3	53	1	1
Simpson, Joe, Kansas City*	0	0	.000	3.00	2	0	0	0	2	0	3.0	4	15	1	1	0	0	0	0	2	0	1	0	0
Slaton, James, Milwaukee	14	6	.700	4.33	46	0	0	0	26	5	112.1	112	490	57	54	12	9	10	3	56	5	38	3	0
Smith, Mark, Oakland	1	0	1.000	6.75	8	1	0	0	2	0	14.2	24	70	11	11	0	1	0	1	6	1	10	1	0
Smithson, B. Mike, Texas	10	14	.417	3.91	33	33	10	0	0	0	223.1	233	960	102	97	14	6	8	8	71	2	135	8	2
Sorensen, Lary, Cleveland	12	11	.522	4.24	36	34	8	1	2	0	222.2	238	941	112	105	21	5	7	2	65	9	76	9	1
Spillner, Daniel, Cleveland	2	9	.182	5.07	60	0	0	0	41	8	92.1	117	418	54	52	7	0	7	2	38	9	48	4	0
Splittorff, Paul, Kansas City*	13	8	.619	3.63	27	27	4	0	0	0	156.0	159	667	77	63	9	3	5	1	52	2	61	3	0
Stanley, Robert, Boston	8	10	.444	2.85	64	0	0	0	53	33	145.1	145	602	56	46	7	11	4	3	38	12	65	4	0
Stanton, Michael, Seattle	2	3	.400	3.32	50	0	0	0	23	7	65.0	65	274	26	24	3	5	2	1	28	5	47	1	3
Steirer, Ricky, California	3	2	.600	4.82	19	5	0	0	7	0	61.2	77	282	40	33	3	3	3	3	18	4	25	1	0
Stewart, David, Texas	5	2	.714	2.14	8	8	2	0	0	0	59.0	50	237	15	14	2	2	1	2	17	0	24	1	0
Stewart, Samuel, Baltimore	9	4	.692	3.62	58	1	0	0	21	7	144.1	138	623	60	58	7	6	3	1	67	4	95	9	0
Stieb, David, Toronto	17	12	.586	3.04	36	36	14	4	0	0	278.0	223	1141	105	94	21	6	9	14	93	6	187	5	1
Stoddard, Robert, Seattle	9	17	.346	4.41	35	23	2	1	4	0	175.2	182	739	95	86	29	9	3	4	58	0	87	5	4
Stoddard, Timothy, Baltimore	4	3	.571	6.09	47	0	0	0	34	9	57.2	65	260	39	39	10	4	4	1	29	4	50	2	1
Sutcliffe, Richard, Cleveland	17	11	.607	4.29	36	35	10	2	0	0	243.1	251	1061	131	116	23	8	9	6	102	5	160	7	3
Sutton, Donald, Milwaukee	8	13	.381	4.08	31	31	4	0	0	0	220.1	209	925	109	100	21	8	7	5	54	2	134	2	0
Swaggerty, William, Baltimore	1	1	.500	2.91	7	2	0	0	3	0	21.2	23	92	8	7	1	0	0	0	6	0	7	0	0
Tanana, Frank, Texas*	7	9	.438	3.16	29	22	3	0	1	0	159.1	144	667	70	56	14	7	3	7	49	5	108	6	1
Tellmann, Thomas, Milwaukee	9	4	.692	2.80	44	0	0	0	26	8	99.2	95	415	34	31	7	8	3	2	35	4	48	2	1
Thomas, Roy, Seattle	3	1	.750	3.45	43	0	0	0	12	1	88.2	95	386	44	34	3	3	4	2	32	3	77	3	0
Tidrow, Richard, Chicago	2	4	.333	4.22	50	1	0	0	27	7	91.2	86	397	50	43	13	4	3	1	34	8	66	1	0
Tobik, David, Texas	2	1	.667	3.68	27	0	0	0	24	9	44.0	36	176	18	18	2	0	1	0	13	3	30	0	0
Travers, William, California*	0	3	.000	5.91	10	7	0	0	2	0	42.2	58	201	32	28	4	2	3	2	19	1	24	4	0
Tudor, John, Boston*	13	12	.520	4.09	34	34	7	2	0	0	242.0	236	1022	122	110	32	5	5	4	81	3	136	8	2
Tufts, Robert, Kansas City*	0	0	.000	8.10	6	0	0	0	3	0	6.2	16	42	8	6	1	0	0	1	5	0	3	1	0
Ujdur, Gerald, Detroit	0	4	.000	7.15	11	6	0	0	4	0	34.0	41	161	33	27	6	0	0	1	20	1	13	2	0
Underwood, Patrick, Detroit*	0	0	.000	8.71	4	0	0	0	2	0	10.1	11	44	10	10	1	0	0	0	6	0	2	1	0
Underwood, Thomas, Oakland*	9	7	.563	4.04	51	15	0	0	15	4	144.2	156	627	69	65	13	1	10	2	50	4	62	7	0
Vande Berg, Edward, Seattle*	2	4	.333	3.36	68	0	0	0	30	5	64.1	59	270	32	24	6	4	3	1	22	6	49	4	1
Viola, Frank, Minnesota*	7	15	.318	5.49	35	34	4	0	0	0	210.0	242	949	141	128	34	5	2	8	92	7	127	6	2

Pitcher and Club	W.	L.	Pct.	ERA.	G.	GS.	CG.	ShO.	GF.	Sv.	IP.	H.	BFP.	R.	ER.	HR.	SH.	SF.	HB.	Tot. BB.	Int. BB.	SO.	WP.	Bk.
Vuckovich, Peter, Milwaukee	0	2	.000	4.91	3	3	0	0	0	0	14.2	15	69	9	8	0	0	0	1	10	1	10	0	0
Waits, M. Richard, Clev.-Milw.*	0	3	.000	4.89	18	2	0	0	5	0	49.2	62	225	33	27	2	3	5	0	20	3	33	3	0
Walters, Michael, Minnesota	1	1	.500	4.12	23	0	0	0	10	2	59.0	52	243	31	27	4	5	2	2	20	4	21	0	1
Warren, Michael, Oakland	5	3	.625	4.11	12	9	3	1	1	0	65.2	51	262	33	30	4	2	4	1	18	1	30	2	0
Welchel, Donald, Baltimore	0	2	.000	5.40	11	0	0	0	3	0	26.2	33	124	18	16	1	2	1	0	10	1	16	1	0
Whitehouse, Leonard, Minnesota*	7	1	.875	4.15	60	0	0	0	27	2	73.2	70	324	34	34	6	6	4	2	44	11	44	6	0
Wilcox, Milton, Detroit	11	10	.524	3.97	26	26	9	2	0	0	186.0	164	775	89	82	19	2	3	4	74	6	101	10	2
Williams, Alberto, Minnesota	11	14	.440	4.14	36	29	4	1	3	1	193.1	196	828	105	89	21	4	4	4	68	6	68	4	3
Williams, Matthew, Toronto	1	1	.500	14.63	4	3	0	0	1	0	8.0	13	45	13	13	5	0	1	1	7	0	5	0	0
Wills, Frank, Kansas City	2	1	.667	4.15	6	4	0	0	1	0	34.2	35	152	17	16	2	0	2	0	15	0	23	3	0
Witt, Michael, California	7	14	.333	4.91	43	19	2	0	15	5	154.0	173	683	90	84	14	5	7	6	75	7	77	8	0
Wortham, Richard, Oakland*	0	0	.000	.....	1	0	0	0	0	0	0.0	3	4	1	1	0	0	0	0	1	0	0	0	0
Wright, J. Richard, Texas*	0	0	.000	0.00	1	0	0	0	0	0	2.0	0	8	0	0	0	2	0	0	1	0	2	0	0
Young, Curtis, Oakland*	0	1	.000	16.00	8	2	0	0	0	0	9.0	17	50	17	16	1	0	0	1	5	0	5	1	0
Young, Matthew, Seattle*	11	15	.423	3.27	33	32	5	2	0	0	203.2	178	851	86	74	17	4	8	7	79	2	130	4	2
Zahn, Geoffrey, California*	9	11	.450	3.33	29	28	11	3	1	0	203.0	212	852	90	75	22	6	8	0	51	2	81	4	0

NOTE—Following pitchers combined to pitch shutout games: Baltimore (6)—Palmer, Davis and F. Martinez, Flanagan and Stewart, Davis and F. Martinez, Flanagan and Stoddard, J.D. Martinez and Stewart, Boddicker, Stewart and F. Martinez; Boston (2)—Ojeda and Stanley, Eckersley and Johnson; California (1)—Kison and Sanchez; Chicago (3)—Burns and Tidrow, Hoyt and Barojas, Dotson, Barojas, Agosto, Koosman and Lamp; Detroit (2)—Bair and Lopez, Berenguer and Rozema; Kansas City (6)—Splittorff and Quisenberry, Splittorff and Armstrong, Splittorff, Creel and Hood, Perry and Quisenberry, Splittorff, Armstrong and Quisenberry, Splittorff, Quisenberry and Armstrong; Milwaukee (3)—Sutton and Tellmann, Haas and Ladd, Sutton and Slaton; Minnesota (2)—Williams and Davis, Filson and Davis; New York (3)—Rawley and Gossage, Howell and May, Fontenot, Frazier, and Gossage; Oakland (6)—Norris, Burgmeier and McCatty 2, Krueger, McCatty, Burgmeier and Beard, Underwood and McCatty, Codiroli and Atherton, Codiroli and Beard; Seattle (2)—Young and Caudill, Moore and Caudill; Texas (3)—Smithson and O. Jones 2, Honeycutt, O. Jones and Tobik; Toronto (1)—Leal and Moffitt.

PITCHERS WITH TWO OR MORE CLUBS

(Alphabetically arranged with pitcher's first club on top)

Pitcher and Club	W.	L.	Pct.	ERA.	G.	GS.	CG.	ShO.	GF.	Sv.	IP.	H.	BFP.	R.	ER.	HR.	SH.	SF.	HB.	Tot. BB.	Int. BB.	SO.	WP.	Bk.
Abbott, W. Glenn, Seattle	5	3	.625	4.59	14	14	2	0	0	0	82.1	103	355	46	42	9	3	2	4	15	2	38	0	2
Abbott, W. Glenn, Detroit	2	1	.667	1.93	7	7	1	1	0	0	46.2	43	186	12	10	5	2	1	0	7	1	11	2	0
Alexander, Doyle, New York	0	2	.000	6.35	8	5	0	0	2	0	28.1	31	121	21	20	6	1	1	0	7	0	17	0	0
Alexander, Doyle, Toronto	7	6	.538	3.93	17	15	5	0	1	0	116.2	126	482	55	51	14	0	3	1	26	1	46	4	0
Easterly, James, Milwaukee*	0	1	.000	3.86	12	0	0	0	5	1	11.2	14	56	7	5	0	3	1	2	10	1	6	0	0
Easterly, James, Cleveland*	4	2	.667	3.63	41	0	0	0	20	3	57.0	69	250	25	23	4	2	1	2	22	4	39	1	0
Keough, Matthew, Oakland	2	3	.400	5.52	14	4	0	0	3	0	44.0	50	210	29	27	7	1	2	0	31	1	28	2	1
Keough, Matthew, New York	3	4	.429	5.17	12	12	0	0	0	0	55.2	59	246	42	32	12	1	1	2	20	0	26	1	0
Perry, Gaylord, Seattle	3	10	.231	4.94	16	16	2	0	0	0	102.0	116	437	60	56	18	3	3	3	23	3	42	1	0
Perry, Gaylord, Kansas City	4	4	.500	4.27	14	14	1	1	0	0	84.1	98	374	48	40	6	8	3	1	26	1	40	4	0
Waits, W. Richard, Cleveland*	0	1	.000	4.58	8	0	0	0	3	0	19.2	23	91	13	10	1	3	4	0	9	2	13	1	0
Waits, W. Richard, Milwaukee*	0	2	.000	5.10	10	2	0	0	2	0	30.0	39	134	20	17	1	0	1	0	11	1	20	2	0

1983 A.L. Pitching Against Each Club

Baltimore—98-64

Pitcher	Bos. W-L	Cal. W-L	Chi. W-L	Clev. W-L	Det. W-L	K.C. W-L	Mil. W-L	Min. W-L	N.Y. W-L	Oak. W-L	Sea. W-L	Tex. W-L	Tor. W-L	Totals W-L
Boddicker...	0-1	1-1	2-0	0-1	1-2	1-1	2-0	2-0	2-1	0-0	1-0	2-0	2-1	16-8
Davis..........	1-1	0-0	0-0	1-1	2-0	2-0	1-0	1-2	0-1	2-0	2-1	1-0	0-1	13-7
Flanagan	1-0	1-0	0-2	1-0	0-1	1-0	1-0	2-0	1-0	2-0	1-0	1-0	0-1	12-4
D. Martinez	1-1	1-2	0-1	1-2	0-2	0-2	1-1	0-1	0-0	2-0	1-1	0-2	0-1	7-16
T. Martinez	0-2	0-0	1-0	0-0	0-0	1-0	2-0	0-0	1-0	0-1	0-0	1-0	3-0	9-3
Morogiello ..	0-0	0-0	0-0	0-0	0-0	0-0	0-0	0-0	0-0	0-1	0-0	0-0	0-0	0-1
McGregor...	1-0	2-1	1-0	2-1	1-1	2-0	1-0	2-1	0-2	1-0	2-1	1-0	2-0	18-7
Palmer........	2-0	0-0	0-0	1-0	0-1	0-1	0-0	1-0	1-0	0-1	0-0	0-0	0-1	5-4
Ramirez......	0-0	2-0	0-1	0-1	0-0	0-0	1-0	0-0	0-0	1-1	0-0	0-1	0-0	4-4
Stewart	1-0	0-0	2-0	0-1	1-1	1-0	0-0	0-0	1-0	0-0	1-1	2-0	0-1	9-4
Stoddard....	0-0	0-0	1-0	0-0	0-0	0-0	2-1	0-0	0-2	0-0	0-0	1-0	0-0	4-3
Swaggerty .	1-0	0-0	0-0	0-0	0-0	0-0	0-0	0-0	0-1	0-0	0-0	0-0	0-0	1-1
Welchel	0-0	0-1	0-1	0-0	0-0	0-0	0-0	0-0	0-0	0-0	0-0	0-0	0-0	0-2
Totals	8-5	7-5	7-5	6-7	5-8	8-4	11-2	8-4	6-7	8-4	8-4	9-3	7-6	98-64

No Decisions—Mirabella.

Boston—78-84

Pitcher	Balt. W-L	Cal. W-L	Chi. W-L	Clev. W-L	Det. W-L	K.C. W-L	Mil. W-L	Min. W-L	N.Y. W-L	Oak. W-L	Sea. W-L	Tex. W-L	Tor. W-L	Totals W-L
Aponte	0-0	1-1	0-0	0-0	0-0	0-1	0-0	0-1	0-0	0-0	2-0	2-0	0-1	5-4
Bird............	0-0	0-0	0-1	0-2	0-0	0-0	0-0	1-0	0-0	0-0	0-1	0-0	0-0	1-4
Boyd	0-1	0-0	1-1	0-1	0-3	1-1	0-0	1-1	0-0	0-0	0-0	1-0	0-0	4-8
Brown.........	0-1	0-0	1-0	0-0	1-0	1-1	1-1	0-0	0-0	0-1	2-2	0-0	0-0	6-6
Clear	0-0	0-1	0-0	1-0	0-0	0-0	1-2	0-0	0-0	1-1	0-0	0-0	1-1	4-5
Eckersley ...	0-1	1-1	0-0	2-0	1-3	0-0	0-1	1-2	0-1	1-0	1-2	1-0	1-2	9-13
Hurst	1-1	0-1	3-1	0-1	0-1	1-1	0-1	0-2	2-2	3-0	0-0	2-0	0-1	12-12
Johnson	0-0	0-0	0-0	1-0	0-0	0-0	0-1	0-0	0-1	0-0	1-0	0-0	1-0	3-2
Nipper.........	0-1	0-0	0-0	1-0	0-0	0-0	0-0	0-0	0-0	0-0	0-0	0-0	0-0	1-1
Ojeda	2-1	0-0	1-1	1-1	1-0	0-1	1-2	2-0	3-0	0-0	0-0	0-1	1-0	12-7
Stanley.......	1-1	3-0	0-0	0-1	0-1	1-0	0-1	0-1	0-0	1-2	0-0	0-3	2-0	8-10
Tudor	1-1	1-2	0-2	1-0	1-1	1-2	1-0	0-0	2-2	2-0	1-0	1-1	1-1	13-12
Totals	5-8	6-6	6-6	7-6	4-9	5-7	4-9	5-7	7-6	8-4	7-5	7-5	7-6	78-84

No Decisions—None.

California—70-92

Pitcher	Balt. W-L	Bos. W-L	Chi. W-L	Clev. W-L	Det. W-L	K.C. W-L	Mil. W-L	Min. W-L	N.Y. W-L	Oak. W-L	Sea. W-L	Tex. W-L	Tor. W-L	Totals W-L
C. Brown	0-0	0-0	0-0	0-0	0-0	0-0	0-0	0-0	0-0	0-0	0-0	0-0	1-1	1-1
S. Brown	0-0	0-0	0-2	0-0	0-0	0-0	0-0	0-1	1-0	0-0	0-0	1-0	0-0	2-3
Corbett	0-0	1-0	0-0	0-0	0-0	0-0	0-0	0-0	0-0	0-0	0-0	0-1	0-0	1-1
Curtis..........	0-0	0-0	0-0	0-0	0-0	0-0	0-0	0-0	0-0	0-0	0-1	1-0	0-1	1-2
Forsch	0-1	1-1	2-2	0-0	0-1	2-0	1-0	1-1	0-2	2-1	2-1	0-2	0-0	11-12
Goltz..........	0-0	0-0	0-0	0-0	0-0	0-0	0-1	0-2	0-1	0-0	0-0	0-0	0-2	0-6
Hassler	0-0	0-1	0-1	0-0	0-0	0-1	0-2	0-0	0-0	0-0	0-0	0-0	0-0	0-5
John............	1-2	1-2	1-3	1-0	0-0	1-2	3-1	0-1	1-1	0-1	2-0	0-0	0-0	11-13
Kison	0-0	2-1	0-0	2-0	1-2	0-1	1-0	3-0	0-0	0-1	1-0	1-0	0-0	11-5
Lacey	0-0	0-0	0-0	0-0	0-0	0-0	0-0	0-0	0-0	0-0	0-0	1-1	0-1	1-2
McLaughlin.	0-1	0-0	0-0	0-0	0-1	1-1	0-0	0-0	0-0	0-0	0-0	0-1	1-0	2-4
Sanchez......	2-0	1-1	0-0	1-2	1-1	0-1	0-0	0-0	1-0	0-1	0-1	2-1	2-0	10-8
Steirer	0-0	0-0	0-0	1-0	0-0	0-1	1-0	1-0	0-0	0-1	0-0	0-0	0-0	3-2
Travers	0-0	0-0	0-0	0-1	0-0	0-0	0-0	0-0	0-0	0-0	0-0	0-1	0-1	0-3
Witt............	1-1	0-0	0-2	2-1	0-2	1-0	0-2	1-1	1-1	1-1	0-2	0-0	0-1	7-14
Zahn...........	1-2	0-0	0-0	1-0	2-1	1-0	0-0	0-1	1-2	2-2	1-2	0-0	0-1	9-11
Totals	5-7	6-6	3-10	8-4	4-8	6-7	6-6	6-7	5-7	5-8	6-7	6-7	4-8	70-92

No Decisions—None.

Chicago—99-63

Pitcher	Balt. W-L	Bos. W-L	Cal. W-L	Clev. W-L	Det. W-L	K.C. W-L	Mil. W-L	Min. W-L	N.Y. W-L	Oak. W-L	Sea. W-L	Tex. W-L	Tor. W-L	Totals W-L
Agosto........	0-0	0-0	0-0	0-0	0-0	1-0	0-1	0-0	0-0	1-0	0-0	0-0	0-1	2-2
Bannister....	2-0	0-2	0-0	1-1	1-0	1-1	1-1	1-0	3-0	1-1	2-1	1-2	2-1	16-10
Barojas.......	1-0	0-0	1-0	0-0	0-0	0-0	0-1	0-2	1-0	0-0	0-0	0-0	0-0	3-3
Burns	0-0	1-1	2-1	1-0	1-1	1-1	0-0	0-2	1-1	1-1	1-0	1-1	0-2	10-11
Dotson........	0-2	1-1	2-0	2-1	1-0	1-0	1-0	3-0	2-1	1-0	3-0	3-1	2-1	22-7
Hickey	0-0	0-0	0-0	0-0	0-0	0-1	0-1	0-0	0-0	1-0	0-0	0-0	0-0	1-2
Hoffman	0-0	0-0	0-0	0-0	0-0	0-0	0-0	1-0	0-0	0-0	0-0	0-0	0-0	1-0
Hoyt............	2-1	2-0	3-0	3-0	2-1	4-0	0-3	2-1	0-1	1-1	3-0	1-1	1-1	24-10
Koosman	0-1	2-1	1-1	1-0	0-2	1-1	1-0	0-0	1-0	1-0	1-0	2-0	0-1	11-7
Lamp	0-3	0-1	0-1	0-1	3-0	0-0	1-0	1-0	0-1	0-0	2-0	0-0	0-0	7-7
Tidrow........	0-0	0-0	1-0	0-1	0-0	0-0	0-1	0-0	0-0	1-2	0-0	0-0	0-0	2-4
Totals	5-7	6-6	10-3	8-4	8-4	9-4	4-8	8-5	8-4	8-5	12-1	8-5	5-7	99-63

No Decisions—Jones, Kern, Martz, Mura.

Cleveland—70-92

Pitcher	Balt. W-L	Bos. W-L	Cal. W-L	Chi. W-L	Det. W-L	K.C. W-L	Mil. W-L	Min. W-L	N.Y. W-L	Oak. W-L	Sea. W-L	Tex. W-L	Tor. W-L	Totals W-L
Anderson	0-1	0-2	0-0	0-0	1-0	0-0	0-1	0-0	0-0	0-0	0-0	0-0	0-2	1-6
Barker	0-1	2-0	0-3	1-1	0-2	2-1	0-1	0-1	0-0	1-1	0-0	1-2	1-0	8-13
Barnes	0-0	1-0	0-0	0-0	0-0	0-0	0-0	0-0	0-1	0-0	0-0	0-0	0-0	1-1
Behenna	0-0	0-0	0-0	0-0	0-1	0-0	0-0	0-0	0-1	0-0	0-0	0-0	0-0	0-2
Blyleven	1-1	1-0	1-0	2-1	0-2	0-0	0-2	2-0	0-1	0-1	0-0	0-1	0-1	7-10
Brennan	1-0	0-0	0-0	0-0	0-0	0-0	0-0	0-1	0-0	0-0	0-0	1-1	0-0	2-2
Camacho	0-0	0-0	0-0	0-0	0-1	0-0	0-0	0-0	0-0	0-0	0-0	0-0	0-0	0-1
Easterly	0-0	0-0	0-0	0-0	0-0	0-0	0-1	1-0	1-1	0-0	1-0	0-0	1-0	4-2
Eichelb'ger	0-0	0-1	0-1	0-2	1-0	0-1	0-2	0-1	0-1	0-0	1-2	0-0	2-0	4-11
Glynn	0-0	0-0	0-0	0-0	0-0	0-0	0-0	0-1	0-0	0-0	0-0	0-1	0-0	0-2
Heaton	2-0	0-2	2-0	0-1	0-0	0-1	0-1	0-0	2-0	1-1	3-0	1-1	0-0	11-7
Jeffcoat	0-0	0-0	0-1	0-0	0-0	0-0	0-0	0-0	1-0	0-1	0-1	0-0	0-0	1-3
Sorensen	1-2	1-1	0-0	0-2	2-1	2-0	1-2	1-0	1-0	2-0	1-0	0-1	0-2	12-11
Spillner	0-0	0-0	0-3	0-0	0-0	0-2	0-0	1-0	0-1	1-0	0-0	0-1	0-2	2-9
Sutcliffe	2-1	1-1	1-0	1-1	1-1	3-0	2-0	1-2	1-1	2-0	2-1	0-1	0-2	17-11
Waits	0-0	0-0	0-0	0-0	0-0	0-0	0-0	0-0	0-0	0-1	0-0	0-0	0-0	0-1
Totals	7-6	6-7	4-8	4-8	5-8	7-5	3-10	6-6	6-7	7-5	8-4	3-9	4-9	70-92

No Decisions—Reed.

Detroit—92-70

Pitcher	Balt. W-L	Bos. W-L	Cal. W-L	Chi. W-L	Clev. W-L	K.C. W-L	Mil. W-L	Min. W-L	N.Y. W-L	Oak. W-L	Sea. W-L	Tex. W-L	Tor. W-L	Totals W-L
Abbott	0-0	0-0	0-0	0-0	1-0	0-0	1-0	0-0	0-0	0-0	0-0	0-1	0-0	2-1
Bailey	0-0	0-0	2-0	0-1	0-0	0-2	0-0	1-0	1-2	1-0	0-0	0-0	0-0	5-5
Bair	2-0	1-0	0-0	0-1	0-0	0-0	0-0	0-0	1-0	1-1	1-1	1-0	0-0	7-3
Berenguer	1-0	3-0	0-0	1-1	0-0	1-0	1-2	1-0	0-1	0-0	0-1	1-0	0-0	9-5
Gumpert	0-1	0-0	0-0	0-0	0-0	0-0	0-0	0-0	0-0	0-0	0-0	0-0	0-1	0-2
Lopez	0-0	0-0	1-1	0-1	0-0	2-0	1-1	1-1	0-1	0-0	1-1	1-0	2-2	9-8
Morris	1-2	1-1	1-0	2-1	3-1	1-1	1-3	2-0	1-1	1-2	2-1	3-0	1-0	20-13
Pashnick	0-0	0-0	0-0	0-0	0-1	0-1	0-0	1-1	0-0	0-0	0-0	0-0	0-0	1-3
Petry	3-1	1-3	2-0	0-1	1-1	1-0	1-1	2-0	2-1	1-1	2-0	1-2	2-0	19-11
Rozema	0-0	1-0	1-1	0-0	1-0	2-1	1-0	0-0	0-1	0-0	1-0	0-0	1-0	8-3
Rucker	0-0	0-0	0-0	0-0	0-0	0-0	0-0	0-0	0-1	1-0	0-0	0-0	0-1	1-2
Ujdur	0-0	0-0	0-0	0-1	0-0	0-0	0-0	0-1	0-0	0-1	0-0	0-1	0-0	0-4
Wilcox	1-1	2-0	1-2	1-1	2-2	0-0	0-0	1-0	0-0	1-1	1-0	1-0	0-3	11-10
Totals	8-5	9-4	8-4	4-8	8-5	7-5	6-7	9-3	5-8	6-6	8-4	8-4	6-7	92-70

No Decisions—James, Martin, Underwood.

Kansas City—79-83

Pitcher	Balt. W-L	Bos. W-L	Cal. W-L	Chi. W-L	Clev. W-L	Det. W-L	Mil. W-L	Min. W-L	N.Y. W-L	Oak. W-L	Sea. W-L	Tex. W-L	Tor. W-L	Totals W-L
Armstrong	0-1	1-1	3-0	0-1	1-1	1-0	0-1	0-1	1-1	2-0	0-0	1-0	0-0	10-7
Black	1-0	0-0	1-2	0-1	0-0	0-1	2-0	1-0	0-0	0-1	1-2	3-0	1-0	10-7
Blue	0-0	0-0	0-1	0-1	0-1	0-0	0-0	0-0	0-1	0-1	0-0	0-0	0-0	0-5
Castro	0-0	0-0	0-0	0-0	0-0	0-0	0-0	1-0	0-0	0-0	1-0	0-0	0-0	2-0
Creel	0-0	1-0	0-1	0-1	0-0	0-0	1-0	0-1	0-0	0-0	0-0	0-1	0-1	2-5
Gura	1-2	0-1	1-0	0-3	0-2	1-1	3-1	1-0	1-2	1-1	1-3	0-0	1-2	11-18
Hood	0-0	0-0	0-0	0-0	1-0	0-2	0-0	0-0	0-0	1-1	0-0	0-0	0-0	2-3
Huismann	0-0	0-0	1-0	0-0	0-0	1-1	0-0	0-0	0-0	0-0	0-0	0-0	0-0	2-1
Jackson	0-0	0-0	0-0	0-0	0-0	0-0	0-0	1-1	0-0	0-0	0-0	0-0	0-0	1-1
Leonard	0-1	2-0	0-0	0-0	0-0	1-0	0-0	0-0	1-1	0-0	0-0	1-0	1-1	6-3
Perry	0-1	2-0	0-1	0-0	1-1	0-0	0-1	0-0	0-0	0-0	0-0	1-0	0-0	4-4
Quisenberry	0-1	0-0	0-0	1-1	0-0	1-0	0-0	0-0	2-0	0-0	1-0	0-0	0-1	5-3
Rasmussen	0-2	1-1	0-0	0-0	0-0	0-0	0-0	0-2	0-0	1-0	0-0	1-1	0-0	3-6
Renko	1-0	0-1	0-0	2-0	0-2	0-1	0-2	1-1	0-0	0-1	0-0	0-2	2-1	6-11
Splittorff	1-0	0-1	1-1	1-1	2-0	0-1	0-1	0-1	1-1	2-0	3-0	1-1	1-0	13-8
Wills	0-0	0-0	0-0	0-0	0-0	0-0	0-0	1-0	0-0	0-1	1-0	0-0	0-0	2-1
Totals	4-8	7-5	7-6	4-9	5-7	5-7	6-6	6-7	6-6	7-6	8-5	8-5	6-6	79-83

No Decisions—Simpson, Tufts.

Milwaukee—87-75

Pitcher	Balt. W-L	Bos. W-L	Cal. W-L	Chi. W-L	Clev. W-L	Det. W-L	K.C. W-L	Minn. W-L	N.Y. W-L	Oak. W-L	Sea. W-L	Tex. W-L	Tor. W-L	Totals W-L
Augustine	0-1	0-0	1-1	0-0	0-0	0-0	0-0	0-0	0-0	0-0	1-0	1-1	0-0	3-3
Cocanower	1-0	0-0	0-0	0-0	0-0	1-0	0-0	0-0	0-0	0-0	0-0	0-0	0-0	2-0
Caldwell	0-1	0-1	1-1	0-0	2-0	0-1	2-0	1-1	0-3	2-0	1-1	1-1	2-1	12-11
Candiotti	0-1	1-0	1-0	0-0	0-2	0-1	0-0	0-0	1-0	0-0	1-0	0-0	0-0	4-4
Easterly	0-0	0-0	0-0	0-0	0-0	0-0	0-0	0-0	0-0	0-1	0-0	0-0	0-0	0-1
Gibson	0-3	1-0	0-0	0-0	0-0	1-0	1-0	0-0	0-1	0-0	0-0	0-0	0-0	3-4
Haas	0-0	2-1	1-0	0-0	1-0	2-0	1-0	2-0	0-1	3-1	0-0	0-0	1-0	13-3
Ladd	0-1	0-1	0-0	2-0	0-0	1-0	0-0	0-1	0-0	0-0	0-0	0-0	0-1	3-4
McClure	0-0	1-0	1-0	2-1	0-0	1-0	1-3	1-1	1-0	0-0	0-1	1-1	0-2	9-9
Porter	0-1	1-0	0-0	0-2	0-1	1-1	0-0	1-0	0-2	0-2	1-0	1-0	2-0	7-9
Slaton	1-0	1-0	1-0	3-0	3-0	0-2	0-1	1-0	1-0	0-1	0-1	1-0	2-1	14-6
Sutton	0-1	1-1	0-3	0-1	3-0	0-0	0-2	2-0	0-1	0-1	0-2	1-1	1-0	8-13
Tellmann	0-2	1-0	0-0	1-0	1-0	0-0	1-0	0-1	1-0	1-0	1-1	2-0	0-0	9-4
Vuckovich	0-0	0-0	0-0	0-0	0-0	0-1	0-0	0-0	0-0	0-0	0-1	0-0	0-0	0-2
Waits	0-0	0-0	0-1	0-0	0-0	0-0	0-0	0-0	0-1	0-0	0-0	0-0	0-0	0-2
Totals	2-11	9-4	6-6	8-4	10-3	7-6	6-6	8-4	4-9	6-6	5-7	8-4	8-5	87-75

No Decisions—Beene.

Minnesota—70-92

Pitcher	Balt. W-L	Bos. W-L	Cal. W-L	Chi. W-L	Clev. W-L	Det. W-L	K.C. W-L	Milw. W-L	N.Y. W-L	Oak. W-L	Sea. W-L	Tex. W-L	Tor. W-L	Totals W-L
Castillo	1-2	0-1	1-1	0-1	1-2	0-1	1-0	0-1	1-1	0-1	2-0	1-0	0-1	8-12
Davis	0-1	1-0	0-0	2-1	0-1	0-0	0-0	1-0	0-1	0-1	0-1	1-1	0-1	5-8
Filson	0-0	0-0	1-0	0-0	0-0	0-0	2-1	0-0	0-0	0-0	0-0	1-0	0-0	4-1
Havens	0-0	1-1	0-1	0-0	1-1	0-1	0-0	1-2	1-0	0-1	1-0	0-1	0-0	5-8
Lysander	0-1	0-1	1-1	0-1	0-1	1-4	0-1	0-0	0-1	0-0	1-0	1-1	1-0	5-12
O'Connor	0-0	0-0	0-0	0-0	0-0	0-0	1-0	0-0	0-2	0-1	1-0	0-0	0-0	2-3
Oelkers	0-0	0-0	0-1	0-1	0-0	0-0	0-0	0-0	0-0	0-0	0-2	0-0	0-1	0-5
Pettibone	0-0	0-0	0-0	0-0	0-0	0-0	0-2	0-0	0-0	0-0	0-0	0-0	0-2	0-4
Schrom	2-2	1-0	2-0	0-2	1-0	1-1	1-1	0-1	1-0	1-0	1-0	1-1	3-0	15-8
Viola	1-1	1-1	0-1	1-2	0-1	0-1	1-1	1-1	0-1	1-2	1-1	0-1	0-1	7-15
Walters	0-0	0-0	0-1	1-0	0-0	0-0	0-0	0-0	0-0	0-0	0-0	0-0	0-0	1-1
Whitehouse	0-0	1-0	2-0	0-0	0-0	0-0	0-0	1-0	1-0	1-1	1-0	0-0	0-0	7-1
Williams	0-1	2-1	0-0	1-0	3-0	1-1	1-0	0-3	0-2	1-2	1-0	0-3	1-1	11-14
Totals	4-8	7-5	7-6	5-8	6-6	3-9	7-6	4-8	4-8	4-9	9-4	5-8	5-7	70-92

No Decisions—Lewis.

New York—91-71

Pitcher	Balt. W-L	Bos. W-L	Cal. W-L	Chi. W-L	Clev. W-L	Det. W-L	K.C. W-L	Milw. W-L	Minn. W-L	Oak. W-L	Sea. W-L	Tex. W-L	Tor. W-L	Totals W-L
Alexander	0-0	0-0	0-0	0-0	0-0	0-0	0-1	0-0	0-1	0-0	0-0	0-0	0-0	0-2
Erickson	0-0	0-0	0-0	0-0	0-0	0-0	0-0	0-0	0-0	0-0	0-1	0-0	0-0	0-1
Fontenot	0-0	0-0	0-0	0-2	1-0	1-0	1-0	2-0	0-0	0-0	1-0	2-0	0-0	8-2
Frazier	0-0	0-0	0-0	0-0	1-1	0-1	0-1	1-0	2-0	0-1	0-0	0-0	0-0	4-4
Gossage	3-0	0-0	1-1	1-0	1-1	2-0	1-2	1-0	1-0	1-0	0-0	1-0	0-1	13-5
Guidry	2-0	1-1	2-0	0-1	2-0	1-2	1-0	1-1	3-1	3-0	3-0	0-2	2-1	21-9
Howell	0-1	1-0	0-0	0-1	0-1	0-0	0-0	0-0	0-1	0-0	0-1	0-0	0-0	1-5
Keough	0-0	1-2	0-0	0-0	0-0	0-1	0-0	1-0	0-0	0-1	0-0	1-0	0-0	3-4
May	0-1	0-0	0-2	0-0	0-0	0-0	0-0	0-1	0-0	1-0	0-0	0-0	0-1	1-5
Montefusco	1-0	1-0	1-0	0-0	1-0	0-0	0-0	0-0	0-0	0-0	1-0	0-0	0-0	5-0
Murray	0-0	0-0	1-0	0-1	0-0	0-1	0-0	0-0	0-1	0-0	0-0	1-0	0-1	2-4
Rawley	0-3	0-2	1-1	0-2	1-0	1-0	2-0	1-1	2-0	2-0	1-1	0-3	3-1	14-14
Righetti	1-1	1-1	1-1	2-1	0-1	3-0	0-1	1-1	0-0	1-1	1-0	2-0	1-0	14-8
Shirley	0-0	1-1	0-0	1-0	0-2	0-0	1-1	1-0	0-0	0-1	0-2	0-0	1-1	5-8
Totals	7-6	6-7	7-5	4-8	7-6	8-5	6-6	9-4	8-4	8-4	7-5	7-5	7-6	91-71

No Decisions—Kaufman, LaRoche.

Oakland—74-88

Pitcher	Balt. W-L	Bos. W-L	Cal. W-L	Chi. W-L	Clev. W-L	Det. W-L	K.C. W-L	Milw. W-L	Minn. W-L	N.Y. W-L	Sea. W-L	Tex. W-L	Tor. W-L	Totals W-L
Atherton	0-0	1-0	0-0	0-1	0-1	0-0	0-1	0-0	1-0	0-0	0-0	0-1	0-1	2-5
Baker	0-1	0-0	0-0	0-0	0-0	1-1	0-0	1-0	1-0	0-0	0-0	0-1	0-0	3-3
Beard	1-0	0-0	2-0	0-0	0-1	0-2	0-0	0-0	1-0	1-1	0-0	0-1	0-0	5-5
Burgmeier	1-0	0-2	1-0	1-1	1-0	1-0	0-1	1-0	0-1	0-2	0-0	0-0	0-0	6-7
Callahan	0-0	0-0	0-0	0-0	0-0	0-0	1-1	0-0	0-0	0-0	0-0	0-1	0-0	1-2
Codiroli	1-1	1-1	1-1	1-2	0-0	2-0	0-0	1-2	3-0	1-1	1-1	0-1	0-2	12-12
Conroy	0-2	0-0	1-0	1-2	0-1	0-1	0-0	1-1	0-1	0-1	2-0	0-1	2-0	7-10
Heimueller	0-1	0-0	1-1	0-0	0-1	0-0	0-1	1-0	1-0	0-0	0-1	0-0	0-0	3-5
Jones	0-0	0-0	0-0	0-0	0-0	0-0	1-1	0-0	0-0	0-0	0-0	0-0	0-0	1-1
Keough	0-0	0-0	0-2	0-0	1-0	0-0	0-0	1-0	0-0	0-0	0-1	0-0	0-0	2-3
Krueger	1-1	1-2	1-0	0-0	0-0	0-0	1-0	0-0	0-1	0-1	2-0	0-1	1-0	7-6
Langford	0-0	0-1	0-0	0-0	0-1	0-1	0-0	0-0	0-0	0-0	0-1	0-0	0-0	0-4
McCatty	0-1	0-1	0-0	0-0	2-1	1-0	0-2	0-1	1-0	0-0	0-0	1-2	1-1	6-9
Norris	0-1	0-1	0-0	0-0	1-0	1-1	0-0	0-0	1-0	0-2	1-0	0-0	0-0	4-5
Smith	0-0	0-0	0-0	0-0	0-0	0-0	1-0	0-0	0-0	0-0	0-0	0-0	0-0	1-0
Underwood	0-0	1-0	1-0	1-1	0-1	0-0	1-0	0-1	0-1	1-0	3-0	0-1	1-2	9-7
Warren	0-0	0-0	0-1	1-1	0-0	0-0	1-0	0-1	0-0	1-0	0-0	1-0	1-0	5-3
Young	0-0	0-0	0-0	0-0	0-0	0-0	0-0	0-0	0-0	0-0	0-0	0-1	0-0	0-1
Totals	4-8	4-8	8-5	5-8	5-7	6-6	6-7	6-6	9-4	4-8	9-4	2-11	6-6	74-88

No Decisions—Bradley, Farmer, Gross, Wortham.

Seattle—60-102

Pitcher	Balt. W-L	Bos. W-L	Cal. W-L	Chi. W-L	Clev. W-L	Det. W-L	K.C. W-L	Milw. W-L	Minn. W-L	N.Y. W-L	Oak. W-L	Tex. W-L	Tor. W-L	Totals W-L
Abbott	0-1	0-1	0-0	1-0	1-0	0-1	1-0	0-0	1-0	0-0	0-0	0-0	1-0	5-3
Beattie	2-2	1-0	0-1	0-2	1-1	1-0	2-0	0-2	0-0	1-1	0-3	0-3	2-0	10-15
Best	0-0	0-0	0-0	0-0	0-1	0-0	0-0	0-0	0-0	0-0	0-0	0-0	0-0	0-1
Caudill	1-0	0-0	0-0	0-1	0-1	0-2	0-1	0-0	0-2	0-0	0-0	1-0	0-1	2-8
Clark	0-0	1-0	1-1	0-2	0-0	0-1	0-1	2-1	0-1	2-2	0-0	1-0	0-1	7-10
Moore	0-0	0-0	1-1	0-1	0-1	2-1	0-0	1-0	0-2	0-1	0-0	2-0	0-1	6-8
G. Nelson	0-0	0-0	0-0	0-0	0-1	0-0	0-1	0-0	0-0	0-0	0-0	0-1	0-0	0-3
Nunez	0-1	0-0	0-0	0-0	0-0	0-1	0-0	0-0	0-1	0-0	0-1	0-0	0-0	0-4
Perry	0-2	1-0	0-1	0-1	0-1	0-0	0-2	1-1	0-2	0-0	1-0	0-0	0-0	3-10
Stanton	0-0	0-1	1-0	0-0	0-0	0-0	1-0	0-0	0-0	0-0	0-1	0-0	0-1	2-3
Stoddard	1-0	1-1	3-1	0-3	1-2	0-1	1-1	1-1	0-0	0-1	0-3	1-1	0-2	9-17
Thomas	0-0	0-0	0-0	0-0	0-0	0-0	0-0	0-0	2-0	0-0	1-0	0-0	0-1	3-1
Vande Berg	0-0	0-3	0-0	0-0	0-0	0-0	0-0	1-0	0-0	0-1	0-0	1-0	0-0	2-4
Young	0-2	1-1	1-1	0-2	1-0	1-1	0-2	1-0	1-1	2-1	2-1	0-2	1-1	11-15
Totals	4-8	5-7	7-6	1-12	4-8	4-8	5-8	7-5	4-9	5-7	4-9	6-7	4-8	60-102

No Decisions—Castillo.

Texas—77-85

Pitcher	Balt. W-L	Bos. W-L	Cal. W-L	Chi. W-L	Clev. W-L	Det. W-L	K.C. W-L	Milw. W-L	Minn. W-L	N.Y. W-L	Oak. W-L	Sea. W-L	Tor. W-L	Totals W-L
Butcher	1-0	1-0	0-1	1-1	0-0	1-2	0-1	1-0	1-0	0-1	0-0	0-0	0-0	6-6
Cruz	0-0	0-1	1-0	0-1	0-0	0-1	0-0	0-0	0-0	0-0	0-0	0-0	0-0	1-3
Darwin	1-0	0-1	1-0	0-0	0-0	1-0	0-3	1-2	1-2	0-0	2-0	1-1	0-4	8-13
Henke	0-0	0-0	1-0	0-0	0-0	0-0	0-0	0-0	0-0	0-0	0-0	0-0	0-0	1-0
Honeycutt	0-0	1-1	1-1	2-0	2-1	0-1	1-0	1-1	1-0	2-1	1-0	1-0	1-2	14-8
Hough	0-2	1-1	1-0	0-2	2-0	1-1	2-1	0-2	2-0	2-1	3-0	1-2	0-1	15-13
O. Jones	0-2	1-0	0-1	0-0	0-0	0-0	0-0	0-1	1-0	0-1	1-0	0-1	0-0	3-6
Lachowicz	0-0	0-0	0-1	0-0	0-0	0-0	0-0	0-0	0-0	0-0	0-0	0-0	0-0	0-1
Mason	0-0	0-1	0-0	0-0	0-1	0-0	0-0	0-0	0-0	0-0	0-0	0-0	0-0	0-2
Matlack	0-0	0-1	0-1	1-0	0-1	0-0	0-1	0-0	0-0	0-0	0-0	0-0	1-0	2-4
Schmidt	0-1	0-0	1-0	0-0	1-0	0-0	0-1	0-0	0-0	0-0	1-0	0-0	0-1	3-3
Smithson	1-2	1-1	0-1	0-2	1-0	0-2	1-0	0-1	1-1	0-2	2-1	2-1	1-0	10-14
Stewart	0-0	0-0	1-0	1-1	0-0	0-0	1-0	0-0	0-1	0-0	0-0	2-0	0-0	5-2
Tanana	0-1	0-0	0-0	0-1	2-0	1-1	0-1	0-1	1-1	1-1	1-1	0-1	1-0	7-9
Tobik	0-1	0-0	0-0	0-0	1-0	0-0	0-0	1-0	0-0	0-0	0-0	0-0	0-0	2-1
Totals	3-9	5-7	7-6	5-8	9-3	4-8	5-8	4-8	8-5	5-7	11-2	7-6	4-8	77-85

No Decisions—R. Wright.

Toronto—89-73

Pitcher	Balt. W-L	Bos. W-L	Cal. W-L	Chi. W-L	Clev. W-L	Det. W-L	K.C. W-L	Milw. W-L	Minn. W-L	N.Y. W-L	Oak. W-L	Sea. W-L	Tex. W-L	Totals W-L
Acker	0-0	1-0	0-0	0-0	0-1	1-0	0-0	0-0	1-0	0-0	1-0	1-0	0-0	5-1
Alexander	1-0	0-1	2-0	0-2	0-1	1-0	0-0	0-2	1-0	0-0	0-0	2-0	0-0	7-6
Clancy	2-0	1-1	1-0	0-0	2-0	0-2	1-1	2-1	1-1	1-2	0-3	1-0	3-0	15-11
Clarke	0-0	0-0	1-1	0-0	0-0	0-0	0-0	0-0	0-0	0-0	0-0	0-0	0-0	1-1
Geisel	0-0	0-0	0-1	0-0	0-0	0-0	0-0	0-1	0-0	0-0	0-0	0-1	0-0	0-3
Gott	1-1	2-0	2-0	1-0	0-0	0-3	0-2	0-1	1-1	0-1	2-1	0-2	0-2	9-14
Jackson	0-1	1-1	0-0	0-0	0-0	1-0	2-1	0-0	0-0	2-0	1-0	1-0	0-0	8-3
Leal	1-1	0-1	1-2	2-2	1-0	2-0	0-1	0-1	2-0	0-1	0-2	2-0	2-1	13-12
Moffitt	0-0	0-1	0-0	0-0	2-1	0-0	2-0	0-0	0-0	0-0	0-0	0-0	2-0	6-2
Morgan	0-1	0-0	0-0	0-0	0-1	0-0	0-0	0-1	0-0	0-0	0-0	0-0	0-0	0-3
McLaughlin	0-2	0-0	0-0	2-0	3-0	1-1	0-0	1-1	0-0	0-0	0-0	0-0	0-0	7-4
Stieb	1-1	1-2	1-0	2-1	1-0	1-0	1-1	2-0	1-3	2-2	2-0	1-1	1-1	17-12
Williams	0-0	0-0	0-0	0-0	0-0	0-0	0-0	0-0	0-0	1-1	0-0	0-0	0-0	1-1
Totals	6-7	6-7	8-4	7-5	9-4	7-6	6-6	5-8	7-5	6-7	6-6	8-4	8-4	89-73

No Decisions—Cooper.

NATIONAL LEAGUE

Including

Team Reviews of 1983 Season

Team Day-by-Day Scores

1983 Standings, Home-Away Records

1983 Official N.L. Batting Averages

1983 Official N.L. Fielding Averages

1983 Official N.L. Pitching Averages

1983 Pitching Against Each Club

John Denny, in his first full National League season since 1979, displayed Cy Young form.

Phillies Weather the Storm

By HAL BODLEY

On July 18, 1983, Phillies General Manager Paul Owens fired Manager Pat Corrales and took over the field job himself.

"I'll win it for you," Owens told Phils President Bill Giles. "I still think this is the best team we've put together."

Bold statements.

The day Corrales was fired, the Phillies were atop the National League's East Division, but only one game over .500 (43-42). They had been inconsistent since the season opened, saved only by the fact that everyone else in the N.L. East was struggling, too.

Owens, 59, had not managed since 1972, when he took over a hapless Phils team at midseason.

In 1983, the man called the Pope was out to produce a league champion—and that's precisely what he did.

The Phillies overcame clubhouse grousing, anemic batting averages (the club was held scoreless in 42 consecutive innings in May), inconsistency and three other contenders to win their fifth East Division title in eight years and first since 1980.

They then polished off the Los Angeles Dodgers in the N.L. Championship Series before losing to the Baltimore Orioles in the World Series.

The ingredients of the N.L. championship year are difficult to dissect.

The bottom line is that the Phillies got hot in September, winning 11 consecutive games (the major leagues' longest victory streak of '83) and going 22-7 overall. They moved into first place for good on September 14 after sweeping the Montreal Expos in a doubleheader. After sharing the lead with the Pirates September 15-16-17, Philadelphia had undisputed control of the top spot the rest of the way.

The Phils compiled the best home record in the league, winning 50 of 81 games at Veterans Stadium (where they drew 2,128,339 fans). Against East Division teams, they were 60-30 overall—and that was a key.

Several times in June the Phils were 5½ games out of first place, the last occurring June 29 after a loss to Montreal in the first game of a doubleheader.

What really turned around this team—a club known as the Wheeze Kids because of such aging players as Pete Rose, Joe Morgan, Tony Perez and Ron Reed—and made it a champion?

Was it the many roster moves?

Recalled from the minors late in the year, Len Matuszek delivered key hits and displaced veteran Pete Rose at first base.

From the start of the season through August 31, 40 players wore Phillie uniforms and eight who joined the team after opening day were on the postseason roster.

Or was it the constant juggling of the lineup?

Outside the pitcher's spot, the Phillies did not use just eight players in a game until July 4. And they employed only eight just five times during the entire season.

On the night of September 6—when the Phillies were in the thick of the division race with Pittsburgh, Montreal and St. Louis—All-Star third baseman Mike Schmidt went public with a complaint, telling a reporter the team lacked direction and stability.

"Nobody is sure who the manager is (a reference to Owens' heavy reliance on his coaches), who is calling the shots," said Schmidt, who finished with 40 home runs

SCORES OF PHILADELPHIA PHILLIES' 1983 GAMES

APRIL

			Winner	Loser
5—At N.Y.	L	0-2	Sisk	Carlton
7—At N.Y.	L	2-6	Swan	Denny
8—At S. Fran.	L	2-3	Breining	Christenson
9—At S. Fran.	W	5-4	Monge	Krukow
10—At S. Fran.	W	10-2	Carlton	Laskey
12—New York	W	4-3*	Reed	Allen
13—New York	W	10-9	Altamirano	Allen
16—Atlanta	W	8-4	Carlton	Niekro
17—Atlanta	L	1-3	Perez	Farmer
18—Chicago	W	8-2	Denny	Moskau
20—Chicago	W	2-0	Carlton	Rainey
22—At Hous.	W	6-3	Monge	Ryan
23—At Hous.	W	7-3	Denny	Niekro
24—At Hous.	L	2-3‡	Madden	Reed
26—At Atlanta	L	4-10	Perez	Christenson
27—At Atlanta	W	6-2	Ruthven	Niekro
29—Houston	L	3-6*	LaCorte	Carlton
30—Houston	W	8-0	Denny	LaCoss

Won 11, Lost 7

MAY

			Winner	Loser
1—Houston	W	11-3	Christenson	Knepper
2—Cincinnati	L	2-5	Power	Ruthven
3—Cincinnati	W	13-7	Monge	Pastore
4—Cincinnati	W	9-4	Carlton	Gale
6—At Mon.	W	5-2	Reed	Smith
7—At Mon.	L	2-3	Gullickson	Altamirano
10—At Cinn.	W	3-1	Carlton	Power
11—At Cinn.	L	0-2	Soto	Denny
12—At Chicago	L	3-6	Rainey	Ruthven
13—At Chicago	L	2-10	Trout	Christenson
15—At Chicago	W	5-3*	Carlton	Smith
17—San Fran.	W	2-1	Denny	McGaffigan
18—San Fran.	L	1-8	Krukow	Ruthven
20—San Diego	L	0-5	Hawkins	Carlton
23—Los Ang.	L	0-2	Valenzuela	Denny
24—Los Ang.	L	0-3	Pena	Christenson
25—Los Ang.	L	1-6	Hooton	Bystrom
27—Montreal	L	4-7	Sanderson	Carlton
28—Montreal	W	5-3	Hernandez	Reardon
29—Montreal	W	5-2	Christenson	Gullickson
30—At L.A.	L	2-5	Hooton	Bystrom
31—At L.A.	L	1-4	Reuss	Hudson

Won 9, Lost 13

JUNE

			Winner	Loser
1—At L.A.	L	0-1	Welch	Carlton
2—At S. Diego	L	1-4	Dravecky	Farmer
3—At S. Diego	L	5-8	Lucas	Farmer
4—At S. Diego	L	4-5	Montefusco	Bystrom
5—At S. Diego	W	2-1	Holland	Whitson
7—St. Louis	L	1-2	Forsch	Carlton
8—St. Louis	W	7-4	Holland	Sutter
9—St. Louis	W	6-5‡	Reed	Von Ohlen
10—Pittsburgh	L	3-4§	Tekulve	Farmer
11—Pittsburgh	W	9-7	Carlton	Scurry
12—Pittsburgh	W	5-4‡	Reed	Scurry
13—At St. L.	W	6-2	Bystrom	LaPoint
14—At St. L.	L	4-5	Sutter	Altamirano
15—At St. L.	L	6-7	Hagen	Carlton
17—At Pitts.	L	1-2	Candelaria	Denny
18—At Pitts.	W	6-4	Bystrom	Rhoden
19—At Pitts.	W	14-2	Hudson	McWilliams
20—At Mon.	L	0-5	Burris	Carlton
21—At Mon.	W	8-1	Denny	Sanderson
21—At Mon.	L	4-5§	Reardon	Altamirano
22—At Mon.	L	0-4	Lea	Bystrom
23—At Mon.	L	3-4	Gullickson	Hudson
24—At N.Y.	W	6-3	Carlton	Swan
25—At N.Y.	W	4-2	Gross	Terrell
26—At N.Y.	W	8-4	McGraw	Seaver
26—At N.Y.	L	1-5	Torrez	Farmer
28—Montreal	T	5-5†	.....	.....
29—Montreal	L	2-5	Rogers	Carlton
29—Montreal	W	3-2	Hudson	Sanderson
30—Montreal	W	3-1	Gross	Burris

Won 14, Lost 15

JULY

			Winner	Loser
1—New York	W	5-1	Denny	Seaver
2—New York	W	6-5	Holland	Orosco
2—New York	L	3-4	Lynch	Farmer
3—New York	W	6-4	Hernandez	Sisk
4—New York	W	4-0	Carlton	Terrell
8—At Cinn.	L	1-3	Price	Denny
9—At Cinn.	L	1-2	Hume	Hernandez
10—At Cinn.	W	2-0	Bystrom	Soto
11—At Cinn.	W	11-7‡	Holland	Hume
12—Atlanta	W	4-1	Denny	Dayley
12—Atlanta	W	7-6	Hernandez	Bedrosian
13—Atlanta	L	2-5	McMurtry	Carlton
14—Atlanta	L	2-5	Bedrosian	Hernandez
15—Cincinnati	L	2-3	Soto	Hudson
16—Cincinnati	W	9-3	Denny	Berenyi
17—Cincinnati	L	2-5	Pastore	Gross
18—Houston	L	2-8	Niekro	Carlton
19—Houston	L	3-7	Knepper	Bystrom
20—Houston	W	10-3	Hudson	Scott
21—At Atlanta	W	10-6	Denny	Camp
22—At Atlanta	L	1-6	McMurtry	Gross
23—At Atlanta	L	5-6	Camp	Hernandez
24—At Atlanta	L	4-12	Perez	Bystrom
26—At Hous.	W	1-0	Hudson	Ryan
27—At Hous.	W	3-1	Denny	Niekro
28—At Hous.	W	6-5	Reed	LaCoss
29—Chicago	W	3-2	Holland	Smith
30—Chicago	L	3-4	Campbell	Hernandez
30—Chicago	W	4-3	Hudson	Trout
31—Chicago	W	5-2	Denny	Ruthven

Won 17, Lost 13

AUGUST

			Winner	Loser
1—Chicago	W	2-1	Carlton	Campbell
2—At Pitts.	L	3-10	McWilliams	Gross
3—At Pitts.	L	2-7	Candelaria	Bystrom
4—At Pitts.	W	5-1	Hudson	Rhoden
5—At St. L.	W	10-7	Denny	Stuper
6—At St. L.	W	1-0‡	Holland	Sutter
7—At St. L.	W	5-2	Bystrom	Allen
8—Pittsburgh	W	14-5	Hudson	Candelaria
9—Pittsburgh	L	1-3	Tekulve	Holland
10—Pittsburgh	W	4-2	Carlton	DeLeon
12—St. Louis	W	5-2	Bystrom	Allen
13—St. Louis	L	2-6	LaPoint	Hudson
14—St. Louis	W	5-1	Denny	Forsch
15—At Chicago	W	5-0	Carlton	Trout
16—At Chicago	L	1-10	Ruthven	Bystrom
16—At Chicago	W	6-2	Hernandez	Proly
17—At S. Diego	L	4-5	Show	Hudson
18—At S. Diego	W	4-2*	Holland	Lucas
19—At L.A.	L	0-3	Pena	Carlton
20—At L.A.	L	3-4	Valenzuela	Bystrom
21—At L.A.	L	0-6	Honeycutt	Gross
22—At S. Fran.	L	5-11	Laskey	Hudson
23—At S. Fran.	L	1-3	Krukow	Holland
24—At S. Fran.	L	3-5	Martin	Carlton
26—Los Ang.	W	4-1	Gross	Valenzuela
27—Los Ang.	L	1-6	Honeycutt	Hudson
28—Los Ang.	L	3-8	Reuss	Denny
29—San Diego	L	5-6	DeLeon	Carlton
29—San Diego	W	8-6	Comer	Monge
30—San Diego	W	6-0	Gross	Hawkins
30—San Diego	L	5-7	Whitson	McGraw
31—San Diego	W	4-3	Holland	Sosa

Won 16, Lost 16

SEPTEMBER

			Winner	Loser
1—San Fran.	W	4-2	Ghelfi	Hammaker
2—San Fran.	W	5-3	Reed	Lavelle
3—San Fran.	L	4-5	Krukow	Carlton
4—San Fran.	L	4-10	McGaffigan	Gross
5—At N.Y.	L	5-6	Orosco	Holland
6—At N.Y.	W	2-0	McGraw	Darling
7—At N.Y.	W	6-1	Denny	Terrell
9—At Pitts.	W	4-3x	Hernandez	Bibby
10—At Pitts.	L	5-6*	Tekulve	Holland
11—At Pitts.	W	5-3	Reed	Guante
12—New York	W	2-1	Denny	Darling
13—New York	L	1-5	Terrell	Ghelfi
14—Montreal	W	9-5	Carlton	Smith
14—Montreal	W	5-0	Bystrom	Burris
15—Montreal	L	1-4	Gullickson	Gross
16—St. Louis	W	3-2x	Hernandez	Baker
17—St. Louis	W	4-1	Denny	Cox
18—St. Louis	W	5-3	Carlton	Andujar
19—Chicago	W	7-6	Reed	Smith
20—Chicago	W	8-5	Hernandez	Patterson
22—At Mon.	W	9-7	Denny	Lea
22—At Mon.	W	7-1	Hudson	Rogers
23—At St. L.	W	6-2	Carlton	Andujar
24—At St. L.	W	9-6	Reed	Sutter
25—At St. L.	W	6-5*	Andersen	Lahti
26—At Chicago	W	5-2	Denny	Rainey
27—At Chicago	L	0-3	Trout	Carlton
28—At Chicago	W	13-6	Hernandez	Ruthven
30—Pittsburgh	W	2-1	Denny	McWilliams

Won 22, Lost 7

OCTOBER

			Winner	Loser
1—Pittsburgh	W	5-3	Altamirano	Guante
2—Pittsburgh	L	0-4	Tunnell	Hudson

Won 1, Lost 1

*10 innings. †10½ innings. ‡11 innings. §12 innings. x13 innings.

and 109 runs batted in. "From day to day, we don't know what the lineup is going to be. You don't know who's going to hit in front of you or behind you.

"Maybe this year will be a mirror of 1980 when we won 19 of the last 27 games to pull it out. I hope so, but I wouldn't bet on it. . . ."

Owens reacted angrily.

"There's too much individualism, too much 'I-ism' and not enough 'we-ism' on this team," he said.

Some players insisted Schmidt's remarks ignited the team, but Giles had a different opinion.

"I really believe the key to our winning the division after struggling most of the year was Pete Rose's attitude," Giles said. "The thing he did when he wasn't playing in September was not complain, and he rooted for the team. Gary Matthews said that made the team pull together."

Rose, 42, batted only .245 in '83 and on August 24 his consecutive-game playing streak ended at 745 (Owens simply decided not to use the healthy Rose). Rose, whose contract was not renewed by the Phillies for '84, ended his 21st season in the majors with 3,990 career hits, 202 shy of breaking Ty Cobb's all-time record.

It was a bewildering season for Pete. Five days before spring training ended, Corrales asked him to play right field instead of first base, the position he had held since signing with the Phillies before the 1979 season. Rose alternated between the outfield and first base for nearly eight weeks as Perez saw considerable playing time at first.

In September, Rose found himself on the bench. After the recall of Len Matuszek from Portland, Rose was used primarily as a pinch-hitter and was effective in that role.

Matuszek hit .275, finishing his season with an eight-game hitting streak in which he batted .382 and drove in 10 runs.

With Matuszek ineligible for postseason play, Rose returned to first base and hit .375 in the N.L. Championship Series and .313 in the World Series (during which he was benched for one game).

"A lot of us became role players after Paul Owens took over as manager," Rose said. "Everyone here knew his role after he arrived, but it took a couple more weeks to accept it."

Role-playing meant extensive platoon duty in the Phillies' outfield, which was manned principally by righthanded hitters Matthews, Garry Maddox and Sixto Lezcano (an August 31 acquisition from the Padres) and lefthanded batters Greg Gross, Joe Lefebvre (obtained from San Diego in May) and Von Hayes.

Ivan DeJesus was a fixture at shortstop, fielding superbly and batting .254. Second baseman Morgan, in danger of losing his job after a 0-for-35 slump in July contributed to a mid-August batting mark of .198, found the range in the stretch run and finished with a .230 average and 16 homers. Morgan celebrated his 40th birthday anniversary September 19 with a two-homer, 4-for-5 performance and came back with four hits the next day.

Schmidt led the majors in homers, the sixth time he had done so. Even though he batted only .255, Schmidt was first in the N.L. in on-base percentage (.399) and topped the majors in walks (128). He slugged 25 of his homers after the All-Star Game.

Catcher Bo Diaz, who hit only .236, provided additional punch with 15 homers and 64 RBIs.

The Phillies were ninth in the league in club batting at .249, but were second only to the Dodgers in team pitching with a 3.34 earned-run average.

"Our pitching kept us in it," said Owens. "We were never out of very many games."

Righthander John Denny led the N.L. with 19 victories and was second in ERA at 2.37. He was 6-0 with a 1.80 ERA in September.

Four-time Cy Young Award winner Steve Carlton had an off year with a 15-16 record. However, he led the majors with 275 strikeouts and became the big leagues' all-time strikeout leader (3,709). And on September 23, Carlton became the 16th pitcher in major league history to post 300 or more career victories.

But had it not been for lefthanded reliever Al Holland, obtained along with Morgan from San Francisco during the off-season, the Phils would not have won. Holland, who shared the N.L.'s Fireman of the Year honor with the Cubs' Lee Smith, set a club record with 25 saves and fashioned a 1.98 ERA after the All-Star break. In his final 15 outings, he allowed only one earned run.

The pitching staff also received lifts from relievers Reed and Willie Hernandez and rookie starter Charles Hudson, all of whom helped Owens to deliver on his pennant vow. Reed compiled a 9-1 record in 61 appearances, finishing with eight saves. Hernandez, obtained from the Cubs on May 22, appeared in 63 games with the Phils and went 8-4 with seven saves. Hudson put together an 8-8 season after his late-May recall from Portland and had a 3.35 ERA.

Catcher Tony Pena was consistent defensively and finished with an impressive .301 average.

Resurgent Pirates Progress

By CHARLEY FEENEY

At the All-Star Game break, the 1983 Pittsburgh Pirates seemed like anything but contenders in the National League East.

Chuck Tanner's Pirates blundered their way to a 23-36 start in '83, regrouped for a nine-game winning streak and then staggered to the break with six losses in eight games. At 34-42, Pittsburgh was fifth in the East Division.

The Pirates, though, won 10 of their first 11 games after the break and by July 21 had seized a half-game lead in the division. They built a 2½-game edge on August 3, fell out of the top spot three days later and then settled into a stretch fight with the Phillies, Expos and Cardinals. Pittsburgh had a share of the lead as late as September 17, but the Phils' 11-game winning streak resolved the issue.

The Bucs finished second with an 84-78 record, six games behind the Phils. Pittsburgh compiled the same won-lost record in '82, a year in which the Pirates placed fourth and finished eight games off the pace.

Among the positive developments in '83 were the progress of three young pitchers, the steady improvement of second-year second baseman Johnny Ray, the consistency of catcher Tony Pena and third baseman Bill Madlock's fourth N.L. batting championship.

In addition, veteran pitchers John Candelaria and Larry McWilliams each won 15 games, Rick Rhoden had 13 victories and reliever Kent Tekulve posted 18 saves and a 1.64 earned-run average.

The young pitchers who developed were Lee Tunnell, who collected nine of his 11 victories after the All-Star Game; Cecilio Guante, who proved a valuable addition to the bullpen (nine saves) after being called up from Hawaii in late May; and Jose DeLeon, who was an instant sensation (he flirted with no-hitters three times in '83) after being brought up from Hawaii in July. DeLeon was 7-3 with a 2.83 ERA.

Ray batted .283, Pena hit .301 and Madlock was the N.L.'s best batsman at .323.

The big pitching disappointment was lefthanded reliever Rod Scurry, who, after a fine start, fell into a slump in May and never recovered. Veteran Jim Bibby flopped as a starter, but was effective at times in relief.

Don Robinson, a 15-game winner in 1982, had another bout with shoulder problems and pitched in only nine games.

Bill Madlock fought off injuries and captured his fourth N.L. batting title.

Manny Sarmiento didn't pitch as effectively as he did in 1982 (when he was a part-time starter), but still fashioned a 2.99 ERA in 52 relief appearances.

First baseman Jason Thompson was a bust on offense in the second half of the season. Still, he finished as the team leader in home runs (18) and runs batted in (76). Shortstop Dale Berra, who started slowly for the second straight year, played exceptionally well in the stretch drive.

When the season opened, Lee Mazzilli, who had been acquired from the New York Yankees, was the regular center fielder and Lee Lacy and Mike Easler made up the platoon twosome in left. Lacy was woeful when it came to driving in runs. He finished with 13 RBIs and had only two after July 14. Easler, who suffered a thumb injury in August and didn't play for more than three weeks, drove in 54 runs.

Mazzilli, who had a .400-plus on-base percentage in June, was lacking on defense and Marvell Wynne was acquired in June from the New York Mets for catcher Junior Ortiz. Wynne batted only .243, but

SCORES OF PITTSBURGH PIRATES' 1983 GAMES

APRIL

			Winner	Loser
5—At St. L.	W	7-1	Candelaria	Forsch
7—At Hous.	W	3-2	Scurry	Knepper
8—At Hous.	W	5-3	Scurry	DiPino
9—At Hous.	W	1-0	McWilliams	Niekro
10—At Hous.	W	10-8	Bibby	Solano
12—St. Louis	L	3-4*	Sutter	Bibby
13—St. Louis	L	1-9	Andujar	Tunnell
16—Chicago	L	5-6	Hernandez	McWilliams
17—Chicago	W	7-0	Candelaria	Trout
20—At N.Y.	L	0-6	Seaver	McWilliams
20—At N.Y.	L	5-7	Diaz	Tekulve
22—Los Ang.	L	2-4	Reuss	Rhoden
23—Los Ang.	L	2-3	Welch	Candelaria
26—San Fran.	W	3-0	McWilliams	Breining
27—San Fran.	L	2-3	Laskey	Rhoden
30—San Diego	L	4-8	Hawkins	Candelaria
30—San Diego	W	2-1	McWilliams	DeLeon

Won 8, Lost 9

MAY

2—At L.A.	W	5-1	Rhoden	Reuss
3—At L.A.	L	4-5	Pena	Bibby
4—At L.A.	L	2-3	Niedenfuer	Sarmiento
6—At S. Fran.	L	1-2	McGaffigan	Candelaria
7—At S. Fran.	L	1-5	Breining	Rhoden
8—At S. Fran.	L	1-12	Laskey	Bibby
9—At S. Diego	W	5-3x	Sarmiento	Couchee
10—At S. Diego	L	1-4	Hawkins	Scurry
12—New York	W	6-2	Candelaria	Torrez
13—New York	W	2-1	Tekulve	Diaz
14—New York	L	2-6	Allen	McWilliams
16—New York	L	4-11	Lynch	Bibby
17—Cincinnati	L	1-2	Soto	Candelaria
18—Cincinnati	W	2-1	Rhoden	Berenyi
20—Houston	W	4-3	McWilliams	Knepper
21—Houston	L	4-6	LaCoss	Niemann
23—At Atlanta	L	3-6	Falcone	Rhoden
24—At Atlanta	W	6-5	McWilliams	Camp
25—At Atlanta	L	0-6	McMurtry	Bibby
26—At Cinn.	W	6-4	Tunnell	Puleo
27—At Cinn.	L	0-9	Soto	Candelaria
28—At Cinn.	L	3-4	Hayes	Scurry
29—At Cinn.	W	8-5	McWilliams	Scherrer
30—Atlanta	W	8-6	Bibby	McMurtry
31—Atlanta	L	2-10	Niekro	Tunnell

Won 10, Lost 15

JUNE

1—Atlanta	L	3-6	Perez	Candelaria
2—At Chicago	L	2-3	Trout	Rhoden
3—At Chicago	L	3-9	Ruthven	Scurry
4—At Chicago	L	2-5	Jenkins	Bibby
5—At Chicago	L	1-3	Lefferts	Tunnell
7—At Mon.	W	3-2	Candelaria	Lea
8—At Mon.	L	4-5	Gullickson	Rhoden
9—At Mon.	W	6-3	McWilliams	Rogers
10—At Phila.	W	4-3‡	Tekulve	Farmer
11—At Phila.	L	7-9	Carlton	Scurry
12—At Phila.	L	4-5†	Reed	Scurry
13—Montreal	W	4-3	Rhoden	Gullickson
14—Montreal	L	3-7	Rogers	McWilliams
15—Montreal	L	4-7	Burris	Bibby
17—Phila.	W	2-1	Candelaria	Denny
18—Phila.	L	4-6	Bystrom	Rhoden
19—Phila.	L	2-14	Hudson	McWilliams
20—Chicago	W	5-4*	Tekulve	Campbell
20—Chicago	W	6-5§	Robinson	Campbell
21—Chicago	W	8-4	Rhoden	Noles
22—Chicago	W	5-2	Candelaria	Rainey
23—Chicago	W	5-2	McWilliams	Trout
24—At St. L.	W	8-2	Bibby	LaPoint
25—At St. L.	W	10-3	Tunnell	Hagen
26—At St. L.	W	5-0	Rhoden	Allen
27—At St. L.	W	6-1	Guante	Andujar
28—At Chicago	L	7-8†	Lefferts	Tekulve
29—At Chicago	L	0-5	Ruthven	Bibby
30—At Chicago	L	3-4	Smith	Sarmiento

Won 14, Lost 15

JULY

			Winner	Loser
1—St. Louis	L	6-13	Andujar	Robinson
2—St. Louis	W	3-1	Candelaria	LaPoint
3—St. Louis	L	3-4	Forsch	Sarmiento
4—St. Louis	W	7-2	Rhoden	Hagen
4—St. Louis	L	4-11	Allen	Bibby
8—At L.A.	W	4-3	Candelaria	Reuss
9—At L.A.	W	3-0	McWilliams	Pena
10—At L.A.	L	3-10	Hooton	Rhoden
11—At S. Fran.	W	3-2	Sarmiento	Breining
12—At S. Fran.	W	6-2	Tunnell	Laskey
13—At S. Fran.	W	7-6	Sarmiento	Minton
14—At S. Diego	W	8-6	Guante	Montefusco
15—At S. Diego	W	4-2	Tekulve	Thurmond
16—At S. Diego	W	3-2	Robinson	Whitson
17—At S. Diego	W	4-3	Tunnell	Show
19—Los Ang.	W	4-1	Candelaria	Reuss
19—Los Ang.	L	2-3†	Howe	Sarmiento
20—Los Ang.	W	7-3	Rhoden	Hooton
21—Los Ang.	W	5-4	Tekulve	Howe
22—San Fran.	L	3-5	Barr	Scurry
23—San Fran.	W	5-2	DeLeon	Martin
24—San Fran.	W	3-1	Scurry	Krukow
24—San Fran.	L	5-8†	Minton	Scurry
25—San Diego	W	6-3	Rhoden	Dravecky
26—San Diego	L	1-6	Thurmond	Robinson
26—San Diego	W	10-5	Tunnell	Whitson
27—San Diego	W	10-1	DeLeon	Show
28—At N.Y.	W	6-2	McWilliams	Swan
29—At N.Y.	W	2-1	Candelaria	Seaver
30—At N.Y.	W	6-3	Scurry	Lynch
31—At N.Y.	L	6-7‡	Orosco	Bibby
31—At N.Y.	L	0-1‡	Orosco	Sarmiento

Won 22, Lost 10

AUGUST

2—Phila.	W	10-3	McWilliams	Gross
3—Phila.	W	7-2	Candelaria	Bystrom
4—Phila.	L	1-5	Hudson	Rhoden
5—Montreal	L	1-7	Gullickson	DeLeon
6—Montreal	L	3-7	Smith	Tunnell
7—Montreal	L	0-6	Rogers	McWilliams
8—At Phila.	L	5-14	Hudson	Candelaria
9—At Phila.	W	3-1	Tekulve	Holland
10—At Phila.	L	2-4	Carlton	DeLeon
12—At Mon.	W	6-3	McWilliams	Rogers
13—At Mon.	W	2-0	Candelaria	Smith
14—At Mon.	W	5-3	Rhoden	Schatzeder
15—New York	W	4-2	DeLeon	Torrez
16—New York	W	3-1	Tunnell	Swan
18—Cincinnati	L	5-6	Hume	Tekulve
19—Cincinnati	L	1-2	Soto	Rhoden
20—Cincinnati	W	4-0	DeLeon	Berenyi
21—Cincinnati	L	4-6	Scherrer	Guante
23—Houston	L	5-6	Ruhle	Tekulve
23—Houston	L	1-2	Niekro	Tunnell
24—Houston	L	4-10	Madden	Rhoden
25—Houston	W	5-3	DeLeon	Knepper
26—Atlanta	W	9-1	McWilliams	Perez
27—Atlanta	W	2-0	Tunnell	Dayley
28—Atlanta	L	1-2	Falcone	Candelaria
29—At Cinn.	W	2-1	Rhoden	Soto
30—At Cinn.	W	5-3	DeLeon	Russell
31—At Hous.	L	1-4	Niekro	Scurry

Won 14, Lost 14

SEPTEMBER

1—At Hous.	L	0-3	Ryan	Guante
2—At Atlanta	W	4-1	Candelaria	Dayley
3—At Atlanta	W	6-2	Bibby	Bedrosian
4—At Atlanta	L	5-6	Forster	Bibby
5—At St. L.	L	4-7	LaPoint	Scurry
5—At St. L.	L	6-7*	Allen	Guante
6—At St. L.	W	5-0	Tunnell	Stuper
7—At St. L.	L	2-5	Cox	Rhoden
9—Phila.	L	3-4§	Hernandez	Bibby
10—Phila.	W	6-5*	Tekulve	Holland
11—Phila.	L	3-5	Reed	Guante
12—St. Louis	W	7-5	Tunnell	Cox
13—St. Louis	W	6-0	Rhoden	Andujar
14—Chicago	W	6-3	Candelaria	Trout
15—Chicago	W	8-4	McWilliams	Rainey
16—Montreal	W	9-0	DeLeon	Lea
17—Montreal	W	5-4§	Bibby	Dixon
18—Montreal	L	2-5	Sanderson	Rhoden
19—At N.Y.	L	4-5*	Diaz	Tekulve
20—At N.Y.	W	4-0	McWillams	Lynch
21—At Chicago	L	6-7	Jenkins	Guante
22—At Chicago	W	8-2	Tunnell	Reuschel
23—At Mon.	W	10-1	Rhoden	Sanderson
24—At Mon.	W	1-0	Candelaria	Smith
25—At Mon.	L	3-5	Gullickson	McWilliams
27—New York	L	3-4	Torrez	DeLeon
28—New York	L	2-4	Darling	Tunnell
29—New York	W	4-2	Rhoden	Holman
30—At Phila.	L	1-2	Denny	McWilliams

Won 15, Lost 14

OCTOBER

1—At Phila.	L	3-5	Altamirano	Guante
2—At Phila.	W	4-0	Tunnell	Hudson

Won 1, Lost 1

*10 innings. †11 innings. ‡12 innings. §13 innings. x14 innings.

Jose DeLeon got his chance in July and made a lasting impression on opposing National League batters.

improved the outfield defense tremendously.

Once a superstar, Dave Parker stumbled through the first half of the season. Parker was batting .242 with three homers and 21 RBIs at the All-Star break, and his play in right field was adequate at best. Parker's bat improved in the second half, but his final figures (.279, 12 homers, 69 RBIs) weren't close to his old-time production.

Jim Morrison and Richie Hebner were valuable reserves. Gene Tenace, signed as a free agent to supply righthanded-hitting power off the bench, batted .177 with six RBIs.

Tanner, who won his 1,000th game as a major league manager in Cincinnati on May 29, deserved an A-plus for patience in 1983 and did a fine job in keeping the club from falling apart.

After starting the season with a 5-0 record, the Pirates lost 14 of their next 18 games. Just when it appeared the Bucs could write off the season—they were 8½ games out of first on June 19—they showed remarkable bounce. But in the end, the Phils showed even more.

Pittsburgh's most significant improvement in '83 was in pitching. The staff had 14 shutouts (compared with seven in 1982), including five in September and one on October 2, the final day of the season. The club ERA at the All-Star break was 4.25; when the season ended, the figure was 3.55 (compared with 3.81 in '82).

Andre Dawson's best offensive season wasn't enough to offset other Expo deficiencies.

Expos Self-Destruct—Again

By IAN MacDONALD

The 1983 season was another painful experience for the Montreal Expos, who have a history of falling short after a big buildup. This time, however, the Expos self-destructed with more of a thud than usual.

While Montreal wasn't mathematically eliminated from the National League East race until September 26 (a night on which the Expos were no-hit victims of St. Louis' Bob Forsch), a doubleheader loss to Philadelphia four nights earlier proved the telling blow. The twin bill had afforded Montreal a chance to tie for the N.L. East lead; instead, the Expos dropped four games back with nine to play.

"When you start the season, you hope you stay close so you have a chance in the final few weeks," Manager Bill Virdon said. "We did that. Then we couldn't put it together—we weren't good enough—in the particularly important days.

"Now, if you do all the other (positive) things all year . . . you're not in that position in the final few weeks."

A weak bullpen and a sizable drop in production from the meat of the batting order put the Expos in their precarious late-season position. Still, Montreal led the East Division as late as September 13, only to lose 12 of its final 20 games and stumble to third place with an 82-80 record—eight games behind the champion Phils.

For Montreal, also the victim of a Phils' doubleheader sweep on September 14, it was the worst deficit since a 14-game gap in 1978. The Expos finished six games out of first in 1982 (after winning the East in the split season of '81), one game behind in '80 and two off the pace in '79.

"This team has all the qualities needed to win a championship," Virdon said in April. "But it is all dependent on those two guys in the bullpen. They have to get the job done."

They didn't.

The two were Woodie Fryman and Jeff Reardon.

There were suspicions that the 43-year-old Fryman's arthritic left elbow simply gave way over the winter (possibly, some wag suggested, as the veteran was signing a $500,000 contract). After two sessions on the disabled list, Fryman ended up pitching three innings in all of '83.

Reardon aggravated a life-long back ailment during the spring. While he went on to post 21 saves and a 3.03 earned-run average, Reardon had enough ineffective stretches to offset his brilliant streaks.

Bill Gullickson (above) tied Steve Rogers for the team lead in victories with 17.

Dan Schatzeder and Bob James stepped into the bullpen breach. Schatzeder was 5-2 with two saves and a 3.21 ERA. James had an outstanding September, collecting five of his seven saves in that month.

Gary Carter, Al Oliver and Tim Wallach had decent statistics in 1983. Nevertheless, the Expos led the big leagues in men left on base, 1,213, and fingers could be pointed at that usually reliable threesome.

In 1982, Carter, Oliver and Wallach totaled 79 home runs and 303 runs batted in while batting a cumulative .297. In 1983, they combined for 44 homers, 233 RBIs and a .280 mark.

"You'd like to think," theorized Virdon, "that those three are capable of doing better. But you simply don't get that big production from your sluggers every year."

It wasn't all negative for the Expos, who are still trying to live up to their "team of the '80s" billing. (The Expos do own the N.L.'s best winning percentage over the

SCORES OF MONTREAL EXPOS' 1983 GAMES

APRIL

			Winner	Loser
6—At Chicago	W	3-0	Rogers	Jenkins
7—At Chicago	W	7-3	Gullickson	Noles
8—At L.A.	W	8-3	Sanderson	Hooton
9—At L.A.	W	7-2	Lea	Welch
10—At L.A.	L	0-3	Valenzuela	Rogers
12—Chicago	L	0-5	Trout	Gullickson
14—Chicago	W	4-3	Sanderson	Rainey
15—At Hous.	L	6-7*	Dawley	Burris
16—At Hous.	W	2-0	Lea	Knepper
17—At Hous.	L	3-6	Ryan	Gullickson
21—St. Louis	W	6-5	Sanderson	Andujar
22—At Cinn.	W	4-0	Rogers	Pastore
24—At Cinn.	W	5-4	Reardon	Soto
26—Houston	L	0-2	Knepper	Gullickson
27—Houston	L	2-4	Ryan	Sanderson
29—Cincinnati	W	9-6	Rogers	Pastore
30—Cincinnati	L	3-4	Gale	Lea

Won 10, Lost 7

MAY

1—Cincinnati	W	5-4	Gullickson	Berenyi
1—Cincinnati	L	3-6	Price	Burris
3—Atlanta	L	2-5	Behenna	Grapenthin
4—Atlanta	W	4-1	Rogers	Camp
6—Phila.	L	2-5	Reed	Smith
7—Phila.	W	3-2	Gullickson	Altamirano
9—At Atlanta	W	5-3	Rogers	Camp
10—At Atlanta	L	2-4	McMurtry	Sanderson
11—At Atlanta	W	8-5‡	Schatzeder	Bedrosian
12—At St. L.	L	0-4	Forsch	Gullickson
13—At St. L.	L	4-5§	Martin	Smith
14—At St. L.	L	2-3‡	Sutter	Reardon
15—At St. L.	L	2-4	Stuper	Sanderson
17—Los Ang.	W	3-2y	Schatzeder	Howe
18—Los Ang.	L	3-13	Stewart	Gullickson
20—San Fran.	W	7-1	Rogers	Breining
21—San Fran.	L	2-5	Laskey	Sanderson
22—San Fran.	W	2-0	Lea	Hammaker
23—San Diego	W	3-1	Gullickson	Dravecky
24—San Diego	W	5-4x	Reardon	DeLeon
25—San Diego	W	2-0	Rogers	Hawkins
27—At Phila.	W	7-4	Sanderson	Carlton
28—At Phila.	L	3-5	Hernandez	Reardon
29—At Phila.	L	2-5	Christenson	Gullickson
30—At S. Diego	L	4-5	Lucas	Rogers
31—At S. Diego	L	3-5	Montefusco	Reardon

Won 12, Lost 14

JUNE

1—At S. Diego	W	8-6	Smith	Sosa
2—At S. Fran.	W	11-4	Burris	McGaffigan
3—At S. Fran.	W	9-2	Gullickson	Krukow
4—At S. Fran.	L	2-4	Lavelle	Reardon
5—At S. Fran.	W	12-9	Schatzeder	Laskey
7—Pittsburgh	L	2-3	Candelaria	Lea
8—Pittsburgh	W	5-4	Gullickson	Rhoden
9—Pittsburgh	L	3-6	McWilliams	Rogers
10—At N.Y.	L	2-4z	Ownbey	Smith
11—At N.Y.	W	5-2	Lerch	Holman
12—At N.Y.	L	1-9	Seaver	Lea
13—At Pitts.	L	3-4	Rhoden	Gullickson
14—At Pitts.	W	7-3	Rogers	McWilliams
15—At Pitts.	W	7-4	Burris	Bibby
17—New York	W	7-2	Lea	Seaver
18—New York	L	1-6	Torrez	Gullickson
19—New York	W	4-3	Rogers	Lynch
20—Phila.	W	5-0	Burris	Carlton
21—Phila.	L	1-8	Denny	Sanderson
21—Phila.	W	5-4§	Reardon	Altamirano
22—Phila.	W	4-0	Lea	Bystrom
23—Phila.	W	4-3	Gullickson	Hudson
24—Chicago	W	4-3	Rogers	Ruthven
25—Chicago	L	1-2§	Brusstar	Welsh
26—Chicago	L	5-9	Noles	Lerch
27—Chicago	W	3-1	Lea	Rainey
28—At Phila.	T	5-5†	....	....
29—At Phila.	W	5-2	Rogers	Carlton
29—At Phila.	L	2-3	Hudson	Sanderson
30—At Phila.	L	1-3	Gross	Burris

Won 17, Lost 12

JULY

			Winner	Loser
1—At Chicago	L	5-7	Noles	Lerch
2—At Chicago	L	2-5	Rainey	Lea
3—At Chicago	L	4-7	Trout	Gullickson
4—At Chicago	W	6-3	Rogers	Ruthven
4—At Chicago	W	4-2	Sanderson	Jenkins
8—Atlanta	L	5-6	McMurtry	Lea
9—Atlanta	L	5-8*	Forster	Smith
10—Atlanta	W	7-6	Reardon	Moore
11—Atlanta	L	4-6	Camp	Fryman
12—At Hous.	L	5-7	Ruhle	Lerch
13—At Hous.	L	4-9	Ryan	Lea
14—At Hous.	L	0-3	Niekro	Rogers
15—At Atlanta	L	3-9	Niekro	Gullickson
16—At Atlanta	L	3-6	Falcone	Burris
17—At Atlanta	W	3-1	Bargar	Dayley
19—Cincinnati	L	2-5	Price	Rogers
20—Cincinnati	W	6-4	Lea	Soto
21—Houston	W	9-4	Gullickson	Ryan
22—Houston	L	8-11	Smith	Fryman
23—Houston	W	4-1	Schatzeder	Knepper
24—Houston	W	7-3	Rogers	LaCoss
25—At Cinn.	L	2-4	Soto	Lea
25—At Cinn.	W	8-1	Burris	Gale
26—At Cinn.	W	5-0	Gullickson	Puleo
27—At Cinn.	W	6-3	Bargar	Pastore
28—St. Louis	L	2-3*	Sutter	Fryman
28—St. Louis	L	1-10	Forsch	Schatzeder
29—St. Louis	W	7-2	Smith	Allen
30—St. Louis	L	2-3	LaPoint	Lea
31—St. Louis	W	6-5	Reardon	Stuper

Won 13, Lost 17

AUGUST

2—At N.Y.	L	2-5	Swan	Rogers
3—At N.Y.	L	1-2	Orosco	Reardon
4—At N.Y.	W	2-1	Lea	Lynch
5—At Pitts.	W	7-1	Gullickson	DeLeon
6—At Pitts.	W	7-3	Smith	Tunnell
7—At Pitts.	W	6-0	Rogers	McWilliams
8—New York	L	5-6*	Orosco	Reardon
9—New York	W	7-3	Lea	Lynch
10—New York	W	5-3	Gullickson	Torrez
12—Pittsburgh	L	3-6	McWilliams	Rogers
13—Pittsburgh	L	0-2	Candelaria	Smith
14—Pittsburgh	L	3-5	Rhoden	Schatzeder
15—At St. L.	W	5-1	Lea	Sutter
16—At St. L.	L	3-4	Allen	Reardon
17—At S. Fran.	W	12-5	Rogers	Martin
18—At S. Fran.	L	3-5	Krukow	Smith
19—At S. Diego	L	5-6	Lollar	Burris
21—At S. Diego	W	3-0	Lea	Dravecky
21—At S. Diego	L	2-5	Thurmond	Gullickson
22—At L.A.	L	1-4	Reuss	Rogers
23—At L.A.	L	3-6	Zachry	Smith
24—At L.A.	L	2-3	Niedenfuer	Reardon
26—San Diego	W	10-4	Gullickson	Dravecky
27—San Diego	W	6-4	Lea	DeLeon
28—San Diego	W	8-0	Rogers	Show
29—San Fran.	W	5-0	Smith	Krukow
30—San Fran.	L	2-13	Davis	Burris
31—San Fran.	W	4-3	Gullickson	Breining

Won 14, Lost 14

SEPTEMBER

1—Los Ang.	W	8-3	Lea	Honeycutt
2—Los Ang.	L	1-4	Reuss	Rogers
3—Los Ang.	L	0-4	Welch	Smith
4—Los Ang.	W	3-2§	Schatzeder	Zachry
5—Chicago	W	7-3	Gullickson	Trout
6—Chicago	W	8-2	Lea	Ruthven
7—Chicago	W	6-1	Rogers	Noles
9—New York	L	4-5	Seaver	Smith
10—New York	W	10-9	Reardon	Orosco
11—New York	W	4-0	Lea	Torrez
12—At Chicago	L	0-8	Ruthven	Rogers
13—At Chicago	W	5-2	James	Noles
14—At Phila.	L	5-9	Carlton	Smith
14—At Phila.	L	0-5	Bystrom	Burris
15—At Phila.	W	4-1	Gullickson	Gross
16—At Pitts.	L	0-9	DeLeon	Lea
17—At Pitts.	L	4-5x	Bibby	Dixon
18—At Pitts.	W	5-2	Sanderson	Rhoden
19—St. Louis	W	3-0	Smith	Allen
19—St. Louis	W	6-3	Reardon	Rucker
20—St. Louis	W	10-1	Gullickson	Forsch
22—Phila.	L	7-9	Denny	Lea
22—Phila.	L	1-7	Hudson	Rogers
23—Pittsburgh	L	1-10	Rhoden	Sanderson
24—Pittsburgh	L	0-1	Candelaria	Smith
25—Pittsburgh	W	5-3	Gullickson	McWilliams
26—At St. L.	L	0-3	Forsch	Rogers
27—At St. L.	W	10-4	Lea	Stuper
28—At St. L.	W	4-0	Smith	Cox

Won 16, Lost 13

OCTOBER

1—At N.Y.	L	4-5	Gaff	Gullickson
2—At N.Y.	L	0-1	Terrell	Lea
2—At N.Y.	L	4-5	Leary	Reardon

Won 0, Lost 3

*10 innings. †10½ innings. ‡11 innings. §12 innings. x13 innings. y15 innings. z17 innings.

Tim Raines became the first National Leaguer in history to steal 70 bases and drive in 70 runs in one season.

last five seasons—but just barely. From 1979 through 1983, Montreal played at a .548 pace, winning 413 games and losing 341. Philadelphia was 413-342, .547, and Los Angeles went 413-346, .544.)

Led by Steve Rogers, Bill Gullickson and Charlie Lea (who totaled 50 victories, the most by any three starters on one N.L. team), Montreal led the N.L. in complete games (38) and tied for the major league lead in shutouts (15). Rogers and Gullickson fashioned 17-12 records and Lea was 16-11.

Bryn Smith, brought out of the bullpen in late July, proved in 12 starts that he will be a factor in the Expos' 1984 rotation. Smith scored five complete-game victories and walked only nine batters in his last 57⅔ innings of work.

Scott Sanderson, out of the rotation for more than two months because of a thumb injury, had only 16 starts and a 6-7 record.

Offensively, the Expos had standouts in Andre Dawson and Tim Raines. The two outfielders combined for 35 percent of the club's runs scored and 83 percent of Montreal's stolen bases.

Dawson carried the Expos for much of the season. He set club records with 32 home runs, 113 RBIs and 18 sacrifice flies and was in the N.L.'s top 10 in nine of 12 major offensive categories.

Raines led the league in stolen bases (90) for the third straight year, drove in 71 runs (becoming the first National Leaguer in history to have 70 steals and 70 RBIs in one season) and hit .368 with runners in scoring position.

The team had trouble establishing a middle-infield combination. Rookie Bryan Little started quickly but was found wanting on defense at both shortstop and second base. Veteran Chris Speier lost a step—and his regular job at shortstop as well.

Doug Flynn was solid at second and took over at shortstop when Manny Trillo was acquired from Cleveland in August.

Montreal ended the season on a sorry note, losing three straight games to the last-place Mets. The Expos probably were thinking of next year, anyway. As in "wait until next year."

Despite tailing off in the second half of the season, George Hendrick remained the Cardinals' top production man.

Shaky Pitching Dooms Cards

By RICK HUMMEL

After winning their first world championship in 15 years in 1982, the Cardinals dropped to an ignominious fourth-place standing in the National League East in 1983 and became the eighth World Series titlists to finish under .500 the next season.

Of his club's 79-83 finish, Manager Whitey Herzog said, "We didn't really play well from opening day."

The Cardinals had several deficiencies, the foremost being their starting pitching. Joaquin Andujar and Bob Forsch, both 15-game winners in 1982, were 16-28 collectively in '83, with Andujar plummeting to 6-16.

"We didn't have a No. 1 or a No. 2 guy," said Herzog. "The year before, we had two guys on the pitching staff who were outstanding all year. Our players knew that they had a helluva chance of winning if they got a few runs.

"That's why we had the long losing streaks (two of eight games and one of seven in 1983). We had no semblance of a No. 1."

The Cardinals' top winners were Dave LaPoint, John Stuper and Neil Allen, all with 12 victories (Allen won 10 with St. Louis and two with New York). As a barometer, Steve Mura was a 12-game winner in '82 as the Cardinals' No. 5 starter.

Herzog deemed the Cardinals' pitching so shaky that he traded star first baseman Keith Hernandez to the Mets on the June 15 trading deadline for pitchers Allen and Rick Ownbey (who was sent to Louisville).

There were other factors involved in the trade, to be sure. Hernandez will make about $1 million in 1984 and the Cardinals didn't want to pay that or sign him after '84. And though he didn't often say so publicly, Herzog never had been a big booster of Hernandez.

Herzog acknowledged that the Cardinals' defensive fundamentals weren't as good without Hernandez.

"Keith's a good ballplayer. I'm not denying that," said Herzog. "But we were going down.

"We were not going to stay in the race unless we got some pitching help. We had to do something. Everybody in the organization felt the same way."

The Cardinals surely missed Hernandez's offense, too. While he had been hitting only .284 and not producing with runners in scoring position before the trade, Hernandez had proved an effective run producer during his career with the Cards and carried a lifetime .299 batting average into the '83 season. And he went on to bat .306 and hit nine home runs for the Mets.

George Hendrick, the Cards' cleanup hitter, was less productive after the trade. He had driven in 48 runs and was hitting .333 in 186 at-bats before the swap. Afterward, he knocked in 49 runs in 343 at-bats and batted .309.

Hendrick's 97 RBIs easily led the club. Sophomore Willie McGee put to rest any doubts of his ability by driving in 75 runs and batting .286.

David Green, who got more playing time after the Hernandez deal, batted .284 with 69 RBIs.

Lonnie Smith had his second consecutive big year for the Cardinals, despite losing a month for drug and alcohol rehabilitation. Smith needed a 3-for-3 or 4-for-5 game on the final day of the season to slip past N.L. batting leader Bill Madlock of Pittsburgh, but he flied out after going 2-for-2 and popped out in his final at-bat to finish as the league runner-up at .321. Lonnie stole a team-high 43 bases.

The Cardinals' 207 steals represented a club record, breaking the 204 mark set by the 1914 team. St. Louis had five players steal 20 or more bases—Lonnie Smith, McGee (39), Ozzie Smith (34), Green (34) and rookie Andy Van Slyke (21).

Van Slyke, called up from Louisville when Hernandez was traded, started at five positions for the Cardinals—all three outfield spots, third base and first base.

Injuries played a part in the Cardinals' decline, especially the knee ailment suffered by second baseman Tom Herr, who was batting .323 before being forced out for the season in early August.

Dane Iorg, St. Louis' top reserve, was limited to just 116 at-bats because of various injuries.

The starting pitching wasn't very good and the relief often wasn't much better. Bruce Sutter, though he had 21 saves and nine victories, had a 4.23 earned-run average as N.L. hitters became more selective when swinging at his dreaded split-fingered fastball.

The Cardinals had only six saves other than Sutter's.

Ozzie Smith probably was the Cardinals' best player. No matter his average, Smith would play consummate shortstop nearly every day and he raised his batting mark from .188 just before the All-Star break to

SCORES OF ST. LOUIS CARDINALS' 1983 GAMES

APRIL

			Winner	Loser
5—Pittsburgh	L	1-7	Candelaria	Forsch
9—At N.Y.	W	5-0	Andujar	Torrez
12—At Pitts.	W	4-3*	Sutter	Bibby
13—At Pitts.	W	9-1	Andujar	Tunnell
14—New York	W	7-1	Forsch	Torrez
15—New York	W	5-2	Stuper	Holman
16—New York	W	6-2	LaPoint	Lynch
21—At Mon.	L	5-6	Sanderson	Andujar
22—San Diego	L	1-4	Dravecky	Forsch
23—San Diego	W	9-5	Martin	Show
24—San Diego	W	2-0	LaPoint	Hawkins
25—Los Ang.	L	0-8	Valenzuela	Andujar
26—Los Ang.	L	1-3	Hooton	Stuper
27—Los Ang.	W	7-6	Sutter	Pena
29—San Fran.	W	6-5xz	Bair	Calvert
30—San Fran.	L	0-5	McGaffigan	Andujar

Won 10, Lost 6

MAY

			Winner	Loser
1—San Fran.	W	10-9	Stuper	Breining
3—At S. Diego	L	3-4	Dravecky	Forsch
4—At S. Diego	L	0-10	Show	Andujar
5—At S. Diego	W	4-3	Sutter	Lucas
6—At L.A.	L	10-16	Stewart	Lahti
7—At L.A.	L	3-5	Howe	Bair
8—At L.A.	L	4-6	Reuss	Andujar
9—At S. Fran.	L	4-5	Lavelle	Sutter
10—At S. Fran.	W	8-4	Stuper	McGaffigan
12—Montreal	W	4-0	Forsch	Gullickson
13—Montreal	W	5-4‡	Martin	Smith
14—Montreal	W	3-2†	Sutter	Reardon
15—Montreal	W	4-2	Stuper	Sanderson
17—Houston	W	8-4	Forsch	Niekro
18—Houston	W	9-5	Andujar	DiPino
20—Atlanta	L	1-2	McMurtry	LaPoint
21—Atlanta	L	1-4	Bedrosian	Stuper
22—Atlanta	L	5-7†	Bedrosian	Sutter
23—At Cinn.	L	1-2	Price	Andujar
24—At Cinn.	W	7-1	LaPoint	Berenyi
25—At Cinn.	W	7-2	Stuper	Power
26—At Hous.	W	5-3	Von Ohlen	LaCoss
27—At Hous.	W	3-1y	Lahti	Knepper
28—At Hous.	L	2-9	Niekro	Martin
29—At Hous.	W	7-3	LaPoint	Scott
30—Cincinnati	W	9-1	Stuper	Power
31—Cincinnati	L	1-2	Puleo	Andujar

Won 15, Lost 12

JUNE

			Winner	Loser
1—Cincinnati	W	8-3	Martin	Soto
2—At Atlanta	L	1-8	Falcone	Forsch
3—At Atlanta	L	3-5	Camp	LaPoint
4—At Atlanta	L	4-6	Moore	Andujar
5—At Atlanta	W	8-3	Stuper	Niekro
7—At Phila.	W	2-1	Forsch	Carlton
8—At Phila.	L	4-7	Holland	Sutter
9—At Phila.	L	5-6†	Reed	Von Ohlen
10—At Chicago	L	0-7	Jenkins	Stuper
11—At Chicago	W	5-4*	Sutter	Smith
12—At Chicago	L	3-6	Rainey	Forsch
13—Phila.	L	2-6	Bystrom	LaPoint
14—Phila.	W	5-4	Sutter	Altamirano
15—Phila.	W	7-6	Hagen	Carlton
17—Chicago	W	7-2	Forsch	Rainey
18—Chicago	L	1-10	Trout	Andujar
19—Chicago	L	1-4	Ruthven	LaPoint
20—At N.Y.	W	3-1	Hagen	Swan
20—At N.Y.	L	4-6	Terrell	Stuper
21—At N.Y.	W	6-0	Allen	Gorman
22—At N.Y.	L	4-6	Seaver	Forsch
22—At N.Y.	L	1-2	Torrez	Andujar
23—At N.Y.	L	5-7	Diaz	Von Ohlen
24—Pittsburgh	L	2-8	Bibby	LaPoint
25—Pittsburgh	L	3-10	Tunnell	Hagen
26—Pittsburgh	L	0-5	Rhoden	Allen
27—Pittsburgh	L	1-6	Guante	Andujar
28—New York	L	1-10	Lynch	Forsch
28—New York	W	8-1	LaPoint	Gorman
29—New York	W	4-3	Sutter	Orosco
30—New York	W	6-1	Allen	Terrell

Won 12, Lost 19

JULY

			Winner	Loser
1—At Pitts.	W	13-6	Andujar	Robinson
2—At Pitts.	L	1-3	Candelaria	LaPoint
3—At Pitts.	W	4-3	Forsch	Sarmiento
4—At Pitts.	L	2-7	Rhoden	Hagen
4—At Pitts.	W	11-4	Allen	Bibby
8—At S. Diego	L	2-3	Lucas	Sutter
9—At S. Diego	W	12-4	LaPoint	Dravecky
10—At S. Diego	W	4-2	Von Ohlen	Lucas
11—At L.A.	L	6-7	Beckwith	Sutter
12—At L.A.	L	1-3	Welch	Stuper
13—At L.A.	W	6-5	Rucker	Howe
14—At S. Fran.	W	6-5	LaPoint	Lavelle
15—At S. Fran.	L	4-5	Barr	Andujar
16—At S. Fran.	W	9-3	Lahti	Breining
17—At S. Fran.	L	1-3	Laskey	Stuper
19—San Diego	W	4-0	Allen	Lollar
20—San Diego	L	4-5	DeLeon	Sutter
21—San Diego	L	2-4	Thurmond	Andujar
22—Los Ang.	L	4-9	Welch	Forsch
23—Los Ang.	L	5-10	Howe	Rucker
24—Los Ang.	W	3-0	Allen	Reuss
25—San Fran.	W	9-4	LaPoint	McGaffigan
26—San Fran.	W	6-5	Rucker	Minton
27—San Fran.	W	7-6	Von Ohlen	Barr
28—At Mon.	W	3-2*	Sutter	Fryman
28—At Mon.	W	10-1	Forsch	Schatzeder
29—At Mon.	L	2-7	Smith	Allen
30—At Mon.	W	3-2	LaPoint	Lea
31—At Mon.	L	5-6	Reardon	Stuper

Won 16, Lost 13

AUGUST

			Winner	Loser
2—Chicago	L	3-5	Noles	Allen
3—Chicago	L	0-4	Rainey	Forsch
4—Chicago	L	6-9	Trout	LaPoint
5—Phila.	L	7-10	Denny	Stuper
6—Phila.	L	0-1†	Holland	Sutter
7—Phila.	L	2-5	Bystrom	Allen
9—At Chicago	L	3-5	Rainey	Forsch
10—At Chicago	W	9-5§	Rucker	Noles
11—At Chicago	L	5-10	Ruthven	Cox
12—At Phila.	L	2-5	Bystrom	Allen
13—At Phila.	W	6-2	LaPoint	Hudson
14—At Phila.	L	1-5	Denny	Forsch
15—Montreal	L	1-5	Lea	Sutter
16—Montreal	W	4-3	Allen	Reardon
18—Houston	W	5-4*	Rucker	Dawley
19—Houston	W	2-0	LaPoint	Madden
20—Houston	W	3-0	Stuper	Knepper
21—Houston	W	5-2	Cox	Ryan
23—Atlanta	W	7-0	Andujar	Falcone
24—Atlanta	L	3-11	Niekro	LaPoint
25—Atlanta	W	2-1	Allen	Bedrosian
26—At Cinn.	L	3-7	Puleo	Cox
27—At Cinn.	W	3-1	Rucker	Power
28—At Cinn.	L	4-5†	Hayes	Sutter
29—At Hous.	W	6-1	Stuper	Madden
30—At Hous.	L	1-3	Ruhle	Cox
31—At Atlanta	W	6-3	Andujar	Barker

Won 12, Lost 15

SEPTEMBER

			Winner	Loser
1—At Atlanta	W	8-3	Forsch	Perez
2—Cincinnati	L	0-4	Pastore	Stuper
3—Cincinnati	L	2-3*	Soto	Rucker
4—Cincinnati	W	5-4	Lahti	Hayes
5—Pittsburgh	W	7-4	LaPoint	Scurry
5—Pittsburgh	W	7-6*	Allen	Guante
6—Pittsburgh	L	0-5	Tunnell	Stuper
7—Pittsburgh	W	5-2	Cox	Rhoden
9—At Chicago	W	6-5*	Sutter	Smith
10—At Chicago	L	5-8	Campbell	Lahti
11—At Chicago	W	2-1	Stuper	Smith
12—At Pitts.	L	5-7	Tunnell	Cox
13—At Pitts.	L	0-6	Rhoden	Andujar
14—At N.Y.	W	2-1	Allen	Seaver
15—At N.Y.	L	4-6	Lynch	LaPoint
16—At Phila.	L	2-3§	Hernandez	Baker
17—At Phila.	L	1-4	Denny	Cox
18—At Phila.	L	3-5	Carlton	Andujar
19—At Mon.	L	0-3	Smith	Allen
19—At Mon.	L	3-6	Reardon	Rucker
20—At Mon.	L	1-10	Gullickson	Forsch
21—New York	W	9-3	Stuper	Torrez
22—New York	W	3-2	Cox	Darling
23—Phila.	L	2-6	Carlton	Andujar
24—Phila.	L	6-9	Reed	Sutter
25—Phila.	L	5-6*	Andersen	Lahti
26—Montreal	W	3-0	Forsch	Rogers
27—Montreal	L	4-10	Lea	Stuper
28—Montreal	L	0-4	Smith	Cox
30—Chicago	W	9-2	Allen	Patterson

Won 12, Lost 18

OCTOBER

			Winner	Loser
1—Chicago	W	3-2	Forsch	Lefferts
2—Chicago	W	9-6	Stuper	Rainey

Won 2, Lost 0

*10 innings. †11 innings. ‡12 innings. §13 innings. x16 innings. y18 innings. zSuspended game, completed April 30.

Lonnie Smith fell just short of winning the N.L. batting title despite missing a month of the season while undergoing rehabilitation.

a final .243. His 50 RBIs ranked fourth among N.L. shortstops.

Despite their uneven play, the Cardinals stayed in the N.L. East race until 2½ weeks remained in the season. But they went 3-10 on a trip to the other five East Division cities, wiping out any hope of defending their title.

The Cardinals didn't even play a spoiler's role. The Phillies, for instance, beat them 14 times in 18 meetings (including six straight times in September).

There were two notable highlights for St. Louis in '83. Forsch became the first man to pitch two no-hitters in his Cardinal career, beating the Montreal Expos, 3-0, on September 26, and the Cards set a club season attendance mark of 2,343,716.

Mel Hall emerged as the top-flight center fielder the Cubs had been seeking.

Hopeful Cubs Sink in the East

By DAVE van DYCK

If the first year of the Cubs' so-called New Tradition was a disappointment, the second year was downright discouraging. The 1983 Cubs, projected to be a .500 team in spring training by General Manager Dallas Green, finished 71-91, which was two games worse than the record of the '82 club. It was a season of little tranquility.

The Cubs were 38-41 and only four games out of first place in the National League East at the All-Star Game break. By August 21, though, they had plummeted to 15 games under .500 and Manager Lee Elia was fired the next day.

Elia's interim replacement, Charlie Fox, finished the season, then returned to the front office and turned the managerial duties over to Mets coach Jim Frey, whose contract runs through 1985.

Jim Finks, who resigned as general manager of football's Chicago Bears, was hired as Cubs team president near the end of the season, a move that stripped Green of some power. Yet the product on the field was still Green's responsibility, and another fifth-place finish didn't make him happy.

"I don't think there's a Cub fan or a person working in the organization who isn't disappointed," said Green.

Chicago's troubles started not long after the season did, with Elia alienating fans with a late-April verbal blast. "Eighty-five percent of the people in this country work," Elia said. "The other 15 percent come out here (Wrigley Field) and boo my players." The remark left hard feelings in Chicago, but it seemed to push the players.

After beginning the season with a 5-14 record, the Cubs won 33 of their next 58 games and moved within one game of .500 at 38-39 before losing a July 4 doubleheader to Montreal.

However, a 3-8 West Coast trip right after the break set the tone for the second half. The Cubs proved agonizingly consistent, going 12-17 overall in July, 12-17 in August and 12-18 in September-October.

No one had a tougher season than Leon Durham, who spent time on the disabled list for a hamstring pull and then several days in the hospital for back spasms. Apparently healthy for the first time, Durham saw his season end September 6 in Montreal when he suffered a thumb fracture. He finished with a .258 average, 12 homers and 55 runs batted in while batting officially only 337 times.

Bill Buckner spent two weeks nursing a sore hamstring and played some left field in 1983. Although he tied for the league lead in doubles with 38, Buckner had an off year with a .280 average and 66 RBIs (compared with a .306 mark and 105 RBIs in 1982).

Green liked the growth of second baseman Ryne Sandberg, who was nurtured as a shortstop and played third base for the Cubs in his rookie season of '82. He liked rookie Mel Hall, who "went through growing periods but gave us a center fielder we never had before." He liked third baseman Ron Cey, who "did everything we asked for and paid for."

And, of course, he liked Lee Smith, who led the N.L. in saves with 29.

The streaky Hall, who spent the first part of the season on the injured list, showed flashes of power. During a late-August spree, he popped five homers in 11 at-bats, finishing the season with 17 homers and a .283 average.

Cey, obtained from the Dodgers over the winter, finished with his most RBIs, 90, since 1977 and slugged 24 homers. Jody Davis also hit 24 homers, the most by a Cub catcher since Gabby Hartnett hit 37 in 1930. Right fielder Keith Moreland finally found a position and a home. He was the Cubs' most consistent player, finishing with a .302 average and 70 RBIs. And Larry Bowa batted .267 and played solidly at shortstop.

The Cubs made only 115 errors in '83 (Texas' total of 113 was the lowest in the majors), and no one made more than 17.

"And some of the young kids came up here and did a pretty decent job," Green said.

Most impressive was first baseman Carmelo Martinez (six homers and 16 RBIs in 89 at-bats).

There was even some potential on the pitching staff. Don Schulze pitched seven innings against the Cardinals on the next-to-last day of the season and allowed only two runs. Reggie Patterson gave up only one earned run in five innings the previous night against the Cards.

Although he finished with a career-high 14 victories and came within one out of pitching a no-hitter against Cincinnati on August 24, veteran Chuck Rainey didn't win after August 30. Ferguson Jenkins went 6-9 and wound up in the bullpen, 16 victories short of 300 for his career. Steve Trout won 10 games, but dropped six of his last eight decisions.

SCORES OF CHICAGO CUBS' 1983 GAMES

APRIL

			Winner	Loser
6—Montreal	L	0-3	Rogers	Jenkins
7—Montreal	L	3-7	Gullickson	Noles
8—At Cinn.	L	3-7	Soto	Trout
9—At Cinn.	L	4-8	Pastore	Rainey
10—At Cinn.	L	2-7	Berenyi	Jenkins
11—At Cinn.	L	1-5	Price	Noles
12—At Mon.	W	5-0	Trout	Gullickson
14—At Mon.	L	3-4	Sanderson	Rainey
16—At Pitts.	W	6-5	Hernandez	McWilliams
17—At Pitts.	L	0-7	Candelaria	Trout
18—At Phila.	L	2-8	Denny	Moskau
20—At Phila.	L	0-2	Carlton	Rainey
22—San Fran.	W	7-2	Jenkins	Laskey
23—San Fran.	L	0-5	Hammaker	Trout
24—San Fran.	W	5-1	Moskau	McGaffigan
26—San Diego	L	8-10	Montefusco	Lefferts
27—San Diego	W	5-4†	Campbell	Lucas
28—San Diego	L	1-3	Show	Trout
29—Los Ang.	L	3-4	Pena	Campbell
30—Los Ang.	W	7-2	Rainey	Valenzuela

Won 6, Lost 14

MAY

1—Los Ang.	L	2-3*	Stewart	Jenkins
3—At S. Fran.	L	4-5	Laskey	Trout
4—At S. Fran.	L	4-7	Hammaker	Moskau
6—At S. Diego	W	3-2	Rainey	Lollar
7—At S. Diego	W	6-4	Campbell	Lucas
8—At S. Diego	L	3-5	Dravecky	Brusstar
9—At L.A.	L	3-4	Stewart	Smith
10—At L.A.	W	3-2	Proly	Welch
12—Phila.	W	6-3	Rainey	Ruthven
13—Phila.	W	10-2	Trout	Christenson
15—Phila.	L	3-5†	Carlton	Smith
17—Atlanta	W	4-3	Rainey	Perez
18—Atlanta	W	5-3	Trout	Behenna
20—Cincinnati	L	5-9	Scherrer	Proly
21—Cincinnati	W	8-4	Moskau	Puleo
22—Cincinnati	L	3-4	Soto	Rainey
23—At Hous.	L	2-3	Niekro	Trout
24—At Hous.	W	5-4	Ruthven	Scott
25—At Hous.	L	0-1	Madden	Lefferts
26—At Atlanta	W	5-1	Moskau	Niekro
27—At Atlanta	W	8-6	Brusstar	Behenna
28—At Atlanta	L	4-6	Moore	Proly
29—At Atlanta	L	2-6	Camp	Ruthven
30—Houston	L	7-9	Dawley	Campbell
31—Houston	L	10-12	LaCorte	Lefferts

Won 11, Lost 14

JUNE

1—Houston	W	3-2	Rainey	Knepper
2—Pittsburgh	W	3-2	Trout	Rhoden
3—Pittsburgh	W	9-3	Ruthven	Scurry
4—Pittsburgh	W	5-2	Jenkins	Bibby
5—Pittsburgh	W	3-1	Lefferts	Tunnell
7—New York	W	6-1	Rainey	Orosco
8—New York	W	2-1	Smith	Torrez
9—New York	L	4-6‡	Orosco	Proly
10—St. Louis	W	7-0	Jenkins	Stuper
11—St. Louis	L	4-5†	Sutter	Smith
12—St. Louis	W	6-3	Rainey	Forsch
13—At N.Y.	W	7-3	Trout	Torrez
14—At N.Y.	L	3-4†	Sisk	Smith
15—At N.Y.	W	7-4†	Smith	Holman
17—At St. L.	L	2-7	Forsch	Rainey
18—At St. L.	W	10-1	Trout	Andujar
19—At St. L.	W	4-1	Ruthven	LaPoint
20—At Pitts.	L	4-5†	Tekulve	Campbell
20—At Pitts.	L	5-6x	Robinson	Campbell
21—At Pitts.	L	4-8	Rhoden	Noles
22—At Pitts.	L	2-5	Candelaria	Rainey
23—At Pitts.	L	2-5	McWilliams	Trout
24—At Mon.	L	3-4	Rogers	Ruthven
25—At Mon.	W	2-1§	Brusstar	Welsh
26—At Mon.	W	9-5	Noles	Lerch
27—At Mon.	L	1-3	Lea	Rainey
28—Pittsburgh	W	8-7‡	Lefferts	Tekulve
29—Pittsburgh	W	5-0	Ruthven	Bibby
30—Pittsburgh	W	4-3	Smith	Sarmiento

Won 18, Lost 11

JULY

			Winner	Loser
1—Montreal	W	7-5	Noles	Lerch
2—Montreal	W	5-2	Rainey	Lea
3—Montreal	W	7-4	Trout	Gullickson
4—Montreal	L	3-6	Rogers	Ruthven
4—Montreal	L	2-4	Sanderson	Jenkins
8—At S. Fran.	L	1-4	Laskey	Noles
9—At S. Fran.	W	4-2	Rainey	Davis
10—At S. Fran.	L	8-10	Lavelle	Campbell
10—At S. Fran.	L	2-4	Hammaker	Ruthven
11—At S. Diego	L	5-6	Montefusco	Jenkins
12—At S. Diego	L	3-5	Show	Noles
13—At S. Diego	L	4-5	Lollar	Rainey
14—At L.A.	L	4-8	Pena	Trout
15—At L.A.	W	8-4	Ruthven	Hooton
16—At L.A.	L	4-7	Valenzuela	Jenkins
17—At L.A.	W	10-0	Noles	Welch
19—San Fran.	L	3-4†	Minton	Campbell
20—San Fran.	L	3-4†	Minton	Smith
21—San Fran.	W	3-2	Ruthven	Hammaker
22—San Diego	W	7-3	Lefferts	Lucas
23—San Diego	L	2-4	Show	Noles
24—San Diego	W	5-2	Rainey	Lollar
25—Los Ang.	W	9-3	Trout	Hooton
26—Los Ang.	L	2-5	Valenzuela	Ruthven
27—Los Ang.	W	2-1	Smith	Welch
29—At Phila.	L	2-3	Holland	Smith
30—At Phila.	W	4-3	Campbell	Hernandez
30—At Phila.	L	3-4	Hudson	Trout
31—At Phila.	L	2-5	Denny	Ruthven

Won 12, Lost 17

AUGUST

1—At Phila.	L	1-2	Carlton	Campbell
2—At St. L.	W	5-3	Noles	Allen
3—At St. L.	W	4-0	Rainey	Forsch
4—At St. L.	W	9-6	Trout	LaPoint
5—New York	L	4-9	Orosco	Proly
6—New York	L	1-4	Terrell	Jenkins
7—New York	L	4-6†	Sisk	Smith
9—St. Louis	W	5-3	Rainey	Forsch
10—St. Louis	L	5-9x	Rucker	Noles
11—St. Louis	W	10-5	Ruthven	Cox
12—At N.Y.	L	0-2	Terrell	Jenkins
13—At N.Y.	L	1-5	Seaver	Bordi
14—At N.Y.	L	2-5	Lynch	Rainey
15—Phila.	L	0-5	Carlton	Trout
16—Phila.	W	10-1	Ruthven	Bystrom
16—Phila.	L	2-6	Hernandez	Proly
18—Atlanta	W	3-0	Jenkins	Falcone
19—Atlanta	L	3-5	Niekro	Rainey
20—Atlanta	L	2-9	Dayley	Trout
21—Atlanta	L	9-11	Camp	Ruthven
22—Cincinnati	W	2-0	Noles	Pastore
23—Cincinnati	L	2-4	Russell	Jenkins
24—Cincinnati	W	3-0	Rainey	Soto
26—At Hous.	L	0-1	Ruhle	Trout
27—At Hous.	W	9-5	Ruthven	Niekro
28—At Hous.	L	2-4	Scott	Noles
29—At Atlanta	W	7-5	Campbell	Garber
30—At Atlanta	W	9-6	Rainey	McMurtry
31—At Cinn.	L	4-6	Gale	Bordi

Won 12, Lost 17

SEPTEMBER

1—At Cinn.	W	3-1	Ruthven	Berenyi
2—Houston	L	5-6	Dawley	Campbell
3—Houston	W	9-3	Jenkins	Madden
4—Houston	W	9-7	Brusstar	Dawley
5—At Mon.	L	3-7	Gullickson	Trout
6—At Mon.	L	2-8	Lea	Ruthven
7—At Mon.	L	1-6	Rogers	Noles
9—St. Louis	L	5-6†	Sutter	Smith
10—St. Louis	W	8-5	Campbell	Lahti
11—St. Louis	L	1-2	Stuper	Smith
12—Montreal	W	8-0	Ruthven	Rogers
13—Montreal	L	2-5	James	Noles
14—At Pitts.	L	3-6	Candelaria	Trout
15—At Pitts.	L	4-8	McWilliams	Rainey
16—At N.Y.	W	7-4	Reuschel	Torrez
17—At N.Y.	W	7-6	Johnson	Orosco
18—At N.Y.	W	6-5	Campbell	Sisk
19—At Phila.	L	6-7	Reed	Smith
20—At Phila.	L	5-8	Hernandez	Patterson
21—Pittsburgh	W	7-6	Jenkins	Guante
22—Pittsburgh	L	2-8	Tunnell	Reuschel
23—New York	W	4-1	Ruthven	Terrell
24—New York	L	6-7	Seaver	Schulze
25—New York	W	11-7	Patterson	Leary
26—Phila.	L	2-5	Denny	Rainey
27—Phila.	W	3-0	Trout	Carlton
28—Phila.	L	6-13	Hernandez	Ruthven
30—At St. L.	L	2-9	Allen	Patterson

Won 12, Lost 16

OCTOBER

1—At St. L.	L	2-3	Forsch	Lefferts
2—At St. L.	L	6-9	Stuper	Rainey

Won 0, Lost 2

*5 innings. †10 innings. ‡11 innings. §12 innings. x13 innings.

Mets Continue Long Struggle

By JACK LANG

At the end of the 1982 season, Mets General Manager Frank Cashen was so distraught with his team's last-place finish that he went to Ireland to get away from it all. When the '83 season ended, Cashen didn't leave town. There was no place far enough away to hide.

Cashen was optimistic about '82 after acquiring George Foster, but he later referred to that season as "a step backward." In that regard, 1983 was two steps to the rear. The Mets finished last again and they did it on merit.

Only in August—when the club posted the best record (16-13) in the East Division—were the Mets respectable. Reliever Jesse Orosco was named the National League's Pitcher of the Month in August after allowing only one earned run in 12 appearances, and rookie Darryl Strawberry smashed nine home runs.

The rest of the season was a litany of losses. New York went 6-11 in April, 10-17 in May, 13-18 in June, 10-19 in July and 10-16 in September before winning its final three games in October.

George Bamberger had returned to manage the Mets for a second season against his wishes and better judgment. Bamberger was coaxed into returning by Cashen, his longtime Baltimore associate.

Cashen appeased Bamberger by revamping the pitching staff. Veterans Tom Seaver and Mike Torrez were brought in, while Pat Zachry, Mike Scott, Pete Falcone, Randy Jones and Charlie Puleo departed. Seaver, brought back after 5½ years of "exile" in Cincinnati, and Torrez were supposed to lend crucial experience to go with the staff's young arms.

The Mets had a starting rotation in April that included youngsters Scott Holman and Rick Ownbey, but by the end of the year, Ownbey was Cardinal property and pitching in Louisville, Holman had a 1-7 record and a new crop of young pitchers was getting the buildup for 1984.

Bamberger tried twice to jump ship early in the season, saying his stomach was acting up and that he no longer could take the losing. Finally, on the morning of June 2, Bamberger called Cashen from the West Coast and told him to get a new man. Cashen pleaded with him to stay one more day until he could find a replacement.

After being told that former Orioles Manager Earl Weaver didn't want to come out of retirement, Cashen flew to Los Angeles and offered the job to Mets coach Frank Howard on an interim basis.

The Mets, 16-30 under Bamberger, responded at first to the enthusiasm and energy of Howard. They went 11-10 in Howard's first three weeks as manager before resuming their losing ways.

In August, the outlook brightened. Orosco saved six games and won five that month and Strawberry started hitting homers in bunches and driving in runs. But Howard's fate already was sealed.

On the final day of the season (during the first game of a doubleheader), the Mets announced Howard wouldn't be back. During the World Series, Cashen introduced former Baltimore second baseman Dave Johnson as the new manager.

Seaver made a dramatic return as a Met. On opening day, 48,682 fans welcomed him back to Shea Stadium and he responded with six innings of shutout ball before giving way to Doug Sisk, who completed a 2-0 shutout of Steve Carlton and the Phillies. Seaver notched eight more victories, but he suffered from the same lack of support that marked most of his previous tour with the Mets. Seaver posted a 9-14 record, never missed a turn and pitched 231 innings. Torrez also was a workhorse, pitching 222⅓ innings and compiling a 10-17 mark.

Orosco wound up as the Mets' winningest pitcher with a 13-7 record and he recorded 17 saves and a 1.47 ERA. Sisk provided bullpen assistance with 11 saves and a 2.24 ERA. Ed Lynch and rookie Walt Terrell had the best records of the starters, going 10-10 and 8-8, respectively.

The Mets had the second-lowest team batting average in the league (.241) in '83 and were last in runs scored (575).

There were some bright spots offensively, though.

Strawberry, called up May 4, emerged as a potential superstar. After a horrible first month, the young right fielder finished with a .257 average, 26 homers, 74 runs batted in and 19 stolen bases.

Slick-fielding and solid-hitting Keith Hernandez, obtained from St. Louis on June 15 for pitchers Neil Allen and Ownbey, batted .306 and hit nine homers in his 95 games as a Met.

Foster, after a dismal '82 performance, batted only .241 but slugged 28 homers and had 90 RBIs. Mookie Wilson stole 54 bases, and Rusty Staub tied a major league record with eight consecutive pinch hits in one season.

One bright spot in the Mets' bleak season was Jesse Orosco, who now ranks among the best relievers in the N.L.

SCORES OF NEW YORK METS' 1983 GAMES

APRIL

			Winner	Loser
5—Phila.	W	2-0	Sisk	Carlton
7—Phila.	W	6-2	Swan	Denny
9—St. Louis	L	0-5	Andujar	Torrez
12—At Phila.	L	3-4*	Reed	Allen
13—At Phila.	L	9-10	Altamirano	Allen
14—At St. L.	L	1-7	Forsch	Torrez
15—At St. L.	L	2-5	Stuper	Holman
16—At St. L.	L	2-6	LaPoint	Lynch
20—Pittsburgh	W	6-0	Seaver	McWilliams
20—Pittsburgh	W	7-5	Diaz	Tekulve
22—At Atlanta	L	4-5	Garber	Allen
24—At Atlanta	L	3-6	Camp	Swan
24—At Atlanta	L	3-5	Bedrosian	Sisk
26—At Cinn.	L	0-7	Berenyi	Seaver
27—At Cinn.	W	2-1	Torrez	Price
29—Atlanta	W	6-5	Lynch	Camp
30—Atlanta	L	1-6	McMurtry	Ownbey

Won 6, Lost 11

MAY

1—Atlanta	L	1-2	Niekro	Seaver
2—Houston	L	2-3	Ryan	Torrez
3—Houston	L	4-7	Niekro	Swan
4—Houston	L	3-4	LaCoss	Ownbey
6—Cincinnati	W	7-4§	Orosco	Scherrer
7—Cincinnati	L	5-7	Berenyi	Torrez
8—Cincinnati	W	10-5	Orosco	Gale
9—At Hous.	L	4-6	Madden	Ownbey
10—At Hous.	L	4-5†	DiPino	Allen
11—At Hous.	W	3-0	Seaver	Scott
12—At Pitts.	L	2-6	Candelaria	Torrez
13—At Pitts.	L	1-2	Tekulve	Diaz
14—At Pitts.	W	6-2	Allen	McWilliams
16—At Pitts.	W	11-4	Lynch	Bibby
17—San Diego	W	6-4	Seaver	Lollar
18—San Diego	W	2-1	Torrez	Dravecky
19—San Diego	L	2-3	Show	Holman
20—Los Ang.	W	4-0	Allen	Reuss
22—Los Ang.	L	0-5	Welch	Seaver
23—San Fran.	W	4-3	Orosco	Minton
24—San Fran.	L	2-6	Krukow	Lynch
25—San Fran.	L	6-7	Martin	Allen
27—At S. Diego	L	0-4	Show	Seaver
28—At S. Diego	L	4-5	Dravecky	Torrez
29—At S. Diego	W	3-2	Lynch	Lollar
30—At S. Fran.	L	0-5	Breining	Allen
31—At S. Fran.	L	1-2	Laskey	Holman

Won 10, Lost 17

JUNE

1—At S. Fran.	L	2-4	Hammaker	Seaver
2—At L.A.	L	4-5x	Zachry	Orosco
3—At L.A.	W	5-2	Lynch	Beckwith
4—At L.A.	L	1-2	Hooton	Allen
5—At L.A.	W	4-2	Holman	Reuss
7—At Chicago	L	1-6	Rainey	Orosco
8—At Chicago	L	1-2	Smith	Torrez
9—At Chicago	W	6-4†	Orosco	Proly
10—Montreal	W	4-2z	Ownbey	Smith
11—Montreal	L	2-5	Lerch	Holman
12—Montreal	W	9-1	Seaver	Lea
13—Chicago	L	3-7	Trout	Torrez
14—Chicago	W	4-3*	Sisk	Smith
15—Chicago	L	4-7*	Smith	Holman
17—At Mon.	L	2-7	Lea	Seaver
18—At Mon.	W	6-1	Torrez	Gullickson
19—At Mon.	L	3-4	Rogers	Lynch
20—St. Louis	L	1-3	Hagen	Swan
20—St. Louis	W	6-4	Terrell	Stuper
21—St. Louis	L	0-6	Allen	Gorman
22—St. Louis	W	6-4	Seaver	Forsch
22—St. Louis	W	2-1	Torrez	Andujar
23—St. Louis	W	7-5	Diaz	Von Ohlen
24—Phila.	L	3-6	Carlton	Swan
25—Phila.	L	2-4	Gross	Terrell
26—Phila.	L	4-8	McGraw	Seaver
26—Phila.	W	5-1	Torrez	Farmer
28—At St. L.	W	10-1	Lynch	Forsch
28—At St. L.	L	1-8	LaPoint	Gorman
29—At St. L.	L	3-4	Sutter	Orosco
30—At St. L.	L	1-6	Allen	Terrell

Won 13, Lost 18

JULY

			Winner	Loser
1—At Phila.	L	1-5	Denny	Seaver
2—At Phila.	L	5-6	Holland	Orosco
2—At Phila.	W	4-3	Lynch	Farmer
3—At Phila.	L	4-6	Hernandez	Sisk
4—At Phila.	L	0-4	Carlton	Terrell
8—Houston	L	3-6	Ryan	Torrez
9—Houston	L	3-7	Niekro	Seaver
10—Houston	W	7-5	Sisk	Dawley
12—Cincinnati	L	2-6	Pastore	Torrez
13—Cincinnati	L	1-3	Price	Terrell
14—Cincinnati	W	7-4	Seaver	Puleo
15—At Hous.	L	0-6	Knepper	Lynch
16—At Hous.	L	1-3	Scott	Torrez
17—At Hous.	W	3-1	Terrell	Ryan
18—At Atlanta	L	4-7	Camp	Gorman
19—At Atlanta	L	7-11	Brizzolara	Orosco
20—At Atlanta	W	3-2	Lynch	Moore
21—At Cinn.	L	1-6	Puleo	Torrez
22—At Cinn.	W	3-2	Orosco	Hayes
23—At Cinn.	L	3-7	Berenyi	Gorman
24—At Cinn.	L	2-4	Price	Seaver
25—Atlanta	W	5-4	Sisk	Bedrosian
26—Atlanta	W	2-1*	Torrez	Dayley
27—Atlanta	L	3-6	McMurtry	Sisk
28—Pittsburgh	L	2-6	McWilliams	Swan
29—Pittsburgh	L	1-2	Candelaria	Seaver
30—Pittsburgh	L	3-6	Scurry	Lynch
31—Pittsburgh	W	7-6‡	Orosco	Bibby
31—Pittsburgh	W	1-0‡	Orosco	Sarmiento

Won 10, Lost 19

AUGUST

2—Montreal	W	5-2	Swan	Rogers
3—Montreal	W	2-1	Orosco	Reardon
4—Montreal	L	1-2	Lea	Lynch
5—At Chicago	W	9-4	Orosco	Proly
6—At Chicago	W	4-1	Terrell	Jenkins
7—At Chicago	W	6-4*	Sisk	Smith
8—At Mon.	W	6-5*	Orosco	Reardon
9—At Mon.	L	3-7	Lea	Lynch
10—At Mon.	L	3-5	Gullickson	Torrez
12—Chicago	W	2-0	Terrell	Jenkins
13—Chicago	W	5-1	Seaver	Bordi
14—Chicago	W	5-2	Lynch	Rainey
15—At Pitts.	L	2-4	DeLeon	Torrez
16—At Pitts.	L	1-3	Tunnell	Swan
17—At L.A.	L	1-4	Welch	Terrell
19—At S. Fran.	W	7-6*	Orosco	Minton
20—At S. Fran.	W	7-2	Lynch	Breining
21—At S. Fran.	W	4-3	Torrez	Hammaker
22—At S. Diego	L	3-4	Show	Swan
23—At S. Diego	W	8-3	Terrell	Montefusco
24—At S. Diego	L	2-3	Lollar	Seaver
26—San Fran.	L	1-12	Breining	Lynch
27—San Fran.	W	6-3	Torrez	Hammaker
28—San Fran.	L	2-7	Barr	Swan
29—Los Ang.	L	1-6	Welch	Seaver
29—Los Ang.	L	3-7	Hooton	Terrell
30—Los Ang.	W	3-2	Orosco	Niedenfuer
30—Los Ang.	L	1-2	Zachry	Holman
31—Los Ang.	W	7-1	Torrez	Valenzuela

Won 16, Lost 13

SEPTEMBER

2—San Diego	W	7-3	Terrell	Show
3—San Diego	W	4-3y	Gorman	Sosa
4—San Diego	L	5-7	Monge	Lynch
5—Phila.	W	6-5	Orosco	Holland
6—Phila.	L	0-2	McGraw	Darling
7—Phila.	L	1-6	Denny	Terrell
9—At Mon.	W	5-4	Seaver	Smith
10—At Mon.	L	9-10	Reardon	Orosco
11—At Mon.	L	0-4	Lea	Torrez
12—At Phila.	L	1-2	Denny	Darling
13—At Phila.	W	5-1	Terrell	Ghelfi
14—St. Louis	L	1-2	Allen	Seaver
15—St. Louis	W	6-4	Lynch	LaPoint
16—Chicago	L	4-7	Reuschel	Torrez
17—Chicago	L	6-7	Johnson	Orosco
18—Chicago	L	5-6	Campbell	Sisk
19—Pittsburgh	W	5-4*	Diaz	Tekulve
20—Pittsburgh	L	0-4	McWilliams	Lynch
21—At St. L.	L	3-9	Stuper	Torrez
22—At St. L.	L	2-3	Cox	Darling
23—At Chicago	L	1-4	Ruthven	Terrell
24—At Chicago	W	7-6	Seaver	Schulze
25—At Chicago	L	7-11	Patterson	Leary
27—At Pitts.	W	4-3	Torrez	DeLeon
28—At Pitts.	W	4-2	Darling	Tunnell
29—At Pitts.	L	2-4	Rhoden	Holman

Won 10, Lost 16

OCTOBER

1—Montreal	W	5-4	Gaff	Gullickson
2—Montreal	W	1-0	Terrell	Lea
2—Montreal	W	5-4	Leary	Reardon

Won 3, Lost 0

*10 innings. †11 innings. ‡12 innings. §13 innings. x14 innings. y15 innings. z17 innings.

Bob Welch, the Dodgers' most consistent starter, posted 15 victories and a 2.65 ERA.

Dodgers Rebuild and Still Win

By GORDON VERRELL

The Los Angeles Dodgers tried an interesting parlay in 1983. They attempted to rebuild and win at the same time.

The Dodgers accomplished their goal, inserting newcomers Greg Brock and Mike Marshall into a lineup in which Steve Garvey and Ron Cey had resided for a decade and then winning the National League West (by three games over Atlanta). But Los Angeles fell in the N.L. Championship Series to Philadelphia, three games to one.

Los Angeles won its division not so much because of Brock and Marshall, but because of a pitching staff that led the league in earned-run average, 3.10. At the All-Star Game break, the Dodgers' team ERA was 2.81.

But even the pitching, which figured to be strong, had to undergo change.

It started in the spring when Alejandro Pena, who had failed as a relief pitcher, was given a spot in the five-man starting rotation. It continued into June when left-handed relief ace Steve Howe, who earlier had received treatment for cocaine abuse, was sidelined again after a relapse. Howe didn't pitch for the Dodgers from May 18 through June 28.

Then, in August, the Dodgers obtained Texas lefthander Rick Honeycutt, who was leading the American League in ERA. But they parted with versatile pitcher Dave Stewart, whose loss would be severely felt in the playoffs against the Phillies.

And, in the critical last 10 days of the season, the Dodgers once more were without Howe, who had 18 saves and a 1.44 ERA. He missed a team charter to Atlanta, joined the club one day later and then returned home and was suspended for the rest of the season.

Howe's problems with drugs and "stress" (as his late-season troubles were diagnosed) were only part of the turmoil the Dodgers had to overcome. Within one week in June, Steve Sax and Bill Russell were burdened by the deaths of their fathers.

Sax had another problem. For some unexplained reason, he couldn't make an accurate throw from second base. By the All-Star break, he had 24 errors, five more than he had in all of 1982, his rookie year. But Sax made only six errors in the second half, and only one was on a bad throw.

The club's top slugger, Pedro Guerrero, had to make a difficult transition from right field to third base. There were skeptics, especially as his misplays mounted. Guerrero finished with 30 errors, the most by any third baseman in the majors. But he also became the first Los Angeles Dodger to hit 30 or more homers (he had 32) in two successive seasons, and he reached 100 runs batted in for the second straight year (he had 103).

Pedro Guerrero continued his slugging ways despite struggling defensively at third base.

The attention at the start of the year, though, focused on Brock, who had slugged 44 homers the year before at Albuquerque (Pacific Coast), and Marshall, who had hit .373 and .388 (in 66 games) in Triple-A in 1981 and 1982.

When Garvey turned down the Dodgers' offer of $5 million for four years and subsequently signed with San Diego, and Cey was traded to the Chicago Cubs one year before his contract expired, the youth movement was in full swing.

The breakup of the Dodgers' infield—the unit had been together for 8½ years—had begun a year earlier when Sax displaced Dave Lopes at second. All that remained now was Russell, the shortstop.

Brock had three spurts of note—his most resounding night was a two-homer, six-RBI game in Montreal on May 18—and finished with 20 homers, the most by a Dodger rookie since Frank Howard hit 23

SCORES OF LOS ANGELES DODGERS' 1983 GAMES

APRIL			Winner	Loser
5—At Hous.	W	16-7	Pena	LaCorte
6—At Hous.	W	4-2	Reuss	Smith
8—Montreal	L	3-8	Sanderson	Hooton
9—Montreal	L	2-7	Lea	Welch
10—Montreal	W	3-0	Valenzuela	Rogers
11—Houston	W	4-3‡	Howe	Solano
12—Houston	W	3-1	Pena	Ruhle
13—Houston	W	5-3y	Zachry	LaCorte
15—San Diego	W	6-2	Valenzuela	Whitson
16—San Diego	W	8-5	Reuss	Chiffer
17—San Diego	L	1-9	Dravecky	Welch
18—At S. Fran.	W	4-3	Niedenfuer	Minton
20—At S. Fran.	L	2-3†	Minton	Valenzuela
22—At Pitts.	W	4-2	Reuss	Rhoden
23—At Pitts.	W	3-2	Welch	Candelaria
25—At St. L.	W	8-0	Valenzuela	Andujar
26—At St. L.	W	3-1	Hooton	Stuper
27—At St. L.	L	6-7	Sutter	Pena
29—At Chicago	W	4-3	Pena	Campbell
30—At Chicago	L	2-7	Rainey	Valenzuela

Won 14, Lost 6

MAY				
1—At Chicago	W	3-2*	Stewart	Jenkins
2—Pittsburgh	L	1-5	Rhoden	Reuss
3—Pittsburgh	W	5-4	Pena	Bibby
4—Pittsburgh	W	3-2	Niedenfuer	Sarmiento
6—St. Louis	W	16-10	Stewart	Lahti
7—St. Louis	W	5-3	Howe	Bair
8—St. Louis	W	6-4	Reuss	Andujar
9—Chicago	W	4-3	Stewart	Smith
10—Chicago	L	2-3	Proly	Welch
12—At S. Diego	W	4-3	Valenzuela	DeLeon
13—At S. Diego	L	4-6	Dravecky	Hooton
14—At S. Diego	W	4-1	Reuss	Show
15—At S. Diego	W	3-2	Welch	Hawkins
17—At Mon.	L	2-3z	Schatzeder	Howe
18—At Mon.	W	13-3	Stewart	Gullickson
20—At N.Y.	L	0-4	Allen	Reuss
22—At N.Y.	W	5-0	Welch	Seaver
23—At Phila.	W	2-0	Valenzuela	Denny
24—At Phila.	W	3-0	Pena	Christenson
25—At Phila.	W	6-1	Hooton	Bystrom
26—San Fran.	L	3-5	Laskey	Reuss
27—San Fran.	L	3-6	Hammaker	Welch
28—San Fran.	W	5-0	Valenzuela	McGaffigan
29—San Fran.	L	4-6	Lavelle	Stewart
30—Phila.	W	5-2	Hooton	Bystrom
31—Phila.	W	4-1	Reuss	Hudson

Won 18, Lost 8

JUNE				
1—Phila.	W	1-0	Welch	Carlton
2—New York	W	5-4y	Zachry	Orosco
3—New York	L	2-5	Lynch	Beckwith
4—New York	W	2-1	Hooton	Allen
5—New York	L	2-4	Holman	Reuss
7—At Atlanta	L	1-4	Perez	Welch
8—At Atlanta	W	11-5	Valenzuela	Camp
9—At Atlanta	W	4-2	Stewart	Forster
10—At Cinn.	L	2-3	Puleo	Reuss
11—At Cinn.	W	3-2	Niedenfuer	Hayes
12—At Cinn.	L	1-3	Soto	Welch
13—At Cinn.	W	5-1	Valenzuela	Price
14—Atlanta	W	4-3	Hooton	McMurtry
15—Atlanta	L	2-3	Garber	Stewart
16—Atlanta	W	6-1	Pena	Camp
17—Cincinnati	W	1-0	Welch	Soto
18—Cincinnati	L	2-3	Price	Valenzuela
19—Cincinnati	W	5-1	Hooton	Berenyi
20—San Diego	L	1-4	Whitson	Reuss
21—San Diego	L	0-2	Lollar	Pena
22—San Diego	L	2-5	Show	Welch
23—San Diego	L	5-7	Dravecky	Valenzuela
24—Houston	W	7-2	Hooton	Niekro
25—Houston	W	2-1‡	Niedenfuer	Dawley
26—Houston	L	7-9	Scott	Pena
28—At S. Diego	W	9-5	Welch	Dravecky
29—At S. Diego	L	2-13	Thurmond	Valenzuela
30—At S. Diego	L	6-7	Montefusco	Howe

Won 14, Lost 14

JULY			Winner	Loser
1—At Hous.	W	5-2†	Pena	LaCorte
2—At Hous.	L	1-3	Ryan	Beckwith
3—At Hous.	L	1-8	Niekro	Welch
4—At Hous.	L	4-5	Smith	Howe
8—Pittsburgh	L	3-4	Candelaria	Reuss
9—Pittsburgh	L	0-3	McWilliams	Pena
10—Pittsburgh	W	10-3	Hooton	Rhoden
11—St. Louis	W	7-6	Beckwith	Sutter
12—St. Louis	W	3-1	Welch	Stuper
13—St. Louis	L	5-6	Rucker	Howe
14—Chicago	W	8-4	Pena	Trout
15—Chicago	L	4-8	Ruthven	Hooton
16—Chicago	W	7-4	Valenzuela	Jenkins
17—Chicago	L	0-10	Noles	Welch
19—At Pitts.	L	1-4	Candelaria	Reuss
19—At Pitts.	W	3-2‡	Howe	Sarmiento
20—At Pitts	L	3-7	Rhoden	Hooton
21—At Pitts.	L	4-5	Tekulve	Howe
22—At St. L.	W	9-4	Welch	Forsch
23—At St. L.	W	10-5	Howe	Rucker
24—At St. L.	L	0-3	Allen	Reuss
25—At Chicago	L	3-9	Trout	Hooton
26—At Chicago	W	5-2	Valenzuela	Ruthven
27—At Chicago	L	1-2	Smith	Welch
29—At S. Fran.	L	2-5	Krukow	Pena
30—At S. Fran.	L	0-8	Davis	Reuss
31—At. S. Fran.	W	2-1	Niedenfuer	Breining
31—At S. Fran.	L	6-8	Barr	Valenzuela

Won 11, Lost 17

AUGUST				
1—Cincinnati	L	2-4†	Hayes	Welch
2—Cincinnati	W	3-1	Pena	Pastore
3—Cincinnati	W	7-4	Zachry	Gale
4—Cincinnati	L	3-4‡	Hayes	Niedenfuer
5—Atlanta	W	2-1	Valenzuela	McMurtry
6—Atlanta	W	4-2	Welch	Camp
7—Atlanta	L	2-5	Perez	Pena
9—At Cinn.	L	4-5	Soto	Howe
10—At Cinn.	L	2-9	Berenyi	Hooton
11—At Cinn.	W	4-3	Niedenfuer	Puleo
12—At Atlanta	W	5-3	Welch	Perez
13—At Atlanta	L	7-8	Bedrosian	Howe
14—At Atlanta	W	5-4	Valenzuela	Niekro
15—San Fran.	L	3-7	Breining	Hooton
16—San Fran.	W	5-1	Reuss	Laskey
17—New York	W	4-1	Welch	Terrell
19—Phila.	W	3-0	Pena	Carlton
20—Phila.	W	4-3	Valenzuela	Bystrom
21—Phila.	W	6-0	Honeycutt	Gross
22—Montreal	W	4-1	Reuss	Rogers
23—Montreal	W	6-3	Zachry	Smith
24—Montreal	W	3-2	Niedenfuer	Reardon
26—At Phila.	L	1-4	Gross	Valenzuela
27—At Phila.	W	6-1	Honeycutt	Hudson
28—At Phila.	W	8-3	Reuss	Denny
29—At N.Y.	W	6-1	Welch	Seaver
29—At N.Y.	W	7-3	Hooton	Terrell
30—At N.Y.	L	2-3	Orosco	Niedenfuer
30—At N.Y.	W	2-1	Zachry	Holman
31—At N.Y.	L	1-7	Torrez	Valenzuela

Won 20, Lost 10

SEPTEMBER				
1—At Mon.	L	3-8	Lea	Honeycutt
2—At Mon.	W	4-1	Reuss	Rogers
3—At Mon.	W	4-0	Welch	Smith
4—At Mon.	L	2-3§	Schatzeder	Zachry
5—San Diego	L	2-5	Thurmond	Valenzuela
6—San Diego	L	3-8	Whitson	Honeycutt
7—Cincinnati	W	7-3†	Niedenfuer	Hayes
8—Cincinnati	W	5-2	Welch	Soto
9—Atlanta	W	3-2	Pena	Niekro
10—Atlanta	L	3-6†	Bedrosian	Beckwith
11—Atlanta	W	7-6	Beckwith	Garber
13—At Hous.	W	5-1	Reuss	Scott
14—At Hous.	L	2-4	Niekro	Welch
15—At Hous.	W	6-0	Pena	Ryan
16—At S. Fran.	L	0-1	Davis	Valenzuela
17—At S. Fran.	L	1-4	Breining	Honeycutt
18—At S. Fran.	L	3-6	Krukow	Reuss
19—Houston	W	9-2	Welch	Niekro
20—Houston	L	2-15	Ryan	Pena
21—Houston	W	2-1	Valenzuela	Ruhle
23—At Atlanta	W	11-2	Reuss	Barker
24—At Atlanta	L	2-3	Perez	Niedenfuer
25—At Atlanta	L	1-7	McMurtry	Pena
26—At Cinn.	W	12-9†	Zachry	Gale
27—At Cinn.	W	7-4	Beckwith	Russell
28—At S. Diego	T	4-4x	.....	.....
29—At S. Diego	L	1-7	Monge	Beckwith
29—At S. Diego	L	1-4	Hawkins	Pena
30—San Fran.	W	4-3	Valenzuela	Garrelts

Won 14, Lost 14

OCTOBER				
1—San Fran.	L	1-4	Davis	Hooton
2—San Fran.	L	3-4	Barr	Fernandez

Won 0, Lost 2

*5 innings. †10 innings. ‡11 innings. §12 innings. x13 innings. y14 innings. z15 innings.

in 1960. But Brock hit only one homer in the final month and batted a disappointing .224.

Marshall was hitting only .212 on June 2 when he caught fire, lifting his average to .292 in just two months. He finished at .284, second only on the Dodgers to Guerrero's .298.

The pitching carried the Dodgers to the top early, then went flat. The Braves slipped in front by one game on July 4 and built a 6½-game bulge by August 1. It was following a 9-2 loss in Cincinnati on August 10 that Dodgers Manager Tom Lasorda, showing more patience than in any of his seven seasons at the helm, staged his one and only outburst. The Dodgers, who had dropped 29 of 47 games from June 20 to that point, responded to go 30-21 in the final 7½ weeks.

Still 6½ games out as late as August 13, Los Angeles seized the West Division lead by August 29. And the Dodgers really jolted the Braves on September 11 when, trailing Atlanta, 6-3, entering the bottom of the ninth, they rallied for four runs and a 7-6 victory that dropped Atlanta three games back.

Bob Welch was the club's most consistent pitcher, winning 15 games and posting a 2.65 ERA. Fernando Valenzuela also finished with 15 victories, but had a 3.75 ERA and was only a 7-8 pitcher after mid-June. Pena (2.75 ERA) and Jerry Reuss were 12-game winners, but Reuss, in the final year of his contract, went 11 weeks without winning. Tom Niedenfuer emerged as the team's most dependable reliever (eight victories, 11 saves).

Burt Hooton won only one of his first eight starts, then won seven consecutive decisions, then lost five straight and wound up in the bullpen.

Veteran left fielder Dusty Baker labored through a poor first half, hitting only .231, but he batted .370 in July. He ended at .260, his lowest average in seven years. Center fielder Ken Landreaux hit 17 homers and batted .281.

The season was a satisfying one, inasmuch as the Dodgers won the division for the fourth time in seven years and drew a major league-leading 3,510,313 fans, the second-highest season attendance in baseball history (surpassed only by Los Angeles' 1982 total of 3,608,881).

But it was a rough year, too, especially because of the turmoil surrounding Howe and the sparks that followed Valenzuela's $1 million arbitration victory.

And Fernando, after all, is as much a part of the youth movement as Brock, 26, and Marshall, 24, are. Valenzuela has been in the big leagues since late 1980—but he's still only 23.

Newcomers Greg Brock (above) and Mike Marshall were inserted into the lineup and the Dodgers kept right on winning.

Center fielder Dale Murphy put together a super season and captured his second straight MVP award.

Late Slide Silences Brave Talk

By TIM TUCKER

It ended with a double-play combination of Paul Zuvella and Paul Runge. It ended with Bruce Benedict playing the part of manager. It ended quietly, unceremoniously.

The Atlanta Braves' 1983 season—one of such promise in March, such excitement in April, May, June and July, such bitter disappointment in late August and September—ended without a championship. The Braves, who had the best record in the big leagues for almost two midsummer months, finished with the majors' eighth-best mark at 88-74, three games behind the National League West champion Los Angeles Dodgers and one game behind Atlanta's division-winning record of 1982.

The Braves were eliminated with two games remaining in the season. "Those were the two longest days of the year for me," said Manager Joe Torre. "The only two games since I've been manager here that didn't mean something. And I don't like those kind of games; I had them for five years in New York (as manager of the Mets)."

To relieve the boredom of two post-elimination games, Torre played the kids, including shortstop Zuvella and second baseman Runge. And in game No. 162, he let catcher Benedict handle all the strategy decisions against the San Diego Padres.

That may have lightened the mood, but it also emphasized the vast difference a year had made. After the 162nd game in 1982, the Braves duly noted their first division championship since 1969 with a wild celebration in the visitors' clubhouse at San Diego Stadium.

The Braves, who began the 1982 season with 13 straight victories, got off to another rousing start in '83, winning seven of their first eight games and 13 of their first 16. At the All-Star Game break, they were 18 games over .500 at 49-31. And as late as August 13, they were 25 games over, 71-46, and 6½ games in front of the second-place Dodgers.

In Atlanta, the mayor formed a "World Series Task Force."

But after August 13, the Braves went downhill fast. On August 15, third baseman Bob Horner, who had a .303 batting average, 20 home runs and 68 runs batted in at the time, broke his right wrist and was sidelined for the remainder of the season. The bullpen soon fell apart. And so did the season. By August 29, Atlanta was in

Youngsters Craig McMurtry (above) and Pascual Perez emerged as the leaders of the Braves' pitching staff.

SCORES OF ATLANTA BRAVES' 1983 GAMES

APRIL

			Winner	Loser
4—At Cinn.	L	4-5	Soto	Bedrosian
6—At Cinn.	W	5-1	Perez	Berenyi
8—San Diego	W	4-2	Bedrosian	Chiffer
9—San Diego	W	6-5	Falcone	Welsh
10—San Diego	W	4-3	McMurtry	Whitson
11—San Diego	W	4-0	Perez	Lollar
12—Cincinnati	W	4-1	Behenna	Soto
13—Cincinnati	W	6-1	Camp	Pastore
16—At Phila.	L	4-8	Carlton	Niekro
17—At Phila.	W	3-1	Perez	Farmer
18—At S. Diego	L	3-10	Show	McMurtry
19—At S. Diego	W	9-2	Camp	Montefusco
22—New York	W	5-4	Garber	Allen
24—New York	W	6-3	Camp	Swan
24—New York	W	5-3	Bedrosian	Sisk
26—Phila.	W	10-4	Perez	Christenson
27—Phila.	L	2-6	Ruthven	Niekro
29—At N.Y.	L	5-6	Lynch	Camp
30—At N.Y.	W	6-1	McMurtry	Ownbey

Won 14, Lost 5

MAY

1—At N.Y.	W	2-1	Niekro	Seaver
3—At Mon.	W	5-2	Behenna	Grapenthin
4—At Mon.	L	1-4	Rogers	Camp
5—Houston	W	6-3	McMurtry	Knepper
6—Houston	L	0-6	DiPino	Niekro
7—Houston	W	10-1	Perez	Niekro
8—Houston	W	4-3	Behenna	LaCoss
9—Montreal	L	3-5	Rogers	Camp
10—Montreal	W	4-2	McMurtry	Sanderson
11—Montreal	L	5-8†	Schatzeder	Bedrosian
12—At Hous.	L	3-4*	DiPino	Falcone
13—At Hous.	L	2-5	LaCoss	Behenna
14—At Hous.	W	4-3*	Forster	Dawley
15—At Hous.	W	9-4	McMurtry	Knepper
17—At Chicago	L	3-4	Rainey	Perez
18—At Chicago	L	3-5	Trout	Behenna
20—At St. L.	W	2-1	McMurtry	LaPoint
21—At St. L	W	4-1	Bedrosian	Stuper
22—At St. L.	W	7-5†	Bedrosian	Sutter
23—Pittsburgh	W	6-3	Falcone	Rhoden
24—Pittsburgh	L	5-6	McWilliams	Camp
25—Pittsburgh	W	6-0	McMurtry	Bibby
26—Chicago	L	1-5	Moskau	Niekro
27—Chicago	L	6-8	Brusstar	Behenna
28—Chicago	W	6-4	Moore	Proly
29—Chicago	W	6-2	Camp	Ruthven
30—At Pitts.	L	6-8	Bibby	McMurtry
31—At Pitts.	W	10-2	Niekro	Tunnell

Won 16, Lost 12

JUNE

1—At Pitts.	W	6-3	Perez	Candelaria
2—St. Louis	W	8-1	Falcone	Forsch
3—St. Louis	W	5-3	Camp	LaPoint
4—St. Louis	W	6-4	Moore	Andujar
5—St. Louis	L	3-8	Stuper	Niekro
7—Los Ang.	W	4-1	Perez	Welch
8—Los Ang.	L	5-11	Valenzuela	Camp
9—Los Ang.	L	2-4	Stewart	Forster
10—San Fran.	L	4-6*	Lavelle	Camp
10—San Fran.	W	7-3	Falcone	Laskey
11—San Fran.	L	6-7	Hammaker	Garber
12—San Fran.	W	3-2	Perez	McGaffigan
14—At L.A.	L	3-4	Hooton	McMurtry
15—At L.A.	W	3-2	Garber	Stewart
16—At L.A.	L	1-6	Pena	Camp
17—At S. Fran.	L	1-2	Hammaker	Perez
18—At S. Fran.	L	4-5	Lavelle	Garber
19—At S. Fran.	L	6-9	Krukow	McMurtry
20—At Hous.	W	7-1	Falcone	Ruhle
21—At Hous.	L	0-5	Scott	Niekro
22—At Hous.	L	3-4	Dawley	Garber
24—At Cinn.	W	3-0	McMurtry	Price
24—At Cinn.	W	10-5	Dayley	Berenyi
25—At Cinn.	W	8-2	Falcone	Puleo
26—At Cinn.	W	5-1	Niekro	Pastore
27—At Cinn.	W	2-1	Perez	Soto
28—Houston	L	3-4	Ryan	Forster
29—Houston	W	11-1	Dayley	Niekro
30—Houston	W	6-4	Bedrosian	DiPino

Won 16, Lost 13

JULY

			Winner	Loser
1—Cincinnati	W	5-2	Niekro	Pastore
2—Cincinnati	W	4-2	Perez	Soto
3—Cincinnati	L	1-2	Price	McMurtry
4—Cincinnati	W	9-5	Falcone	Berenyi
8—At Mon.	W	6-5	McMurtry	Lea
9—At Mon.	W	8-5*	Forster	Smith
10—At Mon.	L	6-7	Reardon	Moore
11—At Mon.	W	6-4	Camp	Fryman
12—At Phila.	L	1-4	Denny	Dayley
12—At Phila.	L	6-7	Hernandez	Bedrosian
13—At Phila.	W	5-2	McMurtry	Carlton
14—At Phila.	W	5-2	Bedrosian	Hernandez
15—Montreal	W	9-3	Niekro	Gullickson
16—Montreal	W	6-3	Falcone	Burris
17—Montreal	L	1-3	Bargar	Dayley
18—New York	W	7-4	Camp	Gorman
19—New York	W	11-7	Brizzolara	Orosco
20—New York	L	2-3	Lynch	Moore
21—Phila.	L	6-10	Denny	Camp
22—Phila.	W	6-1	McMurtry	Gross
23—Phila.	W	6-5	Camp	Hernandez
24—Phila.	W	12-4	Perez	Bystrom
25—At N.Y.	L	4-5	Sisk	Bedrosian
26—At N.Y.	L	1-2*	Torrez	Dayley
27—At N.Y.	W	6-3	McMurtry	Sisk
29—At S. Diego	W	2-1	Perez	Lollar
29—At S. Diego	L	5-6‡	Monge	Moore
30—At S. Diego	W	5-2	Niekro	Dravecky
31—At S. Diego	L	2-5	Thurmond	McMurtry

Won 18, Lost 11

AUGUST

1—At S. Fran.	W	8-3	Camp	McGaffigan
2—At S. Fran.	L	3-7	Krukow	Perez
3—At S. Fran.	W	6-4	Bedrosian	Barr
4—At S. Fran.	W	8-1	Niekro	Breining
5—At L.A.	L	1-2	Valenzuela	McMurtry
6—At L.A.	L	2-4	Welch	Camp
7—At L.A.	W	5-2	Perez	Pena
9—San Fran.	W	7-2	Niekro	Calvert
10—San Fran.	L	4-7	Minton	Bedrosian
11—San Fran.	W	6-4	Dayley	Laskey
12—Los Ang.	L	3-5	Welch	Perez
13—Los Ang.	W	8-7	Bedrosian	Howe
14—Los Ang.	L	4-5	Valenzuela	Niekro
15—San Diego	L	0-4	Dravecky	McMurtry
16—San Diego	L	2-3*	Monge	Bedrosian
18—At Chicago	L	0-3	Jenkins	Falcone
19—At Chicago	W	5-3	Niekro	Rainey
20—At Chicago	W	9-2	Dayley	Trout
21—At Chicago	W	11-9	Camp	Ruthven
23—At St. L.	L	0-7	Andujar	Falcone
24—At St. L.	W	11-3	Niekro	LaPoint
25—At St. L.	L	1-2	Allen	Bedrosian
26—At Pitts.	L	1-9	McWilliams	Perez
27—At Pitts.	L	0-2	Tunnell	Dayley
28—At Pitts.	W	2-1	Falcone	Candelaria
29—Chicago	L	5-7	Campbell	Garber
30—Chicago	L	6-9	Rainey	McMurtry
31—St. Louis	L	3-6	Andujar	Barker

Won 12, Lost 16

SEPTEMBER

1—St. Louis	L	3-8	Forsch	Perez
2—Pittsburgh	L	1-4	Candelaria	Dayley
3—Pittsburgh	L	2-6	Bibby	Bedrosian
4—Pittsburgh	W	6-5	Forster	Bibby
5—Houston	W	7-5	Barker	Niekro
7—At S. Fran.	L	1-2	Garrelts	Perez
8—At S. Fran.	W	12-9	Garber	Minton
9—At L.A.	L	2-3	Pena	Niekro
10—At L.A.	W	6-3*	Bedrosian	Beckwith
11—At L.A.	L	6-7	Beckwith	Garber
13—At Cinn.	L	0-6	Soto	Perez
14—At Cinn.	L	4-6	Pastore	Niekro
16—San Diego	W	6-0	McMurtry	Lollar
17—San Diego	L	1-2	DeLeon	Barker
18—San Diego	L	2-4§	Lucas	Dayley
21—Cincinnati	W	9-1	McMurtry	Puleo
21—Cincinnati	L	3-4	Hume	Bedrosian
22—Cincinnati	L	4-6	Russell	Dayley
23—Los Ang.	L	2-11	Reuss	Barker
24—Los Ang.	W	3-2	Perez	Niedenfuer
25—Los Ang.	W	7-1	McMurtry	Pena
26—San Fran.	W	6-2	Niekro	Calvert
27—San Fran.	L	2-6	Davis	Bedrosian
28—At Hous.	W	3-1	Perez	Scott
28—At Hous.	L	1-5	Niekro	Dayley
29—At Hous.	W	5-4	Garber	Ruhle
30—At S. Diego	L	2-3	Show	Niekro

Won 11, Lost 16

OCTOBER

1—At S. Diego	L	3-4*	Monge	Falcone
2—At S. Diego	W	4-3	Dayley	Booker

Won 1, Lost 1

*10 innings. †11 innings. ‡12 innings. §13 innings.

second place.

In their final 45 games, the Braves were 17-28. The club's top two relievers of 1982, Steve Bedrosian and Gene Garber, had a collective 7.01 earned-run average in the final seven weeks (although Bedrosian managed to record 19 saves in '83). The pitching deteriorated so much after August 13 that the Braves won only four times the rest of the season in games in which they scored fewer than five runs. And without Horner in the lineup, the offense slipped, too.

With 10 games remaining in the season, Atlanta fell 5½ games behind. At that point, Braves Owner Ted Turner sought out Dodgers Manager Tommy Lasorda and wished him well in the playoffs. It was over, and the Braves knew it.

Dale Murphy, the Braves' brilliant center fielder, did all he could to offset the loss of Horner. The particulars:

Murphy batted .302, hit 36 homers (second in the league), drove in a league-leading 121 runs, scored 131 runs (second in the league and a modern Braves record) and stole 30 bases. His 1983 performance marked only the sixth time in N.L. history that a player had hit 30 homers and stolen 30 bases in the same season. And Murphy played superb defense.

Individually, there were other standouts. Young righthanders Craig McMurtry and Pascual Perez won 15 games apiece. Second baseman Glenn Hubbard had his most productive offensive season (.263, 12 homers, 70 RBIs). Rafael Ramirez continued to improve at shortstop and hit .297, and Benedict batted .298. Chris Chambliss had a typically productive year (.280, 20 homers, 78 RBIs). Bob Watson, who had 37 RBIs in only 149 at-bats, made major contributions off the bench. And reliever Terry Forster was excellent with 13 saves and a 2.16 ERA.

So what made the difference in the championship year of '82 and the disappointing season of '83?

1. The bullpen slipped. If the Braves won the division because of their bullpen in '82, they lost out because of their relievers in '83. Only Forster was consistently effective.

2. Starter Phil Niekro slipped. He fell from 17-4 in '82 to 11-10 in '83, and the Braves—in a controversial move—gave the 44-year-old righthander his unconditional release after the season. Niekro's days in a Braves uniform dated to 1964, when the club was still in Milwaukee.

3. Claudell Washington slipped. He was roughly half as productive as the year before, falling from 16 homers to nine and from 80 RBIs to 44. He hit .205 with runners in scoring position and played erratically in right field.

Bob Horner was an offensive force until an August 15 injury ended his season.

4. Horner's injury. Yes, Horner was injured late in the '82 season, too. But he missed only the last two weeks of that season, compared with the last seven weeks of '83. The Braves are not the same team without him.

5. Jerry Royster slipped. Over the last two months of the '82 race, Royster batted .326 and Torre called him "our most valuable player." But after being thrust into an important role because of the injury to Horner, Royster hit only .159 in the final two months of '83.

Otherwise, the Braves had some of the same problems they experienced but overcame in '82. The starters completed only 18 games, compared to 15 the year before, and Atlanta still didn't have the pitching quality or depth it needed. The late-August acquisition of Len Barker from Cleveland did not make a difference in the '83 pennant chase, but the Braves see Barker as one of their top starting pitchers for the next few seasons.

"Hopefully," Torre said minutes after the '83 season ended, "our last two regular-season games won't mean anything next year, either. But hopefully, that will be because we have already clinched the division championship."

Dickie Thon established himself as one of the top shortstops in the National League.

Astro Turnabout Is Fair Play

By HARRY SHATTUCK

It was almost as if the Astros played two seasons in 1983.

The first began in February in ankle-deep mud at Cocoa, Fla., reached its low point in mid-April with an agonizing string of defeats and ended in early June.

Choose any word connoting negatives. Depressing. Stunning. Frustrating. Sickening. All applied. The Astros lost 16 of 19 exhibition games. They tied a National League record by dropping their first nine regular-season games. Combined, that's 25 defeats in 28 outings.

By June 3, Houston was 13½ games out of first place in the N.L. West. Home attendance was more than 300,000 behind the disappointing 1982 pace.

Would Bob Lillis survive his first full year as a major league manager? Would General Manager Al Rosen last until his contract expired in November?

Then came the second season.

Suddenly, the Astros clicked. From June 4 through September 2, they won 50 games and lost 32 and moved within six games of first place. The team which in April was labeled the "worst in baseball" had evolved into one of the best by season's end.

Houston steadily pecked away at the teams ahead of it in the standings. The Astros left Cincinnati far behind, passed San Francisco, then San Diego.

By early September they were, if not in a pennant race, on the periphery, needing only one noteworthy winning streak or a collapse by the Dodgers and Braves to complete a remarkable comeback.

Alas, there was no Cinderella finish for the Astros—only third place. But from the reaction in Houston, it was as if this team, through its never-say-die approach, had won a championship.

And why not? After starting 0-9, the Astros finished 85-77—a gain of 17 games over .500. They trailed N.L. West champion Los Angeles by six games at the end and were just three games behind second-place Atlanta.

Home attendance picked up. Lillis and all five coaches were rewarded with two-year contract extensions. Rosen signed a new three-year agreement.

And the future loomed bright.

In 1983, Houston fielded a middle-infield combination of shortstop Dickie Thon and second baseman Bill Doran which could rate with the best in the game for several years.

The Astros also developed a one-two rookie bullpen punch in lefthander Frank DiPino (20 saves) and righthander Bill Dawley (14 saves), a combination which also figures to stand out in seasons ahead.

Houston's starting pitching, led by Nolan Ryan (14-9) and Joe Niekro (15-14), remained sound. Mike Scott, acquired from the Mets, was 10-6, and rookie Mike Madden went 9-5.

And Houston's offense has seldom been more potent.

Jose Cruz, a talented if unsung performer for nine seasons in Houston, enjoyed his best year ever, hitting .318 and contending for the batting title until the final day.

Ray Knight batted .304, Terry Puhl (who rebounded strongly after two sub-par seasons) hit .292 and Thon finished at .286.

Thon stole 34 bases, hammered 20 home runs, scored 81 times, drove in 79 runs, led the league with 18 game-winning runs batted in and made spectacular plays afield.

But Thon was edged for club most-valuable-player honors by Cruz, who had 92 RBIs, 85 runs scored and 30 steals. Cruz also performed well defensively in left field.

Jerry Mumphrey, acquired from the Yankees in August to replace an unhappy Omar Moreno, hit .336 in 44 games.

Doran, a rookie, proved an ideal leadoff batter, combining 145 hits and 86 walks for an on-base percentage of .372.

Phil Garner, though not a classic cleanup batter and mired in a slump much of the second half, was a key man offensively early in the season—he had knocked in 45 runs by the All-Star Game break—and finished with 79 RBIs.

There were a few disappointments. Catcher Alan Ashby was bothered much of the year by injuries and hit only .229. Pitcher Bob Knepper recorded a 3.19 earned-run average, but his 6-13 record wasn't positive. Garner (third base) and Knight (first base) tackled new positions and understandably endured growing pains. Veteran relievers Dave Smith and Frank LaCorte were troubled by injuries and experienced off years (although Smith managed a 3.10 ERA).

The biggest defensive problem was a familiar one in Houston—an inability to throw out baserunners, who stole 182 times and were caught (excluding pick-offs) only 43 times.

SCORES OF HOUSTON ASTROS' 1983 GAMES

APRIL

			Winner	Loser
5—Los Ang.	L	7-16	Pena	LaCorte
6—Los Ang.	L	2-4	Reuss	Smith
7—Pittsburgh	L	2-3	Scurry	Knepper
8—Pittsburgh	L	3-5	Scurry	DiPino
9—Pittsburgh	L	0-1	McWilliams	Niekro
10—Pittsburgh	L	8-10	Bibby	Solano
11—At L.A.	L	3-4†	Howe	Solano
12—At L.A.	L	1-3	Pena	Ruhle
13—At L.A.	L	3-5§	Zachry	LaCorte
15—Montreal	W	7-6*	Dawley	Burris
16—Montreal	L	0-2	Lea	Knepper
17—Montreal	W	6-3	Ryan	Gullickson
19—Cincinnati	W	6-5	Dawley	Hume
20—Cincinnati	L	4-6	Gale	LaCoss
21—Cincinnati	W	4-3*	LaCorte	Hume
22—Phila.	L	3-6	Monge	Ryan
23—Phila.	L	3-7	Denny	Niekro
24—Phila.	W	3-2†	Madden	Reed
26—At Mon.	W	2-0	Knepper	Gullickson
27—At Mon.	W	4-2	Ryan	Sanderson
29—At Phila.	W	6-3*	LaCorte	Carlton
30—At Phila.	L	0-8	Denny	LaCoss

Won 8, Lost 14

MAY

1—At Phila.	L	3-11	Christenson	Knepper
2—At N.Y.	W	3-2	Ryan	Torrez
3—At N.Y.	W	7-4	Niekro	Swan
4—At N.Y.	W	4-3	LaCoss	Ownbey
5—At Atlanta	L	3-6	McMurtry	Knepper
6—At Atlanta	W	6-0	DiPino	Niekro
7—At Atlanta	L	1-10	Perez	Niekro
8—At Atlanta	L	3-4	Behenna	LaCoss
9—New York	W	6-4	Madden	Ownbey
10—New York	W	5-4†	DiPino	Allen
11—New York	L	0-3	Seaver	Scott
12—Atlanta	W	4-3*	DiPino	Falcone
13—Atlanta	W	5-2	LaCoss	Behenna
14—Atlanta	L	3-4*	Forster	Dawley
15—Atlanta	L	4-9	McMurtry	Knepper
17—At St. L.	L	4-8	Forsch	Niekro
18—At St. L.	L	5-9	Andujar	DiPino
20—At Pitts.	L	3-4	McWilliams	Knepper
21—At Pitts.	W	6-4	LaCoss	Niemann
23—Chicago	W	3-2	Niekro	Trout
24—Chicago	L	4-5	Ruthven	Scott
25—Chicago	W	1-0	Madden	Lefferts
26—St. Louis	L	3-5	Von Ohlen	LaCoss
27—St. Louis	L	1-3x	Lahti	Knepper
28—St. Louis	W	9-2	Niekro	Martin
29—St. Louis	L	3-7	LaPoint	Scott
30—At Chicago	W	9-7	Dawley	Campbell
31—At Chicago	W	12-10	LaCorte	Lefferts

Won 14, Lost 14

JUNE

1—At Chicago	L	2-3	Rainey	Knepper
3—At Cinn.	L	1-3	Price	Niekro
4—At Cinn.	W	13-0	Scott	Berenyi
5—At Cinn.	W	6-3	Ruhle	Scherrer
7—San Fran.	W	4-2	LaCorte	Hammaker
8—San Fran.	W	1-0†	Dawley	Lavelle
9—San Fran.	W	3-0	Knepper	Krukow
10—San Diego	W	2-1	LaCoss	Whitson
11—San Diego	L	4-8	Montefusco	Ruhle
12—San Diego	W	2-0	Ryan	Show
13—San Diego	W	2-0	Niekro	Dravecky
14—At S. Fran.	W	3-2‡	Smith	Minton
15—At S. Fran.	L	1-7	Breining	LaCoss
16—At S. Fran.	W	7-2	Scott	Laskey
17—At S. Diego	W	4-1	Ryan	Show
18—At S. Diego	L	1-2†	Dravecky	LaCorte
19—At S. Diego	L	4-6	Sosa	Knepper
20—Atlanta	L	1-7	Falcone	Ruhle
21—Atlanta	W	5-0	Scott	Niekro
22—Atlanta	W	4-3	Dawley	Garber
24—At L.A.	L	2-7	Hooton	Niekro
25—At L.A.	L	1-2†	Niedenfuer	Dawley
26—At L.A.	W	9-7	Scott	Pena
28—At Atlanta	W	4-3	Ryan	Forster
29—At Atlanta	L	1-11	Dayley	Niekro
30—At Atlanta	L	4-6	Bedrosian	DiPino

Won 15, Lost 11

JULY

			Winner	Loser
1—Los Ang.	L	2-5*	Pena	LaCorte
2—Los Ang.	W	3-1	Ryan	Beckwith
3—Los Ang.	W	8-1	Niekro	Welch
4—Los Ang.	W	5-4	Smith	Howe
8—At N.Y.	W	6-3	Ryan	Torrez
9—At N.Y.	W	7-3	Niekro	Seaver
10—At N.Y.	L	5-7	Sisk	Dawley
12—Montreal	W	7-5	Ruhle	Lerch
13—Montreal	W	9-4	Ryan	Lea
14—Montreal	W	3-0	Niekro	Rogers
15—New York	W	6-0	Knepper	Lynch
16—New York	W	3-1	Scott	Torrez
17—New York	L	1-3	Terrell	Ryan
18—At Phila.	W	8-2	Niekro	Carlton
19—At Phila.	W	7-3	Knepper	Bystrom
20—At Phila.	L	3-10	Hudson	Scott
21—At Mon.	L	4-9	Gullickson	Ryan
22—At Mon.	W	11-8	Smith	Fryman
23—At Mon.	L	1-4	Schatzeder	Knepper
24—At Mon.	L	3-7	Rogers	LaCoss
26—Phila.	L	0-1	Hudson	Ryan
27—Phila.	L	1-3	Denny	Niekro
28—Phila.	L	5-6	Reed	LaCoss
29—Cincinnati	W	4-1	Madden	Price
30—Cincinnati	L	2-3	Soto	Ryan
31—Cincinnati	W	9-2	Niekro	Berenyi

Won 15, Lost 11

AUGUST

1—At S. Diego	L	4-7*	DeLeon	Dawley
2—At S. Diego	W	4-2‡	Ruhle	Monge
3—At S. Diego	W	1-0	Ryan	Lollar
4—At S. Diego	L	2-4	Dravecky	Niekro
5—At S. Fran.	L	1-7	Laskey	Knepper
6—At S. Fran.	W	4-2	Madden	Martin
7—At S. Fran.	W	2-1	Ryan	Minton
9—San Diego	L	2-3	Lollar	Niekro
10—San Diego	W	4-3§	Ruhle	DeLeon
11—San Diego	W	5-1	Scott	Thurmond
12—San Fran.	W	5-2	Ryan	Martin
13—San Fran.	W	4-1	Niekro	Krukow
14—San Fran.	L	2-5	Davis	Madden
15—At Cinn.	W	9-1	Knepper	Berenyi
16—At Cinn.	W	8-5	Scott	Puleo
17—At Cinn.	W	7-6	Ruhle	Pastore
18—At St. L.	L	4-5*	Rucker	Dawley
19—At St. L.	L	0-2	LaPoint	Madden
20—At St. L.	L	0-3	Stuper	Knepper
21—At St. L.	L	2-5	Cox	Ryan
23—At Pitts.	W	6-5	Ruhle	Tekulve
23—At Pitts.	W	2-1	Niekro	Tunnell
24—At Pitts.	W	10-4	Madden	Rhoden
25—At Pitts.	L	3-5	DeLeon	Knepper
26—Chicago	W	1-0	Ruhle	Trout
27—Chicago	L	5-9	Ruthven	Niekro
28—Chicago	W	4-2	Scott	Noles
29—St. Louis	L	1-6	Stuper	Madden
30—St. Louis	W	3-1	Ruhle	Cox
31—Pittsburgh	W	4-1	Niekro	Scurry

Won 18, Lost 12

SEPTEMBER

1—Pittsburgh	W	3-0	Ryan	Guante
2—At Chicago	W	6-5	Dawley	Campbell
3—At Chicago	L	3-9	Jenkins	Madden
4—At Chicago	L	7-9	Brusstar	Dawley
5—At Atlanta	L	5-7	Barker	Niekro
7—At S. Diego	L	7-8	Monge	DiPino
8—At S. Diego	W	3-2*	Madden	DeLeon
9—At S. Fran.	W	7-4	Niekro	Davis
10—At S. Fran.	W	5-3	Heathcock	Breining
11—At S. Fran.	L	2-3	Minton	Ryan
13—Los Ang.	L	1-5	Reuss	Scott
14—Los Ang.	W	4-2	Niekro	Welch
15—Los Ang.	L	0-6	Pena	Ryan
16—At Cinn.	L	3-8	Berenyi	Heathcock
17—At Cinn.	W	4-3	Madden	Russell
18—At Cinn.	W	4-1	Scott	Soto
19—At L.A.	L	2-9	Welch	Niekro
20—At L.A.	W	15-2	Ryan	Pena
21—At L.A.	L	1-2	Valenzuela	Ruhle
23—San Fran.	L	2-3	Breining	Niekro
24—San Fran.	W	6-5	Scott	Krukow
25—San Fran.	L	0-3	Garrelts	Ryan
26—San Diego	W	5-3	Madden	Show
27—San Diego	W	8-5	Knepper	Lollar
28—Atlanta	L	1-3	Perez	Scott
28—Atlanta	W	5-1	Niekro	Dayley
29—Atlanta	L	4-5	Garber	Ruhle
30—Cincinnati	W	3-2	LaCoss	Puleo

Won 14, Lost 14

OCTOBER

1—Cincinnati	L	4-6	Pastore	Madden
2—Cincinnati	W	3-2	Heathcock	Russell

Won 1, Lost 1

*10 innings. †11 innings. ‡12 innings. §14 innings. x18 innings.

Jose Cruz hit .318 and enjoyed the best overall season of a solid career.

The only controversy involved Moreno, who asked to be traded if Lillis wasn't planning to play him every day. Moreno, neither hitting nor fielding well at the time, was benched, then traded.

The Moreno situation became a plus. It seemed to signal a new-found, unified approach within the Astros' management. Rosen strongly backed his manager, Owner John McMullen strongly backed Rosen—and the club seemed the better for it.

Rosen, who stepped into a hornet's nest in October of 1980 when he replaced popular General Manager Tal Smith, finally was judged on his own decisions.

Rosen's trades since taking over for Smith proved significant in the Astros' 1983 performance. They included the dealing of pitcher Ken Forsch to California for Thon; of pitcher Don Sutton to Milwaukee for DiPino, Madden and outfielder Kevin Bass; of outfielder Cesar Cedeno to Cincinnati for Knight; of catcher Alan Knicely to the Reds for Dawley and a minor league outfielder; of outfielder Danny Heep to the Mets for Scott; of second baseman Johnny Ray and two others to Pittsburgh for Garner, and of Moreno for Mumphrey.

For his part, Lillis drew raves, not only for his strategy but for holding the club together during the early crisis. Lillis' low-key approach, refusal to panic and continual optimism were cited as key factors in Houston's improvement.

Lillis, however, preferred to credit his players.

"Nobody ever gave up," Lillis said. "We had a tough spring training (bad drainage made practice fields unplayable for several days), we lost a lot of games early that we could have won and we had some injuries (10 Astros were on the disabled list in '83, including Ryan twice).

"But our players didn't quit. I'm proud of this team. And I'm excited about our future."

Catcher Terry Kennedy put together a solid season and led the Padres in numerous offensive categories.

Padres Pass Survival Test

By PHIL COLLIER

The San Diego Padres continued to make progress in 1983, despite merely duplicating their 81-81 record and fourth-place standing of the previous season.

"We're much further along than we were at the end of 1982," Dick Williams said after his second season as the Padres' manager.

The Padres' front office and San Diego fans thought the signing of free-agent first baseman Steve Garvey to a five-year, $6.5 million contract in December of 1982 would enable the club to field its first legitimate title contender in the franchise's 15-year history.

Garvey did provide the righthanded power that Williams needed so badly, but the veteran became a victim of an injury wave that doomed the Padres to their 15th consecutive fourth-or-lower overall finish in the National League West.

The team could never get untracked after outfielder Tony Gwynn missed most of the first half of the season because of a broken wrist he suffered in winter ball.

Shortstop Garry Templeton, who underwent arthroscopic knee surgery in early March, and pitcher Ed Whitson, who pulled a muscle in his left side, both missed almost all of spring training.

Lefthander Tim Lollar, a 16-game winner in 1982, developed a tender elbow in a season-opening 16-13 victory at San Francisco and, after two more starts totaling 7⅔ innings, was forced to rest for three weeks. Whitson, finally recovered from his side ailment, injured a knee in mid-April, underwent arthroscopic surgery and was lost for six weeks.

Lefthander Dave Dravecky, who posted a 14-10 record and recorded nine complete games, ended his season on a sour note when a shoulder problem sidelined him for the final five weeks.

Garvey was batting .294 with 14 homers and 59 runs batted in when he dislocated his left thumb in a late-July collision at home plate and was lost for the remainder of the season. Garvey's consecutive-game playing streak, which ranked third on the majors' all-time list, thus was snapped at an N.L.-best 1,207.

Garvey's absence made it easier for the opposition to pitch around the other half of the Padres' one-two punch, Terry Kennedy, and yet the strapping catcher led the team in nearly every offensive category: home runs (17), RBIs (98), game-winning RBIs (14), doubles (27) and sacrifice flies (nine). He batted .284.

The injuries forced the Padres to make moves that are likely to serve them well in the future.

Former Yankee outfielder Bobby Brown, called up from Las Vegas to take Garvey's spot on the roster, developed into the leadoff hitter the club had needed. The switch-hitter had a 21-game hitting streak, stole 27 bases and scored 40 runs in his 57 games, batted .267 and contributed five homers.

Outfielder Alan Wiggins, switched to first base in Garvey's absence, set a club record with 66 stolen bases (in 79 tries), batted .276 and led the Padres in runs scored (83).

The injuries to Lollar and Whitson (obtained in a trade with Cleveland) opened a spot in the starting rotation for Mark Thurmond, a rookie lefthander who compiled a 7-3 record and a 2.65 earned-run average after being called up from Las Vegas on June 28.

Management apparently decided early in the season that it would make little or no attempt to retain two veteran outfielders who became eligible for free agency in November. One, Gene Richards, previously had been a fixture in left field; the other, Ruppert Jones, had been an All-Star Game participant in 1982.

The plan was to develop an outfield unit of Wiggins, Gwynn and Kevin McReynolds, the latter a 23-year-old righthanded power hitter who batted .377 at Las Vegas in 1983 with 32 homers and 116 RBIs. McReynolds flunked a midseason major league trial, but hit two homers and batted .269 after being recalled in September.

Gwynn recovered from his wrist injury to lead the Padres in hitting (.309) and set a club record with a late-season 25-game hitting streak, longest in the majors in '83.

The Padres sometimes despaired of third baseman Luis Salazar's defensive play, but Salazar tried to atone for his 21 errors by hitting 14 homers, a club record for third basemen, and stealing 24 bases.

His left knee having improved as the season wore on, Templeton batted .301 in the last seven weeks and finished with a .263 average (highest ever by a San Diego shortstop).

Pitchers Eric Show (15-12) and Andy Hawkins (5-7, 2.93 ERA) combined with Lollar (7-12), Thurmond, Dravecky, Whitson (5-7) and rookie Dennis Rasmussen to create spirited competition for starting jobs.

SCORES OF SAN DIEGO PADRES' 1983 GAMES

APRIL			Winner	Loser
5—At S. Fran.	W	16-13	Lollar	Krukow
6—At S. Fran.	W	5-3	Dravecky	Laskey
8—At Atlanta	L	2-4	Bedrosian	Chiffer
9—At Atlanta	L	5-6	Falcone	Welsh
10—At Atlanta	L	3-4	McMurtry	Whitson
11—At Atlanta	L	0-4	Perez	Lollar
12—San Fran.	L	5-6	Breining	Dravecky
13—San Fran.	W	2-1	Show	Hammaker
14—San Fran.	W	6-4	Montefusco	McGaffigan
15—At L.A.	L	2-6	Valenzuela	Whitson
16—At L.A.	L	5-8	Reuss	Chiffer
17—At L.A.	W	9-1	Dravecky	Welch
18—Atlanta	W	10-3	Show	McMurtry
19—Atlanta	L	2-9	Camp	Montefusco
22—At St. L.	W	4-1	Dravecky	Forsch
23—At St. L.	L	5-9	Martin	Show
24—At St. L.	L	0-2	LaPoint	Hawkins
26—At Chicago	W	10-8	Montefusco	Lefferts
27—At Chicago	L	4-5*	Campbell	Lucas
28—At Chicago	W	3-1	Show	Trout
30—At Pitts.	W	8-4	Hawkins	Candelaria
30—At Pitts.	L	1-2	McWilliams	DeLeon

Won 10, Lost 12

MAY				
3—St. Louis	W	4-3	Dravecky	Forsch
4—St. Louis	W	10-0	Show	Andujar
5—St. Louis	L	3-4	Sutter	Lucas
6—Chicago	L	2-3	Rainey	Lollar
7—Chicago	L	4-6	Campbell	Lucas
8—Chicago	W	5-3	Dravecky	Brusstar
9—Pittsburgh	L	3-5x	Sarmiento	Couchee
10—Pittsburgh	W	4-1	Hawkins	Scurry
12—Los Ang.	L	3-4	Valenzuela	DeLeon
13—Los Ang.	W	6-4	Dravecky	Hooton
14—Los Ang.	L	1-4	Reuss	Show
15—Los Ang.	L	2-3	Welch	Hawkins
17—At N.Y.	L	4-6	Seaver	Lollar
18—At N.Y.	L	1-2	Torrez	Dravecky
19—At N.Y.	W	3-2	Show	Holman
20—At Phila.	W	5-0	Hawkins	Carlton
23—At Mon.	L	1-3	Gullickson	Dravecky
24—At Mon.	L	4-5§	Reardon	DeLeon
25—At Mon.	L	0-2	Rogers	Hawkins
27—New York	W	4-0	Show	Seaver
28—New York	W	5-4	Dravecky	Torrez
29—New York	L	2-3	Lynch	Lollar
30—Montreal	W	5-4	Lucas	Rogers
31—Montreal	W	5-3	Montefusco	Reardon

Won 11, Lost 13

JUNE				
1—Montreal	L	6-8	Smith	Sosa
2—Phila.	W	4-1	Dravecky	Farmer
3—Phila.	W	8-5	Lucas	Farmer
4—Phila.	W	5-4	Montefusco	Bystrom
5—Phila.	L	1-2	Holland	Whitson
7—At Cinn.	W	7-3	Show	Soto
8—At Cinn.	W	5-3	Dravecky	Price
9—At Cinn.	L	1-8	Berenyi	Hawkins
10—At Hous.	L	1-2	LaCoss	Whitson
11—At Hous.	W	8-4	Montefusco	Ruhle
12—At Hous.	L	0-2	Ryan	Show
13—At Hous.	L	0-2	Niekro	Dravecky
14—Cincinnati	L	3-4	Cato	Lucas
15—Cincinnati	W	5-1	Whitson	Puleo
16—Cincinnati	W	3-1	Lollar	Pastore
17—Houston	L	1-4	Ryan	Show
18—Houston	W	2-1†	Dravecky	LaCorte
19—Houston	W	6-4	Sosa	Knepper
20—At L.A.	W	4-1	Whitson	Reuss
21—At L.A.	W	2-0	Lollar	Pena
22—At L.A.	W	5-2	Show	Welch
23—At L.A.	W	7-5	Dravecky	Valenzuela
24—At S. Fran.	L	0-5	Krukow	Hawkins
25—At S. Fran.	W	3-2	Montefusco	Lavelle
26—At S. Fran.	L	0-2	Hammaker	Lollar
26—At S. Fran.	L	3-4	Laskey	Show
28—Los Ang.	L	5-9	Welch	Dravecky
29—Los Ang.	W	13-2	Thurmond	Valenzuela
30—Los Ang.	W	7-6	Montefusco	Howe

Won 17, Lost 12

JULY			Winner	Loser
1—San Fran.	L	3-4	Laskey	Lollar
2—San Fran.	W	5-4*	Lucas	Hammaker
3—San Fran.	W	4-1	Dravecky	Davis
4—San Fran.	W	4-3	Thurmond	Krukow
8—St. Louis	W	3-2	Lucas	Sutter
9—St. Louis	L	4-12	LaPoint	Dravecky
10—St. Louis	L	2-4	Von Ohlen	Lucas
11—Chicago	W	6-5	Montefusco	Jenkins
12—Chicago	W	5-3	Show	Noles
13—Chicago	W	5-4	Lollar	Rainey
14—Pittsburgh	L	6-8	Guante	Montefusco
15—Pittsburgh	L	2-4	Tekulve	Thurmond
16—Pittsburgh	L	2-3	Robinson	Whitson
17—Pittsburgh	L	3-4	Tunnell	Show
19—At St. L.	L	0-4	Allen	Lollar
20—At St. L.	W	5-4	DeLeon	Sutter
21—At St. L.	W	4-2	Thurmond	Andujar
22—At Chicago	L	3-7	Lefferts	Lucas
23—At Chicago	W	4-2	Show	Noles
24—At Chicago	L	2-5	Rainey	Lollar
25—At Pitts.	L	3-6	Rhoden	Dravecky
26—At Pitts.	W	6-1	Thurmond	Robinson
26—At Pitts.	L	5-10	Tunnell	Whitson
27—At Pitts.	L	1-10	DeLeon	Show
29—Atlanta	L	1-2	Perez	Lollar
29—Atlanta	W	6-5‡	Monge	Moore
30—Atlanta	L	2-5	Niekro	Dravecky
31—Atlanta	W	5-2	Thurmond	McMurtry

Won 13, Lost 15

AUGUST				
1—Houston	W	7-4*	DeLeon	Dawley
2—Houston	L	2-4‡	Ruhle	Monge
3—Houston	L	0-1	Ryan	Lollar
4—Houston	W	4-2	Dravecky	Niekro
5—Cincinnati	L	3-4	Power	Sosa
6—Cincinnati	W	11-4	Show	Puleo
6—Cincinnati	W	6-2	Montefusco	Power
7—Cincinnati	L	3-5	Pastore	Whitson
9—At Hous.	W	3-2	Lollar	Niekro
10—At Hous.	L	3-4x	Ruhle	DeLeon
11—At Hous.	L	1-5	Scott	Thurmond
12—At Cinn.	L	5-6	Pastore	Show
13—At Cinn.	L	1-3	Russell	Montefusco
14—At Cinn.	W	10-9*	DeLeon	Hume
15—At Atlanta	W	4-0	Dravecky	McMurtry
16—At Atlanta	W	3-2*	Monge	Bedrosian
17—Phila.	W	5-4	Show	Hudson
18—Phila.	L	2-4*	Holland	Lucas
19—Montreal	W	6-5	Lollar	Burris
21—Montreal	L	0-3	Lea	Dravecky
21—Montreal	W	5-2	Thurmond	Gullickson
22—New York	W	4-3	Show	Swan
23—New York	L	3-8	Terrell	Montefusco
24—New York	W	3-2	Lollar	Seaver
26—At Mon.	L	4-10	Gullickson	Dravecky
27—At Mon.	L	4-6	Lea	DeLeon
28—At Mon.	L	0-8	Rogers	Show
29—At Phila.	W	6-5	DeLeon	Carlton
29—At Phila.	L	6-8	Comer	Monge
30—At Phila.	L	0-6	Gross	Hawkins
30—At Phila.	W	7-5	Whitson	McGraw
31—At Phila.	L	3-4	Holland	Sosa

Won 15, Lost 17

SEPTEMBER				
2—At N.Y.	L	3-7	Terrell	Show
3—At N.Y.	L	3-4y	Gorman	Sosa
4—At N.Y.	W	7-5	Monge	Lynch
5—At L.A.	W	5-2	Thurmond	Valenzuela
6—At L.A.	W	8-3	Whitson	Honeycutt
7—Houston	W	8-7	Monge	DiPino
8—Houston	L	2-3*	Madden	DeLeon
9—Cincinnati	W	8-2	Hawkins	Puleo
11—Cincinnati	L	2-4	Russell	Thurmond
13—San Fran.	W	4-3	Monge	Minton
14—San Fran.	W	7-4	Show	Krukow
16—At Atlanta	L	0-6	McMurtry	Lollar
17—At Atlanta	W	2-1	DeLeon	Barker
18—At Atlanta	W	4-2§	Lucas	Dayley
19—At S. Fran.	W	4-2	Whitson	Garrelts
20—At S. Fran.	L	1-8	Calvert	Show
21—At S. Fran.	L	4-5	Lavelle	Lucas
23—At Cinn.	W	11-8	DeLeon	Hayes
24—At Cinn.	L	2-3	Berenyi	Monge
25—At Cinn.	L	2-5	Puleo	Hawkins
26—At Hous.	L	3-5	Madden	Show
27—At Hous.	L	5-8	Knepper	Lollar
28—Los Ang.	T	4-4§	.....	
29—Los Ang.	W	7-1	Monge	Beckwith
29—Los Ang.	W	4-1	Hawkins	Pena
30—Atlanta	W	3-2	Show	Niekro

Won 14, Lost 11

OCTOBER				
1—Atlanta	W	4-3*	Monge	Falcone
2—Atlanta	L	3-4	Dayley	Booker

Won 1, Lost 1

*10 innings. †11 innings. ‡12 innings. §13 innings. x14 innings. y15 innings.

Eric Show remained healthy and led the Padres with 15 victories.

Rasmussen, a 6-foot-7 lefthander acquired with infielder Edwin Rodriguez in September to complete an August swap that sent veteran righthander John Montefusco to the New York Yankees, was highly impressive in a start against Atlanta. He struck out seven Braves in seven innings.

Veteran relief pitcher Gary Lucas (5-8, 17 saves) improved significantly after the Padres acquired another lefthanded reliever, Sid Monge, from Philadelphia for outfielder Joe Lefebvre in May. As a Padre, Monge won seven of 10 decisions and posted seven saves.

Rookie reliever Marty Decker, a hard-throwing righthander, was impressive late in the season. Decker was one of four minor league pitchers acquired from the Phillies in the August 31 deal for outfielder Sixto Lezcano.

The San Diego bullpen had 44 saves, with Luis DeLeon credited with 13.

The Padres were subpar in double plays (135), next-to-last in the N.L. in homers (93) and averaged only four runs per game. Home attendance dropped from 1,607,516 in 1982 to 1,539,819.

However, the Padres generated interest for 1984 by stealing 179 bases, 125 coming after the All-Star break, and by winning 12 of their 18 games against Los Angeles, including 10 of their last 11 meetings and the last seven games at Dodger Stadium. And San Diego was 7-5 against the N.L. champion Phillies.

Darrell Evans took over first base and became the Giants' power source by hitting 30 home runs.

Giants Show Split Personality

By NICK PETERS

Pennant hopes turned into shattered dreams for the Giants in 1983, the team plunging from contending status in the National League West to fifth place and thereby triggering talk of a major shake-up in the off-season.

The Giants, the hottest team in the majors during the second half of the 1982 season, hoped to improve in '83 despite the absence of Joe Morgan, Al Holland and Reggie Smith (who went to Japan after becoming a free agent), three sources of inspiration during the previous year.

There was individual improvement for Darrell Evans, Jeff Leonard, Johnnie LeMaster and newcomer Joel Youngblood, but the team suffered from key injuries and a lack of leadership and slipped from 87 victories to 79. And the Giants finished 12 games out of first place in '83, compared with their two-game deficit as a third-place club in '82.

"Our biggest problem was inconsistency," summed up Manager Frank Robinson. "We made too many mistakes and we couldn't overcome them. I really didn't know which team would show up at the ballpark."

The Giants clearly exhibited a split personality. They were 13-5 against the West Division champion Dodgers and 7-5 against the N.L. pennant-winning Phillies. They split with the divisional runners-up, the Braves and the Pirates, thus going 35-25 against the four top finishers in the league and 44-58 against the other clubs.

"There's some consolation in knowing you can play with the best because you can build from that," Robinson added. "But it's also frustrating because it makes you wonder what went wrong against the weaker teams."

The Giants were mediocre most of the way, going 39-40 before the All-Star break and 40-43 after it, but they enjoyed one solid month to keep hopes high. San Francisco was 19-7 in May, riding the shoulders of three players.

Evans, who nailed down the first-base job, was a terror in May, batting .423 with nine home runs, 23 runs batted in and a 13-game hitting streak. He was voted N.L. Player of the Month.

Righthander Bill Laskey earned Pitcher of the Month honors in May with a 6-0 record and a 2.83 earned-run average, but was 7-10 the rest of the time. Reliever Gary Lavelle was 2-0 with seven saves during May, finishing with 20 saves.

Evans tailed off following his blazing start, but still enjoyed his finest season since 1973 by belting 30 home runs, driving in 82 runs, scoring 94, totaling 15 game-winning RBIs and posting a .516 slugging percentage.

"It's very gratifying to have this type of season at this point of my career, but I would have traded my stats for the type of feeling we had down the stretch in 1982," said the 36-year-old Evans, voted the Giants' Most Valuable Player by his teammates.

Left fielder Leonard enjoyed his finest major league season with a team-leading 87 RBIs, plus 21 homers and 26 stolen bases, all career highs. He also batted .322 with runners in scoring position and registered 17 assists, 10 on throws to the plate.

"I feel good about the season I had," Leonard said, "but there's still a long way to go because I didn't hit .300, I didn't get 100 runs batted in and I didn't steal 40 bases. We also didn't win."

Utilityman Youngblood, who became a regular in the second half and responded with a .317 average after the break, became the third straight free-agent signee to pace the Giants in hitting (Milt May led in '81, Joe Morgan in '82), batting .292 and contributing 17 home runs.

"Everything turned out real nice," said Youngblood. "I was anxious to have a good year, considering I had a poor one in 1982. I feel that I justified the Giants' faith in me."

The Giants' other regulars had little to be happy about. Jack Clark connected for 20 homers and 66 RBIs, decent for some sluggers but below his standards. Center fielder Chili Davis hit four home runs in his first four games and batted .299 in April, but went .220 the rest of the way (his slump led to a short stint back in the minors) and finished with a .233 average and 11 homers in a poor sophomore season.

Shortstop LeMaster fielded his position well and performed marvelously as the leadoff batter during the first two months. But he slipped to .221 in the second half and finished with a .240 average and 39 steals, two more thefts than he had totaled previously in his major league career.

The Giants' bench generally was weak, but Dave Bergman was one of the best pinch-hitters in the league with a .355 average off the bench (11 for 31, including two homers). Overall, Bergman batted

SCORES OF SAN FRANCISCO GIANTS' 1983 GAMES

APRIL

			Winner	Loser
5—San Diego	L	13-16	Lollar	Krukow
6—San Diego	L	3-5	Dravecky	Laskey
8—Phila.	W	3-2	Breining	Christenson
9—Phila.	L	4-5	Monge	Krukow
10—Phila.	L	2-10	Carlton	Laskey
12—At S. Diego	W	6-5	Breining	Dravecky
13—At S. Diego	L	1-2	Show	Hammaker
14—At S. Diego	L	4-6	Montefusco	McGaffigan
15—Cincinnati	L	1-3	Gale	Laskey
16—Cincinnati	L	3-8	Soto	Breining
17—Cincinnati	W	3-0	Hammaker	Price
17—Cincinnati	L	3-12	Pastore	Calvert
18—Los Ang.	L	3-4	Niedenfuer	Minton
20—Los Ang.	W	3-2*	Minton	Valenzuela
22—At Chicago	L	2-7	Jenkins	Laskey
23—At Chicago	W	5-0	Hammaker	Trout
24—At Chicago	L	1-5	Moskau	McGaffigan
26—At Pitts.	L	0-3	McWilliams	Breining
27—At Pitts.	W	3-2	Laskey	Rhoden
29—At St. L.	L	5-6§x	Bair	Calvert
30—At St. L.	W	5-0	McGaffigan	Andujar

Won 7, Lost 14

MAY

1—At St. L.	L	9-10	Stuper	Breining
3—Chicago	W	5-4	Laskey	Trout
4—Chicago	W	7-4	Hammaker	Moskau
6—Pittsburgh	W	2-1	McGaffigan	Candelaria
7—Pittsburgh	W	5-1	Breining	Rhoden
8—Pittsburgh	W	12-1	Laskey	Bibby
9—St. Louis	W	5-4	Lavelle	Sutter
10—St. Louis	L	4-8	Stuper	McGaffigan
12—At Cinn.	W	4-2	Krukow	Berenyi
13—At Cinn.	W	8-5	Breining	Gale
14—At Cinn.	W	8-7	Laskey	Pastore
15—At Cinn.	W	5-2	Hammaker	Hume
17—At Phila.	L	1-2	Denny	McGaffigan
18—At Phila.	W	8-1	Krukow	Ruthven
20—At Mon.	L	1-7	Rogers	Breining
21—At Mon.	W	5-2	Laskey	Sanderson
22—At Mon.	L	0-2	Lea	Hammaker
23—At N.Y.	L	3-4	Orosco	Minton
24—At N.Y.	W	6-2	Krukow	Lynch
25—At N.Y.	W	7-6	Martin	Allen
26—At L.A.	W	5-3	Laskey	Reuss
27—At L.A.	W	6-3	Hammaker	Welch
28—At L.A.	L	0-5	Valenzuela	McGaffigan
29—At L.A.	W	6-4	Lavelle	Stewart
30—New York	W	5-0	Breining	Allen
31—New York	W	2-1	Laskey	Holman

Won 19, Lost 7

JUNE

1—New York	W	4-2	Hammaker	Seaver
2—Montreal	L	4-11	Burris	McGaffigan
3—Montreal	L	2-9	Gullickson	Krukow
4—Montreal	W	4-2	Lavelle	Reardon
5—Montreal	L	9-12	Schatzeder	Laskey
7—At Hous.	L	2-4	LaCorte	Hammaker
8—At Hous.	L	0-1†	Dawley	Lavelle
9—At Hous.	L	0-3	Knepper	Krukow
10—At Atlanta	W	6-4*	Lavelle	Camp
10—At Atlanta	L	3-7	Falcone	Laskey
11—At Atlanta	W	7-6	Hammaker	Garber
12—At Atlanta	L	2-3	Perez	McGaffigan
14—Houston	L	2-3‡	Smith	Minton
15—Houston	W	7-1	Breining	LaCoss
16—Houston	L	2-7	Scott	Laskey
17—Atlanta	W	2-1	Hammaker	Perez
18—Atlanta	W	5-4	Lavelle	Garber
19—Atlanta	W	9-6	Krukow	McMurtry
20—Cincinnati	W	4-3*	Minton	Power
21—Cincinnati	L	5-6§	Power	Barr
22—Cincinnati	L	2-4	Soto	Davis
24—San Diego	W	5-0	Krukow	Hawkins
25—San Diego	L	2-3	Montefusco	Lavelle
26—San Diego	W	2-0	Hammaker	Lollar
26—San Diego	W	4-3	Laskey	Show
28—At Cinn.	L	4-5	Power	Minton
29—At Cinn.	L	6-7	Power	Minton
30—At Cinn.	L	5-15	Puleo	Breining

Won 12, Lost 16

JULY

			Winner	Loser
1—At S. Diego	W	4-3	Laskey	Lollar
2—At S. Diego	L	4-5*	Lucas	Hammaker
3—At S. Diego	L	1-4	Dravecky	Davis
4—At S. Diego	L	3-4	Thurmond	Krukow
8—Chicago	W	4-1	Laskey	Noles
9—Chicago	L	2-4	Rainey	Davis
10—Chicago	W	10-8	Lavelle	Campbell
10—Chicago	W	4-2	Hammaker	Ruthven
11—Pittsburgh	L	2-3	Sarmiento	Breining
12—Pittsburgh	L	2-6	Tunnell	Laskey
13—Pittsburgh	L	6-7	Sarmiento	Minton
14—St. Louis	L	5-6	LaPoint	Lavelle
15—St. Louis	W	5-4	Barr	Andujar
16—St. Louis	L	3-9	Lahti	Breining
17—St. Louis	W	3-1	Laskey	Stuper
19—At Chicago	W	4-3*	Minton	Campbell
20—At Chicago	W	4-3*	Minton	Smith
21—At Chicago	L	2-3	Ruthven	Hammaker
22—At Pitts.	W	5-3	Barr	Scurry
23—At Pitts.	L	2-5	DeLeon	Martin
24—At Pitts.	L	1-3	Scurry	Krukow
24—At Pitts.	W	8-5†	Minton	Scurry
25—At St. L.	L	4-9	LaPoint	McGaffigan
26—At St. L.	L	5-6	Rucker	Minton
27—At St. L.	L	6-7	Von Ohlen	Barr
29—Los Ang.	W	5-2	Krukow	Pena
30—Los Ang.	W	8-0	Davis	Reuss
31—Los Ang.	L	1-2	Niedenfuer	Breining
31—Los Ang.	W	8-6	Barr	Valenzuela

Won 13, Lost 16

AUGUST

1—Atlanta	L	3-8	Camp	McGaffigan
2—Atlanta	W	7-3	Krukow	Perez
3—Atlanta	L	4-6	Bedrosian	Barr
4—Atlanta	L	1-8	Niekro	Breining
5—Houston	W	7-1	Laskey	Knepper
6—Houston	L	2-4	Madden	Martin
7—Houston	L	1-2	Ryan	Minton
9—At Atlanta	L	2-7	Niekro	Calvert
10—At Atlanta	W	7-4	Minton	Bedrosian
11—At Atlanta	L	4-6	Dayley	Laskey
12—At Hous.	L	2-5	Ryan	Martin
13—At Hous.	L	1-4	Niekro	Krukow
14—At Hous.	W	5-2	Davis	Madden
15—At L.A.	W	7-3	Breining	Hooton
16—At L.A.	L	1-5	Reuss	Laskey
17—Montreal	L	5-12	Rogers	Martin
18—Montreal	W	5-3	Krukow	Smith
19—New York	L	6-7*	Orosco	Minton
20—New York	L	2-7	Lynch	Breining
21—New York	L	3-4	Torrez	Hammaker
22—Phila.	W	11-5	Laskey	Hudson
23—Phila.	W	3-1	Krukow	Holland
24—Phila.	W	5-3	Martin	Carlton
26—At N.Y.	W	12-1	Breining	Lynch
27—At N.Y.	L	3-6	Torrez	Hammaker
28—At N.Y.	W	7-2	Barr	Swan
29—At Mon.	L	0-5	Smith	Krukow
30—At Mon.	W	13-2	Davis	Burris
31—At Mon.	L	3-4	Gullickson	Breining

Won 12, Lost 17

SEPTEMBER

1—At Phila.	L	2-4	Ghelfi	Hammaker
2—At Phila.	L	3-5	Reed	Lavelle
3—At Phila.	W	5-4	Krukow	Carlton
4—At Phila.	W	10-4	McGaffigan	Gross
5—Cincinnati	W	3-2	Breining	Russell
6—Cincinnati	L	1-11	Berenyi	Hammaker
7—Atlanta	W	2-1	Garrelts	Perez
8—Atlanta	L	9-12	Garber	Minton
9—Houston	L	4-7	Niekro	Davis
10—Houston	L	3-5	Heathcock	Breining
11—Houston	W	3-2	Minton	Ryan
13—At S. Diego	L	3-4	Monge	Minton
14—At S. Diego	L	4-7	Show	Krukow
16—Los Ang.	W	1-0	Davis	Valenzuela
17—Los Ang.	W	4-1	Breining	Honeycutt
18—Los Ang.	W	6-3	Krukow	Reuss
19—San Diego	L	2-4	Whitson	Garrelts
20—San Diego	W	8-1	Calvert	Show
21—San Diego	W	5-4	Lavelle	Lucas
23—At Hous.	W	3-2	Breining	Niekro
24—At Hous.	L	5-6	Scott	Krukow
25—At Hous.	W	3-0	Garrelts	Ryan
26—At Atlanta	L	2-6	Niekro	Calvert
27—At Atlanta	W	6-2	Davis	Bedrosian
28—At Cinn.	L	4-5	Soto	Krukow
29—At Cinn.	W	11-7	Lerch	Hayes
30—At L.A.	L	3-4	Valenzuela	Garrelts

Won 14, Lost 13

OCTOBER

1—At L.A.	W	4-1	Davis	Hooton
2—At L.A.	W	4-3	Barr	Fernandez

Won 2, Lost 0

*10 innings. †11 innings. ‡12 innings. §16 innings. xSuspended game, completed April 30.

Atlee Hammaker won the N.L. ERA title despite suffering through a down second half.

.342 with runners in scoring position.

San Francisco equalled its club record with 140 stolen bases. The Giants also generated enough offense to be a winner, ranking second in the N.L. in homers and fourth in runs scored, but those figures were offset by 171 errors, most in the big leagues, and 103 unearned runs allowed, the second-worst total in the majors.

Arm trouble experienced by sophomore starters Atlee Hammaker and Laskey greatly affected the team. They were a combined 18-11 in the first half and a mere 5-8 following the break.

Hammaker, nonetheless, pitched well enough to become the league's ERA king at 2.25 despite going 1-5 in the second half and not posting a victory after July 10 (four days following his All-Star Game pounding). The lefthander became the club's first ERA champion since Juan Marichal in 1969.

Fred Breining was the workhorse of the staff, but his full-time status as a starter weakened the club's long relief, a sore spot. Rookies Mark Davis and Scott Garrelts impressed down the stretch, Davis shutting out the Dodgers in the first 26 innings that he faced them and Garrelts firing a shutout at Houston.

Greg Minton posted 22 saves but wasn't nearly as impressive as he had been in 1982, and the bullpen suffered from Holland's absence.

Tom Haller, the Giants' vice president of baseball operations, was criticized for trading Morgan and Holland to Philadelphia, which won a pennant with them. In return, San Francisco received Mike Krukow (who posted an 11-11 record) and pitcher Davis, who should pay dividends in the future.

The trade weakened the club for 1983, but likely fortified it down the road, a move that front-office executives enjoy and managers abhor.

The highlight of an otherwise dismal Cincinnati season came on September 17 when 53,790 fans turned out to honor retirement-bound Johnny Bench.

Bench Bids Farewell in Style

By EARL LAWSON

Cincinnati fans didn't have much to cheer about during 1983. But a shakeup in the front office and the second managerial change in as many years gave them plenty to talk about.

Also, 1983 will be remembered as the year in which catcher Johnny Bench, a certain Hall of Famer, retired after 16-plus seasons with the Reds.

A sellout crowd of 53,790 turned out September 17 for "Johnny Bench Night" and the Reds' veteran—always exhibiting a flair for the dramatic—rewarded his fans with a game-tying two-run homer. That the Reds wound up 4-3 losers is something fans soon will forget. Bench's homer, the 389th and last of his career, is something they'll always remember.

It was on July 11, about a month after Bench announced his retirement (effective at season's end), that Owners Bill and Jim Williams fired Dick Wagner, the Reds' president and chief executive officer.

Cincinnati fans had been after Wagner's scalp ever since he refused to make an all-out effort to sign Pete Rose before Rose opted for free agency after the 1978 season. Further dismantling of the Big Red Machine—the departures of George Foster and Ken Griffey after the 1981 season, for example—intensified the ill feeling.

The Williams brothers obviously figured the firing of Wagner was the only positive action they could take when, even though the season was just beyond the halfway mark, it became apparent the Reds were doomed to finish in the National League West cellar for the second straight year.

The Reds did just that, finishing with a 74-88 record. The home attendance was 1,190,419, which, excluding the strike-abbreviated 1981 season, was the Reds' lowest since the club moved into Riverfront Stadium in 1970.

Bob Howsam, who had been serving as a Reds vice chairman since giving up his club presidency after the 1977 season, was named Wagner's front-office successor on an interim basis.

However, the Williams brothers soon stripped the "interim" from Howsam's title and gave him a free hand in operating the club.

One of Howsam's first moves was to sign Mario Soto, the club's pitching ace, to a contract that could keep him in a Reds uniform through 1990.

The 27-year-old righthander's contract, which made him the highest-paid player in club history, is guaranteed through 1988. The Reds have the option of renewing it for an additional two years.

While trying to bolster their chances for the future with the Soto signing, the Reds still had to deal with the present. And the 1983 season wasn't too many weeks old before fans began to realize it was going to be another long year. Cincinnati did show a 13-game improvement over 1982 (during which it lost a club-record 101 games), but the bright spots were few and far between.

The Reds posted an 11-10 record in April, but were 11-17 in May and June, 13-14 in July, 15-15 in August and 13-15 in September-October.

As a team, the Reds batted .239, lowest in the major leagues. The pitchers' combined earned-run average was 3.98; only the Chicago Cubs' staff had a poorer N.L. mark.

Veteran first baseman Dan Driessen's .277 batting average was tops among regulars. Surprisingly, second baseman Ron Oester, who batted only .264, led the club in runs batted in with 58.

Veteran shortstop Dave Concepcion, plagued by an ailing left shoulder throughout the season, batted .233. He underwent surgery two days after the season ended.

Tom Hume, who had undergone knee surgery midway through the 1982 season, failed to bounce back as expected. He spent most of the season nursing a sore shoulder and wound up with a 3-5 record, a 4.77 ERA and only nine saves.

Rookies Gary Redus, Dann Bilardello, Nick Esasky and Bill Scherrer provided some hope.

Redus batted only .247, but his 17 homers and 90 runs scored led the club even though injuries kept him out of 37 games. His 39 stolen bases ranked second on the Reds to Eddie Milner's 41.

Esasky, who joined the club in mid-June after being recalled from Indianapolis, batted .265, hit 12 homers and drove home 46 runs in 302 at-bats.

Bilardello, drafted from the Los Angeles Dodgers' organization in December of 1982, emerged as the Reds' No. 1 catcher. He hit just .238, but indicated during the closing weeks that he will improve his offense in '84.

Scherrer, a 25-year-old lefthander, be-

SCORES OF CINCINNATI REDS' 1983 GAMES

APRIL

			Winner	Loser
4—Atlanta	W	5-4	Soto	Bedrosian
6—Atlanta	L	1-5	Perez	Berenyi
8—Chicago	W	7-3	Soto	Trout
9—Chicago	W	8-4	Pastore	Rainey
10—Chicago	W	7-2	Berenyi	Jenkins
11—Chicago	W	5-1	Price	Noles
12—At Atlanta	L	1-4	Behenna	Soto
13—At Atlanta	L	1-6	Camp	Pastore
15—At S. Fran.	W	3-1	Gale	Laskey
16—At S. Fran.	W	8-3	Soto	Breining
17—At S. Fran.	L	0-3	Hammaker	Price
17—At S. Fran.	W	12-3	Pastore	Calvert
19—At Hous.	L	5-6	Dawley	Hume
20—At Hous.	W	6-4	Gale	LaCoss
21—At Hous.	L	3-4*	LaCorte	Hume
22—Montreal	L	0-4	Rogers	Pastore
24—Montreal	L	4-5	Reardon	Soto
26—New York	W	7-0	Berenyi	Seaver
27—New York	L	1-2	Torrez	Price
29—At Mon.	L	6-9	Rogers	Pastore
30—At Mon.	W	4-3	Gale	Lea

Won 11, Lost 10

MAY

1—At Mon.	L	4-5	Gullickson	Berenyi
1—At Mon.	W	6-3	Price	Burris
2—At Phila.	W	5-2	Power	Ruthven
3—At Phila.	L	7-13	Monge	Pastore
4—At Phila.	L	4-9	Carlton	Gale
6—At N.Y.	L	4-7‡	Orosco	Scherrer
7—At N.Y.	W	7-5	Berenyi	Torrez
8—At N.Y.	L	5-10	Orosco	Gale
10—Phila.	L	1-3	Carlton	Power
11—Phila.	W	2-0	Soto	Denny
12—San Fran.	L	2-4	Krukow	Berenyi
13—San Fran.	L	5-8	Breining	Gale
14—San Fran.	L	7-8	Laskey	Pastore
15—San Fran.	L	2-5	Hammaker	Hume
17—At Pitts.	W	2-1	Soto	Candelaria
18—At Pitts.	L	1-2	Rhoden	Berenyi
20—At Chicago	W	9-5	Scherrer	Proly
21—At Chicago	L	4-8	Moskau	Puleo
22—At Chicago	W	4-3	Soto	Rainey
23—St. Louis	W	2-1	Price	Andujar
24—St. Louis	L	1-7	LaPoint	Berenyi
25—St. Louis	L	2-7	Stuper	Power
26—Pittsburgh	L	4-6	Tunnell	Puleo
27—Pittsburgh	W	9-0	Soto	Candelaria
28—Pittsburgh	W	4-3	Hayes	Scurry
29—Pittsburgh	L	5-8	McWilliams	Scherrer
30—At St. L.	L	1-9	Stuper	Power
31—At St. L.	W	2-1	Puleo	Andujar

Won 11, Lost 17

JUNE

1—At St. L.	L	3-8	Martin	Soto
3—Houston	W	3-1	Price	Niekro
4—Houston	L	0-13	Scott	Berenyi
5—Houston	L	3-6	Ruhle	Scherrer
7—San Diego	L	3-7	Show	Soto
8—San Diego	L	3-5	Dravecky	Price
9—San Diego	W	8-1	Berenyi	Hawkins
10—Los Ang.	W	3-2	Puleo	Reuss
11—Los Ang.	L	2-3	Niedenfuer	Hayes
12—Los Ang.	W	3-1	Soto	Welch
13—Los Ang.	L	1-5	Valenzuela	Price
14—At S. Diego	W	4-3	Cato	Lucas
15—At S. Diego	L	1-5	Whitson	Puleo
16—At S. Diego	L	1-3	Lollar	Pastore
17—At L.A.	L	0-1	Welch	Soto
18—At L.A.	W	3-2	Price	Valenzuela
19—At L.A.	L	1-5	Hooton	Berenyi
20—At S. Fran.	L	3-4*	Minton	Power
21—At S. Fran.	W	6-5§	Power	Barr
22—At S. Fran.	W	4-2	Soto	Davis
24—Atlanta	L	0-3	McMurtry	Price
24—Atlanta	L	5-10	Dayley	Berenyi
25—Atlanta	L	2-8	Falcone	Puleo
26—Atlanta	L	1-5	Niekro	Pastore
27—Atlanta	L	1-2	Perez	Soto
28—San Fran.	W	5-4	Power	Minton
29—San Fran.	W	7-6	Power	Minton
30—San Fran.	W	15-5	Puleo	Breining

Won 11, Lost 17

JULY

			Winner	Loser
1—At Atlanta	L	2-5	Niekro	Pastore
2—At Atlanta	L	2-4	Perez	Soto
3—At Atlanta	W	2-1	Price	McMurtry
4—At Atlanta	L	5-9	Falcone	Berenyi
8—Phila.	W	3-1	Price	Denny
9—Phila.	W	2-1	Hume	Hernandez
10—Phila.	L	0-2	Bystrom	Soto
11—Phila.	L	7-11†	Holland	Hume
12—At N.Y.	W	6-2	Pastore	Torrez
13—At N.Y.	W	3-1	Price	Terrell
14—At N.Y.	L	4-7	Seaver	Puleo
15—At Phila.	W	3-2	Soto	Hudson
16—At Phila.	L	3-9	Denny	Berenyi
17—At Phila.	W	5-2	Pastore	Gross
19—At Mon.	W	5-2	Price	Rogers
20—At Mon.	L	4-6	Lea	Soto
21—New York	W	6-1	Puleo	Torrez
22—New York	L	2-3	Orosco	Hayes
23—New York	W	7-3	Berenyi	Gorman
24—New York	W	4-2	Price	Seaver
25—Montreal	W	4-2	Soto	Lea
25—Montreal	L	1-8	Burris	Gale
26—Montreal	L	0-5	Gullickson	Puleo
27—Montreal	L	3-6	Bargar	Pastore
29—At Hous.	L	1-4	Madden	Price
30—At Hous.	W	3-2	Soto	Ryan
31—At Hous.	L	2-9	Niekro	Berenyi

Won 13, Lost 14

AUGUST

1—At L.A.	W	4-2*	Hayes	Welch
2—At L.A.	L	1-3	Pena	Pastore
3—At L.A.	L	4-7	Zachry	Gale
4—At L.A.	W	4-3†	Hayes	Niedenfuer
5—At S. Diego	W	4-3	Power	Sosa
6—At S. Diego	L	4-11	Show	Puleo
6—At S. Diego	L	2-6	Montefusco	Power
7—At S. Diego	W	5-3	Pastore	Whitson
9—Los Ang.	W	5-4	Soto	Howe
10—Los Ang.	W	9-2	Berenyi	Hooton
11—Los Ang.	L	3-4	Niedenfuer	Puleo
12—San Diego	W	6-5	Pastore	Show
13—San Diego	W	3-1	Russell	Montefusco
14—San Diego	L	9-10*	DeLeon	Hume
15—Houston	L	1-9	Knepper	Berenyi
16—Houston	L	5-8	Scott	Puleo
17—Houston	L	6-7	Ruhle	Pastore
18—At Pitts.	W	6-5	Hume	Tekulve
19—At Pitts.	W	2-1	Soto	Rhoden
20—At Pitts.	L	0-4	DeLeon	Berenyi
21—At Pitts.	W	6-4	Scherrer	Guante
22—At Chicago	L	0-2	Noles	Pastore
23—At Chicago	W	4-2	Russell	Jenkins
24—At Chicago	L	0-3	Rainey	Soto
26—St. Louis	W	7-3	Puleo	Cox
27—St. Louis	L	1-3	Rucker	Power
28—St. Louis	W	5-4†	Hayes	Sutter
29—Pittsburgh	L	1-2	Rhoden	Soto
30—Pittsburgh	L	3-5	DeLeon	Russell
31—Chicago	W	6-4	Gale	Bordi

Won 15, Lost 15

SEPTEMBER

1—Chicago	L	1-3	Ruthven	Berenyi
2—At St. L.	W	4-0	Pastore	Stuper
3—At St. L.	W	3-2*	Soto	Rucker
4—At St. L.	L	4-5	Lahti	Hayes
5—At S. Fran.	L	2-3	Breining	Russell
6—At S. Fran.	W	11-1	Berenyi	Hammaker
7—At L.A.	L	3-7*	Niedenfuer	Hayes
8—At L.A.	L	2-5	Welch	Soto
9—At S. Diego	L	2-8	Hawkins	Puleo
11—At S. Diego	W	4-2	Russell	Thurmond
13—Atlanta	W	6-0	Soto	Perez
14—Atlanta	W	6-4	Pastore	Niekro
16—Houston	W	8-3	Berenyi	Heathcock
17—Houston	L	3-4	Madden	Russell
18—Houston	L	1-4	Scott	Soto
21—At Atlanta	L	1-9	McMurtry	Puleo
21—At Atlanta	W	4-3	Hume	Bedrosian
22—At Atlanta	W	6-4	Russell	Dayley
23—San Diego	L	8-11	DeLeon	Hayes
24—San Diego	W	3-2	Berenyi	Monge
25—San Diego	W	5-2	Puleo	Hawkins
26—Los Ang.	L	9-12*	Zachry	Gale
27—Los Ang.	L	4-7	Beckwith	Russell
28—San Fran.	W	5-4	Soto	Krukow
29—San Fran.	L	7-11	Lerch	Hayes
30—At Hous.	L	2-3	LaCoss	Puleo

Won 12, Lost 14

OCTOBER

1—At Hous.	W	6-4	Pastore	Madden
2—At Hous.	L	2-3	Heathcock	Russell

Won 1, Lost 1

*10 innings. †11 innings. ‡13 innings. §16 innings.

Gary Redus batted only .247 and fought off injury problems, but still encouraged fans by hitting 17 home runs.

came the Reds' only dependable relief pitcher, finishing with 10 saves and a 2.74 ERA in 73 appearances.

Soto compiled a 17-13 record and a 2.70 ERA. His 18 complete games led the National League and he ranked second to the Phillies' Steve Carlton with 242 strikeouts.

Lefthander Joe Price, a reliever the previous two seasons, was moved into the starting rotation and responded with a 10-6 record and a 2.88 ERA. Rookie Jeff Russell showed promise in his 10 starts, fashioning a 3.03 ERA while winning four of nine decisions.

Meanwhile, starters Bruce Berenyi, Frank Pastore and Charlie Puleo struggled to a combined 24-38 record.

Obviously seeking a new direction in addition to wanting his own man, Howsam fired Reds Manager Russ Nixon on October 4. Nixon, who had taken over for John McNamara in July of 1982, was replaced by Vern Rapp. Howsam also restructured his scouting system.

The Reds' executive was wasting little time in his effort to turn the fans' chatter into cheers.

National League Averages for 1983

CHAMPIONSHIP WINNERS IN PREVIOUS YEARS

1876—Chicago .788
1877—Boston .646
1878—Boston .683
1879—Providence .705
1880—Chicago .798
1881—Chicago .667
1882—Chicago .655
1883—Boston .643
1884—Providence .750
1885—Chicago .777
1886—Chicago .726
1887—Detroit .637
1888—New York .641
1889—New York .659
1890—Brooklyn .667
1891—Boston .630
1892—Boston .680
1893—Boston .662
1894—Baltimore .695
1895—Baltimore .669
1896—Baltimore .698
1897—Boston .705
1898—Boston .685
1899—Brooklyn .677
1900—Brooklyn .603
1901—Pittsburgh .647
1902—Pittsburgh .741
1903—Pittsburgh .650
1904—New York .693
1905—New York .686
1906—Chicago .763
1907—Chicago .704
1908—Chicago .643
1909—Pittsburgh .724
1910—Chicago .675
1911—New York .647
1912—New York .682
1913—New York .664
1914—Boston .614
1915—Philadelphia .592
1916—Brooklyn .610
1917—New York .636
1918—Chicago .651
1919—Cincinnati .686
1920—Brooklyn .604
1921—New York .614
1922—New York .604
1923—New York .621
1924—New York .608
1925—Pittsburgh .621
1926—St. Louis .578
1927—Pittsburgh .610
1928—St. Louis .617
1929—Chicago .645
1930—St. Louis .597
1931—St. Louis .656
1932—Chicago .584
1933—New York .599
1934—St. Louis .621
1935—Chicago .649
1936—New York .597
1937—New York .625
1938—Chicago .586
1939—Cincinnati .630
1940—Cincinnati .654
1941—Brooklyn .649
1942—St. Louis .688
1943—St. Louis .682
1944—St. Louis .682
1945—Chicago .636
1946—St. Louis* .628
1947—Brooklyn .610
1948—Boston .595
1949—Brooklyn .630
1950—Philadelphia .591
1951—New York† .624
1952—Brooklyn .627
1953—Brooklyn .682
1954—New York .630
1955—Brooklyn .641
1956—Brooklyn .604
1957—Milwaukee .617
1958—Milwaukee .597
1959—Los Angeles‡ .564
1960—Pittsburgh .617
1961—Cincinnati .604
1962—San Francisco§ .624
1963—Los Angeles .611
1964—St. Louis .574
1965—Los Angeles .599
1966—Los Angeles .586
1967—St. Louis .627
1968—St. Louis .599
1969—New York (East)a .617
1970—Cincinnati (West)b .630
1971—Pittsburgh (East)c .599
1972—Cincinnati (West)b .617
1973—New York (East)d .509
1974—Los Angeles (West)b .630
1975—Cincinnati (West)b .667
1976—Cincinnati (West)e .630
1977—Los Angeles (West)e .605
1978—Los Angeles (West)e .586
1979—Pittsburgh (East)d .605
1980—Philadelphia (East)f .562
1981—Los Angeles (West)g .573
1982—St. Louis (East)a .568

*Defeated Brooklyn, two games to none, in playoff for pennant. †Defeated Brooklyn, two games to one, in playoff for pennant. ‡Defeated Milwaukee, two games to none, in playoff for pennant. §Defeated Los Angeles, two games to one, in playoff for pennant. aDefeated Atlanta (West) in Championship Series. bDefeated Pittsburgh (East) in Championship Series. cDefeated San Francisco (West) in Championship Series. dDefeated Cincinnati (West) in Championship series. eDefeated Philadelphia (East) in Championship Series. fDefeated Houston (West) in Championship Series. gDefeated Montreal (East) in Championship Series.

STANDING OF CLUBS AT CLOSE OF SEASON

EAST DIVISION

Club	Phil.	Pitt.	Mon.	St.L.	Chi.	N.Y.	Atl.	Cin.	Hou.	L.A.	S.D.	S.F.	W.	L.	Pct.	G.B.
Philadelphia	..	11	10	14	13	12	5	6	8	1	5	5	90	72	.556	....
Pittsburgh	7	..	10	10	9	9	6	6	6	6	9	6	84	78	.519	6
Montreal	8	8	..	9	11	8	5	8	4	5	8	8	82	80	.506	8
St. Louis	4	8	9	..	8	12	5	6	10	3	6	8	79	83	.488	11
Chicago	5	9	7	10	..	9	7	4	5	6	5	4	71	91	.438	19
New York	6	9	10	6	9	..	4	5	3	5	6	5	68	94	.420	22

WEST DIVISION

Club	L.A.	Atl.	Hou.	S.D.	S.F.	Cin.	Chi.	Mon.	N.Y.	Phil.	Pitt.	St.L.	W.	L.	Pct.	G.B.
Los Angeles	..	11	12	6	5	11	6	7	7	11	6	9	91	71	.562	....
Atlanta	7	..	11	9	9	12	5	7	8	7	6	7	88	74	.543	3
Houston	6	7	..	11	12	13	7	8	9	4	6	2	85	77	.525	6
San Diego	12	9	7	..	11	9	7	4	6	7	3	6	81	81	.500	10
San Francisco	13	9	6	7	..	8	8	4	7	7	6	4	79	83	.488	12
Cincinnati	7	6	5	9	10	..	8	4	7	6	6	6	74	88	.457	17

Tie Games—Montreal vs. Philadelphia, Los Angeles vs. San Diego.
Championship Series—Philadelphia defeated Los Angeles, three games to one.

RECORD AT HOME

EAST DIVISION

Club	Phil.	Mon.	St.L.	Chi.	Pitt.	N.Y.	L.A.	S.D.	Atl.	Hou.	S.F.	Cin.	W.	L.	Pct.
Philadelphia	......	6-3	7-2	8-1	6-3	7-2	1-5	3-3	3-3	3-3	3-3	3-3	50	31	.617
Montreal	5-4	......	6-3	6-3	2-7	6-3	3-3	6-0	2-4	3-3	4-2	3-3	46	35	.568
St. Louis	2-7	6-3	......	4-5	3-6	8-1	2-4	3-3	2-4	6-0	5-1	3-3	44	37	.543
Chicago	4-5	4-5	5-4	......	8-1	4-5	3-3	3-3	3-3	3-3	3-3	3-3	43	38	.531
Pittsburgh	4-5	3-6	4-5	8-1	......	5-4	3-3	4-2	3-3	2-4	3-3	2-4	41	40	.506
New York	4-5	7-2	5-4	4-5	5-4	......	3-4	4-2	3-3	1-5	2-4	3-3	41	41	.500

WEST DIVISION

Club	L.A.	S.D.	Atl.	Hou.	S.F.	Cin.	Phil.	Mon.	St.L.	Chi.	Pitt.	N.Y.	W.	L.	Pct.
Los Angeles	......	2-7	6-3	7-2	3-6	6-3	6-0	4-2	5-1	3-3	3-3	3-2	48	32	.600
San Diego	5-4	......	5-4	5-4	7-2	5-4	4-2	4-2	3-3	4-2	1-5	4-2	47	34	.580
Atlanta	4-5	5-4	......	6-2	5-4	6-3	4-2	3-3	3-3	2-4	3-3	5-1	46	34	.575
Houston	4-5	7-2	5-5	......	6-3	6-3	1-5	5-1	2-4	4-2	2-4	4-2	46	36	.561
San Francisco	7-2	5-4	5-4	3-6	......	3-6	4-2	2-4	3-3	5-1	3-3	3-3	43	38	.531
Cincinnati	4-5	5-4	3-6	2-7	4-5	......	3-3	1-5	3-3	5-1	2-4	4-2	36	45	.444

RECORD ABROAD

EAST DIVISION

Club	Pitt.	Phil.	Mon.	St.L.	Chi.	N.Y.	L.A.	Atl.	Hou.	Cin.	S.F.	S.D.	W.	L.	Pct.
Pittsburgh	......	3-6	7-2	6-3	1-8	4-5	3-3	3-3	4-2	4-2	3-3	5-1	43	38	.531
Philadelphia	5-4	......	4-5	7-2	5-4	5-4	0-6	2-4	5-1	3-3	2-4	2-4	40	41	.494
Montreal	6-3	3-6	......	3-6	5-4	2-7	2-4	3-3	1-5	5-1	4-2	2-4	36	45	.444
St. Louis	5-4	2-7	3-6	......	4-5	4-5	1-5	3-3	4-2	3-3	3-3	3-3	35	46	.432
Chicago	1-8	1-8	3-6	5-4	......	5-4	3-3	4-2	2-4	1-5	1-5	2-4	28	53	.346
New York	4-5	2-7	3-6	1-8	5-4	......	2-3	1-5	2-4	2-4	3-3	2-4	27	53	.338

WEST DIVISION

Club	L.A.	Atl.	Hou.	Cin.	S.F.	S.D.	Pitt.	Phil.	Mon.	St.L.	Chi.	N.Y.	W.	L.	Pct.
Los Angeles	......	5-4	5-4	5-4	2-7	4-5	3-3	5-1	3-3	4-2	3-3	4-3	43	39	.524
Atlanta	3-6	......	5-5	6-3	4-5	4-5	3-3	3-3	4-2	4-2	3-3	3-3	42	40	.512
Houston	2-7	2-6	......	7-2	6-3	4-5	4-2	3-3	3-3	0-6	3-3	5-1	39	41	.488
Cincinnati	3-6	3-6	3-6	......	6-3	4-5	4-2	3-3	3-3	3-3	3-3	3-3	38	43	.469
San Francisco	6-3	4-5	3-6	5-4	......	2-7	3-3	3-3	2-4	1-5	3-3	4-2	36	45	.444
San Diego	7-2	4-5	2-7	4-5	4-5	......	2-4	3-3	0-6	3-3	3-3	2-4	34	47	.420

SHUTOUT GAMES

Club	Pitt.	L.A.	Hou.	S.F.	Chi.	Mon.	Phil.	St.L.	N.Y.	Atl.	Cin.	S.D.	W.	L.	Pct.
Pittsburgh	..	1	1	1	1	3	1	3	1	1	1	0	14	7	.667
Los Angeles	0	..	1	1	0	2	5	1	1	0	1	0	12	7	.632
Houston	1	0	..	2	2	2	0	0	1	2	1	3	14	9	.609
San Francisco	0	2	1	..	1	0	0	1	1	0	1	2	9	6	.600
Chicago	1	1	0	0	..	2	1	2	0	1	2	0	10	8	.556
Montreal	1	0	1	2	1	..	2	2	1	0	2	3	15	13	.536
Philadelphia	0	0	2	0	2	1	..	1	2	0	1	1	10	12	.455
St. Louis	0	1	2	0	0	2	0	..	2	1	0	2	10	12	.455
New York	2	1	1	0	1	1	1	0	..	0	0	0	7	11	.389
Atlanta	1	0	0	0	0	0	0	0	0	..	1	2	4	7	.364
Cincinnati	1	0	0	0	0	0	1	1	1	1	..	0	5	10	.333
San Diego	0	1	0	0	0	0	1	1	1	1	0	..	5	13	.278

OFFICIAL NATIONAL LEAGUE BATTING AVERAGES

Compiled by Elias Sports Bureau

CLUB BATTING

Club	Pct.	G.	AB.	R.	OR.	H.	TB.	2B.	3B.	HR.	RBI.	SH.	SF.	SB.	CS.	LOB.
Atlanta	.272	162	5472	746	640	1489	2187	218	45	130	691	78	46	146	88	1155
St. Louis	.270	162	5550	679	710	1496	2133	262	63	83	636	72	49	207	89	1175
Montreal	.264	163	5611	677	646	1482	2167	297	41	102	632	78	57	138	44	1213
Pittsburgh	.264	162	5531	659	648	1460	2119	238	29	121	612	84	38	124	77	1142
Chicago	.261	162	5512	701	719	1436	2212	272	42	140	649	71	50	84	40	1120
Houston	.257	162	5502	643	646	1412	2062	239	60	97	615	81	54	164	95	1145
San Diego	.250	163	5527	653	653	1384	1938	207	34	93	592	89	45	179	67	1103
Los Angeles	.250	163	5440	654	609	1358	2061	197	34	146	613	86	40	166	76	1104
Phil'phia	.249	163	5426	696	635	1352	2026	209	45	125	649	80	46	143	75	1154
San Fran.	.247	162	5369	687	697	1324	2016	206	30	142	638	64	46	140	78	1104
New York	.241	162	5444	575	680	1314	1874	172	26	112	542	66	32	141	64	1041
Cincinnati	.239	162	5333	623	710	1274	1901	236	35	107	577	72	45	154	77	1090
Totals	.255	974	65717	7993	7993	16781	24696	2753	484	1398	7446	921	548	1786	870	13546

INDIVIDUAL BATTING

(Top Fifteen Qualifiers for Batting Championship—502 or More Plate Appearances)

*Bats lefthanded. †Switch-hitter.

Player and Club	Pct.	G.	AB.	R.	H.	TB.	2B.	3B.	HR.	RBI.	GW.	SH.	SF.	SB.	CS.
Madlock, Bill, Pittsburgh	.323	130	473	68	153	210	21	0	12	68	14	1	5	3	4
Smith, Lonnie, St. Louis	.321	130	492	83	158	223	31	5	8	45	3	1	4	43	18
Cruz, Jose, Houston*	.318	160	594	85	189	275	28	8	14	92	9	1	3	30	16
Hendrick, George, St. Louis	.318	144	529	73	168	261	33	3	18	97	12	0	11	3	4
Knight, C. Ray, Houston	.304	145	507	43	154	225	36	4	9	70	8	3	11	0	3
Murphy, Dale, Atlanta	.302	162	589	131	178	318	24	4	36	121	14	0	6	30	4
Moreland, B. Keith, Chicago	.302	154	533	76	161	245	30	3	16	70	11	5	10	0	3
Pena, Antonio, Pittsburgh	.301	151	542	51	163	236	22	3	15	70	2	6	1	6	7
Oliver, Albert, Montreal*	.300	157	614	70	184	252	38	3	8	84	12	1	3	1	3
Dawson, Andre, Montreal	.299	159	633	104	189	341	36	10	32	113	14	0	18	25	11
Guerrero, Pedro, Los Angeles	.298	160	584	87	174	310	28	6	32	103	13	0	6	23	7

Player and Club	Pct.	G.	AB.	R.	H.	TB.	2B.	3B.	HR.	RBI.	GW.	SH.	SF.	SB.	CS.
Raines, Timothy, Montreal†	.298	156	615	133	183	264	32	8	11	71	13	2	4	90	14
Ramirez, Rafael, Atlanta	.297	152	622	82	185	229	13	5	7	58	10	6	2	16	12
Hernandez, Keith, St. L.-N. Y.*	.297	150	538	77	160	233	23	7	12	63	9	2	3	9	5
Oberkfell, Kenneth, St. Louis*	.293	151	488	62	143	188	26	5	3	38	6	4	3	12	6

DEPARTMENTAL LEADERS: G—Murphy, 162; AB—Wilson, 638; R—Raines, 133; H—Cruz, Dawson, 189; TB—Dawson, 341; 2B—Buckner, Oliver, Ray, 38; 3B—Butler, 13; HR—Schmidt, 40; RBI—Murphy, 121; GW—Thon, 18; SH—Rogers, 20; SF—Dawson, 18; SB—Raines, 90; CS—S. Sax, 30.

(All Players—Listed Alphabetically)

Player and Club	Pct.	G.	AB.	R.	H.	TB.	2B.	3B.	HR.	RBI.	GW.	SH.	SF.	SB.	CS.
Adduci, James, St. Louis*	.050	10	20	0	1	1	0	0	0	0	0	0	0	0	0
Aguayo, Luis, Philadelphia	.250	2	4	1	1	1	0	0	0	0	0	0	0	0	0
Allen, Neil, New York-St. Louis	.102	46	49	2	5	7	2	0	0	3	0	7	0	0	0
Altamirano, Porfirio, Philadelphia	.000	31	2	0	0	0	0	0	0	0	0	0	0	0	0
Andersen, Larry, Philadelphia	.000	17	2	0	0	0	0	0	0	0	0	0	0	0	0
Anderson, David, Los Angeles	.165	61	115	12	19	30	4	2	1	2	0	4	0	6	3
Andujar, Joaquin, St. Louis†	.082	39	73	2	6	7	1	0	0	2	1	5	0	2	1
Ashby, Alan, Houston†	.229	87	275	31	63	107	18	1	8	34	5	1	4	0	0
Ashford, Thomas, New York	.179	35	56	3	10	12	0	1	0	2	0	0	0	0	0
Backman, Walter, New York†	.167	26	42	6	7	9	0	1	0	3	0	1	0	0	0
Bailor, Robert, New York	.250	118	340	33	85	96	8	0	1	30	4	3	4	18	3
Bair, C. Douglas, St. Louis	.000	26	2	0	0	0	0	0	0	0	0	0	0	0	0
Baker, Johnnie, Los Angeles	.260	149	531	71	138	210	25	1	15	73	10	4	7	7	1
Baker, Steven, St. Louis	.000	8	0	0	0	0	0	0	0	0	0	0	0	0	0
Bargar, Gregory, Montreal	.167	8	6	0	1	1	0	0	0	1	0	0	0	0	0
Barker, Leonard, Atlanta	.125	6	8	1	1	1	0	0	0	0	0	2	0	0	0
Barnes, William, Cincinnati	.206	15	34	5	7	10	0	0	1	4	0	0	0	2	2
Barr, James, San Francisco	.133	53	15	0	2	3	1	0	0	0	0	1	0	0	0
Bass, Kevin, Houston†	.236	88	195	25	46	65	7	3	2	18	1	4	1	2	2
Beckwith, T. Joseph, Los Angeles*	.200	42	5	1	1	1	0	0	0	0	0	0	0	0	0
Bedrosian, Stephen, Atlanta	.105	70	19	0	2	2	0	0	0	0	0	1	0	0	0
Behenna, Richard, Atlanta	.333	14	12	1	4	7	0	0	1	2	0	0	0	0	0
Belliard, Rafael, Pittsburgh	.000	4	1	1	0	0	0	0	0	0	0	0	0	0	0
Bench, Johnny, Cincinnati	.255	110	310	32	79	134	15	2	12	54	7	0	0	0	1
Benedict, Bruce, Atlanta	.298	134	423	43	126	147	13	1	2	43	4	4	3	1	3
Berenyi, Bruce, Cincinnati	.218	32	55	5	12	15	3	0	0	5	0	10	0	0	0
Bergman, David, San Francisco*	.286	90	140	16	40	64	4	1	6	24	4	2	0	2	1
Berra, Dale, Pittsburgh	.251	161	537	51	135	192	25	1	10	52	4	7	2	8	5
Bevacqua, Kurt, San Diego	.244	74	156	17	38	51	7	0	2	24	3	2	1	0	3
Bibby, James, Pittsburgh	.111	29	18	0	2	2	0	0	0	0	0	2	0	0	0
Bilardello, Dann, Cincinnati	.238	109	298	27	71	116	18	0	9	38	6	2	4	2	1
Bishop, Michael, New York	.125	3	8	2	1	2	1	0	0	0	0	0	0	0	0
Bjorkman, George, Houston	.227	29	75	8	17	27	4	0	2	14	0	1	0	0	0
Blackwell, Timothy, Montreal†	.200	6	15	0	3	4	1	0	0	2	0	0	0	0	0
Bochy, Bruce, San Diego	.214	23	42	2	9	12	1	1	0	3	0	0	2	0	0
Boggs, Thomas, Atlanta	.000	5	0	0	0	0	0	0	0	0	0	0	0	0	0
Bonilla, Juan, San Diego	.237	152	556	55	132	169	17	4	4	45	6	3	5	3	0
Booker, Gregory, San Diego	.000	6	1	0	0	0	0	0	0	0	0	0	0	0	0
Bordi, Richard, Chicago	.000	11	4	0	0	0	0	0	0	0	0	0	0	0	0
Bosley, Thaddis, Chicago*	.292	43	72	12	21	33	4	1	2	12	1	0	1	1	1
Bowa, Lawrence, Chicago†	.267	147	499	73	133	169	20	5	2	43	8	6	4	7	3
Bradley, Mark, New York	.202	73	104	10	21	34	4	0	3	5	0	0	0	4	2
Braun, Stephen, St. Louis*	.272	78	92	8	25	38	2	1	3	7	1	0	1	0	1
Bream, Sidney, Los Angeles*	.182	15	11	0	2	2	0	0	0	2	0	0	0	0	0
Breining, Fred, San Francisco	.149	32	67	1	10	11	1	0	0	4	0	5	0	0	0
Brenly, Robert, San Francisco	.224	104	281	36	63	100	12	2	7	34	3	1	2	10	7
Brizzolara, Anthony, Atlanta	.000	14	0	0	0	0	0	0	0	0	0	0	0	0	0
Brock, Gregory, Los Angeles*	.224	146	455	64	102	180	14	2	20	66	4	0	4	5	1
Brooks, Hubert, New York	.251	150	586	53	147	188	18	4	5	58	8	7	3	6	4
Brown, Rogers, San Diego†	.267	57	225	40	60	86	5	3	5	22	1	1	1	27	9
Brummer, Glenn, St. Louis	.276	45	87	7	24	31	7	0	0	9	1	2	0	1	3
Brusstar, Warren, Chicago	.000	59	4	0	0	0	0	0	0	0	0	1	0	0	0
Buckner, William, Chicago*	.280	153	626	79	175	273	38	6	16	66	5	4	5	12	4
Burris, B. Ray, Montreal	.231	40	39	2	9	11	2	0	0	2	0	2	0	0	0
Butler, Brett, Atlanta*	.281	151	549	84	154	216	21	13	5	37	2	3	5	39	23
Bystrom, Martin, Philadelphia	.237	24	38	2	9	10	1	0	0	4	0	1	1	0	0
Calvert, Mark, San Francisco	.000	18	8	0	0	0	0	0	0	0	0	1	0	0	0
Camp, Rick, Atlanta	.077	40	39	3	3	4	1	0	0	2	0	3	1	0	0
Campbell, William, Chicago	.100	82	10	0	1	1	0	0	0	1	0	0	0	0	0
Candelaria, John, Pittsburgh†	.138	33	65	4	9	10	1	0	0	2	1	5	0	0	0
Carlton, Steven, Philadelphia*	.196	37	97	9	19	24	5	0	0	1	0	6	0	0	0
Carman, Donald, Philadelphia*	.000	1	0	0	0	0	0	0	0	0	0	0	0	0	0
Carter, Gary, Montreal	.270	145	541	63	146	240	37	3	17	79	5	2	8	1	1
Carter, Joseph, Chicago	.176	23	51	6	9	12	1	1	0	1	0	1	0	1	0
Cato, J. Keefe, Cincinnati	.000	4	0	0	0	0	0	0	0	0	0	1	0	0	0
Cedeno, Cesar, Cincinnati	.232	98	332	40	77	120	16	0	9	39	4	1	6	13	9
Cey, Ronald, Chicago	.275	159	581	73	160	267	33	1	24	90	11	1	9	0	0
Chambliss, C. Christopher, Atlanta*	.280	131	447	59	125	215	24	3	20	78	10	0	3	2	7
Chiffer, Floyd, San Diego	.000	15	1	0	0	0	0	0	0	0	0	0	0	0	0
Chris, Michael, San Francisco*	.000	7	2	0	0	0	0	0	0	0	0	0	0	0	0
Christenson, Larry, Philadelphia	.059	9	17	0	1	2	1	0	0	1	0	1	0	0	0

Player and Club	Pct.	G.	AB.	R.	H.	TB.	2B.	3B.	HR.	RBI.	GW.	SH.	SF.	SB.	CS.
Christmas, Stephen, Cincinnati*	.059	9	17	0	1	1	0	0	0	1	0	0	1	0	0
Citarella, Ralph, St. Louis	.000	6	1	0	0	0	0	0	0	0	0	0	0	0	0
Clark, Jack, San Francisco	.268	135	492	82	132	217	25	0	20	66	11	0	7	5	3
Comer, Steven, Philadelphia*	.000	3	1	0	0	0	0	0	0	0	0	1	0	0	0
Concepcion, David, Cincinnati	.233	143	528	54	123	148	22	0	1	47	8	2	7	14	9
Connally, Fritzie, Chicago	.100	8	10	0	1	1	0	0	0	0	0	0	0	0	0
Corcoran, Timothy, Philadelphia*	.000	3	0	0	0	0	0	0	0	0	0	1	0	0	0
Couchee, Michael, San Diego	.500	8	2	0	1	1	0	0	0	0	0	0	0	0	0
Cox, Danny, St. Louis	.074	12	27	1	2	2	0	0	0	0	0	3	0	0	0
Cromartie, Warren, Montreal*	.278	120	360	37	100	139	26	2	3	43	8	1	5	8	3
Crowley, Terrence, Montreal*	.182	50	44	2	8	8	0	0	0	3	1	0	1	0	0
Cruz, Jose, Houston*	.318	160	594	85	189	275	28	8	14	92	9	1	3	30	16
Darling, Ronald, New York	.100	5	10	0	1	1	0	0	0	0	0	1	0	0	0
Daulton, Darren, Philadelphia*	.333	2	3	1	1	1	0	0	0	0	0	0	0	0	0
Davis, Charles, San Francisco†	.233	137	486	54	113	171	21	2	11	59	9	3	9	10	12
Davis, Gerald, San Diego	.333	5	15	3	5	7	2	0	0	1	0	0	0	1	0
Davis, Jody, Chicago	.271	151	510	56	138	245	31	2	24	84	8	0	5	0	2
Davis, Mark, San Francisco*	.133	20	30	3	4	5	1	0	0	1	0	9	0	0	0
Dawley, William, Houston	.222	48	9	0	2	2	0	0	0	1	0	0	0	0	0
Dawson, Andre, Montreal	.299	159	633	104	189	341	36	10	32	113	14	0	18	25	11
Dayley, Kenneth, Atlanta*	.219	25	32	2	7	7	0	0	0	1	0	5	0	0	0
Decker, D. Martin, San Diego	.000	4	0	0	0	0	0	0	0	0	0	0	0	0	0
Dedmon, Jeffrey, Atlanta	.000	5	0	0	0	0	0	0	0	0	0	0	0	0	0
DeJesus, Ivan, Philadelphia	.254	158	497	60	126	167	15	7	4	45	7	11	4	11	4
DeLeon, Jose, Philadelphia	.059	15	34	2	2	2	0	0	0	0	0	3	0	0	0
DeLeon, Luis, San Diego	.143	65	14	3	2	2	0	0	0	0	0	3	0	0	0
Denny, John, Philadelphia	.169	36	77	7	13	14	1	0	0	2	0	17	0	2	0
Dernier, Robert, Philadelphia	.231	122	221	41	51	64	10	0	1	15	3	5	1	35	7
Diaz, Baudilio, Philadelphia	.236	136	471	49	111	173	17	0	15	64	7	4	1	1	4
Diaz, Carlos, New York	.000	54	5	1	0	0	0	0	0	0	0	1	0	0	0
Diaz, Michael, Chicago	.286	6	7	2	2	3	1	0	0	1	0	0	0	0	0
Dilone, Miguel, Pittsburgh†	.000	7	0	1	0	0	0	0	0	0	0	0	0	2	0
DiPino, Frank, Houston*	.167	53	6	1	1	2	1	0	0	1	0	0	0	0	0
Dixon, Thomas, Montreal	.000	4	0	0	0	0	0	0	0	0	0	0	0	0	0
Doran, William, Houston†	.271	154	535	70	145	195	12	7	8	39	2	7	1	12	12
Doyle, Jeffrey, St. Louis*	.297	13	37	4	11	16	1	2	0	2	0	2	0	0	0
Dravecky, David, San Diego	.098	28	61	4	6	8	2	0	0	1	1	6	0	0	0
Driessen, Daniel, Cincinnati*	.277	122	386	57	107	162	17	1	12	57	8	0	6	6	4
Durham, Leon, Chicago*	.258	100	337	58	87	157	18	8	12	55	5	0	3	12	6
Easler, Michael, Pittsburgh*	.307	115	381	44	117	168	17	2	10	54	8	1	1	4	2
Esasky, Nicholas, Cincinnati	.265	85	302	41	80	136	10	5	12	46	5	0	3	6	2
Espy, Cecil, Los Angeles†	.273	20	11	4	3	4	1	0	0	1	0	0	0	0	0
Evans, Darrell, San Francisco*	.277	142	523	94	145	270	29	3	30	82	15	0	2	6	6
Falcone, Peter, Atlanta*	.115	33	26	0	3	3	0	0	0	2	0	5	1	0	0
Farmer, Edward, Philadelphia	.167	12	6	0	1	1	0	0	0	0	0	1	0	0	0
Fernandez, C. Sid, Los Angeles*	1.000	2	1	0	1	1	0	0	0	0	0	0	0	0	0
Fimple, John, Los Angeles	.250	54	148	16	37	53	8	1	2	22	1	7	1	1	0
Fireovid, Stephen, San Diego†	.000	3	0	0	0	0	0	0	0	0	0	0	0	0	0
Fitzgerald, Michael, New York	.100	8	20	1	2	5	0	0	1	2	0	0	0	0	0
Flannery, Timothy, San Diego*	.234	92	214	24	50	72	7	3	3	19	0	2	4	2	2
Flynn, R. Douglas, Montreal	.237	143	452	44	107	133	18	4	0	26	3	5	1	2	1
Foley, Thomas, Cincinnati*	.204	68	98	7	20	26	4	1	0	9	1	2	0	1	0
Forsch, Robert, St. Louis	.241	37	54	4	13	19	3	0	1	6	1	7	2	0	1
Forster, Terry, Atlanta*	.500	56	8	1	4	5	1	0	0	0	0	1	0	0	0
Foster, George, New York	.241	157	601	74	145	252	19	2	28	90	12	0	4	1	1
Francona, Terry, Montreal*	.257	120	230	21	59	81	11	1	3	22	1	0	2	0	2
Frobel, Douglas, Pittsburgh*	.283	32	60	10	17	32	4	1	3	11	1	0	0	1	1
Fryman, Woodrow, Montreal	.000	6	0	0	0	0	0	0	0	0	0	0	0	0	0
Fuentes, Michael, Montreal	.250	6	4	1	1	1	0	0	0	0	0	0	0	0	0
Gaff, Brent, New York	.000	4	3	0	0	0	0	0	0	0	0	0	0	0	0
Gale, Richard, Cincinnati	.150	33	20	2	3	7	1	0	1	3	0	1	0	0	1
Garber, H. Eugene, Atlanta	.000	43	3	1	0	0	0	0	0	0	0	0	0	0	0
Garcia, Alfonso, Philadelphia	.288	84	118	22	34	49	7	1	2	9	1	3	0	1	2
Gardenhire, Ronald, New York	.063	17	32	1	2	2	0	0	0	1	0	0	0	0	0
Garner, Philip, Houston	.238	154	567	76	135	205	24	2	14	79	10	3	6	18	12
Garrelts, Scott, San Francisco	.222	5	9	1	2	2	0	0	0	0	0	3	0	0	0
Garvey, Steven, San Diego	.294	100	388	76	114	178	22	0	14	59	9	0	5	4	1
Ghelfi, Anthony, Philadelphia	.250	3	4	0	1	1	0	0	0	0	0	0	0	0	0
Giles, Brian, New York	.245	145	400	39	98	119	15	0	2	27	2	4	3	17	10
Gladden, C. Daniel, San Francisco	.222	18	63	6	14	19	2	0	1	9	2	3	1	4	3
Gorman, Thomas, New York*	.250	25	4	0	1	1	0	0	0	0	0	1	0	0	1
Grant, Thomas, Chicago*	.150	16	20	2	3	4	1	0	0	2	0	0	0	0	0
Grapenthin, Richard, Montreal	.000	1	1	0	0	0	0	0	0	0	0	0	0	0	0
Green, David, St. Louis	.284	146	422	52	120	178	14	10	8	69	6	3	4	34	16
Gross, Gregory, Philadelphia*	.302	136	245	25	74	92	12	3	0	29	5	1	3	3	5
Gross, Kevin, Philadelphia	.091	17	33	1	3	4	1	0	0	1	1	1	0	1	0
Guante, Cecilio, Pittsburgh	.091	49	22	1	2	2	0	0	0	0	0	0	0	0	0
Guerrero, Pedro, Los Angeles	.298	160	584	87	174	310	28	6	32	103	13	0	6	23	7
Gullickson, William, Montreal	.134	34	82	10	11	19	5	0	1	3	1	9	0	0	0
Gwosdz, Douglas, San Diego	.109	39	55	7	6	10	1	0	1	4	1	2	0	0	0

Player and Club	Pct.	G.	AB.	R.	H.	TB.	2B.	3B.	HR.	RBI.	GW.	SH.	SF.	SB.	CS.
Gwynn, Anthony, San Diego*	.309	86	304	34	94	113	12	2	1	37	6	4	3	7	4
Hagen, Kevin, St. Louis	.000	9	5	0	0	0	0	0	0	0	0	0	0	0	0
Hall, Albert, Atlanta†	.000	10	8	2	0	0	0	0	0	0	0	0	0	1	1
Hall, Melvin, Chicago*	.283	112	410	60	116	200	23	5	17	56	3	1	2	6	6
Hammaker, C. Atlee, San Francisco	.102	23	59	1	6	6	0	0	0	2	0	3	0	0	0
Hargesheimer, Alan, Chicago	.000	5	0	0	0	0	0	0	0	0	0	0	0	0	0
Harper, Brian, Pittsburgh	.221	61	131	16	29	56	4	1	7	20	1	2	4	0	0
Harper, Terry, Atlanta	.264	80	201	19	53	77	13	1	3	26	4	1	1	6	5
Harris, Greg, Cincinnati†	.000	1	1	0	0	0	0	0	0	0	0	0	0	0	0
Hawkins, M. Andrew, San Diego	.065	21	31	3	2	2	0	0	0	0	0	6	0	0	0
Hayes, Ben, Cincinnati	.000	60	5	0	0	0	0	0	0	0	0	0	0	0	0
Hayes, Von, Philadelphia*	.265	124	351	45	93	130	9	5	6	32	6	0	2	20	12
Heathcock, R. Jeffery, Houston	.000	6	6	0	0	0	0	0	0	0	0	3	0	0	0
Hebner, Richard, Pittsburgh*	.265	78	162	23	43	64	4	1	5	26	3	2	4	8	3
Heep, Daniel, New York*	.253	115	253	30	64	100	12	0	8	21	3	1	5	3	3
Hendrick, George, St. Louis	.318	144	529	73	168	261	33	3	18	97	12	0	11	3	4
Hernandez, Guillermo, Chi-Phil*	.400	74	15	2	6	6	0	0	0	1	0	0	0	1	0
Hernandez, Keith, St.L.-N.Y.*	.297	150	538	77	160	233	23	7	12	63	9	2	3	9	5
Herr, Thomas, St. Louis†	.323	89	313	43	101	129	14	4	2	31	6	8	3	6	8
Hershiser, Orel, Los Angeles	.000	8	0	0	0	0	0	0	0	0	0	0	0	0	0
Hinshaw, George, San Diego	.438	7	16	1	7	8	1	0	0	4	1	1	0	1	0
Hodges, Ronald, New York*	.260	110	250	20	65	77	12	0	0	21	2	2	2	0	3
Holland, Alfred, Philadelphia	.000	68	7	0	0	0	0	0	0	0	0	1	0	0	0
Holman, R. Scott, New York	.217	35	23	1	5	5	0	0	0	2	0	2	0	0	0
Honeycutt, Frederick, Los Angeles*	.083	9	12	1	1	1	0	0	0	1	0	2	0	0	0
Hooton, Burt, Los Angeles	.160	33	50	5	8	10	2	0	0	7	1	4	0	0	0
Horner, J. Robert, Atlanta	.303	104	386	75	117	204	25	1	20	68	10	0	2	4	2
Householder, Paul, Cincinnati†	.255	123	380	40	97	147	24	4	6	43	3	0	1	12	12
Howard, Michael, New York†	.333	1	3	0	1	1	0	0	0	1	1	0	0	0	0
Howe, Steven, Los Angeles*	.125	46	8	1	1	1	0	0	0	0	0	0	0	0	0
Hubbard, Glenn, Atlanta	.263	148	517	65	136	208	24	6	12	70	4	9	7	3	8
Hudson, Charles, Philadelphia	.093	27	54	4	5	5	0	0	0	3	0	5	0	0	0
Hume, Thomas, Cincinnati	.000	48	5	0	0	0	0	0	0	0	0	1	0	0	0
Hurdle, Clinton, New York*	.182	13	33	3	6	8	2	0	0	2	0	0	0	0	0
Iorg, Dane, St. Louis*	.267	58	116	6	31	42	9	1	0	11	1	0	4	1	0
Jacoby, Brook, Atlanta	.000	4	8	0	0	0	0	0	0	0	0	1	0	0	0
James, Robert, Montreal	.286	27	7	0	2	2	0	0	0	1	0	0	0	0	0
Jeltz, L. Steven, Philadelphia	.125	13	8	0	1	3	0	1	0	1	0	1	0	0	0
Jenkins, Ferguson, Chicago	.245	33	53	3	13	17	2	1	0	5	0	5	0	0	0
Johnson, Randall G., Atlanta	.250	86	144	22	36	42	3	0	1	17	5	4	0	1	3
Johnson, Wallace, Mtl-S.F.†	.200	10	10	1	2	2	0	0	0	1	0	0	0	1	0
Johnson, William, Chicago	.000	10	0	0	0	0	0	0	0	0	0	0	0	0	0
Johnstone, John, Chicago*	.257	86	140	16	36	61	7	0	6	22	1	2	0	1	1
Jones, Jeffrey R., Cincinnati	.227	16	44	6	10	13	3	0	0	5	1	0	2	2	0
Jones, Ruppert, San Diego*	.233	133	335	42	78	132	12	3	12	49	8	2	0	11	11
Jorgensen, Michael, N.Y.-Atlanta*	.250	95	72	10	18	28	4	0	2	11	0	0	1	0	1
Kaat, James, St. Louis*	.000	24	4	0	0	0	0	0	0	0	0	1	0	0	0
Keener, Jeffrey, St. Louis*	.000	4	0	0	0	0	0	0	0	0	0	0	0	0	0
Kennedy, Junior, Chicago	.136	17	22	3	3	3	0	0	0	3	0	0	1	0	0
Kennedy, Terrence, San Diego*	.284	149	549	47	156	238	27	2	17	98	14	1	9	1	3
Kingman, Brian, San Francisco	.000	3	0	0	0	0	0	0	0	0	0	0	0	0	0
Kingman, David, New York	.198	100	248	25	49	95	7	0	13	29	1	1	1	2	1
Knepper, Robert, Houston*	.182	35	66	5	12	19	2	1	1	5	1	4	2	0	0
Knicely, Alan, Cincinnati	.224	59	98	11	22	31	3	0	2	10	1	1	0	0	2
Knight, C. Ray, Houston	.304	145	507	43	154	225	36	4	9	70	8	3	11	0	3
Komminsk, Brad, Atlanta	.222	19	36	2	8	10	2	0	0	4	1	0	0	0	0
Krenchicki, Wayne, Cincinnati*	.273	51	77	6	21	23	2	0	0	11	2	0	1	0	0
Krukow, Michael, San Francisco	.254	31	63	3	16	21	2	0	1	8	0	4	2	1	1
Kuiper, Duane, San Francisco*	.250	72	176	14	44	50	2	2	0	14	1	4	2	0	1
LaCorte, Frank, Houston	.200	37	5	0	1	2	1	0	0	1	0	1	1	0	0
LaCoss, Michael, Houston	.086	38	35	1	3	3	0	0	0	1	0	4	0	0	0
Lacy, Leondaus, Pittsburgh	.302	108	288	40	87	117	12	3	4	13	1	3	0	31	13
Lahti, Jeffrey, St. Louis	.000	53	10	0	0	0	0	0	0	0	0	0	0	0	0
Lake, Steven, Chicago	.259	38	85	9	22	31	4	1	1	7	1	0	0	0	0
Landestoy, Rafael, Cin-L.A.†	.159	71	69	6	11	17	1	1	1	1	0	0	0	0	2
Landreaux, Kenneth, Los Ang.*	.281	141	481	63	135	217	25	3	17	66	16	2	5	30	11
Landrum, Terry, St. Louis	.200	6	5	0	1	3	0	1	0	0	0	0	0	1	0
Lansford, Joseph, San Diego	.250	12	8	1	2	5	0	0	1	2	0	0	0	0	0
LaPoint, David, St. Louis*	.153	37	59	4	9	9	0	0	0	5	0	5	0	0	0
Larkin, Patrick, San Francisco*	.000	5	1	0	0	0	0	0	0	0	0	0	0	0	0
Laskey, William, San Francisco	.106	26	47	5	5	5	0	0	0	1	0	1	0	0	1
Lavelle, Gary, San Francisco	.000	56	14	0	0	0	0	0	0	0	0	0	0	0	0
Lea, Charles, Montreal	.114	33	70	6	8	9	1	0	0	3	0	12	0	0	0
Leary, Timothy, New York	.333	2	3	0	1	1	0	0	0	0	0	0	0	0	0
Lefebvre, Joseph, S.D.-Phila.*	.306	119	278	35	85	145	20	8	8	39	7	1	2	5	3
Lefferts, Craig, Chicago*	.111	56	18	1	2	2	0	0	0	0	0	1	0	0	0
LeMaster, Johnnie, San Francisco	.240	141	534	81	128	164	16	1	6	30	1	8	4	39	19
Leonard, Jeffrey, San Francisco	.279	139	516	74	144	238	17	7	21	87	6	0	6	26	7
Lerch, Randy, Mtl-S.F.*	.222	26	9	0	2	3	1	0	0	0	0	1	0	0	0
Lesley, Bradley, Cincinnati	.000	5	0	0	0	0	0	0	0	0	0	1	0	0	0

Player and Club	Pct.	G.	AB.	R.	H.	TB.	2B.	3B.	HR.	RBI.	GW.	SH.	SF.	SB.	CS.
Lezcano, Sixto, San Diego-Phila.	.239	115	356	49	85	125	12	2	8	56	8	5	4	1	0
Little, R. Bryan, Montreal†	.260	106	350	48	91	115	15	3	1	36	4	5	4	4	5
Lollar, W. Timothy, San Diego*	.241	31	58	7	14	20	1	1	1	11	1	0	2	0	0
Loucks, Scott, Houston	.214	7	14	2	3	3	0	0	0	0	0	0	0	2	2
Loviglio, John, Chicago	.000	1	1	0	0	0	0	0	0	0	0	0	0	0	0
Lucas, Gary, San Diego*	.000	62	12	0	0	0	0	0	0	1	0	0	0	0	0
Lynch, Edward, New York	.154	30	52	3	8	8	0	0	0	4	0	11	0	0	0
Lyons, William, St. Louis	.167	42	60	3	10	13	1	1	0	3	0	0	0	3	2
Madden, Michael, Houston*	.045	28	22	0	1	1	0	0	0	2	0	6	0	0	0
Maddox, Garry, Philadelphia	.275	97	324	27	89	119	14	2	4	32	0	2	1	7	6
Madlock, Bill, Pittsburgh	.323	130	473	68	153	210	21	0	12	68	14	1	5	3	4
Mahler, Richard, Atlanta	.000	10	2	0	0	0	0	0	0	0	0	0	0	0	0
Maldonado, Candido, Los Angeles	.194	42	62	5	12	18	1	1	1	6	1	1	0	0	0
Marshall, Michael, Los Angeles	.284	140	465	47	132	202	17	1	17	65	11	0	5	7	3
Martin, D. Renie, San Francisco	.346	37	26	4	9	15	2	2	0	1	0	1	0	1	0
Martin, John, St. Louis†	.222	26	18	1	4	5	1	0	0	4	0	2	0	0	0
Martinez, Carmelo, Chicago	.258	29	89	8	23	44	3	0	6	16	1	0	1	0	0
Matthews, Gary, Philadelphia	.258	132	446	66	115	167	18	2	10	50	3	4	7	13	9
Matuszek, Leonard, Philadelphia*	.275	28	80	12	22	42	6	1	4	16	0	2	1	0	1
May, Milton, San Fran.-Pittsburgh*	.247	73	198	18	49	73	6	0	6	20	4	1	0	2	2
Mazzilli, Lee, Pittsburgh†	.240	109	246	37	59	83	9	0	5	24	5	4	4	15	5
McGaffigan, Andrew, San Fran.	.067	43	30	0	2	4	2	0	0	3	0	2	0	0	1
McGee, Willie, St. Louis†	.286	147	601	75	172	225	22	8	5	75	9	1	3	39	8
McGraw, Frank, Philadelphia	.333	34	3	0	1	1	0	0	0	0	0	2	0	0	0
McMurtry, J. Craig, Atlanta	.086	36	70	2	6	6	0	0	0	3	0	12	0	0	0
McReynolds, W. Kevin, San Diego	.221	39	140	15	31	48	3	1	4	14	2	0	3	2	1
McWilliams, Larry, Pittsburgh*	.114	35	79	5	9	10	1	0	0	4	1	10	0	1	1
Milbourne, Lawrence, Philadelphia†.	.242	41	66	3	16	18	0	1	0	4	2	2	1	2	1
Mills, J. Bradley, Montreal*	.250	14	20	1	5	5	0	0	0	1	0	0	0	0	0
Milner, Eddie, Cincinnati*	.261	146	502	77	131	193	23	6	9	33	1	12	1	41	12
Minton, Gregory, San Francisco†	.545	73	11	4	6	10	1	0	1	3	0	0	0	0	0
Mizerock, John, Houston*	.153	33	85	8	13	22	4	1	1	10	1	1	1	0	0
Molinaro, Robert, Philadelphia*	.111	19	18	1	2	6	1	0	1	3	1	0	1	0	0
Monday, Robert, Los Angeles*	.247	99	178	21	44	71	7	1	6	20	4	0	1	0	0
Monge, Isidro, Phila.-San Diego†	.091	61	11	0	1	1	0	0	0	0	0	1	0	0	0
Montefusco, John, San Diego	.053	31	19	1	1	1	0	0	0	1	0	4	0	0	0
Moore, Donnie, Atlanta*	.500	43	8	0	4	4	0	0	0	3	0	1	0	0	0
Morales, Jose, Los Angeles	.283	47	53	4	15	27	3	0	3	8	1	0	0	0	0
Morales, Julio, Chicago	.195	63	87	11	17	26	9	0	0	11	2	0	1	0	0
Moreland, B. Keith, Chicago	.302	154	533	76	161	245	30	3	16	70	11	5	10	0	3
Moreno, Omar, Houston*	.242	97	405	48	98	132	12	11	0	25	1	0	1	30	13
Morgan, Joe, Philadelphia*	.230	123	404	72	93	163	20	1	16	59	7	1	6	18	2
Morrison, James, Pittsburgh	.304	66	158	16	48	77	7	2	6	25	5	4	1	2	6
Moskau, Paul, Chicago	.182	8	11	2	2	3	1	0	0	0	0	2	0	0	0
Mumphrey, Jerry, Houston†	.336	44	143	17	48	65	10	2	1	17	2	0	1	5	0
Murphy, Dale, Atlanta	.302	162	589	131	178	318	24	4	36	121	14	0	6	30	4
Murray, Richard, San Francisco	.200	4	10	0	2	2	0	0	0	1	0	0	0	0	0
Nicosia, Steven, Pitts.-San Fran.	.215	36	79	8	17	22	2	0	1	7	0	3	0	0	0
Niedenfuer, Thomas, Los Angeles	.000	66	4	1	0	0	0	0	0	0	0	0	0	0	0
Niekro, Joseph, Houston	.094	38	85	1	8	10	2	0	0	2	0	12	0	0	0
Niekro, Philip, Atlanta	.185	34	65	3	12	14	2	0	0	5	0	6	1	0	0
Niemann, Randy, Pittsburgh	.000	8	1	0	0	0	0	0	0	0	0	0	0	0	0
Noles, Dickie, Chicago	.237	24	38	1	9	10	1	0	0	5	0	3	0	0	0
Nordhagen, Wayne, Chicago	.143	21	35	1	5	9	1	0	1	4	0	0	1	0	0
Oberkfell, Kenneth, St. Louis*	.293	151	488	62	143	188	26	5	3	38	6	4	3	12	6
Oester, Ronald, Cincinnati†	.264	157	549	63	145	211	23	5	11	58	5	7	6	2	2
Oliver, Albert, Montreal*	.300	157	614	70	184	252	38	3	8	84	12	1	3	1	3
O'Malley, Thomas, San Francisco*	.259	135	410	40	106	139	16	1	5	45	8	4	3	2	4
Oquendo, Jose, New York	.213	120	328	29	70	80	7	0	1	17	3	3	1	8	9
Orosco, Jesse, New York	.333	62	12	0	4	4	0	0	0	2	0	2	1	0	0
Orsulak, Joseph, Pittsburgh*	.182	7	11	0	2	2	0	0	0	1	0	0	1	0	1
Ortiz, Adalberto, Pitts.-New York	.249	73	193	11	48	53	5	0	0	12	1	2	0	1	0
Owchinko, Robert, Pittsburgh*	.000	1	0	0	0	0	0	0	0	0	0	0	0	0	0
Owen, Dave, Chicago†	.091	16	22	1	2	4	0	1	0	2	0	1	1	1	0
Owen, Lawrence, Atlanta	.118	17	17	0	2	2	0	0	0	1	1	0	0	0	1
Ownbey, Richard, New York	.111	12	9	2	1	1	0	0	0	0	0	1	0	0	0
Paris, Kelly, Cincinnati	.250	56	120	13	30	36	6	0	0	7	0	1	1	8	2
Parker, David, Pittsburgh*	.279	144	552	68	154	227	29	4	12	69	10	0	6	12	9
Pastore, Frank, Cincinnati	.186	36	59	6	11	16	2	0	1	5	1	3	0	0	1
Patterson, Reginald, Chicago*	.000	5	6	1	0	0	0	0	0	0	0	2	0	0	0
Pena, Adalberto, Houston	.125	4	8	0	1	1	0	0	0	0	0	0	0	0	0
Pena, Alejandro, Los Angeles	.100	34	60	2	6	9	0	0	1	4	1	1	0	0	0
Pena, Antonio, Pittsburgh	.301	151	542	51	163	236	22	3	15	70	2	6	1	6	7
Perez, Atanasio, Philadelphia	.241	91	253	18	61	94	11	2	6	43	8	0	3	1	0
Perez, Pascual, Atlanta	.160	33	75	4	12	12	0	0	0	3	0	7	0	0	0
Perry, Gerald, Atlanta*	.359	27	39	5	14	19	2	0	1	6	1	0	1	0	1
Pettini, Joseph, San Francisco	.186	61	86	11	16	18	0	1	0	7	0	1	1	4	1
Phillips, Michael, Montreal*	.000	5	2	0	0	0	0	0	0	0	0	0	0	0	0
Pocoroba, Biff, Atlanta*	.267	55	120	11	32	44	6	0	2	16	1	0	1	0	0
Porter, Darrell, St. Louis*	.262	145	443	57	116	191	24	3	15	66	5	1	3	1	3

Player and Club	Pct.	G.	AB.	R.	H.	TB.	2B.	3B.	HR.	RBI.	GW.	SH.	SF.	SB.	CS.
Power, Ted, Cincinnati	.000	49	16	0	0	0	0	0	0	0	0	3	0	0	0
Price, Joseph, Cincinnati	.098	21	41	0	4	4	0	0	0	0	0	3	0	0	0
Proly, Michael, Chicago	.091	60	11	1	1	1	0	0	0	0	0	2	0	0	0
Pruitt, Ronald, San Francisco	.000	1	1	0	0	0	0	0	0	0	0	0	0	0	0
Puhl, Terry, Houston*	.292	137	465	66	136	199	25	7	8	44	5	5	4	24	11
Pujols, Luis, Houston	.195	40	87	4	17	19	2	0	0	12	4	3	2	0	0
Puleo, Charles, Cincinnati	.100	27	50	4	5	5	0	0	0	3	0	2	0	0	0
Pulido, Alfonso, Pittsburgh*	.000	1	0	0	0	0	0	0	0	0	0	1	0	0	0
Quirk, James, St. Louis*	.209	48	86	3	18	28	2	1	2	11	1	0	0	0	0
Rabb, John, San Francisco	.231	40	104	10	24	36	9	0	1	14	0	1	0	1	0
Raines, Timothy, Montreal†	.298	156	615	133	183	264	32	8	11	71	13	2	4	90	14
Rainey, Charles, Chicago	.161	34	56	4	9	9	0	0	0	0	0	10	0	0	0
Rajsich, Gary, New York*	.333	11	36	5	12	18	3	0	1	3	0	0	0	0	0
Ramirez, Mario, San Diego	.196	55	107	11	21	33	6	3	0	12	0	2	1	0	0
Ramirez, Rafael, Atlanta	.297	152	622	82	185	229	13	5	7	58	10	6	2	16	12
Ramos, Roberto, Montreal	.230	27	61	2	14	19	3	1	0	5	0	0	0	0	0
Ramsey, Michael, St. Louis†	.263	97	175	25	46	59	4	3	1	16	2	1	3	4	2
Ransom, Jeffrey, San Francisco	.200	6	20	3	4	7	0	0	1	3	1	0	0	0	0
Rasmussen, Dennis, San Diego*	.000	4	3	0	0	0	0	0	0	0	0	0	0	0	0
Rasmussen, Eric, St. Louis	.000	6	0	0	0	0	0	0	0	0	0	0	0	0	0
Ray, Johnny, Pittsburgh†	.283	151	576	68	163	230	38	7	5	53	5	10	2	18	9
Rayford, Floyd, St. Louis	.212	56	104	5	22	35	4	0	3	14	2	2	1	1	0
Reardon, Jeffrey, Montreal	.125	66	8	0	1	1	0	0	0	0	0	0	0	0	0
Redus, Gary, Cincinnati	.247	125	453	90	112	201	20	9	17	51	11	2	2	39	14
Reed, Ronald, Philadelphia	.167	61	6	0	1	1	0	0	0	0	0	1	0	0	0
Reuschel, Ricky, Chicago	.143	4	7	0	1	1	0	0	0	0	0	0	0	0	0
Reuss, Jerry, Los Angeles*	.282	32	71	4	20	22	2	0	0	3	0	10	0	0	0
Reyes, Gilberto, Los Angeles	.161	19	31	1	5	7	2	0	0	0	0	0	0	0	0
Reynolds, G. Craig, Houston*	.214	65	98	10	21	27	3	0	1	6	3	0	0	0	1
Reynolds, Robert, Los Angeles†	.236	24	55	5	13	19	0	0	2	11	1	1	2	5	0
Reynolds, Ronn, New York	.197	24	66	4	13	14	1	0	0	2	0	0	1	0	0
Rhoden, Richard, Pittsburgh	.151	36	86	2	13	14	1	0	0	5	0	2	0	0	0
Richards, Eugene, San Diego*	.275	95	233	37	64	90	11	3	3	22	4	0	1	14	5
Rivera, German, Los Angeles	.353	13	17	1	6	7	1	0	0	0	0	0	0	0	1
Robinson, Don, Pittsburgh	.154	10	13	1	2	5	0	0	1	3	1	0	0	0	0
Robinson, William, Philadelphia	.143	10	7	0	1	1	0	0	0	2	0	0	0	0	0
Rodas, Richard, Los Angeles*	.000	7	0	0	0	0	0	0	0	0	0	0	0	0	0
Rodriguez, Edwin, San Diego	.167	7	12	1	2	3	1	0	0	0	0	1	0	0	0
Roenicke, Ronald, Los Angeles†	.221	81	145	12	32	42	4	0	2	12	3	4	1	3	2
Rogers, Stephen, Montreal	.146	36	82	5	12	13	1	0	0	2	1	20	0	0	0
Rohn, Daniel, Chicago*	.387	23	31	3	12	19	3	2	0	6	0	1	0	1	0
Roof, Eugene, St. Louis-Montreal†	.133	14	15	3	2	4	2	0	0	1	0	0	0	0	0
Rose, Peter, Philadelphia†	.245	151	493	52	121	141	14	3	0	45	5	1	7	7	7
Royster, Jeron, Atlanta	.235	91	268	32	63	88	10	3	3	30	3	5	2	11	7
Rucker, David, St. Louis*	.000	34	4	0	0	0	0	0	0	0	0	0	0	0	0
Ruhle, Vernon, Houston	.105	41	19	1	2	2	0	0	0	2	0	4	0	0	0
Runge, Paul, Atlanta	.250	5	8	0	2	2	0	0	0	1	0	1	0	0	0
Russell, Jeffrey, Cincinnati	.143	10	21	1	3	7	1	0	1	3	0	2	0	0	0
Russell, William, Los Angeles	.246	131	451	47	111	129	13	1	1	30	7	12	2	13	9
Ruthven, Richard, Phila.-Chicago	.210	32	62	6	13	15	2	0	0	3	0	7	0	0	0
Ryan, L. Nolan, Houston	.072	29	69	3	5	5	0	0	0	2	0	4	0	0	0
Salazar, Argenis, Montreal	.216	36	37	5	8	11	1	1	0	1	0	1	1	0	0
Salazar, Luis, San Diego	.258	134	481	52	124	186	16	2	14	45	3	8	2	24	9
Samuel, Juan, Philadelphia	.277	18	65	14	18	29	1	2	2	5	0	0	1	3	2
Sanchez, Alejandro, Philadelphia	.286	8	7	2	2	2	0	0	0	2	0	0	0	0	0
Sanchez, Orlando, St. Louis*	.000	6	6	0	0	0	0	0	0	0	0	0	0	0	0
Sandberg, Ryne, Chicago	.261	158	633	94	165	222	25	4	8	48	3	7	5	37	11
Sanderson, Scott, Montreal	.143	18	28	1	4	6	2	0	0	1	0	1	0	0	0
Santana, Rafael, St. Louis	.214	30	14	1	3	3	0	0	0	2	0	0	0	0	1
Sarmiento, Manuel, Pittsburgh	.000	52	10	0	0	0	0	0	0	0	0	2	0	0	0
Sax, David, Los Angeles	.000	7	8	0	0	0	0	0	0	1	0	0	0	0	0
Sax, Stephen, Los Angeles	.281	155	623	94	175	218	18	5	5	41	2	8	2	56	30
Schatzeder, Daniel, Montreal*	.200	58	10	0	2	2	0	0	0	2	0	1	0	0	0
Scherrer, William, Cincinnati*	.091	73	11	0	1	1	0	0	0	0	0	1	0	0	0
Schmidt, Michael, Philadelphia	.255	154	534	104	136	280	16	4	40	109	12	0	4	7	8
Schulze, Donald, Chicago	.000	4	1	0	0	0	0	0	0	0	0	1	0	0	0
Scioscia, Michael, Los Angeles*	.314	12	35	3	11	17	3	0	1	7	1	0	0	0	0
Scott, Anthony, Houston†	.226	80	186	20	42	56	6	1	2	17	3	1	4	5	4
Scott, Michael, Houston	.167	24	48	2	8	10	2	0	0	4	0	8	0	0	0
Scurry, Rodney, Pittsburgh*	.000	61	5	0	0	0	0	0	0	0	0	0	0	0	0
Seaver, G. Thomas, New York	.156	34	64	6	10	14	0	2	0	4	0	6	1	0	0
Sexton, Jimmy, St. Louis	.111	6	9	1	1	2	1	0	0	0	0	0	0	0	0
Shines, A. Raymond, Montreal†	.500	3	2	0	1	1	0	0	0	0	0	0	0	0	0
Show, Eric, San Diego	.172	35	64	3	11	12	1	0	0	2	0	5	0	0	0
Sinatro, Matthew, Atlanta	.167	7	12	0	2	2	0	0	0	2	0	0	0	0	0
Sisk, Douglas, New York	.500	67	6	0	3	3	0	0	0	0	0	1	0	0	0
Smith, Bryn, Montreal	.167	49	30	0	5	5	0	0	0	0	0	7	0	0	0
Smith, Christopher, San Francisco†	.328	22	67	13	22	33	6	1	1	11	1	0	1	0	0
Smith, David, Houston	.000	42	5	0	0	0	0	0	0	0	0	1	0	0	0
Smith, Kenneth, Atlanta*	.167	30	12	2	2	5	0	0	1	2	0	0	0	1	0

Player and Club	Pct.	G.	AB.	R.	H.	TB.	2B.	3B.	HR.	RBI.	GW.	SH.	SF.	SB.	CS.
Smith, Lee, Chicago	.111	66	9	0	1	1	0	0	0	0	0	1	0	0	0
Smith, Lonnie, St. Louis	.321	130	492	83	158	223	31	5	8	45	3	1	4	43	18
Smith, Osborne, St. Louis†	.243	159	552	69	134	185	30	6	3	50	7	7	2	34	7
Solano, Julio, Houston	.000	4	0	0	0	0	0	0	0	0	0	0	0	0	0
Sosa, Elias, San Diego	.143	41	7	0	1	1	0	0	0	1	0	0	0	0	0
Soto, Mario, Cincinnati	.125	35	88	6	11	14	3	0	0	2	0	11	0	0	0
Speier, Chris, Montreal	.257	88	261	31	67	89	12	2	2	22	2	3	3	2	1
Spilman, W. Harry, Houston*	.167	42	78	7	13	19	3	0	1	9	1	0	2	0	0
Staub, Daniel, New York*	.296	104	115	5	34	49	6	0	3	28	3	0	2	0	0
Stearns, John, New York	.000	4	0	2	0	0	0	0	0	0	0	0	0	0	0
Stenhouse, Michael, Montreal*	.125	24	40	2	5	6	1	0	0	2	1	0	0	0	0
Stewart, David, Los Angeles	.143	46	7	0	1	1	0	0	0	1	0	1	0	0	0
Stone, Jeffery, Philadelphia*	.750	9	4	2	3	7	0	2	0	3	1	0	0	4	0
Strawberry, Darryl, New York*	.257	122	420	63	108	215	15	7	26	74	11	0	2	19	6
Stuper, John, St. Louis	.136	40	59	2	8	8	0	0	0	6	2	7	0	0	0
Sularz, Guy, San Francisco	.100	10	20	3	2	2	0	0	0	0	0	0	0	0	0
Summers, John, San Francisco*	.136	29	22	3	3	3	0	0	0	3	0	0	1	0	0
Sutter, H. Bruce, St. Louis	.000	60	7	0	0	0	0	0	0	0	0	1	0	0	0
Swan, Craig, New York	.077	27	26	0	2	2	0	0	0	1	0	1	0	0	0
Taveras, Alejandro, Los Angeles	.000	10	4	0	0	0	0	0	0	0	0	0	0	0	0
Tekulve, Kenton, Pittsburgh	.000	76	8	0	0	0	0	0	0	0	0	1	0	0	0
Templeton, Garry, San Diego†	.263	126	460	39	121	154	20	2	3	40	8	7	2	16	6
Tenace, F. Gene, Pittsburgh	.177	53	62	7	11	16	5	0	0	6	0	0	0	0	1
Terrell, C. Walter, New York*	.182	21	44	3	8	18	1	0	3	8	1	3	0	0	0
Thomas, Derrel, Los Angeles†	.250	118	192	38	48	72	6	6	2	8	0	4	2	9	3
Thompson, Jason, Pittsburgh*	.259	152	517	70	134	210	20	1	18	76	11	0	6	1	0
Thompson, V. Scot, Chicago*	.193	53	88	4	17	22	3	1	0	10	1	0	0	0	0
Thon, Richard, Houston	.286	154	619	81	177	283	28	9	20	79	18	3	8	34	16
Thurmond, Mark, San Diego*	.054	21	37	1	2	3	1	0	0	0	0	6	0	0	0
Tolman, Timothy, Houston	.196	43	56	4	11	21	4	0	2	10	1	0	1	0	1
Tomlin, David, Pittsburgh*	.000	5	0	0	0	0	0	0	0	0	0	0	0	0	0
Torrez, Michael, New York	.046	39	65	2	3	3	0	0	0	2	1	8	0	0	0
Trevino, Alejandro, Cincinnati	.216	74	167	14	36	49	8	1	1	13	0	1	2	0	0
Trillo, J. Manuel, Montreal	.264	31	121	16	32	46	8	0	2	16	3	3	0	0	0
Trout, Steven, Chicago*	.194	34	62	6	12	12	0	0	0	1	0	8	0	0	0
Tunnell, B. Lee, Pittsburgh	.121	35	58	2	7	9	0	1	0	3	0	8	0	0	0
Turner, John, San Diego*	.130	25	23	1	3	3	0	0	0	0	0	0	0	0	0
Vail, Michael, San Fran.-Montreal	.241	52	79	6	19	28	3	0	2	7	2	0	0	0	0
Valenzuela, Fernando, Los Angeles*	.187	36	91	5	17	23	3	0	1	9	1	12	1	0	1
Van Slyke, Andrew, St. Louis*	.262	101	309	51	81	130	15	5	8	38	2	2	3	21	7
Venable, W. McKinley, San Fran.*	.219	94	228	28	50	83	7	4	6	27	3	2	1	15	2
Veryzer, Thomas, Chicago	.205	59	88	5	18	24	3	0	1	3	0	1	0	0	0
Virgil, Osvaldo, Philadelphia	.214	55	140	11	30	55	7	0	6	23	3	0	0	0	2
Von Ohlen, David, St. Louis*	.143	46	7	0	1	1	0	0	0	0	0	1	0	0	0
Walk, Robert, Atlanta	.000	1	1	0	0	0	0	0	0	1	0	0	0	0	0
Walker, Duane, Cincinnati*	.236	109	225	14	53	73	12	1	2	29	3	0	2	6	3
Wallach, Timothy, Montreal	.269	156	581	54	156	252	33	3	19	70	8	0	5	0	3
Walling, Dennis, Houston*	.296	100	135	24	40	60	5	3	3	19	4	1	1	2	2
Washington, Claudell, Atlanta*	.278	134	496	75	138	205	24	8	9	44	5	1	6	31	9
Watson, Robert, Atlanta	.309	65	149	14	46	73	9	0	6	37	7	0	3	0	2
Welch, Robert, Los Angeles	.096	31	73	2	7	11	1	0	1	2	1	3	0	0	1
Wellman, Brad, San Francisco	.214	82	182	15	39	45	3	0	1	16	1	1	2	5	3
Welsh, Christopher, S. D.-Mont.*	.222	23	18	0	4	4	0	0	0	2	1	0	0	0	0
White, Jerome, Montreal†	.147	40	34	4	5	6	1	0	0	0	0	0	0	4	0
White, Larry, Los Angeles	.000	4	0	0	0	0	0	0	0	0	0	0	0	0	0
Whitson, Eddie, San Diego	.182	31	44	1	8	8	0	0	0	3	0	2	0	0	0
Wieghaus, Thomas, Montreal	.000	1	0	0	0	0	0	0	0	0	0	0	0	0	0
Wiggins, Alan, San Diego†	.276	144	503	83	139	163	20	2	0	22	2	16	0	66	13
Williams, Dallas, Cincinnati*	.056	18	36	2	2	2	0	0	0	1	0	2	0	0	0
Wilson, William, New York†	.276	152	638	91	176	234	25	6	7	51	6	2	1	54	16
Winn, James, Pittsburgh	.000	7	0	0	0	0	0	0	0	0	0	0	0	0	0
Wohlford, James, Montreal	.277	83	141	7	39	50	8	0	1	14	0	2	2	0	0
Woods, Gary, Chicago	.242	93	190	25	46	67	9	0	4	22	3	1	1	5	3
Wotus, Ronald, Pittsburgh	.000	5	3	0	0	0	0	0	0	0	0	0	0	0	0
Wright, J. Richard, Los Angeles*	.000	6	0	0	0	0	0	0	0	0	0	0	0	0	0
Wynne, Marvell, Pittsburgh*	.243	103	366	66	89	130	16	2	7	26	3	7	1	12	10
Yeager, Stephen, Los Angeles	.203	113	335	31	68	127	8	3	15	41	6	6	1	1	1
Youngblood, Joel, San Francisco	.292	124	373	59	109	186	20	3	17	53	6	2	2	7	4
Zachry, Patrick, Los Angeles	.500	40	4	0	2	2	0	0	0	0	0	0	0	0	0
Zuvella, Paul, Atlanta	.000	3	5	0	0	0	0	0	0	0	0	0	0	0	0

AWARDED FIRST BASE ON INTERFERENCE: Berra, Pitts. 7 (Owen, Bilardello, Ashby, Reyes, Ortiz (2), Quirk); Van Slyke, St.L. 3 (Mizerock, Diaz, Virgil); Benedict, Atl. 2 (Fimple, Yeager); Bowa, Chi. (May); Chambliss, Atl. (Kennedy); C. Davis, S.F. (Reyes); Gale, Cin. (Ashby); Hendrick, St.L. (Ashby); Oester, Cin. (May); Valenzuela, L.A. (Kennedy); Venable, S.F. (Benedict).

PLAYERS WITH TWO OR MORE CLUBS

(Alphabetically Arranged With Player's First Club on Top)

Player and Club	Pct.	G.	AB.	R.	H.	TB.	2B.	3B.	HR.	RBI.	GW.	SH.	SF.	Tot. BB.	Int. BB.	HP.	SO.	SB.	CS.	GI. DP.
Allen, N.Y.	.000	21	10	0	0	0	0	0	0	0	0	1	0	0	0	0	3	0	0	0
Allen, St.L.	.128	25	39	2	5	7	2	0	0	3	0	6	0	0	0	0	19	0	0	0
Hernandez, Chi.	.500	11	2	0	1	1	0	0	0	0	0	0	0	0	0	0	0	0	0	0
Hernandez, Phila.	.385	63	13	2	5	5	0	0	0	1	0	0	0	0	0	0	5	1	0	0
Hernandez, St.L.	.284	55	218	34	62	94	15	4	3	26	5	0	2	24	5	0	30	1	1	2
Hernandez, N.Y.	.306	95	320	43	98	139	8	3	9	37	4	2	1	64	9	2	42	8	4	5
Johnson, Mtl.	.500	3	2	1	1	1	0	0	0	0	0	0	0	1	0	0	0	1	0	0
Johnson, S.F.	.125	7	8	0	1	1	0	0	0	1	0	0	0	0	0	0	0	0	0	0
Jorgensen, N.Y.	.250	38	24	5	6	12	3	0	1	3	0	0	0	2	0	1	4	0	1	1
Jorgensen, Atl.	.250	57	48	5	12	16	1	0	1	8	0	0	1	8	0	0	8	0	0	1
Landestoy, Cin.	.000	7	5	0	0	0	0	0	0	0	0	0	0	0	0	0	0	0	0	0
Landestoy, L.A.	.172	64	64	6	11	17	1	1	1	1	0	0	0	3	0	0	8	0	2	1
Lefebvre, S.D.	.250	18	20	1	5	5	0	0	0	1	0	0	0	2	0	0	3	0	0	1
Lefebvre, Phila.	.310	101	258	34	80	140	20	8	8	38	7	1	2	31	6	3	46	5	3	8
Lerch, Mtl.	.222	19	9	0	2	3	1	0	0	0	0	1	0	1	0	0	0	0	0	1
Lerch, S.F.	.000	7	0	0	0	0	0	0	0	0	0	0	0	0	0	0	0	0	0	0
Lezcano, S.D.	.233	97	317	41	74	113	11	2	8	49	6	4	4	47	3	1	66	0	0	8
Lezcano, Phila.	.282	18	39	8	11	12	1	0	0	7	2	1	0	5	0	0	9	1	0	0
May, S.F.	.247	66	186	18	46	70	6	0	6	20	4	1	0	21	6	0	23	2	2	6
May, Pitt.	.250	7	12	0	3	3	0	0	0	0	0	0	0	1	1	0	1	0	0	0
Monge, Phila.	.000	14	1	0	0	0	0	0	0	0	0	0	0	0	0	0	0	0	0	0
Monge, S.D.	.100	47	10	0	1	1	0	0	0	0	0	1	0	0	0	0	3	0	0	0
Nicosia, Pitt.	.130	21	46	4	6	11	2	0	1	1	0	2	0	1	0	0	7	0	0	5
Nicosia, S.F.	.333	15	33	4	11	11	0	0	0	6	0	1	0	3	1	0	2	0	0	2
Ortiz, Pitt.	.125	5	8	1	1	1	0	0	0	0	0	1	0	1	0	0	0	0	0	0
Ortiz, N.Y.	.254	68	185	10	47	52	5	0	0	12	1	1	0	3	0	1	34	1	0	1
Roof, St.L.	.000	6	3	1	0	0	0	0	0	0	0	0	0	0	0	0	0	0	0	0
Roof, Mtl.	.167	8	12	2	2	4	2	0	0	1	0	0	0	1	0	0	3	0	0	0
Ruthven, Phila.	.111	7	9	1	1	2	1	0	0	0	0	3	0	0	0	0	3	0	0	0
Ruthven, Chi.	.226	25	53	5	12	13	1	0	0	3	0	4	0	2	0	0	13	0	0	2
Vail, S.F.	.154	18	26	1	4	5	1	0	0	3	0	0	0	0	0	1	7	0	0	0
Vail, Mtl.	.283	34	53	5	15	23	2	0	2	4	2	0	0	8	0	1	10	0	0	1
Welsh, S.D.	.000	7	4	0	0	0	0	0	0	0	0	0	0	0	0	0	1	0	0	0
Welsh, Mtl.	.286	16	14	0	4	4	0	0	0	2	1	0	0	1	0	0	3	0	0	1

OFFICIAL MISCELLANEOUS NATIONAL LEAGUE BATTING RECORDS

CLUB MISCELLANEOUS BATTING RECORDS

Club	Slg. Pct.	G.	Tot. BB.	Int. BB.	HP.	SO.	GIDP.	ShO.
Chicago	.401	162	470	63	29	868	113	8
Atlanta	.400	162	582	72	17	847	129	7
Montreal	.386	163	509	76	38	733	133	13
St. Louis	.384	162	543	66	24	879	117	12
Pittsburgh	.383	162	497	63	19	873	121	7
Los Angeles	.379	163	541	61	22	925	112	7
Houston	.375	162	517	71	19	869	76	9
San Francisco	.375	162	619	63	28	990	129	6
Philadelphia	.373	163	640	75	26	906	132	12
Cincinnati	.356	162	588	69	19	1006	121	10
San Diego	.351	163	482	80	20	822	121	13
New York	.344	162	436	54	31	1031	113	11
Totals	.376	974	6424	813	292	10749	1417	115

INDIVIDUAL MISCELLANEOUS BATTING RECORDS

(Top Ten Qualifiers for Slugging Championship)

Player—Club	Slg. Pct.	Tot. BB.	Int. BB.	HP.	SO.	GI DP.
Murphy, Atl.	.540	90	12	2	110	15
Dawson, Mtl.	.539	38	12	9	81	14
Guerrero, L.A.	.531	72	12	6	110	11
Schmidt, Phila.	.524	128	17	3	148	10
Evans, S.F.	.516	84	12	2	81	8
Hendrick, St.L.	.493	51	15	2	76	12
Chambliss, Atl.	.481	63	15	0	68	8
Davis, Chi.	.480	33	5	2	93	16
Cruz, Hou.	.463	65	10	1	86	4
Leonard, S.F.	.461	35	2	1	116	10

DEPARTMENTAL LEADERS: Tot. BB—Schmidt, 128; Int. BB—Berra, 19; HP—Dawson, Lo. Smith, 9; SO—Schmidt, 148; GIDP—Concepcion, Oliver, 21.

(All Players—Listed Alphabetically)

Player—Club	Slg. Pct.	Tot. BB.	Int. BB.	HP.	SO.	GI DP.
Adduci, St.L.	.050	1	0	0	6	0
Aguayo, Phila.	.250	1	0	0	2	0
Allen, N.Y.-St.L.	.143	0	0	0	22	0
Altamirano, Phila.	.000	0	0	0	0	0
Andersen, Phila.	.000	0	0	0	0	0
Anderson, L.A.	.261	12	1	0	15	1

Player—Club	Slg. Pct.	Tot. BB.	Int. BB.	HP.	SO.	GI DP.
Andujar, St.L.	.096	2	0	0	38	2
Ashby, Hou.	.389	31	4	0	38	12
Ashford, N.Y.	.214	7	1	0	4	1
Backman, N.Y.	.214	2	0	0	8	2
Bailor, N.Y.	.282	20	2	1	23	11
Bair, St.L.	.000	0	0	0	2	0
Baker, L.A.	.395	72	2	2	59	9
Baker, St.L.	.000	0	0	0	0	0
Bargar, Mtl.	.167	0	0	0	4	0
Barker, Atl.	.125	0	0	0	5	0
Barnes, Cin.	.294	7	0	2	3	0
Barr, S.F.	.200	0	0	0	4	1
Bass, Hou.	.333	6	1	0	27	2
Beckwith, L.A.	.200	0	0	0	3	0
Bedrosian, Atl.	.105	0	0	0	7	0
Behenna, Atl.	.583	0	0	0	5	0
Belliard, Pitt.	.000	0	0	0	1	0
Bench, Cin.	.432	24	1	0	38	13
Benedict, Atl.	.348	61	16	1	24	12
Berenyi, Cin.	.273	0	0	0	19	1
Bergman, S.F.	.457	24	2	1	21	5
Berra, Pitt.	.358	61	19	0	84	10
Bevacqua, S.D.	.327	18	1	0	33	3
Bibby, Pitt.	.111	0	0	0	6	0
Bilardello, Cin.	.389	15	3	1	49	9
Bishop, N.Y.	.250	3	0	0	4	0
Bjorkman, Hou.	.360	16	4	1	29	1
Blackwell, Mtl.	.267	1	0	0	3	1
Bochy, S.D.	.286	0	0	0	9	2
Boggs, Atl.	.000	1	0	0	0	0
Bonilla, S.D.	.304	50	11	3	40	19
Booker, S.D.	.000	0	0	0	0	0
Bordi, Chi.	.000	0	0	0	3	0
Bosley, Chi.	.458	10	1	0	12	0
Bowa, Chi.	.339	35	1	0	30	3
Bradley, N.Y.	.327	11	1	0	35	2
Braun, St.L.	.413	21	0	0	7	1
Bream, L.A.	.182	2	0	0	2	1
Breining, S.F.	.164	6	0	0	31	4
Brenly, S.F.	.356	37	6	2	48	12
Brizzolara, Atl.	.000	0	0	0	0	0
Brock, L.A.	.396	83	12	1	81	13
Brooks, N.Y.	.321	24	2	4	96	14
Brown, S.D.	.382	23	0	0	38	1
Brummer, St.L.	.356	10	1	0	11	4
Brusstar, Chi.	.000	0	0	0	3	0
Buckner, Chi.	.436	25	5	5	30	10
Burris, Mtl.	.282	4	0	0	15	0
Butler, Atl.	.393	54	3	2	56	5
Bystrom, Phila.	.263	2	0	0	14	1
Calvert, S.F.	.000	1	0	0	6	0
Camp, Atl.	.103	0	0	2	16	0
Campbell, Chi.	.100	0	0	0	3	1
Candelaria, Pitt.	.154	5	0	0	17	3
Carlton, Phila.	.247	2	0	0	20	2
Carman, Phila.	.000	0	0	0	0	0
Carter, Mtl.	.444	51	7	7	57	14
Carter, Chi.	.235	0	0	0	21	1
Cato, Cin.	.000	0	0	0	0	0
Cedeno, Cin.	.361	33	2	3	53	2
Cey, Chi.	.460	62	11	5	85	20
Chambliss, Atl.	.481	63	15	0	68	8
Chiffer, S.D.	.000	0	0	0	1	0
Chris, S.F.	.000	0	0	0	0	0
Christenson, Phila.	.118	0	0	0	8	0
Christmas, Cin.	.059	1	0	0	3	1
Citarella, St.L.	.000	0	0	0	0	0
Clark, S.F.	.441	74	6	1	79	14
Comer, Phila.	.000	0	0	0	0	0
Concepcion, Cin.	.280	56	9	0	81	21
Connally, Chi.	.100	0	0	0	5	0
Corcoran, Phila.	.000	0	0	0	0	0
Couchee, S.D.	.500	0	0	0	0	0
Cox, St.L.	.074	0	0	0	12	1
Cromartie, Mtl.	.386	43	7	1	48	11
Crowley, Mtl.	.182	9	0	1	4	2
Cruz, Hou.	.463	65	10	1	86	4
Darling, N.Y.	.100	0	0	0	3	0
Daulton, Phila.	.333	1	0	0	1	0

Player—Club	Slg. Pct.	Tot. BB.	Int. BB.	HP.	SO.	GI DP.
C. Davis, S.F.	.352	55	6	0	108	9
Davis, S.D.	.467	3	0	0	4	1
Davis, Chi.	.480	33	5	2	93	16
M. Davis, S.F.	.167	3	0	0	8	0
Dawley, Hou.	.222	0	0	0	3	0
Dawson, Mtl.	.539	38	12	9	81	14
Dayley, Atl.	.219	4	0	0	11	0
Decker, S.D.	.000	0	0	0	0	0
Dedmon, Atl.	.000	0	0	0	0	0
DeJesus, Phila.	.336	53	18	0	77	7
DeLeon, Pitt.	.059	6	0	0	16	1
DeLeon, S.D.	.143	1	0	0	8	0
Denny, Phila.	.182	2	0	0	16	2
Dernier, Phila.	.290	18	0	0	21	2
Diaz, Phila.	.367	38	4	2	57	10
Diaz, N.Y.	.000	1	0	0	2	0
Diaz, Chi.	.429	0	0	0	0	0
Dilone, Pitt.	.000	0	0	0	0	0
DiPino, Hou.	.333	1	0	0	1	0
Dixon, Mtl.	.000	0	0	0	0	0
Doran, Hou.	.364	86	11	0	67	6
Doyle, St.L.	.432	1	1	0	3	2
Dravecky, S.D.	.131	3	0	0	19	1
Driessen, Cin.	.420	75	10	0	51	12
Durham, Chi.	.466	66	12	3	83	4
Easler, Pitt.	.441	22	1	3	64	10
Esasky, Cin.	.450	27	1	3	99	5
Espy, L.A.	.364	1	0	0	2	0
Evans, S.F.	.516	84	12	2	81	8
Falcone, Atl.	.115	0	0	0	5	3
Farmer, Phila.	.167	0	0	0	2	0
Fernandez, L.A.	1.000	0	0	0	0	0
Fimple, L.A.	.358	11	0	0	39	4
Fireovid, S.D.	.000	0	0	0	0	0
Fitzgerald, N.Y.	.250	3	1	0	6	0
Flannery, S.D.	.336	20	8	5	23	4
Flynn, Mtl.	.294	19	8	0	38	12
Foley, Cin.	.265	13	2	0	17	1
Forsch, St.L.	.352	3	0	0	14	0
Forster, Atl.	.625	0	0	0	1	0
Foster, N.Y.	.419	38	5	4	111	19
Francona, Mtl.	.352	6	2	0	20	7
Frobel, Pitt.	.533	4	0	0	17	2
Fryman, Mtl.	.000	0	0	0	0	0
Fuentes, Mtl.	.250	0	0	0	2	0
Gaff, N.Y.	.000	0	0	0	1	0
Gale, Cin.	.350	2	0	0	16	0
Garber, Atl.	.000	2	0	0	2	0
Garcia, Phila.	.415	9	2	1	20	6
Gardenhire, N.Y.	.063	1	0	0	4	1
Garner, Hou.	.362	63	8	5	84	4
Garrelts, S.F.	.222	0	0	0	4	0
Garvey, S.D.	.459	29	11	3	39	16
Ghelfi, Phila.	.250	0	0	0	0	0
Giles, N.Y.	.298	36	1	2	77	8
Gladden, S.F.	.302	5	0	0	11	3
Gorman, N.Y.	.250	0	0	0	2	0
Grant, Chi.	.200	3	0	0	4	0
Grapenthin, Mtl.	.000	0	0	0	0	0
Green, St.L.	.422	26	1	1	76	13
G. Gross, Phila.	.376	34	4	1	16	6
K. Gross, Phila.	.121	1	0	0	14	0
Guante, Pitt.	.091	2	0	0	14	0
Guerrero, L.A.	.531	72	12	2	110	11
Gullickson, Mtl.	.232	4	0	0	27	1
Gwosdz, S.D.	.182	7	0	0	19	2
Gwynn, S.D.	.372	23	5	0	21	9
Hagen, St.L.	.000	0	0	0	4	0
Hall, Atl.	.000	2	0	0	2	0
Hall, Chi.	.488	42	6	3	101	4
Hammaker, S.F.	.102	4	0	1	19	0
Hargesheimer, Chi.	.000	0	0	0	0	0
Harper, Pitt.	.427	2	0	1	15	3
Harper, Atl.	.383	20	0	1	43	6
Harris, Cin.	.000	0	0	0	0	0
Hawkins, S.D.	.065	4	0	0	9	0
Hayes, Cin.	.000	0	0	0	2	0
Hayes, Phila.	.370	36	7	3	55	11
Heathcock, Hou.	.000	0	0	0	4	0

Player—Club	Slg. Pct.	Tot. BB.	Int. BB.	HP.	SO.	GI DP.
Hebner, Pitt.	.395	17	4	1	28	3
Heep, N.Y.	.395	29	6	1	40	5
Hendrick, St.L.	.493	51	15	2	76	12
Hernandez, Chi.-Phila.	.400	0	0	0	5	0
Hernandez, St.L.-N.Y.	.433	88	14	2	72	7
Herr, St.L.	.412	43	2	1	27	7
Hershiser, L.A.	.000	0	0	0	0	0
Hinshaw, S.D.	.500	0	0	0	4	0
Hodges, N.Y.	.308	49	6	2	42	8
Holland, Phila.	.000	0	0	0	5	0
Holman, N.Y.	.217	0	0	0	9	0
Honeycutt, L.A.	.083	0	0	0	0	0
Hooton, L.A.	.200	3	0	0	15	1
Horner, Atl.	.528	50	2	1	63	14
Householder, Cin.	.387	44	5	2	60	7
Howard, N.Y.	.333	0	0	0	1	0
Howe, L.A.	.125	1	0	0	3	0
Hubbard, Atl.	.402	55	2	4	71	12
Hudson, Phila.	.093	2	0	1	32	0
Hume, Cin.	.000	0	0	0	2	0
Hurdle, N.Y.	.242	2	0	0	10	1
Iorg, St.L.	.362	10	2	1	11	6
Jacoby, Atl.	.000	0	0	0	1	0
James, Mtl.	.286	0	0	0	4	0
Jeltz, Phila.	.375	1	0	0	2	2
Jenkins, Chi.	.321	1	0	0	8	0
Johnson, Atl.	.292	20	3	1	27	4
Johnson, Mtl.-S.F.	.200	1	0	0	0	0
Johnson, Chi.	.000	0	0	0	0	0
Johnstone, Chi.	.436	20	6	3	24	4
Jones, Cin.	.295	11	0	1	13	0
Jones, S.D.	.394	35	4	0	58	8
Jorgensen, N.Y.-Atl.	.389	10	0	1	12	2
Kaat, St.L.	.000	0	0	0	2	0
Keener, St.L.	.000	0	0	0	0	0
Kennedy, Chi.	.136	1	0	0	6	2
Kennedy, S.D.	.434	51	15	2	89	10
Kingman, S.F.	.000	0	0	0	0	0
Kingman, N.Y.	.383	22	1	1	57	2
Knepper, Hou.	.288	2	0	0	25	0
Knicely, Cin.	.316	16	3	0	28	5
Knight, Hou.	.444	42	9	4	62	17
Komminsk, Atl.	.278	5	0	0	7	1
Krenchicki, Cin.	.299	8	2	1	4	2
Krukow, S.F.	.333	2	0	0	15	1
Kuiper, S.F.	.284	27	6	2	13	7
LaCorte, Hou.	.400	0	0	0	0	0
LaCoss, Hou.	.086	1	0	0	12	0
Lacy, Pitt.	.406	22	2	0	36	2
Lahti, St.L.	.000	0	0	0	5	0
Lake, Chi.	.365	2	2	1	6	4
Landestoy, Cin.-L.A.	.246	3	0	0	8	1
Landreaux, L.A.	.451	34	5	2	52	9
Landrum, St.L.	.600	1	0	0	2	0
Lansford, S.D.	.625	0	0	0	3	0
LaPoint, St.L.	.153	7	0	0	20	2
Larkin, S.F.	.000	0	0	0	1	0
Laskey, S.F.	.106	7	0	1	21	0
Lavelle, S.F.	.000	0	0	0	7	0
Lea, Mtl.	.129	2	0	0	29	3
Leary, N.Y.	.333	0	0	0	1	0
Lefebvre, S.D.-Phila.	.522	33	6	3	49	9
Lefferts, Chi.	.111	1	0	0	9	0
LeMaster, S.F.	.307	60	3	2	96	3
Leonard, S.F.	.461	35	2	1	116	10
Lerch, Mtl.-S.F.	.333	1	0	0	0	1
Lesley, Cin.	.000	0	0	0	0	0
Lezcano, S.D.-Phila.	.351	52	3	1	75	8
Little, Mtl.	.329	50	1	2	22	10
Lollar, S.D.	.345	5	0	0	12	0
Loucks, Hou.	.214	1	0	0	4	0
Loviglio, Chi.	.000	0	0	0	1	0
Lucas, S.D.	.000	0	0	0	5	0
Lynch, N.Y.	.154	1	0	0	17	0
Lyons, St.L.	.217	1	0	0	11	1
Madden, Hou.	.045	1	0	0	12	0
Maddox, Phila.	.367	17	5	1	31	9
Madlock, Pitt.	.444	49	10	2	24	16
Mahler, Atl.	.000	0	0	0	1	0

Player—Club	Slg. Pct.	Tot. BB.	Int. BB.	HP.	SO.	GI DP.
Maldonado, L.A.	.290	5	0	0	14	1
Marshall, L.A.	.434	43	4	5	127	8
Martin, S.F.	.577	0	0	0	8	0
Martin, St.L.	.278	0	0	0	2	0
Martinez, Chi.	.494	4	0	0	19	3
Matthews, Phila.	.374	69	3	0	81	8
Matuszek, Phila.	.525	4	1	0	14	1
May, S.F.-Pitt.	.369	22	7	0	24	6
Mazzilli, Pitt.	.337	49	1	2	43	8
McGaffigan, S.F.	.133	1	0	0	20	0
McGee, St.L.	.374	26	2	0	98	8
McGraw, Phila.	.333	0	0	0	0	0
McMurtry, Atl.	.086	3	0	0	40	1
McReynolds, S.D.	.343	12	1	0	29	1
McWilliams, Pitt.	.127	1	0	0	32	0
Milbourne, Phila.	.273	4	0	0	7	3
Mills, Mtl.	.250	2	0	0	3	0
Milner, Cin.	.384	68	2	1	60	11
Minton, S.F.	.909	2	0	0	2	0
Mizerock, Hou.	.259	12	2	1	15	2
Molinaro, Phila.	.333	0	0	0	2	0
Monday, L.A.	.399	29	9	0	42	3
Monge, Phila.-S.D.	.091	0	0	0	3	0
Montefusco, S.D.	.053	2	0	0	11	0
Moore, Atl.	.500	0	0	0	2	1
Morales, L.A.	.509	1	0	0	11	2
Morales, Chi.	.299	7	0	0	19	1
Moreland, Chi.	.460	68	8	3	73	16
Moreno, Hou.	.326	22	3	1	72	2
Morgan, Phila.	.403	89	1	4	54	13
Morrison, Pitt.	.487	9	1	2	25	3
Moskau, Chi.	.273	0	0	0	0	0
Mumphrey, Hou.	.455	22	3	1	23	1
Murphy, Atl.	.540	90	12	2	110	15
Murray, S.F.	.200	0	0	0	3	1
Nicosia, Pitt.-S.F.	.278	4	1	0	9	7
Niedenfuer, L.A.	.000	0	0	0	0	0
Niekro, Hou.	.118	0	0	1	22	1
Niekro, Atl.	.215	1	0	0	12	7
Niemann, Pitt.	.000	0	0	0	0	0
Noles, Chi.	.263	1	0	0	17	0
Nordhagen, Chi.	.257	0	0	1	5	2
Oberkfell, St.L.	.385	61	5	1	27	12
Oester, Cin.	.384	49	14	1	106	17
Oliver, Mtl.	.410	44	17	2	44	21
O'Malley, S.F.	.339	52	4	4	47	12
Oquendo, N.Y.	.244	19	2	2	60	10
Orosco, N.Y.	.333	1	0	0	3	0
Orsulak, Pitt.	.182	0	0	0	2	0
Ortiz, Pitt.-N.Y.	.275	4	0	1	34	1
Owchinko, Pitt.	.000	0	0	0	0	0
Owen, Chi.	.182	2	0	0	7	0
Owen, Atl.	.118	0	0	0	2	0
Ownbey, N.Y.	.111	0	0	0	2	0
Paris, Cin.	.300	15	1	1	22	3
Parker, Pitt.	.411	28	6	0	89	11
Pastore, Cin.	.271	2	0	0	19	0
Patterson, Chi.	.000	0	0	0	2	0
Pena, Hou.	.125	2	0	0	2	0
Pena, L.A.	.150	0	0	0	21	2
Pena, Pitt.	.435	31	8	0	73	13
Perez, Phila.	.372	28	1	1	57	9
Perez, Atl.	.160	3	0	0	27	2
Perry, Atl.	.487	5	0	0	4	1
Pettini, S.F.	.209	9	1	0	11	3
Phillips, Mtl.	.000	0	0	0	0	0
Pocoroba, Atl.	.367	12	4	0	7	3
Porter, St.L.	.431	68	12	4	94	8
Power, Cin.	.000	1	0	0	14	0
Price, Cin.	.098	3	0	0	14	0
Proly, Chi.	.091	1	0	0	3	0
Pruitt, S.F.	.000	0	0	0	0	0
Puhl, Hou.	.428	36	2	2	48	4
Pujols, Hou.	.218	5	2	0	14	4
Puleo, Cin.	.100	4	0	0	18	1
Pulido, Pitt.	.000	0	0	0	0	0
Quirk, St.L.	.326	6	0	1	27	2
Rabb, S.F.	.346	9	1	0	17	4
Raines, Mtl.	.429	97	9	2	70	12

Player—Club	Slg. Pct.	Tot. BB.	Int. BB.	HP.	SO.	GI DP.
Rainey, Chi.	.161	6	0	0	20	0
Rajsich, N.Y.	.500	3	1	1	1	1
Ramirez, S.D.	.308	20	1	1	23	2
Ramirez, Atl.	.368	36	4	2	48	8
Ramos, Mtl.	.311	8	1	1	11	0
Ramsey, St.L.	.337	12	2	1	23	4
Ransom, S.F.	.350	4	0	0	7	1
Rasmussen, S.D.	.000	0	0	0	2	0
Rasmussen, St.L.	.000	0	0	0	0	0
Ray, Pitt.	.399	35	3	0	26	11
Rayford, St.L.	.337	10	1	0	27	3
Reardon, Mtl.	.125	0	0	0	3	0
Redus, Cin.	.444	71	4	3	111	6
Reed, Phila.	.167	0	0	0	2	0
Reuschel, Chi.	.143	0	0	0	2	0
Reuss, L.A.	.310	2	0	0	28	1
Reyes, L.A.	.226	0	0	1	5	3
Reynolds, Hou.	.276	6	1	0	10	0
Reynolds, L.A.	.345	3	1	0	11	1
Reynolds, N.Y.	.212	8	1	0	12	2
Rhoden, Pitt.	.163	0	0	0	19	2
Richards, S.D.	.386	17	1	1	17	8
Rivera, L.A.	.412	2	0	0	2	0
Robinson, Pitt.	.385	0	0	0	4	0
Robinson, Phila.	.143	1	0	0	4	1
Rodas, L.A.	.000	0	0	0	0	0
Rodriguez, S.D.	.250	1	0	0	3	0
Roenicke, L.A.	.290	14	1	0	26	5
Rogers, Mtl.	.159	1	0	1	27	0
Rohn, Chi.	.613	2	0	0	2	0
Roof, St.L.-Mtl.	.267	1	0	0	3	0
Rose, Phila.	.286	52	5	2	28	11
Royster, Atl.	.328	28	2	0	35	12
Rucker, St.L.	.000	0	0	0	1	0
Ruhle, Hou.	.105	3	0	0	11	0
Runge, Atl.	.250	1	0	0	4	0
Russell, Cin.	.333	1	0	0	6	1
Russell, L.A.	.286	33	4	4	31	5
Ruthven, Phila.-Chi.	.242	2	0	0	16	2
Ryan, Hou.	.072	2	0	0	29	0
Salazar, Mtl.	.297	1	0	0	8	1
Salazar, S.D.	.387	17	8	2	80	4
Samuel, Phila.	.446	4	1	1	16	1
Sanchez, Phila.	.286	0	0	0	2	1
Sanchez, St.L.	.000	0	0	0	4	0
Sandberg, Chi.	.351	51	3	3	79	8
Sanderson, Mtl.	.214	0	0	0	8	0
Santana, St.L.	.214	2	0	1	2	0
Sarmiento, Pitt.	.000	1	0	0	4	0
D. Sax, L.A.	.000	0	0	0	0	0
S. Sax, L.A.	.350	58	3	1	73	8
Schatzeder, Mtl.	.200	0	0	0	0	0
Scherrer, Cin.	.091	1	0	0	3	0
Schmidt, Phila.	.524	128	17	3	148	10
Schulze, Chi.	.000	1	0	0	1	0
Scioscia, L.A.	.486	5	1	0	2	1
A. Scott, Hou.	.301	11	0	0	39	0
M. Scott, Hou.	.208	1	0	0	17	0
Scurry, Pitt.	.000	0	0	0	4	0
Seaver, N.Y.	.219	6	0	0	26	2
Sexton, St.L.	.222	1	1	0	4	0
Shines, Mtl.	.500	0	0	0	0	0
Show, S.D.	.188	1	0	1	23	0
Sinatro, Atl.	.167	2	0	0	1	0
Sisk, N.Y.	.500	0	0	0	2	0
Smith, Mtl.	.167	2	0	0	5	0
Smith, S.F.	.493	7	1	2	12	0
Smith, Hou.	.000	0	0	0	3	0
Smith, Atl.	.417	1	0	0	5	0
Smith, Chi.	.111	1	0	0	5	0
L. Smith, St.L.	.453	41	2	9	55	11
O. Smith, St.L.	.335	64	9	1	36	10
Solano, Hou.	.000	0	0	0	0	0
Sosa, S.D.	.143	0	0	0	2	0
Soto, Cin.	.159	1	0	0	26	0
Speier, Mtl.	.341	29	4	2	37	4
Spilman, Hou.	.244	5	0	0	12	2
Staub, N.Y.	.426	14	3	1	10	4
Stearns, N.Y.	.000	0	0	0	0	0
Stenhouse, Mtl.	.150	4	0	0	10	2
Stewart, L.A.	.143	0	0	0	3	0
Stone, Phila.	1.750	0	0	0	1	0
Strawberry, N.Y.	.512	47	9	4	128	5
Stuper, St.L.	.136	4	0	0	32	2
Sularz, S.F.	.100	3	0	0	2	1
Summers, S.F.	.136	7	0	0	8	3
Sutter, St.L.	.000	0	0	0	4	0
Swan, N.Y.	.077	0	0	0	11	0
Taveras, L.A.	.000	0	0	0	1	0
Tekulve, Pitt.	.000	0	0	0	4	1
Templeton, S.D.	.335	21	7	0	57	16
Tenace, Pitt.	.258	12	0	4	17	0
Terrell, N.Y.	.409	1	0	0	17	1
Thomas, L.A.	.375	27	2	2	36	4
Thompson, Pitt.	.406	99	7	1	128	14
Thompson, Chi.	.250	3	0	0	14	4
Thon, Hou.	.457	54	10	2	73	12
Thurmond, S.D.	.081	2	0	0	6	1
Tolman, Hou.	.375	6	0	0	9	1
Tomlin, Pitt.	.000	0	0	0	0	0
Torrez, N.Y.	.046	1	0	0	20	1
Trevino, Cin.	.293	17	6	0	20	3
Trillo, Mtl.	.380	10	0	2	18	2
Trout, Chi.	.194	2	0	0	20	0
Tunnell, Pitt.	.155	1	0	0	20	0
Turner, S.D.	.130	1	1	0	8	1
Vail, S.F.-Mtl.	.354	8	0	2	17	1
Valenzuela, L.A.	.253	1	0	0	23	2
Van Slyke, St.L.	.421	46	5	1	64	4
Venable, S.F.	.364	22	1	3	34	3
Veryzer, Chi.	.273	3	1	0	13	1
Virgil, Phila.	.393	8	0	3	34	8
Von Ohlen, St.L.	.143	1	0	0	3	0
Walk, Atl.	.000	0	0	0	0	0
Walker, Cin.	.324	20	4	0	43	0
Wallach, Mtl.	.434	55	8	6	97	9
Walling, Hou.	.444	15	1	0	16	1
Washington, Atl.	.413	35	6	0	103	8
Watson, Atl.	.490	18	3	0	23	5
Welch, L.A.	.151	1	0	1	22	1
Wellman, S.F.	.247	22	1	0	39	5
Welsh, S.D.-Mtl.	.222	1	0	0	4	1
White, Mtl.	.176	12	0	1	8	0
White, L.A.	.000	0	0	0	0	0
Whitson, S.D.	.182	2	0	0	11	0
Wieghaus, Mtl.	.000	0	0	0	0	0
Wiggins, S.D.	.324	65	3	1	43	3
Williams, Cin.	.056	3	0	0	6	0
Wilson, N.Y.	.367	18	3	4	103	6
Winn, Pitt.	.000	0	0	0	0	0
Wohlford, Mtl.	.355	5	0	0	14	4
Woods, Chi.	.353	15	2	0	27	7
Wotus, Pitt.	.000	0	0	0	1	0
Wright, L.A.	.000	0	0	0	0	0
Wynne, Pitt.	.355	38	0	3	52	3
Yeager, L.A.	.379	23	4	1	57	15
Youngblood, S.F.	.499	33	4	5	59	11
Zachry, L.A.	.500	0	0	0	1	0
Zuvella, Atl.	.000	2	0	1	1	0

OFFICIAL NATIONAL LEAGUE FIELDING AVERAGES

CLUB FIELDING

Club	Pct.	G.	PO.	A.	E.	TC.	DP.	TP.	PB.
Chicago	.982	162	4286	1982	115	6383	164	1	24
Pittsburgh	.982	162	4387	1717	115	6219	165	0	9
Montreal	.981	163	4413	1687	116	6216	130	0	8
Cincinnati	.981	162	4324	1624	114	6062	121	0	16
San Diego	.979	163	4403	1729	129	6261	135	1	9
Atlanta	.978	162	4322	1850	137	6309	176	0	6
Houston	.977	162	4399	1839	147	6385	165	0	35
St. Louis	.976	162	4382	1922	152	6456	173	1	19
New York	.976	162	4353	1889	151	6393	171	0	12
Philadelphia	.976	163	4385	1804	152	6341	117	0	13
Los Angeles	.974	163	4392	1805	168	6365	132	0	20
San Francisco	.973	162	4337	1775	171	6283	109	0	11
Totals	.978	974	52383	21623	1667	75673	1758	3	182

INDIVIDUAL FIELDING

*Throws lefthanded.

FIRST BASEMEN

Leader—Club	Pct.	G.	PO.	A.	E.	DP.
DRIESSEN, Cin.	.996	112	917	71	4	73

(Listed Alphabetically)

Player—Club	Pct.	G.	PO.	A.	E.	DP.
Adduci, St.L.	1.000	6	47	4	0	3
Barnes, Cin.	1.000	7	43	6	0	5
Bench, Cin.	.989	32	249	14	3	21
Bergman, S.F.*	.994	50	291	27	2	20
Bevacqua, S.D.	.995	27	185	12	1	14
Bream, L.A.*	1.000	4	8	0	0	1
Brenly, S.F.	.985	10	61	3	1	6
Brock, L.A.	.991	140	1162	106	12	94
Buckner, Chi.*	.992	144	1366	161	13	132
Carter, Mtl.	1.000	1	8	1	0	1
Cedeno, Cin.	1.000	17	120	5	0	7
Chambliss, Atl.	.996	126	1092	89	5	117
Clark, S.F.	1.000	2	13	3	0	2
Concepcion, Cin.	.000	1	0	0	0	0
Corcoran, Phila.*	1.000	3	4	0	0	0
Cromartie, Mtl.*	1.000	1	1	0	0	0
Crowley, Mtl.*	1.000	4	19	0	0	2
Driessen, Cin.	.996	112	917	71	4	73
Durham, Chi.*	1.000	6	35	2	0	2
Evans, S.F.	.993	113	979	88	7	60
Francona, Mtl.*	.990	47	88	7	1	9
Garvey, S.D.	.994	100	888	49	6	69
G. Gross, Phila.*	1.000	1	1	0	0	0
Guerrero, L.A.	.909	2	7	3	1	0
Harper, Pitt.	.000	1	0	0	0	0
Hebner, Pitt.	1.000	7	39	2	0	3
Heep, N.Y.*	1.000	14	69	7	0	11
Hendrick, St.L.	.992	92	819	77	7	72
Hernandez, St.L.-N.Y.*	.992	144	1418	147	13	147
Horner, Atl.	1.000	1	2	0	0	0
Iorg, St.L.	.979	11	90	5	2	11
Jones, Cin.	1.000	1	7	0	0	0
Jones, S.D.*	.957	5	19	3	1	1
Jorgensen, N.Y.-Atl.*	1.000	38	72	6	0	11
Kennedy, S.D.	1.000	4	25	3	0	4
Kingman, N.Y.	.994	50	443	28	3	43
Knicely, Cin.	1.000	2	2	1	0	1
Knight, Hou.	.993	143	1285	73	9	131
Landestoy, Cin.	1.000	2	6	0	0	1
Lansford, S.D.	1.000	8	11	1	0	1
Marshall, L.A.	.992	33	235	18	2	15
Martinez, Chi.	.992	26	231	15	2	18
Matuszek, Phila.	1.000	21	144	9	0	8
Mazzilli, Pitt.	.956	7	43	0	2	5
Mills, Mtl.	.000	1	0	0	1	0
Monday, L.A.*	.950	4	18	1	1	1
Morales, L.A.	.951	4	37	2	2	2
Murray, S.F.	1.000	3	20	1	0	1
Oliver, Mtl.*	.990	153	1207	118	13	93
Paris, Cin.	.917	3	22	0	2	2
Perez, Phil.	.998	69	514	40	1	36
Perry, Atl.	.982	7	55	0	1	5
Rajsich, N.Y.*	1.000	10	94	6	0	9
Robinson, Phila.	1.000	3	3	0	0	0
Rose, Phila.	.990	112	786	74	9	57
Smith, S.F.	.976	15	113	8	3	6
Smith, Atl.	1.000	13	27	6	0	3
Spilman, Hou.	1.000	19	124	7	0	5
Staub, N.Y.	.976	5	36	5	1	6
Stenhouse, Mtl.	1.000	5	29	2	0	3
Tenace, Pitt.	.989	19	83	5	1	6
Thompson, Pitt.*	.993	151	1266	89	9	131
Thompson, Chi.*	.000	1	0	0	0	0
Tolman, Hou.	1.000	7	53	2	0	6
Vail, S.F.-Mtl.*	1.000	5	30	1	0	1
Van Slyke, St.L.	.974	9	71	5	2	13
Walling, Hou.	.992	42	115	8	1	12
Watson, Atl.	.984	34	280	19	5	23
Wiggins, S.D.	.984	45	330	29	6	30

TRIPLE PLAYS: Adduci, St.L.; Bevacqua, S.D.; Buckner, Chi.

FIRST BASEMEN WITH TWO OR MORE CLUBS

Player—Club	Pct.	G.	PO.	A.	E.	DP.
Hernandez, St.L.*	.991	54	581	51	6	62
Hernandez, N.Y.*	.993	90	837	96	7	85
Jorgensen, N.Y.*	1.000	19	36	3	0	5
Jorgensen, Atl.*	1.000	19	36	3	0	6
Vail, S.F.	1.000	4	24	0	0	0
Vail, Mtl.	1.000	1	6	1	0	1

SECOND BASEMEN

Leader—Club	Pct.	G.	PO.	A.	E.	DP.
SANDBERG, Chi.	.986	157	330	571	13	126

(Listed Alphabetically)

Player—Club	Pct.	G.	PO.	A.	E.	DP.
Ashford, N.Y.	1.000	13	8	14	0	4
Backman, N.Y.	1.000	14	11	12	0	2
Bailor, N.Y.	.960	50	73	120	8	25
Bonilla, S.D.	.986	149	335	414	11	95
Brooks, N.Y.	1.000	7	9	14	0	3
Doran, Hou.	.979	153	347	461	17	109
Doyle, St.L.	.966	12	29	28	2	11
Flannery, S.D.	1.000	21	31	49	0	6
Flynn, Mtl.	.986	107	205	290	7	57
Foley, Cin.	1.000	5	6	7	0	1
Garcia, Phila.	.970	52	78	84	5	15
Giles, N.Y.	.980	140	299	380	14	87
Herr, St.L.	.986	86	178	245	6	60
Hinshaw, S.D.	.000	1	0	0	0	0
Hubbard, Atl.	.985	148	313	484	12	103
Jeltz, Phila.	1.000	4	1	1	0	1
Johnson, Atl.	1.000	4	5	3	0	2
Johnson, S.F.	1.000	1	3	2	0	1
Kennedy, Chi.	1.000	7	11	17	0	3
Krenchicki, Cin.	.000	1	0	0	0	0

SECOND BASEMEN—Continued

Player—Club	Pct.	G.	PO.	A.	E.	DP.
Kuiper, S.F.	.988	64	107	140	3	17
Landestoy, L.A.	1.000	14	15	21	0	6
Little, Mtl.	.995	51	77	111	1	17
Lyons, St.L.	.985	23	27	38	1	7
Milbourne, Phila.	.963	27	38	40	3	4
Morgan, Phila.	.971	117	231	331	17	63
Morrison, Pitt.	.973	28	42	65	3	16
Oberkfell, St.L.	.960	32	51	69	5	16
Oester, Cin.	.977	154	315	413	17	80
Paris, Cin.	.975	10	18	21	1	2
Pettini, S.F.	1.000	14	12	28	0	4
Raines, Mtl.	1.000	7	7	2	0	0
Ramsey, St.L.	.968	66	76	106	6	29
Ray, Pitt.	.983	151	319	452	13	102
Reynolds, Hou.	.956	26	25	40	3	7
Rodriguez, S.D.	1.000	5	7	8	0	2
Rohn, Chi.	.923	6	12	12	2	2
Royster, Atl.	.989	26	42	51	1	17
Runge, Atl.	1.000	2	4	3	0	1
Samuel, Phil.	.916	18	44	54	9	9
Sandberg, Chi.	.986	157	330	571	13	126
Santana, St.L.	.857	9	2	4	1	1
S. Sax, L.A.	.961	152	331	399	30	74
Speier, Mtl.	.000	2	0	0	0	0
Taveras, L.A.	1.000	2	3	3	0	0
Thomas, L.A.	.926	9	13	12	2	4
Trevino, Cin.	1.000	1	0	1	0	0
Trillo, Mtl.	.979	31	57	86	3	23
Wellman, S.F.	.965	74	91	160	9	26
Woods, Chi.	.000	1	0	0	0	0
Wotus, Pitt.	1.000	1	1	1	0	1
Youngblood, S.F.	.948	64	97	142	13	26

TRIPLE PLAYS: Doyle, St.L.; Flannery, S.D.; Sandberg, Chi.

THIRD BASEMEN

Leader—Club	Pct.	G.	PO.	A.	E.	DP.
OBERKFELL, St.L.	.960	127	79	231	13	27

(Listed Alphabetically)

Player—Club	Pct.	G.	PO.	A.	E.	DP.
Anderson, L.A.	.000	1	0	0	0	0
Ashford, N.Y.	.957	15	5	17	1	2
Backman, N.Y.	.800	2	5	3	2	0
Bailor, N.Y.	1.000	11	9	14	0	5
Barnes, Cin.	.875	7	2	5	1	2
Bench, Cin.	.933	42	26	58	6	5
Bevacqua, S.D.	.950	12	5	14	1	1
Braun, St.L.	1.000	4	3	4	0	1
Brooks, N.Y.	.950	145	107	289	21	25
Cey, Chi.	.955	157	90	270	17	12
Concepcion, Cin.	1.000	6	2	11	0	0
Connally, Chi.	1.000	3	1	3	0	0
Esasky, Cin.	.935	84	53	133	13	11
Evans, S.F.	.924	32	14	59	6	4
Flannery, S.D.	.969	52	27	99	4	13
Garcia, Phila.	.923	10	3	9	1	1
Garner, Hou.	.945	154	100	311	24	22
Guerrero, L.A.	.934	157	123	305	30	22
Hebner, Pitt.	.967	40	16	43	2	1
Hinshaw, S.D.	1.000	5	6	5	0	0
Horner, Atl.	.958	104	76	153	10	18
Hurdle, N.Y.	.800	9	1	15	4	2
Jacoby, Atl.	1.000	2	0	2	0	0
Jeltz, Phila.	.000	2	0	0	0	0
Johnson, Atl.	.991	53	39	69	1	11
Kennedy, Chi.	.000	4	0	0	0	0
Krenchicki, Cin.	.980	39	7	41	1	3
Landestoy, Cin-L.A.	.909	11	5	5	1	0
Lefebvre, S.D.-Phila.	.840	13	4	17	4	0
Lyons, St.L.	1.000	8	0	3	0	0
Madlock, Pitt.	.958	126	59	193	11	20
Martinez, Chi.	1.000	1	1	2	0	0
Milbourne, Phila.	1.000	3	0	2	0	0
Mills, Mtl.	1.000	3	1	4	0	0
Morrison, Pitt.	.911	26	12	29	4	3
Oberkfell, St.L.	.960	127	79	231	13	27
O'Malley, S.F.	.940	117	70	213	18	12
Owen, Chi.	1.000	3	0	1	0	0
Paris, Cin.	1.000	16	13	27	0	0
Pettini, S.F.	.846	12	3	8	2	0
Phillips, Mtl.	.000	2	0	0	0	0
Quirk, St.L.	1.000	7	0	2	0	0
Ramirez, S.D.	1.000	1	0	1	0	0
Ramsey, St.L.	1.000	8	3	9	0	3
Rayford, St.L.	.883	33	13	40	7	3
Reynolds, Hou.	1.000	15	2	6	0	2
Rivera, L.A.	.929	8	2	11	1	0
Robinson, Phila.	.000	2	0	0	1	0
Rodriguez, S.D.	1.000	1	1	0	0	0
Royster, Atl.	.940	47	26	68	6	5
Salazar, S.D.	.949	118	102	250	19	17
Santana, St.L.	.500	4	0	2	2	1
Schmidt, Phila.	.959	153	107	332	19	29
Sexton, St.L.	1.000	2	2	1	0	0
Smith, S.F.	.000	1	0	0	0	0
Speier, Mtl.	.895	12	10	7	2	1
Sularz, S.F.	1.000	4	0	8	0	1
Taveras, L.A.	1.000	1	0	2	0	1
Thomas, L.A.	.929	7	5	8	1	0
Trevino, Cin.	1.000	4	0	3	0	0
Vail, Mtl.	.000	1	0	0	0	0
Van Slyke, St.L.	.987	30	24	50	1	2
Veryzer, Chi.	1.000	17	4	7	0	1
Wallach, Mtl.	.956	156	151	265	19	25
Walling, Hou.	.906	13	8	21	3	1
Youngblood, S.F.	.923	28	22	38	5	2

TRIPLE PLAYS: Cey, Chi.; Oberkfell, St.L.

THIRD BASEMEN WITH TWO OR MORE CLUBS

Player—Club	Pct.	G.	PO.	A.	E.	DP.
Landestoy, Cin.	.000	1	0	0	0	0
Landestoy, L.A.	.909	10	5	5	1	0
Lefebvre, S.D.	1.000	4	1	4	0	0
Lefebvre, Phil.	.800	9	3	13	4	0

SHORTSTOPS

Leader—Club	Pct.	G.	PO.	A.	E.	DP.
BOWA, Chi.	.984	145	230	464	11	102

(Listed Alphabetically)

Player—Club	Pct.	G.	PO.	A.	E.	DP.
Aguayo, Phila.	1.000	2	3	0	0	0
Anderson, L.A.	.969	53	56	100	5	19
Bailor, N.Y.	.969	75	84	162	8	35
Belliard, Pitt.	1.000	3	1	3	0	1
Berra, Pitt.	.963	161	286	505	30	103
Bowa, Chi.	.984	145	230	464	11	102
Concepcion, Cin.	.979	139	225	376	13	67
DeJesus, Phila.	.966	158	214	438	23	64
Evans, S.F.	.806	9	8	17	6	3
Flannery, S.D.	1.000	7	5	8	0	0
Flynn, Mtl.	.970	37	44	85	4	20
Foley, Cin.	.983	37	48	69	2	15
Garcia, Phila.	1.000	22	13	22	0	2
Gardenhire, N.Y.	1.000	15	13	30	0	4
Giles, N.Y.	1.000	12	10	10	0	3
Jeltz, Phila.	1.000	2	3	4	0	0
Kennedy, Chi.	1.000	1	1	0	0	0
Landestoy, L.A.	1.000	1	0	2	0	0
LeMaster, S.F.	.964	139	215	402	23	58
Little, Mtl.	.968	66	104	137	8	27
Lyons, St.L.	1.000	2	3	3	0	0
Milbourne, Phila.	1.000	8	2	6	0	0
Morrison, Pitt.	1.000	7	2	5	0	2
Oberkfell, St.L.	1.000	1	2	3	0	1
Oquendo, N.Y.	.960	116	182	326	21	65
Owen, Chi.	1.000	14	10	28	0	5

SHORTSTOPS—Continued

Player—Club	Pct.	G.	PO.	A.	E.	DP.
Paris, Cin.	.875	7	7	14	3	3
Pena, Hou.	1.000	4	1	7	0	2
Pettini, S.F.	.949	26	29	46	4	12
Phillips, Mtl.	.000	3	0	0	1	0
Quirk, St.L.	.000	1	0	0	0	0
Ramirez, S.D.	.985	38	50	85	2	14
Ramirez, Atl.	.949	152	232	490	39	116
Ramsey, St.L.	.961	20	15	34	2	2
Reynolds, Hou.	1.000	8	10	11	0	6
Rodriguez, S.D.	.000	2	0	0	0	0
Rohn, Chi.	.000	1	0	0	0	0
Royster, Atl.	.966	13	19	37	2	7
Russell, L.A.	.964	127	192	392	22	61
Salazar, Mtl.	.966	34	28	28	2	9
Salazar, S.D.	.957	19	20	24	2	5
Sandberg, Chi.	1.000	1	0	1	0	0
Santana, St.L.	.750	6	1	2	1	1
Schmidt, Phila.	1.000	2	1	1	0	0
Sexton, St.L.	1.000	4	2	7	0	2
O. Smith, St.L.	.975	158	304	519	21	100
Speier, Mtl.	.962	74	107	196	12	31
Sularz, S.F.	.917	6	10	12	2	2
Taveras, L.A.	.000	3	0	0	0	0
Templeton, S.D.	.960	123	219	355	24	66
Thomas, L.A.	.979	13	19	28	1	7
Thon, Hou.	.966	154	258	533	28	114
Veryzer, Chi.	.978	28	23	65	2	16
Wellman, S.F.	1.000	2	3	7	0	1
Wotus, Pitt.	1.000	2	1	1	0	0
Zuvella, Atl.	.750	2	1	2	1	0

TRIPLE PLAYS: O. Smith, St.L.; Templeton, S.D.

OUTFIELDERS

Leader—Club	Pct.	G.	PO.	A.	E.	DP.
HOUSEHOLDER, Cin.	.991	112	221	5	2	0

(Listed Alphabetically)

Player—Club	Pct.	G.	PO.	A.	E.	DP.
Adduci, St.L.	.000	1	0	0	0	0
Bailor, N.Y.	1.000	3	5	0	0	0
Baker, L.A.	.981	143	249	4	5	2
Bass, Hou.	.945	52	68	1	4	1
Bench, Cin.	.000	1	0	0	0	0
Bergman, S.F.*	1.000	6	8	0	0	0
Bevacqua, S.D.	1.000	12	17	2	0	1
Bosley, Chi.*	1.000	20	27	1	0	1
Bradley, N.Y.	1.000	35	41	2	0	1
Braun, St.L.	1.000	22	23	0	0	0
Brenly, S.F.	1.000	2	1	0	0	0
Brown, S.D.	.963	54	103	1	4	0
Buckner, Chi.*	1.000	15	25	0	0	0
Butler, Atl.*	.987	143	284	13	4	4
Carter, Chi.	1.000	16	26	0	0	0
Cedeno, Cin.	.993	73	138	5	1	1
Clark, S.F.	.967	133	249	17	9	3
Cromartie, Mtl.*	.973	101	208	12	6	2
Cruz, Hou.*	.979	160	322	9	7	1
C. Davis, S.F.	.976	133	357	7	9	1
Davis, S.D.	1.000	5	8	1	0	0
Dawson, Mtl.	.980	157	435	6	9	2
Dernier, Phila.	.988	107	164	3	2	1
Durham, Chi.*	.966	95	168	2	6	0
Easler, Pitt.	.965	105	158	6	6	1
Espy, L.A.	1.000	15	11	0	0	0
Foster, N.Y.	.988	153	314	12	4	3
Francona, Mtl.*	.978	51	84	3	2	1
Frobel, Pitt.	.964	24	27	0	1	0
Gladden, S.F.	1.000	18	53	0	0	0
Grant, Chi.	1.000	10	6	1	0	0
Green, St.L.	.970	136	214	10	7	2
G. Gross, Phila.*	.991	110	104	1	1	0
Gwynn, S.D.*	.994	81	163	9	1	1
Hall, Atl.	.750	4	3	0	1	0
Hall, Chi.*	.988	112	239	8	3	2
Harper, Pitt.	1.000	35	40	0	0	0
Harper, Atl.	.952	60	95	5	5	0
Hayes, Phila.	.972	103	165	7	5	0
Hebner, Pitt.	1.000	7	8	0	0	0
Heep, N.Y.*	1.000	61	90	4	0	1
Hendrick, St.L.	.989	51	85	2	1	0
Householder, Cin.	.991	112	221	5	2	0
Howard, N.Y.	.000	1	0	0	0	0
Hurdle, N.Y.	.000	1	0	0	0	0
Iorg, St.L.	.974	22	37	0	1	0
Johnstone, Chi.	.935	44	55	3	4	1
Jones, Cin.	1.000	13	26	1	0	0
Jones, S.D.*	.981	111	249	3	5	2
Jorgensen, Atl.*	1.000	6	9	0	0	0
Kingman, N.Y.	1.000	5	7	0	0	0
Knicely, Cin.	1.000	8	14	1	0	1
Komminsk, Atl.	.944	13	16	1	1	0
Lacy, Pitt.	1.000	98	167	2	0	0
Landestoy, Cin.-L.A.	.800	11	8	0	2	0
Landreaux, L.A.	.990	137	299	4	3	1
Landrum, St.L.	1.000	5	1	0	0	0
Lefebvre, S.D.-Phila.	.990	80	93	5	1	0
Leonard, S.F.	.975	136	253	17	7	2
Lezcano, S.D.-Phila.	.971	106	189	10	6	1
Loucks, Hou.	1.000	6	12	1	0	0
Maddox, Phila.	.977	95	216	1	5	0
Maldonado, L.A.	1.000	33	26	0	0	0
Marshall, L.A.	.976	109	160	3	4	1
Martinez, Chi.	1.000	1	1	0	0	0
Matthews, Phila.	.974	122	174	11	5	2
Mazzilli, Pitt.	.985	57	130	3	2	1
McGee, St.L.	.987	145	385	7	5	1
McReynolds, S.D.	.989	38	87	4	1	1
Milner, Cin.*	.990	139	392	9	4	0
Monday, L.A.*	.969	44	62	1	2	0
Morales, Chi.	1.000	29	29	1	0	0
Moreland, Chi.	.976	151	236	7	6	1
Moreno, Hou.*	.977	97	251	8	6	3
Mumphrey, Hou.	.990	43	103	1	1	0
Murphy, Atl.	.985	160	373	10	6	0
Nordhagen, Chi.	1.000	7	7	0	0	0
Oliver, Mtl.*	.000	1	0	0	0	0
Orsulak, Pitt.*	1.000	4	2	2	0	0
Parker, Pitt.	.973	142	282	3	8	2
Perry, Atl.	.000	1	0	0	0	0
Puhl, Hou.	.991	124	220	4	2	1
Rabb, S.F.	1.000	2	8	0	0	0
Raines, Mtl.	.988	154	307	21	4	3
Ramsey, St.L.	.000	1	0	0	0	0
Redus, Cin.	.972	120	235	11	7	0
Reynolds, Hou.	.000	1	0	0	0	0
Reynolds, L.A.	.931	18	25	2	2	1
Richards, S.D.*	.980	54	96	2	2	0
Robinson, Phila.	.000	1	0	0	0	0
Roenicke, L.A.	.987	62	75	1	1	0
Roof, St.L.-Mtl.	1.000	6	3	0	0	0
Rose, Phila.	.976	35	41	0	1	0
Royster, Atl.	.962	18	25	0	1	0
Sanchez, Phila.	.500	2	1	0	1	0
T. Scott, Hou.	1.000	61	89	2	0	1
Shines, Mtl.	.000	1	0	0	0	0
Smith, S.F.	1.000	4	5	0	0	0
L. Smith, St.L.	.941	126	225	14	15	4
Staub, N.Y.	.800	5	4	0	1	0
Stenhouse, Mtl.	1.000	9	8	0	0	0
Stone, Phila.	.000	1	0	0	0	0
Strawberry, N.Y.*	.984	117	232	8	4	0
Summers, S.F.	1.000	1	2	0	0	0
Tenace, Pitt.	.000	1	0	0	0	0
Thomas, L.A.	.990	82	97	3	1	0
Thompson, Chi.*	1.000	29	29	0	0	0
Tolman, Hou.	1.000	3	2	0	0	0
Turner, S.D.*	.000	1	0	0	0	0
Vail, S.F.-Mtl.	.960	17	20	4	1	0
Van Slyke, St.L.	.974	69	108	4	3	1
Venable, S.F.	.993	66	141	5	1	0
Walker, Cin.*	.956	60	104	4	5	0
Walling, Hou.	.846	13	11	0	2	0

Player—Club	Pct.	G.	PO.	A.	E.	DP.
Washington, Atl.*	.974	128	218	8	6	3
White, Mtl.	1.000	13	13	0	0	0
Wiggins, S.D.	.992	105	242	6	2	1
Williams, Cin.*	1.000	12	18	0	0	0
Wilson, N.Y.	.984	148	422	5	7	1
Wohlford, Mtl.	.988	61	80	2	1	0
Woods, Chi.	.971	73	97	4	3	2
Wynne, Pitt.*	.983	102	223	3	4	2
Youngblood, S.F.	.968	22	28	2	1	0

OUTFIELDERS WITH TWO OR MORE CLUBS

Player—Club	Pct.	G.	PO.	A.	E.	DP.
Landestoy, Cin.	.000	1	0	0	1	0
Landestoy, L.A.	.889	10	8	0	1	0
Lefebvre, S.D.	1.000	6	1	1	0	0
Lefebvre, Phila.	.990	74	92	4	1	0
Lezcano, S.D.	.968	91	171	8	6	1
Lezcano, Phila.	1.000	15	18	2	0	0
Roof, St.L.	.000	1	0	0	0	0
Roof, Mtl.	1.000	5	3	0	0	0
Vail, S.F.	1.000	2	1	0	0	0
Vail, Mtl.	.958	15	19	4	1	0

CATCHERS

Leader—Club	Pct.	G.	PO.	A.	E.	DP.	PB.
CARTER, Mtl.	.995	144	847	107	5	14	6

(Listed Alphabetically)

Player—Club	Pct.	G.	PO.	A.	E.	DP.	PB.
Ashby, Hou.	.974	85	435	56	13	2	9
Ashford, N.Y.	1.000	1	1	0	0	0	0
Bench, Cin.	.950	5	17	2	1	0	0
Benedict, Atl.	.992	134	738	91	7	12	4
Bilardello, Cin.	.991	105	494	72	5	4	8
Bishop, N.Y.	.944	3	16	1	1	0	0
Bjorkman, Hou.	.993	29	136	16	1	0	4
Blackwell, Mtl.	.935	5	28	1	2	0	0
Bochy, S.D.	1.000	11	51	5	0	0	1
Brenly, S.F.	.983	90	403	70	8	9	9
Brummer, St.L.	.978	41	122	11	3	2	3
Carter, Mtl.	.995	144	847	107	5	14	6
Christmas, Cin.	1.000	7	28	3	0	0	1
Daulton, Phila.	1.000	2	8	0	0	0	0
Davis, Chi.	.984	150	730	75	13	7	21
Diaz, Phila.	.986	134	903	97	14	7	10
Diaz, Chi.	1.000	3	5	0	0	0	1
Fimple, L.A.	.989	54	336	32	4	2	9
Fitzgerald, N.Y.	.957	8	37	8	2	0	0
Gwosdz, S.D.	.971	32	95	5	3	0	1
Hodges, N.Y.	.971	96	360	45	12	4	5
Kennedy, S.D.	.986	143	782	79	12	8	7
Knicely, Cin.	1.000	31	108	11	0	1	3
Lake, Chi.	1.000	32	115	22	0	3	2
Lefebvre, S.D.-Phila.	1.000	5	8	0	0	1	0
May, S.F.-Pitt.	.983	60	308	35	6	5	1
Mizerock, Hou.	.967	33	154	24	6	5	11
Moreland, Chi.	1.000	3	8	0	0	0	0
Nicosia, Pitt.-S.F.	.986	24	131	9	2	0	1
Ortiz, Pitt.-N.Y.	.967	71	293	31	11	2	6
Owen, Atl.	.970	16	30	2	1	1	0
Pena, Pitt.	.992	149	976	90	9	9	7
Pocoroba, Atl.	.983	34	166	12	3	1	1
Porter, St.L.	.989	133	578	70	7	8	14
Pujols, Hou.	.971	39	180	20	6	0	11
Quirk, St.L.	.929	22	68	11	6	1	2
Rabb, S.F.	.973	31	168	13	5	2	2
Ramos, Mtl.	.984	25	111	14	2	0	2
Ransom, S.F.	.946	6	32	3	2	0	0
Reyes, L.A.	.944	19	59	9	4	2	4
Reynolds, N.Y.	.942	24	99	14	7	2	1
Sanchez, St.L.	1.000	1	1	0	0	0	0
D. Sax, L.A.	.917	4	11	0	1	0	1
Scioscia, L.A.	1.000	11	55	4	0	0	0
Sinatro, Atl.	.967	7	24	5	1	0	1
Spilman, Hou.	1.000	6	14	1	0	0	0
Tenace, Pitt.	.944	3	16	1	1	0	0
Trevino, Cin.	.987	63	359	28	5	2	4
Virgil, Phila.	.966	51	228	24	9	2	3
Wieghaus, Mtl.	1.000	1	1	0	0	0	0
Yeager, L.A.	.985	112	579	63	10	10	6

CATCHERS WITH TWO OR MORE CLUBS

Player—Club	Pct.	G.	PO.	A.	E.	DP.	PB.
Lefebvre, S.D.	1.000	2	3	0	0	1	0
Lefebvre, Phila.	1.000	3	5	0	0	0	0
May, S.F.	.981	56	285	32	6	5	0
May, Pitt.	1.000	4	23	3	0	0	1
Nicosia, Pitt.	.988	15	76	3	1	0	1
Nicosia, S.F.	.984	9	55	6	1	0	0
Ortiz, Pitt.	1.000	4	20	0	0	0	0
Ortiz, N.Y.	.965	67	273	31	11	2	6

PITCHERS

Leader—Club	Pct.	G.	PO.	A.	E.	DP.
ROGERS, Mtl.	1.000	36	28	28	0	1

(Listed Alphabetically)

Player—Club	Pct.	G.	PO.	A.	E.	DP.
Allen, N.Y.-St.L.	1.000	46	17	20	0	0
Altamirano, Phila.	1.000	31	2	8	0	0
Andersen, Phila.	1.000	17	2	6	0	0
Andujar, St.L.	.928	39	15	62	6	3
Bair, St.L.	1.000	26	2	3	0	0
Baker, St.L.	1.000	8	1	3	0	0
Bargar, Mtl.	1.000	8	1	1	0	0
Barker, Atl.	.857	6	4	8	2	0
Barr, S.F.	.958	53	10	13	1	0
Beckwith, L.A.	1.000	42	8	13	0	1
Bedrosian, Atl.	1.000	70	4	16	0	2
Behenna, Atl.	1.000	14	2	4	0	0
Berenyi, Cin.	.958	32	5	41	2	2
Bibby, Pitt.	1.000	29	4	10	0	1
Boggs, Atl.	.000	5	0	0	0	0
Booker, S.D.	1.000	6	0	3	0	0
Bordi, Chi.	.750	11	3	3	2	1
Breining, S.F.	.957	32	21	24	2	0
Brizzolara, Atl.	1.000	14	2	0	0	0
Brusstar, Chi.	1.000	59	7	12	0	1
Burris, Mtl.	1.000	40	12	23	0	1
Bystrom, Phila.	.952	24	10	10	1	0
Calvert, S.F.	1.000	18	5	7	0	0
Camp, Atl.	.881	40	14	23	5	1
Campbell, Chi.	.951	82	15	24	2	0
Candelaria, Pitt.*	1.000	33	5	20	0	1
Carlton, Phila.*	.911	37	4	37	4	0
Carman, Phila.*	1.000	1	1	0	0	0
Cato, Cin.	.000	4	0	0	0	0
Chiffer, S.D.	1.000	15	3	4	0	0
Chris, S.F.*	.500	7	0	1	1	0
Christenson, Phila.	.929	9	4	9	1	0
Citarella, St.L.	1.000	6	1	1	0	0
Comer, Phila.	1.000	3	2	0	0	0
Couchee, S.D.	1.000	8	1	1	0	0
Cox, St.L.	.926	12	9	16	2	1
Darling, N.Y.	1.000	5	2	6	0	1
M. Davis, S.F.*	1.000	20	4	13	0	0
Dawley, Hou.	1.000	48	2	5	0	1
Dayley, Atl.*	1.000	24	0	7	0	0
Decker, S.D.	.667	4	0	2	1	0
Dedmon, Atl.	1.000	5	1	1	0	0
DeLeon, Pitt.	.938	15	6	9	1	0
DeLeon, S.D.	.917	63	2	9	1	1
Denny, Phila.	.879	36	16	42	8	6
Diaz, N.Y.*	1.000	54	8	13	0	2
DiPino, Hou.*	1.000	53	5	11	0	1
Dixon, Mtl.	.000	4	0	0	0	0
Dravecky, S.D.*	.977	28	7	35	1	3
Falcone, Atl.*	1.000	33	1	11	0	0

PITCHERS—Continued

Player—Club	Pct.	G.	PO.	A.	E.	DP.
Farmer, Phila.	1.000	12	2	5	0	0
Fernandez, L.A.*	1.000	2	1	1	0	0
Fireovid, S.D.	1.000	3	0	1	0	0
Forsch, St.L.	.977	34	14	29	1	1
Forster, Atl.*	.947	56	3	15	1	1
Fryman, Mtl.*	1.000	6	0	2	0	0
Gaff, N.Y.	.600	4	1	2	2	0
Gale, Cin.	.895	33	7	10	2	0
Garber, Atl.	1.000	43	4	17	0	1
Garrelts, S.F.	1.000	5	1	7	0	1
Ghelfi, Phila.	1.000	3	0	5	0	0
Gorman, N.Y.*	1.000	25	3	7	0	2
Grapenthin, Mtl.	1.000	1	0	1	0	0
K. Gross, Phila.	1.000	17	11	13	0	0
Guante, Pitt.	.875	49	5	9	2	0
Gullickson, Mtl.	.981	34	27	25	1	3
Hagen, St.L.	1.000	9	2	4	0	0
Hammaker, S.F.*	.919	23	3	31	3	2
Hargesheimer, Chi.	.000	5	0	0	0	0
Harris, Cin.	1.000	1	0	1	0	0
Hawkins, S.D.	.969	21	13	18	1	2
Hayes, Cin.	1.000	60	3	11	0	0
Heathcock, Hou.	1.000	6	3	4	0	1
Hernandez, Chi.-Phila*	1.000	74	2	17	0	3
Hershiser, L.A.	1.000	8	0	2	0	1
Holland, Phila.*	1.000	68	0	5	0	0
Holman, N.Y.	.950	35	16	22	2	1
Honeycutt, L.A.*	1.000	9	2	16	0	0
Hooton, L.A.	.941	33	8	24	2	1
Howe, L.A.*	1.000	46	4	15	0	0
Hudson, Phila.	.971	26	14	19	1	3
Hume, Cin.	.944	48	3	14	1	3
James, Mtl.	.889	27	4	12	2	1
Jenkins, Chi.	1.000	33	16	18	0	0
Johnson, Chi.	1.000	10	1	4	0	0
Kaat, St.L.*	.889	24	2	6	1	0
Keener, St.L.	1.000	4	0	1	0	0
Kingman, S.F.	.000	3	0	0	0	0
Knepper, Hou.*	.933	35	2	40	3	4
Krukow, S.F.	.861	31	13	18	5	1
LaCorte, Hou.	1.000	37	1	6	0	0
LaCoss, Hou.	1.000	38	6	27	0	1
Lahti, St.L.	1.000	53	6	14	0	3
LaPoint, St.L.*	1.000	37	11	24	0	1
Larkin, S.F.*	.667	5	0	2	1	0
Laskey, S.F.	.964	25	11	16	1	0
Lavelle, S.F.*	.962	56	5	20	1	2
Lea, Mtl.	.958	33	19	27	2	0
Leary, N.Y.	1.000	2	1	3	0	0
Lefferts, Chi.*	.955	56	8	13	1	0
Lerch, Mtl.-S.F.*	1.000	26	3	6	0	1
Lesley, Cin.	1.000	5	0	1	0	0
Lollar, S.D.*	1.000	30	4	19	0	1
Lucas, S.D.*	.833	62	5	10	3	1
Lynch, N.Y.	1.000	30	10	24	0	0
Madden, Hou.*	.957	28	7	15	1	4
Mahler, Atl.	.667	10	1	1	1	1
Martin, S.F.	1.000	37	15	16	0	0
Martin, St.L.*	.944	26	3	14	1	0
McGaffigan, S.F.	.857	43	8	4	2	0
McGraw, Phila.*	.917	34	1	10	1	1
McMurtry, Atl.	.957	36	15	51	3	3
McWilliams, Pitt.*	.909	35	10	40	5	5
Minton, S.F.	.958	73	5	18	1	0
Monge, Phila.-S.D.*	1.000	61	4	10	0	0
Montefusco, S.D.	.842	31	3	13	3	0
Moore, Atl.	1.000	43	2	8	0	0
Moskau, Chi.	.800	8	3	5	2	0
Niedenfuer, L.A.	.941	66	8	8	1	0
Niekro, Hou.	.918	38	9	36	4	0
Niekro, Atl.	.955	34	15	27	2	6
Niemann, Pitt.*	1.000	8	2	2	0	1
Noles, Chi.	.962	24	11	14	1	0
Orosco, N.Y.*	1.000	62	5	19	0	0
Owchinko, Pitt.*	.000	1	0	0	0	0
Ownbey, N.Y.	.875	10	1	6	1	1
Pastore, Cin.	1.000	36	15	19	0	3
Patterson, Chi.	1.000	5	3	1	0	1
Pena, L.A.	.918	34	13	32	4	4
Perez, Atl.	.934	33	24	33	4	2
Power, Cin.	1.000	49	4	8	0	1
Price, Cin.*	.879	21	8	21	4	3
Proly, Chi.	.952	60	6	14	1	0
Puleo, Cin.	.926	27	11	14	2	1
Pulido, Pitt.*	.000	1	0	0	0	0
Rainey, Chi.	.904	34	28	38	7	2
Rasmussen, S.D.*	1.000	4	0	4	0	1
Rasmussen, St.L.	1.000	6	0	1	0	1
Reardon, Mtl.	.778	66	3	4	2	0
Reed, Phila.	1.000	61	2	7	0	0
Reuschel, Chi.	1.000	4	4	7	0	0
Reuss, L.A.*	.945	32	17	52	4	4
Rhoden, Pitt.	1.000	36	14	38	0	4
Robinson, Pitt.	1.000	9	1	6	0	1
Rodas, L.A.*	1.000	7	1	0	0	0
Rogers, Mtl.	1.000	36	28	28	0	1
Rucker, St.L.*	.909	34	5	5	1	1
Ruhle, Hou.	1.000	41	12	19	0	0
Russell, Cin.	.923	10	2	10	1	0
Ruthven, Phila.-Chi.	.962	32	16	35	2	4
Ryan, Hou.	.941	29	4	28	2	0
Sanderson, Mtl.	.833	18	4	6	2	0
Sarmiento, Pitt.	1.000	52	5	9	0	0
Schatzeder, Mtl.*	.944	58	9	8	1	0
Scherrer, Cin.*	1.000	73	2	18	0	1
Schulze, Chi.	1.000	4	1	2	0	0
M. Scott, Hou.	.952	24	20	20	2	0
Scurry, Pitt.*	1.000	61	2	8	0	0
Seaver, N.Y.	.926	34	22	28	4	0
Show, S.D.	.895	35	7	27	4	0
Sisk, N.Y.	.955	67	7	14	1	1
Smith, Mtl.	1.000	49	10	22	0	3
Smith, Hou.	.778	42	3	4	2	0
Smith, Chi.	1.000	66	8	9	0	0
Solano, Hou.	1.000	4	0	1	0	0
Sosa, S.D.	1.000	41	7	5	0	0
Soto, Cin.	.909	34	22	28	5	1
Stewart, L.A.	.929	46	6	7	1	2
Stuper, St.L.	.911	40	17	24	4	2
Sutter, St.L.	.938	60	11	19	2	1
Swan, N.Y.	1.000	27	4	10	0	0
Tekulve, Pitt.	1.000	76	3	20	0	2
Terrell, N.Y.	1.000	21	16	15	0	2
Thurmond, S.D.*	1.000	21	7	22	0	0
Tomlin, Pitt.*	.000	5	0	0	0	0
Torrez, N.Y.	.964	39	20	33	2	4
Trout, Chi.*	.960	34	8	40	2	3
Tunnell, Pitt.	1.000	35	11	35	0	6
Valenzuela, L.A.*	.974	35	20	54	2	5
Von Ohlen, St.L.*	.929	46	2	11	1	1
Walk, Atl.	1.000	1	0	2	0	0
Welch, L.A.	.932	31	14	27	3	1
Welsh, S.D.-Mtl.*	.900	23	3	15	2	2
White, L.A.	1.000	4	1	1	0	0
Whitson, S.D.	1.000	31	4	6	0	0
Winn, Pitt.	1.000	7	1	2	0	0
Wright, L.A.*	.000	6	0	0	0	0
Zachry, L.A.	.882	40	6	9	2	1

PITCHERS WITH TWO OR MORE CLUBS

Player—Club	Pct.	G.	PO.	A.	E.	DP.
Allen, N.Y.	1.000	21	5	6	0	0
Allen, St.L.	1.000	25	12	14	0	0
Hernandez, Chi.*	1.000	11	1	4	0	1
Hernandez, Phila.*	1.000	63	1	13	0	2
Lerch, Mtl.*	1.000	19	1	5	0	0
Lerch, S.F.*	1.000	7	2	1	0	1
Monge, Phila.*	1.000	14	0	1	0	0
Monge, S.D.*	1.000	47	4	9	0	0
Ruthven, Phil.	1.000	7	1	4	0	2
Ruthven, Chi.	.958	25	15	31	2	2
Welsh, S.D.*	.600	7	1	2	2	0
Welsh, Mtl.*	1.000	16	2	13	0	2

OFFICIAL NATIONAL LEAGUE PITCHING AVERAGES

CLUB PITCHING

Club	ERA.	G.	CG.	ShO.	Sv.	IP.	H.	BFP.	R.	ER.	HR.	SH.	SF.	HB.	Tot. BB.	Int. BB.	SO.	WP.	Bk.
Los Angeles	3.10	163	27	12	40	1464.0	1336	6132	609	505	97	99	45	20	495	78	1000	38	12
Philadelphia	3.34	163	20	10	41	1461.2	1429	6168	635	542	111	65	39	23	464	77	1092	44	18
Houston	3.45	162	22	14	48	1466.1	1276	6117	646	562	94	65	52	27	570	49	904	49	14
Pittsburgh	3.55	162	25	14	41	1462.1	1378	6167	648	577	109	64	46	18	563	67	1061	52	21
Montreal	3.58	163	38	15	34	1471.0	1406	6151	646	585	120	67	37	33	479	50	899	38	9
San Diego	3.62	163	23	5	44	1467.2	1389	6179	653	590	144	96	42	28	528	52	850	33	10
Atlanta	3.67	162	18	4	48	1440.2	1412	6113	640	588	132	75	43	23	540	47	895	34	10
New York	3.68	162	18	7	33	1451.0	1384	6181	680	593	97	83	47	21	615	82	717	46	14
San Francisco	3.70	162	20	9	47	1445.2	1431	6206	697	594	127	78	52	31	520	95	881	53	20
St. Louis	3.79	162	22	10	27	1460.2	1479	6232	710	615	115	88	45	23	525	73	709	55	19
Cincinnati	3.98	162	34	5	29	1441.1	1365	6166	710	638	135	61	58	20	627	60	934	27	9
Chicago	4.08	162	9	10	42	1428.2	1496	6110	719	647	117	80	42	25	498	83	807	43	13
Totals	3.63	974	276	115	474	17461.0	16781	73922	7993	7036	1398	921	548	292	6424	813	10749	512	169

NOTE: Total earned runs for six clubs do not agree with composite total of respective club's pitchers due to provisions of Scoring Rule Section 10.18 (i). The following differences are to be noted: Cincinnati pitchers add to 634, Los Angeles pitchers add to 504, Montreal pitchers add to 584, Philadelphia pitchers add to 540, St. Louis pitchers add to 608, San Francisco pitchers add to 589.

PITCHERS' RECORDS

(Top Fifteen Qualifiers for Earned-Run Leadership—162 or More Innings)

*Throws lefthanded.

Pitcher and Club	W.	L.	Pct.	ERA.	G.	GS.	CG.	ShO.	GF.	Sv.	IP.	H.	BFP.	R.	ER.	HR.	SH.	SF.	HB.	Tot. BB.	Int. BB.	SO.	WP.	Bk.
Hammaker, C. Atlee, San Francisco*	10	9	.526	2.25	23	23	8	3	0	0	172.1	147	695	57	43	9	10	4	3	32	12	127	6	2
Denny, John, Philadelphia	19	6	.760	2.37	36	36	7	1	0	0	242.2	229	983	77	64	9	8	3	4	53	5	139	6	1
Welch, Robert, Los Angeles	15	12	.556	2.65	31	31	4	3	0	0	204.0	164	828	73	60	13	8	7	3	72	4	156	4	6
Soto, Mario, Cincinnati	17	13	.567	2.70	34	34	18	3	0	0	273.2	207	1114	96	82	28	8	9	5	95	6	242	2	2
Pena, Alejandro, Los Angeles	12	9	.571	2.75	34	26	4	3	4	1	177.0	152	730	67	54	7	8	5	1	51	7	120	2	1
Reuss, Jerry, Los Angeles*	12	11	.522	2.94	32	31	7	0	0	0	223.1	233	935	94	73	12	18	6	2	50	5	143	3	2
Ryan, L. Nolan, Houston	14	9	.609	2.98	29	29	5	2	0	0	196.1	134	804	74	65	9	7	5	4	101	3	183	5	1
McMurtry, J. Craig, Atlanta	15	9	.625	3.08	36	35	6	3	0	0	224.2	204	943	86	77	13	9	5	1	88	1	105	1	2
Rhoden, Richard, Pittsburgh	13	13	.500	3.09	36	35	7	2	1	1	244.1	256	1012	95	84	13	8	6	2	68	15	153	6	5
Carlton, Steven, Philadelphia*	15	16	.484	3.11	37	37	8	3	0	0	283.2	277	1183	117	98	20	20	4	3	84	10	275	13	9
Lea, Charles, Montreal	16	11	.593	3.12	33	33	8	4	0	0	222.0	195	917	87	77	15	4	8	1	84	4	137	8	3
Knepper, Robert, Houston*	6	13	.316	3.19	35	29	4	3	2	0	203.0	202	867	93	72	12	9	8	4	71	3	125	3	2
Rogers, Stephen, Montreal	17	12	.586	3.23	36	36	13	5	0	0	273.0	258	1125	108	98	14	12	7	5	78	12	146	6	0
Candelaria, John, Pittsburgh*	15	8	.652	3.23	33	32	2	0	0	0	197.2	191	797	73	71	15	4	4	2	45	3	157	3	2
McWilliams, Larry, Pittsburgh*	15	8	.652	3.25	35	35	8	4	0	0	238.0	205	1002	99	86	19	13	6	3	87	7	199	9	4

DEPARTMENTAL LEADERS: W—Denny, 19; L—Torrez, 17; Pct.—Denny, .760; G—Campbell, 82; CG—Soto, 18; ShO—Rogers, 5; GF—L. Smith, Tekulve, 56; Sv—L. Smith, 29; IP—Carlton, 283.2; H—Carlton, 277; BFP—Carlton, 1,183; R—Valenzuela, 122; ER—Torrez, 108; HR—Soto, 28; SH—Valenzuela, 27; SF—Breining, LaPoint, 11; HB—Bystrom, 7; Tot. BB—Torrez, 113; Int. BB—Campbell, 18; SO—Carlton, 275; WP—J. Niekro, 14; Bk—Carlton, 9.

(All Pitchers—Listed Alphabetically)

Pitcher and Club	W.	L.	Pct.	ERA.	G.	GS.	CG.	ShO.	GF.	Sv.	IP.	H.	BFP.	R.	ER.	HR.	SH.	SF.	HB.	Tot. BB.	Int. BB.	SO.	WP.	Bk.
Allen, Neil, N.Y.-St.L.	12	13	.480	3.94	46	22	5	3	12	2	175.2	179	762	84	77	12	9	2	1	84	9	106	8	1
Altamirano, Porfirio, Philadelphia	2	3	.400	3.70	31	0	0	0	11	0	41.1	38	173	18	17	9	6	1	2	15	3	24	2	1
Andersen, Larry, Philadelphia	1	0	1.000	2.39	17	0	0	0	4	0	26.1	19	106	7	7	0	1	1	0	9	1	14	1	1
Andujar, Joaquin, St. Louis	6	16	.273	4.16	39	34	5	2	3	1	225.0	215	943	112	104	23	12	3	3	75	7	125	5	6
Bair, C. Douglas, St. Louis	1	1	.500	3.03	26	0	0	0	9	1	29.2	24	122	11	10	4	1	1	0	13	3	21	1	0
Baker, Steven, St. Louis	0	1	.000	1.80	8	0	0	0	3	0	10.0	10	43	4	2	0	2	1	1	4	1	1	3	0
Bargar, Gregory, Montreal	2	0	1.000	6.75	8	3	0	0	1	0	20.0	23	94	15	15	6	0	0	1	8	0	9	0	0
Barker, Leonard, Atlanta	1	3	.250	3.82	6	6	0	0	0	0	33.0	31	143	17	14	0	3	1	0	14	2	21	2	0
Barr, James, San Francisco	5	3	.625	3.98	53	0	0	0	23	2	92.2	106	395	47	41	7	4	9	1	20	9	47	1	0
Beckwith, T. Joseph, Los Angeles	3	4	.429	3.55	42	3	0	0	15	1	71.0	73	321	40	28	5	7	1	1	35	11	50	1	0
Bedrosian, Stephen, Atlanta	9	10	.474	3.60	70	1	0	0	52	19	120.0	100	504	50	48	11	8	4	4	51	8	114	2	0
Behenna, Richard, Atlanta	3	3	.500	4.58	14	6	0	0	1	0	37.1	37	160	20	19	7	1	1	1	12	2	17	0	3
Berenyi, Bruce, Cincinnati	9	14	.391	3.86	32	31	4	1	1	0	186.1	173	816	92	80	9	8	4	2	102	3	151	8	0
Bibby, James, Pittsburgh	5	12	.294	6.69	29	12	0	0	6	2	78.0	92	367	60	58	10	1	4	1	51	0	44	2	2
Boggs, Thomas, Atlanta	0	0	.000	5.68	5	0	0	0	1	0	6.1	8	27	4	4	1	1	0	0	1	0	5	1	0
Booker, Gregory, San Diego	0	1	.000	7.71	6	1	0	0	1	0	11.2	18	58	10	10	2	1	0	0	9	0	5	0	0
Bordi, Richard, Chicago	0	2	.000	4.97	11	1	0	0	1	1	25.1	34	119	15	14	2	1	0	0	12	1	20	0	0
Breining, Fred, San Francisco	11	12	.478	3.82	32	32	6	0	0	0	202.2	202	868	97	86	15	13	11	5	60	11	117	4	1
Brizzolara, Anthony, Atlanta	1	0	1.000	3.54	14	0	0	0	2	1	20.1	22	88	8	8	2	3	0	0	6	0	17	0	0
Brusstar, Warren, Chicago	3	1	.750	2.35	59	0	0	0	21	1	80.1	67	335	21	21	1	5	5	2	37	10	46	4	1
Burris, B. Ray, Montreal	4	7	.364	3.68	40	17	2	1	6	0	154.0	139	641	68	63	13	9	5	2	56	4	100	2	1
Bystrom, Martin, Philadelphia	6	9	.400	4.60	24	23	1	1	0	0	119.1	136	540	75	61	6	3	8	7	44	2	87	2	1
Calvert, Mark, San Francisco	1	4	.200	6.27	18	4	0	0	5	0	37.1	46	190	33	26	2	2	1	3	34	4	14	3	1
Camp, Rick, Atlanta	10	9	.526	3.79	40	16	1	0	4	0	140.0	146	590	64	59	16	5	3	4	38	2	61	3	0
Campbell, William, Chicago	6	8	.429	4.49	82	0	0	0	46	8	122.1	128	530	65	61	4	10	5	1	49	18	97	6	1
Candelaria, John, Pittsburgh*	15	8	.652	3.23	33	32	2	0	0	0	197.2	191	797	73	71	15	4	4	2	45	3	157	3	2
Carlton, Steven, Philadelphia*	15	16	.484	3.11	37	37	8	3	0	0	283.2	277	1183	117	98	20	20	4	3	84	10	275	13	9
Carman, Donald, Philadelphia*	0	0	.000	0.00	1	0	0	0	1	1	1.0	0	3	0	0	0	0	0	0	0	0	0	0	0
Cato, J. Keefe, Cincinnati	1	0	1.000	2.45	4	0	0	0	1	0	3.2	2	14	1	1	0	0	0	0	1	0	3	0	0
Chiffer, Floyd, San Diego	0	2	.000	3.18	15	0	0	0	3	1	22.2	17	94	10	8	0	3	0	0	10	1	15	0	1
Chris, Michael, San Francisco*	0	0	.000	8.10	7	0	0	0	0	0	13.1	16	72	14	12	1	1	1	2	16	2	5	1	0
Christenson, Larry, Philadelphia	2	4	.333	3.91	9	9	0	0	0	0	48.1	42	203	25	21	2	1	4	1	17	1	44	2	0
Citarella, Ralph, St. Louis	0	0	.000	1.64	6	0	0	0	2	0	11.0	8	42	2	2	0	0	0	0	3	1	4	1	0
Comer, Steven, Philadelphia	1	0	1.000	5.19	3	1	0	0	0	0	8.2	11	38	6	5	0	0	0	0	3	0	1	0	0
Couchee, Michael, San Diego	0	1	.000	5.14	8	0	0	0	2	0	14.0	12	63	8	8	1	0	1	0	6	1	5	0	1
Cox, Danny, St. Louis	3	6	.333	3.25	12	12	0	0	0	0	83.0	92	352	38	30	6	6	1	0	23	2	36	2	0
Darling, Ronald, New York	1	3	.250	2.80	5	5	1	0	0	0	35.1	31	148	11	11	0	3	0	3	17	1	23	3	2
Davis, Mark, San Francisco*	6	4	.600	3.49	20	20	2	2	0	0	111.0	93	469	51	43	14	2	4	3	50	4	83	8	1
Dawley, William, Houston	6	6	.500	2.82	48	0	0	0	37	14	79.2	51	304	26	25	9	5	0	1	22	4	60	1	0
Dayley, Kenneth, Atlanta*	5	8	.385	4.30	24	16	0	0	3	0	104.2	100	436	59	50	12	3	3	2	39	2	70	3	0
Decker, D. Martin, San Diego	0	0	.000	2.08	4	0	0	0	1	0	8.2	5	34	2	2	1	0	0	1	3	0	9	1	0
Dedmon, Jeffrey, Atlanta	0	0	.000	13.50	5	0	0	0	0	0	4.0	10	23	6	6	1	1	0	0	0	0	3	0	0
DeLeon, Jose, Pittsburgh	7	3	.700	2.83	15	15	3	2	0	0	108.0	75	438	36	34	5	4	3	1	47	2	118	5	2
DeLeon, Luis, San Diego	6	6	.500	2.68	63	0	0	0	34	13	111.0	89	442	34	33	8	7	9	1	27	7	90	1	0
Denny, John, Philadelphia	19	6	.760	2.37	36	36	7	1	0	0	242.2	229	983	77	64	9	8	3	4	53	5	139	6	1
Diaz, Carlos, New York*	3	1	.750	2.05	54	0	0	0	20	2	83.1	62	339	22	19	1	6	3	1	35	13	64	2	0
DiPino, Frank, Houston*	3	4	.429	2.65	53	0	0	0	32	20	71.1	52	279	21	21	2	1	3	1	20	5	67	3	0
Dixon, Thomas, Montreal	0	1	.000	9.82	4	0	0	0	3	0	3.2	6	19	4	4	1	0	1	1	1	0	4	1	0

Pitcher and Club	W.	L.	Pct.	ERA.	G.	GS.	CG.	ShO.	GF.	Sv.	IP.	H.	BFP.	R.	ER.	HR.	SH.	SF.	HB.	Tot. BB.	Int. BB.	SO.	WP.	Bk.
Dravecky, David, San Diego*	14	10	.583	3.58	28	28	9	1	0	0	183.2	181	756	78	73	18	13	4	3	44	4	74	2	1
Falcone, Peter, Atlanta*	9	4	.692	3.63	33	15	2	0	6	0	106.2	102	467	47	43	14	4	4	1	60	2	59	5	0
Farmer, Edward, Philadelphia	0	6	.000	6.08	12	3	0	0	3	0	26.2	35	137	22	18	2	1	1	1	20	8	16	3	0
Fernandez, C. Sid, Los Angeles*	0	1	.000	6.00	2	1	0	0	0	0	6.0	7	33	4	4	0	0	0	1	7	0	9	0	0
Fireovid, Stephen, San Diego	0	0	.000	1.80	3	0	0	0	1	0	5.0	4	20	2	1	0	1	0	0	2	0	1	1	0
Forsch, Robert, St. Louis	10	12	.455	4.28	34	30	6	2	3	0	187.0	190	790	104	89	23	11	8	3	54	2	56	4	1
Forster, Terry, Atlanta*	3	2	.600	2.16	56	0	0	0	29	13	79.1	60	316	19	19	3	7	0	2	31	9	54	2	0
Fryman, Woodrow, Montreal*	0	3	.000	21.00	6	0	0	0	1	0	3.0	8	16	7	7	1	1	0	0	1	0	1	0	0
Gaff, Brent, New York	1	0	1.000	6.10	4	0	0	0	2	0	10.1	18	53	9	7	0	1	1	0	1	1	4	1	0
Gale, Richard, Cincinnati	4	6	.400	5.82	33	7	0	0	6	1	89.2	103	408	64	58	8	2	2	1	43	8	53	3	1
Garber, H. Eugene, Atlanta	4	5	.444	4.60	43	0	0	0	29	9	60.2	72	277	37	31	8	6	6	2	23	7	45	2	1
Garrelts, Scott, San Francisco	2	2	.500	2.52	5	5	1	1	0	0	35.2	33	154	11	10	4	3	0	2	19	4	16	4	1
Ghelfi, Anthony, Philadelphia	1	1	.500	3.14	3	3	0	0	0	0	14.1	15	62	5	5	2	0	0	0	6	0	14	0	1
Gorman, Thomas, New York*	1	4	.200	4.93	25	4	0	0	9	0	49.1	45	204	29	27	3	3	2	0	15	4	30	2	1
Grapenthin, Richard, Montreal	0	1	.000	9.00	1	0	0	0	0	0	4.0	4	16	4	4	2	0	0	0	1	0	3	0	0
Gross, Kevin, Philadelphia	4	6	.400	3.56	17	17	1	1	0	0	96.0	100	418	46	38	13	2	1	3	35	3	66	4	1
Guante, Cecilio, Pittsburgh	2	6	.250	3.32	49	0	0	0	19	9	100.1	90	431	45	37	5	7	2	2	46	6	82	3	0
Gullickson, William, Montreal	17	12	.586	3.75	34	34	10	1	0	0	242.1	230	990	108	101	19	4	7	4	59	4	120	4	1
Hagen, Kevin, St. Louis	2	2	.500	4.84	9	4	0	0	1	0	22.1	34	103	15	12	0	2	0	0	7	0	7	2	0
Hammaker, C. Atlee, San Francisco*	10	9	.526	2.25	23	23	8	3	0	0	172.1	147	695	57	43	9	10	4	3	32	12	127	6	2
Hargesheimer, Alan, Chicago	0	0	.000	9.00	5	0	0	0	2	0	4.0	6	19	4	4	0	1	0	0	2	0	5	0	0
Harris, Greg, Cincinnati	0	0	.000	27.00	1	0	0	0	0	0	1.0	2	9	3	3	0	1	0	1	3	2	1	0	0
Hawkins, M. Andrew, San Diego	5	7	.417	2.93	21	19	4	1	1	0	119.2	106	501	50	39	8	10	4	5	48	4	59	4	1
Hayes, Ben, Cincinnati	4	6	.400	6.49	60	0	0	0	34	7	69.1	82	318	53	50	8	3	5	1	37	6	44	1	1
Heathcock, R. Jeffrey, Houston	2	1	.667	3.21	6	3	0	0	2	1	28.0	19	111	14	10	1	0	1	1	4	0	12	0	1
Hernandez, Guillermo, Chi.-Phila.*	9	4	.692	3.28	74	1	0	0	31	8	115.1	109	478	47	42	9	7	0	1	32	8	93	5	0
Hershiser, Orel, Los Angeles	0	0	.000	3.38	8	0	0	0	4	1	8.0	7	37	6	3	1	1	0	0	6	0	5	1	0
Holland, Alfred, Philadelphia*	8	4	.667	2.26	68	0	0	0	53	25	91.2	63	371	26	23	8	5	1	0	30	12	100	0	0
Holman, R. Scott, New York	1	7	.125	3.74	35	10	0	0	10	0	101.0	90	439	48	42	7	9	5	1	52	8	44	3	1
Honeycutt, Frederick, Los Angeles*	2	3	.400	5.77	9	7	1	0	0	0	39.0	46	172	26	25	6	2	0	2	13	4	18	0	1
Hooton, Burt, Los Angeles	9	8	.529	4.22	33	27	2	0	0	0	160.0	156	684	86	75	21	3	6	2	59	4	87	3	0
Howe, Steven, Los Angeles*	4	7	.364	1.44	46	0	0	0	33	18	68.2	55	274	15	11	2	5	3	1	12	7	52	3	0
Hudson, Charles, Philadelphia	8	8	.500	3.35	26	26	3	0	0	0	169.1	158	701	73	63	13	6	4	0	53	6	101	4	3
Hume, Thomas, Cincinnati	3	5	.375	4.77	48	0	0	0	33	9	66.0	66	301	40	35	8	3	4	3	41	11	34	1	0
James, Robert, Montreal	1	0	1.000	2.88	27	0	0	0	16	7	50.0	37	208	17	16	3	6	0	3	23	2	56	2	1
Jenkins, Ferguson, Chicago	6	9	.400	4.30	33	29	1	1	1	0	167.1	176	705	89	80	19	7	5	6	46	5	96	2	3
Johnson, William, Chicago	1	0	1.000	4.38	10	0	0	0	2	0	12.1	17	55	6	6	0	2	1	0	3	1	4	0	1
Kaat, James, St. Louis*	0	0	.000	3.89	24	0	0	0	9	0	34.2	48	162	19	15	5	4	1	0	10	3	19	0	0
Keener, Jeffrey, St. Louis	0	0	.000	8.31	4	0	0	0	2	0	4.1	6	21	4	4	0	0	1	1	1	0	4	0	1
Kingman, Brian, San Francisco	0	0	.000	7.71	3	0	0	0	2	0	4.2	10	25	6	4	0	0	0	0	1	0	1	0	0
Knepper, Robert, Houston*	6	13	.316	3.19	35	29	4	3	2	0	203.0	202	867	93	72	12	9	8	4	71	3	125	3	2
Krukow, Michael, San Francisco	11	11	.500	3.95	31	31	2	1	0	0	184.1	189	816	95	81	17	9	3	3	76	8	136	8	1
LaCorte, Frank, Houston	4	4	.500	5.06	37	0	0	0	19	3	53.1	35	220	32	30	8	5	1	2	28	3	48	5	0
LaCoss, Michael, Houston	5	7	.417	4.43	38	17	2	0	6	1	138.0	142	590	81	68	10	6	6	2	56	11	53	9	1
Lahti, Jeffrey, St. Louis	3	3	.500	3.16	53	0	0	0	13	0	74.0	64	305	31	26	2	6	2	1	29	12	26	3	2
LaPoint, David, St. Louis*	12	9	.571	3.95	37	29	1	0	1	0	191.1	191	832	92	84	12	17	11	4	84	7	113	11	4
Larkin, Patrick, San Francisco*	0	0	.000	4.35	5	0	0	0	4	0	10.1	13	48	6	5	1	1	1	2	3	1	6	0	2
Laskey, William, San Francisco	13	10	.565	4.19	25	25	1	0	0	0	148.1	151	627	75	69	18	7	4	3	45	4	81	0	1
Lavelle, Gary, San Francisco*	7	4	.636	2.59	56	0	0	0	38	20	87.0	73	349	33	25	4	8	3	0	19	8	68	3	1
Lea, Charles, Montreal	16	11	.593	3.12	33	33	8	4	0	0	222.0	195	917	87	77	15	4	8	1	84	4	137	8	3

Pitcher and Club	W.	L.	Pct.	ERA.	G.	GS.	CG.	ShO.	GF.	Sv.	IP.	H.	BFP.	R.	ER.	HR.	SH.	SF.	HB.	Tot. BB.	Int. BB.	SO.	WP.	Bk.
Leary, Timothy, New York	1	1	.500	3.38	2	2	1	0	0	0	10.2	15	53	10	4	0	1	1	0	4	0	9	0	1
Lefferts, Craig, Chicago*	3	4	.429	3.13	56	5	0	0	10	1	89.0	80	367	35	31	13	7	0	2	29	3	60	2	0
Lerch, Randy, Mtl-S.F.*	2	3	.400	6.02	26	5	0	0	2	0	49.1	54	224	33	33	7	2	2	1	26	3	30	1	0
Lesley, Bradley, Cincinnati	0	0	.000	2.16	5	0	0	0	5	0	8.1	9	32	2	2	1	0	1	0	0	0	5	0	0
Lollar, W. Timothy, San Diego*	7	12	.368	4.61	30	30	1	0	0	0	175.2	170	758	98	90	22	9	2	4	85	1	135	5	1
Lucas, Gary, San Diego*	5	8	.385	2.87	62	0	0	0	41	17	91.0	85	391	38	29	9	7	3	0	34	11	60	1	0
Lynch, Edward, New York	10	10	.500	4.28	30	27	1	0	1	0	174.2	208	749	94	83	17	9	7	3	41	10	44	3	2
Madden, Michael, Houston*	9	5	.643	3.14	28	13	0	0	7	0	94.2	76	387	37	33	4	9	3	1	45	3	44	2	3
Mahler, Richard, Atlanta	0	0	.000	5.02	10	0	0	0	1	0	14.1	16	66	8	8	0	1	2	0	9	1	7	0	0
Martin, D. Renie, San Francisco	2	4	.333	4.20	37	6	0	0	6	1	94.1	95	414	50	44	11	3	3	3	51	9	43	2	2
Martin, John, St. Louis*	3	1	.750	3.53	26	5	0	0	8	0	66.1	60	284	31	26	6	5	3	2	26	4	29	3	0
McGaffigan, Andrew, San Francisco	3	9	.250	4.29	43	16	0	0	11	2	134.1	131	560	67	64	17	5	2	1	39	5	93	8	7
McGraw, Frank, Philadelphia*	2	1	.667	3.56	34	1	0	0	9	0	55.2	58	236	24	22	4	0	3	0	19	4	30	0	0
McMurtry, J. Craig, Atlanta	15	9	.625	3.08	36	35	6	3	0	0	224.2	204	943	86	77	13	9	5	1	88	1	105	1	2
McWilliams, Larry, Pittsburgh*	15	8	.652	3.25	35	35	8	4	0	0	238.0	205	1002	99	86	19	13	6	3	87	7	199	9	4
Minton, Gregory, San Francisco	7	11	.389	3.54	73	0	0	0	52	22	106.2	117	476	51	42	6	10	5	0	47	13	38	5	0
Monge, Isidro, Phil-S.D.*	10	3	.769	3.70	61	0	0	0	32	7	80.1	85	354	34	33	8	7	3	1	37	7	39	3	1
Montefusco, John, San Diego	9	4	.692	3.30	31	10	1	0	9	4	95.1	94	398	38	35	6	9	1	1	32	6	52	1	1
Moore, Donnie, Atlanta	2	3	.400	3.67	43	0	0	0	16	6	68.2	72	276	30	28	6	3	5	0	10	3	41	0	1
Moskau, Paul, Chicago	3	2	.600	6.75	8	8	0	0	0	0	32.0	44	149	25	24	7	2	0	0	14	1	16	2	0
Niedenfuer, Thomas, Los Angeles	8	3	.727	1.90	66	0	0	0	38	11	94.2	55	366	22	20	6	7	5	1	29	11	66	1	0
Niekro, Joseph, Houston	15	14	.517	3.48	38	38	9	1	0	0	263.2	238	1113	115	102	15	13	9	3	101	5	152	14	1
Niekro, Philip, Atlanta	11	10	.524	3.97	34	33	2	0	0	0	201.2	212	888	94	89	18	7	5	2	105	3	128	6	3
Niemann, Randy, Pittsburgh*	0	1	.000	9.22	8	1	0	0	4	0	13.2	20	66	14	14	2	1	1	1	7	1	8	3	0
Noles, Dickie, Chicago	5	10	.333	4.72	24	18	1	1	2	0	116.1	133	506	69	61	9	2	2	1	37	3	59	3	1
Orosco, Jesse, New York*	13	7	.650	1.47	62	0	0	0	42	17	110.0	76	432	27	18	3	4	3	1	38	7	84	1	2
Owchinko, Robert, Pittsburgh*	0	0	.000	....	1	0	0	0	0	0	0.0	2	2	1	1	1	0	0	0	0	0	0	0	0
Ownbey, Richard, New York	1	3	.250	4.67	10	4	0	0	3	0	34.2	31	152	19	18	4	1	0	1	21	0	19	1	2
Pastore, Frank, Cincinnati	9	12	.429	4.88	36	29	4	1	2	0	184.1	207	791	104	100	20	6	6	1	64	3	93	6	3
Patterson, Reginald, Chicago	1	2	.333	4.82	5	2	0	0	0	0	18.2	17	78	12	10	3	0	1	2	6	0	10	1	0
Pena, Alejandro, Los Angeles	12	9	.571	2.75	34	26	4	3	4	1	177.0	152	730	67	54	7	8	5	1	51	7	120	2	1
Perez, Pascual, Atlanta	15	8	.652	3.43	33	33	7	1	0	0	215.1	213	889	88	82	20	12	4	4	51	5	144	7	0
Power, Ted, Cincinnati	5	6	.455	4.54	49	6	1	0	14	2	111.0	120	480	62	56	10	4	6	1	49	3	57	1	0
Price, Joseph, Cincinnati*	10	6	.625	2.88	21	21	5	0	0	0	144.0	118	581	46	46	12	6	4	0	46	2	83	0	0
Proly, Michael, Chicago	1	5	.167	3.58	60	0	0	0	8	1	83.0	79	351	35	33	5	3	4	1	38	13	31	2	1
Puleo, Charles, Cincinnati	6	12	.333	4.89	27	24	0	0	0	0	143.2	145	649	86	78	18	7	6	5	91	9	71	4	1
Pulido, Alfonso, Pittsburgh*	0	0	.000	9.00	1	1	0	0	0	0	2.0	4	11	3	2	2	0	0	0	1	0	1	0	0
Rainey, Charles, Chicago	14	13	.519	4.48	34	34	1	1	0	0	191.0	219	836	109	95	17	10	7	3	74	3	84	7	1
Rasmussen, Dennis, San Diego*	0	0	.000	1.98	4	1	0	0	1	0	13.2	10	58	5	3	1	0	0	0	8	0	13	1	0
Rasmussen, Eric, St. Louis	0	0	.000	11.74	6	0	0	0	5	1	7.2	16	40	11	10	1	0	0	0	4	2	6	2	0
Reardon, Jeffrey, Montreal	7	9	.438	3.03	66	0	0	0	53	21	92.0	87	403	34	31	7	8	2	1	44	9	78	2	0
Reed, Ronald, Philadelphia	9	1	.900	3.48	61	0	0	0	31	8	95.2	89	403	42	37	5	6	3	1	34	14	73	2	0
Reuschel, Ricky, Chicago	1	1	.500	3.92	4	4	0	0	0	0	20.2	18	88	9	9	1	0	1	0	10	2	9	0	0
Reuss, Jerry, Los Angeles*	12	11	.522	2.94	32	31	7	0	0	0	223.1	233	935	94	73	12	18	6	2	50	5	143	3	2
Rhoden, Richard, Pittsburgh	13	13	.500	3.09	36	35	7	2	1	1	244.1	256	1012	95	84	13	8	6	2	68	15	153	6	5
Robinson, Don, Pittsburgh	2	2	.500	4.46	9	6	0	0	2	0	36.1	43	168	21	18	5	2	0	0	21	3	28	2	0
Rodas, Richard, Los Angeles*	0	0	.000	1.93	7	0	0	0	1	0	4.2	4	21	1	1	0	0	0	0	3	1	5	5	1
Rogers, Stephen, Montreal	17	12	.586	3.23	36	36	13	5	0	0	273.0	258	1125	108	98	14	12	7	5	78	12	146	6	0
Rucker, David, St. Louis*	5	3	.625	2.43	34	0	0	0	9	0	37.0	36	158	14	10	1	2	0	1	18	0	22	1	0

Pitcher and Club	W.	L.	Pct.	ERA.	G.	GS.	CG.	ShO.	GF.	Sv.	IP.	H.	BFP.	R.	ER.	HR.	SH.	SF.	HB.	Tot. BB.	Int. BB.	SO.	WP.	Bk.
Ruhle, Vernon, Houston	8	5	.615	3.69	41	9	0	0	11	3	114.2	107	480	49	47	13	6	6	3	36	7	43	1	0
Russell, Jeffrey, Cincinnati	4	5	.444	3.03	10	10	2	0	0	0	68.1	58	282	30	23	7	6	5	0	22	3	40	1	1
Ruthven, Richard, Philadelphia-Chicago	13	12	.520	4.38	32	32	5	2	0	0	183.0	202	775	101	89	22	8	7	3	38	3	99	1	0
Ryan, L. Nolan, Houston	14	9	.609	2.98	29	29	5	2	0	0	196.1	134	804	74	65	9	7	5	4	101	3	183	5	1
Sanderson, Scott, Montreal	6	7	.462	4.65	18	16	0	0	1	1	81.1	98	346	50	42	12	2	1	0	20	0	55	0	0
Sarmiento, Manuel, Pittsburgh	3	5	.375	2.99	52	0	0	0	17	4	84.1	74	356	35	28	8	10	6	0	36	8	49	0	1
Schatzeder, Daniel, Montreal*	5	2	.714	3.21	58	2	0	0	23	2	87.0	88	369	34	31	3	5	2	5	25	6	48	5	0
Scherrer, William, Cincinnati*	2	3	.400	2.74	73	0	0	0	32	10	92.0	73	371	31	28	6	7	6	0	33	4	57	0	0
Schulze, Donald, Chicago	0	1	.000	7.07	4	3	0	0	0	0	14.0	19	67	11	11	1	0	0	1	7	0	8	1	0
Scott, Michael, Houston	10	6	.625	3.72	24	24	2	2	0	0	145.0	143	612	67	60	8	1	5	5	46	0	73	4	4
Scurry, Rodney, Pittsburgh*	4	9	.308	5.56	61	0	0	0	25	7	68.0	63	317	45	42	6	3	4	4	53	7	67	6	0
Seaver, G. Thomas, New York	9	14	.391	3.55	34	34	5	2	0	0	231.0	201	962	104	91	18	9	7	4	86	5	135	10	0
Show, Eric, San Diego	15	12	.556	4.17	35	33	4	2	0	0	200.2	201	857	97	93	25	9	4	6	74	3	120	4	2
Sisk, Douglas, New York	5	4	.556	2.24	67	0	0	0	39	11	104.1	88	447	38	26	1	6	4	4	59	7	33	5	1
Smith, Bryn, Montreal	6	11	.353	2.49	49	12	5	3	17	3	155.1	142	636	51	43	13	14	2	5	43	6	101	5	3
Smith, David, Houston	3	1	.750	3.10	42	0	0	0	24	6	72.2	72	323	32	25	2	3	5	0	36	4	41	1	1
Smith, Lee, Chicago	4	10	.286	1.65	66	0	0	0	56	29	103.1	70	413	23	19	5	9	2	1	41	14	91	5	2
Solano, Julio, Houston	0	2	.000	6.00	4	0	0	0	0	0	6.0	5	27	5	4	1	0	0	0	4	1	3	1	0
Sosa, Elias, San Diego	1	4	.200	4.35	41	1	0	0	9	1	72.1	72	314	41	35	7	7	5	3	30	5	45	4	0
Soto, Mario, Cincinnati	17	13	.567	2.70	34	34	18	3	0	0	273.2	207	1114	96	82	28	8	9	5	95	6	242	2	2
Stewart, David, Los Angeles	5	2	.714	2.96	46	1	0	0	25	8	76.0	67	328	28	25	4	7	3	2	33	7	54	2	0
Stuper, John, St. Louis	12	11	.522	3.68	40	30	6	1	6	1	198.0	202	845	95	81	15	5	4	2	71	3	81	8	2
Sutter, H. Bruce, St. Louis	9	10	.474	4.23	60	0	0	0	46	21	89.1	90	384	45	42	8	7	3	1	30	14	64	2	2
Swan, Craig, New York	2	8	.200	5.51	27	18	0	0	4	1	96.1	112	424	63	59	14	3	4	0	42	3	43	1	1
Tekulve, Kenton, Pittsburgh	7	5	.583	1.64	76	0	0	0	56	18	99.0	78	398	27	18	1	9	4	0	36	12	52	1	0
Terrell, C. Walter, New York	8	8	.500	3.57	21	20	4	2	1	0	133.2	123	561	57	53	7	9	5	2	55	7	59	5	0
Thurmond, Mark, San Diego*	7	3	.700	2.65	21	18	2	0	2	0	115.1	104	466	40	34	7	9	3	2	33	2	49	0	1
Tomlin, David, Pittsburgh*	0	0	.000	6.75	5	0	0	0	0	0	4.0	6	20	4	3	0	0	0	0	1	0	5	0	0
Torrez, Michael, New York	10	17	.370	4.37	39	34	5	0	4	0	222.1	227	972	120	108	16	15	4	1	113	11	94	7	1
Trout, Steven, Chicago*	10	14	.417	4.65	34	32	1	0	0	0	180.0	217	789	105	93	13	11	6	2	59	5	80	7	2
Tunnell, B. Lee, Pittsburgh	11	6	.647	3.65	35	25	5	3	4	0	177.2	167	731	81	72	15	2	6	2	58	3	95	11	5
Valenzuela, Fernando, Los Angeles*	15	10	.600	3.75	35	35	9	4	0	0	257.0	245	1094	122	107	16	27	5	3	99	10	189	12	1
Von Ohlen, David, St. Louis*	3	2	.600	3.29	46	0	0	0	17	2	68.1	71	290	27	25	3	3	5	3	25	8	21	1	0
Walk, Robert, Atlanta	0	0	.000	7.36	1	1	0	0	0	0	3.2	7	20	3	3	0	1	0	0	2	0	4	0	0
Welch, Robert, Los Angeles	15	12	.556	2.65	31	31	4	3	0	0	204.0	164	828	73	60	13	8	7	3	72	4	156	4	6
Welsh, Christopher, S. Diego-Mont.*	0	2	.000	4.42	23	6	0	0	6	0	59.0	59	254	35	29	7	2	1	4	20	1	22	5	0
White, Larry, Los Angeles	0	0	.000	1.29	4	0	0	0	2	0	7.0	4	26	1	1	0	0	0	0	3	0	5	0	0
Whitson, Eddie, San Diego	5	7	.417	4.30	31	21	2	0	4	1	144.1	143	617	73	69	23	3	4	1	50	1	81	2	0
Winn, James, Pittsburgh	0	0	.000	7.36	7	0	0	0	3	0	11.0	12	51	9	9	2	0	0	0	6	0	3	1	0
Wright, J. Richard, Los Angeles*	0	0	.000	2.84	6	0	0	0	3	0	6.1	5	26	2	2	0	1	1	0	2	1	5	1	0
Zachry, Patrick, Los Angeles	6	1	.857	2.49	40	1	0	0	11	0	61.1	63	257	22	17	4	5	3	1	21	6	36	0	0

NOTE—Following pitchers combined to pitch shutout games: Chicago (5)—Jenkins and Smith, Noles and Smith, Rainey, Lefferts, Proly and Campbell, Reuschel, Trout and Smith, Trout and Smith; Houston (6)—Madden, LaCorte, DiPino and Dawley, Niekro and Dawley, Niekro and DiPino, Ryan and DiPino, Ryan, Ruhle and Dawley, M. Scott and DiPino; Los Angeles (2)—Honeycutt and Niedenfuer, Welch and Niedenfuer; Montreal (1)—Lea and Reardon; New York (2)—Seaver and Sisk, Torrez and Orosco; Philadelphia (4)—Bystrom, Reed and Holland, Carlton and Holland, Ghelfi, McGraw and Holland, Hudson and Holland; Pittsburgh (3)—Candelaria and Guante, Candelaria and Rhoden, Candelaria and Tekulve; St. Louis (3)—LaPoint and Sutter 2, Allen and Bair; San Diego (1)—Lollar and DeLeon; San Francisco (2)—Breining, McGaffigan and Barr, McGaffigan and Lavelle.

PITCHERS WITH TWO OR MORE CLUBS

(Alphabetically Arranged With Pitcher's First Club on Top)

Pitcher and Club	W.	L.	Pct.	ERA.	G.	GS.	CG.	ShO.	GF.	Sv.	IP.	H.	BFP.	R.	ER.	HR.	SH.	SF.	HB.	Tot. BB.	Int. BB.	SO.	WP.	Bk.
Allen, New York	2	7	.222	4.50	21	4	1	1	9	2	54.0	57	246	29	27	6	4	1	0	36	5	32	2	0
Allen, St. Louis	10	6	.625	3.70	25	18	4	2	3	0	121.2	122	516	55	50	6	5	1	1	48	4	74	6	1
Hernandez, Chicago*	1	0	1.000	3.20	11	1	0	0	4	1	19.2	16	80	8	7	0	2	0	0	6	1	18	0	0
Hernandez, Philadelphia*	8	4	.667	3.29	63	0	0	0	27	7	95.2	93	398	39	35	9	5	0	1	26	7	75	5	0
Lerch, Montreal*	1	3	.250	6.75	19	5	0	0	1	0	38.2	45	176	29	29	6	2	1	1	18	2	24	1	0
Lerch, San Francisco*	1	0	1.000	3.38	7	0	0	0	1	0	10.2	9	48	4	4	1	0	1	0	8	1	6	0	0
Monge, Philadelphia*	3	0	1.000	6.94	14	0	0	0	4	0	11.2	20	61	10	9	4	1	1	0	6	1	7	0	0
Monge, San Diego*	7	3	.700	3.15	47	0	0	0	28	7	68.2	65	293	24	24	4	6	2	1	31	6	32	3	1
Ruthven, Philadelphia	1	3	.250	5.61	7	7	0	0	0	0	33.2	46	152	23	21	5	0	4	0	10	0	26	0	0
Ruthven, Chicago	12	9	.571	4.10	25	25	5	2	0	0	149.1	156	623	78	68	17	8	3	3	28	3	73	1	0
Welsh, San Diego*	0	1	.000	2.51	7	1	0	0	3	0	14.1	13	59	5	4	2	2	0	0	2	0	5	3	0
Welsh, Montreal*	0	1	.000	5.04	16	5	0	0	3	0	44.2	46	195	30	25	5	0	1	4	18	1	17	2	0

1983 N.L. Pitching Against Each Club

ATLANTA—88-74

Pitcher	Chi. W—L	Cin. W—L	Hou. W—L	L.A. W—L	Mtl. W—L	N.Y. W—L	Phil. W—L	Pitt. W—L	St.L. W—L	S.D. W—L	S.F. W—L	Totals W—L
Barker	0—0	0—0	1—0	0—1	0—0	0—0	0—0	0—0	0—1	0—1	0—0	1—3
Bedrosian	0—0	0—2	1—0	2—0	0—1	1—1	1—1	0—1	2—1	1—1	1—2	9—10
Behenna	0—2	1—0	1—1	0—0	1—0	0—0	0—0	0—0	0—0	0—0	0—0	3—3
Brizzolara	0—0	0—0	0—0	0—0	0—0	1—0	0—0	0—0	0—0	0—0	0—0	1—0
Camp	2—0	1—0	0—0	0—3	1—2	2—1	1—1	0—1	1—0	1—0	1—1	10—9
Dayley	1—0	1—1	1—1	0—0	0—1	0—1	0—1	0—2	0—0	1—1	1—0	5—8
Falcone	0—1	2—0	1—1	0—0	1—0	0—0	0—0	2—0	1—1	1—1	1—0	9—4
Forster	0—0	0—0	1—1	0—1	1—0	0—0	0—0	1—0	0—0	0—0	0—0	3—2
Garber	0—1	0—0	1—1	1—1	0—0	1—0	0—0	0—0	0—0	0—0	1—2	4—5
McMurtry	0—1	2—1	2—0	1—2	2—0	2—0	2—0	1—1	1—0	2—3	0—1	15—9
Moore	1—0	0—0	0—0	0—0	0—1	0—1	0—0	0—0	1—0	0—1	0—0	2—3
Niekro	1—1	2—1	0—2	0—2	1—0	1—0	0—2	1—0	1—1	1—1	3—0	11—10
Perez	0—1	3—1	2—0	3—1	0—0	0—0	3—0	1—1	0—1	2—0	1—3	15—8
Totals	5—7	12—6	11—7	7—11	7—5	8—4	7—5	6—6	7—5	9—9	9—9	88—74

No Decisions—Boggs, Dedmon, Mahler, Walk.

CHICAGO—71-91

Pitcher	Atl. W—L	Cin. W—L	Hou. W—L	L.A. W—L	Mtl. W—L	N.Y. W—L	Phil. W—L	Pitt. W—L	St.L. W—L	S.D. W—L	S.F. W—L	Totals W—L
Bordi	0—0	0—1	0—0	0—0	0—0	0—1	0—0	0—0	0—0	0—0	0—0	0—2
Brusstar	1—0	0—0	1—0	0—0	1—0	0—0	0—0	0—0	0—0	0—1	0—0	3—1
Campbell	1—0	0—0	0—2	0—1	0—0	1—0	1—1	0—2	1—0	2—0	0—2	6—8
Hernandez	0—0	0—0	0—0	0—0	0—0	0—0	0—0	1—0	0—0	0—0	0—0	1—0
Jenkins	1—0	0—2	1—0	0—2	0—2	0—2	0—0	2—0	1—0	0—1	1—0	6—9
Johnson	0—0	0—0	0—0	0—0	0—0	1—0	0—0	0—0	0—0	0—0	0—0	1—0
Lefferts	0—0	0—0	0—2	0—0	0—0	0—0	0—0	2—0	0—1	1—1	0—0	3—4
Moskau	1—0	1—0	0—0	0—0	0—0	0—0	0—1	0—0	0—0	0—0	1—1	3—2
Noles	0—0	1—1	0—1	1—0	2—3	0—0	0—0	0—1	1—1	0—2	0—1	5—10
Patterson	0—0	0—0	0—0	0—0	0—0	1—0	0—1	0—0	0—1	0—0	0—0	1—2
Proly	0—1	0—1	0—0	1—0	0—0	0—2	0—1	0—0	0—0	0—0	0—0	1—5
Rainey	2—1	1—2	1—0	1—0	1—2	1—1	1—2	0—2	3—2	2—1	1—0	14—13
Reuschel	0—0	0—0	0—0	0—0	0—0	1—0	0—0	0—1	0—0	0—0	0—0	1—1
Ruthven	0—2	1—0	2—0	1—1	1—3	1—0	1—2	2—0	2—0	0—0	1—1	12—9
Schulze	0—0	0—0	0—0	0—0	0—0	0—1	0—0	0—0	0—0	0—0	0—0	0—1
Smith	0—0	0—0	0—0	1—1	0—0	2—2	0—3	1—0	0—3	0—0	0—1	4—10
Trout	1—1	0—1	0—2	1—1	2—1	1—0	2—2	1—3	2—0	0—1	0—2	10—14
Totals	7—5	4—8	5—7	6—6	7—11	9—9	5—13	9—9	10—8	5—7	4—8	71—91

No Decisions—Hargesheimer.

CINCINNATI—74-88

Pitcher	Atl. W—L	Chi. W—L	Hou. W—L	L.A. W—L	Mtl. W—L	N.Y. W—L	Phil. W—L	Pitt. W—L	St.L. W—L	S.D. W—L	S.F. W—L	Totals W—L
Berenyi	0—3	1—1	1—3	1—1	0—1	3—0	0—1	0—2	0—1	2—0	1—1	9—14
Cato	0—0	0—0	0—0	0—0	0—0	0—0	0—0	0—0	0—0	1—0	0—0	1—0
Gale	0—0	1—0	1—0	0—2	1—1	0—1	0—1	0—0	0—0	0—0	1—1	4—6
Hayes	0—0	0—0	0—0	2—2	0—0	0—1	0—0	1—0	1—1	0—1	0—1	4—6
Hume	1—0	0—0	0—2	0—0	0—0	0—0	1—1	1—0	0—0	0—1	0—1	3—5
Pastore	1—3	1—1	1—1	0—1	0—3	1—0	1—1	0—0	1—0	2—1	1—1	9—12
Power	0—0	0—0	0—0	0—0	0—0	0—0	1—1	0—0	0—3	1—1	3—1	5—6
Price	1—1	1—0	1—1	1—1	2—0	2—1	1—0	0—0	1—0	0—1	0—1	10—6
Puleo	0—2	0—1	0—2	1—1	0—1	1—1	0—0	0—1	2—0	1—3	1—0	6—12
Russell	1—0	1—0	0—2	0—1	0—0	0—0	0—0	0—1	0—0	2—0	0—1	4—5
Scherrer	0—0	1—0	0—1	0—0	0—0	0—1	0—0	1—1	0—0	0—0	0—0	2—3
Soto	2—3	2—1	1—1	2—2	1—2	0—0	2—1	3—1	1—1	0—1	3—0	17—13
Totals	6—12	8—4	5—13	7—11	4—8	7—5	6—6	6—6	6—6	9—9	10—8	74—88

No Decisions—Lesley.

HOUSTON—85-77

Pitcher	Atl. W—L	Chi. W—L	Cin. W—L	L.A. W—L	Mtl. W—L	N.Y. W—L	Phil. W—L	Pitt. W—L	St.L. W—L	S.D. W—L	S.F. W—L	Totals W—L
Dawley	1—1	2—1	1—0	0—1	1—0	0—1	0—0	0—0	0—1	0—1	1—0	6—6
DiPino	2—1	0—0	0—0	0—0	0—0	1—0	0—0	0—1	0—1	0—1	0—0	3—4
Heathcock	0—0	0—0	1—1	0—0	0—0	0—0	0—0	0—0	0—0	0—0	1—0	2—1
Knepper	0—2	0—1	1—0	0—0	1—2	1—0	1—1	0—3	0—2	1—1	1—1	6—13
LaCorte	0—0	1—0	1—0	0—3	0—0	0—0	1—0	0—0	0—0	0—1	1—0	4—4
LaCoss	1—1	0—0	1—1	0—0	0—1	1—0	0—2	1—0	0—1	1—0	0—1	5—7
Madden	0—0	1—1	2—1	0—0	0—0	1—0	1—0	1—0	0—2	2—0	1—1	9—5
Niekro	1—3	1—1	1—1	2—2	1—0	2—0	1—2	2—1	1—1	1—2	2—1	15—14
Ruhle	0—2	1—0	2—0	0—2	1—0	0—0	0—0	1—0	1—0	2—1	0—0	8—5
Ryan	1—0	0—0	0—1	2—1	3—1	2—1	0—2	1—0	0—1	3—0	2—2	14—9
M. Scott	1—1	1—1	3—0	1—1	0—0	1—1	0—1	0—0	0—1	1—0	2—0	10—6
Smith	0—0	0—0	0—0	1—1	1—0	0—0	0—0	0—0	0—0	0—0	1—0	3—1
Solano	0—0	0—0	0—0	0—1	0—0	0—0	0—0	0—1	0—0	0—0	0—0	0—2
Totals	7—11	7—5	13—5	6—12	8—4	9—3	4—8	6—6	2—10	11—7	12—6	85—77

LOS ANGELES—91-71

Pitcher	Atl. W—L	Chi. W—L	Cin. W—L	Hou. W—L	Mtl. W—L	N.Y. W—L	Phil. W—L	Pitt. W—L	St.L. W—L	S.D. W—L	S.F. W—L	Totals W—L
Beckwith	1—1	0—0	1—0	0—1	0—0	0—1	0—0	0—0	1—0	0—1	0—0	3—4
Fernandez	0—0	0—0	0—0	0—0	0—0	0—0	0—0	0—0	0—0	0—0	0—1	0—1
Honeycutt	0—0	0—0	0—0	0—0	0—1	0—0	2—0	0—0	0—0	0—1	0—1	2—3
Hooton	1—0	0—2	1—1	1—0	0—1	2—0	2—0	1—1	1—0	0—1	0—2	9—8
Howe	0—1	0—0	0—1	1—1	0—1	0—0	0—0	1—1	2—1	0—1	0—0	4—7
Niedenfuer	0—1	0—0	3—1	1—0	1—0	0—1	0—0	1—0	0—0	0—0	2—0	8—3
Pena	2—2	2—0	1—0	4—2	0—0	0—0	2—0	1—1	0—1	0—2	0—1	12—9
Reuss	1—0	0—0	0—1	2—0	2—0	0—2	2—0	1—3	1—1	2—1	1—3	12—11
Stewart	1—1	2—0	0—0	0—0	1—0	0—0	0—0	0—0	1—0	0—0	0—1	5—2
Valenzuela	3—0	2—1	1—1	1—0	1—0	0—1	2—1	0—0	1—0	2—3	2—3	15—10
Welch	2—1	0—3	2—2	1—2	1—1	3—0	1—0	1—0	2—0	2—2	0—1	15—12
Zachry	0—0	0—0	2—0	1—0	1—1	2—0	0—0	0—0	0—0	0—0	0—0	6—1
Totals	11—7	6—6	11—7	12—6	7—5	7—5	11—1	6—6	9—3	6—12	5—13	91—71

No Decisions—Hershiser, Rodas, White, Wright.

MONTREAL—82-80

Pitcher	Atl. W—L	Chi. W—L	Cin. W—L	Hou. W—L	L.A. W—L	N.Y. W—L	Phil. W—L	Pitt. W—L	St.L. W—L	S.D. W—L	S.F. W—L	Totals W—L
Bargar	1—0	0—0	1—0	0—0	0—0	0—0	0—0	0—0	0—0	0—0	0—0	2—0
Burris	0—1	0—0	1—1	0—1	0—0	0—0	1—2	1—0	0—0	0—1	1—1	4—7
Dixon	0—0	0—0	0—0	0—0	0—0	0—0	0—0	0—1	0—0	0—0	0—0	0—1
Fryman	0—1	0—0	0—0	0—1	0—0	0—0	0—0	0—0	0—1	0—0	0—0	0—3
Grapenthin	0—1	0—0	0—0	0—0	0—0	0—0	0—0	0—0	0—0	0—0	0—0	0—1
Gullickson	0—1	2—2	2—0	1—2	0—1	1—2	3—1	3—1	1—1	2—1	2—0	17—12
James	0—0	1—0	0—0	0—0	0—0	0—0	0—0	0—0	0—0	0—0	0—0	1—0
Lea	0—1	2—1	1—2	1—1	2—0	4—2	1—1	0—2	2—1	2—0	1—0	16—11
Lerch	0—0	0—2	0—0	0—1	0—0	1—0	0—0	0—0	0—0	0—0	0—0	1—3
Reardon	1—0	0—0	1—0	0—0	0—1	1—3	1—1	0—0	2—2	1—1	0—1	7—9
Rogers	2—0	4—1	2—1	1—1	0—3	1—1	1—1	2—2	0—1	2—1	2—0	17—12
Sanderson	0—1	2—0	0—0	0—1	1—0	0—0	1—2	1—1	1—1	0—0	0—1	6—7
Schatzeder	1—0	0—0	0—0	1—0	2—0	0—0	0—0	0—1	0—1	0—0	1—0	5—2
Smith	0—1	0—0	0—0	0—0	0—2	0—2	0—2	1—2	3—1	1—0	1—1	6—11
Welsh	0—0	0—1	0—0	0—0	0—0	0—0	0—0	0—0	0—0	0—0	0—0	0—1
Totals	5—7	11—7	8—4	4—8	5—7	8—10	8—10	8—10	9—9	8—4	8—4	82—80

NEW YORK—68-94

Pitcher	Atl. W—L	Chi. W—L	Cin. W—L	Hou. W—L	L.A. W—L	Mtl. W—L	Phil. W—L	Pitt. W—L	St.L. W—L	S.D. W—L	S.F. W—L	Totals W—L
Allen	0—1	0—0	0—0	0—1	1—1	0—0	0—2	1—0	0—0	0—0	0—2	2—7
Darling	0—0	0—0	0—0	0—0	0—0	0—0	0—2	1—0	0—1	0—0	0—0	1—3
Diaz	0—0	0—0	0—0	0—0	0—0	0—0	0—0	2—1	1—0	0—0	0—0	3—1
Gaff	0—0	0—0	0—0	0—0	0—0	1—0	0—0	0—0	0—0	0—0	0—0	1—0
Gorman	0—1	0—0	0—1	0—0	0—0	0—0	0—0	0—0	0—2	1—0	0—0	1—4
Holman	0—0	0—1	0—0	0—0	1—1	0—1	0—0	0—1	0—1	0—1	0—1	1—7
Leary	0—0	0—1	0—0	0—0	0—0	1—0	0—0	0—0	0—0	0—0	0—0	1—1
Lynch	2—0	1—0	0—0	0—1	1—0	0—3	1—0	1—2	2—1	1—1	1—2	10—10
Orosco	0—1	2—2	3—0	0—0	1—1	2—1	1—1	2—0	0—1	0—0	2—0	13—7
Ownbey	0—1	0—0	0—0	0—2	0—0	1—0	0—0	0—0	0—0	0—0	0—0	1—3
Seaver	0—1	2—0	1—2	1—1	0—2	2—1	0—2	1—1	1—1	1—2	0—1	9—14
Sisk	1—2	2—1	0—0	1—0	0—0	0—0	1—1	0—0	0—0	0—0	0—0	5—4
Swan	0—1	0—0	0—0	0—1	0—0	1—0	1—1	0—2	0—1	0—1	0—1	2—8
Terrell	0—0	2—1	0—1	1—0	0—2	1—0	1—3	0—0	1—1	2—0	0—0	8—8
Torrez	1—0	0—3	1—3	0—3	1—0	1—2	1—0	1—2	1—3	1—1	2—0	10—17
Totals	4—8	9—9	5—7	3—9	5—7	10—8	6—12	9—9	6—12	6—6	5—7	68—94

PHILADELPHIA—90-72

Pitcher	Atl. W—L	Chi. W—L	Cin. W—L	Hou. W—L	L.A. W—L	Mtl. W—L	N.Y. W—L	Pitt. W—L	St.L. W—L	S.D. W—L	S.F. W—L	Totals W—L
Altamirano	0—0	0—0	0—0	0—0	0—0	0—2	1—0	1—0	0—1	0—0	0—0	2—3
Andersen	0—0	0—0	0—0	0—0	0—0	0—0	0—0	0—0	1—0	0—0	0—0	1—0
Bystrom	0—1	0—1	1—0	0—1	0—3	1—1	0—0	1—1	3—0	0—1	0—0	6—9
Carlton	1—1	4—1	2—0	0—2	0—2	1—3	2—1	2—0	2—2	0—2	1—2	15—16
Christenson	0—1	0—1	0—0	1—0	0—1	1—0	0—0	0—0	0—0	0—0	0—1	2—4
Comer	0—0	0—0	0—0	0—0	0—0	0—0	0—0	0—0	0—0	1—0	0—0	1—0
Denny	2—0	3—0	1—2	3—0	0—2	2—0	3—1	1—1	3—0	0—0	1—0	19—6
Farmer	0—1	0—0	0—0	0—0	0—0	0—0	0—2	0—1	0—0	0—2	0—0	0—6
Ghelfi	0—0	0—0	0—0	0—0	0—0	0—0	0—1	0—0	0—0	0—0	1—0	1—1
K. Gross	0—1	0—0	0—1	0—0	1—1	1—1	1—0	0—1	0—0	1—0	0—1	4—6
Hernandez	1—2	3—1	0—1	0—0	0—0	1—0	1—0	1—0	1—0	0—0	0—0	8—4
Holland	0—0	1—0	1—0	0—0	0—0	0—0	1—1	0—2	2—0	3—0	0—1	8—4
Hudson	0—0	1—0	0—1	2—0	0—2	2—1	0—0	3—1	0—1	0—1	0—1	8—8
McGraw	0—0	0—0	0—0	0—0	0—0	0—0	2—0	0—0	0—0	0—1	0—0	2—1
Monge	0—0	0—0	1—0	1—0	0—0	0—0	0—0	0—0	0—0	0—0	1—0	3—0
Reed	0—0	1—0	0—0	1—1	0—0	1—0	1—0	2—0	2—0	0—0	1—0	9—1
Ruthven	1—0	0—1	0—1	0—0	0—0	0—0	0—0	0—0	0—0	0—0	0—1	1—3
Totals	5—7	13—5	6—6	8—4	1—11	10—8	12—6	11—7	14—4	5—7	5—7	90—72

No Decisions—Carman.

PITTSBURGH—84-78

Pitcher	Atl. W—L	Chi. W—L	Cin. W—L	Hou. W—L	L.A. W—L	Mtl. W—L	N.Y. W—L	Phil. W—L	St.L. W—L	S.D. W—L	S.F. W—L	Totals W—L
Bibby	2—2	0—2	0—0	1—0	0—1	1—1	0—2	0—1	1—2	0—0	0—1	5—12
Candelaria	1—2	3—0	0—2	0—0	2—1	3—0	2—0	2—1	2—0	0—1	0—1	15—8
DeLeon	0—0	0—0	2—0	1—0	0—0	1—1	1—1	0—1	0—0	1—0	1—0	7—3
Guante	0—0	0—1	0—1	0—1	0—0	0—0	0—0	0—2	1—1	1—0	0—0	2—6
McWilliams	2—0	2—1	1—0	2—0	1—0	2—3	2—2	1—2	0—0	1—0	1—0	15—8
Niemann	0—0	0—0	0—0	0—1	0—0	0—0	0—0	0—0	0—0	0—0	0—0	0—1
Rhoden	0—1	1—1	2—1	0—1	2—2	3—2	1—0	0—2	3—1	1—0	0—2	13—13
Robinson	0—0	1—0	0—0	0—0	0—0	0—0	0—0	0—0	0—1	1—1	0—0	2—2
Sarmiento	0—0	0—1	0—0	0—0	0—2	0—0	0—1	0—0	0—1	1—0	2—0	3—5
Scurry	0—0	0—1	0—1	2—1	0—0	0—0	1—0	0—2	0—1	0—1	1—2	4—9
Tekulve	0—0	1—1	0—1	0—1	1—0	0—0	1—2	3—0	0—0	1—0	0—0	7—5
Tunnell	1—1	1—1	1—0	0—1	0—0	0—1	1—1	1—0	3—1	2—0	1—0	11—6
Totals	6—6	9—9	6—6	6—6	6—6	10—8	9—9	7—11	10—8	9—3	6—6	84—78

No Decisions—Owchinko, Pulido, Tomlin, Winn.

ST. LOUIS—79-83

Pitcher	Atl. W—L	Chi. W—L	Cin. W—L	Hou. W—L	L.A. W—L	Mtl. W—L	N.Y. W—L	Phil. W—L	Pitt. W—L	S.D. W—L	S.F. W—L	Totals W—L
Allen	1—0	1—1	0—0	0—0	1—0	1—2	3—0	0—2	2—1	1—0	0—0	10—6
Andujar	2—1	0—1	0—2	1—0	0—2	0—1	1—1	0—2	2—2	0—2	0—2	6—16
Bair	0—0	0—0	0—0	0—0	0—1	0—0	0—0	0—0	0—0	0—0	1—0	1—1
Baker	0—0	0—0	0—0	0—0	0—0	0—0	0—0	0—1	0—0	0—0	0—0	0—1
Cox	0—0	0—1	0—1	1—1	0—0	0—1	1—0	0—1	1—1	0—0	0—0	3—6
Forsch	1—1	2—3	0—0	1—0	0—1	3—1	1—2	1—1	1—1	0—2	0—0	10—12
Hagen	0—0	0—0	0—0	0—0	0—0	0—0	1—0	1—0	0—2	0—0	0—0	2—2
Lahti	0—0	0—1	1—0	1—0	0—1	0—0	0—0	0—1	0—0	0—0	1—0	3—3
LaPoint	0—3	0—2	1—0	2—0	0—0	1—0	2—1	1—1	1—2	2—0	2—0	12—9
Martin	0—0	0—0	1—0	0—1	0—0	1—0	0—0	0—0	0—0	1—0	0—0	3—1
Rucker	0—0	1—0	1—1	1—0	1—1	0—1	0—0	0—0	0—0	0—0	1—0	5—3
Stuper	1—1	2—1	2—1	2—0	0—2	1—2	2—1	0—1	0—1	0—0	2—1	12—11
Sutter	0—1	2—0	0—1	0—0	1—1	2—1	1—0	1—3	1—0	1—2	0—1	9—10
Von Ohlen	0—0	0—0	0—0	1—0	0—0	0—0	0—1	0—1	0—0	1—0	1—0	3—2
Totals	5—7	8—10	6—6	10—2	3—9	9—9	12—6	4—14	8—10	6—6	8—4	79—83

No Decisions—Citarella, Kaat, Keener, Ownbey, Rasmussen.

SAN DIEGO—81-81

Pitcher	Atl. W—L	Chi. W—L	Cin. W—L	Hou. W—L	L.A. W—L	Mtl. W—L	N.Y. W—L	Phil. W—L	Pitt. W—L	St.L. W—L	S.F. W—L	Totals W—L
Booker	0—1	0—0	0—0	0—0	0—0	0—0	0—0	0—0	0—0	0—0	0—0	0—1
Chiffer	0—1	0—0	0—0	0—0	0—1	0—0	0—0	0—0	0—0	0—0	0—0	0—2
Couchee	0—0	0—0	0—0	0—0	0—0	0—0	0—0	0—0	0—1	0—0	0—0	0—1
DeLeon	1—0	0—0	2—0	1—2	0—1	0—2	0—0	1—0	0—1	1—0	0—0	6—6
Dravecky	1—1	1—0	1—0	2—1	3—1	0—3	1—1	1—0	0—1	2—1	2—1	14—10
Hawkins	0—0	0—0	1—2	0—0	1—1	0—1	0—0	1—1	2—0	0—1	0—1	5—7
Lollar	0—3	1—2	1—0	1—2	1—0	1—0	1—2	0—0	0—0	0—1	1—2	7—12
Lucas	1—0	0—3	0—1	0—0	0—0	1—0	0—0	1—1	0—0	1—2	1—1	5—8
Monge	3—0	0—0	0—1	1—1	1—0	0—0	1—0	0—1	0—0	0—0	1—0	7—3
Montefusco	0—1	2—0	1—1	1—0	1—0	1—0	0—1	1—0	0—1	0—0	2—0	9—4
Show	2—0	3—0	2—1	0—3	1—1	0—1	3—1	1—0	0—2	1—1	2—2	15—12
Sosa	0—0	0—0	0—1	1—0	0—0	0—1	0—1	0—1	0—0	0—0	0—0	1—4
Thurmond	1—0	0—0	0—1	0—1	2—0	1—0	0—0	0—0	1—1	1—0	1—0	7—3
Welsh	0—1	0—0	0—0	0—0	0—0	0—0	0—0	0—0	0—0	0—0	0—0	0—1
Whitson	0—1	0—0	1—1	0—1	2—1	0—0	0—0	1—1	0—2	0—0	1—0	5—7
Totals	9—9	7—5	9—9	7—11	12—6	4—8	6—6	7—5	3—9	6—6	11—7	81—81

No Decisions—Decker, Fireovid, Rasmussen.

SAN FRANCISCO—79-83

Pitcher	Atl. W—L	Chi. W—L	Cin. W—L	Hou. W—L	L.A. W—L	Mtl. W—L	N.Y. W—L	Phil. W—L	Pitt. W—L	St.L. W—L	S.D. W—L	Totals W—L
Barr	0—1	0—0	0—1	0—0	2—0	0—0	1—0	0—0	1—0	1—1	0—0	5—3
Breining	0—1	0—0	2—2	2—1	2—1	0—2	2—1	1—0	1—2	0—2	1—0	11—12
Calvert	0—2	0—0	0—1	0—0	0—0	0—0	0—0	0—0	0—0	0—1	1—0	1—4
M. Davis	1—0	0—1	0—1	1—1	3—0	1—0	0—0	0—0	0—0	0—0	0—1	6—4
Garrelts	1—0	0—0	0—0	1—0	0—1	0—0	0—0	0—0	0—0	0—0	0—1	2—2
Hammaker	2—0	3—1	2—1	0—1	1—0	0—1	1—2	0—1	0—0	0—0	1—2	10—9
Krukow	2—0	0—0	1—1	0—3	2—0	1—2	1—0	3—1	0—1	0—0	1—3	11—11
Laskey	0—2	2—1	1—1	1—1	1—1	1—1	1—0	1—1	2—1	1—0	2—1	13—10
Lavelle	2—0	1—0	0—0	0—1	1—0	1—0	0—0	0—1	0—0	1—1	1—1	7—4
Lerch	0—0	0—0	1—0	0—0	0—0	0—0	0—0	0—0	0—0	0—0	0—0	1—0
Martin	0—0	0—0	0—0	0—2	0—0	0—1	1—0	1—0	0—1	0—0	0—0	2—4
McGaffigan	0—2	0—1	0—0	0—0	0—1	0—1	0—0	1—1	1—0	1—2	0—1	3—9
Minton	1—1	2—0	1—2	1—2	1—1	0—0	0—2	0—0	1—1	0—1	0—1	7—11
Totals	9—9	8—4	8—10	6—12	13—5	4—8	7—5	7—5	6—6	4—8	7—11	79—83

No Decisions—Chris, Kingman, Larkin.

The right arm of Philadelphia's John Denny (above) and the bat of Baltimore's Cal Ripken were the primary reasons their clubs reached their respective League Championship Series.

1983 CHAMPIONSHIP SERIES

Including

American League Review

American League Box Scores

American League Composite Box Score

National League Review

National League Box Scores

National League Composite Box Score

Orioles rookie Mike Boddicker fanned a Championship Series record-tying 14 batters when he shut out the White Sox in Game 2.

O's Pitching Zeroes Sox Sluggers

By LARRY WIGGE

After watching Chicago righthander LaMarr Hoyt mow down his Baltimore teammates, 2-1, on five hits in Game 1 of the 1983 American League Championship Series, Orioles designated hitter Ken Singleton suggested: "We had better win the next three games, guys, because I don't think any of us wants to face Hoyt again in Game 5."

The Orioles took Singleton's suggestion to heart, prevailing by 4-0, 11-1 and 3-0 scores in the next three games to earn the right to face the Philadelphia Phillies in the World Series.

Baltimore pitchers made sure Hoyt wouldn't take the mound again, limiting the White Sox to one run in the final 31 innings of the playoff series. The Orioles' staff combined for a 0.49 earned-run average overall and stymied the heart of the Chicago batting order, holding Carlton Fisk, Greg Luzinski, Ron Kittle, Harold Baines and Tom Paciorek to a combined .183 average on 13 hits in 71 at-bats.

As dominant as Hoyt was in Game 1, Baltimore rookie righthander Mike Boddicker was even more masterful in the second game as he blanked the Sox on five hits and struck out a Championship Series record-tying 14 batters. Boddicker, who went 16-8 after being recalled from Rochester (International) in early May to replace the injured Jim Palmer, tied Detroit's Joe Coleman, who fanned 14 Oakland hitters in 1972, and Pittsburgh's John Candelaria, who had 14 strikeouts against Cincinnati in 1975. The performance led to Boddicker's selection as the A.L. playoffs' Most Valuable Player.

"Good hitters take advantage of pitchers' mistakes," Chicago Manager Tony LaRussa said with a sigh, "but Boddicker didn't make any mistakes."

Gary Roenicke was the offensive star in Game 2, scoring three runs and driving in two with a homer in the sixth inning. Half of Baltimore's left-field combination (he platooned with John Lowenstein), Roenicke doubled and scored on Julio Cruz's error in the second, walked and scored on Singleton's double in the fourth and then belted his homer to climax the scoring.

The scene shifted to Chicago for Game 3, and the Orioles brought out all of their artillery. The Orioles jumped on 22-game winner Richard Dotson in the first inning as Eddie Murray slugged a three-run homer. Murray, held hitless in his previous 29 postseason at-bats (21 in the 1979 World Series and eight in the first two games of this playoff), connected after a double by Jim Dwyer and a single by Cal Ripken.

Gary Roenicke supported Boddicker's pitching gem by scoring three runs and driving home two more.

Al Bumbry's double scored another run in the second, and there was no stopping the Orioles. Baltimore had only eight hits off four Chicago hurlers, but the Sox pitchers walked nine batters. Murray, who drew three bases on balls, scored four

Tito Landrum's three-run blast in the top of the 10th inning of Game 4 clinched the American League pennant for the Orioles.

runs.

Mike Flanagan pitched five innings before his knee stiffened and Sammy Stewart came on to limit the Sox to one hit and no runs over the final four frames to record the save.

Flanagan was part of a full-blown brouhaha when he plunked Kittle on the left knee with a pitch in the fourth inning. Both benches emptied. One inning later, Dotson zinged Ripken in the left side. When Murray followed at the plate and a Dotson delivery buzzed the Baltimore batsman, Murray threatened Dotson and both benches emptied again. Peace was maintained, however.

Though the Orioles led the series, two games to one, the Sox figured they had the edge in the Britt Burns-Storm Davis pitching pairing in Game 4. The matchup turned out to be a dandy.

Davis hurled six innings of scoreless ball before Tippy Martinez took over after Greg Walker singled to open the Chicago seventh. Burns matched zeroes with both as the scoreless duel extended into the 10th inning.

When a game of such importance goes down to the wire, a player least expected to produce often becomes the hero. The name to go down in history this time was Tito Landrum.

Ticketed for the minor leagues in spring training by the St. Louis Cardinals but given a reprieve because of an injury to outfielder Willie McGee, Landrum had only five at-bats with the Cards when he finally was sent to Triple-A in late April. He batted .292 with 18 homers and 77 RBIs at Louisville (American Association), but was frozen in the minors until being obtained by the Orioles on August 31 to complete a June trade of utilityman Floyd Rayford. Landrum batted .310 the remainder of the season for the Orioles as a part-time player.

Landrum, 0-for-5 in the first three games of the playoffs, was in the starting lineup in Games 2 and 4 because right fielder Dan Ford had come up lame in Game 1. Having a 1-for-4 day when he strode to the plate in the 10th inning of the fourth game, the 28-year-old Landrum belted a home run against a brisk wind that had held up numerous long blasts earlier in the game.

"Pinch me a couple of times when I leave here," Landrum told reporters afterward, "to see if I'm really here."

As heartwarming as the story had become for Landrum, a veteran of 11 seasons in the Cardinals' organization, it had evolved into a nightmare for Burns, who was brilliant in holding the Orioles at bay while awaiting the one run that would have made him a winner. Instead, Burns' 147 pitches resulted only in a losing effort.

After Burns departed, the Orioles added two more runs against Salome Barojas. Ripken, Murray and Roenicke stroked successive singles and, after Juan Agosto replaced Barojas, pinch-hitter Benny Ayala scored Murray with a sacrifice fly.

In every big game, there are "what-if" situations. On this occasion, Chicago fans were wondering what would have happened if Sox shortstop Jerry Dybzinski hadn't blundered in the seventh inning. Walker and Vance Law had opened that inning with singles. Dybzinski was asked to bunt the runners along.

On a 3-and-1 count, Dybzinski forced pinch-runner Mike Squires at third base when Oriole catcher Rick Dempsey pounced on the bunt and retired the lead runner. Julio Cruz followed with a single to left, but Dybzinski rounded second base too far and got caught in a rundown. Law was gunned down at the plate on the play, snuffing out the rally.

"I made a big mistake," Dybzinski said. "I had the adrenaline flowing and, well, it was a big mistake."

While the Sox had missed on their first chance at making the World Series since 1959, the Orioles had evaded a second go-round with 24-game winner Hoyt and made it to the World Series for the second time in five years.

GAME OF WEDNESDAY, OCTOBER 5, AT BALTIMORE

Chicago	AB.	R.	H.	RBI.	PO.	A.
R. Law, cf	5	1	3	0	3	0
Fisk, c	5	0	1	0	5	0
Paciorek, 1b-lf	4	1	2	1	9	2
Luzinski, dh	3	0	1	0	0	0
Kittle, lf	3	0	0	0	1	0
Squires, 1b	1	0	0	0	2	0
Baines, rf	4	0	0	0	2	0
V. Law, 3b	3	0	0	0	0	2
Fletcher, ss	2	0	0	0	2	2
J. Cruz, 2b	2	0	0	0	1	6
Hoyt, p	0	0	0	0	2	1
Totals	32	2	7	1	27	13

Baltimore	AB.	R.	H.	RBI.	PO.	A.
Bumbry, cf	4	0	0	0	0	0
Ford, rf	4	0	1	0	1	0
Landrum, pr	0	1	0	0	0	0
Ripken, ss	4	0	1	1	2	2
Murray, 1b	4	0	0	0	10	1
Lowenstein, lf	3	0	0	0	1	0
Singleton, dh	3	0	1	0	0	0
Dauer, 2b	3	0	0	0	5	3
T. Cruz, 3b	3	0	1	0	3	6
Dempsey, c	2	0	1	0	4	2
Dwyer, ph	1	0	0	0	0	0
McGregor, p	0	0	0	0	1	1
Stewart, p	0	0	0	0	0	0
T. Martinez, p	0	0	0	0	0	1
Totals	31	1	5	1	27	16

Chicago	0 0 1	0 0 1	0 0 0—2
Baltimore	0 0 0	0 0 0	0 0 1—1

Chicago	IP.	H.	R.	ER.	BB.	SO.
Hoyt (Winner)	9	5	1	1	0	4

Baltimore	IP.	H.	R.	ER.	BB.	SO.
McGregor (Loser)	6⅔	6	2	1	3	2
Stewart	⅓*	1	0	0	1	1
T. Martinez	2	0	0	0	2	1

*Pitched to two batters in eighth.

Game-winning RBI—Paciorek.

Error—Murray. Double plays—Chicago 1, Baltimore 1. Left on bases—Chicago 10, Baltimore 3. Two-base hits—Luzinski, Singleton, R. Law, Ford. Sacrifice hit—Fletcher. Wild pitch—T. Martinez. Balk—McGregor. Umpires—McKean, Merrill, Bremigan, Evans, Phillips and Reilly. Time—2:38. Attendance—51,289.

GAME OF THURSDAY, OCTOBER 6, AT BALTIMORE (N)

Chicago	AB.	R.	H.	RBI.	PO.	A.
R. Law, cf	4	0	2	0	2	0
Fisk, c	3	0	0	0	6	0
Baines, rf	4	0	0	0	1	0
Dybzinski, ss	0	0	0	0	1	1
Luzinski, dh	3	0	0	0	0	0
Paciorek, 1b	3	0	1	0	9	0
Kittle, lf	3	0	1	0	2	0
V. Law, 3b	2	0	0	0	0	3
Walker, ph	1	0	0	0	0	0
Rodriguez, 3b	0	0	0	0	0	0
Squires, ph	1	0	0	0	0	0
Fletcher, ss	2	0	0	0	1	3
Hairston, ph-rf	1	0	0	0	0	0
J. Cruz, 2b	4	0	1	0	2	1
Bannister, p	0	0	0	0	0	0
Barojas, p	0	0	0	0	0	1
Lamp, p	0	0	0	0	0	0
Totals	31	0	5	0	24	9

Baltimore	AB.	R.	H.	RBI.	PO.	A.
Shelby, cf	4	0	1	0	0	0
Landrum, rf	4	0	0	0	2	0
Ripken, ss	4	1	2	0	0	0
Murray, 1b	4	0	0	0	6	0
Roenicke, lf	2	3	2	2	1	0
Singleton, dh	4	0	1	1	0	0
Dauer, 2b	3	0	0	0	2	3
T. Cruz, 3b	3	0	0	0	1	3
Dempsey, c	3	0	0	0	15	1
Boddicker, p	0	0	0	0	0	1
Totals	31	4	6	3	27	8

Chicago	0 0 0	0 0 0	0 0 0—0
Baltimore	0 1 0	1 0 2	0 0 x—4

Chicago	IP.	H.	R.	ER.	BB.	SO.
Bannister (Loser)	6	5	4	3	1	5
Barojas	1	1	0	0	0	0
Lamp	1	0	0	0	1	0

Baltimore	IP.	H.	R.	ER.	BB.	SO.
Boddicker (Winner)	9	5	0	0	3	14

Game-winning RBI—None.

Errors—V. Law, Rodriguez. Double plays—Chicago 1, Baltimore 1. Left on bases—Chicago 9, Baltimore 5. Two-base hits—Roenicke, Singleton, Ripken. Home run—Roenicke. Stolen bases—R. Law 2, Shelby. Caught stealing—Paciorek. Hit by pitcher—By Boddicker (Paciorek, Luzinski). Umpires—Merrill, Bremigan, Evans, Phillips, Reilly and McKean. Time—2:51. Attendance—52,347.

GAME OF FRIDAY, OCTOBER 7, AT CHICAGO (N)

Baltimore	AB.	R.	H.	RBI.	PO.	A.
Bumbry, cf	4	0	1	1	3	0
Shelby, ph-cf	0	1	0	0	0	0
Dwyer, rf	3	1	1	0	4	0
Landrum, ph-rf	1	0	0	0	2	0
Ripken, ss	4	3	2	0	2	4
Murray, 1b	2	4	1	3	7	2
Lowenstein, lf	3	0	1	2	3	0
Roenicke, ph-lf	0	1	0	1	0	0
Singleton, dh	3	0	1	0	0	0
Palmer, pr	0	0	0	0	0	0
Nolan, ph	0	0	0	1	0	0
Dauer, 2b	4	0	0	1	1	4
T. Cruz, 3b	5	0	1	1	1	1
Dempsey, c	3	1	0	0	2	0
Flanagan, p	0	0	0	0	0	0
Stewart, p	0	0	0	0	2	0
Totals	32	11	8	10	27	11

Chicago	AB.	R.	H.	RBI.	PO.	A.
R. Law, cf	4	0	2	0	3	0
Fisk, c	4	0	1	0	8	2
Paciorek, 1b	4	0	0	0	11	1
Luzinski, dh	4	0	1	0	0	0
Kittle, lf	1	1	1	0	0	0
Hairston, ph-lf	2	0	0	0	0	0
Baines, rf	4	0	0	0	2	1
V. Law, 3b	2	0	1	1	1	1
Squires, ph	1	0	0	0	0	0
Rodriguez, 3b	0	0	0	0	0	0
Fletcher, ss	3	0	0	0	0	3
J. Cruz, 2b	3	0	0	0	1	5
Dotson, p	0	0	0	0	1	1
Tidrow, p	0	0	0	0	0	0
Koosman, p	0	0	0	0	0	0
Lamp, p	0	0	0	0	0	0
Totals	32	1	6	1	27	14

Baltimore	3 1 0	0 2 0	0 1 4—11
Chicago	0 1 0	0 0 0	0 0 0— 1

Baltimore	IP.	H.	R.	ER.	BB.	SO.
Flanagan (Winner)	5	5	1	1	0	1
Stewart (Save)	4	1	0	0	0	1

Chicago	IP.	H.	R.	ER.	BB.	SO.
Dotson (Loser)	5	6	6	6	3	3
Tidrow	3	1	1	1	3	3
Koosman	⅓	1	3	2	2	0
Lamp	⅔	0	1	0	1	1

Game-winning RBI—Murray.

Errors—Dempsey, Hairston. Double plays—Baltimore 1, Chicago 1. Left on bases—Baltimore 6, Chicago 5. Two-base hits—Dwyer, Bumbry, Kittle, Fisk, Lowenstein, Ripken. Home runs—Murray. Stolen base—Murray. Sacrifice flies—Nolan, Dauer. Hit by pitcher—By Flanagan (Kittle); by Dotson (Ripken). Umpires—Bremigan, Evans, Phillips, Reilly, McKean and Merrill. Time—2:58. Attendance—46,635.

GAME OF SATURDAY, OCTOBER 8, AT CHICAGO

Baltimore	AB.	R.	H.	RBI.	PO.	A.
Shelby, cf	5	0	1	0	3	0
Landrum, rf	5	1	2	1	1	0
Ripken, ss	3	1	1	0	3	5
Murray, 1b	5	1	3	0	11	0
Roenicke, lf	2	0	1	1	3	1
Singleton, dh	2	0	0	0	0	0
Bumbry, pr	0	0	0	0	0	0
Ford, ph	1	0	0	0	0	0
Lowenstein, ph	0	0	0	0	0	0
Ayala, ph	0	0	0	1	0	0
Dauer, 2b	4	0	0	0	0	2
T. Cruz, 3b	4	0	0	0	1	3
Dempsey, c	4	0	1	0	8	2
Davis, p	0	0	0	0	0	0
T. Martinez, p	0	0	0	0	0	1
Totals	35	3	9	3	30	14

Chicago	AB.	R.	H.	RBI.	PO.	A.
R. Law, cf	5	0	0	0	2	0
Fisk, c	5	0	1	0	8	1
Baines, rf	4	0	2	0	0	0
Luzinski, dh	5	0	0	0	0	0
Paciorek, lf	5	0	1	0	1	0
Walker, 1b	2	0	1	0	7	1
Squires, pr-1b	1	0	0	0	4	0
V. Law, 3b	4	0	1	0	0	3
Dybzinski, ss	4	0	1	0	2	7
J. Cruz, 2b	3	0	3	0	6	2
Burns, p	0	0	0	0	0	1
Barojas, p	0	0	0	0	0	0
Agosto, p	0	0	0	0	0	0
Lamp, p	0	0	0	0	0	0
Totals	38	0	10	0	30	15

Baltimore	0 0 0	0 0 0	0 0 0	3—3
Chicago	0 0 0	0 0 0	0 0 0	0—0

Baltimore	IP.	H.	R.	ER.	BB.	SO.
Davis	6*	5	0	0	2	2
T. Martinez (Winner)	4	5	0	0	1	4

Chicago	IP.	H.	R.	ER.	BB.	SO.
Burns (Loser)	9⅓	6	1	1	5	8
Barojas	0†	3	2	2	0	0
Agosto	⅓	0	0	0	0	0
Lamp	⅓	0	0	0	0	0

*Pitched to one batter in seventh.
†Pitched to three batters in tenth.

Game-winning RBI—Landrum.

Errors—None. Double plays—Baltimore 1, Chicago 2. Left on bases—Baltimore 10, Chicago 11. Home run—Landrum. Stolen bases—J. Cruz 2. Sacrifice hit—Dauer. Sacrifice fly—Ayala. Hit by pitcher—By Burns (Roenicke). Balk—T. Martinez. Umpires—Evans, Phillips, Reilly, McKean, Merrill and Bremigan. Time—3:41. Attendance—45,477.

BALTIMORE ORIOLES' BATTING AND FIELDING AVERAGES

Player—Position	G.	AB.	R.	H.	TB.	2B.	3B.	HR.	RBI.	B.A.	PO.	A.	E.	F.A.
Roenicke, lf-ph	3	4	4	3	7	1	0	1	4	.750	4	1	0	1.000
Ripken, ss	4	15	5	6	8	2	0	0	1	.400	7	11	0	1.000
Murray, 1b	4	15	5	4	7	0	0	1	3	.267	34	3	1	.974
Singleton, dh	4	12	0	3	5	2	0	0	1	.250	0	0	0	.000
Dwyer, ph-rf	2	4	1	1	2	1	0	0	0	.250	4	0	0	1.000
Shelby, cf-ph	3	9	1	2	2	0	0	0	0	.222	3	0	0	1.000
Landrum, pr-rf-ph	4	10	2	2	5	0	0	1	1	.200	5	0	0	1.000
Ford, rf-ph	2	5	0	1	2	1	0	0	0	.200	1	0	0	1.000
Dempsey, c	4	12	1	2	2	0	0	0	0	.167	29	5	1	.971
Lowenstein, lf-ph	3	6	0	1	2	1	0	0	2	.167	4	0	0	1.000
T. Cruz, 3b	4	15	0	2	2	0	0	0	1	.133	6	13	0	1.000
Bumbry, cf-pr	3	8	0	1	2	1	0	0	1	.125	3	0	0	1.000
T. Martinez, p	2	0	0	0	0	0	0	0	0	.000	0	2	0	1.000
Stewart, p	2	0	0	0	0	0	0	0	0	.000	2	0	0	1.000
Ayala, ph	1	0	0	0	0	0	0	0	1	.000	0	0	0	.000
Boddicker, p	1	0	0	0	0	0	0	0	0	.000	0	1	0	1.000
Davis, p	1	0	0	0	0	0	0	0	0	.000	0	0	0	.000

Player—Position	G.	AB.	R.	H.	TB.	2B.	3B.	HR.	RBI.	B.A.	PO.	A.	E.	F.A.
Flanagan, p	1	0	0	0	0	0	0	0	0	.000	0	0	0	.000
McGregor, p	1	0	0	0	0	0	0	0	0	.000	1	1	0	1.000
Nolan, ph	1	0	0	0	0	0	0	0	1	.000	0	0	0	.000
Palmer, pr	1	0	0	0	0	0	0	0	0	.000	0	0	0	.000
Dauer, 2b	4	14	0	0	0	0	0	0	1	.000	8	12	0	1.000
Totals	4	129	19	28	46	9	0	3	17	.217	111	49	2	.988

CHICAGO WHITE SOX' BATTING AND FIELDING AVERAGES

Player—Position	G.	AB.	R.	H.	TB.	2B.	3B.	HR.	RBI.	B.A.	PO.	A.	E.	F.A.
R. Law, cf	4	18	1	7	8	1	0	0	0	.389	10	0	0	1.000
J. Cruz, 2b	4	12	0	4	4	0	0	0	0	.333	10	14	0	1.000
Walker, ph-1b	2	3	0	1	1	0	0	0	0	.333	7	1	0	1.000
Kittle, lf	3	7	1	2	3	1	0	0	0	.286	3	0	0	1.000
Paciorek, 1b-lf	4	16	1	4	4	0	0	0	1	.250	30	3	0	1.000
Dybzinski, ss	2	4	0	1	1	0	0	0	0	.250	3	8	0	1.000
V. Law, 3b	4	11	0	2	2	0	0	0	1	.182	1	9	1	.909
Fisk, c	4	17	0	3	4	1	0	0	0	.176	27	3	0	1.000
Luzinski, dh	4	15	0	2	3	1	0	0	0	.133	0	0	0	.000
Baines, rf	4	16	0	2	2	0	0	0	0	.125	5	1	0	1.000
Lamp, p	3	0	0	0	0	0	0	0	0	.000	0	0	0	.000
Barojas, p	2	0	0	0	0	0	0	0	0	.000	0	1	0	1.000
Rodriguez, 3b	2	0	0	0	0	0	0	0	0	.000	0	0	1	.000
Agosto, p	1	0	0	0	0	0	0	0	0	.000	0	0	0	.000
Bannister, p	1	0	0	0	0	0	0	0	0	.000	0	0	0	.000
Burns, p	1	0	0	0	0	0	0	0	0	.000	0	1	0	1.000
Dotson, p	1	0	0	0	0	0	0	0	0	.000	1	1	0	1.000
Hoyt, p	1	0	0	0	0	0	0	0	0	.000	2	1	0	1.000
Koosman, p	1	0	0	0	0	0	0	0	0	.000	0	0	0	.000
Tidrow, p	1	0	0	0	0	0	0	0	0	.000	0	0	0	.000
Hairston, ph-rf-lf	2	3	0	0	0	0	0	0	0	.000	0	0	1	.000
Squires, 1b-ph-pr	4	4	0	0	0	0	0	0	0	.000	6	0	0	1.000
Fletcher, ss	3	7	0	0	0	0	0	0	0	.000	3	8	0	1.000
Totals	4	133	3	28	32	4	0	0	2	.211	108	51	3	.981

BALTIMORE ORIOLES' PITCHING RECORDS

Pitcher	G.	GS.	CG.	IP.	H.	R.	ER.	BB.	SO.	HB.	WP.	W.	L.	Pct.	ERA.
Boddicker	1	1	1	9	5	0	0	3	14	2	0	1	0	1.000	0.00
Davis	1	1	0	6	5	0	0	2	2	0	0	0	0	.000	0.00
T. Martinez	2	0	0	6	5	0	0	3	5	0	1	1	0	1.000	0.00
Stewart	2	0	0	4⅓	2	0	0	1	2	0	0	0	0	.000	0.00
McGregor	1	1	0	6⅔	6	2	1	3	2	0	0	0	1	.000	1.35
Flanagan	1	1	0	5	5	1	1	0	1	1	0	1	0	1.000	1.80
Totals	4	4	1	37	28	3	2	12	26	3	1	3	1	.750	0.49

Shutouts—Boddicker, Davis-T. Martinez (combined). Save—Stewart.

CHICAGO WHITE SOX' PITCHING RECORDS

Pitcher	G.	GS.	CG.	IP.	H.	R.	ER.	BB.	SO.	HB.	WP.	W.	L.	Pct.	ERA.
Lamp	3	0	0	2	0	1	0	2	1	0	0	0	0	.000	0.00
Agosto	1	0	0	⅓	0	0	0	0	0	0	0	0	0	.000	0.00
Burns	1	1	0	9⅓	6	1	1	5	8	1	0	0	1	.000	0.96
Hoyt	1	1	1	9	5	1	1	0	4	0	0	1	0	1.000	1.00
Tidrow	1	0	0	3	1	1	1	3	3	0	0	0	0	.000	3.00
Bannister	1	1	0	6	5	4	3	1	5	0	0	0	1	.000	4.50
Dotson	1	1	0	5	6	6	6	3	3	1	0	0	1	.000	10.80
Barojas	2	0	0	1	4	2	2	0	0	0	0	0	0	.000	18.00
Koosman	1	0	0	⅓	1	3	2	2	0	0	0	0	0	.000	54.00
Totals	4	4	1	36	28	19	16	16	24	2	0	1	3	.250	4.00

No shutouts or saves.

COMPOSITE SCORE BY INNINGS

Baltimore	3	2	0	1	2	2	0	1	5	3—19
Chicago	0	1	1	0	0	1	0	0	0	0— 3

Game-winning RBIs—Paciorek, Murray, Landrum.

Sacrifice hits—Fletcher, Dauer.

Sacrifice flies—Nolan, Dauer, Ayala.

Stolen bases—R. Law 2, J. Cruz 2, Shelby, Murray.

Caught stealing—Paciorek.

Double plays—Fletcher, J. Cruz and Paciorek 2; Ripken, Dauer and Murray; Dempsey and T. Cruz; Dybzinski and Paciorek; Dauer, Ripken and Murray; Dybzinski and Walker; Ripken and Murray; V. Law, J. Cruz and Walker.

Left on bases—Baltimore 3, 5, 6, 10—24; Chicago 10, 9, 5, 11—35.

Hit by pitcher—By Boddicker (Paciorek, Luzinski); by Flanagan (Kittle); by Dotson (Ripken); by Burns (Roenicke).

Passed balls—None.

Balks—McGregor, T. Martinez.

Time of games—First game, 2:38; second game, 2:51; third game, 2:58; fourth game, 3:41.

Attendance—First game, 51,289; second game, 52,347; third game, 46,635; fourth game, 45,477.

Umpires—McKean, Merrill, Bremigan, Evans, Phillips and Reilly.

Official scorers—Neal Eskridge; Dave Nightingale, The Sporting News.

Gary Matthews made up for a sub-par regular season by clubbing three home runs and driving home eight more to capture N.L. Championship Series MVP honors.

Phillies, Matthews Get Even

By LARRY WIGGE

When he strolled to the plate in the second inning of the second game of the 1983 National League Championship Series, Gary Matthews did so with considerable trepidation.

Matthews, a .284 career hitter entering the 1983 season and a man who normally produced 15-20 homers and more than 70 runs batted in per year, had fallen off to a .258 average in '83 with only 10 homers and 50 RBIs. He had become a platoon player shortly after Phillies General Manager Paul Owens took over as field manager July 18, spending a lot of time on the bench in the waning months of the season.

Matthews, a righthanded batter, knew very well that many platoon players never become regulars again. And at age 33, he wasn't pleased with the outlook.

The Championship Series, Matthews figured, offered the perfect setting for regaining his starting left-field job. The fact that he was 0-for-4 in Game 1 against Los Angeles lefthander Jerry Reuss hadn't set well with Matthews. And he knew the Dodgers were talking about starting righthanders Bob Welch and Alejandro Pena in Games 3 and 4 when the playoffs shifted from Los Angeles to Philadelphia. If he was going to produce, now was the time.

To that end, Matthews ended a personal 1-for-25 slump in great fashion against lefthander Fernando Valenzuela by blasting a home run into the left-field seats. He wound up with a 2-for-4 game, and his homer was the only offense for the Phillies as they dropped a 4-1 decision to even the Championship Series at one game apiece.

When the playoff resumed two days later, Owens again had penciled Matthews' name into the lineup, even though Welch was on the mound. Gary responded with a 3-for-3 day, including another homer and four RBIs, as the Phillies downed the Dodgers, 7-2.

Now, Matthews was on a roll. There was no keeping him out of the lineup.

In the first inning of Game 4, he clubbed a three-run homer off Reuss (Pena had pitched in relief the day before) and, behind lefthander Steve Carlton, the Phillies won another 7-2 decision to advance to the World Series against the Baltimore Orioles.

"Not playing was the low point in my career," Matthews said solemnly after being named the Most Valuable Player of the N.L. title series. "But I didn't dwell on

Steve Carlton (above) had little trouble with the Dodgers in Game 1 while Phillies reliever Al Holland rejoices after the pennant-clinching Game 4 victory.

The Phillies' Mike Schmidt not only beat the Dodgers with his .467 batting average, he beat them with his glove, too.

it or tear up the clubhouse or sulk. I knew I could still do it, that I wasn't washed up."

Matthews had five straight hits to set an N.L. Championship Series record. His eight RBIs tied a league playoff mark set by the Dodgers' Dusty Baker in 1977, and his homers in three consecutive games equalled Hank Aaron's Championship Series record established in 1969.

Matthews, whose RBI total surpassed his output in the final four weeks of the season and whose three homers were one more than he had hit since the All-Star break, was asked if his playoff success could erase the misfortunes of the regular season.

Matthews took a long sip of champagne as he pondered his answer.

"This doesn't make up for it, if that's what you mean," he said. "I would have rather had a good season and a good playoff. I'm not going to lie to you, this was a tough year.

"I feel I could have had this kind of streak if I had played regularly, but I'm not going to complain. Greg Gross and Joe Lefebvre added a lot to our ballclub. We wouldn't be here if it wasn't for them."

The Phillies also wouldn't have made it to the World Series without the strong pitching of Carlton and Al Holland, who combined for victories in the opener and in the clincher. Reliever Ron Reed also helped out in the finale.

Mike Schmidt's first-inning homer was all the offense the Phillies needed behind Carlton and Holland in Game 1. When Carlton (who permitted only seven hits in $7\frac{2}{3}$ innings) loaded the bases on singles by Steve Sax and Baker and a walk to Pedro Guerrero in the eighth inning, Holland bailed out the veteran by getting Mike Marshall to fly out. Holland then set down the Dodgers in the ninth to preserve the

Phils' 1-0 victory.

The Phillies' bats were unproductive in Game 2 against Valenzuela and reliever Tom Niedenfuer, the Dodgers knotting the playoffs on the strength of Guerrero's two-run triple in the fifth inning and a run-scoring single by Jack Fimple in the eighth.

The Phillies got their first two runs in Game 3 without a hit, scoring on a passed ball and on a groundout by Ivan DeJesus in the second inning. They added another run in the third on Lefebvre's sacrifice fly. Then, after Marshall belted a two-run homer for the Dodgers in the fourth, Matthews took over. He hit a solo homer in the bottom of the fourth, drove in two more runs with a single in the fifth and climaxed the victory with another run-scoring single in the seventh. Meanwhile, rookie Charles Hudson shackled the Dodgers on four hits.

Schmidt and Sixto Lezcano had two-out singles preceding Matthews' three-run blast in the first inning of Game 4. Schmidt, who had three hits in the final game and batted .467 (7-for-15) in the four games, doubled home a run and scored on a groundout by Garry Maddox in the fifth, making the score 5-1. Lezcano increased the lead to 7-1 with a two-run homer in the sixth.

Carlton, Reed and Holland scattered 10 hits in the decisive triumph.

Matthews, Pete Rose, Joe Morgan and others may have been unhappy over some of Owens' strategy during the season, but no one was complaining after the Phillies had won their second N.L. pennant in four years.

GAME OF TUESDAY, OCTOBER 4, AT LOS ANGELES (N)

Philadelphia	AB.	R.	H.	RBI.	PO.	A.
Morgan, 2b	4	0	0	0	3	1
Rose, 1b	4	0	1	0	8	1
Schmidt, 3b	3	1	2	1	0	2
Lezcano, rf	3	0	1	0	2	0
Matthews, lf	4	0	0	0	2	0
Holland, p	0	0	0	0	0	0
Maddox, cf	4	0	1	0	4	0
Diaz, c	3	0	0	0	6	0
DeJesus, ss	3	0	0	0	1	2
Carlton, p	3	0	0	0	1	3
G. Gross, lf	1	0	0	0	0	0
Totals	32	1	5	1	27	9

Los Angeles	AB.	R.	H.	RBI.	PO.	A.
Sax, 2b	4	0	3	0	1	5
Russell, ss	3	0	1	0	0	3
Baker, lf	4	0	1	0	3	0
Guerrero, 3b	2	0	0	0	0	1
Marshall, 1b	4	0	0	0	11	0
Niedenfuer, p	0	0	0	0	0	1
Yeager, c	4	0	0	0	4	0
Landreaux, cf	3	0	0	0	3	0
Morales, ph	1	0	0	0	0	0
Thomas, rf	4	0	2	0	4	0
Reuss, p	1	0	0	0	0	1
Maldonado, ph	1	0	0	0	0	0
Brock, 1b	1	0	0	0	1	0
Totals	32	0	7	0	27	11

Philadelphia	1 0 0	0 0 0	0 0 0—1
Los Angeles	0 0 0	0 0 0	0 0 0—0

Philadelphia	IP.	H.	R.	ER.	BB.	SO.
Carlton (Winner)	7⅔	7	0	0	2	6
Holland (Save)	1⅓	0	0	0	0	0

Los Angeles	IP.	H.	R.	ER.	BB.	SO.
Reuss (Loser)	8	5	1	1	3	3
Niedenfuer	1	0	0	0	1	1

Game-winning RBI—Schmidt.

Error—Schmidt. Left on bases—Philadelphia 8, Los Angeles 9. Home run—Schmidt. Stolen base—Thomas. Sacrifice hits—Reuss, Russell. Wild pitches—Carlton, Reuss. Umpires—Tata, Stello, McSherry, Weyer, Harvey and Crawford. Time—2:17. Attendance—49,963.

GAME OF WEDNESDAY, OCTOBER 5, AT LOS ANGELES (N)

Philadelphia	AB.	R.	H.	RBI.	PO.	A.
Morgan, 2b	3	0	0	0	4	3
Rose, 1b	3	0	0	0	7	0
Schmidt, 3b	4	0	1	0	1	3
Lezcano, rf	4	0	0	0	1	0
Matthews, lf	4	1	2	1	1	0
Maddox, cf	3	0	2	0	4	0
G. Gross, ph	0	0	0	0	0	0
Diaz, c	3	0	0	0	5	1
Lefebvre, ph	1	0	0	0	0	0
DeJesus, ss	2	0	1	0	1	3
Hayes, ph	1	0	0	0	0	0
Denny, p	1	0	0	0	0	0
Perez, ph	1	0	1	0	0	0
Samuel, pr	0	0	0	0	0	0
Reed, p	0	0	0	0	0	1
Virgil, ph	1	0	0	0	0	0
Totals	31	1	7	1	24	11

Los Angeles	AB.	R.	H.	RBI.	PO.	A.
Sax, 2b	4	0	0	0	4	4
Brock, 1b	4	1	0	0	7	0
Thomas, rf	0	0	0	0	0	0
Baker, lf	3	2	0	0	3	0
Guerrero, 3b	3	0	1	2	0	2
Landreaux, cf	3	0	2	1	3	0
Marshall, rf-1b	4	0	0	0	2	0
Russell, ss	3	1	2	0	1	5
Fimple, c	4	0	1	1	6	1
Valenzuela, p	3	0	0	0	1	0
Niedenfuer, p	0	0	0	0	0	0
Totals	31	4	6	4	27	12

Philadelphia	0 1 0	0 0 0	0 0 0—1
Los Angeles	1 0 0	0 2 0	0 1 x—4

Philadelphia	IP.	H.	R.	ER.	BB.	SO.
Denny (Loser)	6	5	3	0	3	3
Reed	2	1	1	1	1	1

Los Angeles	IP.	H.	R.	ER.	BB.	SO.
Valenzuela (Winner)	8*	7	1	1	4	5
Niedenfuer (Save)	1	0	0	0	0	2

*Pitched to two batters in ninth.

Game-winning RBI—Guerrero.

Errors—DeJesus, Maddox, Russell. Double plays—Los Angeles 3. Left on bases—Philadelphia 8, Los Angeles 8. Two-base hit—Maddox. Three-base hit—Guerrero. Home run—Matthews. Stolen bases—Rose, Russell. Sacrifice hit—Denny. Hit by pitcher—By Denny (Guerrero). Wild pitch—Valenzuela. Umpires—Stello, McSherry, Weyer, Harvey, Crawford and Tata. Time—2:44. Attendance—55,967.

GAME OF FRIDAY, OCTOBER 7, AT PHILADELPHIA

Los Angeles	AB.	R.	H.	RBI.	PO.	A.
Sax, 2b	3	0	0	0	1	0
Brock, 1b	4	0	0	0	5	0
Baker, lf	4	1	2	0	2	0
Guerrero, 3b	4	0	0	0	0	4
Landreaux, cf	4	0	0	0	5	0
Marshall, rf	3	1	1	2	4	0
Russell, ss	4	0	0	0	0	0
Fimple, c	3	0	0	0	7	1
Welch, p	0	0	0	0	0	0
Pena, p	1	0	1	0	0	0
Landestoy, ph	1	0	0	0	0	0
Honeycutt, p	0	0	0	0	0	0
Beckwith, p	0	0	0	0	0	0
Thomas, ph	1	0	0	0	0	0
Zachry, p	0	0	0	0	0	0
Totals	32	2	4	2	24	5

Philadelphia	AB.	R.	H.	RBI.	PO.	A.
Morgan, 2b	4	1	1	0	0	2
Rose, 1b	4	2	3	0	7	0
Schmidt, 3b	3	1	1	0	3	1
Lefebvre, rf	1	0	0	1	2	0
Lezcano, ph-rf	2	0	0	0	0	0
Matthews, lf	3	2	3	4	2	0
Dernier, cf	0	0	0	0	0	0
G. Gross, cf-lf	3	1	0	0	4	0
Diaz, c	3	0	0	0	9	0
DeJesus, ss	4	0	1	1	0	2
Hudson, p	4	0	0	0	0	0
Totals	31	7	9	6	27	5

Los Angeles	000	200	000—2
Philadelphia	021	120	10x—7

Los Angeles	IP.	H.	R.	ER.	BB.	SO.
Welch (Loser)	1⅓	0	2	1	2	0
Pena	2⅔	4	2	2	1	3
Honeycutt	⅓	2	2	2	0	0
Beckwith	1⅔	1	0	0	0	3
Zachry	2	2	1	1	1	1

Philadelphia	IP.	H.	R.	ER.	BB.	SO.
Hudson (Winner)	9	4	2	2	2	9

Game-winning RBI—None.

Error—DeJesus. Left on bases—Los Angeles 5, Philadelphia 5. Two-base hits—Baker, Schmidt. Home runs—Marshall, Matthews. Stolen bases—Sax, Matthews. Caught stealing—Rose. Sacrifice flies—Lefebvre. Wild pitches—Pena 2. Passed ball—Fimple. Umpires—McSherry, Weyer, Harvey, Crawford, Tata and Stello. Time—2:51. Attendance—53,490.

GAME OF SATURDAY, OCTOBER 8, AT PHILADELPHIA (N)

Los Angeles	AB.	R.	H.	RBI.	PO.	A.
Sax, 2b	5	0	1	0	5	3
Russell, ss	4	0	1	0	3	2
Guerrero, 3b	3	1	2	0	0	2
Baker, lf	3	1	2	1	1	0
Marshall, 1b	4	0	1	0	5	2
Yeager, c	2	0	1	0	3	1
Monday, ph	0	0	0	0	0	0
Morales, ph	1	0	0	0	0	0
Fimple, c	0	0	0	0	1	0
Landreaux, cf	4	0	0	0	1	0
Thomas, rf	4	0	2	0	3	0
Reuss, p	2	0	0	0	0	0
Beckwith, p	0	0	0	0	0	0
Honeycutt, p	0	0	0	0	1	0
Landestoy, ph	1	0	0	0	0	0
Zachry, p	0	0	0	0	1	0
Maldonado, ph	1	0	0	0	0	0
Totals	34	2	10	1	24	10

Philadelphia	AB.	R.	H.	RBI.	PO.	A.
Morgan, 2b	4	0	0	0	1	1
Rose, 1b	5	1	2	0	7	1
Schmidt, 3b	5	3	3	1	2	1
Lezcano, rf-lf	4	2	3	2	2	1
Matthews, lf	3	1	1	3	1	0
Reed, p	0	0	0	0	0	0
Hayes, rf	1	0	0	0	0	0
Maddox, cf	4	0	0	1	0	0
Diaz, c	4	0	2	0	12	1
DeJesus, ss	3	0	1	0	2	4
Carlton, p	2	0	1	0	0	2
G. Gross, lf	1	0	0	0	0	0
Holland, p	0	0	0	0	0	0
Totals	36	7	13	7	27	11

Los Angeles	000	100	010—2
Philadelphia	300	022	00x—7

Los Angeles	IP.	H.	R.	ER.	BB.	SO.
Reuss (Loser)	4*	9	5	5	0	1
Beckwith	⅔	0	0	0	2	0
Honeycutt	1⅓	2	2	2	0	2
Zachry	2	2	0	0	1	1

Philadelphia	IP.	H.	R.	ER.	BB.	SO.
Carlton (Winner)	6	6	1	1	3	7
Reed	1⅓	3	1	0	0	2
Holland	1⅔	1	0	0	0	3

*Pitched to two batters in fifth.

Game-winning RBI—Matthews.

Error—Lezcano. Left on bases—Los Angeles 9, Philadelphia 10. Two-base hits—Guerrero, Marshall, Schmidt, Yeager, Diaz, Thomas. Home runs—Matthews, Baker, Lezcano. Caught stealing—Sax, Marshall. Sacrifice hits—Carlton, Lezcano. Hit by pitcher—By Carlton (Yeager). Wild pitches—Carlton. Umpires—Weyer, Harvey, Crawford, Tata, Stello and McSherry. Time—2:50. Attendance—64,494.

PHILADELPHIA PHILLIES' BATTING AND FIELDING AVERAGES

Player—Position	G.	AB.	R.	H.	TB.	2B.	3B.	HR.	RBI.	B.A.	PO.	A.	E.	F.A.
Perez, ph	1	1	0	1	1	0	0	0	0	1.000	0	0	0	.000
Schmidt, 3b	4	15	5	7	12	2	0	1	2	.467	6	7	1	.929
Matthews, lf	4	14	4	6	15	0	0	3	8	.429	6	0	0	1.000
Rose, 1b	4	16	3	6	6	0	0	0	0	.375	29	2	0	1.000
Lezcano, rf-ph-lf	4	13	2	4	7	0	0	1	2	.308	5	1	1	.857
Maddox, cf	3	11	0	3	4	1	0	0	1	.273	8	0	1	.889
DeJesus, ss	4	12	0	3	3	0	0	0	1	.250	4	11	2	.882
Carlton, p	2	5	0	1	1	0	0	0	0	.200	1	5	0	1.000
Diaz, c	4	13	0	2	3	1	0	0	0	.154	32	2	0	1.000
Morgan, 2b	4	15	1	1	1	0	0	0	0	.067	8	7	0	1.000
Dernier, cf	1	0	0	0	0	0	0	0	0	.000	0	0	0	.000
Holland, p	2	0	0	0	0	0	0	0	0	.000	0	0	0	.000

Player—Position	G.	AB.	R.	H.	TB.	2B.	3B.	HR.	RBI.	B.A.	PO.	A.	E.	F.A.
Reed, p	2	0	0	0	0	0	0	0	0	.000	0	1	0	1.000
Samuel, pr	1	0	0	0	0	0	0	0	0	.000	0	0	0	.000
Denny, p	1	1	0	0	0	0	0	0	0	.000	0	0	0	.000
Virgil, ph	1	1	0	0	0	0	0	0	0	.000	0	0	0	.000
Hayes, ph-rf	2	2	0	0	0	0	0	0	0	.000	0	0	0	.000
Lefebvre, ph-rf	2	2	0	0	0	0	0	0	1	.000	2	0	0	1.000
Hudson, p	1	4	0	0	0	0	0	0	0	.000	0	0	0	.000
G. Gross, lf-ph-cf	4	5	1	0	0	0	0	0	0	.000	4	0	0	1.000
Totals	4	130	16	34	53	4	0	5	15	.262	105	36	5	.966

LOS ANGELES DODGERS' BATTING AND FIELDING AVERAGES

Player—Position	G.	AB.	R.	H.	TB.	2B.	3B.	HR.	RBI.	B.A.	PO.	A.	E.	F.A.
Pena, p	1	1	0	1	1	0	0	0	0	1.000	0	0	0	.000
Thomas, rf-ph	4	9	0	4	5	1	0	0	0	.444	7	0	0	1.000
Baker, lf	4	14	4	5	9	1	0	1	1	.357	9	0	0	1.000
Russell, ss	4	14	1	4	4	0	0	0	0	.286	4	10	1	.933
S. Sax, 2b	4	16	0	4	4	0	0	0	0	.250	11	12	0	1.000
Guerrero, 3b	4	12	1	3	6	1	1	0	2	.250	0	9	0	1.000
Yeager, c	2	6	0	1	2	1	0	0	0	.167	7	1	0	1.000
Landreaux, cf	4	14	0	2	2	0	0	0	1	.143	12	0	0	1.000
Fimple, c	3	7	0	1	1	0	0	0	1	.143	14	2	0	1.000
Marshall, 1b-rf	4	15	1	2	6	1	0	1	2	.133	22	2	0	1.000
Beckwith, p	2	0	0	0	0	0	0	0	0	.000	0	0	0	.000
Honeycutt, p	2	0	0	0	0	0	0	0	0	.000	1	0	0	1.000
Niedenfuer, p	2	0	0	0	0	0	0	0	0	.000	0	1	0	1.000
Zachry, p	2	0	0	0	0	0	0	0	0	.000	1	0	0	1.000
Monday, ph	1	0	0	0	0	0	0	0	0	.000	0	0	0	.000
Welch, p	1	0	0	0	0	0	0	0	0	.000	0	0	0	.000
Landestoy, ph	2	2	0	0	0	0	0	0	0	.000	0	0	0	.000
Maldonado, ph	2	2	0	0	0	0	0	0	0	.000	0	0	0	.000
Morales, ph	2	2	0	0	0	0	0	0	0	.000	0	0	0	.000
Reuss, p	2	3	0	0	0	0	0	0	0	.000	0	1	0	1.000
Valenzuela, p	1	3	0	0	0	0	0	0	0	.000	1	0	0	1.000
Brock, 1b	3	9	1	0	0	0	0	0	0	.000	13	0	0	1.000
Totals	4	129	8	27	40	5	1	2	7	.209	102	38	1	.993

PHILADELPHIA PHILLIES' PITCHING RECORDS

Pitcher	G.	GS.	CG.	IP.	H.	R.	ER.	BB.	SO.	HB.	WP.	W.	L.	Pct.	ERA.
Denny	1	1	0	6	5	3	0	3	3	1	0	0	1	.000	0.00
Holland	2	0	0	3	1	0	0	0	3	0	0	0	0	.000	0.00
Carlton	2	2	0	13⅔	13	1	1	5	13	1	2	2	0	1.000	0.66
Hudson	1	1	1	9	4	2	2	2	9	0	0	1	0	1.000	2.00
Reed	2	0	0	3⅓	4	2	1	1	3	0	0	0	0	.000	2.70
Totals	4	4	1	35	27	8	4	11	31	2	2	3	1	.750	1.03

Shutout—Carlton-Holland (combined). Save—Holland.

LOS ANGELES DODGERS' PITCHING RECORDS

Pitcher	G.	GS.	CG.	IP.	H.	R.	ER.	BB.	SO.	HB.	WP.	W.	L.	Pct.	ERA.
Beckwith	2	0	0	2⅓	1	0	0	2	3	0	0	0	0	.000	0.00
Niedenfuer	2	0	0	2	0	0	0	1	3	0	0	0	0	.000	0.00
Valenzuela	1	1	0	8	7	1	1	4	5	0	1	1	0	1.000	1.13
Zachry	2	0	0	4	4	1	1	2	2	0	0	0	0	.000	2.25
Reuss	2	2	0	12	14	6	6	3	4	0	1	0	2	.000	4.50
Pena	1	0	0	2⅔	4	2	2	1	3	0	2	0	0	.000	6.75
Welch	1	1	0	1⅓	0	2	1	2	0	0	0	0	1	.000	6.75
Honeycutt	2	0	0	1⅔	4	4	4	0	2	0	0	0	0	.000	21.60
Totals	4	4	0	34	34	16	15	15	22	0	4	1	3	.250	3.97

No shutouts. Save—Niedenfuer.

COMPOSITE SCORE BY INNINGS

Philadelphia	4	3	1	1	4	2	1	0	0	—16
Los Angeles	1	0	0	3	2	0	0	2	0	— 8

Game-winning RBIs—Schmidt, Guerrero, Matthews.
Sacrifice hits—Reuss, Russell, Denny, Carlton, Lezcano.
Sacrifice fly—Lefebvre.
Stolen bases—Thomas, Rose, Russell, Sax, Matthews.
Caught stealing—Rose, Sax, Marshall.
Double plays—Russell, Sax and Brock 2; Russell, Sax and Marshall.
Left on bases—Philadelphia 8, 8, 5, 10—31; Los Angeles 9, 8, 5, 9—31.
Hit by pitcher—By Denny (Guerrero), by Carlton (Yeager).
Passed ball—Fimple.
Balks—None.
Time of games—First game, 2:17; second game, 2:44; third game, 2:51; fourth game, 2:50.
Attendance—First game, 49,963; second game, 55,967; third game, 53,490; fourth game, 64,494.
Umpires—Tata, Stello, McSherry, Weyer, Harvey and Crawford.
Official scorers—Jay Dunn, Trentonian (N.J.); Terry Johnson, Torrance (Cal.) Daily Breeze; Wayne Monroe, Pasadena Star-News.

Winning pitcher Scott McGregor and Orioles catcher Rick Dempsey embrace after Baltimore's Series-clinching 5-0 victory in Game 5. Dempsey was voted the Series' Most Valuable Player.

1983 WORLD SERIES

Including

Review of 1983 Series

Official Play-by-Play, Each Game

Official Composite Box Score

World Series Tables—Attendance, Money, Results

Baltimore outfielder Jim Dwyer got the Series off to a rousing start with a solo homer in the first inning of Game 1.

For O's, History Didn't Repeat

By LARRY WIGGE

You could describe the mood of the Baltimore Orioles as quiet but confident as they filed onto the Veterans Stadium carpet in Philadelphia on October 16 for Game 5 of the 1983 World Series. You might have expected cockiness since the Orioles had beaten the Phillies' Steve Carlton and John Denny in consecutive games on enemy turf for a 3-1 lead in the Series.

But . . . .

Baltimore catcher Rick Dempsey bristled when a reporter asked him what he thought about his team's "imminent" World Series victory. "Listen," he said, obviously perturbed at the nonchalant attitude his questioner used. "The moment we won yesterday, all I could think about was 1979."

End of interview.

Dempsey, Eddie Murray, Ken Singleton, Scott McGregor, Mike Flanagan and 10 other Baltimore players of '83 also were members of the '79 Orioles, who took a 3-1 lead into Game 5 of the World Series against Pittsburgh, only to lose to the Pirates in seven games.

So, no one could blame Baltimore for approaching the fifth game of the '83 classic with some apprehension.

Lead or no lead, the American League champions were feeling some pressure. And it wasn't until Murray completed his turn at bat in the second inning that the tension eased.

Murray had been expected to provide much of the Orioles' punch in the Series, but instead went into an ill-timed October slump. Several of his critics reminded him that he had finished the '79 Series in a 0-for-21 drought and was just 2-for-16 in the first four games of this Series.

But Murray silenced those critics when he ripped a 2-and-2 delivery from Philadelphia righthander Charles Hudson into the right-field bleachers, giving the Orioles a 1-0 lead.

"Eddie did that in Chicago," said Singleton, reflecting on Murray's first-inning, three-run homer in Game 3 of the A.L. Championship Series, a blast that came after a 0-for-8 start. "You never heard 50,000 people shut up so fast. He did the same to almost 70,000 people (67,064) today. We knew we had it when Eddie hit that first one. When he is in a groove, he can carry you for a week."

"The sound," said McGregor, "it was 'thwack,' then 'clunk,' then silence."

A tale of two stars: The Orioles' Eddie Murray (above) eventually broke out of his hitting slump; the Phillies' Mike Schmidt never did, only breaking his bat on his lone Series hit.

"All I had in mind," said Murray, "is that we were up, 1-0, and I had just taken 67,000 people out of the ball game."

Murray then took the Phillies out of the game with a two-run homer in his next time at the plate in the fourth inning, opening up a 4-0 Baltimore cushion. That home-run ball struck the scoreboard in right-center field, crashing near the letter "M" on the message board, where M-U-R-R-A-Y was spelled out among the American League leaders with 111 RBIs.

"It was like fooling with a case of dynamite," said Phillies Manager Paul Owens of Murray. "Somewhere, somehow you knew he was going to explode."

Afterward, Murray, who also had a single in the ninth and went 3-for-4, said he gladly would have taken another hitless day as long as the Orioles won. His attitude epitomized Baltimore's team concept, which the Birds rode to their first World Series title since 1970 and their third since the former St. Louis Browns franchise moved to Baltimore after the 1953 season.

McGregor, for instance, spun a five-hitter in shutting out the Phillies, 5-0, in Game 5. And Dempsey was named the Series' Most Valuable Player for contributing grit and desire, not to mention a .385 average (5-for-13). He set a record with five extra-base hits (four doubles and a homer) in a five-game Series and tied the doubles mark for five games.

The Orioles' only setback came in Game 1. Denny and reliever Al Holland combined on a five-hitter and were backed by solo homers by Joe Morgan in the sixth inning and Garry Maddox in the eighth for a 2-1 decision in a game played in a driving rain. Ironically, Maddox's decisive homer accounted for his only game-winning RBI of the year—regular season or postseason.

Jim Dwyer's first-inning homer, coming in the Oriole right fielder's first career Series at-bat, provided Baltimore with its only run.

Rookie righthander Mike Boddicker and left fielder John Lowenstein were the heroes for Baltimore in a 4-1 victory over the Phillies in Game 2. Boddicker yielded only three hits and a fourth-inning sacrifice fly by Joe Lefebvre.

Meanwhile, Lowenstein, who had three hits in the game, tied the contest at 1-1 with a fifth-inning homer and ignited a three-run outburst in the process. Rich Dauer and Todd Cruz singled before Dempsey doubed across Dauer for a 2-1 lead. Boddicker, batting in a big-league game for the first time, connected for a sacrifice fly.

Baltimore right fielder Dan Ford, who was beaned later in the fifth inning by Phillies reliever Willie Hernandez, contributed a key single in the seventh inning as the Orioles added an insurance run.

Game 3 turned into a series of eventful managerial maneuvers, with the Orioles finally earning a 3-2 victory for a 2-1 edge in the Series.

The first move belonged to Philadelphia's Owens. He pulled a stunner, announcing that Tony Perez—not Pete Rose—would start the contest at first base. It was the first time that Rose, a veteran of five previous classics, had failed to start a Series game.

Move No. 2 for Owens came in the last of the sixth. With the Phillies leading, 2-1, and two runners on base and two out, Owens visited Carlton in the on-deck circle. The manager wanted to know whether his 300-game winner thought he had run out of gas after laboring through six innings; if so, the Phils' skipper was going to pinch-hit for Carlton and try to get more runs. Result: Baltimore veteran righthander Jim Palmer, who would win his first Series game in 12 years, struck out Carlton and the Orioles then rallied against the tiring lefthander after two were out in the seventh for two runs and the victory.

It was the omnipresent Dempsey who ignited the uprising with a double. Baltimore Manager Joe Altobelli then sent up Benny Ayala to pinch-hit. After Dempsey took third on a wild pitch, Ayala responded with a single to left, tying the score, 2-2. Owens decided he had seen enough and called on his relief ace, Holland, who tied with Chicago's Lee Smith for the National League Fireman of the Year award and had a particularly impressive N.L. Championship Series against the Dodgers.

John Shelby greeted Holland with a single, with Ayala stopping at second base. Ford followed with a hard smash at Philadelphia shortstop Ivan DeJesus, who couldn't come up with the ball and let it dribble into short left field. The misplay enabled Ayala to score the game-winning run.

Altobelli, having gotten two solid innings of relief from Palmer, summoned Sammy Stewart and Tippy Martinez from the bullpen over the last three innings and received hitless pitching from the duo to save the contest.

Rose was used as a pinch-hitter in the ninth inning and grounded out. Perez was 1-for-4.

Altobelli took center stage in Game 4 as the Orioles edged the Phillies, 5-4, to seize a 3-1 Series edge.

Light-hitting second baseman Dauer brought home Baltimore's first two runs with a bases-loaded single in the fourth. Philadelphia came back with one run off rookie starter Storm Davis in its half of the inning, with Lefebvre slamming a run-scoring double.

The Phillies then went ahead 3-2 in the fifth on a double by Bo Diaz, an RBI single by starting pitcher Denny and another two-base hit by Rose.

But it was in the sixth that Altobelli earned his keep. The Baltimore manager entered the Series record book by using four consecutive pinch-hitters after Lowenstein had singled with one out and Dauer had doubled him to third.

Altobelli went to Joe Nolan first, using the reserve catcher as a pinch-hitter for third baseman Cruz. Nolan was walked intentionally to load the bases. Singleton was then called on to bat for Dempsey. Owens shunned a relief hurler and Denny proceeded to walk Singleton on four pitches, forcing in the tying run.

Next, Altobelli sent up switch-hitter Shelby to bat for Davis, and Owens countered with Hernandez from the bullpen. Only a leaping catch at the wall by left fielder Gary Matthews deprived Shelby of a "sure" three-run double. But the go-ahead run crossed the plate nonetheless on Shelby's sacrifice fly. Reed relieved Hernandez and retired Ford, who was batting for center fielder Al Bumbry.

"Any time you use four pinch-hitters in an inning, you're going for broke," said Altobelli. "I was after the pot of gold."

Dauer provided insurance with a run-scoring single in the seventh. A pinch single by Ozzie Virgil brought home the Phils' final run in the ninth.

Winning pitcher Davis was not a part of the 1979 Orioles, but he said some of the other Baltimore players already were whispering "Remember '79" in the locker room after Game 4.

But there was no repeat of 1979. Murray saw to that with his two homers in Game 5. And Dempsey saw to it with a homer and a double in the finale. And McGregor saw to it with his five-hit gem.

The Orioles batted only .213 in winning the World Series, but they held the Phillies to a .195 average. Against Orioles pitching, the Phillies managed consecutive hits only twice in the five games.

No, there was no repeat of the Orioles' failure in 1979. And October slumps were long forgotten.

"Amazing," said Murray, "how you can turn hero in one day."

Game 1

At Baltimore October 11

Philadelphia (N.L.)	AB.	R.	H.	PO.	A.	E.
Morgan, 2b	4	1	2	1	5	0
Rose, 1b	4	0	1	11	0	0
Schmidt, 3b	4	0	0	0	1	0
Lezcano, rf	3	0	0	0	0	0
dHayes, rf	1	0	0	0	0	0
Matthews, lf	3	0	1	4	0	0
Maddox, cf	3	1	1	3	0	0
Diaz, c	3	0	0	7	0	0
DeJesus, ss	3	0	0	1	5	0
Denny, p	3	0	0	0	0	0
Holland, p	0	0	0	0	0	0
Totals	31	2	5	27	11	0

Baltimore (A.L.)	AB.	R.	H.	PO.	A.	E.
Bumbry, cf	4	0	1	4	0	0
Stewart, p	0	0	0	0	0	0
T. Martinez, p	0	0	0	0	0	0
Dwyer, rf	3	1	1	2	0	0
cFord, rf	1	0	0	0	0	0
Ripken, ss	4	0	1	1	4	0
Murray, 1b	4	0	1	8	0	0
Lowenstein, lf	3	0	1	2	0	0
eRoenicke	1	0	0	0	0	0
Dauer, 2b	3	0	0	3	1	0
Cruz, 3b	3	0	0	0	3	1
Dempsey, c	2	0	0	6	1	0
aShelby, cf	1	0	0	0	0	0
McGregor, p	2	0	0	0	0	0
bNolan, c	1	0	0	1	0	0
Totals	32	1	5	27	9	1

Philadelphia	000	001	010	—2
Baltimore	100	000	000	—1

Philadelphia	IP.	H.	R.	ER.	BB.	SO.
Denny (W)	7⅔	5	1	1	0	5
Holland (S)	1⅓	0	0	0	0	1

Baltimore	IP.	H.	R.	ER.	BB.	SO.
McGregor (L)	8	4	2	2	0	6
Stewart	⅔	1	0	0	0	1
T. Martinez	⅓	0	0	0	0	0

Base on balls—None.

Strikeouts—By Denny 5 (Lowenstein, Dauer, Cruz, Ripken, Shelby), by Holland 1 (Murray), by McGregor 6 (Rose, Maddox, DeJesus, Lezcano, Denny, Schmidt), by Stewart 1 (Schmidt).

Game-winning RBI—Maddox.

aStruck out for Dempsey in eighth. bGrounded out for McGregor in eighth. cFlied out for Dwyer in eighth. dGrounded out for Lezcano in ninth. eFlied out for Lowenstein in ninth. Runs batted in—Morgan, Maddox, Dwyer. Two-base hit—Bumbry. Home runs—Dwyer, Morgan, Maddox. Caught stealing—Morgan. Double play—Ripken, Dauer and Murray. Left on bases—Philadelphia 2, Baltimore 4. Umpires—Springstead (A.L.) plate, Vargo (N.L.) first, Clark (A.L.) second, Pulli (N.L.) third, Palermo (A.L.) left, Rennert (N.L.) right. Time—2:22. Attendance—52,204.

FIRST INNING

Philadelphia—Cruz went behind the pitcher's mound for Morgan's pop fly, but dropped it for an error. With Rose at the plate, Morgan was caught stealing, Dempsey to Dauer. Rose struck out. Schmidt lined out to Bumbry. No runs, no hits, one error, none left.

Baltimore—Bumbry flied to Maddox. Dwyer belted a 3-2 delivery over the right-field wall for a home run. Ripken bounced out to DeJesus. Murray lined a single to left. Lowenstein struck out. One run, two hits, no errors, one left.

Joe Morgan's sixth-inning blast tied Game 1 at 1-1.

SECOND INNING

Philadelphia—Lezcano lined out to Ripken. Matthews flied out to Bumbry. Maddox struck out. No runs, no hits, no errors, none left.

Baltimore—Dauer struck out. Cruz struck out. Dempsey grounded out to DeJesus. No runs, no hits, no errors, none left.

THIRD INNING

Philadelphia—Diaz grounded out to Cruz. DeJesus struck out. Denny flied to Lowenstein. No runs, no hits, no errors, none left.

Baltimore—McGregor bounced out to Morgan. Bumbry flied to Matthews. Dwyer grounded out to Morgan. No runs, no hits, no errors, none left.

FOURTH INNING

Philadelphia—Morgan singled to center for Philadelphia's first hit. Rose forced Morgan at second base, Cruz to Dauer. Schmidt flied deep to Bumbry near the warning track in center field. Lezcano struck out. No runs, one hit, no errors, one left.

Baltimore—Ripken grounded a single to right. Murray forced Ripken at second base, DeJesus to Morgan. Lowenstein flied to Matthews. With Murray running off first on pitch, Dauer bounced out, DeJesus to Rose. No runs, one hit, no errors, one left.

FIFTH INNING

Philadelphia—Matthews singled to left. Maddox hit a sharp grounder to Ripken, who turned it into a double play, Ripken to Dauer to Murray. Diaz flied to Bumbry. No runs, one hit, no errors, none left.

Baltimore—Cruz grounded out to DeJesus. Schmidt fielded Cruz's high chop behind the third-base bag and made a long throw to Rose for the out. McGregor grounded out to Morgan. No runs, no hits, no errors, none left.

SIXTH INNING

Philadelphia—DeJesus flied to Dwyer. Denny was called out on strikes. Morgan clubbed a 1-2 offering over the 376-foot sign in right field, tying the score at 1-1. Rose grounded out to Ripken. One run, one hit, no errors, none left.

Baltimore—Bumbry flied to Maddox. Dwyer hit a foul pop to Diaz. Ripken struck out on a check swing and was tagged out by Diaz. No runs, no hits, no errors, none left.

SEVENTH INNING

Philadelphia—Schmidt struck out. Ripken ranged to deep short to field Lezcano's grounder and threw him out. Matthews flied to Dwyer. No runs, no hits, no errors, none left.

Baltimore—Murray bounced to Rose, who made the play unassisted. Lowenstein singled to right. Dauer flied to Maddox. Cruz grounded out to Morgan. No runs, one hit, no errors, one left.

EIGHTH INNING

Philadelphia—Maddox blasted McGregor's first pitch into the left-field stands, giving the Phillies a 2-1 lead. Lowenstein made a leaping catch, with his glove draped over the left-field wall, to rob Diaz of a home run. DeJesus grounded out to Ripken. Denny bounced to Cruz. One run, one hit, no errors, none left.

Baltimore—Shelby batted for Dempsey and struck out. Nolan batted for McGregor and grounded out to Morgan. Bumbry doubled into the right-field corner. Holland replaced Denny on the mound for the Phillies. Ford batted for Dwyer and flied to Matthews. No runs, one hit, no errors, one left.

NINTH INNING

Philadelphia—Shelby remained in the game and played center field, Nolan stayed in as the catcher, Ford went into right field and Stewart came in to pitch for the Orioles. Morgan popped out to Murray. Rose singled to right. Schmidt struck out. When Hayes was announced as the pinch-hitter for Lezcano, Baltimore Manager Altobelli brought in Tippy Martinez to pitch. Hayes grounded out to Murray unassisted. No runs, one hit, no errors, one left.

Baltimore—Hayes remained in the game and played right field for the Phillies. Ripken popped out to DeJesus. Murray struck out. Roenicke, batting for Lowenstein, flied out to Matthews in front of the warning track. No runs, no hits, no errors, none left.

Dan Ford was dazed by a Willie Hernandez fastball to the head in Game 2.

Game 2

At Baltimore October 12

Philadelphia (N.L.)	AB.	R.	H.	PO.	A.	E.
Morgan, 2b	4	1	1	1	1	0
Rose, 1b	4	0	0	7	1	0
Schmidt, 3b	4	0	0	0	3	0
Lefebvre, rf	2	0	0	1	0	0
Matthews, lf	3	0	1	2	0	0
G. Gross, cf	3	0	0	5	0	0
Diaz, c	3	0	1	5	1	0
cSamuel	0	0	0	0	0	0
Virgil, c	0	0	0	1	0	0
DeJesus, ss	3	0	0	1	1	0
Hudson, p	1	0	0	0	0	0
Hernandez, p	0	0	0	0	0	0
bHayes	1	0	0	0	0	0
Andersen, p	0	0	0	1	0	0
dPerez	1	0	0	0	0	0
Reed, p	0	0	0	0	0	0
Totals	29	1	3	24	7	0

Baltimore (A.L.)	AB.	R.	H.	PO.	A.	E.
Bumbry, cf	2	0	0	2	0	0
aShelby, cf	2	1	1	1	0	0
Ford, rf	3	0	1	1	0	0
Ripken, ss	3	0	1	1	6	0
Murray, 1b	4	0	0	13	1	1
Lowenstein, lf	4	1	3	0	0	0
eLandrum, lf	0	0	0	0	0	0
Dauer, 2b	4	1	1	2	2	0
Cruz, 3b	4	1	1	0	3	0
Dempsey, c	3	0	1	6	1	0
Boddicker, p	3	0	0	1	2	0
Totals	32	4	9	27	15	1

Philadelphia	000	100	000—1
Baltimore	000	030	10x—4

Philadelphia	IP.	H.	R.	ER.	BB.	SO.
Hudson (L)	4⅓	5	3	3	0	3
Hernandez	⅔	0	0	0	1	1
Andersen	2	3	1	1	0	1
Reed	1	1	0	0	1	1

Baltimore	IP.	H.	R.	ER.	BB.	SO.
Boddicker (W)	9	3	1	0	0	6

Bases on balls—Off Hernandez 1 (Ripken), off Reed 1 (Dempsey).

Strikeouts—By Hudson 3 (Boddicker, Bumbry, Ford), by Hernandez 1 (Shelby), by Andersen 1 (Dempsey), by Reed 1 (Dauer), by Boddicker 6 (Morgan, Rose, Schmidt, Lefebvre, Diaz, Hayes).

Game-winning RBI—Dempsey.

aCalled out on strikes for Bumbry in fifth. bStruck out for Hernandez in sixth. cRan for Diaz in eighth. dGrounded into double play for Andersen in eighth. eRan for Lowenstein in eighth. Runs batted in—Lefebvre, Ripken, Lowenstein, Dempsey, Boddicker. Two-base hits—Lowenstein, Dempsey. Home run—Lowenstein. Stolen bases—Morgan, Landrum. Sacrifice flies—Lefebvre, Boddicker. Hit by pitcher—By Hernandez (Ford). Double play—Dauer, Ripken and Murray. Left on bases—Philadelphia 2, Baltimore 8. Umpires—Vargo (N.L.) plate, Clark (A.L.) first, Pulli (N.L.) second, Palermo (A.L.) third, Rennert (N.L.) left, Springstead (A.L.) right. Time—2:27. Attendance—52,132.

FIRST INNING

Philadelphia—Morgan struck out. Rose was called out on strikes. Schmidt grounded out to Ripken. No runs, no hits, no errors, none left.

Baltimore—Diaz fielded Bumbry's tap in front of the plate and threw to Rose for the out. Ford grounded out to Schmidt. Ripken flied to Lefebvre. No runs, no hits, no errors, none left.

SECOND INNING

Philadelphia—Lefebvre struck out. Matthews grounded out to Cruz. Gross grounded out to Dauer. No runs, no hits, no errors, none left.

Baltimore—Murray filed to Gross. Lowenstein drilled a double into the gap in right-center field. Dauer flied to Matthews, Lowenstein taking third after the catch. Cruz flied to Gross. No runs, one hit, no errors, one left.

THIRD INNING

Philadelphia—Diaz popped out to Murray. DeJesus grounded out to Ripken. Hudson hit dribbler in front of the plate and was thrown out, Boddicker to Murray. No runs, no hits, no errors, none left.

Baltimore—Dempsey popped out to Morgan. Boddicker was called out on strikes. Bumbry also was called out on strikes. No runs, no hits, no errors, none left.

FOURTH INNING

Philadelphia—Morgan reached first base with infield hit when Ripken failed to come up with his grounder in the hole and made no throw. With Rose at the plate, Morgan stole second. Rose bunted, but Morgan had to hold at second when Dempsey charged from behind the plate to field the ball and threw to Murray at first to retire Rose. With Morgan running on pitch, Schmidt hit grounder to Ripken, whose throw to first was dropped by Murray, Morgan stopping at third and Schmidt safe at first on the error. Lefebvre lofted fly ball to Bumbry, Morgan scoring and Schmidt taking second after the catch. Matthews flied to Bumbry. One run, one hit, one error, one left.

Baltimore—Ford struck out. Ripken flied to Gross. Murray grounded out to Schmidt. No runs, no hits, no errors, none left.

FIFTH INNING

Philadelphia—Gross bounced out to Ripken. Diaz was called out on strikes. DeJesus grounded out, Murray to Boddicker. No runs, no hits, no errors, none left.

Baltimore—Lowenstein jumped on a 2-0 delivery and clouted it over the center-field fence for a home run, tying the score at 1-1. Dauer singled to left. Cruz received credit for a hit when he legged out a bunt down the third-base line which Schmidt fielded but had no one to throw to at first base because Morgan was late covering; Dauer stopped at second. Dempsey doubled into the right-field corner, Dauer scoring and Cruz stopping at third. Boddicker lined out to Matthews, Cruz scoring after the catch and Dempsey holding at second. Willie Hernandez replaced Hudson for the Phillies. Shelby batted for Bumbry and was called out on strikes. Ford was hit on the head by a Hernandez delivery. Ford remained in the game and went to first base. Ripken walked, loading the bases. Murray flied to Gross. Three runs, four hits, no errors, three left.

SIXTH INNING

Philadelphia—Shelby remained in the game and played center field for the Orioles. Hayes batted for Hernandez and struck out. Morgan bounced out, Murray unassisted. Rose grounded out to Cruz. No runs, no hits, no errors, none left.

Baltimore—Andersen became the Phillies' third pitcher. Lowenstein grounded out, Rose to Andersen. Dauer lined out to DeJesus. Cruz grounded out to Schmidt. No runs, no hits, no errors, none left.

SEVENTH INNING

Philadelphia—Schmidt flied to Ford. Lefebvre grounded out, Murray unassisted. Matthews singled to right. Gross forced Matthews, Cruz to Dauer. No runs, one hit, no errors, one left.

Baltimore—Dempsey struck out. Boddicker grounded out to DeJesus. Shelby beat out grounder to Morgan for a single. Ford singled to right, Shelby advancing to third. Ripken also singled to right, Shelby scoring and Ford advancing to third. Murray grounded out to Morgan. One run, three hits, no errors, two left.

EIGHTH INNING

Philadelphia—Diaz singled to right. Samuel ran for Diaz. DeJesus forced Samuel at second base, Ripken to Dauer. Perez, batting for Andersen, hit into a double play, Dauer to Ripken to Murray. No runs, one hit, no errors, none left.

Baltimore—Virgil came in to catch and Reed took over on the mound for the Phillies. Lowenstein singled to left. Landrum ran for Lowenstein. Dauer, attempting to sacrifice, bunted foul on third strike. With Cruz at the plate, Landrum stole second. Cruz fouled out to Rose, Landrum holding at second. Dempsey was issued an intentional walk. Boddicker flied to Gross. No runs, one hit, no errors, two left.

NINTH INNING

Philadelphia—Landrum remained in the game and played right field for the Orioles. Morgan flied out to Shelby near the warning track in center field. Rose bounced out, Boddicker to Murray. Schmidt struck out. No runs, no hits, no errors, none left.

Game 3

At Philadelphia
October 14

Baltimore (A.L.)	AB.	R.	H.	PO.	A.	E.
Shelby, cf	4	0	2	5	0	0
Ford, rf	3	1	1	1	1	0
Ripken, ss	3	0	0	1	3	0
Murray, 1b	4	0	0	10	0	0
Roenicke, lf	4	0	0	1	1	0
Dauer, 2b	4	0	0	4	2	0
Cruz, 3b	3	0	0	0	4	1
Dempsey, c	4	1	2	5	2	0
Flanagan, p	1	0	0	0	0	0
aSingleton	1	0	0	0	0	0
Palmer, p	0	0	0	0	0	0
bAyala	1	1	1	0	0	0
Stewart, p	1	0	0	0	0	0
T. Martinez, p	0	0	0	0	0	0
Totals	33	3	6	27	13	1

Philadelphia (N.L.)	AB.	R.	H.	PO.	A.	E.
Morgan, 2b	3	1	1	5	2	0
Lezcano, rf	4	0	1	1	0	0
Hayes, rf	0	0	0	1	0	0
Schmidt, 3b	4	0	0	0	4	1
Matthews, lf	3	1	1	0	0	0
Perez, 1b	4	0	1	8	0	0
Maddox, cf	4	0	0	1	0	0
Diaz, c	3	0	2	11	0	0
cLefebvre	0	0	0	0	0	0
dRose	1	0	0	0	0	0
DeJesus, ss	3	0	2	0	5	1
Carlton, p	3	0	0	0	0	0
Holland, p	0	0	0	0	0	0
eVirgil	1	0	0	0	0	0
Totals	33	2	8	27	11	2

Baltimore	000	001	200—3
Philadelphia	011	000	000—2

Baltimore	IP.	H.	R.	ER.	BB.	SO.
Flanagan	4	6	2	2	1	1
Palmer (W)	2	2	0	0	1	1
Stewart	2	0	0	0	1	3
T. Martinez (S)	1	0	0	0	0	0

Philadelphia	IP.	H.	R.	ER.	BB.	SO.
Carlton (L)	6⅔	5	3	2	3	7
Holland	2⅓	1	0	0	0	4

Bases on balls—Off Flanagan 1 (Matthews), off Palmer 1 (DeJesus), off Stewart 1 (Morgan), off Carlton 3 (Cruz, Ford, Ripken).

Strikeouts—By Flanagan 1 (Maddox), by Palmer 1 (Carlton), by Stewart 3 (Lezcano, Schmidt, Matthews), by Carlton 7 (Shelby 2, Ripken, Murray 2, Flanagan, Singleton), by Holland 4 (Roenicke, Dauer, Dempsey, Stewart).

Game-winning RBI—None.

aCalled out on strikes for Flanagan in fifth. bSingled home one run for Palmer in seventh. cAnnounced as pinch-hitter for Diaz in ninth. dGrounded out for Lefebvre in ninth. eGrounded out for Holland in ninth. Runs batted in—Ford, Ayala, Morgan, Matthews. Two-bases hits—Dempsey 2. Home runs—Matthews, Morgan, Ford. Caught stealing—Morgan. Wild pitches—Palmer, Carlton. Double plays—DeJesus, Morgan and Perez; Schmidt, Morgan and Perez. Left on bases—Baltimore 6, Philadelphia 7. Umpires—Clark (A.L.) plate, Pulli (N.L.) first, Palermo (A.L.) second, Rennert (N.L.) third, Springstead (A.L.) left, Vargo (N.L.) right. Time—2:35. Attendance—65,792.

FIRST INNING

Baltimore—Shelby was called out on strikes. Ford grounded out to DeJesus. Ripken struck out. No runs, no hits, no errors, none left.

Jim Palmer made a rare relief appearance to pick up the win in Game 3.

Philadelphia—Morgan grounded out to Dauer. Lezcano bounced out to Ripken. Schmidt flied to Shelby. No runs, no hits, no errors, none left.

SECOND INNING

Baltimore—Murray struck out. Roenicke grounded out to DeJesus. Dauer also grounded out to DeJesus. No runs, no hits, no errors, none left.

Philadelphia—Matthews homered over the fence in left-center field. Perez singled to center. Maddox flied to Shelby. Diaz also flied to Shelby. DeJesus singled to right; Perez was safe at third and DeJesus advanced to second when Cruz couldn't hold Ford's throw to third base, with Cruz drawing an error on the play. Carlton grounded out, Murray unassisted. One run, three hits, one error, two left.

THIRD INNING

Baltimore—Cruz walked. Dempsey hit into a double play, DeJesus making a backhanded stop in the hole and throwing to Morgan, who relayed to Perez. Flanagan was called out on strikes. No runs, no hits, no errors, none left.

Philadelphia—Morgan belted a 2-1 pitch over the right-field wall for a 2-0 Phillies lead. Lezcano flied to Ford. Schmidt grounded out to Cruz. Matthews walked. Perez flied to Roenicke. One run, one hit, no errors, one left.

FOURTH INNING

Baltimore—Shelby singled to center for the Orioles' first hit. Ford walked. Carlton also walked Ripken, loading the bases. Murray popped out to Morgan. Roenicke grounded into a double play, Schmidt to Morgan to Perez. No runs, one hit, no errors, two left.

Philadelphia—Maddox struck out, but had to be retired Dempsey to Murray when the third strike briefly got away from Dempsey. Diaz singled to left, but was thrown out at second, Roenicke to Dauer, in attempt to stretch the hit into a double. DeJesus was credited with an infield hit when Dauer failed to come up with his bad-hop grounder at second. Carlton bounced out to Dauer. No runs, two hits, no errors, one left.

FIFTH INNING

Baltimore—Dauer grounded out to Schmidt. Cruz also was thrown out by Schmidt, who stabbed a bad-hop grounder and threw to Perez. Dempsey doubled into the left-field corner. Singleton batted for Flanagan and was called out on strikes. No runs, one hit, no errors, one left.

Philadelphia—Palmer came in to pitch for the Orioles. Morgan popped out to Dauer. Lezcano singled to center. Schmidt fouled out to Dempsey. Matthews forced Lezcano at second, Cruz to Dauer. No runs, one hit, no errors, one left.

SIXTH INNING

Baltimore—Shelby struck out. Ford hit Carlton's first pitch over the left-field wall for a home run, cutting the Phillies' lead to 2-1. Ripken grounded to Schmidt, who threw into the dirt at first base for an error. Murray struck out. Roenicke forced Ripken at second, DeJesus to Morgan. One run, one hit, one error, one left.

Philadelphia—Perez flied to Shelby. Maddox grounded out to Ripken. Diaz was credited with an infield hit when Ripken couldn't come up with his high chopper behind the pitcher's mound. Diaz went to second on Palmer's wild pitch. DeJesus walked. After meeting with Phillies Manager Owens in the on-deck circle, Carlton remained in the game to bat for himself. Carlton struck out. No runs, one hit, no errors, two left.

SEVENTH INNING

Baltimore—Dauer flied to Lezcano. Cruz grounded out to Schmidt. Dempsey doubled to the wall in left-center field. Ayala came to the plate as a pinch-hitter for Palmer. Dempsey advanced to third on Carlton's wild pitch. Ayala smacked a single past a diving Schmidt, Dempsey scoring to tie the game, 2-2. Holland replaced Carlton for the Phillies. Shelby singled to left, Ayala stopping at second. Ford grounded to DeJesus, who booted the ball. When the ball rolled into short left field, Ayala scored to give the Orioles a 3-2 lead. Ripken flied to Maddox. Two runs, three hits, one error, two left.

Philadelphia—Stewart became the Orioles' third pitcher. Morgan walked. Lezcano was called out on strikes. With Schmidt at the plate, Morgan was caught stealing, Dempsey to Dauer. Schmidt struck out. No runs, no hits, no errors, none left.

EIGHTH INNING

Baltimore—Hayes went in to play right field for the Phillies. Murray flied to Hayes. Roenicke struck out. Dauer also struck out. No runs, no hits, no errors, none left.

Philadelphia—Matthews became Stewart's third straight strikeout victim. Perez popped out to Ripken. Maddox grounded out to Cruz. No runs, no hits, no errors, none left.

NINTH INNING

Baltimore—Cruz popped out to Morgan. Dempsey was called out on strikes. Stewart struck out. No runs, no hits, no errors, none left.

Philadelphia—When Lefebvre was announced as a pinch-hitter for Diaz, Baltimore Manager Altobelli brought in Tippy Martinez to replace Stewart. Philadelphia Manager Owens countered with Rose as a pinch-hitter for Lefebvre. Rose grounded out to Cruz. DeJesus flied to Shelby. Virgil batted for Holland and grounded out to Ripken. No runs, no hits, no errors, none left.

Game 4

At Philadelphia
October 15

Baltimore (A.L.)	AB.	R.	H.	PO.	A.	E.
Bumbry, cf	3	0	0	3	0	0
eFord	1	0	0	0	0	0
Stewart, p	1	0	0	0	0	0
T. Martinez, p	0	0	0	0	0	0
Dwyer, rf	5	2	2	0	0	0
Landrum, rf	0	0	0	0	0	0
Ripken, ss	5	1	1	0	1	0
Murray, 1b	4	0	1	9	0	0
Lowenstein, lf	4	1	1	2	0	1
Dauer, 2b-3b	4	1	3	3	2	0
Cruz, 3b	2	0	1	0	1	0
aNolan, c	1	0	0	2	0	0
Dempsey, c	1	0	0	3	0	0
bSingleton	0	0	0	0	0	0
cSakata, 2b	1	0	0	2	2	0
Davis, p	2	0	0	0	1	0
dShelby, cf	1	0	1	3	0	0
Totals	35	5	10	27	7	1

Philadelphia (N.L.)	AB.	R.	H.	PO.	A.	E.
Morgan, 2b	5	0	0	1	1	0
Rose, 1b	3	1	2	5	3	0
Schmidt, 3b	4	0	1	0	0	0
Lefebvre, rf	3	0	1	2	0	0
gPerez	1	0	1	0	0	0
hSamuel	0	0	0	0	0	0
Lezcano, rf	0	0	0	1	0	0
Matthews, lf	3	0	1	3	0	0
G. Gross, cf	3	0	0	3	0	0
iMaddox	1	0	0	0	0	0
Diaz, c	4	1	2	7	0	0
jDernier	0	1	0	0	0	0
DeJesus, ss	4	0	0	2	1	0
Denny, p	2	1	1	3	1	0
Hernandez, p	0	0	0	0	0	0
Reed, p	0	0	0	0	0	0
fHayes	1	0	0	0	0	0
Andersen, p	0	0	0	0	1	0
kVirgil	1	0	1	0	0	0
Totals	35	4	10	27	7	0

Baltimore	0 0 0	2 0 2	1 0 0	—5
Philadelphia	0 0 0	1 2 0	0 0 1	—4

Baltimore	IP.	H.	R.	ER.	BB.	SO.
Davis (W)	5	6	3	3	1	3
Stewart	2⅓	1	0	0	1	2
T. Martinez (S)	1⅔	3	1	1	0	0

Philadelphia	IP.	H.	R.	ER.	BB.	SO.
Denny (L)	5⅓	7	4	4	3	4
Hernandez	⅓	0	0	0	0	0
Reed	1⅓	2	1	1	1	3
Andersen	2	1	0	0	0	0

Bases on balls—Off Davis 1 (Matthews), off Stewart 1 (Rose), off Denny 3 (Dempsey, Nolan, Singleton), off Reed 1 (Murray).

Strikeouts—By Davis 3 (Morgan, Rose, Schmidt), by Stewart 2 (Diaz, DeJesus), by Denny 4 (Davis 2, Lowenstein, Cruz), by Reed 3 (Ford, Ripken, Lowenstein).

Game-winning RBI—Shelby.

aWalked intentionally for Cruz in sixth. bWalked, forcing in one run, for Dempsey in sixth. cRan for Singleton in sixth. dHit sacrifice fly for Davis in sixth. eStruck out for Bumbry in sixth. fGrounded out for Reed in seventh. gSingled for Lefebvre in eighth. hRan for Perez in eighth. iGrounded out for G. Gross in ninth. jRan for Diaz in ninth and scored. kSingled home one run for Andersen in ninth. Runs batted in—Dauer 3, Singleton, Shelby, Rose, Lefebvre, Denny, Virgil. Two-base hits—Lefebvre, Diaz, Rose, Dauer, Dwyer. Sacrifice fly—Shelby. Wild pitch—Davis. Balk—Stewart. Double plays—Dauer and Murray; Ripken, Sakata and Murray; Andersen, DeJesus and Morgan. Left on bases—Baltimore 8, Philadelphia 6. Umpires—Pulli (N.L.) plate, Palermo (A.L.), first, Rennert (N.L.) second, Springstead (A.L.) third, Vargo (N.L.) left, Clark (A.L.) right. Time—2:50. Attendance—66,947.

FIRST INNING

Baltimore—Bumbry grounded out, Rose backhanding the ball between first and second and flipping to Denny covering first. Dwyer grounded out to Morgan. Ripken flied to Matthews at the base of the left-field wall. No runs, no hits, no errors, none left.

Philadelphia—Morgan struck out. Rose also struck out. Schmidt was called out on strikes. No runs, no hits, no errors, none left.

SECOND INNING

Baltimore—Murray flied to Lefebvre. Lowenstein lined to Gross. Denny speared Dauer's grounder and threw to Rose for the out. No runs, no hits, no errors, none left.

Philadelphia—Lefebvre flied to Bumbry. Matthews bounced out to Cruz. Gross rapped sharply back to the mound and was retired, Davis to Murray. No runs, no hits, no errors, none left.

THIRD INNING

Baltimore—Cruz hit a bouncer up the middle and beat DeJesus' throw to first for a single. Dempsey flied to Gross. Davis struck out attempting to bunt. Bumbry lined to Matthews. No runs, one hit, no errors, one left.

Philadelphia—Diaz popped out to Dauer. DeJesus lined to Bumbry, who made a fine running catch in right-center field. Denny lined to Lowenstein on the warning track. No runs, no hits, no errors, none left.

FOURTH INNING

Baltimore—Dwyer singled to right. Ripken singled to left, Dwyer stopping at second base. Murray singled to right, loading the bases. Lowenstein struck out. Dauer singled to right, Dwyer and Ripken scoring and Murray advancing to third. Cruz struck out. Dempsey was walked intentionally, loading the bases for the second time in the inning. Davis was called out on strikes. Two runs, four hits, no errors, three left.

Philadelphia—Morgan flied to Bumbry. Rose singled to center, becoming the first Philadelphia baserunner in the game. Schmidt blooped a broken-bat single into left-center field, Rose advancing to third on the play. Lefebvre doubled into the right-field corner, Rose scoring and Schmidt advancing to third to cut the Baltimore lead to 2-1. Matthews walked, loading the bases. Gross bounced into a double play, Dauer stepping on second base and relaying to Murray. One run, three hits, no errors, two left.

FIFTH INNING

Baltimore—For the second time in the game, Rose ranged to his right to backhand grounder by Bumbry and threw to Denny covering first for the out. Rose also handled grounder by Dwyer and threw to Denny covering first. Ripken popped out to Rose. No runs, no hits, no errors, none left.

Philadelphia—Diaz doubled down the left-field line. DeJesus lined out to Murray. With Denny at the plate, Davis uncorked a wild pitch, Diaz advancing to third. Denny helped himself with a single to left, scoring Diaz; Denny went to second when Lowenstein's throw hit Diaz and rolled away for an error on the throw. Morgan grounded out, Murray unassisted, with Denny advancing to third on the play. Rose doubled to left-center field. Denny scoring to give the Phillies a 3-2 lead. Schmidt flied to Lowenstein, who made a fine running catch in left-center field. Two runs, three hits, one error, one left.

SIXTH INNING

Baltimore—Murray flied to Gross. Lowenstein singled to center. Dauer doubled down the left-field line, Lowenstein advancing to third. Nolan batted for Cruz and was walked intentionally, loading the bases. Singleton batted for Dempsey and coaxed a walk, forcing home Lowenstein and leaving the bases loaded. Sakata ran for Singleton. Shelby was announced as a pinch-hitter for Davis. Hernandez then replaced Denny on the mound for the Phillies. Shelby flied to Matthews, who made a superb leaping catch against the wall, Dauer scoring after the catch to give the Orioles a 4-3 lead. Nolan held at second and Sakata at first. Ford was announced as a pinch-hitter for Bumbry and Philadelphia Manager Owens decided to make another pitching change, bringing in Reed to replace Hernandez. Ford struck out. Two runs, two hits, no errors, two left.

Philadelphia—Nolan remained in the game as catcher, Sakata went to second base, Shelby to center field, Dauer to third base and Stewart came on to pitch for the Orioles. Lefebvre flied to Shelby. Matthews singled to center. Gross lined to Shelby. With Diaz at the plate, Stewart committed a balk, Matthews advancing to second. Diaz was called out on strikes. No runs, one hit, no errors, one left.

SEVENTH INNING

Baltimore—Dwyer doubled to the gap in left-center field. Ripken was called out on strikes. Murray walked. Lowenstein struck out. Dauer singled to center, Dwyer scoring and Murray stopping at second. Nolan popped out to DeJesus, who made an over-the-shoulder catch while running into short left field. One run, two hits, no errors, two left.

Philadelphia—DeJesus struck out. Hayes batted for Reed and grounded out, Murray unassisted. Morgan flied to Shelby. No runs, no hits, no errors, none left.

EIGHTH INNING

Baltimore—Andersen was called on as the Phillies' fourth pitcher of the game. Sakata flied to Lefebvre. Shelby singled to right. Stewart, attempting to sacrifice, bunted into a double play, Andersen to DeJesus to Rose. No runs, one hit, no errors, none left.

Philadelphia—Rose walked on four pitches. Schmidt fouled out to Dauer. Tippy Martinez was brought into the game to replace Stewart for the Orioles. Perez batted for Lefebvre and singled to center, Rose stopping at second. Samuel ran for Perez. Matthews grounded into a double play, Ripken to Sakata to Murray. No runs, one hit, no errors, one left.

NINTH INNING

Baltimore—Lezcano went in to play right field for the Phillies. Dwyer grounded out, Rose unassisted. Ripken lined to Lezcano. Murray grounded out, Rose unassisted. No runs, no hits, no errors, none left.

Philadelphia—Maddox batted for Gross and grounded out to Sakata. Diaz singled to right. Dernier ran for Diaz. DeJesus grounded out to Dauer, Dernier taking second on the play. Virgil batted for Andersen and singled to center, Dernier scoring. Morgan lined to Sakata. One run, two hits, no errors, one left.

Game 5

At Philadelphia
October 16

Baltimore (A.L.)	AB.	R.	H.	PO.	A.	E.
Bumbry, cf	2	0	0	3	0	0
cShelby, cf	1	0	0	1	0	0
Ford, rf	4	0	0	3	0	0
Landrum, rf	0	0	0	1	0	0
Ripken, ss	3	1	0	3	0	0
Murray, 1b	4	2	3	6	0	0
Lowenstein, lf	2	0	0	0	0	0
bRoenicke, lf	2	0	0	1	0	0
Dauer, 2b	4	0	0	2	1	0
Cruz, 3b	4	0	0	0	6	0
Dempsey, c	3	2	2	7	0	0
McGregor, p	3	0	0	0	0	0
Totals	32	5	5	27	7	0

Philadelphia (N.L.)	AB.	R.	H.	PO.	A.	E.
Morgan, 2b	3	0	1	0	1	0
Rose, rf	4	0	2	3	0	0
Schmidt, 3b	4	0	0	1	2	0
Matthews, lf	4	0	0	6	0	0
Perez, 1b	4	0	0	5	1	0
Maddox, cf	4	0	2	3	0	0
Diaz, c	2	0	0	7	0	1
DeJesus, ss	3	0	0	1	2	0
Hudson, p	1	0	0	0	0	0
Bystrom, p	0	0	0	0	0	0
aSamuel	1	0	0	0	0	0
Hernandez, p	0	0	0	1	0	0
dLezcano	1	0	0	0	0	0
Reed, p	0	0	0	0	0	0
Totals	31	0	5	27	6	1

Baltimore	0 1 1	2 1 0	0 0 0—5
Philadelphia	0 0 0	0 0 0	0 0 0—0

Baltimore	IP.	H.	R.	ER.	BB.	SO.
McGregor (W)	9	5	0	0	2	6

Philadelphia	IP.	H.	R.	ER.	BB.	SO.
Hudson (L)	4*	4	5	5	1	3
Bystrom	1	0	0	0	0	1
Hernandez	3	0	0	0	0	3
Reed	1	1	0	0	0	0

*Pitched to one batter in fifth.

Bases on balls—Off McGregor 2 (Morgan, Diaz), off Hudson 1 (Ripken).

Strikeouts—By McGregor 6 (Morgan, Perez 2, Hudson, Matthews, Schmidt), by Hudson 3 (Ford 2, Cruz), by Bystrom 1 (Ripken), by Hernandez 3 (Murray, Roenicke, Ford).

Game-winning RBI—Murray.

aFlied out for Bystrom in fifth. bStruck out for Lowenstein in sixth. cFlied out for Bumbry in eighth. dGrounded out for Hernandez in eighth. Runs batted in—Bumbry, Murray 3, Dempsey. Two-base hits—Dempsey, Maddox. Three-base hit—Morgan. Home runs—Murray 2, Dempsey. Sacrifice fly—Bumbry. Wild pitch—Bystrom. Double play—Cruz, Dauer and Murray. Left on bases—Baltimore 2, Philadelphia 6. Umpires—Palermo (A.L.) plate, Rennert (N.L.) first, Springstead (A.L.) second, Vargo (N.L.) third, Clark (A.L.) left, Pulli (N.L.) right. Time—2:21. Attendance—67,064.

FIRST INNING

Baltimore—Bumbry lined to DeJesus. Ford struck out. Ripken lined to Matthews, who made a lunging backhanded catch at the left-field line. No runs, no hits, none left.

Philadelphia—Morgan struck out. Rose lined a single to center. Schmidt flied to Ford. Matthews also flied to Ford. No runs, one hit, no errors, one left.

Rick Dempsey connects for a homer off Charles Hudson in Game 5.

SECOND INNING

Baltimore—Murray blasted a 2-2 delivery over the right-field wall for a home run. Lowenstein flied to Rose on the warning track. Dauer popped to Maddox in short center field. Cruz struck out. One run, one hit, no errors, none left.

Philadelphia—Perez struck out. Maddox flied to Bumbry. Diaz fouled out to Murray. No runs, no hits, no errors, none left.

THIRD INNING

Baltimore—Dempsey belted a 1-0 pitch over the wall in left-center field for a home run and a 2-0 Orioles lead. McGregor lined out to Rose. Bumbry grounded out to DeJesus. Ford struck out. One run, one hit, no errors, none left.

Philadelphia—DeJesus flied to Ford. Hudson struck out. Morgan walked. Rose popped out to Ripken. No runs, no hits, no errors, one left.

FOURTH INNING

Baltimore—Ripken walked. Murray hit a 0-1 pitch far into the stands in right-center field for a home run, giving the Orioles a 4-0 lead. Lowenstein popped out to Schmidt. Dauer lined to Matthews. Cruz flied to Matthews. Two runs, one hit, no errors, none left.

Philadelphia—Schmidt grounded out to Cruz. Matthews struck out, but had to be tagged by Dempsey. Perez flied to Bumbry. No runs, no hits, no errors, none left.

FIFTH INNING

Baltimore—Dempsey doubled off the wall in left-center, giving him a Series-record five extra-base hits in a five-game Series; Dempsey's four doubles tied a five-game record set by Eddie Collins for Philadelphia A's in 1910. Bystrom replaced Hudson on the mound for the Phillies. McGregor bunted and reached first base safely when Diaz dropped the ball for an error, Dempsey holding second on the play. With Bumbry at the plate, Bystrom fired a wild pitch, Dempsey advancing to third and McGregor to second. Bumbry flied to Matthews, Dempsey scoring after the catch for a 5-0 Baltimore lead. Ford grounded out to DeJesus, McGregor holding second. Ripken was called out on strikes. One run, one hit, one error, one left.

Philadelphia—Maddox singled to right-center. Diaz walked on four pitches. DeJesus rapped into a double play, Cruz taking his smash on one hop and throwing to Dauer, who relayed to Murray; Maddox advanced to third. Samuel batted for Bystrom and flied to Bumbry. No runs, one hit, no errors, one left.

SIXTH INNING

Baltimore—Hernandez came in to pitch for Philadelphia. Murray struck out. Roenicke batted for Lowenstein and struck out. Dauer grounded out, Perez to Hernandez covering first base. No runs, no hits, no errors, none left.

Philadelphia—Roenicke stayed in the game and played left field. Morgan popped out to Ripken. Rose singled to right. Schmidt struck out. Matthews forced Rose, Cruz to Dauer. No runs, one hit, no errors, one left.

SEVENTH INNING

Baltimore—Schmidt charged in from his third-base position, barehanded Cruz's chopper and threw to Perez for the putout. Dempsey flied to Matthews. McGregor bounced out to Morgan. No runs, no hits, no errors, none left.

Philadelphia—Perez was called out on strikes. Maddox doubled off the wall in left-center field. Diaz fouled out to Dempsey. DeJesus grounded out to Cruz. No runs, one hit, no errors, one left.

EIGHTH INNING

Baltimore—Shelby, batting for Bumbry, flied to Maddox in short left-center. Ford struck out. Ripken lined to Rose. No runs, no hits, no errors, none left.

Philadelphia—Shelby remained in the game and played center field and Landrum went in to play right field. Lezcano batted for Hernandez and grounded out to Cruz. Morgan tripled down the right-field line. Rose flied to Roenicke, with Morgan tagging after the catch, but McGregor's shutout remained intact when Morgan fell down when he broke for the plate and had to return to third base. Cruz backhanded Schmidt's smash down the third-base line and threw to Murray for the out. No runs, one hit, no errors, one left.

NINTH INNING

Baltimore—Reed came in to pitch for the Phillies. Murray singled to right. Roenicke flied to Maddox, who backed up against the wall to make the catch. Dauer flied to Matthews. Cruz grounded out to Schmidt. No runs, one hit, no errors, one left.

Philadelphia—Matthews flied to Landrum, who caught the ball in the right-field corner after a long run. Perez flied to Shelby. Maddox lined to Ripken. No runs, no hits, no errors, none left.

BALTIMORE ORIOLES' BATTING AND FIELDING AVERAGES

Player—Position	G.	AB.	R.	H.	TB.	2B.	3B.	HR.	RBI.	BB.	IBB.	SO.	B.A.	PO.	A.	E.	F.A.
Ayala, ph	1	1	1	1	1	0	0	0	1	0	0	0	1.000	0	0	0	.000
Shelby, ph-cf	5	9	1	4	4	0	0	0	1	0	0	4	.444	10	0	0	1.000
Dempsey, c	5	13	3	5	12	4	0	1	2	2	2	2	.385	27	4	0	1.000
Lowenstein, lf	4	13	2	5	9	1	0	1	1	0	0	3	.385	4	0	1	.800
Dwyer, rf	2	8	3	3	7	1	0	1	1	0	0	0	.375	2	0	0	1.000
Murray, 1b	5	20	2	5	11	0	0	2	3	1	0	4	.250	46	1	1	.979
Dauer, 2b-3b	5	19	2	4	5	1	0	0	3	0	0	3	.211	14	8	0	1.000
Ripken, ss	5	18	2	3	3	0	0	0	1	3	0	4	.167	6	14	0	1.000
Ford, ph-rf	5	12	1	2	5	0	0	1	1	1	0	5	.167	5	1	0	1.000
Cruz, 3b	5	16	1	2	2	0	0	0	0	1	0	3	.125	0	17	2	.895
Bumbry, cf	4	11	0	1	2	1	0	0	1	0	0	1	.091	12	0	0	1.000
Landrum, pr-lf-rf	3	0	0	0	0	0	0	0	0	0	0	0	.000	1	0	0	1.000
T. Martinez, p	3	0	0	0	0	0	0	0	0	0	0	0	.000	0	0	0	.000
Palmer, p	1	0	0	0	0	0	0	0	0	0	0	0	.000	0	0	0	.000
Flanagan, p	1	1	0	0	0	0	0	0	0	0	0	1	.000	0	0	0	.000
Sakata, pr-2b	1	1	0	0	0	0	0	0	0	0	0	0	.000	2	2	0	1.000
Singleton, ph	2	1	0	0	0	0	0	0	1	1	0	1	.000	0	0	0	.000
Davis, p	1	2	0	0	0	0	0	0	0	0	0	2	.000	0	1	0	1.000
Nolan, ph-c	2	2	0	0	0	0	0	0	0	1	1	0	.000	3	0	0	1.000
Stewart, p	3	2	0	0	0	0	0	0	0	0	0	1	.000	0	0	0	.000
Boddicker, p	1	3	0	0	0	0	0	0	1	0	0	1	.000	1	2	0	1.000
McGregor, p	2	5	0	0	0	0	0	0	0	0	0	0	.000	0	0	0	.000
Roenicke, ph-lf	3	7	0	0	0	0	0	0	0	0	0	2	.000	2	1	0	1.000
Totals	5	164	18	35	61	8	0	6	17	10	3	37	.213	135	51	4	.979

Ayala—Singled home one run for Palmer in seventh inning of third game.

Ford—Flied out for Dwyer in eighth inning of first game; struck out for Bumbry in sixth inning of fourth game.

Landrum—Ran for Lowenstein in eighth inning of second game.

Nolan—Grounded out for McGregor in eighth inning of first game; walked intentionally for Cruz in sixth inning of fourth game.

Roenicke—Flied out for Lowenstein in ninth inning of first game; struck out for Lowenstein in sixth inning of fifth game.

Sakata—Ran for Singleton in sixth inning of fourth game.

Shelby—Struck out for Dempsey in eighth inning of first game; called out on strikes for Bumbry in fifth inning of second game; hit sacrifice fly for Davis in sixth inning of fourth game; flied out for Bumbry in eighth inning of fifth game.

Singleton—Called out on strikes for Flanagan in fifth inning of third game; walked, forcing in one run, for Dempsey in sixth inning of fourth game.

PHILADELPHIA PHILLIES' BATTING AND FIELDING AVERAGES

Player—Position	G.	AB.	R.	H.	TB.	2B.	3B.	HR.	RBI.	BB.	IBB.	SO.	B.A.	PO.	A.	E.	F.A.
Virgil, ph-c	3	2	0	1	1	0	0	0	1	0	0	0	.500	1	0	0	1.000
Diaz, c	5	15	1	5	6	1	0	0	0	1	0	2	.333	37	1	1	.974
Rose, ph-1b-rf	5	16	1	5	6	1	0	0	1	1	0	3	.313	26	4	0	1.000
Morgan, 2b	5	19	3	5	13	0	1	2	2	2	0	3	.263	8	10	0	1.000
Matthews, lf	5	16	1	4	7	0	0	1	1	2	0	2	.250	15	0	0	1.000
Maddox, ph-cf	4	12	1	3	7	1	0	1	1	0	0	2	.250	7	0	0	1.000
Perez, ph-1b	4	10	0	2	2	0	0	0	0	0	0	2	.200	13	1	0	1.000
Denny, p	2	5	1	1	1	0	0	0	1	0	0	1	.200	3	1	0	1.000
Lefebvre, ph-rf	3	5	0	1	2	1	0	0	2	0	0	1	.200	3	0	0	1.000
DeJesus, ss	5	16	0	2	2	0	0	0	0	1	0	2	.125	5	14	1	.950
Lezcano, ph-rf	4	8	0	1	1	0	0	0	0	0	0	2	.125	2	0	0	1.000
Schmidt, 3b	5	20	0	1	1	0	0	0	0	0	0	6	.050	1	10	1	.917
Andersen, p	2	0	0	0	0	0	0	0	0	0	0	0	.000	1	1	0	1.000
Bystrom, p	1	0	0	0	0	0	0	0	0	0	0	0	.000	0	0	0	.000
Dernier, pr	1	0	1	0	0	0	0	0	0	0	0	0	.000	0	0	0	.000
Hernandez, p	3	0	0	0	0	0	0	0	0	0	0	0	.000	1	0	0	1.000
Holland, p	2	0	0	0	0	0	0	0	0	0	0	0	.000	0	0	0	.000
Reed, p	3	0	0	0	0	0	0	0	0	0	0	0	.000	0	0	0	.000
Samuel, pr-ph	3	1	0	0	0	0	0	0	0	0	0	0	.000	0	0	0	.000
Hudson, p	2	2	0	0	0	0	0	0	0	0	0	1	.000	0	0	0	.000
Carlton, p	1	3	0	0	0	0	0	0	0	0	0	1	.000	0	0	0	.000
Hayes, ph-rf	4	3	0	0	0	0	0	0	0	0	0	1	.000	1	0	0	1.000
G. Gross, cf	2	6	0	0	0	0	0	0	0	0	0	0	.000	8	0	0	1.000
Totals	5	159	9	31	49	4	1	4	9	7	0	29	.195	132	42	3	.983

Dernier—Ran for Diaz in ninth inning of fourth game and scored.

Hayes—Grounded out for Lezcano in ninth inning of first game; struck out for Hernandez in sixth inning of second game; grounded out for Reed in seventh inning of fourth game.

Lefebvre—Announced as pinch-hitter for Diaz in ninth inning of third game.

Lezcano—Grounded out for Hernandez in eighth inning of fifth game.

Maddox—Grounded out for G. Gross in ninth inning of fourth game.

Perez—Grounded into double play for Andersen in eighth inning of second game; singled for Lefebvre in eighth inning of fourth game.

Rose—Grounded out for Lefebvre in ninth inning of third game.

Samuel—Ran for Diaz in eighth inning of second game; ran for Perez in eighth inning of fourth game; flied out for Bystrom in fifth inning of fifth game.

Virgil—Grounded out for Holland in ninth inning of third game; singled home one run for Andersen in ninth inning of fourth game.

BALTIMORE ORIOLES' PITCHING RECORDS

Pitcher	G.	GS.	CG.	IP.	H.	R.	ER.	HR.	BB.	IBB.	SO.	HB.	WP.	W.	L.	Pct.	ERA.
Boddicker	1	1	1	9	3	1	0	0	0	0	6	0	0	1	0	1.000	0.00
Stewart	3	0	0	5	2	0	0	0	2	0	6	0	0	0	0	.000	0.00
Palmer	1	0	0	2	2	0	0	0	1	0	1	0	1	1	0	1.000	0.00
McGregor	2	2	1	17	9	2	2	2	2	0	12	0	0	1	1	.500	1.06
T. Martinez	3	0	0	3	3	1	1	0	0	0	0	0	0	0	0	.000	3.00
Flanagan	1	1	0	4	6	2	2	2	1	0	1	0	0	0	0	.000	4.50
Davis	1	1	0	5	6	3	3	0	1	0	3	0	1	1	0	1.000	5.40
Totals	5	5	2	45	31	9	8	4	7	0	29	0	2	4	1	.800	1.60

Shutout—McGregor. Saves—T. Martinez 2.

PHILADELPHIA PHILLIES' PITCHING RECORDS

Pitcher	G.	GS.	CG.	IP.	H.	R.	ER.	HR.	BB.	IBB.	SO.	HB.	WP.	W.	L.	Pct.	ERA.
Hernandez	3	0	0	4	0	0	0	0	1	0	4	1	0	0	0	.000	0.00
Holland	2	0	0	3⅔	1	0	0	0	0	0	5	0	0	0	0	.000	0.00
Bystrom	1	0	0	1	0	0	0	0	0	0	1	0	1	0	0	.000	0.00
Andersen	2	0	0	4	4	1	1	0	0	0	1	0	0	0	0	.000	2.25
Carlton	1	1	0	6⅔	5	3	2	1	3	0	7	0	1	0	1	.000	2.70
Reed	3	0	0	3⅓	4	1	1	0	2	1	4	0	0	0	0	.000	2.70
Denny	2	2	0	13	12	5	5	1	3	2	9	0	0	1	1	.500	3.46
Hudson	2	2	0	8⅓	9	8	8	4	1	0	6	0	0	0	2	.000	8.64
Totals	5	5	0	44	35	18	17	6	10	3	37	1	2	1	4	.200	3.48

No shutouts. Save—Holland.

COMPOSITE SCORE BY INNINGS

Baltimore	1	1	1	4	4	3	4	0	0	—18
Philadelphia	0	1	1	2	2	1	0	1	1	— 9

Game-winning RBI—Dempsey, Shelby, Murray, Maddox.

Sacrifice hits—None.

Sacrifice flies—Boddicker, Shelby, Bumbry, Lefebvre.

Stolen bases—Morgan, Landrum.

Caught stealing—Morgan 2.

Double plays—Ripken, Dauer and Murray; Dauer, Ripken and Murray; Dauer and Murray; Ripken, Sakata and Murray; Cruz, Dauer and Murray; DeJesus, Morgan and Perez; Schmidt, Morgan and Perez; Andersen, DeJesus and Morgan.

Passed balls—None.

Hit by pitcher—By Hernandez (Ford).

Balk—Stewart.

Bases on balls—Off McGregor 2 (Morgan, Diaz), off Stewart 2 (Morgan, Rose), off Flanagan 1 (Matthews), off Palmer 1 (DeJesus), off Davis 1 (Matthews); off Carlton 3 (Cruz, Ford, Ripken), off Denny 3 (Dempsey, Nolan, Singleton), off Reed 2 (Dempsey, Murray), off Hernandez 1 (Ripken), off Hudson 1 (Ripken).

Strikeouts—By McGregor 12 (Perez 2, Schmidt 2, Morgan, Rose, Maddox, DeJesus, Lezcano, Denny, Hudson, Matthews), by Boddicker 6 (Morgan, Rose, Schmidt, Lefebvre, Diaz, Hayes), by Stewart 6 (Schmidt 2, Lezcano, Matthews, Diaz, DeJesus), by Davis 3 (Morgan, Rose, Schmidt), by Flanagan 1 (Maddox), by Palmer 1 (Carlton); by Denny 9 (Lowenstein 2, Davis 2, Cruz 2, Dauer, Ripken, Shelby), by Carlton 7 (Shelby 2, Murray 2, Ripken, Flanagan, Singleton), by Hudson 6 (Ford 3, Boddicker, Bumbry, Cruz), by Holland 5 (Murray, Roenicke, Dauer, Dempsey, Stewart), by Hernandez 4 (Shelby, Murray, Roenicke, Ford), by Reed 4 (Dauer, Ford, Ripken, Lowenstein), by Andersen 1 (Dempsey), by Bystrom 1 (Ripken).

Left on bases—Baltimore 28—4, 8, 6, 8, 2; Philadelphia 23—2, 2, 7, 6, 6.

Time of games—First game, 2:22; second game, 2:27; third game, 2:35; fourth game, 2:50; fifth game, 2:21.

Attendance—First game, 52,204; second game, 52,132; third game, 65,792; fourth game, 66,947; fifth game, 67,064.

Umpires—Springstead (A.L.), Vargo (N.L.), Clark (A.L.), Pulli (N.L.), Palermo (A.L.), Rennert (N.L.).

Official scorers—Bob Kenney, Camden Courier Post; Neal Eskridge, WCBM radio (Baltimore); Phil Collier, San Diego Tribune.

1983 ALL-STAR GAME

Including

Review of 1983 Game

Official Box Score

Official Play-by-Play

Results of Previous Games

California's Fred Lynn became the first player in All-Star Game history to hit a grand slam home run when he connected off San Francisco's Atlee Hammaker in the third inning of the A.L.'s 13-3 romp last season at Chicago's Comiskey Park.

A.L. Breaks All-Star Jinx

By DAVE SLOAN

Fred Lynn had played in every All-Star Game since he broke into the major leagues with the Boston Red Sox in 1975. Eight times he had played and eight times his American League team had lost. After being voted by the fans as the A.L.'s starting center fielder for the 50th anniversary game at Chicago's Comiskey Park in 1983, Lynn was determined to do his part in breaking that streak.

Lynn, who now plays for the California Angels, did his part and more. He slammed a 2-2 pitch from San Francisco lefthander Atlee Hammaker with the bases loaded into the right-field stands in the third inning for the first grand slam in All-Star history. There were still six innings to be played, but for all practical purposes, this game was over.

"Hammaker had me two strikes," said Lynn, who was unanimously voted the game's MVP. "I choked up a bit and spread my stance. I didn't want to strike out. They had walked (Milwaukee's Robin) Yount to get to me.

"When I hit the ball, I knew it was a home run. It was a breaking ball up and that's where I can hit it. I was elated. It was the most emotion I've shown."

Lynn started trotting around the bases with his right fist held high. His emotion symbolized more than one man's personal triumph. The American Leaguers had lost the last 11 All-Star games in succession and 19 of the previous 20. They were tired of people asking them when they were going to win again and if the National is the better league. They were on their way to a 13-3 laugher, setting a new All-Star Game record for most runs scored in the process.

"I sensed something was different about them," said Montreal Expos first baseman Al Oliver, who was playing in his seventh All-Star Game (his fifth as a National Leaguer), about the A.L. squad. "You could see on the field they weren't smiling. They had their game face on."

"This is the greatest thing that has happened to the sport in a long time," said Whitey Herzog, who, ironically, managed the N.L. squad. "I didn't want to lose, don't get me wrong. But this is the best thing that has happened. Now they (the American League) can say they're better than us, I guess, but it's a big joke. It's like spring training. You can never tell the strength of a league by All-Star games."

That the American League would win by a 10-run margin certainly wasn't evident in the early going.

The first inning brought back bad memories to many A.L. veterans. In the top of the first, Los Angeles' Steve Sax, the N.L. leadoff man, hit a topper near the first-base line that Dave Stieb, the American League's starting pitcher, picked up and promptly threw about 10 feet over the head of first baseman Rod Carew. Sax then stole second base. The second batter, Montreal's Tim Raines, also hit a ball fielded by Stieb. The Toronto pitcher threw a perfect strike to first this time, but Carew lost the throw in the sun and it flew by him. Sax scored from second and Raines wound up at third. Stieb proceeded to strike out Andre Dawson, Dale Murphy and Mike Schmidt, but the Nationals already had a run without a hit.

In the bottom of the first, it was the National League's turn to play giveaway. After Carew led off with a single, N.L. starter Mario Soto of Cincinnati struck out Yount and walked Lynn. But Boston's Jim Rice, who was a fellow rookie of Lynn's with the Red Sox back in '75, bounced a double-play grounder to Schmidt at third. Schmidt bobbled the ball for an error, and the sacks were jammed. Kansas City's George Brett then lofted a fly ball to center to score Carew, and the score was tied.

The American League took a 2-1 lead in the bottom of the second by scoring another unearned run. The Yankees' Dave Winfield led off with a double to left. After Cleveland's Manny Trillo bounced a grounder to Sax at second, the Dodger infielder fielded the ball cleanly and fired it in the dirt in front of first baseman Oliver. The Montreal player couldn't come up with the throw and the A.L. had men on first and third. After a sacrifice bunt by Stieb and an intentional walk to Carew, Yount drove Winfield home with a fly to center. All three runs scored at this point were unearned.

"It sure didn't look like any All-Star Game," said Herzog. "They played bad and we played bad."

But things were to get worse for the National League. The A.L. exploded for seven runs in the third inning and took a staggering 9-1 lead. The seven runs were the most scored in one inning in All-Star history, surpassing the six scored by the A.L. in the fifth inning back in 1934. The

Giants' Hammaker gave up a record-setting six hits in the inning.

"It was probably the worst exhibition of pitching you'll ever see," said Hammaker, who entered the contest with a National League-leading ERA of 1.70. "And I couldn't have picked a worse spot for it, either—my first All-Star Game and in front of all these people. I have no excuses. I was too terrible to alibi." Mercifully, Herzog replaced Hammaker with Houston's Bill Dawley after Lynn's blast. Dawley got the final out when Rice popped to Sax.

Ironically, Hammaker was the only pitcher on the N.L. squad who had ever pitched in the American League. He pitched briefly for the Kansas City Royals in 1981 before he was traded to San Francisco in a deal that sent Vida Blue to the Royals in 1982. (Blue, incidentally, was the winning pitcher for the A.L. when they last won the All-Star Game in 1971 while he played for Oakland.) Some American Leaguers hinted that their familiarity with Hammaker might have helped them in their big inning.

The inning started when Rice lined a home run into the left-field bleachers. Brett tripled, but Hammaker got out No. 1 when Simmons popped to second. Winfield singled, scoring Brett, and Trillo also singled. California's Doug DeCinces pinch-hit for Stieb and flied out to center for out No. 2. Carew singled to left to score Winfield and took second when Raines threw home. Yount was then walked intentionally to get to Lynn.

"I was playing the percentages," said Herzog. "I just passed a .400 hitter to get at a .300 hitter."

"The strategy was right," said Lynn, "but I don't have to like it. I take it personally when someone is walked ahead of me."

So Lynn personally saw to it that this game was over early.

NATIONALS	AB.	R.	H.	RBI.	PO.	A.
Sax, (Dodgers), 2b	3	1	1	1	2	0
Hubbard, (Braves), 2b	1	0	1	0	0	0
Raines, (Expos), lf	3	0	0	0	2	0
dMadl'k, (Pirates), 3b.	1	0	0	0	0	0
Dawson, (Expos), cf	3	0	0	0	3	0
Dravecky, (Padres), p.	0	0	0	0	0	1
Perez, (Braves), p	0	0	0	0	0	0
Orosco, (Mets), p	0	0	0	0	0	0
gBench, (Reds), ph	1	0	0	0	0	0
L. Smith, (Cubs), p	0	0	0	0	1	0
Oliver, (Expos), 1b	2	1	1	0	2	1
Evans, (Giants), 1b	1	0	0	0	2	1
Murphy, (Braves), rf	3	0	1	1	0	0
Guer'ro, (Dodg.), 3b-lf.	1	0	0	0	0	0
Schmidt, (Phillies), 3b.	3	0	0	0	0	0
Benedict, (Braves), c	1	0	1	0	5	0
Carter, (Expos), c	2	0	0	0	3	0
Durham, (Cubs), rf	2	0	0	0	0	0
O. Smith, (Cards), ss	2	1	1	0	0	0
McGee, (Cardinals), cf	2	0	1	0	2	0
Soto, (Reds), p	1	0	0	0	2	0
H'maker, (Giants), p	0	0	0	0	0	0
Dawley, (Astros), p	0	0	0	0	0	0
bThon, (Astros), ss	3	0	1	0	0	2
Totals	35	3	8	2	24	5

AMERICANS	AB.	R.	H.	RBI.	PO.	A.
Carew, (Angels), 1b	3	2	2	1	3	0
Murray, (Orioles), 1b	2	0	0	0	4	0
Yount, (Brewers), ss	2	1	0	1	0	1
Ripken, (Orioles), ss	0	0	0	0	1	0
Lynn, (Angels), cf	3	1	1	4	1	0
Wilson, (Royals), cf	1	0	1	1	2	0
Rice, (Red Sox), lf	4	1	2	1	1	0
Oglivie, (Brewers), rf	1	0	0	0	0	0
Young, (Mariners), p	0	0	0	0	0	0
Quisenb'ry, (Royals), p	0	0	0	0	0	0
Brett, (Royals), 3b	4	2	2	1	1	5
Simmons, (Brewers), c	2	0	0	0	4	0
Parrish, (Tigers), c	2	0	0	0	1	0
hCooper, (Brewers), ph	1	1	1	0	0	0
Boone, (Angels), c	0	0	0	0	1	0
Winfield, (Yankees), rf	3	2	3	1	3	0
Kittle, (Chisox), lf-rf	2	1	1	0	1	0
Trillo, (Indians), 2b	3	1	1	0	3	1
eWhitaker, (Tig.), 2b	1	1	1	2	1	0
Stieb, (Blue Jays), p	0	0	0	0	0	2
aDeCinces (Angels), ph	1	0	0	0	0	0
Honeycutt, (Rang.), p	0	0	0	0	0	0
cWard, (Twins), ph	1	0	0	0	0	0
Stanley, (Red Sox), p	0	0	0	0	0	1
fYastr'ski, (R. Sox), ph	1	0	0	0	0	0
Henderson, (A's), lf	1	0	0	1	0	0
Totals	38	13	15	13	27	10

Nationals	100	110	000— 3
Americans	117	000	22x—13

Nationals	IP.	H.	R.	ER.	BB.	SO.
Soto (Reds)	2	2	2	0	2	2
Hammaker (Giants)	⅔	6	7	7	1	0
Dawley (Astros)	1⅓	1	0	0	0	1
Dravecky (Padres)	2	1	0	0	0	2
Perez (Braves)	⅔	3	2	2	1	1
Orosco (Mets)	⅓	0	0	0	0	1
L. Smith (Cubs)	1	2	2	1	0	1

Americans	IP.	H.	R.	ER.	BB.	SO.
Stieb (Blue Jays)	3	0	1	0	1	4
Honeycutt (Rangers)	2	5	2	2	0	0
Stanley (Red Sox)	2	2	0	0	0	0
Young (Mariners)	1	0	0	0	0	1
Quisenberry (Royals)	1	1	0	0	0	1

Winning pitcher—Stieb. Losing pitcher—Soto.

Game-winning RBI—Yount.

aFlied out for Stieb in third. bSingled for Dawley in fifth. cFlied out for Honeycutt in fifth. dFlied out for Raines in seventh. eTripled one run home for Trillo in seventh. fCalled out on strikes for Stanley in seventh. gPopped out for Orosco in eighth. hSingled for Parrish in eighth. Errors—Stieb, Carew, Schmidt, Sax, Guerrero, Double plays—Yount, Trillo and Carew; Brett and Trillo. Left on bases—Nationals 6, Americans 9. Two-base hits—Winfield, Oliver, Wilson, Brett. Three-base hits—Brett, Whitaker. Home runs—Rice, Lynn. Stolen bases—Sax, Raines. Caught stealing—None. Sacrifice hit—Stieb. Sacrifice flies—Brett, Yount, Whitaker. Passed ball—Benedict. Bases on balls—Off Stieb 1 (Oliver), off Soto 2 (Lynn, Carew), off Hammaker 1 (Yount), off Perez 1 (Ripken). Strikeouts—By Stieb 4 (Dawson, Murphy, Schmidt, Raines), by Young 1 (Guerrero), by Quisenberry 1 (Durham), by Soto 2 (Yount, Lynn), by Dawley 1 (Parrish), by Dravecky 2 (Lynn, Brett), by Perez 1 (Yastrzemski), by Orosco 1 (Oglivie), by L. Smith 1 (Kittle). Umpires—Maloney (A.L.) plate, Wendelstedt (N.L.) first base, Hendry (A.L.) second base, Quick (N.L.) third base, Shulock (A.L.) left field, Pallone (N.L.) right field. Time—3:05. Attendance—43,801. Official scorers—Jerome Holtzman, Chicago Tribune; Joe Giuliotti, Boston Herald-American; Randy Minkoff, United Press International (Chicago). Players listed on rosters but not used: N.L.—Hendrick, Kennedy, Lavelle, Rogers, Valenzuela; A.L.—Lopez, T. Martinez, Sutcliffe.

FIRST INNING

Nationals—Sax reached first base safely when Stieb fielded his swinging bunt and threw the ball over the head of first baseman Carew for an error. Raines bounced back to Stieb, whose throw to first went by Carew, who lost the ball in the setting sunlight; Sax scored and Raines raced all the way to third base on the error charged to Carew. Oliver walked. Murphy struck out. Schmidt was called out on strikes. One run, no hits, two errors, one left.

Americans—Carew lined a single to left-center field. Yount struck out. Lynn walked. Rice hit a potential double-play grounder to Schmidt, who bobbled it for an error, loading the bases. Brett lofted a sacrifice fly to Dawson in left-center, Carew scoring after the catch. Simmons bounced to Oliver, who tossed to Soto covering first. One run, one hit, one error, two left.

SECOND INNING

Nationals—Carter flied to Winfield. Ozzie Smith flied to Rice. Soto grounded to Brett. No runs, no hits, no errors, none left.

Americans—Winfield lined a double down the left-field line. Trillo bounced to Sax, who threw the ball into the dirt, pulling Oliver off first base for an error, Winfield taking third. Stieb sacrificed Trillo to second, Soto unassisted with Winfield holding at third on the play. Carew was intentionaly walked to load the bases. Yount hit a sacrifice fly to Dawson, Winfield scoring after the catch. Lynn struck out. One run, one hit, one error, two left.

THIRD INNING

Nationals—Sax bounced out, Stieb to Carew. Raines was called out on strikes. Dawson lined to Winfield. No runs, no hits, no errors, none left.

Americans—Hammaker went in to pitch for the National League. Rice lined a 1-2 pitch into the left-field bleachers for a home run. Brett tripled to center field. Simmons popped to Sax. Winfield bounced a single up the middle, scoring Brett. Trillo singled to left, Winfield stopping at second. DeCinces batted for Stieb and flied to Dawson. Carew singled to left, scoring Winfield, with Trillo racing to third and Carew taking second on the throw to the plate. Yount was intentionally walked to load the bases. Lynn hit a 2-2 pitch into the right-field bleachers for the first grand slam in All-Star history; the six hits allowed by Hammaker was a record for most hits allowed by one pitcher in one inning and the seven runs surpassed the previous one-inning high of six set by the A.L. in the fifth inning in 1934. Dawley relieved Hammaker. Rice popped to Sax. Seven runs, six hits, no errors, none left.

FOURTH INNING

Nationals—Honeycutt took over the pitching chores for the American League while Parrish came on to catch. Oliver doubled down the left-field line. Murphy singled to center, scoring Oliver. Schmidt grounded into a double play, Yount to Trillo to Carew. Carter flied to Lynn. One run, two hits, no errors, none left.

Americans—Brett fouled out to Raines in the left-field corner. Parrish was called out on strikes. Winfield singled to left. Trillo flied to Raines. No runs, one hit, no errors, one left.

FIFTH INNING

Nationals—Ozzie Smith singled to right. Thon, batting for Dawley, singled to center, Smith taking second on the play. Sax singled to left, scoring Smith, with Thon stopping at second. Brett forced Thon at third on Raines' hard grounder and Sax was out at second for a double play when Trillo tagged him after he overslid the bag. Raines stole second base. Dawson flied to Winfield. One run, three hits, no errors, one left.

Americans—Dravecky took over on the mound for the National League, with Hubbard coming in to play at second base and McGee in center field while Thon stayed in the game at shortstop. Ward, pinch-hitting for Honeycutt, flied to McGee. Carew bounced out, Dravecky to Oliver. Yount grounded to Thon. No runs, no hits, no errors, none left.

SIXTH INNING

Nationals—Stanley became the new pitcher for the American League, with Murray taking over at first base and Ripken coming in at shortstop. Oliver grounded out to Brett. Murphy fouled to Murray. Schmidt bounced to Murray, who made the play at first unassisted. No runs, no hits, no errors, none left.

Americans—Evans took over at first base for the National League, Guerrero came in to play third, while Benedict was the new catcher and Durham went into the game in right field. Lynn struck out. Rice singled off Guerrero's glove at third base. Brett struck out. Parrish flied to McGee. No runs, one hit, no errors, one left.

SEVENTH INNING

Nationals—Wilson entered the game for the American League in center field, with Oliver now playing in right field and Kittle in left. Durham bounced back to the mound and was retired, Stanley to Murray. McGee beat Ripken's throw from shortstop for an infield hit. Thon forced McGee at second, Brett to Trillo. Hubbard was credited with another infield hit, Thon advancing to second, when his hard smash to short was too hot to handle for Ripken. Madlock batted for Raines and flied to Kittle. No runs, two hits, no errors, two left.

Americans—Madlock stayed in the game at third base, while Perez became the new pitcher and Guerrero moved to left field. Kittle beat out a grounder to shortstop Thon for an infield single. Whitaker, batting for Trillo, tripled to the center-field wall, scoring Kittle. Yastrzemski, hitting for Stanley, was called out on strikes. Murray bounced to Evans, who made the putout unassisted at first base, with Whitaker holding at third. Ripken walked. Wilson doubled into the right-field corner, scoring Whitaker with Ripken advancing to third. Orosco was called in from the bullpen in relief of Perez. Oglivie struck out. Two runs, three hits, no errors, two left.

EIGHTH INNING

Nationals—Young took over on the mound for the American League, with Whitaker staying in the game at second and Henderson coming in to play left field while Kittle moved to right. Bench batted for Orosco and popped up to Ripken. Evans' bid for an extra-base hit to left-center was snared by Wilson, who made a diving catch of a sinking liner. Guerrero was called out on strikes. No runs, no hits, no errors, none left.

Americans—Lee Smith became the National League's seventh pitcher in the game. Brett stretched a single off second baseman Hubbard's glove into a double when the ball rolled into short right-center field. Cooper batted for Parrish and singled to left, Brett advancing to third. Benedict was charged with a passed ball, with Cooper moving up to second base and Brett holding at third. Guerrero dropped Whitaker's fly ball near the left-field foul line for an error, with Brett scoring, Cooper advancing to third and Whitaker—who was credited with a sacrifice fly—reaching second base on the play. Henderson grounded out, Thon to Evans, with Cooper scoring on the play and Whitaker holding at second base; the 13 runs by the A.L. was the most by one team in All-Star history, breaking the old mark of 12 set by the A.L. in 1946. Murray grounded out, Evans to Lee Smith covering first. Two runs, two hits, one error, one left.

NINTH INNING

Nationals—Quisenberry came on to pitch for the American League with Boone taking over behind the plate. Benedict looped a single to right. Durham struck out. McGee flied to Wilson. Thon forced Benedict at second, Brett to Whitaker for the final out, giving the Americans their first All-Star Game victory since 1971 at Tiger Stadium in Detroit. No runs, one hit, no errors, one left.

RESULTS OF PREVIOUS GAMES

1933—At Comiskey Park, Chicago, July 6. Americans 4, Nationals 2. Managers—Connie Mack, John McGraw. Winning pitcher—Lefty Gomez. Losing pitcher—Bill Hallahan. Attendance—47,595.

1934—At Polo Grounds, New York, July 10. Americans 9, Nationals 7. Managers—Joe Cronin, Bill Terry. Winning pitcher—Mel Harder. Losing pitcher—Van Mungo. Attendance—48,363.

1935—At Municipal Stadium, Cleveland, July 8. Americans 4, Nationals 1. Managers—Mickey Cochrane, Frankie Frisch. Winning pitcher—Lefty Gomez. Losing pitcher—Bill Walker. Attendance—69,831.

1936—At Braves Field, Boston, July 7. Nationals 4, Americans 3. Managers—Charlie Grimm, Joe McCarthy. Winning pitcher—Dizzy Dean. Losing pitcher—Lefty Grove. Attendance—25,556.

1937—At Griffith Stadium, Washington, July 7. Americans 8, Nationals 3. Managers—Joe McCarthy, Bill Terry. Winning pitcher—Lefty Gomez. Losing pitcher—Dizzy Dean. Attendance—31,391.

1938—At Crosley Field, Cincinnati, July 6. Nationals 4, Americans 1. Managers—Bill Terry, Joe McCarthy. Winning pitcher—Johnny Vander Meer. Losing pitcher—Lefty Gomez. Attendance—27,067.

1939—At Yankee Stadium, New York, July 11. Americans 3, Nationals 1. Managers—Joe McCarthy, Gabby Hartnett. Winning pitcher—Tommy Bridges. Losing pitcher—Bill Lee. Attendance—62,892.

1940—At Sportsman's Park, St. Louis, July 9. Nationals 4, Americans 0. Managers—Bill McKechnie, Joe Cronin. Winning pitcher—Paul Derringer. Losing pitcher—Red Ruffing. Attendance—32,373.

1941—At Briggs Stadium, Detroit, July 8. Americans 7, Nationals 5. Managers—Del Baker, Bill McKechnie. Winning pitcher—Ed Smith. Losing pitcher—Claude Passeau. Attendance—54,674.

1942—At Polo Grounds, New York, July 6. Americans 3, Nationals 1. Managers—Joe Cronin, Leo Durocher. Winning pitcher—Spud Chandler. Losing pitcher—Mort Cooper. Attendance—34,178.

1943—At Shibe Park, Philadelphia, July 13 (night game). Americans 5, Nationals 3. Managers—Joe McCarthy, Billy Southworth. Winning pitcher—Dutch Leonard. Losing pitcher—Mort Cooper. Attendance—31,938.

1944—At Forbes Field, Pittsburgh, July 11 (night game). Nationals 7, Americans 1. Managers—Billy Southworth, Joe McCarthy. Winning pitcher—Ken Raffensberger. Losing pitcher—Tex Hughson. Attendance—29,589.

1945—No game played.

1946—At Fenway Park, Boston, July 9. Americans 12, Nationals 0. Managers—Steve O'Neill, Charlie Grimm. Winning pitcher—Bob Feller. Losing pitcher—Claude Passeau. Attendance—34,906.

1947—At Wrigley Field, Chicago, July 8. Americans 2, Nationals 1. Managers—Joe Cronin, Eddie Dyer. Winning pitcher—Frank Shea. Losing pitcher—Johnny Sain. Attendance—41,123.

1948—At Sportsman's Park, St. Louis, July 13. Americans 5, Nationals 2. Managers—Bucky Harris, Leo Durocher. Winning pitcher—Vic Raschi. Losing pitcher—Johnny Schmitz. Attendance—34,009.

1949—At Ebbets Field, Brooklyn, July 12. Americans 11, Nationals 7. Managers—Lou Boudreau, Billy Southworth. Winning pitcher—Virgil Trucks. Losing pitcher—Don Newcombe. Attendance—32,577.

1950—At Comiskey Park, Chicago, July 11. Nationals 4, Americans 3 (14 innings). Managers—Burt Shotton, Casey Stengel. Winning pitcher—Ewell Blackwell. Losing pitcher—Ted Gray. Attendance—46,127.

1951—At Briggs Stadium, Detroit, July 10. Nationals 8, Americans 3. Managers—Eddie Sawyer, Casey Stengel. Winning pitcher—Sal Maglie. Losing pitcher—Ed Lopat. Attendance—52,075.

1952—At Shibe Park, Philadelphia, July 8. Nationals 3, Americans 2 (five innings—rain). Managers—Leo Durocher, Casey Stengel. Winning pitcher—Bob Rush. Losing pitcher—Bob Lemon. Attendance—32,785.

1953—At Crosley Field, Cincinnati, July 14. Nationals 5, Americans 1. Managers—Chuck Dressen, Casey Stengel. Winning pitcher—Warren Spahn. Losing pitcher—Allie Reynolds. Attendance—30,846.

1954—At Municipal Stadium, Cleveland, July 13. Americans 11, Nationals 9. Managers—Casey Stengel, Walter Alston. Winning pitcher—Dean Stone. Losing pitcher—Gene Conley. Attendance—68,751.

1955—At Milwaukee County Stadium, Milwaukee, July 12. Nationals 6, Americans 5 (12 innings). Managers—Leo Durocher, Al Lopez. Winning pitcher—Gene Conley. Losing pitcher—Frank Sullivan. Attendance—45,643.

1956—At Griffith Stadium, Washington, July 10. Nationals 7, Americans 3. Managers—Walter Alston, Casey Stengel. Winning pitcher—Bob Friend. Losing pitcher—Billy Pierce. Attendance—28,843.

1957—At Busch Stadium, St. Louis, July 9.

Americans 6, Nationals 5. Managers—Casey Stengel, Walter Alston. Winning pitcher—Jim Bunning. Losing pitcher—Curt Simmons. Attendance—30,693.

1958—At Memorial Stadium, Baltimore, July 8. Americans 4, Nationals 3. Managers—Casey Stengel, Fred Haney. Winning pitcher—Early Wynn. Losing pitcher—Bob Friend. Attendance—48,829.

1959 (first game)—At Forbes Field, Pittsburgh, July 7. Nationals 5, Americans 4. Managers—Fred Haney, Casey Stengel. Winning pitcher—Johnny Antonelli. Losing pitcher—Whitey Ford. Attendance—35,277.

1959 (second game)—At Memorial Coliseum, Los Angeles, August 3. Americans 5, Nationals 3. Managers—Casey Stengel, Fred Haney. Winning pitcher—Jerry Walker. Losing pitcher—Don Drysdale. Attendance—55,105.

1960 (first game)—At Municipal Stadium, Kansas City, July 11. Nationals 5, Americans 3. Managers—Walter Alston, Al Lopez. Winning pitcher—Bob Friend. Losing pitcher—Bill Monbouquette. Attendance—30,619.

1960 (second game)—At Yankee Stadium, New York, July 13. Nationals 6, Americans 0. Managers—Walter Alston, Al Lopez. Winning pitcher—Vernon Law. Losing pitcher—Whitey Ford. Attendance—38,362.

1961 (first game)—At Candlestick Park, San Francisco, July 11. Nationals 5, Americans 4 (10 innings). Managers—Danny Murtaugh, Paul Richards. Winning pitcher—Stu Miller. Losing pitcher—Hoyt Wilhelm. Attendance—44,115.

1961 (second game)—At Fenway Park, Boston, July 31. Americans 1, Nationals 1 (nine-inning tie, stopped by rain). Managers—Paul Richards, Danny Murtaugh. Attendance—31,851.

1962 (first game)—At District of Columbia Stadium, Washington, July 10. Nationals 3, Americans 1. Managers—Fred Hutchinson, Ralph Houk. Winning pitcher—Juan Marichal. Losing pitcher—Camilo Pascual. Attendance—45,480.

1962 (second game)—At Wrigley Field, Chicago, July 30. Americans 9, Nationals 4. Managers—Ralph Houk, Fred Hutchinson. Winning pitcher—Ray Herbert. Losing pitcher—Art Mahaffey. Attendance—38,359.

1963—At Municipal Stadium, Cleveland, July 9. Nationals 5, Americans 3. Managers—Alvin Dark, Ralph Houk. Winning pitcher—Larry Jackson. Losing pitcher—Jim Bunning. Attendance—44,160.

1964—At Shea Stadium, New York, July 7. Nationals 7, Americans 4. Managers—Walter Alston, Al Lopez. Winning pitcher—Juan Marichal. Losing pitcher—Dick Radatz. Attendance—50,850.

1965—At Metropolitan Stadium, Bloomington (Minnesota), July 13. Nationals 6, Americans 5. Managers—Gene Mauch, Al Lopez. Winning pitcher—Sandy Koufax. Losing pitcher—Sam McDowell. Attendance—46,706.

1966—At Busch Memorial Stadium, St. Louis, July 12. Nationals 2, Americans 1 (10 innings). Managers—Walter Alston, Sam Mele. Winning pitcher—Gaylord Perry. Losing pitcher—Pete Richert. Attendance—49,936.

1967—At Anaheim Stadium, Anaheim (California), July 11. Nationals 2, Americans 1 (15 innings). Managers—Walter Alston, Hank Bauer. Winning pitcher—Don Drysdale. Losing pitcher—Jim Hunter. Attendance—46,309.

1968—At Astrodome, Houston, July 9 (night). Nationals 1, Americans 0. Managers—Red Schoendienst, Dick Williams. Winning pitcher—Don Drysdale. Losing pitcher—Luis Tiant. Attendance—48,321.

1969—At Robert F. Kennedy Memorial Stadium, Washington, July 23. Nationals 9, Americans 3. Managers—Red Schoendienst, Mayo Smith. Winning pitcher—Steve Carlton. Losing pitcher—Mel Stottlemyre. Attendance—45,259.

1970—At Riverfront Stadium, Cincinnati, July 14 (night). Nationals 5, Americans 4 (12 innings). Managers—Gil Hodges, Earl Weaver. Winning pitcher—Claude Osteen. Losing pitcher—Clyde Wright. Attendance—51,838.

1971—At Tiger Stadium, Detroit, July 13 (night). Americans 6, Nationals 4. Managers—Earl Weaver, George (Sparky) Anderson. Winning pitcher—Vida Blue. Losing pitcher—Dock Ellis. Attendance—53,559.

1972—At Atlanta Stadium, Atlanta, July 25 (night). Nationals 4, Americans 3 (10 innings). Managers—Danny Murtaugh, Earl Weaver. Winning pitcher—Tug McGraw. Losing pitcher—Dave McNally. Attendance—53,107.

1973—At Royals Stadium, Kansas City, July 24 (night). Nationals 7, Americans 1. Managers—George (Sparky) Anderson, Dick Williams. Winning pitcher—Rick Wise. Losing pitcher—Bert Blyleven. Attendance—40,849.

1974—At Three Rivers Stadium, Pittsburgh, July 23 (night). Nationals 7, Americans 2. Managers—Yogi Berra, Dick Williams. Winning pitcher—Ken Brett. Losing pitcher—Luis Tiant. Attendance—50,706.

1975—At Milwaukee County Stadium, Milwaukee, July 15 (night). Nationals 6, Americans 3. Managers—Walter Alston, Alvin Dark. Winning pitcher—Jon Matlack. Losing pitcher—Jim Hunter. Attendance—51,480.

1976—At Veterans Stadium, Philadelphia, July 13 (night). Nationals 7, Americans 1. Managers—George (Sparky) Anderson, Darrell Johnson. Winning pitcher— Randy Jones. Losing pitcher—Mark Fidrych. Attendance—63,974.

1977—At Yankee Stadium, New York, July 19 (night). Nationals 7, Americans 5. Managers—Alfred (Billy) Martin, George (Sparky) Anderson. Winning pitcher—Don Sutton. Losing pitcher—Jim Palmer. Attendance—56,683.

1978—At San Diego Stadium, San Diego, July 11. Nationals 7, Americans 3. Managers—Alfred (Billy) Martin, Thomas Lasorda. Winning pitcher—Bruce Sutter. Losing pitcher—Rich Gossage. Attendance—51,549.

1979—At Kingdome, Seattle, July 17, Nationals 7, Americans 6. Managers—Chuck Tanner, Bob Lemon. Winning pitcher—Bruce Sutter. Losing pitcher—Jim Kern. Attendance—58,905.

1980—At Dodger Stadium, Los Angeles, July 8, Nationals 4, Americans 2. Managers—Chuck Tanner, Earl Weaver. Winning pitcher—Jerry Reuss. Losing pitcher—Tommy John. Attendance—56,088.

1981—At Municipal Stadium, Cleveland, August 9, Nationals 5, Americans 4. Managers—Dallas Green, Jim Frey. Winning pitcher—Vida Blue. Losing pitcher—Rollie Fingers. Attendance—72,086.

1982—At Olympic Stadium, Montreal, July 13. Nationals 4, Americans 1. Managers—Thomas Lasorda, Alfred (Billy) Martin. Winning pitcher—Steve Rogers. Losing pitcher—Dennis Eckersley. Attendance—59,057.

Boston's Carl Yastrzemski decided to call it quits after the 1983 season—after 23 years and a major-league record 3,308 games played, all with the Red Sox.

BATTING, PITCHING
FEATURES

Including

Low-Hit Pitching Performances

Top Strikeout Performances

Baseball's Top Firemen

Pitchers Winning 1-0 Games

Multi-Home Run Performances

Batters Hitting Grand Slams

Top One-Game Hitting Performances

Baseball's Top Pinch-Hitters

Top Performances in Debuts

Homers by Parks

Award Winners

Hall of Fame Electees

Hall of Famers List, Years Selected

Dave Righetti didn't make the A.L. All-Star team in '83 but he made history by becoming the first lefthander to pitch a no-hitter in Yankee Stadium.

Three Pitchers Hurl No-Hitters

By JOE HOPPEL

What a difference a year makes.

On July 4, 1982, lefthander Dave Righetti was a member of the International League's Columbus Clippers. Righetti, named The Sporting News' Rookie Pitcher of the Year in the American League in 1981 after he helped New York to the World Series, found himself back at the Triple-A level in midseason of '82 when he encountered nagging control problems. It was his fourth stop in Columbus.

On July 4, 1983, Righetti pitched a no-hitter for the Yankees against the Boston Red Sox. He was a 4-0 winner at Yankee Stadium on the last day before the All-Star Game break.

Righetti's gem was the first no-hitter by a Yankee since Don Larsen's perfect game in the 1956 World Series and the first regular-season no-hitter for the Yankees since Allie Reynolds baffled the Red Sox on September 28, 1951. It also was the first no-hit game by a lefthander in Yankee Stadium history.

On September 26, 1982, righthander Bob Forsch had won 15 games for the Cardinals and St. Louis was one day away from clinching the National League East championship.

On September 26, 1983, Forsch was struggling with an 8-12 record and the Cardinals—bound for a sub-.500 season and a fourth-place finish—already had been eliminated from N.L. East title contention. That night, though, Forsch tossed a no-hitter against the Montreal Expos, winning a 3-0 decision at Busch Memorial Stadium.

Forsch's masterpiece made him the first man ever to pitch two no-hitters for the Cardinals. On April 16, 1978, Forsch had no-hit the Philadelphia Phillies.

On September 29, 1982, righthander Mike Warren was a Class A pitcher. He was coming off a 19-4 year in the California League, a season in which he had been traded from the Milwaukee Brewers' organization to the Oakland A's system. Property of the A's earlier in his career and drafted originally by the Detroit Tigers, Warren, despite his banner season, must have been wondering where else the baseball trail might take him.

On September 29, 1983, Warren fashioned a no-hitter against the A.L. West champion Chicago White Sox, pitching the A's to a 3-0 triumph at the Oakland Coliseum. The victory was Warren's fifth in the big leagues.

Righetti's No-Hitter

Boston	AB.	R.	H.	RBI.	E.
Remy, 2b	4	0	0	0	0
Boggs, 3b	4	0	0	0	1
Rice, lf	1	0	0	0	0
Armas, cf	3	0	0	0	0
D. Evans, rf	3	0	0	0	0
Nichols, dh	2	0	0	0	0
Stapleton, 1b	3	0	0	0	0
Newman, c	2	0	0	0	0
Hoffman, ss	3	0	0	0	0
Totals	25	0	0	0	1

New York	AB.	R.	H.	RBI.	E.
Campaneris, 3b	3	0	2	0	0
Mattingly, 1b	4	0	0	0	0
Winfield, cf	3	1	1	0	0
Piniella, lf	4	0	0	0	0
Baylor, dh	3	2	1	1	0
Wynegar, c	3	0	0	0	0
Kemp, rf	4	1	2	2	0
Smalley, ss	4	0	1	0	0
Robertson, 2b	3	0	1	1	0
Totals	31	4	8	4	0

Boston	000	000	000—0
New York	000	011	02x—4

Boston	IP.	H.	R.	ER.	BB.	SO.
Tudor (L. 5-5)	7⅔	8	4	4	4	2
Stanley	⅓	0	0	0	0	0

New York	IP.	H.	R.	ER.	BB.	SO.
RIGHETTI (W. 10-3)	9	0	0	0	4	9

Game-winning RBI—Robertson.
DP—Boston 2, New York 1.
LOB—Boston 2, New York 7. HR—Baylor (9). SB—Campaneris. T—2:33. A—41,077.

Warren's no-hitter was the first by a major league rookie since Jim Bibby of the Texas Rangers threw one against Oakland on July 30, 1973. Rookie Steve Busby of the Kansas City Royals also hurled a no-hitter that season, his coming on April 27 against Detroit.

Entering the '83 season, major league baseball had not seen a no-hitter since Houston's Nolan Ryan pitched his record fifth no-hit game on September 26, 1981, against the Los Angeles Dodgers. Righetti got things rolling again, though, against the Red Sox.

Having been left off the A.L. All-Star team, Righetti was an angry young man when he took the mound July 4 with a 9-3 record.

"Instead of going crazy, I channeled my anger and took it out on the Red Sox," said the 24-year-old pitcher, who five days earlier had notched his first big-league shutout (against Baltimore). "I deserved to be on the team, no doubt about it."

Boston's Wade Boggs, the '83 A.L. batting champion, was hitting .357 when he went to the plate with two out in the ninth

A dismal season for Bob Forsch ended on a high note when he no-hit Montreal in the final week.

inning. The count went to 2-2 before Boggs struck out on a slider.

"After Boggs swung and missed, I went blank for a split second," said Righetti. "Then I saw Butch (Wynegar, the Yankees' catcher) coming at me and I grabbed on to him. I didn't want to get knocked to the ground."

Preceding his game-ending strikeout, Boggs lined twice to center field on probably the hardest-hit balls of the day. However, balls hit by Tony Armas, Glenn Hoffman and Dwight Evans provided the greatest drama going into the ninth.

Yankee third baseman Bert Campaneris had to charge Armas' slow grounder in the fourth inning, but he made the play. Shortstop Roy Smalley had to dash into left field to grap Hoffman's sixth-inning popup, and Steve Kemp had to leap against the wall down the right-field line to snare Evans' eighth-inning foul fly. Kemp's play was perhaps the key, cutting short the at-bat of one of Boston' most dangerous hitters.

Righetti finished with nine strikeouts and four walks. And he didn't have to worry about pitching for Columbus again.

Forsch, shunted to the bullpen briefly earlier in the season, added some life to the Cardinals' disappointing season when he shut down the Expos.

"Just one no-hitter is quite an accomplishment," said the 33-year-old Forsch. "I'd never really thought about two no-hitters, especially the way I've been pitching."

In Forsch's 1978 no-hitter, an eighth-inning scoring decision gave St. Louis third baseman Ken Reitz an error on a ball hit by Philadelphia's Garry Maddox—and the questionable ruling was hotly disputed by the Phillies.

"A lot of people said it (his first no-hitter) was tainted," Forsch recalled. "This one I don't think there was any question about. Now they know I'm capable of pitching a no-hitter."

Forsch struck out six Expos and retired the last 22 Montreal batters, the final out

Forsch's No-Hitter

Montreal	AB.	R.	H.	RBI.	E.
Francona, rf	4	0	0	0	0
Trillo, 2b	4	0	0	0	0
Dawson, cf	3	0	0	0	0
Oliver, 1b	3	0	0	0	0
Raines, lf	3	0	0	0	0
Carter, c	2	0	0	0	0
Speier, 3b	3	0	0	0	0
Salazar, ss	2	0	0	0	0
Roof, ph	1	0	0	0	0
Flynn, ss	0	0	0	0	0
Rogers, p	1	0	0	0	0
Cromartie, ph	1	0	0	0	0
Schatzeder, p	0	0	0	0	0
Burris, p	0	0	0	0	0
Reardon, p	0	0	0	0	0
Crowley, ph	1	0	0	0	0
Totals	28	0	0	0	0

St. Louis	AB.	R.	H.	RBI.	E.
L. Smith, lf	4	1	2	1	0
Lyons, 2b-3b	0	0	0	0	0
Oberkfell, 2b-3b	3	0	1	0	1
McGee, cf	4	0	2	1	0
Porter, c	4	0	0	0	0
Van Slyke, 3b	3	0	0	0	0
Green, rf	2	1	0	0	0
Adduci, 1b	3	0	0	0	0
O. Smith, ss	3	1	1	1	0
Forsch, p	3	0	0	0	0
Totals	29	3	6	3	1

Montreal	0 0 0	0 0 0	0 0 0	—0
St. Louis	0 0 0	0 3 0	0 0 x	—3

Montreal	IP.	H.	R.	ER.	BB.	SO.
Rogers (L. 17-12)	5	6	3	3	2	3
Schatzeder	0*	0	0	0	0	0
Burris	2	0	0	0	1	1
Reardon	1	0	0	0	0	1

St. Louis	IP.	H.	R.	ER.	BB.	SO.
FORSCH (W. 9-12)	9	0	0	0	0	6

*Schatzeder pitched to one batter in the sixth.

Game-winning RBI—O. Smith.

LOB—Montreal 2, St. Louis 6. 2B—L. Smith. 3B—Oberkfell. SB—McGee, Van Slyke. HBP—By FORSCH (Carter), by Schatzeder (Van Slyke). T—2:15. A—12,457.

Warren's No-Hitter

Chicago	AB.	R.	H.	RBI.	E.
R. Law, cf	4	0	0	0	0
Fisk, c	4	0	0	0	0
Baines, rf	3	0	0	0	0
Luzinski, dh	3	0	0	0	0
Paciorek, 1b	2	0	0	0	0
Kittle, lf	3	0	0	0	0
Rodriguez, 3b	2	0	0	0	0
Squires, ph	1	0	0	0	0
Dybzinski, 3b	0	0	0	0	0
Fletcher, ss	1	0	0	0	0
Hairston, ph	0	0	0	0	0
Hulett, 2b	2	0	0	0	0
Walker, p	1	0	0	0	0
Totals	26	0	0	0	0

Oakland	AB.	R.	H.	RBI.	E.
R. Henderson, lf	3	1	1	0	0
Peters, cf	4	0	1	0	0
Lopes, 2b	3	1	2	1	0
M. Davis, rf	0	0	0	0	0
Burroughs, dh	4	1	2	2	0
McNealy, pr	0	0	0	0	0
Heath, c	4	0	1	0	0
Almon, 3b	2	0	0	0	0
Gross, 3b	0	0	0	0	0
Phillips, ss	3	0	0	0	0
Meyer, 1b	2	0	0	0	0
Quinones, rf	3	0	0	0	0
D. Hill, ss	0	0	0	0	0
Totals	28	3	7	3	0

Chicago	000	000	000	—0
Oakland	102	000	00x	—3

Chicago	IP.	H.	R.	ER.	BB.	SO.
Burns (L. 10-11)	8	7	3	3	3	2

Oakland	IP.	H.	R.	ER.	BB.	SO.
WARREN (W. 5-3)	9	0	0	0	3	5

Game-winning RBI—Lopes.

LOB—Chicago 2, Oakland 5. 2B—Lopes 2, Heath. HR—Burroughs (10). HBP—By Burns (M. Davis). T—2:20. A—9,058.

A's rookie Mike Warren no-hit A.L. West division champ Chicago in just his ninth big-league start.

coming on Manny Trillo's broken-bat grounder to Ken Oberkfell at third base. Earlier, Oberkfell had erred on a ball hit by Chris Speier, enabling the Expos to get one of their two baserunners of the night.

"It (Speier's second-inning smash) hit off the end of the bat and had a tough spin on it," said Oberkfell, who started the game at second base and moved to third in the eighth inning. "I put my glove down, but it went right through my legs. It was definitely an error. I'm glad it was an error this time.

"I was just hoping I wouldn't make an error on the last one."

Gary Carter was Montreal's other baserunner, also in the second inning. He was hit by a pitch.

Forsch was the beneficiary of two fine plays by center fielder Willie McGee, who caught up with early long drives by Andre Dawson and Tim Raines.

Warren walked three batters and fanned five in his no-hitter against Chicago, against whom he had made his first major league appearance on June 12. In that debut, Warren fired a wild pitch on his first delivery and yielded three hits (including a home run) and two runs in 1⅔ innings of relief.

It was a different story three days before the end of the season as the 22-year-old Warren had only one close call—pinch-hitter Mike Squires' drive to the warning track to end the eighth inning.

In the White Sox's ninth, Jerry Hairston (who ruined a perfect-game bid by Detroit's Milt Wilcox in April with a two-out single in the ninth) walked as a pinch-hitter. Another pinch batsman, Greg Walker, flied to center and Rudy Law struck out. Then Carlton Fisk flied out to Rickey Henderson in left to end the game. Warren had thrown a no-hitter in his ninth big-league start.

"This is really crazy," said Warren, who sandwiched stints at Class AA Albany and Class AAA Tacoma around his June call-up before being summoned to Oakland again in August. "It's kind of mind-boggling to pitch in Modesto one year and then get all this attention the next. I can't believe it."

McWilliams Led Low-Hit Parade

By JOE HOPPEL

Pitching a one-hit game proved agonizing yet rewarding for the Tigers' Milt Wilcox and the Cubs' Chuck Rainey in 1983, but it was another story for Richard Dotson of the White Sox. Dotson experienced only misery.

Wilcox lost his bid for a perfect game with two out in the ninth inning of an April 15 game against Chicago when White Sox pinch-hitter Jerry Hairston singled. Instead of a place in the record books (which Dave Righetti of the Yankees, Bob Forsch of the Cardinals and Mike Warren of the A's achieved with their '83 no-hitters), Wilcox was forced to settle for a one-hit, 6-0 triumph.

Rainey pitched no-hit ball for 8⅔ innings in an August 24 game against Cincinnati before Eddie Milner singled. Rainey finished with a one-hit, 3-0 victory.

While flirting with baseball acclaim and just missing out was painful for Wilcox and Rainey, the veteran pitchers nevertheless could savor success. Not Dotson.

Dotson was pitching no-hit ball in a 0-0 game against Baltimore on May 18 when the Orioles' Dan Ford came to bat with one out in the eighth inning. Ford quickly ended the shutout—and the no-hitter—by blasting a home run. The run stood up, saddling Dotson with a one-hit, 1-0 setback.

Other major league pitchers throwing complete-game one-hitters in 1983 were Charlie Lea of the Expos, Larry McWilliams of the Pirates, Bob Welch of the Dodgers, Nolan Ryan of the Astros, John Tudor of the Red Sox, John Butcher of the Rangers, Britt Burns of the White Sox and Jim Beattie of the Mariners. Beattie's one-hit effort was the first in Mariners' history.

There were 54 one- and two-hit games overall in the majors in '83, with 29 coming in the National League.

Pittsburgh's McWilliams pitched four of the low-hit games, tossing two-hit shutouts against Houston (April 9), Los Angeles (July 9) and New York (September 20) and the one-hitter against San Francisco (April 26).

Seattle's Matt Young blanked the Yankees on a two-hitter on June 3, went 8⅓ innings in a victorious two-hit performance on April 21 against Minnesota and worked 6⅓ innings in a two-hit loss to Baltimore on July 10.

San Francisco duplicated the Orioles' feat of winning twice while being low-hit victims. The Giants needed only two hits to beat San Diego on June 26 and just two safeties to defeat Cincinnati on September 5.

Detroit's Milt Wilcox came within one out of a perfect game against the White Sox on April 15.

Tom Seaver of the Mets made two consecutive starts in which his club was victimized by two-hitters, losing to Welch and the Dodgers on May 22 and to Eric Show and the Padres on May 27. In each instance, Seaver collected New York's first hit of the game. He singled in the fifth inning against Welch and singled in the sixth against Show.

A complete list of one- and two-hit games for 1983 follows:

NATIONAL LEAGUE

One-Hit Games

April 16—Lea, Montreal vs. Houston, 2-0—Puhl, single in eighth.
April 26—McWilliams, Pittsburgh vs. San Francisco, 3-0—Brenly, single in fifth.
June 1—Welch, Los Angeles vs. Philadelphia, 1-0—Hayes, single in fourth.
Aug. 3—Ryan, Houston vs. San Diego, 1-0—Flannery, single in third.
Aug. 24—Rainey, Chicago vs. Cincinnati, 3-0—Milner, single in ninth.

Two-Hit Games

April 9—McWilliams, Pittsburgh vs. Houston, 1-0—Knight, single in second; Thon, single in fourth.
April 11—Price, Cincinnati vs. Chicago, 5-1—Davis, single in sixth; Nordhagen, homer in seventh.

April 17—Hammaker, San Francisco vs. Cincinnati, 3-0 (first game)—Bench, single in eighth; Bilardello, single in ninth.

April 30—Denny, Philadelphia vs. Houston, 8-0—T. Scott, single in first; Thon, single in third.

May 6—M. Scott (four innings) and DiPino (five innings), Houston vs. Atlanta, 6-0—Murphy, single in second; Hubbard, single in third.

May 12—Krukow (six innings), Barr (two and two-thirds innings) and Lavelle (one-third inning), San Francisco vs. Cincinnati, 4-2—Oester, triple in eighth; Concepcion, single in ninth.

May 22—Welch, Los Angeles vs. New York, 5-0—Seaver, single in fifth; Heep, double in ninth.

May 27—Show, San Diego vs. New York, 4-0—Seaver, single in sixth; Foster, single in seventh.

May 28—Valenzuela, Los Angeles vs. San Francisco, 5-0—LeMaster, double in first; Martin, double in third.

June 7—Forsch, St. Louis vs. Philadelphia, 2-1—Schmidt, homer in second; Diaz, single in eighth.

June 9—Knepper, Houston vs. San Francisco, 3-0—O'Malley, single in fifth; LeMaster, single in eighth.

June 19—Ruthven, Chicago vs. St. Louis, 4-1—Hendrick, single in second; Braun, homer in fifth.

June 21—Lollar (eight innings) and DeLeon (one inning), San Diego vs. Los Angeles, 2-0—Baker, single in seventh; Russell, single in ninth.

June 24—Krukow, San Francisco vs. San Diego, 5-0—Salazar, double in first; Salazar, single in third.

June 26—Lollar (seven innings) and Hawkins (one inning), San Diego vs. San Francisco, 0-2 (first game)—Evans, single in seventh; Clark, double in seventh.

July 1—Denny, Philadelphia vs. New York, 5-1—Foster, double in second; Hodges, single in second.

July 9—McWilliams, Pittsburgh vs. Los Angeles, 3-0—Anderson, single in third; Baker, single in seventh.

July 17—Pastore, Cincinnati vs. Philadelphia, 5-2—Diaz, homer in second; Schmidt, homer in fifth.

Aug. 7—Rogers, Montreal vs. Pittsburgh, 6-0—Easler, single in fifth; Wynne, single in sixth.

Aug. 20—DeLeon, Pittsburgh vs. Cincinnati, 4-0—Driessen, double in seventh; Milner, single in ninth.

Aug. 26—Ryan (two and two-thirds innings), Ruhle (five innings) and Dawley (one and one-third innings), Houston vs. Chicago, 1-0—Bowa, single in third; Bowa, single in fifth.

Sept. 5—Russell, Cincinnati vs. San Francisco, 2-3—Youngblood, double in eighth; Bergman, homer in eighth.

Sept. 16—M. Davis, San Francisco vs. Los Angeles, 1-0—Guerrero, single in second; Rivera, single in fifth.

Sept. 20—McWilliams, Pittsburgh vs. New York, 4-0—Foster, single in second; Brooks, single in sixth.

AMERICAN LEAGUE

One-Hit Games

April 15—Wilcox, Detroit vs. Chicago, 6-0—Hairston, single in ninth.

May 14—Leal (five innings) and Jackson (four innings), Toronto vs. Cleveland, 8-1—Bando, single in eighth.

May 18—Dotson, Chicago vs. Baltimore, 0-1—Ford, homer in eighth.

May 27—Tudor, Boston vs. Toronto, 2-0—Collins, single in fourth.

Aug. 16—Butcher, Texas vs. Baltimore, 2-0—Bumbry, single in third.

Sept. 9—Burns, Chicago vs. California, 11-0—M. Brown, single in seventh.

Sept. 27—Beattie, Seattle vs. Kansas City, 4-0—Washington, single in third.

Oct. 2—Boddicker (five innings), Stewart (two innings) and T. Martinez (two innings), Baltimore vs. New York, 2-0—Griffey, single in fourth.

Two-Hit Games

April 17—Lamp, Chicago vs. Detroit, 6-1—Whitaker, single in first; Herndon, homer in fifth.

April 18—Guidry, New York vs. Toronto, 3-0—Collins, single in first; Martinez, single in sixth.

April 21—Young (eight and one-third innings) and Caudill (two-thirds inning), Seattle vs. Minnesota, 2-0—Castino, single in first; Brown, single in ninth.

April 22—Blyleven, Cleveland vs. Chicago, 5-1—Fletcher, double in third; Fletcher, single in sixth.

May 11—Sutcliffe, Cleveland vs. Kansas City, 2-0—McRae, single in second; Simpson, single in ninth.

May 26—Honeycutt (eight innings) and O. Jones (one inning), Texas vs. Chicago, 3-1—R. Law, single in first; Hill, homer in eighth.

May 28—McGregor, Baltimore vs. Kansas City, 1-0—Wathan, single in fourth; Concepcion, single in eighth.

June 3—Young, Seattle vs. New York, 5-0—Griffey, double in sixth; Piniella, single in seventh.

June 26—Davis (eight innings) and T. Martinez (one inning), Baltimore vs. Detroit, 3-1—Leach, homer in ninth; Cabell, single in ninth.

June 27—Kison (seven innings) and Sanchez (two innings), California vs. Texas, 8-0—Rivers, double in first; Wright, single in second.

July 10—Young (six and one-third innings) and Stanton (one and two-thirds innings), Seattle vs. Baltimore, 0-2—Ayala, double in fifth; Murray, single in seventh.

July 14—Leal, Toronto vs. Chicago, 8-0—Luzinski, single in fourth; Baines, single in fourth.

July 15—Splittorff (seven innings), Creel (one inning) and Hood (one inning), Kansas City vs. Cleveland, 10-0—Harrah, double in first; Bannister, single in eighth.

July 23—Stoddard, Seattle vs. Boston, 5-0—Gedman, single in eighth; Boggs, single in ninth.

Aug. 23—Moore, Seattle vs. Milwaukee, 5-0—Moore, single in third; Yount, single in fourth.

Sept. 16—Bannister, Chicago vs. Seattle, 7-0—Owen, single in third; Putnam, single in eighth.

Sept. 24—Burns, Chicago vs. California, 2-0—Pettis, single in first; Lubratich, single in first.

Carlton No. 1 in Strikeout Feats

By JOE HOPPEL

When Giants lefthander Atlee Hammaker had 14 strikeouts after 7⅔ innings of a September 11 game against the Astros, it seemed likely that the major leagues would have at least one 15-strikeout performance for the 25th straight season.

It wasn't to be.

Hammaker, who posted 10 victories in 1983 but didn't win after July 10, was replaced by Greg Minton as Houston struck for two eighth-inning runs. Minton earned the victory as San Francisco rallied for three runs in the ninth for a 3-2 triumph at Candlestick Park.

The losing pitcher was Houston's Nolan Ryan, who struck out 11 batters in 8⅓ innings to increase his major league record of 10-or-more-strikeout games to 151.

Not since 1958—when St. Louis' Sam Jones and Detroit's Jim Bunning paced the National League and American League, respectively, with 14-strikeout efforts—had the majors gone without a 15-strikeout game.

Philadelphia's Steve Carlton, who led the big leagues with 275 strikeouts in '83, fanned 10 or more batters in nine games. Ryan and Mario Soto of the Reds reached the 10-strikeout plateau six times each, and Detroit's Jack Morris (the A.L. strikeout king at 232) attained that level on four occasions.

Pittsburgh rookie Jose DeLeon struck out 13 Reds on August 20 while tossing a two-hit shutout, and Carlton (three times), Ryan (twice), Hammaker, Morris, Soto, Floyd Bannister of the White Sox, Tim Lollar of the Padres and Mike Boddicker of the Orioles recorded 12-strikeout games.

N.L. pitchers continued to dominate A.L. hurlers in attaining the 10-strikeout figure. The N.L. had 41 such performances in '83, compared with 18 in the A.L. In the last four seasons, the N.L. has accounted for 152 of the 214 outings in which pitchers struck out 10 or more batters.

Following is a list of all pitchers who achieved 10 strikeouts in a game in 1983, with the number of times the feat was accomplished:

AMERICAN LEAGUE: Baltimore (1)—Boddicker. Boston—None. California (1)—Kison. Chicago (2)—Bannister 2. Cleveland (3)—Blyleven 2, Sutcliffe. Detroit (5)—Morris 4, Berenguer. Kansas City—None. Milwaukee (1)—Porter. Minnesota—None. New York (2)—Righetti 2. Oakland (1)—Norris. Seattle—None. Texas—None. Toronto (2)—Stieb 2.

NATIONAL LEAGUE: Atlanta (3)—Perez 2, Falcone. Chicago—None. Cincinnati (7)—Soto 6, Berenyi. Houston (7)—Ryan 6, Knepper. Los Angeles (3)—Reuss, Valenzuela, Welch. Montreal—None. New York—None. Philadelphia (10)—Carlton 9, Denny. Pittsburgh (5)—DeLeon 3, Candelaria, McWilliams. St. Louis—None. San Diego (2)—Hawkins, Lollar. San Francisco (4)—Hammaker 3, Krukow.

Steve Carlton's 275 strikeouts in 1983 helped him become baseball's all-time strikeout king. He ended the season with 3,709 whiffs.

Quisenberry Tops Firemen Again

By LARRY WIGGE

Kansas City relief ace Dan Quisenberry said he wouldn't be satisfied just to break the major league record for saves—he wanted to put a number in the record books that would be extremely difficult to surpass.

"I don't want to stop here," Quisenberry said after retiring the final two batters to preserve a 4-3 victory for the Royals over the California Angels on September 13. "I want it to be hard for the next guy."

Bud Black had taken a one-hitter into the ninth inning of that American League contest before yielding two singles and a home run by Ron Jackson. Quisenberry came on and put out the fire for his 39th save of the season, erasing the record of 38 set by Detroit's John Hiller in 1973.

Quisenberry, the righthander with the baffling underhand delivery, went on to record 45 saves in 1983 and posted five victories in relief. As a result, he won the Fireman of the Year Award from The Sporting News for the third time in the last four seasons.

Quisenberry's 50 points—one for each save and each relief win—easily outdistanced runner-up Bob Stanley's total of 41. The Red Sox pitcher amassed 33 saves and eight victories.

Minnesota's Ron Davis and Rich Gossage of the Yankees tied for third place with 35 points. Davis' 30 saves gave the A.L. the only three hurlers to reach that figure in 1983.

The National League Fireman Award was shared by Al Holland of the Phillies and Lee Smith of the Cubs. Holland had 25 saves and eight wins for 33 points, while Smith finished with 29 saves and four triumphs. Jesse Orosco of the Mets and Bruce Sutter of the Cardinals were next with 30 points apiece.

AMERICAN LEAGUE

Pitcher—Club	Saves	Relief Wins	Tot. Pts.
Quisenberry, Kansas City	45	5	50
Stanley, Boston	33	8	41
Davis, Minnesota	30	5	35
Gossage, New York	22	13	35
T. Martinez, Baltimore	21	9	30
Caudill, Seattle	26	2	28
Ladd, Milwaukee	25	3	28
Lopez, Detroit	18	9	27
Lamp, Chicago	15	4	19
Slaton, Milwaukee	5	14	19
Sanchez, California	7	10	17
Tellmann, Milwaukee	8	9	17
McLaughlin, Toronto	9	7	16
Moffitt, Toronto	10	6	16
Stewart, Baltimore	7	9	16
Barojas, Chicago	12	3	15
Beard, Oakland	10	5	15
Jackson, Toronto	7	8	15
Armstrong, Kansas City	3	10	13
O. Jones, Texas	10	3	13
Stoddard, Baltimore	9	4	13
Frazier, New York	8	4	12
Heaton, Cleveland	7	4	11
Tobik, Texas	9	2	11
Bair, Detroit	4	6	10
Burgmeier, Oakland	4	6	10
Spillner, Cleveland	8	2	10
Agosto, Chicago	7	2	9
Stanton, Seattle	7	2	9
Tidrow, Chicago	7	2	9
Whitehouse, Minnesota	2	7	9
Anderson, Cleveland	7	1	8
Aponte, Boston	3	5	8
Baker, Oakland	5	3	8
Butcher, Texas	5	3	8
Clear, Boston	4	4	8
Easterly, Milwaukee-Cleveland	4	4	8
Underwood, Oakland	4	4	8
Witt, California	5	3	8
Lysander, Minnesota	3	4	7
Vande Berg, Seattle	5	2	7
Atherton, Oakland	4	2	6
V. Cruz, Texas	5	1	6
Curtis, California	5	1	6
Hickey, Chicago	5	1	6
Geisel, Toronto	5	0	5
Kison, California	2	3	5
McCatty, Oakland	5	0	5
Schmidt, Texas	2	3	5
Bailey, Detroit	0	4	4
Clark, Seattle	0	4	4
Hassler, California	4	0	4
Johnson, Boston	1	3	4
Thomas, Seattle	1	3	4
Acker, Toronto	1	2	3
Augustine, Milwaukee	2	1	3
Berenguer, Detroit	1	2	3
Gibson, Milwaukee	2	1	3
Koosman, Chicago	2	1	3
Murray, New York	1	2	3
Rozema, Detroit	2	1	3
Walters, Minnesota	2	1	3
Castro, Kansas City	0	2	2
Codiroli, Oakland	1	1	2
Conroy, Oakland	0	2	2
Filson, Minnesota	1	1	2
Gumpert, Detroit	2	0	2
Henke, Texas	1	1	2
Hood, Kansas City	0	2	2
Huismann, Kansas City	0	2	2
Keough, Oakland-New York	0	2	2
Steirer, California	0	2	2
Williams, Minnesota	1	1	2

One save—Bird, Boston; Martin, Detroit; Morogiello, Baltimore; Rawley, New York; Renko, Kansas City.

One relief win—Alexander, Toronto; Barnes, Cleveland; C. Brown, California; S. Brown, California; Burns, Chicago; Clarke, Toronto; Corbett, California; Eichelberger, Cleveland; Gura, Kansas City; Hoffman, Chicago; Hough, Texas; Jackson, Kansas City; Jeffcoat, Cleveland; Jones, Oakland; Krueger, Oakland; Lacey, California; D. Martinez, Baltimore; May, New York; O'Connor, Minnesota; Pashnick, Detroit; Schrom, Minnesota; Shirley, New York; Smith, Oakland; Stoddard, Seattle; Sutcliffe, Cleveland; Swaggerty, Baltimore; Tanana, Texas.

Quisenberry had a 5-3 won-lost record with an impeccable 1.94 earned-run average. Kansas City Manager Dick Howser called on him 54 times in save situations in '83, meaning the Royals' standout did his job more than 80 percent of the time.

Holland picked up nine saves in September, playing a large role in Philadelphia's winning of the N.L. East title. It was Holland's first season with the Phillies after a trade brought him over from San Francisco, where he spent the three previous years. The 6-foot-5, 220-pound Smith was an overpowering force out of the Cubs' bullpen, becoming the most menacing relief pitcher since Dick Radatz of the Red Sox in the early 1960s.

The tie between Holland and Smith was only the third since The Sporting News began the Fireman Award in 1960. Minnesota's Mike Marshall and Jim Kern of Texas tied in the A.L. in 1979, and one year later Rollie Fingers of San Diego and Tom Hume of Cincinnati shared the N.L. honor.

Quisenberry, who first won the Fireman Award in 1980 and then won again in 1982, defended his title in grand fashion. The 1982 N.L. winner was the Cardinals' Sutter.

Al Holland was Philadelphia's main man out of the bullpen.

NATIONAL LEAGUE

Pitcher—Club	Saves	Relief Wins	Tot. Pts.	Pitcher—Club	Saves	Relief Wins	Tot. Pts.
Holland, Philadelphia	25	8	33	Barr, San Francisco	2	5	7
Smith, Chicago	29	4	33	LaCorte, Houston	3	4	7
Orosco, New York	17	13	30	Sarmiento, Pittsburgh	4	3	7
Sutter, St. Louis	21	9	30	Power, Cincinnati	2	4	6
Minton, San Francisco	22	7	29	Schatzeder, Montreal	2	4	6
Bedrosian, Atlanta	19	9	28	Allen, New York-St. Louis	2	3	5
Reardon, Montreal	21	7	28	Bibby, Pittsburgh	2	3	5
Lavelle, San Francisco	20	7	27	Diaz, New York	2	3	5
Tekulve, Pittsburgh	18	7	25	Rucker, St. Louis	0	5	5
DiPino, Houston	20	3	23	Von Ohlen, St. Louis	2	3	5
Howe, Los Angeles	18	4	22	Zachry, Los Angeles	0	5	5
Lucas, San Diego	17	5	22	Beckwith, Los Angeles	1	3	4
Dawley, Houston	14	6	20	Brusstar, Chicago	1	3	4
DeLeon, San Diego	13	6	19	Camp, Atlanta	0	4	4
Niedenfuer, Los Angeles	11	8	19	Smith, Montreal	3	1	4
Hernandez, Chicago-Philadelphia	8	9	17	Gale, Cincinnati	1	2	3
Monge, Philadelphia-San Diego	7	10	17	Lahti, St. Louis	0	3	3
Reed, Philadelphia	8	9	17	Lefferts, Chicago	1	2	3
Forster, Atlanta	13	3	16	Madden, Houston	0	3	3
Sisk, New York	11	5	16	Martin, San Francisco	1	2	3
Campbell, Chicago	8	6	14	McGaffigan, San Francisco	2	1	3
Garber, Atlanta	9	4	13	Pena, Los Angeles	1	2	3
Stewart, Los Angeles	8	5	13	Altamirano, Philadelphia	0	2	2
Hume, Cincinnati	9	3	12	Bair, St. Louis	1	1	2
Scherrer, Cincinnati	10	2	12	Brizzolara, Atlanta	1	1	2
Guante, Pittsburgh	9	2	11	Falcone, Atlanta	0	2	2
Hayes, Cincinnati	7	4	11	Heathcock, Houston	1	1	2
Scurry, Pittsburgh	7	4	11	LaPoint, St. Louis	0	2	2
Montefusco, San Diego	4	6	10	Martin, St. Louis	0	2	2
Ruhle, Houston	3	7	10	McGraw, Philadelphia	0	2	2
Smith, Houston	6	3	9	Proly, Chicago	1	1	2
James, Montreal	7	1	8	Sosa, San Diego	1	1	2
Moore, Atlanta	6	2	8	Stuper, St. Louis	1	1	2

One save—Andujar, St. Louis; Bordi, Chicago; Carman, Philadelphia; Chiffer, San Diego; Hershiser, Los Angeles; LaCoss, Houston; Rasmussen, St. Louis; Rhoden, Pittsburgh; Sanderson, Montreal; Swan, New York; Whitson, San Diego.

One relief win—Andersen, Philadelphia; Burris, Montreal; Cato, Cincinnati; Dayley, Atlanta; Forsch, St. Louis; Gaff, New York; Gorman, New York; Hagen, St. Louis; Jenkins, Chicago; Johnson, Chicago; Knepper, Houston; Lerch, San Francisco; Lynch, New York; Ownbey, New York; Robinson, Pittsburgh; Trout, Chicago; Tunnell, Pittsburgh.

O's, Astros Take Four 1-0 Wins

By DAVE SLOAN

Pitchers are notorious for complaining about losing games in which they perform well but receive little batting support. Bob Welch of Los Angeles had this lack-of-offense problem on June 17, so he took matters into his own hands.

In a game against Cincinnati, Welch belted a sixth-inning home run off Mario Soto and pitched a six-hit shutout to beat the Reds, 1-0. It was Welch's second 1-0 victory of the month. On June 1, the hard-throwing Dodger pitched a one-hitter against the Philadelphia Phillies and their ace lefthander, Steve Carlton. The only hit off Welch was a fourth-inning single by Von Hayes.

On May 18, Richard Dotson of the White Sox also threw a one-hitter—but he lost, 1-0, to the Baltimore Orioles on Dan Ford's eighth-inning homer. The White Sox got only three hits off Storm Davis and one against Tippy Martinez.

Baltimore was the only American League club to win four 1-0 games, with Mike Flanagan getting two of the victories. Flanagan beat Seattle on May 11 and edged Minnesota on September 2 when the Orioles scored the winning run in the ninth. Martinez notched the win in Dotson's one-hitter, and Scott McGregor picked up Baltimore's other 1-0 triumph on May 28 against Kansas City.

The Houston Astros were the only National League team to record four 1-0 triumphs and the only major league team involved in six such games. Mike Madden, Bill Dawley, Nolan Ryan and Vern Ruhle were Houston's winning pitchers, with Madden (May 25) and Ruhle (August 26) beating the Chicago Cubs and Dawley earning the decision against San Francisco on June 8. Ryan's win on August 3 was a one-hitter against San Diego. Tim Flannery's third-inning single was the Padres' only hit.

The Astros lost the season's first 1-0 game, to Pittsburgh's Larry McWilliams on April 9, and on July 26 they fell to rookie Charles Hudson of Philadelphia.

Only the Atlanta Braves and Toronto Blue Jays were not involved in a 1-0 game in 1983. The California Angels had the dubious distinction of losing all three of the 1-0 games involving them.

Eight of the majors' 32 1-0 outcomes were decided by home runs—three by Baltimore hitters. Ford connected on May 18, Eddie Murray on May 28 and Ken Singleton on September 2. Wayne Gross of Oakland (on May 8 against the Orioles) and Kansas City's Pat Sheridan (in an August 7 game with Boston) were the other A.L. batters to accomplish the feat.

Welch, Joe Morgan of the Phillies (on July 26 against Houston) and Danny Heep of the Mets (on October 2 against Montreal) were the National League players to do it.

The complete list of 1-0 games, including the winning and losing pitchers and the inning in which the run was scored, follows:

AMERICAN LEAGUE (19)

Date	Winner	Loser	Inning
APRIL—			
17	—*Jones, Tex.	*Stanley, Bos.	14
MAY—			
8	—*Krueger, Oak.	*T.Martinez, Balt.	8
11	— Flanagan, Balt.	Perry, Sea.	5
18	—*T. Martinez, Balt.	Dotson, Chi.	8
19	— Young, Sea.	Forsch, Cal.	8
21	—*Rawley, N.Y.	Norris, Oak.	9
28	— McGregor, Balt.	*Armstrong, K.C.	7
JUNE—			
8	—*Smithson, Tex.	Young, Sea.	7
19	— Burns, Chi.	*Underwood, Oak.	4
JULY—			
16	— Moore, Sea.	*Lopez, Det.	9
AUGUST—			
7	—*Perry, K.C.	Boyd, Bos.	4
15	— Burns, Chi.	Righetti, N.Y.	1
24	— Heaton, Clev.	Conroy, Oak.	4
24	—*Slaton, Mil.	*Hassler, Cal.	14
28	— Hough, Tex.	*Renko, K.C.	4
SEPTEMBER—			
2	—*Flanagan, Balt.	*Viola, Minn.	9
12	—*Fontenot, N.Y.	Porter, Mil.	5
14	—*Armstrong, K.C.	*Steirer, Cal.	14
14	—*Davis, Minn.	Burns, Chi.	9

NATIONAL LEAGUE (13)

Date	Winner	Loser	Inning
APRIL—			
9	— McWilliams, Pitts.	Niekro, Hou.	1
MAY—			
25	—*Madden, Hou.	*Lefferts, Chi.	2
JUNE—			
1	— Welch, L.A.	*Carlton, Phila.	4
8	—*Dawley, Hou.	*Lavelle, S.F.	11
17	— Welch, L.A.	Soto, Cin.	6
JULY—			
26	—*Hudson, Phila.	*Ryan, Hou.	4
31‡	—*Orosco, N.Y.	*Sarmiento, Pitts.	12
AUGUST—			
3	— Ryan, Hou.	*Lollar, S.D.	1
6	—*Holland, Phila.	*Sutter, St.L.	11
26	—*Ruhle, Hou.	*Trout, Chi.	7
SEPTEMBER—			
16	— M. Davis, S.F.	*Valenzuela, L.A.	6
24	—*Candelaria, Pitts.	*Smith, Mont.	5
OCTOBER—			
2†	— Terrell, N.Y.	Lea, Mont.	1

*Did not pitch complete game.
†First game of doubleheader.
‡Second game of doubleheader.

5 Players Attain 3-Homer Plateau

By JOE HOPPEL

Walloping three home runs in one game is a notable achievement for any major leaguer, regardless of the circumstances. However, the dramatic manner in which George Brett, Jim Rice and Ben Oglivie capped three-homer games in 1983—plus the usual situation surrounding Dan Ford's spree—added considerably to the magnitude of those players' feats.

Kansas City's Brett was the first of five big leaguers to slug three home runs in one game in '83, breaking loose on April 20 in Detroit. Having hit two homers earlier in the game against the Tigers, Brett strode to the plate in the ninth inning with a man on base and the Royals trailing, 7-6.

Detroit Manager Sparky Anderson brought in lefthander Howard Bailey to face the lefthanded-hitting Brett, and the Royals' third baseman drilled homer No. 3 for an 8-7 Kansas City triumph.

The three-homer game was the second of Brett's career in regular-season play. Brett hit three homers in a 1979 American League game, and he also had a three-homer salvo in Game 3 of the 1978 A.L. Championship Series.

Rice of the Red Sox produced in a situation identical to Brett's. With his club down, 7-6, in the second game of an August 29 doubleheader in Toronto, Rice lashed a two-run homer—his third home run of the game—in the ninth inning, giving Boston an 8-7 victory.

Rice, who had a three-homer game in the A.L. in 1977, drove in six runs against the Blue Jays.

Milwaukee's Oglivie didn't win the Brewers' May 14 game against Boston with a ninth-inning homer, but he did the next-best thing. The Red Sox were ahead, 6-4, in the bottom of the ninth at Milwaukee when Oglivie cracked his third homer of the night, a two-run drive, to send the game into extra innings. The Brewers went on to win, 8-7, in 10 innings.

Baltimore's Ford came off 28 days on the disabled list on July 20 at Seattle—and belted three bases-empty homers to mark his return. Ford's outburst sparked the Orioles to a 4-2 victory over the Mariners.

While Darrell Evans' three-homer, six-RBI performance for the Giants in a June 15 game against Houston lacked the theatrics of the other three-homer shows (the Giants won, 7-1), Evans' big day in San Francisco did represent a breakthrough for the National League. It had been nearly three years (June 22, 1980) since Claudell Washington, then with the Mets, had turned in the N.L.'s last three-homer game.

For Ford and Evans, the three-homer games were career firsts.

Boston's Rice and Tony Armas and Atlanta's Dale Murphy topped the majors in 1983 with six multi-homer games each.

Following is a list of players who had multi-homer games in '83 and the number of times they did it:

AMERICAN LEAGUE: Baltimore (7)—Murray 2, Ripken 2, Ford, Roenicke, Singleton. Boston (14)—Armas 6, Rice 6, Evans 2. California (4)—DeCinces 2, Grich, Valentine. Chicago (5)—Luzinski 3, Baines, Fisk. Cleveland (2)—Harrah, Thornton. Detroit (3)—Lemon, Trammell, Wilson. Kansas City (5)—Aikens 2, Brett 2, White. Milwaukee (3)—Cooper 2, Oglivie. Minnesota (9)—Brunansky 4, Hrbek 2, Bush, Teufel, Ward. New York (7)—Winfield 3, Griffey 2, Nettles, Smalley. Oakland (4)—Gross, Lansford, Lopes, Moore. Seattle (8)—S. Henderson 2, Zisk 2, Cowens, T. Cruz, D. Henderson, Putnam. Texas (3)—Parrish 2, Hostetler. Toronto (11)—Barfield 4, Moseby 3, Whitt 2, Johnson, Klutts.

NATIONAL LEAGUE: Atlanta (10)—Murphy 6, Chambliss 3, Horner. Chicago (9)—Hall 4, Cey 2, Davis 2, Buckner. Cincinnati (1)—Redus. Houston (5)—Thon 3, Ashby, Cruz. Los Angeles (9)—Guerrero 2, Yeager 2, Baker, Brock, Marshall, Monday, Roenicke. Montreal (6)—Dawson 3, Carter 2, Oliver. New York (7)—Strawbery 4, Foster, Kingman, Terrell. Philadelphia (9)—Schmidt 5, Morgan 3, Diaz. Pittsburgh (3)—Berra, Pena, Ray. St. Louis (4)—Hendrick 2, Porter, L. Smith. San Diego (0). San Francisco (11)—Evans 4, C. Davis 2, Bergman, Clark, LeMaster, Leonard, Youngblood.

A recap of the three-homer games:

Date	Player—Club—Opp.	Place	AB.	R.	H.	2B.	3B.	HR.	RBI.	Result
Apr. 20	Brett, Royals vs Tigers	A	5	3	4	0	0	3	7	W 8-7
May 14	Oglivie, Brewers vs. Red Sox (10 inn.)	H	4	3	3	0	0	3	5	W 8-7
June 15	Evans, Giants vs. Astros	H	4	3	3	0	0	3	6	W 7-1
July 20	Ford, Orioles vs. Mariners	A	4	3	4	0	0	3	3	W 4-2
Aug. 29*	Rice, Red Sox vs. Blue Jays	A	5	3	3	0	0	3	6	W 8-7

*Second game a doubleheader.

O's Slammed Way to Division Title

By DAVE SLOAN

At the halfway point of their 1983 schedule, the Baltimore Orioles were tied for second place in the American League East with a 45-36 record and had yet to hit a bases-loaded home run.

How things changed.

Baltimore went on a 53-28 surge the rest of the season and won the East Division crown, displaying timely muscle in the process. The Orioles slugged eight grand slams in the second half of the season, with the first coming off the bat of Cal Ripken on July 13 in game No. 82. Baltimore's outburst marked the second straight season that the Orioles had hit eight grand slams.

The major league record for team grand slams in a season is 10, set by the 1938 Tigers, and the N.L. mark is nine, established by the 1929 Cubs.

There were 78 grand slams in the majors in '83, 40 in the American League.

The California Angels also hit eight slams, belting six in the first two months of the season. California batters hit three of the season's first five bases-full homers, with two coming in one game. Fred Lynn and Daryl Sconiers connected against Detroit on April 27 to lead the Angels to a 13-3 victory. It was the 32nd time in big-league history that two grand slams had been hit by one team in the same game.

Sconiers was one of 10 hitters to hit two slams in 1983. Dwayne Murphy of Oakland, Don Baylor of New York, Lance Parrish of Detroit and John Lowenstein of Baltimore were the other American Leaguers to accomplish the feat in regular-season play. In addition to his April wallop, Lynn hit the first grand slam in All-Star Game history in July.

Parrish and Lowenstein were the only A.L. players to deliver game-winning grand slams in the ninth inning. Parrish's decisive smash came at home on July 10 to cap a five-run Tiger rally that beat Oakland, 5-3. Lowenstein's blow also came at Detroit in the Orioles' 7-3 victory in the second game of a September 21 doubleheader.

Lowenstein struck his first slam of the season September 10 in the opener of a doubleheader at New York off the Yankees' Rich Gossage. It was one of only three pinch-hit grand slams in the American League in 1983. John Wockenfuss of the Tigers got the first on July 3 at Detroit and Alan Bannister of the Indians hit the last against the Brewers on September 21 at Cleveland. Bannister's blow was the third slam hit off Milwaukee pitching in four days.

Tom Brunansky of the Twins was the only American Leaguer to hit a second home run in his grand-slam game. Brunansky's two homers came in Minnesota's 11-0 blowout of the Red Sox at Boston on September 1.

Four National League players—Greg Brock of the Dodgers, Mike Schmidt of the Phillies, Mel Hall of the Cubs and Gary Carter of the Expos—had two-homer games that included a slam.

Brock's two homers came on May 18 at Montreal in a 13-3 L.A. triumph, and Hall's blasts came in Chicago's 7-5 victory over the Braves at Atlanta on August 29. Brock and Hall were rookies in '83. Schmidt hit his two on July 11 at Cincinnati, and Carter connected on September 10 at Montreal against the New York Mets.

Al Oliver and Tim Raines of Montreal, George Foster of New York, Mike Easler of Pittsburgh and Schmidt were the N.L. players to hit two slams in 1983.

One of Raines' slams, on June 22 at home against Al Holland of the Phillies, came with two out in the ninth and accounted for all the runs in the game, the only time that occurred in '83. Philadelphia's Bo Diaz (April 13) and Ozzie Virgil (September 2) also hit N.L. game-winning slams in the ninth inning, with both coming in Philadelphia. Diaz's drive beat the Mets, 10-9, and Virgil's pinch-hit smash upended the Giants, 5-3.

Easler's first slam came in a pinch-hitting role against the Braves' Steve Bedrosian in a 6-2 Pirate victory on September 3 in Atlanta. Three other pinch slams—by Virgil, Kurt Bevacqua of San Diego and Richie Hebner of Pittsburgh—were hit in the N.L.

Foster's two slams were the only ones hit by Met batters in 1983 and they came in the same week. On August 14, Foster hit one off Chuck Rainey of the Cubs in New York and on August 20 he slugged his second at San Francisco off the Giants' Mark Calvert.

Jeff Leonard of the Giants, Mike Marshall of the Dodgers, Baylor and Schmidt hit extra-inning slams that proved decisive in '83.

Every team yielded at least one slam in '83, with the Cubs and Detroit Tigers giving up the most, six. Kansas City and

The Orioles' John Lowenstein is congratulated after his grand slam against the Yankees on September 10.

Texas were the only clubs not to hit any.

The complete list of grand slams, with the inning in which each was hit in parentheses, follows:

AMERICAN LEAGUE (40)

APRIL—
9 —Carew, California vs. Keough, Oakland (5)
9 —Vukovich, Cleveland vs. T. Martinez, Baltimore (8)
27 —Lynn, California vs. Wilcox, Detroit (3)
27 —Sconiers, California vs. James, Detroit (7)

MAY—
1 —Bonnell, Toronto vs. Tidrow, Chicago (7)
7 —Armas, Boston vs. Caudill, Seattle (7)
12 —Murphy, Oakland vs. Petry, Detroit (5)
28 —Sconiers, California vs. Barker, Cleveland (1)

JUNE—
2 —Valentine, California vs. Murray, New York (6)
5 —Martinez, Toronto vs. Stoddard, Baltimore (6)
6 —Ro. Jackson, California vs. McClure, Mil. (8)
15 —Lopes, Oakland vs. Geisel, Toronto (5)
16 —Baylor, New York vs. Blyleven, Cleveland (3)
29 —Lansford, Oakland vs. Splittorff, Kansas City (1)

JULY—
3 —Wockenfuss, Detroit vs. Morogiello, Baltimore (8)
4 —Oglivie, Milwaukee vs. Barker, Cleveland (1)
10 —Parrish, Detroit vs. Jones, Oakland (9)
13 —Ripken, Baltimore vs. Conroy, Oakland (4)
22 —Grich, California vs. Bair, Detroit (7)
26 —Balboni, New York vs. Tanana, Texas (4)
29 —Parrish, Detroit vs. Gura, Kansas City (3)
31 —Baylor, New York vs. Lamp, Chicago (11)

AUGUST—
8 —Nolan, Baltimore vs. Sutcliffe, Cleveland (4)
8† —Griffey, New York vs. Williams, Toronto (1)
13 —Bernazard, Seattle vs. Forsch, California (5)
17 —Beniquez, California vs. Warren, Oakland (7)
20 —Rice, Boston vs. Stieb, Toronto (3)
29 —Shelby, Baltimore vs. Creel, Kansas City (9)

SEPTEMBER—
1* —Brunansky, Minnesota vs. Aponte, Boston (7)
3 —Singleton, Baltimore vs. Whitehouse, Minnesota (3)
3 —Murphy, Oakland vs. Heaton, Cleveland (4)
10* —Lowenstein, Baltimore vs. Gossage, New York (9)
11 —Upshaw, Toronto vs. Codiroli, Oakland (1)
13† —Roenicke, Baltimore vs. Johnson, Boston (8)
15 —Baines, Chicago vs. Best, Seattle (6)
18 —Murray, Baltimore vs. Ladd, Milwaukee (8)
20 —Fischlin, Cleveland vs. Caldwell, Milwaukee (2)
21 —Bannister, Cleveland vs. Waits, Milwaukee (8)
21† —Lowenstein, Baltimore vs. Lopez, Detroit (9)

OCTOBER—
1 —Howell, Milwaukee vs. Bailey, Detroit (7)

NATIONAL LEAGUE (38)

APRIL—
13 —Diaz, Philadelphia vs. Allen, New York (9)

MAY—
18 —Brock, Los Angeles vs. Gullickson, Montreal (5)
18 —Clark, San Francisco vs. Altamirano, Phila. (7)
20 —Concepcion, Cincinnati vs. Campbell, Chicago (8)
31 —Sandberg, Chicago vs. LaCorte, Houston (6)

JUNE—
2 —Chambliss, Atlanta vs. Kaat, St. Louis (8)
12 —Davis, Chicago vs. Forsch, St. Louis (4)
20 —Hubbard, Atlanta vs. LaCorte, Houston (5)
22 —Raines, Montreal vs. Holland, Philadelphia (9)
26 —Davis, Chicago vs. Lerch, Montreal (2)
28 —Guerrero, Los Angeles vs. Sosa, San Diego (4)

JULY—
3 —Garvey, San Diego vs. M. Davis, San Francisco (5)
4† —Porter, St. Louis vs. Bibby, Pittsburgh (3)
11 —Flannery, San Diego vs. Jenkins, Chicago (1)
11 —Schmidt, Philadelphia vs. Hume, Cincinnati (11)
14 —Bevacqua, San Diego vs. Scurry, Pittsburgh (7)
20 —Lefebrve, Philadelphia vs. M. Scott, Houston (1)
23 —Landreaux, Los Angeles vs. Sutter, St. Louis (8)
24† —Leonard, San Francsico vs. Sarmiento, Pitts. (11)
31* —Thompson, Pittsburgh vs. Terrell, New York (1)

AUGUST—
6* —Brown, San Diego vs. Hume, Cincinnati (8)
7 —Raines, Montreal vs. McWilliams, Pittsburgh (2)
11 —Durham, Chicago vs. Cox, St. Louis (3)
14 —Foster, New York vs. Rainey, Chicago (3)
15 —Schmidt, Philadelphia vs. Smith, Chicago (8)
20 —Foster, New York vs. Calvert, San Francisco (5)
28 —Oliver, Montreal vs. Lucas, San Diego (7)
29 —Hall, Chicago vs. Niekro, Atlanta (5)

SEPTEMBER—
2 —Virgil, Philadelphia vs. Lavelle, San Francisco (9)
3 —Easler, Pittsburgh vs. Bedrosian, Atlanta (7)
5 —Oliver, Montreal vs. Proly, Chicago (6)
7 —Marshall, Los Angeles vs. Hayes, Cincinnati (10)
10 —Carter, Montreal vs. Lynch, New York (1)
14 —Esasky, Cincinnati vs. Bedrosian, Atlanta (7)
15 —Hebner, Pittsburgh vs. Smith, Chicago (8)
16 —Wynne, Pittsburgh vs. Reardon, Montreal (8)
20 —Cruz, Houston vs. Hooton, Los Angeles (2)
23 —Easler, Pittsburgh vs. Sanderson, Montreal (1)

*First game of doubleheader.
†Second game of doubleheader.

Dawson Led Five-Hit Batters

By JOE HOPPEL

Tim Teufel, rookie infielder of the Twins, wasted little time in making his mark in the majors. In his 10th big-league game after being recalled from Minnesota's Triple-A farm club at Toledo, Teufel collected five hits in a September 16 contest against the Blue Jays.

Teufel, a .323 hitter at Toledo, slugged his first two homers in the major leagues, two singles and a triple.

Twelve days later, Bo Diaz of the Phillies turned in the 23rd and last five-hit performance of the 1983 major league season.

One major leaguer, Andre Dawson of the Expos, enjoyed two five-hit games in '83. Dawson went on his sprees against the Dodgers on April 8 (in Montreal's third game of the season) and against the Giants on June 5.

For the Rangers' Jim Sundberg, a five-hit salvo was hardly indicative of his season. While Sundberg had five hits in an 11-inning game against the Orioles on May 14, he ended up with a season batting average of .201—two points above his low-water mark in the big leagues.

Jerry Mumphrey and Manny Trillo posted four-hit games in each major league during the '83 season. Mumphrey accomplished the four-hit feat for the Yankees in the American League and, after an August 10 trade, did it for the Astros in the N.L.; Trillo, dealt to the N.L. in mid-August, had four-hit games for the A.L.'s Indians and for Montreal. Keith Hernandez, swapped by the Cardinals on June 15, had four-hit efforts for both St. Louis and the Mets.

Cal Ripken of the Orioles and Rod Carew of the Angels led the majors with six games of four or more hits.

Ripken was the only big leaguer who had both a five-hit game and a batting streak of at least 15 games. Ripken cracked five hits against the Twins on September 3, three days before the start of his 16-game batting streak.

Tony Gwynn of the Padres had the majors' longest batting streak of '83, hitting in 25 straight games from August 21 through September 18. Another San Diego player, Bobby Brown, had the N.L.'s second-longest streak at 21 games.

Two Blue Jays, Damaso Garcia and Lloyd Moseby, paced the A.L. with 21-game strings. Of the majors' 25 hitting streaks of 15 or more games, 21 were achieved by American Leaguers.

Toronto teammates Lloyd Moseby (above) and Damaso Garcia each had 21-game hitting streaks.

Buddy Bell of the Rangers and Mickey Hatcher of the Twins each had two batting streaks of 15 or more games. Bell's streaks covered 17 and 15 games, and Hatcher's were for 16 and 15. Hatcher's

16-game streak was the majors' longest in terms of time span, running from July 20 through August 27 because the Minnesota player spent three weeks on the supplemental disabled list.

George Brett's 19-game streak for the Royals started on opening day, while Rick Manning's 17-game streak for Cleveland came in his final 17 contests with the Indians. Traded to Milwaukee on June 6 with his streak intact, Manning went 0-for-4 on June 7 in his first game with the Brewers.

Streaks of 15 or more games also were recorded by these major leaguers in '83: 19 games—Harold Baines, White Sox; Carney Lansford, A's; Jose Cruz, Astros; Willie McGee, Cardinals; 18 games—Gary Gaetti, Twins; Lou Whitaker, Tigers; 17 games—Willie Wilson, Royals; 16 games—Ben Oglivie, Brewers; Tom Paciorek, White Sox; Willie Randolph, Yankees; Ted Simmons, Brewers; 15 games—Don Mattingly, Yankees; Jim Rice, Red Sox; Wayne Tolleson, Rangers.

The complete list of players with four or more hits in one game follows:

AMERICAN LEAGUE: Baltimore (17)—Ripken 6, Murray 3, Singleton 2, Dauer, Dwyer, Ford, Lowenstein, Roenicke, Shelby. Boston (14)—Boggs 4, Hoffman 2, Remy 2, Allenson, Armas, Evans, Nichols, Rice, Stapleton. California (13)—Carew 6, Grich 2, Beniquez, DeCinces, Downing, Pettis, Sconiers. Chicago (7)—R. Law 3, Fisk 2, Luzinski, Paciorek. Cleveland (8)—Harrah 2, Hargrove, Hassey, McBride, Thornton, Trillo, Vukovich. Detroit (17)—Whitaker 5, Herndon 4, Brookens 2, Cabell 2, Trammell 2, Lemon, Parrish. Kansas City (15)—Sheridan 3, Brett 2, McRae 2, Slaught 2, Washington 2, Wilson 2, Geronimo, White. Milwaukee (15)—Cooper 3, Gantner 3, Molitor 2, Brouhard, Howell, Moore, Ready, Romero, Simmons, Yount. Minnesota (12)—Ward 4, Brown 3, Brunansky, Castino, Engle, Gaetti, Teufel. New York (10)—Winfield 3, Smalley 2, Campaneris, Gamble, Kemp, Mumphrey, Nettles. Oakland (5)—Davis, Hancock, Kearney, Lansford, Murphy. Seattle (3)—Putnam 2, S. Henderson. Texas (16)—Parrish 3, Sample 3, Dent 2, Anderson, Bell, Johnson, B. Jones, Rivers, Sundberg, Tolleson, Wright. Toronto (14)—Collins 3, Barfield 2, Moseby 2, Upshaw 2, Bell, Bonnell, Iorg, Martinez, Whitt.

NATIONAL LEAGUE: Atlanta (12)—Butler 3, Murphy 3, Ramirez 2, Washington 2, Harper, Horner. Chicago (10)—Bowa 2, Buckner 2, Davis 2, Cey, Hall, Lake, Sandberg. Cincinnati (5)—Milner 2, Driessen, Oester, Redus. Houston (12)—Cruz 3, Knight 3, Moreno 2, Ashby, Doran, Mumphrey, Thon. Los Angeles (16)—Baker 4, S. Sax 3, Brock 2, Guerrero 2, Landreaux 2, Marshall, Russell, Thomas. Montreal (11)—Cromartie 2, Dawson 2, Oliver 2, Raines 2, Francona, Little, Trillo. New York (6)—Brooks, Foster, Giles, Hernandez, Kingman, Wilson. Philadelphia (10)—Morgan 3, Diaz 2, Rose 2, DeJesus, Dernier, Matthews. Pittsburgh (13)—Ray 4, Pena 2, Thompson 2, Berra, Hebner, Lacy, Parker, Wynne. St. Louis (16)—Hendrick 5, Oberkfell 3, O. Smith 3, L. Smith 2, Hernandez, Herr, McGee. San Diego (7)—Bonilla 2, Garvey, Gwynn, Hinshaw, Salazar, Templeton. San Francisco (7)—Clark 2, Evans 2, Bergman, C. Davis, Leonard.

The records of all players with five or more hits in a game follow:

Date	Player—Club—Opp.	Place	AB.	R.	H.	2B.	3B.	HR.	RBI.	Result
April 8	Dawson, Expos vs. Dodgers	A	5	1	5	1	1	0	2	W 8-3
April 13	Hendrick, Cardinals vs. Pirates	A	5	2	5	0	0	2	4	W 9-1
April 13	Hoffman, Red Sox vs. Royals	A	6	2	5	1	0	0	1	W 18-4
April 22	Carew, Angels vs. Orioles (11 innings)	H	7	1	5	1	0	0	3	W 6-5
May 9	Thompson, Pirates vs. Padres (14 innings)	A	7	0	5	2	0	0	2	W 5-3
May 9	Cromartie, Expos vs. Braves	A	5	0	5	1	0	0	1	W 5-3
May 14	Sundberg, Rangers vs. Orioles (11 innings)	H	6	2	5	1	0	0	1	L 11-14
June 5	Dawson, Expos vs. Giants	A	5	4	5	2	0	1	1	W 12-9
June 28*	Brooks, Mets vs. Cardinals	A	6	2	5	1	0	0	1	W 10-1
July 3	B. Jones, Rangers vs. A's (15 innings)	A	8	2	5	3	0	0	4	W 16-4
July 10	Butler, Braves vs. Expos	A	6	2	5	0	1	0	0	L 6-7
July 11	Herndon, Tigers vs. Angels	H	6	4	5	2	0	1	3	W 12-6
July 20	Landreaux, Dodgers vs. Pirates	A	5	0	5	1	0	0	1	L 3-7
July 21	Dernier, Phillies vs. Braves	A	5	2	5	0	0	0	3	W 10-6
July 22	Clark, Giants vs. Pirates	A	5	2	5	0	0	0	0	W 5-3
July 24	Trammell, Tigers vs. Angels (12 innings)	A	5	0	5	1	0	0	1	W 4-3
July 27	Molitor, Brewers vs. Twins	A	5	4	5	1	0	0	0	W 13-9
July 31	Harrah, Indians vs. Blue Jays	A	5	1	5	2	0	0	3	W 16-11
Aug. 2	Ray, Pirates vs. Phillies	H	5	1	5	0	0	0	3	W 10-3
Sept. 3	Ripken, Orioles vs. Twins	A	6	3	5	2	0	2	4	W 13-0
Sept. 8	Ramirez, Braves vs. Giants	A	6	2	5	0	1	1	3	W 12-9
Sept. 16	Teufel, Twins vs. Blue Jays	H	5	5	5	0	1	2	3	W 11-4
Sept. 28	Diaz, Phillies vs. Cubs	A	5	4	5	0	0	2	3	W 13-6

*First game of doubleheader.

Easler Again Led in Pinch-Hits

By JOE HOPPEL

When the Pittsburgh Pirates needed someone to deliver in the clutch during the last two seasons, they had just the man—Mike Easler. Now, the Bucs will have to look elsewhere in tough situations.

Easler, with eight hits in 17 at-bats and a .471 average, topped the National League in pinch-hitting (10 at-bats are needed to qualify) for the second straight season in 1983. The N.L. runner-up was Gerald Perry, who batted .438 (7-for-16) in the pinch for the Atlanta Braves.

Easler, whose .500 mark (5-for-10) paced the N.L. in 1982, was traded by the Pirates to the Boston Red Sox two months after the close of the '83 season.

Garry Hancock of the Oakland A's and Alan Bannister of the Cleveland Indians shared the American League pinch-hitting championship last season with .500 averages. Hancock went 7-for-14, and Bannister was 5-for-10.

Rusty Staub of the New York Mets established two major league pinch-hitting records in '83 by appearing in 94 games and totaling 81 at-bats.

Staub also tied a big-league mark by collecting eight consecutive pinch-hits in one season, achieving the feat from June 11 through the first game of a June 26 doubleheader.

N.L. batters set a major league record by belting 55 pinch homers in '83, surpassing the mark of 53 attained by the A.L. in 1980. And the Mets tied the 1957 Cincinnati Reds' record of 12 pinch homers in one season.

Following is a list of all pinch-hitters with at least 10 at-bats in 1983:

NATIONAL LEAGUE PINCH-HITTING
(Compiled by Elias Sports Bureau)

Club Pinch-Hitting

Club	AB.	H.	HR.	RBI.	Pct.	Club	AB.	H.	HR.	RBI.	Pct.
Atlanta	181	50	4	37	.276	New York	301	68	12	50	.226
San Francisco	198	50	3	38	.253	Cincinnati	229	51	5	37	.223
Philadelphia	227	55	4	35	.242	Pittsburgh	211	44	5	29	.209
Montreal	211	50	0	25	.237	Los Angeles	226	47	8	31	.208
San Diego	214	49	2	31	.229	Chicago	249	50	4	39	.201
St. Louis	228	52	4	28	.228	Houston	200	39	4	29	.195
						Totals	2675	605	55	409	.226

Individual Pinch-Hitting
(10 or More At-Bats)

Player-Club	AB.	H.	HR.	RBI.	Pct.	Player-Club	AB.	H.	HR.	RBI.	Pct.
Easler, Pitts.	17	8	1	7	.471	Hayes, Phila.	21	5	0	2	.238
Perry, Atlanta	16	7	0	2	.438	May, S.F.-Pitts.	13	3	0	1	.231
Hodges, New York.	14	6	0	5	.429	Roenicke, L.A.	22	5	0	1	.227
Bevacqua, S. D.	34	14	1	16	.412	Harper, Pittsburgh	27	6	1	6	.222
Watson, Atlanta	27	11	2	13	.407	Bosley, Chicago	18	4	1	6	.222
Cromartie, Mon.	22	8	0	7	.364	Walling, Houston	37	8	1	8	.216
Rose, Philadelphia.	22	8	0	2	.364	Thompson, Chi.	28	6	0	1	.214
Lezcano, S.D.-Phil.	14	5	0	5	.357	G. Gross, Phila.	33	7	0	5	.212
Bergman, S.F.	31	11	2	9	.355	Francona, Mon.	38	8	0	2	.211
Wohlford, Mon.	31	11	0	9	.355	Flannery, S.D.	19	4	0	1	.211
Rohn, Chicago	17	6	0	2	.353	Knicely, Cincinnati	19	4	0	3	.211
Walker, Cincinnati	48	16	0	11	.333	Perez, Philadelphia	19	4	0	3	.211
Bochy, San Diego	12	4	0	0	.333	Vail, S.F.-Mon.	25	5	0	3	.200
Johnson, Atlanta	25	8	0	4	.320	Foley, Cincinnati	20	4	0	0	.200
Porter, St. Louis	19	6	0	5	.316	Youngblood, S. F.	20	4	0	3	.200
Braun, St. Louis	48	15	2	5	.313	Bream, L.A.	10	2	0	2	.200
Morales, L.A.	40	12	3	8	.300	Cedeno, Cincinnati.	10	2	2	3	.200
Green, St. Louis	20	6	0	2	.300	Kuiper, S.F.	10	2	0	0	.200
Iorg, St. Louis	20	6	0	4	.300	Morales, Chicago	41	8	0	8	.195
Lacy, Pittsburgh	20	6	0	0	.300	Woods, Chicago	31	6	1	6	.194
Morgan, Phila.	10	3	0	2	.300	Rayford, St. Louis	26	5	2	5	.192
Staub, New York	81	24	3	25	.296	Monday, L.A.	42	8	0	7	.190
O'Malley, S.F.	17	5	0	7	.294	Backman, N. Y.	16	3	0	1	.188
Heep, New York	40	11	4	6	.275	Thomas, L.A.	16	3	1	1	.188
Lefebvre, S.D.-Phil	40	11	2	4	.275	T. Scott, Houston	27	5	0	3	.185
Venable, S.F.	22	6	1	3	.273	Kingman, N. Y.	39	7	1	5	.179
Maddox, Phila.	11	3	0	1	.273	Bradley, New York	34	6	2	2	.176
Veryzer, Chicago	11	3	0	0	.273	Householder, Cin.	17	3	0	0	.176
Jorgensen, NY-Atl.	45	12	2	9	.267	Crowley, Montreal.	35	6	0	3	.171
Morrison, Pitts.	15	4	0	0	.267	Richards, S.D.	36	6	0	3	.167
Puhl, Houston	15	4	0	0	.267	Harper, Atlanta	18	3	0	0	.167
Bench, Cincinnati	34	9	2	11	.265	Jones, San Diego	18	3	0	3	.167
Hebner, Pittsburgh	27	7	2	7	.259	Reynolds, Houston.	12	2	0	0	.167
Bass, Houston	43	11	0	6	.256	Johnstone, Chicago	38	6	1	8	.158

Individual Pinch-Hitting—Continued
(10 or More At-Bats)

Player-Club	AB.	H.	HR.	RBI.	Pct.
Brenly, S.F.	13	2	0	2	.154
Summers, S.F.	20	3	0	3	.150
Mazzilli, Pitts.	41	6	0	1	.146
Tolman, Houston	30	4	2	5	.133
Nordhagen, Chi.	15	2	0	2	.133
Turner, San Diego	23	3	0	0	.130
Landestoy, Cin-LA	33	4	0	0	.121
Molinaro, Phila.	18	2	1	3	.111
Tenace, Pittsburgh	29	3	0	3	.103
Ashford, New York	10	1	0	0	.100
Krenchicki, Cin.	11	1	0	2	.091
Lyons, St. Louis	11	1	0	1	.091
Paris, Cincinnati	11	1	0	1	.091
White, Montreal	23	2	0	0	.087
Quirk, St. Louis	17	1	0	0	.059
Pocoroba, Atlanta	20	1	0	2	.050
Spilman, Houston	20	1	1	4	.050
Ramirez, S.D.	15	0	0	0	.000

AMERICAN LEAGUE PINCH-HITTING
(Compiled by Sports Information Center)

Club Pinch-Hitting

Club	AB.	H.	HR.	RBI.	Pct.
Boston	103	34	0	19	.330
Kansas City	76	23	0	17	.303
Oakland	115	34	0	16	.296
Toronto	200	58	5	42	.290
California	101	28	4	22	.277
Cleveland	100	27	1	17	.270
Chicago	179	48	2	33	.268
Detroit	153	40	3	28	.261
Milwaukee	81	21	2	15	.259
Texas	118	29	2	20	.246
Seattle	159	39	2	28	.245
New York	95	23	3	12	.242
Minnesota	99	23	2	16	.232
Baltimore	191	43	4	36	.225
Totals	1770	470	30	321	.266

Individual Pinch-Hitting
(10 or More At-Bats)

Player-Club	AB.	H.	HR.	RBI.	Pct.
Hancock, Oakland	14	7	0	3	.500
Bannister, Cleve.	10	5	1	7	.500
Miller, Boston	35	16	0	9	.457
Mulliniks, Toronto	23	10	1	8	.435
Romero, Milw.	14	6	0	2	.429
R. Nelson, Seattle	12	5	0	6	.417
Rivers, Texas	20	8	0	0	.400
Sweet, Seattle	20	8	0	4	.400
Hatcher, Minn.	15	6	1	4	.400
Grubb, Detroit	10	4	1	4	.400
Burroughs, Oak.	13	5	0	2	.385
Barfield, Toronto	16	6	0	0	.375
Walker, Chicago	35	13	1	15	.371
Cabell, Detroit	11	4	0	1	.364
Carew, California	17	6	0	1	.353
Stein, Texas	18	6	1	9	.333
Martinez, Toronto	12	4	1	4	.333
Putnam, Seattle	12	4	1	4	.333
Nichols, Boston	19	6	0	1	.316
Iorg, Toronto	16	5	0	4	.313
R. Law, Chicago	13	4	0	3	.308
Roberts, Kan. City	13	4	0	2	.308
Engle, Minnesota	20	6	1	4	.300
Gamble, New York	20	6	0	0	.300
Lopes, Oakland	10	3	0	1	.300
Oglivie, Milwaukee	10	3	0	3	.300
Piniella, New York	10	3	0	2	.300
Whitt, Toronto	17	5	1	6	.294
Wockenfuss, Det.	24	7	1	10	.292
Sconiers, Calif.	28	8	2	9	.286
Ayala, Baltimore	14	4	0	1	.286
Collins, Toronto	18	5	0	2	.278
Hairston, Chicago	62	17	1	9	.274
Phelps, Seattle	11	3	0	2	.273
Vukovich, Cleve.	11	3	0	0	.273
Lowenstein, Balt.	15	4	1	8	.267
Gedman, Boston	19	5	0	2	.263
Sheridan, Kan. C.	19	5	0	3	.263
Shelby, Baltimore	27	7	0	2	.259
Biittner, Texas	31	8	0	7	.258
Gibson, Detroit	20	5	0	5	.250
Howell, Milwaukee	16	4	1	5	.250
Bumbry, Balt.	12	3	0	2	.250
Page, Oakland	12	3	0	0	.250
Dwyer, Baltimore	33	8	1	9	.242
Castillo, Seattle	29	7	0	5	.241
Mitchell, Minn.	13	3	0	1	.231
Leach, Detroit	18	4	1	1	.222
Almon, Oakland	14	3	0	3	.214
Roenicke, Balt.	38	8	1	6	.211
Bush, Minnesota	19	4	0	2	.211
Jones, Detroit	15	3	0	1	.200
Re. Jackson, Calif.	10	2	1	3	.200
McBride, Cleve.	10	2	0	0	.200
Yastrzemski, Bos.	10	2	0	2	.200
Zisk, Seattle	10	2	0	0	.200
Orta, Toronto	26	5	0	3	.192
Perkins, Cleveland	28	5	0	3	.179
B. Jones, Texas	23	4	1	4	.174
Squires, Chicago	23	4	0	0	.174
Johnson, Toronto	24	4	1	4	.167
Ro. Jackson, Calif.	12	2	0	4	.167
Nolan, Baltimore	12	2	0	1	.167
Powell, Toronto	12	2	0	2	.167
Brookens, Detroit	10	1	0	2	.100
Money, Milwaukee	12	1	0	0	.083

PINCH-HOMERS FOR 1983

NATIONAL LEAGUE: Atlanta (4)—Watson 2, Jorgensen, Washington. Chicago (4)—Bosley, Hall, Johnstone, Woods. Cincinnati (5)—Bench 2, Cedeno 2, Driessen. Houston (4)—Tolman 2, Spilman, Walling. Los Angeles (8)—Morales 3, Reynolds 2, Anderson, Maldonado, Thomas. Montreal (0). New York (12)—Heep 4, Staub 3, Bradley 2, Foster, Jorgensen, Kingman. Philadelphia (4)—Lefebvre 2, Molinaro, Virgil. Pittsburgh (5)—Hebner 2, Easler, Harper, Ray. St. Louis (4)—Braun 2, Rayford 2. San Diego (2)—Bevacqua, Lansford. San Francisco (3)—Bergman 2, Venable.

AMERICAN LEAGUE: Baltimore (4)—Dwyer, Lowenstein, Roenicke, Singleton. Boston (0). California (4)—Sconiers 2, Re. Jackson, Wilfong. Chicago (2)—Hairston, Walker. Cleveland (1)—Bannister. Detroit (3)—Grubb, Leach, Wockenfuss. Kansas City (0). Milwaukee (2)—Brouhard, Howell. Minnesota (2)—Engle, Hatcher. New York (3)—Baylor, Nettles, Smalley. Oakland (0). Seattle (2)—Maler, Putnam. Texas (2)—B. Jones, Stein. Toronto (5)—Johnson, Klutts, Martinez, Mulliniks, Whitt.

Four Players Homer in Debuts

By DAVE SLOAN

If 23-year-old righthander Danny Cox of the St. Louis Cardinals was more than just a little nervous when he made his major league debut on August 6, it could have been expected.

Cox, who started the 1983 season with St. Petersburg of the Class A Florida State League, took the mound for the defending world champion Cardinals against the Philadelphia Phillies and Steve Carlton, who became baseball's all-time strikeout king earlier in the season and later in the year captured his 300th career victory.

The Phillies didn't get a run off Cox during his 10 innings of work, the rookie allowing only seven hits and two walks to go with eight strikeouts. But St. Louis didn't score off Carlton in the veteran's nine innings of work and the Cards lost the game, 1-0, in 11 innings, when the Phils pushed across a run off reliever Bruce Sutter.

Cox, who also pitched for Class AA Arkansas and Class AAA Louisville prior to his call-up, was one of 158 players who made major league debuts in 1983, 70 of them pitchers. Two pitchers made their debuts in the same game. Jay Pettibone of the Minnesota Twins pitched a complete game against Kansas City on September 11 but lost, 3-1, giving up homers to Butch Davis and Willie Aikens. Royals lefthander Danny Jackson, who made his debut by pitching three scoreless innings in relief, picked up the victory.

Darryl Strawberry made his debut on May 6 and stayed around long enough to capture N.L. Rookie of the Year honors.

Four players hit home runs in their first games, including Mike Fitzgerald of the New York Mets, who tied a major league record on September 13 by homering in his first plate appearance. His shot came off Philadelphia rookie Tony Ghelfi and helped New York to a 5-1 triumph. Carmelo Martinez of the Chicago Cubs, after walking in his first plate appearance, homered off Cincinnati's Frank Pastore in his first official at-bat in the Cubs' 2-0 victory on August 22. It was the same day Manager Lee Elia was fired by the Cubs and replaced by Charlie Fox.

Kevin McReynolds of the San Diego Padres, on June 2, and Jamie Nelson of the Seattle Mariners, on July 21, also homered in their first games. McReynolds' blast came off Philadelphia's Ron Reed in a 4-1 Padre victory while Nelson connected against Boston's Bob Ojeda in a 10-inning 14-13 Mariner loss.

Nelson's Seattle teammate, Al Chambers, also had a memorable debut. Chambers, the No. 1 pick in the June 1979 free-agent draft, first appeared in a major league game on July 23 and singled home two runs in each of his first two at-bats against the Red Sox. Seattle won, 5-0.

Three players named Brown made their debuts in '83 and, ironically, all played with the California Angels. Curtis and Steve, both pitchers, made their debuts on June 10 and August 1, respectively, while Michael, an outfielder, first appeared in an Angels game on July 21.

Brothers Spike and Dave Owen, both shortstops, also made their debuts last season. Spike of the Mariners played his first game on June 25, and Dave made his debut for the Cubs on September 6.

An alphabetical list of the players who made their debuts in '83 follows:

Player	Pos.	Club	Date and Place of Birth	Debut
Acker, James Justin	P	Toronto	9-24-58—Freer, Tex.	4- 7
Adduci, James David	PH	St. Louis	8- 9-59—Chicago, Ill.	9-12
Allen, James Bradley	3B	Seattle	5-29-58—Yakima, Wash.	5- 1
Allen, Roderick Bernet	PH	Seattle	10- 5-59—Los Angeles, Calif.	4- 7
Anderson, David Carter	SS	Los Angeles	8- 1-60—Louisville, Ky.	5- 8
Atherton, Keith Rowe	P	Oakland	2-19-59—Mathews, Va.	7-14
Bargar, Gregory Robert	P	Montreal	1-27-59—Inglewood, Calif.	7-17
Barnes, William Henry	1B	Cincinnati	3- 7-57—Cincinnati, O.	9- 6
Beene, Ramon Andrew	P	Milwaukee	10-13-56—Freeport, Tex.	9-22
Behenna, Richard Kipp	P	Atlanta	3- 6-60—Miami, Fla.	4-12
Best, Karl Jon	P	Seattle	3- 6-59—Aberdeen, Wash.	8-19
Bilardello, Dann James	C	Cincinnati	5-26-59—Santa Cruz, Calif.	4-11
Bishop, Michael David	C	New York N. L.	11- 5-58—Santa Maria, Calif.	4-16
Bjorkman, George Anton	C	Houston	8-26-56—Ontario, Calif.	7-10
Booker, Gregory Scott	P	San Diego	6-22-60—Lynchburg, Va.	9-11
Bradley, Philip Poole	PH-OF	Seattle	3-11-59—Bloomington, Ind.	9- 2
Bradley, Steven Bert	P	Oakland	12-23-56—Athens, Ga.	9- 3
Bream, Sidney Eugene	PH	Los Angeles	8- 3-60—Carlisle, Pa.	9- 1
Brown, Curtis Steven	P	California	1-15-60—Ft. Lauderdale, Fla.	6-10
Brown, Michael Charles	OF	California	12-29-59—San Francisco, Calif.	7-21
Brown, Steven Elbert	P	California	2-12-57—San Francisco, Calif.	8- 1
Callahan, Benjamin Franklin	P	Oakland	5-19-58—Mt. Airy, N. C.	6-22
Calvert, Mark	P	San Francisco	9-29-56—Tulsa, Okla.	4-17
Candiotti, Thomas Caesar	P	Milwaukee	8-31-57—Walnut Creek, Calif.	8- 8
Carman, Donald Wayne	P	Philadelphia	8-14-59—Oklahoma City, Okla.	10- 1
Carter, Joseph	PR	Chicago N. L.	3- 7-60—Oklahoma City, Okla.	7-30
Cato, John Keefe	P	Cincinnati	5- 6-58—Yonkers, N. Y.	6-13
Chambers, Albert Eugene	DH	Seattle	3-24-61—Harrisburg, Pa.	7-23
Christmas, Stephen Randall	PH-C	Cincinnati	12- 9-57—Orlando, Fla.	9- 1
Cias, Darryl Richard	C	Oakland	4-23-57—New York, N. Y.	4-27
Citarella, Ralph Alexander	P	St. Louis	2- 7-58—East Orange, N. J.	9-13
Clarke, Stanley Martin	P	Toronto	8- 9-60—Toledo, O.	6- 7
Cocanower, James Stanley	P	Milwaukee	2-14-57—Balboa Hts., C. Zone	9- 7
Coles, Darnell	PH	Seattle	6- 2-62—San Bernardino, Calif.	9- 4
Connally, Fritzie Lee	PH	Chicago N. L.	5-19-58—Bryan, Tex.	9- 9
Couchee, Michael Eugene	P	San Diego	12- 4-57—San Jose, Calif.	4- 5
Cox, Danny Bradford	P	St. Louis	9-21-59—Northhampton, Eng.	8- 6
Culmer, Wilfred Hillard	DH	Cleveland	11-11-58—Nassau, Bahamas	4-12
Darling, Ronald Maurice	P	New York N. L.	8-19-60—Honolulu, Hawaii	9- 6
Daulton, Darren Arthur	C	Philadelphia	1- 3-62—Arkansas City, Kan.	9-25
Davis, Gerald Edward	OF	San Diego	12-25-58—Trenton, N. J.	9-20
Davis, Wallace McArthur	OF	Kansas City	6-19-58—Martin County, N. C.	8-23
Dawley, William Chester	P	Houston	2- 6-58—Norwich, Conn.	4-15
Dayett, Brian Kelly	OF	New York A. L.	1-22-57—New London, Conn.	9-11
Decker, Dee Marty	P	San Diego	6- 7-57—Upland, Calif.	9-20
Dedmon, Jeffrey Linden	P	Atlanta	3- 4-60—Torrance, Calif.	9- 2
DeLeon, Jose	P	Pittsburgh	12-20-60—LaVega, D. R.	7-23
Diaz, Michael Anthony	PH	Chicago N. L.	4-15-60—San Francisco, Calif.	9-15
Doyle, Jeffrey Donald	PH	St. Louis	10- 2-56—Havre, Mont.	9-13
Dunbar, Thomas Jerome	DH	Texas	11-24-59—Graniteville, S. C.	9- 7
Esasky, Nicholas Andrew	3B	Cincinnati	2-24-60—Hialeah, Fla.	6-19
Espy, Cecil Edward	OF	Los Angeles	1-20-63—San Diego, Calif.	9- 2
Fernandez, Charles Sid	P	Los Angeles	10-12-62—Honolulu, Hawaii	9-20
Fernandez, Octavio A.	PR-DH	Toronto	8- 6-62—S. P. de Macoris, D. R.	9- 2
Fimple, John Joseph	C	Los Angeles	2-10-59—Darby, Pa.	7-30
Fitzgerald, Michael Roy	C	New York N.L.	7-13-60—Long Beach, Calif.	9-13
Foley, Thomas Michael	SS	Cincinnati	9- 9-59—Columbus, Ga.	4- 9
Fontenot, Silton Ray	P	New York A.L.	8- 8-57—Lake Charles, La.	6-30
Fuentes, Michael Jay	PH	Montreal	7-11-58—Miami, Fla.	9- 2
Gagne, Gregory Carpenter	SS	Minnesota	11-12-61—Fall River, Mass.	6- 5
Ghelfi, Anthony Paul	P	Philadelphia	8-23-61—La Crosse, Wis.	9- 1
Gibson, Robert Louis	P	Milwaukee	6-19-57—Philadelphia, Pa.	4-13
Gladden, Clinton Daniel	OF	San Francisco	7- 7-57—San Jose, Calif.	9- 5
Graham, Lee Willard	PR	Boston	9-22-59—Summerfield, Fla.	9- 3
Grant, Thomas Raymond	PH	Chicago N.L.	5-28-57—Worcester, Mass.	6-17
Grapenthin, Richard Ray	P	Montreal	4-16-58—Linn Grove, Ia.	5- 3
Gross, Kevin Frank	P	Philadelphia	6- 8-61—Downey, Calif.	6-25
Gutierrez, Joaquin Fernando	SS	Boston	6-27-60—Cartagena, Columbia	9- 6
Hagen, Kevin Eugene	P	St. Louis	3- 8-60—Renton, Wash.	6- 4
Heathcock, Ronald Jeffrey	P	Houston	11-18-59—West Covina, Calif.	9- 3
Heimueller, Gorman John	P	Oakland	9-24-55—Los Angeles, Calif.	7-12
Hershiser, Orel Leonard	P	Los Angeles	9-16-58—Buffalo, N.Y.	9- 1
Hill, Donald Earl	SS	Oakland	11-20-60—Pomona, Calif.	7-25
Hudgens, David Mark	1B	Oakland	12- 5-56—Oroville, Calif.	9- 4
Hudson, Charles Lynn	P	Philadelphia	3-16-59—Ennis, Tex.	5-31
Huismann, Mark Lawrence	P	Kansas City	5-11-58—Lincoln, Neb.	8-16
Hulett, Timothy Craig	2B	Chicago A.L.	1-12-60—Springfield, Ill.	9-15
Huppert, David Blain	C	Baltimore	4- 1-57—Southgate, Calif.	9-15
Jackson, Danny Lynn	P	Kansas City	1- 5-62—San Antonio, Tex.	9-11
James, Dion	OF	Milwaukee	11- 9-62—Philadelphia, Pa.	9-16

Player	Pos.	Club	Date and Place of Birth	Debut
Jeffcoat, James Michael	P	Cleveland	8- 3-59—Pine Bluff, Ark.	8-21
Jeltz, Larry Steven	2B	Philadelphia	5-28-59—Paris, France	7-17
Jimenez, Alfonso	SS	Minnesota	10-30-57—Navojoa, Sonora, Mex.	6-13
Johnson, William C.	P	Chicago N.L.	10- 6-60—Wilmington, Del.	9- 6
Jones, Alfornia	P	Chicago A.L.	2-10-59—Charleston, Miss.	8- 6
Jones, Jeffry Raymond	OF	Cincinnati	10-22-57—Philadelphia, Pa.	4- 4
Komminsk, Brad Lynn	PH-OF	Atlanta	4- 4-61—Lima, O.	8-14
Krueger, William Culp	P	Oakland	4-24-58—Waukegan, Ill.	4-10
Lachowicz, Allen Robert	P	Texas	9- 6-60—Pittsburgh, Pa.	9-13
Lake, Steven Michael	C	Chicago N.L.	3-14-57—Inglewood, Calif.	4- 9
Larkin, Patrick Clibborn	P	San Francisco	6-14-60—Arcadia, Calif.	7-16
Lefferts, Craig Lindsey	P	Chicago N.L.	9-29-57—Munich, West Germany	4- 7
Lyons, William Allen	PH	St. Louis	4-26-58—Alton, Ill.	7-20
Madden, Michael Anthony	P	Houston	1-13-58—Denver, Colo.	4- 5
Martinez, Carmelo	1B	Chicago N.L.	7-28-60—Dorado, P.R.	8-22
McMurtry, Joe Craig	P	Atlanta	11- 5-59—Troy, Tex.	4-10
McNealy, Robert Lee	OF	Oakland	8-12-58—Sacramento, Calif.	9- 4
McReynolds, Walter Kevin	OF	San Diego	10-16-59—Little Rock, Ark.	6- 2
Meacham, Robert Andrew	SS	New York A.L.	8-25-60—Los Angeles, Calif.	6-30
Mizerock, John Joseph	C	Houston	12- 8-60—Punxsutawney, Pa.	4-12
Morogiello, Daniel Joseph	P	Baltimore	3-26-55—Brooklyn, N.Y.	5-20
Nelson, James Victor	C	Seattle	9- 5-59—Clinton, Okla.	7-21
Nelson, Ricky Lee	OF	Seattle	5- 8-59—Eloy, Ariz.	5-17
Nipper, Albert Samuel	P	Boston	4- 2-59—San Diego, Calif.	9- 6
Nixon, Otis Junior	PR	New York A.L.	1- 9-59—Columbus County, N.C.	9- 9
Oelkers, Bryan Alois	P	Minnesota	3- 1-61—Zaragoza, Spain	4- 9
Oquendo, Jose Manuel	PH	New York N.L.	7- 4-63—Rio Piedras, P.R.	5- 2
Orsulak, Joseph Michael	PH	Pittsburgh	5-31-62—Parsippany, N.J.	9- 1
Owen, Dave	SS	Chicago N.L.	4-25-58—Cleburne, Tex.	9- 6
Owen, Spike Dee	SS	Seattle	4-19-61—Cleburne, Tex.	6-25
Pastornicky, Clifford Scott	3B	Kansas City	11-18-58—Seattle, Wash.	6-14
Perry, Gerald June	1B	Atlanta	10-30-60—Savannah, Ga.	8-11
Pettibone, Harry Jonathan	P	Minnesota	6-21-57—Mt. Clemens, Mich.	9-11
Pulido, Alfonso	P	Pittsburgh	1-23-59—Vera Cruz, Mexico	9- 5
Quinones, Luis Raul	OF	Oakland	4-28-62—Ponce, P.R.	5-27
Ramirez, Daniel Allan	P	Baltimore	5- 1-57—Victoria, Tex.	6- 8
Rasmussen, Dennis Lee	P	San Diego	4-18-59—Los Angeles, Calif.	9-16
Ready, Randy Max	PH	Milwaukee	1- 8-60—Fremont, Calif.	9- 4
Reyes, Gilberto R.	C	Los Angeles	12-10-63—Santo Domingo, D.R.	6-11
Reynolds, Harold Craig	PR	Seattle	11-26-60—Eugene, Ore.	9- 2
Reynolds, Robert James	PH	Los Angeles	4-19-59—Sacramento, Calif.	9- 1
Rivera, German	3B	Los Angeles	7- 6-60—Santurce, P.R.	9- 2
Rodas, Richard Martin	P	Los Angeles	11- 7-59—Roseville, Calif.	9- 6
Rohn, Daniel Jay	2B	Chicago N.L.	1-10-56—Alpena, Mich.	9- 2
Russell, Jeffrey Lee	P	Cincinnati	9- 2-61—Cincinnati, O.	8-13
Salazar, Argenis Antonio	SS	Montreal	11- 4-61—El Tigre, Venezuela	8-10
Samuel, Juan Milton	2B	Philadelphia	12- 9-60—S. P. de Macoris, D.R.	8-24
Santana, Rafael Francisco	3B	St. Louis	1-31-58—La Romana, D.R.	4- 5
Schofield, Richard Craig	SS	California	11-21-62—Springfield, Ill.	9- 8
Schroeder, Alfred William	C	Milwaukee	9- 7-58—Baltimore, Md.	7-13
Schulze, Donald Arthur	P	Chicago N.L.	9-27-62—Roselle, Ill.	9-13
Scott, Donald Malcolm	C	Texas	8-16-61—Dunedin, Fla.	9-30
Shines, Anthony Raymond	PH	Montreal	7-18-56—Durham, N.C.	9- 9
Skinner, Joel Patrick	C	Chicago A.L.	2-21-61—San Diego, Calif.	6-12
Smith, Mark Christopher	P	Oakland	11-23-55—Arlington, Va.	8-12
Solano, Julio Cesar	P	Houston	1- 8-60—Agua Blanca, D.R.	4- 5
Stefero, John Robert	C	Baltimore	9-22-59—Sumter, S.C.	6-24
Stone, Jeffrey Glen	PR	Philadelphia	12-26-60—Kennett, Mo.	9- 9
Strawberry, Darryl Eugene	OF	New York N.L.	3-12-62—Los Angeles, Calif.	5- 6
Swaggerty, William David	P	Baltimore	12- 5-56—Sanford, Fla.	8-13
Teufel, Timothy Shawn	2B	Minnesota	7- 7-58—Greenwich, Conn.	9- 3
Thurmond, Mark Anthony	P	San Diego	9-12-56—Houston, Tex.	5-14
Ullger, Scott Matthew	DH	Minnesota	6-10-56—New York, N.Y.	4-17
Van Slyke, Andrew James	OF	St. Louis	12-21-60—Utica, N.Y.	6-17
Von Ohlen, David	P	St. Louis	10-25-58—Flushing, N.Y.	5-13
Walters, Michael Charles	P	Minnesota	10-18-57—St. Louis, Mo.	7- 8
Warren, Michael Bruce	P	Oakland	3-26-61—Inglewood, Calif.	6-12
Webster, Mitchell Dean	OF	Toronto	5-16-59—Larned, Kan.	9- 2
White, Larry David	P	Los Angeles	9-25-58—San Fernando, Calif.	9-20
Wilkerson, Curtis Vernon	SS	Texas	4-26-61—Petersburg, Va.	9-10
Williams, Matthew Evan	P	Toronto	7-25-59—Houston, Tex.	8- 2
Wills, Frank Lee	P	Kansas City	10-26-58—New Orleans, La.	7-31
Wilson, Michael	PR	Minnesota	5-16-56—Shreveport, La.	4- 9
Winn, James Francis	P	Pittsburgh	9-23-59—Stockton, Calif.	4-10
Wotus, Ronald Allan	SS	Pittsburgh	3- 3-61—Colchester, Conn.	9- 3
Wynne, Marvell	OF	Pittsburgh	12-17-59—Chicago, Ill.	6-15
Young, Curtis Allen	P	Oakland	4-16-60—Saginaw, Mich.	6-24
Young, Matthew John	P	Seattle	8- 9-58—Pasadena, Calif.	4- 6

Homers by Parks for 1983

National League

	At Atl.	At Chi.	At Cin.	At Hou.	At L.A.	At Mont.	At N.Y.	At Phil.	At Pitt.	At St.L.	At S.D.	At S.F.	Totals 1983	Totals 1982
Atlanta	66	3	7	3	5	7	6	5	5	2	8	13	130	146
Chicago	11	71	4	4	3	6	2	7	9	10	10	3	140	102
Cincinnati	6	5	52	2	5	8	3	9	3	2	6	6	107	82
Houston	6	8	11	26	5	4	7	5	6	4	9	6	97	74
Los Angeles	13	4	9	3	74	5	4	3	5	8	12	6	146	138
Montreal	3	9	7	5	2	40	1	7	11	5	5	7	102	133
New York	4	7	3	1	2	3	63	9	5	4	6	5	112	97
Philadelphia	7	10	2	3	2	8	7	61	7	6	7	5	125	112
Pittsburgh	5	3	3	3	5	6	4	6	60	13	8	5	121	134
St. Louis	3	8	2	2	2	3	7	2	6	38	2	8	83	67
San Diego	1	6	7	0	8	3	4	3	2	3	53	3	93	81
San Francisco	12	6	9	2	10	3	8	5	4	1	9	73	142	133
1983 Totals	137	140	116	54	123	96	116	122	123	96	135	140	1398	....
1982 Totals	181	115	84	57	92	124	108	103	142	75	109	109	....	1299

AT ATLANTA (137): Atlanta (66)—Murphy 17, Horner 12, Chambliss 9, Hubbard 6, Butler 4, Washington 4, Watson 3, Harper 2, Pocoroba 2, Ramirez 2, Royster 2, Behenna, Benedict, Johnson. **Chicago (11)**—Hall 3, Buckner 2, Davis 2, Cey, Johnstone, Martinez, Moreland. **Cincinnati (6)**—Esasky 3, Redus 2, Driessen. **Houston (6)**—Knight 3, Thon 2, Doran. **Los Angeles (13)**—Guerrero 5, Baker 3, Landreaux 2, Brock, Monday, Valenzuela. **Montreal (3)**—Carter, Dawson, Wallach. **New York (4)**—Strawberry 2, Foster, Kingman. **Philadelphia (7)**—Schmidt 5, Garcia, Hayes. **Pittsburgh (5)**—Easler, Madlock, Mazzilli, Nicosia, Parker. **St. Louis (3)**—Hendrick 2, O. Smith. **San Diego (1)**—Jones. **San Francisco (12)**—Evans 4, Youngblood 4, Clark, Minton, O'Malley, Venable.

AT CHICAGO (140): Atlanta (3)—Hubbard, Murphy, Perry. **Chicago (71)**—Davis 15, Cey 11, Durham 9, Moreland 8, Buckner 6, Hall 6, Johnstone 4, Sandberg 4, Martinez 2, Woods 2, Bosley, Bowa, Lake, Veryzer. **Cincinnati (5)**—Bench, Concepcion, Milner, Redus, Russell. **Houston (8)**—Cruz 2, Doran 2, Ashby, Garner, Puhl, Tolman. **Los Angeles (4)**—Landreaux 2, Marshall 2. **Montreal (9)**—Carter 2, Dawson 2, Oliver 2, Raines, Speier, Wohlford. **New York (7)**—Foster 2, Terrell 2, Giles, Rajsich, Strawberry. **Philadelphia (10)**—Diaz 3, Schmidt 2, DeJesus, Lefebvre, Maddox, Matuszek, Perez. **Pittsburgh (3)**—Berra, Hebner, Wynne. **St. Louis (8)**—Hendrick 2, Green, McGee, Oberkfell, Ramsey, L. Smith, Van Slyke. **San Diego (6)**—Kennedy 3, Flannery, Garvey, Jones. **San Francisco (6)**—Brenly, Clark, C. Davis, Leonard, May, Venable.

AT CINCINNATI (116): Atlanta (7)—Murphy 2, Butler, Chambliss, Horner, Hubbard, Ramirez. **Chicago (4)**—Hall 2, Martinez, Nordhagen. **Cincinnati (52)**—Bilardello 7, Cedeno 7, Oester 6, Redus 6, Bench 5, Esasky 5, Householder 5, Driessen 3, Milner 3, Knicely 2, Barnes, Gale, Walker. **Houston (11)**—Cruz 4, Ashby 3, Garner, Knight, Mizerock, Puhl. **Los Angeles (9)**—Fimple 2, Marshall 2, Brock, Guerrero, Russell, S. Sax, Yeager. **Montreal (7)**—Dawson 4, Carter 2, Wallach. **New York (3)**—Foster, Hernandez, Strawberry. **Philadelphia (2)**—Schmidt 2. **Pittsburgh (3)**—Easler, Parker, Wynne. **St. Louis (2)**—Oberkfell, Porter. **San Diego (7)**—Kennedy 2, Gwynn, Jones, Lezcano, Lollar, McReynolds. **San Francisco (9)**—Evans 3, Youngblood 2, Leonard, O'Malley, Ransom, Smith.

AT HOUSTON (54): Atlanta (3)—Murphy 2, Hubbard. **Chicago (4)**—Cey, Davis, Durham, Martinez. **Cincinnati (2)**—Driessen 2. **Houston (26)**—Garner 4, Thon 4, Cruz 3, Knight 3, Ashby 2, Bass 2, Bjorkman, Doran, Mumphrey, Puhl, Reynolds, T. Scott, Spilman, Walling. **Los Angeles (3)**—Guerrero, Morales, Yeager. **Montreal (5)**—Dawson 3, Carter, Wallach. **New York (1)**—Kingman. **Philadelphia (3)**—Schmidt 2, Morgan. **Pittsburgh (3)**—Berra, Mazzilli, Thompson. **St. Louis (2)**—Hendrick, Quirk. **San Diego**—None. **San Francisco (2)**—Evans, Leonard.

AT LOS ANGELES (123): Atlanta (5)—Murphy 3, Chambliss, Horner. **Chicago (3)**—Buckner, Davis, Sandberg. **Cincinnati (5)**—Oester 2, Cedeno, Driessen, Esasky. **Houston (5)**—Thon 3, Cruz, Puhl. **Los Angeles (74)**—Brock 14, Guerrero 13, Landreaux 10, Marshall 9, Baker 8, Yeager 7, Monday 4, S. Sax 3, Roenicke 2, Anderson, Maldonado, Reynolds, Welch. **Montreal (2)**—Dawson 2. **New York (2)**—Bradley, Foster. **Philadelphia (2)**—Schmidt, Virgil. **Pittsburgh (5)**—Madlock, Morrison, Parker, Pena, Wynne. **St. Louis (2)**—Porter, Rayford. **San Diego (8)**— Kennedy 3, Bonilla, Garvey, Jones, Salazar, Templeton. **San Francisco (10)**—Evans 3, Leonard 3, Clark 2, May, Youngblood.

AT MONTREAL (96): Atlanta (7)—Chambliss 4, Horner 2, Ramirez. **Chicago (6)**—Moreland 2, Buckner, Cey, Davis, Durham. **Cincinnati (8)**—Bench 2, Cedeno, Driessen, Esasky, Milner, Oester, Walker. **Houston (4)**—Bjorkman, Cruz, Garner, Puhl. **Los Angeles (5)**—Brock 2, Baker, Guerrero, Landestoy. **Montreal (40)**—Dawson 10, Wallach 9, Carter 6, Oliver 5, Raines 5, Trillo 2, Francona, Gullickson, Speier. **New York (3)**—Staub, Strawberry, Wilson. **Philadelphia (8)**—Schmidt 3, DeJesus, Matthews, Morgan, Perez, Virgil. **Pittsburgh (6)**—Pena 4, Berra, Easler. **St. Louis (3)**—Quirk, L. Smith, Van Slyke. **San Diego (3)**—Brown, Garvey, Jones. **San Francisco (3)**—Bergman 2, Clark.

AT NEW YORK (116): Atlanta (6)—Murphy 3, Chambliss, Jorgensen, Washington. **Chicago (2)**—Buckner Hall. **Cincinnati (3)**—Driessen, Oester, Redus. **Houston (7)**—Thon 2, Doran, Garner, Knight, Puhl, T. Scott. **Los Angeles (4)**—Yeager 2, Brock, Marshall. **Montreal (1)**—Carter. **New York (63)**—Foster 17, Strawberry 10, Hernandez 8, Kingman 8, Heep 6, Brooks 4, Wilson 4, Bradley 2, Staub 2, Giles, Jorgensen. **Philadelphia (7)**—Schmidt 2, Dernier, Diaz, Lefebvre, Matthews, Molinaro. **Pittsburgh (4)**—Easler, Parker, Pena, Thompson. **St. Louis (7)**—Van Slyke 3, Porter 2, Green, L. Smith. **San Diego (4)**—Kennedy 2, Flannery, Garvey. **San Francisco (8)**—Clark 2, Leonard 2, C. Davis, Evans, LeMaster, Youngblood.

AT PHILADELPHIA (122): Atlanta (5)—Horner 2, Chambliss, Murphy, Washington. **Chicago (7)**—Cey 3, Buckner 2, Davis, Woods. **Cincinnati (9)**—Driessen 2, Milner 2, Redus 2, Bench, Esasky, Trevino. **Houston (5)**—Ashby, Garner, Thon, Tolman, Walling. **Los Angeles (3)**—Guerrero 2, Marshall. **Montreal (7)**—Dawson 2, Vail 2, Carter, Francona, Oliver. **New York (9)**—Strawberry 3, Kingman 2, Bailor, Fitzgerald, Foster, Heep. **Philadelphia (61)**—Schmidt 19, Diaz 9, Morgan 9, Lefebvre 5, Hayes 3, Matthews 3, Perez 3, DeJesus 2, Maddox 2, Matuszek 2, Virgil 2, Garcia, Samuel. **Pittsburgh (6)**—Thompson 2, Easler, Madlock, Parker, Wynne. **St. Louis (2)**—Hendrick, Porter. **San Diego (3)**—Salazar 2, Lezcano. **San Francisco (5)**—Clark 2, Bergman, Brenly, Evans.

AT PITTSBURGH (123): Atlanta (5)—Watson 2, Harper, Horner, Murphy. **Chicago (9)**—Cey 3, Moreland 3, Buckner, Davis, Sandberg. **Cincinnati (3)**—Redus 2, Bench. **Houston (6)**—Thon 2, Ashby, Doran, Garner, Walling. **Los Angeles (5)**—Guerrero 2, Baker, Monday, S. Sax. **Montreal (11)**—Dawson 4, Raines 3, Wallach 2, Carter, Cromartie. **New York (5)**—Strawberry 3, Foster, Wilson. **Philadelphia (7)**—Matthews 2, Virgil 2, Lefebvre, Morgan, Samuel. **Pittsburgh (60)**—Thompson 10, Madlock 8, Pena 8, Parker 6, Berra 5, Harper 5, Frobel 3, Hebner 3, Ray 3, Wynne 3, Easler 2, Morrison 2, Lacy, Mazzilli. **St. Louis (6)**—Braun 2, Hendrick 2, Porter 2. **San Diego (2)**—Garvey Jones. **San Francisco (4)**—Leonard 2, Evans, Youngblood.

AT ST. LOUIS (96): Atlanta (2)—Hubbard, Ramirez. **Chicago (10)**—Hall 3, Bosley, Buckner, Cey, Davis, Johnstone, Martinez, Woods. **Cincinnati (2)**—Bench, Redus. **Houston (4)**—Cruz, Garner, Puhl, Thon. **Los Angeles (8)**—Yeager 2, Baker, Guerrero, Landreaux, Marshall, Morales, Pena. **Montreal (5)**—Carter, Cromartie, Francona, Raines, Wallach. **New York (4)**—Strawberry 2, Brooks, Heep. **Philadelphia (6)**—Morgan 2, Schmidt 2, Hayes, Matuszek. **Pittsburgh (13)**—Berra 2, Lacy 2, Morrison 2, Thompson 2, Easler, Harper, Hebner, Madlock, Mazzilli. **St. Louis (38)**—Hendrick 10, Green 5, Porter 5, McGee 4, L. Smith 4, Van Slyke 3, Hernandez 2, Braun, Forsch, Herr, Rayford, O. Smith. **San Diego (3)**—Garvey, Jones, Salazar. **San Francisco (1)**—Rabb.

AT SAN DIEGO (135): Atlanta (8)—Hubbard 2, Benedict, Chambliss, Murphy, Smith, Washington, Watson. **Chicago (10)**—Cey 2, Hall 2, Moreland 2, Bowa, Davis, Durham, Sandberg. **Cincinnati (6)**—Bilardello, Esasky, Householder, Milner, Oester, Pastore. **Houston (9)**—Thon 4, Garner 2, Doran, Knight, Puhl. **Los Angeles (12)**—Guerrero 5, Yeager 2, Brock, Marshall, Morales, Scioscia, Thomas. **Montreal (5)**—Wallach 3, Little, Raines. **New York (6)**—Strawberry 2, Foster, Kingman, Terrell, Wilson. **Philadelphia (7)**—Morgan 2, Diaz, Maddox, Matthews, Perez, Schmidt. **Pittsburgh (8)**—Thompson 2, Mazzilli, Morrison, Parker, Pena, Ray, Robinson. **St. Louis (2)**—Hernandez, L. Smith. **San Diego (53)**—Salazar 10, Garvey 8, Kennedy 7, Lezcano 6, Jones 5, Brown 4, Bonilla 3, McReynolds 3, Bevacqua 2, Richards 2, Flannery, Gwosdz, Templeton. **San Francisco (9)**—C. Davis 2, Leonard 2, Youngblood 2, Krukow, LeMaster, Venable.

AT SAN FRANCISCO (140): Atlanta (13)—Murphy 5, Chambliss 2, Ramirez 2, Washington 2, Horner, Royster. **Chicago (3)**—Buckner, Cey, Sandberg. **Cincinnati (6)**—Redus 2, Bench, Bilardello, Driessen, Milner. **Houston (6)**—Cruz 2, Doran, Garner, Knepper, Thon. **Los Angeles (6)**—Landreaux 2, Baker, Guerrero, Reynolds, Thomas. **Montreal (7)**—Dawson 4, Carter, Cromartie, Wallach. **New York (5)**—Foster 3, Oquendo, Strawberry. **Philadelphia (5)**—Matthews 2, Diaz, Hayes, Schmidt. **Pittsburgh (5)**—Easler 2, Harper, Lacy, Ray. **St. Louis (8)**—Porter 3, Green, Herr, Oberkfell, Rayford, O. Smith. **San Diego (3)**—Lansford, Richards, Templeton. **San Francisco (73)**—Evans 16, Clark 11, Leonard 9, C. Davis 7, Youngblood 6, Brenly 5, LeMaster 4, May 4, Bergman 3, O'Malley 3, Venable 3, Gladden, Wellman.

American League

	At Balt.	At Bos.	At Cal.	At Chi.	At Clev.	At Det.	At K.C.	At Mil.	At Min.	At N.Y.	At Oak.	At Sea.	At Tex.	At Tor.	Totals 1983	Totals 1982
Baltimore	79	5	5	7	6	15	7	4	14	4	5	6	5	6	168	179
Boston	2	65	6	6	10	4	3	3	8	10	8	6	1	10	142	136
California	5	5	86	3	7	4	7	8	10	5	2	2	4	6	154	186
Chicago	5	8	4	84	5	6	10	4	4	3	6	10	2	6	157	136
Cleveland	1	4	3	4	48	1	3	6	4	1	4	4	2	1	86	109
Detroit	10	8	7	6	4	83	5	3	4	4	1	5	5	11	156	177
Kansas City	7	3	3	3	4	10	50	4	3	3	4	6	1	8	109	132
Milwaukee	6	6	3	6	9	9	4	64	7	2	6	6	1	3	132	216
Minnesota	9	10	8	9	7	4	7	2	56	6	2	11	5	5	141	148
New York	4	6	8	7	10	10	3	6	9	67	1	7	6	9	153	161
Oakland	6	6	4	5	3	7	3	1	9	3	60	7	1	6	121	149
Seattle	2	3	6	0	3	4	7	7	4	5	2	64	0	4	111	130
Texas	3	5	7	1	2	6	2	5	6	4	8	3	45	9	106	115
Toronto	6	7	3	7	1	7	5	4	9	5	5	7	0	101	167	106
1983 Totals	145	141	153	148	119	170	116	121	147	122	114	144	78	185	1903	....
1982 Totals	174	149	168	94	113	208	125	153	191	128	154	182	109	132	....	2080

AT BALTIMORE (145): Baltimore (79)—Murray 16, Ripken 12, Roenicke 10, Singleton 8, Lowenstein 7, Hernandez 5, Ayala 4, Dempsey 3, Dwyer 3, Ford 3, Bumbry 2, Dauer 2, Nolan 2, Sakata 2. **Boston (2)**—Nichols, Rice. **California (5)**—DeCinces 2, Clark, Downing, Grich. **Chicago (5)**—Luzinski 3, Baines 2. **Cleveland (1)**—Thornton. **Detroit (10)**—Lemon 3, Cabell 2, Herndon 2, Leach 2, Parrish. **Kansas City (7)**—McRae 2, Aikens, Brett, Martin, Roberts, Washington. **Milwaukee (6)**—Brouhard 2, Gantner 2, Yost, Yount. **Minnesota (9)**—Brunansky 3, Ward 2, Castino, Engle, Gaetti, Hrbek. **New York (4)**—Nettles 2, Mumphrey, Smalley. **Oakland (6)**—Gross, Henderson, Kearney, Lansford, Lopes, Moore. **Seattle (2)**—J. Allen, Cowens. **Texas (3)**—Hostetler 2, Sample. **Toronto (6)**—Johnson 3, Bonnell, Martinez, Whitt.

AT BOSTON (141): Baltimore (5)—Roenicke 3, Ripken, Shelby. **Boston (65)**—Armas 17, Rice 16, Evans 12, Yastrzemski 6, Stapleton 5, Hoffman 3, Nichols 3, Boggs 2, Allenson. **California (5)**—Clark 2,

Valentine 2, Downing. **Chicago (8)**—Kittle 5, Fisk 2, V. Law. **Cleveland (4)**—Bannister, Harrah, Thomas, Thornton. **Detroit (8)**—Whitaker 2, Cabell, Gibson, Lemon, Parrish, Trammell, Wockenfuss. **Kansas City (3)**—McRae 2, Roberts. **Milwaukee (6)**—Molitor 3, Cooper 2, Oglivie. **Minnesota (10)**—Brunansky 4, Castino 2, Gaetti 2, Faedo, Washington. **New York (6)**—Balboni, Baylor, Kemp, Mattingly, Mumphrey, Smalley. **Oakland (6)**—Almon, Burroughs, Gross, Hancock, Lansford, Lopes. **Seattle (3)**—J. Allen, R. Nelson, Owen. **Texas (5)**—Sample 2, O'Brien, Parrish, G. Wright. **Toronto (7)**—Upshaw 2, Barfield, Iorg, Johnson, Mulliniks, Whitt.

AT CALIFORNIA (153): Baltimore (5)—Bumbry, Lowenstein, Murray, Ripken, Shelby. **Boston (6)**—Armas 2, Allenson, Gedman, Miller, Stapleton. **California (86)**—Lynn 14, DeCinces 10, Downing 10, Grich 8, Re. Jackson 7, Boone 6, Valentine 6, Ro. Jackson 5, Sconiers 5, M. Brown 3, Pettis 3, Schofield 2, Adams, Beniquez, Carew, Clark, Foli, O'Berry, Wilfong. **Chicago (4)**—Kittle, Luzinski, Paciorek, Walker. **Cleveland (3)**—Essian, Harrah, Thomas. **Detroit (7)**—Herndon 2, Parrish 2, Grubb, Trammell, Whitaker. **Kansas City (3)**—Brett 2, Aikens. **Milwaukee (3)**—Simmons, Thomas, Yount. **Minnesota (8)**—Gaetti 2, Hrbek 2, Ward 2, Brunansky, Engle. **New York (8)**—Griffey 2, Smalley 2, Baylor, Gamble, Mattingly, Nettles. **Oakland (4)**—Hancock 2, Heath, Henderson. **Seattle (6)**—D. Henderson 2, Bernazard, Phelps, Putnam, Zisk. **Texas (7)**—Parrish 2, Bell, Dent, Hostetler, Johnson, O'Brien. **Toronto (3)**—Orta, Upshaw, Whitt.

AT CHICAGO (148): Baltimore (7)—Ripken 2, Roenicke 2, Dauer, Shelby, Singleton. **Boston (6)**—Armas 2, Rice 2, Evans, Stapleton. **California (3)**—Boone, Ro. Jackson, Schofield. **Chicago (84)**—Kittle 18, Luzinski 18, Fisk 17, Baines 12, Paciorek 4, Walker 4, Hairston 3, Bernazard 2, Fletcher, Gray, Hill, R. Law, V. Law, Nyman. **Cleveland (4)**—Tabler 2, Franco, Thomas. **Detroit (6)**—Herndon 3, Gibson 2, Parrish. **Kansas City (3)**—Washington 2, Brett. **Milwaukee (6)**—Cooper 2, Yount 2, Molitor, Oglivie. **Minnesota (9)**—Brunansky 4, Ward 2, Bush, Kuntz, Laudner. **New York (7)**—Winfield 2, Baylor, Kemp, Mumphrey, Smalley, Wynegar. **Oakland (5)**—Gross 2, Hill, Lopes, Phillips. **Seattle**—None. **Texas (1)**—Sample. **Toronto (7)**—Johnson 3, Martinez, Moseby, Mulliniks, Upshaw.

AT CLEVELAND (119): Baltimore (6)—Murray 2, Dempsey, Hernandez, Roenicke, Singleton. **Boston (10)**—Evans 3, Rice 3, Armas, Miller, Stapleton, Yastrzemski. **California (7)**—Re. Jackson 2, Beniquez, Downing, Lynn, Sconiers, Wilfong. **Chicago (5)**—Paciorek 2, Baines, Fisk, Kittle. **Cleveland (48)**—Thomas 8, Harrah 7, Franco 6, Thornton 6, Bando 4, Hassey 4, Tabler 3, Vukovich 3, Bannister 2, Fischlin 2, Castillo, Essian, Trillo. **Detroit (4)**—Gibson 2, Parrish 2. **Kansas City (4)**—Brett 2, McRae, Sheridan. **Milwaukee (9)**—Cooper 2, Gantner, Manning, Molitor, Oglivie, Ready, Simmons, Yount. **Minnesota (7)**—Gaetti 2, Bush, Castino, Hrbek, Laudner, Ward. **New York (10)**—Winfield 4, Balboni, Baylor, Kemp, Mumphrey, Nettles, Smalley. **Oakland (3)**—Gross, Henderson, Lopes. **Seattle (3)**—D. Henderson 2, S. Henderson. **Texas (2)**—Bell, Hostetler. **Toronto (1)**—Orta.

AT DETROIT (170): Baltimore (15)—Murray 6, Dwyer 2, Lowenstein 2, Ripken 2, Cruz, Dauer, Nolan. **BOSTON (4)**—Armas 2, Evans, Rice. **California (4)**—DeCinces, Downing, Lynn, Sconiers. **Chicago (6)**—Kittle 2, R. Law, V. Law, Paciorek, Walker. **Cleveland (1)**—Hargrove. **Detroit (83)**—Lemon 14, Parrish 12, Wilson 9, Trammell 8, Wockenfuss 8, Herndon 7, Whitaker 7, Brookens 5, Gibson 5, Grubb 3, Johnson 2, Cabell, Krenchicki, Leach. **Kansas City (10)**—Aikens 3, Brett 3, Sheridan 2, Roberts, Washington. **Milwaukee (9)**—Cooper 3, Howell 2, Yount 2, Schroeder, Simmons. **Minnesota (4)**—Gaetti 2, Hrbek, Washington. **New York (10)**—Winfield 5, Kemp 2, Griffey, Mumphrey, Randolph. **Oakland (7)**—Moore 3, Hancock, Lansford, Lopes, Murphy. **Seattle (4)**—Putnam 2, Bernazard, Edler. **Texas (6)**—Parrish 2, Hostetler, Johnson, Sample, G. Wright. **Toronto (7)**—Garcia 2, Moseby 2, Johnson, Mulliniks, Whitt.

AT KANSAS CITY (116): Baltimore (7)—Murray 2, Ripken 2, Roenicke, Shelby, Singleton. **Boston (3)**—Armas, Gedman, Rice. **California (7)**—Downing 2, Grich 2, Valentine 2, Adams. **Chicago (10)**—Luzinski 4, Baines 2, Cruz, Hairston, Kittle, Paciorek. **Cleveland (3)**—Franco, Thomas, Thornton. **Detroit (5)**—Castillo, Herndon, Lemon, Parrish, Trammell. **Kansas City (50)**—Aikens 11, White 8, Brett 7, McRae 5, Sheridan 4, Otis 3, Motley 2, Pastornicky 2, Roberts 2, Wathan 2, Wilson 2, Martin, Washington. **Milwaukee (4)**—Cooper, Molitor, Thomas, Yount. **Minnesota (7)**—Hatcher 2, Brunansky, Bush, Hrbek, Laudner, Ward. **New York (3)**—Balboni, Baylor, Winfield. **Oakland (3)**—Burroughs, Davis, Lansford. **Seattle (7)**—S. Henderson 2, Putnam 2, Coles, D. Henderson, Zisk. **Texas (2)**—Hostetler, Parrish. **Toronto (5)**—Barfield, Bell, Bonnell, Collins, Martinez.

AT MILWAUKEE (121): Baltimore (4)—Ripken 2, Dwyer, Nolan. **Boston (3)**—Newman, Nichols, Stapleton. **California (8)**—Lynn 3, Boone, Foli, Grich. Re. Jackson, Ro. Jackson. **Chicago (4)**—Luzinski 2, Fisk, Kittle. **Cleveland (6)**—Thornton 3, Thomas 2, McBride. **Detroit (3)**—Castillo, Herndon, Lemon. **Kansas City (4)**—McRae, Otis, Roberts, White. **Milwaukee (64)**—Cooper 14, Molitor 9, Oglivie 8, Simmons 8, Yount 6, Gantner 5, Brouhard 4, Manning 2, Schroeder 2, Thomas 2, Yost 2, Money, Moore. **Minnesota (2)**—Castino, Hatcher. **New York (6)**—Baylor 3, Nettles 2, Espino. **Oakland (1)**—Murphy. **Seattle (7)**—Cowens 2, J. Allen, T. Cruz, S. Henderson, R. Nelson, Roenicke. **Texas (5)**—Hostetler 2, Parrish 2, G. Wright. **Toronto (4)**—Barfield, Griffin, Johnson, Martinez.

AT MINNESOTA (147): Baltimore (14)—Murray 3, Ripken 3, Singleton 2, Dauer, Ford, Landrum, Nolan, Roenicke, Shelby. **Boston (8)**—Armas 4, Rice 3, Nichols. **California (10)**—Re. Jackson 3, Grich 2, Lynn 2, Boone, DeCinces, Ro. Jackson. **Chicago (4)**—Walker 2, Fletcher, Luzinski. **Cleveland (4)**—Bannister, Tabler, Thomas, Thornton. **Detroit (4)**—Herndon 2, Cabell, Lemon. **Kansas City (3)**—Aikens, Davis, White. **Milwaukee (7)**—Cooper 2, Oglivie 2, Gantner, Yost, Yount. **Minnesota (56)**—Brunansky 8, Gaetti 7, Hrbek 7, Ward 7, Hatcher 6, Bush 4, Castino 4, Engle 4, Teufel 3, Kuntz 2, Laudner 2, Mitchell, Washington. **New York (9)**—Smalley 2, Winfield 2, Balboni, Cerone, Gamble, Kemp, Piniella. **Oakland (9)**—Kearney 3, Burroughs 2, Davis, Gross, Hancock, Phillips. **Seattle (4)**—Putnam 2, J. Cruz, S. Henderson. **Texas (6)**—Bell 2, G. Wright 2, Johnson, Tolleson. **Toronto (9)**—Upshaw 4, Barfield, Griffin, Johnson, Mulliniks, Whitt.

AT NEW YORK (122): Baltimore (4)—Lowenstein, Roenicke, Sakata, Singleton. **Boston (10)**—Rice 5, Allenson, Armas, Evans, Newman, Yastrzemski. **California (5)**—DeCinces 2, Grich, Sconiers, Valentine. **Chicago (3)**—Kittle 2, R. Law. **Cleveland (1)**—Hassey. **Detroit (4)**—Brookens, Gibson, Parrish, Wilson. **Kansas City (3)**—Brett 2, Roberts. **Milwaukee (2)**—Brouhard, Yount. **Minnesota (6)**—Engle 2, Ward 2, Castino, Gaetti. **New York (67)**—Winfield 13, Nettles 11, Baylor 10, Griffey 8, Smalley 7, Gamble 5, Wynegar 4, Kemp 3, Moreno, Mumphrey, Murcer, Piniella, Randolph, Robertson. **Oakland (3)**—Burroughs 2, Murphy. **Seattle (5)**—Cowens 2, Zisk 2, R. Nelson. **Texas (4)**—Parrish 3, G. Wright. **Toronto (5)**—Johnson 2, Bonnell, Moseby, Upshaw.

AT OAKLAND (114): Baltimore (5)—Murray 2, Cruz, Dwyer, Ripken. **Boston (8)**—Evans 3, Boggs 2, Armas, Rice, Yastrzemski. **California (2)**—Beniquez, Carew. **Chicago (6)**—Walker 2, Hairston, Luzinski, Nyman, Squires. **Cleveland (4)**—Thornton 2, Hassey, Thomas. **Detroit (1)**—Lemon. **Kansas City (4)**—Aikens, Brett, Davis, Roberts. **Milwaukee (6)**—Cooper 2, Yost 2, Howell, Moore. **Minnesota (2)**—Laudner, Ward. **New York (1)**—Smalley. **Oakland (60)**—Murphy 12, Lopes 10, Heath 5, Henderson 5, Gross 4, Kearney 4, Lansford 4, Almon 3, Burroughs 3, Davis 3, Hancock 3, Hill, Meyer, Moore, Phillips. **Seattle (2)**—D. Henderson, Roenicke. **Texas (8)**—Parrish 3, G. Wright 3, Bell, Dent. **Toronto (5)**—Upshaw 2, Barfield, Moseby, Mulliniks.

AT SEATTLE (144): Baltimore (6)—Ford 3, Lowenstein, Ripken, Singleton. **Boston (6)**—Armas 3, Boggs, Rice, Stapleton. **California (2)**—Downing, Valentine. **Chicago (10)**—Fisk 2, Kittle 2, Luzinski 2, Baines, Fletcher, V. Law, Rodriguez. **Cleveland (4)**—Bannister, Hargrove, Manning, Thornton. **Detroit (5)**—Parrish 2, Herndon, Trammell, Whitaker. **Kansas City (6)**—Aikens 3, Brett, Motley, White. **Milwaukee (6)**—Simmons 2, Cooper, Gantner, Romero, Thomas. **Minnesota (11)**—Brunansky 4, Gaetti 3, Bush 2, Castino, Hrbek. **New York (7)**—Winfield 4, Kemp 2, Wynegar. **Oakland (7)**—Lansford 2, Burroughs, Davis, Gross, Murphy, Phillips. **Seattle (64)**—Putman 11, D. Henderson 9, Zisk 8, T. Cruz 6, Phelps 6, S. Henderson 5, Bernazard 4, Cowens 2, Ramos 2, Roenicke 2, J. Allen, Chambers, J. Cruz, Maler, Mercado, J. Nelson, R. Nelson, Owen, Sweet. **Texas (3)**—O'Brien, Sundberg, G. Wright. **Toronto (7)**—Klutts 2, Bonnell, Martinez, Mulliniks, Orta, Whitt.

AT TEXAS (78): Baltimore (5)—Lowenstein 3, Singleton 2. **Boston (1)**—Hoffman. **California (4)**—Downing 2, Clark, Narron. **Chicago (2)**—Dybzinski, Fisk. **Cleveland (2)**—Hargrove, Thornton. **Detroit (5)**—Gibson, Herndon, Parrish, Trammell, Whitaker. **Kansas City (1)**—Aikens. **Milwaukee (1)**—Howell. **Minnesota (5)**—Brunansky 2, Gaetti, Ward, Washington. **New York (6)**—Baylor 2, Balboni, Cerone, Mumphrey, Nettles. **Oakland (1)**—Lopes. **Seattle**—None. **Texas (45)**—Parrish 10, Bell 8, G. Wright 7, Sample 6, O'Brien 4, Hostetler 2, Johnson 2, Stein 2, Tolleson 2, B. Jones, Richardt. **Toronto**—None.

AT TORONTO (185): Baltimore (6)—Ford 2, Cruz, Dwyer, Murray, Singleton. **Boston (10)**—Rice 5, Armas 2, Evans, Newman, Yastrzemski. **California (6)**—DeCinces 2, Grich, Re. Jackson, Lynn, Valentine. **Chicago (6)**—Baines 2, Fisk 2, Kittle 2. **Cleveland (1)**—Thomas. **Detroit (11)**—Gibson 3, Parrish 3, Lemon 2, Johnson, Trammell, Wilson. **Kansas City (8)**—Brett 5, Aikens, McRae, Pryor. **Milwaukee (3)**—Cooper, Gantner, Yount. **Minnesota (5)**—Bush 2, Hrbek 2, Brunansky. **New York (9)**—Mattingly 2, Nettles 2, Smalley 2, Baylor, Kemp, Winfield. **Oakland (6)**—Davis 2, Gross, Henderson, Lopes, Murphy. **Seattle (4)**—D. Henderson 2, R. Nelson, Putnam. **Texas (9)**—Parrish 2, Bell, Hostetler, O'Brien, Rivers, Sample, Sundberg, G. Wright. **Toronto (101)**—Barfield 22, Upshaw 16, Moseby 13, Whitt 11, Johnson 10, Orta 7, Bonnell 6, Martinez 5, Mulliniks 4, Griffin 2, Bell, Garcia, Iorg, Klutts, Powell.

The Sporting News AWARDS

THE SPORTING NEWS MVP AWARDS

Year	AMERICAN LEAGUE Player, Club	Points	NATIONAL LEAGUE Player, Club	Points
1929	Al Simmons, Philadelphia, of	40	No selection	
1930	Joseph Cronin, Washington, ss	52	William Terry, New York, 1b	47
1931	H. Louis Gehrig, New York, 1b	40	Charles Klein, Philadelphia, of	40
1932	James Foxx, Philadelphia, 1b	46	Charles Klein, Philadelphia, of	46
1933	James Foxx, Philadelphia, 1b	49	Carl Hubbell, New York, p	64
1934	H. Louis Gehrig, New York, 1b	51	Jerome Dean, St. Louis, p	57
1935	Henry Greenberg, Detroit, 1b	64	J. Floyd Vaughan, Pittsburgh, ss	42
1936	H. Louis Gehrig, New York, 1b	55	Carl Hubbell, New York, p	61
1937	Charles Gehringer, Detroit, 2b	78	Joseph Medwick, St. Louis, of	70
1938	James Foxx, Boston, 1b	304	Ernest Lombardi, Cincinnati, c	229
1939	Joseph DiMaggio, New York, of	280	William Walters, Cincinnati, p	303
1940	Henry Greenberg, Detroit, of	292	Frank McCormick, Cincinnati, 1b	274
1941	Joseph DiMaggio, New York, of	291	Adolph Camilli, Brooklyn, 1b	300
1942	Joseph Gordon, New York, 2b	270	Morton Cooper, St. Louis, p	263
1943	Spurgeon Chandler, New York, p	246	Stanley Musial, St. Louis, of	267
1944	Robert Doerr, Boston, 2b		Martin Marion, St. Louis, ss	
1945	Edward J. Mayo, Detroit, 2b		Thomas Holmes, Boston, of	

THE SPORTING NEWS PLAYER, PITCHER OF YEAR

Year	AMERICAN LEAGUE Player, Club	NATIONAL LEAGUE Player, Club
1948	Louis Boudreau, Cleveland, ss Robert Lemon, Cleveland, p	Stanley Musial, St. Louis, of-1b John Sain, Boston, p
1949	Theodore Williams, Boston, of Ellis Kinder, Boston, p	Enos Slaughter, St. Louis, of Howard Pollet, St. Louis, p
1950	Philip Rizzuto, New York, ss Robert Lemon, Cleveland, p	Ralph Kiner, Pittsburgh, of C. James Konstanty, Philadelphia, p
1951	Ferris Fain, Philadelphia, 1b Robert Feller, Cleveland, p	Stanley Musial, St. Louis, of Elwin Roe, Brooklyn, p
1952	Luscious Easter, Cleveland, 1b Robert Shantz, Philadelphia, p	Henry Sauer, Chicago, of Robin Roberts, Philadelphia, p
1953	Albert Rosen, Cleveland, 3b Erv (Bob) Porterfield, Washington, p	Roy Campanella, Brooklyn, c Warren Spahn, Milwaukee, p
1954	Roberto Avila, Cleveland, 2b Robert Lemon, Cleveland, p	Willie Mays, New York, of John Antonelli, New York, p
1955	Albert Kaline, Detroit, of Edward Ford, New York, p	Edwin Snider, Brooklyn, of Robin Roberts, Philadelphia, p
1956	Mickey Mantle, New York, of W. William Pierce, Chicago, p	Henry Aaron, Milwaukee, of Donald Newcombe, Brooklyn, p
1957	Theodore Williams, Boston, of W. William Pierce, Chicago, p	Stanley Musial, St. Louis, 1b Warren Spahn, Milwaukee, p
1958	Jack Jensen, Boston, of Robert Turley, New York, p	Ernest Banks, Chicago, ss Warren Spahn, Milwaukee, p
1959	J. Nelson Fox, Chicago, 2b Early Wynn, Chicago, p	Ernest Banks, Chicago, ss Samuel Jones, San Francisco, p
1960	Roger Maris, New York, of Charles Estrada, Baltimore, p	Richard Groat, Pittsburgh, ss Vernon Law, Pittsburgh, p
1961	Roger Maris, New York, of Edward Ford, New York, p	Frank Robinson, Cincinnati, of Warren Spahn, Milwaukee, p
1962	Mickey Mantle, New York, of Richard Donovan, Cleveland, p	Maurice Wills, Los Angeles, ss Donald Drysdale, Los Angeles, p
1963	Albert Kaline, Detroit, of Edward Ford, New York, p	Henry Aaron, Milwaukee, of Sanford Koufax, Los Angeles, p
1964	Brooks Robinson, Baltimore, 3b Dean Chance, Los Angeles, p	Kenton Boyer, St. Louis, 3b Sanford Koufax, Los Angeles, p
1965	Pedro (Tony) Oliva, Minnesota, of James Grant, Minnesota, p	Willie Mays, San Francisco, of Sanford Koufax, Los Angeles, p
1966	Frank Robinson, Baltimore, of James Kaat, Minnesota, p	Roberto Clemente, Pittsburgh, of Sanford Koufax, Los Angeles, p
1967	Carl Yastrzemski, Boston, of Jim Lonborg, Boston, p	Orlando Cepeda, St. Louis, 1b Mike McCormick, San Francisco, p
1968	Ken Harrelson, Boston, of Denny McLain, Detroit, p	Pete Rose, Cincinnati, of Bob Gibson, St. Louis, p
1969	Harmon Killebrew, Minnesota, 1b-3b Denny McLain, Detroit, p	Willie McCovey, San Francisco, 1b Tom Seaver, New York, p
1970	Harmon Killebrew, Minnesota, 3b Sam McDowell, Cleveland, p	Johnny Bench, Cincinnati, c Bob Gibson, St. Louis, p
1971	Pedro (Tony) Oliva, Minnesota, of Vida Blue, Oakland, p	Joe Torre, St. Louis, 3b Ferguson Jenkins, Chicago, p
1972	Richie Allen, Chicago, 1b Wilbur Wood, Chicago, p	Billy Williams, Chicago, of Steve Carlton, Philadelphia, p

PLAYER, PITCHER OF YEAR—Continued

Year	AMERICAN LEAGUE Player, Club	NATIONAL LEAGUE Player, Club
1973	Reggie Jackson, Oakland, of	Bobby Bonds, San Francisco, of
	Jim Palmer, Baltimore, p	Ron Bryant, San Francisco, p
1974	Jeff Burroughs, Texas, of	Lou Brock, St. Louis, of
	Jim Hunter, Oakland, p	Mike Marshall, Los Angeles, p
1975	Fred Lynn, Boston, of	Joe Morgan, Cincinnati, 2b
	Jim Palmer, Baltimore, p	Tom Seaver, New York, p
1976	Thurman Munson, New York, c	George Foster, Cincinnati, of
	Jim Palmer, Baltimore, p	Randy Jones, San Diego, p
1977	Rod Carew, Minnesota, 1b	George Foster, Cincinnati, of
	Nolan Ryan, California, p	Steve Carlton, Philadelphia, p
1978	Jim Rice, Boston, of	Dave Parker, Pittsburgh, of
	Ron Guidry, New York, p	Vida Blue, San Francisco, p
1979	Don Baylor, California, of	Keith Hernandez, St. Louis, 1b
	Mike Flanagan, Baltimore, p	Joe Niekro, Houston, p
1980	George Brett, Kansas City, 3b	Mike Schmidt, Philadelphia, 3b
	Steve Stone, Baltimore, p	Steve Carlton, Philadelphia, p
1981	Tony Armas, Oakland, of	Andre Dawson, Montreal, of
	Jack Morris, Detroit, p	Fernando Valenzuela, Los Angeles, p
1982	Robin Yount, Milwaukee, ss	Dale Murphy, Atlanta, of
	Dave Stieb, Toronto, p	Steve Carlton, Philadelphia, p
1983	Cal Ripken, Baltimore, ss	Dale Murphy, Atlanta, of
	LaMarr Hoyt, Chicago, p	John Denny, Philadelphia, p

FIREMAN (Relief Pitcher) OF THE YEAR

Year	Player, Club	Player, Club
1960	Mike Fornieles, Boston	Lindy McDaniel, St. Louis
1961	Luis Arroyo, New York	Stu Miller, San Francisco
1962	Dick Radatz, Boston	Roy Face, Pittsburgh
1963	Stu Miller, Baltimore	Lindy McDaniel, Chicago
1964	Dick Radatz, Boston	Al McBean, Pittsburgh
1965	Eddie Fisher, Chicago	Ted Abernathy, Chicago
1966	Jack Aker, Kansas City	Phil Regan, Los Angeles
1967	Minnie Rojas, California	Ted Abernathy, Cincinnati
1968	Wilbur Wood, Chicago	Phil Regan, L.A.-Chicago
1969	Ron Perranoski, Minnesota	Wayne Granger, Cincinnati
1970	Ron Perranoski, Minnesota	Wayne Granger, Cincinnati
1971	Ken Sanders, Milwaukee	Dave Giusti, Pittsburgh
1972	Sparky Lyle, New York	Clay Carroll, Cincinnati
1973	John Hiller, Detroit	Mike Marshall, Montreal
1974	Terry Forster, Chicago	Mike Marshall, Los Angeles
1975	Rich Gossage, Chicago	Al Hrabosky, St. Louis
1976	Bill Campbell, Minnesota	Rawly Eastwick, Cincinnati
1977	Bill Campbell, Boston	Rollie Fingers, San Diego
1978	Rich Gossage, New York	Rollie Fingers, San Diego
1979	Mike Marshall, Minnesota	Bruce Sutter, Chicago
	Jim Kern, Texas	
1980	Dan Quisenberry, Kansas City	Rollie Fingers, San Diego
		Tom Hume, Cincinnati
1981	Rollie Fingers, Milwaukee	Bruce Sutter, St. Louis
1982	Dan Quisenberry, Kansas City	Bruce Sutter, St. Louis
1983	Dan Quisenberry, Kansas City	Al Holland, Philadelphia
		Lee Smith, Chicago

THE SPORTING NEWS ROOKIE AWARDS

1946—Combined selection—Delmer Ennis, Philadelphia, N. L., of
1947—Combined selection—Jack Robinson, Brooklyn, 1b
1948—Combined selection—Richie Ashburn, Philadelphia, N. L., of

Year	Player, Club	Player, Club
1949	Roy Sievers, St. Louis, of	Donald Newcombe, Brooklyn, p
1950	Combined selection—Edward Ford, New York, A. L., p	
1951	Orestes Minoso, Chicago, of	Willie Mays, New York, of
1952	Clinton Courtney, St. Louis, c	Joseph Black, Brooklyn, p
1953	Harvey Kuenn, Detroit, ss	James Gilliam, Brooklyn, 2b
1954	Robert Grim, New York, p	Wallace Moon, St. Louis, of
1955	Herbert Score, Cleveland, p	William Virdon, St. Louis, of
1956	Luis Aparicio, Chicago, ss	Frank Robinson, Cincinnati, of
1957	Anthony Kubek, New York, inf-of	Edward Bouchee, Philadelphia, 1b
	(No pitcher named)	Jack Sanford, Philadelphia, p
1958	Albert Pearson, Washington, of	Orlando Cepeda, San Francisco, 1b
	Ryne Duren, New York, p	Carlton Willey, Milwaukee, p
1959	W. Robert Allison, Washington, of	Willie McCovey, San Francisco, 1b
1960	Ronald Hansen, Baltimore, ss	Frank Howard, Los Angeles, of
1961	Richard Howser, Kansas City, ss	Billy Williams, Chicago, of
	Donald Schwall, Boston, p	Kenneth Hunt, Cincinnati, p
1962	Thomas Tresh, New York, of-ss	Kenneth Hubbs, Chicago, 2b

THE SPORTING NEWS ROOKIE AWARDS—Continued

Year	AMERICAN LEAGUE Player, Club	NATIONAL LEAGUE Player, Club
1963	Peter Ward, Chicago, 3b	Peter Rose, Cincinnati, 2b
	Gary Peters, Chicago, p	Raymond Culp, Philadelphia, p
1964	Pedro (Tony) Oliva, Minnesota, of	Richard Allen, Philadelphia, 3b
	Wallace Bunker, Baltimore, p	William McCool, Cincinnati, p
1965	Curtis Blefary, Baltimore, of	Joseph Morgan, Houston, 2b
	Marcelino Lopez, California, p	Frank Linzy, San Francisco, p
1966	Tommie Agee, Chicago, of	Tommy Helms, Cincinnati, 3b
	James Nash, Kansas City, p	Donald Sutton, Los Angeles, p
1967	Rod Carew, Minnesota, 2b	Lee May, Cincinnati, 1b
	Tom Phoebus, Baltimore, p	Dick Hughes, St. Louis, p
1968	Del Unser, Washington, of	Johnny Bench, Cincinnati, c
	Stan Bahnsen, New York, p	Jerry Koosman, New York, p
1969	Carlos May, Chicago, of	Coco Laboy, Montreal, 3b
	Mike Nagy, Boston, p	Tom Griffin, Houston, p
1970	Roy Foster, Cleveland, of	Bernie Carbo, Cincinnati, of
	Bert Blyleven, Minnesota, p	Carl Morton, Montreal, p
1971	Chris Chambliss, Cleveland, 1b	Earl Williams, Atlanta, c
	Bill Parsons, Milwaukee, p	Reggie Cleveland, St. Louis, p
1972	Carlton Fisk, Boston, c	Dave Rader, San Francisco, c
	Dick Tidrow, Cleveland, p	Jon Matlack, New York, p
1973	Al Bumbry, Baltimore, of	Gary Matthews, San Francisco, of
	Steve Busby, Kansas City, p	Steve Rogers, Montreal, p
1974	Mike Hargrove, Texas, 1b	Greg Gross, Houston, of
	Frank Tanana, California, p	John D'Acquisto, San Francisco, p
1975	Fred Lynn, Boston, of	Gary Carter, Montreal, of-c
	Dennis Eckersley, Cleveland, p	John Montefusco, San Francisco, p
1976	Butch Wynegar, Minnesota, c	Larry Herndon, San Francisco, of
	Mark Fidrych, Detroit, p	Butch Metzger, San Diego, p
1977	Mitchell Page, Oakland, of	Andre Dawson, Montreal, of
	Dave Rozema, Detroit, p	Bob Owchinko, San Diego, p
1978	Paul Molitor, Milwaukee, 2b	Bob Horner, Atlanta, 3b
	Rich Gale, Kansas City, p	Don Robinson, Pittsburgh, p
1979	Pat Putnam, Texas, 1b	Jeff Leonard, Houston, of
	Mark Clear, California, p	Rick Sutcliffe, Los Angeles, p
1980	Joe Charboneau, Cleveland, of	Lonnie Smith, Philadelphia, of
	Britt Burns, Chicago, p	Bill Gullickson, Montreal, p
1981	Rich Gedman, Boston, c	Tim Raines, Montreal, of
	Dave Righetti, New York, p	Fernando Valenzuela, Los Angeles, p
1982	Cal Ripken, Baltimore, ss-3b	Johnny Ray, Pittsburgh, 2b
	Ed Vande Berg, Seattle, p	Steve Bedrosian, Atlanta, p
1983	Ron Kittle, Chicago, of	Darryl Strawberry, New York, of
	Mike Boddicker, Baltimore, p	Craig McMurtry, Atlanta, p

MAJOR LEAGUE EXECUTIVE

Year Executive Club

1936—Branch Rickey, St. Louis NL
1937—Edward Barrow, New York AL
1938—Warren Giles, Cincinnati NL
1939—Larry MacPhail, Brooklyn NL
1940—W. O. Briggs, Sr., Detroit AL
1941—Edward Barrow, New York AL
1942—Branch Rickey, St. Louis NL
1943—Clark Griffith, Washington AL
1944—Wm. O. DeWitt, St. Louis AL
1945—Philip K. Wrigley, Chicago NL
1946—Thomas A. Yawkey, Boston AL
1947—Branch Rickey, Brooklyn NL
1948—Bill Veeck, Cleveland AL
1949—Robt. Carpenter, Phila'phia NL
1950—George Weiss, New York AL
1951—George Weiss, New York AL
1952—George Weiss, New York AL
1953—Louis Perini, Milwaukee NL
1954—Horace Stoneham, N. York NL
1955—Walter O'Malley, Brooklyn NL
1956—Gabe Paul, Cincinnati NL
1957—Frank Lane, St. Louis NL
1958—Joe L. Brown, Pittsburgh NL
1959—E. J. (Buzzie) Bavasi, L.A. NL
1960—George Weiss, New York AL
1961—Dan Topping, New York AL
1962—Fred Haney, Los Angeles AL
1963—Vaughan (Bing) Devine, St.L.NL
1964—Vaughan (Bing) Devine, St.L.NL
1965—Calvin Griffith, Minnesota AL
1966—Lee MacPhail, Commissioner's Office
1967—Dick O'Connell, Boston AL
1968—James Campbell, Detroit AL
1969—John Murphy, New York NL
1970—Harry Dalton, Baltimore AL
1971—Cedric Tallis, Kansas City AL
1972—Roland Hemond, Chicago AL
1973—Bob Howsam, Cincinnati NL
1974—Gabe Paul, New York AL
1975—Dick O'Connell, Boston AL
1976—Joe Burke, Kansas City AL
1977—Bill Veeck, Chicago AL
1978—Spec Richardson, San Fran. NL
1979—Hank Peters, Baltimore AL
1980—Tal Smith, Houston NL
1981—John McHale, Montreal NL
1982—Harry Dalton, Milwaukee AL
1983—Hank Peters, Baltimore AL

MAJOR LEAGUE MANAGER

Year Manager Club
1936—Joe McCarthy, New York AL
1937—Bill McKechnie, Boston NL
1938—Joe McCarthy, New York AL
1939—Leo Durocher, Brooklyn NL
1940—Bill McKechnie, Cincinnati NL
1941—Billy Southworth, St. Louis NL
1942—Billy Southworth, St. Louis NL
1943—Joe McCarthy, New York AL
1944—Luke Sewell, St. Louis AL
1945—Ossie Bluege, Washington AL
1946—Eddie Dyer, St. Louis NL
1947—Bucky Harris, New York AL
1948—Bill Meyer, Pittsburgh NL
1949—Casey Stengel, New York AL
1950—Red Rolfe, Detroit AL
1951—Leo Durocher, New York NL
1952—Eddie Stanky, St. Louis NL
1953—Casey Stengel, New York AL
1954—Leo Durocher, New York NL
1955—Walter Alston, Brooklyn NL
1956—Birdie Tebbetts, Cincinnati NL
1957—Fred Hutchinson, St. Louis NL
1958—Casey Stengel, New York AL
1959—Walter Alston, Los Angeles NL

Year Manager Club
1960—Danny Murtaugh, Pitts. NL
1961—Ralph Houk, New York AL
1962—Bill Rigney, Los Angeles AL
1963—Walter Alston, Los Angeles NL
1964—Johnny Keane, St. Louis NL
1965—Sam Mele, Minnesota AL
1966—Hank Bauer, Baltimore AL
1967—Dick Williams, Boston AL
1968—Mayo Smith, Detroit AL
1969—Gil Hodges, New York NL
1970—Danny Murtaugh, Pittsb'gh NL
1971—Charlie Fox, San Francisco NL
1972—Chuck Tanner, Chicago AL
1973—Gene Mauch, Montreal NL
1974—Bill Virdon, New York AL
1975—Darrell Johnson, Boston AL
1976—Danny Ozark, Philadelphia NL
1977—Earl Weaver, Baltimore AL
1978—George Bamberger, Milw'kee AL
1979—Earl Weaver, Baltimore AL
1980—Bill Virdon, Houston NL
1981—Billy Martin, Oakland AL
1982—Whitey Herzog, St. Louis NL
1983—Tony LaRussa, Chicago AL

MAJOR LEAGUE PLAYER

Year Player Club
1936—Carl Hubbell, New York NL
1937—Johnny Allen, Cleveland AL
1938—Johnny Vander Meer, Cinn. NL
1939—Joe DiMaggio, New York AL
1940—Bob Feller, Cleveland AL
1941—Ted Williams, Boston AL
1942—Ted Williams, Boston AL
1943—Spud Chandler, New York AL
1944—Marty Marion, St. Louis NL
1945—Hal Newhouser, Detroit AL
1946—Stan Musial, St. Louis NL
1947—Ted Williams, Boston AL
1948—Lou Boudreau, Cleveland AL
1949—Ted Williams, Boston AL
1950—Phil Rizzuto, New York AL
1951—Stan Musial, St. Louis NL
1952—Robin Roberts, Philadelphia NL
1953—Al Rosen, Cleveland AL
1954—Willie Mays, New York NL
1955—Duke Snider, Brooklyn NL
1956—Mickey Mantle, New York AL
1957—Ted Williams, Boston AL
1958—Bob Turley, New York AL
1959—Early Wynn, Chicago AL
1960—Bill Mazeroski, Pittsburgh NL

Year Player Club
1961—Roger Maris, New York AL
1962—Maury Wills, Los Angeles NL
Don Drysdale, Los Angeles NL
1963—Sandy Koufax, Los Angeles NL
1964—Ken Boyer, St. Louis NL
1965—Sandy Koufax, Los Angeles NL
1966—Frank Robinson, Baltimore AL
1967—Carl Yastrzemski, Boston AL
1968—Denny McLain, Detroit AL
1969—Willie McCovey, San Fran. NL
1970—Johnny Bench, Cin. NL
1971—Joe Torre, St. Louis NL
1972—Billy Williams, Chicago NL
1973—Reggie Jackson, Oakland AL
1974—Lou Brock, St. Louis NL
1975—Joe Morgan, Cincinnati NL
1976—Joe Morgan, Cincinnati NL
1977—Rod Carew, Minnesota AL
1978—Ron Guidry, New York AL
1979—Willie Stargell, Pittsburgh NL
1980—George Brett, Kansas City AL
1981—Fernando Valenzuela, Los Angeles NL
1982—Robin Yount, Milwaukee AL
1983—Cal Ripken, Baltimore AL

MINOR LEAGUE EXECUTIVE (HIGHER CLASSIFICATIONS)

(Restricted to Class AAA Starting in 1963)

Year Executive Club
1936—Earl Mann, Atlanta, Southern
1937—Robt. LaMotte, Savannah, Sally
1938—Louis McKenna, St. Paul, A.A.
1939—Bruce Dudley, Louisville, A.A.
1940—Roy Hamey, Kansas City, A.A.
1941—Emil Sick, Seattle, PCL
1942—Bill Veeck, Milwaukee, A.A.
1943—Clar. Rowland, Los Angeles, PCL
1944—William Mulligan, Seattle, PCL
1945—Bruce Dudley, Louisville, A.A.
1946—Earl Mann, Atlanta, Southern
1947—Wm. Purnhage, Waterloo, I.I.I.
1948—Ed. Glennon, Bir'ham, Southern
1949—Ted Sullivan, Indianapolis, A.A.
1950—Cl. (Brick) Laws, Oakland, PCL
1951—Robert Howsam, Denver, West.
1952—Jack Cooke, Toronto, Int.
1953—Richard Burnett, Dallas, Texas
1954—Edward Stumpf, Indpls., A.A.
1955—Dewey Soriano, Seattle, PCL
1956—Robert Howsam, Denver, A.A.
1957—John Stiglmeier, Buffalo, Int.
1958—Ed. Glennon, Bir'ham, Southern
1959—Ed. Leishman, Salt Lake, PCL

Year Executive Club
1960—Ray Winder, Little Rock, Sou.
1961—Elten Schiller, Omaha, A.A.
1962—Geo. Sisler, Jr., Rochester, Int.
1963—Lewis Matlin, Hawaii, PCL
1964—Ed. Leishman, San Diego, PCL
1965—Harold Cooper, Columbus, Int.
1966—John Quinn, Jr., Hawaii, PCL
1967—Hillman Lyons, Richmond, Int.
1968—Gabe Paul, Jr., Tulsa, PCL
1969—Bill Gardner, Louisville, Int.
1970—Dick King, Wichita, A.A.
1971—Carl Steinfeldt, Jr., Roch'ter, Int.
1972—Don Labbruzzo, Evansville, A.A.
1973—Merle Miller, Tucson, PCL
1974—John Carbray, Sacramento, PCL
1975—Stan Naccarato, Tacoma, PCL
1976—Art Teece, Salt Lake City, PCL
1977—George Sisler, Jr., Col'bus, Int.
1978—Willie Sanchez, Albu'que, PCL
1979—George Sisler, Jr., Col'bus, Int.
1980—Jim Burris, Denver, A.A.
1981—Pat McKernan, Albuquerque, PCL
1982—A. Ray Smith, Louisville, A.A.
1983—A. Ray Smith, Louisville, A.A.

MINOR LEAGUE EXECUTIVE (LOWER CLASSIFICATIONS)

(Separate Awards for Class AA and Class A Started in 1963)

Year Executive Club
1950—H. Cooper, Hutch'son, West. A.
1951—O. W. (Bill) Hayes, T'ple, B.S.
1952—Hillman Lyons, Danville, MOV
1953—Carl Roth, Peoria, III
1954—James Meaghan, Cedar R., III
1955—John Petrakis, Dubuque, MOV
1956—Marvin Milkes, Fresno, Calif.
1957—Richard Wagner, L'coln, West.
1958—Gerald Waring, Macon, Sally
1959—Clay Dennis, Des Moines, III
1960—Hubert Kittle, Yakima, Northw.
1961—David Steele, Fresno, California
1962—John Quinn, Jr., S. Jose, Calif.
1963—Hugh Finnerty, Tulsa, Texas
Ben Jewell, M. Valley, Pioneer
1964—Glynn West, Birmingham, Sou.
Jas. Bayens, Rock Hill, W. Car.
1965—Dick Butler, Dallas-Ft.W., Tex.
Ken. Blackman, Quad C., Midw.
1966—Tom Fleming, Evansville, South.
Cappy Harada, Lodi, California
1967—Robt. Quinn, Reading, East.
Pat Williams, Spar'burg, W. C.
1968—Phil Howser, Charlotte, South.
Merle Miller, Burlington, Midw.
1969—Charlie Blaney, Albuq., Texas
Bill Gorman, Visalia, Calif.
1970—Carl Sawatski, Arkansas, Texas
Bob Williams, Bakersfield, Calif.

Year Executive Club
1971—Miles Wolff, Savannah, Dixie A.
Ed Holtz, Appleton, Midwest
1972—John Begzos, S. Antonio, Texas
Bob Piccinini, Modesto, Calif.
1973—Dick Kravitz, Jacksonville, Sou.
Fritz Colschen, Clinton, Midw.
1974—Jim Paul, El Paso, Texas
Bing Russell, Portland, N'west
1975—Jim Paul, El Paso, Texas
Cordy Jensen, Eugene, N'west
1976—Woodrow Reid, Chat'ooga, Sou.
Don Buchheister, Ced. Rap., Mid.
1977—Jim Paul, El Paso, Texas
Harry Pells, Quad Cities, Midw.
1978—Larry Schmittou, Nashville, Sou.
Dave Hersh, Appleton, Midwest
1979—Bill Rigney Jr., Midland, Tex.
Tom Romenesko, G'sboro, W.C.
1980—Frances Crockett, C'lotte, Sou.
Tom Romenesko, G'sboro, W.C.
1981—Allie Prescott, Memphis, Southern
Dan Overstreet, Hagerstown, Caro.
1982—Art Clarkson, Birmingham, Sou.
Bob Carruesco, Stockton, Calif.
1983—Edward Kenney, New Britain, East.
Terry Reynolds, Vero Beach, Fla. St.

MINOR LEAGUE MANAGER

Year Manager Club
1936—Al Sothoron, Milwaukee, A.A.
1937—Jake Flowers, Salis'y, East. Sh.
1938—Paul Richards, Atlanta, South.
1939—Bill Meyer, Kansas City, A.A.
1940—Larry Gilbert, Nashville, South.
1941—Burt Shotton, Columbus, A.A.
1942—Eddie Dyer, Columbus, A.A.
1943—Nick Cullop, Columbus, A.A.
1944—Al Thomas, Baltimore, Int.
1945—Lefty O'Doul, San Fran., PCL
1946—Clay Hopper, Montreal, Int.
1947—Nick Cullop, Milwaukee, A.A.
1948—Casey Stengel, Oakland, PCL
1949—Fred Haney, Hollywood, PCL
1950—Rollie Hemsley, Columbus, A.A.
1951—Charlie Grimm, Milw., A.A.
1952—Luke Appling, Memphis, South.
1953—Bobby Bragan, Hollywood, PCL
1954—Kerby Farrell, Indpls., A.A.
1955—Bill Rigney, Minneapolis, A.A.
1956—Kerby Farrell, Indpls., A.A.
1957—Ben Geraghty, Wichita, A.A.
1958—Cal Ermer, Birmingham, South.
1959—Pete Reiser, Victoria, Texas

Year Manager Club
1960—Mel McGaha, Toronto, Int.
1961—Kerby Farrell, Buffalo, Int.
1962—Ben Geraghty, Jackson'le, Int.
1963—Rollie Hemsley, Indpls., Int.
1964—Harry Walker, Jacks'vle., Int.
1965—Grady Hatton, Okla. City, PCL
1966—Bob Lemon, Seattle, PCL
1967—Bob Skinner, San Diego, PCL
1968—Jack Tighe, Toledo, Int.
1969—Clyde McCullough, Tide., Int.
1970—Tom Lasorda, Spokane, PCL
1971—Del Rice, Salt Lake City, PCL
1972—Hank Bauer, Tidewater, Int.
1973—Joe Morgan, Charleston, Int.
1974—Joe Altobelli, Rochester, Int.
1975—Joe Frazier, Tidewater, Int.
1976—Vern Rapp, Denver, A.A.
1977—Tommy Thompson, Arkan., Tex.
1978—Les Moss, Evansville, A.A.
1979—Vern Benson, Syracuse, Int.
1980—Hal Lanier, Springfield, A.A.
1981—Del Crandall, Albuquerque, PCL
1982—George Scherger, Indianapolis, A.A.
1983—Bill Dancy, Reading, East.

MINOR LEAGUE PLAYER

Year Player Club
1936—Jn. Vander Meer, Durham, Pied.
1937—Charlie Keller, Newark, Int.
1938—Fred Hutchinson, Seattle, PCL
1939—Lou Novikoff, Tulsa-Los A'les.
1940—Phil Rizzuto, Kansas City, A.A.
1941—John Lindell, Newark, Int.
1942—Dick Barrett, Seattle, PCL
1943—Chet Covington, Scranton, East.
1944—Rip Collins, Albany, Eastern
1945—Gil Coan, Chattanooga, South.
1946—Sibby Sisti, Indianapolis, A.A.
1947—Hank Sauer, Syracuse, Int.
1948—Gene Woodling, S. F., PCL
1949—Orie Arntzen, Albany, Eastern
1950—Frank Saucier, San Ant'o, Tex.
1951—Gene Conley, Hartford, Eastern
1952—Bill Skowron, Kans. City, A.A.
1953—Gene Conley, Toledo, A.A.
1954—Herb Score, Indianapolis, A.A.
1955—John Murff, Dallas, Texas

Year Player Club
1956—Steve Bilko, Los Angeles, PCL
1957—Norm Siebern, Denver, A.A.
1958—Jim O'Toole, Nashville, South.
1959—Frank Howard, Victoria-Spok.
1960—Willie Davis, Spokane, PCL
1961—Howie Koplitz, Bir'ham, South.
1962—Bob Bailey, Columbus, Int.
1963—Don Buford, Indianapolis, Int.
1964—Mel Stottlemyre, Richm'd., Int.
1965—Joe Foy, Toronto, International
1966—Mike Epstein, Rochester, Int.
1967—Johnny Bench, Buffalo, Int.
1968—Merv Rettenmund, Roch'ter, Int.
1969—Danny Walton, Okla. City, A.A.
1970—Don Baylor, Rochester, Int.
1971—Bobby Grich, Rochester, Int.
1972—Tom Paciorek, Albuq'que, PCL
1973—Steve Ontiveros, Phoenix, PCL
1974—Jim Rice, Pawtucket, Int.
1975—Hector Cruz, Tulsa, A.A.

MINOR LEAGUE PLAYER—Cont.

Year	Player	Club
1976	Pat Putnam	Asheville, W. Car.
1977	Ken Landreaux	S.L.C., PCL-El Paso, Tex.
1978	Champ Summers	Indi'polis, A.A.
1979	Mark Bomback	Vancouver, PCL
1980	Tim Raines	Denver, A.A.
1981	Mike Marshall	Albuquerque, PCL
1982	Ron Kittle	Edmonton, PCL
1983	Kevin McReynolds	Las Vegas, PCL

Baseball Writers' Association Awards

Most Valuable Player Citations

CHALMERS AWARD

Year	AMERICAN LEAGUE Player, Club	Points	NATIONAL LEAGUE Player, Club	Points
1911	Tyrus Cobb, Detroit, of	64	Frank Schulte, Chicago, of	29
1912	Tristram Speaker, Boston, of	59	Lawrence Doyle, New York, 2b	48
1913	Walter Johnson, Washington, p	54	Jacob Daubert, Brooklyn, 1b	50
1914	Edward Collins, Philadelphia, 2b	63	John Evers, Boston, 2b	50

LEAGUE AWARDS

Year	AMERICAN LEAGUE Player, Club	Points	NATIONAL LEAGUE Player, Club	Points
1922	George Sisler, St. Louis, 1b	59	No selection	
1923	George Ruth, New York, of	64	No selection	
1924	Walter Johnson, Washington, p	55	Arthur Vance, Brooklyn, p	74
1925	Roger Peckinpaugh, Washington, ss	45	Rogers Hornsby, St. Louis, 2b	73
1926	George Burns, Cleveland, 1b	63	Robert O'Farrell, St. Louis, c	79
1927	H. Louis Gehrig, New York, 1b	56	Paul Waner, Pittsburgh, of	72
1928	Gordon Cochrane, Philadelphia, c	53	James Bottomley, St. Louis, 1b	76
1929	No selection		Rogers Hornsby, Chicago, 2b	60

BASEBALL WRITERS' ASSOCIATION MVP AWARDS

Year	AMERICAN LEAGUE Player, Club	Points	NATIONAL LEAGUE Player, Club	Points
1931	Robert Grove, Philadelphia, p	78	Frank Frisch, St. Louis, 2b	65
1932	James Foxx, Philadelphia, 1b	75	Charles Klein, Philadelphia, of	78
1933	James Foxx, Philadelphia, 1b	74	Carl Hubbell, New York, p	77
1934	Gordon Cochrane, Detroit, c	67	Jerome Dean, St. Louis, p	78
1935	Henry Greenberg, Detroit, 1b	*80	Charles Hartnett, Chicago, c	75
1936	H. Louis Gehrig, New York, 1b	73	Carl Hubbell, New York, p	60
1937	Charles Gehringer, Detroit, 2b	78	Joseph Medwick, St. Louis, of	70
1938	James Foxx, Boston, 1b	305	Ernest Lombardi, Cincinnati, c	229
1939	Joseph DiMaggio, New York, of	280	William Walters, Cincinnati, p	303
1940	Henry Greenberg, Detroit, of	292	Frank McCormick, Cincinnati, 1b	274
1941	Joseph DiMaggio, New York, of	291	Adolph Camilli, Brooklyn, 1b	300
1942	Joseph Gordon, New York, 2b	270	Morton Cooper, St. Louis, p	263
1943	Spurgeon Chandler, New York, p	246	Stanley Musial, St. Louis, of	267
1944	Harold Newhouser, Detroit, p	236	Martin Marion, St. Louis, ss	190
1945	Harold Newhouser, Detroit, p	236	Philip Cavarretta, Chicago, 1b	279
1946	Theodore Williams, Boston, of	224	Stanley Musial, St. Louis, 1b	319
1947	Joseph DiMaggio, New York, of	202	Robert Elliott, Boston, 3b	205
1948	Louis Boudreau, Cleveland, ss	324	Stanley Musial, St. Louis, of	303
1949	Theodore Williams, Boston, of	272	Jack Robinson, Brooklyn, 2b	264
1950	Philip Rizzuto, New York, ss	284	C. James Konstanty, Philadelphia, p	286
1951	Lawrence Berra, New York, c	184	Roy Campanella, Brooklyn, c	243
1952	Robert Shantz, Philadelphia, p	280	Henry Sauer, Chicago, of	226
1953	Albert Rosen, Cleveland, 3b	*336	Roy Campanella, Brooklyn, c	297
1954	Lawrence Berra, New York, c	230	Willie Mays, New York, of	283
1955	Lawrence Berra, New York, c	218	Roy Campanella, Brooklyn, c	226
1956	Mickey Mantle, New York, of	*336	Donald Newcombe, Brooklyn, p	223
1957	Mickey Mantle, New York, of	233	Henry Aaron, Milwaukee, of	239
1958	Jack Jensen, Boston, of	233	Ernest Banks, Chicago, ss	283
1959	J. Nelson Fox, Chicago, 2b	295	Ernest Banks, Chicago, ss	232½
1960	Roger Maris, New York, of	225	Richard Groat, Pittsburgh, ss	276
1961	Roger Maris, New York, of	202	Frank Robinson, Cincinnati, of	219
1962	Mickey Mantle, New York, of	234	Maurice Wills, Los Angeles, ss	209
1963	Elston Howard, New York, c	248	Sanford Koufax, Los Angeles, p	237
1964	Brooks Robinson, Baltimore, 3b	269	Kenton Boyer, St. Louis, 3b	243
1965	Zoilo Versalles, Minnesota, ss	275	Willie Mays, San Francisco, of	224
1966	Frank Robinson, Baltimore, of	*280	Roberto Clemente, Pittsburgh, of	218
1967	Carl Yastrzemski, Boston, of	275	Orlando Cepeda, St. Louis, 1b	*280
1968	Dennis McLain, Detroit, p	*280	Robert Gibson, St. Louis, p	242
1969	Harmon Killebrew, Minnesota, 1-3b	294	Willie McCovey, San Francisco, 1b	265
1970	John (Boog) Powell, Baltimore, 1b	234	Johnny Bench, Cincinnati, c	326
1971	Vida Blue, Oakland, p	268	Joseph Torre, St. Louis, 3b	318

BASEBALL WRITERS' ASSOCIATION MVP AWARDS—Cont.

Year	AMERICAN LEAGUE Player, Club	Points	NATIONAL LEAGUE Player, Club	Points
1972	Richie Allen, Chicago, 1b	321	Johnny Bench, Cincinnati, c	263
1973	Reggie Jackson, Oakland, of	*336	Pete Rose, Cincinnati, of	274
1974	Jeff Burroughs, Texas, of	248	Steve Garvey, Los Angeles, 1b	270
1975	Fred Lynn, Boston, of	326	Joe Morgan, Cincinnati, 2b	321½
1976	Thurman Munson, New York, c	304	Joe Morgan, Cincinnati, 2b	311
1977	Rod Carew, Minnesota, 1b	273	George Foster, Cincinnati, of	291
1978	Jim Rice, Boston, of	352	Dave Parker, Pittsburgh, of	320
1979	Don Baylor, California, of	347	Willie Stargell, Pittsburgh, 1b	216
			Keith Hernandez, St. Louis, 1b	216
1980	George Brett, Kansas City, 3b	335	Mike Schmidt, Philadelphia, 3b	*336
1981	Rollie Fingers, Milwaukee, p	319	Mike Schmidt, Philadelphia, 3b	321
1982	Robin Yount, Milwaukee, ss	385	Dale Murphy, Atlanta, of	283
1983	Cal Ripken, Baltimore, ss	322	Dale Murphy, Atlanta, of	318

*Unanimous selection.

BASEBALL WRITERS' ASSOCIATION ROOKIE AWARDS

1947—Combined selection—Jack Robinson, Brooklyn, 1b.
1948—Combined selection—Alvin Dark, Boston, N. L., ss.

Year	Player, Club	Votes	Player, Club	Votes
1949	Roy Sievers, St. Louis, of	10	Donald Newcombe, Brooklyn, p	21
1950	Walter Dropo, Boston, 1b	15	Samuel Jethroe, Boston, of	11
1951	Gilbert McDougald, New York, 3b	13	Willie Mays, New York, of	18
1952	Harry Byrd, Philadelphia, p	9	Joseph Black, Brooklyn, p	19
1953	Harvey Kuenn, Detroit, ss	23	James Gilliam, Brooklyn, 2b	11
1954	Robert Grim, New York, p	15	Wallace Moon, St. Louis, of	17
1955	Herbert Score, Cleveland, p	18	William Virdon, St. Louis, of	15
1956	Luis Aparicio, Chicago, ss	22	Frank Robinson, Cincinnati, of	*24
1957	Anthony Kubek, New York, inf-of	23	John Sanford, Philadelphia, p	16
1958	Albert Pearson, Washington, of	14	Orlando Cepeda, San Francisco, 1b	*†21
1959	W. Robert Allison, Washington, of	18	Willie McCovey, San Francisco, 1b	*24
1960	Ronald Hansen, Baltimore, ss	22	Frank Howard, Los Angeles, of	12
1961	Donald Schwall, Boston, p	7	Billy Williams, Chicago, of	10
1962	Thomas Tresh, New York, of-ss	13	Kenneth Hubbs, Chicago, 2b	19
1963	Gary Peters, Chicago, p	10	Peter Rose, Cincinnati, 2b	17
1964	Pedro (Tony) Oliva, Minnesota, of	19	Richard Allen, Philadelphia, 3b	18
1965	Curtis Blefary, Baltimore, of	12	James Lefebvre, Los Angeles, 2b	13
1966	Tommie Agee, Chicago, of	16	Tommy Helms, Cincinnati, 3b	12
1967	Rod Carew, Minnesota, 2b	19	Tom Seaver, New York, p	11
1968	Stan Bahnsen, New York, p	17	Johnny Bench, Cincinnati, c	10½
1969	Lou Piniella, Kansas City, of	9	Ted Sizemore, Los Angeles, 2b	14
1970	Thurman Munson, New York, c	23	Carl Morton, Montreal, p	11
1971	Chris Chambliss, Cleveland, 1b	11	Earl Williams, Atlanta, c	18
1972	Carlton Fisk, Boston, c	*24	Jon Matlack, New York, p	19
1973	Al Bumbry, Baltimore, of	13½	Gary Matthews, San Francisco, of	11
1974	Mike Hargrove, Texas, 1b	16½	Bake McBride, St. Louis, of	16
1975	Fred Lynn, Boston, of	23	John Montefusco, San Francisco, p	12
1976	Mark Fidrych, Detroit, p	22	Butch Metzger, San Diego, p	11
			Pat Zachry, Cincinnati, p	11
1977	Eddie Murray, Baltimore, dh-1b	12½	Andre Dawson, Montreal, of	10
1978	Lou Whitaker, Detroit, 2b	21	Bob Horner, Atlanta, 3b	12½
1979	John Castino, Minnesota, 3b	7	Rick Sutcliffe, Los Angeles, p	20
	Alfredo Griffin, Toronto, ss	7		
1980	Joe Charboneau, Cleveland, of	103	Steve Howe, Los Angeles, p	80
1981	Dave Righetti, New York, p	127	Fernando Valenzuela, Los Angeles, p	107
1982	Cal Ripken, Baltimore, ss-3b	132	Steve Sax, Los Angeles, 2b	63
1983	Ron Kittle, Chicago, of	104	Darryl Strawberry, New York, of	109

*Unanimous selection. †Three writers did not vote.

LaMarr Hoyt's 24 wins in '83 ranked as the most by any big-league pitcher in the last three seasons.

CY YOUNG MEMORIAL AWARD

1956—Donald Newcombe, Brooklyn 10
1957—Warren Spahn, Milwaukee.................. 15
1958—Robert Turley, New York, A.L. 5
1959—Early Wynn, Chicago, A.L.................. 13
1960—Vernon Law, Pittsburgh...................... 8
1961—Edward Ford, New York, A.L. 9
1962—Don Drysdale, Los Angeles, N.L. 14
1963—Sanford Koufax, Los Angeles, N.L..... *20
1964—Dean Chance, Los Angeles, A.L. 17
1965—Sanford Koufax, Los Angeles, N.L..... *20
1966—Sanford Koufax, Los Angeles, N.L. ... *20

Year Pitcher Club Votes
1967—A. L.—Jim Lonborg, Boston 18
N. L.—M. McCormick, San Francisco 18
1968—A. L.—Dennis McLain, Detroit *20
N. L.—Bob Gibson, St. Louis *20
1969—A. L.—Dennis McLain, Detroit 10
Mike Cuellar, Baltimore 10
N. L.—Tom Seaver, New York............. 23

Year Pitcher Club Votes
1970—A. L.—Jim Perry, Minnesota .... †55
N. L.—Bob Gibson, St. Louis .... †118
1971—A. L.—Vida Blue, Oakland.................... †98
N. L.—Fergy Jenkins, Chicago .... †97
1972—A. L.—Gaylord Perry, Cleveland......... †64
N. L.—Steve Carlton, Philadelphia . *†120
1973—A. L.—Jim Palmer, Baltimore............ †88
N. L.—Tom Seaver, New York............ †71
1974—A. L.—Jim Hunter, Oakland .... †90
N. L.—Mike Marshall, Los Angeles..... †96
1975—A. L.—Jim Palmer, Baltimore............ †98
N. L.—Tom Seaver, New York............ †98
1976—A. L.—Jim Palmer, Baltimore........... †108
N. L.—Randy Jones, San Diego............ †96
1977—A. L.—Sparky Lyle, New York......... †56½
N. L.—Steve Carlton, Philadelphia . *†104
1978—A. L.—Ron Guidry, New York .... *†140
N. L.—Gaylord Perry, San Diego ....‡116
1979—A. L.—Mike Flanagan, Baltimore..... †136
N. L.—Bruce Sutter, Chicago .... †72
1980—A. L.—Steve Stone, Baltimore.............. 100
N. L.—Steve Carlton, Philadelphia 118
1981—A. L.—Rollie Fingers, Milwaukee 126
N. L.—Fernando Valenzuela, Los Ang. 70
1982—A. L.—Pete Vuckovich, Milwaukee 87
N. L.—Steve Carlton, Philadelphia 112
1983—A. L.—LaMarr Hoyt, Chicago.............. 116
N. L.—John Denny, Philadelphia......... 103

*Unanimous selection. †Point system used.

3 More Inductees For Hall

By JOE HOPPEL

To say they were contemporaries would be to understate the case. And to say they collectively epitomized defense, speed, pitching and power would be to do likewise.

While Luis Aparicio, Don Drysdale and Harmon Killebrew, elected to the Baseball Hall of Fame in 1984 by the Baseball Writers' Association of America, possessed diverse skills on the baseball field, the time frame in which they played surely makes them kindred spirits.

For example, when Aparicio and Drysdale reflect on their first games in the major leagues, they think back to the very same afternoon in 1956. It was April 17 of that year when Aparicio, nearing his 22nd birthday, made his big-league debut for the White Sox at Comiskey Park in Chicago. Approximately 800 miles away, at Brooklyn's Ebbets Field, the 19-year-old Drysdale broke into the majors with one inning of relief work.

And at Washington's Griffith Stadium on the same afternoon, the 19-year-old Killebrew, two months away from completing his mandatory two-year bonus-baby stint on the Senators' roster, played in only his 48th major league game. He appeared as a pinch-hitter.

What transpired on that season-opening day 28 years ago gave hint of what was to come.

Aparicio, a slick-fielding shortstop from Venezuela, handled four chances flawlessly against Cleveland and his speed proved crucial as Chicago notched a 2-1 triumph.

With the score tied 1-1, Sherman Lollar and Aparicio led off the seventh inning with singles against the Indians' Bob Lemon. Chicago pitcher Billy Pierce then tapped to Lemon, who tried to force Aparicio at second base. Lemon, though, misjudged the rookie's speed and Aparicio beat the throw, setting up a bases-loaded, no-out situation. Jim Rivera then coaxed a walk from Lemon, forcing in the decisive run.

Aparicio had made things happen. Such would be his trademark over 18 years in the majors with the White Sox, Orioles and Red Sox.

Drysdale pitched the ninth inning in the Dodgers' 8-6 loss to the Phillies. A Sporting News account of the game took note of the rookie pitcher's poise and said Drysdale "pitched calmly and effectively."

Effectively, of course, is just the way the 6-foot-6 Dodger pitched for 14 big-league seasons.

Killebrew struck out against the Yankees' Don Larsen that day. It was his 35th strikeout in 94 official at-bats since joining the Senators at age 17 in 1954. But even that proved indicative, showing that the ever-so-raw power hitter was a true free swinger.

When Killebrew connected, the results would be devastating (as 573 lifetime homers, fifth on the all-time list, proved); when he didn't, the results would be futile (as 1,699 career strikeouts, seventh on the all-time chart, showed).

Aparicio was the leading vote-getter in the '84 balloting, receiving 341 votes, or 84.6 percent of the 403 ballots cast. To gain election, a candidate must be listed on at least 75 percent of the ballots cast.

Killebrew received 335 votes and Drysdale was third at 316. Falling 13 votes shy of the necessary total of 303 was pitcher Hoyt Wilhelm, while Nellie Fox, who was Aparicio's keystone partner on the American League pennant-winning Go-Go Sox of 1959, attracted 246 votes.

Aparicio led A.L. shortstops in fielding percentage for eight straight seasons and topped the league in stolen bases nine consecutive times. He holds big-league shortstop records for most games played (2,581), most assists (8,016), most chances (12,564) and most double plays (1,553).

"I realize that I didn't have big numbers," said Aparicio, a career .262 hitter, "but it (his election to Cooperstown) may remind people that there's a lot more to playing shortstop than having a batting average."

Drysdale won 209 games for the Dodgers, 187 of them after the club moved to Los Angeles in 1958. His most notable feat came in 1968 when he pitched six straight shutouts and 58 consecutive scoreless innings, both big-league records.

Drysdale's side-wheeling delivery, blazing speed and willingness to use the brush-back pitch helped him fashion a career earned-run average of 2.95, lead the National League in strikeouts three times and compile a 25-9 record in his Cy Young Award-winning season of 1962.

"It's something like Fantasy Island," Drysdale said of his election. "I feel up on cloud nine."

Killebrew, a .256 career hitter, led the A.L. or shared the league lead in homers six times. In his first full season of play in the majors, 1959, he walloped 42 home runs and drove in 105 runs for the Sena-

Luis Aparicio

Harmon Killebrew

Don Drysdale

tors. He really flexed his muscles when the franchise moved to Minnesota in 1961, hitting 45 or more homers in his first four seasons with the Twins.

Killebrew, who drove in 100 or more runs nine times (with a high of 140 in his A.L. Most Valuable Player season of 1969), called his election "the ultimate dream."

The addition of Aparicio, Drysdale and Killebrew—coming after the Veterans Committee's election of George Kell and Walter Alston in March of 1983—brought the Hall of Fame membership to 187.

The complete 1984 voting totals follow:

Aparicio, 341; Killebrew, 335; Drysdale, 316; Wilhelm, 290; Fox, 246; Billy Williams, 202; Jim Bunning, 201, Orlando Cepeda, 124; Tony Oliva, 124; Roger Maris, 107; Harvey Kuenn, 106, Maury Wills, 104; Lew Burdette, 97; Bill Mazeroski, 74; Roy Face, 65; Elston Howard, 45; Joe Torre, 45; Thurman Munson, 29; Don Larsen, 25; Wilbur Wood, 14; Jim Fregosi, 4; Jim Bouton, 3; Dave Johnson, 3; Mickey Stanley, 2; Bob Bailey, 1; Clay Carroll, 1. (Failing to receive votes were Ron Fairly, Nelson Briles and Jim Colborn.)

Following is a complete list of those enshrined in the Hall of Fame prior to 1984 with the vote by which each enrollee was elected:

1936—Tyrus Cobb (222), John (Honus) Wagner (215), George (Babe) Ruth (215), Christy Mathewson (205), Walter Johnson (189), named by Baseball Writers' Association of America. Total ballots cast, 226.

1937—Napoleon Lajoie (168), Tristram Speaker (165), Denton (Cy) Young (153), named by the BBWAA. Total ballots cast, 201. George Wright, Morgan G. Bulkeley, Byron Bancroft Johnson, John J. McGraw, Cornelius McGillicuddy (Connie Mack), named by Centennial Commission.

1938—Grover C. Alexander (212), named by BBWAA. Total ballots, 262. Henry Chadwick, Alexander J. Cartwright, named by Centennial Commission.

1939—George Sisler (235), Edward Collins (213), William Keeler (207), Louis Gehrig, named by BBWAA (Gehrig by special election after retirement from game was announced). Total ballots cast, 274. Albert G. Spalding, Adrian C. Anson, Charles A. Comiskey, William (Buck) Ewing, Charles Radbourn, William A. (Candy) Cummings, named by committee of old-time players and writers.

1942—Rogers Hornsby (182), named by BBWAA. Total ballots cast, 233.

1944—Judge Kenesaw M. Landis, named by committee on old-timers.

1945—Hugh Duffy, Jimmy Collins, Hugh Jennings, Ed Delahanty, Fred Clarke, Mike Kelly, Wilbert Robinson, Jim O'Rourke, Dennis (Dan) Brouthers and Roger Bresnahan, named by committee on old-timers.

1946—Jesse Burkett, Frank Chance, Jack Chesbro, Johnny Evers, Clark Griffith, Tom McCarthy, Joe McGinnity, Eddie Plank, Joe Tinker, Rube Waddell and Ed Walsh, named by committee on old-timers.

1947—Carl Hubbell (140), Frank Frisch (136), Gordon (Mickey) Cochrane (128) and Robert (Lefty) Grove (123), named by BBWAA. Total ballots, 161.

1948—Herbert J. Pennock (94) and Harold (Pie) Traynor (93), named by BBWAA. Total ballots cast, 121.

1949—Charles Gehringer (159), named by BBWAA in runoff election. Total ballots cast, 187. Charles (Kid) Nichols and Mordecai (Three-Finger) Brown, named by committee on old timers.

1951—Mel Ott (197) and Jimmie Foxx (179), named by BBWAA. Total ballots cast, 226.

1952—Harry Heilmann (203) and Paul Waner (195), named by BBWAA. Total ballots cast, 234.

1953—Jerome (Dizzy) Dean (209) and Al

Simmons (199), named by BBWAA. Total ballots cast, 264. Charles Albert (Chief) Bender, Roderick (Bobby) Wallace, William Klem, Tom Connolly, Edward G. Barrow and William Henry (Harry) Wright, named by the new Committee on Veterans.

1954—Walter (Rabbit) Maranville (209), William Dickey (202) and William Terry (195), named by BBWAA. Total ballots cast, 252.

1955—Joe DiMaggio (223), Ted Lyons (217), Arthur (Dazzy) Vance (205) and Charles (Gabby) Hartnett (195), named by BBWAA. Total ballots cast, 251. J. Franklin (Home Run) Baker and Ray Schalk, named by Committee on Veterans.

1956—Hank Greenberg (164) and Joe Cronin (152), named by BBWAA. Total ballots cast, 193.

1957—Joseph V. McCarthy and Sam Crawford, named by Committee on Veterans.

1959—Zachariah (Zack) Wheat, named by Committee on Veterans.

1961—Max Carey and William Hamilton, named by Committee on Veterans.

1962—Bob Feller (150) and Jackie Robinson (124), named by BBWAA. Total ballots cast, 160. Bill McKechnie and Edd Roush, named by Committee on Veterans.

1963—Eppa Rixey, Edgar (Sam) Rice, Elmer Flick and John Clarkson, named by Committee on Veterans.

1964—Luke Appling (189), named by BBWAA in runoff election. Total ballots cast, 225. Urban (Red) Faber, Burleigh Grimes, Tim Keefe, Heinie Manush, Miller Huggins and John Montgomery Ward, named by Committee on Veterans.

1965—James (Pud) Galvin, named by Committee on Veterans.

1966—Ted Williams (282), named by BBWAA. Total ballots cast, 302. Casey Stengel, named by Committee on Veterans.

1967—Charles (Red) Ruffing (266), named by BBWAA in runoff election. Total ballots cast, 306. Branch Rickey and Lloyd Waner, named by Committee on Veterans.

1968—Joseph (Ducky) Medwick (240), named by BBWAA. Total ballots cast, 283. Leon (Goose) Goslin and Hazen (Kiki) Cuyler, named by Committee on Veterans.

1969—Stan (The Man) Musial (317) and Roy Campanella (270), named by BBWAA. Total ballots cast, 340. Stan Coveleski and Waite Hoyt, named by Committee on Veterans.

1970—Lou Boudreau (232), named by BBWAA. Total ballots cast, 300. Earle Combs, Jesse Haines and Ford Frick, named by Committee on Veterans.

1971—Chick Hafey, Rube Marquard, Joe Kelley, Dave Bancroft, Harry Hooper, Jake Beckley and George Weiss, named by Committee on Veterans. Satchel Paige, named by Special Committee on Negro Leagues.

1972—Sandy Koufax (344), Yogi Berra (339) and Early Wynn (301), named by BBWAA. Total ballots cast, 396. Lefty Gomez, Will Harridge and Ross Youngs, named by Committee on Veterans. Josh Gibson and Walter (Buck) Leonard, named by Special Committee on Negro Leagues.

1973—Warren Spahn (316), named by BBWAA. Total ballots cast, 380. Roberto Clemente (393), in special election by BBWAA in which 424 ballots were cast. Billy Evans, George Kelly and Mickey Welch, named by Committee on Veterans. Monte Irvin, named by Special Committee on Negro Leagues.

1974—Mickey Mantle (322) and Whitey Ford (284), named by BBWAA. Total ballots cast, 365. Jim Bottomley, Sam Thompson and Jocko Conlan, named by Committee on Veterans. James (Cool Papa) Bell, named by Special Committee on Negro Leagues.

1975—Ralph Kiner (273), named by BBWAA. Total ballots cast, 362. Earl Averill, Bucky Harris and Billy Herman, named by Committee on Veterans. William (Judy) Johnson, named by Special Committee on Negro Leagues.

1976—Robin Roberts (337) and Bob Lemon (305), named by BBWAA. Total ballots cast, 388. Roger Connor, Cal Hubbard and Fred Lindstrom, named by Committee on Veterans. Oscar Charleston, named by Special Committee on Negro Leagues.

1977—Ernie Banks (321), named by BBWAA. Total ballots cast, 383. Joe Sewell, Al Lopez and Amos Rusie, named by Committee on Veterans. Martin Dihigo and John Henry Lloyd, named by Special Committee on Negro Leagues.

1978—Eddie Mathews (301), named by BBWAA. Total ballots cast, 379. Larry MacPhail and Addie Joss, named by Committee on Veterans.

1979—Willie Mays (409), named by BBWAA. Total ballots cast, 432. Hack Wilson and Warren Giles, named by Committee on Veterans.

1980—Al Kaline (340) and Duke Snider (333), named by BBWAA. Total ballots cast, 385. Chuck Klein and Tom Yawkey, named by Committee on Veterans.

1981—Bob Gibson (337), named by BBWAA. Total ballots cast, 401. Johnny Mize and Rube Foster, named by Committee on Veterans.

1982—Henry Aaron (406) and Frank Robinson (370), named by BBWAA. Total ballots cast, 415. Albert B. (Happy) Chandler and Travis Jackson, named by Committee on Veterans.

1983—Brooks Robinson (344) and Juan Marichal (313), named by BBWAA. Total ballots cast, 374. George Kell and Walter Alston, named by Committee on Veterans.

BASEBALL RE-ENTRY DRAFT

MINOR LEAGUE DRAFT

MAJOR LEAGUE TRANSACTIONS

NECROLOGY

Whether or not outfielder Dave Parker can become the dominating player in Cincinnati he was six years ago in Pittsburgh remains to be seen. New Reds Manager Vern Rapp (right) certainly hopes so.

Goose Lands in San Diego

By JOE HOPPEL

The San Diego Padres, who led a low-profile existence through their first 14 years in the National League, have paid the price in the last two off-seasons to bolster their identity and strengthen their club.

And they have paid mightily—in greenbacks.

On December 21, 1982, the Padres signed former Los Angeles Dodger star Steve Garvey, one of the plums of the '82 re-entry draft, to a five-year contract worth $6.5 million. Garvey not only provided the sock that San Diego had wanted (14 homers and 59 runs batted in before suffering a season-ending thumb injury in late July), but gave the club a true "name" player.

The signing process after the 1983 re-entry draft again put the Padres in the spotlight. Standout relief pitcher Goose Gossage was chosen by 12 clubs (including his own team, the Yankees) in the November 7 draft proceedings at the New York Sheraton and, after 8½ weeks of negotiations, cast his lot with San Diego.

Gossage, who has notched 206 saves in the big leagues, reportedly received a $6.25 million package from the Padres, who have yet to finish above fourth place in the N.L. West since their entry into the league in 1969. The contract is guaranteed for five years, with an option for a sixth season.

Gossage was among 45 players eligible for the re-entry draft and ranked as the third most popular selection. First baseman Darrell Evans, coming off a 30-homer season with San Francisco, was drafted by 17 other clubs and his rights also were retained by the Giants. Longtime Pittsburgh reliever Kent Tekulve was named by 13 clubs, including the Pirates.

Fourteen players, including seven-time American League batting champion Rod Carew, were not picked by any team and 15 others were chosen by fewer than four clubs (excluding their own), meaning 29 of the 45 available players were free to negotiate with any club.

The Texas Rangers made the most selections, 13, while the Minnesota Twins and the New York Mets passed on the entire field.

George Steinbrenner's Yankees, usually the No. 1 investors in the draft, chose only one player, Evans, this time around and failed to sign him. Steinbrenner nevertheless landed a big-name free agent—although not of the re-entry variety—when he signed veteran knuckleball pitcher Phil Niekro early in 1984. Niekro had been released by the Atlanta Braves.

Evans, a lefthanded pull hitter who sought a long-term deal, signed with Detroit after the A.L. club offered a contract of more than three years (exact terms weren't disclosed). The Tigers think Evans, 36, will find Tiger Stadium's cozy right-field wall to his liking.

Tekulve, who has pitched in 647 Pirate games since reaching the majors in 1974, decided to stay in Pittsburgh, signing a four-year contract worth nearly $900,000 for each of the first three years. The salary for his fourth season will depend on his performance in the third year.

While the Bucs retained their ace reliever, they lost outfielder Dave Parker. A two-time N.L. batting champion, Parker signed a two-year contract with his hometown team, the Cincinnati Reds.

Carew, while overlooked, wasn't unappreciated. The Angels re-signed the veteran first baseman to a two-year contract at a reported $900,000 per season. As hefty as the salary is, though, it still represents a cut from Carew's $1.1 million pay figure of '83.

Other prominent free agents staying put after participating in the draft were Detroit pitcher Milt Wilcox, Milwaukee catcher Ted Simmons and second baseman Julio Cruz and pitcher Jerry Koosman, both of the White Sox.

Other notable free agents changing clubs included second baseman Manny Trillo, who went from Montreal to San Francisco; pitcher Dennis Lamp, who signed with Toronto after recording a club-high 15 saves for the A.L. West champion White Sox; pitcher Frank LaCorte, who switched from Houston to California; outfielder Amos Otis, who moved to Pittsburgh from Kansas City, and first baseman Bruce Bochte, who joined Oakland after last playing with Seattle in '82. Disenchanted with baseball, Bochte sat out the '83 season after going through the re-entry draft at the end of the previous year.

Lamp, like Tekulve and Wilcox, was a Type A free agent. A club losing a Type A player receives compensation in the form of a professional player chosen from a special pool, plus an amateur draft choice.

Trillo was a Type B free agent, compensation for which is two amateur draft picks.

Warren Cromartie, a lifetime .280 hitter

in 1,038 games with the Expos, was picked by three teams but the 30-year-old outfielder opted to play in Japan in '84.

Following is a list of the 45 players eligible for the 1983 re-entry draft. The number in parentheses following a player's name indicates the number of clubs selecting that player. Those clubs choosing to retain rights to a free agent are listed in capital letters:

Type A Players

Doug Bair (2)—Indians, Pirates.

Dennis Lamp (6)—Orioles, WHITE SOX, Indians, Cardinals, Rangers, Blue Jays.

Kent Tekulve (13)—Braves, Orioles, Cubs, White Sox, Reds, Indians, Expos, A's, Phillies, PIRATES, Padres, Rangers, Blue Jays.

Tom Underwood (1)—Indians.

Milt Wilcox (8)—Cubs, White Sox, TIGERS, A's, Pirates, Padres, Rangers, Blue Jays.

Type B Players

Ruppert Jones (3)—Reds, Indians, Mariners.

Manny Trillo (1)—White Sox.

Others

Jim Bibby (1)—Expos.

Doug Bird (0)—None.

Enos Cabell (6)—TIGERS, Astros, Royals, Dodgers, Mariners, Rangers.

Bert Campaneris (0)—None.

Rod Carew (0)—None.

Warren Cromartie (3)—Red Sox, Giants, Mariners.

Julio Cruz (7)—Orioles, Angels, WHITE SOX, Indians, Expos, Giants, Rangers.

Miguel Dilone (0)—None.

Jamie Easterly (0)—None.

Darrell Evans (18)—Orioles, Red Sox, White Sox, Reds, Tigers, Astros, Royals, Dodgers, Brewers, Expos, Yankees, A's, Pirates, Padres, GIANTS, Mariners, Rangers, Blue Jays.

Dan Ford (6)—ORIOLES, Indians, Expos, A's, Pirates, Mariners.

Oscar Gamble (8)—Orioles, Red Sox, White Sox, Brewers, Expos, YANKEES, A's, Blue Jays.

Rich Gossage (12)—Braves, Orioles, Angels, White Sox, Indians, YANKEES, A's, Pirates, Padres, Giants, Rangers, Blue Jays.

Richie Hebner (1)—Seattle.

Steve Henderson (2)—Indians, Rangers.

Don Hood (0)—None.

Art Howe (0)—None.

Jerry Koosman (8)—WHITE SOX, Expos, A's, Phillies, Pirates, Cardinals, Rangers, Blue Jays.

Frank LaCorte (8)—Angels, ASTROS, Phillies, Pirates, Giants, Mariners, Rangers, Blue Jays.

Jerry Martin (0)—None.

Bake McBride (1)—Expos.

Randy Moffitt (0)—None.

Dale Murray (2)—Cubs, Blue Jays.

Amos Otis (1)—Orioles.

Dave Parker (2)—Reds, Mariners.

Rob Picciolo (1)—Giants.

J. R. Richard (0)—None.

Gene Richards (4)—Royals, Expos, Giants, Mariners.

Aurelio Rodriguez (0)—None.

Eighteen clubs drafted slugger Darrell Evans, but the Tigers eventually won his services.

Dan Schatzeder (9)—Angels, Reds, Dodgers, EXPOS, Phillies, Pirates, Mariners, Rangers, Blue Jays.

Ted Simmons (2)—Pirates, Giants.

Lary Sorensen (8)—Angels, Cubs, INDIANS, A's, Padres, Mariners, Rangers, Blue Jays.

Elias Sosa (1)—Mariners.

Derrel Thomas (7)—Cubs, White Sox, Astros, Brewers, Expos, Cardinals, Padres.

Dave Tomlin (0)—None.

Mark Wagner (0)—None.

Denny Walling (9)—Cubs, White Sox, ASTROS, Royals, Dodgers, Expos, Pirates, Giants, Rangers.

Jerry White (0)—None.

NOTE—The following players, selected by fewer than four clubs (excluding a player's former club), were free to negotiate with any club: Bair, Bibby, Bird, Campaneris, Carew, Cromartie, Dilone, Easterly, Hebner, Henderson, Hood, Howe, Jones, Martin, McBride, Moffitt, Murray, Otis, Parker, Picciolo, Richard, Rodriguez, Simmons, Sosa, Tomlin, Trillo, Underwood, Wagner, White.

Blue Jays Select Two in Draft

By JOE HOPPEL

More than half of the clubs in the big leagues usually bypass the annual major league draft, apparently believing that players left unprotected by other teams would be of little value to them.

The Toronto Blue Jays obviously don't share that philosophy.

For the fourth straight year, the Blue Jays selected two players in the grab bag. Choosing from the 19th position in the first round of the 1983 draft conducted December 5 at baseball's winter meetings in Nashville, Tenn., Toronto picked infielder Kelly Gruber from the Indians' organization. Then, making the only selection of round two, the Blue Jays opted for catcher Terry Cormack of the Braves' farm system.

Eleven players, including six pitchers, were taken in the draft. Players with three years in the minors who were left off their parent clubs' 40-man rosters were eligible to be purchased by another major league club for $25,000.

With clubs drafting in inverse order of their 1983 records and alternating by leagues, the Mariners chose first and tabbed lefthanded pitcher Dave Geisel from the Blue Jays' organization. Geisel made 47 relief appearances for the Jays in '83, compiling a 0-3 record and a 4.64 earned-run average.

Cleveland, choosing after the Mets passed, took Braves farmhand Tom Waddell, a reliever who was 13-2 overall with 10 saves at Class AA Savannah and Class AAA Richmond. The Cubs, in the No. 4 spot, then selected pitcher Johnny Abrego of the Phillies' system.

Besides Geisel, other draftees with major league experience were infielder Fran Mullins (chosen by the Giants), pitcher Pat Underwood (taken by the Rangers) and catchers Orlando Sanchez and Jamie Nelson (picked by the Royals and Brewers, respectively).

Draft choices in order of selection:

FIRST ROUND

Mariners—Pitcher Dave Geisel from Syracuse (International) of the Blue Jays' organization.

Indians—Pitcher Tom Waddell from Richmond (International) of the Braves' organization.

Cubs—Pitcher Johnny Abrego from Portland (Pacific Coast) of the Phillies' organization.

A's—Pitcher Jeff Bettendorf from Tidewater (International) of the Mets' organization.

Giants—Infielder Fran Mullins from Indianapolis (American Association) of the Reds' organization.

Rangers—Pitcher Pat Underwood from Evansville (American Association) of the Tigers' organization.

Royals—Catcher Orlando Sanchez from Louisville (American Association) of the Cardinals' organization.

Brewers—Catcher Jamie Nelson from Salt Lake City (Pacific Coast) of the Mariners' organization.

Blue Jays—Infielder Kelly Gruber from Charleston, W. Va. (International) of the Indians' organization.

Phillies—Pitcher Jay Tibbs from Tidewater (International) of the Mets' organization.

SECOND ROUND

Blue Jays—Catcher Terry Cormack from Richmond (International) of the Braves' organization.

Major League Attendance for 1983

NATIONAL LEAGUE

	Home	Away
Atlanta	2,119,935	1,855,862
Chicago	1,479,717	1,744,178
Cincinnati	1,190,419	1,698,328
Houston	1,351,962	1,640,827
Los Angeles	3,510,313	2,235,950
Montreal	2,320,651	1,634,092
New York	1,112,774	1,634,417
Philadelphia	2,128,339	1,870,883
Pittsburgh	1,225,916	1,812,294
St. Louis	2,317,914	1,914,537
San Diego	1,539,815	1,693,146
San Francisco	1,251,530	1,814,771
Total	21,549,285	21,549,285

AMERICAN LEAGUE

	Home	Away
Baltimore	2,042,071	1,854,401
Boston	1,782,285	1,793,459
California	2,555,016	1,882,234
Chicago	2,132,821	1,596,873
Cleveland	768,941	1,551,992
Detroit	1,829,636	1,793,315
Kansas City	1,963,875	1,599,182
Milwaukee	2,397,131	1,885,884
Minnesota	858,939	1,502,733
New York	2,257,976	2,291,280
Oakland	1,294,941	1,557,202
Seattle	813,537	1,492,526
Texas	1,363,469	1,476,670
Toronto	1,930,415	1,713,302
Total	23,991,053	23,991,053

Few Major Deals Pulled Off in '83

By CARL CLARK

Complicated long-term contracts with no-trade clauses are making it increasingly difficult to put together a blockbuster deal, complain baseball's general managers. And it's hard to disagree with that assessment.

There were few stop-the-presses trades in 1983. Gorman Thomas, Ron Cey and Keith Hernandez were traded—Thomas twice—but to second-division teams. Not much happened overall at the winter meetings in Nashville, Tenn., either. The Rangers made the most news that week, trading catcher Jim Sundberg and landing Minnesota slugger Gary Ward in separate deals.

Texas traded Sundberg, who had won six Gold Gloves in his 10 seasons with the Rangers, to Milwaukee for catcher Ned Yost and minor league pitcher Dan Scarpetta. At the previous year's winter meetings, Sundberg had rejected a trade to the Dodgers.

To get Ward, who belted 28 homers in 1982 and 19 in '83, the Rangers gave up pitchers Mike Smithson and John Butcher and minor league catcher Sam Sorce. Smithson had a 10-14 record for the Rangers. Butcher, working mostly in relief, split 12 decisions and recorded five saves.

The only other attention-grabber in Nashville—besides a deal that would have sent Dodger outfielder Dusty Baker to the A's for two minor leaguers, had Baker agreed—involved the Padres, Cubs and Expos. Lefthander Gary Lucas, who saved 17 games for San Diego in 1983, was traded to the Expos, who sent righthander Scott Sanderson to Chicago. Sanderson, a 16-game winner in 1980, was out of the rotation for more than two months in '83 because of a thumb injury and finished 6-7. The Cubs dealt pitcher Craig Lefferts, first baseman Carmelo Martinez and third baseman Fritz Connally to San Diego. Martinez hit 31 homers at Iowa and six for the Cubs in 89 at-bats. Connally hit 22 homers at Iowa.

"There are people who think Martinez is going to be another Orlando Cepeda," said Padres General Manager Jack McKeon.

While the Cubs disposed of a promising slugger in Martinez late in the year, they acquired a proven power hitter early in '83. On January 19, Chicago obtained veteran Ron Cey from the Dodgers for two minor leaguers.

As usual, a few players were smuggled across league lines in August, prompting calls for tightening of the waiver rules. The Dodgers and Braves, scrapping for the National League West title, turned to the American League for stretch-run pitching help. Each team paid dearly and

The Twins will be expecting a lot from pitchers John Butcher (above) and Mike Smithson, acquired from Texas for slugger Gary Ward.

Manny Trillo (above) and Gorman Thomas both wanted out of Cleveland and had their wishes met by the Indians' management.

got unsatisfactory results.

The Dodgers sent pitchers Dave Stewart and Ricky Wright to Texas for 29-year-old lefthander Rick Honeycutt. The Dodgers awarded Honeycutt, who would have been eligible for free agency following the season, a five-year, $3.75 million contract. In his first start for Los Angeles, Honeycutt, 14-8 for the Rangers and the A.L. leader in earned-run average with a 2.42 mark, combined with Tom Niedenfuer to shut out the Phillies. He won only one of his six other starts, however, and finished with a 2-3 record and a 5.77 ERA.

Nine days after the Dodgers acquired Honeycutt, the Braves, too, found a team unwilling to meet the salary demands of a potential free agent. The Indians were looking for a taker for 28-year-old righthander Len Barker, the A.L. strikeout leader in 1980 and 1981 but the owner of an 8-13 record and a 5.11 ERA for Cleveland in '83. Barker, after winning a five-year, $4 million contract from the Braves, won only one of four decisions for Atlanta.

The Indians were promised three players for Barker, all to be delivered after the season had ended. But the identities of the players—outfielder Brett Butler and two minor leaguers, pitcher Rick Behenna and third baseman Brook Jacoby—soon became public knowledge.

The leak proved costly to Braves Owner Ted Turner. When Butler asked Turner about the rumors in mid-September, Turner confirmed the makeup of the deal as reported. ("I knew that was an Indian instead of a Brave on my bag," Butler cracked.) The result was a $25,000 fine levied by Commissioner Bowie Kuhn. Turner took the penalty gracefully; he had feared that Kuhn might order Butler, the Braves' left fielder and leadoff man, to report to Cleveland immediately.

Behenna officially became an Indian on September 2, and Butler and Jacoby (.315, 25 homers, 100 runs batted in at Richmond) became official Cleveland property in October.

The Indians also traded second baseman Manny Trillo to a National League club in August. They had obtained the four-time Gold Glove winner from the Phillies only the previous December but considered his contract demands out of line. The Expos were willing to hand over minor league outfielder Don Carter and an undisclosed amount of cash for the opportunity to dicker with Trillo before he would become a free agent. Trillo, though, wouldn't budge after playing 31 games for Montreal and eventually signed with the Giants over the winter.

The next big name to leave Cleveland was Thomas, whom the Tribe had acquired from Milwaukee on June 6 for Rick Manning (like Thomas, a center fielder). Thomas had averaged 35 homers a season for the Brewers over the previous five years but, hampered by a bad knee, slumped to 22 (5 for Milwaukee, 17 for Cleveland) in '83 and batted .209 overall. When Gorman exercised his contractual right to demand a trade, the Indians arranged a deal with the Mariners at the winter meetings, packaging Thomas and second baseman Jack Perconte for Tony Bernazard, who was expected to replace Trillo at second.

Cardinals' wheeler-dealer Whitey Herzog sat on his hands at Nashville, even though the St. Louis manager had watched his 1982 world champions fall to fourth place in the N.L. East.

Herzog, working with Cards General Manager Joe McDonald, had made his big trade in June when he dealt Hernandez, N.L. batting champion in 1979 and a five-time Gold Glove winner at first base, to the Mets for pitchers Neil Allen and Rick Ownbey. The Redbirds needed pitching, Herzog said, and with a promising group of young outfielders, he felt he could move George Hendrick from right field to first base.

The 25-year-old Allen, who was 2-7 for the Mets in '83 and 25-40 for his career preceding the trade, was 10-6 for the Cardinals. He appeared in 25 games for St. Louis and completed four of 18 starts. The Cardinals assigned Ownbey, 1-3 for the Mets, to Louisville, where he was 7-5 with a 3.63 ERA.

Each American League playoff team plugged a hole in its infield via trade or purchase. The Orioles obtained third baseman Todd Cruz from the Mariners (for whom he played shortstop) on June 30 after he had been placed on waivers, while the White Sox acquired shortstops Scott Fletcher and Jerry Dybzinski in trades with the Cubs and Indians, respectively.

Cruz drove in 27 runs in 81 games with Baltimore. At the winter meetings, though, the Orioles traded reliever Tim Stoddard to the A's for third baseman Wayne Gross, a lefthanded hitter with more power than Cruz. The 1983 world champions planned to platoon Gross and Cruz in 1984.

Fletcher came to the White Sox in a January 25 deal that also netted pitchers Dick Tidrow and Randy Martz and infielder Pat Tabler. The Cubs received pitchers Steve Trout and Warren Brusstar. The White Sox traded Tabler to the Indians on April 1 for Dybzinski.

The Phillies, who became N.L. East champions for the fifth time in eight years, made a couple of key moves on May 22. They traded lefthanded reliever Sid Monge to the Padres for outfielder Joe Lefebvre and replaced Monge with Willie Hernandez, obtained from the Cubs for pitchers Dick Ruthven and Bill Johnson (the latter a minor leaguer).

In 101 games with the Phillies, Lefebvre batted .310, hit eight home runs and collected 38 RBIs, seven of them game-winners. Hernandez was 8-4 with seven saves after joining the Phillies. He made 63 appearances and struck out 75 batters in 95⅔ innings.

A handful of flickering stars were released, and 45-year-old Gaylord Perry retired after his fourth straight losing season (7-14, 4.64 ERA for the Royals and Mariners).

Kansas City released 34-year-old Vida Blue (0-5) on August 5, and Atlanta dismissed 44-year-old Phil Niekro (11-10, 3.97) at season's end. Perry, Blue and Niekro had won a total of 773 games in the majors.

The Phillies, on the heels of their World Series defeat, released Pete Rose and Joe Morgan. Rose, at age 42, had experienced the worst season of his career, hitting only .245 and spending an uncustomary amount of time on the bench. Morgan surged in September (.337 average, five homers and 18 RBIs that month), but still hit only .230 for the season.

The former Cincinnati standouts were undaunted, however. Morgan, 40, an Oakland resident since he was 4, signed a one-year contract with the A's, and Rose was confident that he would be resuming his pursuit of Ty Cobb's career hits record in 1984.

January 5 —Braves released pitcher Tom Hausman.

January 5 —Reds traded outfielder Mike Vail to Giants for pitcher Rich Gale.

January 6 —Mets purchased pitcher Joe Georger from Mariners; assigned him to Jackson.

January 10 —Angels traded first baseman John Harris to Reds for catcher Mike O'Berry. Harris was assigned to Indianapolis; O'Berry on Indianapolis roster, was assigned to Edmonton.

January 12 —Twins traded pitcher Bob Veselic to Astros for pitcher Rick Lysander. Lysander was assigned to Toledo; Veselic, on Toledo roster, was assigned to Tucson.

January 13 —Red Sox traded pitcher Mike Torrez to Mets for a player to be named; Red Sox acquired third baseman Mike Davis to complete deal, February 15.

January 14 —Cubs signed pitcher Paul Moskau, a free agent.

January 14 —Mariners re-signed outfielder Al Cowens, a re-entry free agent.

January 14 —Twins released first baseman Greg (Boomer) Wells.

January 17 —A's traded pitcher Brian Kingman to Red Sox for a player to be named.

January 18 —Cardinals purchased pitcher Jerry Garvin from Blue Jays' Syracuse affiliate and assigned him to Louisville.

January 18 —A's signed infielder Bill Almon, a re-entry free agent formerly with the White Sox.

January 19 —Dodgers traded third baseman Ron Cey to Cubs for outfielder Dan Cataline and pitcher Vance Lovelace, who were assigned to Vero Beach.

January 20 —Orioles re-signed catcher Joe Nolan, a re-entry free agent.

January 21 —Mariners traded catcher Jim Essian to Indians for a player to be named.

January 21 —Yankees signed pitcher Steve Comer, a free agent.

January 21 —Mets released catcher Bruce Bochy.

January 24 —Angels signed outfielder Ellis Valentine, a re-entry free agent formerly with the Mets.

January 25 —Cubs traded pitchers Dick Tidrow and Randy Martz and infielders Scott Fletcher and Pat Tabler to White Sox for pitchers Steve Trout and Warren Brusstar.

January 26 —White Sox selected Cardinals pitcher Steve Mura as compensation for the loss of Type A free-agent outfielder Steve Kemp, who signed with the Yankees.

January 27 —Braves signed pitcher Pete Falcone, a re-entry free agent formerly with the Mets.

January 27 —Rangers traded pitcher Bob Babcock, on Denver roster, to Mariners for shortstop Vance McHenry, on Salt Lake City roster.

January 28 —Pirates signed pitcher Nino Espinosa, a free agent, and assigned him to Hawaii.

January 31 —Phillies re-signed outfielder Bill Robinson, a re-entry free agent.

January 31 —Phillies signed first baseman Tony Perez, a free agent.

February 1 —Indians re-signed infielder-outfielder Alan Bannister, a free agent.

February 2 —Giants traded outfielder Jim Wohlford to Expos for infielder Chris Smith.

February 2 —Angels released pitcher Steve Renko.

February 3 —Orioles signed third baseman Aurelio Rodriguez, a re-entry free agent formerly with the White Sox.

February 4 —Mets traded outfielder Jorge Orta to Blue Jays for pitcher Steve Senteney; Mets assigned Senteney to Tidewater.

February 5 —Blue Jays traded outfielder Leon Roberts to Royals for first baseman Cecil Fielder; Fielder, on Butte roster, was assigned to Florence.

February 6 —Mets re-signed catcher Ron Hodges, a re-entry free agent.

February 7 —Giants signed outfielder Joel Youngblood, a re-entry free agent formerly with the Expos.

February 7 —Indians signed outfielder Otto Velez, a free agent, and assigned him to Charleston, W. Va.

February 9 —Royals signed pitcher Steve Renko, a free agent.

February 9 —Indians re-signed outfielder Miguel Dilone, a re-entry free agent.

February 14 —A's signed outfielder Thad Bosley, a free agent, and assigned him to Tacoma.

February 15 —Cubs conditionally purchased pitcher Sandy Wihtol from Indians; returned him March 27.

February 15 —Blue Jays signed pitcher Randy Moffitt, a re-entry free agent formerly with the Astros.

February 16 —Cardinals signed catcher Jamie Quirk, a re-entry free agent formerly with the Royals.

February 17 —Angels' Edmonton affiliate purchased first baseman Gary Gray from Mariners' Salt Lake City affiliate.

February 21 —Tigers signed first baseman Dave Revering, a free agent, and assigned him to Evansville.

February 23 —Blue Jays signed third baseman Mickey Klutts, a free agent.

February 23 —Padres signed catcher Bruce Bochy, a free agent, and assigned him to Las Vegas.

February 24 —Yankees signed infielder Bert Campaneris, a free agent, and assigned him to Columbus, O.

February 24 —Orioles re-signed outfielder John Lowenstein, a re-entry free agent.

February 28 —Padres signed outfielder Jerry Turner, a free agent, and assigned him to Las Vegas.

February 28 —Yankees signed outfielder Rowland Office, a free agent, and assigned him to Columbus, O.

March 1 —Tigers signed catcher Bill Nahorodny, a free agent, and assigned him to Evansville.

March 1 —Phillies signed shortstop Kiko Garcia, a free agent, and assigned him to Portland.

March 8 —Pirates signed pitcher Tom Hausman, a free agent, and assigned him to Hawaii.

March 15 —Tigers signed infielder Julio Gonzalez, a free agent, and assigned him to Evansville.

March 16 —Cardinals traded catcher George Bjorkman to Astros for pitcher Jeff Meadows. Bjorkman was assigned to Columbus, Ga., and Meadows was assigned to Macon.

March 20 —Cubs released pitcher Allen Ripley.

March 23 —Angels released infielder Mick Kelleher.

March 24 —Yankees released first baseman John Mayberry.

March 24 —Tigers traded pitcher Dave Tobik to Rangers for outfielder Johnny Grubb.

March 25 —Twins released pitcher Pete Redfern.

March 25 —Yankees released catcher Barry Foote.

March 25 —Tigers released pitcher Kevin Saucier.

March 25 —Red Sox released pitcher Brian Kingman.

March 25 —Twins traded catcher Sal Butera to Tigers for catcher Stine Poole, who was assigned to Toledo.

March 26 —Rangers released pitcher Paul Mirabella.

March 27 —Pirates released pitcher Randy Jones.

March 27 —Padres released pitcher Mike Griffin.

March 28 —Yankees released pitcher Steve Comer.

March 28 —Brewers released pitcher Dwight Bernard.

March 28 —A's released pitchers Bob Owchinko and John D'Acquisto and outfielder Al Woods.

March 28 —Pirates released pitcher Ross

Baumgarten, outfielder Dick Davis and first baseman John Milner.

March 28 —Mariners released outfielder Bobby Brown.

March 28 —Padres returned pitcher Ray Searage, conditionally purchased on December 15, 1982, to Indians' organization.

March 29 —Twins traded shortstop Ivan Mesa to Dodgers for outfielder Mike (Tack) Wilson; Dodgers assigned Mesa to San Antonio.

March 29 —Dodgers traded outfielder Mark Bradley to Mets for pitchers Jody Johnston and Steve Walker. Mets assigned Bradley to Tidewater and Dodgers assigned Johnston to San Antonio.

March 31 —Mariners purchased first baseman Ken Phelps from Expos.

March 31 —Rangers released first baseman Lamar Johnson.

March 31 —Cardinals traded infielder Kelly Paris to Reds for pitcher Jim Strichek; Reds assigned Paris to Indianapolis and Cardinals assigned Strichek to Macon.

March 31 —Reds traded pitcher Bill Dawley and outfielder Anthony Walker to Astros for catcher Alan Knicely; Astros assigned Dawley to Tucson and Walker to Columbus, Ga.

April 1 —Indians traded shortstop Jerry Dybzinski to White Sox for infielder Pat Tabler.

April 1 —Royals released outfielder Bombo Rivera.

April 1 —Brewers traded catcher Steve Lake to Cubs for a player to be named; Brewers acquired pitcher Rich Buonantony and assigned him to Vancouver to complete deal, October 24.

April 2 —White Sox released outfielder Ron LeFlore.

April 2 —Mets traded infielder Tom Veryzer to Cubs for pitchers Bob Schilling and Craig Weissman; Schilling was assigned to Jackson, Weissman to Columbia.

April 4 —Orioles released first baseman Terry Crowley.

April 4 —Cardinals signed outfielder-third baseman Steve Braun, a free agent.

April 5 —Blue Jays returned third baseman Tucker Ashford to Yankees, from whom they had conditionally purchased him October 27, 1982.

April 7 —Mets signed outfielder Clint Hurdle, a free agent, and assigned him to Tidewater.

April 8 —White Sox signed pitcher Al Hrabosky, a free agent, and assigned him to Denver.

April 11 —Mariners signed pitcher Steve Comer, a free agent, and assigned him to Salt Lake City.

April 14 —Giants released catcher-outfielder Ron Pruitt.

April 18 —Yankees traded third baseman Tucker Ashford to Mets for pitcher Steve Ray and a player to be named. Ashford, on Columbus (O.) roster, was assigned to Tidewater; Ray, on Columbia roster, was assigned to Greensboro. To complete the deal, Yankees acquired infielder Felix Perdomo, on Columbia roster, on May 3 and assigned him to Greensboro.

April 19 —Padres signed outfielder Bobby Brown, a free agent, and assigned him to Las Vegas.

May 1 —Giants signed pitcher Brian Kingman, a free agent, and assigned him to Phoenix.

May 3 —Expos purchased pitcher Bob James from Tigers; assigned him to Wichita.

May 4 —Expos purchased pitcher Chris Welsh from Padres.

May 9 —Reds traded infielder Rafael Landestoy to Dodgers for pitchers Brett Wise and John Franco. Wise and Franco, on Albuquerque roster, were assigned to Indianapolis.

May 16 —Tigers released first baseman Mike Ivie.

May 17 —Phillies released infielder-outfielder Dave Roberts.

May 22 —Phillies traded pitcher Sid Monge to Padres for outfielder Joe Lefebvre.

May 22 —Phillies traded pitchers Dick Ruthven and Bill Johnson to Cubs for pitcher Willie Hernandez; Johnson, on Reading roster, was assigned to Midland.

May 25 —Expos signed first baseman Terry Crowley, a free agent.

May 25 —Giants traded outfielder Mike Vail to Expos for infielder Wallace Johnson.

May 31 —Expos released catcher Tim Blackwell.

May 31 —Yankees released pitcher Doyle Alexander.

June 6 —Brewers traded outfielder Gorman Thomas and pitchers Jamie Easterly and Ernie Camacho to Indians for outfielder Rick Manning and pitcher Rick Waits; Camacho, on Vancouver roster, was assigned to Charleston, W. Va.

June 6 —Phillies released outfielder Bob Molinaro.

June 9 —Yankees released pitcher Rick Reuschel.

June 9 —Phillies released outfielder-first baseman Bill Robinson.

June 9 —Cubs released outfielder Wayne Nordhagen.

June 14 —Orioles traded infielder Floyd Rayford, on Rochester roster, to Cardinals for a player to be named; Orioles acquired outfielder Tito Landrum, on Louisville roster, to complete deal, August 31.

June 14 —Pirates traded catcher Junior Ortiz and pitcher Arthur Ray to Mets for outfielder Marvell Wynne and pitcher Steve Senteney. Mets assigned Ray to Lynchburg, and Pirates assigned Senteney to Hawaii.

June 15 —Mariners traded second baseman Julio Cruz to White Sox for second baseman Tony Bernazard.

June 15 —Cardinals traded first baseman Keith Hernandez to Mets for pitchers Neil Allen and Rick Ownbey; Ownbey was assigned to Louisville.

June 15 —Braves purchased first baseman-outfielder Mike Jorgensen from Mets.

June 15 —A's traded pitcher Matt Keough to Yankees for first baseman Marshall Brant and pitcher Ben Callahan. Brant, on Columbus (O.) roster, was assigned to Tacoma; Callahan, on Nashville roster, joined A's.

June 16 —Mariners' Salt Lake City affiliate released pitcher Steve Comer.

June 20 —Yankees released outfielder Bobby Murcer.

June 21 —Cardinals traded pitcher Doug Bair to Tigers for a player to be named; Cardinals acquired pitcher Dave Rucker to complete deal July 5.

June 21 —Blue Jays signed pitcher Doyle Alexander, a free agent, and assigned him to Kinston.

June 21 —White Sox traded outfielder Rusty Kuntz to Twins for third baseman Mike Sodders; White Sox assigned Sodders, on Orlando roster, to Glens Falls.

June 22 —Phillies signed pitcher Steve Comer, a free agent, and assigned him to Portland.

June 27—Mariners released pitcher Gaylord Perry.

June 28—Cubs signed pitcher Rick Reuschel, a free agent, and assigned him to Quad City.

June 30—Orioles purchased infielder Todd Cruz from Mariners.

June 30—Tigers traded pitcher Pat Underwood to Reds for third baseman Wayne Krenchicki; Reds assigned Underwood to Indianapolis.

July 6—Cardinals released pitcher Jim Kaat.

July 6—Angels released catcher Joe Ferguson and pitcher Dave Goltz.

July 6—Royals signed pitcher Gaylord Perry, a free agent.

July 8—Royals released pitcher Bill Castro.

July 10—Blue Jays released outfielder Hosken Powell.

July 15—Brewers signed pitcher Bill Castro, a free agent, and assigned him to Vancouver.

July 16—Yankees purchased infielder Larry Milbourne from Phillies.

July 18—Dodgers released outfielder Ron Roenicke.

July 19—Angels released pitcher Bill Travers.

July 21—Cardinals signed third baseman Ken Reitz, a free agent, and assigned him to Louisville.

July 26—Mariners signed outfielder Ron Roenicke, a free agent.

July 26—Padres released outfielder Jerry Turner.

July 28—Expos released pitcher Randy Lerch.

July 29—Phillies purchased pitcher Larry Andersen from Mariners; Andersen was on Portland roster, on loan.

August 1—Cubs released second baseman Junior Kennedy.

August 2—Pirates purchased pitcher Dave Tomlin from Expos' Wichita affiliate.

August 2—Royals purchased pitcher Eric Rasmussen from Cardinals' Louisville affiliate.

August 4—Tigers purchased pitcher John Martin from Cardinals.

August 5—Royals released pitcher Vida Blue.

August 5—Tigers released catcher Bill Fahey.

August 8—Cubs' organization released pitcher Paul Moskau, on Iowa roster.

August 10—Yankees traded outfielder Jerry Mumphrey to Astros. for outfielder Omar Moreno.

August 13—Phillies released pitcher Ed Farmer.

August 13—Orioles released third baseman Aurelio Rodriguez.

August 17—Indians traded second baseman Manny Trillo to Expos for outfielder Don Carter and cash; Indians assigned Carter, on Memphis roster, to Buffalo.

August 19—Pirates traded catcher Steve Nicosia to Giants for catcher Milt May and cash.

August 19—Rangers traded pitcher Rick Honeycutt to Dodgers for pitcher Dave Stewart and a player to be named; Rangers acquired pitcher Ricky Wright to complete deal, September 16.

August 23—Expos signed infielder Mike Phillips, a free agent, and assigned him to Wichita.

August 23—Tigers purchased pitcher Glenn Abbott from Mariners.

August 25—Indians acquired pitcher Richard Barnes from White Sox's Denver affiliate for a player to be named. Indians assigned Barnes to Charleston, W. Va., and White Sox acquired outfielder Miguel Dilone to complete deal, September 1.

August 26—Padres traded pitcher John Montefusco to Yankees for two players to be named; Padres acquired pitcher Dennis Rasmussen and infielder Edwin Rodriguez to complete deal, September 12.

August 28—Indians traded pitcher Len Barker to Braves for three players to be named; Indians acquired pitcher Rick Behenna on September 2 and outfielder Brett Butler and third baseman Brook Jacoby on October 21.

August 31—White Sox signed infielder Aurelio Rodriguez, a free agent.

August 31—Padres traded outfielder Sixto Lezcano and a player to be named to Phillies for four players to be named. Padres acquired pitchers Marty Decker (on Portland roster), Ed Wojna (Reading), Darren Burroughs (Reading) and Lance McCullers (Spartanburg) on September 20; Phillies acquired pitcher Steve Fireovid on October 11 and assigned him to Portland.

September 1—Tigers signed outfielder Bob Molinaro, a free agent.

September 2—A's traded pitcher Steve Baker, on Tacoma roster, to Cardinals for two players to be named; A's acquired pitchers Tom Dozier, on St. Petersburg roster, and Jim Strichek, on Macon roster, September 16 and assigned them to Modesto.

September 7—White Sox traded outfielder Miguel Dilone and pitcher Mike Maitland to Pirates for pitcher Randy Niemann; Pirates assigned Maitland, on Denver roster, to Hawaii.

September 16—Expos released infielder Mike Phillips.

September 16—Expos purchased outfielder Gene Roof from Cardinals.

September 27—Expos purchased pitcher Greg Harris from Reds.

September 30—Cubs released outfielder Jerry Morales.

September 30—Cubs purchased pitcher Mike Chris from Giants.

October 3—Royals released pitcher Steve Renko.

October 4—Braves released pitcher Tommy Boggs.

October 7—Braves released pitcher Phil Niekro.

October 7—Expos released pitcher Woodie Fryman and first baseman Terry Crowley.

October 10—Royals released outfielder Cesar Geronimo.

October 17—Royals released pitcher Eric Rasmussen.

October 19—Phillies released first baseman-outfielder Pete Rose.

October 21—Tigers released outfielder Bob Molinaro and catchers Sal Butera and Bill Nahorodny.

October 27—Giants released outfielder-first baseman Chris Smith.

October 28—Orioles released catcher Dave Huppert.

October 28—A's released outfielder Joe Rudi.

October 31—Phillies released second baseman Joe Morgan.

October 31—Tigers signed infielder Jimmy Smith, a free agent.

October 31—White Sox released pitcher Dick Tidrow.

November 1—Rangers released pitcher Jon

Matlack and outfielder-first baseman Larry Biittner.

November 2—White Sox released first baseman Chris Nyman, who signed with Nankai Hawks of Japanese Pacific League.

November 3—Phillies released pitcher Larry Christenson.

November 4—Reds signed catcher Brad Gulden, a free agent.

November 8—Angels released pitcher Mickey Mahler.

November 9—Reds released pitcher Rich Gale.

November 9—Yankees released outfielder Rowland Office.

November 12—Reds purchased pitcher Bob Owchinko from Pirates.

November 14—A's signed first baseman-outfielder Bruce Bochte, a free agent.

November 18—Reds purchased third baseman Wayne Krenchicki from Tigers.

November 21—Yankees re-signed pitcher Dale Murray, a re-entry free agent.

November 21—Indians released outfielder Karl Pagel.

November 21—Reds traded catcher Steve Christmas to White Sox for infielder Fran Mullins.

November 21—Mariners traded pitcher Bill Caudill and a player to be named to A's for pitcher Dave Beard and catcher Bob Kearney; A's acquired pitcher, Darrel Akerfelds to complete deal, December 6.

November 22—Angels re-signed first baseman Rod Carew, a re-entry free agent.

November 22—Pirates signed pitchers Jeff Little and Andy Rincon, free agents, and assigned them to Hawaii.

November 28—White Sox purchased infielder Kelly Paris from Reds.

December 2—White Sox re-signed pitcher Jerry Koosman, a re-entry free agent.

December 2—A's released first baseman Marshall Brant.

December 5—Angels released pitcher Byron McLaughlin.

December 5—Phillies traded first baseman Tony Perez to Reds for a player to be named.

December 5—Indians traded catcher Jim Essian to A's for a player to be named; Indians acquired infielder Luis Quinones to complete deal, December 8.

December 5—Tigers traded pitcher Larry Pashnick to Twins for outfielder Rusty Kuntz.

December 5—Phillies traded pitcher Ron Reed to White Sox for a player to be named.

December 5—Giants traded outfielder-first baseman Champ Summers to Padres for infielder Joe Pittman and a player to be named; Giants acquired outfielder Tommy Francis, on Miami roster, to complete deal, December 7.

December 6—Pirates traded outfielder Mike Easler to Red Sox for pitcher John Tudor.

December 6—Royals signed outfielder Lynn Jones, a free agent.

December 7—Reds signed outfielder Dave Parker, a re-entry free agent formerly with the Pirates.

December 7—In three-team deal, Padres traded pitcher Gary Lucas to Expos, Cubs sent pitcher Craig Lefferts, first baseman Carmelo Martinez and third baseman Fritz Connally to the Padres, and Expos dealt pitcher Scott Sanderson to Cubs.

December 7—Indians traded outfielder Gorman Thomas and second baseman Jack Perconte to Mariners for second baseman Tony Bernazard.

December 7—Twins traded outfielder Gary Ward to Rangers for pitchers Mike Smithson and John Butcher and catcher Sam Sorce, on Burlington roster.

December 8—Rangers traded catcher Jim Sundberg to Brewers for catcher Ned Yost and pitcher Dan Scarpetta, who was assigned from Beloit to Burlington.

December 8—Yankees signed catcher Mike O'Berry, a free agent.

December 8—Angels traded shortstop Tim Foli to Yankees for pitcher Curt Kaufman and cash.

December 8—Expos traded pitcher Ray Burris to A's for outfielder Rusty McNealy and cash.

December 8—Yankees traded pitcher Roger Erickson and first baseman Steve Balboni to Royals for pitcher Mike Armstrong and catcher Duane Dewey.

December 8—Angels signed pitcher Frank LaCorte, a re-entry free agent formerly with the Astros.

December 8—Dodgers traded pitcher Sid Fernandez and infielder Ross Jones to Mets for pitcher Carlos Diaz and a player to be named; Dodgers acquired infielder Bob Bailor to complete deal, December 12.

December 8—Dodgers traded pitcher Joe Beckwith to Royals for three minor leaguers, catcher Joe Szekely and pitchers Jose Torres and John Serritella.

December 9—Royals signed catcher Don Werner, a free agent.

December 9—A's traded third baseman-first baseman Wayne Gross to Orioles for pitcher Tim Stoddard.

December 9—Mariners traded pitcher Bryan Clark to Blue Jays for outfielder Barry Bonnell.

December 13—A's signed second baseman Joe Morgan, a free agent.

December 15—Cardinals released infielder Jeff Doyle.

December 18—Tigers signed infielder Darrell Evans, a re-entry free agent formerly with the Giants.

December 19—Pirates signed outfielder Amos Otis, a re-entry free agent formerly with the Royals.

December 19—Royals traded first baseman Willie Aikens to Blue Jays for outfielder Jorge Orta.

December 19—Expos re-signed pitcher Dan Schatzeder, a re-entry free agent.

December 19—Yankees traded pitcher Mike Browning, on Columbus (O.) roster, to Angels for pitcher Curt Brown, who was assigned to Columbus.

December 20—Brewers traded pitcher Jim Slaton to Angels for outfielder Bobby Clark.

December 20—Astros re-signed first baseman-outfielder Dennis Walling, a re-entry free agent.

December 20—Yankees traded pitcher Tim Burke to Expos for outfielder Pat Rooney.

December 21—Giants signed second baseman Manny Trillo, a re-entry free agent formerly with the Expos.

December 23—Pirates re-signed pitcher Kent Tekulve, a re-entry free agent.

December 24—Tigers re-signed pitcher Doug Bair, a re-entry free agent.

December 29—Tigers re-signed pitcher Milt Wilcox, a re-entry free agent.

Grimm, Averill Died in 1983

By CARL CLARK

Baseball lost its jester when Charlie Grimm died. Jolly Cholly, whose japes as a player and manager delighted fans and nettled umpires for more than 40 years, succumbed on November 15, 1983, at Scottsdale (Ariz.) Memorial Hospital, where he was being treated for Hodgkin's disease. He was 85.

Grimm signed his first professional contract with the Philadelphia Athletics in 1916 at age 17 and played in 12 games for Connie Mack's club that year. Two years later, he appeared in 50 games for the St. Louis Cardinals, who subsequently sold him to the Pittsburgh Pirates for $3,500. He was the Pirates' first baseman from 1920 through 1924.

Following the '24 season, Grimm, a left-handed hitter and thrower, was traded with infielder Rabbit Maranville and pitcher Wilbur Cooper to the Chicago Cubs for second baseman George Grantham, pitcher Vic Aldridge and first baseman Albert Niehaus. Grimm had hit .345 and driven in 99 runs in 1923 but fell to .288 and 63 RBIs the next year.

For Grimm, the trade was the beginning of a long, though not unbroken, association with the Cubs that lasted until the Wrigley family sold the franchise in 1981. He was the Cubs' regular first baseman from 1925 through 1933 and saw sporadic duty in the 1934, '35 and '36 seasons. He finished his playing career with a .290 average, 79 home runs and 1,083 RBIs. He holds the modern National League career records for most putouts by a first baseman, most chances accepted and most games at the position. He led or tied for the lead in fielding percentage at first base in nine seasons.

In 1932, Grimm began the first of his three stints as manager of the Cubs, replacing Rogers Hornsby with 57 games remaining and the club in second place. Charlie brought the team home in front, four games ahead of Pittsburgh. Included in Chicago's 37-20 run under Grimm was a 14-game winning streak.

The Cubs won one more flag, in 1935, before Grimm resigned in mid-1938, saying he had lost control of his players. He climbed the stairs to the broadcasting booth and did not return to the field until 1941 when he became a coach for the Cubs. He soon quit, however, to become manager of the Milwaukee club in the American Association. His success—the Brewers won the pennant in 1943—and

Charlie Grimm was a first baseman during his playing days and later a successful manager.

exaggerated German accent helped him establish a great rapport with the burghers of Milwaukee. Showman Bill Veeck Jr., a kindred soul and owner of the Brewers, said of Grimm: "We'd book Charlie into the old Wisconsin and Riverview theaters during the off-season. He was a wonderful entertainer. He would sing and play the banjo, and he was a great storyteller. Many of us always believed he could have been a professional vaudevillian."

Grimm returned to Chicago to pilot the Cubs in May of 1944 and lifted them from the cellar to fourth place. A year later, the Cubs won their last pennant. Grimm directed the club until Frankie Frisch succeeded him in June of 1949.

After a brief and unsatisfying stab at front-office work, Charlie returned to Milwaukee in 1951 and guided the Class AAA Brewers to the Little World Series championship. He was named manager of the Boston Braves on May 31, 1952, and stayed aboard when the franchise moved to Milwaukee in 1953. The Braves were in fifth place when he was fired 46 games into the 1956 campaign.

P.K. Wrigley brought Grimm back to the Cubs as a vice president in 1957, and Charlie took a final fling at managing in 1960. But early in May, he and broadcaster Lou Boudreau traded places. Grimm remained in the Cubs' organization in one capacity or another for 20 more years and was popular on the banquet circuit.

In accordance with Grimm's wishes, his body was cremated and the ashes scattered over Wrigley Field.

Earl Averill, favorite son of Snohomish, Wash., was the only member of the Hall of Fame who died in 1983. An outfield standout for the Cleveland Indians in the 1930s, Averill died of pneumonia at an Everett, Wash., hospital on August 15. He was 81.

The Earl of Snohomish had a career batting average of .318 and drove in more than 100 runs in five of his 10-plus seasons with the Indians, including 143 in 1931. He also played for Detroit in 1939 and 1940 and the Boston Braves in 1941. He finished his career with 2,019 hits, 238 of them homers. In 1936, Averill led the American League in hits (232), tied for the lead in triples (15), finished fifth in homers (28) and second in batting (.378 to Luke Appling's .388).

It was Averill who lined a pitch off the foot of Dizzy Dean in the 1937 All-Star Game at Washington, one of five midsummer classics in which Averill played. The drive fractured Dean's toe, shortening his career.

"It wasn't me that put him (Dean) out of commission for good; it was the Cardinals," Averill maintained. "They pitched him too soon after he got hurt."

A son, Earl Douglas Averill, was a major leaguer in the 1950s and '60s, but familial ties didn't mitigate the father's view of the players of that era. "In my day," he said, "most of us stood close to the plate. They don't do that nowadays and are dead on outside pitches. You got to be close. Ever see Ruth bat? His foot was out in front of the batter's box."

The townspeople of Snohomish, who once took up a collection to send Averill to Seattle for a tryout with that city's Pacific Coast League club, stumped for his election to the Hall of Fame and their efforts finally paid off in 1975 when the Veterans Committee acted unanimously.

Vic Wertz, an outfielder and first baseman who slugged 266 major league homers, most of them for Detroit and Cleveland, died on July 7 at a Detroit hospital while undergoing heart surgery. He was 58.

Wertz drove in 133 runs for the Tigers in 1949 and 123 runs the following season. He was struck by polio in 1955 but came back to hit 32 homers for the Indians in 1956.

Wertz is best remembered, though, as the batter whom Willie Mays foiled with his great eighth-inning catch at the Polo Grounds in Game 1 of the 1954 World Series. With Cleveland runners at first and second, none out and the score tied 2-2, Wertz belted a pitch from the Giants' Don Liddle to deep center field. Mays made a running, over-the-shoulder catch 460 feet from home plate. The Giants won the game in 10 innings, 5-2, and won the world championship in four games. Wertz went 4-for-5 in Game 1 and 8-for-16 in the Series.

Emil (Dutch) Leonard, who used a knuckleball to record 191 victories in the majors, died at Springfield, Ill., April 17. He was 74.

Leonard toiled for the Brooklyn Dodgers, Washington Senators, Philadelphia Phillies and Chicago Cubs from 1933 through 1953, interrupted only by a 1936-37 stint in the minors. He enjoyed his greatest success with the Senators, posting records of 20-8 in 1939 and 17-7 in 1945.

Leonard, of Belgian ancestry but called Dutch after former big-league pitcher Hubert (Dutch) Leonard, once had a terrific fastball but lost it after jamming his shoulder while playing basketball. He credited Paul Richards, his catcher at Atlanta (Southern Association) in '36 and '37, with saving his career by encouraging him to develop the knuckler.

Leonard's 4-1 victory for Washington over Detroit on the final day of the 1944 season, coupled with St. Louis' 5-2 triumph over the New York Yankees, gave the Browns their only American League pennant. After the game—before which he had received a phone call from a man who offered him $20,000 for a subpar performance—Leonard got a call from Dizzy Dean, who was broadcasting for the Browns. Said Leonard: "He wouldn't let me get off the phone until I promised to go to St. Louis for a big party they were going to have. When I got there, they put me in a big easy chair and told me to sit back and relax and have anything I wanted to eat or drink."

It was a rare moment of appreciation for Leonard, who spent most of his career with second-division teams. "Sure, if I had been with better teams, I always figured I could have won 75 or 80 more games," he said. "But I look at it this way: I never had to dig coal for a living the way my father did. I've thanked the good Lord for that many times."

Chet Laabs, who keyed the Browns' pennant-clinching victory in '44 with a pair of two-run homers, died January 26. He was 70.

Among the other baseball personalities who died in 1983 were Willie (Puddin' Head) Jones, third baseman for the 1950 Philadelphia Phillies "Whiz Kids," who won the National League pennant; H. Roy Hamey, former general manager of the Yankees, Pirates and Phillies; Fred Schulte, outfielder for the Browns, Senators and Pirates from 1927 through 1937; George (Kiddo) Davis, center fielder who batted .368 for the New York Giants in their 1933 World Series triumph over Washington; Ray Sanders, first baseman for the St. Louis Cardinals and Boston Braves in the 1940s; Del Rice, major league catcher for 17 seasons, The Sporting News' Minor League Manager of the Year in 1971 and manager of the California Angels in 1972; Carl Morton, National League Rookie of the Year after winning 18 games for the Montreal Expos in 1970; F.J. (Steve) O'Neill, board chairman and majority owner of the Indians since 1978; Mel Wright, pitching coach for the Montreal Expos; Phil Piton, president and treasurer of the National Association from 1963 through 1971; and Tony Latham, a 21-year-old outfielder in the Boston Red Sox organization who drowned in a boating accident near the Florida coast.

An alphabetical list of baseball deaths in 1983 follows:

Howard Earl Averill, 81, Hall of Fame outfielder for the Cleveland Indians and a .318 batter during his 13-year major league career, of pneumonia, at an Everett, Wash., hospital on August 15; drove in more than 100 runs in five of his 10-plus seasons with the Indians (1929-1939), including 143 in 1931; played for Detroit in 1939 and 1940 and the Boston Braves in 1941; finished his career with 2,019 hits, including 238 homers, in 1,669 major league games; led the American League in hits (232) and tied for the lead in triples (15) in 1936, and batted .378 that season with 28 homers; appeared in five All-Star Games—in the 1937 classic in Washington, he lined a pitch off the foot of Dizzy Dean, fracturing the pitcher's toe; the nagging injury forced Dean to alter his pitching motion, leading to a career-shortening arm injury for Dean; though Averill never received more than 14 Hall of Fame votes from the Baseball Writers' Association of America, he was a unanimous shrine pick by the Veterans Committee in 1975; a son, Earl Douglas Averill, played a total of 449 games, most as a utilityman, for five major league clubs from 1956 through 1963.

David Barnhill, 68, righthanded pitcher in the old Negro leagues for the New York Cubans, Kansas City Monarchs and Chicago American Giants, at Miami on January 8; pitched for Minneapolis of the American Association from 1949 through 1952.

Joseph Stanley Beggs, 72, righthanded pitcher for the New York Yankees in 1938, Cincinnati from 1940 through 1944 and in 1946 and 1947, and the New York Giants in 1947 and 1948, at Indianapolis on July 19; in 1940, a world championship year for the Reds, he was 12-3 and had a nine-game winning streak in relief; appeared in 238 games in the majors, as a reliever in nearly 200 of them, and compiled a 48-35 record, with a 2.96 earned-run average.

Joe Bowen, 66, director of scouting for the Cincinnati Reds for 15 years until his retirement in 1983, at Cincinnati on May 13; scouted for various organizations, beginning in 1948 with Brooklyn; moved to Pittsburgh with Branch Rickey in 1951 and joined the Reds in 1967.

Stephen Gilbert (Gil) Britton, 91, shortstop who played three games for Pittsburgh in 1913, at Parsons, Kan., June 27.

Joseph Francis (Joe) Cicero, 72, outfielder who appeared in a total of 40 games for the Boston Red Sox in 1929 and 1930 and the Philadelphia Athletics in 1945, at Clearwater, Fla., March 30; scouted for Brooklyn in 1953 and 1954.

Rufus Rivers (Rufe) Clarke, 82, righthander who compiled a 1-1 record in seven appearances for Detroit in 1923 and 1924, at Columbia, S.C., February 8; brother of third baseman-outfielder Sumpter Clarke, who played 47 games in the majors in the early '20s.

John Edgar (Zip) Collins, 91, outfielder who batted .253 in 286 games with Pittsburgh, the Boston Braves and the Philadelphia Athletics starting in 1914 and ending in 1921, of a heart ailment, at Manassas, Va., December 19; his best season was 1915, when he hit .293 in 111 games.

Frank Lloyd Colman, 64, outfielder and first baseman for Pittsburgh from 1942 through June 1946, and the New York Yankees in 1946 and 1947, at London, Ont., February 21; batted .228 in 271 games.

James John Cronin, 77, infielder who batted .232 in 25 games for the Philadelphia Athletics in 1929, at Richmond, Calif., June 10.

Clyde Elsworth (Bucky) Crouse, 86, catcher for the Chicago White Sox from 1923 through 1930, at Muncie, Ind., October 23; batted .262 in 470 games; International League's Most Valuable Player as playing manager at Baltimore in 1937.

Arthur Joseph (Cookie) Cuccurullo, 64, left-handed pitcher for Pittsburgh from 1943 through 1945, at West Orange, N.J., January 23; posted a 3-5 record in 62 games.

Al Daniels, 60, scout for the Seattle Mariners, at Portland, Ore., April 6; he previously had scouted for Cleveland, Montreal and Pittsburgh.

George Willis (Kiddo) Davis, 81, outfielder who had a .282 average over seven seasons in the 1930s with five big-league clubs, at Bridgeport, Conn., February 4; played one game for the New York Yankees in 1926 but didn't reach the majors again until 1932, when he batted .309 and scored 100 runs for the Philadelphia Phillies; he was the center fielder for the 1933 New York Giants, who defeated Washington in the World Series as Davis batted .368 (7-for-19); played for the St. Louis Cardinals and Phillies in 1934, then rejoined the Giants for the 1935 and 1936 seasons, making another World Series appearance in '36; in 1937, he was traded to the Cincinnati Reds, with whom he concluded his career a year later.

Connie Desmond, 75, sportscaster who teamed with Mel Allen on accounts of New York Yankees games and with Red Barber in play-by-play coverage of the Brooklyn Dodgers in the 1940s and '50s, at Toledo on March 10.

Everett Joseph Fagan, 65, righthanded pitcher who was 2-7 in 38 appearances for the Philadelphia Athletics in 1943 and 1946, at Morristown,

N.J., February 16.

Frank Forbes, 92, scout for the New York Giants from 1951 through 1957 and for the San Francisco Giants in 1958 and a shortstop for such Negro league teams as the Lincoln Giants, Chicago American Giants and Brooklyn Royal Giants, at Philadelphia on August 19.

Carl Alexander (Jake) Freeze, 83, righthander who pitched two games for the Chicago White Sox in 1925, at San Angelo, Tex., June 9.

William A. (Bill) Gardner, 63, The Sporting News' Minor League Executive of the Year in 1969, the first of his four years as owner of the Louisville Colonels of the International League, at Louisville, Ky., July 10; nephew of Tom Yawkey, late owner of the Boston Red Sox, Gardner purchased the Colonels from the I.L. on the eve of the '69 opener after the franchise had been lifted from Walter Dilbeck, who had unpaid debts of $170,000; the Kentucky State Fair Board evicted the Colonels after the 1972 season in order to remodel the fairgrounds stadium, used as the baseball club's home field, for the University of Louisville football program.

Samuel Braxton Gibson, 83, lefthanded pitcher for Detroit from 1926 through 1928, the New York Yankees in 1930 and the New York Giants in 1932, at High Point, N.C., January 31; 32-38 in 131 games, his only winning season was 1926, when he was 12-9; had six 20-victory seasons for the San Francisco Seals of the Pacific Coast League; scouted briefly for the St. Louis Browns.

Danny Goodman, 71, director of souvenirs and advertising for the Los Angeles Dodgers since 1958, at Los Angeles on June 16.

Nelson George Greene, 82, lefthanded pitcher who won two of three decisions for Brooklyn in 1924 and 1925, at Lebanon, Pa., April 6.

Charles John (Jolly Cholly) Grimm, 85, major league first baseman for 20 years and a man who served three terms as manager of the Chicago Cubs, of Hodgkin's disease, at Scottsdale, Ariz., November 15; played for the Philadelphia Athletics in 1916, the St. Louis Cardinals in 1918, Pittsburgh from 1919 through 1924 and the Cubs from 1925 through 1936; in 2,166 games, he batted .290, with 79 home runs and 1,083 runs batted in; his best year was 1923, when he hit .345 and drove in 99 runs; holds modern N.L. career records for most putouts by a first baseman, most chances accepted and most games at the position—he led or tied for the lead in fielding percentage at first base in nine seasons; became playing manager for the Cubs in 1932, replacing Rogers Hornsby with 57 games remaining and the Cubs in second place—thanks to a 37-20 stretch run, which included a 14-game winning streak, Chicago won the N.L. pennant; Grimm managed the Cubs to one more pennant in 1935, before resigning in the middle of the 1938 season, saying he had lost control of his players—he spent the next 2½ seasons in the broadcasting booth, then returned as a Cub coach in 1941; he quit in June of '41 to become manager of the Milwaukee club in the American Association, but returned to the Cubs' helm in May 1944; Cubs won their last flag under Grimm in 1945; he remained as manager until June 1949, when he was fired and succeeded by Frankie Frisch; managed the Braves from 1952 through the early stages of the 1956 campaign; returned to the Cubs' organization and served in the front office and as a broadcaster for another 15 years; took a final fling at managing in 1960 (6-11 record before pulling a dugout-broadcast booth switch with Lou Boudreau); Grimm's overall managerial record in the majors was 1,287 victories and 1,069 defeats (.546).

George Stanley Halas, 88, legendary patriarch of the National Football League and longtime coach of the Chicago Bears who played 12 games as an outfielder for the New York Yankees in 1919, at Chicago on October 31.

Robert Lewis (Bob) Hall, 59, pitcher for the Boston Braves in 1949 and 1950 and Pittsburgh in 1953, after being struck by an auto while directing traffic at a construction site, at St. Petersburg, Fla., March 12; primarily a relief pitcher, he was 6-4 in '49 and 0-2 the following season; appeared in 37 games for the Pirates in 1953, 17 as a starter, and had a 3-12 record.

H. Roy Hamey, 81, general manager of the New York Yankees, Philadelphia Phillies and Pittsburgh during a career as a baseball executive that covered nearly 40 years, of a heart attack, at Tucson, Ariz., December 14; his longtime off-and-on association with New York was highlighted by three straight Yankee pennants and two world championships while he served as general manager from 1961 through 1963, which offset not-so-productive G.M. stints with Pittsburgh in the '40s and Philadelphia in the '50s; deteriorating health forced his retirement before the 1964 season, but he recovered sufficiently to become head of the Yankees' West Coast scouting operation in 1966 and was still listed as an active scout at the time of his death.

Minter Carney (Jackie) Hayes, 76, infielder for Washington from 1927 through 1931 and the Chicago White Sox from 1932 through 1940, at Birmingham, Ala., February 9; batted .265 in 962 games; best season was 1936, when he hit .312 and drove in 84 runs; career ended when glaucoma caused blindness in one eye; three years later, he lost the sight in the other eye.

Berlyn Dale Horne, 83, righthanded pitcher who was 1-1 in 11 games for the Chicago Cubs in 1929, at Franklin, O., February 3.

Rudolfo (Rudy) Hoyos, 66, co-announcer for the Los Angeles Dodgers' Spanish-language broadcasts from 1975 through 1981, at Los Angeles on April 15.

Bob (Rupe) Hughes, 86, former scout for Brooklyn, Pittsburgh and the St. Louis Cardinals, at Long Beach, Calif., July 27.

Clifford K. Jaffe, 64, public relations director for the Chicago Cubs from 1948 through 1959, at Highland Park, Ill., April 21; before joining the Cubs, he was sports editor of the old Chicago Herald-American.

Chester Lillis (Chet) Johnson, 65, lefthanded pitcher for the St. Louis Browns in 1946, at Seattle on April 10; won more than 200 games in the minors between 1939 and 1959; a younger brother, Earl, had a 40-32 record with the Boston Red Sox and Detroit Tigers in the 1940s and early '50s.

Harry L. Jones, 62, radio and TV play-by-play announcer for the Cleveland Indians from 1961 through 1976, at Sedona, Ariz., August 10; spent 20 years with the Cleveland Plain Dealer, 13 of them covering the Indians, before launching his broadcast career.

Willie Edward (Puddin' Head) Jones, 58, third baseman for the 1950 Philadelphia Phillies "Whiz Kids," of cancer of the lymph glands, at Cincinnati on October 18; played for the Phillies from 1947 until the middle of the 1959 season, when he was traded to Cleveland; a month later, he was back in the National League at Cincinnati, where he finished his career in 1961; he batted .267 in 1950, hitting 25 homers and driving in 88 runs, as the Phillies won their first pennant in 35 years before being swept by New York in the World Series; in 1,691 major league games, he batted .258, with 190 homers and 812 RBIs.

William Aulton (Bill) Kennedy, 62, lefthanded pitcher who had a 15-28 record with five major league clubs spanning eight seasons between 1948

Willie "Puddin' Head" Jones hit 25 homers and drove in 88 runs playing third base for the Philadelphia Phillies' "Whiz Kids" of 1950.

Montreal's Carl Morton captured National League Rookie of the Year honors in 1970 with an 18-11 record.

and 1957, at Seattle on April 9; pitched for Cleveland in 1948, the St. Louis Browns from 1948 through 1951, the Chicago White Sox in 1952, the Boston Red Sox in 1953 and Cincinnati in 1956 and 1957.

Peter C. Kramer, 59, scout for Washington in 1970, Oakland in 1973 and Texas in 1980, of a heart attack, at St. Paul, Minn., February 19.

Calvin W. Kunz Jr., 63, former president of the Denver Bears (American Association, 1962, and Pacific Coast League, 1963 through 1965), at Denver on January 26.

Chester Peter (Chet) Laabs, 70, outfielder who hit a pair of two-run homers on the final day of the 1944 season to boost the St. Louis Browns to their only American League pennant, of a pulmonary embolism, at Warren, Mich., January 26; he batted only .234 in the Browns' championship season and had hit only three homers entering the final game, but he hit two against the New York Yankees and the Browns won, 5-2 (St. Louis became the A.L. champion when the Detroit Tigers, with whom the Browns had been tied, lost to Washington, 4-1); played for Detroit from 1937 until the 1939 season, during which he was traded to the Browns; played for the Browns through 1946 and finished his career with the Philadelphia Athletics the next season; led the A.L. in pinch-hits (14) in 1940; in his most productive season, 1942, he drilled 27 homers and knocked in 99 runs.

Jesse Glenn Landrum, 70, scout for the Chicago Cubs, Detroit, the New York Yankees and the Philadelphia Phillies from 1953 through 1970, at Beaumont, Tex., June 27; appeared in four games as an infielder for the Chicago White Sox in 1938.

Anthony (Tony) Latham, 21, outfielder in the Boston Red Sox organization who played at Winston-Salem (Carolina) in 1983, drowned following a boating accident near the Florida coast in the Gulf of Mexico on October 30; Latham was one of four persons aboard a 15-foot pleasure boat that sank as it was heading back from a fishing trip; the boat's owner, Mark Zastrowmy of Punta Gorda, Fla., was never found, while two other Boston farmhands who were playing for the Red

Sox's Florida Instructional League team in Sarasota, Scott Skripko and John Mitchell, survived, clinging to debris until they were rescued the next morning.

Emil John (Dutch) Leonard, 74, righthanded knuckleballer who pitched in the majors for 20 years, of heart disease, at Springfield, Ill., April 17; pitched for Brooklyn from 1933 to 1936, Washington from 1938 through 1946, the Philadelphia Phillies in 1947 and 1948 and the Chicago Cubs from 1949 through 1953; pitching for second-division clubs for most of his career, he nevertheless fashioned a 191-181 record, with a 3.25 earned-run average and 30 shutouts; best seasons were 1939, when he was 20-8, and 1945, when he was 17-7; one of four knuckleballers on the Senators' 1944 staff, he was 14-14 that year—and on the last day of the season, his 4-1 victory over Detroit, combined with St. Louis' 5-2 victory over New York, gave the Browns their only American League pennant; though he was 12-17 for the Phillies in 1948, his 2.51 ERA was second best in the N.L.; served as pitching coach for the Cubs from 1954 through 1956.

Thompson Orville (Mickey) Livingston, 66, catcher for Washington, the Philadelphia Phillies, Chicago Cubs, New York Giants, Boston Braves and Brooklyn between 1938 and 1951, at Houston on April 3; batted .238 in 561 major league games; hit .364 in the Cubs' 1945 World Series loss to Detroit.

Carl Alan Manda, 94, a second baseman who appeared in nine games for the Chicago White Sox in 1914, at Artesia, N.M., March 9.

Elwood Goode (Speed) Martin, 89, righthanded pitcher for the St. Louis Browns in 1917 and the Chicago Cubs from 1918 through 1922, at Lemon Grove, Calif., June 14; he was one of the heroes of the Cubs' drive to the National League pennant in 1918, winning six of eight decisions after joining the club in August; he was 30-42 in 126 major league games, with a 3.78 earned-run average.

Gus Mauch, 81, trainer for the New York Yankees and New York Mets during Casey Stengel's tenure as manager of the two clubs, of congestive heart failure, at St. Petersburg, Fla., April 16; joined the Yankees as an assistant trainer in 1943 and became head trainer in 1947; stayed with the Yankees until 1962, when he joined Stengel with the expansion Mets; retired after the 1969 season.

William Joseph (Bill) McCarren, 87, scout for the Boston Red Sox since 1944 and a third baseman for Brooklyn in 1923, at Denver on October 2; batted .245 for the Dodgers in 69 games.

Michael William (Mike) Menosky, 88, outfielder for Pittsburgh of the old Federal League in 1914 and 1915, Washington in 1916, 1917 and 1919, and the Boston Red Sox from 1920 through 1923, at Detroit on April 11; counting his years in the Federal League, he batted .278 in 809 games; made the last out for Washington in 1917 game in which Boston's Ernie Shore pitched a perfect game in relief of Babe Ruth (who was ejected after walking the game's first batter).

Carl Wendle Morton, 39, National League Rookie of the Year in 1970 when he compiled an 18-11 record for Montreal, of a heart attack, at Tulsa on April 12; a righthander who began his career as an outfielder in the Atlanta organization, he was selected by the Expos in the 1968 expansion draft after posting a 13-5 record at Shreveport that year; after slipping to records of 10-18 in 1971 and 7-13 in 1972, he was traded to Atlanta for pitcher Pat Jarvis; he had three consecutive winning seasons at Atlanta (48-38 overall), but slumped to 4-9 in 1976, his last year in the majors; finished 87-92 in 255 games, with an earned-run average of 3.73.

Frank J. Oceak, 70, a coach for Pittsburgh from 1958 through 1964 and from 1970 through 1972 and for Cincinnati in 1965, at Johnstown, Pa., March 19; though he never played above Class A, he developed a reputation as a good tutor of young players and managed in the Pirates' minor league system for many years, beginning in 1938.

F. J. (Steve) O'Neill, 83, board chairman and majority owner of the Cleveland Indians since 1978, after apparently suffering a heart attack, at Hunting Valley, O., August 30; he once had a financial interest in the New York Yankees.

Edwin Henry (Eddie) Palmer, 89, infielder who appeared in 16 games for the Philadelphia Athletics in 1917, at Marlow, Okla., January 9.

Stanley F. Perry, 54, scout for the New York Yankees, of a heart attack, at San Diego on September 9; pitched in the Yankee farm system and in the late '70s was general manager at Ogden, then the Triple-A farm club of the Oakland A's.

Clarence Douglas Pickrel, 72, a righthander who worked in relief in 18 of his 19 appearances with the Philadelphia Phillies and Boston Braves in 1933 and 1934, at Rocky Mount, Va., December 9; won his only big-league decision in '33.

Phil Piton, 79, president-treasurer of the National Association of Professional Baseball Leagues from 1963 through 1971, at Columbus, O., January 23; during his tenure, the minor leagues grew from 130 clubs to 150.

Chester Jennings (Jinx) Poindexter, 72, lefthander who was 0-2 in 14 appearances with the Boston Red Sox in 1936 and the Philadelphia Phillies in 1939, at Norman, Okla., March 3.

Robert H. (Bob) Potter, 80, a righthander who pitched in one game for Washington in 1923, at Ashland, Ky., January 27.

Ellis Foree (Mike) Powers, 77, outfielder for Cleveland in 1932 and 1933, at Louisville, Ky., December 2; batted .238 in 38 games.

Donald Russell Rader, 89, infielder who played briefly for the Chicago White Sox in 1913 and the Philadelphia Phillies in 1921, at Walla Walla, Wash., June 28.

Delbert W. (Del) Rice, 60, major league catcher for 17 seasons and manager of the California Angels in 1972, at Buena Park, Calif., January 26; broke in with the St. Louis Cardinals in 1945 and spent 10-plus seasons with the club; he was traded to Milwaukee in June 1955 and played for the Braves through 1959, then spent the 1960 season with the Chicago Cubs, Cardinals and Baltimore before finishing his playing career in 1961 with the Los Angeles Angels; coached in the majors and managed in the minors before piloting the Angels in '72—in 1971 he was named Minor League Manager of the Year by The Sporting News after his Salt Lake City club won the Pacific Coast League championship; played professional basketball for the Rochester Royals from 1942 through 1946.

Allen I. (Dutch) Romberger, 56, a righthanded pitcher who was 1-1 in 10 games for the Philadelphia Athletics in 1954, at Weikert, Pa., May 26.

Harry Salmon, 87, pitcher for the Birmingham Black Barons and Pittsburgh Crawfords of the old Negro leagues, at Pittsburgh in June.

Raymond Floyd (Ray) Sanders, 66, first baseman for the St. Louis Cardinals from 1942 through 1945 and the Boston Braves in 1946, 1948 and 1949, in a traffic accident, at Washington, Mo., October 28; played for pennant winners in '42, '43, '44 and '48 and batted .275 in 14 World Series games; a .274 career hitter, he enjoyed his finest season in 1944 when he batted .295, hit 12 homers, scored 87 runs and drove in 102; following his playing days, which were cut short by an arm injury suffered in August 1946 (he played only 14 regular-season games in the majors thereafter but did make a pinch-hitting appearance in the '48 Series), Sanders scouted briefly for Cleveland.

William F. (Bill) Sarni, 55, catcher for the St. Louis Cardinals and New York Giants whose playing career was ended by a heart attack he suffered as a 29-year-old, at St. Louis on April 14; played 312 games for the Cardinals in five seasons and hit .300 with 70 RBIs in 1954; joined the Giants in the June 1956 trade involving Red Schoendienst and Alvin Dark; suffered heart attack at the Giants' spring-training camp in Phoenix in 1957; became the youngest player in Pacific Coast League history when he signed with the Los Angeles Angels as a 15-year-old high school student.

Michael (Lefty) Schemer, 65, first baseman who played 32 games for the New York Giants in 1945 and 1946, at Miami on April 22; batted .333 in 31 games in '45.

Fred William Schulte, 82, outfielder for the St. Louis Browns from 1927 through 1932, Washington from 1933 through 1935 and Pittsburgh in 1936 and 1937, at Belvidere, Ill., May 20; in 1933, he scored 98 runs and drove in 87 for Washington's American League champs, then batted .333 in a World Series that the Senators lost to the New York Giants in five games; hit .292 in 1,178 major league games; managed and coached in the minors, and at various times from 1947 through 1964 he scouted for Cincinnati, the Chicago White Sox, Cleveland and the Milwaukee Braves.

Lee Scott, 77, traveling secretary for the Dodgers in Brooklyn and Los Angeles for 28 years prior to his retirement early in 1979, at Duarte, Calif., November 24.

Peter M. Seitz, 78, professional labor arbitrator whose 1975 ruling signaled the end of the reserve clause, at New York City on October 17, following spinal surgery; his decision released Andy Messersmith and Dave McNally from their obligations to pitch for clubs with whom their contracts had expired, ushering in the age of free agency.

Daniel Frank Seremba, 80, scout for the St. Louis Cardinals and Baltimore Orioles during the 1940s and '50s, at Jersey City, N.J., October 9.

David Orvis Short, 66, outfielder who played in seven games for the Chicago White Sox in 1940 and 1941, found beaten to death in the trunk of his car on the parking lot at a Marshall, Tex., motel on December 1; an agent for a life insurance company and a resident of Shreveport, La., 30 miles east of Marshall, Short was last seen by his family November 22.

Hilton Smith, 71, star pitcher who also played the outfield and pinch-hit for the Kansas City Monarchs in the Negro American League during the 1930s and '40s, at Kansas City on November 18; threw a no-hitter against the Chicago American Giants in 1937 and didn't lose a game in 1938, according to John (Buck) O'Neil, a '38 teammate.

Stanley Orvil (Stan) Spence, 67, slick-fielding outfielder for the Boston Red Sox (1940-41-48-49), Washington (1942 through 1944, 1946 and 1947) and the St. Louis Browns (1949), at Kinston, N.C., January 9; had his best years with the Senators, batting .323 in 1942 and .316 with 18 homers and 100 RBIs in 1944; led the American League in triples (15) in 1942.

Bob Stamsos, 67, scout for the San Diego Padres since 1978, at Portland, Ore., March 5.

Frank Tule Tabacchi, 73, American League umpire from 1956 through 1959, at Hoboken, N.J., October 26.

John Martin Tobin, 76, outfielder who appeared in one game for the New York Giants in 1932, at Rhinebeck, N.Y., August 8.

George Edward Turbeville, 69, righthander who was 2-12 in 62 appearances for the Philadelphia Athletics from 1935 through 1937, at Salisbury, N.C., October 5; in the second of his 15 major league starts, he blanked Cleveland for 14 innings before giving up a two-out, two-run homer to Earl Averill in the 15th.

James Charles (Jimmy) Wasdell, 69, outfielder-first baseman for five major league clubs between 1937 and 1947, at Newport Richey, Fla., August 6; batted .273 in 888 games for Washington, Brooklyn, Pittsburgh, the Philadelphia Phillies and Cleveland.

Harry A. Weaver, 91, righthanded pitcher for the Philadelphia Athletics in 1915 and 1916 and the Chicago Cubs from 1917 through 1919, at Rochester, N.Y., May 30; appeared in 19 games and posted a 3-6 record.

Victor Woodrow Wertz, 58, outfielder-first baseman who had a .277 average, 266 home runs and 1,178 RBIs in 17 major league seasons, at a Detroit hospital on July 7 while undergoing surgery to replace a heart valve; best remembered for making one of the most famous outs in World Series history—Willie Mays' over-the-shoulder catch of his long drive in the 1954 opener at the Polo Grounds; came up with Detroit in 1947 and also played for the St. Louis Browns, Baltimore, Cleveland, the Boston Red Sox and Minnesota before retiring in 1963; drove in 133 runs for the Tigers in 1949 and 123 the following season; collected eight hits (including four in Game 1) in 16 at-bats in the '54 Series, but the Giants beat the Indians in four games; in 1962, back in Detroit, he led the A.L. with 17 pinch-hits; in apparent good health until suffering a heart attack June 23, he had operated a highly successful beer distributorship in Detroit for many years.

Paul E. Williams, 71, sportscaster on the first regular telecasts of the Detroit Tigers (in 1947), of a heart attack, at Detroit on March 27.

Harold James (Whitey) Wiltse, 80, lefthanded pitcher who was 20-40 in 102 major league appearances, 65 of them as a starter, at Bunkie, La., November 2; he had an 18-33 mark for the Boston Red Sox in 1926 and 1927, was 2-7 the following season for Boston and the St. Louis Browns and worked in one game for the Philadelphia Phillies in 1931.

Melvn James (Mel) Wright, 55, pitching coach for the Montreal Expos, of heart failure, at Houston on May 16; he had been suffering from cancer; a righthander, he pitched for the St. Louis Cardinals in 1954 and 1955 and the Chicago Cubs in 1960 and 1961; in 58 big-league games, all in relief, he was 2-4; led the American Association in winning percentage in 1953, posting a 13-2 mark (.867) for Kansas City; from 1963 through 1972 he served the Cubs as a coach, minor league instructor and manager, and scout; pitching coach for Pittsburgh in 1973, the New York Yankees in 1974 and 1975, Houston from 1976 through 1982 and the Expos in 1983 until he was hospitalized in early April.

Archie Joseph Yelle, 90, catcher who batted .161 in 86 games for Detroit from 1917 through 1919, at Woodland, Calif., May 2.

Norman Robert (Babe) Young, 68, a first baseman who hit .273, slugged 79 home runs and drove in 415 runs in a 728-game big-league career that began in 1936 and concluded in 1948, of a heart attack, at Everett, Mass., December 25 while visiting a daughter for the holidays; enjoyed big seasons with the New York Giants in 1940 (17 home runs and 101 RBIs) and 1941 (25 homers and 104 RBIs) and later played for Cincinnati and the St. Louis Cardinals.

LEAGUE AND CLUB INFORMATION

Including

Major League Directory

American League Directory

American League Team Directories

National League Directory

National League Team Directories

Major League Players Association Directory

Major League Farm Systems

Minor League Presidents

Directory of Organized Baseball

MAJOR LEAGUES

COMMISSIONER—Bowie K. Kuhn
SECRETARY-TREASURER & GENERAL COUNSEL—Alexander H. Hadden
HEADQUARTERS—350 Park Avenue
New York, N. Y. 10022
Telephone—371-7800 (area code 212)
Teletype—710-581-4279

EXECUTIVE COUNCIL—Bowie K. Kuhn, Commissioner; Robert W. Brown, President of American League; Charles S. Feeney, President of National League; Roy Eisenhardt, Jerry Reinsdorf, Allan H. Selig and Edward Bennett Williams, representatives of American League, and Nelson Doubleday, Daniel M. Galbreath, Peter F. O'Malley and Ballard F. Smith, Jr., representatives of National League.

ADMINISTRATOR—William A. Murray
DIRECTOR OF BROADCASTING—Bryan L. Burns
DIRECTOR OF INFORMATION—Robert A. Wirz
DIRECTOR OF SECURITY—Horace J. (Harry) Gibbs
CONTROLLER—Donald C. Marr, Jr.
ASSISTANTS TO ADMINISTRATIVE OFFICER—
George E. Pfister, Miguel A. Rodriguez
(Winter League Baseball Coordinators)
ASSISTANT COUNSEL—Edwin M. Durso
ASSOCIATE DIRECTOR OF INFORMATION, MEDIA—Charles B. Adams
ASSISTANT DIRECTOR OF INFORMATION—Richard Cerrone
OFFICE MANAGER—Mary Ann Burns
BOOKKEEPER—Rita Datz

NATIONAL ASSOCIATION REPRESENTATIVES—John Johnson, President of the National Association, and members of National Association Executive Committee.

NATIONAL ASSOCIATION OF PROFESSIONAL BASEBALL LEAGUES

PRESIDENT-TREASURER—John H. Johnson
ADMINISTRATOR—Sal Artiaga
VICE-PRESIDENT—George G. MacDonald, Jr.
LEGAL COUNSEL—Charles J. Crist, Jr.
DIRECTOR OF PROMOTIONS—Bob Sparks
HEADQUARTERS—201 Bayshore Dr. S.E., P. O. Box A
St. Petersburg, Fla. 33731
Telephone—822-6937 (area code 813)
Teletype—810-863-0361

EXECUTIVE COMMITTEE—George G. MacDonald, Jr., Chairman, President of the Florida State League; Jimmy Bragan, President of the Southern League, Bill Cutler, President of the Pacific Coast League.

American League

Organized 1900

ROBERT W. BROWN
President

JOSEPH E. CRONIN
Chairman

CALVIN R. GRIFFITH, JOHN E. FETZER, GENE AUTRY
Vice-Presidents

ROBERT O. FISHEL
Executive Vice President

DONALD C. MARR, Jr.
Controller

RICHARD BUTLER
Supervisor of Umpires

ROBERT F. HOLBROOK
Special Assistant

STEPHANIE VARDAVAS
Manager, Waivers & Player Records Department

PHYLLIS MERHIGE
Director of Public Relations

TESS BASTA, DAVID GLAZIER
Administrators

Headquarters—350 Park Avenue, New York, N. Y. 10022

Telephone—371-7600 (area code 212)

ASSISTANT SUPERVISORS OF UMPIRES—William Haller, Henry Soar, Larry Napp.

UMPIRES—Lawrence Barnett, Nicholas Bremigan, Joseph Brinkman, Alan Clark, Drew Coble, Terrance Cooney, Derryl Cousins, Donald Denkinger, James Evans, Dale Ford, Richard Garcia, Russell Goetz, Ted Hendry, Kenneth Kaiser, Greg Kosc, William Kunkel, George Maloney, Tim McClelland, Larry McCoy, James McKean, Durwood Merrill, Dan Morrison, Jerome Neudecker, Stephen Palermo, David Phillips, Rick Reed, Michael Reilly, John (Rocky) Roe, John Shulock, Martin Springstead, Vic Voltaggio.

OFFICIAL STATISTICIANS—Sports Information Center, 1776 Heritage Drive, No. Quincy, Mass. 02171. Telephone—(617) 328-4674.

Players cannot be transferred from one major league to another after June 15 to close of the championship season except through regular waiver channels.

WAIVER PRICE, $20,000. Interleague waivers, $20,000, except for selected players and draft-excluded players.

American League President Robert W. Brown

BALTIMORE ORIOLES

Chairman of the Board and President—Edward Bennett Williams

Executive Vice-President, General Manager—Henry J. Peters
Vice-President, Secretary, General Counsel—Lawrence Lucchino
Vice-President, Stadium Operations—Jack Dunn, III
Vice-President, Finance—Joseph P. Hamper, Jr.
Directors—Edward Bennett Williams, Joseph P. DiMaggio, Jack Dunn, III, Jay Emmett, Robert J. Flanagan, Gerald T. Gabrys, Charles H. Hoffberger, Jerold C. Hoffberger, Zanvyl Krieger, Lawrence Lucchino, Henry J. Peters, Peter P. Weidenbruch, Jr.
Special Assistant to the General Manager—James J. Russo
Director of Business Affairs—Robert R. Aylward
Director of Public Relations—Robert W. Brown
Director, Player Development and Scouting—Thomas A. Giordano
Traveling Secretary—Philip E. Itzoe
Executive Sales Director—Louis I. Michaelson
Promotions Director—Drew M. Sheinman
Ticket Office Manager—Timothy Geraghty
Director, Media Information—John C. Blake
Assistant Director, Player Development and Scouting—John J. McCall
Assistant Ticket Manager—Joseph B. Codd
Major Accounts Coordinator—Daniel J. O'Dowd
Special Projects Coordinator—Kenneth E. Nigro
Baltimore Sales Representative—Martin J. Smith
Washington Office Coordinator—Joseph D. Felperin
President, Orioles Foundation—Herbert E. Armstrong
Manager—Joseph S. Altobelli
Club Physician—Dr. Leonard Wallenstein
Executive Offices—Memorial Stadium, Baltimore, Md. 21218
Telephone—243-9800 (area code 301)

SCOUTS—(Major League)—Jim Russo, John Stokoe, Bill Werle. (Regular)—Jack Baker, Joe Bowman, Dan Cressman, Ray Crone, Ed Crosby, Joe DeLucca, Jim Driscoll, Jose Garcia, Jim Gilbert, John Hagemann, Len Johnston, Mark Just, Bill Lawlor, George Lauzerique, Earl MacKenzie, Minnie Mendoza, Lamar North, Jim Pamlanye, Jack Sanford, William Teed, Tommy Thompson, Herman Welsh, Al Zarilla, Jerry Zimmerman.

PARK LOCATION—Memorial Stadium, 33rd Street, Ellerslie Avenue, 36th Street and Ednor Road.

Seating capacity—53,197.

FIELD DIMENSIONS—Home plate to left field at foul line, 309 feet; to center field, 405 feet; to right field at foul line, 309 feet.

BOSTON RED SOX

President—Jean R. Yawkey

Executive Vice-President, General Manager—Haywood C. Sullivan
Executive Vice-President, Administration—Edward G. LeRoux, Jr.
Treasurer—James M. Olivier, Jr.
Comptroller—Robert C. Furbush
V. P., Player Development Director—Edward F. Kenney
Asst. Player Development Director—Edward Kenney, Jr.
Scouting Director—Edward M. Kasko
Traveling Secretary—John J. Rogers
Public Relations Director—George Sullivan
Publicity Director—Richard L. Bresciani
Marketing Director—James P. Healey
Group Sales Director—Leslie Cargill
Executive Assistant—Joseph F. McDermott
Assistant Treasurer—John J. Reilly
Ticket Director—Arthur J. Moscato
Consultant, Player Relations—John L. Harrington
Consultant, Organizational Hitting Instructor—Theodore S. Williams
Superintendent, Grounds & Maintenance—Joseph Mooney
Manager—Ralph G. Houk
Club Physician—Dr. Arthur M. Pappas
Executive Offices—24 Yawkey Way, Boston, Mass. 02215
Telephone—267-9440 (area code 617)

SCOUTS—Milton Bolling, Ray Boone, Wayne Britton, George Digby, Howard (Danny) Doyle, Bill Enos, Larry Flynn, Earl Johnson, Charles Koney, Wilfrid (Lefty) Lefebvre, Don Lenhardt, Tommy McDonald, Felix Maldonado, Frank Malzone, Sam Mele, Joe Morgan, Ramon Naranjo, Willie Paffen, Peter Randall, Philip Rossi, Edward Scott, Matt Sczesny, Joe Stephenson, Larry Thomas, Charlie Wagner.

PARK LOCATION—Fenway Park, Yawkey Way, Lansdowne Street and Ipswich Street.

Seating capacity—33,583.

FIELD DIMENSIONS—Home plate to left field at foul line, 315 feet; to center field, 420 feet; to right field at foul line, 302 feet; average right-field distance, 382 feet.

CALIFORNIA ANGELS

President and Chairman of the Board—Gene Autry

Executive Vice-President—E.J. Bavasi
Assistant to the Chairman of the Board—Arthur E. Patterson
Vice-President and Chief Administrative Officer—Mike Port
Director Public Relations and Promotions—Tom Seeberg
Director of Accounting—Jim Kaczmarek
Director Scouting & Player Development—Larry Himes
Director of Minor League Operations—Bill Bavasi
Director Ticket Development—Carl Gordon
Director Group Sales—Lynn Kirchmann Biggs
Director Stadium Operations—Jean (Corky) Lippert
Traveling Secretary—Frank Sims
Assistant Director Public Relations—Tim Mead
Assistant Ticket Director—Bob Terzes
Stadium Operations—Kevin Uhlich
Film Coordinator and Special Statistics—George Goodale
Medical Director—Dr. Robert K. Kerlan
Orthopedist—Dr. Lewis Yocum
Trainers—Rick Smith, Ned Bergert
Manager—John McNamara
Executive Offices—Anaheim Stadium, 2000 State College Blvd., Anaheim, Calif. 92806
Telephone—937-6700 (area code 714) or 625-1123 (area code 213)

SCOUTS—Edmundo Borrome, Vince Capece, Joe Carpenter, Lloyd Christopher, Alex Cosmidis, Pompeyo Davillo, Jack Deutch, Preston Douglas, Bob Gardner, Al Goldis, Steve Gruwell, Rick Ingalls, Nick Kamzic, Eusebio Perez, Vic Power, Philip Rizzo, Cookie Rojas, Rich Schlenker, Lou Snipp, Mark Snipp, Hank Weaver.

PARK LOCATION—Anaheim Stadium, 2000 State College Blvd.

Seating capacity—65,158.

FIELD DIMENSIONS—Home plate to left field at foul line, 333 feet; to center field, 404 feet; to right field at foul line, 333 feet.

CHICAGO WHITE SOX

Chairman, Board of Directors—Jerry M. Reinsdorf
President—Eddie M. Einhorn
Executive Vice-President, General Manager—Roland A. Hemond
Executive Vice-President—Howard C. Pizer
Vice-President, Marketing—Michael D. McClure
Vice-President, Broadcasting and Special Projects—Laureen Ong Fadil
Vice-President, Baseball Administration—Jack Gould
Assistant General Manager—David Dombrowski
Director of Player Development—Bob Winkles
Assistant to Vice-President, Marketing—Stephen M. Schanwald
Director of Public Relations—Charles A. Shriver
Sales Manager—Millie Johnson
Director, Season Sales—Jeff Overton
Director of Broadcast Sales—Edwin M. Doody
Controller—Timothy L. Buzard
Traveling Secretary—Glen Rosenbaum
Ticket Manager—Robert K. Devoy
Director, Group Sales and Park Entertainment—M. Scott Smith
Assistant Director of Public Relations—Kenneth M. Valdiserri
Director of Latin American Baseball Operations—Angel Vasquez
Administrative Assistants, Baseball Operations—Daniel Evans, Brian Boles
General Counsel—Allan B. Muchin
Trainer—Herman Schneider
Assistant Trainer—Brandt McFarlin
Team Physicians—Drs. Richard D. Corzatt, James B. Boscardin, Hugo Cuadros
Manager—Tony LaRussa
Equipment/Club House Mgr., White Sox—Willie Thompson
Equipment/Club House Mgr., Visitors—John MacNamara, Jr.
Director of Park Operations—David M. Schaffer
Groundskeepers—Gene and Roger Bossard
P.A. Announcer—Wayne Mesmer
Organist—Nancy Faust
Executive Offices—Comiskey Park, Dan Ryan at 35th Street, Chicago, Ill. 60616
Telephone—924-1000 (area code 312)

SCOUTS—(Advance)—Bart Johnson. (Special Assignment)—Jerry Krause, Jim Mahoney, Fred Shaffer. (Supervisor)—Walt Widmayer. (Regular)—James Busby, Bobby Gardner, Jr., Bill Gayton, Eric Gluck, Joseph Ingalls, Leo Labossiere, Marvin Lane, Dario Lodigiani, Terry Logan, Larry Monroe, Rich Morales, Carlos Pena, Silvano Quezada, Jorge Read, Thomas Roberts, Cucho Rodriguez, Mark Servais, Duane Shaffer, George Sobek, Lynn Squires, Kenneth Stauffer, Angel Vazquez (Castro), Carver White, Stan Zielinski.

PARK LOCATION—Comiskey Park, Dan Ryan at 35th Street, Chicago, Ill. 60616.

Seating capacity—44,432.

FIELD DIMENSIONS—Home plate to left field at foul line, 341 feet; to center field, 401 feet; to right field at foul line, 341 feet.

CLEVELAND INDIANS

President and Chief Executive Officer—Gabe Paul

Chairman of the Board—Patrick J. O'Neill
Directors—Dudley S. Blossom, III, Alva T. Bonda, G.E. DiGeronimo, Michael J. Fetchko, Bernard S. Goldfarb, Walter Laich, Patrick J. O'Neill, Gabriel H. Paul, Arnold R. Pinkney, Robert E. Quinn, Phillip D. Seghi, Maurice L. Stonehill
Vice-President and General Manager—Phillip D. Seghi
Secretary and Club Legal Counsel—Edward C. Crouch
Manager—Pat Corrales
Traveling Secretary—Mike Seghi
Director of Public Relations—Bob DiBiasio
Director of Sales and Marketing—Tom Pulchinski
Director of Stadium Operations—Dan Zerbey
Ticket Director—Jerry Waring
Controller—Jason Rosenthal
Public Relations—Bob Feller
Special Assistant to the President—Ron Mottl
Special Assistant to the General Manager—Dan Carnevale
Special Assignment Representative—Birdie Tebbetts
Asst. Public Relations Director—Pete Spudich
Minor League Administrator—Joe Pavia
Asst. Farm Director—Phil Thomas
Trainer—Jim Warfield
Club Physicians—Drs. William Wilder, William Bohl
Club Dentist—Dr. Marvin Schermer
Equipment Manager—Cy Buynak
Groundskeeper—Jim Anglea
Executive Offices—Cleveland Stadium, Cleveland, Ohio 44114
Telephone—861-1200 (area code 216)

SCOUTS—Hector Acevedo, Eddie Bane, Dan Carnevale, Jack Cassini, Tom Couston, Red Gaskill, Leon Hamilton, Luis Issac, Frank Lucchesi, Bobby Malkmus, Bill Meyer, Jim Miller, Woody Smith, Gary Sutherland, Birdie Tebbetts, Jack Vallely, Gene Wooding.

PARK LOCATION—Cleveland Stadium, Boudreau Blvd.

Seating capacity—74,208.

FIELD DIMENSIONS—Home plate to left field at foul line, 320 feet; to center field, 400 feet; to right field at foul line, 320 feet.

DETROIT TIGERS

Chairman of the Board—John E. Fetzer

Vice-Chairman—Thomas S. Monaghan
President & Chief Executive Officer—James A. Campbell
Executive Vice-President & Chief Operating Officer—William E. Haase
Vice-President & General Manager—William R. Lajoie
Vice-President/Finance—Alexander C. Callam
Director of Public Relations—Dan Ewald
Director of Radio & TV—Neal Fenkell
Director of Stadium Operations—Ralph E. Snyder
Director of Minor League Operations—Dave Miller
Director of Ticket Sales—Jerry Bucholtz
Director of Concession Operations (Bismarck Corp.)—Bob Sherman
Executive Secretary/Baseball—Alice Sloane
Executive Secretary/Operations—Hazel McLane
Traveling Secretary—Bill Brown
Executive Consultant—Rick Ferrell
Special Assignment Scout—Walter A. Evers
Field Director, Minor Leagues—Frank Franchi
Scouting Coordinator—George Bradley
Box Office Treasurer—William H. Willis
Assistant Director of Public Relations—Bob Miller
Assistant Director of Public Relations/Special Events/Scoreboard—Lew Matlin
Assistant Director of Public Relations/Community Relations—Vince Desmond
Group Sales Coordinator—Irwin Cohen
Assistant Director of Stadium Operations/Grounds Maintenance—Frank Feneck
Assistant Director of Stadium Operations/Grounds Maintenance—Ed Goward
Manager—Sparky Anderson
Club Physician—Clarence S. Livingood M.D.
Orthopedic Consultant—Robert A. Teitge M.D.
Orthopedic Consultant—Lawrence V. Tkach M.D.
Executive Offices—Tiger Stadium, Detroit, Mich. 48216
Telephone—962-4000 (area code 313)

SCOUTS—Rick Arnold, John Barkley, Ray Bellino, Wayne Blackburn, Joe Henderson, Roger Jongewaard, Joe Lewis, Orlando Pena, Jax Robertson, Paul Robinson, Bill Schudlich, Jack Tighe, Marti Wolever.

PARK LOCATION—Tiger Stadium, Michigan Avenue, Cochrane Avenue, Kaline Drive and Trumbull Avenue.

Seating capacity—52,806.

FIELD DIMENSIONS—Home plate to left field at foul line, 340 feet; to center field, 440 feet; to right field at foul line, 325 feet.

KANSAS CITY ROYALS

Board of Directors
Joe Burke, William Deramus, III, Avron Fogelman, Charles Hughes,
Ewing Kauffman, Mrs. Ewing Kauffman, Earl Smith

Chairman of the Board—Ewing Kauffman
Vice Chairman of the Board—Avron Fogelman
President—Joe Burke
Executive Vice-President and General Manager—John Schuerholz
Executive Vice-President, Administration—Spencer (Herk) Robinson
Vice-President, Controller—Dale Rohr
Vice-President and Legal Counsel—Phil Koury
Director of Public Relations—Dean Vogelaar
Director of Marketing and Broadcasting—Dennis Cryder
Traveling Secretary/Lancer Coordinator—Will Rudd
Assistant Director of Public Relations—Jeffrey Coy
Director of Scouting and Player Development—Dick Balderson
Assistant Director of Scouting and Player Development—Dean Taylor
Administrative Assistant of Scouting & Player Development—Joe Kasunick
Assistant Director of Marketing—Scott Pederson
Director of Ticket Operations—Stacy Sherrow
Director of Season Ticket Sales—Joe Grigoli
Season Ticket Coordinator—Debbie Donahue
Director of Event Personnel—Chris Muehlbach
Stadium Engineer—George Humphrey
Stadium Maintenance Coordinator—Bob Frank
Accountants—Tom Pfannenstiel, Ken Willeke
Manager—Dick Howser
Equipment Manager—Al Zych
Groundskeeper—George Toma
Team Physician—Dr. Paul Meyer
Trainers—Mickey Cobb, Paul McGannon
Executive Offices—Royals Stadium, Harry S Truman Sports Complex
Mailing Address—P. O. Box 1969, Kansas City, Mo. 64141
Telephone—921-2200 (area code 816)

SCOUTS—Carl Blando, Al Diez, Tom Ferrick, Rosey Gilhousen, Ken Gonzales, Ron Hopkins, Al Kubski, Chuck McMichael, Brian Murphy, George Noga, Jerry Stephens, Art Stewart, Roy Tanner, Jerry Terrell, Red Whitsett.

PARK LOCATION—Royals Stadium, Harry S Truman Sports Complex.

Seating capacity—40,625.

FIELD DIMENSIONS—Home plate to left field at foul line, 330 feet; to center field, 410 feet; to right field at foul line, 330 feet.

MILWAUKEE BREWERS

President, Chief Executive Officer—Allan H. (Bud) Selig

Executive Vice-President, General Manager—Harry Dalton
Vice-President, Marketing—Richard Hackett
Vice-President, Broadcast Operations—William Haig
Vice-President, Finance—Richard Hoffmann
Vice-President, Stadium Operations—Gabe Paul, Jr.
Assistant General Manager—Walter Shannon
Special Assistants to the General Manager—Dee Fondy, Sal Bando
Traveling Secretary—Jimmy Bank
Director of Player Procurement—Ray Poitevint
Coordinator of Player Development—Bob Humphreys
Coordinator of Minor League Operations—Bruce Manno
Administrative Assistant for Scouting and Player Development—Dan Duquette
Director of Publicity—Tom Skibosh
Assistant Director of Stadium Operations and Advertising—Jack Hutchinson
Ticket Sales Director—Tim Trovato
Director of the Speakers Bureau—John Counsell
Assistant Director of Publicity—Mario Ziino
Ticket Office Manager—John Barnes
Director of Ticket Office Computer Operations—Alice Boettcher
Director of Special Events—Mark Paget
Manager—Rene Lachemann
Club Physician—Dr. Paul Jacobs
Trainer—John Adam
Superintendent of Grounds and Maintenance—Harry Gill
Assistant Groundskeeper—Gary Vandenberg
Equipment Manager—Bob Sullivan
P.A. Announcer—Bob Betts
Organist—Frank Charles
Executive Offices—Milwaukee Brewers Baseball Club
Milwaukee County Stadium, Milwaukee, Wis. 53214
Telephone—933-1818 (area code 414)

SCOUTS—Scouting supervisors: Julio Blanco-Herrera, Nelson Burbrink, Felix Delgado, Tom Gamboa, Roland LeBlanc, Walter Youse. Regular scouts: Fred Beene, Tom Bourque, Ken Califano, Gerry Craft, Dick Ehrig, Charles Fitzgerald, Dick Foster, Hy Gomberg, Larry Hisle, Gene Kerns, Frank Kolarek, Billy Moffitt, Johnny Neun, Ken Richardson, Lee Sigman, Harry Smith, Milt Sobel, Sam Suplizio, Paul Tretiak.

PARK LOCATION—Milwaukee County Stadium, S. 46th St. off Bluemound Rd.

Seating capacity—53,192.

FIELD DIMENSIONS—Home plate to left field at foul line, 315 feet; to center field, 402 feet; to right field at foul line, 315 feet.

MINNESOTA TWINS

Chairman of Board, President—Calvin R. Griffith

Vice-President—Mrs. Thelma Griffith Haynes
Executive Vice-President—Clark Griffith
Executive Vice-President—Bruce G. Haynes
Director—H. Gabriel Murphy
Director—Eugene V. Young
Director—Wheelock Whitney
Executive Vice-President—Howard T. Fox, Jr.
Vice-President—William S. Robertson
Vice-President—James K. Robertson
Vice-President, Farm Director—George Brophy
Assistant Farm Director—Jim Rantz
Controller—Jack Alexander
Director of Public Relations—Tom Mee
Director of Sales—Gil Lansdale
Traveling Secretary—Mike Robertson
Manager—Billy Gardner
Club Physicians—Dr. Leonard J. Michienzi and Dr. Harvey O'Phelan
Executive Offices—Hubert H. Humphrey Metrodome, 501 Chicago Ave. South, Minneapolis, Minn. 55415
Telephone—375-1366 (area code 612)

SCOUTS—Floyd Baker, Vern Borning, Ellsworth Brown, Buck Chamberlin, Spud Chandler, Ellis Clary, Edward Dunn, Jesse Flores, Jr., Jesse Flores, Sr., Angelo Giuliani, Lee Irwin, Hank Izquierdo, Vern McKee, Bobby Morlan, Marvin Olson, Spencer (Red) Robbins, Stanley Rogers, Herb Stein, Harry Warner.

PARK LOCATION—Hubert H. Humphrey Metrodome, 501 Chicago Ave. South.

Seating capacity—55,122.

FIELD DIMENSIONS—Home plate to left field at foul line, 343 feet; to center field, 408 feet; to right field at foul line, 327 feet.

NEW YORK YANKEES

Principal Owner—George M. Steinbrenner, III

Limited Partners—Harold Bowman, Lester Crown, Michael Friedman, Marvin Goldklang, Barry Halper, Harvey Leighton, Daniel McCarthy, Harry Nederlander, Robert Nederlander, William Rose, Edward Rosenthal, Jack Satter, Charlotte Witkind, Richard Witkind
President—Eugene J. McHale
General Manager/Executive Vice-President—Murray Cook
Manager—Yogi Berra
Administrative Vice-President and Treasurer—David Weidler
Vice-President, Baseball Operations—Bill Bergesch
Vice-President—Ed Weaver
Vice-President/General Counsel—Mel Southard, Jr.
Director of Minor League Operations—David Hersh
Director of Scouting—Bobby Hofman
Traveling Secretary—Bill Kane
Administrative Assistant—Richard Kraft
Director of Media Relations—Joseph V. Safety
Director of Publications—David Szen
Asst. Director of Publications—Kip Ingle
Publications Assistant—Ken Wittcoff
Director of Public Relations—John Fugazy
Stadium Manager—Patrick Kelly
Executive Director of Ticket Operations—Frank Swaine
Ticket Director—Michael Rendine
Assistant Ticket Director—Jim Hodge
Director, Customer Services and Asst. Stadium Manager—Jim Naples
Assistant Scouting Director—Roy Krasik
Assistant Minor League Director—John Dato
Baseball Operations Assistants—Mike Barnett, Doug Melvin
Director of Group Sales—Jim Aldrich
Director of Accounting—Bill Nahabedian
Club Physician—Dr. John J. Bonamo
P.A. Announcer—Bob Sheppard
Organist—Eddie Layton
Executive Offices—Yankee Stadium, Bronx, N.Y. 10451
Telephone—293-4300 (area code 212)
Ticket Information—293-6000 (area code 212)

SCOUTS—Luis Arroyo, Hank Bauer, Joe Begani, Howard Cassady, David Cook, Al Cuccinello, Whitey DeHart, Joe DiCarlo, Henry Dotterer, Fred Ferreira, Whitey Ford, Orrin Freeman, Tom Greenwade, Dick Groch, Jim Gruzdis, Roy Hamey, Jim Hegan, Gary Hughes, Grover Jones, John Kennedy, Clyde King, Bob Lemon, Don Lindeberg, Bill Livesey, Jack Llewellyn, Gene Michael, Jim Naples, Sr., Don Nichols, Bob Nieman, Frank O'Rourke, Greg Orr, Meade Palmer, Eddie Robinson, Russ Sehon, Robert Shaw, Moose Skowron, Ron Walters, Dick Wilson.

PARK LOCATION—Yankee Stadium, E. 161st St. and River Ave., Bronx, N.Y. 10451.

Seating capacity—57,545.

FIELD DIMENSIONS—Home plate to left field at foul line, 312 feet; to center field, 417 feet; to right field at foul line, 310 feet.

OAKLAND A's

President—Roy Eisenhardt

Executive Vice-President—Walter J. Haas
Vice-President of Baseball Operations—Sandy Alderson
Vice-President, Business Operations—Andy Dolich
Vice-President, Finance—Kathleen McCracken
Assistant to the President, Baseball Matters—Bill Rigney
Director of Scouting—Dick Wiencek
Director of Player Development—Karl Kuehl
Director of Baseball Administration—Walt Jocketty
Director of Latin American Scouting—Juan Marichal
Director of Medical Services—Hirsch Handmaker
Director of Press Relations and Team Travel—Mickey Morabito
Director of Media Relations—Rick Moxley
Director of Sales and Telecommunications—David Rubinstein
Director of Marketing and Merchandising—Roger Moskowitz
Director of Ticket Operations—Raymond B. Krise Jr.
Director of Special Projects—Earl Robinson
Director of Stadium Operations—Jorge Costa
Director of Publications—Art Worthington
Managing Editor, Publications—David Azevedo
Consultant, Baseball Administration—Carl Finley
Executive Assistant—Sharon Jones
Business Operations Coordinator/Promotions Director—Sharon Kelly
Ticket Manager—Bettina Flores
Director of Broadcast Operations—Bill King
Director of Ticket Sales—Steve Page
Assistant Director of Press Relations-Statistician—Jay Alves
Manager—Steve Boros
Trainer—Barry Weinberg, Larry Davis
Equipment Manager—Frank Ciensczyk
Visiting Clubhouse Manager—Steve Vucinich
Marketing Representatives—Tom Cordova, Clarence Jackson, Doris Messina, Will Davis, Tony Stevens
Executive Offices—Oakland-Alameda County Coliseum, Oakland, Calif. 94621
Telephone—638-4900 (area code 415)

SCOUTS—Albert Elliott, Jr., Grady Fuson, Fred Hatfield, Juan Marichal, Edwin Mathews, Jethro McIntyre, Charlie Metro, Mel Nelson, Camilo Pascual, James Perry, Ed Stevens, Mike Wallace, Gary Wiencek, Del Wilber.

PARK LOCATION—Oakland-Alameda County Coliseum, Nimitz Freeway and Hegenberger Road.

Seating capacity—50,219.

FIELD DIMENSIONS—Home plate to left field at foul line, 330 feet; to center field, 397 feet; to right field at foul line, 330 feet.

SEATTLE MARINERS

Owner & Chairman of the Board—George L. Argyros

President—Charles G. Armstrong
Vice President, Baseball Operations & General Manager—Hal Keller
Vice President, Sales and Marketing—Bill Long
Vice President, Finance—Brian Beggs
Director of Marketing Services—Randy Adamack
Director of Sales—Al (Moose) Clausen
Director of Publicity—Bob Porter
Director of Team Travel—Lee Pelekoudas
Director of Stadium Operations—Jeff Klein
Director of Player Development—Jeff Scott
Director of Ticket Services—Doug Hopkins
Assistant Director of Player Development, Instruction—Bill Haywood
Assistant Director of Player Development, Scouting—Gary Pellant
Assistant Director of Publicity—Craig Detwiler
Assistant Director of Ticket Services—Mark Mitchell
Manager of Sales and Promotion—Larry Sindall
Manager of Broadcast Services—Melody Tucker
Manager of Communications and Youth Marketing—Randy Stearnes
Controller—Denise Podosek
Office Manager—Janet Croft
Manager—Del Crandall
Club Physicians—Drs. Larry Pedegana, James Trombold
Club Dentist—Dr. Richard Leshgold
Head Groundskeeper—Wilbur Loo
P.A. Announcer—Gary Spinnell
Executive Offices—P.O. Box 4100
100 South King Street, Suite 300, Seattle, Washington 98104
Telephone—628-3555 (area code 206)

SCOUTS—David Blume, Bob Harrison, Bill Kearns, Coco Laboy, Jeff Malinoff, Whitey Piurek, Bill Tracy, Rip Tutor, Steve Vrablik.

PARK LOCATION—Kingdome, 201 South King Street, Seattle, Washington.

Seating capacity—59,438.

FIELD DIMENSIONS—Home plate to left field at foul line, 316 feet; to center field, 410 feet; to right field at foul line, 316 feet.

TEXAS RANGERS

Chairman of the Board, Chief Executive Officer—Eddie Chiles

President—Mike Stone
Vice President, General Counsel, Secretary—Dee J. Kelly
Vice President and General Manager—Joe Klein
Vice President, Marketing and Administration—Larry Schmittou
Vice President, Treasurer—Charles F. Wangner
Vice President, Director of Minor League System—Tom Grieve
Directors—Eddie Chiles, Georgeann Carter, Dee J. Kelly, William H. Seay
Executive Director, Texas Rangers Network—Roy Parks
Assistant to the General Manager—Wayne Krivsky
Special Assistant to the General Manager—Paul Richards
Director of Media Relations—Burton Hawkins
Director of Public Relations—Bobby Bragan
Director of Promotions—Dave Fendrick
Director of Ticket Management—Mary Ann Bosher
Stadium Manager—John Welaj
Assistant Stadium Manager—Mat Stolley
Medical Director—Dr. B.J. Mycoskie
Public Address Announcer—Chuck Morgan
Director of Physical Fitness Programs—Mike Fitzsimmons
Sabremetrician—Craig Wright
Traveling Secretary—Dan Schimek
Manager—Doug Rader
Field Superintendent—John Oliveria
Concessions Manager—Dave Wood
Home Clubhouse and Equipment Manager—Joe Macko
Visiting Clubhouse Manager—Mike Wallace
Executive Offices—1200 Copeland Road, Arlington, Tex. 76011
Arlington Stadium—1500 Copeland Road, P.O. Box 1111, Arlington, Tex. 76010
Telephone—273-5222 (area code 817)

SCOUTS—Harley Anderson, Lee Anthony, Joseph Branzell, Jackie Brathwaite, Paddy Cottrell, Dick Gernert, Cesar Guttierez, Andy Hancock, Sid Hudson, Stan Jakubowski, Gary Johnson, Joseph Lewis, Joseph Marchese, Steve Minor, Cotton Nix, Connie Ryan, Rick Schroeder, Fred Velasquez.

PARK LOCATION—Arlington Stadium, 1500 Copeland Road, Arlington, Tex.

Seating capacity—43,508.

FIELD DIMENSIONS—Home plate to left field at foul line, 330 feet; to center field, 400 feet; to right field at foul line, 330 feet.

TORONTO BLUE JAYS

Chief Executive Officer—N. E. Hardy

Board of Directors—John Craig Eaton, L. G. Greenwood, N. E. Hardy, R. Howard Webster, P. N. T. Widdrington
Chairman of the Board—R. Howard Webster
Vice-President, Business Operations—Paul Beeston
Vice-President, Baseball Operations—Pat Gillick
Executive Coordinator, Baseball Operations—Bobby Mattick
Director, Public Relations—Howard Starkman
Director, Operations—Ken Erskine
Director, Ticket Operations—George Holm
Trainer-Director, Team Travel—Ken Carson
Director, Group Sales—Maureen Haffey
Director, Player Development—Billy Smith
Director, Canadian Scouting—Bob Prentice
Assistant Director, Public Relations—Gary Oswald
Assistant Director, Operations—Gord Ash
Assistant Director, Ticket Operations—Len Frejlich
Director, Security—Fred Wootton
Equipment Manager—Jeff Ross
Coordinator, Promotions & Group Services—John MacLachlan
Supervisor, Grounds—Dave Hamilton
Manager—Bobby Cox
Team Physician—Dr. Ron Taylor
Executive Offices—Exhibition Stadium, Exhibition Place, Toronto, Ontario
Mailing Address—Box 7777, Adelaide St. P. O., Toronto, Ont. M5C 2K7
Telephone—595-0077 (area code 416)

SCOUTS—Ellis Dungan, Robert Engle (Eastern Regional Scouting Director), Joe Ford, Epy Guerrero, Jack Hayes, Jim Hughes, Al LaMacchia (Senior Scouting Supervisor), Duane Larson (off-season), Larry Maxie, Ben McLure, Wayne Morgan (Western Regional Scouting Director), Paul Ricciarini, Don Welke, Bob Wilber, Tim Wilken, Dave Yoakum.

PARK LOCATION—Exhibition Stadium on the grounds of Exhibition Place. Entrances to Exhibition Place via Lakeshore Boulevard, Queen Elizabeth Way Highway and Dufferin and Bathurst Streets.

Seating capacity—43,737.

FIELD DIMENSIONS—Home plate to left field at foul line, 330 feet; to center field, 400 feet; to right field at foul line, 330 feet.

National League

Organized 1876

CHARLES S. FEENEY
President and Treasurer

JOHN J. McHALE
Vice-President

PHYLLIS B. COLLINS
Secretary

BLAKE CULLEN
Administrator and Public Relations Director

KATY FEENEY
Assistant Public Relations Director

LOUIS H. KREMS
Business Manager

JOSEPHINE TROY
Administrative Assistant

Headquarters—350 Park Avenue, New York, N. Y. 10022

Telephone—371-7300 (area code 212)

UMPIRES—Fred Brocklander, Jerry Crawford, Jerry Dale, David Davidson, Robert Davidson, Robert Engel, Bruce Froemming, Eric Gregg, Lanny Harris, H. Douglas Harvey, John Kibler, Randy Marsh, John McSherry, Ed Montague, Dave Pallone, Frank Pulli, Jim Quick, Lawrence (Dutch) Rennert, Paul Runge, Dick Stello, Terry Tata, Harry Wendelstedt, Joe West, Lee Weyer, Charles Williams, William G. Williams.

OFFICIAL STATISTICIANS—Elias Sports Bureau, Inc., 500 5th Ave., Suite 2114, New York, N. Y. 10036. Telephone (212) 869-1530.

Players cannot be transferred from one major league club to another after June 15 to the close of the championship season except through regular waiver channels.

WAIVER PRICE, $20,000. Interleague waivers, $20,000, except for selected players and draft-excluded players.

National League President Charles S. Feeney.

ATLANTA BRAVES

Chairman of the Board—William C. Bartholomay

President—R.E. (Ted) Turner, III
Executive Vice-President—Allison Thornwell, Jr.
Vice-President and General Manager—John W. Mullen
Vice-President and Business Manager—Charles S. Sanders
Vice-President, Player Development—Henry L. Aaron
Assistant Vice-President, Scouting—Paul L. Snyder, Jr.
Assistant Vice-President, Baseball—Patrick R. Nugent
Director of Broadcasting—Ernie Johnson
Manager of Broadcast Sales and Administration—Wayne Long
Ticket Distribution Manager—Ed Newman
Director of Public Relations, Promotions—Wayne Minshew
Director of Publications and Publicity Manager—Bob Korch
Director of Stadium Operations and Security—Joe Shirley
Director of Matrix Operations—Bob Larson
Assistant Controller—Martin Mathews
Traveling Secretary and Equipment Manager—Bill Acree
Director of Ticket Sales—Andre DeLorenzo
Manager—Joe Torre
Club Physician—Dr. David T. Watson
Executive Offices—P.O. Box 4064, Atlanta, Ga. 30302
Telephone—522-7630 (area code 404)

SCOUTS—Mike Arbuckle, Sam Berry, Forrest (Smoky) Burgess, Stu Cann, Joe Caputo, Harold Cronin, Tony DeMacio, Lou Fitzgerald, Rod Gilbreath, Pedro Gonzalez, John Groth, Gene Hassell, Herb Hippauf, Ray Holton, Jim Johnson, Burney R. (Dickey) Martin, Bob Mavis, Rance Pless, Bob Scruggs, Bill Serena, Charles Smith, Tony Stiel, Bob Turzilli, Bob Wadsworth, Wesley Westrum, William R. Wight, Don Williams, H.F. (Red) Wooten.

PARK LOCATION—Atlanta-Fulton County Stadium, on Capitol Avenue at the junction of Interstate Highways 20, 75 and 85.

Seating capacity—53,046.

FIELD DIMENSIONS—Home plate to left field at foul line, 330 feet; to center field, 402 feet; to right field at foul line, 330 feet.

CHICAGO CUBS

Chairman of the Board—Andrew J. McKenna
President and Chief Executive Officer—James E. Finks
Executive Vice President and General Manager—Dallas Green
Vice President, Business Operations—Terry Barthelmas
Director of Minor Leagues and Scouting—Gordon Goldsberry
Vice President, Planning and Special Projects—Mark McGuire
Vice President, Marketing—Jeff Odenwald
Vice President, Special Assignments—Jack Brickhouse
Chief Financial Officer—Leo M. Breen
Special Baseball Consultant to Exec. V. P. and G. M.—Charlie Fox
Special Assistant to Exec. V. P. and V. P., Business Operations—E.R. Saltwell
Assistant to the Exec. V. P. and Traveling Secretary—John Cox
Director of Scouting—A.B. "Vedie" Himsl
Chief Accounting Officer—Joseph A. Kirchen
Secretary—Stanley J. Gradowski, Jr.
Director, Public Relations and Publications—Bob Ibach
Director, Ticket Sales—Frank Maloney
Director, Stadium Operations—Robert Hubberts
Director, Ticket Services—Lamar Vernon
Director, Promotions and Sales—John McDonough
Director, Community Services—Mary Beth Hughes
Manager, Group Sales—Bob Farrell
Associate Director, Minor Leagues—William Harford
Assistant Director, Publications and Statistics—Ned Colletti
Assistant Director, Stadium Operations/Facilities—Lubie Veal
Manager—Jim Frey
Executive Offices—Wrigley Field, N. Clark and Addison Streets, Chicago, Ill. 60613
Telephone—281-5050 (area code 312)

SCOUTS—(Major League)—Charlie Fox, Scott Reid, Eric Soderholm. (Supervisors)—Brandon Davis, Frank DeMoss, Gene Handley, Gary Nickels. (Regular)—Billy Blitzer, William Capps, Billy Champion, Tom Davis, Edward DiRamio, Walt Dixon, Nino Espinosa, John Hennessy, Ron Hollingsworth, Roy Johnson, John "Spider" Jorgensen, Doug Laumann, Doug Mapson, Julio Navarro, John "Buck" O'Neil, Andrew Pienovi, Evo Pusich, Joaquin Velilla, H.D. Wilson, Earl Winn, Harold Younghans, James Zerilla.

PARK LOCATION—Wrigley Field, Addison Street, N. Clark Street, Waveland Avenue and Sheffield Avenue.

Seating capacity—37,242.

FIELD DIMENSIONS—Home plate to left field at foul line, 355 feet; to center field, 400 feet; to right field at foul line, 353 feet.

CINCINNATI REDS

Chairmen—James R. Williams, William J. Williams

President and Chief Executive Officer—Robert L. Howsam, Sr.
Assistant General Manager—Woody Woodward
Vice-President, Marketing—Robert L. Howsam, Jr.
Vice-President, Player Development—Sheldon Bender
Vice-President, Controller—D.L. Porco
Vice-President, Publicity—Jim Ferguson
Business Manager—Doug Bureman
Director, Scouting—Larry Doughty
Director, Stadium Operations—Doug Duennes
Director, Promotions—Greg McCollam
Director, Ticket Department—Bill Stewart
Director, Season Tickets and Customer Relations—Janet Wendel
Director, Group Sales—Willard Bailey
Director, Broadcasting—Jim Winters
Director of Speakers Bureau—Gordy Coleman
Traveling Secretary—Steve Cobb
Assistant Scout—Jim Stewart
Assistant Director, Player Development and Scouting—Greg Riddoch
Assistant, Player Development and Scouting—Joe Nichols
Assistant Publicity Director—Jon Braude
Assistant Controller—Chris Krabbe
Assistant Ticket Director—John O'Brien
Chairman Emeritus—Louis Nippert
Manager—Vern Rapp
Executive Offices—100 Riverfront Stadium, Cincinnati, O. 45202
Telephone—421-4510 (area code 513)

SCOUTS—Larry Barton, Jr., Gene Bennett, Cameron Bonifay, Dave Calaway, Bill Clark, Martin Daily, Roger Ferguson, Elmer Gray, Edwin Howsam, Jeff McKay, Julian Mock, Chet Montgomery, Robert Myer, Ed Roebuck, Tom Severtson, Johnny Sierra, Larry Smith, Neil Summers, Fred Uhlman, Mickey White, George Zuraw.

PARK LOCATION—Riverfront Stadium, downtown Cincinnati, bounded by Second Street to Ohio River and from Walnut Street to Broadway.

Seating capacity—52,392.

FIELD DIMENSIONS—Home plate to left field at foul line, 330 feet; to center field, 404 feet; to right field at foul line, 330 feet.

HOUSTON ASTROS

Board of Directors—John J. McMullen, Jack T. Trotter, T.H. Neyland

President and General Manager—Albert L. Rosen
Vice-President, Baseball Operations—Bob Kennedy
Administrative Asst. to the President and Traveling Secretary—Donald Davidson
Assistant to the General Manager—Andy MacPhail
Director of Minor League Operations—William J. Wood
Director of Scouting—Lynwood Stallings
Assistant, Minor League Operations and Scouting—Dan O'Brien, Jr.
Director of Public Relations—Mike Ryan
Asst. Director of Public Relations—Rick Rivers
Director of Broadcasting and Promotions—Art Elliott
Scoreboard Operations—Paul Darst
Broadcast and Promotions Sales—Hugh Pickett, Lou Korpas
Director of Ticket Sales—Larry Serota
Manager, Season Ticket Sales—M.M. (Buddy) Hancken
Manager, Group Sales—Donna deGruyter
Administrative Asst., Major League Operations—Sandra Zimmerman
Secretary, Public Relations—Beverly Rains
Club Physician—Dr. William Bryan
Public Address Announcer—J. Fred Duckett
Manager—Bob Lillis
Executive Offices—Astrodome, P.O. Box 288
Houston, Tex. 77001
Telephone—799-9500 (area code 713)
HOUSTON SPORTS ASSOCIATION, INC.
President and Chief Operating Officer—Robert G. Harter
Executive Vice-President—Neal Gunn
Vice-President, Engineering—W. Gary Keller
Senior Vice-President, Marketing and Sales—Mike Storen
Vice-President, Corporate Affairs—Jim McConn
Executive Vice-President, Event Sales and Management—Jimmie Fore
Director, Special Projects—Jim Weidler
Director, Service and Administration—Bill Boyd
Treasurer—A. Eugene Stoffel
Controller—Adam C. Richards
Financial Analyst—Bill Boyd
Ticket Manager—Charles T. Wall

SCOUTS—Clary Anderson, Stan Benjamin, Jack Bloomfield, Joe Campise, C.V. Davis, Doug Deutsch, Ben Galante, Carl Greene, Bill Hallauer, Bob Hartsfield, Bob Kennedy, Jr., David Lakey, Gordon Lakey, Julio Linares, Walter Matthews, William Melendez, Domingo Mercedes, Carlos Muro, Dan O'Brien, Jr., Tony Pacheco, Victor Ramirez, Adriano Rodriguez, Lynwood Stallings, Reggie Waller, Paul Weaver, Harrison Wickel.

PARK LOCATION—Astrodome, Kirby and Interstate Loop 610

Seating capacity—45,000.

FIELD DIMENSIONS—Home plate to left field at foul line, 340 feet; to center field, 406 feet; to right field at foul line, 340 feet.

LOS ANGELES DODGERS

Board of Directors—Peter O'Malley, President; Harry M. Bardt;
Roland Seidler, Jr., Vice-President and Treasurer;
Mrs. Roland (Terry) Seidler, Secretary

President—Peter O'Malley
Executive Vice-President—Fred Claire
Vice-President, Player Personnel—Al Campanis
Vice-President, Minor League Operations—William P. Schweppe
Vice-President, Marketing—Merritt Willey
Special Consultant—Walter Alston
Controller and Assistant Treasurer—Ken Hasemann
Assistant Secretary—Irene Tanji
Resident Council—Santiago Fernandez
Director, Advertising, Novelties and Souvenirs—Jim Campbell
Director, Dodgertown—Charles Blaney
Director, Stadium Operations—Bob Smith
Director, Ticket Department—Walter Nash
Director, Stadium Club and Transportation—Bob Schenz
Director, Dodger Network—David Van de Walker
Director, Scouting—Ben Wade
Director, Publicity—Steve Brener
Director, Publications—Toby Zwikel
Director, Community Relations—Don Newcombe
Community Relations—Roy Campanella, Lou Johnson
Director, Ticket Marketing and Promotions—Barry Stockhamer
Director, Community Services and Special Events—Bill Shumard
Assistant to the President—Ike Ikuhara
Traveling Secretary—Billy DeLury
Auditor—Michael Strange
Manager—Tom Lasorda
Club Physicians—Dr. Frank Jobe, Dr. Robert Woods
Executive Offices—Dodger Stadium, 1000 Elysian Park Avenue,
Los Angeles, Calif. 90012
Telephone—224-1500 (area code 213)

SCOUTS—Eleodoro Arias, Rafael Avila, Boyd Bartley, Bob Bishop, Gib Bodet, Mike Brito, Bob Darwin, Paul Duval, Eddie Fajardo, Sergio Ferrer, Jim Garland, Dick Hanlon, Dennis Haren, Gail Henley, Elvio Jimenez, Tony John, Tim Johnson, Hank Jones, John Keenan, Ron King, Steve Lembo, Ed Liberatore, Carl Lowenstine, Dale McReynolds, Tommy Mixon, John O'Neil, Regie Otero, Bill Pleis, Tomas Silverio, Jerry Stephenson, Dick Teed, Corito Varona, Guy Wellman.

PARK LOCATION—Dodger Stadium, 1000 Elysian Park Avenue.

Seating capacity—56,000.

FIELD DIMENSIONS—Home plate to left field at foul line, 330 feet; to center field, 395 feet; to right field at foul line, 330 feet.

MONTREAL EXPOS

Board of Directors—Charles R. Bronfman, Lorne C. Webster, John J. McHale, Sydney Maislin, Hugh Hallward, E. Leo Kolber, Melvin W. Griffin, Louis R. Desmarais, Arnold Ludwick, Honorary Treasurer

Chairman of the Board—Charles R. Bronfman
President and Chief Executive Officer—John J. McHale
Vice-President, Player Development, Scouting—Jim Fanning
Assistant to the President—Bill Stoneman
Director of Minor League Operations—Bob Gebhard
Director, Team Travel—Peter Durso
Group Vice-President—Pierre Gauvreau
Vice-President, Business Operations—Gerry Trudeau
Vice-President, Marketing & Public Affairs—Rene Guimond
Director of Finance—Dennis Bodin
Publicists—Monique Giroux, Richard Griffin
Field Coordinator, Player Development—Pat Daugherty
Coordinator, Spring Training—Kevin McHale
Manager—Bill Virdon
Club Physician—Dr. Robert Brodrick
Mailing Address—P. O. Box 500, Station M, Montreal, Quebec, Canada H1V 3P2
Telephone—253-3434 (area code 514)

SCOUTS—(Special assignment)—Eddie Lyons, Carroll (Whitey) Lockman, Ed Lopat; (Supervisors)—Danny Menendez, Bob Fontaine, Jr.; (Regular)—Bill Adair, Jesus Alou, Terry Boyle, Harry Bright, Cliff Ditto, Mercer Harris, Tom Hinkle, Dick Lemay, Roy McMillan, Walter Millies, John (Red) Murff, Herb Newberry, Bob Oldis, Frank Perez, Ron Piche, Harry Pritikin, Earl Rapp, Bob Rogers.

PARK LOCATION—Olympic Stadium, 4545 Pierre de Coubertin, Montreal, Quebec, Canada H1V 3N7.

Seating capacity—59,149.

FIELD DIMENSIONS—Home plate to left field at foul line, 325 feet; to center field, 404 feet; to right field at foul line, 325 feet.

NEW YORK METS

Chairman of the Board—Nelson Doubleday

Directors—Nelson Doubleday, Fred Wilpon, Walter E. Freese
John W. O'Donnell, John T. Sargent
President & Chief Executive Officer—Fred Wilpon
Exec. Vice-President, G.M. & Chief Operating Officer—J. Frank Cashen
Vice-President, Baseball Operations—James Lou Gorman
Vice-President, Operations—Bob Mandt
Vice-President—Alan E. Harazin
Vice-President, Finance and Administration—Harold W. O'Shaughnessy
Special Asst. to the G.M. & Team Travel Director—Arthur Richman
Director of Scouting—Joseph McIlvaine
Ticket Manager—Bill Ianniciello
Director of Minor League Operations—Stephen Schryver
Director of Public Relations—Jay Horwitz
Director of Promotions—Tim Hamilton
Stadium Manager—John McCarthy
Manager—Dave Johnson
Club Physician—Dr. James C. Parkes II
Team Trainer—Steve Garland
Executive Offices—William A. Shea Stadium, Roosevelt
Avenue and 126th Street, Flushing, N.Y. 11368
Telephone—507-6387 (area code 212)

SCOUTS—Carmen Fusco, Roland Johnson, Dean Jongewaard, Buddy Kerr, Dave Madison, Joe Mason, Rich Miller, Harry Minor, Robert Minor, Danny Monzon, Julian Morgan, Roy Partee, Carlos Pascual, Junior Roman, Terry Ryan, Bob Scheffing, Marvin Scott, Jim Terrell, Eddy Toledo, Bob Wellman, Len Zanke, Jack Zduriencik.

PARK LOCATION—William A. Shea Stadium, Roosevelt Avenue and 126th Street, Flushing, N. Y. 11368.

Seating capacity—55,601.

FIELD DIMENSIONS—Home plate to left field at foul line, 338 feet; to center field, 410 feet; to right field at foul line, 338 feet.

PHILADELPHIA PHILLIES

President—Bill Giles

Partners—The Taft Broadcasting Co., John Drew Betz, Tri-Play Associates, Fitz Eugene Dixon Jr., Mrs. Rochelle Levy
Vice-President—Paul Owens
Vice-President, Baseball Administration—Tony Siegle
Executive Vice-President—David Montgomery
Vice-President, Finance—Jerry Clothier
Vice-President, Public Relations—Larry Shenk
Secretary and Counsel—William Y. Webb
Vice-President, Director of Player Development—Jim Baumer
Player Personnel Advisor—Hugh Alexander
Assistant to the President—Mrs. Cathy Halpin
Ticket Manager—Ray Krise
Director of Promotions—Frank Sullivan
Director of Advertising—Tom Hudson
Traveling Secretary—Eddie Ferenz
Director of Ticket Sales—Richard Deats
Asst. Director of Minor Leagues and Scouting—Jack Pastore
Director of Community Relations and Broadcaster—Chris Wheeler
Assistant Public Relations Director—Vince Nauss
Director of Marketing—Dennis Lehman
Director of Stadium Operations—Mike DiMuzio
Executive Secretary to Minor Leagues—Bill Gargano
Club Physician—Dr. Phillip Marone
Club Trainer—Jeff Cooper
Strength and Flexibility Instructor—Gus Hoefling
Manager—Paul Owens
Executive Offices—Philadelphia Veterans Stadium
Mailing Address—P.O. Box 7575, Philadelphia, Pa. 19101
Telephone—463-6000 (area code 215)

SCOUTS—(Special assignment)—Hugh Alexander, Wilbur Johnson and Ray Shore. (Regular)—Francisco Acevedo, Oliver Bidwell, Edward Bockman, Carlos Cervo, George Farson, Doug Gassaway, Charles Gault, Bill Harper, Dick Lawlor, Anthony Lucadello, Gene Martin, Fred Mazuca, Luis Peraza, Bob Reasonover, Joe Reilly, Jay Robertson, Tony Roig, Andy Seminick, Rudy Terrasas, Elmer Valo, Randy Waddill, Don Williams.

PARK LOCATION—Philadelphia Veterans Stadium, Broad Street and Pattison Avenue.

Seating capacity—65,454.

FIELD DIMENSIONS—Home plate to left field at foul line, 330 feet; to center field, 408 feet; to right field at foul line, 330 feet.

PITTSBURGH PIRATES

President—Daniel M. Galbreath

Chairman of the Board—John W. Galbreath
Directors—Daniel M. Galbreath, James W. Phillips,
Deane F. Johnson, Caesar P. Kimmel
Executive Vice-President—Caesar P. Kimmel
Executive Vice-President—Harding Peterson
Vice-President Administration—Joseph M. O'Toole
Vice-President Public Relations and Marketing—Jack Schrom
Treasurer/Assistant Secretary—Douglas G. McCormick
Secretary—James W. Phillips
Assistant to Vice-President for Sales and Promotions—Steve Greenberg
Director of Publicity—Edward A. Wade
Assistant Directors of Publicity—Sally O'Leary, Greg Johnson
Director of Scouting—Milt Graff
Minor League Director—Branch B. Rickey
Special Assistant to the Executive Vice-President—Willie Stargell
Assistant Minor League Director—Tom Kayser
Assistant Director of Scouting—Jon Neiderer
Traveling Secretary—Charles Muse
Radio and TV Coordinator—Greg Brown
Director of Promotions—Frank Gilbert
Assistant Directors of Promotions—Kathy Saba, Patty Paytas
Community Relations Director—Patty Paytas
Assistant to the Treasurer—Kenneth C. Curcio
Ticket Manager—Richard C. Holland
Director of Season and Group Sales—Steve Greenberg
Manager—Chuck Tanner
Club Physicians—Drs. Joseph Coroso, Jack Failla
Team Trainer—Tony Bartirome, Kent Biggerstaff
Equipment Manager—John Hallahan
Executive Offices—Three Rivers Stadium, 600 Stadium Circle, Pittsburgh, PA 15212
Telephone—323-5000 (area code 412)

SCOUTS—(Scouting Supervisors)—Gene Baker, Kelvin Bowles, Bart Braun, Joe L. Brown, Bill Bryk, Joe Consoli, Pablo Cruz, Larry D'Amato, George Detore, Angel Figueroa, Jerry Gardner, Pete Gebrian, Fred Goodman, Howie Haak, Carlton Keller, Jim Maxwell, Lenny Yochim. (Associate Scouts)—Bob Johnson, Jose Luna, Boyd Odom, Steve Oleschuk, Mark Tanner, Bob Whalen.

PARK LOCATION—Three Rivers Stadium, 600 Stadium Circle.

Seating capacity—58,365.

FIELD DIMENSIONS—Home plate to left field at foul line, 335 feet; to center field, 400 feet; to right field at foul line, 335 feet.

ST. LOUIS CARDINALS

Chairman of the Board, President and Chief Executive Officer—
August A. Busch, Jr.

Vice-Presidents—August A. Busch, III, Fred L. Kuhlmann, Margaret S. Busch
Senior Vice-President—Stan Musial
Secretary and Treasurer—John L. Hayward
Assistant Secretary—Richard Schwartz
Assistant Treasurer—H. F. Suellentrop
Board of Directors—Adolphus A. Busch, IV, August A. Busch, Jr.,
August A. Busch, III, Margaret S. Busch, Frederic E. Giersch, Jr., Louis B. Hager,
John Hayward, Ben Kerner, Fred L. Kuhlmann, J.W. McAfee, Stanley F. Musial,
W.R. Persons, Walter C. Reisinger, Louis B. Susman
General Manager—Joe McDonald
Manager—Whitey Herzog
Vice-President, Business Operations—Gary Blase
Controller—John McMinn
Director of Administration—Joe McShane
Director of Player Development—Lee Thomas
Director of Scouting—Fred McAlister
Director of Minor League Operations—Paul Fauks
Director of Promotions—Marty Hendin
Director of Public Relations—Jim Toomey
Assistant Director of Public Relations—Robin Monsky
Director of Sales—Joe Cunningham
Director of Season Ticket Sales—Sue Ann McClaren
Director of Tickets and Operations—Mike Bertani
Assistant Director of Tickets—Josephine Arnold
Administrative Assistant to G.M.—Judy Lovelace
Traveling Secretary—C.J. Cherre
Club Physician—Dr. Stan London
Executive Offices—Busch Stadium, 250 Stadium Plaza,
St. Louis, Mo. 63102
Telephone—421-3060 (area code 314)

SCOUTS—(Special Assignment)—Joe Frazier. (Supervisors)—Jim Belz, Vern Benson, Willie Calvino, Steve Flores, Rich Hacker, Jim Johnston, Hank Kelly, Marty Keough, Marty Maier, Tom McCormack, Mo Mozzali, Mike Roberts, Hal Smith, Charles (Tim) Thompson. (Regular)—Ted Baker, James Brown, Walker Cress, Roberto Diaz, Jim Dreyer, Cecil Espy, Bob Geels, Ray Goodman, Manuel Guerra, Jim Holden, Ray King, Henry Krause, Thornton Lee, Bill Lohr, Juan Melo, Virgil Melvin, Albert Osorio, Bob Parks, Medaro Perez, Joe Popek, Bart Shelly, John Skurski, Kenneth Thomas, Bill Warren.

PARK LOCATION—Busch Stadium, Broadway, Walnut Street, Stadium Plaza and Spruce Street.

Seating capacity—50,100.

FIELD DIMENSIONS—Home plate to left field at foul line, 330 feet; to center field, 414 feet; to right field at foul line, 330 feet.

SAN DIEGO PADRES

Board of Directors—Joan Kroc, Ballard F. Smith, Jr.

President and Treasurer—Ballard F. Smith, Jr.
Senior Vice-President, Business Operations—Elten F. Schiller
Vice-President, Baseball Operations—Jack McKeon
Administrative Assistant—Rhoda Polley
Vice-President, Administration—Dick Freeman
Accounting Dept. Supervisor—Sondra Welch
Director of Scouting—Sandy Johnson
Major League Scout, Special Assignments—Dick Hager
Administrator, Minor Leagues and Scouting—Tom Romenesko
Director of Media Relations—Bill Beck
Administrative Assistant—Mil Chip
Media Relations Assistant—Be Barnes
Asst. Dir. Community Relations/Publications—Jim Geschke
Director of Broadcasting—Jerry Coleman
Director of Group Sales—Tom Mulcahy
Director of Promotions—Andy Strasberg
Director of Business Development—Fred Whitacre
Director of Ticket Sales—Dave Gilmore
Traveling Secretary—John Mattei
Manager—Dick Williams
Club Physician—Scripps Clinic
Executive Offices—P. O. Box 2000, San Diego, Calif. 92120
Telephone—283-4494 (area code 619)

SCOUTS—Dave Bartosch, Ken Bracey, Alfonso (Chico) Carrasquel, Billy Castell, Ray Coley, Manny Crespo, Grisha Davida, Bill Earnhart, Denny Galehouse, Dick Hager, Al Heist, Donald Hennelly, Edgar Jewell, Earl Jones, Jim Marshall, Abe Martinez, Bill McKeon, Luis Rosa, Brad Sloan, Vince Valecce, Bob Warner, John Young, Hank Zacharias.

PARK LOCATION—San Diego Stadium, 9949 Friars Road.

Seating capacity—58,671.

FIELD DIMENSIONS—Home plate to left field at foul line, 330 feet; to center field, 405 feet; to right field at foul line, 330 feet.

SAN FRANCISCO GIANTS

President—Robert A. Lurie

Executive Vice-President, Baseball Operations—Thomas F. Haller
Vice-President, Business Operations—Patrick J. Gallagher
Executive Vice-President, Administration—Corey Busch
Asst. Vice-President, Baseball Operations/Minor Leagues—Ralph E. Nelson, Jr.
Director of Player Personnel and Scouting—Bob Fontaine
Field Director of Player Development—Jim Lefebvre
Minor League Consultant—Jack Schwarz
Asst. Field Director of Player Personnel and Development—Robert L. Miller
Director of Publicity—Duffy Jennings
Director of Community and Public Relations—Stu Smith
Director of Marketing—Dale Kaetzel
Director of Stadium Operations—Don Foreman
Ticket Manager—Arthur Schulze
Accounting Manager—Jeannie Adamo
Director of Sales—Bob Gaillard
Traveling Secretary—Dirk Smith
Speakers Bureau—Joe Orengo
Community Representative—Mike Sadek
Team Photographer—Dennis Desprois
Manager—Frank Robinson
Executive Offices—Candlestick Park, San Francisco, Calif. 94124
Telephone—468-3700 (area code 415)

SCOUTS—Everett (Rocky) Bridges, Edward A. Barberis, Mark Conkin, Harry Craft, Dutch Deutsch, Jack DiGrace, Ruben Decena, Nino Escalera, Jack French, Robert Folkins, Maurice D. Fisher, George M. Genovese, Grady Hatton, Carl Hubbell, Herman Hannah, Richard Klaus, Harvey Koepf, Andy Korenek, Reggie Lewis, Jim Lyke, Marty Miller, Bob Miller, Frank Ontiveros, Bill Parese, Ken (Squeaky) Parker, Walt Ripley, Hank Sauer, Marvin Stendel, John Shafer, Gene Thompson, Mike Toomey, Jack Uhey, Joe Winstead, Tom Zimmer.

PARK LOCATION—Candlestick Point, Bayshore Freeway.

Seating capacity—58,000.

FIELD DIMENSIONS—Home plate to left field at foul line, 335 feet; to center field, 400 feet; to right field at foul line, 335 feet.

CAL RIPKEN
• BALTIMORE ORIOLES•
MAJOR LEAGUE
PLAYER OF THE YEAR

HANK PETERS
• BALTIMORE ORIOLES•
MAJOR LEAGUE EXECUTIVE

TONY LaRUSSA
• CHICAGO WHITE SOX•
MAJOR LEAGUE MANAGER

The Sporting News

No. 1 MEN of 1983

KEVIN McREYNOLDS
• LAS VEGAS•
MINOR LEAGUE PLAYER

BILL DANCY
• READING•
MINOR LEAGUE MANAGER

A. RAY SMITH
• LOUISVILLE •
MINOR LEAGUE EXECUTIVE
IN CLASS AAA

ED KENNEY
• NEW BRITAIN•
MINOR LEAGUE EXECUTIVE
IN CLASS AA

TERRY REYNOLDS
• VERO BEACH•
MINOR LEAGUE EXECUTIVE
IN CLASS A

Major League Players Association

805 Third Avenue
New York, N.Y. 10022
Telephone—(212) 826-0808

Acting Executive Director &
General Counsel—Donald Fehr
Special Assistant—Mark Belanger
Counsel—Arthur Schack
Staff—Joyce Reiss and Margaret Westwell

EXECUTIVE BOARD

Steve Renko—American League Representative
Phil Garner—National League Representative
Ted Simmons—Pension Committee
Steve Rogers—Pension Committee
Plus all remaining player representatives

NATIONAL LEAGUE PLAYER REPRESENTATIVES

Dale Murphy—Atlanta Braves
Bill Buckner—Chicago Cubs
Frank Pastore—Cincinnati Reds
Bob Knepper—Houston Astros
Burt Hooton—Los Angeles Dodgers
Steve Rogers—Montreal Expos
Ed Lynch—New York Mets
Greg Gross—Philadelphia Phillies
Kent Tekulve—Pittsburgh Pirates
Tommy Herr—St. Louis Cardinals
Dave Dravecky—San Diego Padres
Gary Lavelle—San Francisco Giants

AMERICAN LEAGUE PLAYER REPRESENTATIVES

Scott McGregor—Baltimore Orioles
Rick Miller—Boston Red Sox
Bruce Kison—California Angels
Greg Luzinski—Chicago White Sox
Mike Hargrove—Cleveland Indians
Jack Morris—Detroit Tigers
Dan Quisenberry—Kansas City Royals
Ted Simmons—Milwaukee Brewers
Ron Davis—Minnesota Twins
Dave Winfield—New York Yankees
Tom Burgmeier—Oakland A's
Jim Beattie—Seattle Mariners
Billy Sample—Texas Rangers
Buck Martinez—Toronto Blue Jays

Major League Farm Systems for '84

AMERICAN LEAGUE

BALTIMORE (5): AAA—Rochester. AA—Charlotte. A—Hagerstown, Newark. Rookie—Bluefield.

BOSTON (5): AAA—Pawtucket. AA—New Britain, Conn. A—Elmira, Winston-Salem, Winter Haven.

CALIFORNIA (5): AAA—Edmonton. AA—Waterbury. A—Peoria, Redwood, Salem.

CHICAGO (5): AAA—Denver. AA—Glens Falls. A—Appleton, Niagara Falls. Rookie—Sarasota.

CLEVELAND (4): AAA—Old Orchard Beach, Me. AA—Buffalo. A—Batavia, Waterloo.

DETROIT (4): AAA—Evansville. AA—Birmingham. A—Lakeland. Rookie—Bristol, Va.

KANSAS CITY (5): AAA—Omaha. AA—Memphis. A—Eugene, Fort Myers, Charleston, S. C.

MILWAUKEE (5): AAA—Vancouver. AA—El Paso. A—Beloit, Stockton. Rookie—Paintsville.

MINNESOTA (4): AAA—Toledo. AA—Orlando. A—Visalia. Rookie—Elizabethton.

NEW YORK (5): AAA—Columbus, O. AA—Nashville. A—Ft. Lauderdale, Greensboro, Oneonta.

OAKLAND (5): AAA—Tacoma. AA—Albany. A—Idaho Falls, Medford, Modesto.

SEATTLE (6): AAA—Salt Lake City. AA—Chattanooga. A—Butte, Bellingham, Wausau, Salinas.

TEXAS (6): AAA—Oklahoma City. AA—Tulsa. A—Burlington, Salem, Tri-Cities. Rookie—Sarasota.

TORONTO (6): AAA—Syracuse. AA—Knoxville. A—Florence, Kinston. Rookie—Bradenton, Medicine Hat.

NATIONAL LEAGUE

ATLANTA (5): AAA—Richmond. AA—Greenville. A—Anderson, Durham. Rookie—Bradenton.

CHICAGO (6): AAA—Iowa. AA—Midland. A—Geneva, Quad Cities, Lodi. Rookie—Pikeville.

CINCINNATI (6): AAA—Wichita. AA—Burlington, Vt. A—Cedar Rapids, Tampa, Sarasota. Rookie—Billings.

HOUSTON (6): AAA—Tucson. AA—Columbus, Ga. A—Asheville, Auburn, Daytona Beach. Rookie—Sarasota.

LOS ANGELES (6): AAA—Albuquerque. AA—San Antonio. A—Bakersfield, Vero Beach. Rookie—Lethbridge, Bradenton.

MONTREAL (6): AAA—Indianapolis. AA—Jacksonville. A—Gastonia, Jamestown, West Palm Beach. Rookie—Calgary.

NEW YORK (6): AAA—Tidewater. AA—Jackson. A—Columbia, S.C., Little Falls, Lynchburg. Rookie—Kingsport.

PHILADELPHIA (6): AAA—Portland. AA—Reading. A—Peninsula, Spartanburg. Rookie—Bend, Helena.

PITTSBURGH (6): AAA—Hawaii. AA—Nashua. A—Prince William, Macon, Watertown. Rookie—Bradenton.

ST. LOUIS (7): AAA—Louisville. AA—Arkansas. A—Erie, St. Petersburg, Savannah, Springfield. Rookie—Johnson City.

SAN DIEGO (5): AAA—Las Vegas. AA—Beaumont, Tex. A—Miami, Reno. Rookie—Spokane.

SAN FRANCISCO (5): AAA—Phoenix. AA—Shreveport. A—Clinton. Fresno. Rookie—Everett, Wash.

Minor League Presidents for '84

CLASS AAA

American Association—Joe Ryan, P. O. Box 382, Wichita, Kan. 67201

International League—Harold Cooper, Box 608, Grove City, Ohio 43123

Mexican League—Pedro Treto Cisneros, Angel Pola No. 16, Col. del Periodista, Mexico 10, D. F., Mexico

Pacific Coast League—Bill Cutler, 2101 E. Broadway Rd., Tempe, Ariz. 85282

CLASS AA

Eastern League—Charles Eshbach, Box 716, Plainville, Conn. 06062

Southern League—Jimmy Bragan, 235 Main St., Suite 200, Trussville, Ala. 35173

Texas League—Carl Sawatski, 1501 N. University, Suite 412, Little Rock, Ark. 72207

CLASS A

California League—Joe Gagliardi, 1060 Willow, San Jose, Calif. 95125

Carolina League—John Hopkins, 4241 United Street, Greensboro, N.C. 27407

Florida State League—George MacDonald, Jr., P. O. Box 414, Lakeland, Fla. 33802

Midwest League—William K. Walters, P. O. Box 444, Burlington, Ia. 52601

New York-Pennsylvania League—Vincent M. McNamara, 220 Brookside Drive, Buffalo, N. Y. 14220.

Northwest League—Bob Freitas, 1840 Tabor Street, Eugene, Ore. 97401

South Atlantic League—John H. Moss, P. O. Box 49, Kings Mountain, N. C. 28086

ROOKIE CLASSIFICATION

Appalachian League—Bill Halstead, 157 Carson Lane, Bristol, Va. 24201

Gulf Coast League—Thomas J. Saffell, 420 Golden Gate Point, Apt. 18, Sarasota, Fla. 33577

Pioneer League—Ralph C. Nelles, P. O. Box 1144, Billings, Mont. 59103

OFFICIAL MINOR LEAGUE AVERAGES

Including

Official Averages of All Class AAA, Class AA, Class A and Rookie Leagues

National Association President John Johnson.

American Association

CLASS AAA

Leading Batter
MICHAEL STENHOUSE
Wichita

League President
JOE RYAN

Leading Pitcher
CRAIG EATON
Evansville

CHAMPIONSHIP WINNERS IN PREVIOUS YEARS

Year	Club	Pct.
1902	Indianapolis	.683
1903	St. Paul	.657
1904	St. Paul	.646
1905	Columbus	.658
1906	Columbus	.615
1907	Columbus	.584
1908	Indianapolis	.601
1909	Louisville	.554
1910	Minneapolis	.637
1911	Minneapolis	.600
1912	Minneapolis	.636
1913	Milwaukee	.599
1914	Milwaukee	.590
1915	Minneapolis	.597
1916	Louisville	.605
1917	Indianapolis	.588
1918	Kansas City	.589
1919	St. Paul	.610
1920	St. Paul	.701
1921	Louisville	.583
1922	St. Paul	.641
1923	Kansas City	.675
1924	St. Paul	.578
1925	Louisville	.635
1926	Louisville	.629
1927	Toledo	.601
1928	Indianapolis	.593
1929	Kansas City	.665
1930	Louisville	.608
1931	St. Paul	.623
1932	Minneapolis	.595
1933	Columbus*	.604
	Minneapolis	.562
1934	Minneapolis	.570
	Columbus*	.556
1935	Minneapolis	.591
1936	Milwaukee†	.584
1937	Columbus†	.584
1938	St. Paul	.596
	Kansas City (2nd)‡	.556
1939	Kansas City	.695
	Louisville (4th)‡	.490
1940	Kansas City	.625
	Louisville (4th)‡	.500
1941	Columbus†	.621
1942	Kansas City	.549
	Columbus (3rd)‡	.532
1943	Milwaukee	.596
	Columbus (3rd)‡	.532
1944	Milwaukee	.667
	Louisville (3rd)‡	.574
1945	Milwaukee	.604
	Louisville (3rd)‡	.545
1946	Louisville†	601
1947	Kansas City	.608
	Milwaukee (3rd)‡	.513
1948	Indianapolis	.649
	St. Paul (3rd)‡	.558
1949	St. Paul	.608
	Indianapolis (2nd)‡	.604
1950	Minneapolis	.584
	Columbus (3rd)‡	.549
1951	Milwaukee†	.623
1952	Milwaukee	.656
	Kansas City (2nd)‡	.578
1953	Toledo	.584
	Kansas City (2nd)‡	.571
1954	Indianapolis	.625
	Louisville (2nd)‡	.556
1955	Minneapolis†	.597
1956	Indianapolis†	.597
1957	Wichita	.604
	Denver (2nd)‡	.584
1958	Charleston	.589
	Minneapolis (3rd)‡	.536
1959	Louisville§	.599
	Omaha§	.516
	Minneapolis (2nd)‡	.586
1960	Denver	.571
	Louisville (2nd)‡	.556
1961	Indianapolis	.573
	Louisville (2nd)‡	.533
1962	Indianapolis	.605
	Louisville (4th)‡	.486
1963-1968	Did not operate.	
1969	Omaha	.607
1970	Omaha*	.529
	Denver	.504
1971	Indianapolis	.604
	Denver*	.521
1972	Wichita	.621
	Evansville*	.593
1973	Iowa	.610
	Tulsa*	.504
1974	Indianapolis	.578
	Tulsa*	.567
1975	Evansville*	.566
	Denver	.596
1976	Denver*	.632
	Omaha	.574
1977	Omaha	.563
	Denver*	.522
1978	Indianapolis	.578
	Omaha*	.489
1979	Evansville*	.574
	Oklahoma City	.533
1980	Denver	.676
	Springfield*	.551
1981	Omaha	.581
	Denver*	.559
1982	Indianapolis*	.551
	Omaha	.518

*Won playoff (East vs. West). †Won championship and four-team playoff. ‡Won four-team playoff. §Respective Eastern and Western division winners.

STANDING OF CLUBS AT CLOSE OF SEASON, AUGUST 31

EASTERN DIVISION

Club	W.	L.	T.	Pct.	G.B.
Louisville (Cardinals)	78	57	0	.578	....
Iowa (Cubs)	71	65	0	.522	7½
Indianapolis (Reds)	64	72	0	.471	14½
Evansville (Tigers)	61	75	0	.449	17½

WESTERN DIVISION

Club	W.	L.	T.	Pct.	G.B.
Denver (White Sox)	73	61	0	.545	....
Oklahoma City (Rangers)	66	69	0	.489	7½
Wichita (Expos)	65	71	0	.478	9
Omaha (Royals)	64	72	0	.471	10

COMPOSITE STANDING OF CLUBS AT CLOSE OF SEASON, AUGUST 31

Club	LOU.	DEN.	IOWA	OKLA.	WICH.	OMA.	IND.	EVAN.	W.	L.	T.	Pct.	G.B.
Louisville (Cardinals)	....	9	14	11	9	8	12	15	78	57	0	.578	....
Denver (White Sox)	6	....	9	9	14	16	12	7	73	61	0	.545	4½
Iowa (Cubs)	10	7	....	7	10	9	15	13	71	65	0	.522	7½
Oklahoma City (Rangers)	5	14	9	....	9	14	8	7	66	69	0	.489	12
Wichita (Expos)	7	10	6	15	....	11	7	9	65	71	0	.478	13½
Omaha (Royals)	8	8	7	10	13	...	9	9	64	72	0	.471	14½
Indianapolis (Reds)	12	4	9	8	9	7	....	15	64	72	0	.471	14½
Evansville (Tigers)	9	9	11	9	7	7	9	....	61	75	0	.449	17½

Iowa club represented Des Moines, Iowa.

Major league affiliations in parentheses.

Playoffs—Denver defeated Iowa three games to one; Louisville defeated Oklahoma City three games to two and Denver defeated Louisville four games to none to win league championship. Denver represented American Association in AAA World Series.

Regular-Season Attendance—Denver, 442,870; Evansville, 120,703; Indianapolis, 227,595; Iowa, 255,830; Louisville, 1,052,438; Oklahoma City, 226,079; Omaha, 137,545; Wichita, 128,756. Total, 2,591,816.

Managers—Denver, Jim Mahoney; Evansville, Gordy MacKenzie; Indianapolis, Roy Hartsfield; Iowa, Jim Napier; Louisville, Jim Fregosi; Oklahoma City, Tom Burgess; Omaha, Joe Sparks; Wichita, Felipe Alou.

All-Star Team—1B—Mike Stenhouse, Wichita; 2B—Dan Rohn, Iowa; 3B—Fritz Connally, Iowa; SS—Curtis Wilkerson, Oklahoma City; OF—Mike Fuentes, Wichita; Dave Stegman, Denver; Joe Carter, Iowa; C—Joel Skinner, Iowa; DH—Bill Nahorodny, Evansville; RHP—Dan Larson, Iowa; LHP—Rich Barnes, Denver; Manager of the Year—Jim Fregosi, Louisville.

(Compiled by Howe News Bureau, Boston, Mass.)

CLUB BATTING

Club	Pct.	G.	AB.	R.	OR.	H.	TB.	2B.	3B.	HR.	RBI.	GW.	SH.	SF.	HP.	BB.	Int. BB.	SO.	SB.	CS.	LOB.
Denver	.289	134	4410	748	673	1273	2063	216	50	158	695	67	24	49	32	539	29	713	55	35	976
Wichita	.288	136	4518	732	778	1299	1965	257	35	113	679	53	36	40	27	496	23	583	104	62	938
Louisville	.284	135	4605	771	653	1307	1979	245	50	109	713	67	63	40	31	520	26	758	133	66	960
Indianapolis	.277	136	4558	676	685	1263	1845	207	42	97	615	57	66	32	17	473	30	754	120	67	960
Iowa	.276	136	4575	710	664	1264	2049	233	39	158	668	59	59	35	22	503	34	857	179	97	918
Oklahoma City	.267	135	4418	608	672	1179	1681	213	35	73	567	60	53	40	31	513	21	650	70	62	969
Evansville	.263	136	4447	584	663	1169	1860	232	30	133	538	55	32	30	27	405	20	753	57	45	906
Omaha	.259	136	4350	588	629	1127	1735	216	43	102	538	56	33	38	30	408	22	668	94	47	856

INDIVIDUAL BATTING

(Leading Qualifiers for Batting Championship—367 or More Plate Appearances)

*Bats lefthanded. †Switch-hitter.

Player and Club	Pct.	G.	AB.	R.	H.	TB.	2B.	3B.	HR.	RBI.	GW.	SH.	SF.	HP.	BB.	Int. BB.	SO.	SB.	CS.
Stenhouse, Michael, Wichita*	.355	109	361	93	128	246	33	5	25	93	4	1	6	7	95	4	55	6	5
Barnes, William, Indianapolis	.337	109	377	67	127	179	19	6	7	56	6	3	2	0	26	2	42	10	5
Nahorodny, William, Evansville	.335	127	463	70	155	257	37	1	21	94	5	0	4	2	42	2	55	2	3
Stegman, David, Denver	.334	111	395	94	132	195	30	6	7	54	3	1	7	3	100	0	55	4	2
Williams, Dallas, Indianapolis*	.328	132	512	75	168	247	30	8	11	75	7	4	4	1	28	3	50	14	13
Garbey, Barbaro, Evansville	.321	101	377	60	121	196	21	6	14	59	5	2	4	6	28	1	24	7	3
Nyman, Christopher, Denver	.319	107	398	69	127	228	18	7	23	90	11	0	6	1	55	1	62	10	4
Hammond, Steven, Omaha*	.318	111	400	65	127	196	37	4	8	57	7	1	3	2	29	7	35	1	1
Johnson, Ronald, Omaha	.317	104	356	47	113	166	21	1	10	49	7	0	3	1	49	1	48	0	1
Rohn, Daniel, Iowa*	.315	117	413	84	130	193	29	5	8	56	8	9	5	0	71	1	46	23	17

Departmental Leaders: G—Dunbar, 135; AB—Carter, 522; R—Fuentes, 96; H—Williams, 168; TB—Carter, 265; 2B—Hammond, Nahorodny, 37; 3B—Landrum, 12; HR—Martinez, 31; RBI—Adduci, 101; GWRBI—Adduci, 14; SH—Gonzalez, 14; SF—Hulett, 9; HP—Jirschele, Mullins, Nieto, 8; BB—Stegman, 100; IBB—Grant, 16; SO—Adduci, Carter, Fuentes, 103; SB—Lawless, 46; CS—Cotto, Rohn, 17.

(All Players—Listed Alphabetically)

Player and Club	Pct.	G.	AB.	R.	H.	TB.	2B.	3B.	HR.	RBI.	GW.	SH.	SF.	HP.	BB.	Int. BB.	SO.	SB.	CS.
Adduci, James, Louisville*	.281	129	467	81	131	249	29	7	25	101	14	1	4	4	60	3	103	3	1
Ayer, Jonathan, Louisville	.200	8	30	3	6	7	1	0	0	3	1	1	0	0	5	0	3	0	2
Babitt, Mack, Wichita	.284	73	218	34	62	86	11	5	1	22	2	1	1	0	20	0	10	12	3
Baker, Kenneth, Evansville*	.192	9	26	3	5	13	2	0	2	2	0	0	0	0	2	0	3	0	0
Bargar, Gregory, Wichita	.000	12	4	0	0	0	0	0	0	0	0	0	0	0	1	0	4	0	0
Barnes, William, Indianapolis	.337	109	377	67	127	179	19	6	7	56	6	3	2	0	26	2	42	10	5
Barranca, German, Evansville	.163	19	43	4	7	10	3	0	0	1	0	1	0	1	6	0	11	3	2
Benton, Alfred, Wichita	.298	125	460	66	137	197	29	2	9	51	3	0	0	4	12	0	41	5	6
Bertoni, Jeffery, Evansville	.250	58	192	31	48	75	10	1	5	18	1	2	0	0	25	1	46	3	2
Biancalana, Roland, Omaha†	.223	113	367	41	82	116	13	3	5	39	6	7	5	1	36	2	70	17	6
Bogener, Terry, Oklahoma City*	.272	109	345	44	94	130	7	7	5	51	6	5	1	6	38	1	39	3	8
Bonaparte, Elijah, Louisville*	.000	1	4	0	0	0	0	0	0	0	0	0	0	0	0	0	0	0	0
Bosley, Thaddis, Iowa*	.290	39	124	22	36	68	11	0	7	24	1	0	1	0	12	2	29	3	5
Boston, Daryl, Denver*	.255	14	51	11	13	25	4	1	2	7	0	0	0	0	7	0	14	0	0
Brewer, Michael, Omaha	.252	120	412	63	104	160	23	3	9	42	4	4	1	4	49	3	77	28	7
Buchanan, Robert, Indianapolis*	.000	31	9	2	0	0	0	0	0	0	0	0	0	0	1	0	2	0	0
Buechele, Steven, Oklahoma City	.265	9	34	6	9	17	5	0	1	4	1	0	0	0	4	0	6	0	0
Butera, Salvatore, Evansville	.297	67	219	23	65	82	11	0	2	21	6	1	0	2	28	0	26	1	0
Calise, Michael, Louisville	.230	37	122	23	28	59	2	1	9	30	2	0	3	0	14	0	44	0	1
Capra, Nick, Oklahoma City	.256	124	441	84	113	177	17	4	13	41	4	2	3	3	69	0	66	27	10
Carlucci, Richard, Indianapolis*	.000	43	3	3	0	0	0	0	0	1	0	0	0	0	3	0	2	0	0
Carter, Joseph, Iowa	.307	124	522	82	160	265	27	6	22	83	4	6	1	0	17	3	103	40	12
Castillo, Martin, Evansville	.269	54	186	29	50	88	2	0	12	29	2	2	2	0	25	3	32	1	3
Castro, Jose, Denver	.250	88	288	42	72	108	10	1	8	37	2	3	4	1	24	1	40	2	2

Player and Club	Pct.	G.	AB.	R.	H.	TB.	2B.	3B.	HR.	RBI.	GW.	SH.	SF.	HP.	BB.	Int. BB.	SO.	SB.	CS.
Cato, J. Keefe, Indianapolis	.167	18	12	1	2	3	1	0	0	1	0	1	0	0	0	0	4	0	0
Christmas, Stephen, Indianapolis*	.245	31	98	14	24	44	6	1	4	20	4	0	1	0	15	2	5	1	0
Connally, Fritzie, Iowa	.288	128	451	74	130	225	25	2	22	85	5	2	1	4	49	0	78	1	5
Corbett, Raymond, Indianapolis	.113	26	62	5	7	7	0	0	0	2	0	1	0	1	7	0	17	0	0
Cotto, Henry, Iowa	.261	104	426	52	111	138	7	10	0	35	3	7	2	4	35	1	67	32	17
Cowger, Tracy, Oklahoma City	.195	14	41	4	8	11	0	0	1	3	0	0	0	0	3	0	7	0	1
Cox, Jeffrey, Omaha	.242	53	128	14	31	33	2	0	0	10	3	1	2	1	13	0	18	0	2
Davis, Eric, Indianapolis	.299	19	77	18	23	48	4	0	7	19	1	1	0	2	8	0	22	9	2
Davis, Wallace, Omaha	.316	46	171	27	54	85	10	3	5	21	4	1	0	1	18	0	36	13	5
DeJohn, Mark, Evansville†	.206	88	277	23	57	72	8	2	1	17	1	7	1	3	26	1	37	1	5
Desa, Joseph, Louisville*	.295	27	105	12	31	42	6	1	1	14	2	1	1	0	9	0	11	0	1
Dewey, Duane, Omaha	.206	25	63	4	13	14	1	0	0	3	1	2	0	0	2	0	24	1	0
Diaz, Michael, Iowa	.324	74	238	43	77	141	13	3	15	47	2	1	1	0	31	2	47	3	4
Dilks, Darren, Wichita*	.200	32	5	1	1	4	0	0	1	2	0	0	0	0	0	0	0	0	0
Dixon, Thomas, Wichita	.143	28	7	1	1	2	1	0	0	2	0	1	0	0	0	0	5	0	0
Dotson, J. Eugene, Louisville	.246	60	195	37	48	80	9	1	7	33	2	1	2	0	32	2	53	6	3
Dowless, Michael, Indianapolis	.107	17	28	1	3	3	0	0	0	2	0	1	1	0	2	0	17	0	0
Doyle, Jeffrey, Louisville†	.300	127	474	87	142	194	25	6	5	65	7	10	4	1	73	4	51	17	6
Dunbar, Thomas, Oklahoma City*	.281	135	498	73	140	196	34	5	4	65	8	2	5	1	66	2	68	10	10
Edelen, B. Joe, Indianapolis	.333	9	6	0	2	3	1	0	0	0	0	0	0	0	0	0	0	0	1
Esasky, Nicholas, Indianapolis	.278	49	158	33	44	91	5	0	14	37	3	1	3	1	38	2	42	6	2
Fahey, William, Evansville*	.304	8	23	4	7	12	2	0	1	6	1	0	1	0	2	0	2	0	0
Foley, Marvis, Denver*	.319	78	257	44	82	127	11	2	10	43	5	1	1	3	31	4	35	0	0
Franco, John, Indianapolis*	.395	23	38	7	15	24	2	2	1	10	0	1	0	0	1	0	6	1	2
Franklin, Glen, Indianapolis*	.322	72	208	33	67	100	8	5	5	29	5	3	1	1	25	1	34	4	2
Fucci, Dominic, 15 Den.-29 Evns.*	.239	44	117	13	28	47	5	1	4	9	1	0	0	1	21	1	48	0	2
Fuentes, Michael, Wichita	.299	132	448	96	134	253	23	3	30	91	8	0	4	5	86	3	103	15	4
Funderburk, Mark, Omaha	.169	17	59	4	10	16	0	0	2	4	0	0	0	2	1	0	7	0	1
Garbey, Barbaro, Evansville	.321	101	377	60	121	196	21	6	14	59	5	2	4	6	28	1	24	7	3
Gates, Michael, Wichita*	.274	126	431	69	118	158	24	2	4	43	4	9	3	0	47	3	37	9	9
Gilbert, Mark, Indianapolis†	.279	117	445	73	124	145	16	1	1	62	3	6	0	3	55	2	57	18	5
Glynn, Eugene, Wichita	.198	61	111	14	22	29	3	2	0	17	0	2	1	1	11	0	11	5	0
Gomez, Jorge, Oklahoma City	.236	18	55	5	13	22	3	0	2	15	1	1	4	0	8	0	7	0	1
Gonzalez, Jose, Louisville†	.284	122	423	64	120	160	19	6	3	44	4	14	3	2	35	3	45	26	10
Gonzalez, Julio, Evansville	.236	59	199	17	47	57	8	1	0	27	2	3	1	0	13	0	39	1	3
Grandas, Robert, Evansville	.250	101	288	50	72	108	14	2	6	19	1	5	2	4	32	0	34	13	6
Grant, Thomas, Iowa*	.312	112	394	68	123	200	24	1	17	59	7	3	4	4	69	16	81	16	12
Grapenthin, Richard, Wichita	.500	40	2	0	1	1	0	0	0	0	0	0	0	0	0	0	0	0	0
Gray, Lorenzo, Denver	.331	42	169	26	56	84	8	4	4	31	1	0	2	3	14	0	28	9	2
Guin, Gregory, Louisville*	.222	58	203	23	45	65	9	1	3	23	1	3	0	1	7	0	29	3	2
Hammond, Steven, Omaha*	.318	111	400	65	127	196	37	4	8	57	7	1	3	2	29	7	35	1	1
Harris, Greg, Indianapolis	.313	35	32	6	10	13	1	1	0	4	1	2	0	0	5	0	3	0	1
Harris, John, Indianapolis*	.295	116	420	52	124	191	30	2	11	66	3	3	7	0	42	9	71	2	1
Harris, Michael, Louisville	.250	9	16	5	4	4	0	0	0	2	0	1	0	0	0	0	3	0	0
Hart, J. Michael, Denver†	.319	50	138	31	44	70	7	2	5	19	0	1	3	0	20	4	32	1	0
Hayes, Ben, Indianapolis	.000	6	1	0	0	0	0	0	0	0	0	0	0	0	0	0	0	0	0
Hayes, William, Iowa	.257	102	331	43	85	142	16	1	13	55	7	4	4	3	46	2	62	3	2
Heath, Kelly, Omaha	.239	129	460	71	110	177	16	6	13	61	3	6	5	2	56	2	74	16	8
Hegman, Robert, Omaha	.000	4	4	2	0	0	0	0	0	0	0	0	0	0	3	0	0	0	0
Heidenreich, Curtis, Indianapolis	.000	7	4	0	0	0	0	0	0	0	0	0	0	0	0	0	4	0	0
Hicks, Joseph, Iowa	.238	78	244	34	58	101	12	2	9	29	3	4	2	0	29	3	80	7	3
Hulett, Timothy, Denver	.273	133	477	77	130	220	19	4	21	88	6	2	9	2	61	3	64	5	3
Iorg, Dane, Louisville*	.200	3	10	2	2	2	0	0	0	0	0	0	0	0	0	0	0	0	0
Isales, Orlando, Indianapolis	.272	113	390	38	106	150	18	4	6	61	9	5	5	1	35	2	63	3	2
James, Robert, Wichita	.000	22	2	0	0	0	0	0	0	0	0	0	0	0	0	0	2	0	0
Jirschele, Michael, Oklahoma City	.242	115	347	37	84	115	12	2	5	38	4	13	1	8	29	0	64	7	4
Johnson, Howard, Evansville†	.222	3	9	1	2	3	1	0	0	0	0	0	0	0	4	0	2	0	1
Johnson, Jerry, Louisville	.000	5	2	0	0	0	0	0	0	0	0	0	0	0	0	0	0	0	0
Johnson, Ronald, Omaha	.317	104	356	47	113	166	21	1	10	49	7	0	3	1	49	1	48	0	1
Johnson, Roy, Wichita*	.290	79	248	39	72	102	13	1	5	43	5	0	2	0	35	4	27	11	4
Johnson, Wallace, Wichita†	.264	16	53	7	14	19	3	1	0	6	1	1	1	0	9	0	4	2	3
Jones, Robert, Oklahoma City†	.357	46	171	25	61	93	14	3	4	29	4	1	3	1	19	1	18	0	1
Jones, Jeffrey, Indianapolis	.187	31	75	12	14	24	1	0	3	12	1	1	0	1	14	0	30	0	0
Kenaga, Jeffrey, Evansville*	.282	112	365	43	103	176	21	5	14	36	7	1	1	2	22	4	73	1	0
Kuntz, Russell, Denver	.349	13	43	6	15	22	2	1	1	8	0	0	0	1	6	0	7	1	2
Laga, Michael, Evansville*	.231	105	355	46	82	156	24	1	16	58	8	0	5	2	44	7	97	2	1
Lancellotti, Richard, 31 W-33 OC*	.206	64	218	27	45	80	11	0	8	35	3	1	1	2	19	2	28	2	3
Landrum, T. William, Indianapolis	.500	15	4	0	2	2	0	0	0	0	0	0	0	0	0	0	1	0	0
Landrum, Terry, Louisville	.292	111	431	79	126	227	23	12	18	77	4	6	2	3	38	4	86	15	6
Lawless, Thomas, Indianapolis	.279	115	423	93	118	186	23	3	13	35	4	6	1	0	47	0	77	46	14
Leeper, David, Omaha*	.277	106	405	52	112	175	20	8	9	58	6	3	7	1	14	2	56	3	2
Leibrandt, Charles, 11 Ind.-16 Oma.	.241	27	29	3	7	11	1	0	1	4	0	0	0	0	1	0	6	0	1
Lesley, Bradley, Indianapolis	.000	13	1	0	0	0	0	0	0	0	0	0	0	0	0	0	1	0	0
Lezcano, Carlos, Iowa	.186	32	118	13	22	40	4	1	4	13	2	1	0	0	9	0	39	1	2
Little, Ronald, Indianapolis*	.218	26	55	5	12	19	1	0	2	4	1	0	0	0	6	0	17	0	1
Lopez, Juan, Evansville	.202	109	332	32	67	108	12	4	7	30	3	1	2	1	33	0	42	0	3
Loviglio, John, Iowa	.227	24	66	6	15	19	2	1	0	8	0	1	1	0	3	0	6	5	1
Lozado, William, Indianapolis	.249	133	449	56	112	141	18	4	1	32	3	6	3	3	50	4	83	3	8
Lyons, William, Louisville	.271	77	266	60	72	103	14	1	5	25	2	7	0	4	48	2	43	21	3
Mackanin, Peter, Oklahoma City	.269	129	479	71	129	196	32	1	11	91	9	0	2	3	45	5	89	0	0
Manuel, Jerry, Iowa	.265	85	279	37	74	103	14	3	3	33	4	8	3	1	22	0	46	6	2
Martinez, Carmelo, Iowa	.251	123	458	76	115	235	25	1	31	94	9	2	6	2	61	1	85	8	8
McHenry, Vance, Oklahoma City	.229	15	48	6	11	12	1	0	0	4	1	0	0	0	4	0	13	0	2
Melvin, Robert, Evansville	.190	45	142	10	27	39	6	0	2	11	0	2	0	0	7	0	41	0	1
Mills, J. Bradley, Wichita*	.317	81	271	47	86	131	21	0	8	46	6	1	6	2	32	5	20	3	5
Molinaro, Robert, Indianapolis*	.265	52	151	24	40	60	3	4	3	23	0	1	0	2	23	2	11	1	2
Motley, Darryl, Evansville	.281	130	506	89	142	232	32	5	16	60	8	4	1	3	37	1	71	19	7
Mullins, Francis, Denver	.270	100	355	65	96	172	18	2	18	55	7	6	3	8	48	0	72	9	4
Murphy, Daniel, Oklahoma City*	.250	1	4	0	1	1	0	0	0	0	0	0	0	0	0	0	0	0	0
Mustad, Eric, Wichita	.000	26	5	0	0	0	0	0	0	0	0	0	0	0	1	0	2	0	0
Nahorodny, William, Evansville	.335	127	463	70	155	257	37	1	21	94	5	0	4	2	42	2	55	2	3
Newman, Albert, Wichita†	.242	38	124	20	30	38	6	1	0	16	1	3	2	1	21	1	8	2	2
Nieto, Thomas, Louisville	.272	115	383	44	104	138	17	1	5	52	2	7	3	8	41	0	78	0	2

Player and Club	Pct.	G.	AB.	R.	H.	TB.	2B.	3B.	HR.	RBI.	GW.	SH.	SF.	HP.	BB.	Int. BB.	SO.	SB.	CS.
Nyman, Christopher, Denver	.319	107	398	69	127	228	18	7	23	90	11	0	6	1	55	1	62	10	4
Owen, Dave, Iowa†	.259	126	425	67	110	155	21	3	6	39	3	11	2	4	46	2	77	30	6
Paris, Kelly, Indianapolis†	.314	8	35	9	11	18	1	0	2	9	0	0	0	0	5	0	7	0	0
Parsons, Casey, Denver*	.300	134	520	89	156	257	27	7	20	95	12	1	3	0	62	8	59	4	4
Pastornicky, Clifford, Omaha	.270	108	404	51	109	169	23	2	11	52	4	2	7	4	15	0	45	6	4
Phillips, Michael, Wichita	.340	14	47	7	16	21	2	0	1	12	0	0	1	0	1	0	3	1	0
Poldberg, Brian, Omaha	.194	64	180	17	35	59	6	0	6	18	0	2	0	4	26	1	30	0	0
Ramler, Steven, Wichita	.500	6	6	3	3	3	0	0	0	0	0	0	0	0	2	0	1	1	0
Ramos, Richard, Wichita	.000	24	3	0	0	0	0	0	0	1	0	0	0	0	1	0	0	0	0
Reitz, Kenneth, Louisville	.143	3	7	0	1	1	0	0	0	0	0	0	0	0	0	0	2	0	0
Richardt, Michael, Oklahoma City	.267	30	116	7	31	42	5	0	2	13	2	1	1	0	10	0	12	3	5
Rivera, Jesus, 68 Oma.-23 Lou.	.197	91	300	40	59	100	12	1	9	40	2	0	1	3	42	1	73	4	4
Rohn, Daniel, Iowa*	.315	117	413	84	130	193	29	5	8	56	8	9	5	0	71	1	46	23	17
Rollin, Rondal, Evansville	.291	62	230	29	67	109	12	0	10	34	3	0	5	1	5	0	55	1	2
Roof, Eugene, Louisville†	.309	114	450	74	139	181	23	5	3	60	9	5	5	2	65	3	54	15	15
Rooney, Patrick, Wichita	.275	113	425	57	117	186	20	2	15	71	5	1	2	0	20	1	93	7	3
Royster, Willie, Evansville	.152	13	33	3	5	10	2	0	1	5	1	0	1	0	1	0	9	1	0
Rubel, Michael, Oklahoma City	.250	50	180	26	45	68	11	0	4	18	1	0	1	2	20	2	38	0	0
Russell, Jeffrey, Indianapolis	.152	18	33	2	5	8	1	1	0	2	1	3	0	0	1	0	10	0	1
Ryal, Mark, Omaha*	.260	132	454	61	118	183	28	5	9	57	5	2	1	2	31	3	62	4	4
Salazar, Argenis, Wichita	.302	98	341	47	103	143	23	7	1	54	6	7	6	1	15	0	40	12	5
Sanchez, Orlando, Louisville*	.295	116	424	70	125	204	27	2	16	89	9	3	7	1	30	4	54	4	2
Santana, Rafael, Louisville	.281	45	167	19	47	58	9	1	0	20	1	1	3	2	5	1	24	3	7
Sattler, William, Wichita	.500	41	8	1	4	4	0	0	0	0	0	0	0	0	0	0	1	0	0
Scott, Donald, Oklahoma City†	.253	112	371	44	94	126	14	3	4	54	8	8	7	1	45	3	67	0	1
Scott, Rodney, Wichita†	.307	48	189	32	58	71	8	1	1	17	2	3	2	0	25	0	21	5	6
Sexton, Jimmy, 23 Den.-13 Lou.	.300	36	130	19	39	60	4	1	5	17	2	0	2	0	11	0	24	4	2
Sheridan, Patrick, Omaha*	.307	20	75	16	23	49	4	5	4	14	2	1	0	1	9	0	12	2	1
Shines, Anthony, Wichita†	.277	29	112	14	31	42	6	1	1	11	0	0	1	0	3	0	11	1	1
Skinner, Joel, Denver	.260	108	361	55	94	155	15	5	12	50	5	4	1	1	31	0	79	1	1
Smith, James, Denver	.292	94	319	55	93	139	17	4	7	45	7	3	5	7	35	2	53	0	3
Stegman, David, Denver	.334	111	395	94	132	195	30	6	7	54	3	1	7	3	100	0	55	4	2
Stenhouse, Michael, Wichita*	.355	109	361	93	128	246	33	5	25	93	4	1	6	7	95	4	55	6	5
Stennett, Renaldo, Wichita	.309	55	165	20	51	65	11	0	1	23	2	0	0	0	8	0	17	1	1
Stephans, Russell, Omaha	.240	61	175	25	42	59	4	2	3	22	2	1	3	3	27	0	18	1	2
Stockstill, David, Oklahoma City*	.230	88	265	32	61	92	9	2	6	32	3	3	1	0	30	4	33	2	4
Strain, Joseph, Oklahoma City	.262	86	336	45	88	103	9	3	0	27	3	3	3	2	38	0	16	3	5
Tarnow, Greg, Denver	.000	3	5	0	0	0	0	0	0	0	0	0	0	0	0	0	1	0	0
Thompson, V. Scot, Iowa*	.209	25	86	9	18	24	3	0	1	8	1	0	2	0	3	1	11	1	1
Toliver, Freddie, Indianapolis	.273	26	33	6	9	9	0	0	0	1	0	7	0	0	1	0	5	0	0
Tomlin, David, Wichita*	.000	41	3	0	0	0	0	0	0	0	0	0	0	0	0	0	2	0	0
Tufts, Robert, 5 Oma.-25 Ind.*	.000	30	2	0	0	0	0	0	0	0	0	0	0	0	0	0	1	0	0
Underwood, Patrick 9 Evns.-11 Ind.*	.143	20	7	0	1	1	0	0	0	0	0	0	0	0	1	0	4	0	0
Van Gorder, David, Indianapolis	.226	117	380	38	86	118	17	0	5	48	5	10	4	1	33	1	60	2	4
Van Slyke, Andrew, Louisville*	.368	54	220	52	81	128	21	4	6	41	4	1	2	1	31	0	30	13	3
Wagner, Mark, Evansville	.208	36	106	8	22	26	2	1	0	5	0	1	0	0	10	0	24	1	3
Waller, E. Tyrone, Denver	.259	87	293	40	76	120	14	3	8	39	5	1	3	0	11	0	53	8	4
Welsh, Christopher, Wichita*	.000	11	2	0	0	0	0	0	0	0	0	0	0	0	0	0	2	0	0
Werner, Donald, Oklahoma City	.289	76	232	39	67	101	14	1	6	38	0	3	3	1	38	1	38	1	1
Werth, Dennis, Louisville	.245	34	94	17	23	35	4	1	2	19	3	1	1	0	12	0	22	2	0
White, Jerome, Wichita†	.248	32	101	18	25	39	7	2	1	8	1	0	0	1	19	0	11	4	0
Wieghaus, Thomas, Wichita	.242	82	260	28	63	81	9	0	3	28	2	6	2	3	21	1	39	0	2
Wilkerson, Curtis, Oklahoma City	.312	89	343	51	107	143	19	4	3	31	3	10	4	3	38	1	55	14	9
Williams, Dallas, Indianapolis*	.328	132	512	75	168	247	30	8	11	75	7	4	4	1	28	3	50	14	13
Wise, Brett, Indianapolis	.000	18	1	0	0	0	0	0	0	0	0	0	0	0	0	0	0	0	0
Yobs, David, Denver*	.251	60	219	28	55	85	12	0	6	20	1	1	0	1	18	5	24	0	1

The following pitchers, listed alphabetically by club, with games in parentheses, had no plate appearances, primarily through use of designated hitters:

DENVER—Agosto, Juan (19); Arroyo, Fernando (23); Atkinson, William (12); Barnes, Richard (22); D'Acquisto, John (6); Fallon, Robert (24); Hoffman, Guy (32); Hrabosky, Alan (26); Johnson, Charles (36); Martz, Randy (21); Mura, Stephen (19); Ratzer, Steven (37); Siwy, James (21); Umbarger, James (3).

EVANSVILLE—Baumgarten, Ross (7); Cary, Charles (15); Dacko, Mark (24); Dixon, Troy (2); Eaton, Craig (53); Gumpert, David (14); Jones, Larry (18); Kelly, Bryan (14); Luebber, Steven (31); Mason, Roger (11); Nail, Charlie (25); O'Neal, Randall (23); Pashnick, Larry (23); Rucker, David (18); Ujdur, Gerald (18); Wilcox, Milton (2).

INDIANAPOLIS—Robinson, Ronald (4); Ryder, Brian (5).

IOWA—Bordi, Richard (18); Earley, William (46); Filer, Thomas (27); Hargesheimer, Alan (49); Jones, Larry (11); Kyles, Stanley (4); Larson, Daniel (27); Moskau, Paul (11); Patterson, Reginald (28); Perlman, Jonathan (31); Pryce, Kenneth (16); Schulze, Donald (25); Stein, Randoph (28).

LOUISVILLE—Brito, Jose (26); Citarella, Ralph (37); Cox, Daniel (2); Fulgham, John (5); Hagen, Kevin (21); Horton, Ricky (30); Keener, Jeffrey (60); Kepshire, Kurt (21); Lahti, Jeff (1); Miller, Dyar (32); Ownbey, Richard (16); Pimentel, Rafael (3); Rasmussen, Eric (11); Rhodes, Michael (47); Riggins, Mark (5); Rincon, Andrew (6); Thurberg, Thomas (10); Von Ohlen, David (12); Worrell, Todd (15).

OKLAHOMA CITY—Boitano, Danny (29); Cook, Glenn (3); Cruz, Victor (30); Davis, Ted (3); Farr, James (20); Fossas, Anthony (10); Griffin, Michael (35); Henke, Thomas (47); Lachowicz, Allen (17); Mason, Michael (16); Mengwasser, Bradley (26); Mercer, Mark (6); Musselman, Ronald (28); Rajsich, David (46); Semall, Paul (14); Tobik, David (12); Zwolensky, Mitchell (2).

OMAHA—Alvarez, Evelio (4); Black, Harry (5); Botelho, Derek (25); Brown, Scott (14); Creel, Keith (7); Hood, Donald (5); Huismann, Mark (17); Jackson, Danny (23); Keeton, Rickey (20); Parrott, Michael (44); Schuler, David (38); Shaw, Theodore (1); St. Clair, Daniel (43); Wills, Frank (16); Yuhas, Vincent (19).

WICHITA—Abone, Joseph (9); Hesketh, Joseph (15); Kinnunen, Michael (13); Quintana, Luis (21); Schuler, Mark (20); Shimp, Tommy Joe (11); Stoll, Richard (2); Tenenini, Robert (2).

GRAND-SLAM HOME RUNS—Adduci, Fuentes, Mackanin, Smith, Williams, 2 each; Benton, Diaz, Foley, Gilbert, Grandas, Heath, Ron Johnson, Landrum, Nahorodny, Nyman, Rollin, Roof, Rooney, 1 each.

AWARDED FIRST BASE ON CATCHER'S INTERFERENCE—Barnes 7 (Butera 2, Dewey, Nieto, Poldberg, Scott, Skinner); Harris 2 (Butera, Hayes); Adduci (Stephans); Bertoni (Nieto); Calise (Scott); Fucci (Scott); Gilbert (Poldberg); Wagner (Poldberg).

CLUB FIELDING

Club	Pct.	G.	PO.	A.	E.	DP.	PB.
Denver	.975	134	3351	1529	125	127	5
Iowa	.974	136	3574	1617	138	132	13
Oklahoma City	.973	135	3476	1431	136	134	23
Wichita	.973	136	3438	1386	134	124	9
Indianapolis	.971	136	3513	1433	149	133	9
Evansville	.969	136	3424	1410	157	126	13
Omaha	.969	136	3400	1417	153	119	7
Louisville	.967	135	3564	1465	170	147	7

INDIVIDUAL FIELDING

*Throws lefthanded.

FIRST BASEMEN

Player and Club	Pct.	G.	PO.	A.	E.	DP.
Adduci, Louisville*	.986	15	134	7	2	21
Ayer, Louisville	1.000	1	10	0	0	0
Barnes, Indianapolis	.993	19	131	11	1	11
Benton, Wichita	.958	8	43	3	2	2
Bertoni, Evansville	1.000	1	7	1	0	0
Calise, Louisville	.971	9	66	2	2	8
Christmas, Indianapolis	.988	10	80	4	1	10
Connally, Iowa	1.000	1	6	0	0	1
De Sa, Louisville*	.995	19	164	20	1	17
Diaz, Iowa	1.000	1	3	0	0	0
Foley, Denver	1.000	11	93	3	0	9
Fucci, Evansville*	1.000	3	17	1	0	0
Funderburk, Omaha	.967	17	172	3	6	14
Garbey, Evansville	1.000	1	2	0	0	0
Guin, Louisville*	.996	54	441	30	2	39
Hammond, Omaha	.985	36	300	18	5	25
HARRIS, Indianapolis*	.996	114	900	73	4	94
Hicks, Iowa	.983	14	107	10	2	12
Iorg, Louisville	1.000	3	21	0	0	3
Johnson, Omaha	.990	87	716	49	8	64
J. Jones, Indianapolis	.926	6	24	1	2	4
R. Jones, Oklahoma City*	.993	29	268	22	2	30
Laga, Evansville*	.988	101	835	62	11	81
Lancellotti, 22 Wi.-19 OkC.*	.986	41	329	25	5	34
Lopez, Evansville	.667	2	2	0	1	0
Lyons, Louisville	1.000	3	20	2	0	2
Mackanin, Oklahoma City	.979	29	211	19	5	15
Martinez, Iowa	.993	120	1191	83	9	99
Melvin, Evansville	1.000	7	61	1	0	5
Mills, Wichita	1.000	11	82	4	0	11
Nahorodny, Evansville	1.000	27	236	14	0	22
Nyman, Denver	.994	107	1041	81	7	99
Royster, Evansville	.833	1	5	0	1	1
Rubel, Oklahoma City	.993	49	402	29	3	44
Ryal, Omaha*	1.000	1	1	0	0	0
Santana, Louisville	1.000	2	13	0	0	2
Sexton, Louisville	1.000	1	8	0	0	2
Shines, Wichita	.995	27	187	16	1	17
Stenhouse, Wichita	.991	81	629	47	6	61
Stockstill, Oklahoma City	.992	16	115	7	1	12
Thompson, Iowa*	1.000	5	45	2	0	5
Van Slyke, Louisville	.981	14	145	11	3	20
Waller, Denver	.980	16	136	14	3	14
Werth, Louisville	.990	28	182	14	2	16

SECOND BASEMEN

Player and Club	Pct.	G.	PO.	A.	E.	DP.
Babitt, Wichita	.982	35	64	96	3	21
Barnes, Indianapolis	1.000	3	10	5	0	3
Barranca, Evansville	.968	15	24	37	2	8
Bertoni, Evansville	.985	16	34	32	1	8
Buechele, Oklahoma City	.974	9	17	21	1	3
Cox, Omaha	.963	35	81	75	6	20
DeJohn, Evansville	.976	7	18	23	1	6
Doyle, Louisville	.973	121	279	344	17	97
Franklin, Indianapolis	.951	34	55	82	7	16
Gates, Wichita	.989	60	113	145	3	27
Gonzalez, Evansville	1.000	8	16	20	0	8
Harris, Louisville	.714	2	2	3	2	1
Heath, Omaha	.985	106	223	296	8	65
Hulett, Denver	.973	133	286	424	20	88
Jirschele, Oklahoma City	.900	9	14	22	4	3
Lawless, Indianapolis	.970	109	255	303	17	74
Lopez, Evansville	.980	108	193	297	10	69
Loviglio, Iowa	.987	18	24	51	1	8
Lyons, Louisville	1.000	7	18	15	0	3
Mackanin, Oklahoma City	1.000	2	2	5	0	1
Manuel, Iowa	.963	28	51	79	5	19
McHenry, Oklahoma City	.938	15	42	34	5	12
Mullins, Denver	1.000	1	2	1	0	0
Newman, Wichita	.971	36	73	96	5	24
Paris, Indianapolis	1.000	2	4	4	0	3
Richardt, Oklahoma City	.980	20	40	60	2	14
ROHN, Iowa	.990	103	186	313	5	56
Santana, Louisville	.976	9	16	25	1	1
Scott, Wichita	.974	15	41	34	2	12
Stennett, Wichita	1.000	9	15	18	0	4
Strain, Oklahoma City	.978	86	182	224	9	53

THIRD BASEMEN

Player and Club	Pct.	G.	PO.	A.	E.	DP.
Barnes, Indianapolis	.925	68	37	124	13	11
Barranca, Evansville	1.000	1	1	4	0	1
Bertoni, Evansville	.939	31	18	59	5	2
Buechele, Oklahoma City	1.000	1	0	1	0	0
Castillo, Evansville	.941	39	30	66	6	8
Castro, Denver	.926	63	39	124	13	10
CONNALLY, Iowa	.947	127	104	234	19	16
Cowger, Oklahoma City	1.000	4	3	4	0	2
Cox, Omaha	.909	5	5	5	1	0
DeJohn, Evansville	.953	14	12	29	2	4
Dotson, Louisville	.667	1	1	1	1	0
Esasky, Indianapolis	.875	48	27	71	14	9
Franklin, Indianapolis	.898	26	12	41	6	4
Garbey, Evansville	.935	34	25	47	5	3
Gates, Wichita	.935	58	37	93	9	14
Glynn, Wichita	.853	14	8	21	5	2
Gomez, Oklahoma City	.976	18	11	30	1	2
Gonzalez, Evansville	.955	24	22	42	3	5
Gray, Denver	.956	17	6	37	2	3
Hammond, Omaha	.914	27	15	49	6	4
Hegman, Omaha	.750	4	1	2	1	0
Jirschele, Oklahoma City	.977	60	41	127	4	11
Johnson, Evansville	.857	3	1	11	2	2
Lyons, Louisville	.952	53	54	103	8	5
Mackanin, Oklahoma City	.926	53	45	80	10	7
Manuel, Iowa	.955	10	7	14	1	1
Mills, Wichita	.977	67	58	111	4	8
Mullins, Denver	.945	56	28	92	7	5
Paris, Indianapolis	1.000	2	0	3	0	0
Pastornicky, Omaha	.906	106	62	198	27	13
Reitz, Louisville	.500	2	1	0	1	0
Rohn, Iowa	.833	5	3	2	1	0
Santana, Louisville	.938	32	25	80	7	9
Scott, Wichita	.900	5	4	5	1	0
Sexton, 1 Den.-12 Lou.	.828	13	6	18	5	3
Stennett, Wichita	.828	11	7	17	5	2
Stockstill, Oklahoma City	.846	5	3	8	2	0
Van Slyke, Louisville	.893	38	42	67	13	5
Wagner, Evansville	1.000	1	1	0	0	0
Waller, Denver	1.000	1	1	0	0	0
Werner, Oklahoma City	.857	6	4	8	2	0

SHORTSTOPS

Player and Club	Pct.	G.	PO.	A.	E.	DP.
Bertoni, Evansville	.933	15	17	39	4	11
Biancalana, Omaha	.958	113	184	341	23	65
Castillo, Evansville	.889	3	3	5	1	0
DeJohn, Evansville	.956	68	102	202	14	39
Franklin, Indianapolis	.000	1	0	0	1	0
Gates, Wichita	1.000	12	15	26	0	4
Glynn, Wichita	1.000	11	12	10	0	4
Jo. Gonzalez, Louisville	.950	122	206	425	33	90
Ju. Gonzalez, Evansville	.905	26	31	74	11	14
Harris, Louisville	.913	4	7	14	2	2
Heath, Omaha	.958	26	40	75	5	14
Jirschele, Oklahoma City	.955	48	83	151	11	26
Lozado, Indianapolis	.961	132	227	395	25	87
Lyons, Louisville	.938	8	11	19	2	4
Manuel, Iowa	.969	12	17	45	2	8
Mullins, Denver	.940	37	68	105	11	26
OWEN, Iowa	.962	125	203	431	25	82
Paris, Indianapolis	1.000	6	6	19	0	3
Phillips, Wichita	.833	14	22	33	11	6
Salazar, Wichita	.944	97	152	256	24	54
Santana, Louisville	.900	4	6	12	2	2
Scott, Wichita	.931	22	31	50	6	13
Sexton, Denver	1.000	8	9	22	0	4
Smith, Denver	.960	92	148	287	18	63
Wagner, Evansville	.947	34	65	79	8	19
Wilkerson, Oklahoma City	.955	89	135	272	19	54

OUTFIELDERS

Player and Club	Pct.	G.	PO.	A.	E.	DP.
Adduci, Louisville*	.944	113	193	10	12	5
Ayer, Louisville	.933	8	14	0	1	0
Babitt, Wichita	1.000	31	60	2	0	0
Baker, Evansville*	1.000	4	11	0	0	0
Barnes, Indianapolis	.926	15	25	0	2	0
Benton, Wichita	1.000	29	28	2	0	0
Bogener, Oklahoma City*	.954	73	118	6	6	3
Bonaparte, Louisville*	1.000	1	3	0	0	0
Bosley, Iowa*	.750	4	3	0	1	0
Boston, Denver*	.844	14	26	1	5	0
Brewer, Omaha	.957	117	233	10	11	3
Capra, Oklahoma City	.967	123	307	12	11	5
Carter, Iowa	.947	120	204	9	12	2
Corbett, Indianapolis	1.000	2	2	0	0	0
Cotto, Iowa	.974	104	253	8	7	1
Cowger, Oklahoma City	.875	5	6	1	1	0
E. Davis, Indianapolis	.984	19	61	1	1	0
W. Davis, Omaha	.909	9	10	0	1	0
De Sa, Louisville*	1.000	9	12	1	0	1
Dotson, Louisville	.947	44	69	2	4	0
Dunbar, Oklahoma City*	.981	135	244	13	5	1
Fucci, Evansville*	.897	17	26	0	3	0
Fuentes, Wichita	.977	126	244	13	6	2
Garbey, Evansville	.948	71	120	8	7	2
Gilbert, Indianapolis	.987	114	212	11	3	3
Glynn, Wichita	1.000	32	56	0	0	0
Grandas, Evansville	.971	96	190	8	6	1
Grant, Iowa	.979	109	177	6	4	3
Gray, Denver	.909	7	10	0	1	0
Guin, Louisville*	1.000	3	5	2	0	1
Hammond, Omaha	.985	40	62	3	1	1
Hart, Denver	.987	47	70	6	1	1
Hicks, Iowa	.889	11	7	1	1	0
Isales, Indianapolis	.958	106	168	13	8	6
Roy Johnson, Wichita*	.968	44	89	1	3	1
W. Johnson, Wichita	.929	14	26	0	2	0
Jones, Indianapolis	.900	18	25	2	3	0
Kenaga, Evansville	.940	68	107	3	7	0
Kuntz, Denver	.962	13	25	0	1	0
Lancellotti, Wichita*	1.000	4	5	0	0	0
Landrum, Louisville	.974	109	286	8	8	3
Leeper, Omaha*	.961	102	199	0	8	0
Lezcano, Iowa	.987	32	73	3	1	0
Little, Indianapolis*	1.000	18	32	1	0	0
Lyons, Louisville	1.000	5	10	0	0	0
Manuel, Iowa	.983	28	54	5	1	1
Molinaro, Indianapolis	1.000	7	6	1	0	0
Motley, Evansville	.983	130	282	14	5	5
Murphy, Oklahoma City*	1.000	1	3	0	0	0
Parsons, Denver	.970	134	248	12	8	0
Richardt, Oklahoma City	1.000	2	2	0	0	0
Rivera, 2 Oma.-15 Lou.	.933	17	25	3	2	1
Rollin, Evansville	.956	58	130	1	6	0
ROOF, Louisville	.991	111	221	3	2	0
Rooney, Wichita	.965	107	206	13	8	0
Ryal, Omaha*	.964	128	202	11	8	2
Sanchez, Louisville	1.000	1	3	0	0	0
Scott, Wichita	1.000	6	10	1	0	0
Sheridan, Omaha	1.000	20	53	2	0	0
Stegman, Denver	.988	111	231	11	3	2
Stenhouse, Wichita	.964	30	52	1	2	0
Stockstill, Oklahoma City	.970	56	92	4	3	2
Thompson, Iowa*	1.000	6	11	0	0	0
Van Gorder, Indianapolis	1.000	2	7	1	0	0
Van Slyke, Louisville	1.000	3	14	0	0	0
Waller, Denver	.976	51	76	4	2	1
Werner, Oklahoma City	.978	23	43	2	1	0
White, Wichita	1.000	22	45	2	0	1
Williams, Indianapolis*	.956	128	264	16	13	3
Yobs, Denver*	.931	37	50	4	4	0

CATCHERS

Player and Club	Pct.	G.	PO.	A.	E.	DP.	PB.
Benton, Wichita	.984	60	333	39	6	2	2
Butera, Evansville	.967	60	300	26	11	6	5
Castillo, Evansville	.972	13	58	12	2	2	0
Christmas, Indianapolis	.983	17	107	12	2	3	0
Corbett, Indianapolis	.980	19	90	7	2	0	2
Cowger, Oklahoma City	1.000	2	14	1	0	1	0
Dewey, Omaha	.991	24	104	7	1	1	1
Diaz, Iowa	.951	41	220	14	12	0	7
Fahey, Evansville	1.000	8	42	3	0	1	2
Foley, Denver	1.000	28	117	17	0	2	0
Hayes, Iowa	.987	98	537	49	8	8	6
Melvin, Evansville	.994	34	152	15	1	2	2
Nahorodny, Evansville	.982	19	102	10	2	2	2
Nieto, Louisville	.978	113	605	71	15	9	6
Poldberg, Omaha	.986	64	337	28	5	4	3
Ramler, Wichita	1.000	3	14	0	0	0	0
Royster, Evansville	.951	9	53	5	3	0	2
Sanchez, Louisville	.959	25	151	11	7	3	1
Scott, Oklahoma City	.982	100	596	74	12	11	22
Shines, Wichita	1.000	3	9	2	0	1	1
Skinner, Denver	.992	108	550	54	5	5	5
Stephans, Omaha	.981	60	327	42	7	9	3
Tarnow, Denver	1.000	3	2	0	0	0	0
VAN GORDER, Indianapolis	.9959	112	666	67	3	14	7
Werner, Oklahoma City	.986	38	194	10	3	1	1
Werth, Louisville	.857	2	5	1	1	0	0
Wieghaus, Wichita	.9956	80	419	42	2	4	6

PITCHERS

Player and Club	Pct.	G.	PO.	A.	E.	DP.
Abone, Wichita	1.000	9	0	2	0	0
Agosto, Denver*	1.000	19	1	4	0	0
Alvarez, Omaha	.857	4	1	5	1	1
ARROYO, Denver	1.000	23	24	50	0	9
Atkinson, Denver	1.000	12	0	3	0	1
Bargar, Wichita	.889	12	4	4	1	0
Barnes, Denver*	.943	22	7	26	2	3
Baumgarten, Evansville*	.000	7	0	0	1	0
Black, Omaha*	1.000	5	2	9	0	2
Boitano, Oklahoma City	1.000	29	6	14	0	2
Bordi, Iowa	.917	18	6	16	2	0
Botelho, Omaha	.909	25	7	23	3	1
Brito, Louisville	.769	26	2	8	3	0
Brown, Omaha	.800	14	3	1	1	0
Buchanan, Indianapolis*	1.000	30	2	11	0	1
Carlucci, Indianapolis	1.000	43	7	12	0	1
Cary, Evansville*	1.000	15	1	4	0	1
Cato, Indianapolis	.923	18	1	11	1	1
Citarella, Louisville	.913	37	7	14	2	2
Cook, Oklahoma City	1.000	3	3	4	0	1
Cox, Louisville	1.000	2	1	2	0	0
Creel, Omaha	1.000	7	0	10	0	1
Cruz, Oklahoma City	1.000	30	2	4	0	0
D'Acquisto, Denver	1.000	6	1	0	0	0
Dacko, Evansville	.923	24	10	14	2	0
Davis, Oklahoma City	1.000	3	0	2	0	0
Dilks, Wichita*	.917	32	7	15	2	1
Th. Dixon, Wichita	.952	28	11	29	2	0
Tr. Dixon, Evansville	1.000	2	1	0	0	0
Dowless, Indianapolis	.875	17	7	7	2	0
Earley, Iowa*	1.000	46	7	21	0	0
Eaton, Evansville	.955	53	10	11	1	0
Edelen, Indianapolis	1.000	9	2	1	0	0
Fallon, Denver*	.914	24	3	29	3	1
Farr, Oklahoma City	1.000	20	8	15	0	2
Filer, Iowa	.955	27	7	35	2	4
Fossas, Oklahoma City	1.000	10	1	2	0	0
Franco, Indianapolis*	.920	23	7	16	2	2
Fulgham, Louisville	1.000	5	0	2	0	0
Grapenthin, Wichita	1.000	40	3	14	0	2
Griffin, Oklahoma City	.923	35	8	28	3	2
Gumpert, Evansville	1.000	14	3	7	0	0
Hagen, Louisville	.939	21	13	18	2	1
Hargesheimer, Iowa	1.000	49	2	25	0	3
Harris, Indianapolis	.946	28	12	23	2	0
Hayes, Indianapolis	1.000	6	0	1	0	0
Heidenreich, Indianapolis	.833	7	3	7	2	0
Henke, Oklahoma City	.857	47	5	13	3	0
Hesketh, Wichita*	.960	15	8	16	1	1
Hoffman, Denver*	1.000	32	3	7	0	0
Hood, Omaha*	1.000	5	0	6	0	0
Horton, Louisville*	.962	30	5	20	1	4
Hrabosky, Denver*	1.000	26	6	20	0	1
Huismann, Omaha	1.000	17	1	5	0	0
Jackson, Omaha*	.960	23	8	16	1	1
James, Wichita	1.000	22	0	1	0	0
C. Johnson, Denver	.955	36	4	17	1	2
J. Johnson, Louisville	.800	5	2	2	1	0
L. Jones, 11 Iowa-18 Evns.	1.000	29	9	12	0	2
Keener, Louisville	.923	60	6	18	2	2
Keeton, Omaha	.967	19	8	21	1	0
Kelly, Evansville	941	14	5	11	1	2
Kepshire, Louisville	1.000	21	3	7	0	0
Kinnunen, Wichita*	1.000	13	0	2	0	0
Kyles, Iowa	.875	4	0	7	1	1
Lachowicz, Oklahoma City	1.000	17	8	18	0	1
Landrum, Indianapolis	1.000	15	1	1	0	0
Larson, Iowa	.909	27	12	28	4	2
Leibrandt, 11 Ind.-16 Oma.*	.965	27	10	45	2	3
Lesley, Indianapolis	1.000	13	1	3	0	0

PITCHERS—Continued

Player and Club	Pct.	G.	PO.	A.	E.	DP.
Luebber, Evansville	.971	31	14	19	1	1
Martz, Denver	.932	21	12	29	3	1
M. Mason, Oklahoma City*	.957	16	6	16	1	2
R. Mason, Evansville	.923	11	1	11	1	1
Mengwasser, Oklahoma City	.926	26	7	18	2	2
Mercer, Oklahoma City*	1.000	6	1	2	0	2
Miller, Louisville	1.000	32	3	8	0	0
Moskau, Iowa	1.000	11	6	14	0	0
Mura, Denver	.973	19	12	24	1	1
Musselman, Oklahoma City	.846	28	12	10	4	1
Mustad, Wichita	.935	26	6	23	2	3
Nail, Evansville	1.000	25	8	4	0	0
O'Neal, Evansville	1.000	23	5	22	0	1
Ownbey, Louisville	1.000	16	11	10	0	1
Parrott, Omaha	1.000	44	10	19	0	1
Pashnick, Evansville	.947	23	3	15	1	1
Patterson, Iowa	.952	28	12	28	2	1
Perlman, Iowa	.925	31	13	36	4	4
Pimentel, Louisville	1.000	3	1	1	0	0
Pryce, Iowa	.750	16	2	4	2	0
Quintana, Wichita*	.923	21	2	10	1	0
Rajsich, Oklahoma City*	1.000	46	3	11	0	1
Ramos, Wichita	1.000	24	9	9	0	1
Rasmussen, Louisville	1.000	11	5	5	0	0
Ratzer, Denver	.913	37	10	11	2	0
Rhodes, Louisville*	.833	47	1	4	1	0
Riggins, Louisville*	.750	5	0	3	1	0
Rincon, Louisville	1.000	6	4	4	0	0
Robinson, Indianapolis	.800	4	2	2	1	0
Rucker, Evansville*	.636	18	0	7	4	0
Russell, Indianapolis	.905	18	7	12	2	2
Ryder, Indianapolis	1.000	5	2	1	0	0
Sattler, Wichita	.935	41	12	17	2	1
D. Schuler, Omaha*	.952	38	7	13	1	0
M. Schuler, Wichita	1.000	20	4	5	0	1
Schulze, Iowa	.922	25	15	32	4	2
Semall, Oklahoma City	1.000	14	6	14	0	2
Shimp, Wichita	1.000	11	3	7	0	0
Siwy, Denver	.882	21	6	9	2	1
St. Clair, Omaha	.875	43	4	10	2	0
Stein, Iowa	1.000	28	2	9	0	1
Thurberg, Louisville	1.000	10	2	4	0	0
Tobik, Oklahoma City	1.000	12	2	1	0	0
Toliver, Indianapolis	.927	26	12	26	3	2
Tomlin, Wichita*	.941	41	4	12	1	3
Tufts, 50 Oma.-25 Ind.*	.429	30	1	2	4	1
Ujdur, Evansville	.913	18	5	16	2	0
Umbarger, Denver*	1.000	3	0	1	0	0
Underwood, 9 Evns.-11 Ind.*	.926	20	7	18	2	0
Von Ohlen, Louisville*	1.000	12	0	2	0	0
Welsh, Wichita*	.938	11	8	7	1	0
Wilcox, Evansville	1.000	2	1	0	0	0
Wills, Omaha	.955	16	2	19	1	1
Wise, Indianapolis	.889	18	3	5	1	0
Worrell, Louisville	1.000	15	7	9	0	0
Yuhas, Omaha	.933	19	11	17	2	1
Zwolensky, Oklahoma City	1.000	2	0	1	0	0

The following players had no accepted recorded chances at the positions indicated; therefore, are not listed in the fielding averages for those particular positions: Benton, 3b; Bertoni, p; Diaz, of; Ron Johnson, c; Lahti, p; Lozado, of; Martinez, 2b; Pastornicky, ss; Poldberg, 1b; Rohn, ss, of, p; Shaw, p; Stennett, of; Stoll, p; Tenenini, p; Wieghaus, p.

CLUB PITCHING

Club	ERA.	G.	CG.	ShO.	Sv.	IP.	H.	R.	ER.	HR.	HB.	BB.	Int. BB.	SO.	WP.	Bk.
Omaha	4.22	136	32	8	24	1133.1	1128	629	532	106	25	499	26	725	30	22
Louisville	4.27	135	23	9	32	1188.0	1185	653	563	126	36	513	35	708	63	23
Iowa	4.34	136	27	5	28	1191.1	1307	664	575	113	37	475	38	709	58	16
Evansville	4.43	136	23	5	22	1141.1	1242	663	562	91	22	459	24	672	41	6
Oklahoma City	4.47	135	14	2	26	1158.2	1267	672	576	96	30	427	33	773	61	4
Indianapolis	4.60	136	30	5	24	1171.0	1240	685	599	132	14	486	21	806	35	9
Denver	4.81	134	32	6	26	1117.0	1228	673	597	114	18	448	8	623	54	10
Wichita	5.55	136	22	6	32	1146.0	1284	778	707	165	35	550	20	720	43	6

PITCHERS' RECORDS

(Leading Qualifiers for Earned-Run Average Leadership — 109 or More Innings)

*Throws lefthanded.

Pitcher—Club	W.	L.	Pct.	ERA.	G.	GS.	CG.	GF.	ShO.	Sv.	IP.	H.	R.	ER.	HR.	HB.	BB.	Int. BB.	SO.	WP.
Eaton, Evansville	7	6	.538	2.64	53	3	0	43	0	10	109.0	110	39	32	7	1	30	9	64	1
Lachowicz, Oklahoma City	5	3	.625	2.97	17	16	3	1	0	0	115.1	101	48	38	7	3	52	1	96	7
Russell, Indianapolis	5	5	.500	3.55	18	17	5	1	0	1	119.0	106	51	47	7	0	44	3	98	3
Luebber, Evansville	6	8	.429	3.68	31	8	1	12	0	2	127.1	125	62	52	8	3	42	3	108	7
Jackson, Omaha*	7	8	.467	3.97	23	22	5	1	2	0	136.0	126	74	60	14	4	73	2	93	2
Larson, Iowa	13	7	.650	4.05	27	25	5	1	0	0	186.2	203	100	84	21	10	74	1	122	16
Harris, Indianapolis	9	12	.429	4.14	28	21	5	3	0	0	152.1	155	83	70	17	2	66	3	146	6
Arroyo, Denver	14	4	.778	4.15	23	23	6	0	1	0	162.2	188	80	75	15	1	30	0	43	2
Barnes, Denver*	11	6	.647	4.17	22	22	8	0	0	0	131.2	133	73	61	9	5	69	0	62	8
Griffin, Oklahoma City	7	8	.467	4.23	35	15	1	7	0	2	144.2	155	79	68	6	1	43	3	87	7
O'Neal, Evansville	8	10	.444	4.23	23	23	3	0	0	0	140.1	159	80	66	13	1	45	1	70	6

Departmental Leaders: G—Keener, 60; W—Arroyo, 14; L—Botelho, 14; Pct.—Arroyo, .778; GS—Patterson, 28; CG—Dacko, 9; GF—Eaton, 43; ShO—many players, 2; Sv.—Cruz, 14; IP—Larson, 186.2; H—Larson, 203; R—Patterson, 116; ER—Dixon, 103; HR—Dixon, Sattler, 23; HB—Larson, 10; BB—Toliver, 110; IBB—Keener, 15; SO—Harris, 146; WP—Hrabosky, 19.

(All Pitchers—Listed Alphabetically)

Pitcher—Club	W.	L.	Pct.	ERA.	G.	GS.	CG.	GF.	ShO.	Sv.	IP.	H.	R.	ER.	HR.	HB.	BB.	Int. BB.	SO.	WP.
Abone, Wichita	0	0	.000	11.78	9	0	0	3	0	0	18.1	35	27	24	4	2	11	1	7	2
Agosto, Denver*	4	1	.800	2.08	19	0	0	16	0	7	26.0	19	8	6	1	2	10	1	19	1
Alvarez, Omaha	0	2	.000	10.80	4	1	0	0	0	0	8.1	19	16	10	2	1	5	1	1	0
Arroyo, Denver	14	4	.778	4.15	23	23	6	0	1	0	162.2	188	80	75	15	1	30	0	43	2
Atkinson, Denver	0	3	.000	4.05	12	0	0	9	0	1	26.2	21	14	12	9	0	10	0	21	0
Bargar, Wichita	6	2	.750	4.66	12	11	2	0	0	0	73.1	78	41	38	10	1	32	0	53	4
Barnes, Denver*	11	6	.647	4.17	22	22	8	0	0	0	131.2	133	73	61	9	5	69	0	62	8
Baumgarten, Evansville*	0	3	.000	12.10	7	2	0	1	0	0	9.2	21	20	13	0	0	8	0	1	0
Bertoni, Evansville	0	0	.000	0.00	1	0	0	1	0	0	3.0	1	0	0	0	1	0	0	1	0
Black, Omaha*	3	1	.750	3.34	5	5	3	0	0	0	35.0	31	13	13	1	0	13	0	32	0
Boitano, Oklahoma City	5	5	.500	5.83	29	12	1	7	0	2	109.2	122	77	71	16	6	51	2	74	13
Bordi, Iowa	7	2	.778	4.61	18	17	6	1	0	0	111.1	134	62	57	16	1	21	2	80	2
Botelho, Omaha	10	14	.417	5.42	25	25	6	0	1	0	152.2	155	105	92	18	3	73	1	101	1
Brito, Louisville	3	3	.500	5.49	26	6	1	4	0	0	77.0	82	50	47	13	2	45	0	56	6
Brown, Omaha	0	0	.000	8.39	14	0	0	9	0	0	24.2	29	23	23	7	1	13	0	3	1
Buchanan, Indianapolis*	1	6	.143	6.61	30	1	0	11	0	1	49.0	69	42	36	7	1	31	2	22	1
Carlucci, Indianapolis	3	1	.750	3.58	43	0	0	23	0	11	70.1	74	34	28	6	1	21	2	52	2
Cary, Evansville*	1	1	.500	4.41	15	1	0	6	0	1	16.1	21	10	8	2	0	8	1	8	1
Cato, Indianapolis	3	3	.500	3.65	18	6	1	6	0	1	69.0	78	31	28	11	2	21	1	38	0
Citarella, Louisville	7	6	.538	4.76	37	13	3	16	0	7	109.2	122	67	58	13	4	41	4	64	5
Cook, Oklahoma City	0	1	.000	4.50	3	3	0	0	0	0	20.0	16	10	10	3	0	7	0	16	0

Pitcher—Club	W.	L.	Pct.	ERA.	G.	GS.	CG.	GF.	ShO.	Sv.	IP.	H.	R.	ER.	HR.	HB.	BB.	Int. BB.	SO.	WP.
Cox, Louisville	0	0	.000	2.45	2	2	0	0	0	0	11.0	10	3	3	1	1	0	0	8	1
Creel, Omaha	4	2	.667	3.04	7	7	2	0	1	0	53.1	44	18	18	2	1	24	0	41	3
Cruz, Oklahoma City	4	3	.571	2.16	30	0	0	24	0	14	33.1	22	8	8	0	0	9	1	35	6
D'Acquisto, Denver	0	3	.000	9.53	6	3	1	1	0	0	17.0	31	20	18	2	1	10	0	10	2
Dacko, Evansville	6	12	.333	5.29	24	22	9	1	2	0	143.0	167	97	84	13	1	50	3	74	3
Davis, Oklahoma City	1	0	1.000	4.91	3	0	0	2	0	0	7.1	9	4	4	1	0	4	0	3	0
Dilks, Wichita*	4	6	.400	6.27	32	12	2	7	1	2	99.0	110	71	69	14	6	58	2	64	4
Th. Dixon, Wichita	12	9	.571	5.33	28	27	8	0	2	0	174.0	187	114	103	23	7	72	2	105	10
Tr. Dixon, Evansville	0	0	.000	18.00	2	0	0	0	0	0	2.0	8	5	4	0	0	1	0	4	1
Dowless, Indianapolis	2	5	.286	6.78	17	14	2	2	0	0	78.1	89	64	59	17	0	32	1	49	1
Earley, Iowa*	5	6	.455	3.94	46	0	0	17	0	2	80.0	87	39	35	3	3	34	7	56	5
Eaton, Evansville	7	6	.538	2.64	53	3	0	43	0	10	109.0	110	39	32	7	1	30	9	64	1
Edelen, Indianapolis	1	1	.500	6.05	9	0	0	3	0	0	19.1	28	22	13	8	0	5	1	8	1
Fallon, Denver*	10	5	.667	4.29	24	23	2	0	0	0	138.1	119	74	66	6	0	73	0	105	4
Farr, Oklahoma City	4	8	.333	5.81	20	16	3	0	1	0	93.0	123	67	60	7	3	29	1	38	2
Filer, Iowa	5	6	.455	4.17	27	13	1	7	0	1	108.0	128	56	50	8	4	44	5	56	3
Fossas, Oklahoma City*	1	2	.333	7.90	10	5	0	2	0	0	35.1	55	33	31	2	1	12	0	23	2
Franco, Indianapolis*	6	10	.375	4.85	23	18	2	4	0	2	115.0	148	69	62	10	3	42	3	54	2
Fulgham, Louisville	1	2	.333	6.27	5	5	0	0	0	0	18.2	26	18	13	3	0	8	0	11	0
Grapenthin, Wichita	5	5	.500	3.84	40	0	0	23	0	8	70.1	72	35	30	8	2	26	1	33	0
Griffin, Oklahoma City	7	8	.467	4.23	35	15	1	7	0	2	144.2	155	79	68	6	1	43	3	87	7
Gumpert, Evansville	5	1	.833	2.28	14	0	0	10	0	2	27.2	23	8	7	0	0	9	1	17	0
Hagen, Louisville	6	9	.400	4.32	21	20	8	1	2	0	131.1	122	72	63	11	8	46	2	60	7
Hargesheimer, Iowa	7	4	.636	3.45	49	0	0	39	0	11	78.1	78	35	30	4	3	48	9	50	4
Harris, Indianapolis	9	12	.429	4.14	28	21	5	3	0	0	152.1	155	83	70	17	2	66	3	146	6
Hayes, Indianapolis	2	0	1.000	4.70	6	0	0	6	0	0	7.2	4	5	4	2	0	4	0	4	0
Heidenreich, Indianapolis	3	3	.500	4.57	7	7	2	0	1	0	41.1	45	27	21	1	2	16	0	23	3
Henke, Oklahoma City	9	6	.600	3.01	47	0	0	31	0	2	77.2	71	33	26	2	2	33	6	90	1
Hesketh, Wichita*	5	5	.500	5.09	15	15	2	0	2	0	88.1	98	53	50	8	0	46	0	41	1
Hoffman, Denver*	5	3	.625	3.76	32	1	0	22	0	5	52.2	49	23	22	1	0	23	3	50	2
Hood, Omaha*	0	1	.000	3.86	5	0	0	3	0	3	9.1	7	7	4	2	1	2	0	5	0
Horton, Louisville*	10	6	.625	4.82	30	24	3	1	1	0	157.0	177	99	84	20	2	58	0	92	8
Hrabosky, Denver*	7	6	.538	5.82	26	15	5	6	1	1	116.0	135	78	75	14	2	64	0	54	19
Huismann, Omaha	0	2	.000	1.85	17	0	0	17	0	8	24.1	16	7	5	2	1	9	2	25	1
Jackson, Omaha*	7	8	.467	3.97	23	22	5	1	2	0	136.0	126	74	60	14	4	73	2	93	2
James, Wichita	4	2	.667	4.65	22	2	0	14	0	3	31.0	27	17	16	3	1	25	1	40	2
C. Johnson, Denver	5	2	.714	4.81	36	0	0	17	0	6	82.1	100	55	44	14	0	24	0	39	1
J. Johnson, Louisville	2	2	.500	2.15	5	4	1	1	1	1	29.1	24	13	7	3	0	8	0	18	1
Jones, 11 Iowa-18 Evns	5	2	.714	4.19	29	4	1	9	1	1	92.1	101	50	43	9	2	30	1	59	3
Keener, Louisville	11	5	.688	3.92	60	0	0	42	0	12	96.1	84	43	42	5	4	70	15	69	5
Keeton, Omaha	6	3	.667	4.09	19	10	1	2	0	1	88.0	93	45	40	8	2	43	4	42	2
Kelly, Evansville	2	4	.333	6.16	14	11	0	2	0	0	57.0	64	50	39	4	3	60	1	41	7
Kepshire, Louisville	6	2	.750	3.67	21	10	1	5	1	0	83.1	88	44	34	10	0	24	1	52	6
Kinnunen, Wichita*	0	1	.000	7.97	13	0	0	7	0	0	20.1	24	20	18	3	1	13	0	9	1
Kyles, Iowa	2	1	.667	3.24	4	4	1	0	0	0	25.0	16	9	9	0	2	10	0	9	4
Lachowicz, Oklahoma City	5	3	.625	2.97	17	16	3	1	0	0	115.1	101	48	38	7	3	52	1	96	7
Lahti, Louisville	0	0	.000	4.50	1	1	0	0	0	0	2.0	2	1	1	0	0	0	0	0	0
Landrum, Indianapolis	1	3	.250	3.06	15	0	0	12	0	2	17.2	20	6	6	2	0	6	1	21	1
Larson, Iowa	13	7	.650	4.05	27	25	5	1	0	0	186.2	203	100	84	21	10	74	1	122	16
Leibrandt, 11 Ind.-16 Oma.*	9	10	.474	4.27	27	27	6	0	1	0	185.1	181	113	88	11	1	77	2	128	3
Lesley, Indianapolis	3	1	.750	2.55	13	0	0	10	0	3	17.2	11	5	5	2	0	5	0	19	0
Luebber, Evansville	6	8	.429	3.68	31	8	1	12	0	2	127.1	125	62	52	8	3	42	3	108	7
Martz, Denver	8	7	.533	5.12	21	21	5	0	1	0	128.1	158	79	73	15	2	44	0	60	7
M. Mason, Oklahoma City*	5	5	.500	4.16	16	16	1	0	0	0	88.2	100	50	41	7	1	26	1	50	4
R. Mason, Evansville	5	5	.500	4.23	11	11	2	0	0	0	78.2	84	39	37	6	0	21	0	43	4
Mengwasser, Oklahoma City	4	10	.286	4.68	26	16	2	7	0	0	117.1	138	72	61	11	3	43	7	77	4
Mercer, Oklahoma City*	0	0	.000	6.43	6	1	0	4	0	0	7.0	13	5	5	1	1	5	2	2	0
Miller, Louisville	5	3	.625	3.56	32	1	0	19	0	6	73.1	70	34	29	6	3	26	3	30	1
Moskau, Iowa	2	2	.500	5.93	11	11	0	0	0	0	54.2	57	36	36	8	0	27	0	26	3
Mura, Denver	3	11	.214	4.82	19	19	4	0	0	0	121.1	121	73	65	14	1	49	0	85	6
Musselman, Oklahoma City	9	12	.429	5.49	28	21	2	4	0	0	137.2	166	99	84	20	5	50	3	85	4
Mustad, Wichita	6	10	.375	4.53	26	23	3	1	0	0	139.0	148	84	70	9	2	76	4	86	5
Nail, Evansville	8	10	.444	4.90	25	23	3	0	0	0	145.0	167	85	79	16	4	54	0	79	5
O'Neal, Evansville	8	10	.444	4.23	23	23	3	0	0	0	140.1	159	80	66	13	1	45	1	70	6
Ownbey, Louisville	7	5	.583	3.63	16	15	3	0	1	0	104.0	100	47	42	7	5	51	2	77	3
Parrott, Omaha	7	7	.500	3.08	44	7	1	23	1	6	99.1	97	40	34	7	3	40	5	72	4
Pashnick, Evansville	4	1	.800	2.84	23	3	1	17	0	5	50.2	42	19	16	3	3	16	0	36	0
Patterson, Iowa	10	10	.500	5.23	28	28	4	0	2	0	172.0	201	116	100	18	6	84	3	114	12
Perlman, Iowa	4	11	.267	4.51	31	13	3	9	0	3	115.2	138	78	58	8	2	29	1	34	1
Pimentel, Louisville	1	2	.333	6.14	3	0	0	2	0	0	7.1	5	5	5	1	0	6	0	3	0
Pryce, Iowa	1	2	.333	2.35	16	0	0	14	0	6	23.0	23	8	6	0	1	5	2	14	0
Quintana, Wichita*	2	2	.500	4.00	21	1	0	4	0	1	36.0	40	18	16	4	2	19	1	26	0
Rajsich, Oklahoma City*	5	1	.833	2.32	46	0	0	25	0	6	66.0	63	25	17	0	2	26	4	42	6
Ramos, Wichita	4	6	.400	6.09	24	15	1	5	0	0	88.2	121	71	60	22	0	23	1	48	0
Rasmussen, Louisville	8	1	.889	2.28	11	11	1	0	1	0	71.0	60	21	18	6	2	18	1	46	1
Ratzer, Denver	3	6	.333	6.75	37	2	1	22	0	1	61.1	90	52	46	8	1	16	3	36	2
Rhodes, Louisville*	4	4	.500	3.56	47	0	0	8	0	1	48.0	50	25	19	7	0	12	1	19	3
Riggins, Louisville*	0	0	.000	4.85	5	1	0	1	0	0	13.0	15	10	7	0	0	10	2	5	2
Rincon, Louisville	1	2	.333	4.65	6	5	1	0	0	0	31.0	26	18	16	5	1	17	1	14	1
Robinson, Indianapolis	4	0	1.000	3.23	4	4	2	0	0	0	30.2	22	13	11	3	0	7	0	20	0
Rohn, Iowa	0	0	.000	13.50	1	0	0	1	0	0	3.1	11	8	5	2	0	3	0	1	0
Rucker, Evansville*	2	4	.333	3.34	18	2	0	13	0	2	29.2	25	12	11	1	0	21	3	30	0
Russell, Indianapolis	5	5	.500	3.55	18	17	5	1	0	1	119.0	106	51	47	7	0	44	3	98	3
Ryder, Indianapolis	0	0	.000	10.29	5	0	0	1	0	0	7.0	10	11	8	1	0	7	0	4	2
Sattler, Wichita	5	10	.333	5.93	41	12	3	16	1	8	120.0	131	86	79	23	7	44	2	91	6
D. Schuler, Omaha*	6	7	.462	3.26	38	9	4	18	1	5	107.2	99	45	39	9	4	32	5	59	0
M. Schuler, Wichita	1	1	.500	7.81	20	0	0	7	0	2	27.2	34	25	24	7	2	22	0	18	0
Schulze, Iowa	11	9	.550	4.27	25	25	7	0	2	0	168.2	170	88	80	16	3	63	0	103	4
Semall, Oklahoma City	4	5	.444	4.79	14	14	1	0	0	0	82.2	98	54	44	12	2	27	1	39	4
Shimp, Wichita	4	4	.500	7.83	11	9	0	1	0	0	46.0	56	42	40	14	1	31	1	25	0
Siwy, Denver	3	3	.500	6.14	21	5	0	8	0	5	51.1	60	41	35	4	3	25	1	36	0
St. Clair, Omaha	4	1	.800	3.81	43	0	0	27	0	1	85.0	88	45	36	8	3	38	2	44	5
Stein, Iowa	2	4	.333	3.16	28	0	0	17	0	4	37.0	33	15	13	5	1	19	7	24	2

Pitcher—Club	W.	L.	Pct.	ERA.	G.	GS.	CG.	GF.	ShO.	Sv.	IP.	H.	R.	ER.	HR.	HB.	BB.	Int. BB.	SO.	WP.
Stoll, Wichita	0	1	.000	15.00	2	1	0	0	0	0	3.0	5	6	5	1	0	4	0	3	0
Tenenini, Wichita	0	0	.000	0.00	2	0	0	2	0	1	1.0	1	0	0	0	0	1	0	0	0
Thurberg, Louisville	1	3	.250	7.58	10	3	0	4	0	0	29.2	30	26	25	6	2	26	1	25	4
Tobik, Oklahoma City	3	0	1.000	3.54	12	0	0	6	0	0	20.1	13	8	8	1	0	10	1	14	1
Toliver, Indianapolis	8	10	.444	4.54	26	26	6	0	1	0	166.2	151	93	84	7	2	110	0	112	6
Tomlin, Wichita*	4	1	.800	3.61	41	0	0	22	0	6	52.1	44	21	21	5	0	18	3	44	2
Tufts, 5 Oma.-25 Ind.*	2	3	.400	5.98	30	0	0	19	0	2	40.2	52	29	27	6	0	12	1	24	1
Ujdur, Evansville	3	7	.300	6.24	18	18	3	0	0	0	106.2	122	87	74	12	3	59	1	46	1
Umbarger, Denver*	0	1	.000	20.25	3	0	0	1	0	0	1.1	4	3	3	2	0	1	0	3	0
Underwood, 9 Evns.-11 Ind.*	7	4	.636	4.09	20	14	3	1	1	0	94.2	96	48	43	10	0	27	1	51	6
Von Ohlen, Louisville*	1	0	1.000	4.70	12	0	0	8	0	5	15.1	16	8	8	1	0	5	1	13	1
Welsh, Wichita*	3	6	.333	6.99	11	8	1	1	0	1	56.2	72	47	44	7	1	29	1	27	6
Wieghaus, Wichita	0	0	.000	0.00	1	0	0	1	0	0	1.0	1	0	0	0	0	0	0	0	0
Wilcox, Evansville	0	1	.000	3.38	2	2	0	0	0	0	8.0	8	5	3	0	1	6	0	5	1
Wills, Omaha	4	11	.267	4.74	16	16	4	0	1	0	95.0	96	56	50	8	1	45	2	65	6
Wise, Indianapolis	2	2	.500	8.25	18	0	0	9	0	1	24.0	39	22	22	12	0	10	2	16	3
Worrell, Louisville	4	2	.667	4.74	15	14	1	0	0	0	79.2	76	49	42	8	2	42	1	46	8
Yuhas, Omaha	7	7	.500	4.65	19	18	2	0	0	0	102.2	112	61	53	11	0	45	1	65	2
Zwolensky, Oklahoma City	0	0	.000	0.00	2	0	0	1	0	0	2.2	2	0	0	0	0	0	0	2	0

BALKS—Horton, 7; Ownbey, 5; Hargesheimer, Worrell, 4 each; Leibrandt, Parrott, St. Clair, Wills, Yuhas, 3 each; Arroyo, Barnes, Botelho, Earley, Fallon, Hesketh, Keeton, Moskau, Nail, Schulze, Toliver, 2 each; Black, Bordi, Buchanan, Citarella, Cox, Creel, Dixon, Dowless, Franco, Heidenreich, Hoffman, Hrabosky, James, J. Johnson, Jones, Keener, Kelly, Kepshire, Kyles, Lachowicz, Larson, Martz, Mason, Mengwasser, Musselman, Pashnick, Patterson, Perlman, Rhodes, Russell, Sattler, Siwy, Thurberg, Welsh, Zwolensky, 1 each.

COMBINATION SHUTOUTS—Martz-Hoffman, Barnes-Ratzer, Fallon-Hoffman, Denver; Underwood-Gumpert, O'Neal-Eaton, Evansville; Franco-Carlucci, Indianapolis; Patterson-Earley-Price, Iowa; Citarella-Keener, Kepshire-Keener, Louisville; Mengwasser-Rajsich, Oklahoma City; Keeton-Huismann, Omaha.

NO-HIT GAME—None.

International League

CLASS AAA

Leading Batter
JOHN PERCONTE
Charleston

League President
HAROLD COOPER

Leading Pitcher
THOMAS BRENNAN
Charleston

CHAMPIONSHIP WINNERS IN PREVIOUS YEARS

Year	Team	Pct.
1884	Trenton	.520
1885	Syracuse	.584
1886	Utica	.646
1887	Toronto	.644
1888	Syracuse	.723
1889	Detroit	.649
1890	Detroit	.617
1891	Buffalo (reg. season)	.727
	Buffalo (supplem'l)	.680
1892	Providence	.615
	Binghamton*	.667
1893	Erie	.606
1894	Providence	.696
1895	Springfield	.687
1896	Providence	.602
1897	Syracuse	.632
1898	Montreal	.586
1899	Rochester	.624
1900	Providence	.616
1901	Rochester	.642
1902	Toronto	.669
1903	Jersey City	.642
1904	Buffalo	.657
1905	Providence	.638
1906	Buffalo	.607
1907	Toronto	.619
1908	Baltimore	.593
1909	Rochester	.596
1910	Rochester	.601
1911	Rochester	.645
1912	Toronto	.595
1913	Newark	.625
1914	Providence	.617
1915	Buffalo	.632
1916	Buffalo	.586
1917	Toronto	.604
1918	Toronto	.693
1919	Baltimore	.671
1920	Baltimore	.719
1921	Baltimore	.717
1922	Baltimore	.689
1923	Baltimore	.677
1924	Baltimore	.709
1925	Baltimore	.633
1926	Toronto	.657
1927	Buffalo	.667
1928	Rochester	.549
1929	Rochester	.613
1930	Rochester	.629
1931	Rochester	.601
1932	Newark	.649
1933	Newark	.622
	Buffalo (4th)†	.494
1934	Newark	.608
	Toronto (3rd)†	.559
1935	Montreal	.597
	Syracuse (2nd)†	.565
1936	Buffalo‡	.610
1937	Newark‡	.717
1938	Newark‡	.684
1939	Jersey City	.582
	Rochester (2nd)†	.556
1940	Rochester	.611
	Newark (2nd)†	.594
1941	Newark	.649
	Montreal (2nd)†	.584
1942	Newark	.601
	Syracuse (3rd)†	.513
1943	Toronto	.625
	Syracuse (3rd)†	.536
1944	Baltimore‡	.553
1945	Montreal	.621
	Newark (2nd)†	.582
1946	Montreal‡	.649
1947	Jersey City	.610
	Syracuse (3rd)†	.575
1948	Montreal‡	.614
1949	Buffalo	.584
	Montreal (3rd)†	.545
1950	Rochester	.609
	Baltimore (3rd)†	.556
1951	Montreal‡	.617
1952	Montreal	.629
	Rochester (3rd)†	.619
1953	Rochester	.630
	Montreal (2nd)†	.586
1954	Toronto	.630
	Syracuse (4th)§	.510
1955	Montreal	.617
	Rochester (4th)†	.497
1956	Toronto	.566
	Rochester (2nd)†	.553
1957	Toronto	.575
	Buffalo (2nd)†	.571
1958	Montreal‡	.588
1959	Buffalo	.582
	Havana (3rd)†	.523
1960	Toronto‡	.649
1961	Columbus	.597
	Buffalo (3rd)†	.559
1962	Jacksonville	.610
	Atlanta (3rd)†	.539
1963	Syracuse x	.533
	Indianapolis‡	.562
1964	Jacksonville	.589
	Rochester (4th)†	.532
1965	Columbus	.582
	Toronto (3rd)†	.556
1966	Rochester	.565
	Toronto (2nd-tied)†	.558
1967	Richmond	.574
	Toledo (3rd)†	.525
1968	Toledo	.565
	Jacksonville (4th)†	.514
1969	Tidewater	.563
	Syracuse (3rd)†	.536
1970	Syracuse‡	.600
1971	Rochester‡	.614
1972	Louisville	.563
	Tidewater (3rd)†	.545
1973	Charleston	.586
	Pawtucket y†	.534
1974	Memphis	.613
	Rochester x‡	.611
1975	Tidewater‡	.610
1976	Rochester	.638
	Syracuse (2nd)†	.590
1977	Pawtucket	.571
	Charleston (2nd)‡	.557
1978	Charleston	.607
	Richmond (4th)†	.511
1979	Columbus‡	.612
1980	Columbus‡	.593
1981	Columbus‡	.633
1982	Tidewater (3rd)†	.540
	Rochester	.514

*Won split-season playoff. †Won four-team playoff. ‡Won championship and four-team playoff. §Defeated Havana in game to decide fourth place, then won four-team playoff. xLeague was divided into Northern, Southern divisions. yLeague divided into American, National divisions. (NOTE—Known as Eastern League in 1884, New York State League in 1885, International League in 1886-87, International Association in 1888, International League in 1889-90, Eastern Association in 1891, and Eastern League from 1892 until 1912.)

STANDING OF CLUBS AT CLOSE OF SEASON, SEPTEMBER 2

Club	Col.	Rich.	Char.	Tide.	Tol.	Roch.	Syr.	Paw.	W.	L.	T.	Pct.	G.B.
Columbus (Yankees)	....	8	9	11	15	14	10	16	83	57	0	.593	....
Richmond (Braves)	12	....	13	13	12	8	10	12	80	59	0	.576	2½
Charleston (Indians)	11	7	....	13	13	11	10	9	74	66	0	.529	9
Tidewater (Mets)	9	7	7	....	13	10	13	12	71	68	0	.511	11½
Toledo (Twins)	5	8	7	7	....	12	15	14	68	72	0	.486	15
Rochester (Orioles)	6	12	9	10	8	....	11	9	65	75	0	.464	18
Syracuse (Blue Jays)	10	9	10	7	5	9	....	11	61	78	0	.439	21½
Pawtucket (Red Sox)	4	8	11	7	6	11	9	....	56	83	0	.403	26½

Major League affiliations in parentheses.

Tidewater club represented Norfolk and Portsmouth, Va.

Playoffs—Richmond defeated Charleston, three games to none; Tidewater defeated Columbus, three games to two; Tidewater defeated Richmond, three games to one, to win Governors Cup; and Tidewater won AAA World Series in a round-robin playoff against Denver (American Association) and Portland (Pacific Coast).

Regular-Season Attendance—Charleston, 103,977; Columbus, 367,480; Pawtucket, 188,186; Richmond, 293,328; Rochester, 284,046; Syracuse, 166,030; Tidewater, 147,584; Toledo, 164,269; Total, 1,714,920; All-Star Game, 11,032.

Managers—Charleston, Doc Edwards; Columbus, Johnny Oates; Pawtucket, Tony Torchia; Richmond, Eddie Haas; Rochester, Lance Nichols; Syracuse, Jim Beauchamp; Tidewater, Davey Johnson; Toledo, Cal Ermer.

All-Star Team—1B—Gerald Perry, Richmond; 2B—Tim Teufel, Toledo; 3B—Brook Jacoby, Richmond; SS—Tony Fernandez, Syracuse; OF—Brian Dayett, Columbus; Brad Komminsk, Richmond; Otis Nixon, Columbus; C—Gene Petralli, Syracuse; DH—Karl Pagel, Charleston; Starting Pitcher—Walt Terrell, Tidewater; Relief Pitcher—Don Cooper, Syracuse; Manager-of-the-Year—Doc Edwards, Charleston.

(Compiled by Howe News Bureau, Boston, Mass.)

CLUB BATTING

Club	Pct.	G.	AB.	R.	OR.	H.	TB.	2B.	3B.	HR.	RBI.	GW.	SH.	SF.	HP.	BB.	Int. BB.	SO.	SB.	CS.	LOB.
Charleston	.281	140	4614	753	756	1296	1837	182	31	99	684	58	58	46	34	682	39	728	119	80	1088
Richmond	.281	139	4578	809	694	1285	1988	210	50	131	745	73	25	43	30	599	25	705	151	73	962
Columbus	.277	140	4754	898	788	1317	2165	210	46	182	826	74	39	62	37	741	24	914	137	59	1081
Toledo	.276	140	4504	722	722	1244	1893	193	33	130	657	59	44	46	34	641	22	711	119	61	994
Tidewater	.273	139	4544	694	635	1239	1816	199	36	102	633	63	26	39	27	576	29	795	175	77	1014
Rochester	.261	140	4485	666	696	1170	1826	203	48	119	604	59	48	38	26	623	27	892	97	62	1014
Syracuse	.259	139	4514	578	684	1170	1758	196	43	102	526	52	44	29	21	464	22	785	107	61	965
Pawtucket	.254	139	4487	653	798	1141	1710	178	23	115	603	49	30	46	21	569	28	793	148	72	934

INDIVIDUAL BATTING

(Leading Qualifiers for Batting Championship—378 or More Plate Appearances)

*Bats lefthanded. †Switch-hitter.

Player and Club	Pct.	G.	AB.	R.	H.	TB.	2B.	3B.	HR.	RBI.	GW.	SH.	SF.	HP.	BB.	Int. BB.	SO.	SB.	CS.
Perconte, John, Charleston*	.346	94	341	76	118	151	17	2	4	45	4	4	2	2	83	4	34	13	6
Meier, David, Toledo	.336	126	426	63	143	200	21	6	8	68	5	2	6	1	55	2	54	1	2
Komminsk, Brad, Richmond	.334	117	413	94	138	246	24	6	24	103	14	2	8	0	78	3	70	26	5
Wilson, Michael, Toledo	.325	109	416	71	135	170	20	3	3	33	1	6	0	2	55	3	36	53	26
Pagel, Karl, Charleston*	.325	124	381	78	124	202	12	3	20	82	8	1	1	2	109	9	96	5	3
Teufel, Timothy, Toledo	.323	136	471	103	152	272	27	6	27	100	10	4	9	1	102	2	71	13	4
Backman, Walter, Tidewater†	.316	101	361	69	114	134	11	3	1	28	0	0	2	0	68	2	47	37	15
Jacoby, Brook, Richmond	.315	133	489	88	154	265	32	2	25	100	7	0	3	3	56	4	102	1	4
Perry, Gerald, Richmond*	.314	113	423	81	133	209	21	8	13	71	8	3	5	2	73	2	55	26	13
Rhomberg, Kevin, Charleston	.311	133	508	102	158	192	17	7	1	60	4	6	4	4	87	0	55	27	21
Gulliver, Glenn, Rochester*	.309	123	411	86	127	194	28	3	11	63	8	3	4	5	117	5	37	7	7

Departmental Leaders: G—D. Baker, 140; AB—Nixon, 557; R—Nixon, 129; H—Nixon, 162; TB—Dayett, 181; 2B—Hurdle, 33; 3B—Hall, 11; HR—Dayett, 35; RBI—Dayett, 108; GWRBI—Hurdle, Komminsk, 14; SH—DeLeon, 15; SF—Burgess, 12; HP—Lisi, Rajsich, 9; BB—Gulliver, 117; IBB—Hurdle, 12; SO—Reynolds, 123; SB—Nixon, 94; CS—Nixon, 29.

Player and Club	Pct.	G.	AB.	R.	H.	TB.	2B.	3B.	HR.	RBI.	GW.	SH.	SF.	HP.	BB.	Int. BB.	SO.	SB.	CS.
Aponte, Edwin, Charleston	.320	52	175	20	56	71	12	0	1	33	4	4	4	2	14	0	13	3	2
Ashford, Thomas, Tidewater	.327	12	49	8	16	22	3	0	1	8	2	0	1	1	2	0	5	0	1
Austin, Richard, Toledo	.144	58	146	12	21	30	1	1	2	13	2	2	2	2	14	0	32	1	1
Backman, Walter, Tidewater†	.316	101	361	69	114	134	11	3	1	28	0	0	2	0	68	2	47	37	15
Baker, David, Toledo*	.278	140	518	71	144	210	22	1	14	88	13	2	7	6	57	4	98	5	1
Balboni, Stephen, Columbus	.274	84	317	72	87	182	14	0	27	81	10	0	7	6	48	2	91	1	1
Barranca, German, Rochester	.230	62	217	34	50	86	5	2	9	27	3	2	3	1	36	1	47	18	8
Barrett, Martin, Pawtucket	.345	36	119	24	41	52	4	2	1	18	1	2	1	0	38	2	8	5	2
Barrios, Jose, Rochester	.265	55	185	30	49	93	10	2	10	30	5	0	1	0	30	0	49	0	0
Bell, Jorge, Syracuse	.271	85	317	37	86	150	11	4	15	59	4	1	5	1	23	0	54	5	3
Bishop, Michael, Tidewater	.203	27	74	6	15	24	6	0	1	11	1	0	1	1	15	0	16	1	1
Blocker, Terry, Tidewater*	.305	72	239	26	73	90	7	2	2	32	6	4	0	0	10	1	41	24	6
Bonaparte, Elijah, Rochester*	.273	114	403	53	110	149	13	7	4	48	4	7	4	0	47	1	56	17	15
Bonner, Robert, Rochester	.222	61	198	36	44	57	6	2	1	15	4	6	0	4	8	0	21	7	1
Brant, Marshall, Columbus	.193	37	119	21	23	48	2	1	7	19	0	0	0	3	10	0	38	0	0
Brown, Darrell, Toledo	.217	5	23	8	5	6	1	0	0	5	1	0	1	0	1	0	3	6	0
Burgess, Gus, Pawtucket*	.269	130	449	62	121	168	11	6	8	66	6	2	12	1	49	5	73	21	9
Bustabad, Juan, Pawtucket*	.214	71	215	26	46	61	8	2	1	24	0	3	1	0	20	0	30	3	5
Calise, Michael, Rochester	.254	60	181	31	46	93	6	1	13	34	6	0	2	0	39	2	64	0	0
Campaneris, Dagoberto, Columbus	.333	13	45	7	15	22	2	1	1	7	1	1	0	1	5	0	5	3	0
Castillo, M. Carmelo, Charleston	.270	36	148	29	40	61	5	2	4	22	3	3	1	0	9	0	25	4	1
Chapman, Kelvin, Tidewater	.274	72	223	41	61	87	8	3	4	28	4	0	2	3	36	0	35	14	2
Christensen, John, Tidewater	.263	20	80	12	21	27	0	0	2	15	0	1	1	0	5	0	9	0	0
Craig, Rodney, Charleston†	.266	121	413	86	110	163	20	0	11	56	1	4	4	6	75	5	70	27	19
Culmer, Wilfred, Charleston	.245	87	286	39	70	109	14	2	7	29	5	3	3	3	26	2	65	8	6
David, Andre, Toledo*	.290	116	403	59	117	152	15	1	6	54	3	6	6	4	50	1	35	5	7
Davis, Michael, Pawtucket	.228	77	246	24	56	80	9	0	5	35	2	1	6	0	21	0	34	2	2
Dayett, Brian, Columbus	.288	128	479	105	138	281	28	5	35	108	9	0	8	7	76	4	101	1	2
DeLeon, Luis, Charleston†	.231	129	464	50	107	122	9	3	0	27	2	15	4	2	20	0	70	6	4
Dempsey, Patrick, Rochester	.000	1	3	0	0	0	0	0	0	0	0	0	0	0	0	0	0	0	0
Dilone, Miguel, Charleston†	.340	34	141	39	48	54	4	1	0	14	1	2	0	0	20	0	11	18	5
Dye, Scott, Tidewater	.000	27	1	0	0	0	0	0	0	0	0	0	0	0	0	0	1	0	0
Espino, Juan, Columbus	.280	77	211	35	59	101	10	1	10	42	2	2	1	5	41	2	34	0	1

Player and Club	Pct.	G.	AB.	R.	H.	TB.	2B.	3B.	HR.	RBI.	GW.	SH.	SF.	HP.	BB.	Int. BB.	SO.	SB.	CS.
Evans, Barry, Columbus	.266	62	218	41	58	87	9	1	6	39	3	1	7	1	41	0	27	0	2
Falcone, David, Rochester*	.250	2	8	1	2	3	1	0	0	2	0	0	0	0	1	0	3	0	0
Fernandez, O. Antonio, Syracuse†	.300	117	437	65	131	176	18	6	5	38	4	2	1	1	57	3	27	35	16
Fitzgerald, Michael, Tidewater	.284	111	370	64	105	166	17	1	14	65	8	3	3	3	73	3	57	2	3
Flores, Gilberto, Tidewater	.312	88	317	57	99	118	11	1	2	34	1	0	5	3	29	0	33	17	9
Gaff, Brent, Tidewater	.000	37	1	0	0	0	0	0	0	0	0	0	0	0	0	0	1	0	0
Gagne, Gregory, Toledo	.255	119	392	61	100	181	22	4	17	66	5	6	3	3	36	0	70	6	3
Gardenhire, Ronald, Tidewater	.287	102	387	63	111	155	20	6	4	39	3	5	2	2	34	0	54	9	7
Gentile, Gene, Pawtucket*	.227	104	331	46	75	108	10	1	7	37	2	0	5	0	39	2	89	3	4
Graham, Lee, Pawtucket*	.276	136	507	78	140	202	23	3	11	59	7	5	4	2	54	2	46	51	14
Gulden, Bradley, Columbus*	.316	94	275	45	87	132	16	1	9	47	6	0	3	2	35	1	39	0	2
Gulliver, Glenn, Rochester*	.309	123	411	86	127	194	28	3	11	63	8	3	4	5	117	5	37	7	7
Gutierrez, Joaquin, Pawtucket	.266	66	233	30	62	78	11	1	1	17	0	2	1	0	28	0	39	5	4
Hall, Albert, Richmond†	.294	130	521	120	153	206	28	11	1	42	2	3	3	5	66	0	52	46	16
Hart, Michael L., Toledo*	.290	137	487	95	141	224	18	7	17	66	4	8	4	2	96	2	78	13	5
Hazewood, Drungo, Rochester	.224	47	125	18	28	46	7	1	3	18	1	0	0	1	32	0	42	6	4
Hernańdez, Leonardo, Rochester	.343	57	201	24	69	110	13	2	8	25	3	0	1	1	8	0	22	0	3
Hernandez, Tobias, Syracuse	.266	66	203	19	54	72	13	1	1	14	1	5	0	2	9	0	42	1	0
Hobson, Clell, Columbus	.245	112	379	68	93	175	17	4	19	63	7	4	8	1	56	4	76	2	2
Howard, Michael, Tidewater†	.194	65	216	26	42	66	10	1	4	30	3	0	2	2	29	0	47	12	4
Hudler, Rex, Columbus	.305	40	118	17	36	44	5	0	1	11	0	2	0	1	6	0	25	1	0
Hundhammer, Paul, Pawtucket	.223	115	390	65	87	133	15	2	9	45	5	6	2	3	53	1	87	18	10
Huppert, David, Rochester	.194	68	155	21	30	41	7	2	0	11	0	12	4	0	28	0	46	0	1
Hurdle, Clinton, Tidewater*	.285	139	477	82	136	243	33	4	22	105	14	0	6	1	105	12	109	0	2
Jacoby, Brook, Richmond	.315	133	489	88	154	265	32	2	25	100	7	0	3	3	56	4	102	1	4
Jimenez, Alfonso, Toledo	.250	22	64	13	16	28	3	0	3	6	0	0	0	0	12	0	14	2	2
Johnson, Anthony, Syracuse	.293	98	328	46	96	128	18	1	4	24	2	3	2	1	28	3	70	11	4
Johnson, Randall, Toledo*	.237	96	279	45	66	112	12	2	10	39	2	2	2	2	48	1	57	0	0
Johnston, Christopher, Syracuse	.213	56	202	25	43	88	10	1	11	36	3	3	1	1	16	0	45	0	1
Jones, Ricky, Rochester	.230	95	339	28	78	117	16	1	7	38	1	5	5	0	18	0	61	4	3
Klutts, Gene, Syracuse	.375	12	32	3	12	14	2	0	0	6	0	0	0	0	1	0	7	0	0
Komminsk, Brad, Richmond	.334	117	413	94	138	246	24	6	24	103	14	2	8	0	78	3	70	26	5
Koza, David, Pawtucket	.266	94	316	46	84	139	11	1	14	44	7	0	0	5	28	1	60	0	0
LaFrancois, Roger, Pawtucket*	.226	75	235	25	53	86	10	1	7	39	5	0	1	0	10	4	36	2	0
Leach, Terry, Tidewater	.000	37	1	0	0	0	0	0	0	0	0	0	0	0	0	0	0	0	0
Lickert, John, Pawtucket	.263	69	213	28	56	81	13	0	4	30	2	4	3	1	23	1	29	0	0
Linares, Rufino, Richmond	.224	29	107	10	24	37	6	2	1	24	5	0	3	0	3	0	12	1	0
Lindsey, William, Columbus	.000	1	4	1	0	0	0	0	0	0	0	0	0	0	0	0	0	0	0
Lisi, Riccardo, Rochester	.252	126	476	81	120	169	20	10	3	37	3	5	0	9	63	1	87	15	9
Logan, H. Daniel, Rochester*	.269	110	353	41	95	143	11	2	11	56	6	2	2	1	36	5	75	1	1
LoGrande, Angelo, Charleston	.249	124	473	55	118	175	20	2	11	73	4	2	7	1	20	4	75	2	1
MacWhorter, Keith, Pawtucket	.000	49	4	0	0	0	0	0	0	0	0	0	0	0	0	0	4	0	0
Manrique, Fred, Syracuse	.268	128	485	55	130	198	22	8	10	50	8	8	4	2	22	0	75	3	8
Mattingly, Donald, Columbus*	.340	43	159	35	54	95	11	3	8	37	6	3	2	0	29	2	14	2	1
McCain, Michael, Toledo*	.244	33	86	8	21	25	2	1	0	10	1	0	0	0	13	0	17	0	0
McMullen, Ricky, Tidewater	.224	28	98	6	22	26	2	1	0	7	0	1	1	0	7	0	7	5	0
Meacham, Robert, Columbus†	.262	120	423	58	111	162	18	3	9	60	3	7	4	1	35	1	74	13	5
Meier, David, Toledo	.336	126	426	63	143	200	21	6	8	68	5	2	6	1	55	2	54	1	2
Moloney, William, Pawtucket*	.000	46	3	0	0	0	0	0	0	0	0	2	0	0	0	0	0	0	0
Moore, Kelvin, Tidewater	.208	30	101	11	21	32	3	1	2	14	3	0	2	0	6	0	39	1	1
Nandin, Robert, Syracuse†	.267	105	341	42	91	106	8	2	1	29	3	2	2	0	36	2	23	15	8
Nixon, Otis, Columbus	.291	138	557	129	162	185	11	6	0	41	1	12	5	1	96	1	83	94	29
Norrid, Timothy, Charleston*	.259	121	425	54	110	160	15	4	9	84	6	4	9	4	75	5	49	3	4
Office, Rowland, Columbus*	.297	87	212	37	63	109	14	4	8	45	4	2	1	0	24	3	30	1	2
Oquendo, Jose, Tidewater†	.118	13	34	3	4	4	0	0	0	3	0	1	2	0	5	0	6	2	0
Owen, Lawrence, Richmond	.417	5	12	4	5	10	0	1	1	2	0	0	0	0	2	0	2	0	0
Pacho, Juan, Charleston	.268	43	142	17	38	39	1	0	0	21	0	5	2	1	10	0	14	3	3
Pagel, Karl, Charleston*	.325	124	381	78	124	202	12	3	20	82	8	1	1	2	109	9	96	5	3
Pardo, Alberto, Rochester†	.255	69	220	25	56	74	11	2	1	31	3	2	2	1	28	1	42	2	1
Pasqua, Daniel, Columbus*	.000	1	3	0	0	0	0	0	0	0	0	0	0	0	1	0	2	0	0
Patterson, Michael, Columbus*	.285	80	256	45	73	130	17	5	10	54	5	1	3	1	39	1	51	5	3
Pautt, Juan, Pawtucket	.275	78	229	39	63	91	13	0	5	31	3	0	2	4	47	2	46	1	1
Perconte, John, Charleston*	.346	94	341	76	118	151	17	2	4	45	4	4	2	2	83	4	34	13	6
Perry, Gerald, Richmond*	.314	113	423	81	133	209	21	8	13	71	8	3	5	2	73	2	55	26	13
Petralli, Eugene, Syracuse†	.245	104	327	39	80	102	9	2	3	40	3	3	3	0	54	4	37	0	1
Poole, Mark, Syracuse	.185	19	54	7	10	19	1	1	2	7	0	2	1	0	9	0	8	0	0
Poole, Stine, Toledo	.202	93	267	35	54	88	10	0	8	27	2	3	1	1	18	1	85	0	1
Porter, Robert, Richmond*	.244	80	238	39	58	94	19	1	5	37	0	1	2	1	26	2	34	0	1
Purpura, Daniel, Rochester	.239	28	67	7	16	23	3	2	0	6	0	1	0	0	8	0	15	1	1
Rajsich, Gary, Tidewater*	.270	129	430	68	116	219	15	2	28	83	4	3	2	9	52	9	78	7	7
Ramie, Vernon, Syracuse*	.217	62	180	21	39	69	7	1	7	28	2	0	1	1	36	3	46	1	0
Rayford, Floyd, Rochester	.371	42	140	24	52	76	16	1	2	38	3	1	1	0	16	0	30	0	1
Reed, Jeffrey, Toledo*	.171	14	41	5	7	10	1	1	0	3	0	0	0	2	5	0	9	0	0
Rey, Everett, Charleston	.139	13	36	2	5	5	0	0	0	5	0	0	0	0	2	0	8	0	0
Reynolds, Jeffrey, Syracuse	.219	128	434	46	95	151	15	1	13	50	5	2	1	3	32	0	123	1	3
Reynolds, Ronn, Tidewater	.211	40	128	8	27	35	8	0	0	9	2	1	0	0	6	0	27	0	0
Rhomberg, Kevin, Charleston	.311	133	508	102	158	192	17	7	1	60	4	6	4	4	87	0	55	27	21
Richardson, Billy Joe, Pawtucket	.071	6	14	1	1	1	0	0	0	0	0	0	0	0	0	0	6	0	0
Rios, Carlos, Richmond	.286	15	49	11	14	17	0	0	1	11	0	0	2	0	4	0	4	0	2
Rodriguez, Edwin, Columbus	.249	112	393	73	98	127	7	8	2	54	6	3	9	3	69	0	83	12	7
Ruiz, Manuel, Richmond	.176	28	68	6	12	13	1	0	0	6	3	0	2	0	6	0	11	0	0
Runge, Paul, Richmond	.273	137	472	76	129	199	17	4	15	72	5	4	2	2	84	4	82	6	10
Saavedra, Edwin, Charleston	.000	1	4	0	0	0	0	0	0	0	0	0	0	0	0	0	1	0	0
Schmitz, Daniel, 48 Tide.-19 Tol.*	.242	67	149	15	36	38	2	0	0	8	1	3	1	1	22	1	6	2	2
Schoppee, David, Pawtucket	.000	42	1	0	0	0	0	0	0	0	0	0	0	0	0	0	1	0	0
Scott, Richard, Columbus	.000	1	2	0	0	0	0	0	0	0	0	0	0	0	0	0	1	0	0
Sheets, Larry, Rochester*	.154	3	13	1	2	3	1	0	0	2	0	0	0	0	0	0	4	0	0
Shepherd, Ronald, Syracuse	.272	119	404	60	110	175	20	3	13	62	7	3	1	4	29	0	108	12	8
Shields, Stephen, Pawtucket	.000	36	2	0	0	0	0	0	0	0	0	0	0	0	0	0	0	0	0
Showalter, William, Columbus*	.238	18	63	9	15	21	3	0	1	8	1	1	0	1	7	0	3	1	0
Simunic, Douglas, Charleston	.224	42	125	16	28	46	5	2	3	12	3	1	0	1	16	0	30	0	0
Sinatro, Matthew, Richmond	.211	110	365	36	77	102	11	1	4	41	5	6	2	1	28	1	61	6	6
Smith, Kenneth, Richmond*	.282	52	174	36	49	73	8	2	4	31	5	1	1	2	31	4	45	6	2

Player and Club	Pct.	G.	AB.	R.	H.	TB.	2B.	3B.	HR.	RBI.	GW.	SH.	SF.	HP.	BB.	Int. BB.	SO.	SB.	CS.
Sosa, Miguel, Richmond	.333	2	9	2	3	4	1	0	0	2	0	0	0	0	0	0	2	0	0
Stefero, John, Rochester*	.196	35	97	13	19	30	5	0	2	5	0	1	1	0	17	1	27	0	0
Strawberry, Darryl, Tidewater*	.333	16	57	12	19	34	4	1	3	13	2	0	0	0	14	0	18	7	1
Stroughter, Stephen, Syracuse*	.203	22	64	7	13	21	5	0	1	4	0	0	1	1	10	0	16	0	0
Sullivan, Marc, Pawtucket	.186	27	70	9	13	19	3	0	1	7	0	0	1	0	11	0	12	2	0
Swisher, Steven, Richmond	.218	41	101	13	22	39	1	2	4	20	1	2	2	1	9	0	23	0	0
Tabler, Patrick, Charleston	.214	4	14	2	3	5	0	1	0	2	0	0	0	0	4	1	2	0	0
Tarver, Laschelle, Tidewater*	.500	3	10	4	5	6	1	0	0	0	0	0	0	0	0	0	0	2	1
Teufel, Timothy, Toledo	.323	136	471	103	152	272	27	6	27	100	10	4	9	1	102	2	71	13	4
Thompson, Milton, Richmond*	.250	12	32	12	8	9	1	0	0	3	1	0	0	1	10	0	5	6	1
Thompson, Timothy, Syracuse*	.294	16	51	9	15	32	5	0	4	10	3	0	1	0	4	0	12	0	0
Tillman, Kerry, Tidewater	.255	126	483	67	123	181	20	7	8	63	8	4	4	1	34	0	111	23	0
Valle, John, Rochester	.222	102	320	50	71	141	10	0	20	52	2	1	3	2	35	2	71	1	2
Vargas, Leonel, Richmond	.289	112	408	69	118	196	19	1	19	75	4	0	3	3	26	0	56	9	4
Vega, Jesus, Toledo	.253	130	455	69	115	178	18	0	15	77	10	2	4	8	75	6	50	14	9
Velez, Otoniel, Charleston	.310	48	142	27	44	80	9	0	9	42	5	0	2	1	32	2	34	0	1
Walker, Cleotha, Pawtucket†	.269	125	442	78	119	193	18	1	18	56	5	3	3	1	68	4	80	27	14
Webster, Mitchell, Syracuse†	.260	135	462	77	120	189	26	8	9	45	4	8	5	4	67	5	60	21	8
Werth, Dennis, Columbus	.211	30	90	11	19	21	2	0	0	11	0	0	1	0	11	0	24	0	0
Whisenton, Larry, Richmond	.245	93	282	59	69	115	8	7	8	41	5	0	3	2	69	4	55	14	5
Whittemore, Reginald, Pawtucket	.274	119	413	68	113	203	18	3	22	84	4	0	3	4	76	4	101	7	6
Willard, Gerald, Charleston*	.301	127	396	61	119	202	22	2	19	77	8	4	3	5	80	7	76	0	4
Wilson, James, Pawtucket	.200	21	55	4	11	15	1	0	1	11	0	0	1	0	4	0	12	1	1
Wilson, Michael, Toledo	.325	109	416	71	135	170	20	3	3	33	1	6	0	2	55	3	36	53	26
Winningham, Herman, Tidewater*	.265	29	113	18	30	42	5	2	1	11	1	0	0	0	10	0	29	6	2
Winters, Matthew, Columbus*	.292	133	431	89	126	243	24	3	29	99	10	0	3	3	112	3	113	1	2
Wood, Andre, Syracuse	.150	18	40	2	6	6	0	0	0	1	0	1	0	0	4	0	8	1	0
Woods, Alvis, Syracuse*	.255	47	153	18	39	62	6	4	3	23	3	1	0	0	27	2	24	1	1
Wynne, Marvell, Tidewater*	.286	51	175	32	50	74	13	1	3	29	0	1	3	0	18	1	21	4	5
Young, Michael, Rochester†	.284	102	373	62	106	178	14	8	14	66	7	0	5	1	56	8	93	18	5
Zuvella, Paul, Richmond	.287	117	415	53	119	154	13	2	6	64	8	3	2	7	28	1	34	4	4

The following pitchers, listed alphabetically by club, with games in parentheses, had no plate appearances, primarily through use of designated hitters:

CHARLESTON—Anderson, Karl (13); Baller, Jay (20); Barkley, Jeffrey (24); Barnes, Richard (2); Bohnet, John (5); Brennan, Thomas (21); Camacho, Ernie (24); Glaser, Gordon (11); Glynn, Edward (37); Hrynko, Lawrence (45); Jeffcoat, Michael (26); Narleski, Steven (5); Reed, Jerry (21); Searage, Raymond (31); Smith, Leroy (27); Wihtol, Alexander (34).

COLUMBUS—Browning, Michael (14); Burke, Timothy (4); Callahan, Benjamin (9); Christiansen, Clay (32); Elston, Guy (40); Erickson, Roger (24); Fontenot, Ray (26); Hernaiz, Jesus (26); Kaufman, Curt (50); King, Michael (10); Kneuer, Frank (1); LaRoche, David (7); May, Rudolph (4); Olwine, Edward (8); Patterson, Scott (15); Rasmussen, Dennis (28); Reuschel, Ricky (4); Solomon, Eddie (7); Wehrmeister, David (13); Werly, James (17); Wever, Stefan (7).

PAWTUCKET—Birrell, Robert (22); Bolton, Thomas (6); Boyd, Dennis (20); Burtt, Dennis (23); Crawford, Steve (27); Denman, Brian (26); Dorsey, James (29); Fidrych, Mark (12); Nipper, Albert (18).

RICHMOND—Alvarez, Jose (33); Behenna, Richard (17); Boggs, Thomas (4); Brizzolara, Anthony (21); Cowley, Joseph (28); Dayley, Kenneth (14); Dedmon, Jeffrey (21); Field, Gregory (20); Fore, Charles (33); Johnson, Joseph (1); Jones, Craig (1); Mahler, Richard (24); Moore, Donnie (12); North, Roy (3); Reiter, Gary (33); Ruiz, August (14); Waddell, Thomas (13); Walk, Robert (28).

ROCHESTER—Arnold, Tony (3); Boddicker, Michael (4); Brown, Mark (19); Dixon, Kenneth (11); Flinn, John (49); Ford, David (14); Fore, Charles (33); Gonzalez, Julian (12); King, Jerome (4); Minetto, Craig (52); Mirabella, Paul (19); Morogiello, Daniel (17); Ramirez, Allan (15); Smith, Mark (21); Snell, Nathaniel (39); Speck, Clifford (29); Swaggerty, William (25); Welchel, Donald (18).

SYRACUSE—Baker, James (43); Bomback, Mark (27); Clarke, Stanley (33); Cooper, Donald (46); Eichhorn, Mark (7); Howard, Dennis (22); Key, James (16); Knapp, Christian (8); Lukish, Thomas (39); McLaughlin, Colin (25); Morgan, Michael (5); Schneider, Jeffery (37); Shipanoff, David (8); Walker, Keith (13); Williams, Matthew (20).

TIDEWATER—Anderson, Richard (15); Biercevicz, Gregory (23); Bittiger, Jeffrey (28); Bullinger, Matthews (24); Darling, Ronald (27); Gorman, Thomas (10); Leary, Timothy (27); Pickett, Richard (26); Semprini, John (16); Senteney, Steve (20); Terrell, Walter (12).

TOLEDO—Boris, Paul (24); Broersma, Eric (21); Felton, Terry (23); Filson, Peter (2); Flannery, Kevin (30); Giordano, Michael (16); Havens, Bradley (11); Hodge, Eddie (28); Korczyk, Steven (33); Lewis, James (38); Little, Jeffrey (23); Mulligan, Robert (29); O'Connor, Jack (15); Oelkers, Bryan (17); Pettibone, Harry (4); Schrom, Kenneth (5); Walters, Michael (27).

GRAND SLAM HOME RUNS—Craig, Jacoby, 3 each; Brant, Hobson, Patterson, Shepherd, Zuvella, 2 each; Baker, Barranca, Calise, Espino, Gagne, Gentile, Graham, Johnson, R. Jones, Komminsk, Lisi, Mattingly, Meacham, Meier, Reynolds, K. Smith, Teufel, Valle, Velez, Willard, J. Wilson, Winters, 1 each.

AWARDED FIRST BASE ON CATCHER'S INTERFERENCE—Webster, 5 (Bishop 2, LaFrancois, Rey, Willard); Craig (T. Hernandez); Manrique (Poole); Willard (LaFrancois).

CLUB FIELDING

Club	Pct.	G.	PO.	A.	E.	DP.	PB.
Richmond	.976	139	3530	1407	123	123	7
Toledo	.972	140	3545	1557	147	150	16
Charleston	.970	140	3607	1507	157	130	8
Columbus	.970	140	3687	1469	160	131	16
Tidewater	.970	139	3505	1456	152	135	11
Rochester	.968	140	3525	1460	163	134	6
Pawtucket	.965	139	3535	1604	187	143	7
Syracuse	.965	139	3517	1502	182	150	14

Triple plays—Rochester, Toledo.

INDIVIDUAL FIELDING

*Throws lefthanded.

FIRST BASEMEN

Player and Club	Pct.	G.	PO.	A.	E.	DP.
Balboni, Columbus	.980	60	479	47	11	51
Barrios, Rochester	.983	34	261	29	5	23
Bishop, Tidewater	1.000	6	48	2	0	3
Brant, Columbus	.989	11	81	6	1	12
David, Toledo*	.957	4	22	0	1	2
Dayett, Columbus	.875	1	5	2	1	0
Falcone, Rochester	1.000	2	10	0	0	0
Fitzgerald, Tidewater	.984	6	56	6	1	3
Hobson, Columbus	.933	2	14	0	1	3
Howard, Tidewater	1.000	1	1	0	0	0
Hurdle, Tidewater	.987	9	68	6	1	5
R. Johnson, Toledo*	.979	23	127	11	3	22
Johnston, Syracuse	.979	55	475	29	11	53
Koza, Pawtucket*	.985	41	311	25	5	32
LaFrancois, Pawtucket	.944	2	17	0	1	0
Logan, Rochester*	.994	92	751	46	5	74
LoGrande, Charleston	.985	115	990	72	16	92
Mattingly, Columbus*	.997	36	313	29	1	22
Moore, Tidewater*	.978	8	42	2	1	5
Norrid, Charleston	.996	26	222	20	1	27
Pagel, Charleston	.947	4	34	2	2	2
Perry, Richmond	.989	110	943	88	11	86
Petralli, Syracuse	.987	19	131	19	2	17
Porter, Richmond*	1.000	1	2	0	0	1
RAJSICH, Tidewater*	.991	120	924	120	10	109
Ramie, Syracuse	.988	43	370	25	5	34

FIRST BASEMEN—Continued

Player and Club	Pct.	G.	PO.	A.	E.	DP.
Reynolds, Syracuse	.986	13	64	8	1	11
Showalter, Columbus*	.994	16	139	14	1	9
Smith, Richmond	.993	29	275	16	2	22
Stroughter, Syracuse	.882	2	14	1	2	1
Sullivan, Pawtucket	.963	6	47	5	2	5
Thompson, Syracuse*	.993	14	128	7	1	13
Valle, Rochester	.995	27	193	12	1	21
Vega, Toledo	.989	124	1074	68	13	112
Velez, Charleston	1.000	2	1	1	0	0
Webster, Syracuse*	.970	6	30	2	1	3
Werth, Columbus	.975	21	180	18	5	20
Whittemore, Pawtucket	.984	98	839	80	15	73

Triple plays—Logan, Vega.

SECOND BASEMEN

Player and Club	Pct.	G.	PO.	A.	E.	DP.
Backman, Tidewater	.975	85	154	233	10	51
Barranca, Rochester	.967	50	111	154	9	31
Barrett, Pawtucket	.995	36	70	115	1	19
Bonner, Rochester	.995	41	93	124	1	28
Campaneris, Columbus	1.000	3	3	2	0	0
Chapman, Tidewater	.990	20	37	58	1	16
Evans, Columbus	.950	21	41	54	5	14
Gulliver, Rochester	.941	34	59	100	10	17
Hernandez, Rochester	1.000	1	1	3	0	0
Howard, Tidewater	1.000	1	2	2	0	1
Hudler, Columbus	.972	30	53	87	4	20
Hundhammer, Pawtucket	.971	97	238	334	17	74
Lisi, Rochester	.938	5	15	15	2	4
Manrique, Syracuse	.953	101	171	276	22	76
McCain, Toledo	1.000	10	17	28	0	6
McMullen, Tidewater	.967	28	51	65	4	14
Nandin, Syracuse	.985	50	78	122	3	25
Nixon, Columbus	.976	9	22	19	1	1
Norrid, Charleston	1.000	6	11	16	0	1
Pacho, Charleston	.981	23	47	57	2	12
PERCONTE, Charleston	.988	93	176	322	6	63
Poole, Syracuse	1.000	1	0	2	0	0
Purpura, Rochester	1.000	9	13	13	0	2
Rayford, Rochester	.933	12	15	27	3	3
Rhomberg, Charleston	.952	25	53	65	6	18
Rodriguez, Columbus	.957	90	180	267	20	53
Ruiz, Richmond	1.000	1	2	3	0	0
Runge, Richmond	.979	137	269	392	14	85
Schmitz, Tidewater	.973	19	33	40	2	10
Sosa, Richmond	1.000	2	5	8	0	2
Teufel, Toledo	.982	132	304	394	13	109
Walker, Pawtucket	.943	10	14	19	2	4
Wood, Syracuse	1.000	2	0	1	0	0

Triple play—Teufel.

THIRD BASEMEN

Player and Club	Pct.	G.	PO.	A.	E.	DP.
Aponte, Charleston	.956	51	32	99	6	13
Ashford, Tidewater	.971	12	14	20	1	1
Backman, Tidewater	.900	4	3	6	1	1
Baker, Toledo	.946	140	82	305	22	27
Bishop, Tidewater	.833	5	3	7	2	0
Campaneris, Columbus	.913	11	4	17	2	0
Chapman, Tidewater	1.000	1	0	1	0	1
Davis, Pawtucket	.885	66	43	95	18	17
DeLeon, Charleston	1.000	5	1	6	0	1
Evans, Columbus	.985	35	13	53	1	6
Fitzgerald, Tidewater	1.000	1	1	3	0	0
Gulliver, Rochester	.949	91	65	177	13	17
Hernandez, Rochester	.927	41	28	61	7	12
HOBSON, Columbus	.958	95	77	149	10	6
Hudler, Columbus	1.000	9	2	8	0	1
Hundhammer, Pawtucket	.919	15	10	24	3	3
Hurdle, Tidewater	.910	115	59	143	20	13
Jacoby, Richmond	.945	132	62	247	18	17
Klutts, Syracuse	1.000	4	0	6	0	1
Manrique, Syracuse	1.000	1	0	1	0	0
McCain, Toledo	1.000	1	0	1	0	1
Nandin, Syracuse	.914	24	18	35	5	2
Norrid, Charleston	.917	48	28	72	9	6
Pacho, Charleston	1.000	1	0	1	0	0
Pautt, Pawtucket	1.000	2	1	0	0	0
Perconte, Charleston	1.000	1	1	1	0	0
Rayford, Rochester	.950	10	5	14	1	0
Rey, Charleston	.800	1	1	3	1	0
Reynolds, Syracuse	.914	119	80	197	26	22
Rhomberg, Charleston	.877	34	14	50	9	2
Rios, Richmond	1.000	1	1	6	0	2
Rodriguez, Columbus	1.000	1	0	1	0	1
Ruiz, Richmond	.842	6	2	14	3	0
Schmitz, Tidewater	.950	16	1	18	1	0
Tabler, Charleston	.667	4	2	4	3	0
Valle, Rochester	1.000	2	1	3	0	0
Walker, Pawtucket	.918	59	45	89	12	5
Werth, Columbus	1.000	3	0	1	0	0
Willard, Charleston	.333	2	0	1	2	0
Wilson, Pawtucket	.889	13	7	25	4	2

SHORTSTOPS

Player and Club	Pct.	G.	PO.	A.	E.	DP.
Backman, Tidewater	.966	12	18	39	2	13
Barranca, Rochester	.957	15	21	46	3	9
Bonner, Rochester	.969	20	38	57	3	10
Bustabad, Pawtucket	.960	71	122	194	13	14
DeLeon, Charleston	.943	125	191	357	33	72
Evans, Columbus	1.000	3	0	2	0	0
Fernandez, Syracuse	.957	111	211	361	26	87
Gagne, Toledo	.943	116	201	364	34	84
Gardenhire, Tidewater	.951	102	202	321	27	77
Gutierrez, Pawtucket	.941	66	109	211	20	41
Hall, Richmond	1.000	1	2	2	0	0
Howard, Tidewater	.400	2	1	1	3	0
Jimenez, Toledo	.967	20	31	56	3	14
Jones, Rochester	.950	94	151	265	22	69
Manrique, Syracuse	.890	33	39	74	14	18
Meacham, Columbus	.949	120	206	348	30	79
Oquendo, Tidewater	.915	13	20	23	4	4
Pacho, Charleston	.988	19	32	50	1	14
Purpura, Rochester	.952	15	22	37	3	7
Reynolds, Syracuse	1.000	3	3	6	0	2
Rios, Richmond	.985	14	24	42	1	11
Rodriguez, Columbus	.946	20	27	61	5	9
Ruiz, Richmond	1.000	13	7	16	0	2
Schmitz, 15 Tide.-5 Tol.	.953	20	29	53	4	9
Scott, Columbus	1.000	1	2	0	0	0
Teufel, Toledo	.900	2	2	7	1	0
Walker, Pawtucket	.935	11	14	15	2	7
Wood, Syracuse	1.000	1	2	5	0	1
ZUVELLA, Richmond	.965	117	169	324	18	72

Triple plays—Gagne, Purpura.

OUTFIELDERS

Player and Club	Pct.	G.	PO.	A.	E.	DP.
Barrios, Rochester	.955	16	20	1	1	0
Bell, Syracuse	.961	85	135	12	6	4
Bishop, Tidewater	1.000	3	7	1	0	0
Blocker, Tidewater*	.958	70	133	4	6	2
Bonaparte, Rochester*	.964	108	211	6	8	3
Brown, Toledo	.933	5	13	1	1	0
Burgess, Pawtucket*	.963	129	195	16	8	2
Castillo, Charleston	.938	36	85	6	6	1
Christensen, Tidewater	.935	19	28	1	2	0
Craig, Charleston	.972	120	270	4	8	0
Culmer, Charleston	.956	73	102	7	5	0
David, Toledo*	.968	66	85	7	3	0
Dayett, Columbus	.978	121	219	8	5	0
Dilone, Charleston	.986	32	69	1	1	0
Fitzgerald, Tidewater	1.000	1	1	0	0	0
Flores, Tidewater	.956	59	106	3	5	0
Gentile, Pawtucket*	.947	68	99	9	6	1
Graham, Pawtucket*	.977	134	242	15	6	1
Hall, Richmond	.960	129	278	8	12	3
Hart, Toledo*	.970	137	311	12	10	3
Hazewood, Rochester	.931	40	67	0	5	0
Hernandez, Rochester	.909	12	28	2	3	1
Howard, Tidewater	1.000	56	100	2	0	1
Hundhammer, Pawtucket	1.000	2	2	1	0	0
Hurdle, Tidewater	.750	6	3	0	1	0
A. Johnson, Syracuse	.953	74	113	8	6	1

OUTFIELDERS—Continued

Player and Club	Pct.	G.	PO.	A.	E.	DP.
R. Johnson, Toledo*	1.000	5	14	0	0	0
Komminsk, Richmond	.984	97	179	4	3	2
Koza, Pawtucket*	1.000	3	4	1	0	1
Linares, Richmond	.955	13	20	1	1	0
Lisi, Rochester	.965	122	237	10	9	4
Manrique, Syracuse	1.000	1	1	0	0	0
Mattingly, Columbus*	1.000	7	12	0	0	0
McCain, Toledo	1.000	1	2	0	0	0
Meier, Toledo	.970	123	224	6	7	3
NIXON, Columbus	.992	127	363	5	3	2
Norrid, Charleston	.986	40	71	0	1	0
Office, Columbus*	.975	53	75	3	2	0
Pagel, Charleston	.968	50	89	3	3	0
Pasqua, Columbus*	1.000	1	5	0	0	0
Patterson, Columbus	.954	52	83	0	4	0
Pautt, Pawtucket	.917	72	95	4	9	1
Porter, Richmond*	.920	14	23	0	2	0
Rajsich, Tidewater*	1.000	4	3	0	0	0
Rhomberg, Charleston	.996	81	223	4	1	3
Ruiz, Richmond	1.000	1	2	0	0	0
Saavedra, Charleston	1.000	1	1	0	0	0
Sheets, Rochester	.833	3	5	0	1	0
Shepherd, Syracuse	.985	108	254	6	4	0
Smith, Richmond	1.000	3	6	0	0	0
Strawberry, Tidewater*	.846	14	22	0	4	0
Stroughter, Syracuse	1.000	7	3	1	0	0
Thompson, Richmond	.968	12	30	0	1	0
Tillman, Tidewater	.971	125	220	13	7	3
Valle, Rochester	.984	35	63	0	1	0
Vargas, Richmond	.965	102	189	3	7	1
Walker, Pawtucket	1.000	36	49	3	0	0
Webster, Syracuse*	.965	133	236	14	9	2
Whisenton, Richmond	.971	65	99	2	3	2
Whittemore, Pawtucket	1.000	3	1	0	0	0
Willard, Charleston	.500	2	1	0	1	0
J. Wilson, Pawtucket	1.000	7	9	2	0	0
M. Wilson, Toledo	.971	97	191	10	6	2
Winningham, Tidewater	.959	29	70	1	3	0
Winters, Columbus	.987	92	150	2	2	0
Wood, Syracuse	.909	6	9	1	1	0
Woods, Syracuse*	.917	16	22	0	2	0
Wynne, Tidewater*	.983	51	114	5	2	3
Young, Rochester	.971	100	198	4	6	0

CATCHERS

Player and Club	Pct.	G.	PO.	A.	E.	DP.	PB.
Austin, Toledo	.980	57	264	29	6	2	4
Bishop, Tidewater	.980	14	86	10	2	0	1
Dempsey, Rochester	1.000	1	3	1	0	0	0
Espino, Columbus	.981	75	326	42	7	6	10
Fitzgerald, Tidewater	.988	90	530	53	7	4	5
Gulden, Columbus	.977	88	512	45	13	2	6
Hernandez, Syracuse	.984	59	317	43	6	5	7
Howard, Tidewater	1.000	2	5	1	0	0	0
Huppert, Rochester	.979	66	367	58	9	3	5
Kneuer, Columbus	1.000	1	1	0	0	0	0
LaFrancois, Pawtucket	.972	70	379	65	13	12	2
Lickert, Pawtucket	.983	69	404	57	8	12	3
Lindsey, Columbus	1.000	1	2	0	0	0	0
Owen, Richmond	1.000	5	20	0	0	0	0
Pardo, Rochester	.964	45	223	18	9	4	0
Petralli, Syracuse	.989	70	410	49	5	6	6
M. Poole, Syracuse	.993	18	128	11	1	0	1
S. POOLE, Toledo	.990	91	450	64	5	10	10
Rayford, Rochester	.974	9	34	3	1	0	1
Reed, Toledo	.988	14	77	6	1	2	2
Rey, Charleston	.938	10	58	2	4	2	1
Reynolds, Tidewater	.996	39	209	27	1	4	5
Richardson, Pawtucket	1.000	1	3	0	0	0	0
Simunic, Charleston	.991	22	95	14	1	1	0
Sinatro, Richmond	.989	108	642	60	8	10	6
Stefero, Rochester	.978	32	153	26	4	2	0
Sullivan, Pawtucket	1.000	17	60	9	0	0	2
Swisher, Richmond	.990	36	191	4	2	1	1
Willard, Charleston	.987	118	612	78	9	5	7

PITCHERS

Player and Club	Pct.	G.	PO.	A.	E.	DP.
Alvarez, Richmond	1.000	33	10	6	0	0
K. Anderson, Charleston	1.000	13	1	0	0	0
R. Anderson, Tidewater	1.000	15	3	6	0	0
Arnold, Rochester	1.000	3	1	5	0	0
Baker, Syracuse	.902	43	10	27	4	3
Baller, Charleston	.778	20	2	12	4	1
Barkley, Charleston	1.000	24	4	2	0	1
Barnes, Charleston*	1.000	2	2	3	0	0
Behenna, Richmond	.882	17	4	11	2	0
Biercevicz, Tidewater	.955	23	8	13	1	0
Birrell, Pawtucket*	.857	22	1	5	1	0
Bittiger, Tidewater	.857	28	15	21	6	0
Boddicker, Rochester	.889	4	2	6	1	0
Boggs, Richmond	1.000	4	0	1	0	0
Bohnet, Charleston*	.857	5	3	3	1	0
Bolton, Pawtucket*	1.000	6	0	9	0	0
Bomback, Syracuse	.861	27	10	21	5	2
Boris, Toledo	1.000	24	2	3	0	0
Boyd, Pawtucket	.909	20	11	19	3	0
Brennan, Charleston	.979	21	16	30	1	2
Brizzolara, Richmond	.933	21	10	18	2	0
Broersma, Toledo	1.000	21	3	6	0	0
Brown, Rochester	.833	19	1	4	1	0
Browning, Columbus	.786	14	4	7	3	3
Bullinger, Tidewater*	1.000	24	1	4	0	1
Burke, Columbus	1.000	4	3	4	0	1
Burtt, Pawtucket	.962	23	9	16	1	1
Callahan, Columbus	.882	9	5	10	2	0
Camacho, Charleston	.800	24	1	7	2	1
Christiansen, Columbus	.833	32	15	25	8	0
Clarke, Syracuse*	1.000	33	4	5	0	0
Cooper, Syracuse	.941	46	8	8	1	0
Cowley, Richmond	.973	28	17	19	1	2
Crawford, Pawtucket	.895	27	15	19	4	1
Darling, Tidewater	.966	27	26	30	2	5
Dayley, Richmond*	1.000	14	2	16	0	0
Dedmon, Richmond	.929	21	4	9	1	0
Denman, Pawtucket	.978	26	21	23	1	3
Dixon, Rochester	1.000	11	3	6	0	0
Dorsey, Pawtucket	.750	29	4	5	3	0
Dye, Tidewater	1.000	27	3	6	0	1
Eichhorn, Syracuse	.833	7	1	4	1	0
Elston, Columbus	1.000	40	2	5	0	0
ERICKSON, Columbus	1.000	24	17	26	0	1
Felton, Toledo	.920	23	7	16	2	2
Fidrych, Pawtucket	1.000	12	1	8	0	1
Field, Richmond	.833	20	2	8	2	0
Filson, Toledo*	1.000	2	0	2	0	0
Flannery, Toledo	1.000	30	2	11	0	1
Flinn, Rochester	.846	49	5	6	2	1
Fontenot, Columbus*	.800	26	0	4	1	1
Ford, Rochester	.900	14	2	7	1	0
Fore, Richmond	.923	33	6	6	1	0
Gaff, Tidewater	.885	37	10	13	3	1
Giordano, Toledo	.833	16	0	5	1	0
Glaser, Charleston	.947	11	9	9	1	2
Glynn, Charleston*	.800	37	0	4	1	0
Gonzalez, Rochester*	.800	12	1	7	2	0
Gorman, Tidewater*	.867	10	3	10	2	2
Havens, Toledo*	.833	11	0	10	2	0
Hernaiz, Columbus	1.000	26	8	18	0	3
Hodge, Toledo*	.967	28	4	25	1	1
Howard, Syracuse	.906	22	10	19	3	1
Hrynko, Charleston	.957	45	3	19	1	1
Jeffcoat, Charleston*	.917	26	10	34	4	2
Johnson, Richmond	1.000	1	1	1	0	1
Kaufman, Columbus	.867	50	6	7	2	1
Key, Syracuse*	.923	16	6	18	2	0
M. King, Columbus*	1.000	10	0	1	0	0
Knapp, Syracuse	1.000	8	4	3	0	0
Korczyk, Toledo	1.000	33	2	10	0	1
LaRoche, Columbus*	1.000	7	0	2	0	2
Leach, Tidewater	.947	37	16	20	2	0
Leary, Tidewater	.951	27	14	25	2	1
Lewis, Toledo	.788	38	10	16	7	1
Little, Toledo*	1.000	23	1	2	0	0
Lukish, Syracuse	.923	39	4	20	2	2
MacWhorter, Pawtucket	.885	48	10	13	3	1
Mahler, Richmond	.902	24	16	21	4	2
McLaughlin, Syracuse	.923	25	3	9	1	0
Minetto, Rochester*	.923	52	4	8	1	1
Mirabella, Rochester*	.909	19	2	18	2	0
Moloney, Pawtucket*	.920	44	6	17	2	0
Moore, Richmond	.800	12	2	2	1	1
Morgan, Syracuse	1.000	5	1	4	0	0
Morogiello, Rochester*	1.000	17	0	1	0	0
Mulligan, Toledo*	.970	29	7	25	1	1
Narleski, Charleston	1.000	5	0	1	0	0
Nipper, Pawtucket	.973	18	14	22	1	5
North, Richmond	1.000	3	3	3	0	0
O'Connor, Toledo*	1.000	15	1	3	0	0
Oelkers, Toledo*	.955	17	2	19	1	1
Olwine, Columbus*	1.000	8	0	1	0	1
Patterson, Columbus	.947	15	6	12	1	1

PITCHERS—Continued

Player and Club	Pct.	G.	PO.	A.	E.	DP.
Pettibone, Toledo	1.000	4	1	5	0	1
Pickett, Tidewater*	.875	26	2	5	1	0
Ramirez, Rochester	.944	15	6	11	1	0
Rasmussen, Columbus*	.914	28	8	24	3	1
Reed, Charleston	1.000	21	16	25	0	2
Reiter, Richmond*	1.000	33	1	8	0	0
Reuschel, Columbus	1.000	4	2	4	0	0
Ruiz, Richmond*	1.000	14	2	6	0	0
Schneider, Syracuse*	.933	37	5	9	1	1
Schoppee, Pawtucket	.950	41	5	14	1	2
Schrom, Toledo	1.000	5	3	3	0	0
Searage, Charleston*	.875	31	9	19	4	1
Semprini, Tidewater	.750	16	0	3	1	0
Senteney, Tidewater	1.000	20	3	6	0	0
Shields, Pawtucket	.938	36	9	21	2	0
Shipanoff, Syracuse	1.000	8	0	1	0	0
Showalter, Columbus*	1.000	1	0	1	0	0
L. Smith, Charleston	1.000	27	16	12	0	1
M. Smith, Rochester	.800	21	2	2	1	0
Snell, Rochester	.947	39	5	13	1	3
Solomon, Columbus	1.000	7	2	3	0	1
Speck, Rochester	.972	29	16	19	1	1
Swaggerty, Rochester	.963	25	8	18	1	0
Terrell, Tidewater	1.000	12	4	20	0	2
Walk, Richmond	.930	28	8	32	3	3
Walker, Syracuse*	.889	13	0	8	1	1
Walters, Toledo	1.000	27	2	11	0	1
Wehrmeister, Columbus	.905	13	9	10	2	1
Welchel, Rochester	.880	18	5	17	3	2
Werly, Columbus	.900	17	9	9	2	3
Wever, Columbus	.889	7	2	6	1	0
Wihtol, Charleston	.923	34	3	9	1	0
Williams, Syracuse	.943	21	9	24	2	0

The following players do not have any recorded accepted chances at the positions indicated and therefore are not listed in the fielding averages for those particular positions: M. Davis, ss; Dayett, 3b; Hudler, ss; C. Jones, p; J. King, p; Klutts, 2b; Koza, p; R. May, p; Meier, p; Nandin, c; Ramie, of; Rey, of; Simunic, of; Waddell, p.

CLUB PITCHING

Club	ERA.	G.	CG.	ShO.	Sv.	IP.	H.	R.	ER.	HR.	HB.	BB.	Int. BB.	SO.	WP.	Bk.
Tidewater	4.18	139	27	8	34	1168.1	1165	635	543	99	21	571	22	787	60	10
Syracuse	4.39	139	16	7	31	1172.1	1124	684	572	114	31	640	25	828	84	8
Rochester	4.54	140	19	5	25	1175.0	1222	696	593	130	22	578	28	759	53	7
Richmond	4.69	139	31	9	32	1176.2	1150	694	613	113	37	626	11	829	73	4
Toledo	4.79	140	22	6	30	1181.2	1259	722	629	130	24	629	25	757	49	8
Charleston	5.01	140	31	11	31	1202.1	1290	756	669	121	39	543	25	730	59	5
Columbus	5.08	140	25	5	45	1229.0	1329	788	694	131	30	638	32	820	65	10
Pawtucket	5.25	139	22	2	20	1178.1	1323	798	687	142	26	670	48	813	56	8

PITCHERS' RECORDS

(Leading Qualifiers for Earned-Run Average Leadership—112 or More Innings)

*Throws lefthanded.

Pitcher—Club	W.	L.	Pct.	ERA.	G.	GS.	CG.	GF.	ShO.	Sv.	IP.	H.	R.	ER.	HR.	HB.	BB.	Int. BB.	SO.	WP.
Brennan, Charleston	9	5	.643	3.31	21	12	6	4	2	1	114.1	105	44	42	11	2	29	2	72	1
Biercevicz, Tidewater	8	8	.500	3.40	23	18	4	3	1	3	121.2	115	51	46	12	2	28	1	82	1
Williams, Syracuse	7	8	.467	3.54	20	20	6	0	0	0	139.2	100	60	55	15	3	64	0	110	9
Reed, Charleston	10	6	.625	3.59	21	21	7	0	2	0	145.1	141	70	58	16	1	67	1	57	5
Howard, Syracuse	9	7	.563	3.69	22	21	5	0	1	0	114.2	114	72	47	7	2	63	0	64	10
Brizzolara, Richmond	9	7	.563	3.74	21	19	3	1	1	0	127.2	136	58	53	7	2	44	0	90	6
Bomback, Syracuse	13	11	.542	3.84	27	26	2	0	1	0	168.2	160	83	72	13	4	76	3	123	8
Hodge, Toledo*	11	6	.647	3.97	28	25	2	1	0	0	143.0	137	72	63	17	3	64	0	72	5
Darling, Tidewater	10	9	.526	4.02	27	27	5	0	1	0	159.0	137	83	71	12	1	102	1	107	10
Mulligan, Toledo*	6	10	.375	4.03	29	23	2	3	1	0	145.1	163	80	65	11	2	53	1	50	2

Departmental Leaders: G—Minetto, 52; W—Bomback, Rasmussen, 13; L—Leary, 16; Pct.—Terrell, .909; GS—Bittiger, Rasmussen, Walk, 28; CG—Walk, 11; GF—Cooper, Kaufman, 41; ShO—Cowley, 4; Sv.—Kaufman, 25; IP—Walk, 185; H—Christiansen, 196; R—Walk, 119; ER—Walk, 107; HR—Felton, Walk, 22; HB—Baller, 12; BB—Bittiger, 111; IBB—Schoppee, 9; SO—Rasmussen, 187; WP—Christiansen, 16.

(All Pitchers—Listed Alphabetically)

Pitcher—Club	W.	L.	Pct.	ERA.	G.	GS.	CG.	GF.	ShO.	Sv.	IP.	H.	R.	ER.	HR.	HB.	BB.	Int. BB.	SO.	WP.
Alvarez, Richmond	8	2	.800	5.29	33	7	1	18	0	1	81.2	67	50	48	5	5	53	1	61	5
K. Anderson, Charleston	1	0	1.000	3.60	13	0	0	11	0	2	20.0	21	11	8	0	0	9	1	15	3
R. Anderson, Tidewater	2	1	.667	4.05	15	1	0	8	0	2	40.0	37	19	18	1	0	22	1	23	2
Arnold, Rochester	0	1	.000	3.52	3	1	0	1	0	0	7.2	10	5	3	0	0	5	1	5	1
Baker, Syracuse	1	4	.200	4.62	43	7	0	14	0	1	113.0	117	70	58	10	2	49	5	64	4
Baller, Charleston	4	12	.250	8.81	20	16	2	3	0	2	78.2	91	79	77	9	12	66	0	62	6
Barkley, Charleston	3	1	.750	4.63	24	1	0	11	0	3	58.1	64	32	30	7	0	23	2	51	3
Barnes, Charleston*	1	0	1.000	3.65	2	2	0	0	0	0	12.1	9	5	5	0	0	9	0	3	2
Behenna, Richmond	6	5	.545	4.47	17	16	1	1	0	0	94.2	91	55	47	7	10	61	1	50	7
Biercevicz, Tidewater	8	8	.500	3.40	23	18	4	3	1	3	121.2	115	51	46	12	2	28	1	82	1
Birrell, Pawtucket*	0	3	.000	8.55	22	3	0	5	0	0	33.2	42	36	32	3	0	32	5	29	3
Bittiger, Tidewater	12	10	.545	4.36	28	28	1	0	1	0	163.0	175	90	79	15	2	111	0	110	6
Boddicker, Rochester	3	1	.750	1.90	4	4	1	0	1	0	23.2	17	6	5	1	0	13	0	18	0
Boggs, Richmond	0	4	.000	14.25	4	4	0	0	0	0	12.0	19	20	19	3	1	9	0	5	0
Bohnet, Charleston*	0	3	.000	5.40	5	5	0	0	0	0	25.0	30	20	15	2	0	15	1	18	0
Bolton, Pawtucket*	0	5	.000	6.52	6	6	0	0	0	0	29.0	33	26	21	4	1	25	0	20	1
Bomback, Syracuse	13	11	.542	3.84	27	26	2	0	1	0	168.2	160	83	72	13	4	76	3	123	8
Boris, Toledo	5	4	.556	7.39	24	8	0	7	0	0	63.1	84	56	52	8	0	35	2	57	3
Boyd, Pawtucket	5	8	.385	4.04	20	17	9	3	0	1	122.2	119	69	55	17	1	41	2	129	5
Brennan, Charleston	9	5	.643	3.31	21	12	6	4	2	1	114.1	105	44	42	11	2	29	2	72	1
Brizzolara, Richmond	9	7	.563	3.74	21	19	3	1	1	0	127.2	136	58	53	7	2	44	0	90	6
Broersma, Toledo	1	1	.500	4.66	21	2	0	8	0	1	58.0	62	31	30	8	1	30	1	46	1
Brown, Rochester	6	1	.857	3.54	19	4	1	13	1	5	53.1	41	23	21	3	0	20	2	44	1
Browning, Columbus	5	1	.833	5.23	14	0	0	5	0	0	43.0	71	32	25	4	1	15	0	12	5
Bullinger, Tidewater*	0	1	.000	3.41	24	0	0	10	0	0	31.2	27	17	12	3	0	22	4	15	5
Burke, Columbus	1	0	1.000	6.75	4	0	0	0	0	0	12.0	15	9	9	0	0	8	1	6	1
Burtt, Pawtucket	4	5	.444	5.30	23	20	1	3	0	0	110.1	109	72	65	16	1	75	2	66	4
Callahan, Columbus	3	2	.600	6.24	9	9	0	0	0	0	53.1	57	42	37	7	2	37	1	22	0
Camacho, Charleston	4	0	1.000	1.35	24	0	0	15	0	4	33.1	19	5	5	1	0	17	3	27	0
Christiansen, Columbus	8	9	.471	5.44	32	19	1	2	0	0	160.1	196	118	97	15	4	81	5	92	16
Clarke, Syracuse*	0	3	.000	2.89	33	0	0	18	0	2	53.0	39	26	17	4	1	34	4	58	3
Cooper, Syracuse	10	5	.667	3.21	46	1	0	41	0	22	87.0	69	33	31	7	3	33	2	73	2
Cowley, Richmond	9	7	.563	4.40	28	18	4	7	4	2	124.2	106	69	61	11	5	72	0	108	8

Pitcher—Club	W.	L.	Pct.	ERA.	G.	GS.	CG.	GF.	ShO.	Sv.	IP.	H.	R.	ER.	HR.	HB.	BB.	Int. BB.	SO.	WP.
Crawford, Pawtucket	8	11	.421	5.18	27	27	4	0	1	0	154.2	181	98	89	17	3	80	4	104	7
Darling, Tidewater	10	9	.526	4.02	27	27	5	0	1	0	159.0	137	83	71	12	1	102	1	107	10
Dayley, Richmond*	9	3	.750	3.28	14	14	4	0	1	0	90.2	79	39	33	7	0	49	0	74	4
Dedmon, Richmond	2	2	.500	1.75	21	0	0	18	0	10	36.0	28	9	7	1	0	14	0	33	2
Denman, Pawtucket	8	11	.421	5.02	26	25	3	1	0	0	154.1	182	99	86	21	1	66	2	76	3
Dixon, Rochester	3	6	.333	4.48	11	11	1	0	0	0	64.1	65	41	32	9	2	26	0	34	2
Dorsey, Pawtucket	5	7	.417	4.01	29	1	0	24	0	8	67.1	59	33	30	9	1	40	3	63	6
Dye, Tidewater	1	3	.250	6.08	27	0	0	21	0	5	37.0	47	26	25	4	1	20	6	23	1
Eichhorn, Syracuse	0	5	.000	7.92	7	5	0	1	0	0	30.2	36	32	27	8	2	21	1	12	1
Elston, Columbus	4	2	.667	4.50	40	0	0	24	0	7	64.0	60	34	32	9	1	29	0	53	4
Erickson, Columbus	9	7	.563	6.04	24	18	5	1	1	0	134.0	175	99	90	21	3	59	3	59	5
Felton, Toledo	3	10	.231	5.24	23	17	4	3	0	1	115.0	117	81	67	22	4	72	2	77	5
Fidrych, Pawtucket	2	5	.286	9.68	12	8	0	1	0	0	48.1	85	55	52	7	1	37	1	27	5
Field, Richmond	2	1	.667	4.40	20	1	0	10	0	2	47.0	56	30	23	4	2	17	1	26	3
Filson, Toledo*	0	1	.000	7.71	2	1	0	0	0	0	7.0	8	6	6	2	0	3	0	6	1
Flannery, Toledo	6	4	.600	5.34	30	10	3	10	0	0	97.2	117	66	58	7	0	49	3	57	2
Flinn, Rochester	5	7	.417	4.89	49	1	0	29	0	5	88.1	93	55	48	15	4	45	5	60	3
Fontenot, Columbus*	3	2	.600	2.83	26	0	0	18	0	8	35.0	25	16	11	1	1	17	2	36	2
Ford, Rochester	3	2	.600	6.54	14	12	0	2	0	0	63.1	89	56	46	16	2	22	0	30	1
Fore, Richmond	6	3	.667	5.67	33	5	1	13	0	3	87.1	90	62	55	7	4	52	2	69	3
Gaff, Tidewater	6	7	.462	6.04	37	11	1	16	0	5	111.2	132	87	75	13	1	43	1	60	10
Giordano, Toledo	1	2	.333	5.21	16	0	0	9	0	3	19.0	20	13	11	2	1	14	2	10	1
Glaser, Charleston	4	4	.500	4.86	11	10	3	0	0	0	66.2	89	48	36	6	0	12	0	15	1
Glynn, Charleston*	3	5	.375	4.98	37	0	0	21	0	10	47.0	43	30	26	5	0	28	3	51	3
Gonzalez, Rochester*	5	3	.625	4.43	12	12	1	0	0	0	67.0	55	39	33	7	0	42	0	61	6
Gorman, Tidewater*	6	1	.857	2.92	10	8	1	1	1	0	61.2	54	25	20	6	1	18	0	58	3
Havens, Toledo*	6	3	.667	3.88	11	11	4	0	0	0	69.2	60	34	30	4	0	37	0	64	6
Hernaiz, Columbus	4	5	.444	4.79	26	10	2	6	1	1	97.2	103	60	52	6	0	42	4	49	3
Hodge, Toledo*	11	6	.647	3.97	28	25	2	1	0	0	143.0	137	72	63	17	3	64	0	72	5
Howard, Syracuse	9	7	.563	3.69	22	21	5	0	1	0	114.2	114	72	47	7	2	63	0	64	10
Hrynko, Charleston	3	2	.600	8.34	45	1	1	19	0	4	77.2	109	79	72	10	1	38	6	49	4
Jeffcoat, Charleston*	12	8	.600	4.53	26	25	6	1	0	0	167.0	187	95	84	8	10	46	3	96	7
Johnson, Richmond	0	0	.000	7.20	1	1	0	0	0	0	5.0	7	4	4	1	0	3	0	2	0
Jones, Richmond	0	1	.000	3.00	1	0	0	1	0	0	3.0	2	1	1	0	0	0	0	1	0
Kaufman, Columbus	6	3	.667	2.75	50	0	0	41	0	25	78.2	60	24	24	6	1	33	4	93	3
Key, Syracuse*	4	8	.333	4.13	16	15	2	1	0	0	89.1	87	58	41	14	3	33	2	71	6
J. King, Rochester	0	2	.000	11.57	4	3	0	0	0	0	16.1	28	22	21	6	0	10	0	8	1
M. King, Columbus*	2	0	1.000	5.60	10	1	1	3	0	0	17.2	18	15	11	1	1	19	2	9	1
Knapp, Syracuse	0	4	.000	6.00	8	4	0	1	0	0	27.0	33	20	18	2	2	20	0	12	2
Korczyk, Toledo	3	9	.250	4.53	33	0	0	15	0	3	59.2	60	32	30	6	2	41	7	44	1
Koza, Pawtucket	0	0	.000	5.40	1	0	0	1	0	0	1.2	1	1	1	1	0	1	0	0	0
LaRoche, Columbus*	1	1	.500	5.40	7	0	0	4	0	2	8.1	11	5	5	1	3	7	4	8	0
Leach, Tidewater	5	7	.417	4.46	37	7	2	18	0	6	113.0	120	66	56	10	4	42	5	66	555
Leary, Tidewater	8	16	.333	4.38	27	27	8	0	1	0	160.1	170	100	78	11	7	73	1	106	10
Lewis, Toledo	11	9	.550	5.05	38	12	2	21	0	4	123.0	128	81	69	14	7	86	3	76	6
Little, Toledo*	2	4	.333	7.91	23	1	0	9	0	2	33.0	40	33	29	6	1	39	0	34	5
Lukish, Syracuse	6	5	.545	4.40	39	12	1	22	0	2	114.2	125	61	56	11	4	51	3	69	7
MacWhorter, Pawtucket	5	6	.455	5.55	48	0	0	31	0	5	86.0	95	60	53	6	5	58	7	63	4
Mahler, Richmond	12	7	.632	4.92	24	24	6	0	0	0	162.2	165	102	89	17	4	85	2	103	11
May, Columbus*	0	0	.000	2.45	4	1	0	2	0	0	7.1	5	2	2	0	0	3	0	6	2
McLaughlin, Syracuse	4	6	.400	6.08	25	13	0	6	0	0	84.1	78	64	57	5	1	92	1	62	12
Meier, Toledo	0	0	.000	9.00	1	0	0	1	0	0	1.0	2	1	1	0	0	0	0	0	0
Minetto, Rochester*	3	6	.333	3.59	52	1	0	25	0	2	95.1	99	52	38	5	4	48	6	76	2
Mirabella, Rochester*	3	5	.375	3.66	19	13	0	3	0	1	76.1	87	44	31	6	3	29	0	32	2
Moloney, Pawtucket*	3	4	.429	4.82	44	1	0	13	0	0	52.1	61	33	28	6	1	41	7	31	1
Moore, Richmond	0	2	.000	3.24	12	0	0	12	0	8	16.2	12	6	6	2	0	7	0	9	2
Morgan, Syracuse	0	3	.000	5.59	5	4	0	1	0	1	19.1	20	12	12	1	0	13	0	17	3
Morogiello, Rochester*	1	1	.500	5.73	17	1	0	7	0	2	33.0	41	24	21	3	0	12	4	16	0
Mulligan, Toledo*	6	10	.375	4.03	29	23	2	3	1	0	145.1	163	80	65	11	2	53	1	50	2
Narleski, Charleston	0	0	.000	4.50	5	0	0	2	0	0	10.0	7	5	5	2	0	3	0	6	1
Nipper, Pawtucket	9	4	.692	4.45	18	17	4	1	1	0	109.1	108	62	54	11	2	54	1	58	1
North, Richmond	0	1	.000	7.58	3	2	0	1	0	0	19.0	21	16	16	6	0	11	0	7	0
O'Connor, Toledo*	2	1	.667	4.98	14	6	0	6	0	4	43.1	52	30	24	7	0	23	1	39	3
Oelkers, Toledo*	5	7	.417	5.18	17	17	5	0	0	0	104.1	121	68	60	6	0	49	1	60	7
Olwine, Columbus*	2	0	1.000	9.58	8	0	0	4	0	0	10.1	21	11	11	3	1	6	0	11	1
Patterson, Columbus	6	2	.750	5.92	15	15	2	0	1	0	89.2	113	65	59	14	2	47	1	43	4
Pettibone, Toledo	0	0	.000	3.32	4	2	0	1	0	0	21.2	21	9	8	3	2	3	0	16	0
Pickett, Tidewater*	1	0	1.000	3.98	26	0	0	12	0	5	31.2	31	16	14	1	0	18	0	27	1
Ramirez, Rochester	4	5	.444	3.80	15	15	4	0	0	0	90.0	76	42	38	11	1	55	0	78	4
Rasmussen, Columbus*	13	10	.565	4.57	28	28	8	0	1	0	181.0	161	106	92	16	2	108	1	187	5
Reed, Charleston	10	6	.625	3.59	21	21	7	0	2	0	145.1	141	70	58	16	1	67	1	57	5
Reiter, Richmond*	1	1	.500	5.00	33	0	0	9	0	3	36.0	36	22	20	7	0	28	1	26	3
Reuschel, Columbus	0	1	.000	5.06	4	4	0	0	0	0	16.0	21	9	9	2	0	6	0	7	0
Ruiz, Richmond*	0	1	.000	5.09	14	0	0	6	0	0	23.0	30	20	13	0	0	13	1	13	4
Schneider, Syracuse*	4	4	.500	5.13	37	4	0	14	0	3	66.2	63	41	38	5	2	60	3	52	10
Schoppee, Pawtucket	3	2	.600	6.58	41	1	0	25	0	5	65.2	77	60	48	12	1	57	9	32	5
Schrom, Toledo	3	1	.750	4.55	5	5	0	0	0	0	31.2	30	19	16	4	1	14	1	20	0
Searage, Charleston*	7	7	.500	5.64	31	20	2	4	2	1	134.0	146	94	84	16	4	76	1	77	12
Semprini, Tidewater	2	1	.667	4.32	16	0	0	9	0	2	16.2	19	9	8	1	1	8	1	13	0
Senteney, Tidewater	0	3	.000	2.88	20	0	0	14	0	6	34.1	25	12	11	1	1	20	1	39	4
Shields, Pawtucket	4	12	.250	4.66	36	13	1	9	0	1	143.0	171	94	74	12	8	63	5	115	11
Shipanoff, Syracuse	0	1	.000	3.27	8	0	0	4	0	0	11.0	9	4	4	1	0	9	0	18	0
Showalter, Columbus*	0	0	.000	0.00	1	0	0	1	0	0	2.0	0	0	0	0	0	0	0	2	0
L. Smith, Charleston	6	8	.429	5.16	27	27	4	0	2	0	155.1	166	101	89	21	7	75	2	95	4
M. Smith, Rochester	2	3	.400	5.33	21	2	1	6	0	1	49.0	50	31	29	8	2	46	1	35	7
Snell, Rochester	6	2	.750	3.60	39	1	1	32	0	9	70.0	71	29	28	6	0	17	2	46	4
Solomon, Columbus	2	1	.667	5.79	7	1	0	3	0	2	14.0	12	9	9	1	0	7	1	4	0
Speck, Rochester	8	12	.400	5.04	29	24	3	2	1	0	148.1	136	95	83	14	2	105	5	130	12
Swaggerty, Rochester	9	6	.600	4.64	25	17	3	1	0	0	118.1	136	67	61	9	1	37	2	25	2
Terrell, Tidewater	10	1	.909	3.12	12	12	5	0	1	0	86.2	76	34	30	9	0	44	0	58	6
Waddell, Richmond	5	0	1.000	4.38	13	0	0	11	0	3	24.2	26	12	12	6	0	6	0	29	1
Walk, Richmond	11	12	.478	5.21	28	28	11	0	2	0	185.0	179	119	107	22	4	102	2	123	14
Walker, Syracuse*	2	4	.333	7.60	13	6	0	0	0	0	45.0	68	47	38	11	2	22	1	17	7

Pitcher—Club	W.	L.	Pct.	ERA.	G.	GS.	CG.	GF.	ShO.	Sv.	IP.	H.	R.	ER.	HR.	HB.	BB.	Int. BB.	SO.	WP.
Walters, Toledo	3	0	1.000	1.96	27	0	0	24	0	12	46.0	37	10	10	3	0	17	1	29	1
Wehrmeister, Columbus	4	5	.444	4.32	13	11	0	1	0	0	75.0	62	41	36	6	4	50	2	41	6
Welchel, Rochester	4	12	.250	4.64	18	18	3	0	0	0	110.2	128	65	57	11	1	46	0	61	5
Werly, Columbus	9	2	.818	4.89	17	17	6	0	0	0	106.2	111	64	58	14	3	45	0	70	6
Wever, Columbus	1	4	.200	9.78	7	6	0	0	0	0	23.0	32	27	25	4	1	19	1	10	1
Wihtol, Charleston	7	5	.583	5.18	34	0	0	18	0	4	57.1	63	38	33	7	2	30	0	36	7
Williams, Syracuse	8	8	.500	3.41	21	21	6	0	0	0	148.0	106	61	56	15	3	64	0	116	9

BALKS—Biercevicz, 3; Baker, Barkley, Bomback, Christiansen, Denman, Flannery, Leary, Minetto, Moloney, Oelkers, Pickett, 2 each; K. Anderson, Behenna, Bolton, Boris, Boyd, Broersma, Brown, Browning, Callahan, Clarke, Cooper, Cowley, Darling, Eichhorn, Elston, Erickson, Fontenot, Gaff, Hodge, Jeffcoat, M. King, Little, Mahler, McLaughlin, Nipper, Patterson, Ramirez, Rasmussen, Searage, Shields, M. Smith, Speck, Swaggerty, Terrell, Walk, 1 each.

COMBINATION SHUTOUTS—Brennan-Camacho-Glynn, Brennan-Camacho, Reed-Wihtol, Charleston; Wever-Fontenot, Columbus; Dayley-Alvarez, Richmond; Ford-Flinn, Mirabella-Snell, Rochester; McLaughlin-Cooper 2, Bomback-Cooper, Bomback-Lukish, Bomback-Clarke, Syracuse; Biercevicz-Gaff, Biercevicz-Pickett, Tidewater; Schrom-Walters, Hodge-Walters, Hodge-Boris, Hodge-Korczyk, Hodge-O'Connor, Toledo.

NO-HIT GAME—None.

Mexican League

CLASS AAA

CHAMPIONSHIP WINNERS IN PREVIOUS YEARS

Year	Club	Pct.
1955	Mexico City Tigers*	.539
1956	Mexico City Reds	.692
1957	Yucatan	.567
	Mex. C. Reds (2nd)†	.550
1958	Nuevo Laredo	.625
1959	Poza Rica	.575
	Mex. C. Reds (3rd)†	.507
1960	Mexico City Tigers	.538
1961	Veracruz	.575
1962	Monterrey	.592
1963	Puebla	.606
1964	Mexico City Reds	.586
1965	Mexico City Tigers	.590
1966	Mexico City Tigers‡	.614
	Mexico City Reds	.571
1967	Jalisco	.607
1968	Mexico City Reds	.586
1969	Reynosa	.591
1970	Aguila§	.580
	Mexico City Reds	.607
1971	Jalisco§	.558
	Saltillo	.593
1972	Saltillo	.636
	Cordoba§	.541
1973	Saltillo	.656
	Mexico City Reds x	.590
1974	Jalisco	.627
	Mexico City Reds x	.551
1975	Tampico x	.541
	Cordoba	.649
1976	Mexico City Reds x	.543
	Union Laguna	.547
1977	Mexico City Reds	.623
	Nuevo Laredo x	.507
1978	Aguascalientes x	.589
	Union Laguna	.523
1979	Saltillo	.704
	Puebla x	.628
1980	No champion y	
1981	Mexico City Reds	.615
	Reynosa	.492
1982	Ciudad Juarez x	.570
	Mexico City Tigers	.508

*Defeated Nuevo Laredo, two games to none, in playoff for pennant. †Won four-team playoff. ‡Won split-season playoff. §League divided into Northern, Southern divisions; won two-team playoff. xLeague divided into Northern, Southern zones; sub-divided into Eastern, Western divisions, won eight-team playoff. yA players strike on July 1 forced the cancellation of the regular season and playoff schedule.

STANDING OF CLUBS AT CLOSE OF SEASON

NORTHERN ZONE

Club	Ags.	CJ	Tam.	Sal.	NL	Leo.	Mon.	Mva	MR	Cam.	MT	Yuc.	Ctz.	Tab.	Ver.	PR	W.	L.	T.	Pct.	G.B.
Aguascalientes	....	6	5	7	7	6	7	7	1	3	3	2	2	2	2	4	64	54	0	.542	....
Ciudad Juarez	6	....	5	7	6	6	6	9	1	3	4	1	4	1	1	2	62	54	2	.535	1
Tampico	7	6	....	5	5	7	7	7	1	0	1	2	3	3	1	2	57	55	3	.509	4
Saltillo	5	7	7	....	6	9	4	9	0	1	2	2	1	2	2	3	60	58	0	.508	4
Nuevo Laredo	5	5	7	6	....	6	7	8	1	4	1	1	2	1	2	2	58	59	1	.496	5½
Leon	8	6	5	3	6	....	5	5	1	1	2	2	3	3	3	2	55	61	0	.474	8
Monterrey	5	6	6	8	5	7	....	3	1	1	2	1	1	1	1	2	50	67	0	.427	13½
Monclova	5	3	5	3	6	7	9	....	1	1	0	1	1	4	2	1	49	69	0	.415	15

SOUTHERN ZONE

Club	Ags.	CJ	Tam.	Sal.	NL	Leo.	Mon.	Mva.	MR	Cam.	MT	Yuc.	Ctz.	Tab.	Ver.	PR	W.	L.	T.	Pct.	G.B.
Mexico City Reds	3	3	3	4	3	2	3	3	....	5	8	6	8	6	7	10	74	37	3	.667	....
Campeche	1	1	3	3	0	3	3	3	6	....	8	8	7	9	9	6	70	44	1	.614	5½
Mexico City Tigers	1	0	2	2	3	2	2	4	6	4	....	11	7	6	6	9	65	51	1	.560	11½
Yucatan	2	3	2	2	3	1	3	3	5	6	1	....	10	8	7	4	60	55	1	.522	16
Coatzacoalcos	2	0	1	3	2	1	3	3	4	5	4	2	....	8	5	11	54	63	0	.462	23
Tabasco	2	3	1	2	3	1	3	0	5	3	6	4	6	....	6	8	53	62	0	.461	23
Veracruz	2	3	1	2	2	1	3	2	2	2	6	5	7	6	....	7	51	61	2	.455	23½
Poza Rica	0	2	2	1	2	2	2	3	2	5	3	7	1	2	7	....	41	73	0	.360	34½

Playoffs—The top eight teams during regular-season play, four in the Northern Zone and four in the Southern Zone, qualified for postseason play. Each team played 18 games, with the two teams having the best records (one from each zone) meeting in the championship series. Campeche won the Southern Zone title with a 13-5 record; Ciudad Juarez defeated Saltillo in a one-game playoff for the Northern Zone title after the two teams finished with 11-7 records. Campeche defeated Ciudad Juarez, four games to three, in the final series to capture the league championship.

Regular-Season Attendance—Aguascalientes, 235,998; Campeche, 287,749; Ciudad Juarez, 156,388; Coatzacoalcos, 98,306; Leon, 132,629; Mexico City Reds, 254,900; Mexico City Tigers, 216,913; Monclova, 108,526; Monterrey, 125,315; Nuevo Laredo, 154,798; Poza Rica, 105,479; Saltillo, 163,760; Tabasco, 176,304; Tampico, 178,123; Veracruz, 85,650; Yucatan, 400,978. Total, 2,881,816.

Managers—Aguascalientes, Eladio Urias; Campeche, Francisco Estrada; Ciudad Juarez, Jose Guerrero; Coatzacoalcos, Ramon Arano; Leon, Abraham Rivera, Benjamin Valenzuela; Mexico City Reds, Benjamin Reyes; Mexico City Tigers, Gregorio Luque, Fernando Remes Garza; Monclova, Lee Sigman, Adolfo Cabrera; Monterrey, Mario Pelaez; Nuevo Laredo, Moises Camacho, Jorge Calvo; Poza Rica, David Garcia, Aaron Flores; Saltillo, Cesar Gutierrez, Juan Navarrete; Tabasco, Mario Saldana, Mario Salazar; Tampico, Felipe Hernandez, Roberto Castellon; Veracruz, Jose Luis Garcia Cobos; Yucatan, Carlos Paz.

All-Star Team—Northern Zone: 1B—John Evans, Aguascalientes; Carlos Soto, Nuevo Laredo; Rafael Batista, Tampico. 2B—Juan Navarrete, Saltillo; Antonio Briones, Ciudad Juarez. 3B—Alejandro Ortiz, Nuevo Laredo; Enrique Aguilar, Aguascalientes. SS—Ali Uscanga, Monterrey; Victor Quintero, Saltillo. OF—Andres Mora, Nuevo Laredo; Ron Arnold, Nuevo Laredo; Henry Cruz, Leon; Rosario Zambrano, Monterrey. C—Julio Benitez, Saltillo; Andy Pasillas, Tampico. P—Miguel Solis, Saltillo; Leonel Urrea, Saltillo; Teodore Higueras, Ciudad Juarez; Gabriel Low, Aguascalientes; Guadalupe Chavez, Tampico; Carlos Ibarra, Leon; Arturo Gonzalez, Monterrey; Mario Rodriguez, Monclova. Southern Zone: 1B—Gary Gray, Mexico City Reds; Guillermo Rodriguez, Campeche. 2B—Armando Sanchez, Mexico City Reds; Leo Guerrero, Campeche. 3B—Juan Bernhardt, Campeche; Nelson Barrera, Mexico City Reds. SS—Juan Hernandez, Mexico City Reds; Fernando Villaescusa, Yucatan. OF—Derek Bryant, Mexico City Tigers; Paul Herring, Tabasco; Matias Carrillo, Poza Rica; John Tutt, Veracruz; Miguel Suarez, Tabasco. C—Pedro Bazan, Yucatan; Juan Alvarez, Mexico City Tigers. P—Alfonso Pulido, Mexico City Reds; Max Leon, Mexico City Reds; Vicente Romo, Mexico City Tigers; Jesus Mundo, Veracruz; Herminio Dominguez, Campeche; Chuck Rogers, Tabasco; Pilar Rodriguez, Yucatan; Salvador Colorado, Coatzacoalcos.

(Compiled by Ana Luisa Perea Talarico, League Statistician, Mexico, D.F.)

CLUB BATTING

Club	Pct.	G.	AB.	R.	OR.	H.	TB.	2B.	3B.	HR.	RBI.	GW.	SH.	SF.	HP.	BB.	Int. BB.	SO.	SB.	CS.	LOB.
Aguascalientes	.280	118	3795	558	505	1061	1428	169	33	44	492	53	51	43	43	457	33	458	33	30	823
Mexico City Tigers	.279	117	3699	476	389	1032	1359	108	42	45	415	57	65	46	21	405	38	420	142	86	767
Campeche	.276	115	3657	469	337	1008	1322	138	34	36	408	52	72	36	39	373	40	357	102	57	831
Mexico City Reds	.274	114	3749	525	359	1028	1390	126	34	56	464	61	47	44	22	383	18	519	136	56	764
Yucatan	.270	116	3636	411	424	981	1248	113	26	34	363	42	57	27	38	389	28	475	89	57	876
Leon	.269	116	3743	499	550	1007	1379	126	27	64	437	37	59	30	39	424	38	436	90	38	853
Saltillo	.266	118	3660	467	465	974	1259	129	21	38	433	60	68	37	23	450	25	462	108	67	753
Tabasco	.265	115	3729	344	431	988	1231	117	24	26	291	39	60	24	26	265	34	381	51	58	808
Ciudad Juarez	.264	118	3675	441	419	971	1243	129	34	25	397	52	72	25	37	446	34	409	97	61	806
Nuevo Laredo	.262	118	3641	478	439	955	1364	122	28	77	437	50	69	30	41	387	37	494	72	48	792
Poza Rica	.256	114	3521	382	472	901	1164	110	45	21	338	38	72	27	16	384	26	474	73	42	771
Monclova	.253	118	3701	398	515	936	1190	129	25	25	357	38	57	25	27	374	27	463	80	51	853
Tampico	.252	115	3637	449	421	917	1239	134	40	36	382	49	68	36	20	355	35	539	56	28	801
Monterrey	.248	117	3671	359	466	909	1167	116	32	26	317	35	56	22	21	360	25	532	31	23	802
Coatzacoalcos	.247	117	3644	388	407	901	1115	122	19	18	308	32	69	17	25	377	28	541	79	44	827
Veracruz	.244	114	3543	319	364	866	1079	96	24	23	268	42	53	13	24	275	23	451	50	37	747

INDIVIDUAL BATTING

(Leading Qualifiers for Batting Championship—319 or More Plate Appearances)

*Bats lefthanded. †Switch-hitter.

Player and Club	Pct.	G.	AB.	R.	H.	TB.	2B.	3B.	HR.	RBI.	GW.	SH.	SF.	HP.	BB.	Int. BB.	SO.	SB.	CS.
Duran, Ricardo, Ciudad Juarez	.377	79	257	42	97	142	19	1	8	53	2	0	1	6	56	9	21	1	2
Olivares, Oswaldo, Ciudad Juarez*	.366	84	295	63	108	129	10	4	1	26	4	5	1	2	52	2	27	12	10
Bryant, Derek, Mexico City Tigers	.345	114	400	73	138	204	22	7	10	64	7	3	10	2	53	3	39	16	15
Lora, Ramon, Campeche	.337	93	326	55	110	168	15	5	11	72	7	1	7	5	44	6	29	6	5
Monreal, Luis, Mexico City Reds*	.332	96	343	59	114	128	10	2	0	29	3	4	2	0	37	5	27	15	4
Navarrete, Juan, Saltillo*	.329	118	419	60	138	149	9	1	0	40	2	8	2	1	58	4	19	21	7
Arnold, Ron, Nuevo Laredo	.329	118	404	92	133	190	21	3	10	47	2	4	1	6	81	6	43	24	10
Herring, Paul, Tabasco	.328	115	433	48	142	181	23	2	4	36	3	5	3	0	32	4	33	5	9
Bellacetin, Jose Juan, Campeche*	.324	102	340	69	110	128	8	5	0	37	7	4	3	1	80	3	22	21	10
Sanchez, Armando, MC Reds*	.322	106	376	60	121	145	18	3	0	41	7	8	6	3	42	0	27	26	4
Villaescusa, Fernando, Yucatan*	.322	102	401	56	129	148	10	3	1	24	2	7	1	2	28	1	24	20	11
Bazan, Pedro, Yucatan	.321	113	364	41	117	152	15	4	4	54	6	6	4	4	48	6	35	2	8
Suarez, Miguel, Tabasco*	.320	113	438	39	140	153	9	2	0	20	2	5	2	7	31	5	13	3	11

Departmental Leaders: G—Arnold, Burke, Mora, J. Navarrete, 118; AB—J.F. Rodriguez, 460; R—Arnold, 92; H—Herring, 142; TB—C. Soto, 218; 2B—Rod. Rodriguez, 26; 3B—Villela, 14; HR—C. Soto, 22; RBI—Aguilar, 89; GWRBI—M. Ramirez, 13; SH—Montiel, 17; SF—Aguilar, 11; HP—Evans, 10; BB—Evans, 110; IBB—Beamon, 20; SO—Batista, 80; SB—M. Alexander, 73; CS—M. Alexander, 28.

(All Players—Listed Alphabetically)

Player and Club	Pct.	G.	AB.	R.	H.	TB.	2B.	3B.	HR.	RBI.	GW.	SH.	SF.	HP.	BB.	Int. BB.	SO.	SB.	CS.
Aceves, Alfredo, Yucatan	.276	88	254	38	70	91	6	3	3	30	5	1	2	5	43	0	50	12	0
Acosta, Fernando, Veracruz	.167	7	6	0	1	1	0	0	0	1	0	0	0	0	0	0	3	0	0
Acosta, Leonardo, Tampico	.263	15	38	5	10	12	2	0	0	2	0	1	0	0	3	0	15	0	0
Adams, Calvin, 18 Mont-91 Monc	.296	109	379	52	110	136	12	3	2	42	3	4	3	4	62	3	26	24	13
Aguilar, Enrique, Aguascalientes	.273	110	410	66	112	181	22	1	15	89	12	2	11	6	28	4	22	7	7
Alcaraz, Florencio, Leon	.500	2	2	0	1	1	0	0	0	1	1	0	0	0	0	0	1	0	0
Alexander, Gary, Coatzacoalcos	.271	40	133	12	36	53	7	2	2	17	2	0	0	0	19	0	33	1	0
Alexander, Matthew, MC Tigers†	.312	116	433	68	135	155	12	1	2	31	4	1	3	1	78	8	43	73	28
Alexander, Robert, Poza Rica	.270	41	126	16	34	40	2	2	0	5	1	4	0	1	7	0	19	6	5
Almeida, Reynaldo, Leon	.186	54	113	12	21	28	2	1	1	4	0	2	0	0	14	0	28	4	1
Alonso, Hermilo, Campeche	.259	42	81	10	21	22	1	0	0	4	0	2	1	1	8	0	9	1	1
Alvarado, Natanael, Coatzacoalcos	.227	108	419	60	95	117	13	3	1	25	3	11	1	3	34	1	63	7	4
Alvarez, Juan Carlos, MC Tigers	.271	99	310	28	84	103	9	2	2	32	6	11	5	1	23	1	50	3	3
Alvarez, Jorge, Tabasco	.200	5	15	0	3	3	0	0	0	2	0	1	0	0	1	0	4	0	0
Andrade, Reynaldo, Tampico	.281	67	203	30	57	72	8	2	1	17	2	9	2	1	29	2	24	6	3
Aranda, Severo, Poza Rica	.333	5	9	3	3	3	0	0	0	2	1	0	0	0	1	0	3	0	0
Arano, Wilfredo, Coatzacoalcos	.000	2	3	1	0	0	0	0	0	0	0	0	0	0	1	0	1	0	0
Arce, Fco. Javier, Leon	.100	6	10	0	1	1	0	0	0	0	0	0	0	0	0	0	1	0	0
Arnold, Ron, Nuevo Laredo	.329	118	404	92	133	190	21	3	10	47	2	4	1	6	81	6	43	24	10
Arzate, Martin, 8 NL-86 Monc	.265	94	272	25	72	89	13	2	0	21	1	4	1	1	32	2	43	4	5
Avila, Ruben, Tampico	.256	72	215	24	55	76	7	1	4	25	4	2	3	1	11	1	41	3	0
Avina, Fco. Javier, Campeche	.333	11	30	4	10	12	0	1	0	1	0	0	1	0	0	0	3	1	2
Ayala, Javier, Monterrey	.171	61	146	11	25	29	4	0	0	4	0	7	0	2	7	0	37	0	0
Baca, Manuel, Veracruz	.177	34	79	1	14	16	2	0	0	4	0	4	0	0	4	0	13	0	1
Barrera, Jose Antonio, Nuevo Laredo	.269	87	201	22	54	62	6	1	0	15	3	10	1	2	6	0	24	2	1
Barrera, Nelson, Mexico City Reds	.312	108	391	52	122	180	14	4	12	60	11	5	6	3	31	1	70	12	6
Batista, Rafael, Tampico*	.256	105	348	53	89	141	17	1	11	46	5	4	4	3	65	11	80	2	0
Bazan, Pedro, Yucatan*	.321	113	364	41	117	152	15	4	4	54	6	6	4	4	48	6	35	2	8
Beamon, Charles, Campeche	.296	103	345	46	102	132	13	4	3	45	6	2	4	7	44	20	33	5	4
Bellacetin, Jose Juan, Campeche*	.324	102	340	69	110	128	8	5	0	37	7	4	3	1	80	3	22	21	10
Benitez, J.L. 16 Tam.-41 MC Tig.	.245	57	139	4	34	36	2	0	0	15	2	5	5	1	14	0	18	0	1
Benitez, Julio Cesar, Saltillo	.220	98	296	34	65	79	7	2	1	33	7	6	3	7	23	1	39	4	2
Bernal, Cosme, Aguascalientes	.114	17	35	4	4	7	0	0	1	3	0	1	0	0	5	0	7	0	0
Bernhardt, Juan, 46 Cam.-46 Vera.	.279	92	323	27	90	108	12	0	2	35	7	6	4	1	19	2	23	3	2
Blanks, Larvell, 68 Coatz.-27 Tab.	.262	95	332	37	87	106	12	2	1	38	6	9	5	0	36	6	36	4	7
Bobadilla, Manuel, Ciudad Juarez	.220	89	273	34	60	67	7	0	0	20	1	10	1	5	52	1	33	10	6
Bojorquez, Jose, Nuevo Laredo	.229	40	118	6	27	34	1	0	2	10	2	4	2	2	14	1	25	2	1
Bosley, Thad, Mexico City Tigers	.327	31	107	24	35	60	7	3	4	18	2	1	2	0	18	0	16	3	0
Briones, Antonio, Ciudad Juarez	.227	117	374	41	85	107	7	6	1	37	5	10	0	2	45	1	25	22	9
Bryant, Derek, Mexico City Tigers	.345	114	400	73	138	204	22	7	10	64	7	3	10	2	53	3	39	16	15
Buenrostro, Jose Luis, Yucatan	.216	51	51	4	11	11	0	0	0	2	0	0	0	2	3	0	19	0	0
Burke, Norberto, Saltillo	.256	118	348	43	89	119	21	0	3	48	12	10	3	5	71	4	39	2	10
Burton, Juan, Leon	.267	9	30	2	8	10	2	0	0	1	0	1	0	0	2	0	4	0	0
Cabrales, Sergio, Poza Rica	.182	21	11	4	2	2	0	0	0	1	0	0	0	0	1	0	2	0	0
Cage, Wayne, Yucatan*	.247	95	295	27	73	104	13	0	6	34	4	1	4	1	49	8	56	1	2
Canedo, Donald, 41 Tam.-49 Monc.	.264	100	314	43	83	118	17	3	4	29	2	3	1	2	54	5	55	9	4
Carreno, Luis Alberto, Monclova	.221	21	68	8	15	16	1	0	0	6	0	1	1	0	7	1	8	1	2
Carrillo, Francisco, Aguascalientes	.230	43	61	12	14	15	1	0	0	7	1	2	1	2	10	0	13	0	0
Carrillo, Matias, Poza Rica*	.311	91	360	54	112	165	13	11	6	39	3	4	2	2	34	7	56	25	11

Player and Club	Pct.	G.	AB.	R.	H.	TB.	2B.	3B.	HR.	RBI.	GW.	SH.	SF.	HP.	BB.	Int. BB.	SO.	SB.	CS.
Castelan, Miguel Angel, Campeche*	.257	91	288	39	74	92	8	5	0	19	1	5	1	1	35	0	37	22	3
Castro, Antonio, 19 Tig.-97 Tam.*	.271	116	405	49	110	152	21	6	3	43	4	7	3	0	56	8	36	6	10
Castro, Arnoldo, Veracruz	.000	5	6	0	0	0	0	0	0	0	0	0	0	0	0	0	2	0	0
Castro, Efren, Tabasco	.149	47	94	5	14	24	1	0	3	6	0	3	1	2	7	0	20	0	0
Castro, Fernando, Yucatan	.213	27	61	5	13	15	2	0	0	3	0	0	0	0	3	0	7	1	1
Castro, Jose Antonio, Veracruz	.194	78	252	15	49	56	7	0	0	18	4	7	1	2	18	0	39	1	2
Cervantes, Eduardo, Aguascalientes	.304	116	415	62	126	160	23	4	1	51	3	8	2	7	55	1	40	3	3
Cesena, Jose Isabel, Saltillo	.500	1	2	0	1	1	0	0	0	0	0	0	0	0	0	0	1	0	0
Chavez Baeza, Guadalupe, Saltillo*	.190	72	211	14	40	42	2	0	0	15	3	10	2	1	22	1	25	3	1
Chavez, Jose Santos, Nuevo Laredo*	.218	61	170	26	37	44	5	1	0	6	1	2	0	0	26	1	37	2	2
Chavez, Juan de Dios, Monclova	.217	93	300	25	65	77	9	0	1	22	2	12	2	2	27	0	51	5	3
Collins, James, Coatzacoalcos*	.296	117	432	52	128	158	18	3	2	46	1	0	2	3	42	10	53	39	12
Collins, Silvester, Coatzacoalcos*	.286	10	21	3	6	8	2	0	0	4	0	2	1	0	0	0	2	0	1
Contreras, Juan Carlos, Tampico	.164	35	61	9	10	10	0	0	0	2	1	3	0	0	10	2	9	1	1
Cordova, Ignacio, Poza Rica	.400	8	15	2	6	6	0	0	0	1	0	0	0	0	4	1	5	0	0
Cosey, Donald Ray, Saltillo*	.270	113	404	51	109	156	25	2	6	61	9	5	10	1	28	2	47	7	4
Cotes, Eugenio, Saltillo	.308	78	286	34	88	107	12	2	1	40	3	3	3	0	23	1	33	20	10
Covarrubias, Hector, MC Reds	.500	2	2	0	1	1	0	0	0	0	0	0	0	0	0	0	0	0	0
Cruz De La O, Domingo, Tabasco	.250	88	292	23	73	85	6	3	0	25	4	6	2	4	19	4	24	5	3
Cruz, Henry, Leon*	.302	116	391	57	118	181	21	3	12	63	1	1	4	6	64	14	28	5	2
Daut, Manuel, Monterrey	.192	37	104	10	20	20	0	0	0	3	0	2	0	2	3	0	22	1	0
Davis, Stanley, Ciudad Juarez	.220	60	209	20	46	62	8	1	2	17	4	2	1	0	24	7	29	18	2
DeFreites, Arturo, Tabasco	.272	113	427	51	116	164	15	3	9	57	11	2	8	4	19	4	55	5	6
Deliza, Juan Ernesto, Poza Rica	.267	12	45	3	12	13	1	0	0	10	2	2	0	0	2	0	5	0	0
De Los Santos, Carlos E., Coatz.	.300	18	40	5	12	13	1	0	0	1	0	1	0	0	3	0	4	1	0
Diaz, Albino, Campeche	.300	67	223	38	67	92	10	3	3	25	2	9	4	3	19	0	16	8	4
Diaz, Gustavo, Tabasco	.088	29	34	5	3	3	0	0	0	0	0	0	0	0	3	0	2	0	0
Duncan, Taylor, 24 Ctz-89 Poza Rica	.288	113	400	37	115	152	22	3	3	47	3	2	2	1	59	6	22	3	4
Duran, Ricardo, Ciudad Juarez	.377	79	257	42	97	142	19	1	8	53	2	0	1	6	56	9	21	1	2
Duran, Roberto, Yucatan	.200	30	55	6	11	12	1	0	0	4	0	0	1	3	5	1	9	1	0
Dyes, Andy, Yucatan	.303	35	122	17	37	61	5	2	5	21	1	0	0	0	17	1	30	0	1
Edwards, Dave, Monterrey	.274	49	164	22	45	64	8	1	3	16	2	2	1	2	31	4	26	6	4
Elizondo, Fernando, Veracruz	.255	112	427	36	109	131	14	4	0	19	3	10	1	1	29	0	39	2	7
Esparza, Julio, Poza Rica	.143	6	7	1	1	1	0	0	0	0	0	0	0	0	0	0	2	0	0
Espino, Hector, Monterrey	.246	70	244	14	60	73	7	0	2	20	1	0	1	5	24	6	19	1	1
Espinosa Ramos, Ernesto, Coatz.*	.195	38	82	7	16	18	2	0	0	5	2	1	0	0	5	0	12	0	1
Estrada, Francisco, Campeche	.249	81	245	23	61	73	9	0	1	24	4	8	2	2	31	5	15	3	2
Evans, John, Aguascalientes	.301	114	345	81	104	165	22	3	11	64	4	1	6	10	110	3	56	3	4
Fabela, Lorenzo, Saltillo	.000	11	4	4	0	0	0	0	0	0	0	0	0	0	0	0	1	0	0
Felix, Alfredo, Coatzacoalcos	.195	29	77	7	15	22	5	1	0	9	1	1	1	3	3	0	17	0	0
Felix, Victor Manuel, Saltillo	.270	86	248	41	67	88	9	0	4	15	0	10	3	1	48	1	43	6	3
Fernandez, Daniel, Mexico City Reds	.000	5	2	0	0	0	0	0	0	0	0	0	0	0	0	0	0	0	0
Fierro, Javier, Mexico City Tigers	.222	6	18	1	4	0	0	0	0	2	0	1	1	0	1	0	1	0	0
Figueroa, Leobardo, Ciudad Juarez	.282	56	170	26	48	59	7	2	0	20	4	2	1	9	35	2	21	3	6
Firova, Dan, Nuevo Laredo	.239	72	218	17	52	63	3	1	2	14	2	4	3	1	6	0	33	0	1
Flores, Mario, Yucatan	.156	19	45	2	7	9	2	0	0	4	1	2	1	0	4	0	5	1	1
Flores, Rodolfo, Monclova	.183	27	82	6	15	18	3	0	0	5	0	0	1	2	4	0	15	0	1
Fobs, Terry, Tabasco	.261	7	23	0	6	7	1	0	0	2	0	0	0	0	5	0	2	0	0
Ford, Lambert, Poza Rica*	.280	44	150	19	42	50	4	2	0	14	0	3	2	0	21	2	19	5	2
Franco, Francisco, Poza Rica	.000	2	5	0	0	0	0	0	0	0	0	0	0	0	0	0	1	0	0
Frias, Jesus, Tampico	.270	103	397	45	107	127	11	3	1	37	4	6	1	3	18	1	41	8	4
Funderburk, Mark, MC Tigers	.364	36	129	24	47	80	7	1	8	33	7	0	2	1	12	2	26	1	1
Gage, Ralph, 36 Yuc.-72 Mont.*	.282	108	376	44	106	142	13	7	3	42	8	1	2	0	59	9	42	3	4
Gamundi, Timoteo, Poza Rica	.266	104	339	49	90	118	9	5	3	41	4	10	4	4	40	1	48	9	5
Garcia, Enrique, Leon	.000	1	0	0	0	0	0	0	0	0	0	0	0	0	1	0	0	0	0
Garcia, Sabino, Poza Rica	.207	13	29	9	6	9	1	1	0	3	1	0	0	0	4	0	6	1	0
Garza, Adolfo, 17 Yuc.-86 Tab.	.282	103	340	30	96	126	15	3	3	30	3	2	2	1	32	10	40	2	1
Garza, Carlos, Mexico City Tigers*	.227	108	330	37	75	107	11	6	3	38	4	3	4	1	56	10	44	2	5
Garzon, Felix, Coatzacoalcos	.279	104	337	28	94	116	18	2	0	32	2	5	4	1	34	2	69	0	2
Gomez, Alejandro, Nuevo Laredo	.208	82	289	20	60	68	2	3	0	24	7	9	2	3	15	0	19	14	5
Gomez, Arturo, Tabasco	.000	2	6	0	0	0	0	0	0	0	0	0	0	0	0	0	1	0	0
Gomez, Graciano, Monclova	.232	111	431	43	100	122	11	4	1	27	1	7	1	4	25	0	35	16	7
Gomez, Marcos, Aguascalientes	.302	53	192	41	58	82	9	6	1	27	6	4	4	5	26	0	23	6	2
Gonzalez, Arturo, Monclova	.254	101	338	47	86	103	7	2	2	34	3	5	2	3	23	2	41	9	1
Gonzalez, Efrain, Yucatan	.333	10	15	3	5	6	1	0	0	1	0	0	0	0	1	0	0	0	0
Gonzalez, Fernando, Tampico	.290	88	317	45	92	126	21	2	3	38	8	1	3	2	31	1	29	10	1
Gonzalez, Jesus, Coatzacoalcos	.262	108	404	32	106	124	13	1	1	27	3	7	0	4	15	0	30	2	3
Gonzalez, Mario, Tabasco	.227	12	22	1	5	7	2	0	0	1	0	0	0	0	5	0	3	0	1
Gonzalez, Moe, Mexico City Tigers	.231	83	238	27	55	67	4	4	0	18	1	9	3	1	16	0	41	6	2
Gonzalez, Ricardo, Ciudad Juarez	.227	95	304	27	69	82	9	2	0	39	8	3	5	4	27	2	55	7	3
Gray, Gary, Mexico City Reds	.318	96	355	56	113	184	15	4	16	77	12	0	6	2	38	3	71	7	3
Greene, Altar, Coatzacoalcos*	.252	106	306	49	77	120	11	1	10	49	4	2	3	3	95	8	71	10	4
Guerra, Ricardo, 43 Reds-59 Yuc	.268	102	351	52	94	129	13	2	6	50	7	3	7	6	61	2	47	9	6
Guerrero, Leobardo, Tabasco	.285	112	425	47	121	139	14	2	0	12	2	11	0	1	28	0	29	17	9
Guzman, Andres, Campeche	.271	57	155	18	42	61	9	2	2	22	5	0	1	2	9	0	19	0	4
Guzman, Marco Antonio, MC Reds	.200	44	120	16	24	35	5	0	2	10	0	0	1	0	15	0	20	1	2
Hansen, John, Aguascalientes	.211	40	142	12	30	37	5	1	0	9	1	2	1	0	3	1	32	0	1
Harris, Dario, 22 Tabasco-37 PR*	.245	59	204	31	50	75	5	7	2	15	1	4	1	0	23	3	23	7	5
Hazzard, Rick, Aguascalientes*	.222	18	63	9	14	24	2	1	2	7	1	0	0	0	7	2	20	0	1
Heras, Roberto, Coatzacoalcos	.048	13	21	1	1	2	1	0	0	0	0	0	0	0	0	0	5	0	0
Hernandez, Gustavo, MC Reds	.200	3	5	0	1	1	0	0	0	0	0	0	0	0	0	0	1	0	0
Hernandez, Jorge Luis, Campeche	.209	100	320	23	69	79	10	1	0	14	2	9	1	6	15	0	33	3	0
Hernandez, Juan, Mexico City Reds	.266	113	425	60	113	137	10	7	0	22	4	11	2	1	36	0	73	36	18
Hernandez, Loreto, Yucatan	.113	49	71	8	8	9	1	0	0	6	1	2	1	2	7	0	21	1	0
Hernandez, Miguel, Coatzacoalcos	.214	103	290	26	62	67	5	0	0	17	2	6	0	4	33	0	35	4	5
Hernandez, Pedro, Monclova	.175	62	154	19	27	36	5	2	0	10	0	3	0	2	18	1	8	1	3
Hernandez, Rodolfo, Yucatan	.202	32	89	2	18	21	3	0	0	5	0	2	1	1	8	1	11	0	0
Hernandez, Rogelio, Leon	.000	1	2	0	0	0	0	0	0	0	0	0	0	0	0	0	2	0	0
Herrera, Ricardo, Campeche	.249	99	358	41	89	117	19	3	1	27	3	7	1	1	40	2	40	19	10
Herring, Paul, Tabasco	.328	115	433	48	142	181	23	2	4	36	3	5	3	0	32	4	33	5	9
Horton, Willie, Nuevo Laredo	.324	49	170	17	55	66	5	0	2	33	1	1	6	0	13	1	30	2	5
Howard, Wilbur, Yucatan	.303	36	122	7	37	40	3	0	0	15	1	3	1	0	5	0	12	7	4
Huerta, Juan Pedro, Monclova	.194	20	36	1	7	7	0	0	0	3	0	1	0	0	0	0	4	0	0

Player and Club	Pct.	G.	AB.	R.	H.	TB.	2B.	3B.	HR.	RBI.	GW.	SH.	SF.	HP.	BB.	Int. BB.	SO.	SB.	CS.
Irvine, Edward, Nuevo Laredo*	.272	112	445	55	121	140	11	4	0	29	6	6	2	2	38	3	27	23	13
Jimenez, German, Campeche*	.000	1	1	0	0	0	0	0	0	0	0	0	0	0	0	0	0	0	0
Jimenez, Leopoldo, Tampico	.235	62	183	13	43	53	8	1	0	22	4	1	3	2	17	1	29	1	2
Johnson, Lorenzo, Nuevo Laredo	.181	50	144	13	26	36	2	1	2	13	1	3	1	2	15	1	31	5	1
Lara, Francisco, Veracruz	.217	88	254	16	55	61	3	0	1	15	2	7	2	4	8	0	17	1	2
Lazaro, Manuel, Poza Rica	.137	27	51	5	7	7	0	0	0	2	0	1	0	0	5	0	14	0	0
Leal, Jose Guadalupe, Tampico*	.249	62	173	23	43	60	3	1	4	25	5	3	4	1	21	5	29	2	0
Leon, Juan Carlos, Yucatan	.233	80	202	21	47	63	5	4	1	14	1	12	0	5	16	0	51	2	1
Limon, Arturo, 21 Tab.-19 Ver	.237	40	76	9	18	18	0	0	0	2	0	1	0	1	4	0	12	1	1
Limon, Salvador, Leon	.231	7	13	3	3	3	0	0	0	0	0	0	0	0	1	0	0	0	0
Lizarraga, Alejandro, MC Reds	.247	87	299	31	74	91	6	4	1	29	0	5	2	1	12	1	15	7	2
Llanes, Ramon Ernesto, Aguas.	.000	3	1	0	0	0	0	0	0	0	0	0	0	0	0	0	0	0	0
Lopez, Carlos, Yucatan	.315	98	337	58	106	145	16	1	7	41	4	1	1	4	29	4	31	20	8
Lopez, Jaime, E., Ciudad Juarez*	.298	103	376	50	112	150	14	3	6	40	3	7	4	1	20	3	15	1	1
Lopez, Victor Manuel, Campeche	.236	18	55	3	13	16	1	1	0	8	0	0	0	0	5	0	8	0	0
Lora, Ramon, Campeche	.337	93	326	55	110	168	15	5	11	72	7	1	7	5	44	6	29	6	5
Lugo, Gabriel, Aguascalientes	.264	76	220	17	58	71	8	1	1	31	0	1	3	2	24	5	17	1	0
Lugo, Pedro, Poza Rica	.231	72	186	11	43	51	8	0	0	16	3	5	1	0	5	0	20	0	1
Luna, Jose Luis, 7 CJ-58 Monclova	.197	65	183	14	36	45	6	0	1	16	2	5	1	0	10	0	24	0	1
Madero, Carlos, Poza Rica	.261	50	111	8	29	34	2	0	1	7	2	4	0	0	12	0	11	0	0
Marquez, Francisco, Veracruz	.235	6	17	2	4	4	0	0	0	0	0	0	0	0	0	0	2	0	0
Martinez, Alfonso, Tampico	.000	1	1	0	0	0	0	0	0	0	0	0	0	0	0	0	1	0	0
Martinez, Francisco, Coatzacoalcos	.207	89	237	16	49	54	5	0	0	11	3	19	0	1	5	0	33	2	1
Martinez, Oscar, 15 Reds-25 Ctz	.209	40	91	11	19	22	1	1	0	5	0	0	0	0	12	0	9	0	1
Martinez, Raul, Leon	.172	65	174	10	30	33	1	1	0	9	1	6	0	1	23	0	27	0	0
Martinez, Teodoro, Campeche	.260	31	104	10	27	34	2	1	1	8	0	2	1	0	9	1	8	3	0
McDonald, Anthony, Tabasco	.250	51	172	16	43	49	4	1	0	16	1	6	1	2	14	1	11	3	7
McDonald, James, Veracruz*	.300	109	390	58	117	178	19	6	10	51	7	1	1	4	33	8	37	5	4
Mendez, Roberto, Mexico City Tigers	.141	39	85	8	12	14	2	0	0	5	1	6	1	2	22	0	16	1	1
Mendoza, Margarito, Ciudad Juarez	.267	8	15	2	4	4	0	0	0	1	0	1	0	0	2	0	0	0	1
Mendoza, Porfirio, Campeche	.296	59	152	19	45	63	4	1	4	19	1	4	2	1	14	0	17	0	2
Mendoza, Ricardo, Tampico	.000	4	0	1	0	0	0	0	0	0	0	0	0	0	0	0	0	0	0
Mendoza, Santiago, Tabasco	.117	61	120	7	14	19	2	0	1	9	1	3	0	1	10	0	28	0	0
Mendoza, Saul, Poza Rica	.242	106	343	27	83	96	8	1	1	33	3	9	7	3	41	1	43	4	3
Molina, Jose Maria, 43 Tab-17 PR	.203	60	158	7	32	42	5	1	1	19	1	5	2	0	5	0	24	0	0
Monreal, Luis, Mexico City Reds*	.332	96	343	59	114	128	10	2	0	29	3	4	2	0	37	5	27	15	4
Montano, Nicolas, Ciudad Juarez*	.272	5	11	0	3	3	0	0	0	1	0	2	0	0	3	0	3	0	0
Montiel, Julio, 38 Monc.-75 Yuc	.241	113	381	31	92	104	10	1	0	21	3	17	2	3	25	0	33	3	2
Montoya, Ramon, Mexico City Reds	.500	4	6	0	3	3	0	0	0	2	0	0	0	0	0	0	0	0	1
Moore, Alvin, Mexico City Tigers	.301	84	289	53	87	135	6	3	12	50	5	1	2	1	40	7	15	6	2
Moore, Stephen, Saltillo*	.281	111	405	74	114	150	12	9	2	40	5	6	0	2	71	2	52	36	17
Mora, Andres, Nuevo Laredo	.304	118	401	64	122	193	14	0	19	75	8	2	6	7	64	10	34	6	5
Morales, Carlos, Saltillo	.146	16	48	4	7	9	2	0	0	2	0	0	0	0	3	1	10	0	0
Morales, Manuel, Mexico City Tigers	.283	114	368	43	104	122	10	4	0	31	6	14	3	5	24	0	22	17	7
Moreno, Jose, Mexico City Reds*	.228	47	162	25	37	56	5	1	4	25	7	0	2	0	29	1	26	13	2
Morris, Angel, Monclova	.212	18	52	5	11	12	1	0	0	6	0	1	0	0	9	0	13	0	1
Munoz, Eduardo, Yucatan	.246	89	289	22	71	86	5	2	2	32	1	5	3	4	27	0	23	4	4
Munoz, Jose Luis, Monterrey	.224	86	255	20	57	62	3	1	0	14	1	7	0	0	31	0	40	1	2
Murrell, Ivan, Leon	.291	96	354	69	103	179	14	1	20	73	3	0	3	8	37	3	63	7	2
Navarrete, Juan, Saltillo*	.329	118	419	60	138	149	9	1	0	40	2	8	2	1	58	4	19	21	7
Nunez, Arturo, Veracruz	.106	40	94	6	10	12	0	1	0	3	0	0	0	2	7	0	31	1	0
Ochoa, Porfirio, Nuevo Laredo	.000	1	0	1	0	0	0	0	0	0	0	0	0	0	0	0	0	0	0
Olivares, Oswaldo, 36 Ctz-48 CJ*	.366	84	295	63	108	129	10	4	1	26	4	5	1	2	52	2	27	12	10
Ortiz, Alejandro, Nuevo Laredo*	.259	117	386	65	101	163	21	1	13	64	5	8	4	6	59	3	54	7	4
Ortiz, Alfredo, Mexico City Reds*	.444	15	18	0	8	11	3	0	0	4	0	1	0	0	1	0	2	0	0
Ortiz, Jose Manuel, Veracruz	.264	113	394	37	104	120	16	0	0	28	3	7	2	3	23	2	37	2	2
Osuna, Elpidio, Ciudad Juarez	.000	1	1	0	0	0	0	0	0	0	0	0	0	0	0	0	0	0	0
Pacheco, Claudio, Mexico City Tigers	.246	63	171	20	42	52	3	2	1	12	1	2	1	1	12	1	22	2	3
Paredes, Jesus, 63 Tig-28 NL	.239	91	309	28	74	91	4	5	1	34	5	4	1	4	19	1	38	6	5
Parra, Salomon, Monclova	.229	58	166	11	38	48	5	1	1	18	3	1	0	0	12	1	27	1	1
Pasillas, Andy, 10 Tig-83 Tampico	.256	93	270	33	69	92	7	2	4	30	1	6	5	3	24	1	28	1	3
Peralta, Amado, Monclova	.176	85	222	22	39	55	6	2	2	14	0	6	1	1	35	2	67	0	0
Peraza, Jose, Yucatan	.167	11	6	0	1	1	0	0	0	1	0	0	0	0	0	0	2	0	1
Perez, Alfredo, 50 Poza Rica-20 Ctz	.266	70	199	19	53	57	4	0	0	11	0	0	0	1	23	2	28	1	1
Perez, Jose Luis, Aguascalientes*	.290	114	396	47	115	167	20	4	8	74	8	1	3	3	29	12	48	6	3
Petters, Jay, Monclova	.288	82	274	49	79	139	17	5	11	45	7	1	1	4	52	8	69	7	2
Pierce, Jack, 15 Ca-48 Vr-48 Sal.*	.246	111	378	40	93	153	13	1	15	51	8	0	5	3	37	9	52	2	1
Poe, Richard, Leon*	.278	107	374	56	104	155	15	3	10	60	10	3	7	1	48	9	51	3	1
Prevost, Eric, Monterrey	.000	1	2	0	0	0	0	0	0	0	0	1	0	0	0	0	0	0	0
Purata, Julio, Poza Rica	.000	1	0	1	0	0	0	0	0	0	0	0	0	0	0	0	0	0	0
Quintero, Victor, Saltillo	.286	76	227	21	65	70	5	0	0	23	3	2	2	2	24	0	26	2	6
Quinonez, Ventura, 8 Mt.-49 Mc.	.217	57	129	11	28	33	3	1	0	4	0	7	0	1	6	0	14	3	1
Quiroz, Jose Julian, Nuevo Laredo*	.256	99	317	41	81	118	11	7	4	28	5	8	1	6	25	3	51	1	4
Ramirez, Manuel, Monclova	.314	101	366	34	115	140	15	2	2	65	13	2	9	0	27	2	21	7	6
Raymundo, Oscar, Yucatan	.200	2	5	1	1	2	1	0	0	1	0	0	0	0	2	0	2	0	0
Rendon, Josue, Saltillo	.274	82	263	31	72	99	6	0	7	40	5	3	0	0	27	4	52	3	4
Reyes, Enrique, Nuevo Laredo	.159	30	82	5	13	14	1	0	0	5	0	4	0	0	8	3	16	0	1
Reyes, Gerardo, Mexico City Tigers	.385	7	13	3	5	6	1	0	0	2	0	0	0	1	1	0	2	1	1
Reyes, Juan, Aguascalientes*	.273	63	172	23	47	69	9	2	3	21	3	0	4	1	9	0	43	3	0
Rios, Carlos, Mexico City Tigers	253	105	391	32	99	119	7	5	1	34	7	5	6	1	10	4	34	3	8
Rivera, Carlos, Tabasco	.252	96	314	28	79	103	11	2	3	27	5	6	5	1	27	4	53	9	1
Rivera, Eduardo, Ciudad Juarez	.268	98	291	24	78	101	10	2	3	39	4	11	5	4	27	0	22	0	4
Rivero, Gener, Leon	.241	113	345	38	83	91	8	0	0	19	1	13	1	2	43	0	24	7	4
Robles, Humberto, Monterrey	.293	109	351	30	103	145	16	7	4	37	5	3	3	2	35	2	64	3	2
Robles, Sergio, Mexico City Reds	.236	88	301	31	71	82	8	0	1	32	4	4	3	0	5	0	23	3	2
Rodriguez, I. Francisco, Aguas	.273	115	432	60	118	132	12	1	0	33	6	15	1	1	50	1	32	0	3
Rodriguez, Genaro, Ciudad Juarez	.063	11	16	1	1	1	0	0	0	0	0	0	0	0	1	0	5	1	0
Rodriguez, Guillermo, Campeche	.270	111	408	50	110	156	21	2	7	55	8	13	3	7	11	1	50	9	9
Rodriguez, Jaime, Leon	.303	116	435	36	132	180	21	3	7	63	7	7	2	5	16	2	30	5	6
Rodriguez, Jose de Jesus, Poza Rica	.230	96	300	35	69	93	4	7	2	28	4	7	0	2	15	0	38	4	4
Rodriguez, Juan Francisco, Leon	.274	115	460	74	126	145	12	2	1	33	4	11	3	2	48	0	20	30	8
Rodriguez, C. Leonardo, Saltillo†	.239	93	259	31	62	90	13	3	3	34	5	4	4	1	34	1	36	4	3
Rodriguez, Roberto, Yucatan*	.250	62	236	27	59	72	4	3	1	19	5	5	1	0	27	1	17	9	8

Player and Club	Pct.	G.	AB.	R.	H.	TB.	2B.	3B.	HR.	RBI.	GW.	SH.	SF.	HP.	BB.	Int. BB.	SO.	SB.	CS.
Rodriguez, Rodolfo, Aguascalientes*	.319	117	442	82	141	180	26	5	1	35	5	5	1	2	65	3	36	3	3
Rojas, Omar, Monterrey	.209	95	292	20	61	85	12	3	2	30	3	7	4	0	10	0	65	0	1
Rojo, Gonzalo, Saltillo	.240	37	75	2	18	24	1	1	1	11	2	1	1	0	3	0	15	0	0
Rosas, Clemente, Aguascalientes	.277	89	292	26	81	92	7	2	0	30	1	2	4	2	21	0	43	1	3
Romero, Felipe, Monterrey	.000	1	1	0	0	0	0	0	0	0	0	0	0	0	0	0	1	0	0
Romero, Pedro, Poza Rica	.143	5	7	3	1	1	0	0	0	0	0	0	0	0	0	0	1	0	0
Romo, Jose Maria, Poza Rica	.212	83	212	13	45	64	11	1	2	15	2	4	1	1	29	0	33	0	2
Rubio, Arturo, Tabasco	.229	72	157	13	36	42	2	2	0	9	0	5	0	0	15	1	12	1	2
Ruiz, Demetrio, Coatzacoalcos	.148	20	54	4	8	9	1	0	0	1	0	1	0	0	2	0	6	0	0
Ruiz, Porfirio, 37 Leon-45 Vera	.207	82	242	18	50	59	7	1	0	18	2	4	1	1	28	2	26	2	1
Rush, Lawrence, Ciudad Juarez*	.182	23	77	10	14	23	5	2	0	12	2	0	1	0	12	1	17	2	2
Saenz, Ricardo, Leon	.333	68	183	20	61	85	6	3	4	30	4	2	4	1	13	0	18	5	1
Saiz, Herminio, Ciudad Juarez	.185	35	65	5	12	16	2	1	0	7	1	3	0	0	11	0	13	0	0
Salais, Ricardo, Nuevo Laredo	.308	4	13	3	4	4	0	0	0	1	0	1	0	0	2	0	2	0	0
Salazar, Ronaldo, Leon	.307	49	176	32	54	64	8	1	0	20	0	4	2	3	26	4	21	8	4
Sanchez, Armando, MC Reds*	.322	106	376	60	121	145	18	3	0	41	7	8	6	3	42	0	27	26	4
Sanchez, Gerardo, Nuevo Laredo	.217	88	226	23	49	66	4	5	1	19	2	7	1	2	13	0	39	4	4
Sarabia, Antonio, Veracruz	.246	77	236	17	58	76	4	7	0	14	3	2	1	1	30	3	48	7	5
Sauceda, Victor Manuel, C. Juarez	.271	84	258	32	70	91	9	3	2	22	5	3	1	2	6	0	38	0	2
Scott, George, 83 PR-31 Veracruz	.223	114	391	30	87	120	14	2	5	52	8	0	3	1	62	7	58	0	1
Serna, Joel, Monterrey	.255	114	377	47	96	122	13	2	3	40	5	6	5	1	54	3	65	1	1
Serratos, Miguel, Coatzacoalcos	.216	68	204	15	44	54	5	1	1	14	2	3	0	2	10	0	47	0	1
Silva, Eduardo, Ciudad Juarez	.000	1	1	0	0	0	0	0	0	0	0	0	0	0	0	0	1	0	0
Sommers, Jesus, 67 Reds-37 Leon	.221	104	367	43	81	126	11	2	10	48	4	1	2	0	44	3	53	3	2
Sosa, Arturo, Tampico*	.163	20	43	3	7	5	2	0	0	4	0	1	1	0	4	1	6	0	0
Sotelo, Emilio, Leon	.273	95	330	54	90	110	6	7	0	20	1	6	2	6	45	2	56	14	7
Soto, Carlos, Nuevo Laredo	.299	112	402	52	120	218	24	4	22	75	9	0	1	2	34	7	43	2	3
Soto, Gregorio, Veracruz	.253	113	387	34	98	112	10	2	0	35	8	5	2	4	23	0	47	6	5
Soto, Jorge, Saltillo	.125	5	8	0	1	1	0	0	0	0	0	0	0	0	1	0	3	0	0
Stenholm, Richard, MC Reds*	.292	35	113	17	33	63	4	1	8	30	2	0	2	2	23	4	20	3	1
Suarez, Miguel, Tabasco	.320	113	438	39	140	153	9	2	0	20	2	5	2	7	31	5	13	3	11
Tapia, Noe, Mexico City Reds	.263	7	19	2	5	8	1	1	0	6	0	0	0	0	4	0	1	0	2
Tiburcio, Zeferino, Poza Rica	.192	13	26	1	5	6	1	0	0	1	0	0	0	0	0	0	3	0	0
Tisdale, Alfred, Veracruz*	.179	18	67	6	12	19	1	0	2	11	0	1	1	0	5	1	14	0	0
Torres, Antonio, Tampico	.234	65	167	25	39	47	8	0	0	8	4	5	1	0	7	0	26	5	3
Torres,Nemesio, Monterrey	.254	39	114	11	29	35	4	1	0	7	0	0	0	2	5	0	7	1	1
Torres, Rafael, Aguascalientes	.219	28	64	9	14	15	1	0	0	2	1	1	1	2	8	0	10	0	0
Torres, Raymundo, Mexico City Reds.	.217	96	290	41	63	101	10	5	6	33	5	3	6	7	39	2	67	5	3
Tutt, John Edward, Veracruz	.320	48	175	24	56	65	1	1	2	8	0	1	0	2	10	1	24	12	6
Uresti, Guadalupe, Leon	.069	11	29	0	2	2	0	0	0	1	0	0	0	0	1	0	11	0	0
Urias, Reyes, Campeche	.000	1	2	0	0	0	0	0	0	0	0	0	0	0	0	0	0	0	0
Uzcanga, Ali, Monterrey	.269	114	458	50	123	157	14	7	2	42	8	6	2	2	24	0	34	6	4
Valdez, Baltazar, Monclova	.268	35	123	10	33	45	6	0	2	10	0	0	2	0	14	3	19	0	0
Valenzuela, Ricardo, Mex. City Tigers	.000	5	9	0	0	0	0	0	0	0	0	0	0	0	0	0	3	0	0
Valle, Guadalupe, Ciudad Juarez	.258	115	361	39	93	124	15	5	2	41	6	8	2	1	56	3	71	6	5
Vargas, Antonio, Monclova	.241	18	58	6	14	17	1	1	0	5	1	0	1	1	1	0	12	0	0
Vazquez, Nicolas, Monclova	.174	18	46	3	8	9	1	0	0	1	0	0	0	1	5	1	3	0	0
Vazquez, Rafael, Poza Rica	.000	1	0	1	0	0	0	0	0	0	0	0	0	0	0	0	0	0	0
Vega, Abelardo, Mexico City Reds	.307	42	101	23	31	40	6	0	1	11	1	2	0	0	12	0	14	1	2
Vega, Ramon, Aguascalientes	.221	45	113	7	25	31	2	2	0	9	1	6	1	0	7	1	16	0	0
Velarde, Roman, Tabasco	.228	60	136	8	31	38	5	1	0	15	3	1	0	2	5	0	16	0	2
Vergara, Salvador, Veracruz	.174	34	86	6	15	15	0	0	0	3	0	2	0	0	8	0	15	4	0
Vidana, Alejandro, Saltillo	.000	1	0	1	0	0	0	0	0	0	0	0	0	0	0	0	0	0	0
Villaescusa, Fernando, Yucatan	.322	102	401	56	129	148	10	3	1	24	2	7	1	2	28	1	24	20	11
Villagomez, David, Tampico	.253	91	305	31	77	98	9	6	0	37	5	5	3	4	24	1	48	2	2
Villalobos, Juan Enrique, Leon	.184	51	98	8	18	27	1	1	2	9	1	2	1	3	9	0	23	1	0
Villela, Carlos, Tampico	.234	112	432	55	101	150	6	14	5	39	2	12	1	0	32	0	74	7	2
Villela, Rigoberto P., Monterrey	.229	58	175	14	40	54	8	0	2	17	1	2	1	1	19	1	17	1	1
Williams, Ellis, Monterry*	.336	38	119	11	40	49	3	0	2	18	2	1	0	0	4	0	16	0	1
Yepez, Francisco, Poza Rica	.269	91	268	32	72	97	5	7	2	19	5	11	3	0	37	1	37	10	1
Zaguren, Andres, Monterrey	.000	1	0	0	0	0	0	0	0	0	0	0	0	0	0	0	0	0	0
Zambrano, Rosario, Monterrey*	.262	95	340	37	89	101	8	2	0	16	4	2	2	0	22	0	16	4	5
Zamora, Roberto, 3 Tigers-36 Vera.	.148	39	81	6	12	17	3	1	0	7	1	2	0	1	12	0	18	3	0
Zavala, Marcos, Tabasco	.200	3	5	1	1	1	0	0	0	0	0	0	0	0	0	0	4	0	0

The following pitchers, listed alphabetically by club, with games in parentheses, had no plate appearances, primarily through use of designated hitters:

AGUASCALIENTES—Abarca, David (16); Alcala, Santo (15); Brunet, George (24); Canedo, Guillermo (5); Casas, Arturo (1); Castillejos, Jose (29); Contreras, Patricio (3); Cordova, Ernesto (17); Delgadillo, Gustavo (2); Feola, Larry (2); Guzman, Jose (15); Hinrichs, Phillip (5); Jackson, Darrell (6); Low, Gabriel (24); Madrigal, Hector (10); Martinez, Gabriel (25); Morales, Mario (35); Moreno, Jesus (27); Mundo, Jesus (21); Munez, Miguel (5); Palacios, Vicente (22); Pena, Hipolito (17); Ramirez, Pedro (1); Valdez, Humberto (23); Vazquez, Jessie (33); Villegas, David (17); Villegas, Mike (21); Zamudio, Aurelio (15).

CAMPECHE—Diaz, Anibal (20); Divison, Julie (35); Dominguez, Herminio (26); Gamez, Carlos (1); Guzman, Gelasio (3); Moreno, Domingo (2); Ontiveros, Juan (3); Orozco, Jaime (25); Peralta, Alvaro (26); Preciado, Ignacio (13).

CIUDAD JUAREZ—Alicea, Miguel (32); Castillo, Humberto (11); Dorin, Matt (9); Gutierrez, Perfirio (26); Higueras, Teodoro (27); Martinez, Francisco (16); Montenegro, Francisco (24); Quinonez, Rene (6); Serna, Ramon (27).

COATZACOALCOS—Arano, Ramon (27); Armas, Isidro (5); Colorado, Salvador (23); Diaz, Cesar (23); Guzman, Jose (4); Miranda, Francisco (29); Ochea, Domingo (29); Ponce, Jorge (4); Quijada, Armando (9); Solis, Ricardo (27); Tejeda, Felix (24); Torres, Martin (16); Vazquez, Marco (10).

LEON—Beltran, Jorge (13); Corona, Benjamin (2); Gomez, Fernando (2); Ibarra, Carlos (18); Inzunza, Sergio (40); Jefferson, Jesse (16); Madrigal, Hector (3); Matus, Nelson (7); Milanez, Luis (9); Munoz, Emeterio (7); Partida, Gustavo (2); Ramirez, Jose (22); Raygoza, Jose (5); Rios, Rogelio (9); Rodriguez, Arturo (46); Solis, Jesus (1); Soto, Alvaro (10); Zambrano, Rogelio (8).

MEXICO CITY REDS—Escarrega, Ernesto (19); Hernandez, Martin (1); Howard, Fred (3); Ibarra, Carlos (7); Leon, Maximino (20); Mendez, Luis (27); Pruneda, Armando (20); Pulido, Alfonso (29); Pulido, Antonio (40); Rios, Rogelio (5); Rodriguez, Antonio (2); Schattinger, Jeff (6); Soto, Alvaro (21); Tiant, Luis (5); Vazquez, Marco (5).

MEXICO CITY TIGERS—Aguilar, Jose (21); Casas, Arturo (3); Dimas, Rodolfo (42); Jamie, Ismael (16); Lopez, Hector (16); Montano, Francisco (29); Moore, Edmond (4); Palafox, Juan (21); Pena, Jose (26); Romo, Vicente (26); Sauceda, Ramiro (11); Velasquez, Ildefonso (17); Villanueva, Luis (29); Villegas Ramon (25).

MONCLOVA—Bloonfiels, Mark (5); Bordley, Bill (2); Cutty, Francis (30); Ellis, Duane (7); Garcia, Rogelio (42); Guzman, Ramon (39); Jimenez, Raymundo (23); Juarez, Esteban (11); Ontiveros, Francisco (8); Pena, Manuel (6); Rivas, Lorenzo (20); Rodriguez, Mario (24); Ruiz, Pablo (20); Sigman, Lee (2).

MONTERREY—Cruz, Victor (32); Crysler, Joel (5); Chevolek, Tom (8); Delfin, Juan (22); Gaxiola, Fernando (24); Gonzalez, Arturo (23); Gonzalez, Carlos (30); Gonzalez, Isidro (4); Lopez, Tomas (11); Mariscal, Tomas (26); Ramirez, Hermenegildo (20).

NUEVO LAREDO—Castillo, Luis (15); Garcia, Leonel (22); Garcia, Victor (21); Greene, Steve (19); Hallgreen, Tim (4); Huerta, Luis (4); Meza, Rigobert (2); Navarro, Adolfo (12); Ochoa, Julio (27); Pettigren, William (6); Randolph, Robert (3); Rios, Hector (10); Rodriguez, Jose (28); Salas, Ernesto (1); Sanchez, Felipe (24); Smith, Billy (8); Solomon, Eddie (5); Valdez, Humberto (12); Widales, Oscar (1).

POZA RICA—Acosta, Cecilio (27); Baruch, Matias (28); Garduza, Jose (4); Garduza, Jose (7); Lopez, Eduardo (2); Madrigal, Jose (22); Posadas, Rafael (20); Rodriguez, Ramon (32); Tinajero, Juan (7).

SALTILLO—Alcala, Santo (7); Castaneda, Mario (7); Lopez, Filiberto (4); Lopez, Hector (17); Menendez, Rolando (27); Moreno, Cesar (21); Moya, Ramon (16); Pellorena, Antonio (23); Solis, Miguel (26); Urrea, Leonel (37); Valenzuela, Jairo (25).

TABASCO—Beltran, Jorge (9); Chevez, Carlos (4); Dominguez, Manuel (1); Feola, Larry (11); Franco, David (3); Matus, Nelson (18); Nunez, Mario (22); Palacios, Raul (9); Perez, Cipriano (19); Pollorena, Oscar (8); Raygoza, Jose (7); Rivera, Abraham (22); Rogers, Charles (26); Serafin, Hector (27); Uribe, Carlos (4); Yucupicio, Javier (25).

TAMPICO—Aguilar, Rafael (16); Ayala, David (21); Beltran, Eleazar (20); Contreras, Roberto (4); Chavez, Guadalupe (25); Galindo, Jose (15); Greene, Steve (1); Hernandez, Angel (20); Juarez, Esteban (12); Luna, Jose (19); Munoz, Emeterio (1); Palomares, Hernan (3); Perez, Americo (6); Rivas, Martin (46); Sauceda, Ramiro (10); Sosa, Carlos (26); Vega, Gustavo (5).

VERACRUZ—Esquivel, Leonardo (3); Feola, Larry (5); Figueroa, Miguel (4); Garcia, Jorge (25).

YUCATAN—Aguilar, Vinicio (3); Arceo, Luis (4); Chavez, Enrique (8); Figueroa, Eduardo (9); Granillo, Carlos (20); Greene, Steve (3); Lopez, Tomas (2); Navarrete, Jorge (2); Ponce, Javier (6); Rincon, Juan (20); Rodriguez, Pilar (37); Salinas, Guadalupe (13); Segui, Diego (22); Tiant, Luis (12); Valenzuela, Humberto (19); Velazquez, Agustin (8); Velazquez, Luis (23); Villalobos, Ernesto (20).

GRAND SLAM HOME RUNS—E. Aguilar, Murrell, Saenz, 2 each; Briones, Cosey, Gamundi, Greene, Hazzard, Saul Mendoza, Mora, Ale, Ortiz, Parra, J. Perez, Rendon, Gu. Rodriguez, Ja. Rodriguez, Serna, C. Soto, 1 each.

AWARDED FIRST BASE ON CATCHER'S INTERFERENCE—C. Lopez 2 (Rojas, P. Lugo); Canedo (Rosas); F. Castro (Luna); Firova (J.L. Benitez).

CLUB FIELDING

Club	Pct.	G.	PO.	A.	E.	DP.	PB.
Ciudad Juarez	.984	118	2976	1273	69	108	14
Veracruz	.979	114	2858	1403	93	110	9
Yucatan	.978	116	2896	1295	94	83	8
Mexico City Reds	.978	114	2982	1485	101	126	4
Leon	.977	116	2935	1310	102	119	16
Mexico City Tigers	.976	117	2979	1386	106	94	14
Aguascalientes	.974	118	2974	1304	112	118	9
Monclova	.973	118	2982	1318	118	84	9
Campeche	.973	115	2935	1325	117	68	9
Saltillo	.973	118	2941	1316	117	111	12
Coatzacoalcos	.973	117	2927	1273	117	68	13
Tampico	.972	115	2933	1334	114	102	6
Tabasco	.971	115	2913	1335	128	79	17
Monterrey	.971	117	2904	1243	126	103	19
Poza Rica	.969	114	2849	1241	129	81	13
Nuevo Laredo	.967	118	2939	1359	147	120	16

Triple Plays—Aguascalientes, Poza Rica, Tabasco.

INDIVIDUAL FIELDING

*Throws lefthanded.

FIRST BASEMEN

Player and Club	Pct.	G.	PO.	A.	E.	DP.
An. Castro, Mexico City Tigers*	1.000	12	121	6	0	6
Vergara, Veracruz	1.000	13	98	7	0	5
Gray, Mexico City Reds	.998	58	568	57	1	50
CLAYTON, Saltillo	.998	81	859	43	2	70
Avila, Tampico	.998	72	797	42	2	76
J. Lopez, Ciudad Juarez*	.998	54	386	29	1	25
Aceves, Yucatan	.998	42	376	26	1	26
Ri. Duran, Ciudad Juarez	.997	75	748	47	2	83
Evans, Aguascalientes	.997	87	696	43	2	63
Cage, Yucatan	.997	88	688	30	2	48
Batista, Tampico*	.997	54	336	18	1	26
H. Cruz, Leon	.997	114	989	66	3	78
C. Garza, Mexico City Tigers	.997	99	925	66	3	76
G. Gomez, Monclova	.997	83	869	58	3	76
McDonald, Veracruz	.997	21	266	21	1	18
DeFreites, Tabasco	.996	55	495	39	2	34
Espino, Monterrey	.996	28	215	28	1	15
H. Robles, Monterrey	.995	86	788	15	4	69
C. Soto, Nuevo Laredo	.994	98	989	66	6	89
Garzon, Coatzacoalcos	.994	104	992	32	6	57
Scott, 83 PR-16 Veracruz	.993	99	1050	50	7	73
Pierce, 15 Cam-46 Vera-48 Sal	.993	109	816	56	6	77
J. Reyes, Aguascalientes*	.993	32	256	22	2	41
Sommers, 46 Reds-2 Leon	.993	48	535	42	4	53
A. Garza, 15 Yuc.-68 Tab.	.993	83	750	55	6	49
R. Lora, Campeche	.992	43	473	12	4	35
Zamora, Veracruz	.990	18	92	3	1	6
Gu. Rodriguez, Campeche	.989	42	354	18	4	20
G. Lugo, Aguascalientes	.987	26	130	18	2	8
Duncan, 24 Ctz-22 PR	.986	46	194	18	3	18
B. Valdez, Monclova	.986	35	249	29	4	8
Bojorquez, Nuevo Laredo	.981	40	289	29	6	16
Tiburcio, Poza Rica	.977	13	76	8	2	6
Beamon, Campeche	.974	16	68	6	2	6
Peralta, Monterrey	.972	28	76	28	3	16

(Fewer Than Ten Games)

Player and Club	Pct.	G.	PO.	A.	E.	DP.
Lara, Veracruz	1.000	9	76	6	0	5
M. Mendoza, Ciudad Juarez	1.000	8	68	6	0	0
Guerra, Mexico City Reds	1.000	9	63	1	0	8
V.M. Lopez, Campeche	1.000	6	30	2	0	0
Pacheco, Mexico City Tigers	1.000	5	24	1	0	4
Monreal, Mexico City Reds	1.000	2	20	2	0	1
Poe, Leon	1.000	4	11	0	0	0
Stenholm, Mexico City Reds	1.000	1	6	0	0	0
Alf. Ortiz, Mexico City Reds*	1.000	1	5	0	0	0
Gage, Yucatan	.986	8	67	6	1	2
Funderburk, Mexico City Tigers.	.973	5	69	2	2	1

SECOND BASEMEN

Player and Club	Pct.	G.	PO.	A.	E.	DP.
N. Barrera, Mexico City Reds	1.000	13	23	30	0	8
J. ORTIZ, Veracruz	.990	113	221	295	5	68
Mendez, Mexico City Tigers	.987	33	79	70	2	8
Villaescusa, Yucatan	.985	88	235	296	8	36
Briones, Ciudad Juarez	.982	117	230	359	11	78
J.L. Hernandez, Campeche	.981	100	214	305	10	31
A. Sanchez, Mexico City Reds	.980	103	251	335	12	80
J. Navarrete, Saltillo	.979	117	238	359	13	81
N. Torres, Monterrey	.978	39	78	99	4	9
Rios, Mexico City Tigers	.970	86	214	238	14	46
A. Gonzalez, Monclova	.969	31	59	66	4	28
Herrera, Campeche	.969	11	34	28	2	8
O. Martinez, 6 Reds-15 Ctz.	.967	21	24	65	3	3
Cervantes, Aguascalientes	.967	116	232	328	19	68
Villela, Tampico	.965	112	239	286	19	69
Lazaro, Poza Rica	.964	22	74	89	6	8
J.F. Rodriguez, Leon	.964	115	223	309	20	78
Johnson, Nuevo Laredo	.960	50	96	118	9	26
J. Chavez, Monclova	.957	93	199	221	19	58
Limon, Veracruz	.957	15	30	58	4	6
Guerrero, Tabasco	.953	109	208	315	26	63
J.J. Rodriguez, Poza Rica	.951	96	219	267	25	68
F. Martinez, Coatzacoalcos	.949	89	189	198	21	59
J.A. Barrera, Nuevo Laredo	.945	48	89	116	12	38
J.L. Munoz, Monterrey	.941	86	197	205	25	56
Sanchez, Nuevo Laredo	.934	88	76	95	12	44
F. Gonzalez, Tampico	.919	11	21	36	5	3
DeFreites, Tabasco	.919	11	43	48	8	5
J. Gonzalez, Coatzacoalcos	.912	26	14	48	6	8
L. Hernandez, Yucatan	.891	33	16	33	6	5
Leon, Yucatan	.871	13	9	18	4	6

SECOND BASEMEN—Continued

(Fewer Than Ten Games)

Player and Club	Pct.	G.	PO.	A.	E.	DP.
Avina, Campeche	1.000	8	28	21	0	0
Rod. Hernandez, Yucatan	1.000	3	8	11	0	0
Moreno, Mexico City Reds	1.000	1	2	9	0	0
N. Gonzalez, Mexico City Tigers.	1.000	2	5	3	0	0
T. Martinez, Campeche	1.000	1	4	3	0	1

Player and Club	Pct.	G.	PO.	A.	E.	DP.
Saiz, Campeche	1.000	1	0	5	0	0
Fierro, Mexico City Tigers	.967	6	9	20	1	2
Llanes, Aguascalientes	.929	3	11	15	2	2
Almeida, Leon	.853	4	8	21	5	2

THIRD BASEMEN

Player and Club	Pct.	G.	PO.	A.	E.	DP.
N. Gonzalez, Mexico City Tigers.	.978	75	57	122	4	14
F. RODRIGUEZ, Aguas	.976	103	112	136	6	9
Saul Mendoza, Poza Rica	.975	36	32	45	4	2
Guerrero, Tabasco	.971	15	21	47	3	3
Saiz, Ciudad Juarez	.968	35	22	39	2	1
T. Martinez, Campeche	.968	32	52	68	4	3
Garzon, Coatzacoalcos	.968	11	26	34	2	2
Saenz, Leon	.963	60	61	92	6	7
A. Vega, Mexico City Reds	.957	30	31	36	3	1
Guerra, Yucatan	.954	18	21	41	3	3
Sarabia, Veracruz	.951	25	33	45	4	7
Bernhardt, 43 Cam.-27 Vera.	.949	70	61	127	10	6
J.A. Castro, Veracruz	.949	64	43	58	6	3
P. Mendoza, Campeche	.943	11	9	41	3	0
Alonso, Campeche	.941	35	12	38	3	3
Bobadilla, Ciudad Juarez	.939	89	98	116	14	11
C. Rivera, Tabasco	.938	96	63	117	12	7
N. Barrera, Mexico City Reds	.935	98	82	192	19	21
F. Castro, Yucatan	.926	18	8	17	2	1

Player and Club	Pct.	G.	PO.	A.	E.	DP.
A. Moore, Mexico City Tigers	.926	31	22	65	7	2
de Los Santos, Coatzacoalcos	.923	18	8	16	2	2
Zamora, 3 Tig.-16 Veracruz	.922	19	23	48	6	2
F. Gonzalez, Tampico	.922	80	83	105	16	11
Ale. Ortiz, Nuevo Laredo	.916	117	116	178	27	29
J. Gonzalez, Coatzacoalcos	.916	89	98	107	19	19
Leon, Yucatan	.911	58	28	54	8	3
Villalobos, Leon	.909	38	18	32	5	2
Duncan, Poza Rica	.906	89	87	86	18	19
Ramirez, Monclova	.906	101	111	167	29	23
Burke, Saltillo	.903	118	103	176	30	19
Serna, Monterrey	.900	114	98	126	25	28
Rod. Hernandez, Yucatan	.886	30	26	44	9	3
Rios, Mexico City Tigers	.872	17	13	28	6	1
Velarde, Tabasco	.871	11	11	16	4	2
L. Jimenez, Tampico	.843	62	41	46	18	5
E. Aguilar, Aguascalientes	.822	18	11	26	8	7
Almeida, Leon	.795	23	9	22	8	0

(Fewer Than Ten Games)

Player and Club	Pct.	G.	PO.	A.	E.	DP.
Llanes, Aguascalientes	1.000	3	2	4	0	0
Sommers, Leon	1.000	2	0	6	0	0
R. Torres, Aguascalientes	.1000	2	0	4	0	0
L. Hernandez, Yucatan	1.000	2	0	2	0	0
A. Sanchez, Mexico City Reds	1.000	1	1	1	0	0
N. Torres, Monterrey	.931	8	6	21	2	0

Player and Club	Pct.	G.	PO.	A.	E.	DP.
Herrera, Campeche	.929	8	8	18	2	2
Zavala, Tabasco	.889	3	2	6	1	0
Salazar, Leon	.889	8	3	5	1	0
Fobbs, Tabasco	.846	7	3	8	2	0
J.A. Barrera, Nuevo Laredo	.667	5	3	5	4	0

SHORTSTOPS

Player and Club	Pct.	G.	PO.	A.	E.	DP.
E. Aguilar, Aguascalientes	.972	65	105	168	8	63
RIVERO, Leon	.969	113	221	414	20	68
J. Hernandez, Mexico City Reds.	.968	111	213	448	22	82
Valle, Ciudad Juarez	.968	115	239	389	21	68
Elizondo, Veracruz	.967	112	193	426	21	63
Montiel, 38 Monc.-74 Yuc.	.966	112	81	149	8	34
Leon, Yucatan	.965	18	42	97	5	11
Frias, Tampico	.965	103	201	347	20	63
Saul Mendoza, Poza Rica	.964	98	209	247	17	58
L. Jimenez, Tampico	.964	16	20	33	2	2
Blanks, 68 Coatz.-27 Tab.	.963	95	169	244	16	45
Uzcanga, Monterrey	.960	114	289	415	29	86
J. Gonzalez, Coatzacoalcos	.960	65	194	266	19	57
Ale. Gomez, Nuevo Laredo	.959	82	189	345	23	58
Quintero, Saltillo	.958	76	189	307	22	59
Villaescusa, Yucatan	.957	34	62	118	8	11
A. Gonzalez, Monclova	.957	89	145	189	15	37

Player and Club	Pct.	G.	PO.	A.	E.	DP.
Velarde, Tabasco	.952	16	23	41	3	8
Canedo, 41 Tam.-49 Monc.	.953	90	143	201	17	55
G. Chavez, Saltillo	.952	72	92	106	10	39
M. Morales, Mexico City Tigers	.951	110	195	428	32	61
McDonald, Tabasco	.951	51	85	146	12	39
Herrera, Campeche	.946	81	197	378	33	46
M. Gomez, Aguascalientes	.946	53	109	186	17	41
J.A. Barrera, Nuevo Laredo	.941	41	76	98	11	16
F. Rodriguez, Aguascalientes	.940	11	23	55	5	6
R. Alexander, Poza Rica	.939	41	67	119	12	36
Quinonez, 8 Mont.-49 Monc.	.938	57	79	104	12	11
G. Diaz, Tabasco	.915	25	19	46	6	6
Flores, Yucatan	.907	19	13	55	7	5
Huerta, Monclova	.904	20	11	36	5	6
P. Mendoza, Campeche	.903	38	58	52	13	19
Saenz, Leon	.895	11	8	26	4	3
Fabela, Saltillo	.864	11	8	11	3	6

(Fewer Than Ten Games)

Player and Club	Pct.	G.	PO.	A.	E.	DP.
F. Castro, Yucatan	1.000	4	2	8	0	1
N. Gonzalez, Mexico City Tigers.	1.000	2	2	5	0	1
A. Sanchez, Mexico City Reds	1.000	1	3	3	0	0
L. Hernandez, Yucatan	1.000	1	0	5	0	0
A. Vega, Mexico City Reds	1.000	1	1	1	0	0
Rios, Mexico City Tigers	.971	6	12	22	1	3

Player and Club	Pct.	G.	PO.	A.	E.	DP.
Saiz, Ciudad Juarez	.941	5	5	11	1	0
M. Gonzalez, Tabasco	.923	7	10	26	3	1
Valenzuela, Mexico City Tigers	.917	3	2	9	1	1
Esparza, Poza Rica	.909	6	8	32	4	2
J.A. Castro, Veracruz	.843	6	15	28	8	4
O. Martinez, Mexico City Reds	.833	1	3	2	1	0

OUTFIELDERS

Player and Club	Pct.	G.	PO.	A.	E.	DP.
ARNOLD, Nuevo Laredo	1.000	118	136	20	0	0
Olivares, 24 Coatz.-47 CJ	1.000	71	131	7	0	0
A. Torres, Tampico	1.000	65	104	11	0	0
Moreno, Mexico City Reds	1.000	42	105	6	0	0
Lara, Veracruz	1.000	45	81	6	0	0
Williams, Monterrey	1.000	28	75	4	0	0
Guerra, 30 Reds-36 Yuc.	1.000	66	75	3	0	1
Salazar, Leon	1.000	49	61	4	0	1
Flores, Monclova	1.000	27	48	7	0	0
G. Alexander, Coatzacoalcos	1.000	40	45	3	0	0
G. Gomez, Monclova	1.000	58	41	6	0	0
Vargas, Monclova	1.000	18	36	2	0	0
Rob. Rodriguez, Yucatan	1.000	58	36	1	0	0
Howard, Yucatan	1.000	36	29	3	0	0
Tisdale, Veracruz	1.000	14	21	6	0	0
Bosley, Mexico City Tigers	1.000	16	24	1	0	0
Carreno, Monclova	1.000	21	24	1	0	0
L. Acosta, Tampico	1.000	15	20	2	0	0
Espinosa, Coatzacoalcos	1.000	38	18	2	0	0

Player and Club	Pct.	G.	PO.	A.	E.	DP.
Rush, Ciudad Juarez	1.000	23	18	2	0	0
M.A. Guzman, Mexico City Reds	1.000	11	15	3	0	0
Serratos, Coatzacoalcos	1.000	49	15	1	0	0
Collins, Coatzacoalcos	1.000	10	15	0	0	0
R. Duran, Yucatan	1.000	20	12	1	0	1
S. Garcia, Poza Rica	1.000	13	11	1	0	0
C. Morales, Saltillo	1.000	16	11	0	0	0
Cabrales, Poza Rica	1.000	21	9	0	0	0
F. Castro, Yucatan	1.000	10	8	0	0	0
Uresti, Leon	1.000	10	8	0	0	0
N. Vazquez, Monclova	1.000	18	6	0	0	0
Harris, Poza Rica	1.000	10	6	0	0	0
Herring, Tabasco	.996	115	229	14	1	2
Rod. Rodriguez, Aguascalientes.	.996	116	210	16	1	3
Suarez, Tabasco	.995	113	201	11	1	1
Gage, 31 Yuc.-72 Mont.	.995	103	182	18	1	0
Collins, Coatzacoalcos*	.995	117	176	21	1	2
Castelan, Campeche*	.995	92	173	8	1	2
Adams, 18 Mont.-91 Monc.	.994	109	151	21	1	2

OUTFIELDERS—Continued

Player and Club	Pct.	G.	PO.	A.	E.	DP.
V. Sauceda, Ciudad Juarez	.994	84	156	12	1	1
Ant. Castro, 8 MCT-97 Tam.*	.994	105	137	24	1	2
Poe, Leon	.994	107	146	13	1	2
Ja. Rodriguez, Leon	.994	84	143	11	1	1
Cosey, Saltillo	.993	113	136	12	1	0
Carrillo, Poza Rica	.993	91	128	12	1	0
Arzate, 8 Lar.-86 Monc.	.993	94	120	14	1	0
Alvarado, Coatzacoalcos	.992	108	118	12	1	2
Greene, Coatzacoalcos	.992	81	116	11	1	0
C. Lopez, Yucatan	.992	49	111	15	1	2
Cotes, Saltillo	.991	78	106	8	1	1
V.M. Felix, Saltillo	.991	85	101	9	1	0
Rubio, Tabasco	.991	65	98	8	1	0
Gamundi, Poza Rica	.991	104	189	21	2	0
Rendon, Saltillo	.991	82	99	6	1	0
Mora, Nuevo Laredo	.991	114	189	20	2	0
S. Moore, Saltillo	.990	111	186	19	2	2
Ford, Poza Rica	.990	44	86	11	1	0
Villela, Monterrey	.990	58	89	6	1	0
Bellacetin, Campeche*	.989	93	166	14	1	2
J.L. Perez, Aguascalientes*	.989	112	169	10	2	2
Villagomez, Tampico	.989	91	156	21	2	2
D. Cruz, Tabasco	.989	44	75	11	1	1
Edwards, Monterrey	.988	49	78	7	1	0
L. Figueroa, Ciudad Juarez	.988	30	78	4	1	0
Davis, Ciudad Juarez	.988	60	78	3	1	0
Irvine, Ciudad Juarez	.987	112	136	17	2	1
Andrade, Tampico	.987	67	69	7	1	0
McDonald, Veracruz	.987	85	136	14	2	2
Petters, Monclova	.987	82	126	22	2	2
Paredes, 49 Tig.-28 Lar.	.986	77	139	7	2	0
E. Munoz, Yucatan	.986	86	126	11	2	2
G. Soto, Veracruz	.985	110	189	14	3	1
Zambrano, Monterrey*	.985	93	116	18	2	0

Player and Club	Pct.	G.	PO.	A.	E.	DP.
Hansen, Aguascalientes	.984	36	58	5	1	1
Sotelo, Leon	.984	95	115	8	2	0
Leal, Tampico*	.984	62	103	18	2	0
Murrell, Leon	.983	96	158	12	3	0
Romo, Poza Rica	.981	83	141	16	3	1
Bryant, Mexico City Tigers	.981	103	149	3	3	0
H. Robles, Monterrey	.980	36	46	4	1	0
Tutt, Veracruz	.980	43	91	8	2	0
Aceves, Yucatan	.977	18	41	2	1	0
Parra, Monclova	.977	48	69	15	2	1
A. Moore, Mexico City Tigers	.977	24	40	2	1	0
Quiroz, Nuevo Laredo	.976	99	111	10	3	1
R. Torres, Mexico City Reds	.976	94	185	15	5	6
Monreal, Mexico City Reds	.976	89	147	13	4	0
Lizarraga, Mexico City Reds	.976	75	112	8	3	0
A. Perez, 50 PR-20 Coatz.	.975	70	75	3	2	0
J. Ayala, Monterrey	.975	61	38	1	1	0
E. Aguilar, Aguascalientes	.975	22	66	11	2	2
M. Alexander, MC Tigers	.975	110	222	8	6	1
Almeida, Leon	.972	40	31	4	1	0
Pacheco, Mexico City Tigers	.971	45	63	3	2	1
A. Diaz, Campeche	.968	58	56	4	2	1
Baca, Veracruz	.968	32	28	2	1	0
Hazzard, Aguascalientes	.967	18	26	3	1	0
Buenrostro, Yucatan	.964	51	26	1	1	0
Beamon, Campeche	.964	88	124	9	5	1
Carrillo, Aguascalientes	.962	43	70	6	3	1
Bernal, Aguascalientes	.960	15	23	1	1	0
Vergara, Veracruz	.958	21	23	0	1	1
Dyes, Yucatan	.946	14	33	2	2	1
Gu. Rodriguez, Campeche	.945	33	65	4	4	0
A. Felix, Coatzacoalcos	.929	29	11	2	1	0
R. Torres, Aguascalientes	.900	19	15	3	2	0

(Fewer Than Ten Games)

Player and Club	Pct.	G.	PO.	A.	E.	DP.
G. Reyes, Mexico City Tigers	1.000	7	12	1	0	0
Limon, Leon	1.000	7	11	0	0	0
Tapia, Mexico City Reds	1.000	5	8	1	0	0
Saenz, Leon	1.000	8	6	0	0	0
Burton, Leon	1.000	8	5	0	0	0
Defreites, Tabasco	1.000	6	4	1	0	0
Funderburk, Mexico City Tigers	1.000	9	4	0	0	0
Horton, Nuevo Laredo	1.000	3	4	0	0	0

Player and Club	Pct.	G.	PO.	A.	E.	DP.
G. Hernandez, Mexico City Reds	1.000	1	3	0	0	0
D. Fernandez, Mexico City Reds	1.000	4	2	0	0	0
A. Gomez, Tabasco	1.000	2	2	0	0	0
Osuna, Ciudad Juarez	1.000	1	2	0	0	0
Montano, Ciudad Juarez	1.000	5	2	0	0	0
F. Acosta, Veracruz	.800	6	8	1	1	0
N. Barrera, Mexico City Reds	.800	3	4	0	1	0

CATCHERS

Player and Club	Pct.	G.	PO.	A.	E.	DP.	PB.
M.A. Guzman, MC Reds	1.000	31	110	20	0	2	2
R. Lora, Campeche	1.000	12	92	8	0	1	1
ESTRADA, Campeche	.995	74	392	48	2	6	6
Nunez, Veracruz	.994	40	160	16	1	0	4
E. Rivera, Ciudad Juarez	.994	98	426	38	3	6	8
Pasillas, 3 Tig.-81 Tam.	.993	84	393	43	3	0	3
Bazan, Yucatan	.991	110	488	59	5	2	4
R. Martinez, Leon	.991	63	386	34	3	3	10
J.C. Benitez, Saltillo	.986	98	378	46	6	3	8
Sant. Mendoza, Tabasco	.986	61	295	46	5	3	11
Luna, 7 CJ-58 Monc.	.985	65	309	29	5	0	5
P. Hernandez, Monclova	.985	62	248	21	4	0	5
Rosas, Aguascalientes	.985	85	478	58	8	6	6
P. Ruiz, 37 Leon-45 Vera.	.985	82	422	45	7	6	7
M. Hernandez, Coatzacoalcos	.985	103	389	56	7	0	8
Sosa, Tampico	.984	20	115	11	2	1	1
Rojas, Monterrey	.984	95	346	26	6	0	8
Villalobos, Leon	.984	28	105	18	2	0	2
S. Robles, Mexico City Reds	.984	85	374	52	7	5	2

Player and Club	Pct.	G.	PO.	A.	E.	DP.	PB.
J.C. Alvarez, MC Tigers	.984	94	424	59	8	10	13
E. Castro, Tabasco	.983	47	158	11	3	2	5
J.L. Benitez, 16 Tam-37 Tig.	.978	53	157	23	4	1	3
Lugo, Poza Rica	.975	72	209	21	6	0	8
Madero, Poza Rica	.974	50	178	46	6	0	3
E. Gonzalez, Yucatan	.973	10	28	8	1	1	1
Firoba, Nuevo Laredo	.972	72	318	34	10	3	11
Sarabia, Veracruz	.972	24	61	9	2	1	1
A. Guzman, Campeche	.971	30	118	14	4	0	2
Peralta, Monterrey	.968	41	96	26	4	0	5
Molina, 43 Tab.-17 PR	.964	60	184	29	8	1	3
Ri. Gonzalez, Ciu. Juarez	.963	15	86	19	2	0	4
D. Ruiz, Coatzacoalcos	.959	20	86	8	4	0	3
C. Soto, Nuevo Laredo	.959	16	48	22	3	1	0
E. Reyes, Nuevo Laredo	.957	30	112	21	6	1	5
Rojo, Saltillo	.955	35	95	12	5	1	4
Daut, Monterrey	.955	37	87	18	5	1	6
R. Vega, Aguascalientes	.951	40	105	11	6	1	3
Morris, Monclova	.931	18	46	8	4	0	1

(Fewer Than Ten Games)

Player and Club	Pct.	G.	PO.	A.	E.	DP.	PB.
Raymundo, Yucatan	1.000	2	8	5	0	0	2
Marquez, Veracruz	.976	5	29	12	1	0	1
Heras, Coatzacoalcos	.957	13	40	4	2	0	2

Player and Club	Pct.	G.	PO.	A.	E.	DP.	PB.
Peraza, Yucatan	.926	5	19	6	2	0	1
J. Alvarez, Tabasco	.920	5	16	7	2	0	0

PITCHERS

Player and Club	Pct.	G.	PO.	A.	E.	DP.
Romo, Mexico City Tigers	1.000	26	5	42	0	1
M. Rivas, Tampico	1.000	46	8	38	0	0
Cutty, Monclova	1.000	30	8	28	0	0
Rogers, Tabasco	1.000	26	11	25	0	2
R. Guzman, Monclova	1.000	39	5	29	0	0
Silva, Ciudad Juarez	1.000	22	7	26	0	0
A. Rivera, Tabasco	1.000	22	8	21	0	0
Juarez, 11 Monc.-12 Tampico	1.000	23	6	23	0	0
P. Ruiz, Monclova*	1.000	20	7	21	0	0
Baruch, Poza Rica	1.000	28	4	23	0	0
C. Gonzalez, Monterrey	1.000	30	5	21	0	0
A. Gonzalez, Monterrey	1.000	23	4	22	0	0
H. Lopez, 16 Tigers-17 Saltillo	1.000	33	6	18	0	0

Player and Club	Pct.	G.	PO.	A.	E.	DP.
R. Arano, Coatzacoalcos	1.000	27	5	19	0	0
A. Hernandez, Tampico	1.000	20	0	22	0	0
E. Cordova, Aguascalientes	1.000	17	4	18	0	0
Higueras, Ciudad Juarez*	1.000	27	8	11	0	0
Low, Aguascalientes	1.000	24	4	12	0	0
A. Diaz, Campeche	1.000	20	4	11	0	0
R. Jimenez, Monclova	1.000	23	1	14	0	1
F. Sanchez, Nuevo Laredo	1.000	24	2	13	0	1
H. Ramirez, Monterrey	1.000	20	4	11	0	1
Raygoza, 7 Tabasco-5 Leon	1.000	12	4	11	0	0
Urias, Campeche	1.000	27	4	11	0	0
Uresti, Leon	1.000	16	3	11	0	0
F. Martinez, Ciudad Juarez	1.000	16	3	11	0	1

PITCHERS—Continued

Player and Club	Pct.	G.	PO.	A.	E.	DP.
Salinas, Yucatan	1.000	13	2	11	0	1
Mariscal, Monterrey	1.000	26	4	8	0	1
A. Navarro, Nuevo Laredo	1.000	12	0	11	0	0
D. Abarca, Monclova	1.000	16	0	11	0	2
R. Solis, Coatzacoalcos	1.000	27	0	11	0	1
Galindo, Tampico	1.000	15	0	11	0	0
Zamudio, Veracruz	1.000	15	0	11	0	1
H. Madrigal, 10 Vera.-3 Leon	1.000	13	4	7	0	0
T. Lopez, 2 Yucatan-11 Mont.	1.000	13	0	11	0	1
Rios, Nuevo Laredo	1.000	10	0	8	0	0
M. Torres, Coatzacoalcos	1.000	16	0	8	0	0
J.R. Guzman, 15 Vera.-4 Ctz.	1.000	19	0	7	0	0
Jaime, Mexico City Tigers	1.000	16	1	5	0	0
Romero, Monterrey	1.000	15	1	5	0	0
J.M. Aguilar, Mexico City Tigers	1.000	21	0	1	0	0
Pollorena, Saltillo	.980	23	11	37	1	2
J. Vazquez, Aguascalientes	.979	33	10	36	1	2
G. Jimenez, Campeche	.978	25	8	36	1	3
Ricon, Yucatan	.976	20	8	33	1	1
Alf. Ortiz, Mexico City Reds*	.976	26	6	35	1	1
P. Ochoa, Nuevo Laredo	.976	41	6	34	1	0
P. Rodriguez, Yucatan	.974	37	9	28	1	1
J.L. Garcia, Veracruz	.974	25	9	28	1	1
Brunet, Veracruz*	.971	24	7	27	1	1
Castillejos, Aguascalientes	.971	29	9	25	1	0
Alicea, Ciudad Juarez	.971	32	6	27	1	1
J. Pena, Mexico City Tigers	.971	26	4	29	1	1
E. Beltran, Tampico	.970	20	5	31	1	2
Inzunza, Leon	.969	40	3	28	1	0
Ibarra, 18 Leon-7 MC Reds	.969	25	12	19	1	0
Serafin, Tabasco	.969	27	2	29	1	0
Palacios, Veracruz	.968	22	8	22	1	2
R. Vazquez, Poza Rica	.967	27	8	21	1	0
C. Acosta, Poza Rica	.967	27	8	21	1	0
Villanueva, Mexico City Tigers*	.967	29	6	23	1	1
Segui, Yucatan	.966	22	6	22	1	1
R. Rodriguez, Poza Rica	.966	32	6	22	1	0
S. Alcala, 7 Saltillo-15 Aguas	.964	22	5	22	1	0
J. Ramirez, Leon	.964	22	4	23	1	0
G. Chavez, Tampico	.964	25	8	19	1	0
J.M. Rodriguez, Nuevo Laredo*	.964	28	8	19	1	0
Dimas, Mexico City Tigers	.963	42	4	22	1	1
M.A. Vazquez, 10 Ctz.-5 Reds	.963	15	6	20	1	0
J. Ochoa, Nuevo Laredo	.962	27	3	22	1	0
Pruneda, Mexico City Reds	.962	20	3	22	1	1
Art. Rodriguez, Leon	.961	46	8	41	2	1
Moralez, Veracruz	.960	35	5	19	1	0
J. Beltran, 9 Tabasco-13 Leon	.960	22	3	21	2	0
A. Soto, 21 Reds-10 Leon	.960	31	3	21	1	0
Montenegro, Ciudad Juarez	.960	24	3	21	1	0
Greene, 3 Yuc.-1 Tam.-19 NL	.958	23	4	19	1	0
H. Dominguez, Campeche	.958	26	4	19	1	0
Ant. Pulido, 31 Ctz.-9 Reds	.957	40	12	33	2	1
H. Valenzuela, Yucatan	.957	19	4	18	1	1
L. Rivas, Monclova	.957	20	4	18	1	0
Purata, Poza Rica	.955	28	5	16	1	0
Urrea, Saltillo	.953	37	8	33	2	0
Vidana, 18 Leon-9 Saltillo	.950	27	0	19	1	0
C. Diaz, Coatzacoalcos	.949	23	8	29	2	0

Player and Club	Pct.	G.	PO.	A.	E.	DP.
D. Ochoa, Coatzacoalcos	.947	29	9	27	2	0
R. Villegas, Mexico City Tigers	.947	25	8	28	2	1
Granillo, Yucatan	.947	20	7	11	1	1
Preciado, Campeche	.947	13	6	12	1	0
Leon, Mexico City Reds	.946	20	10	43	3	4
R. Garcia, Monclova	.944	42	6	28	2	0
Franco, Poza Rica	.944	27	6	11	1	0
Palafox, Mexico City Tigers	.944	21	6	11	1	1
Cosena, Saltillo	.944	16	7	10	1	0
Alf. Pulido, Mexico City Reds*	.943	29	13	37	3	2
Villalobos, Yucatan	.943	20	7	26	2	0
G. Martinez, Aguascalientes	.943	25	6	27	2	1
Tejeda, Coatzacoalcos	.941	24	5	11	1	0
Yucupicio, Tabasco	.938	25	3	27	2	0
Gutierrez, Ciudad Juarez	.938	26	11	19	2	0
D. Ayala, Tampico	.938	21	4	11	1	0
C. Sosa, Tampico	.938	26	4	11	1	0
L. Garcia, Nuevo Laredo	.938	22	4	11	1	0
I. Velazquez, Mexico City Tigers	.938	17	4	11	1	2
Miranda, Coatzacoalcos	.935	29	8	21	2	1
C. Perez, Tabasco	.933	19	5	9	1	0
Colorado, Coatzacoalcos	.931	23	6	21	2	0
Nunez, Tabasco	.931	22	5	22	2	0
J. Madrigal, Poza Rica	.931	22	8	19	2	0
Prozco, Campeche	.931	25	8	19	2	0
Gaxiola, Monterrey	.929	24	5	21	2	0
Mundo, Veracruz	.926	21	4	21	2	0
Serna, Ciudad Juarez	.926	27	9	16	2	0
V. Cruz, Monterrey	.923	32	11	25	3	1
H. Valdez, Veracruz	.923	23	5	19	2	0
M.A. Rodriguez, Monclova	.923	24	5	19	2	0
V. Garcia, Nuevo Laredo	.923	21	5	19	2	0
D. Villegas, Aguascalientes	.923	17	6	6	1	0
Matus, 7 Leon-18 Tabasco	.920	25	7	16	2	0
Prevost, Monterrey	.917	25	3	19	2	0
Posadas, Poza Rica	.917	20	4	18	2	0
R. Sauceda, 11 Tigers-10 Tam.	.917	21	2	9	1	0
F. Montano, Mexico City Tigers.	.914	29	10	22	3	1
E. Garcia, Leon	.913	29	6	15	2	1
Rios, 5 MC Reds-9 Leon	.909	14	2	8	1	0
Divison, Campeche	.909	35	4	6	1	1
Solis, Saltillo	.900	26	8	18	3	1
Tiant, 5 Reds-12 Yucatan	.900	17	6	12	2	2
L.T. Castillo, Nuevo Laredo	.900	15	1	8	1	0
J. Moreno, Veracruz	.897	27	8	18	3	1
M. Villegas, Aguascalientes	.895	21	4	13	2	0
L.F. Mendez, Mexico City Reds	.895	27	4	13	2	1
Feola, 2 Aguas-5 Vera-11 Tab.	.895	18	2	15	2	0
H. Pena, Aguascalientes	.889	17	6	10	2	0
Moya, Saltillo	.889	16	0	8	1	0
Jefferson, Leon	.882	16	4	11	2	1
R. Menendez, Saltillo	.880	27	5	17	3	0
R. Aguilar, Tampico	.875	16	0	7	1	0
Moreno, Saltillo	.870	21	4	16	3	0
Luna, Tampico	.846	18	2	9	2	0
H. Valdez, Nuevo Laredo	.846	12	2	9	2	0
Escarrega, Mexico City Reds	.844	19	13	14	5	1
Peralta, Campeche	.840	26	2	19	4	0
J. Valenzuela, Saltillo	.824	25	4	10	3	1

(Fewer Than Ten Games)

Player and Club	Pct.	G.	PO.	A.	E.	DP.
Dorin, Ciudad Juarez	1.000	9	3	18	0	0
Chevolek, Monterrey	1.000	8	2	9	0	0
Quinonez, Ciudad Juarez	1.000	6	1	9	0	0
A. Velazquez, Yucatan	1.000	8	3	7	0	1
Pena, Monclova	1.000	6	0	8	0	0
Howard, Mexico City Reds	1.000	3	2	6	0	0
Castaneda, Saltillo	1.000	7	0	7	0	0
E. Figueroa, Yucatan	1.000	9	0	6	0	0
Zambrano, Leon	1.000	8	0	6	0	0
F. Ontiveros, Monclova	1.000	8	0	5	0	0
Quijada, Coatzacoalcos	1.000	9	0	4	0	0
Hinrichs, Aguascalientes	1.000	5	1	3	0	0
Crysley, Monterrey	1.000	5	0	4	0	0
Milanez, Leon	1.000	9	0	3	0	0
A. Perez, Tampico	1.000	6	0	3	0	0
Ponce, Yucatan	1.000	6	0	3	0	0
F. Lopez, Saltillo	1.000	4	0	3	0	0
I. Gonzalez, Monterrey	1.000	4	0	3	0	0

Player and Club	Pct.	G.	PO.	A.	E.	DP.
D. Franco, Tabasco	1.000	3	0	3	0	0
E. Moore, Mexico City Tigers	1.000	4	0	2	0	0
V. Aguilar, Yucatan	1.000	3	0	2	0	0
Jo. Navarrete, Yucatan	1.000	2	0	2	0	0
Schattinger, Mexico City Reds	1.000	6	0	1	0	0
L. Arceo, Yucatan	1.000	4	0	1	0	0
G. Guzman, Campeche	1.000	3	0	1	0	0
A. Rodriguez, Mexico City Reds	1.000	2	1	0	0	0
D. Moreno, Campeche	1.000	2	0	1	0	0
Pollorena, Tabasco	.900	8	0	9	1	0
Jackson, Aguascalientes	.900	6	5	4	1	0
M. Munoz, Aguascalientes	.875	5	3	4	1	0
Smith, Nuevo Laredo	.875	8	1	6	1	0
C. Chavez, Yucatan	.833	8	1	4	1	0
R. Palacios, Tabasco	.800	9	0	4	1	0
Uribe, Tabasco	.750	4	0	3	1	0
Canedo, Aguascalientes	.667	5	4	0	2	0

CLUB PITCHING

Club	ERA.	G.	CG.	ShO.	Sv.	IP.	H.	R.	ER.	HR.	HB.	BB.	Int. BB.	SO.	WP.	Bk.
Campeche	2.53	115	51	15	23	978.1	909	337	275	34	25	373	21	534	34	1
Mexico City Reds	2.82	114	52	20	14	994.0	998	359	311	31	17	276	29	412	25	2
Veracruz	2.92	114	44	21	15	952.2	856	364	309	23	20	374	27	488	46	6
Tabasco	2.97	115	51	7	9	971.0	946	431	320	29	40	376	31	493	40	2
Mexico City Tigers	3.05	117	32	12	17	993.0	978	389	336	33	27	290	26	452	45	1

CLUB PITCHING

Club	ERA.	G.	CG.	ShO.	Sv.	IP.	H.	R.	ER.	HR.	HB.	BB.	Int. BB.	SO.	WP.	Bk.
Tampico	3.06	115	32	16	17	974.0	883	421	331	23	17	469	40	446	37	4
Ciudad Juarez	3.22	118	43	12	17	992.0	944	419	355	35	40	431	18	550	31	2
Yucatan	3.24	116	47	19	11	965.1	934	424	348	37	32	364	28	423	33	0
Coatzacoalcos	3.25	117	42	15	15	975.2	968	407	352	28	24	314	54	539	33	2
Monterrey	3.30	117	44	10	9	968.0	982	466	355	36	27	401	30	474	30	4
Nueva Laredo	3.35	118	32	12	16	979.2	955	439	365	32	33	421	41	411	40	2
Saltillo	3.62	118	46	8	15	980.1	979	465	394	59	42	381	37	453	25	0
Poza Rica	3.73	114	46	7	8	949.2	1042	472	394	29	36	307	29	384	28	3
Aguascalientes	3.74	118	48	4	14	991.1	1058	505	412	54	22	386	27	472	18	2
Monclova	3.97	118	32	6	14	994.0	965	515	439	48	38	497	15	478	65	1
Leon	4.32	116	30	11	19	978.1	1038	550	470	63	22	444	36	402	55	2

PITCHERS' RECORDS

(Leading Qualifiers for Earned-Run Average Leadership—94 or More Innings)

*Throws lefthanded.

Pitcher—Club	W.	L.	Pct.	ERA.	G.	GS.	CG.	GF.	ShO.	Sv.	IP.	H.	R.	ER.	HR.	HB.	BB.	Int. BB.	SO.	WP.
G. A. Gonzalez, Monterrey	12	8	.600	1.92	23	23	15	0	3	0	173.1	135	52	37	2	3	33	3	104	3
Brunet, Veracruz*	9	12	.429	1.93	24	24	14	0	6	0	186.1	160	56	40	5	2	61	2	124	9
Alf. Pulido, MC Reds*	17	3	.850	2.02	29	23	15	4	6	2	187.1	170	46	42	4	0	31	1	83	2
Higueras, Ciudad Juarez*	17	8	.680	2.03	27	27	18	0	3	0	222.0	177	61	50	6	3	68	1	165	5
Rogers, Tabasco	13	11	.542	2.05	26	26	18	0	2	0	202.0	194	67	46	4	5	44	4	126	6
Ayala, Tampico	7	5	.583	2.11	21	17	6	3	3	1	102.1	91	33	24	1	0	47	5	60	6
Leon, Mexico City Reds	13	1	.929	2.11	20	20	9	0	7	0	153.1	127	41	36	3	4	32	1	63	1
Orozco, Campeche	13	6	.684	2.13	25	23	15	1	4	1	186.0	158	58	44	6	1	45	0	119	4
H. Dominguez, Campeche*	16	7	.696	2.13	26	26	10	0	4	0	194.0	179	55	46	8	3	72	3	104	5
M. Rivas, Tampico	9	10	.474	2.14	46	1	0	37	0	14	96.2	67	32	23	0	2	41	3	61	2

Departmental Leaders: G—M. Rivas, 46; W—Higueras, Alf. Pulido, 17; L—C. Acosta, Prevost, 15; Pct.—Leon, .929; GS—C. Acosta, Higueras, Serna, 27; CG—Higueras, Rogers, 18; GF—M. Rivas, 37; ShO—Leon, 7; Sv.—Divison, 20; IP—Higueras, 222; H—C. Acosta, 202; R—Gutierrez, 90; ER—M. A. Rodriguez, 77; HR—Alcala, R. Garcia, Menendez, J. Valenzuela, M. Villegas, 13; HB—M. Solis, 12; BB—Peralta, 89; IBB—Mendez, 15; SO—Higueras, 165; WP—Ibarra 15.

(All Pitchers—Listed Alphabetically)

Pitcher—Club	W.	L.	Pct.	ERA.	G.	GS.	CG.	GF.	ShO.	Sv.	IP.	H.	R.	ER.	HR.	HB.	BB.	Int. BB.	SO.	WP.
Abarca, Aguascalientes	3	9	.250	4.80	16	15	3	0	0	0	86.1	90	57	46	6	0	41	1	29	4
C. Acosta, Poza Rica	8	15	.348	4.16	27	27	12	0	0	0	160.0	202	87	74	5	9	54	5	55	2
F. Acosta, Veracruz	0	0	.000	9.00	1	0	0	0	0	0	1.0	0	1	1	0	0	0	0	0	0
J. Aguilar, MC Tigers	1	0	1.000	2.82	21	2	0	6	0	2	22.1	24	10	7	0	0	11	1	6	0
R. Aguilar, Tampico	1	5	.167	6.59	16	3	0	7	0	0	28.2	43	23	21	0	0	16	3	7	3
V. Aguilar, Yucatan	0	0	.000	6.30	3	0	0	2	0	0	10.0	11	8	7	1	0	6	0	8	0
Alcala, 7 Saltillo-15 Ags	10	4	.667	3.72	22	20	9	1	0	0	128.1	130	69	53	13	4	46	3	74	1
Alicea, Ciudad Juarez	4	2	.667	2.36	32	0	0	27	0	14	61.0	52	20	16	1	1	14	2	37	2
Arano, Coatzacoalcos	8	14	.364	3.48	27	25	10	1	2	0	163.0	173	74	63	8	2	27	6	66	3
Arceo, Yucatan	0	0	.000	16.87	4	0	0	1	0	0	2.2	8	6	5	2	1	5	0	0	1
Armas, Coatzacoalcos	0	0	.000	4.50	5	0	0	1	0	0	6.0	3	3	3	0	1	10	0	2	0
Arzate, Monclova	0	0	.000	0.00	1	0	0	0	0	0	1.0	0	0	0	0	0	0	0	0	0
Ayala, Tampico	7	5	.583	2.11	21	17	6	3	3	1	102.1	91	33	24	1	0	47	5	60	6
Baruch, Poza Rica	0	4	.000	4.76	28	1	1	16	0	0	62.1	73	36	33	4	2	23	2	38	1
E. Beltran, Tampico	6	8	.429	2.80	20	18	5	2	3	0	112.2	90	45	35	5	3	49	6	47	2
J. Beltran, 9 Tabasco-13 Leon	6	8	.429	4.98	22	18	3	0	0	0	103.0	111	68	57	6	1	56	5	31	5
Bloonfiels, Monclova	0	2	.000	6.00	5	3	0	2	0	0	12.0	14	10	8	0	1	11	0	5	0
Bordley, Monclova	0	1	.000	12.00	2	2	0	0	0	0	3.0	3	5	4	0	1	11	0	1	2
Brunet, Veracruz*	9	12	.429	1.93	24	24	14	0	6	0	186.1	160	56	40	5	2	61	2	124	9
Canedo, Aguascalientes	0	1	.000	5.40	5	0	0	3	0	0	11.2	17	9	7	0	0	3	0	5	0
Casas, 1 Ags-3 Tigers	0	0	.000	12.27	4	0	0	2	0	0	3.2	10	6	5	0	0	0	0	2	0
Castaneda, Saltillo	0	1	.000	2.57	7	1	0	4	0	0	14.0	16	4	4	0	1	8	0	4	1
Castillejos, Aguascalientes	6	4	.600	4.38	29	4	2	16	1	5	72.0	91	41	35	4	2	21	4	32	1
H. Castillo, Ciudad Juarez	0	1	.000	4.72	11	3	0	4	0	0	26.2	28	16	14	1	4	28	2	7	0
L. Castillo, Nuevo Laredo	3	2	.600	3.12	15	9	0	2	0	2	66.1	51	26	23	0	2	33	2	36	4
Cesena, Saltillo	1	2	.333	5.77	16	3	0	5	0	0	34.1	33	23	22	4	3	31	3	19	1
C. Chavez, Tabasco	1	2	.333	6.00	4	4	0	0	0	0	15.0	14	11	10	1	0	10	0	6	1
E. Chavez, Yucatan	0	0	.000	7.02	8	0	0	6	0	0	16.2	22	18	13	2	3	3	0	10	0
G. Chavez, Tampico	7	4	.636	3.20	25	20	6	2	1	0	143.1	130	66	51	4	2	79	6	75	3
Chevolek, Monterrey	2	2	.500	1.82	8	1	0	7	0	2	24.2	12	6	5	1	0	7	1	18	1
Collins, Coatzacoalcos*	0	0	.000	9.00	1	0	0	1	0	0	2.0	2	2	2	0	0	2	0	1	0
Colorado, Coatzacoalcos	14	8	.636	2.61	23	23	16	0	3	0	186.0	172	63	54	1	1	35	4	119	6
P. Contreras, Veracruz	1	2	.333	3.55	3	1	0	1	0	0	12.2	13	5	5	0	0	5	0	7	1
R. Contreras, Tampico	0	1	.000	2.61	4	2	0	2	0	0	10.1	9	3	3	0	0	2	0	3	1
Cordova, Aguascalientes	6	8	.429	3.80	17	17	5	0	0	0	106.2	124	55	45	6	1	32	4	24	0
Corona, Leon	0	0	.000	0.00	2	0	0	1	0	0	4.2	3	1	0	0	1	1	0	1	0
Cruz, Monterrey	8	5	.615	2.71	32	4	3	20	0	3	73.0	78	28	22	5	4	28	6	15	2
Crysler, Monterrey	1	2	.333	6.27	5	5	1	0	0	0	18.2	28	16	13	2	0	11	1	14	0
Cutty, Monclova	10	10	.500	2.67	30	17	10	9	1	1	155.1	118	59	46	3	5	85	4	96	9
Delfin, Monterrey	1	4	.200	3.51	22	2	1	5	0	0	69.1	75	38	27	4	1	35	2	29	1
Delgadillo, Aguascalientes	0	0	.000	2.70	2	0	0	1	0	0	3.1	4	1	1	0	0	1	0	2	0
A. Diaz, Campeche	3	2	.600	3.02	20	3	0	7	0	0	53.2	50	21	18	2	4	32	1	21	2
C. Diaz, Coatzacoalcos	10	7	.588	3.91	23	22	4	0	3	0	129.0	142	61	56	5	9	48	9	56	4
Dimas, Mexico City Tigers	5	6	.455	2.29	42	0	0	24	0	6	74.2	77	23	19	0	3	22	5	31	5
Divison, Campeche	3	2	.600	0.77	35	0	0	34	0	20	46.2	36	7	4	0	3	12	6	30	2
H. Dominguez, Campeche*	16	7	.696	2.13	26	26	10	0	4	0	194.0	179	55	46	8	3	72	3	104	5
M. Dominguez, Tabasco	0	0	.000	3.00	1	0	0	1	0	1	3.0	0	1	1	0	0	3	0	0	0
Dorin, Ciudad Juarez	3	3	.500	3.81	9	7	1	2	0	1	52.0	54	25	22	2	4	36	1	13	1
Ellis, Monclova	3	4	.429	4.21	7	7	4	0	0	0	47.0	41	26	22	3	1	29	1	42	4
Escarrega, Mexico City Reds	9	9	.500	3.56	19	19	9	0	2	0	131.1	147	57	52	9	3	27	2	46	1
Esquivel, Veracruz	0	0	.000	2.25	3	0	0	1	0	0	4.0	5	1	1	0	1	3	0	1	0
Feola, 2 Ags-5 Vera-11 Tab	1	5	.167	6.75	18	7	0	4	0	0	50.2	62	47	38	1	0	46	1	34	5
E. Figueroa, Yucatan	4	5	.444	3.50	9	9	2	0	0	0	54.0	60	27	21	0	0	32	1	16	2
M. Figueroa, Veracruz	0	0	.000	13.50	4	0	0	1	0	0	4.2	6	7	7	0	0	5	0	2	1
D. Franco, Tabasco	0	3	.000	5.28	3	3	1	0	0	0	15.1	11	9	9	1	0	4	0	5	0
F. Franco, Poza Rica	7	12	.368	4.10	27	19	3	5	1	1	129.2	141	69	59	6	5	52	7	42	3

Pitcher—Club	W.	L.	Pct.	ERA.	G.	GS.	CG.	GF.	ShO.	Sv.	IP.	H.	R.	ER.	HR.	HB.	BB.	Int. BB.	SO.	WP.
Galindo, Tampico	0	0	.000	3.35	15	1	0	6	0	0	45.2	47	19	17	2	1	17	2	6	3
Gamez, Campeche	0	0	.000	10.80	1	0	0	1	0	0	1.2	4	2	2	0	0	0	0	0	0
Gamundi, Poza Rica	0	0	.000	1.42	2	0	0	0	0	0	6.1	6	3	1	0	0	2	0	3	1
E. Garcia, Leon	8	9	.471	4.23	29	23	5	4	2	0	151.0	175	81	71	12	4	50	6	46	5
J. Garcia, Veracruz	2	8	.200	3.44	25	8	2	12	1	2	81.0	79	37	31	1	2	36	6	42	4
L. Garcia, Nuevo Laredo	10	10	.500	2.91	22	21	9	0	4	0	142.1	126	56	46	1	0	71	5	91	7
R. Garcia, Monclova	5	4	.556	3.50	42	0	0	23	0	1	92.2	86	42	36	13	6	37	2	43	9
V. Garcia, Nuevo Laredo	7	6	.538	3.63	21	19	3	1	0	0	119.0	111	53	48	8	4	37	0	30	6
J.A. Garduza, Poza Rica	0	2	.000	6.05	7	3	0	2	0	0	19.1	20	19	13	0	4	12	1	7	1
J.M. Garduza, Poza Rica	0	0	.000	5.23	4	2	0	0	0	0	10.1	15	8	6	0	1	6	0	5	1
Gaxiola, Monterrey	8	11	.421	2.77	24	23	7	1	1	0	166.0	166	69	51	4	3	72	4	74	6
Gomez, Leon	0	0	.000	8.31	2	0	0	0	0	0	4.1	9	4	4	1	1	1	1	3	0
C. Gonzalez, Monterrey	3	7	.300	4.33	30	7	0	10	0	0	79.0	89	51	38	5	3	38	2	19	1
G.A. Gonzalez, Monclova	0	0	.000	6.75	5	0	0	2	0	2	5.1	6	4	4	0	1	4	0	3	1
I. Gonzalez, Monterrey	0	1	.000	5.00	4	1	0	3	0	0	9.0	7	6	5	0	0	7	0	7	0
M.A. Gonzalez, Monterrey	12	8	.600	1.92	23	23	15	0	3	0	173.1	135	52	37	2	3	33	3	104	3
Granillo, Yucatan*	1	3	.250	4.30	20	2	0	10	0	0	46.0	52	29	22	1	0	23	2	15	1
Greene, 3 Yuc-1 Tam-19 NL	9	9	.500	3.33	23	22	10	0	2	0	143.1	158	64	53	5	6	31	6	39	3
Gutierrez, Ciudad Juarez	6	10	.375	4.29	26	26	6	0	0	0	155.1	166	90	74	5	8	88	2	76	4
G. Guzman, Campeche	0	2	.000	4.50	3	1	0	1	0	0	6.0	13	6	3	0	1	1	0	1	1
J. Guzman, 15 Vera-4 Ctz*	0	1	.000	5.81	19	2	0	7	0	0	26.1	30	24	17	0	1	27	0	8	9
R. Guzman, Monclova	5	3	.625	1.86	39	0	0	31	0	12	67.2	48	17	14	1	1	32	2	34	10
Hallgreen, Nuevo Laredo	0	0	.000	6.46	4	4	0	0	0	0	15.1	25	20	11	0	0	14	0	4	2
A. Hernandez, Tampico	3	4	.429	3.86	20	1	0	10	0	2	44.1	47	21	19	0	1	15	6	25	1
M. Hernandez, Mex C Reds	0	0	.000	20.25	1	0	0	0	0	0	1.1	2	3	3	1	0	2	0	0	2
Higueras, Ciudad Juarez*	17	8	.680	2.03	27	27	18	0	3	0	222.0	177	61	50	6	3	68	1	165	5
Hinrichs, Aguascalientes	2	3	.400	1.73	5	5	3	0	1	0	36.1	34	9	7	0	1	17	2	13	0
Howard, Mexico City Reds	0	3	.000	6.61	3	3	1	0	0	0	16.1	22	12	12	1	0	3	0	6	0
Huerta, Nuevo Laredo	0	0	.000	2.25	4	0	0	2	0	0	4.0	4	1	1	0	0	2	0	1	2
Ibarra, 18 Leon-7 MC Reds	13	10	.565	3.78	25	25	9	0	0	0	173.2	178	88	73	7	5	71	6	76	15
Inzunza, Leon	2	1	.667	5.80	40	0	0	13	0	0	49.2	56	37	32	8	0	23	3	17	0
Jackson, Aguascalientes*	3	2	.600	4.18	6	6	3	0	0	0	32.1	40	19	15	2	0	14	0	11	1
Jaime, Mexico City Tigers	1	4	.200	7.66	16	0	0	7	0	1	22.1	24	20	19	2	0	12	2	14	0
Jefferson, Leon	10	6	.625	2.65	16	16	7	0	3	0	112.0	101	38	33	2	1	25	1	58	3
G. Jimemez, Campeche*	13	9	.591	2.40	25	25	9	0	0	0	184.0	183	64	49	5	6	75	4	114	6
R. Jimenez, Monclova	5	3	.625	4.13	23	8	3	3	2	0	72.0	76	36	33	1	3	36	0	24	3
Juarez, 11 Mva-12 Tampico	6	9	.400	4.21	23	20	5	3	2	0	124.0	145	70	58	8	4	36	3	37	4
Leon, Mexico City Reds	13	1	.929	2.11	20	20	9	0	7	0	153.1	127	41	36	3	4	32	1	63	1
E. Lopez, Poza Rica	0	0	.000	5.63	2	0	0	0	0	0	8.0	11	5	5	0	0	1	0	0	0
F. Lopez, Saltillo	0	0	.000	1.08	4	0	0	3	0	2	8.1	9	2	1	0	0	7	0	2	0
H. Lopez, 16 Tig-17 Saltillo	4	9	.308	4.31	33	0	0	22	0	6	48.0	56	26	23	2	2	19	3	30	2
T. Lopez, 2 Yuc-11 Mon	3	1	.750	5.01	13	8	1	1	1	0	50.1	61	34	28	3	2	20	4	22	2
Low, Aguascalientes	9	9	.500	3.52	24	24	7	0	1	0	150.2	168	72	59	9	2	64	2	94	0
Luna, Tampico	6	4	.600	3.10	18	14	2	1	0	0	104.2	91	47	36	2	3	64	3	31	1
H. Madrigal, 10 Vera-3 Leon	4	5	.444	3.19	13	13	2	0	1	0	59.1	58	23	21	2	2	25	1	26	1
J. Madrigal, Poza Rica	7	10	.412	3.35	22	20	11	1	1	0	131.2	133	61	49	4	4	33	2	53	4
Mariscal, Monterrey	2	7	.222	4.00	26	12	3	8	0	3	78.2	85	46	35	3	5	40	2	24	3
F. Martinez, Ciudad Juarez*	2	2	.500	3.70	16	1	0	5	0	2	24.1	24	12	10	1	1	7	0	9	0
G. Martinez, Aguascalientes	10	7	.588	2.98	25	21	8	3	0	1	163.1	169	68	54	3	6	76	3	66	5
Matus, 7 Leon-18 Tabasco	12	9	.571	2.86	25	23	11	2	0	1	160.1	184	70	51	6	4	64	9	68	2
Mendez, Mexico City Reds	5	8	.385	1.86	27	1	1	21	1	2	87.0	74	25	18	2	0	38	15	46	7
Menendez, Saltillo	10	10	.500	3.82	27	25	6	2	2	0	167.1	184	96	71	13	5	69	3	70	5
Meza, Nuevo Laredo	0	0	.000	1.80	2	1	0	1	0	0	5.0	7	2	1	0	0	0	0	2	0
Milanez, Leon	0	0	.000	8.27	9	0	0	5	0	0	16.1	19	18	15	1	2	12	1	4	2
Miranda, Coatzacoalcos	2	1	.667	2.26	29	0	0	12	0	2	63.2	57	20	16	0	2	37	11	28	7
F. Montano, MC Tigers	7	8	.467	3.33	29	11	1	12	0	2	108.0	102	48	40	4	1	33	3	44	4
N. Montano, Ciudad Juarez	9	5	.643	2.97	27	11	2	13	0	0	94.0	88	33	31	5	4	40	1	20	2
Montenegro, Ciudad Juarez	3	7	.300	5.10	24	4	1	15	0	0	54.2	59	34	31	6	1	24	3	15	4
Moore, Mexico City Tigers	0	0	.000	1.93	4	0	0	3	0	0	4.2	3	1	1	0	0	3	0	1	0
Morales, Veracruz	5	6	.455	2.20	35	2	0	26	0	11	81.2	75	25	20	3	2	30	8	23	1
C. Moreno, Saltillo	3	4	.429	4.98	21	7	3	5	0	0	72.1	76	48	40	8	6	48	3	38	8
D. Moreno, Campeche	0	0	.000	2.70	2	0	0	2	0	0	1.2	3	1	1	0	0	0	0	1	0
J. Moreno, Veracruz	2	7	.222	3.80	27	9	3	9	0	1	73.1	80	35	31	1	0	25	2	39	2
Moya, Saltillo	1	2	.333	5.76	16	1	0	7	0	0	29.2	44	21	19	0	0	25	1	10	0
Mundo, Veracruz	10	5	.667	2.27	21	19	8	1	4	0	134.2	113	41	34	5	3	43	1	50	5
E. Munoz, 7 Leon-1 Tampico	1	0	1.000	5.40	8	1	0	3	0	0	13.1	15	10	8	3	1	8	0	4	6
M. Munoz, Aguascalientes	1	0	1.000	10.24	5	1	0	1	0	0	9.2	16	11	11	0	3	7	0	2	1
Navarrete, Yucatan	0	0	.000	3.60	2	0	0	2	0	0	5.0	7	3	2	0	0	4	0	2	1
Navarro, Laredo	2	1	.667	3.00	12	2	1	2	0	0	39.0	33	16	13	1	3	24	3	28	3
Nunez, Tabasco	7	6	.539	3.89	22	6	1	14	1	2	69.1	59	36	30	2	4	39	1	47	4
D. Ochoa, Coatzacoalcos	0	8	.000	2.31	29	7	1	13	0	0	85.2	88	25	22	1	3	24	8	58	0
J. Ochoa, Nuevo Laredo	3	3	.500	1.33	27	1	0	24	0	5	54.0	40	11	8	1	1	15	6	22	1
P. Ochoa, Nuevo Laredo	5	2	.714	2.53	41	0	0	25	0	4	78.1	69	24	22	3	3	31	1	26	2
F. Ontiveros, Monclova	1	2	.333	7.16	8	5	0	1	0	0	32.2	42	28	26	1	0	19	1	10	2
J. Ontiveros, Campeche	1	1	.500	4.97	3	2	2	0	0	0	12.2	15	7	7	0	0	4	0	6	1
Orozco, Campeche	13	6	.684	2.13	25	23	15	1	4	1	186.0	158	58	44	6	1	45	0	119	4
Ortiz, Mexico City Reds*	9	7	.563	3.24	26	23	9	1	2	0	147.0	178	65	53	3	1	29	1	48	4
R. Palacios, Tabasco	3	3	.500	2.29	9	7	5	2	1	0	55.0	42	17	14	4	3	15	2	20	1
V. Palacios, Veracruz	12	6	.667	2.61	22	22	10	0	3	0	165.1	121	53	48	6	4	60	3	125	6
Palafox, Mex. City Tigers	1	1	.500	2.59	21	5	0	10	0	0	59.0	63	18	17	1	0	22	2	33	8
Palomares, Tampico	0	0	.000	10.12	3	0	0	1	0	0	2.2	1	3	3	1	0	2	0	1	0
Partida, Leon	0	0	.000	9.00	2	0	0	1	0	0	6.0	7	6	6	0	0	5	0	1	0
H. Pena, Aguascalientes	1	4	.200	4.35	17	3	0	9	0	2	39.1	26	25	19	2	1	23	0	18	1
J. Pena, Mex. City Tigers	12	8	.600	3.32	26	24	8	1	1	0	154.2	161	66	57	4	6	48	2	52	5
M. Pena, Monclova*	1	0	1.000	13.50	6	0	0	1	0	0	6.2	15	10	10	0	0	3	0	1	0
Peralta, Campeche*	10	5	.667	3.09	26	25	10	0	3	0	157.1	149	62	54	6	2	89	3	92	6
A. Perez, Tampico	0	1	.000	10.22	6	0	0	1	0	0	12.1	13	15	14	1	0	12	0	5	2
C. Perez, Tabasco*	5	9	.357	3.61	19	17	6	1	1	0	124.2	139	60	50	2	3	29	3	68	2
Petters, Monclova	0	0	.000	0.00	1	0	0	1	0	0	1.0	3	0	0	0	0	0	0	0	0
Pettigren, Nuevo Laredo	1	3	.250	3.86	6	6	1	0	0	0	32.2	41	22	14	2	1	19	1	11	1
Poe, Leon	0	0	.000	5.40	1	0	0	1	0	0	1.2	2	1	1	0	0	0	0	0	0
A. Pollorena, Saltillo	12	7	.632	2.44	23	23	11	0	3	0	165.2	153	57	45	4	5	37	6	83	2
O. Pollorena, Tabasco	0	0	.000	5.17	8	0	0	5	0	0	15.2	23	12	9	0	1	9	0	2	0

Pitcher—Club	W.	L.	Pct.	ERA.	G.	GS.	CG.	GF.	ShO.	Sv.	IP.	H.	R.	ER.	HR.	HB.	BB.	Int. BB.	SO.	WP.
Ja. Ponce, Yucatan	0	0	.000	6.00	6	0	0	1	0	0	9.0	14	6	6	1	1	4	0	4	0
Jo. Ponce, Coatzacoalcos	0	3	.000	5.93	4	4	1	0	0	0	13.2	16	10	9	1	1	5	0	6	0
Posadas, Poza Rica	2	4	.333	3.49	20	2	1	8	0	0	69.2	84	33	27	4	1	18	1	23	4
Preciado, Campeche	4	2	.667	3.26	13	9	4	1	1	0	69.0	62	30	25	4	4	18	2	13	0
Prevost, Monterrey	8	15	.348	3.31	25	25	11	0	4	0	165.2	175	80	61	2	2	70	4	128	6
Pruneda, Mexico City Reds	10	1	.909	3.04	20	12	5	3	1	0	112.1	114	44	38	3	3	54	3	60	2
Alf. Pulido, M City Reds*	17	3	.850	2.02	29	23	15	4	6	2	187.1	170	46	42	4	6	31	1	83	2
Ant. Pulido, 31 Ctz.-9 Reds	7	5	.583	2.13	40	0	0	32	0	10	67.2	62	20	16	1	1	27	11	51	3
Purata, Poza Rica*	8	10	.444	3.61	28	18	5	6	1	2	122.0	128	57	49	1	4	44	5	68	7
Quijada, Coatzacoalcos	2	4	.333	3.38	9	4	1	4	1	0	34.2	24	17	13	3	0	15	3	5	1
Quinonez, Ciudad Juarez	3	3	.500	2.49	6	6	5	0	1	0	47.0	35	15	13	0	2	16	0	52	2
Quiroz, Nuevo Laredo	2	0	1.000	3.00	6	0	0	5	0	1	9	7	3	3	0	1	5	1	7	0
H. Ramirez, Monterrey	1	3	.250	4.05	20	3	1	10	1	1	33.1	38	20	15	3	2	17	2	11	1
J. Ramirez, Leon	5	7	.417	5.19	22	11	2	3	1	0	86.2	94	55	50	6	2	53	3	37	6
P. Ramirez, Veracruz	0	0	.000	0.00	1	0	0	1	0	0	1.0	0	0	0	0	0	0	0	1	0
Randolph, Nuevo Laredo	0	3	.000	5.87	3	3	0	0	0	0	15.1	17	10	10	1	1	5	1	6	0
Raygoza, 7 Tab.-5 Leon	1	2	.333	6.29	12	0	0	4	0	0	24.1	36	26	17	1	1	23	0	7	6
Rincon, Yucatan	7	9	.438	3.86	20	19	5	1	4	0	111.2	101	60	48	7	8	41	3	52	5
H. Rios, Nuevo Laredo	3	5	.375	3.95	10	8	3	2	1	0	54.2	55	27	24	2	1	28	1	15	1
R. Rios, 5 Reds-9 Leon	0	3	.000	4.50	14	5	0	2	0	1	38.0	43	23	19	2	2	21	2	13	1
L. Rivas, Monclova	4	3	.571	2.85	20	9	2	9	0	0	85.1	84	37	27	6	3	29	0	33	7
M. Rivas, Tampico	9	10	.474	2.14	46	1	0	37	0	14	96.2	67	32	23	0	2	41	3	61	2
Rivera, Tabasco	6	10	.375	2.74	22	20	6	1	0	1	141.0	113	61	43	6	10	65	6	74	10
An. Rodriguez, MC Reds	0	0	.000	2.70	2	0	0	2	0	0	6.2	3	2	2	0	1	3	0	1	0
Ar. Rodriguez, Leon	4	3	.571	2.58	46	0	0	40	0	16	76.2	72	25	22	2	1	33	3	46	1
J. Rodriguez, N. Laredo*	4	4	.500	4.06	28	6	2	9	0	1	62.0	68	33	28	2	3	29	0	26	3
M. Rodriguez, Monclova	8	10	.444	4.35	24	24	7	0	2	0	159.1	173	85	77	7	9	58	3	70	2
P. Rodriguez, Yucatan	6	4	.600	2.59	37	0	0	31	0	11	62.2	70	22	18	2	5	26	6	27	2
R. Rodriguez, Poza Rica	1	3	.250	3.05	32	0	0	21	0	3	59.0	64	22	20	0	2	22	2	20	2
Rogers, Tabasco	13	11	.542	2.05	26	26	18	0	2	0	202.0	194	67	46	4	5	44	4	126	6
Romero, Monterrey	1	1	.500	7.06	15	3	1	8	0	0	29.1	37	26	23	2	2	25	0	10	4
Romo, Mexico City Tigers	14	6	.700	2.48	26	26	12	0	4	0	181.1	160	57	50	4	5	33	3	119	10
Ruiz, Monclova*	4	11	.267	4.06	20	19	1	0	0	0	108.2	96	60	49	1	3	84	0	73	10
Salas, Nuevo Laredo	0	0	.000	0.00	1	0	0	1	0	0	.1	1	0	0	0	0	0	0	1	1
Salinas, Yucatan	3	7	.300	2.67	13	12	5	0	1	0	77.2	77	33	23	4	0	27	4	32	4
Sanchez, Nuevo Laredo	5	3	.625	4.29	24	5	1	8	0	2	56.2	63	29	27	4	3	31	7	11	1
Sauceda, 11 MCT-10 Tam.	3	3	.500	3.86	21	0	0	11	0	1	44.1	41	21	19	3	3	19	4	20	2
Schattinger, M. City Reds	0	0	.000	2.70	6	0	0	5	0	2	3.1	3	1	1	0	0	2	1	0	0
Segui, Yucatan	12	5	.706	2.53	22	22	12	0	5	0	152.2	135	45	43	6	1	30	1	88	3
Serafin, Tabasco	4	5	.444	4.03	27	3	1	15	0	4	60.1	68	39	27	2	2	27	4	33	7
Serna, Ciudad Juarez	14	8	.636	3.34	27	27	8	0	4	0	183.1	183	81	68	5	9	82	2	141	9
Sigman, Monclova	0	1	.000	1.13	2	1	0	1	0	0	8.0	6	1	1	0	0	1	0	1	0
Silva, Ciudad Juarez	1	5	.167	3.27	21	6	2	9	0	0	71.2	78	32	26	3	3	28	4	15	2
Smith, Nuevo Laredo	4	1	.800	1.84	8	7	2	0	1	0	49.0	41	11	10	0	1	18	4	22	0
J. Solis, Leon	0	0	.000	0.00	1	0	0	0	0	0	1.0	1	0	0	0	0	2	0	1	0
M. Solis, Saltillo	13	9	.591	2.95	26	26	16	0	3	0	195.1	176	67	64	12	12	54	8	75	4
R. Solis, Coatzacoalcos	4	5	.444	3.29	27	14	6	3	3	1	93.0	92	35	34	2	2	33	1	60	4
Solomon, Nuevo Laredo	1	4	.200	5.40	5	5	0	0	0	0	28.1	35	22	17	2	2	11	1	17	0
Sosa, Tampico	9	8	.529	2.59	26	25	10	0	3	0	163.2	141	64	47	3	5	88	2	80	9
Soto, 21 Reds-10 Leon	7	4	.636	2.50	31	9	5	15	1	4	108.0	93	33	30	4	4	41	5	42	6
Tejeda, Coatzacoalcos*	5	4	.556	3.64	24	8	2	7	2	3	76.2	80	38	31	6	0	20	1	59	1
Tiant, 5 Reds-12 Yucatan	8	6	.571	3.36	17	17	6	0	1	0	112.2	109	47	42	2	2	34	1	75	1
Tinajero, Poza Rica	0	0	.000	0.00	7	0	0	3	0	0	6.0	7	1	0	0	0	1	1	2	1
Torres, Coatzacoalcos	0	0	.000	4.87	16	1	0	6	0	0	20.1	19	11	11	0	0	11	1	10	2
Uresti, Leon	5	4	.556	2.42	16	8	3	5	1	2	63.1	65	22	17	2	1	31	1	26	7
Urias, Campeche	7	8	.467	3.02	27	1	1	17	0	2	65.2	57	24	22	3	1	25	2	33	7
Uribe, Tabasco	0	1	.000	3.55	4	1	0	0	0	0	12.2	12	7	5	0	1	5	0	0	1
Urrea, Saltillo	5	6	.455	3.74	37	0	0	29	0	10	55.1	57	24	23	1	0	25	8	37	0
H. Valdez, Veracruz	6	7	.462	2.76	23	13	5	8	2	1	101.0	90	37	31	1	4	41	4	28	4
H. Valdez, Nuevo Laredo	0	4	.000	5.79	12	3	1	3	0	1	28.0	29	24	18	1	3	24	3	18	3
H. Valenzuela, Yucatan	9	7	.563	2.75	19	18	7	0	3	0	117.2	105	43	36	5	3	45	0	32	1
J. Valenzuela, Saltillo	9	10	.474	3.50	25	25	8	0	0	0	164.2	150	72	64	13	4	41	2	66	2
J. Vazquez, Aguascalientes	3	4	.429	5.64	33	1	0	24	0	6	59.0	68	41	37	1	0	26	7	33	1
M. Vazquez, 10 Ctz.-5 Reds	4	5	.444	4.37	15	9	1	3	0	0	55.2	56	31	27	1	2	24	1	33	2
R. Vasquez, Poza Rica	8	13	.381	3.16	27	22	13	5	2	2	165.1	158	71	58	5	4	39	3	68	1
Vega, Tampico	0	0	.000	7.20	5	0	0	3	0	0	5.0	6	4	4	1	0	4	0	2	0
A. Velazquez, Yucatan	1	0	1.000	3.52	8	0	0	3	0	0	15.1	21	10	6	0	0	6	1	9	0
I. Velazquez, MC Tigers	9	1	.900	2.15	17	11	1	1	1	0	75.1	69	23	18	3	4	35	2	24	1
L. Velazquez, Yucatan	1	3	.250	4.12	23	3	1	9	1	0	59.0	60	28	27	1	2	30	2	23	4
Vergara, Veracruz	0	0	.000	0.00	1	0	0	0	0	0	1.0	1	0	0	0	0	2	0	0	0
Vidana, 18 Leon-9 Saltillo	1	7	.125	5.73	27	6	0	10	0	1	59.2	72	50	38	4	2	24	3	24	2
Villalobos, Yucatan	8	7	.533	2.27	20	16	8	3	4	0	111.0	87	37	28	2	4	48	5	35	8
Villanueva, MC Tigers*	5	7	.417	3.54	29	13	2	6	0	2	81.1	78	39	32	3	4	25	0	36	6
D. Villegas, Aguascalientes	3	1	.750	5.12	17	0	0	11	0	0	38.2	47	25	22	4	0	20	2	22	5
M. Villegas, Aguascalientes	12	7	.632	2.91	21	21	13	0	0	0	157.2	137	64	51	13	4	48	2	91	1
R. Villegas, MC Tigers	9	5	.643	2.85	25	25	8	0	1	0	164.1	163	59	52	8	1	29	2	70	2
Widales, Nuevo Laredo	0	0	.000	0.00	1	0	0	1	0	0	.1	0	0	0	0	0	0	0	0	0
Yucupicio, Tabasco	2	1	.667	2.38	25	2	1	13	0	0	45.1	38	18	12	3	6	15	0	17	1
Zambrano, Leon	0	0	.000	11.37	8	0	0	4	0	0	12.2	18	16	16	3	0	10	0	9	2
Zamudio, Veracruz	0	0	.000	5.53	15	1	0	5	0	0	27.2	28	17	17	0	0	15	0	10	2

BALKS—V. Palacios, 3; H. Pena, H. Ramirez, 2 each; C. Acosta, E. Beltran, Brunet, Cutty, Delfin, C. Diaz, Escarrega, Galindo, C. Gonzalez, Gutierrez, Higueras, Ibarra, G. Jimenez, J. Madrigal, Mendez, F. Montano, Morales, Mundo, P. Ochoa, Quijada, J. Ramirez, M. Rivas, Rogers, Serafin, Sosa, H. Valdez (Nuevo Laredo), R. Vazquez, 1 each.

COMBINATION SHUTOUTS—S. Alcala—J. Vazquez, Aguascalientes; H. Dominquez-Divison 2, G. Jimenez-Divison, Campeche; H. Castillo-F. Martinez-N. Montano, Higueras-Alicea, N. Montano-Dorin, Ciudad Juarez; M.A. Vasquez-Tejeda-Ant. Pulido, Coatzacoalcos; Jefferson-Vidana, Matus-Art. Rodriguez, Uresti-Art. Rodriguez, Leon; Leon-Alf. Pulido, Mexico City Reds; F. Montano-L. Villanueva-H. Lopez, R. Villegas-L. Villanueva, J. Pena-F. Montano-Dimas, J. Pena-F. Montano, J.M. Aguilar-L. Villanueva-I. Velazquez-F. Montano, Mexico City Tigers; V. Garcia-P. Ochoa, J.M. Rodriguez-P. Ochoa, F. Sanchez-L.T. Castillo, L.T. Castillo-P. Ochoa, Nuevo Laredo; J. Madrigal-F. Franco, Purata-R. Rodriguez, Poza Rica; A. Rivera-Serafin, A. Rivera-Matus, Tabasco; G. Chavez-R. Aguilar, Luna-M. Rivas, Ayala-M. Rivas, E. Juarez-M. Rivas, Tampico; Mundo-M. Morales, H. Madrigal-J.L. Garcia, Brunet-M. Morales, H. Valdez-M. Morales, Veracruz.

NO-HIT GAMES—H. Madrigal, Veracruz, defeated Ciudad Juarez, 7-0, May 12; A. Soto, Leon, defeated Monterrey, 5-0 (seven innings), July 21.

Pacific Coast League

CLASS AAA

Leading Batter
CHRIS SMITH
Phoenix

League President
BILL CUTLER

Leading Pitcher
JOSE DeLEON
Hawaii

CHAMPIONSHIP WINNERS IN PREVIOUS YEARS

1903—Los Angeles	.630
1904—Tacoma	.589
Tacoma§	.571
Los Angeles§	.571
1905—Tacoma	.583
Los Angeles*	.604
1906—Portland	.657
1907—Los Angeles	.608
1908—Los Angeles	.585
1909—San Francisco	.623
1910—Portland	.567
1911—Portland	.589
1912—Oakland	.591
1913—Portland	.559
1914—Portland	.574
1915—San Francisco	.570
1916—Los Angeles	.601
1917—San Francisco	.561
1918—Vernon	.569
Los Angeles (2nd) x	.548
1919—Vernon	.613
1920—Vernon	.556
1921—Los Angeles	.574
1922—San Francisco	.638
1923—San Francisco	.617
1924—Seattle	.545
1925—San Francisco	.643
1926—Los Angeles	.599
1927—Oakland	.615
1928—San Francisco*	.630
Sacramento§§	.626
San Francisco§§	.626
1929—Mission	.643
Hollywood*	.592
1930—Los Angeles	.576
Hollywood*	.650
1931—Hollywood	.626
San Francisco*	.608
1932—Portland	.587
1933—Los Angeles	.610

1934—Los Angeles z	.786
Los Angeles z	.689
1935—Los Angeles	.648
San Francisco*	.608
1936—Portland‡	.549
1937—Sacramento	.573
San Diego (3rd)†	.545
1938—Los Angeles	.590
Sacramento (3rd)†	.537
1939—Seattle	.589
Sacramento (4th)†	.500
1940—Seattle‡	.629
1941—Seattle‡	.598
1942—Sacramento	.590
Seattle (3rd)†	.539
1943—Los Angeles	.710
S. Francisco (2nd)†	.574
1944—Los Angeles	.586
S. Francisco (3rd)†	.509
1945—Portland	.622
S. Francisco (4th)†	.525
1946—San Francisco‡	.628
1947—Los Angeles††	.567
1948—Oakland‡	.606
1949—Hollywood‡	.583
1950—Oakland	.590
1951—Seattle‡	.593
1952—Hollywood	.606
1953—Hollywood	.589
1954—San Diego y	.604
1955—Seattle	.552
1956—Los Angeles	.637
1957—San Francisco	.601
1958—Phoenix	.578
1959—Salt Lake City	.552
1960—Spokane	.601
1961—Tacoma	.630
1962—San Diego	.604
1963—Spokane	.620
Oklahoma City a	.632

1964—Arkansas	.609
San Diego a	.576
1965—Oklahoma City a	.628
Portland	.547
1966—Seattle a	.561
Tulsa	.578
1967—San Diego a	.574
Spokane	.541
1968—Tulsa a	.642
Spokane	.586
1969—Tacoma a	.589
Eugene	.603
1970—Spokane a	.644
Hawaii	.671
1971—Salt Lake City	.534
Tacoma	.545
1972—Albuquerque	.622
Eugene	.534
1973—Tucson	.583
Spokane a	.563
1974—Spokane a	.549
Albuqerque	.535
1975—Salt Lake City	.556
Hawaii a	.611
1976—Salt Lake City	.625
Hawaii a	.531
1977—Phoenix a	.579
Hawaii	.541
1978—Tacoma b	.584
Albuquerque b	.557
1979—Albuquerque	.581
Salt Lake City c	.541
1980—Albuquerque*	.578
Hawaii	.539
1981—Albuquerque*	.712
Tacoma	.561
1982—Albuquerque*	.594
Spokane	.545

*Won split-season playoff. †Won four-team playoff. ‡Won pennant and four-team playoff. §Tied for second-half title with Tacoma winning playoff. §§Tied for second-half title, with Sacramento winning playoff. ††Ended regular season in tie with San Francisco and won one-game playoff for pennant, then won four-club playoff. xWon playoff from first-place Vernon and awarded championship. yDefeated Hollywood in one-game playoff for pennant. zWon both halves, no playoff. aLeague was divided into Northern, Southern divisions in 1963, 1969-70-71, and Eastern, Western divisions in 1964 through 1968 and 1972 through 1977, won two-team playoff. bLeague divided into Eastern and Western divisions, Tacoma and Albuquerque declared co-champions following cancellation of four-team playoff due to continuing rain and wet grounds. cWon second-half title and defeated Hawaii in four-team playoff.

STANDING OF CLUBS AT CLOSE OF FIRST HALF, JUNE 21

NORTHERN DIVISION

Club	W.	L.	T.	Pct.	G.B.
Edmonton (Angels)	37	33	0	.529	....
Tacoma (A's)	37	35	0	.514	1
Portland (Phillies)	34	38	0	.472	4
Salt Lake City (Mariners)	33	39	0	.458	5
Vancouver (Brewers)	31	39	0	.443	6

SOUTHERN DIVISION

Club	W.	L.	T.	Pct.	G.B.
Las Vegas (Padres)	45	26	0	.634	....
Albuquerque (Dodgers)	41	30	0	.577	4
Tucson (Astros)	34	36	0	.486	10½
Hawaii (Pirates)	32	40	0	.444	13½
Phoenix (Giants)	32	40	0	.444	13½

STANDING OF CLUBS AT CLOSE OF SECOND HALF, SEPTEMBER 1

NORTHERN DIVISION

Club	W.	L.	T.	Pct.	G.B.
Portland (Phillies)	41	29	0	.586	....
Edmonton (Angels)	38	34	0	.528	4
Salt Lake City (Mariners)	34	36	0	.486	7
Vancouver (Brewers)	29	41	0	.414	12
Tacoma (A's)	28	42	0	.400	13

SOUTHERN DIVISION

Club	W.	L.	T.	Pct.	G.B.
Albuquerque (Dodgers)	44	28	0	.611	....
Hawaii (Pirates)	40	31	0	.563	3½
Las Vegas (Padres)	38	34	0	.528	6
Tucson (Astros)	34	38	0	.472	10
Phoenix (Giants)	29	42	0	.408	14½

COMPOSITE STANDING OF CLUBS AT CLOSE OF SEASON, SEPTEMBER 1

Club	Edm.	Port.	SLC	Tac.	Van.	Alb.	LV	Haw.	Tuc.	Phx.	W.	L.	T.	Pct.	G.B.
NORTHERN DIVISION															
Edmonton (Angels)	....	8	9	8	9	7	9	9	9	7	75	67	0	.528	....
Portland (Phillies)	8	....	6	8	11	6	8	9	8	11	75	67	0	.528	....
Salt Lake City (Mariners)	7	9	....	8	5	8	5	7	7	11	67	75	0	.472	8
Tacoma (A's)	8	8	7	....	5	6	6	7	9	9	65	77	0	.458	10
Vancouver (Brewers)	7	4	11	11	....	5	4	5	4	9	60	80	0	.429	14
SOUTHERN DIVISION															
Albuquerque (Dodgers)	8	10	8	10	11	....	8	8	10	12	85	58	0	.594	....
Las Vegas (Padres)	7	8	11	10	11	8	....	11	10	7	83	60	0	.580	2
Hawaii (Pirates)	7	7	9	9	10	8	5	....	9	8	72	71	0	.503	13
Tucson (Astros)	6	8	9	7	11	6	6	7	....	8	68	74	0	.479	16½
Phoenix (Giants)	9	5	5	6	7	4	9	8	8	....	61	82	0	.427	24

Hawaii club represented Honolulu, Hawaii.

Major league affiliations in parentheses.

Playoffs—Portland defeated Edmonton, three games to one; Albuquerque defeated Las Vegas, three games to two; Portland defeated Albuquerque, three games to none, to win league championship.

Regular-Season Attendance—Albuquerque, 295,094; Edmonton, 224,822; Hawaii, 145,880; Las Vegas, 365,848; Phoenix, 189,713; Portland, 283,688; Salt Lake City, 280,130; Tacoma, 215,049; Tucson, 167,231; Vancouver, 179,337. Total, 2,346,792.

Managers—Albuquerque, Del Crandall, Terry Collins; Edmonton, Moose Stubing; Hawaii, Tom Treblehorn; Las Vegas, Harry Dunlop, Bob Cluck; Phoenix, Jack Mull; Portland, John Felske; Salt Lake City, Bobby Floyd; Tacoma, Bob Didier; Tucson, Matt Galante; Vancouver, Dick Phillips, Tony Muser.

All-Star Team: 1B—Sid Bream, Albuquerque; 2B—Juan Samuel, Portland; 3B—Randy Ready, Vancouver; SS—Dick Schofield, Edmonton; OF—Kevin McReynolds, Las Vegas; Mike Brown, Edmonton; Gerald Davis, Las Vegas; C—Bill Schroeder, Vancouver; RHP—Jose DeLeon, Hawaii; LHP—Rich Rodas, Albuquerque; DH—Chris Smith, Phoenix; Manager—John Felske, Portland.

(Compiled by William J. Weiss, League Statistician, San Mateo, Calif.)

CLUB BATTING

Club	Pct.	G.	AB.	R.	OR.	H.	TB.	2B.	3B.	HR.	RBI.	GW.	SH.	SF.	HP.	BB.	Int. BB.	SO.	SB.	CS.	LOB.
Albuquerque	.307	143	4874	960	842	1495	2380	275	56	166	890	72	43	74	32	626	18	704	153	79	1043
Edmonton	.300	142	4869	943	871	1459	2373	277	50	179	868	69	21	59	46	587	34	769	125	37	1039
Phoenix	.299	143	4816	827	935	1439	2108	239	56	106	751	54	33	53	25	512	23	626	189	59	1017
Salt Lake City	.296	142	4706	894	856	1392	2143	250	66	123	804	64	43	52	43	635	37	696	225	84	1029
Las Vegas	.290	143	4945	911	894	1433	2342	271	61	172	846	77	38	60	36	582	36	893	174	74	1014
Portland	.281	142	4716	786	764	1327	2187	259	62	159	731	69	21	45	48	502	26	779	169	59	958
Vancouver	.274	140	4609	703	808	1262	1963	217	44	132	649	54	48	37	39	609	27	767	104	64	1072
Hawaii	.271	143	4739	698	688	1282	1944	202	65	110	629	67	28	48	27	467	25	830	169	65	949
Tacoma	.270	142	4748	704	728	1284	1925	197	27	130	642	55	43	46	28	578	37	809	196	86	1036
Tucson	.270	142	4671	745	785	1259	1910	261	57	92	682	56	44	45	43	590	32	780	163	68	1013

INDIVIDUAL BATTING

(Leading Qualifiers for Batting Championship—389 or More Plate Appearances)

*Bats lefthanded. †Switch-hitter.

Player and Club	Pct.	G.	AB.	R.	H.	TB.	2B.	3B.	HR.	RBI.	GW.	SH.	SF.	HP.	BB.	Int. BB.	SO.	SB.	CS.
Smith, Christopher, Phoenix†	.379	123	449	88	170	274	31	5	21	102	6	0	8	2	58	6	40	4	1
McReynolds, Kevin, Las Vegas	.377	113	446	98	168	328	46	9	32	116	11	0	7	1	41	6	55	14	2
Brown, Michael, Edmonton	.355	115	442	91	157	274	39	6	22	106	7	1	4	7	51	2	57	4	4
James, Dion, Vancouver*	.336	129	467	84	157	220	29	5	8	68	7	6	8	4	63	5	33	22	8
Chambers, Albert, Salt Lake City*	.331	99	347	77	115	189	26	6	12	75	6	1	4	1	61	6	87	20	7
Brown, Rogers, Las Vegas†	.331	97	405	85	134	220	27	7	15	70	4	0	3	1	34	5	54	44	8
Miller, Lemmie, Albuquerque	.330	136	545	122	180	251	31	5	10	66	6	4	4	2	72	1	60	52	27
Matuszek, Leonard, Portland*	.330	113	412	82	136	248	28	6	24	92	13	0	7	3	46	9	58	12	6
Ready, Randy, Vancouver	.329	116	407	82	134	203	28	1	13	59	5	3	4	6	99	5	59	24	6
Rivera, German, Albuquerque	.328	138	515	109	169	278	27	5	24	103	6	1	3	6	41	1	56	13	8

Departmental Leaders: G—Miscik, 142; AB—Pittman, 550; R—Pettis, 138; H—L. Miller, 180; TB—McReynolds, 328; 2B—McReynolds, 46; 3B—Loucks, Orsulak, 13; HR—Bream, McReynolds, 32; RBI—Bream, 118; GWRBI—Brewer, 14; SH—Reynolds, 14; SF—Brewer, 12; HP—G. Davis, E. Miller, 12; BB—Ready, 99; IBB—Narron, 15; SO—Clements, 155; SB—Loucks, 71; CS—L. Miller, 27.

(All Players—Listed Alphabetically)

Player and Club	Pct.	G.	AB.	R.	H.	TB.	2B.	3B.	HR.	RBI.	GW.	SH.	SF.	HP.	BB.	Int. BB.	SO.	SB.	CS.
Adams, Ricky, Edmonton	.313	54	208	38	65	101	10	4	6	38	5	2	2	3	21	0	29	8	1
Aguayo, Luis, Portland	.284	71	229	38	65	100	14	3	5	33	2	1	0	5	24	0	39	7	5
Allen, James, Salt Lake City	.338	20	65	15	22	39	6	1	3	13	0	0	1	1	15	2	9	1	0
Allen, Robert, Albuquerque	.250	1	4	0	1	1	0	0	0	0	0	0	0	0	0	0	1	0	0
Allen, Roderick, Salt Lake City	.324	81	290	48	94	155	17	4	12	69	6	0	4	1	24	0	60	10	2

Player and Club	Pct.	G.	AB.	R.	H.	TB.	2B.	3B.	HR.	RBI.	GW.	SH.	SF.	HP.	BB.	Int. BB.	SO.	SB.	CS.
Amelung, Edward, Albuquerque*	.294	135	534	90	157	240	37	8	10	85	3	8	8	1	30	2	68	13	8
Anderson, David Carter, Albuquerque	.407	9	27	10	11	14	1	1	0	3	0	0	1	1	8	0	3	4	1
Asselstine, Brian, Phoenix*	.313	116	399	57	125	176	31	1	6	60	5	0	2	4	41	3	46	4	3
Augustine, David, Hawaii	.209	26	67	6	14	24	3	2	1	8	0	2	0	0	6	1	8	2	0
Aviles, Ramon, Portland	.256	69	227	21	58	74	7	3	1	17	1	0	0	1	15	0	17	0	3
Bathe, William, Tacoma	.253	116	399	56	101	169	18	1	16	62	3	5	5	1	34	4	66	4	4
Bennett, James, Tacoma*	.241	47	166	25	40	77	11	1	8	29	3	0	1	1	12	1	34	4	0
Bernard, Dwight, Tucson	.000	28	4	0	0	0	0	0	0	0	0	0	0	0	0	0	0	0	0
Beyers, Thomas, Albuquerque*	.400	1	5	2	2	5	0	0	1	2	1	0	0	0	0	0	1	0	0
Bjorkman, George, Tucson	.228	17	57	7	13	18	5	0	0	4	1	1	0	0	5	0	9	0	1
Blackwell, Timothy, Edmonton†	.245	59	192	29	47	63	5	1	3	24	0	3	3	0	34	1	35	1	1
Bochy, Bruce, Las Vegas	.303	42	145	28	44	87	8	1	11	33	1	0	4	1	15	1	25	3	1
Bonine, Eddie, Tucson	.077	27	13	1	1	1	0	0	0	0	0	1	0	0	1	0	3	0	0
Booker, Gregory, Las Vegas	.222	46	9	3	2	5	0	0	1	4	0	2	0	0	0	0	1	0	0
Boone, Daniel, 29 Tuc.-14 Van.*	.000	43	1	0	0	0	0	0	0	0	0	0	0	0	0	0	0	0	0
Borbon, Ernesto, Albuquerque	1.000	39	1	0	1	2	1	0	0	1	0	0	0	0	0	0	0	0	0
Bourjos, Christopher, Portland	.300	44	110	22	33	61	7	3	5	20	0	1	1	2	6	0	13	3	0
Bradley, Phillip, Salt Lake City	.323	130	458	100	148	176	14	4	2	41	2	8	0	6	73	2	41	36	10
Bradley, Bert, Tacoma†	.000	66	1	1	0	0	0	0	0	0	0	0	0	0	0	0	0	0	0
Brant, Marshall, Tacoma	.232	49	164	20	38	74	6	0	10	25	5	0	2	5	21	1	44	1	2
Bream, Sidney, Albuquerque*	.307	138	485	115	149	276	23	4	32	118	10	1	7	1	93	9	80	5	4
Brewer, Anthony, Albuquerque	.315	130	467	99	147	258	29	5	24	96	14	4	12	5	72	2	64	10	6
Brouhard, Mark, Vancouver	.321	45	165	23	53	83	15	0	5	30	1	0	1	4	18	1	26	1	0
Brown, Lawrence, Las Vegas	.000	26	3	0	0	0	0	0	0	0	0	0	0	0	0	0	1	0	0
Brown, Michael, Edmonton	.355	115	442	91	157	274	39	6	22	106	7	1	4	7	51	2	57	4	4
Brown, Rogers, Las Vegas†	.331	97	405	85	134	220	27	7	15	70	4	0	3	1	34	5	54	44	8
Bulling, Terry, Salt Lake City	.262	61	168	27	44	64	9	1	3	25	0	2	1	2	33	1	32	2	0
Burleson, Richard, Edmonton	.196	14	51	3	10	13	3	0	0	4	0	0	0	0	4	0	11	2	0
Calvert, Mark, Phoenix	.154	14	13	1	2	2	0	0	0	2	0	0	1	0	0	0	3	0	0
Chambers, Albert, Salt Lake City*	.331	99	347	77	115	189	26	6	12	75	6	1	4	1	61	6	87	20	7
Chiffer, Floyd, Las Vegas	.000	42	4	0	0	0	0	0	0	0	0	0	0	0	0	0	2	0	0
Chris, Michael, Phoenix*	.333	30	33	5	11	19	2	0	2	4	0	0	0	0	1	0	9	0	0
Christensen, James, Tacoma	.286	126	427	70	122	192	18	2	16	58	4	2	5	6	47	5	74	6	8
Christmas, Stephen, Tucson*	.287	48	164	18	47	59	6	0	2	18	2	1	1	1	18	4	14	2	2
Cias, Darryl, Tacoma	.136	34	88	8	12	15	0	0	1	5	1	1	0	0	14	0	17	2	0
Clark, Christopher, Edmonton†	.315	111	381	70	120	207	29	2	18	77	4	1	7	3	63	6	74	3	2
Clark, Robert, Edmonton	.258	7	31	3	8	16	2	0	2	7	1	0	0	1	1	0	8	0	1
Clements, Wesley, Tucson	.256	132	480	83	123	231	38	5	20	89	6	0	3	3	63	1	155	2	3
Colbert, Richard, Tucson	.254	19	59	9	15	23	5	0	1	10	0	1	1	2	6	0	11	0	0
Coles, Darnell, Salt Lake City	.316	61	234	43	74	126	12	5	10	41	5	0	1	5	20	0	19	11	2
Cook, Timothy, Las Vegas	.000	27	8	1	0	0	0	0	0	0	0	1	0	0	0	0	6	0	0
Corcoran, Timothy, Portland*	.311	128	454	75	141	212	30	7	9	93	12	2	8	1	62	7	32	2	2
Corey, Mark, Vancouver	.273	87	260	36	71	149	15	3	19	64	2	0	2	1	33	0	74	1	0
Cornell, Jeffery, Phoenix*	.000	45	3	1	0	0	0	0	0	0	0	0	0	0	1	0	2	0	0
Couchee, Michael, Las Vegas	.000	19	1	0	0	0	0	0	0	0	0	0	0	0	0	0	1	0	0
Crone, William, Salt Lake City	.269	68	186	37	50	72	9	2	3	19	1	4	2	1	24	0	28	10	2
Cypret, Gregory, Tucson	.297	137	468	71	139	177	18	7	2	75	9	4	6	2	68	2	35	0	3
Davidsmeier, Daniel, Vancouver	.237	122	393	49	93	153	22	4	10	41	3	7	2	4	29	0	64	4	8
Davis, Charles, Phoenix†	.295	10	44	12	13	21	2	0	2	9	0	0	1	1	4	0	6	5	0
Davis, Gerald, Las Vegas	.298	139	503	113	150	264	29	8	23	100	12	3	8	12	99	5	92	11	5
Davis, Glenn, Tucson	.211	15	57	5	12	18	3	0	1	8	0	0	1	1	3	0	10	0	1
Davis, Mark, Phoenix*	.200	15	15	2	3	5	0	1	0	1	0	1	0	0	0	0	2	0	0
Davis, Richard, Portland	.328	87	329	44	108	162	25	4	7	49	2	1	5	3	28	1	43	1	4
Davis, Trench, Hawaii*	.256	79	277	41	71	95	6	9	0	23	1	2	2	1	33	4	50	19	9
Debus, Jon, Albuquerque	.298	14	47	10	14	22	3	1	1	6	0	0	0	0	3	0	7	1	0
DeLeon, Jose, Hawaii	.000	20	15	0	0	0	0	0	0	0	0	0	0	0	0	0	5	0	0
Dempsey, Mark, Phoenix	.267	24	15	3	4	7	1	1	0	1	0	0	0	0	0	0	4	0	0
DeSimone, Gerald, Las Vegas†	.287	106	369	70	106	169	21	6	10	55	3	5	7	0	51	2	60	10	6
Edler, David, Salt Lake City	.306	64	245	49	75	120	14	5	7	53	4	0	2	1	40	3	45	5	2
Estrada, Manuel, Salt Lake City	.438	5	16	3	7	7	0	0	0	0	0	0	0	0	0	0	3	1	0
Farmer, Edward, 9 Port.-6 Tac.	.000	15	1	0	0	0	0	0	0	0	0	0	0	0	0	0	0	0	0
Fick, Charles, Tacoma	.400	19	25	3	10	10	0	0	0	3	0	0	0	0	3	0	7	1	2
Fimple, John, Albuquerque	.247	80	235	44	58	106	12	3	10	51	6	2	10	0	36	1	51	2	3
Fireovid, Steven, Las Vegas	.067	28	15	1	1	1	0	0	0	0	0	1	0	0	1	0	5	0	0
Foley, William, Vancouver	.241	9	29	3	7	14	1	0	2	3	0	1	0	0	0	0	7	0	0
Ford, Kenneth, Hawaii	.205	13	44	6	9	15	1	1	1	6	1	0	0	0	4	0	12	1	0
Fowler, Don, Hawaii	.286	28	21	0	6	6	0	0	0	1	0	0	0	0	3	0	3	0	0
Fowlkes, Alan, Phoenix	.346	28	26	4	9	12	0	0	1	4	0	0	0	0	1	0	1	0	0
Frobel, Douglas, Hawaii*	.304	101	378	66	115	217	18	6	24	80	9	0	0	2	40	5	82	23	8
Frost, David, 6 Haw.-14 Port.	.000	20	1	0	0	0	0	0	0	0	0	0	0	0	0	0	1	0	0
Fryer, Paul, Portland	.171	15	35	4	6	7	1	0	0	2	0	0	0	0	2	0	7	2	0
Gallego, Michael, Tacoma	.000	2	2	0	0	0	0	0	0	0	0	0	0	0	0	0	1	0	0
Garcia, Alfonso, Portland	.345	35	113	19	39	51	7	1	1	16	0	1	2	0	18	1	12	1	2
Garrelts, Scott, Phoenix	.000	21	5	0	0	0	0	0	0	0	0	0	0	0	1	0	3	0	0
Garrett, Lynn, Tacoma	.281	82	160	17	45	72	10	1	5	24	4	1	2	1	14	1	42	2	1
Gerber, Craig, Edmonton	.167	2	6	2	1	1	0	0	0	0	0	0	0	0	1	0	0	0	0
Gladden, Daniel, Phoenix†	.303	127	505	113	153	237	30	9	12	80	4	5	7	1	54	4	68	50	10
Gonzales, Daniel, Portland*	.183	23	60	5	11	18	5	1	0	5	0	0	0	0	5	1	1	0	0
Gonzalez, Denio, Hawaii	.269	125	449	76	121	182	18	8	9	48	3	4	3	4	54	1	98	32	8
Goodwin, Danny, Tacoma*	.305	140	469	71	143	234	20	4	21	96	7	2	8	0	80	9	93	10	5
Green, Christopher, Hawaii*	.000	13	5	0	0	0	0	0	0	0	0	0	0	0	1	0	3	0	0
Guante, Cecilio, Hawaii	.000	15	1	0	0	0	0	0	0	0	0	0	0	0	0	0	0	0	0
Gwynn, Anthony, Las Vegas*	.342	17	73	15	25	31	6	0	0	7	1	0	1	0	6	1	5	3	1
Hamm, Timothy, Las Vegas	.308	23	13	1	4	4	0	0	0	2	0	3	0	0	0	0	3	0	0
Hamric, Russell, Portland	.178	54	146	17	26	29	3	0	0	12	2	2	2	1	18	0	19	12	6
Harlow, Larry, Las Vegas*	.255	74	200	31	51	70	7	3	2	27	2	5	2	1	35	1	47	3	8
Hausman, Thomas, Hawaii	.000	4	3	1	0	0	0	0	0	0	0	0	0	0	0	0	1	0	0
Hawkins, Andrew, Las Vegas	167	14	6	0	1	1	0	0	0	0	0	0	0	0	0	0	3	0	0
Heathcock, Jeffrey, Tucson	.000	15	6	1	0	0	0	0	0	0	0	1	0	0	4	0	5	0	0
Hershiser, Orel, Albuquerque	.000	49	2	0	0	0	0	0	0	0	0	0	0	0	0	0	0	0	0
Herz, Steven, Hawaii	.267	87	266	37	71	110	21	0	6	27	1	2	4	7	23	0	44	4	1
Hill, Donald, Tacoma†	.314	93	322	45	101	166	19	2	14	63	6	1	4	2	40	3	36	9	5

Player and Club	Pct.	G.	AB.	R.	H.	TB.	2B.	3B.	HR.	RBI.	GW.	SH.	SF.	HP.	BB.	Int. BB.	SO.	SB.	CS.
Hinrichs, Phillip, 5 Phx.-2 Van.	.000	7	1	0	0	0	0	0	0	0	0	0	0	0	0	0	1	0	0
Hinshaw, George, Las Vegas	.283	133	480	92	136	213	19	5	16	67	6	4	5	11	42	3	82	16	8
Holman, Dale, Albuquerque*	.277	20	47	10	13	19	2	2	0	8	0	0	0	1	13	0	9	1	1
Holton, Brian, Albuquerque	.000	20	2	0	0	0	0	0	0	0	0	0	0	0	0	0	1	0	0
Hotchkiss, John, Tacoma	.239	127	356	39	85	110	13	0	4	40	1	8	3	3	34	1	52	11	5
Hudgens, David, Tacoma*	.279	125	416	59	116	206	23	2	21	72	6	1	4	2	43	6	83	8	4
James, Dion, Vancouver*	.336	129	467	84	157	220	29	5	8	68	7	6	8	4	63	5	33	22	8
Jeltz, Steven, Portland†	.265	71	181	34	48	56	6	1	0	16	1	3	2	2	25	0	30	15	4
Johnson, Jerry, Las Vegas	.259	52	143	21	37	60	9	1	4	20	3	0	1	1	11	0	33	2	0
Johnson, Wallace, Phoenix†	.288	63	229	42	66	84	8	2	2	26	3	1	0	0	29	0	11	17	10
Jones, Christopher, Tucson*	.282	86	234	41	66	93	8	5	3	21	1	1	3	1	23	2	28	13	3
Jones, Ross, Albuquerque	.273	131	469	67	128	171	18	8	3	56	3	7	1	2	56	0	83	17	5
Keedy, Patrick, Edmonton	.224	66	210	38	47	104	13	1	14	40	3	0	1	2	25	0	64	7	0
Keeton, Rickey, Tucson	.000	13	1	0	0	0	0	0	0	0	0	0	0	0	0	0	1	0	0
Keller, Charles, Portland	.273	119	396	69	108	215	21	1	28	75	8	1	6	1	55	2	95	1	1
Kelleher, Michael, Las Vegas	.331	66	242	34	80	94	11	0	1	39	7	2	2	1	27	2	32	3	1
Kennedy, Kevin, Albuquerque	.000	2	3	1	0	0	0	0	0	2	0	0	1	0	1	0	0	0	0
Kingman, Brian, Phoenix	.000	25	8	1	0	0	0	0	0	0	0	0	0	0	1	0	6	0	0
Kingsolver, Kurtis, Vancouver	.233	22	60	10	14	18	4	0	0	3	1	0	0	1	7	0	15	2	0
Koenigsfeld, Ronald, Vancouver	.256	134	469	65	120	171	17	11	4	51	5	9	3	1	62	0	94	8	10
Kolotka, Charles, Las Vegas	.000	6	1	0	0	0	0	0	0	0	0	0	0	0	0	0	1	0	0
Krauss, Timothy, Edmonton*	.325	111	379	83	123	190	18	5	13	70	4	1	3	4	48	1	41	6	3
Krawczyk, Raymond, Hawaii	.000	41	8	0	0	0	0	0	0	0	0	0	0	0	0	0	5	0	0
Kutcher, Randy, Phoenix	.273	104	275	45	75	103	11	4	3	45	0	2	5	1	20	0	37	16	5
Lamonde, Lawrence, Hawaii	.160	32	25	3	4	6	0	1	0	1	0	0	0	0	1	0	7	0	1
Lancellotti, Richard, Las Vegas*	.302	30	116	21	35	70	8	0	9	32	1	0	0	1	14	1	18	0	0
Lansford, Joseph, Las Vegas	.254	140	528	111	134	246	23	4	27	116	8	0	11	2	76	3	117	10	6
Lerch, Randy, Phoenix*	.000	5	1	0	0	0	0	0	0	0	0	0	0	0	0	0	1	0	0
Littleton, Larry, Portland	.235	25	51	8	12	20	2	0	2	7	1	0	0	0	14	1	15	1	1
Loman, Douglas, Vancouver*	.262	130	465	69	122	207	20	4	19	78	11	2	5	5	49	4	71	5	7
Long, William, Las Vegas	.000	18	9	1	0	0	0	0	0	0	0	0	0	0	0	0	3	0	0
Loucks, Scott, Tucson	.287	138	541	107	155	238	33	13	8	58	6	10	4	2	66	1	83	71	19
Lubratich, Steven, Edmonton	.321	90	380	69	122	177	23	1	10	78	8	2	6	7	22	2	24	7	5
Luebber, Stephen, Las Vegas	.000	3	1	0	0	0	0	0	0	0	0	1	0	0	0	0	1	0	0
MacDonald, James, Tucson	.000	10	7	0	0	0	0	0	0	0	0	1	0	1	0	0	2	0	0
Madden, Michael, Tucson*	.000	4	2	0	0	0	0	0	0	0	0	0	0	0	0	0	2	0	0
Madison, Scotti, Albuquerque†	.292	23	65	10	19	27	2	0	2	12	1	1	2	0	13	0	6	2	0
Maldonado, Candido, Albuquerque	.319	38	144	23	46	66	6	1	4	20	0	0	0	2	14	0	23	3	0
Maler, James, Salt Lake City	.332	68	247	52	82	121	21	0	6	51	4	0	3	8	36	0	19	9	2
Mangual, Jose, Edmonton	.311	32	90	30	28	58	6	0	8	16	1	1	1	0	20	1	24	3	4
Martin, Michael, Las Vegas*	.258	36	120	14	31	45	5	0	3	19	3	0	0	0	22	0	24	0	2
Mathis, Ronald, Tucson	.000	28	14	0	0	0	0	0	0	0	0	1	0	0	1	0	4	0	0
Matuszek, Leonard, Portland*	.330	113	412	82	136	248	28	6	24	92	13	0	7	3	46	9	58	12	6
McKay, David, Tacoma†	.256	50	121	27	31	49	4	1	4	11	1	4	3	0	22	1	28	5	2
McLaughlin, Michael, Las Vegas	.273	13	11	1	3	3	0	0	0	2	0	0	0	0	0	0	6	0	0
McNealy, Robert, Tacoma*	.266	134	425	89	113	137	20	2	0	42	5	3	2	2	71	3	57	43	10
McReynolds, Kevin, Las Vegas	.377	113	446	98	168	328	46	9	32	116	11	0	7	1	41	6	55	14	2
Mendoza, Mario, Hawaii	.185	62	173	18	32	36	2	1	0	12	0	2	1	1	13	0	25	1	0
Mercado, Orlando, Salt Lake City	.227	26	88	12	20	30	2	1	2	12	3	0	1	1	5	0	13	0	0
Meridith, Ronald, Tucson*	.000	39	3	0	0	0	0	0	0	0	0	0	0	0	0	0	1	0	0
Michael, Steven, Vancouver*	.257	128	428	59	110	160	21	1	9	54	6	4	1	1	71	7	76	9	4
Miller, Darrell, Edmonton	.303	51	142	29	43	56	5	1	2	23	2	0	1	2	6	0	28	4	0
Miller, Edward, Portland†	.264	109	382	76	101	159	21	11	5	41	1	4	0	12	34	0	83	39	10
Miller, Lemmie, Albuquerque	.330	136	545	122	180	251	31	5	10	66	6	4	4	2	72	1	60	52	27
Miscik, Robert, Hawaii	.279	142	524	70	146	198	18	2	10	83	11	3	6	2	55	4	68	1	6
Mitchell, Robert, Hawaii*	.243	114	337	41	82	110	12	5	2	32	4	6	4	1	34	3	38	18	11
Mizerock, John, Tucson*	.261	53	176	18	46	77	12	2	5	31	3	1	2	1	20	3	29	1	1
Mohorcic, Dale, Hawaii	.143	15	7	1	1	1	0	0	0	0	0	0	0	0	0	0	0	0	0
Monasterio, Juan, Edmonton	.314	112	423	68	133	216	22	5	17	80	7	2	8	2	9	0	38	6	1
Moore, Kelvin, Tacoma	.279	35	122	17	34	58	3	3	5	22	2	0	1	0	17	0	43	0	3
Moore, Michael, Salt Lake City	.500	11	4	1	2	2	0	0	0	0	0	0	0	0	0	0	0	0	0
Moreno, Jose, Edmonton†	.230	44	165	22	38	70	8	3	6	34	4	0	1	2	24	1	26	8	2
Moses, John, Salt Lake City†	.262	16	65	14	17	21	4	0	0	10	0	0	0	0	10	0	10	4	1
Murray, Richard, Phoenix	.299	120	431	68	129	213	23	2	19	82	7	0	4	2	44	0	62	8	5
Nanni, Tito, Salt Lake City*	.240	122	416	64	100	161	18	5	11	57	6	3	6	4	35	6	78	28	12
Narron, Jerry, Edmonton*	.301	139	532	93	160	281	30	5	27	102	5	0	8	4	66	15	50	1	3
Nelson, James, Salt Lake City	.247	80	231	41	57	84	7	1	6	36	0	4	2	1	54	1	38	2	4
Nelson, Ricky, Salt Lake City*	.333	29	102	20	34	61	6	3	5	27	3	2	3	1	11	3	12	4	6
Niemann, Randy, Hawaii	.000	16	10	0	0	0	0	0	0	0	0	0	0	0	0	0	2	0	0
O'Berry, Michael, Edmonton	.307	57	179	43	55	77	8	1	4	24	2	2	1	0	38	0	31	4	1
Oroz, Felix, Las Vegas*	.000	32	9	0	0	0	0	0	0	0	0	1	0	0	0	0	6	0	0
Orsulak, Joseph, Hawaii*	.286	139	538	87	154	222	12	13	10	58	6	3	5	5	48	2	41	38	8
Owchinko, Robert, Hawaii*	.105	22	19	5	2	3	1	0	0	0	0	0	0	0	3	0	5	0	0
Owen, Spike, Salt Lake City	.266	72	256	58	68	97	8	9	1	32	3	4	2	0	57	2	23	22	7
Pankovits, James, Tucson	.287	126	450	77	129	199	25	6	11	62	2	5	3	4	55	5	66	32	3
Pate, Robert, Tucson	.272	122	423	78	115	183	24	4	12	67	5	1	6	2	74	5	54	21	6
Pederson, Stuart, Albuquerque*	.000	1	2	0	0	0	0	0	0	0	0	0	0	0	0	0	0	0	0
Pena, Adalberto, Tucson	.246	112	382	45	94	136	21	3	5	63	5	4	5	6	31	1	66	2	5
Perry, Stephen, Albuquerque*	.000	17	1	0	0	0	0	0	0	0	0	0	0	0	1	0	0	0	0
Peters, Richard, Tacoma†	.297	66	232	50	69	87	9	3	1	19	3	2	1	3	54	0	33	36	15
Pettis, Gary, Edmonton†	.285	132	529	138	151	227	27	8	11	52	6	4	5	5	81	3	121	52	6
Peyton, Eric, Vancouver*	.207	72	271	36	56	99	11	1	10	29	2	1	2	2	26	2	52	9	3
Phelps, Kenneth, Salt Lake City*	.341	74	270	81	92	205	29	6	24	82	10	0	3	2	54	4	35	4	0
Pisel, Ronald, Phoenix	.200	13	5	0	1	2	1	0	0	1	0	0	0	0	1	0	1	0	0
Pittman, Joseph, Las Vegas	.282	129	550	92	155	205	27	7	3	52	9	6	1	2	53	0	73	38	18
Plante, Daniel, Vancouver	.259	54	147	26	38	51	3	2	2	18	0	3	1	1	19	0	25	0	0
Powell, Hosken, Vancouver*	.281	38	139	19	39	53	5	0	3	19	0	3	3	0	12	0	9	2	1
Pruitt, Ronald, Portland	.281	101	352	50	99	159	19	4	11	47	4	2	0	3	62	0	41	2	2
Pujols, Luis, Tucson	.250	33	112	18	28	38	7	0	1	9	0	0	2	2	11	1	20	0	0
Quinones, Luis, Tacoma†	.263	45	133	14	35	46	3	1	2	14	1	2	1	0	15	0	11	5	5
Rabb, John, Phoenix	.343	62	216	50	74	117	11	1	10	51	4	2	3	2	27	1	40	8	1
Ramirez, Mario, Las Vegas	.222	16	54	7	12	21	2	2	1	8	2	0	0	0	5	1	13	0	2
Ransom, Jeffrey, Phoenix†	.225	102	289	43	65	101	13	1	7	37	0	7	1	1	52	3	63	8	1

Player and Club	Pct.	G.	AB.	R.	H.	TB.	2B.	3B.	HR.	RBI.	GW.	SH.	SF.	HP.	BB.	Int. BB.	SO.	SB.	CS.
Ray, Larry, Tucson*	.307	117	404	73	124	198	28	5	12	80	7	0	0	3	64	5	62	1	5
Ready, Randy, Vancouver	.329	116	407	82	134	203	28	1	13	59	5	3	4	6	99	5	59	24	6
Rennicke, Dean, Albuquerque	.000	32	1	1	0	0	0	0	0	0	0	0	0	0	1	0	1	0	0
Reyes, Gilberto, Albuquerque	.306	20	62	8	19	30	1	2	2	15	0	2	2	0	2	0	13	1	0
Reynolds, Harold, Salt Lake City†	.309	136	534	84	165	206	20	9	1	72	5	14	6	5	47	4	43	54	19
Rivera, German, Albuquerque	.328	138	515	109	169	278	27	5	24	103	6	1	3	6	41	1	56	13	8
Roberge, Bertrand, Tucson	.333	47	3	0	1	1	0	0	0	1	0	1	0	0	1	0	2	0	0
Robinson, Bruce, Hawaii*	.243	58	181	20	44	58	8	0	2	28	4	2	2	0	15	0	33	0	0
Robles, Ruben, Tucson	.279	50	172	30	48	83	10	5	5	33	4	1	0	5	10	0	40	9	2
Rodriguez, Luis, Portland	.133	28	30	9	4	8	1	0	1	2	1	1	0	0	3	0	10	1	2
Ronan, Kernan, Phoenix	.000	43	4	0	0	0	0	0	0	0	0	0	0	0	0	0	3	0	0
Rothschild, Lawrence, Las Vegas*	.000	38	4	0	0	0	0	0	0	0	0	0	0	0	0	0	1	0	0
Ruiz, Cecilio, Las Vegas*	.125	32	8	0	1	1	0	0	0	1	0	1	0	0	0	0	2	0	0
Runnells, Thomas, Phoenix†	.303	74	244	43	74	96	11	4	1	28	4	1	4	1	24	1	24	7	3
Rush, Lawrence, Hawaii	.259	70	228	33	59	108	11	4	10	36	3	0	1	0	25	2	60	9	3
Russell, John, Portland	.254	128	445	71	113	223	23	3	27	76	8	0	2	2	42	1	109	3	3
Samuel, Juan, Portland	.330	65	261	59	86	161	14	8	15	52	5	0	2	4	22	2	46	33	6
Sanchez, Alejandro, Portland	.247	125	458	75	113	195	21	5	17	74	8	2	8	6	18	0	105	33	1
Sax, David, Albuquerque	.343	75	280	59	96	148	22	3	8	59	5	1	4	2	31	0	38	4	3
Schofield, Richard, Edmonton	.284	139	521	91	148	240	30	7	16	94	10	2	8	4	71	2	106	9	5
Schroeder, William, Vancouver	.286	82	304	51	87	166	13	3	20	70	6	1	2	7	37	2	79	2	1
Schu, Richard, Portland	.379	9	29	7	11	18	2	1	1	3	0	0	0	1	3	0	1	0	1
Schultz, Greg, Albuquerque	.320	98	291	58	93	147	19	1	11	55	4	4	9	7	27	0	31	6	2
Segelke, Herman, Phoenix	.286	35	7	0	2	2	0	0	0	1	0	0	0	0	0	0	3	0	0
Senteney, Steven, Hawaii	1.000	25	1	1	1	1	0	0	0	0	0	0	0	0	0	0	0	0	0
Sherow, Dennis, Tacoma	.281	118	395	47	111	136	13	3	2	29	1	7	1	2	24	1	66	26	5
Skorochocki, John, Vancouver*	.278	99	309	50	86	108	4	3	4	38	2	3	2	1	43	1	28	7	4
Skube, Robert, Vancouver*	.209	40	129	15	27	39	3	0	3	8	1	1	1	1	18	0	26	4	4
Smith, Bobby, Vancouver*	.296	43	162	26	48	69	6	6	1	19	2	1	0	0	21	0	26	5	7
Smith, Christopher, Phoenix†	.379	123	449	88	170	274	31	5	21	102	6	0	8	2	58	6	40	4	1
Smith, David, Edmonton	.000	23	0	1	0	0	0	0	0	0	0	0	0	0	1	0	0	0	0
Solano, Julio, Tucson	.176	29	17	1	3	3	0	0	0	1	0	1	0	0	1	0	8	0	0
Stanhouse, Donald, Hawaii	.000	39	3	0	0	0	0	0	0	0	0	0	0	0	0	0	2	0	0
Stassi, James, Phoenix	.278	39	97	14	27	33	3	0	1	10	2	3	1	0	12	0	18	1	1
Steels, James, Las Vegas*	.242	28	95	17	23	33	5	1	1	14	2	2	1	0	8	0	11	5	1
Stubbs, Franklin, Albuquerque*	.277	76	267	49	74	144	16	3	16	58	4	0	5	1	41	2	53	3	3
Sularz, Guy, Phoenix	.316	134	484	76	153	205	23	7	5	58	5	1	4	5	52	3	37	14	6
Taveras, Alejandro, Albuquerque	.321	110	361	71	116	173	25	4	8	74	9	8	5	1	70	1	48	14	10
Thomas, Jimmy, Las Vegas	.125	2	8	0	1	1	0	0	0	0	0	0	0	0	0	0	2	0	0
Thurmond, Mark, Las Vegas*	.000	19	1	0	0	0	0	0	0	0	0	0	0	0	0	0	0	0	0
Tingley, Ronald, Las Vegas	.282	92	294	44	83	140	15	6	10	48	1	1	3	1	39	2	85	9	4
Todd, Jackson, Tucson	.000	21	7	0	0	0	0	0	0	0	0	0	0	0	0	0	3	0	0
Tolman, Timothy, Tucson	.375	7	24	4	9	14	2	0	1	6	1	0	1	2	3	1	2	0	2
Torres, Alfredo, Hawaii	.186	18	59	7	11	20	2	2	1	7	2	0	0	0	8	0	16	1	1
Torve, Kelvin, Phoenix	.260	115	392	58	102	145	21	5	4	54	5	4	7	1	34	2	33	6	4
Turner, John, 23 Las Vegas-6 Port.*	.288	29	80	10	23	39	5	1	3	20	1	0	4	1	6	2	14	3	1
Valentine, Ellis, Edmonton	.222	3	9	2	2	2	0	0	0	0	0	0	0	0	1	0	2	0	0
Vargas, Hediberto, Hawaii	.348	53	204	30	71	126	19	0	12	46	5	0	2	1	15	0	55	1	1
Veselic, Robert, Tucson	.167	13	6	0	1	1	0	0	0	0	0	2	0	0	1	0	2	0	0
Voigt, Paul, Albuquerque	.500	29	2	0	1	1	0	0	0	0	0	0	0	0	0	0	0	0	0
Walker, Glen, Salt Lake City	.262	124	481	68	126	207	28	4	15	86	6	0	11	3	31	3	91	3	6
Walton, Reginald, Hawaii	.299	117	428	55	128	196	22	5	12	71	10	0	9	2	23	2	86	11	3
Wellman, Brad, Phoenix	.311	45	167	32	52	72	6	4	2	28	3	1	2	1	13	0	23	8	3
Wherry, Clifton, Tucson	.246	108	349	57	86	114	15	2	3	44	3	5	7	5	58	1	50	10	8
White, Larry, Albuquerque†	.000	31	4	2	0	0	0	0	0	0	0	0	0	0	1	0	1	0	0
Whitson, Eddie, Las Vegas	.000	3	1	0	0	0	0	0	0	0	0	0	0	0	0	0	1	0	0
Wilborn, Thaddeaus, Phoenix†	.288	125	417	60	120	166	9	8	7	64	7	4	3	1	33	1	70	30	5
Williams, Frank, Phoenix	.000	25	4	0	0	0	0	0	0	0	0	1	0	0	1	0	2	0	0
Williams, Jamie, Tucson	.129	10	31	1	4	5	1	0	0	1	1	1	0	0	4	0	9	0	0
Winn, James, Hawaii	.000	31	2	0	0	0	0	0	0	0	0	0	0	0	0	0	2	0	0
Woodard, Michael, Tacoma*	.241	122	323	45	78	87	7	1	0	27	2	4	3	0	35	1	17	25	8
Wotus, Ronald, Hawaii	.301	125	465	94	140	210	28	6	10	62	7	2	9	1	63	1	72	8	3
Wright, Richard, Albuquerque*	.000	34	1	0	0	0	0	0	0	0	0	0	0	0	0	0	0	0	0
Zacher, Todd, Phoenix*	.265	12	34	8	9	16	2	1	1	2	0	0	0	0	8	0	7	2	0

The following pitchers, listed alphabetically by club, with games in parentheses, had no plate appearances, primarily through use of designated hitters:

ALBUQUERQUE—Anderson, David Carl (1); Franco, John (11); Geiger, Burwell (39); Howell, Kenneth (1); Redfern, Peter (6); Rodas, Richard (27); Wise, Brett (7).

EDMONTON—Brown, Curtis (40); Brown, Steven (20); Calderon, Jose (10); Corbett, Douglas (32); Finch, Steven (28); Jefferson, Jesse (3); Kibbe, Jay (27); Lacey, Robert (54); Mahler, Michael (1); Marshall, Michael (1); McLaughlin, Byron (14); Monteagudo, Aurelio (4); Mooneyham, William (7); Moreno, Angel (27); Smith, David (31); Steirer, Ricky (28); Travers, William (3).

HAWAII—Edge, Claude (9); Semall, Paul (9); Taylor, Johnny (1); Umbarger, James (14); Zaske, Jeffrey (6).

LAS VEGAS—House, Thomas (2).

PHOENIX—Chamberlain, Craig (7); Larkin, Patrick (4).

PORTLAND—Altamirano, Porfirio (25); Andersen, Larry (52); Bahnsen, Stanley (15); Bradford, Larry (43); Burroughs, Darren (11); Comer, Steven (12); Davisson, Jay (1); Decker, Martin (58); Downs, Kelly (29); Faulk, Kelly (10); Ghelfi, Anthony (8); Gross, Kevin (15); Hanna, Preston (16); Hudson, Charles (10); Mirabella, Paul (5); Money, Kyle (19); Rasmussen, James (16); Riley, George (9); Wehrmeister, David (15).

SALT LAKE CITY—Abbott, Glenn (4); Adair, Richard (50); Allard, Brian (35); Babcock, Robert (60); Barnhouse, Scott (1); Beattie, James (3); Best, Karl (51); Comer, Steven (17); Decker, George (13); Gleaton, Jerry (25); Murray, Jed (3); Nelson, Eugene (16); Nunez, Edwin (14); Snyder, Brian (28); Stranski, Scott (29); Sutton, Johnny (23).

TACOMA—Atherton, Keith (26); Baker, Steven (13); Baumgarten, Ross (12); Buice, DeWayne (32); Callahan, Benjamin (15); Dye, Scott (16); Ford, David (8); Hanna, Preston (2); Heaverlo, David (3); Heimueller, Gorman (20); Hensley, Charles (59); Jones, Jeffrey (26); King, Jerome (25); Marietta, Louis (3); McDonald, Russell (3); Myers, Edward (7); Norris, Michael (1); Retzer, Edwin (3); Rodriguez, Ricardo (10); Smith, Mark (11); Warren, Michael (11); Young, Curtis (27).

TUCSON—Morris, Jeffrey (1); Pladson, Gordon (5); Ross, Mark (6); Sprowl, Robert (16); Welborn, Sammye (8).

VANCOUVER—Anderson, Michael (43); Beene, Andrew (26); Burns, Daniel (26); Camacho, Ernie (11); Candiotti, Thomas (15); Castro, William (18); Cocanower, James (23); Jones, Douglas (3); Kranitz, Richard (7); Ladd, Peter (12); Martinez, Alfredo (28); Mueller, Willard (40); Olsen, Richard (6); Porter, Charles (7); Roberts, Scott (21); Seaman, Kim (6); Stablein, George (22).

GRAND SLAM HOME RUNS—Brewer, 3; Bream, C. Clark, J. Moreno, 2 each; R. Allen, Amelung, Bathe, M. Brown, Clements, Corey, Edler, Gladden, Goodwin, Hill, Keedy, Krauss, Maler, Mangual, Matuszek, McReynolds, E. Miller, Monasterio, Narron, Ready, Reyes, Rivera, Robles, Sanchez, Schroeder, Schultz, Turner, Walker, Walton, 1 each.

AWARDED FIRST BASE ON CATCHER'S INTERFERENCE—Asselstine 4 (Blackwell, Colbert, J. Nelson, Reyes); Bradley 3 (Colbert, Fimple, Kingsolver); Wotus 3 (Bathe, Plante, Russell); Krauss 2 (Fimple, Keller); Skorochocki 2 (Fimple, Stassi); Aguayo (Blackwell); Aviles (McKay); M. Brown (Schroeder); Hardgrave (J. Nelson); Johnson (Blackwell); Loucks (Reyes); McNealy (Fimple); Nanni (Bathe); Peters (Madison); Quinones (Mercado); Runnells (Sax); Wilborn (Fimple).

CLUB FIELDING

Club	Pct.	G.	PO.	A.	E.	DP.	PB.
Edmonton	.972	142	3603	1542	149	139	23
Portland	.970	142	3594	1401	157	103	20
Tucson	.969	142	3617	1427	161	121	9
Hawaii	.969	143	3664	1471	166	127	26
Las Vegas	.968	143	3770	1584	175	160	13
Vancouver	.968	140	3549	1549	170	133	26
Tacoma	.965	142	3688	1444	185	110	13
Albuquerque	.964	143	3684	1764	206	150	29
Salt Lake City	.963	142	3542	1500	195	143	23
Phoenix	.962	143	3579	1405	199	105	15

Triple plays—Hawaii 2, Phoenix, Tacoma.

INDIVIDUAL FIELDING

*Throws lefthanded.

FIRST BASEMEN

Player and Club	Pct.	G.	PO.	A.	E.	DP.
Bathe, Tacoma	1.000	1	1	0	0	0
Brant, Tacoma	.985	39	306	26	5	19
Bream, Albuquerque*	.983	136	1264	123	24	129
Bulling, Salt Lake City	1.000	1	8	4	0	0
Christmas, Tucson	.971	4	31	3	1	1
C. Clark, Edmonton*	.994	20	153	9	1	9
Clements, Tucson	.979	125	1061	100	25	103
Corcoran, Portland*	.990	40	267	25	3	21
Corey, Vancouver	.978	14	86	4	2	8
Cypret, Tucson	1.000	8	45	3	0	4
G. Davis, Tucson	1.000	4	35	3	0	1
T. Davis, Hawaii*	1.000	1	2	0	0	0
Edler, Salt Lake City	1.000	1	0	1	0	0
Fick, Tacoma	1.000	1	1	0	0	0
Garcia, Portland	1.000	1	9	1	0	0
Goodwin, Tacoma	.976	66	526	48	14	43
Herz, Hawaii	1.000	1	3	0	0	0
Hudgens, Tacoma*	.994	20	147	11	1	9
Keedy, Edmonton	1.000	1	5	0	0	0
Keller, Portland	1.000	16	105	7	0	8
Lancellotti, Las Vegas	.953	4	39	2	2	3
LANSFORD, Las Vegas	.994	136	1272	104	9	142
Lubratich, Edmonton	1.000	1	8	1	0	1
Maler, Salt Lake City	.996	52	430	41	2	54
Matuszek, Portland	.989	95	807	67	10	63
McKay, Tacoma	1.000	2	3	0	0	1
Michael, Vancouver*	.986	125	1107	83	17	108
Miller, Edmonton	.976	11	75	5	2	7
Mitchell, Hawaii	1.000	1	1	0	0	1
Mizerock, Tucson	1.000	1	6	4	0	1
Moore, Tacoma*	.972	29	191	17	6	11
Murray, Phoenix	.987	50	365	28	5	32
Nanni, Salt Lake City*	.987	27	213	13	3	20
Narron, Edmonton	.990	119	1074	59	12	104
J. Nelson, Salt Lake City	1.000	1	6	2	0	0
Phelps, Salt Lake City*	.988	61	535	37	7	50
Pruitt, Portland	1.000	1	6	0	0	0
Runnells, Phoenix	1.000	1	4	1	0	0
Rush, Hawaii	.988	55	455	34	6	45
Sax, Albuquerque	1.000	3	29	3	0	4
Schultz, Albuquerque	.984	8	58	5	1	4
Skorochocki, Vancouver	1.000	6	26	2	0	3
Skube, Vancouver*	1.000	1	15	1	0	0
Smith, Phoenix	.983	9	48	9	1	4
Steels, Las Vegas*	1.000	3	32	4	0	1
Stubbs, Albuquerque*	.955	4	20	1	1	1
Tolman, Tucson	1.000	4	28	3	0	2
Torres, Hawaii	1.000	2	18	0	0	0
Torve, Phoenix	.987	98	730	53	10	56
Vargas, Hawaii	.979	38	312	13	7	26
Walton, Hawaii	.983	49	389	26	7	27
Wotus, Hawaii	1.000	9	43	3	0	2

Triple plays—Brant, Rush, Torve.

SECOND BASEMEN

Player and Club	Pct.	G.	PO.	A.	E.	DP.
Adams, Edmonton	.960	16	36	36	3	9
Aguayo, Portland	.984	16	26	37	1	9
Aviles, Portland	1.000	1	0	1	0	0
Christensen, Tacoma	.981	58	86	123	4	20
Crone, Salt Lake City	1.000	7	13	17	0	8
Cypret, Tucson	1.000	2	0	2	0	0
Davidsmeier, Vancouver	.979	118	251	351	13	73
DeSimone, Las Vegas	.990	20	38	62	1	14
Gallego, Tacoma	1.000	1	0	1	0	0
Gonzalez, Hawaii	.969	42	85	101	6	25
Hamric, Portland	.974	54	89	140	6	27
Jeltz, Portland	.989	24	39	49	1	6
J. Johnson, Las Vegas	1.000	1	2	0	0	0
W. Johnson, Phoenix	.944	53	105	150	15	30
Jones, Albuquerque	.974	12	29	46	2	11
Keedy, Edmonton	1.000	1	0	1	0	0
Koenigsfeld, Vancouver	1.000	3	6	7	0	1
KRAUSS, Edmonton	.983	106	216	301	9	67
Kutcher, Phoenix	.909	7	5	15	2	2
Lubratich, Edmonton	1.000	33	57	98	0	20
McKay, Tacoma	1.000	7	10	15	0	1
Mendoza, Hawaii	.967	15	22	37	2	10
Mitchell, Hawaii	.958	7	9	14	1	1
Pankovits, Tucson	.956	113	215	322	25	71
Pittman, Las Vegas	.963	124	234	371	23	96
Quinones, Tacoma	1.000	3	3	8	0	2
Reynolds, Salt Lake City	.963	136	286	410	27	92
Runnells, Phoenix	1.000	2	2	3	0	0
Samuel, Portland	.949	65	110	168	15	36
Schultz, Albuquerque	.953	53	77	125	10	28
Skorochocki, Vancouver	.925	38	52	72	10	16
Sularz, Phoenix	1.000	2	7	3	0	0
Taveras, Albuquerque	.967	95	194	277	16	55
Wellman, Phoenix	.980	43	79	120	4	21
Wherry, Tucson	.968	35	62	118	6	13
Wilborn, Phoenix	.935	37	74	70	10	20
Woodard, Tacoma	.973	110	120	235	12	54
Wotus, Hawaii	.980	86	206	236	9	53
Zacher, Phoenix	.913	10	20	22	4	2

Triple play—Wotus.

THIRD BASEMEN

Player and Club	Pct.	G.	PO.	A.	E.	DP.
Adams, Edmonton	.981	16	11	40	1	4
J. Allen, Salt Lake City	.926	20	12	38	4	7
R. Allen, Albuquerque	1.000	1	2	0	0	0
Aviles, Portland	.974	33	20	56	2	3
Christensen, Tacoma	.864	41	21	49	11	7
Crone, Salt Lake City	.934	42	19	66	6	5
Cypret, Tucson	.909	118	91	190	28	18
DeSimone, Las Vegas	1.000	4	3	4	0	2
Edler, Salt Lake City	.924	57	47	99	12	10
Fryer, Portland	.821	14	16	16	7	4
Garcia, Portland	1.000	8	5	15	0	1
Gerber, Edmonton	1.000	2	1	6	0	1
Hinshaw, Las Vegas	.891	130	86	249	41	22
Hotchkiss, Tacoma	.919	127	85	233	28	25
Jeltz, Portland	.933	30	16	26	3	2
Johnson, Las Vegas	1.000	19	13	25	0	2
Keedy, Edmonton	.903	58	37	121	17	14
Kutcher, Phoenix	.941	50	91	115	13	23
Lubratich, Edmonton	.974	62	41	108	4	9
Madison, Albuquerque	.600	1	1	2	2	0
Maldonado, Albuquerque	.857	3	1	5	1	0
Maler, Salt Lake City	1.000	4	2	6	0	2
McKay, Tacoma	.909	9	2	8	1	1
Mendoza, Hawaii	.833	2	4	1	1	0
Mercado, Salt Lake City	1.000	2	0	4	0	1
Miller, Edmonton	.833	8	3	12	3	0
MISCIK, Hawaii	.942	142	139	266	25	29
Mitchell, Hawaii	1.000	1	0	1	0	0

THIRD BASEMEN—Continued

Player and Club	Pct.	G.	PO.	A.	E.	DP.
Murray, Phoenix	.872	46	37	72	16	5
J. Nelson, Salt Lake City	.923	15	9	27	3	1
Plante, Vancouver	.500	1	1	0	1	1
Pruitt, Portland	.889	79	57	111	21	6
Ransom, Phoenix	1.000	1	0	1	0	0
Ready, Vancouver	.939	115	136	231	24	17
Rivera, Albuquerque	.929	133	111	333	34	31
Rush, Hawaii	1.000	3	2	4	0	0
Russell, Portland	.867	7	3	10	2	1
Schofield, Edmonton	.864	10	8	11	3	2
Schu, Portland	.923	8	4	8	1	0
Schultz, Albuquerque	.857	13	5	7	2	0
Skorochocki, Vancouver	.971	25	20	46	2	5
Sularz, Phoenix	.931	103	67	188	19	13
Walker, Salt Lake City	.724	11	8	13	8	2
Wherry, Tucson	.983	28	14	43	1	5

Triple play—Miscik.

SHORTSTOPS

Player and Club	Pct.	G.	PO.	A.	E.	DP.
Adams, Edmonton	1.000	5	7	11	0	4
Aguayo, Portland	.968	58	95	179	9	32
Anderson, Albuquerque	.977	9	17	26	1	10
Aviles, Portland	.982	40	70	97	3	17
Burleson, Edmonton	.917	11	17	16	3	4
Christensen, Tacoma	.951	24	25	52	4	7
Coles, Salt Lake City	.917	61	100	178	25	37
Crone, Salt Lake City	.925	10	16	21	3	8
Davidsmeier, Vancouver	.739	5	6	11	6	2
DeSimone, Las Vegas	.935	65	124	208	23	58
Garcia, Portland	.969	26	33	60	3	12
Gonzalez, Hawaii	.921	80	108	218	28	45
Hill, Tacoma	.957	90	148	256	18	43
Jeltz, Portland	.913	18	26	37	6	5
Jones, Albuquerque	.944	122	188	388	34	78
Keedy, Edmonton	1.000	1	0	1	0	0
Kelleher, Las Vegas	.976	62	127	193	8	50
Koenigsfeld, Vancouver	.947	131	233	411	36	89
Kutcher, Phoenix	.941	50	91	115	13	23
Littleton, Portland	1.000	1	0	2	0	0
McKay, Tacoma	1.000	2	1	4	0	1
Mendoza, Hawaii	956	37	57	96	7	16
Owen, Salt Lake City	.958	72	111	212	14	47
PENA, Tucson	.960	111	166	290	19	58
Pruitt, Portland	1.000	1	3	6	0	2
Quinones, Tacoma	.940	36	52	89	9	16
Ramirez, Las Vegas	.986	16	25	46	1	5
Reynolds, Salt Lake City	1.000	1	1	0	0	0
Rivera, Albuquerque	1.000	3	5	10	0	3
Rodriguez, Portland	.884	15	16	22	5	4
Runnells, Phoenix	.958	67	113	184	13	35
Schofield, Edmonton	.957	135	212	391	27	69
Schu, Portland	.857	2	2	4	1	0
Skorochocki, Vancouver	.875	6	5	16	3	1
Sularz, Phoenix	.924	35	43	102	12	13
Taveras, Albuquerque	.971	22	29	38	2	9
Wellman, Phoenix	1.000	2	0	3	0	0
Wherry, Tucson	.967	44	52	95	5	15
Woodard, Tacoma	1.000	1	0	1	0	0
Wotus, Hawaii	.924	30	37	85	10	13

Triple plays—Gonzalez, Quinones, Runnells.

OUTFIELDERS

Player and Club	Pct.	G.	PO.	A.	E.	DP.
Adams, Edmonton	.947	16	15	3	1	0
R. Allen, Salt Lake City	.982	31	55	1	1	0
Amelung, Albuquerque*	.975	128	256	15	7	3
Asselstine, Phoenix	.978	102	171	6	4	1
Augustine, Hawaii	1.000	10	12	0	0	0
Bennett, Tacoma*	.986	33	65	4	1	0
Bourjos, Portland	.936	36	44	0	3	0
P. BRADLEY, Salt Lake City	.997	130	284	13	1	0
Brewer, Albuquerque	.978	111	158	16	4	1
Brouhard, Vancouver	.967	37	57	2	2	0
M. Brown, Edmonton	.990	99	190	11	2	2
R. Brown, Las Vegas	.971	81	166	4	5	2
Chambers, Salt Lake City*	.922	55	71	0	6	0
C. Clark, Edmonton*	1.000	23	27	1	0	1
R. Clark, Edmonton	1.000	3	7	0	0	0
Corcoran, Portland*	.983	86	170	7	3	0
Corey, Vancouver	1.000	8	10	0	0	0
Crone, Salt Lake City	1.000	1	1	0	0	0
C. Davis, Phoenix	.882	6	15	0	2	0
Ge. Davis, Las Vegas	.972	137	296	17	9	4
Gl. Davis, Tucson	.900	11	17	1	2	0
R. Davis, Portland	1.000	28	53	0	0	0
T. Davis, Hawaii*	.981	76	145	9	3	2
Edler, Salt Lake City	1.000	3	6	0	0	0
Ford, Hawaii	1.000	5	6	2	0	1
Frobel, Hawaii	.952	97	169	11	9	6
Fryer, Portland	.000	1	0	0	1	0
Garrett, Tacoma	.985	56	65	1	1	0
Gladden, Phoenix	.979	127	319	6	7	0
Gonzales, Portland	1.000	16	13	2	0	0
Goodwin, Tacoma	.963	63	97	6	4	0
Gwynn, Las Vegas*	.893	17	23	2	3	0
Harlow, Las Vegas*	.940	63	92	2	6	0
Holman, Albuquerque	1.000	7	6	0	0	0
Hudgens, Tacoma*	.941	31	47	1	3	0
James, Vancouver*	.993	117	289	6	2	0
Jeltz, Portland	.963	13	25	1	1	0
Johnson, Las Vegas	.949	21	35	2	2	0
Jones, Tucson*	1.000	62	119	2	0	0
Keedy, Edmonton	1.000	4	4	0	0	0
Kutcher, Phoenix	1.000	34	50	5	0	0
Lancellotti, Las Vegas*	1.000	5	8	1	0	0
Lansford, Las Vegas	1.000	4	8	0	0	0
Littleton, Portland	1.000	15	15	0	0	0
Loman, Vancouver*	.976	101	199	6	5	2
Loucks, Tucson	.975	136	338	12	9	3
Maldonado, Albuquerque	.959	32	65	6	3	2
Mangual, Edmonton	1.000	6	5	0	0	0
Matuszek, Portland	1.000	3	4	0	0	0
McKay, Tacoma	1.000	7	8	2	0	1
McNealy, Tacoma*	.969	132	271	12	9	2
McReynolds, Las Vegas	.967	110	257	3	9	0
D. Miller, Edmonton	.857	16	12	0	2	0
E. Miller, Portland	.967	105	228	9	8	3
L. Miller, Albuquerque	.960	117	180	13	8	1
Mitchell, Hawaii	.960	61	95	1	4	0
Monasterio, Edmonton	.954	108	176	10	9	1
J. Moreno, Edmonton	.938	39	71	4	5	0
Moses, Salt Lake City*	1.000	15	26	0	0	0
Murray, Phoenix	.944	14	16	1	1	0
Nanni, Salt Lake City*	.960	84	134	11	6	2
R. Nelson, Salt Lake City	.983	28	55	4	1	2
Orsulak, Hawaii*	.978	139	341	18	8	8
Pate, Tucson	.989	94	173	4	2	1
Peters, Tacoma	.982	65	166	1	3	0
Pettis, Edmonton	.985	131	325	10	5	4
Peyton, Vancouver*	.979	65	126	12	3	3
Powell, Vancouver*	1.000	34	51	4	0	1
Quinones, Tacoma	1.000	4	7	0	0	0
Rabb, Phoenix	.960	12	24	0	1	0
Ransom, Phoenix	.824	20	25	3	6	0
Ray, Tucson	.980	87	137	9	3	0
Robles, Tucson	.980	49	94	5	2	1
Rodriguez, Portland	.667	7	2	0	1	0
Rush, Hawaii	1.000	2	1	0	0	0
Russell, Portland	.988	45	75	4	1	1
Sanchez, Portland	.952	125	219	18	12	2
Segelke, Phoenix	1.000	1	1	0	0	0
Sherow, Tacoma	.969	110	208	9	7	3
Skorochocki, Vancouver	1.000	1	2	0	0	0
Skube, Vancouver*	.990	34	89	6	1	2
B. Smith, Vancouver*	.933	28	40	2	3	1
C. Smith, Phoenix	.960	77	118	2	5	0
Steels, Las Vegas*	1.000	7	15	0	0	0
Stubbs, Albuquerque*	.946	56	86	2	5	0
Tolman, Tucson	1.000	3	3	0	0	0
Turner, Las Vegas*	1.000	1	2	0	0	0
Valentine, Edmonton	1.000	3	3	0	0	0
Vargas, Hawaii	.750	3	6	0	2	0
Walker, Salt Lake City	.970	101	176	18	6	3
Walton, Hawaii	.947	49	66	6	4	1
Wilborn, Phoenix	.975	89	147	8	4	0

Triple plays—Sherow, Walton.

CATCHERS

Player and Club	Pct.	G.	PO.	A.	E.	DP.	PB.
Bathe, Tacoma	.979	107	632	55	15	9	8
Bjorkman, Tucson	1.000	16	72	6	0	0	0
Blackwell, Edmonton	.965	59	272	31	11	7	9
Bochy, Las Vegas	.983	29	157	21	3	6	1
Bulling, Salt Lake City	.973	60	324	34	10	4	6
Christmas, Tucson	.967	22	128	18	5	5	0
Cias, Tacoma	.981	32	144	11	3	1	5
Colbert, Tucson	.983	19	108	11	2	2	3
Debus, Albuquerque	1.000	12	45	1	0	0	5
Edler, Salt Lake City	1.000	5	23	1	0	1	6
Fick, Tacoma	1.000	17	38	1	0	0	0
Fimple, Albuquerque	.971	79	397	73	14	3	10
Foley, Vancouver	.979	7	41	5	1	1	4
Herz, Hawaii	.986	83	469	55	7	5	7
Johnson, Las Vegas	1.000	4	6	0	0	0	1
Keller, Portland	.977	53	285	16	7	1	6
Kennedy, Albuquerque	1.000	1	9	0	0	0	1
Kingsolver, Vancouver	.975	19	73	6	2	2	3
Kutcher, Phoenix	1.000	2	2	1	0	0	1
Madison, Albuquerque	.959	20	102	16	5	1	4
Martin, Las Vegas	.990	36	175	17	2	1	3
McKay, Tacoma	.968	12	28	2	1	0	0
Mercado, Salt Lake City	.986	24	131	9	2	1	4
Miller, Edmonton	.984	13	56	7	1	1	1
Mizerock, Tucson	.984	49	292	25	5	2	3
Narron, Edmonton	.996	23	224	11	1	0	0
J. Nelson, Salt Lake City	.958	64	360	48	18	6	7
O'Berry, Edmonton	.975	57	289	19	8	6	13
Plante, Vancouver	.991	44	195	24	2	3	5
Pruitt, Portland	.967	16	82	7	3	1	1
Pujols, Tacoma	.990	29	189	14	2	3	2
Rabb, Phoenix	.986	49	267	17	4	1	4
Ransom, Phoenix	.970	78	415	41	14	3	5
Reyes, Albuquerque	938	19	103	17	8	1	4
Robinson, Hawaii	.985	54	293	32	5	9	13
Russell, Portland	.983	83	473	44	9	2	13
Sax, Albuquerque	980	28	130	15	3	2	5
SCHROEDER, Vancouver	.987	76	399	68	6	7	13
Skorochocki, Vancouver	1.000	1	2	0	0	0	1
Stassi, Phoenix	.980	30	138	10	3	1	5
Thomas, Las Vegas	1.000	2	8	1	0	0	0
Tingley, Las Vegas	.977	83	449	55	12	2	8
Torres, Hawaii	.990	14	89	7	1	1	6
Williams, Tucson	.980	10	43	6	1	0	1

Triple play—Herz.

PITCHERS

Player and Club	Pct.	G.	PO.	A.	E.	DP.
Abbott, Salt Lake City	.833	4	1	4	1	0
Adair, Salt Lake City*	.875	50	6	15	3	0
Allard, Salt Lake City	.950	35	16	22	2	3
Altamirano, Portland	1.000	25	1	3	0	0
Andersen, Portland	.950	52	9	10	1	2
Anderson, Vancouver*	.896	43	12	31	5	3
Atherton, Tacoma	.792	26	9	10	5	1
Babcock, Salt Lake City	.917	60	1	10	1	0
Bahnsen, Portland	1.000	15	3	4	0	1
Baker, Tacoma	.944	13	9	8	1	0
Baumgarten, Tacoma*	1.000	12	0	4	0	0
Beattie, Salt Lake City	1.000	3	0	1	0	0
Beene, Vancouver	.946	26	9	26	2	0
Bernard, Tucson	.929	28	5	8	1	1
Best, Salt Lake City	.909	51	1	9	1	0
Bonine, Tucson	.939	27	15	16	2	1
Booker, Las Vegas	.895	46	9	8	2	1
Boone, 29 Tuc.-14 Van.*	.941	43	5	11	1	1
Borbon, Albuquerque*	.955	39	5	16	1	0
Bradford, Portland	1.000	43	1	7	0	0
Bradley, Tacoma	1.000	65	4	11	0	0
C. Brown, Edmonton	1.000	40	2	8	0	2
L. Brown, Las Vegas	1.000	26	5	11	0	0
S. Brown, Edmonton	.933	20	8	20	2	4
Buice, Tacoma	.933	32	8	6	1	0
Burns, Vancouver	.929	26	5	8	1	1
Burroughs, Portland*	1.000	11	3	8	0	0
Callahan, Tacoma	1.000	15	1	3	0	0
Calvert, Phoenix	1.000	14	2	17	0	0
Camacho, Vancouver	.875	11	0	7	1	2
Candiotti, Vancouver	.969	15	11	20	1	4
Castro, Vancouver	1.000	18	1	0	0	0
Chamberlain, Phoenix	1.000	7	1	1	0	0
Chiffer, Las Vegas	.833	42	1	9	2	1
Chris, Phoenix*	.857	24	7	23	5	0
Cocanower, Vancouver	.877	23	18	39	8	3
Comer, 17 SLC-12 Port.	.967	29	8	21	1	1
Cook, Las Vegas	1.000	27	7	15	0	2
Corbett, Edmonton	.867	32	3	10	2	1
Cornell, Phoenix	.909	45	4	6	1	0
Couchee, Las Vegas	1.000	19	1	7	0	0
M. Davis, Phoenix*	1.000	13	4	10	0	0
Davisson, Portland	1.000	1	1	1	0	0
G. Decker, Salt Lake City	1.000	13	2	5	0	0
M. Decker, Portland	1.000	58	5	9	0	0
DeLeon, Hawaii	.917	20	8	14	2	0
Dempsey, Phoenix	1.000	24	7	14	0	1
Downs, Portland	.955	29	9	12	1	0
Dye, Tacoma	.833	16	3	2	1	0
Edge, Hawaii	1.000	9	1	1	0	0
Farmer, 9 Port.-6 Tac.	1.000	15	0	3	0	0
Faulk, Portland	1.000	10	0	3	0	0
Finch, Edmonton	.900	28	10	26	4	4
Fireovid, Las Vegas	.974	28	13	24	1	3
Ford, Tacoma	1.000	8	1	1	0	0
FOWLER, Hawaii	1.000	28	21	24	0	3
Fowlkes, Phoenix	.892	27	12	21	4	2
Franco, Albuquerque*	.857	11	1	5	1	1
Frost, 6 Haw.-14 Port.	.875	20	2	5	1	2
Garrelts, Phoenix	.895	21	5	12	2	2
Geiger, Albuquerque	.900	39	7	11	2	1
Ghelfi, Portland	.900	8	4	5	1	0
Gleaton, Salt Lake City*	.963	24	7	19	1	2
Green, Hawaii*	.893	13	2	23	3	0
Gross, Portland	1.000	15	8	14	0	1
Guante, Hawaii	1.000	15	1	4	0	0
Hamm, Las Vegas	.828	23	9	15	5	2
Hanna, 2 Tac.-16 Port.	1.000	18	3	7	0	0
Hausman, Hawaii	1.000	4	0	3	0	0
Hawkins, Las Vegas	.923	14	3	9	1	0
Heathcock, Tucson	.909	15	7	13	2	1
Heaverlo, Tacoma	1.000	3	0	1	0	0
Heimueller, Tacoma*	.953	20	13	28	2	2
Hensley, Tacoma*	.857	59	6	24	5	0
Hershiser, Albuquerque	.936	49	18	26	3	3
Hinrichs, 5 Phx.-2 Van.	.600	7	3	0	2	0
Holton, Albuquerque	1.000	20	11	18	0	4
Howell, Albuquerque	1.000	1	0	1	0	0
Hudson, Portland	1.000	10	6	13	0	1
Jefferson, Edmonton	1.000	3	1	4	0	0
Jones, Tacoma	.909	26	9	11	2	2
Keeton, Tucson	1.000	13	5	3	0	0
Kibbe, Edmonton	1.000	27	9	23	0	0
King, Tacoma	.800	25	2	6	2	0
Kingman, Phoenix	.889	25	5	11	2	0
Kolotka, Las Vegas	1.000	6	0	1	0	0
Kranitz, Vancouver	.500	7	1	1	2	0
Krawczyk, Hawaii	.963	41	4	22	1	2
Lacey, Edmonton*	1.000	54	1	18	0	0
Ladd, Vancouver	.000	12	0	0	1	0
Lamonde, Hawaii	.880	29	11	33	6	2
Larkin, Phoenix*	.667	4	0	2	1	0
Lerch, Phoenix*	1.000	5	0	1	0	0
Long, Las Vegas	.944	18	4	13	1	1
Luebber, Las Vegas	1.000	3	1	0	0	0
MacDonald, Tucson	1.000	10	2	6	0	1
Madden, Tucson*	1.000	4	1	5	0	1
Mahler, Edmonton*	1.000	1	0	1	0	0
Martinez, Vancouver	.852	28	10	13	4	0
Mathis, Tucson	.967	28	15	14	1	1
McDonald, Tacoma	1.000	3	1	0	0	0
B. McLaughlin, Edmonton	.875	14	1	6	1	0
M. McLaughlin, Las Vegas	.950	13	4	15	1	1
Meridith, Tucson*	.941	37	4	12	1	0
Mirabella, Portland*	1.000	5	0	4	0	0
Mohorcic, Hawaii	.917	15	1	10	1	1
Money, Portland	.857	19	2	10	2	0
Monteagudo, Edmonton	1.000	4	0	1	0	0
Mooneyham, Edmonton	.714	7	0	5	2	0
Moore, Salt Lake City	.867	11	8	18	4	1
A. Moreno, Edmonton*	.879	27	6	23	4	0
Morris, Tucson*	1.000	1	1	1	0	1
Mueller, Vancouver	1.000	40	4	7	0	1
Murray, Salt Lake City	1.000	3	1	3	0	0
Myers, Tacoma	.500	7	0	1	1	0
E. Nelson, Salt Lake City	.909	16	11	9	2	0
Niemann, Hawaii*	1.000	16	4	10	0	1
Norris, Tacoma	.000	1	0	0	1	0
Nunez, Salt Lake City	.833	14	6	9	3	1
Olsen, Vancouver	1.000	5	1	1	0	0
Oroz, Las Vegas*	.939	32	5	26	2	2
Owchinko, Hawaii*	1.000	22	3	26	0	2
Perry, Albuquerque	.952	17	7	13	1	1
Pisel, Phoenix	.929	13	2	11	1	0

PITCHERS—Continued

Player and Club	Pct.	G.	PO.	A.	E.	DP.
Pladson, Tucson	.600	5	3	0	2	0
Plante, Vancouver	1.000	1	0	1	0	0
Porter, Vancouver	1.000	7	0	2	0	0
Rasmussen, Portland	.889	16	8	8	2	1
Redfern, Albuquerque	1.000	6	1	0	0	0
Rennicke, Albuquerque	1.000	32	8	15	0	3
Riley, Portland*	.938	9	5	10	1	0
Roberge, Tucson	1.000	47	5	7	0	0
Roberts, Vancouver	.824	21	4	10	3	1
Rodas, Albuquerque*	.929	27	6	33	3	2
L. Rodriguez, Portland	1.000	3	1	1	0	0
R. Rodriguez, Tacoma	.778	10	4	3	2	0
Ronan, Phoenix	1.000	42	3	11	0	1
Ross, Tucson	1.000	6	1	4	0	0
Rothschild, Las Vegas	1.000	38	4	10	0	0
Ruiz, Las Vegas*	1.000	32	2	6	0	1
Seaman, Vancouver*	1.000	6	0	1	0	0
Segelke, Phoenix	.957	34	9	13	1	0
Semall, Hawaii	1.000	9	3	0	0	0
Senteney, Hawaii	1.000	25	3	5	0	0
D. A. Smith, Edmonton	.909	31	3	17	2	0
D. W. Smith, Edmonton	.875	23	3	4	1	0
M. Smith, Tacoma	1.000	11	4	5	0	1
Snyder, Salt Lake City*	.900	28	2	7	1	0
Solano, Tucson	.821	29	8	15	5	1
Sprowl, Tucson*	1.000	16	1	2	0	0
Stablein, Vancouver	1.000	22	4	3	0	1
Stanhouse, Hawaii	1.000	39	6	9	0	0
Steirer, Edmonton	1.000	28	3	16	0	1
Stranski, Salt Lake City	.846	29	12	21	6	2
Sutton, Salt Lake City	1.000	23	3	9	0	1
Thurmond, Las Vegas*	1.000	19	4	13	0	0
Todd, Tucson	.947	21	9	9	1	0
Travers, Edmonton*	1.000	3	1	1	0	0
Umbarger, Hawaii*	1.000	14	0	1	0	0
Veselic, Tucson	.947	13	5	13	1	1
Voigt, Albuquerque	.960	29	25	23	2	4
Warren, Tacoma	1.000	11	4	2	0	0
Wehrmeister, Portland	1.000	15	6	6	0	0
Welborn, Tucson	1.000	8	1	3	0	0
White, Albuquerque	.902	29	19	27	5	4
Whitson, Las Vegas	1.000	3	1	1	0	0
Williams, Phoenix	.882	25	6	9	2	0
Winn, Hawaii	.900	31	1	8	1	0
Wise, Albuquerque	1.000	7	2	0	0	0
Wright, Albuquerque*	.935	33	8	21	2	2
Young, Tacoma*	.949	27	11	26	2	1

The following players do not have any recorded accepted chances at the positions indicated and therefore are not listed in the fielding averages for those particular positions: Anderson, p; Barnhouse, p; B. Bradley, of; Calderon, p; Christensen, of; Corcoran, p; Corey, 3b; Crone, p; Gl. Davis, 3b; Estrada, 2b; Fick, p; Hinshaw, of; House, p; Jones, p; Kennedy, p; Lubratich, p; Marietta, p; Marshall, p; Mendoza, p; R. Nelson, 3b; O'Berry, 3b; Pederson, of; Powell, 1b; Retzer, p; Taylor, p; Woodard, 3b, of; Zacher, 3b; Zaske, p.

CLUB PITCHING

Club	ERA.	G.	CG.	ShO.	Sv.	IP.	H.	R.	ER.	HR.	HB.	BB.	Int. BB.	SO.	WP.	Bk.
Hawaii	4.28	143	21	9	22	1221.1	1231	688	581	111	26	596	35	801	68	8
Tacoma	4.47	142	20	3	25	1229.1	1256	728	610	125	36	535	42	814	68	13
Portland	4.91	142	13	6	41	1198.0	1262	764	653	127	37	587	29	797	73	4
Tucson	5.05	142	25	8	32	1205.2	1369	785	676	116	31	516	39	809	73	6
Albuquerque	5.17	143	24	4	37	1228.0	1408	842	705	146	41	586	44	773	83	13
Vancouver	5.34	140	20	8	24	1183.0	1332	808	702	125	40	598	16	676	54	6
Las Vegas	5.46	143	20	5	32	1256.2	1514	894	762	180	32	508	11	724	62	10
Salt Lake City	5.60	142	24	7	24	1180.2	1424	856	735	117	34	650	32	796	75	10
Edmonton	5.64	142	14	3	23	1201.0	1421	871	752	171	35	502	21	695	50	7
Phoenix	5.70	143	23	5	31	1193.0	1416	935	755	151	54	610	28	770	74	9

PITCHERS' RECORDS

(Leading Qualifiers for Earned-Run Average Leadership—115 or More Innings)

*Throws lefthanded.

Pitcher—Club	W.	L.	Pct.	ERA.	G.	GS.	CG.	GF.	ShO.	Sv.	IP.	H.	R.	ER.	HR.	HB.	BB.	Int. BB.	SO.	WP.
DeLeon, Hawaii	11	6	.647	3.04	20	20	6	0	1	0	127.1	90	50	43	9	2	68	2	128	2
Heimueller, Tacoma*	8	4	.667	3.54	20	18	2	1	1	0	117.0	126	61	46	4	3	55	3	61	10
J. Jones, Tacoma	6	9	.400	3.56	26	19	3	2	0	0	121.1	123	69	48	11	5	38	3	80	7
White, Albuquerque	13	8	.619	3.75	29	27	5	1	1	0	184.2	201	96	77	16	10	93	7	135	10
Comer, 17 SLC-12 Port.	8	4	.667	3.76	29	15	1	7	0	2	122.0	137	65	51	7	2	38	4	59	3
Atherton, Tacoma	3	8	.273	3.96	26	14	1	6	0	2	120.1	117	60	53	14	2	44	7	93	2
Hershiser, Albuquerque	10	8	.556	4.09	49	10	6	32	0	16	134.1	132	73	61	16	8	57	8	95	10
Rodas, Albuquerque*	16	4	.800	4.16	27	27	7	0	1	0	186.0	202	99	86	16	5	69	4	157	9
Anderson, Vancouver*	10	11	.476	4.16	43	12	3	16	2	1	155.2	162	88	72	9	4	90	0	101	5
Owchinko, Hawaii*	10	6	.625	4.25	22	21	3	0	1	0	137.2	150	86	65	11	0	56	2	124	11

Departmental Leaders: G—B. Bradley, 65; W—Rodas, 16; L—Downs, Mathis, Moreno, 13; Pct.—Rodas, .800; GS—Downs, Lamonde, Stranski, 29; CG—Dempsey, 9; GF—Babcock, 56; ShO—Mathis, 3; Sv.—Andersen, 22; IP—Rodas, 186; H—Fireovid, 212; R—Kibbe, 127; ER—Allard, 111; HR—Dempsey, 35; HB—White, 10; BB—Stranski, 112; IBB—Hershiser, 8; SO—Rodas, 157; WP—Segelke, 20.

(All Pitchers—Listed Alphabetically)

Pitcher—Club	W.	L.	Pct.	ERA.	G.	GS.	CG.	GF.	ShO.	Sv.	IP.	H.	R.	ER.	HR.	HB.	BB.	Int. BB.	SO.	WP.
Abbott, Salt Lake City	0	2	.000	6.08	4	4	0	0	0	0	23.2	33	21	16	3	2	6	0	12	1
Adair, Salt Lake City*	2	6	.250	5.05	50	3	0	23	0	2	67.2	77	44	38	8	1	30	3	53	3
Allard, Salt Lake City	10	10	.500	6.07	35	26	3	2	2	1	164.2	203	124	111	7	3	85	4	75	12
Altamirano, Portland	5	4	.556	2.88	25	0	0	21	0	9	40.2	37	13	13	3	2	18	3	39	2
Andersen, Portland	7	8	.467	2.05	52	0	0	46	0	22	70.1	63	35	16	6	0	30	5	64	10
D. Carl Anderson, Alb.	1	0	1.000	9.00	1	0	0	1	0	0	3.0	3	3	3	0	1	2	0	4	0
M. Anderson, Vancouver*	10	11	.476	4.16	43	12	3	16	2	1	155.2	162	88	72	9	4	90	0	101	5
Atherton, Tacoma	3	8	.273	3.96	26	14	1	6	0	2	120.1	117	60	53	14	2	44	7	93	2
Babcock, Salt Lake City	3	10	.231	3.92	60	0	0	56	0	15	66.2	86	39	29	4	2	38	7	48	5
Baker, Tacoma	4	9	.308	4.55	13	13	6	0	1	0	85.0	75	49	43	6	3	30	2	67	4
Bahnsen, Portland	0	3	.000	9.59	15	2	0	4	0	0	25.1	41	32	27	8	1	11	0	10	3
Barnhouse, Salt Lake City	0	0	.000	0.00	1	0	0	0	0	0	0.2	0	0	0	0	0	3	0	1	0
Baumgarten, Tacoma*	0	1	.000	5.63	12	3	0	4	0	1	24.0	30	17	15	1	0	15	1	13	3
Beattie, Salt Lake City	2	1	.667	5.94	3	3	0	0	0	0	16.2	19	12	11	2	0	8	0	13	1
Beene, Vancouver	13	6	.684	5.03	26	26	3	0	1	0	154.0	138	94	86	17	4	104	0	95	9
Bernard, Tucson	4	0	1.000	2.73	28	1	0	12	0	3	62.2	64	27	19	0	0	31	4	25	2
Best, Salt Lake City	7	4	.636	4.82	51	1	0	12	0	2	84.0	86	51	45	10	3	64	7	108	8
Bonine, Tucson	12	11	.522	4.71	27	27	7	0	0	0	174.0	194	109	91	19	3	84	4	121	6
Booker, Las Vegas	5	6	.455	5.54	46	6	0	18	0	1	102.1	120	77	63	9	3	68	0	58	9
Boone, 29 Tuc.-14 Van.*	7	6	.538	5.02	43	0	0	34	0	11	75.1	96	49	42	6	1	10	2	58	3
Borbon, Albuquerque*	4	3	.571	4.54	39	0	0	24	0	6	71.1	97	54	36	11	1	30	5	28	5
Bradford, Portland*	0	2	.000	5.92	43	0	0	17	0	1	51.2	62	35	34	7	2	36	3	48	4
Bradley, Tacoma	6	5	.545	2.76	65	0	0	42	0	14	84.2	72	35	26	7	4	29	6	45	3
C. Brown, Edmonton	3	4	.429	4.08	40	0	0	29	0	2	57.1	66	37	26	12	5	16	1	32	3
L. Brown, Las Vegas	3	2	.600	5.95	26	1	1	15	0	6	42.1	48	32	28	4	1	19	0	34	2

Pitcher—Club	W.	L.	Pct.	ERA.	G.	GS.	CG.	GF.	ShO.	Sv.	IP.	H.	R.	ER.	HR.	HB.	BB.	Int. BB.	SO.	WP.
S. Brown, Edmonton	10	4	.714	6.15	20	20	3	0	0	0	124.1	154	95	85	22	2	48	3	64	1
Buice, Tacoma	5	3	.625	3.44	32	0	0	16	0	3	52.1	44	27	20	8	1	22	2	41	1
Burns, Vancouver	2	6	.250	7.63	26	1	0	21	0	6	46.0	59	40	39	9	3	19	2	18	3
Burroughs, Portland*	2	3	.400	5.23	11	9	0	0	0	0	43.0	46	36	25	6	3	39	1	23	7
Calderon, Edmonton*	1	0	1.000	5.19	10	0	0	3	0	1	8.2	9	6	5	0	0	9	1	10	1
Callahan, Tacoma	2	4	.333	7.67	15	5	0	1	0	0	31.2	37	32	27	4	2	31	0	15	4
Calvert, Phoenix	4	5	.444	5.88	14	14	2	0	0	0	85.2	115	69	56	10	2	31	0	33	3
Camacho, Vancouver	0	2	.000	6.85	11	3	0	5	0	0	23.2	31	21	18	1	2	12	0	16	3
Candiotti, Vancouver	6	4	.600	2.81	15	14	5	1	2	0	99.1	87	35	31	6	3	16	0	61	1
Castro, Vancouver	1	2	.333	3.70	18	1	0	11	0	3	41.1	42	17	17	7	0	6	1	20	1
Chamberlain, Phoenix	1	1	.500	8.84	7	0	0	4	0	0	19.1	26	20	19	2	0	11	0	13	0
Chiffer, Las Vegas	10	4	.714	3.22	42	0	0	32	0	14	78.1	74	38	28	6	2	33	2	62	7
Chris, Phoenix*	3	12	.200	5.77	24	23	5	0	0	0	145.0	171	115	93	20	5	82	2	94	4
Cocanower, Vancouver	10	10	.500	4.81	23	23	5	0	0	0	153.1	177	100	82	16	9	59	1	79	9
Comer, 17 SLC-12 Port.	8	4	.667	3.76	29	15	1	7	0	2	122.0	137	65	51	7	2	38	4	59	3
Cook, Las Vegas	6	5	.545	6.07	27	16	0	5	0	0	99.1	113	74	67	18	3	56	2	56	7
Corbett, Edmonton	6	6	.500	4.66	32	8	0	11	0	1	83.0	95	55	43	9	1	29	1	61	4
Corcoran, Portland*	0	0	.000	18.00	1	0	0	1	0	0	1.0	3	2	2	1	0	0	0	0	0
Cornell, Phoenix	3	9	.250	3.30	45	0	0	39	0	18	73.2	66	36	27	6	0	37	3	61	7
Couchee, Las Vegas	2	0	1.000	4.05	19	0	0	10	0	4	26.2	39	13	12	3	1	6	0	25	0
Crone, Salt Lake City	0	0	.000	9.00	1	0	0	1	0	0	1.0	1	2	1	0	1	1	0	1	0
Davis, Phoenix*	6	3	.667	6.32	13	13	1	0	1	0	72.2	89	57	51	7	0	33	1	64	4
Davisson, Portland	1	0	1.000	0.00	1	1	1	0	0	0	7.0	6	1	0	0	1	1	0	1	0
G. Decker, Salt Lake City	1	2	.333	8.05	13	1	0	4	0	0	34.2	42	34	31	7	1	22	2	26	3
M. Decker, Portland	8	3	.727	6.66	58	0	0	15	0	3	96.0	105	77	71	12	2	65	6	102	12
DeLeon, Hawaii	11	6	.647	3.04	20	20	6	0	1	0	127.1	90	50	43	9	2	68	2	128	2
Dempsey, Phoenix	9	9	.500	5.78	24	23	9	1	1	0	148.0	162	105	95	35	5	50	0	105	1
Downs, Portland	9	13	.409	4.46	29	29	5	0	1	0	159.1	186	98	79	14	3	61	0	71	8
Dye, Tacoma	1	0	1.000	3.97	16	1	0	1	0	0	34.0	34	17	15	4	1	9	1	20	0
Edge, Hawaii	0	2	.000	4.94	9	0	0	6	0	1	23.2	20	13	13	2	0	9	0	18	3
Farmer, 9 Port.-6 Tac.	1	1	.500	4.94	15	0	0	8	0	1	23.2	29	18	13	1	1	8	0	16	1
Faulk, Portland	1	1	.500	4.30	10	0	0	3	0	1	14.2	18	9	7	2	1	6	0	5	2
Fick, Tacoma	0	0	.000	0.00	1	0	0	1	0	0	1.0	0	0	0	0	0	1	0	1	0
Finch, Edmonton	7	9	.438	6.20	28	28	0	0	0	0	158.1	205	126	109	29	2	60	2	70	4
Fireovid, Las Vegas	14	10	.583	4.78	28	28	6	0	2	0	184.2	212	124	98	20	5	63	0	80	13
Ford, Tacoma	0	2	.000	7.23	8	3	0	0	0	0	18.2	26	17	15	2	0	6	0	6	0
Fowler, Hawaii	13	11	.542	4.64	28	28	2	0	0	0	172.2	178	106	89	19	3	72	1	64	6
Fowlkes, Phoenix	9	11	.450	6.51	27	20	3	4	0	0	134.0	181	118	97	21	7	58	4	78	3
Franco, Albuquerque*	0	0	.000	5.40	11	0	0	6	0	0	15.0	10	11	9	3	0	11	2	8	4
Frost, 6 Haw.-14 Port.	4	1	.800	5.50	20	3	0	5	0	1	55.2	56	36	34	7	3	23	1	26	0
Garrelts, Phoenix	5	5	.500	4.61	21	20	2	0	1	0	97.2	86	64	50	7	7	81	2	89	11
Geiger, Albuquerque	2	3	.400	6.85	39	2	0	19	0	3	93.1	113	84	71	12	4	51	3	45	9
Ghelfi, Portland	1	2	.333	6.19	8	8	0	0	0	0	32.0	45	25	22	3	0	21	0	28	3
Gleaton, Salt Lake City*	9	9	.500	6.68	24	23	2	0	0	0	137.1	189	112	102	19	0	81	0	73	9
Green, Hawaii*	0	9	.000	5.24	13	12	1	0	0	0	77.1	94	53	45	7	1	36	0	49	2
Gross, Portland	3	5	.375	6.75	15	15	0	0	0	0	80.0	82	60	60	9	3	45	1	61	4
Guante, Hawaii	2	1	.667	3.51	15	0	0	12	0	3	25.2	22	12	10	1	0	12	2	24	1
Hamm, Las Vegas	3	9	.250	6.42	23	19	3	2	0	0	101.0	140	90	72	22	2	25	1	49	2
Hanna, 2 Tac.-16 Port.	3	2	.600	5.79	18	6	0	5	0	2	51.1	53	39	33	4	3	28	3	32	5
Hausman, Hawaii	2	1	.667	1.59	4	4	0	0	0	0	17.0	10	6	3	2	0	8	0	7	0
Hawkins, Las Vegas	6	4	.600	6.43	14	14	4	0	1	0	85.1	110	67	61	13	4	27	1	50	1
Heathcock, Tucson	10	3	.769	2.77	15	15	5	0	0	0	110.1	104	45	34	6	2	26	1	65	7
Heaverlo, Tacoma	0	0	.000	3.00	3	0	0	3	0	0	6.0	5	3	2	1	0	2	0	1	1
Heimueller, Tacoma*	8	4	.667	3.54	20	18	2	1	1	0	117.0	126	61	46	4	3	55	3	61	10
Hensley, Tacoma*	4	8	.333	5.52	59	4	0	27	0	3	76.2	88	58	47	13	3	29	7	40	5
Hershiser, Albuquerque	10	8	.556	4.09	49	10	6	32	0	16	134.1	132	73	61	16	8	57	8	95	10
Hinrichs, 5 Phx.-2 Van.	0	1	.000	7.79	7	0	0	6	0	1	17.1	26	17	15	1	0	5	1	10	0
Holton, Albuquerque	7	5	.583	6.36	20	19	0	0	0	0	97.2	113	76	69	10	0	50	2	70	4
House, Las Vegas*	0	0	.000	3.00	2	0	0	2	0	0	3.0	1	1	1	0	1	2	0	0	0
Howell, Albuquerque	0	0	.000	9.00	1	0	0	0	0	0	3.0	4	3	3	1	0	1	0	1	1
Hudson, Portland	6	3	.667	2.67	10	9	3	0	0	0	64.0	48	19	19	4	0	16	1	51	1
Jefferson, Edmonton	0	1	.000	5.40	3	2	0	0	0	0	13.1	19	8	8	3	0	3	0	4	0
D. Jones, Vancouver	0	1	.000	10.29	3	1	0	2	0	0	7.0	10	8	8	2	1	5	0	4	0
J. Jones, Tacoma	6	9	.400	3.56	26	19	3	2	0	0	121.1	123	69	48	11	5	38	3	80	7
Keeton, Tucson	1	1	.500	10.17	13	0	0	4	0	0	25.2	40	30	29	6	0	17	3	16	1
Kennedy, Albuquerque	0	0	.000	0.00	1	0	0	1	0	0	1.1	1	0	0	0	0	0	0	0	0
Kibbe, Edmonton	10	11	.476	5.32	27	27	6	0	0	0	174.1	194	127	103	33	3	79	2	73	10
King, Tacoma	5	2	.714	6.11	25	7	1	6	1	2	63.1	69	45	43	9	1	38	0	39	4
Kingman, Phoenix	6	6	.500	5.53	25	14	0	8	0	2	94.1	106	65	58	7	2	42	4	56	7
Kolotka, Las Vegas	0	0	.000	9.35	6	0	0	3	0	1	8.2	11	9	9	3	0	4	0	3	1
Kranitz, Vancouver	1	3	.250	5.29	7	4	0	1	0	0	32.1	35	22	19	5	2	29	0	24	2
Krawczyk, Hawaii	5	7	.417	3.76	41	3	0	27	0	7	88.2	80	46	37	9	2	33	5	88	2
Lacey, Edmonton*	7	3	.700	4.72	54	2	0	40	0	12	101.0	117	60	53	7	1	30	5	71	3
Ladd, Vancouver	0	0	.000	1.35	12	0	0	12	0	5	13.1	10	2	2	1	1	4	0	16	0
Lamonde, Hawaii	10	12	.455	4.68	29	29	6	0	2	0	177.0	179	105	92	21	6	104	3	58	14
Larkin, Phoenix*	1	0	1.000	2.89	4	0	0	2	0	1	9.1	12	5	3	0	1	8	1	8	1
Lerch, Phoenix*	0	0	.000	3.24	5	0	0	5	0	0	8.1	8	5	3	0	0	3	0	7	2
Long, Las Vegas	5	5	.500	7.65	18	11	0	1	0	0	62.1	99	66	53	8	1	28	2	41	3
Lubratich, Edmonton	0	0	.000	0.00	1	0	0	1	0	0	1.0	0	0	0	0	1	0	0	0	0
Luebber, Las Vegas	0	1	.000	1.80	3	1	0	1	0	0	10.0	10	4	2	0	0	4	0	12	0
MacDonald, Tucson	1	4	.200	4.72	10	4	0	3	0	0	34.1	31	19	18	1	1	12	2	13	0
Madden, Tucson*	1	1	.500	3.68	4	4	0	0	0	0	22.0	25	9	9	1	0	8	0	15	2
Mahler, Edmonton*	1	0	1.000	3.60	1	1	0	0	0	0	5.0	3	2	2	0	0	2	0	3	0
Marietta, Tacoma	0	1	.000	12.15	3	2	0	1	0	0	6.2	14	10	9	1	0	8	0	2	0
Marshall, Edmonton	0	0	.000	60.75	1	0	0	0	0	0	1.1	9	9	9	0	0	5	0	0	1
Martinez, Vancouver	5	11	.313	6.51	28	26	2	0	0	0	149.1	174	125	108	15	2	91	1	84	10
Mathis, Tucson	11	13	.458	4.34	28	28	8	0	3	0	182.2	179	101	88	18	3	73	3	137	5
McDonald, Tacoma	0	0	.000	9.00	3	0	0	1	0	0	6.0	7	7	6	0	0	7	1	4	1
B. McLaughlin, Edmonton	1	2	.333	5.83	14	6	0	5	0	1	46.1	51	33	30	7	1	15	0	42	2
M. McLaughlin, Las Vegas	3	3	.500	7.04	13	10	1	0	0	0	62.2	88	55	49	6	2	19	1	32	7
Mendoza, Hawaii	0	0	.000	0.00	1	0	0	1	0	0	1.0	0	0	0	0	0	0	0	0	0
Meridith, Tucson*	2	3	.400	6.43	37	8	0	16	0	5	91.0	128	74	65	10	0	33	2	59	3
Mirabella, Portland*	0	1	.000	7.53	5	2	0	2	0	1	14.1	19	13	12	0	1	10	1	11	1

Pitcher—Club	W.	L.	Pct.	ERA.	G.	GS.	CG.	GF.	ShO.	Sv.	IP.	H.	R.	ER.	HR.	HB.	BB.	Int. BB	SO.	WP.
Mohorcic, Hawaii	6	6	.500	4.96	15	10	2	2	1	0	69.0	90	42	38	10	2	21	0	30	3
Money, Portland	5	7	.417	4.19	19	14	1	2	0	0	88.0	74	49	41	10	4	54	1	50	4
Monteagudo, Edmonton	1	0	1.000	2.53	4	0	0	4	0	0	10.2	12	3	3	2	0	6	1	9	0
Mooneyham, Edmonton	2	0	1.000	9.84	7	7	0	0	0	0	35.2	51	39	39	7	1	22	0	26	3
Moore, Salt Lake City	4	4	.500	3.61	11	11	4	0	1	0	82.1	78	48	33	3	4	54	1	80	8
Moreno, Edmonton*	8	13	.381	5.73	27	27	3	0	0	0	163.1	182	113	104	20	1	76	1	102	9
Morris, Tucson*	0	1	.000	10.38	1	1	0	0	0	0	4.1	9	5	5	0	0	2	0	2	0
Mueller, Vancouver	2	4	.333	6.87	40	0	0	26	0	5	74.2	102	67	57	11	4	40	6	26	1
Murray, Salt Lake City	0	1	.000	5.63	3	3	0	0	0	0	16.0	20	10	10	3	0	6	0	11	1
Myers, Tacoma	0	1	.000	10.05	7	1	0	1	0	0	14.1	19	16	16	1	1	17	1	10	1
Nelson, Salt Lake City	9	4	.692	5.18	16	16	7	0	2	0	99.0	115	65	57	11	1	28	0	74	1
Niemann, Hawaii*	2	3	.400	4.50	16	14	0	1	0	0	82.0	95	49	41	4	5	45	2	52	8
Norris, Tacoma	0	0	.000	9.00	1	1	0	0	0	0	4.0	6	6	4	1	0	1	0	3	0
Nunez, Salt Lake City	4	4	.500	7.10	14	12	3	2	0	0	77.1	99	70	61	16	5	36	0	52	3
Olsen, Vancouver	0	4	.000	8.57	5	4	0	0	0	0	21.0	24	23	20	3	1	13	1	12	4
Oroz, Las Vegas*	7	4	.636	4.36	32	13	4	7	1	0	132.0	141	77	64	20	1	53	0	71	5
Owchinko, Hawaii*	10	6	.625	4.25	22	21	3	0	1	0	137.2	150	86	65	11	0	56	2	124	11
Perry, Albuquerque	6	4	.600	7.43	17	10	0	3	0	0	63.0	81	59	52	14	4	40	3	39	3
Pisel, Phoenix	0	0	.000	5.59	13	3	0	2	0	0	48.1	60	47	30	7	3	36	0	34	5
Pladson, Tucson	0	2	.000	7.29	5	4	0	0	0	0	21.0	27	21	17	2	1	12	0	13	2
Plante, Vancouver	0	0	.000	10.13	1	0	0	0	0	0	2.2	5	3	3	0	0	0	0	2	1
Porter, Vancouver	0	1	.000	4.74	7	1	0	4	0	1	19.0	30	15	10	2	0	12	0	10	0
Rasmussen, Portland	0	5	.000	6.03	16	11	0	3	0	0	71.2	92	55	48	10	2	28	0	43	1
Redfern, Albuquerque	0	0	.000	11.25	6	2	0	2	0	0	8.0	14	10	10	1	0	7	0	2	2
Rennicke, Albuquerque	9	4	.692	6.79	32	14	1	2	0	0	118.0	165	100	89	20	1	37	1	48	1
Retzer, Tacoma	0	0	.000	2.70	3	0	0	1	0	0	3.1	0	1	1	0	0	4	0	2	0
Riley, Portland*	5	2	.714	6.32	9	8	0	0	0	0	47.0	48	36	33	4	1	32	1	27	0
Roberge, Tucson	3	8	.273	4.59	47	0	0	38	0	14	68.2	66	37	35	4	4	30	7	63	13
Roberts, Vancouver	6	10	.375	6.36	21	21	2	0	2	0	109.0	135	90	77	15	1	63	1	69	2
Rodas, Albuquerque*	16	4	.800	4.16	27	27	7	0	1	0	186.0	202	99	86	16	5	69	4	157	9
L. Rodriguez, Portland	0	0	.000	13.50	3	0	0	2	0	0	6.0	9	12	9	0	0	7	0	0	0
R. Rodriguez, Tacoma	1	4	.200	3.88	10	9	0	0	0	0	58.0	61	32	25	7	2	28	1	25	5
Ronan, Phoenix	3	8	.273	6.95	42	0	0	25	0	3	79.0	114	73	61	12	7	43	6	31	5
Ross, Tucson	0	2	.000	9.95	6	0	0	4	0	0	6.1	14	10	7	1	0	4	1	2	2
Rothschild, Las Vegas	9	2	.818	5.09	38	0	0	16	0	2	74.1	88	43	42	10	2	34	1	39	0
Ruiz, Las Vegas*	3	4	.429	6.75	32	15	0	1	0	0	108.0	142	87	81	27	3	37	1	62	4
Seaman, Vancouver*	0	0	.000	1.23	6	0	0	2	0	0	7.1	4	1	1	0	0	3	0	5	1
Segelke, Phoenix	6	9	.400	7.18	34	13	1	8	0	0	114.0	155	125	91	14	8	70	3	51	20
Semall, Hawaii	1	0	1.000	2.49	9	1	1	4	0	2	25.1	18	8	7	2	0	13	2	15	0
Senteney, Hawaii	4	4	.500	4.70	25	0	0	12	0	3	51.2	54	30	27	4	2	19	3	55	1
D. A. Smith, Edmonton	4	4	.500	7.54	31	4	0	9	0	1	74.0	111	71	62	3	7	38	1	39	2
D. W. Smith, Edmonton	6	3	.667	5.17	23	0	0	15	0	4	38.1	40	24	22	5	2	23	1	26	5
M. Smith, Tacoma	2	2	.500	3.74	11	4	1	2	0	0	43.1	33	21	18	3	0	20	0	34	3
Snyder, Salt Lake City*	5	2	.714	4.38	28	6	0	5	0	1	49.1	53	25	24	0	3	31	4	37	5
Solano, Tucson	10	7	.588	4.95	29	24	2	3	1	1	161.2	183	104	89	17	7	71	4	123	10
Sprowl, Tucson*	0	0	.000	7.77	16	0	0	6	0	0	22.0	25	20	19	2	1	14	1	11	2
Stablein, Vancouver	1	4	.200	4.95	22	3	0	9	0	1	56.1	75	37	31	4	1	24	1	18	2
Stanhouse, Hawaii	4	2	.667	3.15	39	0	0	28	0	3	68.2	54	27	24	5	0	41	7	32	4
Steirer, Edmonton	7	7	.500	3.84	28	7	2	11	1	1	86.2	85	50	37	10	7	33	2	58	1
Stranski, Salt Lake City	7	11	.389	5.28	29	29	5	0	1	0	177.1	198	121	104	19	4	112	1	93	10
Sutton, Salt Lake City	2	2	.500	8.32	23	1	0	6	0	1	44.1	71	50	41	5	2	38	1	24	5
Taylor, Hawaii	0	0	.000	12.00	1	0	0	1	0	0	3.0	6	4	4	2	0	2	0	4	0
Thurmond, Las Vegas*	6	1	.857	3.29	19	6	1	10	0	4	63.0	63	28	23	6	2	24	1	38	1
Todd, Tucson	4	10	.286	7.35	21	13	1	2	0	0	82.0	113	73	67	14	2	38	2	47	10
Travers, Edmonton*	1	0	1.000	5.50	3	3	0	0	0	0	18.0	18	13	11	2	1	8	0	8	1
Umbarger, Hawaii*	1	0	1.000	5.57	14	0	0	4	0	0	21.0	23	16	13	1	0	25	2	22	5
Veselic, Tucson	4	3	.571	6.06	13	13	2	0	0	0	71.1	88	53	48	10	1	42	4	44	3
Voigt, Albuquerque	9	12	.429	5.17	29	25	4	2	0	1	155.0	183	107	89	18	5	69	1	70	10
Warren, Tacoma	6	3	.667	3.53	11	11	3	0	0	0	79.0	72	34	31	6	2	36	0	85	7
Wehrmeister, Portland	8	2	.800	4.20	15	15	2	0	1	0	98.2	93	51	46	9	5	34	1	64	5
Welborn, Tucson	1	0	1.000	6.17	8	0	0	4	0	0	11.2	7	13	8	0	0	16	0	10	1
White, Albuquerque	13	8	.619	3.75	29	27	5	1	1	0	184.2	201	96	77	16	10	93	7	135	10
Whitson, Las Vegas	1	0	1.000	6.75	3	3	0	0	0	0	12.0	15	9	9	0	0	5	0	11	0
Williams, Phoenix	5	3	.625	3.59	25	0	0	17	0	6	47.2	45	22	19	1	3	24	2	37	1
Winn, Hawaii	0	1	.000	3.96	31	1	0	19	0	3	38.2	49	23	17	1	3	22	1	22	5
Wise, Albuquerque	1	1	.500	4.91	7	0	0	4	0	0	11.0	13	7	6	2	0	11	1	3	2
Wright, Albuquerque*	7	6	.538	4.86	33	7	1	22	0	11	83.1	75	60	45	6	2	58	7	68	13
Young, Tacoma*	12	9	.571	5.05	27	25	2	1	0	0	158.2	175	94	89	21	4	52	6	109	5
Zaske, Hawaii	1	0	1.000	6.00	6	0	0	2	0	0	6.0	6	4	4	1	0	6	1	4	0

BALKS—Moreno, Segelke, 4 each; B. Bradley, Hensley, Oroz, Voigt, White, 3 each; Adair, Atherton, Beene, L. Brown, Calvert, Coconower, Downs, Green, Krawczyk, Niemann, Nunez, Perry, Ruiz, Senteney, Stranski, Young, 2 each; Baumgarten, Best, Bonine, Borbon, Camacho, Comer, Cook, Corcoran, M. Davis, Fowlkes, Geiger, Gross, Heathcock, Heimueller, Holton, Jefferson, Kibbe, King, Mathis, M. McLaughlin, Meridith, Money, Mooneyham, Nelson, Owchinko, Pisel, Ronan, Ross, Rothschild, M. Smith, Solano, Stablein, Sutton, Wright, 1 each.

COMBINATION SHUTOUTS—Voigt-Hershiser, White-Hershiser, Albuquerque; McLaughlin-Corbett, Finch-Steirer, Edmonton; DeLeon-Krawczyk, Fowler-Krawczyk, Fowler-Senteney, Lamonde-Krawczyk, Hawaii; Ruiz-Chiffer, Las Vegas; Kingman-Cornell, Kingman-Williams, Phoenix; Comer-Altamirano-Bradford-Decker, Comer-Decker, Gross-Hudson-Altamirano, Hudson-Rasmussen, Portland; Snyder-Allard-Adair-Babcock, Salt Lake City; Bonine-Meridith, MacDonald-Meridith, Mathis-Roberge, Todd-Roberge, Tucson; Beene-Porter, Vancouver.

NO-HIT GAMES—Wright, Albuquerque, defeated Portland, 4-2, May 4; Garrelts, Phoenix, defeated Tacoma, 1-0 (seven innings), August 20.

Eastern League

CLASS AA

Leading Batter
DAVID GALLAGHER
Buffalo

League President
CHARLES ESHBACH

Leading Pitcher
STEVEN FARR
Buffalo

CHAMPIONSHIP WINNERS IN PREVIOUS YEARS

1923	Williamsport	.661
1924	Williamsport	.654
1925	York§	.583
	Williamsport§	.583
1926	Scranton	.627
1927	Harrisburg	.630
1928	Harrisburg	.603
1929	Binghamton	.597
1930	Wilkes-Barre	.572
1931	Harrisburg	.597
1932	Wilkes-Barre	.561
1933	Binghamton	.690
1934	Binghamton	.694
	Williamsport*	.603
1935	Scranton	.657
	Binghamton*	.580
1936	Scranton*	.609
	Elmira	.629
1937	Elmira†	.622
1938	Binghamton	.622
	Elmira (3rd)‡	.522
1939	Scranton†	.571
1940	Scranton	.568
	Binghamton (2nd)‡	.554
1941	Wilkes-Barre	.630
	Elmira (3rd)‡	.514
1942	Albany	.600
	Scranton (2nd)‡	.593
1943	Scranton	.630
	Elmira (2nd)‡	.568
1944	Hartford	.723
	Binghamton (4th)‡	.474
1945	Utica	.615
	Albany (3rd)‡	.564
1946	Scranton†	.691
1947	Utica†	.652
1948	Scranton†	.636
1949	Albany	.664
	Binghamton (4th)‡	.500
1950	Wilkes-Barre‡	.652
1951	Wilkes-Barre	.612
	Scranton (2nd)†	.562
1952	Albany	.603
	Binghamton (2nd)‡	.562
1953	Reading	.682
	Binghamton (2nd)‡	.636
1954	Wilkes-Barre	.576
	Albany (3rd)‡	.540
1955	Reading	.613
	Allentown (2nd)‡	.565
1956	Schenectady†	.609
1957	Binghamton	.607
	Reading (3rd)‡	.529
1958	Lancaster x	.568
	Binghamton (6th)‡	.493
1959	Springfield†	.607
1960	Williamsport y	.551
	Springfield (3rd)y	.496
1961	Springfield	.612
1962	Williamsport	.593
	Elmira (2nd)‡	.514
1963	Charleston	.593
1964	Elmira	.586
1965	Pittsfield	.607
1966	Elmira	.633
1967	Binghamton z	.586
	Elmira	.532
1968	Pittsfield	.604
	Reading (2nd)‡	.579
1969	York	.640
1970	Waterbury a	.560
	Reading a	.553
1971	Three Rivers	.569
	Elmira b	.561
1972	West Haven b	.600
	Three Rivers	.559
1973	Reading b	.551
	Pittsfield	.551
1974	Thetford Mines (2nd)c	.536
	Pittsfield (2nd)	.496
1975	Reading	.613
	Bristol*	.587
1976	Three Rivers	.601
	West Haven d	.576
1977	West Haven e	.623
	Three Rivers	.551
1978	Reading	.642
	Bristol*	.580
1979	West Haven f	.597
1980	Holyoke*	.561
	Waterbury	.540
1981	Glens Falls	.615
	Bristol*	.577
1982	West Haven*	.614
	Lynn	.590

*Won split-season playoff. †Won championship and four-team playoff. ‡Won four-team playoff. §Tied for pennant, York winning playoff. xLeague was divided into Northern, Southern divisions and played a split season; Lancaster over-all season leader. yPlayoff finals canceled after one game because of rain with Williamsport and Springfield declared playoff co-champions. zLeague was divided into Eastern, Western divisions; Binghamton won playoff. aTied for pennant, Waterbury winning playoff. bLeague was divided into American, National divisions; won playoff. cLeague was divided into American and National divisions; won four-team playoff. dLeague was divided into Northern, Southern divisions, won playoff. eLeague was divided into New England and Canadian-American divisions; won playoff. fWon both halves of split season (no playoffs). (NOTE—Known as New York-Pennsylvania League prior to 1938.)

STANDING OF CLUBS AT CLOSE OF SEASON, SEPTEMBER 3

Club	Read.	Lynn	Buff.	NB	Alb.	Nash.	Wat.	GF	W.	L.	T.	Pct.	G.B.
Reading (Phillies)	....	17	9	14	10	17	11	18	96	44	0	.686	....
Lynn (Pirates)	3	....	13	13	13	15	10	10	77	62	0	.554	18½
Buffalo (Indians)	11	7	....	11	12	9	10	14	74	65	0	.532	21½
New Britain (Red Sox)	6	7	8	....	12	11	16	12	72	67	0	.518	23½
Albany (Athletics)	10	7	8	8	....	10	12	8	63	73	0	.463	31
Nashua (Angels)	3	5	11	9	10	....	11	11	60	80	0	.429	36
Waterbury (Reds)	9	9	10	4	8	9	....	10	59	80	0	.424	36½
Glens Falls (White Sox)	2	10	6	8	8	9	10	....	53	83	0	.390	41

Major league affiliations in parentheses.

Playoffs—New Britain defeated Reading, two games to one; Lynn defeated Buffalo, two games to none; and New Britain defeated Lynn, three games to one, to win league championship.

Regular-Season Attendance—Albany, 200,126; Buffalo, 200,531; Glens Falls, 64,562; Lynn, 31,575; Nashua, 138,030; New Britain, 130,433; Reading, 88,484; Waterbury, 55,274. Total, 909,015. Playoffs, 16,581.

Managers—Albany, Pete Whisenant; Buffalo, Al Gallagher; Glens Falls, Adrian Garrett; Lynn, Tommy Sandt; Nashua, Winston Llenas; New Britain, Rac Slider; Reading, Bill Dancy; Waterbury, Jim Lett.

All-Star Team—1B—Francisco Melendez, Reading; 2B—Shanie Dugas, Buffalo; 3B—Timothy Pyznarski, Albany; SS—Rafael Belliard, Lynn; OF—Benito Distefano, Lynn; Thomas Romano, Albany; Jeffrey Stone, Reading; C—Darren Daulton, Reading; RHP—Curtis Heidenreich, Waterbury; LHP—Donald Carman, Reading; Manager of the Year—Bill Dancy, Reading.

(Compiled by Howe News Bureau, Boston, Mass.)

CLUB BATTING

Club	Pct.	G.	AB.	R.	OR.	H.	TB.	2B.	3B.	HR.	RBI.	GW.	SH.	SF.	HP.	BB.	Int. BB.	SO.	SB.	CS.	LOB.
Reading	.278	140	4509	801	601	1254	1875	207	42	110	701	78	56	38	33	597	26	828	272	86	959
Buffalo	.277	139	4402	710	625	1220	1908	204	26	144	643	65	53	29	33	613	27	787	158	66	1001
Albany	.264	136	4307	706	717	1135	1829	180	23	156	657	54	64	43	35	631	19	656	166	77	962
Lynn	.261	139	4335	633	620	1133	1696	178	29	109	568	63	36	31	40	575	20	606	97	63	1002
Nashua	.248	140	4441	559	673	1103	1515	188	25	58	506	54	51	40	36	513	22	634	88	74	948
New Britain	.246	139	4322	627	542	1065	1521	186	33	68	568	67	43	42	34	670	21	743	199	70	996
Glens Falls	.244	136	4201	609	798	1023	1612	184	18	123	555	44	40	48	23	610	14	886	58	54	925
Waterbury	.239	139	4370	543	612	1046	1571	168	27	101	494	56	49	25	33	466	21	814	127	54	890

INDIVIDUAL BATTING

(Leading Qualifiers for Batting Championship—378 or More Plate Appearances)

*Bats lefthanded. †Switch-hitter.

Player and Club	Pct.	G.	AB.	R.	H.	TB.	2B.	3B.	HR.	RBI.	GW.	SH.	SF.	HP.	BB.	Int. BB.	SO.	SB.	CS.
Gallagher, David, Buffalo	.338	107	376	64	127	160	21	3	2	47	4	8	0	3	83	1	21	12	9
Cecchetti, George, Buffalo*	.323	123	390	65	126	177	23	2	8	57	6	2	3	1	61	10	65	7	5
Romano, Thomas, Albany	.320	134	512	90	164	278	28	7	24	89	9	2	4	3	38	3	67	33	10
Stone, Jeffrey, Reading*	.317	125	492	109	156	228	25	10	9	67	6	6	3	9	42	0	85	90	13
Malkin, John, Lynn	.307	104	339	43	104	159	20	1	11	61	5	1	2	5	47	3	62	1	0
Taylor, Dwight, Buffalo*	.302	131	451	95	136	181	13	4	8	38	5	8	2	5	59	2	63	95	21
Melendez, Francisco, Reading*	.298	126	450	81	134	174	17	4	5	75	12	5	6	0	55	2	56	12	2
Patterson, Larry, Nashua	.298	110	352	57	105	125	13	2	1	49	4	3	7	9	72	0	47	3	5
Dowell, Kenneth, Reading	.294	126	367	64	108	129	13	1	2	42	2	7	3	2	65	1	48	8	5
Harrison, Ronald, Albany*	.291	106	398	65	116	172	17	3	11	50	2	12	3	2	20	1	43	19	10
Wilson, James, Buffalo	.290	136	496	84	144	247	25	0	26	105	14	0	4	10	59	2	114	1	1

Departmental Leaders: G—Distefano, 137; AB—Romano, 512; R—Stone, 109; H—Romano, 164; TB—Romano, 278; 2B—Salava, Stephenson, 30; 3B—Garcia, 11; HR—Darkis, 31; RBI—J. Wilson, 105; GWRBI—Darkis, 16; SH—Harrison, Kiefer, 12; SF—Daulton, Stephenson, 10; HP—J. Wilson, 10; BB—Stephenson, 114; IBB—Cecchetti, 10; SO—Boston, 133; SB—D. Taylor, 95; CS—McGehee, 22.

(All Players—Listed Alphabetically)

Player and Club	Pct.	G.	AB.	R.	H.	TB.	2B.	3B.	HR.	RBI.	GW.	SH.	SF.	HP.	BB.	Int. BB.	SO.	SB.	CS.
Alonzo, Raymond, Albany*	.293	52	167	32	49	89	8	1	10	33	2	0	3	3	25	0	16	11	6
Anderson, Jesse, Albany	.000	31	1	0	0	0	0	0	0	0	0	0	0	0	0	0	0	0	0
Arnold, Ronald, Albany	.270	10	37	4	10	16	3	0	1	5	0	0	1	0	3	0	6	1	0
Ashman, Michael, Albany*	.257	113	369	51	95	144	13	0	12	63	7	2	2	3	53	1	41	3	4
Aulenback, James, Lynn	.375	3	8	2	3	6	0	0	1	3	0	1	0	0	0	0	2	0	0
Beal, Anthony, New Britain	.278	125	414	72	115	156	13	5	6	51	6	9	5	8	67	1	105	38	10
Belliard, Rafael, Lynn†	.262	127	431	63	113	136	13	2	2	37	3	11	3	5	30	0	54	12	12
Beltre, Sergio, Nashua	.221	23	77	11	17	29	3	0	3	12	1	0	0	0	6	1	23	0	1
Beswick, James, Nashua†	.258	134	476	60	123	180	29	2	8	59	3	4	4	0	61	5	70	0	2
Boddy, William, Waterbury	.059	8	17	1	1	1	0	0	0	1	0	0	0	0	1	0	2	0	0
Boston, Daryl, Glens Falls*	.239	113	435	65	104	175	15	1	18	50	2	4	4	3	51	1	133	21	13
Bravo, Luis, Albany	.236	57	191	27	45	69	6	3	4	26	1	6	1	6	26	2	19	7	3
Brooks, Craig, New Britain*	.225	59	160	21	36	59	12	1	3	20	3	1	1	2	39	4	52	2	1
Brown, Jeffrey, Glens Falls	.239	65	197	25	47	64	9	1	2	24	2	4	4	0	35	0	22	5	5
Browning, Thomas, Waterbury*	.250	18	16	0	4	4	0	0	0	0	0	0	0	0	0	0	4	0	0
Bryant, Erwin, New Britain	.216	80	232	30	50	63	11	1	0	23	4	7	2	1	33	0	23	6	3
Bustabad, Juan, New Britain*	.265	67	215	26	57	63	4	1	0	19	6	6	3	0	24	1	17	17	5
Carman, Donald, Reading*	.000	56	2	0	0	0	0	0	0	0	0	0	0	0	0	0	0	0	0
Carter, Don, Buffalo*	.267	16	60	10	16	21	1	2	0	10	2	2	1	0	9	1	8	10	2
Cato, J. Keefe, Waterbury	.313	7	16	3	5	8	1	1	0	1	0	1	0	1	2	0	4	0	1
Cecchetti, George, Buffalo*	.323	123	390	65	126	177	23	2	8	57	6	2	3	1	61	10	65	7	5
Charboneau, Joseph, Buffalo	.200	11	35	3	7	13	0	0	2	3	1	0	1	1	3	0	5	0	0
Ciampa, Michael, New Britain*	.261	112	387	57	101	115	7	2	1	24	2	10	4	4	62	0	36	42	13
Cipolloni, Joseph, Reading	.364	3	11	2	4	5	1	0	0	2	1	0	0	1	0	0	5	2	0
Cliburn, Stanley, Lynn	.260	121	412	48	107	173	17	2	15	68	10	1	5	6	55	1	55	0	3
Cliburn, Stewart, Nashua	.000	40	1	0	0	0	0	0	0	0	0	0	0	0	0	0	0	0	0
Corbett, Raymond, Waterbury	.198	35	96	11	19	26	2	1	1	6	1	4	0	1	17	0	31	0	1
Darkis, William, Reading	.277	110	379	76	105	224	20	3	31	102	16	1	4	4	53	5	103	4	8
Daulton, Darren, Reading*	.262	113	362	77	95	176	16	4	19	83	10	1	10	4	106	6	87	28	11
Davis, Eric, Waterbury	.290	89	293	56	85	145	13	1	15	43	4	0	3	5	65	3	75	39	12
Davis, Trench, Lynn*	.279	59	219	37	61	82	7	4	2	16	2	0	0	2	21	0	25	22	6
Day, G. Dexter, Waterbury†	.140	36	93	12	13	18	2	0	1	8	3	0	2	2	16	1	23	8	1
DeLaRosa, Nelson, Lynn*	.231	4	13	1	3	4	1	0	0	1	0	0	0	0	0	0	3	0	0
Dernier, Robert, Reading	.232	14	56	8	13	19	1	1	1	4	2	0	0	0	8	0	8	6	1

Player and Club	Pct.	G.	AB.	R.	H.	TB.	2B.	3B.	HR.	RBI.	GW.	SH.	SF.	HP.	BB.	Int. BB.	SO.	SB.	CS.
Distefano, Benito, Lynn*	.271	137	480	71	130	238	19	7	25	92	10	2	6	5	63	5	40	2	4
Dodd, Thomas, Glens Falls	.242	94	314	38	76	134	15	2	13	56	1	0	4	2	22	0	89	2	1
Dodson, Patrick, New Britain*	.261	118	383	55	100	163	25	1	12	70	8	0	4	1	84	2	86	4	2
Dowell, Kenneth, Reading	.294	126	367	64	108	129	13	1	2	42	2	7	3	2	65	1	48	8	5
Dowless, Michael, Waterbury	.000	13	1	0	0	0	0	0	0	0	0	1	0	0	0	0	1	0	0
Dugas, Shanie, Buffalo*	.259	133	437	87	113	223	20	3	28	85	11	5	5	0	91	8	130	6	4
Durrman, James, Albany*	.240	90	258	29	62	84	13	0	3	27	3	0	2	0	43	4	23	1	3
Ender, Scot, Waterbury	.000	14	8	0	0	0	0	0	0	0	0	1	0	0	1	0	1	0	0
Feliz, L. Adolfo, Waterbury	.200	10	20	5	4	4	0	0	0	1	0	0	0	1	7	0	6	1	0
Fellows, Mark, Albany	.000	25	1	0	0	0	0	0	0	0	0	0	0	0	0	0	1	0	0
Fick, Charles, Albany	.116	18	43	7	5	8	0	0	1	6	1	1	0	0	15	0	6	4	1
Ford, Kenneth, Lynn	.262	87	317	55	83	141	15	2	13	54	5	1	2	2	29	2	56	3	1
Francis, Harry, Nashua	.198	90	262	25	52	72	9	1	3	26	3	4	4	1	18	0	63	3	2
Franklin, Glen, Waterbury*	.278	26	79	10	22	25	3	0	0	4	0	0	0	1	6	0	4	5	0
Fryer, Paul, Reading	.269	113	401	64	108	164	21	4	9	52	6	5	2	0	40	2	95	12	7
Funk, Bryan, Waterbury	.125	43	8	1	1	1	0	0	0	0	0	0	0	0	2	0	2	0	0
Gallagher, David, Buffalo	.338	107	376	64	127	160	21	3	2	47	4	8	0	3	83	1	21	12	9
Gallego, Michael, Albany	.223	90	274	31	61	67	6	0	0	18	2	10	0	3	43	1	25	3	6
Garcia, A. Leonardo, Waterbury*	.257	131	498	65	128	190	25	11	5	47	4	6	7	1	31	5	70	16	9
Gaynor, Richard, Reading	.667	34	3	0	2	3	1	0	0	0	0	0	0	0	0	0	0	0	0
Gerber, Craig, Nashua*	.237	132	502	65	119	158	18	9	1	40	6	8	1	5	48	0	31	16	14
Glass, Timothy, Buffalo	.256	118	395	58	101	167	18	0	16	61	6	6	2	3	52	0	103	1	2
Goldthorn, Burk, Lynn*	.333	7	18	3	6	7	1	0	0	0	0	0	0	1	2	0	1	0	0
Gonzales, Fernando, Lynn	.333	15	3	0	1	1	0	0	0	0	0	0	0	0	0	0	2	0	0
Gruber, Kelly, Buffalo	.263	111	403	60	106	179	20	4	15	54	4	3	2	5	23	0	45	15	8
Gutierrez, Joaquin, New Britain	.278	67	248	36	69	92	7	2	4	25	2	1	3	1	34	1	29	12	10
Guzman, Ruben, Waterbury	.159	20	44	5	7	10	0	0	1	5	1	1	0	1	6	0	11	0	0
Hall, Jeffrey, New Britain	.245	15	53	6	13	18	2	0	1	8	2	0	0	0	5	0	11	0	0
Hamric, Russell, Reading	.254	71	256	37	65	81	8	1	2	34	5	8	4	4	33	1	32	18	11
Harrison, Ronald, Albany*	.291	106	398	65	116	172	17	3	11	50	2	12	3	2	20	1	43	19	10
Heidenreich, Curtis, Waterbury	.091	17	33	4	3	5	2	0	0	3	0	1	0	0	3	0	14	0	0
Holt, David, New Britain*	.211	29	90	15	19	30	2	0	3	15	0	0	2	0	19	0	20	0	0
Hundhammer, Paul, New Britain	.218	15	55	12	12	15	3	0	0	6	0	2	1	3	9	0	6	2	1
Jones, Jeffrey, Waterbury	.235	91	298	52	70	128	7	0	17	50	5	2	0	5	57	2	108	7	3
Jones, Kenneth, Waterbury	.125	29	8	0	1	1	0	0	0	0	0	0	0	0	2	0	0	0	0
Kelly, D. Patrick, Glens Falls	.180	21	61	4	11	14	3	0	0	4	0	0	1	0	7	0	14	0	0
Kent, Wesley, Glens Falls	.167	21	72	4	12	16	1	0	1	7	0	0	2	0	5	0	37	0	0
Khalifa, Sam, Lynn	.200	5	15	1	3	3	0	0	0	1	0	0	1	0	0	0	1	1	0
Kiefer, Steven, Albany	.246	123	415	68	102	179	18	1	19	81	6	12	5	1	43	2	111	25	4
Kirsch, Paul, Waterbury*	.265	51	155	11	41	52	6	1	1	16	4	1	1	2	9	1	11	4	0
Kravec, Kenneth, Albany*	.000	35	3	0	0	0	0	0	0	0	0	0	0	0	0	0	2	0	0
Landrum, T. William, Waterbury	.000	17	2	0	0	0	0	0	0	0	0	1	0	0	0	0	1	0	0
Lavalliere, Michael, Reading*	.294	81	218	24	64	96	16	2	4	43	2	1	1	0	32	4	26	1	2
Legg, Gregory, Reading	.306	90	284	44	87	115	14	1	4	49	6	7	1	1	26	0	30	5	1
Liddle, Steven, Nashua	.223	117	381	46	85	115	15	0	5	45	5	5	7	5	52	1	72	4	4
Little, Ronald, Waterbury*	.220	101	318	35	70	108	11	0	9	40	7	3	3	1	31	1	95	3	4
Llenas, Winston, Nashua	.000	1	2	0	0	0	0	0	0	0	0	0	0	0	0	0	1	0	0
Lyons, Stephen, New Britain*	.246	132	456	83	112	171	24	7	7	62	7	1	3	6	77	6	65	47	18
Malkin, John, 22 Buff.-82 Lynn	.307	104	339	43	104	159	20	1	11	61	5	1	2	5	47	3	62	1	0
Malpeso, David, New Britain	.258	120	430	54	111	163	19	3	9	72	9	0	3	2	38	0	67	3	3
Marcheskie, Lee, Lynn	.000	25	2	0	0	0	0	0	0	0	0	0	0	0	0	0	1	0	0
McAbee, Monte, Glens Falls*	.258	126	422	58	109	189	17	3	19	72	7	3	7	2	71	4	57	4	3
McClendon, Lloyd, Waterbury	.263	123	434	58	114	182	19	2	15	57	5	3	1	5	42	2	64	4	6
McGehee, C. Connor, Lynn*	.243	125	399	73	97	132	14	3	5	34	2	1	2	3	101	0	89	46	22
Meier, Scott, Glens Falls	.230	71	187	30	43	56	5	1	2	17	0	4	1	0	62	0	38	0	2
Melendez, Francisco, Reading*	.298	126	450	81	134	174	17	4	5	75	12	5	6	0	55	2	56	12	2
Miles, J. Edward, Glens Falls	.213	60	216	31	46	79	8	2	7	40	3	2	4	1	25	0	53	1	5
Miley, David, Waterbury*	.242	65	186	19	45	68	11	0	4	24	4	1	1	0	36	1	7	1	1
Miller-Jones, Gary, New Britain†	.198	125	429	53	85	118	15	3	4	45	4	2	5	2	47	3	71	5	1
Mitchell, Charles, New Britain	.000	49	1	0	0	0	0	0	0	0	0	1	0	0	0	0	1	0	0
Monasterio, Juan, Nashua	.353	9	34	8	12	24	0	0	4	9	1	0	0	0	2	1	4	1	0
Morman, Russell, Glens Falls	.245	71	233	29	57	77	9	1	3	32	4	0	3	5	40	0	65	8	3
Moronko, Jeffrey, Buffalo	.269	124	386	51	104	166	20	3	12	49	3	9	2	2	41	0	80	2	6
Morse, Michael, Glens Falls	.220	130	468	96	103	166	19	1	14	45	4	5	6	3	63	0	91	7	9
Nix, David, Glens Falls*	.255	132	474	72	121	193	23	2	15	64	8	2	3	4	53	2	64	2	1
Norman, Nelson, Lynn	.268	122	410	77	110	148	13	5	5	53	7	5	4	1	85	3	25	2	4
O'Brien, Charles, Albany	.291	92	285	50	83	139	12	1	14	56	8	6	4	6	52	1	39	3	4
O'Neill, Paul, Waterbury*	.279	14	43	6	12	12	0	0	0	6	0	0	0	0	6	0	8	2	1
Pacheco, Hillario, Nashua	.063	6	16	0	1	1	0	0	0	0	0	0	0	0	4	0	6	1	0
Pacho, Juan, Buffalo	.146	37	96	10	14	18	4	0	0	6	0	2	0	0	6	0	9	0	0
Pastors, Gregory, Lynn	.183	79	202	22	37	52	9	0	2	15	4	6	2	1	23	1	42	1	2
Pastrovich, Steven, Glens Falls	.000	47	1	0	0	0	0	0	0	0	0	0	0	0	0	0	1	0	0
Patterson, Larry, Nashua	.298	110	352	57	105	125	13	2	1	49	4	3	7	9	72	0	47	3	5
Perez, Julio, Reading†	.192	8	26	2	5	10	2	0	1	6	0	1	0	0	4	0	3	0	2
Pettibone, James, Waterbury	.158	18	19	1	3	3	0	0	0	1	0	3	0	0	4	0	7	0	0
Polidor, Gustavo, Nashua	.210	105	329	32	69	80	7	2	0	21	2	8	1	1	17	2	32	4	6
Porte, Carlos, Waterbury	.247	112	385	40	95	131	11	5	5	42	3	3	0	0	31	2	38	10	4
Pyle, Scot, Albany	.165	36	91	21	15	25	1	0	3	11	2	3	2	1	27	1	20	3	1
Pyznarski, Timothy, Albany	.279	124	416	84	116	226	15	4	29	79	7	1	4	1	68	0	118	20	7
Quinones, Luis, Albany†	.239	56	213	35	51	74	5	0	6	23	0	2	0	0	25	2	20	8	4
Quinones, Rene, Buffalo†	.299	36	97	10	29	45	6	2	2	14	1	0	2	0	4	0	16	1	2
Randall, James, Nashua†	.276	133	456	78	126	202	26	4	14	88	8	5	3	2	81	5	76	19	6
Reed, Curtis, Glens Falls*	.271	122	402	56	109	163	21	0	11	51	3	3	3	1	59	4	81	2	5
Rende, Salvatore, Buffalo*	.253	63	170	31	43	77	4	0	10	32	3	3	1	0	34	1	33	1	1
Renteria, Richard, Lynn	.285	115	424	47	121	158	25	0	4	40	5	2	3	4	31	2	45	3	2
Rey, Everett, Buffalo	.271	19	59	4	16	24	3	1	1	8	0	1	0	0	2	0	14	1	0
Rincones, Hector, Waterbury	.229	135	494	50	113	137	14	2	2	34	4	4	2	2	20	0	52	17	3
Robinson, Donald, Lynn	.364	5	11	0	4	5	1	0	0	0	0	0	0	0	0	0	1	0	0
Robinson, Ronald, Waterbury	.200	20	30	2	6	7	1	0	0	2	0	6	0	0	2	0	11	0	0
Rodriguez, Jose, Lynn	.246	40	130	19	32	51	4	0	5	18	0	2	1	1	14	0	43	2	4
Rollins, Rip, Reading	1.000	20	1	0	1	1	0	0	0	0	0	0	0	0	0	0	0	0	0
Romanick, Ronald, Nashua	.000	27	3	0	0	0	0	0	0	0	0	0	0	0	1	0	0	0	0
Romano, Thomas, Albany	.320	134	512	90	164	278	28	7	24	89	9	2	4	3	38	3	67	33	10

Player and Club	Pct.	G.	AB.	R.	H.	TB.	2B.	3B.	HR.	RBI.	GW.	SH.	SF.	HP.	BB.	Int. BB.	SO.	SB.	CS.
Romero, E. Albert, Nashua	.235	113	366	36	86	122	19	1	5	47	5	3	8	3	26	1	63	9	7
Romero, Ramon, Glens Falls†	.251	69	199	26	50	71	11	2	2	20	1	6	2	1	30	0	36	0	3
Romine, Kevin, New Britain	.261	132	467	74	122	191	26	5	11	80	8	2	6	1	76	2	91	20	1
Rothey, Mark, Waterbury*	.000	43	2	0	0	0	0	0	0	0	0	1	0	0	1	0	2	0	0
Rowdon, Wade, Waterbury	.233	135	480	62	112	206	29	1	21	76	9	2	3	3	47	0	119	6	3
Rowe, Peter, Lynn	.221	26	86	5	19	29	5	1	1	15	2	1	1	1	3	0	3	0	0
Ryder, Brian, Waterbury	.045	23	22	1	1	1	0	0	0	0	0	0	0	0	0	0	13	0	0
Saatzer, Michael, Nashua*	.208	37	48	5	10	21	2	0	3	6	1	0	0	0	6	0	15	0	0
Saavedra, Edwin, Buffalo	.255	84	274	44	70	108	13	2	7	40	4	3	2	1	45	1	26	4	3
Salava, Randy, Reading*	.280	136	478	98	134	216	30	8	12	69	7	2	0	6	78	5	104	26	8
Samuel, Juan, Reading	.234	47	184	36	43	86	10	0	11	39	1	1	2	1	8	0	50	19	2
Sandt, Thomas, Lynn	.091	6	11	1	1	4	0	0	1	2	0	1	0	0	8	0	1	0	0
Scarpace, Kenneth, Waterbury*	.267	83	266	33	71	98	11	2	4	27	2	3	2	2	20	3	26	4	5
Schaive, John, Lynn	.230	115	379	56	87	151	12	2	16	54	6	2	0	2	48	2	46	2	2
Simunic, Douglas, Buffalo	.281	44	146	19	41	63	7	0	5	21	0	0	1	2	21	1	31	1	1
Smith, Michael, Waterbury	.000	22	4	0	0	0	0	0	0	0	0	1	0	0	0	0	3	0	0
Sodders, Michael, Glens Falls	.251	68	215	30	54	92	10	2	8	36	4	3	2	1	35	0	43	1	0
Stephens, Darryl, Nashua*	.245	105	347	40	85	119	14	1	6	40	4	1	0	1	43	3	51	4	4
Stephenson, Phillip, Albany*	.280	133	436	90	122	215	30	3	19	77	4	4	10	3	114	1	66	17	7
Stone, Jeffrey, Reading*	.317	125	492	109	156	228	25	10	9	67	6	6	3	9	42	0	85	90	13
Straker, Lester, Waterbury	.000	3	2	0	0	0	0	0	0	0	0	0	0	0	1	0	1	0	0
Sullivan, Marc, New Britain	.229	73	231	30	53	91	15	1	7	43	5	0	0	2	53	1	47	1	2
Tarnow, Greg, Glens Falls	.188	11	32	4	6	6	0	0	0	2	0	1	0	0	5	0	16	0	0
Taylor, Dwight, Buffalo*	.302	131	451	95	136	181	13	4	8	38	5	8	2	5	59	2	63	95	21
Taylor, Johnny, Glens Falls	.286	3	7	1	2	2	0	0	0	1	0	0	0	0	0	0	2	0	0
Thomas, Vernon, Glens Falls	.195	15	41	5	8	10	2	0	0	6	0	0	0	0	7	0	4	2	0
Tyler, David, New Britain	.000	41	2	0	0	0	0	0	0	0	0	0	0	0	0	0	2	0	0
Valdez, Julio, New Britain†	.145	21	69	3	10	13	1	1	0	5	1	1	0	1	3	0	14	0	0
Valley, Charles, Buffalo†	.000	13	3	0	0	0	0	0	0	0	0	0	0	0	0	0	2	0	0
Vargas, Hediberto, Lynn	.310	20	71	13	22	33	5	0	2	13	2	0	0	1	16	1	20	0	1
Vilorio, Francisco, Nashua	.236	121	406	38	96	117	18	0	1	33	6	7	3	6	35	1	25	14	9
Wabeke, Douglas, Lynn	.107	10	28	2	3	4	1	0	0	2	1	0	0	0	6	0	3	0	0
Washington, Keith, Reading†	.244	132	468	73	114	129	11	2	0	33	2	9	2	0	43	0	72	40	12
West, Reginald, Nashua*	.316	85	313	47	99	121	8	1	4	29	5	3	1	2	34	2	33	5	13
White, Devon, Nashua	.257	17	70	11	18	29	7	2	0	2	0	0	1	1	7	0	22	5	1
Williams, Melvin, Reading	.232	29	69	6	16	19	1	1	0	1	0	1	0	1	4	0	23	1	1
Wilson, James, Buffalo	.290	136	496	84	144	247	25	0	26	105	14	0	4	10	59	2	114	1	1
Wilson, Phillip, Buffalo	.236	21	55	9	13	18	2	0	1	2	0	0	0	0	13	0	8	1	1
Wojna, Edward, Reading	.000	28	2	0	0	0	0	0	0	0	0	1	0	0	0	0	1	0	0
Woods, Vincent, Glens Falls	.171	14	41	4	7	7	0	0	0	0	0	3	0	0	5	1	19	2	0
Yobs, David, Glens Falls*	.315	54	184	31	58	98	16	0	8	28	5	0	2	0	35	2	21	1	3
Young, Selwyn, Albany†	.198	74	197	22	39	44	5	0	0	13	0	3	2	3	35	0	33	8	7

The following pitchers, listed alphabetically by club, with games in parentheses, had no plate appearances, primarily through use of designated hitters:

ALBANY—Abraham, Brian (3); Edwards, Allen (34); Ferguson, Mark (22); Herron, Anthony (8); Josephson, Paul (50); Law, Joseph (2); Lynes, Michael (47); McDonald, Russell (19); Ontiveros, Steven (33); Vantrease, Robert (1); Warren, Micheal (10); Wex, Gary (6); Wortham, Richard (4); Zmudosky, Thomas (2).

BUFFALO—Baller, Jay (16); Bohnet, John (21); Doyle, Richard (18); Farr, Steven (18); Fuson, Robin (29); Glaser, Gordon (25); Green, Jeffrey (4); Johnson, Wayne (22); Keeler, Jay (9); McDonald, Rodney (12); Owens, Thomas (3); Perry, Patrick (5); Romero, Ramon (44); Santarelli, Calvin (13); Thompson, Richard (43).

GLENS FALLS—Babcock, William (3); Brennan, Thomas (22); Desjarlais, Keith (26); Hardy, John (8); Howard, Fred (2); Maitland, Michael (35); Moncrief, Homer (29); Moore, Robert (24); Mullen, Thomas (42); Ruzek, Donald (12); Schuckert, Wayne (26); Tanner, Bruce (5); Tanzi, Michael (5); Umbarger, James (9); Withrow, Michael (25).

LYNN—Bielecki, Michael (25); Cacciatore, Paul (3); Cordoba, Wilfredo (33); Green, Christopher (23); Lackey, John (27); Mohorcic, Dale (18); Peterson, Eric (2); Pippin, Craig (37); Susce, Steven (4); Taylor, Johnny (5); Thibodeaux, Keith (19); Wheeler, Timothy (26); Zaske, Jeffrey (48).

NASHUA—Bastian, Robert (34); Boxberger, Rodney (25); Buckley, Brian (18); Conner, Jeffrey (27); McCaskill, Kirk (13); McKenzie, Douglas (4); Mooneyham, William (20); Smith, David A. (2); Smith, David W. (24); Sylvia, Ronald (43).

NEW BRITAIN—Birrell, Robert (1); Bolton, Thomas (16); Clemens, Roger (7); Dale, Charles (33); Davis, Charles (16); Gering, Scott (3); Gnacinski, Paul (34); Greco, George (22); Johnson, Clinton (25); Kane, Kevin (9); Mecerod, George (23); Nipper, Albert (10); Woody, Harley (22).

READING—Bartholow, Foster (16); Burroughs, Darren (15); Cole, William (1); Davisson, Jay (20); Ghelfi, Anthony (16); Griffin, Frankie (21); Johnson, William (11); Maddux, Michael (1); Palmieri, John (4); Riley, George (27); Surhoff, Richard (40); Thomas, Dennis (17).

WATERBURY—Buchanan, Robert (14); Wise, Brett (14).

GRAND SLAM HOME RUNS—Ashman, Cliburn, Nix, Stone, 2 each; Bravo, E. Davis, Ford, Hamric, Kiefer, Legg, Malpeso, Pyznarski, Saavedra, Sullivan, J. Wilson, 1 each.

AWARDED FIRST BASE ON CATCHER'S INTERFERENCE—Ender (Malkin); Garcia (Lavalliere); Little (O'Brien); L. Quinones (Dodd).

CLUB FIELDING

Club	Pct.	G.	PO.	A.	E.	DP.	PB.
New Britain	.973	139	3486	1548	139	122	18
Lynn	.970	139	3409	1296	146	128	16
Waterbury	.970	139	3483	1317	149	90	14
Reading	.968	140	3552	1479	165	131	16
Buffalo	.967	139	3446	1347	164	122	27
Nashua	.966	140	3546	1615	179	152	20
Albany	.961	136	3402	1504	201	121	11
Glens Falls	.960	136	3326	1353	196	110	20

Triple play—New Britain.

INDIVIDUAL FIELDING

*Throws lefthanded

FIRST BASEMEN

Player and Club	Pct.	G.	PO.	A.	E.	DP.
Ashman, Albany	.984	51	425	19	7	35
Bryant, New Britain	.900	1	7	2	1	0
Cecchetti, Buffalo*	.987	28	209	15	3	24
Darkis, Reading	1.000	7	42	5	0	3
Daulton, Reading	.964	7	54	0	2	5
Davis, Lynn*	1.000	1	5	0	0	0
Day, Waterbury	.944	2	17	0	1	1
Distefano, Lynn*	1.000	6	40	2	0	2
Dodson, New Britain*	.988	94	815	54	11	69
Durrman, Albany	1.000	3	4	0	0	0
Francis, Nashua	1.000	8	41	1	0	6
Fryer, Reading	.983	7	57	0	1	3

FIRST BASEMEN—Continued

Player and Club	Pct.	G.	PO.	A.	E.	DP.
Glass, Buffalo	1.000	1	2	0	0	1
Jones, Waterbury	.985	61	429	34	7	34
Kent, Glens Falls	.968	6	57	3	2	5
Kirsch, Waterbury*	1.000	34	243	17	0	10
Legg, Reading	1.000	1	3	0	0	0
Llenas, Nashua	1.000	1	7	0	0	0
Malpeso, New Britain	.962	12	97	5	4	7
McAbee, Glens Falls*	.972	59	447	44	14	38
McClendon, Waterbury	.989	24	164	13	2	10
Melendez, Reading*	.990	126	1081	73	12	99
Morman, Glens Falls	.989	71	591	43	7	50
O'Brien, Albany	1.000	1	1	0	0	0
Patterson, Nashua	1.000	6	51	3	0	6
Randall, Nashua*	.988	39	296	37	4	33
Rende, Buffalo*	.992	33	239	11	2	23
Rowdon, Waterbury	.975	5	38	1	1	2
Rowe, Lynn	.976	7	38	3	1	4
Saatzer, Nashua	1.000	9	68	4	0	8
Salava, Reading	.818	1	7	2	2	1
Sandt, Lynn	1.000	1	9	0	0	1
Scarpace, Waterbury*	.990	23	185	10	2	16
SCHAIVE, Lynn	.995	107	841	85	5	86
Simunic, Buffalo	1.000	2	13	4	0	0
Sodders, Glens Falls	1.000	3	17	2	0	1
Stephens, Nashua*	.991	90	729	77	7	81
Stephenson, Albany*	.983	94	709	84	14	68
Sullivan, New Britain	.984	30	296	7	5	29
Valdez, New Britain	1.000	9	76	10	0	5
Vargas, Lynn	.981	17	141	12	3	17
Wabeke, Lynn	.967	5	27	2	1	2
Wilson, Buffalo	.983	82	701	57	13	60

Triple play—Dodson.

SECOND BASEMEN

Player and Club	Pct.	G.	PO.	A.	E.	DP.
Ashman, Albany	1.000	2	0	4	0	0
Belliard, Lynn	.966	15	23	33	2	6
Brown, Glens Falls	.963	6	16	10	1	1
Bryant, New Britain	.981	13	25	27	1	6
Dowell, Reading	.980	13	19	29	1	7
Dugas, Buffalo	.965	132	245	364	22	64
Feliz, Waterbury	1.000	2	2	1	0	0
Francis, Nashua	1.000	1	0	1	0	0
Franklin, Waterbury	.971	8	13	21	1	5
Gallego, Albany	.991	89	183	259	4	59
GERBER, Nashua	.987	132	311	441	10	107
Hamric, Reading	.981	71	149	169	6	41
Legg, Reading	.976	14	32	49	2	11
Miller-Jones, New Britain	.977	125	235	360	14	72
Moronko, Buffalo	1.000	3	5	9	0	2
Morse, Glens Falls	.976	26	54	67	3	18
Nix, Glens Falls	.937	103	216	246	31	54
Norman, Lynn	.970	100	190	267	14	55
Pacho, Buffalo	.880	7	11	11	3	2
Pastors, Lynn	.981	31	40	65	2	12
Porte, Waterbury	.949	109	207	243	24	49
Pyle, Albany	.971	15	30	37	2	10
Quinones, Albany	.945	31	55	66	7	7
Romero, Glens Falls	1.000	5	10	11	0	2
Rowdon, Waterbury	.958	26	49	66	5	11
Samuel, Reading	.947	47	121	127	14	34
Valdez, New Britain	1.000	4	6	4	0	0
Vilorio, Nashua	1.000	13	20	30	0	7
Wabeke, Lynn	1.000	1	3	0	0	0
Young, Albany	.800	10	5	11	4	3

Triple play—Miller-Jones.

THIRD BASEMEN

Player and Club	Pct.	G.	PO.	A.	E.	DP.
Ashman, Albany	.972	21	9	26	1	2
Brown, Glens Falls	1.000	3	1	3	0	2
Bryant, New Britain	.948	40	16	57	4	10
Dowell, Reading	1.000	6	1	13	0	2
Feliz, Waterbury	.800	4	3	5	2	0
Francis, Nashua	.929	78	61	110	13	11
Franklin, Waterbury	.850	7	6	11	3	1
Fryer, Reading	.917	96	68	185	23	19
Gallagher, Buffalo	1.000	1	1	1	0	0
Gruber, Buffalo	.916	107	89	163	23	15
Hundhammer, New Britain	.872	15	13	28	6	5
Kiefer, Albany	.800	6	4	4	2	1
Lavalliere, Reading	.968	15	5	25	1	4
Legg, Reading	.982	26	15	40	1	3
Lyons, New Britain	.949	87	61	197	14	10
Malpeso, New Britain	1.000	1	3	0	0	0
McClendon, Waterbury	.914	29	25	39	6	5
Moronko, Buffalo	.929	17	18	21	3	2
Morse, Glens Falls	.947	54	44	116	9	9
Nix, Glens Falls	.930	30	31	62	7	4
Pacho, Buffalo	1.000	4	0	3	0	0
Pastors, Lynn	.966	25	24	32	2	4
Patterson, Nashua	.800	14	11	13	6	2
Perez, Reading	.917	7	7	15	2	1
Polidor, Nashua	1.000	1	0	2	0	0
Pyle, Albany	1.000	7	7	11	0	0
Pyznarski, Albany	.893	109	90	210	36	24
Quinones, Buffalo	1.000	9	5	14	0	1
Renteria, Lynn	.930	113	83	170	19	20
Rey, Buffalo	.909	4	4	6	1	0
Romero, Nashua	.714	5	3	2	2	0
ROWDON, Waterbury	.940	104	86	164	16	21
Salava, Reading	.500	1	0	2	2	0
Sodders, Glens Falls	.949	52	50	116	9	13
Valdez, New Britain	1.000	5	1	10	0	0
Vilorio, Nashua	.935	64	46	98	10	11
Wabeke, Lynn	.750	2	2	1	1	0
Wilson, Buffalo	.833	7	1	4	1	0
Young, Albany	1.000	3	0	6	0	1

Triple play—Lyons.

SHORTSTOPS

Player and Club	Pct.	G.	PO.	A.	E.	DP.
Ashman, Albany	1.000	5	5	11	0	4
Belliard, Lynn	.950	114	180	274	24	69
Brown, Glens Falls	.943	29	41	59	6	16
Bryant, New Britain	.938	6	12	18	2	4
Bustabad, New Britain	.976	64	105	177	7	36
DOWELL, Reading	.957	108	179	335	23	68
Franklin, Waterbury	1.000	7	10	23	0	7
Fryer, Reading	.981	13	14	39	1	4
Gallego, Albany	1.000	2	1	1	0	1
Gerber, Nashua	1.000	1	0	1	0	0
Gruber, Buffalo	.800	5	9	7	4	1
Gutierrez, New Britain	.960	67	116	194	13	41
Khalifa, Lynn	1.000	5	8	9	0	3
Kiefer, Albany	.931	115	182	302	36	55
Legg, Reading	.908	29	25	74	10	11
Lyons, New Britain	1.000	2	4	3	0	1
Moronko, Buffalo	.941	100	147	284	27	58
Morse, Glens Falls	.906	49	76	136	22	20
Norman, Lynn	.956	23	25	40	3	5
Pacho, Buffalo	.965	25	34	49	3	7
Pastors, Lynn	1.000	3	0	4	0	0
Polidor, Nashua	.930	104	208	281	37	69
Pyle, Albany	.915	10	11	32	4	5
L. Quinones, Albany	.967	9	18	71	3	6
R. Quinones, Buffalo	.989	21	30	60	1	14
Rincones, Waterbury	.956	132	248	342	27	48
Romero, Glens Falls	.953	60	96	147	12	30
Valdez, New Britain	.952	5	8	12	1	0
Vilorio, Nashua	.961	47	88	132	9	36
Young, Albany	.955	5	10	11	1	2

OUTFIELDERS

Player and Club	Pct.	G.	PO.	A.	E.	DP.
Alonzo, Albany*	.957	35	39	6	2	1
Arnold, Albany	.882	10	14	1	2	0
Beal, New Britain	.932	120	227	19	18	2
Beltre, Nashua	.895	22	33	1	4	0
Beswick, Nashua	.965	132	218	4	8	0
Boston, Glens Falls*	.955	113	271	8	13	2
Bravo, Albany	.926	55	86	1	7	0
Brooks, New Britain	.667	10	5	1	3	0
Brown, Glens Falls	.978	18	44	0	1	0
Carter, Buffalo	.967	16	29	0	1	0

OUTFIELDERS—Continued

Player and Club	Pct.	G.	PO.	A.	E.	DP.
Cecchetti, Buffalo*	.981	88	142	9	3	2
Charboneau, Buffalo	1.000	8	9	0	0	0
CIAMPA, New Britain*	.997	111	281	5	1	1
Darkis, Reading	.976	22	40	1	1	0
Daulton, Reading	1.000	1	1	0	0	0
E. Davis, Waterbury	.991	84	214	8	2	2
T. Davis, Lynn*	.957	59	105	7	5	1
Day, Waterbury	.954	27	60	2	3	1
DeLaRosa, Lynn*	1.000	3	5	0	0	0
Dernier, Reading	1.000	14	36	0	0	0
Distefano, Lynn*	.949	130	231	11	13	1
Dodd, Glens Falls	.968	46	87	5	3	2
Feliz, Waterbury	1.000	2	4	0	0	0
Ford, Lynn	.947	72	116	9	7	2
Francis, Nashua	1.000	1	1	0	0	0
Gallagher, Buffalo	.979	107	222	12	5	4
Garcia, Waterbury*	.980	130	233	13	5	2
Guzman, Waterbury	.895	15	17	0	2	0
Hall, New Britain	1.000	3	5	1	0	0
Harrison, Albany	.954	100	215	12	11	3
Jones, Waterbury	.973	23	32	4	1	1
Liddle, Nashua	1.000	2	4	0	0	0
Little, Waterbury*	.981	95	192	10	4	1
Lyons, New Britain	.967	47	80	7	3	0
Malpeso, New Britain	.929	8	12	1	1	0
McGehee, Lynn*	.964	115	210	5	8	1
Melendez, Reading*	1.000	2	1	0	0	0
Miles, Glens Falls	.935	59	94	7	7	2
Monasterio, Nashua	1.000	9	16	0	0	0
Moronko, Buffalo	1.000	7	7	0	0	0
O'Neill, Waterbury	1.000	14	26	0	0	0
Pacheco, Nashua	1.000	3	3	0	0	0
Pastors, Lynn	1.000	18	24	0	0	0
Pyznarski, Albany	.833	5	5	0	1	0
L. Quinones, Albany	.906	19	28	1	3	0
Randall, Nashua*	.921	76	111	17	11	2
Reed, Glens Falls	.981	93	144	8	3	0
Rodriguez, Lynn	.943	30	63	3	4	0
Romano, Albany	.961	135	287	8	12	2
Romero, Nashua	.930	87	142	4	11	0
Romine, New Britain	.982	131	211	12	4	4
Saavedra, Buffalo	.965	79	132	7	5	0
Salava, Reading	.972	128	239	8	7	2
Scarpace, Waterbury*	.991	45	102	6	1	2
Simunic, Buffalo	1.000	1	1	0	0	0
Sodders, Glens Falls	1.000	9	13	0	0	0
Stephenson, Albany*	1.000	40	62	1	0	0
Stone, Reading	.963	125	226	6	9	3
Taylor, Buffalo*	.963	126	223	10	9	1
Thomas, Glens Falls	.947	8	17	1	1	0
Valley, Buffalo*	1.000	1	1	0	0	0
Washington, Reading	.982	131	308	23	6	4
West, Nashua	.971	84	160	7	5	0
White, Nashua	.925	17	37	0	3	0
Williams, Reading	.923	13	11	1	1	0
Wilson, Buffalo	1.000	3	5	0	0	0
Woods, Glens Falls	.952	14	17	3	1	1
Yobs, Glens Falls*	.977	53	81	3	2	0
Young, Albany	.931	26	24	3	2	0

CATCHERS

Player and Club	Pct.	G.	PO.	A.	E.	DP.	PB.
Ashman, Albany	1.000	2	2	0	0	0	0
Aulenback, Lynn	.941	3	16	0	1	1	2
Boddy, Waterbury	.952	8	35	5	2	0	0
Cipolloni, Reading	1.000	2	7	3	0	0	0
CLIBURN, Lynn	.990	84	522	46	6	10	5
Corbett, Waterbury	.984	32	163	20	3	1	6
Daulton, Reading	.979	94	502	57	12	7	12
Dodd, Glens Falls	.985	36	168	23	3	1	10
Durrman, Albany	.989	55	251	28	3	5	3
Fick, Albany	.971	14	60	7	2	2	1
Gerber, Nashua	1.000	1	5	0	0	0	0
Glass, Buffalo	.987	77	435	25	6	7	14
Goldthorn, Lynn	1.000	7	35	2	0	0	0
Holt, New Britain	.974	11	32	5	1	0	4
Kelly, Glens Falls	.963	19	117	12	5	1	1
Lavalliere, Reading	.989	49	236	34	3	2	4
Liddle, Nashua	.970	97	530	86	19	11	11
Malkin, 21 Buff.-39 Lynn	.985	60	353	36	6	6	14
Malpeso, New Britain	.975	89	443	73	13	6	12
McClendon, Waterbury	1.000	48	277	47	0	3	3
Meier, Glens Falls	.970	71	373	42	13	4	8
Miley, Waterbury	.983	60	346	48	7	6	5
O'Brien, Albany	.981	79	477	82	11	8	7
Patterson, Nashua	.990	35	173	30	2	1	5
Rey, Buffalo	.976	15	78	3	2	3	2
Romero, Nashua	1.000	13	61	7	0	0	4
Rowe, Lynn	.990	12	89	9	1	1	1
Simunic, Buffalo	.954	21	126	20	7	1	3
Sullivan, New Britain	.991	43	207	25	2	1	2
Tarnow, Glens Falls	.985	11	59	7	1	1	1
Taylor, Glens Falls	1.000	2	15	0	0	0	0
Wilson, Buffalo	.989	13	81	6	1	0	2

PITCHERS

Player and Club	Pct.	G.	PO.	A.	E.	DP.
Abraham, Albany*	1.000	3	0	2	0	0
Anderson, Albany	.786	30	5	6	3	1
Babcock, Glens Falls*	1.000	3	0	2	0	0
Baller, Buffalo	1.000	16	2	3	0	0
Bartholow, Reading	1.000	16	2	6	0	1
Bastian, Nashua	.963	34	11	15	1	0
Bielecki, Lynn	.857	25	9	27	6	2
Birrell, New Britain*	1.000	1	0	1	0	0
Bohnet, Buffalo*	1.000	21	3	19	0	2
Bolton, New Britain*	1.000	16	12	31	0	2
Boxberger, Nashua	.923	25	11	25	3	4
Brennan, Glens Falls*	.875	22	1	6	1	0
Browning, Waterbury*	.882	18	4	11	2	1
Buchanan, Waterbury*	1.000	14	0	3	0	0
Buckley, Nashua	.882	18	2	13	2	2
Burroughs, Reading*	.846	15	2	9	2	0
Cacciatore, Lynn	1.000	3	0	10	0	0
Carman, Reading*	.938	56	4	11	1	0
Cato, Waterbury	.889	7	2	6	1	0
Clemens, New Britain	1.000	7	3	5	0	1
Cliburn, Nashua	1.000	39	12	24	0	4
CONNER, Nashua*	1.000	27	20	52	0	4
Cordoba, Lynn	.963	33	7	19	1	3
Dale, New Britain	1.000	33	6	10	0	0
Davis, New Britain	.926	16	8	17	2	0
Davisson, Reading	.903	20	6	22	3	6
Desjarlais, Glens Falls	.973	26	13	23	1	0
Dowless, Waterbury	.944	13	4	13	1	1
Doyle, Buffalo	.944	18	4	13	1	2
Edwards, Albany	.914	32	18	14	3	2
Ender, Waterbury	.947	14	5	13	1	1
Farr, Buffalo	.857	18	7	11	3	0
Fellows, Albany	.935	25	14	29	3	0
Ferguson, Albany	.913	22	5	16	2	0
Funk, Waterbury	.941	43	6	10	1	0
Fuson, Buffalo	.956	28	20	23	2	2
Gaynor, Reading	.919	33	16	18	3	2
Gering, New Britain	1.000	3	1	2	0	0
Ghelfi, Reading	.842	16	6	10	3	1
Glaser, Buffalo	1.000	25	15	19	0	1
Gnacinski, New Britain	1.000	34	10	24	0	2
Gonzales, Lynn	.864	15	4	15	3	1
Greco, New Britain*	1.000	22	1	20	0	0
C. Green, Lynn*	.864	23	5	14	3	1
J. Green, Buffalo	1.000	4	3	0	0	0
Griffin, Reading*	.944	20	3	14	1	0
Hardy, Glens Falls	1.000	8	3	9	0	1
Heidenreich, Waterbury	.933	17	9	19	2	0
Herron, Albany*	.933	8	5	9	1	1
Howard, Glens Falls	1.000	2	0	1	0	0
C. Johnson, New Britain	1.000	25	9	17	0	3
Wa. Johnson, Buffalo*	.769	22	7	13	6	3
Wi. Johnson, Reading	.800	11	0	4	1	0
Jones, Waterbury	.952	28	5	15	1	1
Josephson, Albany	.900	50	11	16	3	3
Kane, New Britain	.846	9	5	6	2	0
Keeler, Buffalo	.750	8	1	2	1	0
Kravec, Albany*	1.000	35	8	17	0	2
Lackey, Lynn	.960	27	4	20	1	4
Landrum, Waterbury	1.000	17	1	4	0	0
Lavalliere, Reading	1.000	4	2	0	0	1
Law, Albany	1.000	2	0	1	0	0
Lynes, Albany*	.914	47	16	16	3	0
Maddux, Reading	1.000	1	0	2	0	0
Maitland, Glens Falls*	.941	35	4	12	1	0
Marcheskie, Lynn	.875	25	2	12	2	2
McCaskill, Nashua	.966	13	8	20	1	0
Ro. McDonald, Buffalo	.867	12	2	11	2	1
Ru. McDonald, Albany	.920	19	6	17	2	0
McKenzie, Nashua	1.000	4	6	5	0	0
Mecerod, New Britain	.897	23	11	24	4	4
Mitchell, New Britain	.975	49	10	29	1	2
Mohorcic, Lynn	.917	18	1	10	1	0
Moncrief, Glens Falls	.925	29	17	20	3	2

PITCHERS—Continued

Player and Club	Pct.	G.	PO.	A.	E.	DP.
Mooneyham, Nashua	.920	19	7	16	2	2
Moore, Glens Falls	.900	24	2	7	1	0
Mullen, Glens Falls	.947	42	8	10	1	1
Nipper, New Britain	1.000	10	4	22	0	2
Ontiveros, Albany	.975	32	8	31	1	3
Owens, Buffalo	.000	3	0	0	1	0
Palmieri, Reading*	1.000	4	3	6	0	1
Pastrovich, Glens Falls	.846	47	8	14	4	0
Perry, Buffalo*	1.000	4	0	2	0	0
Pettibone, Waterbury	.667	18	3	7	5	1
Pippin, Lynn	.958	37	12	11	1	0
Riley, Reading*	.947	27	3	15	1	1
R. Robinson, Waterbury	.931	20	4	23	2	1
Rollins, Reading	.923	20	2	10	1	1
Romanick, Nashua	.978	27	18	26	1	3
Romero, Buffalo*	1.000	44	4	13	0	3
Rothey, Waterbury*	.941	41	3	13	1	0
Ruzek, Glens Falls	1.000	12	9	14	0	2
Ryder, Waterbury	.857	23	6	18	4	0
Saatzer, Nashua	.885	22	8	15	3	1
Santarelli, Buffalo	1.000	13	2	7	0	0
Schuckert, Glens Falls*	.931	26	6	21	2	0
D. A. Smith, Nashua	1.000	2	1	0	0	0
D. W. Smith, Nashua	.778	24	2	5	2	3
M. Smith, Waterbury	1.000	22	2	4	0	0
Straker, Waterbury	.800	3	1	3	1	0
Surhoff, Reading	.750	40	2	4	2	0
Susce, Lynn	1.000	4	0	3	0	0
Sylvia, Nashua	.842	43	6	10	3	1
Tanzi, Glens Falls*	.833	5	1	9	2	0
Taylor, Lynn	1.000	5	2	1	0	0
Thibodeaux, Lynn	1.000	18	5	13	0	0
D. Thomas, Reading	1.000	17	1	0	0	0
Thompson, Buffalo	.938	43	2	13	1	0
Tyler, New Britain	.909	41	3	7	1	1
Umbarger, Glens Falls*	1.000	9	2	7	0	0
Valley, Buffalo*	1.000	12	1	6	0	0
Vantrease, Albany*	.667	1	1	1	1	0
Warren, Albany	1.000	10	4	6	0	1
Wex, Albany	.750	6	0	3	1	0
Wheeler, Lynn	.955	26	20	22	2	2
Wise, Waterbury	1.000	14	2	2	0	0
Withrow, Glens Falls	.826	25	5	14	4	2
Wojna, Reading	.904	28	14	33	5	4
Woody, New Britain*	1.000	22	4	19	0	1
Wortham, Albany*	.750	4	1	2	1	1
Zaske, Lynn	1.000	48	9	9	0	4
Zmudosky, Albany	1.000	2	1	3	0	0

The following players do not have any recorded accepted chances at the positions indicated and therefore are not listed in the fielding averages for those particular positions: Ashman, of, p; Brown, 1b; Cliburn, of; Cole, p; Dodd, p; Fick, 1b; Francis, ss; Fryer, 2b; Gallego, 3b; Gruber, of; Kiefer, of; Kravec, of; Liddle, 1b; Lyons, p; McAbee, p; Miles, p; Norman, 1b; Peterson, p; R. Quinones, of; Rende, p, of; D. Robinson, p; R. Romero (Glens Falls) p; Schaive, of, p; Stephens, p; Tanner, p; V. Thomas, p; Valley, 1b; Washington, p.

CLUB PITCHING

Club	ERA.	G.	CG.	ShO.	Sv.	IP.	H.	R.	ER.	HR.	HB.	BB.	Int. BB.	SO.	WP.	Bk.
New Britain	3.53	139	25	7	24	1162.0	1045	542	456	82	30	496	25	660	57	9
Reading	3.92	140	29	18	42	1184.0	1079	601	516	104	35	592	30	712	61	6
Waterbury	3.94	139	36	12	22	1161.0	1080	612	508	88	30	625	26	764	46	6
Buffalo	4.00	139	39	5	22	1148.2	1131	625	511	131	35	617	16	782	60	10
Nashua	4.32	140	38	9	21	1182.0	1201	673	567	71	36	625	26	713	45	9
Lynn	4.33	139	29	9	34	1136.1	1075	620	547	120	38	581	24	854	67	18
Albany	4.66	136	30	6	20	1134.0	1179	717	587	138	33	532	17	758	44	8
Glens Falls	5.31	136	27	3	15	1108.2	1189	798	654	135	30	607	6	711	66	8

PITCHERS' RECORDS

(Leading Qualifiers for Earned-Run Average Leadership — 112 or More Innings)

*Throws lefthanded.

Pitcher — Club	W.	L.	Pct.	ERA.	G.	GS.	CG.	GF.	ShO.	Sv.	IP.	H.	R.	ER.	HR.	HB.	BB.	Int. BB.	SO.	WP.
Farr, Buffalo	13	1	.929	1.61	18	15	5	2	2	1	112.0	88	28	20	8	3	50	1	108	3
Heidenreich, Waterbury	11	4	.733	1.73	17	17	8	0	4	0	119.1	84	29	23	4	4	56	1	98	4
Gaynor, Reading	13	3	.813	2.48	33	19	5	4	3	1	149.0	113	49	41	9	2	71	2	100	5
Carman, Reading*	8	5	.615	2.97	56	7	0	37	0	23	124.1	85	51	41	11	5	71	7	93	2
Bielecki, Lynn	15	7	.682	3.19	25	25	7	0	1	0	163.2	126	73	58	11	5	69	1	143	10
Bastian, Nashua	4	3	.571	3.29	34	3	0	12	0	1	120.1	115	57	44	10	6	39	4	72	2
Gnacinski, New Britain	12	11	.522	3.40	34	20	8	10	1	0	145.2	133	70	55	9	4	64	4	78	6
Davisson, Reading	15	4	.789	3.46	20	20	4	0	2	0	130.0	131	57	50	9	1	48	0	44	2
Browning, Waterbury*	4	10	.286	3.53	18	18	3	0	1	0	117.1	100	62	46	6	3	63	0	101	3
Conner, Nashua*	10	11	.476	3.59	27	27	10	0	3	0	188.0	182	84	75	11	6	78	1	87	2

Departmental Leaders: G—Carman, 56; W—Bielecki, Davisson, 15; L—Withrow, 14; Pct.—Farr, .929; GS—Conner, Romanick, 27; CG—Fuson, 12; GF—Zaske, 44; ShO—Heidenreich, 4; Sv.—Zaske, 24; IP—Conner, 180; H—Romanick, 200; R—Desjarlais, 122; ER—Desjarlais, 100; HR—Edwards, Wheeler, 22; HB—Wojna, 9; BB—Boxberger, 97; IBB—Funk, 8; SO—Bielecki, 143; WP—Pippin, 15.

(All Pitchers—Listed Alphabetically)

Pitcher — Club	W.	L.	Pct.	ERA.	G.	GS.	CG.	GF.	ShO.	Sv.	IP.	H.	R.	ER.	HR.	HB.	BB.	Int. BB.	SO.	WP.
Abraham, Albany*	1	0	1.000	12.27	3	0	0	2	0	0	3.2	5	6	5	1	0	1	0	1	1
Anderson, Albany	4	7	.364	5.18	30	4	0	17	0	3	66.0	70	44	38	7	2	38	2	51	2
Ashman, Albany	0	0	.000	8.53	5	0	0	4	0	0	6.1	8	6	6	1	0	3	0	4	0
Babcock, Glens Falls*	0	2	.000	21.81	3	3	0	0	0	0	8.2	20	21	21	4	0	11	0	5	2
Baller, Buffalo	1	2	.333	7.53	16	1	0	11	0	1	34.2	32	34	29	3	3	35	0	35	6
Bartholow, Reading	2	2	.500	9.35	16	0	0	7	0	1	26.0	34	32	27	4	0	21	6	15	5
Bastian, Nashua	4	3	.571	3.29	34	3	0	12	0	1	120.1	115	57	44	10	6	39	4	72	2
Bielecki, Lynn	15	7	.682	3.19	25	25	7	0	1	0	163.2	126	73	58	11	5	69	1	143	10
Birrell, New Britain*	0	1	.000	2.45	1	1	0	0	0	0	3.2	3	1	1	1	0	5	0	0	0
Bohnet, Buffalo*	4	5	.444	3.89	21	17	6	1	0	0	113.1	117	64	49	17	3	43	1	60	6
Bolton, New Britain*	7	3	.700	2.89	16	16	2	0	1	0	99.2	93	36	32	7	1	41	0	62	5
Boxberger, Nashua	5	10	.333	5.43	25	24	3	0	0	0	127.2	136	94	77	11	5	97	3	84	7
Brennan, Glens Falls*	2	0	1.000	4.61	22	0	0	9	0	0	27.1	36	16	14	3	2	15	0	18	1
Browning, Waterbury*	4	10	.286	3.53	18	18	3	0	1	0	117.1	100	62	46	6	3	63	0	101	3
Buchanan, Waterbury*	0	1	.000	6.50	14	0	0	11	0	2	18.0	19	13	13	2	0	9	1	12	1
Buckley, Nashua	3	2	.600	2.70	18	0	0	10	0	2	36.2	27	17	11	0	0	23	1	32	2
Burroughs, Reading	8	3	.727	2.82	15	15	4	0	2	0	99.0	70	39	31	6	3	50	0	74	5
Cacciatore, Lynn	1	1	.500	4.50	3	2	0	0	0	0	14.0	9	7	7	2	1	7	0	21	0
Carman, Reading*	8	5	.615	2.97	56	7	0	37	0	23	124.1	85	51	41	11	5	71	7	93	2
Cato, Waterbury	3	1	.750	3.18	7	7	3	0	2	0	51.0	37	18	18	4	1	9	0	40	2
Clemens, New Britain	4	1	.800	1.38	7	7	1	0	1	0	52.0	31	8	8	1	2	12	0	59	0
Cliburn, Nashua	6	7	.462	3.74	39	6	2	24	0	5	98.2	94	45	41	3	3	31	3	40	4
Cole, Reading	1	0	1.000	0.00	1	1	1	0	1	0	7.0	4	0	0	0	0	0	0	3	0
Conner, Nashua*	10	11	.476	3.59	27	27	10	0	3	0	188.0	182	84	75	11	6	78	1	87	2
Cordoba, Lynn	2	1	.667	3.49	33	0	0	17	0	0	69.2	48	32	27	5	2	57	4	55	3

Pitcher—Club	W.	L.	Pct.	ERA.	G.	GS.	CG.	GF.	ShO.	Sv.	IP.	H.	R.	ER.	HR.	HB.	BB.	Int. BB.	SO.	WP.
Dale, New Britain	4	3	.571	2.31	33	0	0	20	0	5	66.1	58	18	17	4	3	19	3	38	2
Davis, New Britain	5	8	.385	3.77	16	14	2	1	0	0	86.0	90	43	36	6	2	45	7	34	3
Davisson, Reading	15	4	.789	3.46	20	20	4	0	2	0	130.0	131	57	50	9	1	48	0	44	2
Desjarlais, Glens Falls	5	12	.294	6.55	26	24	2	0	0	0	137.1	167	122	100	16	2	76	0	81	12
Dodd, Glens Falls	0	0	.000	0.00	2	0	0	2	0	0	3.1	1	0	0	0	0	0	0	1	0
Dowless, Waterbury	4	4	.500	2.85	13	11	0	2	0	1	75.2	66	29	24	7	1	26	2	55	1
Doyle, Buffalo	5	7	.417	4.65	18	18	4	0	0	0	98.2	95	55	51	13	3	50	0	80	2
Edwards, Albany	7	11	.389	5.22	32	21	5	8	1	1	141.1	142	98	82	22	4	83	2	102	8
Ender, Waterbury	6	4	.600	4.38	14	10	4	0	2	0	74.0	66	39	36	2	1	46	0	58	3
Farr, Buffalo	13	1	.929	1.61	18	15	5	2	2	1	112.0	88	28	20	8	3	50	1	108	3
Fellows, Albany	6	10	.375	4.44	25	21	3	3	0	2	135.2	153	83	67	11	1	55	1	53	7
Ferguson, Albany	8	8	.500	5.11	22	21	6	0	2	0	118.0	116	79	67	13	5	64	2	75	5
Funk, Waterbury	2	6	.250	4.06	43	4	3	22	1	5	84.1	96	48	38	5	2	37	8	50	5
Fuson, Buffalo	13	11	.542	3.97	28	25	12	0	2	0	183.2	184	95	81	20	3	92	3	114	8
Gaynor, Reading	13	3	.813	2.48	33	19	5	4	3	1	149.0	113	49	41	9	2	71	2	100	5
Gering, New Britain	1	1	.500	2.70	3	2	1	0	0	0	16.2	12	6	5	1	1	3	0	9	1
Ghelfi, Reading	10	3	.769	3.68	16	16	4	0	1	0	110.0	99	48	45	11	4	42	0	96	1
Glaser, Buffalo	8	3	.727	3.99	25	9	6	10	0	2	108.1	119	53	48	18	3	24	1	40	1
Gnacinski, New Britain	12	11	.522	3.40	34	20	8	10	1	0	145.2	133	70	55	9	4	64	4	78	6
Gonzales, Lynn	5	7	.417	5.94	15	14	1	1	0	0	80.1	86	56	53	11	3	56	0	54	2
Greco, New Britain*	1	4	.200	4.81	22	4	1	8	0	2	43.0	49	32	23	4	1	30	2	17	1
C. Green, Lynn*	5	6	.455	3.98	23	9	4	14	0	6	74.2	76	38	33	8	2	31	0	73	2
J. Green, Buffalo	1	0	1.000	5.79	4	0	0	3	0	0	4.2	5	3	3	1	0	5	0	4	0
Griffin, Reading*	6	5	.545	5.94	20	15	4	3	0	0	94.0	94	67	62	12	4	55	1	44	8
Hardy, Glens Falls	1	1	.500	4.46	8	8	1	0	0	0	36.1	30	23	18	7	2	11	0	22	1
Heidenreich, Waterbury	11	4	.733	1.73	17	17	8	0	4	0	119.1	84	29	23	4	4	56	1	98	4
Herron, Albany*	4	2	.667	2.53	8	8	3	0	2	0	42.2	42	17	12	3	0	18	0	33	1
Howard, Glens Falls	0	2	.000	9.00	2	2	0	0	0	0	9.0	21	16	9	2	0	3	0	4	1
C. Johnson, New Britain	7	7	.500	4.89	25	16	1	3	1	0	112.1	111	72	61	9	1	61	2	58	8
Wa. Johnson, Buffalo*	7	7	.500	4.08	22	21	2	1	1	0	119.0	125	73	54	12	4	74	1	64	8
Wi. Johnson, Reading	1	1	.500	4.20	11	0	0	8	0	5	15.0	14	11	7	2	1	10	1	11	0
Jones, Waterbury	4	5	.444	5.32	28	7	1	7	0	0	91.1	89	70	54	9	3	67	2	55	5
Josephson, Albany	6	1	.857	3.98	50	0	0	20	0	2	95.0	100	56	42	15	6	37	2	53	4
Kane, New Britain	4	4	.500	3.54	9	9	1	0	0	0	61.0	54	26	24	8	0	15	0	30	1
Keeler, Buffalo	0	2	.000	6.85	8	3	1	3	0	0	23.2	29	21	18	6	1	20	1	14	2
Kravec, Albany*	3	7	.300	4.85	35	8	1	17	0	3	78.0	81	53	42	6	5	47	0	53	2
Lackey, Lynn	10	9	.526	4.75	27	24	4	0	0	0	142.0	157	87	75	17	3	54	1	67	9
Landrum, Waterbury	1	1	.500	1.52	17	0	0	12	0	3	29.2	17	5	5	0	2	14	2	33	2
Lavalliere, Reading	0	0	.000	5.40	4	0	0	3	0	0	3.1	3	3	2	1	0	2	0	2	0
Law, Albany	0	0	.000	3.00	2	0	0	1	0	0	3.0	1	1	1	0	0	3	0	2	0
Lynes, Albany*	3	6	.333	5.15	47	6	0	18	0	3	101.1	125	68	58	14	1	43	2	53	3
Lyons, New Britain	1	0	1.000	2.45	3	0	0	3	0	0	3.2	3	1	1	1	0	1	0	2	0
Maddux, Reading	0	0	.000	6.00	1	1	0	0	0	0	3.0	4	2	2	0	0	1	0	2	0
Maitland, Glens Falls*	4	7	.364	7.36	35	5	0	18	0	1	69.2	79	60	57	11	3	48	0	47	7
Marcheskie, Lynn	4	2	.667	5.51	25	4	0	5	0	0	80.0	85	53	49	9	5	30	2	69	7
McAbee, Glens Falls	0	0	.000	30.38	1	0	0	0	0	0	2.2	10	10	9	1	1	1	0	2	0
McCaskill, Nashua	4	8	.333	4.45	13	13	3	0	0	0	87.0	90	47	43	8	3	43	3	63	5
Ro. McDonald, Buffalo	4	6	.400	5.64	12	9	1	2	0	0	60.2	68	48	38	6	4	33	0	31	2
Ru. McDonald, Albany	7	8	.467	3.77	19	17	1	1	0	1	105.0	97	52	44	13	4	40	3	79	3
McKenzie, Nashua	2	2	.500	5.25	4	4	2	0	0	0	24.0	30	16	14	1	1	12	0	17	2
Mecerod, New Britain	12	7	.632	3.60	23	21	4	1	1	0	147.2	132	67	59	7	7	56	2	75	9
Miles, Glens Falls	0	0	.000	27.00	1	0	0	1	0	0	1.0	4	3	3	1	0	1	0	2	1
Mitchell, New Britain	2	4	.333	2.88	49	3	0	41	0	13	100.0	82	39	32	3	3	36	1	54	6
Mohorcic, Lynn	3	1	.750	3.63	18	0	0	12	0	2	34.2	35	20	14	2	1	17	3	13	4
Moncrief, Glens Falls	6	13	.316	5.50	29	22	8	4	1	0	150.2	157	102	92	18	4	73	1	89	13
Mooneyham, Nashua	8	6	.571	4.58	19	19	6	0	3	0	110.0	99	67	56	3	5	83	2	76	5
Moore, Glens Falls	2	6	.250	6.57	24	2	0	8	0	0	63.0	82	54	46	6	1	40	0	59	3
Mullen, Glens Falls	5	0	1.000	2.93	42	0	0	32	0	10	67.2	44	26	22	5	2	28	2	50	7
Nipper, New Britain	4	3	.571	2.82	10	9	3	0	1	0	67.0	46	26	21	3	1	25	1	42	1
Ontiveros, Albany	8	4	.667	3.75	32	13	5	12	0	5	129.2	131	62	54	11	0	36	2	91	3
Owens, Buffalo	0	2	.000	15.43	3	3	0	0	0	0	7.0	14	13	12	1	1	10	0	3	3
Palmieri, Reading*	1	2	.333	4.64	4	4	0	0	0	0	21.1	15	13	11	2	3	16	0	7	1
Pastrovich, Glens Falls	5	6	.455	4.91	47	0	0	26	0	3	84.1	87	58	46	11	6	39	2	65	5
Perry, Buffalo*	0	0	.000	6.75	4	0	0	0	0	0	5.1	8	5	4	2	0	4	0	4	1
Peterson, Lynn*	0	0	.000	27.00	2	1	0	1	0	0	3.0	8	9	9	1	2	5	0	3	1
Pettibone, Waterbury	4	8	.333	5.72	18	18	2	0	1	0	91.1	95	65	58	12	2	63	0	54	6
Pippin, Lynn	13	3	.813	3.61	37	10	2	10	2	1	102.1	78	49	41	4	3	76	2	88	15
Rende, Buffalo	0	0	.000	9.00	1	0	0	1	0	0	1.0	2	1	1	0	0	1	0	0	0
Riley, Reading*	8	3	.727	2.42	27	8	3	12	2	4	81.2	69	27	22	9	2	44	1	58	7
D. Robinson, Lynn	0	1	.000	8.10	2	2	0	0	0	0	6.2	9	6	6	2	1	2	0	5	0
R. Robinson, Waterbury	7	9	.438	3.60	20	20	6	0	0	0	142.2	132	66	57	15	4	60	0	82	3
Rollins, Reading	3	4	.429	8.05	20	5	0	4	0	0	57.0	85	58	51	8	1	30	2	30	13
Romanick, Nashua	9	12	.429	4.86	27	27	10	0	2	0	174.0	200	105	94	8	5	80	3	112	5
R. Romero, Glens Falls	0	0	.000	6.75	3	0	0	3	0	0	6.2	7	6	5	3	0	2	0	3	0
R. Romero, Buffalo*	10	4	.714	3.95	44	5	1	26	0	4	98.0	85	50	43	8	2	77	2	92	5
Rothey, Waterbury*	2	7	.222	4.57	41	1	0	20	0	1	67.0	76	45	34	7	3	50	5	45	4
Ruzek, Glens Falls	5	3	.625	2.03	12	12	7	0	1	0	84.1	72	23	19	5	0	26	0	52	0
Ryder, Waterbury	7	10	.412	4.81	23	23	6	0	1	0	136.2	143	84	73	12	2	79	0	49	3
Saatzer, Nashua	3	10	.231	5.93	22	16	2	4	1	0	95.2	99	76	63	8	0	68	1	41	1
Santarelli, Buffalo	3	7	.300	3.70	13	12	1	1	0	0	58.1	55	37	24	5	1	42	1	48	4
Schaive, Lynn	0	0	.000	0.00	1	0	0	1	0	0	1.0	1	0	0	0	0	0	0	0	0
Schuckert, Glens Falls*	7	12	.368	5.77	26	20	4	2	0	0	126.1	150	107	81	15	2	88	1	80	6
D.A. Smith, Nashua	0	0	.000	7.94	2	1	0	1	0	0	5.2	10	6	5	0	0	2	0	6	1
D.W. Smith, Nashua	2	2	.500	1.98	24	0	0	23	0	8	36.1	32	9	8	2	0	15	0	30	3
M. Smith, Waterbury	2	5	.286	2.83	22	0	0	18	0	7	28.2	18	13	9	0	2	25	2	16	2
Stephens, Nashua	0	0	.000	0.00	2	0	0	2	0	0	2.0	2	0	0	0	0	3	0	0	1
Straker, Waterbury	0	2	.000	9.00	3	3	0	0	0	0	10.0	16	10	10	2	0	6	0	5	0
Surhoff, Reading	5	1	.833	3.14	40	0	0	21	0	8	63.0	58	24	22	6	0	26	7	36	4
Susce, Lynn	2	1	.667	1.90	4	4	2	0	0	0	23.2	18	6	5	3	1	12	0	14	0
Sylvia, Nashua	4	7	.364	4.26	43	0	0	26	0	5	76.0	85	50	36	6	2	51	5	53	5
Tanner, Glens Falls	0	0	.000	1.50	5	0	0	3	0	1	6.0	2	1	1	0	0	5	0	1	0
Tanzi, Glens Falls*	2	2	.500	5.48	5	4	0	0	0	0	23.0	23	19	14	3	0	19	0	9	2
Taylor, Lynn	0	1	.000	12.96	5	1	0	4	0	0	8.1	11	12	12	3	0	6	0	7	1

Pitcher—Club	W.	L.	Pct.	ERA.	G.	GS.	CG.	GF.	ShO.	Sv.	IP.	H.	R.	ER.	HR.	HB.	BB.	Int. BB.	SO.	WP.
Thibodeaux, Lynn	2	10	.167	6.51	18	18	1	0	1	0	92.2	97	70	67	17	4	63	4	73	1
D. Thomas, Reading	2	1	.667	9.17	17	3	0	10	0	0	34.1	50	39	35	8	0	24	1	14	2
V. Thomas, Glens Falls	0	0	.000	0.00	1	0	0	1	0	0	3.0	2	0	0	0	0	0	0	0	0
Thompson, Buffalo	3	7	.300	2.86	43	0	0	32	0	13	78.2	67	33	25	7	2	46	5	61	7
Tyler, New Britain	4	3	.571	4.72	41	5	0	21	0	2	74.1	70	46	39	8	0	41	2	53	8
Umbarger, Glens Falls*	4	3	.571	2.82	9	9	4	0	0	0	60.2	45	22	19	6	2	28	0	45	0
Valley, Buffalo*	2	1	.667	2.38	12	1	0	7	0	1	41.2	38	12	11	4	2	11	0	24	2
Vantrease, Albany*	0	1	.000	6.23	1	1	0	0	0	0	4.1	6	6	3	1	1	2	0	4	0
Warren, Albany	6	2	.750	3.25	10	10	6	0	0	0	72.0	56	38	26	12	4	33	1	87	0
Washington, Reading	0	0	.000	2.08	3	0	0	2	0	0	4.1	4	1	1	0	0	3	0	0	1
Wex, Albany	0	2	.000	11.40	6	1	0	3	0	0	15.0	26	25	19	3	0	11	0	8	4
Wheeler, Lynn	10	9	.526	3.93	26	25	8	1	1	1	169.1	177	82	74	22	5	58	3	97	3
Wise, Waterbury	2	3	.400	3.75	14	0	0	11	0	3	24.0	26	16	10	1	0	15	3	11	2
Withrow, Glens Falls	5	14	.263	5.10	25	25	1	0	0	0	137.2	150	109	78	18	3	93	0	76	5
Wojna, Reading	13	7	.650	3.67	28	26	4	0	1	0	161.2	147	80	66	6	9	78	2	83	5
Woody, New Britain*	4	7	.364	4.55	22	12	1	6	0	2	83.0	78	51	42	10	4	42	1	49	6
Wortham, Albany*	0	3	.000	11.45	4	3	0	0	0	0	11.0	11	15	14	4	0	16	0	6	1
Zaske, Lynn	5	3	.625	2.18	48	0	0	44	0	24	70.1	54	20	17	3	0	38	4	72	9
Zmudosky, Albany	0	1	.000	10.50	2	2	0	0	0	0	6.0	9	8	7	1	0	2	0	3	0

BALKS—Gonzales, 6; Heidenreich, Wa. Johnson, Mecerod, Mooneyham, Withrow, 3 each; Bielecki, Ender, Fellows, Fuson, Gaynor, C. Johnson, Marcheskie, R. McDonald, Pippin, Romanick, Sylvia, Wheeler, 2 each; Ashman, Burroughs, Conner, Davisson, Doyle, Edwards, Farr, Gnacinski, Greco, C. Green, Herron, Kane, Kravec, Lackey, McCaskill, Moncrief, Moore, Ontiveros, Pastrovich, Rollins, R. Romero (Buffalo), Ruzek, Susce, Tyler, Umbarger, Warren, Wise, Wojna, Zaske, 1 each.

COMBINATION SHUTOUTS—Herron-Anderson, Albany; Withrow-Mullen, Glens Falls; Wheeler-Zaske, Gonzales-Zaske, Lackey-Mohorcic, Bielecki-Cordoba, Lynn; Bolton-Mitchell, New Britain; Gaynor-Carman 2, Burroughs-Johnson-Riley, Wojna-Carman, Riley-Thomas, Davisson-Carman, Reading.

NO-HIT GAMES—Ferguson, Albany, defeated Nashua, 9-0 (first game), June 5; Doyle, Buffalo, defeated Albany, 6-1 (first game), June 7; Gaynor, Reading, defeated Nashua, 6-0 (second game), August 12.

Southern League

CLASS AA

Leading Batter
IVAN CALDERON
Chattanooga

League President
JIMMY BRAGAN

Leading Pitcher
ROGER MASON
Birmingham

CHAMPIONSHIP WINNERS IN PREVIOUS YEARS

1904—Macon	.598
1905—Macon	.625
1906—Savannah	.637
1907—Charleston	.620
1908—Jacksonville	.694
1909—Chattanooga*	.738
Augusta	.702
1910—Columbus	.588
1911—Columbus*	.681
Columbia	.710
1912—Jacksonville*	.679
Columbus	.632
1913—Savannah	.754
Savannah	.593
1914—Savannah*	.667
Albany	.650
1915—Macon	.588
Columbus*	.686
1916—Augusta*	.617
Columbia	.631
1917—Charleston	.741
Columbia*	.667
1918—Did not operate.	
1919—Columbia	.585
1920—Columbia	.633
1921—Columbia	.642
1922—Charleston	.625
1923—Charlotte*	.653
Macon	.580
1924—Augusta	.612
1925—Spartanburg	.620
1926—Greenville	.662
1927—Greenville	.622
1928—Asheville	.664
1929—Asheville	.605
Knoxville*	.634
1930—Greenville*	.620
Macon	.643
1931-35—Did not operate.	
1936—Jacksonville	.652
Columbus*	.650
1937—Columbus	.572
Savannah (3rd)†	.565
1938—Savannah	.574
Macon (2nd)†	.570
1939—Columbus	.601
Augusta (2nd)†	.597
1940—Savannah	.627
Columbus (2nd)†	.583
1941—Macon	.643
Columbia (2nd)†	.636
1942—Charleston	.620
Macon (2nd)†	.585
1943-45—Did not operate.	
1946—Columbus	.568
Augusta (4th)†	.547
1947—Columbus	.575
Savannah (2nd)†	.563
1948—Charleston	.572
Greenville (3rd)†	.549
1949—Macon‡	.623
1950—Macon‡	.588
1951—Montgomery	.607
1952—Columbia	.649
Montgomery (3rd)†	.558
1953—Jacksonville	.679
Savannah (2nd)†	.571
1954—Jacksonville	.593
Savannah (2nd)†	.571
1955—Columbia	.636
Augusta (3rd)†	.543
1956—Jacksonville‡	.621
1957—Augusta	.636
Charlotte (2nd)†	.562
1958—Augusta	.550
Macon (3rd)†	.500
1959—Knoxville	.557
Gastonia (4th)†	.504
1960—Columbia	.597
Savannah (3rd)†	.561
1961—Asheville	.635
1962—Savannah	.662
Macon (3rd)†	.576
1963—Augusta*	.661
Lynchburg	.662
1964—Lynchburg	.579
1965—Columbus	.572
1966—Mobile	.629
1967—Birmingham	.604
1968—Asheville	.614
1969—Charlotte	.579
1970—Columbus	.569
1971—Did not operate as league—clubs were members of Dixie Association.	
1972—Asheville	.583
Montgomery§	.561
1973—Montgomery§	.580
Jacksonville	.559
1974—Jacksonville	.565
Knoxville§	.533
1975—Orlando	.587
Montgomery§	.545
1976—Montgomery x	.591
Orlando	.540
1977—Montgomery x	.628
Jacksonville	.522
1978—Knoxville x	.611
Savannah	.500
1979—Columbus	.587
Nashville x	.576
1980—Memphis	.576
Charlotte x	.500
1981—Nashville	.566
Orlando x	.556
1982—Jacksonville	.576
Nashville x	.535

*Won split-season playoff. †Won four-club playoff. ‡Won championship and four-club playoff. §League was divided into Eastern and Western divisions; won playoff. xLeague was divided into Eastern and Western divisions and played split-season; won playoff.

STANDING OF CLUBS AT CLOSE OF FIRST HALF, JUNE 19

EASTERN DIVISION

Club	W.	L.	T.	Pct.	G.B.
Savannah (Braves)	40	30	0	.571	....
Jacksonville (Royals)	36	36	0	.500	5
Orlando (Twins)	35	37	0	.486	6
Charlotte (Orioles)	33	39	0	.458	8
Columbus (Astros)	30	40	0	.429	10

WESTERN DIVISION

Club	W.	L.	T.	Pct.	G.B.
Birmingham (Tigers)	45	28	1	.616	....
Nashville (Yankees)	40	32	1	.556	4½
Memphis (Expos)	36	35	0	.507	8
Knoxville (Blue Jays)	32	39	0	.451	12
Chattanooga (Mariners)	30	41	0	.423	14

STANDING OF CLUBS AT CLOSE OF SECOND HALF, SEPTEMBER 1

EASTERN DIVISION

Club	W.	L.	T.	Pct.	G.B.
Jacksonville (Royals)	41	32	0	.562	....
Savannah (Braves)	41	34	0	.547	1
Charlotte (Orioles)	36	38	0	.486	5½
Columbus (Astros)	34	39	0	.466	7
Orlando (Twins)	27	46	0	.370	14

WESTERN DIVISION

Club	W.	L.	T.	Pct.	G.B.
Nashville (Yankees)	48	26	0	.649	....
Birmingham (Tigers)	46	26	1	.639	1
Chattanooga (Mariners)	38	34	0	.528	9
Knoxville (Blue Jays)	32	43	1	.427	16½
Memphis (Expos)	25	50	0	.333	23½

COMPOSITE STANDING OF CLUBS AT CLOSE OF SEASON, SEPTEMBER 1

Club	Bir.	Nash.	Sav.	Jax.	Chat.	Char.	Col.	Knox.	Orl.	Mem.	W.	L.	T.	Pct.	G.B.
Birmingham (Tigers)	....	7	11	8	10	7	15	10	10	13	91	54	2	.628	....
Nashville (Yankees)	7	....	9	9	7	10	11	13	8	14	88	58	1	.603	3½
Savannah (Braves)	4	7	....	6	10	19	12	6	10	7	81	64	0	.559	10
Jacksonville (Royals)	8	5	6	....	8	9	6	11	13	11	77	68	0	.531	14
Chattanooga (Mariners)	6	9	6	8	....	5	4	13	7	10	68	75	0	.476	22
Charlotte (Orioles)	7	6	5	7	9	....	10	7	10	8	69	77	0	.473	22½
Columbus (Astros)	9	3	4	10	7	6	....	8	8	9	64	79	0	.448	26
Knoxville (Blue Jays)	6	3	8	5	11	7	8	....	11	5	64	82	1	.438	27½
Orlando (Twins)	4	8	6	10	9	6	6	5	....	7	62	83	0	.428	29
Memphis (Expos)	3	10	9	5	4	8	7	9	6	....	61	85	0	.418	30½

Major league affiliations in parentheses.

Playoffs—Jacksonville defeated Savannah, three games to one; Birmingham defeated Nashville, three games to two; and Birmingham defeated Jacksonville, three games to one, to win league championship.

Regular-Season Attendance—Birmingham, 241,253; Charlotte, 113,450; Chattanooga, 150,473; Columbus, 118,102; Jacksonville, 137,480; Knoxville, 107,304; Memphis, 213,183; Nashville, 490,002; Orlando, 70,202; Savannah, 66,057. Total, 1,707,506. Playoffs, 24,119. All-Star Game, 1,221.

Managers—Birmingham, Roy Majtyka; Charlotte, Grady Little; Chattanooga, Mickey Bowers (to May 29) and Bill Haywood; Columbus, Jack Hiatt; Jacksonville, Gene Lamont; Knoxville, John McLaren; Memphis, Rick Renick; Nashville, Doug Holmquist; Orlando, Phil Roof; Savannah, Bobby Dews.

All-Star Team—1B-Alvin Davis, Chattanooga; 2B-Victor Rodriguez, Charlotte; 3B-George Foussianes, Birmingham; SS-Douglas Baker, Birmingham; OF-Ivan Calderon, Chattanooga; Glenn Davis, Columbus; John Morris, Jacksonville; C-Jeffrey Reed, Orlando; DH-Gerry Lomastro, Orlando; RHP-Donald Heinkel, Birmingham; LHP-Mark Langston, Chattanooga; Manager of Year-Roy Majtyka, Birmingham.

(Compiled by Howe News Bureau, Boston, Mass.)

CLUB BATTING

Club	Pct.	G.	AB.	R.	OR.	H.	TB.	2B.	3B.	HR.	RBI.	GW.	SH.	SF.	HP.	BB.	Int. BB.	SO.	SB.	CS.	LOB.
Birmingham	.276	147	4811	765	610	1326	1975	230	46	109	687	75	63	48	38	609	32	686	121	76	1066
Chattanooga	.276	143	4644	705	799	1282	1930	239	62	95	638	63	46	44	23	567	28	689	130	88	982
Nashville	.272	147	4736	731	605	1290	1889	205	47	100	650	79	40	43	48	579	30	723	111	70	1039
Charlotte	.267	146	4810	706	726	1285	2017	241	37	139	635	62	42	37	21	517	20	736	88	53	991
Savannah	.267	145	4583	709	647	1224	1769	210	31	91	615	72	49	49	40	640	31	700	203	78	1040
Memphis	.266	146	4779	635	710	1272	1749	217	22	72	554	49	71	34	40	505	24	625	116	74	1054
Orlando	.264	145	4736	709	685	1251	1843	237	44	89	651	52	57	58	52	671	22	697	129	59	1109
Knoxville	.256	147	4692	570	692	1201	1678	189	39	70	512	54	36	49	20	475	18	859	71	61	989
Columbus	.253	143	4621	615	697	1171	1803	201	31	123	554	57	47	35	29	575	39	809	99	82	1010
Jacksonville	.249	145	4708	631	605	1173	1706	189	37	90	562	66	52	37	26	605	19	834	159	60	1062

INDIVIDUAL BATTING

(Leading Qualifiers for Batting Championship—394 or More Plate Appearances)

*Bats lefthanded. †Switch-hitter.

Player and Club	Pct.	G.	AB.	R.	H.	TB.	2B.	3B.	HR.	RBI.	GW.	SH.	SF.	HP.	BB.	Int. BB.	SO.	SB.	CS.
Calderon, Ivan, Chattanooga	.311	139	546	92	170	267	34	15	11	80	3	2	4	3	34	2	70	25	13
Younger, Stanley, Birmingham*	.309	131	530	91	164	208	24	4	4	54	7	7	3	0	43	2	72	43	18
Mata, Victor, Nashville	.303	130	465	79	141	200	19	5	10	63	8	4	6	10	43	0	63	6	9
Estes, Frank, Savannah*	.303	131	445	62	135	189	28	7	4	58	3	2	6	2	55	12	54	10	4
Carter, Don, Memphis*	.303	112	423	61	128	139	7	2	0	30	2	17	0	2	42	0	41	29	20
Thompson, Milton, Savannah*	.303	115	386	84	117	161	21	4	5	36	5	3	1	3	83	4	76	46	10
Tartabull, Danilo, Chattanooga	.301	128	481	95	145	230	32	7	13	66	11	3	4	1	47	2	63	25	13
Norman, Gregory, Birmingham	.300	134	460	61	138	209	31	2	12	80	6	4	9	3	71	0	48	4	7
Negron, Miguel, Chattanooga*	.300	116	427	55	128	167	15	3	6	55	5	5	4	1	29	3	39	6	2
Lomastro, Gerardo, Orlando	.299	142	528	89	158	267	36	5	21	92	7	0	9	8	65	3	90	2	3
Davis, Glenn, Columbus	.299	118	445	68	133	233	19	3	25	85	9	0	5	9	40	6	87	4	2

Departmental Leaders: G—D. Baker, 146; AB—Rodriguez, 571; R—Foussianes, 106; H—Calderon, Rodriguez, 170; TB—Calderon, Lomastro, 267; 2B—Sheets, 37; 3B—Calderon, 15; HR—G. Davis, Sheets, 25; RBI—Sosa, 93; GWRBI—Foussianes, 13; SH—D. Baker, 18; SF—A. Davis, 12; HP—D. Baker, 13; BB—A. Davis, 120; IBB—Estes, 12; SO—Ferris, 143; SB—Cole, 75; CS—Cole, 25.

(All Players—Listed Alphabetically)

Player and Club	Pct.	G.	AB.	R.	H.	TB.	2B.	3B.	HR.	RBI.	GW.	SH.	SF.	HP.	BB.	Int. BB.	SO.	SB.	CS.
Aitcheson, James, Knoxville*	.229	126	428	47	98	151	12	7	9	54	8	0	6	0	31	2	53	7	7
Alfaro, Jesus, Charlotte	.286	139	535	69	153	250	32	4	19	82	11	3	5	1	55	1	69	1	3
Alvarez, Evelio, Jacksonville	.000	30	1	0	0	0	0	0	0	0	0	0	0	0	0	0	1	0	0
Ashmore, W. Mitchell, Jacksonville	.210	80	267	29	56	72	8	1	2	25	3	6	1	2	38	0	59	3	2
Auten, James, Memphis	.251	140	522	57	131	204	30	2	13	66	8	3	5	3	33	3	75	4	5
Babitt, Mack, Memphis	.320	48	181	26	58	74	12	2	0	25	2	4	2	0	17	0	9	7	6
Baez, Jesse, Chattanooga	.183	40	109	12	20	22	2	0	0	6	0	1	0	1	28	1	17	0	2
Baker, Douglas, Birmingham†	.241	146	452	72	109	148	18	3	5	51	5	18	2	13	65	1	51	14	5

Player and Club	Pct.	G.	AB.	R.	H.	TB.	2B.	3B.	HR.	RBI.	GW.	SH.	SF.	HP.	BB.	Int. BB.	SO.	SB.	CS.
Baker, Kenneth, Birmingham*	.284	103	363	71	103	167	17	4	13	67	10	1	9	0	71	9	27	7	9
Barrios, Jose, Charleston	.250	4	12	1	3	7	1	0	1	1	0	0	0	0	2	0	3	0	0
Benson, Steven, Columbus	.239	42	134	16	32	45	4	0	3	18	3	3	4	0	13	0	18	1	3
Best, William, Jacksonville*	.247	117	385	52	95	162	19	6	12	55	9	4	2	1	63	3	57	14	6
Bjorkman, George, Columbus	.252	70	230	36	58	116	16	3	12	36	5	2	3	3	46	1	52	3	5
Blaser, Mark, Nashville	.294	17	51	9	15	30	4	1	3	6	2	0	0	1	5	0	15	1	1
Blume, David, Chattanooga*	.000	3	4	0	0	0	0	0	0	1	0	0	0	0	2	0	2	0	0
Bockhorn, Glen, Savannah	.287	129	442	80	127	210	23	0	20	80	12	0	5	4	72	4	78	1	1
Borucki, Raymond, Birmingham	.296	67	162	17	48	60	9	0	1	19	1	4	2	0	19	2	16	0	1
Bradley, Scott, Nashville*	.270	137	525	83	142	207	33	4	8	76	11	1	8	10	40	9	16	3	2
Briggs, Kenneth, Chattanooga	.163	25	86	9	14	26	4	1	2	9	2	2	1	0	5	0	19	1	0
Broersma, Eric, Orlando	1.000	31	1	0	1	1	0	0	0	0	0	0	0	0	0	0	0	0	0
Brunson, Eddie, Charlotte	.258	106	365	67	94	156	18	4	12	48	4	0	3	1	41	2	49	16	10
Bucci, Michael, Chattanooga	.246	22	61	9	15	18	3	0	0	5	0	2	0	0	11	0	9	7	4
Bullock, Eric, Columbus*	.276	130	475	65	131	185	15	6	9	59	4	2	6	3	69	6	63	35	11
Cadahia, Aurelio, Orlando	.260	56	146	17	38	50	9	0	1	10	0	0	1	0	20	0	13	3	0
Calderon, Ivan, Chattanooga	.311	139	546	92	170	267	34	15	11	80	3	2	4	3	34	2	70	25	13
Candaele, Casey, Memphis†	.211	5	19	4	4	5	1	0	0	1	0	0	0	0	1	0	3	1	0
Carl, Jeffrey, Memphis	.257	57	179	41	46	84	9	1	9	21	3	0	2	3	32	0	47	2	0
Carrion, Leonel, Memphis	.276	98	341	47	94	138	18	1	8	48	4	1	1	4	57	1	52	2	4
Carroll, Carson, Orlando	.202	63	168	15	34	42	5	0	1	16	2	3	2	1	13	0	35	9	1
Carter, Don, Memphis*	.303	112	423	61	128	139	7	2	0	30	2	17	0	2	42	0	41	29	20
Chappas, Harry, Savannah	.231	19	52	12	12	23	3	1	2	5	2	4	2	0	8	0	4	4	3
Chavez, Pedro, Birmingham	.224	20	49	7	11	12	1	0	0	3	0	3	1	0	5	0	7	1	0
Colbert, Richard, Columbus	.223	64	188	18	42	75	14	2	5	22	3	2	2	1	26	0	65	1	2
Cole, Michael, Savannah*	.285	137	470	87	134	166	21	4	1	36	4	8	2	11	95	1	61	75	25
Coles, Darnell, Chattanooga	.287	72	261	49	75	108	10	4	5	24	4	3	1	3	41	1	39	12	10
Cruz, Jose, Memphis*	.274	115	401	47	110	141	17	4	2	36	4	3	4	4	40	3	48	10	6
Csefalvay, John, Columbus*	.288	113	372	51	107	169	24	4	10	61	7	2	2	0	49	4	41	1	4
Cuervo, Edward, Columbus*	.130	10	23	4	3	6	0	0	1	2	0	0	0	0	0	0	3	0	1
Curry, Stephen, Savannah	.248	103	335	55	83	129	17	1	9	39	4	4	4	2	57	0	67	8	2
D'Onofrio, Gary, Columbus†	.203	63	197	19	40	59	7	0	4	22	2	4	2	1	28	4	28	2	1
Dalena, Peter, Nashville*	.322	89	335	52	108	178	23	4	13	59	10	1	1	0	29	1	36	0	1
Damon, John, Memphis	.238	90	303	37	72	86	9	1	1	37	4	5	2	3	34	1	60	11	3
Datz, Jeffrey, Columbus	.194	39	124	15	24	38	3	1	3	11	2	1	0	0	6	0	29	3	1
Davis, Alvin, Chattanooga*	.296	131	422	87	125	209	24	3	18	83	9	1	12	1	120	9	57	7	0
Davis, Wallace, Jacksonville	.317	90	331	51	105	176	15	7	14	63	9	2	6	0	36	2	78	29	7
Davis, Glenn, Columbus	.299	118	445	68	133	233	19	3	25	85	9	0	5	9	40	6	87	4	2
Demeter, Todd, Nashville	.173	34	110	14	19	34	3	0	4	13	3	0	0	2	13	0	44	0	0
Dempsey, Patrick, Charlotte	.264	122	443	56	117	166	25	3	6	63	3	2	2	0	21	1	59	13	1
Denman, John, Charlotte	.130	9	23	3	3	5	2	0	0	2	0	1	0	0	4	0	8	1	0
Dennis, Eduardo, Knoxville	.265	119	415	57	110	129	13	3	0	31	4	1	2	2	31	1	45	5	12
Dewey, Duane, Jacksonville	.153	58	176	18	27	39	6	0	2	16	1	2	1	2	23	0	38	4	2
Diaz, Mario, Chattanooga	.270	33	111	18	30	52	6	5	2	13	0	0	0	0	5	0	15	0	1
Dodd, Thomas, Nashville	.225	22	71	10	16	27	2	0	3	11	1	0	1	1	10	0	20	1	1
Dukes, Kevin, Chattanooga*	.000	37	1	0	0	0	0	0	0	0	0	0	0	0	1	0	1	0	0
Dumouchelle, Patrick, Charlotte	.194	43	139	13	27	31	1	0	1	9	0	1	3	0	16	1	19	1	2
Earl, W. Scott, Birmingham	.261	144	529	96	138	210	22	10	10	60	5	13	5	2	73	2	84	36	15
Estepa, Ramon, Chattanooga	.272	128	449	55	122	194	32	5	10	76	12	5	3	5	53	3	69	10	7
Estes, Frank, Savannah*	.303	131	445	62	135	189	28	7	4	58	3	2	6	2	55	12	54	10	4
Faedo, Leonardo, Orlando	.212	15	52	2	11	12	1	0	0	4	0	0	0	0	2	0	5	0	1
Falcone, David, Charlotte*	.265	101	306	67	81	142	17	4	12	44	5	7	1	2	55	3	56	2	2
Ferris, Robert, Jacksonville	.238	132	445	62	106	166	24	0	12	56	6	0	5	2	83	3	143	5	3
Figueroa, Jesus, Knoxville*	.285	114	438	58	125	156	14	4	3	33	4	3	4	2	38	4	40	12	6
Flores, James, Orlando†	.000	2	6	0	0	0	0	0	0	0	0	0	0	0	0	0	1	0	0
Followell, Vernon, Columbus†	.240	92	308	27	74	86	9	0	1	21	1	6	0	0	48	4	33	2	2
Foster, Kenneth, Orlando	.270	135	493	69	133	203	30	5	10	83	7	6	8	4	52	1	37	2	1
Foussianes, George, Brimingham	.270	138	452	106	122	227	31	4	22	81	13	1	4	7	98	1	97	3	1
Fucci, Dominic, Birmingham*	.111	11	27	2	3	3	0	0	0	2	0	0	0	0	7	0	12	1	0
Gainey, Telmanch, Columbus*	.270	110	397	65	107	151	15	1	9	43	4	4	2	2	40	2	83	24	19
Gallegos, Matthew, Nashville†	.274	129	493	59	135	161	14	6	0	62	5	6	3	2	63	2	36	11	13
Giordano, Michael, Orlando	.000	32	1	0	0	0	0	0	0	0	0	0	0	0	0	0	0	0	0
Glynn, Eugene, Memphis	.125	7	24	0	3	3	0	0	0	1	0	0	0	0	3	0	2	0	2
Gonzales, Rene, Memphis	.269	144	476	67	128	150	12	2	2	44	3	16	2	3	40	1	53	5	2
Grace, Michael, Columbus	.243	119	395	50	96	156	19	1	13	39	3	3	4	1	44	3	82	2	3
Griffin, Gregory, Knoxville	.274	144	525	74	144	196	22	9	4	48	4	6	6	3	52	0	111	21	15
Guerrero, Inocencio, Savannah	.235	71	247	23	58	95	14	1	7	31	4	0	1	1	27	0	52	0	2
Hagman, Keith, Savannah*	.252	41	123	29	31	46	4	1	3	12	1	2	1	2	29	2	9	1	1
Hansen, Roger, Jacksonville	.333	1	3	0	1	1	0	0	0	0	0	0	0	0	1	0	0	0	0
Harris, Garry, Knoxville	.224	118	419	55	94	146	16	6	8	41	4	0	4	2	23	1	89	5	5
Harris, Tracy, Chattanooga	.250	10	4	0	1	1	0	0	0	0	0	0	0	0	0	0	2	0	0
Hatcher, Harold, Jacksonville	.237	52	194	25	46	76	9	3	5	32	3	1	0	2	17	2	32	1	1
Hayes, Thomas, Savannah	.225	114	338	54	76	125	15	2	10	44	4	9	4	5	43	0	56	5	2
Hegman, Robert, Jacksonville	.238	74	235	33	56	69	8	1	1	26	1	3	0	0	29	0	39	5	1
Hill, D. Clay, Chattanooga*	.280	118	403	53	113	138	9	8	0	40	1	7	2	1	57	3	57	4	14
Hodgson, Paul, Knoxville	.297	108	347	37	103	136	15	3	4	38	2	3	2	4	50	1	58	3	5
Hoeksema, David, Memphis	.256	107	403	47	103	164	30	2	9	65	9	2	3	3	31	1	54	6	3
Holland, John, Savannah	.221	94	289	37	64	90	12	1	4	46	4	5	7	2	28	1	42	0	0
Hood, Scott, Savannah*	.214	9	28	0	6	6	0	0	0	1	0	0	0	0	2	0	3	0	0
Ingle, Randy, Savannah	.143	12	35	1	5	5	0	0	0	0	0	0	0	0	3	0	7	0	0
Jabalera, Francisco, Columbus*	.255	82	274	46	70	83	7	3	0	19	0	5	0	2	44	1	40	11	12
Johnson, Rondin, Jacksonville†	.265	140	555	74	147	169	12	5	0	30	5	13	5	0	36	0	51	25	11
Johnston, Christopher, Knoxville	.318	87	314	35	100	147	20	0	9	50	6	0	7	2	27	1	78	0	1
King, Kevin, Chattanooga†	.265	75	245	40	65	115	14	3	10	36	2	1	2	1	19	1	63	13	7
Kneuer, Frank, Nashville	.234	57	171	24	40	62	8	1	4	28	6	1	2	1	26	0	19	2	1
Knight, Timothy, Nashville*	.278	132	439	66	122	181	22	2	11	64	5	1	2	9	59	6	90	13	8
Krzanik, Andrew, Memphis	.000	41	1	0	0	0	0	0	0	0	0	0	0	0	0	0	0	0	0
Leeper, David, Jacksonville*	.293	36	147	22	43	63	9	1	3	25	1	1	4	0	9	0	18	2	1
Lindsey, William, Nashville	.273	3	11	1	3	3	0	0	0	0	0	0	0	0	1	0	1	0	0
Little, D. Jeffrey, Orlando	.000	10	1	0	0	0	0	0	0	0	0	0	0	0	0	0	1	0	0
Lomastro, Gerardo, Orlando	.299	142	528	89	158	267	36	5	21	92	7	0	9	8	65	3	90	2	3
Lombardozzi, Stephen, Orlando	.291	137	492	76	143	187	23	6	3	52	6	6	5	7	83	1	51	11	6
Long, Robert, Chattanooga	.000	34	3	1	0	0	0	0	0	0	0	1	0	0	1	0	1	0	0

Player and Club	Pct.	G.	AB.	R.	H.	TB.	2B.	3B.	HR.	RBI.	GW.	SH.	SF.	HP.	BB.	Int. BB.	SO.	SB.	CS.
Lowry, Dwight, Birmingham*	.267	90	288	42	77	117	9	2	9	44	4	2	2	1	32	3	34	3	2
Mariano, Robert, Charlotte*	.265	64	196	22	52	71	10	0	3	28	2	2	2	2	28	2	32	2	0
Martin, Victor, Chattanooga	.000	49	14	0	0	0	0	0	0	0	0	0	0	0	0	0	6	0	0
Mata, Victor, Nashville	.303	130	465	79	141	200	19	5	10	63	8	4	6	10	43	0	63	6	9
McCain, Michael, Orlando*	.308	56	208	41	64	96	15	1	5	42	3	0	8	3	42	2	26	1	2
McNealy, Derwin, Nashville*	.242	127	421	75	102	134	11	6	3	37	7	15	2	1	48	1	76	39	13
Melvin, Robert, Birmingham	.288	78	285	43	82	130	14	2	10	56	6	0	4	2	18	2	54	0	3
Morris, John, Jacksonville*	.288	140	490	96	141	253	27	8	23	92	6	0	2	4	109	1	107	30	4
Nealeigh, Rodney, Memphis*	.252	127	432	60	109	141	18	1	4	40	1	4	3	3	47	8	53	14	9
Negron, Miguel, Chattanooga*	.300	116	427	55	128	167	15	3	6	55	5	5	4	1	29	3	39	6	2
Newman, Albert, Memphis†	.253	52	194	18	49	58	5	2	0	13	4	9	1	1	21	0	12	16	7
Norman, Gregory, Birmingham	.300	134	460	61	138	209	31	2	12	80	6	4	9	3	71	0	48	4	7
Ortiz, Leopoldo, Birmingham	.222	11	27	4	6	13	1	0	2	5	0	0	2	0	2	0	3	0	0
Pagliarulo, Michael, Nashville†	.260	135	450	82	117	201	19	4	19	80	7	0	8	3	59	2	100	8	4
Palica, John, Orlando	.269	116	401	61	108	163	20	1	11	63	1	5	5	3	47	3	51	7	3
Pardo, Alberto, Charlotte†	.312	37	141	20	44	73	11	3	4	19	3	1	0	1	10	0	20	1	2
Pecota, William, Jacksonville	.242	72	260	38	63	89	9	1	5	25	3	1	2	0	33	1	39	9	6
Peterson, Erik, Nashville	.303	61	195	26	59	96	10	3	7	43	2	1	4	1	20	4	31	0	0
Pilla, Antonio, Orlando	.280	134	436	58	122	150	18	5	0	41	4	10	2	8	85	0	85	7	5
Pinkham, William, Knoxville	.252	72	250	23	63	107	14	0	10	41	3	5	4	0	12	1	53	0	0
Pirruccello, Mark, Jacksonville*	.222	5	9	1	2	2	0	0	0	2	0	0	1	0	2	1	1	0	0
Presley, James, Chattanooga	.265	131	461	70	122	205	31	5	14	90	10	5	9	2	56	2	101	9	3
Ramie, Vernon, Knoxville*	.250	49	148	30	37	80	11	1	10	35	1	0	1	0	32	3	49	1	0
Ramler, Steven, Memphis	.315	30	92	14	29	36	4	0	1	16	0	0	1	2	13	0	13	0	0
Ramppen, Frank, Orlando	.210	56	162	14	34	54	9	1	3	21	0	4	1	0	20	0	40	5	5
Randolph, Robert, Chattanooga	.000	9	1	0	0	0	0	0	0	0	0	0	0	0	0	0	0	0	0
Reddish, Michael, Nashville	.285	67	221	31	63	100	13	3	6	31	3	0	1	2	24	0	35	2	3
Reed, Jeffrey, Orlando*	.264	118	379	52	100	144	16	5	6	45	1	5	5	8	76	6	40	2	3
Reynolds, Michael, Savannah*	.279	51	154	25	43	50	7	0	0	20	5	3	0	0	21	0	18	5	1
Rios, Carlos, Savannah	.292	103	359	51	105	135	15	3	3	59	6	5	6	5	50	5	31	17	13
Rizzo, Richard, Jacksonville	.214	97	350	48	75	114	10	1	9	34	7	1	1	3	35	2	54	20	7
Rodriguez, Victor, Charlotte	.298	140	571	80	170	240	26	1	14	77	6	7	3	0	26	1	44	2	5
Rosario, Simon, Savannah	.266	98	323	42	86	119	9	6	4	42	5	0	1	0	25	1	36	4	2
Santovenia, Nelson, Memphis	.242	94	318	27	77	99	13	0	3	44	3	3	3	1	33	0	36	1	1
Schaefer, Jeffrey, Charlotte	.236	51	182	20	43	60	7	2	2	28	1	3	1	0	5	0	25	4	4
Schmidt, August, Knoxville	.266	135	482	65	128	172	28	2	4	54	11	2	7	0	57	1	65	6	4
Scranton, James, Jacksonville	.218	141	450	43	98	116	10	1	2	31	4	14	3	7	42	0	73	8	8
Serna, Paul, Chattanooga	.251	99	375	40	94	115	12	3	1	32	3	8	1	1	33	1	29	11	11
Shaddy, J. Christopher, Knoxville	.200	127	385	39	77	99	7	3	3	30	5	3	3	0	55	0	101	4	2
Sheets, Larry, Charlotte*	.288	138	503	72	145	263	37	3	25	87	10	1	4	4	45	6	102	1	2
Sherman, James, Columbus	.211	95	323	28	68	95	7	1	6	33	1	2	3	2	33	1	67	1	4
Shimp, Tommy Joe, Memphis	.000	19	2	0	0	0	0	0	0	0	0	0	0	0	0	0	0	0	0
Shines, Anthony, Memphis†	.286	109	388	72	111	202	27	2	20	63	2	2	4	8	55	6	59	7	5
Showalter, William, Nashville	.276	89	297	35	82	106	13	4	1	37	7	4	4	1	39	3	22	1	3
Simcox, Larry, Columbus	.234	41	128	20	30	34	4	0	0	9	1	4	1	0	12	0	10	0	1
Simmons, Nelson, Birmingham†	.272	118	404	57	110	162	17	1	11	64	9	0	3	1	52	6	83	2	4
Simons, Neil, Columbus*	.225	13	40	4	9	13	4	0	0	2	1	1	0	0	3	0	4	0	0
Smith, Keith, Nashville	.258	141	426	78	110	150	8	4	8	38	2	6	1	4	92	2	103	22	11
Smith, Mark, Birmingham	.265	76	260	26	69	104	20	3	3	28	2	7	1	4	16	1	31	2	6
Snider, Van, Jacksonville*	.182	13	33	2	6	9	3	0	0	2	0	1	0	0	4	0	7	1	0
Sodders, Michael, Orlando	.231	67	242	37	56	96	9	2	9	41	3	2	3	5	29	0	61	5	3
Soriano, Hilario, Knoxville	.155	18	58	2	9	12	3	0	0	2	0	2	0	0	2	1	13	0	0
Sosa, Miguel, Savannah	.245	125	490	54	120	187	16	0	17	93	11	3	9	2	21	0	94	26	11
Stefero, John, Charlotte*	.307	61	205	33	63	120	9	0	16	34	4	2	1	1	33	1	38	0	0
Stellern, Michael, Columbus	.333	10	24	7	8	13	2	0	1	1	0	0	0	0	1	0	9	0	0
Strucher, Mark, Columbus	.271	118	373	54	101	199	25	5	21	61	9	5	0	4	51	6	69	5	3
Sutton, Johnny, Chattanooga	.250	11	4	0	1	1	0	0	0	0	0	0	0	0	1	0	2	0	0
Tartabull, Danilo, Chattanooga	.301	128	481	95	145	230	32	7	13	66	11	3	4	1	47	2	63	25	13
Teegarden, Robert, Nashville	.291	20	55	7	16	19	3	0	0	2	0	0	0	0	8	0	16	2	0
Thompson, Milton, Savannah*	.303	115	386	84	117	161	21	4	5	36	5	3	1	3	83	4	76	46	10
Thompson, Tommy, Savannah*	.328	25	67	13	22	33	5	0	2	13	2	1	0	1	20	1	12	1	1
Tiefenthaler, Dennis, Charlotte	.000	3	7	0	0	0	0	0	0	0	0	0	0	0	1	0	1	0	0
Timko, Andrew, Charlotte*	.233	82	257	31	60	76	14	1	0	23	4	6	8	1	31	0	15	5	2
Tovar, Raul, Birmingham	.289	131	461	58	133	181	14	11	4	60	6	3	0	4	28	1	60	4	5
Tutt, Johnny, Charlotte	.280	68	218	47	61	85	7	4	3	21	3	2	3	5	34	0	32	15	6
Tyner, Matthew, Charlotte	.219	89	278	49	61	117	14	0	14	35	3	0	1	2	60	2	82	5	2
Valle, David, Chattanooga	.239	53	176	20	42	62	11	0	3	22	1	0	1	3	24	0	28	0	1
Walker, Anthony, Columbus†	.222	44	171	22	38	47	7	1	0	10	2	1	1	1	22	1	26	4	8
Weaver, James, Orlando*	.247	138	497	85	123	197	25	2	15	84	11	6	6	3	62	5	85	42	14
Weislak, Kenneth, Memphis	.250	25	80	8	20	25	5	0	0	4	0	2	1	0	6	0	8	1	0
Whitfield, Robert, Charlotte	.500	2	4	0	2	2	0	0	0	0	0	0	0	0	0	0	0	0	0
Whitmer, Daniel, Knoxville	.245	84	253	24	62	88	11	0	5	33	2	6	1	4	34	1	50	0	1
Wilkerson, Martin, Jacksonville*	.281	110	377	37	106	130	20	2	0	48	8	3	4	3	45	4	37	3	1
Williams, Daniel, Birmingham*	.210	22	62	12	13	24	2	0	3	13	1	0	1	1	9	2	7	1	0
Williams, Jeffrey, Charlotte*	.249	124	425	56	106	153	10	8	7	34	3	4	0	1	50	0	82	19	12
Williams, Kevin, Orlando	.241	135	523	91	126	181	21	11	4	57	7	10	3	2	74	1	76	33	12
Wood, Andre, Knoxville	.222	81	230	23	51	59	3	1	1	22	0	5	2	1	31	1	54	7	3
Younger, Stanley, Birmingham*	.309	131	530	91	164	208	24	4	4	54	7	7	3	0	43	2	72	43	18

The following pitchers, listed alphabetically by club, with games in parentheses, had no plate appearances, primarily through the use of designated hitters:

BIRMINGHAM—Cary, Charles (17); Comstock, Keith (37); Davis, Ted (7); Dixon, Troy (40); Furman, Kevin (9); Garcia, Alejandro (1); Gordon, Donald (43); Harvey, Randall (17); Heinkel, Donald (30); Kelly, Bryan (4); Mason, Roger (17); Monteleone, Richard (3); Moya, Ernest (1); Robbins, Bruce (16); Schattinger, Jeffrey (6); Tabor, Scott (31); Ward, Colin (26); Willis, Carl (14).

CHARLOTTE—Arias, Juan (12); Arnold, Tony (44); Bradley, Thomas (9); Butler, Mark (16); Cabassa, Carlos (18); Dixon, Kenneth (20); Engle, Richard (7); Gonzalez, Julian (17); King, Jerome (6); Konopa, Robert (8); Kucharski, Joseph (27); Leiter, Kurt (11); Marietta, Louis (9); McCullock, Alec (6); Mitcheltree, John (61); Oliveras, Francisco (25); Pacella, John (10); Riggins, Mark (5); Rooney, James (4); Snell, Nathaniel (15); Willsher, Christopher (23).

CHATTANOOGA—Brennan, Thomas (13); Burden, John (4); Cahill, Mark (26); Hudson, Robert (7); Hunger, Christopher (6); Langston, Mark (28); Nielson, Scott (13); Owens, Thomas (7); Rowe, Thomas (20); Steger, Kevin (13); Stottlemyre, Jeffrey (46); Whitmer, Joseph (26).

COLUMBUS—Acker, Larry (1); Calhoun, Jeffrey (27); Everett, Conrad (9); Foley, Rickey (36); Heathcock, Jeffrey (14); Knudson, Mark

(13); MacDonald, James (27); Meckes, Timothy (45); Paris, Zacarias (23); Perry, Patrick (11); Pladson, Gordon (7); Regalado, Uvaldo (14); Ross, Mark (13); Smith, Jack (18); Snyder, Benjamin (28); Sprowl, Robert (29); Veselic, Robert (9).

JACKSONVILLE—Ferreira, Anthony (35); Fischer, Daniel (16); Gubicza, Mark (28); Harsh, Nicholas (18); Huismann, Mark (37); Martinez, Arthur (6); Olson, Michael (11); Perez, Valerio (1); Ray, Glenn (26); Saberhagen, Bret (11); Shaw, Theodore (16); Strode, Lester (25); Wills, Frank (8); Wong, David (50).

KNOXVILLE—Blackmon, Thomas (29); Cerutti, John (29); Clarke, Stanley (27); Cullen, Michael (9); Davis, Steven (4); Eichhorn, Mark (21); Esquer, Mercedes (21); Key, James (14); McKnight, Jonathan (30); Phillips, Christopher (11); Reish, Stephen (38); Shipanoff, David (61); Stemberger, Brian (16); Valenzuela, Guillermo (28); Walker, Keith (13).

MEMPHIS—Abone, Joseph (4); Bargar, Gregory (9); Cates, Timothy (30); Chapin, Peter (10); Glasscock, Larry (44); Hesketh, Joseph (12); Johnson, Gregory (9); Kinnunen, Michael (38); Neely, Alex (5); Pladson, Gordon (4); Schuler, Mark (30); Taylor, Jeffrey (23); Tenenini, Robert (49); Torres, Miguel (21); Williams, Mark (9); Yanus, Raymond (8); Yenser, Steven (5).

NASHVILLE—Bersano, Mark (10); Browning, Michael (22); Burke, Timothy (20); Callahan, Benjamin (2); Coffman, James (1); Faulk, Kelly (4); Hernaiz, Jesus (7); Hernandez, Carlo (5); King, Michael (6); Olwine, Edward (29); Patterson, Scott (13); Pettaway, Felix (16); Raftice, Robert (13); Rasmussen, James (13); Rijo, Jose (5); Scott, Kelly (26); Shiflett, Mark (24); Silva, Mark (37); Szymczak, David (11); Tewksbury, Robert (7); Werly, James (11).

ORLANDO—Arney, Jeffrey (3); Boris, Paul (13); Gibson, Paul (40); Guerrero, Anthony (28); Hobbs, John (31); Konopa, Robert (4); Korczyk, Steven (14); Kromy, Ted (29); Krueger, Kirby (46); Pena, Manuel (27); Pettibone, Harry (27); Yett, Richard (24).

SAVANNAH—Clay, David (21); Cole, Timothy (16); Dedmon, Jeffrey (21); Dooner, Glenn (48); Fisher, Brian (27); Gibson, James (46); Johnson, Joseph (26); Jones, Craig (27); North, Roy (23); Payne, Michael (25); Treadway, Andre (32); Waddell, Thomas (29).

GRAND SLAM HOME RUNS—K. Smith, Sosa, 2 each; Bockhorn, Csefalvay, Falcone, Griffin, G. Harris, Hatcher, Hoeksema, Mariano, Mata, McNealy, Pardo, Peterson, Ramppen, Rizzo, Sheets, Simmons, Sodders, T. Thompson, Weaver, K. Williams, Younger, 1 each.

AWARDED FIRST BASE ON CATCHER'S INTERFERENCE—Scranton 8 (Dempsey 2, Hill 2, Bjorkman, Colbert, Holland, Reed); Rizzo 5 (Colbert, Lowry, Pinkham, Santovenia, Valle); Lombardozzi 2 (Bjorkman, Hatcher); Cruz (Bjorkman); Damon (Cahill); Jabalera (Ashmore); Leeper (Whitmer.)

CLUB FIELDING

Club	Pct.	G.	PO.	A.	E.	DP.	PB.
Jacksonville	.970	145	3764	1612	166	138	26
Birmingham	.969	147	3801	1690	178	131	9
Orlando	.968	145	3722	1532	173	139	12
Savannah	.968	145	3632	1508	170	119	19
Nashville	.966	147	3722	1647	188	131	17
Charlotte	.965	146	3712	1574	189	138	17
Knoxville	.965	147	3689	1592	194	140	12
Memphis	.965	146	3706	1616	194	160	29
Columbus	.964	143	3660	1770	200	163	28
Chattanooga	.961	143	3630	1752	220	147	20

Triple plays—Columbus, Knoxville.

INDIVIDUAL FIELDING

*Throws lefthanded.

FIRST BASEMEN

Player and Club	Pct.	G.	PO.	A.	E.	DP.
Aitcheson, Knoxville	1.000	1	11	0	0	0
Barrios, Charlotte	1.000	3	28	1	0	0
Bjorkman, Columbus	1.000	8	58	6	0	5
Bockhorn, Savannah	.990	56	486	19	5	43
Brunson, Charlotte	1.000	1	6	1	0	0
Cadahia, Orlando	1.000	14	83	14	0	6
Carrion, Memphis	1.000	1	10	2	0	1
Carroll, Orlando	1.000	3	10	0	0	0
Chavez, Birmingham	1.000	1	8	0	0	0
Csefalvay, Columbus*	.981	69	635	43	13	67
Dalena, Nashville	.992	88	823	56	7	67
A. Davis, Chattanooga	.988	129	1233	99	16	118
W. Davis, Jacksonville	1.000	3	16	3	0	0
Demeter, Nashville	.993	33	284	21	2	30
Dempsey, Charlotte	.967	14	112	5	4	8
Dumouchelle, Charlotte	.985	26	187	16	3	23
Estepa, Chattanooga	1.000	2	17	1	0	2
Estes, Savannah*	1.000	3	3	0	0	0
Falcone, Charlotte	.984	96	831	37	14	72
Ferris, Jacksonville	.989	116	1015	52	12	104
Foster, Orlando	.989	91	760	48	9	69
Foussianes, Birmingham	.988	47	310	19	4	28
Fucci, Birmingham*	.988	9	80	1	1	13
Grace, Columbus	.978	9	83	7	2	11
Guerrero, Savannah	.972	40	325	20	10	30
Hagman, Savannah*	1.000	25	193	15	0	13
Hatcher, Jacksonville	.979	22	208	22	5	14
Hill, Chattanooga	.981	11	98	8	2	11
Hodgson, Knoxville	.996	29	221	10	1	22
Hoeksema, Memphis	.980	5	46	3	1	5
Johnston, Knoxville	.985	86	727	55	12	74
Mariano, Charlotte	.967	3	27	2	1	7
Mata, Nashville	1.000	1	4	0	0	0
Melvin, Birmingham	1.000	5	38	4	0	6
NEALEIGH, Memphis*	.992	101	804	55	7	100
Norman, Birmingham	.983	98	840	73	16	67
Peterson, Nashville	.974	16	144	4	4	6
Pinkham, Knoxville	1.000	1	4	1	0	0
Ramie, Knoxville	1.000	38	244	66	0	25
Sheets, Charlotte	1.000	18	123	5	0	10
Shines, Memphis	.985	45	413	37	7	32
Showalter, Nashville*	.991	15	109	6	1	9
Simons, Columbus*	.933	3	14	0	1	1
Sodders, Orlando	.995	47	399	21	2	46
Strucher, Columbus	.991	67	568	60	6	62
M. Thompson, Savannah	.989	10	86	7	1	9
T. Thompson, Savannah	.989	20	163	11	2	18
Valle, Chattanooga	1.000	3	30	1	0	6
Whitfjeld, Charlotte	1.000	2	15	0	0	0
Wilkerson, Jacksonville	1.000	11	104	9	0	4
Williams, Birmingham*	.973	9	62	10	2	6

Triple plays—Csefalvay, Johnston.

SECOND BASEMEN

Player and Club	Pct.	G.	PO.	A.	E.	DP.
Alfaro, Charlotte	1.000	4	7	10	0	1
Babitt, Memphis	.930	28	56	77	10	16
Benson, Columbus	.898	9	24	20	5	4
Borucki, Birmingham	1.000	11	22	27	0	12
Bucci, Chattanooga	1.000	1	3	1	0	0
Carroll, Orlando	.962	38	73	80	6	9
Chavez, Birmingham	.667	2	1	3	2	0
Cuervo, Columbus	1.000	2	5	6	0	1
Curry, Savannah	.989	50	127	139	3	29
D'Onofrio, Columbus	.969	55	122	187	10	41
Damon, Memphis	.957	67	118	193	14	49
Dennis, Knoxville	.000	1	0	0	1	0
Dumouchelle, Charlotte	1.000	1	4	1	0	0
Earl, Birmingham	.959	143	318	416	31	86
Flores, Orlando	1.000	1	0	2	0	0
Foster, Orlando	1.000	2	5	1	0	0
Gallegos, Nashville	.939	98	165	251	27	48
Glynn, Memphis	1.000	6	11	26	0	7
Grace, Columbus	.977	86	197	267	11	65
Harris, Knoxville	.963	110	235	262	20	62
Hegman, Jacksonville	.970	6	14	18	1	5
Hoeksema, Memphis	1.000	6	9	15	0	3
Ingle, Savannah	1.000	9	14	24	0	3
JOHNSON, Jacksonville	.975	140	274	416	18	87
Lombardozzi, Orlando	.938	18	29	47	5	6
Mata, Nashville	.929	56	109	152	20	34
McCain, Orlando	.971	9	15	18	1	4
Melvin, Birmingham	1.000	1	0	1	0	0
Newman, Memphis	.944	45	111	123	14	34
Pilla, Orlando	.959	90	200	248	19	62
Ramppen, Orlando	1.000	2	3	3	0	1
Reynolds, Savannah	.944	5	9	8	1	1
Rios, Savannah	1.000	2	0	2	0	1
Rodriguez, Charlotte	.974	115	270	341	16	85
Schaefer, Charlotte	.978	26	65	70	3	19
Serna, Chattanooga	.954	26	55	91	7	19
Smith, Nashville	1.000	4	7	5	0	3
Sosa, Savannah	.974	85	157	217	10	45
Tartabull, Chattanooga	.966	119	252	405	23	74
Weislak, Memphis	1.000	1	0	4	0	0
Williams, Orlando	1.000	1	3	1	0	1
Wood, Knoxville	.969	41	101	117	7	35

Triple play—Grace.

THIRD BASEMEN

Player and Club	Pct.	G.	PO.	A.	E.	DP.
Alfaro, Charlotte	.955	88	66	165	11	17
Ashmore, Jacksonville	.000	1	0	0	1	0
Babitt, Memphis	.941	5	4	12	1	2
Benson, Columbus	.806	11	5	24	7	5
Borucki, Birmingham	.976	51	36	86	3	8
Bradley, Nashville	.909	17	12	38	5	4
Bucci, Chattanooga	1.000	2	0	7	0	0
Cadahia, Orlando	1.000	1	0	1	0	0
Calderon, Chattanooga	.878	25	15	50	9	2
Candaele, Memphis	1.000	5	2	11	0	1
Carl, Memphis	.787	13	13	24	10	2
Carroll, Orlando	.949	15	16	21	2	1
Chavez, Birmingham	.900	15	13	32	5	3
Colbert, Columbus	1.000	2	2	6	0	1
Cole, Savannah	1.000	1	7	0	0	0
Curry, Savannah	.922	33	22	61	7	2
Damon, Memphis	.926	9	4	21	2	1
Dennis, Knoxville	.942	59	51	94	9	10
Dumouchelle, Charlotte	.800	8	1	11	3	0
Ferris, Jacksonville	1.000	1	1	1	0	0
Foster, Orlando	.846	13	6	16	4	2
Foussianes, Birmingham	.922	102	66	204	23	19
Grace, Columbus	.920	28	21	48	6	3
Hayes, Savannah	.893	88	69	174	29	11
Hegman, Jacksonville	.938	33	17	58	5	6
Hoeksema, Memphis	.934	96	62	151	15	23
Mariano, Charlotte	.939	34	33	60	6	7
McCain, Orlando	.960	50	45	100	6	11
PAGLIARULO, Nashville	.954	133	98	315	20	17
Pecota, Jacksonville	.912	69	52	134	18	11
Peterson, Nashville	.800	3	3	5	2	0
Pilla, Orlando	.949	12	11	26	2	4
Presley, Chattanooga	.927	110	82	250	26	29
Ramppen, Orlando	.931	49	45	103	11	10
Reynolds, Savannah	.966	33	21	64	3	6
Rodriguez, Charlotte	.957	25	21	45	3	6
Serna, Chattanooga	.933	10	8	20	2	0
Shaddy, Knoxville	.920	76	53	142	17	16
Sherman, Columbus	.879	85	60	157	30	13
Shines, Memphis	.727	4	3	5	3	0
Sodders, Orlando	.942	20	13	36	3	2
Strucher, Columbus	.914	38	25	60	8	4
Weislak, Memphis	.864	23	15	42	9	2
Wilkerson, Jacksonville	.960	52	48	96	6	10
Wood, Knoxville	.971	22	12	55	2	6

Triple play—Shaddy.

SHORTSTOPS

Player and Club	Pct.	G.	PO.	A.	E.	DP.
Alfaro, Charlotte	.974	42	59	130	5	23
Babitt, Memphis	1.000	2	2	3	0	1
Baker, Birmingham	.964	146	238	482	27	88
Benson, Columbus	.862	10	10	15	4	3
Calderon, Chattanooga	.750	1	2	1	1	1
Carroll, Orlando	.500	1	1	0	1	0
Chappas, Savannah	.971	16	18	48	2	7
Chavez, Birmingham	1.000	2	1	2	0	0
Coles, Chattanooga	.924	72	131	232	30	49
D'Onofrio, Columbus	1.000	9	12	11	0	1
Diaz, Chattanooga	.928	27	48	80	10	16
Dumouchelle, Charlotte	.813	3	5	8	3	0
Earl, Birmingham	.938	7	7	8	1	2
Faedo, Orlando	.968	14	19	42	2	5
Flores, Orlando	1.000	1	1	2	0	2
Followell, Columbus	.968	92	178	331	17	70
Gallegos, Nashville	.979	11	14	33	1	6
GONZALES, Memphis	.972	144	258	449	20	102
Hegman, Jacksonville	.964	8	9	18	1	2
Hoeksema, Memphis	1.000	3	4	5	0	3
Ingle, Savannah	.933	3	5	9	1	0
Lombardozzi, Orlando	.946	109	174	317	28	69
McCain, Orlando	.500	1	1	0	1	0
Pecota, Jacksonville	.750	1	2	1	1	1
Pilla, Orlando	.939	31	36	71	7	9
Presley, Chattanooga	.992	21	40	79	1	15
Reynolds, Savannah	.778	2	3	4	2	1
Rios, Savannah	.949	101	140	284	23	48
Schaefer, Charlotte	.943	25	37	96	8	14
Schmidt, Knoxville	.936	97	143	282	29	51
Scranton, Jacksonville	.944	140	211	469	40	87
Serna, Chattanooga	.959	30	47	71	5	12
Shaddy, Knoxville	.922	50	80	144	19	36
Simcox, Columbus	.943	41	61	139	12	35
Smith, Nashville	.948	137	233	440	37	76
Sosa, Savannah	.904	31	39	74	12	15
Timko, Charlotte	.937	80	134	221	24	42
Wood, Knoxville	1.000	2	3	2	0	0

Triple play—Followell.

OUTFIELDERS

Player and Club	Pct.	G.	PO.	A.	E.	DP.
Aitcheson, Knoxville	.979	119	269	9	6	2
Auten, Memphis	.957	135	231	13	11	3
Baez, Chattanooga	1.000	2	1	0	0	0
Baker, Birmingham*	.983	104	213	12	4	2
Barrios, Charlotte	1.000	2	1	0	0	0
Benson, Columbus	1.000	4	4	0	0	0
Best, Jacksonville	.978	100	161	13	4	1
Bockhorn, Savannah	1.000	1	2	0	0	0
Briggs, Chattanooga	.967	25	58	1	2	0
Brunson, Charlotte	.976	93	193	11	5	1
Bucci, Chattanooga	1.000	10	9	2	0	0
Bullock, Columbus*	.986	124	196	9	3	3
Calderon, Chattanooga	.953	106	251	10	13	3
Carl, Memphis	.972	25	33	2	1	0
Carrion, Memphis	.969	69	121	4	4	0
Carroll, Orlando	1.000	5	8	0	0	0
Carter, Memphis	.986	111	269	13	4	2
Colbert, Columbus	1.000	4	4	0	0	0
Cole, Savannah	.976	135	265	18	7	1
Cruz, Memphis*	.949	100	180	8	10	3
Csefalvay, Columbus*	.980	34	46	2	1	0
Curry, Savannah	.950	9	12	7	1	2
G. Davis, Columbus	.958	113	186	17	9	2
W. Davis, Jacksonville	.962	51	101	1	4	0
Denman, Charlotte	1.000	9	18	1	0	0
Dennis, Knoxville	.958	62	103	10	5	0
Dodd, Nashville	1.000	17	29	2	0	1
Dumouchelle, Charlotte	1.000	4	5	0	0	0
Estepa, Chattanooga	.954	121	177	8	9	4
Estes, Savannah*	.980	128	226	13	5	2
Figueroa, Knoxville*	.950	106	200	10	11	2
Foster, Orlando	.800	3	4	0	1	0
Gainey, Columbus	1.000	26	56	1	0	0
Gallegos, Nashville	.943	17	31	2	2	1
Griffin, Knoxville	.977	143	316	19	8	2
Hayes, Savannah	1.000	10	9	2	0	0
Hegman, Jacksonville	.969	20	31	0	1	0
Hill, Chattanooga	1.000	23	25	1	0	0
Hodgson, Knoxville	.952	12	20	0	1	0
Jabalera, Columbus*	.975	64	146	7	4	2
King, Chattanooga*	.925	62	87	12	8	2
Knight, Nashville*	.961	128	203	20	9	2
Leeper, Jacksonville*	1.000	32	58	5	0	1
Lomastro, Orlando	.968	112	174	9	6	0
Long, Chattanooga	1.000	1	2	0	0	0
Mariano, Charlotte	1.000	12	27	1	0	0
Martin, Chattanooga	1.000	1	5	0	0	0
Mata, Nashville	.948	74	144	2	8	0
McNealy, Nashville*	.979	126	314	7	7	2
MORRIS, Jacksonville*	.989	135	260	8	3	1
Nealeigh, Memphis*	.875	14	17	4	3	0
Negron, Chattanooga*	.944	79	130	6	8	0
Palica, Orlando*	.994	78	161	6	1	1
Peterson, Nashville	1.000	16	18	0	0	0
Ramie, Knoxville	.941	7	15	1	1	0
Reddish, Nashville	.951	59	94	4	5	1
Reynolds, Savannah	1.000	10	12	2	0	0
Rizzo, Jacksonville	.975	92	227	7	6	2
Rosario, Savannah	.939	67	101	6	7	1
Serna, Chattanooga	.913	11	19	2	2	0
Sheets, Charlotte	.953	99	133	10	7	2
Sherman, Columbus	.938	19	15	0	1	0
Showalter, Nashville*	.947	15	18	0	1	0
Simmons, Birmingham	.930	102	174	11	14	1
Simons, Columbus*	1.000	10	17	1	0	0
Smith, Birmingham	.971	64	99	3	3	0
Snider, Jacksonville	.933	13	28	0	2	0
Soriano, Knoxville	.833	3	4	1	1	0
Stellern, Columbus	.941	9	15	1	1	0
Teegarden, Nashville	.943	14	33	0	2	0
M. Thompson, Savannah	.973	99	209	8	6	1
T. Thompson, Savannah	1.000	3	7	0	0	0
Tovar, Birmingham	.970	130	250	8	8	2
Tutt, Charlotte	.944	68	146	7	9	2
Tyner, Charlotte	.933	70	108	4	8	2
Walker, Columbus	1.000	44	83	4	0	1
Weaver, Orlando*	.969	129	259	20	9	4
Wilkerson, Jacksonville	.913	11	20	1	2	0
J. Williams, Charlotte*	.954	117	245	26	13	1
K. Williams, Orlando	.976	118	316	9	8	3
Wood, Knoxville	1.000	7	10	0	0	0
Younger, Birmingham*	.990	59	95	8	1	0

CATCHERS

Player and Club	Pct.	G.	PO.	A.	E.	DP.	PB.
Ashmore, Jacksonville	.988	70	401	26	5	4	16
Baez, Chattanooga	.964	34	159	27	7	6	4
Benson, Columbus	1.000	1	1	2	0	1	0
Bjorkman, Columbus	.968	54	286	48	11	7	12
Blume, Chattanooga	1.000	2	7	0	0	0	1
Bockhorn, Savannah	.975	52	288	22	8	1	10
Bradley, Nashville	.985	93	463	50	8	7	12
Bucci, Chattanooga	1.000	1	3	0	0	0	0
Cadahia, Orlando	.982	30	150	10	3	1	5
Colbert, Columbus	.972	54	267	45	9	2	9
Cuervo, Columbus	.964	5	25	2	1	0	2
D'Onofrio, Columbus	1.000	2	2	4	0	0	1
Datz, Columbus	.965	38	130	35	6	3	4
Dempsey, Charlotte	.977	71	346	40	9	3	8
Dewey, Jacksonville	.982	56	304	23	6	1	4
Dodd, Nashville	1.000	2	12	0	0	1	0
Dumouchelle, Charlotte	1.000	3	6	0	0	0	0
Hansen, Jacksonville	1.000	1	6	0	0	0	0
Hatcher, Jacksonville	.972	18	91	12	3	1	5
Hill, Chattanooga	.978	66	315	34	8	6	11
Holland, Savannah	.976	91	507	56	14	5	7
Hood, Savannah	.976	9	35	6	1	0	2
Kneuer, Nashville	.986	53	262	26	4	6	3
Lindsey, Nashville	1.000	3	13	7	0	0	2
Lowry, Birmingham	.988	84	424	51	6	4	4
Melvin, Birmingham	.995	66	366	25	2	0	3
Ortiz, Birmingham	.982	8	52	4	1	0	2
Pardo, Charlotte	.974	27	129	18	4	2	1
Pinkham, Knoxville	.984	53	280	37	5	6	4
Ramler, Memphis	.966	30	143	25	6	3	5
Ramppen, Orlando	.966	6	22	6	1	0	0
REED, Orlando	.989	116	618	88	8	12	7
Santovenia, Memphis	.974	89	490	69	15	3	21
Serna, Chattanooga	1.000	2	8	0	0	0	3
Shines, Memphis	.959	34	195	41	10	4	3
Soriano, Knoxville	.988	15	73	8	1	2	3
Stefero, Charlotte	.962	51	261	40	12	1	8
Valle, Chattanooga	.983	43	209	23	4	2	1
Whitmer, Knoxville	.986	84	439	50	7	6	5
Wilkerson, Jacksonville	1.000	6	28	4	0	2	1

PITCHERS

Player and Club	Pct.	G.	PO.	A.	E.	DP.
Abone, Memphis	1.000	4	0	2	0	0
Alvarez, Jacksonville	1.000	30	8	21	0	1
Arias, Charlotte	1.000	12	2	4	0	0
Arnold, Charlotte	.962	44	7	18	1	2
Bargar, Memphis	.833	8	3	7	2	1
Bersano, Nashville	1.000	10	2	2	0	0
Blackmon, Knoxville	.930	29	14	26	3	2
Boris, Orlando	.667	13	2	2	2	0
Bradley, Charlotte	1.000	9	1	1	0	0
Brennan, Chattanooga*	1.000	13	0	4	0	0
Broersma, Orlando	1.000	31	4	8	0	1
Browning, Nashville	1.000	22	1	7	0	0
Burden, Chattanooga	1.000	4	0	2	0	0
Burke, Nashville	.957	20	5	17	1	3
Butler, Charlotte*	1.000	16	0	1	0	0
Cabassa, Charlotte*	.857	18	2	4	1	0
Cahill, Chattanooga	.964	26	11	16	1	3
Calhoun, Columbus*	.929	27	11	28	3	1
Callahan, Nashville	1.000	2	1	7	0	3
Cary, Birmingham*	.913	17	4	17	2	0
Cates, Memphis	.806	28	7	22	7	3
Cerutti, Knoxville*	.941	29	12	20	2	3
Chapin, Memphis	1.000	10	1	4	0	0
Clarke, Knoxville*	.857	26	0	6	1	0
Clay, Savannah	.857	21	5	13	3	2
Cole, Savannah*	1.000	16	0	4	0	0
Comstock, Birmingham*	.913	37	5	16	2	0
Cullen, Knoxville	1.000	9	1	0	0	0
S. Davis, Knoxville*	1.000	4	0	1	0	0
T. Davis, Birmingham	1.000	7	3	3	0	0
Dedmon, Savannah	.941	21	6	10	1	0
K. Dixon, Charlotte	.897	20	11	15	3	0
T. Dixon, Birmingham	.895	40	6	11	2	1
Dooner, Savannah	1.000	48	3	11	0	0
Dukes, Chattanooga*	.886	36	12	19	4	1
Eichhorn, Knoxville	.929	21	10	16	2	2
Engle, Charlotte*	1.000	7	0	6	0	1
Esquer, Knoxville*	.909	21	3	17	2	1
Everett, Columbus	1.000	9	2	3	0	0
Faulk, Nashville	1.000	4	1	3	0	0
Ferreira, Jacksonville*	.893	35	4	21	3	2
Fischer, Jacksonville	.900	16	3	6	1	1
Fisher, Savannah	.974	27	10	27	1	1
Foley, Columbus	.923	36	3	9	1	0
Furman, Birmingham	.857	9	2	4	1	1
J. Gibson, Savannah*	1.000	46	4	20	0	3
P. Gibson, Orlando*	.625	40	2	3	3	0
Giordano, Orlando	1.000	32	1	7	0	3
Glasscock, Memphis*	1.000	44	4	6	0	3
Gonzalez, Charlotte*	.923	17	0	12	1	1
Gordon, Birmingham	.909	43	3	27	3	2
Gubicza, Jacksonville	.925	28	11	38	4	1
Guerrero, Orlando*	.969	24	6	25	1	3
Harris, Chattanooga	.867	9	4	9	2	1
Harsh, Jacksonville	.952	18	8	12	1	0
Harvey, Birmingham*	1.000	17	1	1	0	0
Heathcock, Columbus	.962	14	8	17	1	2
Heinkel, Birmingham	.981	30	19	32	1	3
Hernaiz, Nashville	1.000	7	3	7	0	2
Hernandez, Nashville*	1.000	5	0	7	0	0
Hesketh, Memphis	1.000	11	5	15	0	0
Hobbs, Orlando*	.931	31	5	22	2	2
Hudson, Chattanooga	.933	7	3	11	1	0
Huismann, Jacksonville	.938	37	2	13	1	1
Hunger, Chattanooga	1.000	6	1	0	0	0
G. Johnson, Memphis	1.000	9	3	6	0	1
J. Johnson, Savannah	.970	26	10	22	1	1
Jones, Savannah	.900	27	9	18	3	1
Kelly, Birmingham	.500	4	1	1	2	0
Key, Knoxville*	.865	14	7	25	5	0
J. King, Charlotte	1.000	6	1	5	0	0
M. King, Nashville*	1.000	6	0	4	0	0
Kinnunen, Memphis*	.947	38	5	13	1	3
Knudson, Columbus	1.000	13	7	10	0	1
Konopa, 4 Orl.-8 Char.*	1.000	12	3	5	0	0
Korczyk, Orlando	.889	14	3	5	1	1
Kromy, Orlando	.903	29	5	23	3	0
Krueger, Orlando	.800	46	8	16	6	2
Krzanik, Memphis	.857	41	4	2	1	1
Kucharski, Charlotte	.941	27	13	35	3	2
Langston, Chattanooga*	.894	28	8	51	7	4
Leiter, Charlotte	.895	11	6	11	2	0
Little, Orlando*	1.000	10	0	2	0	1
Long, Chattanooga	.750	33	4	5	3	1
MacDonald, Columbus	.971	27	9	25	1	4
Marietta, Charlotte	1.000	9	1	4	0	1
Martin, Chattanooga	.950	45	8	11	1	2
Martinez, Jacksonville	1.000	6	1	1	0	0
Mason, Birmingham	.931	17	16	11	2	1
McCullock, Charlotte	1.000	6	0	1	0	1
McKnight, Knoxville	.848	30	7	32	7	0
Meckes, Columbus	.871	45	7	20	4	0
Mitcheltree, Charlotte	.900	61	4	14	2	1
Neely, Memphis	1.000	5	0	3	0	0
Nielson, Chattanooga	1.000	13	3	16	0	0
NORTH, Savannah	1.000	23	11	19	0	0
Oliveras, Charlotte	.882	25	5	25	4	2
Olson, Jacksonville	.958	11	4	19	1	3
Olwine, Nashville*	.867	29	5	8	2	1
Owens, Chattanooga	.800	7	2	2	1	0
Pacella, Charlotte	1.000	10	0	3	0	0
Paris, Columbus	.941	23	11	21	2	3
Patterson, Nashville	.909	13	7	13	2	1
Payne, Savannah	1.000	25	3	26	0	4
Pena, Orlando*	.889	27	5	11	2	4
Perry, Columbus*	1.000	11	3	5	0	1
Pettaway, Nashville	1.000	16	0	5	0	0
Pettibone, Orlando	.921	26	14	21	3	1
Phillips, Knoxville	1.000	11	1	2	0	0
Pladson, 7 Col.-4 Mem.	.913	11	12	9	2	0
Raftice, Nashville*	1.000	13	1	2	0	0
Randolph, Chattanooga	.833	9	1	9	2	0
Rasmussen, Nashville*	1.000	13	9	10	0	0
Ray, Jacksonville	.943	26	10	23	2	4
Regalado, Columbus	.879	14	11	18	4	3
Reish, Knoxville	.826	38	5	14	4	1
Riggins, Charlotte*	1.000	5	0	4	0	1
Rijo, Nashville	1.000	5	6	1	0	1
Robbins, Birmingham*	.840	16	3	18	4	2
Rooney, Charlotte*	1.000	4	0	4	0	1
Ross, Columbus	1.000	13	3	2	0	0
Rowe, Chattanooga	.946	20	13	22	2	0
Saberhagen, Jacksonville	1.000	11	11	9	0	1
Schattinger, Birmingham	1.000	6	2	1	0	0
Schuler, Memphis	1.000	30	5	10	0	3
Scott, Nashville	.936	26	13	31	3	2
Shaw, Jacksonville	.893	16	5	20	3	0
Shiflett, Nashville*	.918	24	9	47	5	2
Shimp, Memphis	1.000	19	7	9	0	0
Shipanoff, Knoxville	1.000	61	6	7	0	0
Silva, Nashville	1.000	37	4	11	0	0
Smith, Columbus	.875	18	4	10	2	0
Snell, Charlotte	1.000	15	0	6	0	0
Snyder, Columbus	.909	28	13	17	3	2
Sprowl, Columbus*	1.000	29	2	11	0	0
Steger, Chattanooga	1.000	13	5	6	0	2

PITCHERS—Continued

Player and Club	Pct.	G.	PO.	A.	E.	DP.
Stemberger, Knoxville	.923	16	2	10	1	1
Stottlemyre, Chattanooga	1.000	46	9	17	0	2
Strode, Jacksonville*	.833	25	6	9	3	1
Sutton, Chattanooga	1.000	10	1	3	0	0
Szymczak, Nashville	1.000	11	2	8	0	1
Tabor, Birmingham	.912	31	9	22	3	2
Taylor, Memphis*	.938	23	2	13	1	0
Tenenini, Memphis	1.000	49	5	15	0	1
Tewksbury, Nashville	.938	7	7	8	1	0
Torres, Memphis	.946	21	13	22	2	2
Treadway, Savannah	.958	32	7	16	1	2
Valenzuela, Knoxville	.846	28	4	7	2	0
Veselic, Columbus	1.000	9	1	5	0	0
Waddell, Savannah	1.000	29	4	2	0	1
Walker, Knoxville*	.833	13	3	7	2	0
Ward, Birmingham*	.978	26	13	31	1	1
Werly, Nashville	.833	11	7	3	2	0
Whitmer, Chattanooga	.939	26	19	27	3	3
M. Williams, Memphis	.950	9	7	12	1	1
Willis, Birmingham	.857	14	1	5	1	0
Wills, Jacksonville	.909	8	1	9	1	1
Willsher, Charlotte	.957	23	7	15	1	0
Wong, Jacksonville	.895	50	3	14	2	0
Yanus, Memphis	.889	8	2	6	1	0
Yenser, Memphis	1.000	5	3	7	0	0
Yett, Orlando	.867	24	7	19	4	0

The following players do not have any recorded accepted chances at the positions indicated and therefore are not listed in the fielding averages for those particular positions: Acker, p; Arney, p; K. Baker, p; Blume, of; Borucki, ss; Coffman, p; Cole, 2b; Cuervo, ss; Curry, 1b; Damon, of; A. Davis, of; Dempsey, of; Dennis, p; Falcone, of; Foussianes, of; Garcia, p; Hill, p; Lowry, of; Monteleone, p; Moya, p; Perez, p; Pirruccello, 1b, c; Rios, 3b; Showalter, p; Sodders, of; Stefero, of; Strucher, ss; Teegarden, p; Thompson, 3b; D. Williams, p.

CLUB PITCHING

Club	ERA.	G.	CG.	ShO.	Sv.	IP.	H.	R.	ER.	HR.	HB.	BB.	Int. BB.	SO.	WP.	Bk.
Jacksonville	3.55	145	27	11	32	1254.2	1145	605	495	89	39	578	30	773	58	9
Nashville	3.56	147	63	13	12	1240.2	1188	605	491	85	35	488	11	708	64	11
Birmingham	3.69	147	35	12	30	1267.0	1253	610	519	119	35	579	19	789	55	8
Savannah	4.10	145	32	11	26	1210.2	1248	647	552	92	32	494	19	792	55	4
Columbus	4.13	143	31	12	23	1220.0	1239	697	560	89	31	619	40	668	85	2
Knoxville	4.20	147	29	9	27	1229.2	1234	692	574	96	23	562	28	750	60	7
Orlando	4.24	145	23	5	33	1240.2	1293	685	585	102	24	558	16	749	70	3
Memphis	4.24	146	29	2	21	1235.1	1227	710	582	119	35	636	39	803	77	11
Charlotte	4.44	146	26	10	27	1237.1	1300	726	610	121	27	610	38	682	58	19
Chattanooga	4.78	143	25	6	28	1210.0	1348	799	642	66	56	619	23	644	77	16

PITCHERS' RECORDS

(Leading Qualifiers for Earned-Run Average Leadership—117 or More Innings)

*Throws lefthanded.

Pitcher—Club	W.	L.	Pct.	ERA.	G.	GS.	CG.	GF.	ShO.	Sv.	IP.	H.	R.	ER.	HR.	HB.	BB.	Int. BB.	SO.	WP.
Mason, Birmingham	7	4	.636	2.06	17	17	4	0	1	0	126.2	116	45	29	10	7	43	0	83	3
Tenenini, Memphis	6	6	.500	2.51	49	3	0	26	0	2	122.0	113	43	34	8	0	50	9	64	5
Scott, Nashville	14	7	.667	2.92	26	26	12	0	3	0	188.0	189	74	61	11	4	48	0	113	5
Gubicza, Jacksonville	14	12	.538	3.08	28	28	5	0	0	0	196.0	146	81	67	10	4	93	5	146	14
Strode, Jacksonville*	7	5	.583	3.20	25	18	3	5	1	0	118.0	98	58	42	9	5	50	1	95	4
Comstock, Birmingham	12	3	.800	3.21	37	14	4	12	3	1	145.2	130	58	52	14	2	63	0	136	5
Burke, Nashville	12	4	.750	3.21	20	20	8	0	2	0	129.0	124	63	46	5	2	37	0	64	6
Heinkel, Birmingham	19	6	.760	3.39	30	30	13	0	2	0	207.1	212	87	78	26	5	57	2	113	9
Cerutti, Knoxville*	9	13	.409	3.43	29	28	9	1	3	1	188.2	182	89	72	16	1	65	3	131	10
Shiflett, Nashville*	11	6	.647	3.45	24	24	11	0	3	0	151.1	134	73	58	8	1	68	0	76	3
North, Savannah	9	7	.563	3.48	23	23	7	0	2	0	145.0	136	66	56	7	1	60	2	78	6

Departmental Leaders: G—Mitcheltree, Shipanoff, 61; W—Heinkel, 19; L—Oliveras, 14; Pct.—Comstock, Waddell, .800; GS—Heinkel, 30; CG—Heinkel, 13; GF—Shipanoff, 46; ShO—by several players, 3; Sv.—Shipanoff, 18; IP—Heinkel, 207.1; H—Heinkel, 212; R—Cates, 105; ER—Cates, 89; HR—Heinkel, 26; HB—Wong, 9; BB—Ward, 109; IBB—Tenenini, 9; SO—Gubicza, 146; WP—Snyder, 21.

(All Pitchers—Listed Alphabetically)

Pitcher—Club	W.	L.	Pct.	ERA.	G.	GS.	CG.	GF.	ShO.	Sv.	IP.	H.	R.	ER.	HR.	HB.	BB.	Int. BB.	SO.	WP.
Abone, Memphis	2	0	1.000	0.00	4	1	1	2	1	1	9.1	3	1	0	0	0	5	0	9	0
Acker, Columbus*	0	1	.000	4.26	1	1	0	0	0	0	6.1	8	3	3	0	0	1	1	1	0
Alvarez, Jacksonville	6	7	.462	2.07	30	6	1	23	0	11	87.0	76	31	20	5	2	30	2	47	1
Arias, Charlotte	1	1	.500	7.81	12	1	0	4	0	0	27.2	34	25	24	4	3	17	0	10	3
Arney, Orlando	0	1	.000	7.53	3	3	0	0	0	0	14.1	20	13	12	1	1	9	0	14	1
Arnold, Charlotte	7	5	.583	3.29	44	2	0	26	0	12	106.2	122	47	39	2	0	36	7	48	1
Baker, Birmingham*	0	0	.000	9.00	1	0	0	1	0	0	1.0	3	1	1	0	0	0	0	0	0
Bargar, Memphis	4	4	.500	3.05	8	8	5	0	0	0	59.0	51	25	20	0	4	28	0	50	6
Bersano, Nashville	0	1	.000	3.38	10	1	0	5	0	1	26.2	28	10	10	2	4	9	1	8	0
Blackmon, Knoxville	7	12	.368	3.83	29	23	5	1	1	0	157.1	153	93	67	12	1	58	0	79	9
Boris, Orlando	1	3	.250	5.19	13	0	0	7	0	2	26.0	29	18	15	3	1	10	0	16	1
Bradley, Charlotte	1	0	1.000	6.94	9	0	0	6	0	0	11.2	18	11	9	0	0	10	1	8	0
Brennan, Chattanooga*	2	1	.667	3.57	13	0	0	5	0	0	22.2	26	9	9	1	0	7	2	13	2
Broersma, Orlando	5	1	.833	3.15	31	0	0	19	0	8	60.0	45	21	21	4	4	22	1	38	5
Browning, Nashville	5	7	.417	4.64	22	0	0	17	0	0	33.0	35	18	17	5	3	17	4	22	5
Burden, Chattanooga	2	0	1.000	0.90	4	0	0	2	0	0	10.0	12	2	1	0	0	4	0	6	1
Burke, Nashville	12	4	.750	3.21	20	20	8	0	2	0	129.0	124	63	46	5	2	37	0	64	6
Butler, Charlotte*	1	2	.333	5.95	16	0	0	8	0	1	19.2	21	14	13	3	1	11	1	4	0
Cabassa, Charlotte*	1	2	.333	6.69	18	2	0	7	0	1	36.1	44	33	27	7	0	21	0	18	1
Cahill, Chattanooga	4	6	.400	6.86	26	11	0	6	0	0	85.1	129	80	65	4	3	37	0	17	3
Calhoun, Columbus	6	11	.353	4.64	27	25	4	1	1	0	151.1	157	103	78	15	4	83	1	93	16
Callahan, Nashville	2	0	1.000	1.50	2	2	2	0	1	0	18.0	17	3	3	0	0	7	0	5	0
Cary, Birmingham*	6	8	.429	3.61	17	17	5	0	1	0	104.2	103	50	42	14	4	42	0	69	3
Cates, Memphis	7	12	.368	5.21	28	28	6	0	0	0	153.2	147	105	89	24	2	96	2	92	10
Cerutti, Knoxville*	9	13	.409	3.43	29	28	9	1	3	1	188.2	182	89	72	16	1	65	3	131	10
Chapin, Memphis	0	7	.000	6.24	10	10	1	0	0	0	49.0	61	43	34	8	4	30	1	30	2
Clarke, Knoxville*	2	4	.333	2.49	26	0	0	17	0	4	43.1	30	18	12	2	1	20	2	51	4
Clay, Savannah	5	2	.714	4.18	21	5	1	9	0	1	71.0	74	38	33	4	5	29	2	23	3
Coffman, Nashville	0	0	.000	16.20	1	0	0	1	0	0	1.2	4	3	3	1	0	0	0	0	1
Cole, Savannah*	2	1	.667	4.29	16	0	0	12	0	2	21.0	13	10	10	4	2	17	0	22	0
Comstock, Birmingham	12	3	.800	3.21	37	14	4	12	3	1	145.2	130	58	52	14	2	63	0	136	5
Cullen, Knoxville	0	0	.000	11.05	9	0	0	5	0	1	7.1	8	10	9	0	0	10	0	6	3
S. Davis, Knoxville*	1	3	.250	6.95	4	4	1	0	0	0	22.0	26	17	17	2	0	14	0	18	2
T. Davis, Birmingham	0	0	.000	5.74	7	3	0	1	0	0	26.2	37	19	17	6	0	16	1	13	0
Dedmon, Savannah	4	1	.800	2.88	21	0	0	12	0	3	50.0	46	18	16	3	2	16	1	26	2

Pitcher—Club	W.	L.	Pct.	ERA.	G.	GS.	CG.	GF.	ShO.	Sv.	IP.	H.	R.	ER.	HR.	HB.	BB.	Int. BB.	SO.	WP.
Dennis, Knoxville	0	0	.000	0.00	1	0	0	1	0	0	1.1	0	0	0	0	0	0	0	0	0
K. Dixon, Charlotte	8	7	.533	3.95	20	20	6	0	2	0	130.0	123	64	57	12	3	70	4	73	5
T. Dixon, Birmingham	7	6	.538	4.07	40	3	0	19	0	7	95.0	95	50	43	6	5	57	3	71	10
Dooner, Savannah	4	6	.400	4.97	48	0	0	27	0	8	83.1	103	52	46	4	6	23	4	49	1
Dukes, Chattanooga*	4	8	.333	4.91	36	14	3	16	0	5	102.2	99	63	56	8	5	77	2	54	10
Eichhorn, Knoxville	6	12	.333	4.33	21	20	3	1	0	0	120.2	124	65	58	17	1	47	0	54	4
Engle, Charlotte*	2	2	.500	7.23	7	3	0	2	0	0	18.2	23	16	15	2	0	14	0	7	0
Esquer, Knoxville	6	7	.462	5.27	21	15	2	4	0	0	100.2	134	70	59	4	5	33	0	74	4
Everett, Columbus	0	3	.000	10.24	9	0	0	3	0	0	19.1	28	22	22	1	0	18	0	6	1
Faulk, Nashville	0	0	.000	4.50	4	0	0	2	0	0	8.0	3	4	4	0	1	7	2	2	1
Ferreira, Jacksonville*	7	11	.389	4.22	35	20	5	8	1	2	136.1	122	77	64	7	4	68	5	85	5
Fischer, Jacksonville	3	3	.500	3.83	16	0	0	7	0	0	56.1	61	27	24	5	2	26	2	37	0
Fisher, Savannah	8	11	.421	5.22	27	27	3	0	1	0	150.0	172	101	87	16	3	56	0	103	4
Foley, Columbus	4	3	.571	3.34	36	0	0	28	0	8	70.0	51	31	36	5	1	56	6	56	5
Furman, Birmingham	2	1	.667	6.94	9	1	0	7	0	1	11.2	13	10	9	2	0	7	0	5	3
Garcia, Birmingham*	0	1	.000	54.00	1	0	0	0	0	0	0.1	2	2	2	0	0	0	0	0	0
J. Gibson, Savannah*	2	2	.500	4.11	46	0	0	18	0	3	76.2	81	48	35	4	5	46	2	46	6
P. Gibson, Orlando*	1	7	.125	6.10	40	5	0	16	0	3	76.2	91	59	52	8	1	56	2	45	7
Giordano, Orlando	3	2	.600	1.05	31	0	0	23	0	12	43.0	33	6	5	0	0	13	2	29	3
Glasscock, Memphis*	2	4	.333	4.35	44	3	0	21	0	2	72.1	66	40	35	5	5	40	3	61	8
Gonzalez, Charlotte*	10	6	.625	3.32	17	17	3	0	0	0	105.2	88	49	39	10	1	71	2	105	9
Gordon, Birmingham	9	5	.643	3.42	43	2	2	30	1	10	102.2	104	50	39	8	1	23	4	50	2
Gubicza, Jacksonville	14	12	.538	3.08	28	28	5	0	0	0	196.0	146	81	67	10	4	93	5	146	14
Guerrero, Orlando*	7	13	.350	4.78	24	24	4	0	1	0	130.0	154	78	69	10	2	64	1	90	8
Harris, Chattanooga	2	5	.286	5.91	9	9	1	0	0	0	56.1	68	53	37	5	7	39	1	29	6
Harsh, Jacksonville	3	3	.500	3.26	18	9	1	2	0	1	80.0	76	37	29	5	4	37	2	31	5
Harvey, Birmingham*	3	2	.600	4.13	17	1	0	10	0	3	28.1	29	14	13	4	0	15	3	17	0
Heathcock, Columbus	4	4	.500	2.27	14	13	6	1	3	1	91.1	82	32	23	3	3	22	2	69	2
Heinkel, Birmingham	19	6	.760	3.39	30	30	13	0	2	0	207.1	212	87	78	26	5	57	2	113	9
Hernaiz, Nashville	2	3	.400	3.54	7	4	0	1	0	0	28.0	27	11	11	2	0	8	0	14	4
Hernandez, Nashville*	1	2	.333	6.00	5	5	0	0	0	0	24.0	27	19	16	2	1	17	0	14	3
Hesketh, Memphis	6	4	.600	3.04	11	11	4	0	0	0	74.0	82	38	25	4	1	25	0	22	1
Hill, Chattanooga	0	0	.000	0.00	1	0	0	1	0	0	0.1	1	0	0	0	0	1	0	0	0
Hobbs, Orlando*	4	8	.333	4.15	31	12	3	10	0	1	123.2	142	72	57	13	3	52	1	64	8
Hudson, Chattanooga	2	3	.400	5.66	7	7	1	0	0	0	35.0	43	27	22	3	2	15	0	19	1
Huismann, Jacksonville	6	3	.667	3.23	37	0	0	31	0	10	61.1	60	25	22	1	3	25	3	46	6
Hunger, Chattanooga	0	0	.000	13.50	6	0	0	2	0	0	7.1	18	15	11	1	0	7	0	4	3
G. Johnson, Memphis	2	4	.333	5.08	9	5	3	1	0	0	39.0	39	27	22	5	3	20	1	15	1
J. Johnson, Savannah	10	9	.526	3.78	26	26	7	0	2	0	157.1	162	82	66	9	2	59	3	94	8
Jones, Savannah	11	7	.611	4.59	27	24	7	2	1	0	137.1	144	79	70	20	3	46	1	106	7
Kelly, Birmingham	1	2	.333	4.68	4	4	0	0	0	0	25.0	23	17	13	2	1	22	0	20	0
Key, Knoxville*	6	5	.545	2.85	14	14	2	0	0	0	101.0	86	35	32	4	5	40	1	57	6
J. King, Charlotte	2	1	.667	5.34	6	5	2	0	0	0	32.0	32	20	19	7	1	12	0	19	1
M. King, Nashville*	3	3	.500	3.51	6	6	2	0	0	0	41.0	37	20	16	1	0	25	0	34	1
Kinnunen, Memphis*	6	4	.600	2.57	38	0	0	22	0	6	63.0	52	29	18	8	0	27	3	46	4
Knudson, Columbus	4	5	.444	4.26	13	13	3	0	0	0	69.2	82	40	33	8	2	21	1	28	3
Konopa, 4 Orl.-8 Char.*	2	4	.333	7.36	12	5	0	1	0	0	33.0	40	29	27	1	2	26	1	24	3
Korczyk, Orlando	2	1	.667	0.71	15	0	0	13	0	2	25.1	26	5	2	1	0	10	0	14	0
Kromy, Orlando	7	10	.412	4.00	29	25	5	1	1	0	157.2	157	81	70	9	3	46	0	80	7
Krueger, Orlando	4	7	.364	3.83	46	1	0	22	0	1	115.0	119	62	49	8	4	49	6	64	3
Krzanik, Memphis	3	6	.333	4.21	41	0	0	28	0	6	68.1	74	34	32	7	0	30	7	49	7
Kucharski, Charlotte	9	13	.409	3.93	27	27	6	0	2	0	185.2	181	97	81	14	1	73	6	86	4
Langston, Chattanooga*	14	9	.609	3.59	28	28	10	0	0	0	198.0	187	104	79	8	8	102	6	142	13
Leiter, Charlotte	4	4	.500	4.48	11	10	3	0	1	0	64.1	70	35	32	2	2	24	4	23	6
Little, Orlando*	0	0	.000	2.89	10	0	0	7	0	3	9.1	5	3	3	0	0	8	0	11	2
Long, Chattanooga	4	5	.444	3.33	33	0	0	27	0	12	48.2	31	21	18	2	5	26	3	44	2
MacDonald, Columbus	4	6	.400	3.47	27	11	3	10	0	2	109.0	108	59	42	10	3	37	1	60	3
Marietta, Charlotte	1	2	.333	5.84	9	2	0	5	0	0	12.1	18	13	8	1	2	8	1	5	3
Martin, Chattanooga	4	7	.364	5.20	45	3	0	22	0	3	88.1	107	64	51	9	1	50	4	51	7
Martinez, Jacksonville	0	0	.000	9.82	6	0	0	3	0	1	7.1	10	8	8	1	0	5	0	5	3
Mason, Birmingham	7	4	.636	2.06	17	17	4	0	1	0	126.2	116	45	29	10	7	43	0	83	3
McCullock, Charlotte	0	0	.000	1.74	6	0	0	4	0	0	10.1	8	4	2	2	0	5	1	8	1
McKnight, Knoxville	8	12	.400	4.13	30	28	5	1	1	1	172.0	162	97	79	12	2	107	3	96	8
Meckes, Columbus	5	9	.357	4.63	45	0	0	28	0	5	89.1	95	53	46	7	3	53	8	51	6
Mitcheltree, Charlotte	6	2	.750	4.16	61	4	0	33	0	8	127.2	131	74	59	11	5	59	4	80	6
Monteleone, Birmingham	1	1	.500	7.20	3	3	0	0	0	0	15.0	25	12	12	4	0	6	0	9	0
Moya, Birmingham	0	0	.000	12.00	1	1	0	0	0	0	3.0	5	4	4	0	1	4	0	2	1
Neely, Memphis	0	1	.000	9.35	5	0	0	0	0	0	8.2	9	15	9	3	0	9	1	4	1
Nielson, Chattanooga	2	4	.333	6.39	13	9	1	2	0	0	63.1	81	49	45	2	2	27	1	24	7
North, Savannah	9	7	.563	3.48	23	23	7	0	2	0	145.0	136	66	56	7	1	60	2	78	6
Oliveras, Charlotte	8	14	.364	4.64	25	25	5	0	2	0	151.1	173	94	78	23	3	73	3	89	5
Olson, Jacksonville	5	3	.625	2.62	11	11	3	0	2	0	82.1	80	29	24	5	0	25	1	38	1
Olwine, Nashville*	2	4	.333	4.35	29	6	1	9	0	0	82.2	90	53	40	7	5	38	1	66	6
Owens, Chattanooga	1	3	.250	4.94	7	2	0	1	0	0	23.2	29	15	13	1	2	9	0	14	0
Pacella, Charlotte	0	5	.000	6.35	10	6	0	2	0	0	28.1	34	30	20	2	2	28	0	17	6
Paris, Columbus	7	6	.538	5.79	23	16	1	3	0	0	107.1	106	78	69	10	4	72	3	63	6
Patterson, Nashville	8	4	.667	2.75	13	13	8	0	0	0	98.1	88	37	30	4	4	30	0	40	6
Payne, Savannah	10	7	.588	3.91	25	24	4	1	2	0	145.0	144	71	63	5	1	80	1	97	10
Pena, Orlando*	6	10	.375	5.47	27	22	2	4	0	1	121.2	140	90	74	11	1	67	0	73	5
Perez, Jacksonville	0	0	.000	0.00	1	0	0	0	0	0	0.0	1	3	3	0	0	2	0	0	0
Perry, Columbus*	5	2	.714	4.04	11	7	0	1	0	0	49.0	60	30	22	1	1	21	1	27	3
Pettaway, Nashville	2	2	.500	4.50	16	0	0	13	0	2	28.0	26	17	14	3	2	12	2	19	2
Pettibone, Orlando	13	7	.650	3.97	25	25	4	0	2	0	161.0	157	78	71	17	2	61	1	105	3
Phillips, Knoxville	1	1	.500	11.17	11	1	0	5	0	0	19.1	31	24	24	5	0	20	0	9	0
Pladson, 7 Col.-4 Mem.	2	7	.222	5.69	11	10	0	0	0	0	61.2	71	43	39	8	1	30	0	34	2
Raftice, Nashville*	0	2	.000	9.53	13	0	0	9	0	2	11.1	14	12	12	1	0	14	0	11	1
Randolph, Chattanooga	1	4	.200	7.14	9	9	0	0	0	0	46.2	53	50	37	4	3	32	1	26	2
Rasmussen, Nashville*	6	4	.600	4.88	13	12	4	1	0	1	75.2	77	47	41	8	3	27	0	54	6
Ray, Jacksonville	5	7	.417	5.54	26	18	2	4	0	0	115.1	142	87	71	14	3	62	3	44	5
Regalado, Columbus	4	6	.400	3.58	14	12	2	0	0	0	75.1	72	39	30	4	1	34	1	16	5
Reish, Knoxville	7	4	.636	5.03	38	0	0	15	0	2	59.0	66	38	33	4	1	38	8	33	4
Riggins, Charlotte*	0	2	.000	7.66	5	4	1	0	0	0	22.1	28	20	19	7	0	10	1	7	1

Pitcher—Club	W.	L.	Pct	ERA.	G.	GS.	CG.	GF.	ShO.	Sv.	IP.	H.	R.	ER.	HR.	HB.	BB.	Int. BB.	SO.	WP.
Rijo, Nashville	3	2	.600	2.68	5	5	3	0	0	0	40.1	31	12	12	1	0	22	0	32	0
Robbins, Birmingham*	4	6	.400	5.12	16	16	1	0	1	0	82.2	97	55	47	6	2	57	0	44	6
Rooney, Charlotte*	0	4	.000	9.20	4	4	0	0	0	0	14.2	25	16	15	2	0	7	0	6	1
Ross, Columbus	1	1	.500	2.63	13	0	0	10	0	5	27.1	27	8	8	0	0	16	3	12	2
Rowe, Chattanooga	8	6	.571	3.49	20	19	5	1	0	0	121.1	113	56	47	5	5	47	0	69	5
Saberhagen, Jacksonville	6	2	.750	2.91	11	11	2	0	1	0	77.1	66	31	25	7	1	29	2	48	2
Schattinger, Birmingham	1	0	1.000	1.23	6	0	0	4	0	0	7.1	2	1	1	0	1	8	1	2	0
Schuler, Memphis	1	5	.167	5.00	30	0	0	12	0	2	54.0	56	33	30	7	3	41	8	43	2
Scott, Nashville	14	7	.667	2.92	26	26	12	0	3	0	188.0	189	74	61	11	4	48	0	113	5
Shaw, Jacksonville	5	7	.417	4.43	16	16	3	0	1	0	105.2	102	60	52	10	1	69	2	68	6
Shiflett, Nashville*	11	6	.647	3.45	24	24	11	0	3	0	151.1	134	73	58	8	1	68	0	76	3
Shimp, Memphis	7	4	.636	3.56	19	13	3	1	0	1	103.2	98	48	41	6	3	31	1	77	3
Shipanoff, Knoxville	6	3	.667	3.36	61	0	0	46	0	18	69.2	53	32	26	3	3	51	7	73	3
Showalter, Nashville	0	0	.000	9.00	1	0	0	1	0	0	1.0	2	1	1	0	0	0	0	1	1
Silva, Nashville	5	1	.833	3.11	37	3	2	23	1	6	81.0	74	41	28	6	1	37	1	53	3
Smith, Columbus	1	1	.500	4.12	18	0	0	9	0	0	43.2	47	21	20	6	1	26	1	40	4
Snell, Charlotte	1	0	1.000	0.00	15	1	0	14	0	5	22.2	15	0	0	0	0	6	1	7	1
Snyder, Columbus	7	13	.350	3.70	28	28	8	0	3	0	175.1	177	101	72	13	5	84	3	53	21
Sprowl, Columbus*	6	2	.750	4.47	29	2	1	18	0	2	44.1	41	25	22	1	2	34	6	37	5
Steger, Chattanooga	0	0	.000	5.95	13	0	0	7	0	1	19.2	29	19	13	1	0	13	0	13	0
Stemberger, Knoxville	0	1	.000	8.44	16	0	0	5	0	0	26.2	31	27	25	2	0	20	0	10	1
Stottlemyre, Chattanooga	7	6	.538	6.08	46	6	0	19	0	5	97.2	125	78	66	6	4	39	1	37	7
Strode, Jacksonville*	7	5	.583	3.20	25	18	3	5	1	0	118.0	98	58	42	9	5	50	1	95	4
Sutton, Chattanooga	1	0	1.000	3.60	10	0	0	7	0	2	15.0	15	8	6	0	1	8	1	6	0
Szymczak, Nashville	1	2	.333	6.09	11	2	0	2	0	0	34.0	50	29	23	3	0	17	0	6	4
Tabor, Birmingham	6	5	.545	3.15	31	9	2	19	1	6	111.1	101	45	39	6	4	43	4	67	1
Taylor, Memphis*	6	7	.462	4.84	23	23	0	0	0	0	115.1	103	68	62	5	3	106	0	126	9
Teegarden, Nashville	0	0	.000	0.00	2	0	0	0	0	0	6.2	3	4	0	0	0	5	0	4	1
Tenenini, Memphis	6	6	.500	2.51	49	3	0	26	0	2	122.0	113	43	34	8	0	50	9	64	5
Tewksbury, Nashville	5	1	.833	2.82	7	7	3	0	0	0	51.0	49	20	16	6	1	10	0	15	0
Torres, Memphis	6	8	.429	4.08	21	21	3	0	1	0	123.2	124	67	56	14	4	45	0	67	4
Treadway, Savannah	8	9	.471	4.37	32	16	3	7	1	2	129.2	141	71	63	15	1	49	2	108	7
Valenzuela, Knoxville	0	1	.000	4.48	28	2	0	15	0	0	64.1	72	40	32	8	2	21	2	26	1
Veselic, Columbus	4	2	.667	4.31	9	9	3	0	2	0	48.0	57	29	23	0	0	23	2	27	2
Waddell, Savannah	8	2	.800	1.42	29	0	0	25	0	7	44.1	32	11	7	1	1	13	1	40	1
Walker, Knoxville*	5	4	.556	3.42	13	12	2	1	1	0	76.1	76	37	29	5	1	18	2	33	1
Ward, Birmingham*	10	3	.769	4.12	26	26	4	0	1	0	150.2	139	81	69	11	2	109	1	71	10
Werly, Nashville	6	3	.667	3.18	11	11	7	0	1	0	82.0	59	34	29	9	3	33	0	55	5
Whitmer, Chattanooga	10	8	.556	3.54	26	26	4	0	2	0	168.0	182	86	66	6	8	79	1	76	8
D. Williams, Birmingham	0	0	.000	0.00	2	0	0	1	0	0	1.2	1	0	0	0	0	0	0	4	0
M. Williams, Memphis	2	3	.400	3.41	9	9	2	0	0	0	58.0	54	31	22	7	3	18	2	25	4
Willis, Birmingham	3	1	.750	3.98	14	0	0	8	0	2	20.1	16	9	9	0	0	7	0	13	2
Wills, Jacksonville	5	2	.714	2.48	8	8	2	0	0	0	54.1	44	19	15	3	1	23	1	40	4
Willsher, Charlotte	6	4	.600	4.34	23	12	0	8	0	0	91.1	94	52	44	10	2	42	1	51	3
Wong, Jacksonville	5	3	.625	3.38	50	0	0	35	0	7	77.1	61	32	29	7	9	34	1	43	2
Yanus, Memphis	0	0	.000	9.37	8	2	0	4	0	1	16.1	31	21	17	4	0	8	1	4	2
Yenser, Memphis	1	3	.250	5.86	5	5	1	0	0	0	27.2	34	22	18	1	0	15	0	14	7
Yett, Orlando	8	10	.444	3.78	24	24	5	0	0	0	162.0	153	82	68	16	1	78	2	93	15

BALKS—Gonzalez, 9; Shiflett, 6; Dukes, 5; Gubicza, 4; Heinkel, Schuler, Whitmer, 3 each; Chapin, Fisher, Langston, McKnight, Oliveras, Pacella, Strode, Tabor, Torres, Walker, 2 each; Arnold, Blackmon, Brennan, Cary, Cates, K. Dixon, Dooner, Giordano, Gordon, Guerrero, Hernandez, Hesketh, Key, Konopa, Kucharski, Leiter, Martin, Mason, Meckes, Pena, Perry, Raftice, Randolph, Rijo, Saberhagen, Shimp, Shipanoff, Steger, Stottlemyre, Sutton, Szymczak, Taylor, Treadway, Werly, Wills, Willsher, Wong, 1 each.

COMBINATION SHUTOUTS—Mason-Furman, Birmingham; Snell-Arnold, Gonzalez-Mitcheltree, Kucharski-Willsher-Cabassa, Charlotte; Rowe-Martin, Hudson-Martin, Rowe-Long, Whitmer-Long, Chattanooga; Regalado-MacDonald-Sprowl, Knudson-Ross, Paris-Ross, Columbus; Gubicza-Huismann, Gubicza-Wong, Harsh-Ray-Huismann, Harsh-Huismann, Harsh-Wong, Jacksonville; Key-Shipanoff, Key-Clarke, Eichhorn-Reish, Knoxville; Hernaiz-Raftice, Burke-Faulk, Nashville; Guerrero-Giordano, Orlando; Johnson-Waddell, Clay-Waddell, Savannah.

NO-HIT GAMES—Ferreira, Jacksonville, defeated Knoxville, 6-0, July 9; Veselic, Columbus, defeated Nashville, 2-0, August 25.

Texas League

CLASS AA

Leading Batter
EARNEST RILES
El Paso

League President
CARL SAWATSKI

Leading Pitcher
SID FERNANDEZ
San Antonio

CHAMPIONSHIP WINNERS IN PREVIOUS YEARS

Year	Club	Pct.
1888	Dallas	.671
1889	Houston	.551
1890	Galveston	.705
1892	Houston	.741
	Houston	.613
1895	Dallas	.754
	Fort Worth*	.750
1896	Fort Worth	.757
	Houston*	.679
	Galveston	.548
1897	San Antonio†	.657
	Galveston†	.717
1898	League disbanded.	
1899	Galveston	.632
	Galveston	.762
1900-01	Did not operate.	
1902	Corsicana	.866
	Corsicana	.682
1903	Paris-Waco	.615
	Dallas*	.648
1904	Corsicana*	.615
	Fort Worth	.800
1905	Fort Worth	.545
1906	Fort Worth	.677
	Cleburne x	.609
1907	Austin	.629
1908	San Antonio	.664
1909	Houston	.601
1910	Dallas†	.586
	Houston†	.586
1911	Austin	.575
1912	Houston	.626
1913	Houston	.620
1914	Houston†	.671
	Waco†	.671
1915	Waco	.592
1916	Waco	.587
1917	Dallas	.600
1918	Dallas	.584
1919	Shreveport*	.677
	Fort Worth	.651
1920	Fort Worth	.703
	Fort Worth	.750
1921	Fort Worth	.691
	Fort Worth	.662
1922	Fort Worth	.694
	Fort Worth	.711
1923	Fort Worth	.632
1924	Fort Worth	.689
	Fort Worth	.763
1925	Fort Worth	.711
	Fort Worth y	.653
1926	Dallas	.574
1927	Wichita Falls	.654
1928	Houston*	.679
	Wichita Falls	.731
1929	Dallas*	.588
	Wichita Falls	.620
1930	Wichita Falls	.697
	Fort Worth*	.632
1931	Houston a	.625
	Houston	.734
1932	Beaumont*	.640
	Dallas	.727
1933	Houston	.623
	San Antonio (4th)§	.523
1934	Galveston‡	.579
1935	Oklahoma City‡	.590
1936	Dallas	.604
	Tulsa (3rd)§	.519
1937	Oklahoma City	.635
	Fort Worth (3rd)§	.535
1938	Beaumont	.635
1939	Houston	.606
	Fort Worth (4th)§	.540
1940	Houston‡	.652
1941	Houston	.673
	Dallas (4th)§	.519
1942	Beaumont	.605
	Shreveport (2nd)§	.576
1943-44-45	Did not operate.	
1946	Fort Worth	.656
	Dallas (2nd)§	.591
1947	Houston‡	.623
1948	Fort Worth‡	.601
1949	Fort Worth	.649
	Tulsa (2nd)§	.584
1950	Beaumont	.595
	San Antonio (4th)§	.513
1951	Houston‡	.619
1952	Dallas	.571
	Shreveport (3rd)§	.522
1953	Dallas‡	.571
1954	Shreveport	.559
	Houston (2nd)§	.553
1955	Dallas	.581
	Shreveport (3rd)§	.540
1956	Houston‡	.623
1957	Dallas	.662
	Houston (2nd)§	.630
1958	Fort Worth	.582
	Cor. Christi (3rd)§	.507
1959	Victoria	.589
	Austin (2nd)§	.548
1960	Rio Grande Valley	.590
	Tulsa (3rd)	.528
1961	Amarillo	.643
	San Antonio (3rd)§	.532
1962	El Paso	.571
	Tulsa (2nd)§	.550
1963	San Antonio	.564
	Tulsa (3rd)§	.529
1964	San Antonio‡	.607
1965	Tulsa	.574
	Albuquerque b	.550
1966	Arkansas	.579
1967	Albuquerque	.557
1968	Arkansas	.586
	El Paso b	.562
1969	Amarillo	.593
	Memphis b	.504
1970	Albuquerque a	.615
	Memphis	.507
1971	Did not operate as league—clubs were members of Dixie Association.	
1972	Alexandria	.600
	El Paso b	.557
1973	San Antonio	.590
	Memphis b	.558
1974	Victoria b	.581
	El Paso	.555
1975	Lafayette c	.558
	Midland c	.604
1976	Amarillo b	.600
	Shreveport	.515
1977	El Paso	.600
	Arkansas d	.485
1978	El Paso d	.593
	Jackson	.567
1979	Arkansas d	.571
	Midland	.563
1980	Arkansas d	.596
	San Antonio	.544
1981	San Antonio	.571
	Jackson d	.507
1982	El Paso	.559
	Tulsa d	.515

*Won split-season playoff. †No playoff for title. ‡Finished first and won four-club playoff. §Won four-club playoff. xTitle to Cleburne by default. yTied with Dallas in second half and won playoff for championship. zFort Worth disbanded. aTied with Beaumont at end of first half and won title in best-of-five series played as part of second half schedule. bLeague divided into Eastern, Western divisions; won two-team playoff. cLeague divided into Eastern, Western divisions; declared co-champions when playoffs were not completed. dLeague divided into Eastern and Western divisions and played split-season; won playoffs. NOTE—Championship awarded to winner of four-team playoff, 1933-51; first-place team and playoff winner co-champions, 1952-64.

STANDING OF CLUBS AT CLOSE OF FIRST HALF, JUNE 18

EASTERN DIVISION

Club	W.	L.	T.	Pct.	G.B.
Jackson (Mets)	37	30	0	.552	....
Shreveport (Giants)	36	32	0	.529	1½
Tulsa (Rangers)	30	37	0	.448	7
Arkansas (Cardinals)	30	38	0	.441	7½

WESTERN DIVISION

Club	W.	L.	T.	Pct.	G.B.
Beaumont (Padres)	37	30	0	.552	....
El Paso (Brewers)	35	33	0	.515	2½
San Antonio (Dodgers)	33	34	0	.493	4
Midland (Cubs)	32	36	0	.471	5½

STANDING OF CLUBS AT CLOSE OF SECOND HALF, AUGUST 31

EASTERN DIVISION

Club	W.	L.	T.	Pct.	G.B.
Arkansas (Cardinals)	39	29	0	.574	....
Shreveport (Giants)	36	32	0	.529	3
Tulsa (Rangers)	33	36	0	.478	6½
Jackson (Mets)	32	37	0	.464	7½

WESTERN DIVISION

Club	W.	L.	T.	Pct.	G.B.
El Paso (Brewers)	39	29	0	.574	....
San Antonio (Dodgers)	33	36	0	.478	6½
Midland (Cubs)	31	37	0	.456	8
Beaumont (Padres)	31	38	0	.449	8½

COMPOSITE STANDINGS OF CLUBS AT CLOSE OF SEASON, AUGUST 31

EASTERN DIVISION

Club	Shrev.	Ark.	Jax.	Tul.	Beau.	EIP.	Mid.	S.A.	W.	L.	T.	Pct.	G.B.
Shreveport (Giants)	....	18	15	18	6	5	6	4	72	64	0	.529	....
Arkansas (Cardinals)	14	....	20	15	7	3	7	3	69	67	0	.507	3
Jackson (Mets)	17	12	....	18	3	6	7	6	69	67	0	.507	3
Tulsa (Rangers)	14	17	14	....	2	4	6	6	63	73	0	.463	9

WESTERN DIVISION

Club	EIP.	Beau.	S.A.	Mid.	Ark.	Jax.	Shrev.	Tul.	W.	L.	T.	Pct.	G.B.
El Paso (Brewers)	....	16	16	20	7	4	5	6	74	62	0	.544	....
Beaumont (Padres)	16	....	17	13	3	7	4	8	68	68	0	.500	6
San Antonio (Dodgers)	16	15	....	14	7	4	6	4	66	70	0	.485	8
Midland (Cubs)	12	19	18	....	3	3	4	4	63	73	0	.463	11

Arkansas club represented Little Rock, Ark.

Major league affiliations in parentheses.

Playoffs—Beaumont defeated El Paso, two games to one; Jackson defeated Arkansas, two games to none; and Beaumont defeated Jackson, three games to none, to win league championship.

Regular-Season Attendance—Arkansas, 214,460; Beaumont, 129,214; El Paso, 282,272; Jackson, 105,456; Midland, 124,144; San Antonio, 100,283; Shreveport, 41,963; Tulsa, 92,347. Total, 1,090,139. Playoffs, 16,299. All-Star Game, 8,093.

Managers: Arkansas, Nick Leyva; Beaumont, Jack Maloof; El Paso, Tony Muser and Lee Sigman; Jackson, Bob Schaefer; Midland, Tom Harmon; San Antonio, Terry Collins (½ season), and co-managers Rick Ollar and Dave Wallace; Shreveport, Duane Espy; Tulsa, Marty Scott.

All-Star Team: 1B—Ponce, El Paso; 2B—Brooks, Midland; 3B—Max, El Paso; SS—Riles, El Paso; OF—Buckley, Tulsa; Reynolds, San Antonio; Kruk, Beaumont; C—Gibbons, Jackson; DH—Gillaspie, Beaumont; LHP—Fernandez, San Antonio; RHP—Georger, Jackson; Manager of the Year—Nick Leyva, Arkansas.

CLUB BATTING

Club	Pct.	G.	AB.	R.	OR.	H.	TB.	2B.	3B.	HR.	RBI.	GW.	SH.	SF.	HP.	BB.	Int. BB.	SO.	SB.	CS.	LOB.
El Paso	.314	136	4666	953	948	1464	2209	261	38	136	871	68	36	58	29	666	20	703	223	76	1032
San Antonio	.2864	136	4496	711	715	1288	1922	220	54	102	634	61	41	41	35	490	25	611	152	55	973
Beaumont	.2861	136	4547	793	774	1301	1961	278	50	94	703	61	47	63	42	578	28	678	135	65	1023
Midland	.281	136	4530	806	834	1273	1933	231	57	105	725	56	35	55	45	609	21	803	238	86	972
Jackson	.277	136	4501	693	686	1246	1776	201	28	91	629	63	15	58	39	487	17	775	157	76	936
Arkansas	.270	136	4420	652	629	1195	1681	218	26	72	572	63	46	39	30	475	29	656	155	79	915
Shreveport	.267	136	4293	676	647	1147	1838	226	18	143	621	62	25	41	35	606	23	827	115	57	954
Tulsa	.266	136	4410	687	738	1173	1916	212	33	155	641	59	42	35	49	557	26	820	151	74	952

INDIVIDUAL BATTING

(Leading Qualifiers for Batting Championship—367 or More Plate Appearances)

*Bats lefthanded. †Switch-hitter.

Player and Club	Pct.	G.	AB.	R.	H.	TB.	2B.	3B.	HR.	RBI.	GW.	SH.	SF.	HP.	BB.	Int. BB.	SO.	SB.	CS.
Riles, Earnest, El Paso*	.349	130	476	109	166	242	31	3	13	91	7	1	4	3	86	5	54	9	11
Ponce, Carlos, El Paso	.348	129	506	114	176	299	50	5	21	111	8	1	8	2	45	3	57	16	8
Kruk, John, Beaumont*	.341	133	498	94	170	259	41	9	10	88	4	4	13	2	69	1	54	13	5
Reynolds, Robert, San Antonio†	.337	133	504	103	170	255	25	3	18	89	10	2	2	1	55	2	60	43	8
Max, William, El Paso	.336	121	456	117	153	272	27	4	28	112	12	3	3	3	74	0	91	6	3
Christensen, John, Jackson	.3333	109	405	76	135	201	26	2	12	72	11	0	6	6	48	3	53	12	6
Gillaspie, Mark, Beaumont†	.3326	131	454	94	151	264	35	3	24	122	13	0	6	8	99	14	109	10	4
Paciorek, James, El Paso	.326	118	435	90	142	195	24	1	9	85	4	2	2	5	56	0	64	6	1
Stevenson, John, Shreveport	.319	104	398	63	127	169	26	2	4	37	5	4	1	5	40	1	54	5	12
Tarver, LaSchelle, Jackson*	.316	121	481	95	152	175	19	2	0	36	1	2	3	2	52	3	46	16	6

Departmental Leaders: G—Schuster, 136; AB—Espy, 564; R—Hatcher, 132; H—Ponce, 176; TB—Ponce, 299; 2B—Ponce, 50; 3B—Baker, 15; HR—Deer, 35; RBI—Gillaspie, 122; GWRBI—Deer, Gillaspie, 13; SH—Tabor, 15; SF—Kruk, 13; HP—See, 16; BB—Gillaspie, 99; IBB—Gillaspie, 14; SO—Deer, 185; SB—Felder, 71; CS—Castillo, 17.

(All Players—Listed Alphabetically)

Player and Club	Pct.	G.	AB.	R.	H.	TB.	2B.	3B.	HR.	RBI.	GW.	SH.	SF.	HP.	BB.	Int. BB.	SO.	SB.	CS.
Alexander, Roberto, San Antonio	.000	60	1	0	0	0	0	0	0	0	0	0	0	0	0	0	0	0	0
Allen, Robert, San Antonio	.266	113	346	46	92	142	18	7	6	55	7	6	3	2	44	1	52	3	2
Anderson, David, San Antonio	.333	21	3	0	1	2	1	0	0	0	0	0	0	0	0	0	0	0	0
Anicich, Michael, Midland	.249	110	382	62	95	188	26	2	21	86	8	1	7	7	70	2	76	2	0
Arigoni, Scott, Arkansas*	.000	5	1	0	0	0	0	0	0	0	0	0	0	0	0	0	1	0	0
Asadoor, Randall, Tulsa	.274	46	157	15	43	79	12	0	8	28	4	1	1	1	13	1	39	2	1

Player and Club	Pct.	G.	AB.	R.	H.	TB.	2B.	3B.	HR.	RBI.	GW.	SH.	SF.	HP.	BB.	Int. BB.	SO.	SB.	CS.
Ayer, Jonathan, Arkansas	.313	110	380	58	119	171	29	1	7	55	4	1	4	7	53	5	46	17	4
Bailey, Robert, San Antonio	.232	78	185	17	43	57	5	3	1	20	3	1	2	1	20	0	18	1	2
Baker, Ricky, Midland†	.303	131	525	101	159	214	16	15	3	64	3	7	6	8	61	2	67	59	12
Ball, Robert, Tulsa	.156	50	179	24	28	39	4	2	1	10	0	3	0	0	17	1	34	20	4
Ballard, Byron, Jackson	.000	53	1	0	0	0	0	0	0	0	0	0	0	0	0	0	1	0	0
Barba, Michael, Arkansas	1.000	29	1	0	1	1	0	0	0	0	0	0	0	0	0	0	0	0	0
Barranca, German, Arkansas*	.291	32	110	19	32	53	6	0	5	19	2	0	3	0	12	2	13	8	4
Bates, Kevin, Shreveport*	.278	60	209	46	58	74	11	1	1	15	2	0	2	4	46	2	37	7	3
Batista, Francisco, Arkansas	.161	20	56	8	9	10	1	0	0	3	0	0	1	0	2	0	16	3	0
Beane, William, Jackson†	.246	121	423	53	104	153	14	1	11	75	5	1	7	2	29	1	129	5	5
Beltre, Sergio, Jackson	.250	46	172	25	43	60	7	2	2	20	0	0	3	2	12	0	41	7	3
Benson, Steve, Beaumont	.296	22	71	12	21	34	5	1	2	9	0	2	0	0	13	0	11	3	1
Beyers, Tom, San Antonio*	.309	130	498	63	154	221	34	6	7	54	8	0	0	2	28	3	34	4	3
Bishop, Michael, Jackson	.280	66	207	40	58	112	15	0	13	43	4	1	1	1	58	1	48	3	1
Blocker, Terry, Jackson*	.308	66	263	38	81	120	16	7	3	54	5	0	6	1	17	0	40	18	7
Booker, Roderick, Arkansas*	.273	127	469	75	128	158	15	3	3	60	10	6	4	2	47	2	46	20	12
Borges, George, Midland	.204	34	93	9	19	26	4	0	1	7	0	1	2	0	8	0	26	1	2
Borbon, Ernesto, San Antonio*	.000	9	1	0	0	0	0	0	0	0	0	1	0	0	0	0	0	0	0
Brooks, Fred, Midland	.268	118	440	72	118	188	28	3	12	81	8	0	6	0	65	3	75	14	10
Brower, Robert, Tulsa	.234	69	252	41	59	74	4	1	3	17	2	0	0	4	36	1	68	22	4
Brown, Christopher, Shreveport	.273	102	322	44	88	139	21	0	10	58	3	1	5	8	42	0	49	19	3
Buckley, Kevin, Tulsa	.293	134	512	73	150	280	30	2	32	104	4	1	3	4	38	2	123	4	3
Buechele, Steven, Tulsa	.277	117	437	62	121	183	12	4	14	62	5	4	6	5	54	2	69	5	5
Canady, Chuckie, Tulsa	.296	132	486	100	144	248	21	4	25	80	9	4	6	9	65	3	90	27	15
Casey, Patrick, Beaumont	.279	120	430	74	120	209	29	6	16	95	8	0	8	4	67	2	73	8	5
Castillo, Juan, El Paso†	.271	123	461	79	125	177	24	2	8	62	4	13	7	2	60	1	85	33	17
Castro, Frank, Beaumont	.250	2	8	2	2	3	1	0	0	1	0	0	0	0	0	0	1	1	0
Chaney, Bruce, Midland	.229	40	131	23	30	48	7	1	3	14	2	2	2	0	22	0	38	2	0
Christensen, John, Jackson	.333	109	405	76	135	201	26	2	12	72	11	0	6	6	48	3	53	12	6
Cowger, Tracy, Tulsa	.245	37	106	11	26	42	4	0	4	9	0	2	0	2	7	0	24	1	2
Cummings, Robert, Shreveport	.245	95	282	42	69	122	13	2	12	41	4	2	1	1	45	1	67	4	2
Davenport, Gary, Shreveport	.206	9	34	5	7	8	1	0	0	2	0	0	0	0	1	0	7	0	0
Davis, Douglas, Tulsa	.228	29	92	10	21	35	8	0	2	9	1	1	0	1	10	0	14	1	3
Davis, Stanley, El Paso*	.347	63	222	57	77	153	9	2	21	70	8	0	5	1	23	4	41	12	4
Debus, Jon, San Antonio	.269	7	26	2	7	8	1	0	0	4	0	1	0	0	1	0	4	0	0
Deer, Robert, Shreveport	.217	132	448	89	97	219	15	1	35	99	13	0	6	5	85	4	185	18	8
Dillard, Ronald, Tulsa	.241	14	29	8	7	7	0	0	0	4	0	0	0	1	4	0	4	8	1
Duff, David, Jackson	.193	62	187	16	36	47	5	0	2	18	0	0	1	1	20	0	27	1	1
Espy, Cecil, San Antonio†	.268	133	564	88	151	201	16	11	4	38	5	3	4	1	39	2	77	51	16
Felder, Michael, El Paso†	.282	133	554	108	156	226	23	10	9	78	6	2	4	3	79	1	71	71	10
Fernandez, Sid, San Antonio*	.000	24	4	0	0	0	0	0	0	0	0	0	0	0	0	0	1	0	0
Foit, James, Tulsa	.209	66	196	19	41	51	5	1	1	13	1	6	0	2	18	1	33	7	8
Garcia, Steven, Beaumont*	.291	110	440	80	128	163	16	8	1	51	9	8	8	3	30	3	35	35	7
Gergen, Robert, Tulsa	.154	4	13	3	2	5	0	0	1	1	0	0	0	0	3	0	2	0	0
Gibbons, John, Jackson	.298	110	373	63	111	192	25	1	18	67	6	0	3	9	39	2	84	6	7
Gillaspie, Mark, Beaumont†	.333	131	454	94	151	264	35	3	24	122	13	0	6	8	99	14	109	10	4
Gomez, Jorge, Tulsa	.332	87	277	55	92	180	26	1	20	61	6	2	3	4	53	2	47	2	1
Gomez, Randall, Shreveport	.278	119	418	57	116	151	18	1	5	48	5	2	8	1	47	0	41	6	3
Guillen, Oswaldo, Beaumont†	.295	114	427	62	126	160	20	4	2	48	3	11	5	0	15	2	29	7	5
Guin, Greg, Arkansas*	.332	60	199	31	66	99	11	2	6	35	4	0	0	4	23	1	18	2	1
Hall, Melvin, Midland*	.474	6	19	9	9	22	2	1	3	7	1	0	0	0	5	0	2	2	0
Hance, William, Tulsa*	.286	7	21	2	6	8	2	0	0	2	1	0	1	0	4	0	1	0	0
Harris, Michael, Arkansas	.293	73	239	29	70	78	8	0	0	13	3	4	0	0	11	0	35	10	6
Hatcher, William, Midland	.299	135	545	132	163	248	33	11	10	80	11	3	4	12	65	1	61	56	8
Hearn, Edward, Jackson	.300	5	20	4	6	7	1	0	0	2	0	0	0	0	2	0	5	1	0
Helsom, Robert, Arkansas*	.253	64	194	26	49	88	10	1	9	37	5	0	4	4	42	1	44	0	3
Henderson, Joseph, El Paso†	.278	92	291	38	81	114	14	2	5	56	3	3	6	0	48	0	75	5	4
Herr, Thomas, Arkansas†	.444	3	9	0	4	7	3	0	0	1	0	0	0	0	1	0	1	0	0
Hicks, Robert, Tulsa	.191	46	136	18	26	44	2	2	4	16	1	0	1	3	13	1	40	3	1
Hill, Anthony, Midland	.282	109	394	69	111	142	22	3	1	45	1	5	2	2	24	1	51	19	7
Holman, Dale, San Antonio*	.296	79	267	36	79	127	15	0	11	39	3	0	3	2	32	5	64	2	2
Howard, Michael, Jackson†	.267	3	15	2	4	4	0	0	0	2	1	0	0	0	2	0	2	0	0
Howell, Kenneth, San Antonio	.000	27	3	0	0	0	0	0	0	0	0	1	0	0	0	0	2	0	0
Hunsinger, Alan, Arkansas	.213	77	272	40	58	92	19	0	5	30	4	2	2	3	25	0	57	0	3
Hunt, James, Arkansas	.225	105	338	36	76	113	21	2	4	51	4	3	5	1	40	0	57	7	2
Hyman, Donald, Midland	.251	117	371	49	93	133	19	0	7	55	3	6	5	3	59	1	75	2	4
Incaviglia, Tony, Beaumont	.308	36	130	25	40	62	12	2	2	19	0	1	1	3	14	1	30	2	3
Johnson, Jerry, Beaumont	.222	3	9	1	2	2	0	0	0	0	0	0	0	0	2	0	2	1	0
Johnson, Steven, Beaumont	.233	113	377	77	88	132	13	8	5	26	7	4	2	5	66	0	105	23	16
Johnson, Thomas, Midland	.232	29	95	18	22	28	6	0	0	11	0	1	4	1	19	0	22	3	2
Johnston, Jody, San Antonio	.000	30	2	0	0	0	0	0	0	0	0	0	0	0	0	0	1	0	0
Kaczmarski, Randy, Beaumont	.205	40	112	16	23	40	4	2	3	21	1	3	2	1	15	0	7	1	2
Kain, Martin, Beaumont	.000	50	0	0	0	0	0	0	0	0	0	0	0	0	1	0	0	0	0
Kingsolver, Kurt, El Paso	.200	13	40	8	8	16	2	0	2	7	0	0	0	1	13	0	7	0	0
Kruk, John, Beaumont*	.341	133	498	94	170	259	41	9	10	88	4	4	13	2	69	1	54	13	5
Kunkel, Jeffrey, Tulsa	.285	37	130	21	37	66	14	0	5	25	4	0	2	3	4	0	24	4	2
Kyles, Stanley, Midland	.000	23	1	0	0	0	0	0	0	0	0	0	0	0	0	0	0	0	0
Larkin, Patrick, Shreveport*	.000	41	1	0	0	0	0	0	0	0	0	0	0	0	0	0	1	0	0
Lavigne, Randall, Midland	.309	116	405	71	125	195	17	7	13	72	6	2	4	6	56	0	93	27	8
Leopold, James, Beaumont	.000	26	2	0	0	0	0	0	0	0	0	0	0	0	0	0	0	0	0
Levi, Stanley, El Paso*	.295	78	278	56	82	115	15	3	4	54	4	3	1	5	35	2	26	18	3
Lezcano, Carlos, Midland	.290	71	255	44	74	134	18	3	12	42	1	0	3	1	29	2	71	8	4
Lombarski, Thomas, Midland*	.300	134	487	83	146	227	23	5	16	119	9	2	8	1	90	9	82	25	15
Long, Dennis, 30 Tulsa-13 Jack	.000	43	1	0	0	0	0	0	0	0	0	0	0	0	0	0	1	0	0
Loviglio, John, Midland	.313	35	144	22	45	57	2	2	2	13	0	2	2	1	14	0	18	10	7
Madison, Charles, San Antonio†	.305	80	259	54	79	131	11	4	11	57	9	1	5	0	47	5	27	5	1
Martin, Michael, Beaumont*	.318	57	220	41	70	108	21	1	5	32	3	2	2	1	23	2	38	1	0
Martin, Steven, San Antonio	.000	22	2	0	0	0	0	0	0	0	0	0	0	0	1	0	1	0	0
Max, William, El Paso	.336	121	456	117	153	272	27	4	28	112	12	3	3	3	74	0	91	6	3
Mazzilli, Donald, Shreveport*	.281	103	320	44	90	132	16	4	6	40	1	1	1	1	56	1	50	12	4
McGee, Willie, Arkansas†	.276	7	29	5	8	11	1	1	0	2	0	0	0	0	4	1	6	1	0
McHenry, Vance, Jackson	.269	48	171	18	46	55	4	1	1	22	5	0	1	2	15	0	20	2	1
McLaughlin, Byron, Beaumont	.000	12	2	0	0	0	0	0	0	0	0	0	0	0	0	0	2	0	0

Player and Club	Pct.	G.	AB.	R.	H.	TB.	2B.	3B.	HR.	RBI.	GW.	SH.	SF.	HP.	BB.	Int. BB.	SO.	SB.	CS.
McMullen, Ricky, Jackson	.249	71	265	38	66	83	12	1	1	25	3	5	6	1	26	1	14	4	4
Mesa, Ivan, San Antonio	.206	84	238	23	49	53	4	0	0	14	0	5	3	1	22	1	27	7	2
Mills, Gotay, Arkansas	.284	130	483	89	137	186	17	4	8	50	3	9	4	1	70	1	90	44	16
Mitchell, Kevin, Jackson	.299	120	441	75	132	206	25	2	15	85	9	1	5	2	48	1	84	11	5
Murphy, Daniel, Tulsa*	.277	120	430	72	119	181	25	5	9	55	5	0	8	2	60	7	54	13	9
Murray, Steven, Beaumont	.289	14	38	7	11	14	3	0	0	4	0	0	0	1	5	0	14	1	1
Nago, Garrett, El Paso†	.265	56	166	20	44	54	7	0	1	17	2	0	1	1	38	1	24	2	2
Neufang, Gerald, Tulsa	.230	110	326	35	75	97	10	3	2	42	5	3	2	0	60	1	36	1	3
Oberbruner, James, Beaumont	.000	15	2	0	0	0	0	0	0	0	0	0	0	0	0	0	0	0	0
O'Connor, Robert, Shreveport	.284	76	222	30	63	96	7	1	8	24	4	4	1	0	24	0	56	11	3
Ojeda, Luis, Arkansas	.269	100	316	32	85	102	15	1	0	43	4	1	3	1	33	1	32	9	6
Paciorek, James, El Paso	.326	118	435	90	142	195	24	1	9	85	4	2	2	5	56	0	64	6	1
Parent, Mark, Beaumont	.252	81	282	38	71	116	22	1	7	33	3	1	2	1	33	2	35	1	1
Patterson, Robert, Beaumont*	.333	43	3	0	1	1	0	0	0	2	1	1	0	0	0	0	2	0	0
Pederson, Stuart, San Antonio*	.308	120	406	92	125	200	21	12	10	66	3	8	3	2	74	3	69	10	5
Pedrique, Alfredo, Jackson	.239	102	326	43	78	87	7	1	0	27	2	3	5	5	35	1	33	6	6
Pendleton, Terry, Arkansas†	.276	48	185	29	51	79	10	3	4	20	2	0	1	1	9	2	26	7	3
Perry, Stephen, San Antonio	.000	15	1	0	0	0	0	0	0	0	0	0	0	0	0	0	0	0	0
Peyton, Eric, El Paso*	.343	54	210	38	72	112	8	4	8	40	5	0	2	0	13	0	32	9	2
Pierce, Walter, Arkansas	.333	23	3	1	1	2	1	0	0	0	0	0	0	0	0	0	1	0	0
Plante, Daniel, El Paso	.333	4	9	4	3	6	0	0	1	2	0	0	0	0	1	0	2	0	0
Poe, Richard, Jackson*	.180	25	89	5	16	22	3	0	1	9	1	0	2	0	8	2	18	1	2
Ponce, Carlos, El Paso	.348	129	506	114	176	299	50	5	21	111	8	1	8	2	45	3	57	16	8
Pott, Lawrence, Beaumont	.232	22	69	8	16	21	5	0	0	6	1	1	0	0	8	0	15	0	1
Purpura, Daniel, Beaumont	.265	66	230	42	61	71	10	0	0	22	1	6	1	1	45	0	31	6	4
Redfield, Joseph, Jackson	.197	36	127	16	25	37	4	1	2	12	1	0	1	1	17	0	43	0	2
Reid, Jessie, Shreveport*	.260	125	389	59	101	162	22	0	13	50	4	1	0	3	58	5	65	14	7
Reyes, Gilberto, San Antonio	.282	33	124	10	35	45	7	0	1	16	2	0	3	0	3	0	18	0	1
Reynolds, Larry, Arkansas	.238	99	303	50	72	85	6	2	1	28	8	8	4	1	22	1	28	15	10
Reynolds, Robert, San Antonio†	.337	133	504	103	170	255	25	3	18	89	10	2	2	1	55	2	60	43	8
Riles, Earnest, El Paso*	.349	130	476	109	166	242	31	3	13	91	7	1	4	3	86	5	54	9	11
Ronk, Jeffrey, Beaumont	.272	115	427	63	116	163	24	1	7	63	3	0	7	10	49	0	40	3	6
Rubel, Michael, Tulsa	.302	72	245	58	74	162	19	0	23	61	4	0	1	4	54	2	58	1	2
Rutledge, Jeffrey, Midland	.230	25	87	8	20	26	2	2	0	7	2	3	0	0	6	0	17	3	3
Salas, Mark, Arkansas*	.304	131	473	76	144	237	25	4	20	82	8	4	3	2	42	12	56	7	5
Sayler, Barry, Arkansas	.191	42	110	19	21	29	6	1	0	12	0	2	0	2	16	0	27	3	1
Schefsky, Steve, Beaumont	.000	9	1	0	0	0	0	0	0	0	0	1	0	0	0	0	0	0	0
Schuster, Mark, Shreveport*	.303	136	479	87	145	273	35	3	29	100	11	3	8	1	60	3	76	11	2
See, Laurence, San Antonio	.292	132	445	72	130	223	38	2	17	91	4	5	6	16	57	0	78	2	3
Sheehy, Mark, San Antonio	.268	123	444	70	119	153	16	3	4	39	2	5	6	5	38	0	46	19	8
Smith, Bobby, El Paso*	.322	74	295	56	95	127	14	0	6	54	2	1	5	1	41	2	38	17	2
Snyder, Bryan, Shreveport*	.242	121	426	56	103	170	24	2	13	67	7	4	3	3	54	3	88	6	7
Stassi, James, Shreveport	.273	19	44	5	12	19	1	0	2	12	1	0	1	0	4	0	2	0	1
Steels, James, Beaumont*	.268	83	313	57	84	139	17	4	10	61	4	2	6	2	24	1	43	19	4
Stevenson, John, Shreveport	.319	104	398	63	127	169	26	2	4	37	5	4	1	5	40	1	54	5	12
Stubbs, Franklin, San Antonio	.312	47	173	35	54	104	8	3	12	52	5	2	1	2	29	3	32	5	2
Sutton, Mark, Tulsa	.188	6	16	3	3	3	0	0	0	2	0	0	0	0	5	0	2	0	0
Tabor, Gregory, Tulsa	.268	112	370	57	99	132	14	8	1	40	7	15	1	4	39	2	58	30	10
Tarver, LaSchelle, Jackson*	.316	121	481	95	152	175	19	2	0	36	1	2	3	2	52	3	46	16	6
Thomas, Deron, Arkansas†	.221	33	104	9	23	27	2	1	0	7	0	4	0	1	7	0	28	0	2
Thomas, Franklin, El Paso	.315	91	267	59	84	101	13	2	0	32	3	7	9	2	54	1	36	19	9
Thurberg, Thomas, Arkansas	.333	10	3	1	1	1	0	0	0	0	0	0	0	0	0	0	2	0	0
Toerner, Sean, Shreveport	.236	92	301	49	71	104	16	1	5	28	2	6	5	3	44	3	49	2	2
Tramble, Otis, Midland†	.333	6	24	3	8	8	0	0	0	1	0	0	0	0	1	0	4	0	1
Vanderbush, Walter, Beaumont	.000	26	2	0	0	0	0	0	0	0	0	0	0	0	0	0	2	0	0
Wabeke, Douglas, Arkansas	.273	24	77	14	21	29	8	0	0	21	1	1	1	0	7	0	3	0	1
Wallace, Timothy, Arkansas	.483	8	29	3	14	18	4	0	0	6	0	0	0	0	1	0	8	0	0
Walsh, James, Midland	.273	35	132	31	36	49	6	2	1	21	1	0	0	3	15	0	25	5	3
Winningham, Herman, Jackson*	.354	78	288	54	102	139	13	6	4	41	7	1	3	1	43	1	44	17	7
Wolters, Michael, Arkansas	.135	16	37	2	5	5	0	0	0	6	1	1	0	0	8	0	17	2	0
Woodward, James, Jackson	.207	83	246	32	51	76	5	1	6	22	2	1	5	3	16	1	42	7	3

The following pitchers, listed alphabetically by club, with games in parentheses, had no plate appearances, primarily through use of designated hitters:

ARKANSAS—Adams, John (23); Brito, Jose (3); Carranza, Javier (9); Clark, Terry (52); Cox, Danny (11); Gotay, Ruben (16); Johnson, Jerry (22); Kepshire, Kurt (19); Martin, John (2); Morlock, Allan (6); Pimentel, Rafael (5); Rhodes, Michael (13); Thomas, William (14); Winfield, Steven (55); Worrell, Todd (10).

BEAUMONT—Coffman, James (9); Gerhardt, William (2); Hardwick, Willie (17); Hayward, Raymond (10); Long, William (10); Ricci, Frank (24); Smith, Wesley (9); Stablein, George (5); Towers, Kevin (3); Vosberg, Edward (1); Williamson, Mark (47).

EL PASO—Alicea, Miguel (11); Bradley, Leonard (4); Burns, Daniel (11); Candiotti, Thomas (7); Clutterbuck, Bryan (27); Crews, Timothy (27); Duquette, Bryan (37); Effrig, Mark (12); Gallo, Raymond (43); Grier, David (13); Hinrichs, Phillip (18); Kranitz, Richard (6); Lazorko, Jack (46); McCoy, Kevin (14); Parrott, Stephen (36); Quinones, Rene (23); Schroeck, Robert (21); Wood, Johnson (2).

JACKSON—Anderson, Richard (13); Bettendorf, Jeffrey (6); Bullinger, Matthew (27); Georger, Joseph (26); Huffman, Phillip (17); Kolbe, Brian (13); Latham, William (12); Lockenmeyer, Mark (23); McDowell, Roger (27); Miller, Thomas (9); Myles, Rick (5); Randolph, Robert (5); Schilling, Robert (27); Schiraldi, Calvin (7); Semprini, John (30); Vaughn, DeWayne (12).

MIDLAND—Banks, Darryl (27); Boudreau, James (3); Bryant, Neil (10); Buonantony, Richard (4); Capel, Michael (3); Gerlach, James (45); Gil, Carlos (30); Housey, Joseph (7); Johnson, William (45); Millner, Timothy (13); Pryce, Kenneth (24); Richardson, Ronald (22); Soff, Raymond (45); Welenc, Douglas (26); Wright, James (12).

SAN ANTONIO—Felt, Richard (16); Grant, Mark (26); Hammond, Shayne (18); Jones, Charles (12); Kenyon, Robert (14); Klawitter, Thomas (7); Madden, Morris (27); Meeks, Timothy (1); Moscaret, Jeffrey (36); Tejeda, Felix (3).

SHREVEPORT—Barling, Glenn (5); Biggus, Bengie (24); Blobaum, Jeffrey (23); Brecht, Michael (1); Chamberlain, Craig (17); Gendron, Robert (25); Grant, Mark (26); Lusted, Charles (6); Manderfield, Steven (3); McKenna, Kevin (23); Reelhorn, Jonathan (3); Schafer, Dennis (6); Violette, John (54); Weibel, Randy (6); Wilhelmi, David (23); Williams, Franklin (21).

TULSA—Brosious, Frank (6); Buckley, John (24); Clark, Robert (23); Cook, Glen (11); Fossas, Emilio (24); Hartman, Albert (19); Henry, Dwayne (9); Henry, Timothy (10); Hudson, Anthony (29); Johnson, Terrance (4); Killingsworth, Kirk (22); Leach, Martin (13); McLane, Larry (47); Mengwasser, Bradley (4); Smith, Daryl (6); Taylor, William (21); Teutsch, Mark (7); Zwolensky, Mitchell (26).

GRAND SLAM HOME RUNS—Felder, 3; Gillaspie, J. Gomez, Ponce, Snyder, 2 each; Asadoor, Barranca, Beane, Brooks, Buechele, Gibbons, Helsom, Henderson, Hunsinger, Lavigne, Madison, Nago, Schuster, See, Steels, 1 each.

AWARDED FIRST BASE ON CATCHER'S INTERFERENCE—Schuster 3 (Hunt, D. Davis, Duff); S. Davis 2 (M. Martin, R. Gomez); Sheehy (Hunt, M. Martin); Casey (Hyman); Chaney (Henderson); Foit (M. Martin); Guin (D. Davis); Hyman (Reyes); Mills (Gibbons); Murphy (R. Gomez.)

CLUB FIELDING

Club	Pct.	G.	PO.	A.	E.	DP.	PB.
Shreveport	.9699	136	3385	1448	150	109	12
Arkansas	.9698	136	3450	1433	152	149	22
Jackson	.9687	136	3479	1544	162	114	9
El Paso	.9636	136	3488	1518	189	126	40
Midland	.9634	136	3487	1541	191	141	22
Tulsa	.9632	136	3448	1474	188	125	10
San Antonio	.962	136	3394	1428	190	123	33
Beaumont	.961	136	3467	1405	197	125	19

Triple plays—Midland 2, Beaumont, Tulsa.

INDIVIDUAL FIELDING

*Throws lefthanded.

FIRST BASEMEN

Player and Club	Pct.	G.	PO.	A.	E.	DP.
Anicich, Midland	.981	88	831	66	17	77
Ayer, Arkansas	.989	26	171	10	2	19
Bailey, San Antonio	.967	24	76	11	3	8
Beane, Jackson	.970	23	213	17	7	13
Beyers, San Antonio*	.982	60	440	44	9	35
Bishop, Jackson	.998	54	481	47	1	40
K. Buckley, Tulsa	.982	74	612	56	12	63
Casey, Beaumont	.980	114	1010	58	22	95
Christensen, Jackson	.988	36	307	26	4	24
Duff, Jackson	1.000	13	84	6	0	2
Guin, Arkansas*	.993	48	388	30	3	31
Hearn, Jackson	.971	3	33	1	1	4
Holman, San Antonio	.967	22	137	11	5	12
Hunsinger, Arkansas	.992	40	354	15	3	42
Tom Johnson, Midland	.977	25	244	9	6	18
Kruk, Beaumont*	.990	12	90	9	1	5
Lombarski, Midland	.986	24	192	13	3	24
J.M. Martin, Beaumont	.949	4	37	0	2	4
Max, El Paso	.923	1	12	0	1	0
Murphy, Tulsa*	.978	11	81	7	2	5
Poe, Jackson*	1.000	17	112	11	0	12
Ponce, El Paso	.982	126	1133	69	22	99
Pott, Beaumont	1.000	1	6	0	0	0
Purpura, Beaumont	1.000	1	10	0	0	1
Redfield, Jackson	1.000	1	8	1	0	0
Rubel, Tulsa	.987	54	504	39	7	39
Sayler, Arkansas	.981	40	290	16	6	35
SCHUSTER, Shreveport*	.988	136	1201	91	16	89
See, San Antonio	.982	7	52	4	1	6
Steels, Beaumont*	.981	6	48	3	1	6
Stubbs, San Antonio	.989	44	418	23	5	46
F. Thomas, El Paso	1.000	11	99	5	0	13
Wolters, Arkansas	1.000	1	2	0	0	1

Triple plays—K. Buckley, Casey, T. Johnson.

SECOND BASEMEN

Player and Club	Pct.	G.	PO.	A.	E.	DP.
Allen, San Antonio	1.000	5	11	13	0	4
Barranca, Arkansas	1.000	11	19	20	0	8
Bates, Shreveport	.959	33	55	84	6	21
Benson, Beaumont	.955	6	9	12	1	3
Booker, Arkansas	.985	28	42	87	2	17
Brooks, Midland	.967	110	231	352	20	73
Buechele, Tulsa	.964	74	145	176	12	45
Castillo, El Paso	.957	112	247	360	27	79
Dillard, Tulsa	1.000	9	10	22	0	4
Felder, El Paso	1.000	2	2	6	0	0
Garcia, Beaumont	.970	37	72	89	5	13
Harris, Arkansas	.846	4	5	6	2	2
Herr, Arkansas	1.000	3	4	9	0	2
Hill, Midland	1.000	2	8	6	0	1
Kaczmarski, Beaumont	1.000	1	0	2	0	1
Loviglio, Midland	.955	26	34	94	6	13
McHenry, Jackson	1.000	1	3	3	0	0
McMullen, Jackson	.974	67	146	191	9	30
Mesa, San Antonio	.969	20	25	38	2	10
Mills, Arkansas	1.000	3	2	0	0	0
O'Connor, Shreveport	.900	27	32	58	10	4
Pedrique, Jackson	.986	33	67	78	2	13
Pendleton, Arkansas	.970	48	94	135	7	28
Purpura, Beaumont	.963	29	60	71	5	18
Ronk, Beaumont	.954	68	150	183	16	40
SHEEHY, San Antonio	.979	117	240	315	12	74
Sutton, Tulsa	1.000	5	8	12	0	5
Tabor, Tulsa	.975	59	129	178	8	44
D. Thomas, Arkansas	.944	33	66	85	9	29
F. Thomas, El Paso	.950	28	56	76	7	11
Toerner, Shreveport	.975	86	166	231	10	43
Wabeke, Arkansas	.960	12	15	33	2	3
Wolters, Arkansas	1.000	11	21	36	0	5
Woodward, Jackson	.961	48	90	134	9	30

Triple plays—Brooks, Buechele, Purpura.

THIRD BASEMEN

Player and Club	Pct.	G.	PO.	A.	E.	DP.
Allen, San Antonio	.950	9	3	16	1	1
Asadoor, Tulsa	.882	39	25	65	12	6
Ayer, Arkansas	.955	9	9	12	1	4
Barranca, Arkansas	1.000	7	3	15	0	2
Bates, Shreveport	.958	7	2	21	1	2
Benson, Beaumont	1.000	2	0	4	0	0
Bishop, Jackson	1.000	6	4	2	0	1
Booker, Arkansas	.903	29	16	40	6	7
Brown, Shreveport	.935	99	63	182	17	8
Buechele, Tulsa	.952	46	37	83	6	7
Casey, Beaumont	1.000	1	0	1	0	0
Chaney, Midland	.900	3	3	6	1	1
Christensen, Jackson	.846	9	7	15	4	1
Cowger, Tulsa	.818	4	4	5	2	0
Garcia, Beaumont	.925	50	40	84	10	8
Gergen, Tulsa	1.000	3	0	10	0	0
J. Gomez, Tulsa	.930	48	36	83	9	8
Henderson, El Paso	.857	6	0	6	1	0
Hill, Midland	.933	23	19	37	4	2
Howard, Jackson	1.000	1	0	1	0	1
Hyman, Midland	1.000	3	4	4	0	0
J. Johnson, Beaumont	1.000	3	0	2	0	0
Kaczmarski, Beaumont	.929	25	19	33	4	3
LOMBARSKI, Midland	.939	100	67	179	16	21
Loviglio, Midland	.966	10	4	24	1	2
Madison, San Antonio	.800	3	1	3	1	0
Max, El Paso	.915	111	92	166	24	24
Mesa, San Antonio	1.000	4	3	6	0	1
Mitchell, Jackson	.933	114	70	224	21	18
O'Connor, Shreveport	.915	41	22	53	7	3
Ojeda, Arkansas	.960	89	67	149	9	16
Pedrique, Jackson	1.000	3	1	7	0	1
Pott, Beaumont	1.000	3	3	5	0	0
Purpura, Beaumont	.933	20	10	46	4	4
Ronk, Beaumont	.941	36	33	78	7	3
Rubel, Tulsa	.714	1	1	4	2	1
See, San Antonio	.884	126	98	191	38	14
Tabor, Tulsa	1.000	1	0	1	0	0
F. Thomas, El Paso	.983	27	23	35	1	0
Tramble, Midland	.857	1	1	5	1	1
Wabeke, Arkansas	.893	11	9	16	3	3
Wolters, Arkansas	.917	3	4	7	1	0
Woodward, Jackson	.927	21	8	30	3	1

Triple play—Lombarski.

SHORTSTOPS

Player and Club	Pct.	G.	PO.	A.	E.	DP.
Allen, San Antonio	.946	93	139	264	23	52
Asadoor, Tulsa	1.000	1	1	0	0	0
Barranca, Arkansas	.846	2	5	6	2	2
Bates, Shreveport	.961	20	35	38	3	10
Benson, Beaumont	.895	5	9	8	2	2
Booker, Arkansas	.966	72	95	216	11	43
Brooks, Midland	1.000	1	1	2	0	0
Castillo, El Paso	.800	2	2	2	1	0
Chaney, Midland	.922	35	65	112	15	21
Davenport, Shreveport	.962	9	18	32	2	5
Foit, Tulsa	.944	65	82	203	17	28
Garcia, Beaumont	.917	7	8	14	2	2
Gergen, Tulsa	.800	1	3	1	1	0
Guillen, Beaumont	.931	114	185	327	38	58
Harris, Arkansas	.940	66	114	197	20	45
Hill, Midland	.935	71	130	199	23	50
Howard, Jackson	1.000	1	0	1	0	0
Kunkel, Tulsa	.951	35	68	106	9	28
Lombarski, Midland	1.000	1	1	1	0	0
McHenry, Jackson	.941	42	59	117	11	20
Mesa, San Antonio	.969	51	62	125	6	22
Pedrique, Jackson	.947	68	114	207	18	36
Purpura, Beaumont	.920	15	22	59	7	13
Redfield, Jackson	.916	28	38	93	12	11
RILES, El Paso	.952	130	193	445	32	77
Rutledge, Midland	.957	25	51	81	6	23
Stevenson, Shreveport	.944	104	155	336	29	46
Tabor, Tulsa	.924	51	54	116	14	19
F. Thomas, El Paso	.898	10	18	26	5	3
Toerner, Shreveport	.824	4	8	6	3	1
Tramble, Midland	.919	5	12	22	3	8
Woodward, Jackson	1.000	4	2	10	0	2

Triple Play—Guillen.

OUTFIELDERS

Player and Club	Pct.	G.	PO.	A.	E.	DP.
Allen, San Antonio	1.000	3	3	0	0	0
Ayer, Arkansas	.969	86	119	4	4	0
Baker, Midland	.969	120	276	10	9	2
Ball, Tulsa	.981	50	100	1	2	0
Barranca, Arkansas	1.000	5	8	1	0	0
Batista, Arkansas	.978	20	42	2	1	1
BEANE, Jackson	.994	94	169	7	1	1
Beltre, Jackson	.970	38	60	5	2	2
Beyers, San Antonio*	.980	32	47	3	1	0
Blocker, Jackson*	.951	53	92	5	5	0
Brower, Tulsa	.973	67	138	4	4	1
K. Buckley, Tulsa	1.000	4	3	3	0	0
Canady, Tulsa	.948	130	230	7	13	1
Castillo, El Paso	1.000	1	1	1	0	0
Christensen, Jackson	.974	59	103	8	3	1
Cummings, Shreveport	1.000	8	3	1	0	0
S. Davis, El Paso	1.000	10	16	1	0	0
Deer, Shreveport	.974	131	252	13	7	5
Espy, San Antonio	.964	127	258	12	10	2
Felder, El Paso	.964	131	332	18	13	3
Gillaspie, Beaumont	.904	67	100	4	11	2
J. Gomez, Tulsa	.929	26	24	2	2	1
Guin, Arkansas*	1.000	4	2	2	0	0
Hall, Midland*	1.000	4	8	0	0	0
Hatcher, Midland	.959	131	286	17	13	2
Helsom, Arkansas	.972	50	65	5	2	1
Hicks, Tulsa	.910	39	69	2	7	1
Holman, San Antonio	.960	17	24	0	1	0
Howard, Jackson	1.000	3	9	1	0	0
Hunsinger, Arkansas	1.000	1	1	0	0	0
Hunt, Arkansas	1.000	2	2	0	0	0
Incaviglia, Beaumont	.926	34	60	3	5	1
S. Johnson, Beaumont	.977	113	251	9	6	2
Kruk, Beaumont*	.970	111	214	11	7	4
Lavigne, Midland	.960	64	85	10	4	5
Levi, El Paso*	.951	56	109	8	6	1
Lezcano, Midland	.985	64	121	7	2	2
Lombarski, Midland	1.000	1	1	1	0	0
Mazzilli, Shreveport*	.960	54	92	5	4	0
McGee, Arkansas	1.000	4	7	0	0	0
Mills, Arkansas	.968	129	286	13	10	3
Mitchell, Jackson	1.000	4	11	0	0	0
Murphy, Tulsa*	.985	102	187	13	3	4
Murray, Beaumont	1.000	11	20	2	0	0
Nago, El Paso	1.000	5	3	1	0	0
Paciorek, El Paso	.972	112	196	14	6	1
Pederson, San Antonio*	.984	113	169	14	3	2
Peyton, El Paso*	.965	54	101	10	4	1
Poe, Jackson*	.957	13	21	1	1	0
Redfield, Jackson	1.000	2	1	0	0	0
Reid, Shreveport*	.976	106	157	7	4	1
L. Reynolds, Arkansas	.986	90	124	12	2	4
R.J. Reynolds, San Antonio	.958	125	255	18	12	8
Salas, Arkansas	.987	47	72	5	1	1
B.G. Smith, El Paso*	.962	44	73	3	3	0
Snyder, Shreveport*	.981	119	244	12	5	6
Steels, Beaumont*	.961	76	140	7	6	1
Stubbs, San Antonio	1.000	7	7	0	0	0
Tabor, Tulsa	1.000	9	16	0	0	0
Tarver, Jackson*	.949	79	127	3	7	0
Walsh, Midland	.982	26	52	2	1	0
Winningham, Jackson	.964	76	157	5	6	1
Woodward, Jackson	1.000	8	3	0	0	0

CATCHERS

Player and Club	Pct.	G.	PO.	A.	E.	DP.	PB.
Bailey, San Antonio	.966	42	233	23	9	3	5
Borges, Midland	.948	29	116	11	7	1	3
Castro, Beaumont	.800	2	11	1	3	0	0
Cowger, Tulsa	.927	10	35	3	3	0	2
Cummings, Shreveport	1.000	12	38	6	0	1	3
D. Davis, Tulsa	.948	22	121	26	8	4	4
Debus, San Antonio	.971	6	29	5	1	0	3
Duff, Jackson	.974	41	195	30	6	1	6
Gibbons, Jackson	.982	103	575	62	12	7	3
R. Gomez, Shreveport	.982	113	699	98	15	12	7
Hance, Tulsa	1.000	6	27	2	0	0	0
Hearn, Jackson	1.000	1	7	0	0	0	0
Henderson, El Paso	.971	85	394	35	13	2	30
Hunt, Arkansas	.968	90	541	67	20	8	16
Hyman, Midland	.980	117	567	84	13	10	19
Kingsolver, El Paso	.962	13	68	8	3	1	4
Madison, San Antonio	.979	67	422	52	10	3	16
M. Martin, Beaumont	.969	45	257	23	9	2	7
Nago, El Paso	.982	44	240	32	5	5	5
Neufang, Tulsa	.977	110	606	80	16	14	4
PARENT, Beaumont	.982	79	464	71	10	3	11
Plante, El Paso	1.000	3	4	0	0	0	1
Pott, Beaumont	1.000	13	64	4	0	0	1
Reyes, San Antonio	.975	31	167	30	5	3	9
Salas, Arkansas	.990	49	262	36	3	5	4
Stassi, Shreveport	.986	12	64	4	1	0	2
Wallace, Arkansas	1.000	6	52	3	0	0	2

Triple play—Martin.

PITCHERS

Player and Club	Pct.	G.	PO.	A.	E.	DP.
Adams, Arkansas	1.000	23	2	9	0	1
Alexander, San Antonio	1.000	60	5	14	0	1
Alicea, El Paso	1.000	11	0	2	0	0
D. Anderson, San Antonio	.857	21	4	14	3	0
R. Anderson, Jackson	1.000	13	8	15	0	0
Ballard, Jackson	1.000	53	13	5	0	0
Banks, Midland	.919	27	8	26	3	2
Barba, Arkansas	.931	29	7	20	2	4
Barling, Shreveport	1.000	5	0	1	0	0
Bettendorf, Jackson	1.000	6	3	6	0	0
Beyers, San Antonio*	.000	4	0	0	1	0
Biggus, Shreveport	.952	24	13	27	2	2
Blobaum, Shreveport	1.000	23	1	4	0	0
Borbon, San Antonio*	1.000	9	0	2	0	0
Boudreau, Midland*	1.000	3	0	4	0	0
Bradley, El Paso	1.000	4	0	2	0	0
Brito, Arkansas	1.000	3	1	5	0	2
Brosious, Tulsa	.909	6	4	6	1	1
Bryant, Midland*	1.000	10	3	4	0	0
J. Buckley, Tulsa	.714	24	4	1	2	0
K. Buckley, Tulsa	1.000	4	1	2	0	1
Bullinger, Jackson*	1.000	27	1	3	0	0
Buonantony, Midland	1.000	4	2	5	0	0
Burns, El Paso	.882	11	6	9	2	1
Candiotti, El Paso	1.000	7	2	2	0	0
Capel, Midland	1.000	3	0	3	0	2
Carranza, Arkansas*	1.000	9	1	1	0	0
Chamberlain, Shreveport	.944	17	3	14	1	0
R. Clark, Tulsa*	.971	23	9	24	1	1
T. Clark, Arkansas	1.000	52	9	9	0	1
Clutterbuck, El Paso	.939	27	12	34	3	0
Coffman, Beaumont	1.000	9	1	1	0	0
Cook, Tulsa	.846	11	3	8	2	0
Cox, Arkansas	.875	11	8	13	3	1
Crews, El Paso	.964	27	6	21	1	1
Duquette, El Paso*	1.000	37	1	13	0	1
Effrig, El Paso	.875	12	1	6	1	0
Felt, San Antonio*	.953	16	9	32	2	1
Fernandez, San Antonio*	.826	24	5	14	4	1
Fossas, Tulsa*	1.000	24	5	24	0	1
Gallo, El Paso*	1.000	43	4	13	0	1
Gendron, Shreveport	.973	25	9	27	1	2
Georger, Jackson	.936	26	17	27	3	2
Gerhardt, Beaumont*	1.000	2	0	1	0	0
Gerlach, Midland	.917	45	7	15	2	1
Gil, Midland	.864	30	5	14	3	2
Gotay, Arkansas	.857	16	2	4	1	1
Grant, Shreveport	.931	26	12	15	2	0
Grier, El Paso	1.000	13	6	15	0	2
Hammond, San Antonio*	.833	18	1	4	1	0
Hardwick, Beaumont	1.000	17	5	11	0	0
Hartman, Tulsa	.895	19	8	9	2	0
Hayward, Beaumont*	1.000	10	2	14	0	0
D. Henry, Tulsa	1.000	9	1	1	0	0
T. Henry, Tulsa*	.875	10	2	5	1	0
Hinrichs, El Paso	.833	18	2	3	1	0
Housey, Midland	1.000	7	0	4	0	0
Howell, San Antonio	.912	27	16	36	5	4
Hudson, Tulsa	1.000	29	6	4	0	0
Huffman, Jackson	.957	17	9	13	1	2
J.D. Johnson, Arkansas	.957	22	9	13	1	2
Terry Johnson, Tulsa*	.750	4	0	3	1	0
W. Johnson, Midland	1.000	45	5	15	0	2
Johnston, San Antonio	.929	30	5	8	1	0
Jones, San Antonio	.889	12	2	6	1	0
Kain, Beaumont	.962	50	7	18	1	3
Kenyon, San Antonio	1.000	14	1	3	0	0
Kepshire, Arkansas	.750	19	2	4	2	0
Killingsworth, Tulsa	1.000	22	2	6	0	0
Klawitter, San Antonio*	.333	7	0	2	4	0
Kolbe, Jackson	1.000	13	2	4	0	0
Kranitz, El Paso	1.000	6	1	5	0	1
Kruk, Beaumont*	1.000	3	0	2	0	0
Kyles, Midland	.891	23	12	29	5	2

PITCHERS—Continued

Player and Club	Pct.	G.	PO.	A.	E.	DP.
Larkin, Shreveport*	1.000	41	4	12	0	1
Latham, Jackson*	1.000	12	4	17	0	1
Lazorko, El Paso	.893	46	8	17	3	3
Leach, Tulsa	.950	13	6	13	1	0
Leopold, Beaumont	.914	26	9	23	3	2
Lockenmeyer, Jackson	1.000	23	0	5	0	0
D. Long, 30 Tulsa-13 Jack.	.939	43	10	21	2	2
W. Long, Beaumont	.913	10	3	18	2	0
Lusted, Shreveport	.667	6	1	1	1	0
Madden, San Antonio*	.941	27	10	22	2	1
Manderfield, Shreveport*	1.000	3	0	1	0	0
S. Martin, San Antonio	.894	21	10	32	5	2
McCoy, El Paso	1.000	14	2	3	0	0
McDowell, Jackson	.928	27	19	45	5	5
McKenna, Shreveport	.966	23	10	18	1	2
McLane, Tulsa*	.944	47	3	14	1	1
McLaughlin, Beaumont	1.000	12	1	8	0	1
Meeks, San Antonio	1.000	1	1	1	0	0
Mengwasser, Tulsa	1.000	4	1	3	0	0
Miller, Jackson*	1.000	9	3	4	0	0
Millner, Midland	1.000	13	0	3	0	0
Morlock, Arkansas	1.000	6	2	2	0	0
Moscaret, San Antonio*	.857	36	5	7	2	0
Myles, Jackson*	1.000	5	2	3	0	0
Nago, El Paso	1.000	1	0	1	0	0
Oberbruner, Beaumont	.800	15	0	8	2	0
Parrott, El Paso	1.000	36	8	21	0	2
Patterson, Beaumont*	1.000	43	4	16	0	1
Perry, San Antonio	.917	15	1	10	1	0
Pierce, Arkansas	.943	23	10	23	2	1
Pimentel, Arkansas	1.000	5	3	2	0	1
Poe, Jackson*	1.000	2	0	1	0	0
Pryce, Midland	1.000	24	4	10	0	0
Quinones, El Paso	.867	23	11	15	4	2
Randolph, Jackson	1.000	5	2	4	0	1
Reelhorn, Shreveport	1.000	3	0	1	0	0
Rhodes, Arkansas*	.833	13	0	5	1	0
Ricci, Beaumont	.929	24	10	16	2	2
Richardson, Midland	.769	22	9	1	3	0
Schafer, Shreveport	1.000	6	3	1	0	0
Schefsky, Beaumont	1.000	9	2	3	0	0
Schilling, Jackson	1.000	27	10	19	0	2
Schiraldi, Jackson	.714	7	0	5	2	0
Schroeck, El Paso*	1.000	21	3	9	0	0
Semprini, Jackson	.900	30	4	5	1	0
D. Smith, Tulsa	1.000	6	1	2	0	0
W. Smith, Beaumont	1.000	9	0	1	0	0
Soff, Midland	.933	45	9	19	2	3
Stablein, Beaumont	1.000	5	4	5	0	1
Taylor, Tulsa	.800	21	4	4	2	0
Teutsch, Tulsa	1.000	7	2	0	0	0
W. Thomas, Arkansas	.700	14	2	5	3	1
Thurberg, Arkansas	.818	9	3	6	2	0
Towers, Beaumont	.800	3	0	4	1	0
Vanderbush, Beaumont	.920	26	8	15	2	1
Vaughn, Jackson	.765	12	4	9	4	1
Violette, Shreveport	.960	54	8	16	1	0
Vosberg, Beaumont*	1.000	1	1	2	0	0
Weibel, Shreveport	1.000	6	0	4	0	0
Welenc, Midland	.967	26	9	20	1	1
Wilhelmi, Shreveport	.958	23	10	13	1	1
Williams, Shreveport	1.000	21	4	15	0	0
Williamson, Beaumont	1.000	47	8	17	0	0
Winfield, Arkansas	.944	55	6	11	1	1
Worrell, Arkansas	.889	10	5	11	2	2
Wright, Midland	.950	12	4	15	1	0
ZWOLENSKY, Tulsa	1.000	26	13	19	0	0

The following players do not have any recorded accepted chances at the positions indicated and therefore are not listed in the fielding averages for those particular positions: Arigoni, p; Brecht, p; D. Davis, of; Duff, 3b, p; J. Gomez, p; Hicks, p; Hill, p; Howard, 1b, 2b c, p; Kaczmarski, of; Kunkel, 2b; J.R. Martin, p; McMullen, 3b; O'Connor, of; Purpura, p; Sayler, 2b; Snyder, p; Stassi, of; Tejada, p; Toerner, of; Wood, p.

CLUB PITCHING

Club	ERA.	G.	CG.	ShO.	Sv.	IP.	H.	R.	ER.	HR.	HB.	BB.	Int. BB.	SO.	WP.	Bk.
Arkansas	4.12	136	30	7	27	1150	1145	629	527	104	33	491	25	807	73	3
Shreveport	4.43	136	20	6	24	1128.1	1245	647	555	128	22	419	7	730	41	8
Jackson	4.52	136	20	7	30	1159.2	1190	686	583	107	39	569	32	729	47	9
Tulsa	4.84	136	27	9	24	1149.1	1202	738	618	99	44	583	12	760	57	7
San Antonio	4.86	136	12	6	31	1131.1	1204	715	611	89	42	691	33	805	92	12
Beaumont	5.09	136	21	7	28	1155.2	1263	774	653	79	44	612	32	759	69	6
Midland	5.56	136	18	2	18	1162.1	1354	834	718	134	46	573	30	622	82	3
El Paso	6.22	136	14	4	36	1162.2	1484	948	804	158	34	530	18	661	74	14

PITCHERS' RECORDS

(Leading Qualifiers for Earned-Run Average Leadership — 109 or More Innings)

*Throws lefthanded.

Pitcher—Club	W.	L.	Pct.	ERA.	G.	GS.	CG.	GF.	ShO.	Sv.	IP.	H.	R.	ER.	HR.	HB.	BB.	Int. BB.	SO.	WP.
Fernandez, San Antonio*	13	4	.765	2.82	24	24	4	0	1	0	153.0	111	61	48	11	8	96	0	209	4
Pierce, Arkansas	11	6	.647	3.02	23	22	6	0	2	0	146.0	143	64	49	12	3	43	1	64	2
Biggus, Shreveport	12	6	.667	3.21	24	23	6	1	1	0	165.2	175	71	59	14	2	50	1	87	6
Zwolensky, Tulsa	12	10	.545	3.33	26	24	10	1	2	1	162.1	158	81	60	10	4	61	0	101	2
R. Clark, Tulsa*	12	3	.800	3.60	23	21	5	1	3	0	145.0	126	67	58	16	1	40	0	88	4
Grant, Shreveport	10	8	.556	3.66	26	26	7	0	2	0	186.2	182	83	76	19	3	71	0	159	7
Kyles, Midland	7	11	.389	3.82	23	23	7	0	1	0	155.1	164	79	66	16	5	67	0	74	13
Huffman, Jackson	7	8	.467	3.88	17	17	5	0	1	0	113.2	105	56	49	13	5	44	2	88	6
Patterson, Beaumont*	8	4	.667	4.01	43	9	2	27	0	11	116.2	107	61	52	10	1	36	2	97	1
D. Anderson, San Antonio	8	8	.500	4.03	21	21	2	0	1	0	120.2	123	70	54	8	5	62	2	88	10

Departmental Leaders: G—Alexander, 60; W—Fernandez, Georger, 13; L—Vanderbush, 13; Pct.—R. Clark, .800; GS—Banks, Clutterbuck, Howell, 27; CG—Zwolensky, 10; GF—Alexander, 51; ShO—R. Clark, 3; Sv.—Alexander, 22; IP—Grant, 186.2; H—Crews, 207; R—Crews, 129; ER—Crews, 119; HR—Crews, 25; HB—Hartman, Winfield, 9; BB—Vanderbush, 119; IBB—Alexander, 11; SO—Fernandez, 209; WP—Vanderbush, 21.

(All Pitchers—Listed Alphabetically)

Pitcher—Club	W.	L.	Pct.	ERA.	G.	GS.	CG.	GF.	ShO.	Sv.	IP.	H.	R.	ER.	HR.	HB.	BB.	Int. BB.	SO.	WP.
Adams, Arkansas	5	10	.333	5.30	23	20	2	1	0	0	124.0	137	82	73	10	6	66	1	116	7
Alexander, San Antonio	6	5	.545	2.42	60	0	0	51	0	22	85.2	78	25	23	2	2	32	11	36	2
Alicea, El Paso	1	1	.500	9.69	11	0	0	9	0	0	13.0	28	20	14	2	0	14	0	3	3
D. Anderson, San Antonio	8	8	.500	4.03	21	21	2	0	1	0	120.2	123	70	54	8	5	62	2	88	10
R. Anderson, Jackson	5	1	.833	3.59	13	12	1	1	0	1	77.2	77	40	31	7	4	29	1	48	2
Arigoni, Arkansas*	0	3	.000	10.13	5	1	0	4	0	0	8.0	16	9	9	2	0	9	0	6	2
Ballard, Jackson	4	6	.400	4.09	53	2	0	38	0	9	99.0	88	53	45	10	2	54	5	58	9
Banks, Midland	12	11	.522	5.47	27	27	5	0	0	0	163.0	187	109	99	19	7	71	3	97	6
Barba, Arkansas	5	7	.417	4.58	29	13	2	4	1	0	120.0	117	72	61	10	5	70	1	82	9
Barling, Shreveport	0	2	.000	9.37	5	5	0	0	0	0	16.1	20	19	17	0	2	15	0	16	0
Bettendorf, Jackson	3	0	1.000	3.16	6	5	0	0	0	0	31.1	31	15	11	4	2	17	1	24	3
Beyers, San Antonio*	0	0	.000	7.36	4	0	0	4	0	0	3.2	7	3	3	0	0	0	0	2	0

Pitcher—Club	W.	L.	Pct.	ERA.	G.	GS.	CG.	GF.	ShO.	Sv.	IP.	H.	R.	ER.	HR.	HB.	BB.	Int. BB.	SO.	WP.
Biggus, Shreveport	12	6	.667	3.21	24	23	6	1	1	0	165.2	175	71	59	14	2	50	1	87	6
Blobaum, Shreveport	7	1	.875	1.31	23	0	0	21	0	5	34.1	22	5	5	2	0	10	0	36	1
Borbon, San Antonio*	1	1	.500	4.02	9	0	0	7	0	1	15.2	19	7	7	2	0	5	0	8	0
Boudreau, Midland*	3	0	1.000	3.32	3	3	0	0	0	0	19.0	21	7	7	2	0	9	0	11	2
Bradley, El Paso	0	0	.000	5.06	4	0	0	2	0	0	5.1	11	8	3	1	0	3	0	4	0
Brecht, Shreveport*	0	1	.000	....	1	1	0	0	0	0	0.0	0	1	1	0	0	1	0	0	0
Brito, Arkansas	2	1	.667	2.89	3	3	0	0	0	0	18.2	11	7	6	0	1	17	0	19	3
Brosious, Tulsa	1	5	.167	4.84	6	6	0	0	0	0	35.1	46	22	19	2	0	15	0	7	1
Bryant, Midland*	1	1	.500	7.06	10	1	0	2	0	0	21.2	15	18	17	1	1	17	0	9	3
J. Buckley, Tulsa	3	3	.500	3.79	24	0	0	15	0	3	35.2	30	16	15	6	4	16	1	16	3
K. Buckley, Tulsa	0	0	.000	5.40	4	0	0	4	0	0	5.0	7	4	3	0	0	1	0	5	0
Bullinger, Jackson*	3	1	.750	3.69	27	0	0	22	0	10	31.2	26	14	13	3	1	23	1	22	0
Buonantony, Midland	1	1	.500	5.47	4	4	0	0	0	0	24.2	24	15	15	3	0	20	0	13	3
Burns, El Paso	2	5	.286	6.59	11	9	1	1	0	1	56.0	89	51	41	7	1	9	0	30	1
Candiotti, El Paso	1	0	1.000	2.92	7	0	0	3	0	2	24.2	23	10	8	1	1	7	0	18	0
Capel, Midland	1	1	.500	6.91	3	3	0	0	0	0	14.1	22	12	11	3	0	8	0	8	2
Carranza, Arkansas*	0	0	.000	5.59	9	0	0	3	0	0	9.2	11	6	6	1	0	8	2	10	0
Chamberlain, Shreveport	3	8	.273	7.15	17	17	0	0	0	0	90.2	138	82	72	19	4	31	0	29	4
R. Clark, Tulsa*	12	3	.800	3.60	23	21	5	1	3	0	145.0	126	67	58	16	1	40	0	88	4
T. Clark, Arkansas	6	6	.500	3.21	52	0	0	39	0	15	81.1	68	31	29	9	2	19	4	63	4
Clutterbuck, El Paso	11	7	.611	5.19	27	27	4	0	1	0	166.1	204	118	96	20	2	78	2	86	13
Coffman, Beaumont	1	1	.500	8.10	9	0	0	6	0	0	16.2	31	23	15	3	0	12	1	14	2
Cook, Tulsa	4	6	.400	3.13	11	11	3	0	0	0	72.0	60	33	25	3	2	26	0	70	2
Cox, Arkansas	8	3	.727	2.29	11	11	7	0	1	0	86.1	60	31	22	4	1	24	0	73	0
Crews, El Paso	9	8	.529	6.56	27	26	2	0	0	0	163.1	207	129	119	25	4	53	0	99	6
Duff, Jackson	0	0	.000	0.00	1	1	0	0	0	0	1.0	0	0	0	0	0	3	0	0	0
Duquette, El Paso*	2	2	.500	5.83	37	0	0	26	0	9	46.1	52	35	30	10	0	30	1	36	7
Effrig, El Paso	4	2	.667	7.54	12	8	0	0	0	0	45.1	58	44	38	8	0	36	0	24	4
Felt, San Antonio*	4	4	.500	6.01	16	15	1	0	0	0	85.1	108	66	57	8	2	53	1	52	5
Fernandez, San Antonio*	13	4	.765	2.82	24	24	4	0	1	0	153.0	111	61	48	11	8	96	0	209	4
Fossas, Tulsa*	8	7	.533	4.20	24	16	6	4	1	0	133.0	123	77	62	11	3	46	0	103	3
Gallo, El Paso*	4	6	.400	7.57	43	8	0	13	0	2	82.0	117	79	69	12	1	39	2	51	11
Gendron, Shreveport	8	11	.421	4.72	25	23	5	1	0	0	139.1	165	83	73	18	1	50	0	74	4
Georger, Jackson	13	5	.722	4.44	26	18	3	3	1	0	133.2	139	75	66	11	7	57	3	88	3
Gerhardt, Beaumont*	0	0	.000	6.00	2	0	0	1	0	0	6.0	6	5	4	0	0	5	0	3	0
Gerlach, Midland	5	4	.556	5.79	45	0	0	24	0	3	91.2	106	65	59	16	5	41	3	60	9
Gil, Midland	5	6	.455	5.42	30	12	3	5	0	0	114.2	135	80	69	20	2	57	4	42	7
J. Gomez, Tulsa	0	0	.000	0.00	2	0	0	2	0	0	2.1	1	0	0	0	0	1	0	2	0
Gotay, Arkansas	0	5	.000	4.92	16	8	1	3	0	1	56.2	52	35	31	5	1	34	0	45	5
Grant, Shreveport	10	8	.556	3.66	26	26	7	0	2	0	186.2	182	83	76	19	3	71	0	159	7
Grier, El Paso	4	6	.400	7.70	13	12	1	1	0	0	66.2	109	65	57	14	0	18	0	27	2
Hammond, San Antonio*	1	1	.500	7.50	18	0	0	7	0	1	24.0	30	21	20	0	2	20	2	14	2
Hardwick, Beaumont	5	6	.455	4.71	17	14	3	0	1	0	86.0	80	53	45	6	2	53	0	65	6
Hartman, Tulsa	3	6	.333	9.40	19	14	1	2	0	0	59.1	68	70	62	6	9	73	0	26	4
Hayward, Beaumont*	5	1	.833	1.76	10	10	5	0	2	0	66.1	45	16	13	3	2	30	0	71	2
D. Henry, Tulsa	0	0	.000	5.79	9	2	0	3	0	1	14.0	16	14	9	2	0	19	0	14	0
T. Henry, Tulsa*	0	4	.000	7.07	10	8	0	1	0	0	35.2	39	36	28	3	0	45	1	29	2
Hicks, Tulsa	0	0	.000	0.00	1	0	0	1	0	0	2.0	0	0	0	0	0	1	0	0	0
Hill, Midland	0	0	.000	0.00	1	0	0	1	0	0	2.0	2	1	0	0	0	0	0	0	0
Hinrichs, El Paso	0	4	.000	6.45	18	0	0	13	0	7	22.1	31	20	16	3	0	8	1	6	2
Housey, Midland	1	4	.200	7.29	7	7	0	0	0	0	33.1	49	29	27	3	2	16	1	23	2
Howard, Jackson	0	1	.000	54.00	1	0	0	0	0	0	1.0	3	6	6	1	1	2	0	2	0
Howell, San Antonio	8	11	.421	4.41	27	27	4	0	1	0	169.1	171	98	83	11	3	101	0	116	18
Hudson, Tulsa	2	3	.400	7.20	29	0	0	20	0	6	35.0	48	32	28	6	0	22	3	18	10
Huffman, Jackson	7	8	.467	3.88	17	17	5	0	1	0	113.2	105	56	49	13	5	44	2	88	6
J. Johnson, Arkansas	6	12	.333	5.34	22	20	4	0	0	0	121.1	146	83	72	12	1	37	1	69	7
T. Johnson, Tulsa*	1	2	.333	5.40	4	4	0	0	0	0	21.2	29	15	13	1	1	12	0	19	3
W. Johnson, Midland	6	6	.500	4.81	45	0	0	38	0	13	63.2	76	39	34	4	2	31	7	22	9
Johnston, San Antonio	4	8	.333	8.11	30	14	0	11	0	0	91.0	140	84	82	14	4	57	4	47	10
Jones, San Antonio	2	2	.500	6.35	12	4	0	4	0	0	34.0	41	31	24	3	1	27	1	21	3
Kain, Beaumont	5	6	.455	3.43	50	0	0	34	0	13	86.2	97	44	33	5	0	23	6	42	3
Kenyon, San Antonio	1	3	.250	8.80	14	0	0	2	0	0	30.2	43	37	30	4	1	17	1	9	6
Kepshire, Arkansas	3	2	.600	3.53	19	0	0	14	0	4	35.2	35	17	14	5	0	5	1	23	2
Killingsworth, Tulsa	1	0	1.000	6.23	22	0	0	9	0	3	34.2	39	26	24	3	1	24	0	30	3
Klawitter, San Antonio*	1	0	1.000	6.75	7	0	0	1	0	1	17.1	21	16	13	2	2	19	0	3	1
Kolbe, Jackson	2	4	.333	8.27	13	3	0	1	0	0	32.2	44	32	30	3	0	27	1	18	1
Kranitz, El Paso	4	2	.667	2.57	6	6	3	0	0	0	42.0	39	22	12	4	3	17	0	41	0
Kruk, Beaumont*	0	0	.000	0.00	3	0	0	2	0	0	5.0	5	0	0	0	1	2	0	3	0
Kyles, Midland	7	11	.389	3.82	23	23	7	0	1	0	155.1	164	79	66	16	5	67	0	74	13
Larkin, Shreveport*	3	4	.429	1.83	41	0	0	38	0	12	54.0	51	19	11	5	0	23	2	39	2
Latham, Jackson*	4	4	.500	4.33	12	11	1	0	0	0	72.2	72	38	35	7	1	35	1	37	1
Lazorko, El Paso	7	1	.875	5.94	46	0	0	31	0	9	80.1	102	62	53	8	3	34	4	55	5
Leach, Tulsa	2	3	.400	5.47	13	3	0	3	0	1	54.1	66	38	33	4	0	21	3	23	1
Leopold, Beaumont	9	8	.529	5.96	26	25	2	0	0	0	136.0	153	106	90	14	6	89	1	60	5
Lockenmeyer, Jackson	3	3	.500	5.18	23	0	0	13	0	1	41.2	44	26	24	3	1	26	5	28	2
D. Long, 30 Tulsa-13 Jack.	3	5	.375	5.51	43	4	0	20	0	5	112.2	144	79	69	9	4	43	2	49	2
W. Long, Beaumont	2	5	.286	5.65	10	10	1	0	0	0	65.1	80	47	41	1	2	28	2	33	2
Lusted, Shreveport	1	1	.500	7.71	6	0	0	2	0	0	11.2	14	12	10	3	1	4	0	13	0
Madden, San Antonio*	6	5	.545	5.47	27	6	1	9	0	1	72.1	77	49	44	6	3	59	3	60	11
Manderfield, Shreveport*	0	0	.000	7.56	3	0	0	1	0	0	8.1	13	7	7	1	0	3	0	5	3
J. Martin, Arkansas*	1	0	1.000	3.09	2	2	0	0	0	0	11.2	13	4	4	0	0	9	0	10	1
S. Martin, San Antonio	5	10	.333	4.66	21	20	0	1	0	0	112.0	114	73	58	8	5	75	0	56	12
McCoy, El Paso	4	1	.800	8.90	14	2	0	7	0	2	31.1	43	33	31	6	2	18	0	12	4
McDowell, Jackson	11	12	.478	4.86	27	26	9	0	1	0	172.1	203	111	93	10	6	71	2	115	7
McKenna, Shreveport	3	5	.375	5.58	23	16	0	2	0	0	100.0	125	70	62	14	1	34	0	43	2
McLane, Tulsa*	4	8	.333	3.55	47	6	1	20	1	5	91.1	90	47	36	7	5	47	1	61	10
McLaughlin, Beaumont	4	2	.667	6.66	12	6	0	2	0	0	50.0	71	40	37	4	6	21	0	30	5
Meeks, San Antonio	1	0	1.000	2.57	1	1	0	0	0	0	7.0	4	2	2	1	0	2	0	3	0
Mengwasser, Tulsa	2	0	1.000	7.08	4	4	1	0	0	0	20.1	19	16	16	3	33	17	0	19	4
Miller, Jackson*	1	0	1.000	6.00	9	1	0	2	0	0	24.0	27	17	16	3	0	12	0	20	0
Millner, Midland	1	2	.333	6.68	13	0	0	6	0	0	32.1	39	32	24	3	2	19	2	23	0
Morlock, Arkansas	3	0	1.000	4.68	6	5	2	0	0	0	32.2	37	18	17	2	1	10	0	17	3
Moscaret, San Antonio*	1	4	.200	4.47	36	0	0	24	0	4	58.1	60	35	29	4	2	40	7	47	5

Pitcher—Club	W.	L.	Pct.	ERA.	G.	GS.	CG.	GF.	ShO.	Sv.	IP.	H.	R.	ER.	HR.	HB.	BB.	Int. BB.	SO.	WP.
Myles, Jackson*	1	1	.500	3.12	5	3	0	1	0	0	17.1	9	7	6	1	0	7	0	10	0
Nago, El Paso	0	0	.000	0.00	1	0	0	1	0	0	2.0	6	5	0	1	0	0	0	0	0
Oberbruner, Beaumont	1	4	.200	6.34	15	1	0	5	0	1	44.0	70	41	31	3	3	26	2	14	3
Parrott, El Paso	3	8	.273	7.11	36	9	0	10	0	2	106.1	127	91	84	13	5	60	6	53	3
Patterson, Beaumont*	8	4	.667	4.01	43	9	2	27	0	11	116.2	107	61	52	10	1	36	2	97	1
Perry, San Antonio	3	2	.600	6.28	15	3	0	3	0	1	43.0	48	33	30	4	2	20	1	31	3
Pierce, Arkansas	11	6	.647	3.02	23	22	6	0	2	0	146.0	143	64	49	12	3	43	1	64	2
Pimentel, Arkansas	2	2	.500	4.22	5	5	0	0	0	0	21.1	20	15	10	2	1	14	0	19	2
Poe, Jackson*	0	0	.000	0.00	2	0	0	1	0	0	5.0	2	0	0	0	0	0	0	4	0
Pryce, Midland	5	2	.714	3.68	24	6	0	10	0	0	80.2	95	44	33	5	2	18	4	49	0
Purpura, Beaumont	0	0	.000	24.00	1	0	0	0	0	0	3.0	10	11	8	2	0	2	0	1	0
Quinones, El Paso	12	4	.750	4.65	23	22	1	0	1	0	133.2	147	88	69	15	8	57	1	78	6
Randolph, Jackson	0	0	.000	2.40	5	2	0	3	0	1	15.0	9	4	4	1	0	11	0	2	0
Reelhorn, Shreveport	0	0	.000	6.75	3	0	0	1	0	0	4.0	4	3	3	0	1	1	0	4	1
Rhodes, Arkansas*	2	0	1.000	3.75	13	0	0	4	0	0	12.0	12	5	5	1	0	8	3	8	1
Ricci, Beaumont	6	6	.500	4.83	24	14	1	5	0	0	113.2	122	72	61	4	4	61	5	66	7
Richardson, Midland	3	10	.231	8.60	22	22	1	0	0	0	96.1	108	110	92	11	6	93	0	56	6
Schafer, Shreveport	0	0	.000	4.20	6	1	0	3	0	0	15.0	17	8	7	2	0	5	0	9	1
Schefsky, Beaumont	3	3	.500	6.98	9	9	1	0	0	0	49.0	51	40	38	4	1	36	3	24	1
Schilling, Jackson	5	9	.357	4.42	27	17	1	5	0	0	124.1	133	73	61	11	2	63	6	66	4
Schiraldi, Jackson	3	3	.500	5.82	7	7	0	0	0	0	38.2	41	28	25	2	2	29	0	26	2
Schroeck, El Paso*	6	3	.667	6.43	21	5	2	5	0	2	70.0	76	53	50	7	3	41	1	36	6
Semprini, Jackson	1	1	.500	3.68	30	0	0	18	0	6	44.0	40	30	18	7	4	29	3	37	2
D. Smith, Tulsa	0	0	.000	1.88	6	1	0	2	0	0	14.1	14	3	3	1	0	6	1	5	0
W. Smith, Beaumont	1	1	.500	8.35	9	2	0	3	0	0	18.1	29	17	17	3	3	10	1	13	3
Snyder, Shreveport*	0	0	.000	0.00	1	0	0	1	0	0	2.0	1	0	0	0	0	0	0	3	0
Soff, Midland	4	3	.571	6.84	45	3	0	30	0	2	76.1	98	63	58	9	5	37	3	41	16
Stablein, Beaumont	1	3	.250	6.14	5	5	0	0	0	0	29.1	42	20	20	1	0	13	1	14	4
Taylor, Tulsa	5	8	.385	6.87	21	12	0	3	0	0	76.0	86	65	58	7	7	51	1	75	4
Tejada, San Antonio*	1	2	.333	4.32	3	1	0	0	0	0	8.1	9	4	4	1	0	6	0	3	0
Teutsch, Tulsa	0	1	.000	6.75	7	0	0	6	0	1	9.1	14	7	7	1	0	3	0	8	0
W. Thomas, Arkansas	2	2	.500	5.22	14	8	0	3	0	0	58.2	77	45	34	8	0	26	0	20	4
Thurberg, Arkansas	2	2	.500	6.00	9	8	2	1	0	0	48.0	44	32	32	8	1	28	1	50	9
Towers, Beaumont	1	2	.333	5.52	3	3	0	0	0	0	14.2	13	13	9	0	4	14	0	9	0
Vanderbush, Beaumont	9	13	.409	5.76	26	26	5	0	1	0	159.1	159	118	102	8	6	119	3	160	21
Vaughn, Jackson	3	7	.300	6.49	12	11	0	0	0	0	61.0	76	51	44	8	1	23	0	28	4
Violette, Shreveport	7	6	.538	4.42	54	0	0	28	0	5	114.0	123	64	56	16	2	29	3	99	3
Vosberg, Beaumont*	1	0	1.000	0.00	1	1	1	0	1	0	7.0	2	0	0	0	0	2	0	1	0
Weibel, Shreveport	2	1	.667	4.61	6	1	0	2	0	0	13.2	15	7	7	2	0	6	0	2	0
Welenc, Midland	3	8	.273	6.39	26	14	2	2	0	0	98.2	131	88	70	14	4	36	1	51	3
Wilhelmi, Shreveport	9	8	.529	5.58	23	23	2	0	1	0	130.2	158	99	81	10	3	61	1	68	7
Williams, Shreveport	7	2	.778	1.71	21	0	0	15	0	2	42.0	22	14	8	3	2	25	0	54	0
Williamson, Beaumont	6	3	.667	4.03	47	1	0	30	0	3	82.2	90	45	37	8	3	30	5	39	4
Winfield, Arkansas	6	4	.600	2.98	55	0	0	30	0	7	87.2	89	40	29	6	9	27	7	39	6
Wood, El Paso	0	2	.000	22.24	2	2	0	0	0	0	5.2	15	15	14	1	1	8	0	2	1
Worrell, Arkansas	5	2	.714	3.07	10	10	4	0	0	0	70.1	57	33	24	7	1	37	3	74	6
Wright, Midland	5	3	.625	4.82	12	11	0	0	0	0	74.2	82	43	40	5	3	33	2	43	1
Zwolensky, Tulsa	12	10	.545	3.33	26	24	10	1	2	1	162.1	158	81	60	10	4	61	0	101	2

BALKS—Barling, Crews, 4 each; Ballard, Fernandez, 3 each; D. Anderson, Gallo, Howell, Johnston, Quinones, Williamson, Wright, Zwolensky, 2 each; Adams, Brosious, Candiotti, Clutterbuck, Effrig, Gendron, Gil, Gotay, Grant, Hardwick, Hartman, Huffman, Kenyon, Kolbe, D. Long, W. Long, McCoy, McDowell, McLane, Moscaret, Myles, Patterson, Perry, Pierce, Ricci, Schiraldi, Schroeck, Semprini, Taylor, Violette, Wilhelmi, Wood, 1 each.

COMBINATION SHUTOUTS—Gotay-Kepshire, Cox-Kepshire, Pierce-T. Clark, Arkansas; Vanderbush-Kain, Hayward-Patterson, Beaumont; Quinones-Lazorko 2, El Paso; McDowell-Bullinger, Vaughn-Bullinger, Huffman-Lockenmeyer-Schilling, Randolph-Lockenmeyer, Jackson; Banks-W. Johnson, Midland; S. Martin-Alexander, Fernandez-Alexander, Felt-Moscaret, San Antonio; Grant-Larkin, Biggus-Violette, Shreveport; Zwolensky-McLane, D. Henry-D. Long, Tulsa.

PERFECT GAME—Wilhelmi, Shreveport, defeated Arkansas, 7-0, May 5. (First perfect game in Texas League since 1935.)

California League

CLASS A

CHAMPIONSHIP WINNERS IN PREVIOUS YEARS

1914—Fresno	.571
1915—Modesto	.857
1916-40—Did not operate.	
1941—Fresno	.643
S. Barbara (2nd)*	.597
1942—Santa Barbara†	.642
1943-44-45—Did not operate.	
1946—Stockton‡	.600
1947—Stockton‡	.679
1948—Fresno	.607
S. Barbara (3rd)*	.529
1949—Bakersfield	.612
San Jose (4th)*	.543
1950—Ventura	.607
Modesto (2nd)*	.586
1951—Santa Barbara‡	.599
1952—Fresno‡	.629
1953—San Jose‡	.664
1954—Modesto‡	.623
1955—Stockton	.733
Fresno§	.718
1956—Fresno‡	.650
1957—Visalia x	.622
Salinas (4th)*	.504
1958—Fresno*	.639
Bakersfield	.672
1959—Bakersfield	.592
Modesto§	.643
1960—Reno	.614
Reno	.657
1961—Reno	.743
Reno	.643
1962—San Jose§	.686
Reno	.587
1963—Modesto	.589
Stockton§	.687
1964—Fresno	.638
Fresno	.600
1965—San Jose	.586
Stockton§	.614
1966—Modesto	.577
Modesto	.671
1967—San Jose§	.676
Modesto	.586
1968—San Jose	.629
Fresno§	.623
1969—Stockton§	.600
Visalia	.614
1970—Bakersfield	.667
Bakersfield	.671
1971—Visalia§	.583
Fresno	.500
1972—Modesto§	.547
Bakersfield	.629
1973—Lodi§	.657
Bakersfield	.571
1974—Fresno§	.607
San Jose	.579
1975—Reno	.614
Reno	.614
1976—Salinas	.650
Reno§	.547
1977—Salinas	.564
Lodi§	.579
1978—Visalia§	.698
Lodi	.607
1979—San Jose§	.636
Reno	.525
1980—Stockton§	.638
Visalia	.507
1981—Visalia	.621
Lodi§	.521
1982—Modesto§	.671
Visalia	.586

*Won four-club playoff. †League disbanded June 28. ‡Won championship and four-club playoff. §Won split-season playoff. xWon both halves of split-season.

STANDING OF CLUBS AT CLOSE OF FIRST HALF, JUNE 19

NORTHERN DIVISION

Club	W.	L.	T.	Pct.	G.B.
Stockton (Brewers)	44	24	0	.647	....
Modesto (A's)	39	30	0	.565	5½
Redwood (Angels)	33	35	0	.485	11
Reno (Padres)	33	36	0	.478	11½
Lodi (Dodgers)	29	39	0	.426	15

SOUTHERN DIVISION

Club	W.	L.	T.	Pct.	G.B.
Visalia (Twins)	45	25	0	.643	....
Fresno (Giants)	37	33	0	.529	8
Bakersfield (Mariners)	30	40	0	.429	15
Salinas (Cubs)	29	41	0	.414	16
San Jose (Orioles)	27	43	0	.386	18

STANDING OF CLUBS AT CLOSE OF SECOND HALF, AUGUST 28

NORTHERN DIVISION

Club	W.	L.	T.	Pct.	G.B.
Redwood (Angels)	40	30	0	.571	....
Modesto (A's)	36	34	0	.514	4
Stockton (Brewers)	35	35	0	.500	5
Lodi (Dodgers)	31	39	0	.443	9
Reno (Padres)	30	40	0	.429	10

SOUTHERN DIVISION

Club	W.	L.	T.	Pct.	G.B.
Visalia (Twins)	42	28	0	.600	....
Fresno (Giants)	41	29	0	.586	1
Bakersfield (Mariners)	38	32	0	.543	4
San Jose (Orioles)	29	41	0	.414	13
Salinas (Cubs)	28	42	0	.400	14

COMPOSITE STANDING OF CLUBS AT CLOSE OF SEASON, AUGUST 28

Club	Sto.	Mod.	Red.	Reno	Lodi	Vis.	Fr.	Bak.	Sal.	S.J.	W.	L.	T.	Pct.	G.B.
NORTHERN DIVISION															
Stockton (Brewers)	...	8	13	15	9	4	6	5	11	8	79	59	0	.572	....
Modesto (A's)	10	...	4	12	12	6	7	7	8	9	75	64	0	.540	4½
Redwood (Angels)	7	15	...	12	8	7	3	8	7	6	73	65	0	.529	6
Reno (Padres)	7	8	7	...	14	4	4	4	6	9	63	76	0	.453	16½
Lodi (Dodgers)	9	8	12	6	...	6	2	6	7	4	60	78	0	.435	19
SOUTHERN DIVISION															
Visalia (Twins)	8	6	5	8	6	...	12	14	14	14	87	53	0	.621	....
Fresno (Giants)	6	5	9	8	10	8	...	9	12	11	78	62	0	.557	9
Bakersfield (Mariners)	7	7	4	4	6	6	11	...	10	13	68	72	0	.486	19
Salinas (Cubs)	1	4	5	8	5	6	8	10	...	10	57	83	0	.407	30
San Jose (Orioles)	4	3	6	3	8	6	9	9	8	...	56	84	0	.400	31

Major league affiliations in parentheses.

Playoffs—Redwood defeated Stockton, two games to one, and defeated Visalia, three games to one, to win league championship.

Regular-Season Attendance:—Bakersfield, 95,896; Fresno, 87,174; Lodi, 67,668; Modesto, 76,664; Redwood, 41,682; Reno, 62,749; Salinas, 48,850; San Jose, 51,802; Stockton, 89,701; Visalia, 69,728. Total, 692,114.

Managers—Bakersfield, Greg Mahlberg; Fresno, Wendell Kim; Lodi, Don LeJohn; Modesto, George Mitterwald; Redwood, Jack Lind; Reno, Jim Skaalen; Salinas, George Enright; San Jose, Frank Verdi; Stockton, Terry Bevington; Visalia, Harry Warner.

All-Star Team—1B—Greg Smith, Lodi; 2B—Matt Sferrazza, Stockton; 3B—Donell Nixon, Bakersfield; SS—Alvaro Espinoza, Visalia; OF—Dave Klipstein, Stockton; Kirby Puckett, Visalia; Mike Madril, Redwood, Brian Williams, Lodi (tie); C—Matt Nokes, Fresno; P—Bill Wegman, Stockton; Tim Meeks, Lodi; Lee Guetterman, Bakersfield; Tim Kammeyer, Redwood; Manager—Harry Warner, Visalia.

(Compiled by William J. Weiss, League Statistician, San Mateo, Calif.)

CLUB BATTING

Club	Pct.	G.	AB.	R.	OR.	H.	TB.	2B.	3B.	HR.	RBI.	GW.	SH.	SF.	HP.	BB.	Int. BB.	SO.	SB.	CS.	LOB.
Visalia	.277	140	4708	717	605	1305	1804	183	32	84	635	79	62	42	35	487	31	686	159	62	1026
Reno	.270	139	4552	688	799	1229	1786	195	55	84	614	56	52	46	48	523	16	866	126	64	1018
Bakersfield	.265	140	4627	654	585	1225	1716	180	25	87	560	57	65	47	20	539	15	711	265	83	1013
Lodi	.265	138	4523	617	713	1198	1617	180	28	61	552	48	54	48	44	457	27	795	84	51	998
Stockton	.264	138	4539	607	527	1200	1588	189	32	45	523	72	56	42	22	490	8	780	158	81	971
Modesto	.263	139	4473	650	600	1177	1645	194	32	70	551	67	53	53	24	613	28	732	120	65	1073
Fresno	.259	140	4482	676	583	1162	1628	170	31	78	598	69	40	37	37	650	17	974	159	74	1057
San Jose	.253	140	4521	619	784	1146	1507	176	34	39	535	52	58	43	45	542	12	869	130	42	1035
Redwood	.253	138	4418	676	573	1119	1587	181	28	77	594	70	33	43	40	530	15	876	130	62	954
Salinas	.251	140	4584	543	678	1152	1479	146	41	33	468	44	53	35	29	464	18	866	211	85	1029

INDIVIDUAL BATTING

(Leading Qualifiers for Batting Championship—378 or More Plate Appearances)

*Bats lefthanded. †Switch-hitter.

Player and Club	Pct.	G.	AB.	R.	H.	TB.	2B.	3B.	HR.	RBI.	GW.	SH.	SF.	HP.	BB.	Int. BB.	SO.	SB.	CS.
Klipstein, David, Stockton	.341	135	543	89	185	216	19	3	2	54	13	5	1	4	54	0	63	21	17
Nokes, Matthew, Fresno*	.322	125	429	62	138	218	26	6	14	82	6	0	3	6	60	5	92	0	0
Nixon, Donell, Bakersfield	.321	135	542	116	174	221	27	4	4	51	5	12	2	1	63	2	82	144	24
Espinoza, Alvaro, Visalia	.319	130	486	57	155	189	20	1	4	57	5	8	1	1	14	1	50	6	4
Smith, Gregory, Lodi*	.317	138	521	89	165	252	22	4	19	109	9	2	3	5	37	9	100	2	3
Puckett, Kirby, Visalia	.314	138	548	105	172	242	29	7	9	97	15	3	5	2	46	2	62	48	11
Vavra, Joseph, Lodi*	.312	110	420	58	131	154	19	2	0	37	0	0	5	1	37	2	26	6	4
Sferrazza, Matthew, Stockton	.309	132	485	79	150	191	18	4	5	56	2	8	7	5	53	1	77	29	10
Smith, Brick, Bakersfield	.304	137	493	84	150	237	26	2	19	88	11	1	6	1	86	5	64	5	8
Holmes, Stanley, Visalia	.302	140	500	89	151	293	27	2	37	115	11	1	5	3	79	11	101	2	4

Departmental Leaders: G—Holmes, 140; AB—Puckett, 548; R—Nixon, 116; H—Klipstein, 185; TB—Holmes, 293; 2B—Howe, 30; 3B—Varsho, 13; HR—Holmes, 37; RBI—Holmes, 115; GWRBI—Bathe, 17; SH—Howe, 16; SF—Cordova, 13; HP—E. Williams, 14; BB—Copeland, 96; IBB—Holmes, 11; SO—Penigar, 136; SB—Nixon, 144; CS—Nixon, 24.

(All Players—Listed Alphabetically)

Player and Club	Pct.	G.	AB.	R.	H.	TB.	2B.	3B.	HR.	RBI.	GW.	SH.	SF.	HP.	BB.	Int. BB.	SO.	SB.	CS.
Abe, Osamu, San Jose*	.271	115	329	51	89	119	18	3	2	51	4	4	3	3	43	1	63	2	1
Akiyama, Koji, San Jose	.253	88	308	45	78	118	9	5	7	43	2	1	1	5	27	1	55	7	3
Aldrete, Michael, Fresno*	.206	20	68	5	14	21	4	0	1	12	1	0	1	2	11	1	17	2	0
Alvarez, Carmelo, Lodi†	.056	7	18	0	1	1	0	0	0	1	0	0	0	0	4	0	5	0	0
Amador, Bruce, Modesto†	.252	116	436	58	110	141	19	3	2	40	4	6	8	1	36	1	60	7	2
Anderson, Willie, Reno	.136	11	22	2	3	6	1	1	0	1	0	0	1	0	1	0	6	0	0
Aragon, Steven, Visalia	.251	123	462	74	116	164	16	1	10	54	10	6	4	2	38	1	56	3	1
Austin, Terry, Salinas	.265	103	324	46	86	102	9	2	1	18	2	0	0	0	37	4	64	19	7
Barragan, Gerardo, San Jose†	.118	4	17	0	2	2	0	0	0	1	1	0	0	0	0	0	4	0	0
Bates, Kevin, Fresno*	.267	51	165	30	44	55	6	1	1	20	1	2	0	0	34	0	22	8	7
Bathe, Robert, Modesto	.267	123	415	74	111	181	23	1	15	82	17	3	7	5	86	4	63	20	12
Beard, Charles, Lodi	.308	30	13	2	4	5	1	0	0	2	0	0	0	0	1	0	3	0	0
Benson, Steven, Reno	.338	20	74	16	25	32	4	0	1	5	0	2	0	2	5	1	7	2	0
Bertucio, Charles, San Jose†	.216	23	74	6	16	20	4	0	0	8	1	2	0	0	8	0	24	0	0
Bogart, Fred, Bakersfield	.210	88	262	29	55	94	6	0	11	37	6	3	2	0	51	1	90	9	8
Bonner, Mark, Redwood	.260	114	362	62	94	156	12	1	16	68	8	1	4	3	52	1	92	2	7
Borowsky, Erez, Visalia	.225	111	311	34	70	81	6	1	1	43	7	5	5	4	54	1	36	3	1
Brady, David, Redwood*	.209	71	201	19	42	49	4	0	1	22	1	0	4	0	25	2	36	1	0
Brantley, Michael, Bakersfield	.297	53	185	33	55	88	9	3	6	29	2	2	0	0	15	0	28	5	0
Brassil, Thomas, Reno	.272	115	416	56	113	145	17	6	1	36	3	3	4	7	32	2	38	4	6
Brown, Renard, Bakersfield	.269	108	375	55	101	122	10	1	3	36	5	8	2	1	43	1	46	24	9
Carrasco, Norman, Redwood	.237	132	473	56	112	167	29	4	6	59	10	5	6	4	29	3	95	30	15
Cartwright, Alan, Stockton*	.277	133	506	70	140	168	16	3	2	64	11	6	8	0	30	1	66	32	6
Castro, Edgar, Reno*	.229	42	140	25	32	56	7	1	5	27	2	0	2	1	22	1	29	0	1
Castro, Frank, Reno	.269	98	349	45	94	133	16	1	7	47	4	5	4	1	33	1	65	2	2
Chavez, Pedro, San Jose	.277	107	401	56	111	147	12	3	6	42	6	8	4	4	23	1	60	23	6
Chinn, Gregory, Lodi	.202	80	248	24	50	65	4	1	3	28	2	3	2	3	24	2	80	3	1
Cimo, Matthew, Fresno	.180	30	89	7	16	19	3	0	0	10	1	0	1	1	11	0	22	3	2
Copeland, Thomas, Modesto*	.294	124	408	72	120	151	15	2	4	34	3	5	2	2	96	1	33	12	9
Cordova, Antonio, Salinas	.232	105	371	32	86	130	17	0	9	69	5	2	13	6	19	1	80	2	4
Coughlon, Kevin, Modesto	.285	130	470	78	134	191	27	6	6	58	6	3	4	0	52	1	56	9	3
Crabtree, Gary, Fresno	.202	108	297	40	60	94	13	0	7	36	5	4	2	2	54	0	96	10	8
Daugherty, John, San Jose†	.261	116	364	46	95	122	17	2	2	45	2	3	4	1	55	1	71	2	1
Daugherty, William, Reno	.224	19	49	8	11	12	1	0	0	6	0	0	1	1	9	0	13	1	0
Davis, Kevin, Redwood	.211	48	152	24	32	35	3	0	0	13	3	5	1	1	25	0	38	4	2
Davis, Rodney, Lodi*	.221	100	303	42	67	94	9	0	6	40	5	5	5	1	54	3	75	10	4
Debus, Jon, Lodi	.274	104	354	64	97	144	22	2	7	56	4	2	8	2	69	1	73	3	4
DeCosta, Robert, Visalia	.281	94	320	43	90	105	7	1	2	39	3	8	3	2	28	3	36	3	3
DeFazio, Steven, Fresno	.270	24	63	2	17	18	1	0	0	4	1	1	0	0	4	0	8	0	0
Denman, John, Reno	.266	56	192	51	51	103	8	4	12	33	4	3	2	1	40	1	63	15	1
DeSantis, Frank, Salinas	.253	90	288	19	73	80	7	0	0	35	3	3	3	0	28	1	49	3	4
Diaz, Jorge, Modesto	.286	7	14	1	4	5	1	0	0	3	1	1	2	0	3	0	3	0	0
Diaz, Mario, Bakersfield	.240	51	171	23	41	48	5	1	0	10	0	4	0	0	10	0	26	3	1
Doggett, Geoffrey, Salinas†	.228	125	469	68	107	117	6	2	0	27	4	8	0	0	73	1	103	39	21
Dunlop, David, San Jose	.248	36	101	17	25	29	4	0	0	12	0	1	0	1	17	0	19	0	1
Dunn, Michael, Fresno	.261	130	448	46	117	158	22	2	5	54	5	6	5	1	45	0	76	11	3
Dye, Mark, San Jose	.087	7	23	1	2	4	2	0	0	3	0	0	0	0	5	0	9	1	1
Eakes, Steven, Redwood	.225	37	111	12	25	31	6	0	0	7	0	4	1	0	9	1	16	1	1
Eppard, James, Modesto*	.283	134	488	68	138	176	18	4	4	45	3	7	2	0	42	6	40	14	4
Erdahl, Jay, Bakersfield*	.248	132	476	62	118	188	22	6	12	56	4	1	7	3	44	0	69	6	8
Espinoza, Alvaro, Visalia	.319	130	486	57	155	189	20	1	4	57	5	8	1	1	14	1	50	6	4
Etchebarren, Raymond, Reno	.281	71	267	34	75	99	12	0	4	37	5	5	4	3	26	0	29	2	4
Ferraro, Robert, San Jose	.198	59	162	21	32	40	5	0	1	19	3	5	0	2	23	0	38	0	0
Ferrigno, Mario, Visalia	.258	43	151	20	39	46	4	0	1	18	2	0	0	4	15	0	16	0	0
Fick, Charles, Modesto	.210	33	81	12	17	20	3	0	0	10	2	2	2	1	19	0	18	0	1
Fields, Bruce, San Jose*	.273	123	450	80	123	162	21	6	2	45	7	2	2	6	54	2	74	26	11
Flammang, Christopher, Bakersfield*	.190	57	184	19	35	43	2	0	2	17	1	2	3	2	22	1	33	3	0
Flores, Richard, Lodi†	.180	44	128	12	23	26	3	0	0	10	0	4	0	1	21	0	23	4	3

Player and Club	Pct.	G.	AB.	R.	H.	TB.	2B.	3B.	HR.	RBI.	GW.	SH.	SF.	HP.	BB.	Int. BB.	SO.	SB.	CS.
Franko, Philip, Visalia*	.234	51	111	15	26	30	4	0	0	6	1	1	0	1	10	0	9	1	1
Freeman, Donald, Reno	.158	28	76	9	12	17	1	2	0	4	1	2	2	0	11	0	21	2	0
Garza, Lonnie, Redwood†	.205	65	166	21	34	41	3	2	0	13	1	7	0	1	22	0	35	1	2
Gatewood, Henry, Lodi	.226	79	252	26	57	66	9	0	0	21	6	10	2	1	24	0	22	0	2
Gibbons, John, Stockton*	.266	103	323	47	86	119	16	4	3	33	1	3	4	2	50	0	45	14	10
Gilbert, Dennis, Redwood	.289	78	270	37	78	144	16	1	16	59	5	0	0	1	32	1	70	0	0
Gobbo, Michael, Stockton	.259	21	58	5	15	16	1	0	0	6	1	2	0	0	9	0	10	2	0
Gomez, Ernesto, Bakersfield†	.240	105	350	32	84	108	13	4	1	27	1	7	6	1	28	0	46	8	1
Gomez, Freddy, Reno	.000	3	4	0	0	0	0	0	0	0	0	0	0	0	0	0	2	0	0
Gonzalez, Jose, Lodi	.294	76	310	48	91	134	17	4	6	36	2	3	2	3	24	1	83	21	9
Graham, Brian, Modesto	.272	33	114	9	31	38	4	0	1	6	1	3	0	1	8	0	14	2	2
Graham, Everett, Fresno*	.274	114	394	64	108	127	8	4	1	33	6	4	3	3	55	2	62	16	12
Granger, Lee, San Jose†	.287	127	474	72	136	184	18	6	6	82	9	2	6	9	30	3	92	50	7
Greer, Brian, Reno	.205	73	244	32	50	76	10	2	4	31	4	1	4	0	35	2	107	5	3
Griggs, David, Stockton†	.278	5	18	3	5	8	3	0	0	4	0	0	0	0	1	0	1	1	0
Gutierrez, Felipe, Lodi	.261	95	360	51	94	129	14	0	7	43	5	9	6	7	20	0	42	1	2
Hamilton, Jeffrey, Lodi	.199	44	141	15	28	32	4	0	0	10	1	0	2	1	14	1	42	2	0
Hanggie, Daniel, Bakersfield†	.255	81	298	48	76	140	15	2	15	56	7	3	5	4	43	1	57	4	2
Hardgrave, Eric, Reno	.261	20	69	3	18	23	0	1	1	5	0	0	0	2	4	1	17	1	1
Harper, Therron, Redwood	.253	110	376	45	95	137	15	0	9	64	7	0	9	1	40	1	39	0	1
Hazewood, Drungo, San Jose	.288	21	73	17	21	31	4	0	2	13	2	0	1	0	17	0	23	1	0
Henderson, Wendell, Salinas	.281	112	381	46	107	126	13	0	2	35	4	1	2	1	45	4	43	2	1
Hennell, John, Stockton*	.249	104	329	38	82	131	21	2	8	49	8	2	4	2	37	2	52	7	4
Hill, Roger, Bakersfield*	.254	134	496	61	126	154	18	2	2	63	7	12	6	2	47	2	53	48	9
Hobbs, Rodney, Modesto	.290	93	328	54	95	139	20	3	6	42	5	1	2	1	41	2	83	20	7
Holmes, Stanley, Visalia	.302	140	500	89	151	293	27	2	37	115	11	1	5	3	79	11	101	2	4
Hoskins, Osbe, Reno	.259	124	483	71	125	156	18	5	1	48	3	6	4	4	58	1	68	33	19
Howe, Gregory, Visalia	.294	133	494	84	145	195	30	4	4	55	6	16	6	7	62	2	95	54	19
Hudson, Lance, Lodi†	.213	25	61	6	13	16	3	0	0	7	1	1	1	0	2	0	8	4	2
Hummel, Dean, Fresno*	.000	20	1	0	0	0	0	0	0	0	0	0	0	0	0	0	0	0	0
Isherwood, Michael, Bakersfield	.311	77	254	22	79	92	7	0	2	31	2	2	3	1	27	0	30	3	8
Jackson, Darrin, Salinas	.248	129	509	70	126	172	18	5	6	54	10	9	4	4	38	0	111	36	12
Johnson, Thomas, Salinas	.265	84	283	46	75	114	11	5	6	35	2	2	1	1	50	2	70	16	7
Johnston, Mark, Stockton*	.282	20	71	9	20	32	7	1	1	10	1	0	2	0	6	0	11	1	0
Jones, Glenn, Fresno	.270	127	452	81	122	191	15	3	16	74	5	2	4	10	44	4	95	19	2
Jones, Michael, Fresno*	.333	40	117	30	39	64	8	1	5	18	2	0	0	1	35	1	21	9	2
Junker, Lance, Redwood	.262	85	229	29	60	74	5	0	3	32	3	0	3	1	31	1	43	4	2
Kaiser, Jeffrey, Modesto	.000	25	3	0	0	0	0	0	0	1	0	0	0	0	0	0	1	0	0
Key, Gregory, Redwood	.251	107	338	62	85	117	21	1	3	48	7	4	1	8	41	0	73	25	7
Klipstein, David, Stockton	.341	135	543	89	185	216	19	3	2	54	13	5	1	4	54	0	63	21	17
Komazaki, Yukiichi, San Jose*	.197	50	122	9	24	32	2	3	0	10	1	1	1	1	8	0	26	0	1
Koontz, James, Stockton	.000	54	1	0	0	0	0	0	0	0	0	0	0	0	0	0	1	0	0
Kubit, Joseph, Visalia	.287	136	505	82	145	211	19	10	9	69	11	5	5	5	47	4	84	10	5
Kwiecinski, Michael, Reno	.250	106	348	47	87	131	10	5	8	47	6	7	3	6	33	0	64	3	3
Loard, Billy, Fresno	.000	5	6	0	0	0	0	0	0	0	0	0	0	0	0	0	4	0	0
Lucido, John, Fresno	.193	23	57	6	11	11	0	0	0	6	1	1	0	1	5	0	18	1	0
Madril, Michael, Redwood†	.282	117	383	88	108	128	12	4	0	33	9	2	3	11	45	0	43	39	14
McInerny, Daniel, San Jose*	.240	36	100	17	24	37	5	1	2	9	0	4	1	1	20	0	14	2	1
McKay, David, Modesto†	.186	24	86	11	16	25	3	0	2	9	1	0	1	0	8	1	20	2	0
McNair, Robert, Reno*	.282	85	298	48	84	143	19	5	10	52	9	3	2	1	30	5	71	3	0
Miller, Scott, Salinas*	.161	31	93	5	15	21	1	1	1	4	0	1	0	0	10	0	23	1	3
Miranda, Manuel, San Jose	.209	83	187	18	39	60	9	0	4	18	2	3	2	0	32	0	41	1	1
Moncerratt, Pablo, Bakersfield*	.000	4	5	1	0	0	0	0	0	1	0	0	0	0	1	0	3	0	0
Montanari, David, Salinas*	.225	82	276	25	62	74	9	0	1	32	6	7	1	1	26	2	25	3	5
Morales, Joseph, Stockton†	.236	87	246	26	58	77	8	1	3	27	3	7	1	0	26	0	44	7	3
Moran, Mitchell, Lodi	.196	65	214	21	42	56	6	1	2	27	4	1	3	6	25	0	57	6	2
Morris, Angel, Stockton	.200	14	25	2	5	6	1	0	0	3	1	0	0	1	6	0	5	0	0
Murphy, Roderick, Modesto	.246	72	175	29	43	55	6	0	2	18	1	6	3	0	33	0	15	8	7
Nago, Garrett, Stockton†	.178	26	73	6	13	13	0	0	0	6	0	2	1	2	10	0	23	0	2
Nichols, Carl, San Jose	.204	54	152	16	31	38	4	0	1	12	0	0	3	3	21	1	42	2	0
Nixon, Donell, Bakersfield	.321	135	542	116	174	221	27	4	4	51	5	12	2	1	63	2	82	144	24
Noce, Paul, Reno	.308	61	237	48	73	111	16	2	6	30	1	3	0	2	26	0	51	8	4
Nokes, Matthew, Fresno*	.322	125	429	62	138	218	26	6	14	82	6	0	3	6	60	5	92	0	0
Olson, Randy, Reno	.333	5	12	1	4	4	0	0	0	0	0	0	0	0	1	0	1	0	0
Orejas, Reinaldo, Visalia*	.167	17	24	2	4	5	1	0	0	2	0	0	0	0	2	0	8	0	0
Ott, Edward, Redwood*	.333	2	3	1	1	1	0	0	0	0	0	0	0	0	0	0	0	0	0
Ouellette, Philip, Fresno†	.271	71	210	37	57	83	7	2	5	35	5	3	1	1	49	1	26	1	1
Parsons, Scott, Reno	.000	29	3	0	0	0	0	0	0	0	0	0	0	0	0	0	0	0	0
Penigar, Charles, Fresno†	.257	118	439	76	113	144	14	4	3	37	2	3	0	0	67	1	136	41	19
Perna, Robert, Fresno	.163	37	92	9	15	15	0	0	0	7	0	2	2	1	7	0	27	4	1
Peterson, David, Modesto*	.251	119	375	46	94	138	11	3	9	54	5	6	8	2	41	4	78	3	6
Piper, Brian, Lodi	.000	26	1	1	0	0	0	0	0	0	0	1	0	0	1	0	0	0	0
Portugal, Mark, Visalia	.000	31	0	2	0	0	0	0	0	0	0	0	0	0	0	0	0	0	0
Pott, Lawrence, Reno	.347	41	124	20	43	58	8	2	1	25	4	0	1	2	15	0	19	1	2
Priessman, Kraig, San Jose	.235	37	102	7	24	29	5	0	0	4	1	2	1	0	3	0	30	0	0
Puckett, Kirby, Visalia	.314	138	548	105	172	242	29	7	9	97	15	3	5	2	46	2	62	48	11
Ramppen, Frank, Visalia	.247	70	239	37	59	73	3	1	3	28	3	4	4	2	28	0	33	13	2
Ramsey, Michael, Lodi	.400	28	20	4	8	8	0	0	0	1	0	0	0	0	3	0	2	2	1
Reade, Curtis, Lodi	.000	31	1	0	0	0	0	0	0	0	0	0	0	0	0	0	1	0	0
Reynolds, Mark, Lodi*	.238	39	130	22	31	48	8	0	3	18	4	2	2	0	21	3	17	0	1
Richie, Bennie, Visalia†	.245	118	380	48	93	120	12	3	3	33	3	4	1	1	36	3	67	10	8
Rodriguez, David, Bakersfield	.333	3	3	0	1	1	0	0	0	0	0	0	0	0	0	0	2	0	0
Rojas, Octavio, 25 Mod.-1 SJ*	.250	26	44	4	11	17	3	0	1	5	1	0	0	1	6	1	14	0	0
Rosales, Arturo, Stockton	.227	89	264	37	60	82	7	0	5	36	4	2	3	3	22	1	51	7	4
Rosenhahn, David, Salinas	.206	72	214	21	44	53	5	2	0	21	1	2	2	4	17	0	21	4	2
Rupe, Brian, Visalia*	.232	52	168	23	39	48	4	1	1	18	2	1	2	0	27	3	31	6	3
Rutledge, Jeffrey, Salinas	.272	98	349	38	95	126	18	2	3	38	2	5	0	0	28	1	69	12	3
Samuel, Michael, Stockton	.188	78	176	26	33	39	2	2	0	6	1	8	1	0	35	1	57	8	5
Sferrazza, Matthew, Stockton	.309	132	485	79	150	191	18	4	5	56	2	8	7	5	53	1	77	29	10
Shields, Steven, Lodi	.333	7	3	1	1	1	0	0	0	0	0	0	0	0	1	0	2	0	0
Shirahata, Katsuhiro, San Jose*	.284	112	282	47	80	99	10	0	3	34	3	4	3	2	38	0	44	0	1
Smelko, Mark, Redwood†	.198	36	101	13	20	27	4	0	1	5	0	0	0	0	18	1	19	0	1
Smith, Brick, Bakersfield	.304	137	493	84	150	237	26	2	19	88	11	1	6	1	86	5	64	5	8

Player and Club	Pct.	G.	AB.	R.	H.	TB.	2B.	3B.	HR.	RBI.	GW.	SH.	SF.	HP.	BB.	Int. BB.	SO.	SB.	CS.
Smith, Gregory, Lodi*	.317	138	521	89	165	252	22	4	19	109	9	2	3	5	37	9	100	2	3
Soma, Katsuya, San Jose	.147	46	75	6	11	12	1	0	0	4	0	2	1	0	12	0	31	0	0
Sowards, Van, Fresno	.339	55	171	32	58	67	9	0	0	30	6	0	5	0	30	0	16	4	1
Springer, Gary, San Jose*	.254	128	401	46	102	121	13	3	0	44	3	10	6	5	58	2	55	2	3
Stanicek, Stephen, Fresno	.242	126	438	68	106	175	15	3	16	77	12	1	7	2	75	0	118	3	3
Steen, Gregory, Redwood	.250	3	8	1	2	2	0	0	0	1	0	0	1	0	1	0	2	1	0
Stewart, Charles, Salinas†	.318	7	22	2	7	7	0	0	0	0	0	1	0	0	2	0	6	1	0
Strom, Phillip, Modesto	.182	36	77	12	14	19	2	0	1	9	1	0	2	0	18	0	23	0	0
Stromer, Richard, Redwood	.321	54	168	41	54	92	11	0	9	47	8	0	3	2	37	1	21	0	1
Sveum, Dale, Stockton†	.261	135	533	70	139	190	26	5	5	70	9	4	4	0	29	0	73	15	8
Tanabe, Collin, Stockton	.255	105	333	36	85	116	13	3	4	37	9	3	4	0	37	0	48	5	6
Tettleton, Mickey, Modesto†	.243	124	378	55	92	135	18	2	7	62	9	1	5	1	82	4	71	1	2
Thoma, Raymond, Modesto	.256	132	469	54	120	183	19	7	10	62	5	7	5	8	19	2	113	11	5
Thomas, Jimmy, Reno	.272	132	459	71	125	212	22	10	15	83	6	4	7	4	77	1	87	1	3
Thomas, Richard, 44 Mod.-52 SJ	.230	96	256	29	59	69	6	2	0	28	4	3	1	2	41	1	54	12	7
Thompson, Robert, Fresno	.259	64	220	33	57	79	8	1	4	23	3	5	0	1	18	0	62	4	6
Thompson, Scott, Reno	.270	117	378	55	102	132	12	3	4	44	3	4	0	8	27	0	63	21	8
Thrower, Keith, San Jose†	.301	32	83	18	25	34	4	1	1	8	0	3	2	1	9	0	8	10	2
Tiefenthaler, Dennis, San Jose	.271	28	85	7	23	28	5	0	0	9	1	0	0	0	19	0	19	0	0
Tramble, Otis, Salinas†	.292	73	236	30	69	82	7	3	0	13	0	2	0	2	20	0	24	24	4
Tryon, Michael, Visalia	.111	6	9	1	1	2	1	0	0	1	0	0	0	0	1	0	2	0	0
Turner, Richard, Redwood	.242	61	161	24	39	43	4	0	0	10	0	1	2	0	9	0	31	4	0
Van Burkleo, Tyler, Stockton*	.205	111	347	42	71	121	23	3	7	37	4	3	1	2	40	1	117	8	3
Vanderburg, Michael, San Jose†	.083	5	12	0	1	1	0	0	0	1	1	0	1	0	1	0	0	0	0
Varsho, Gary, Salinas*	.263	131	490	69	129	180	16	13	3	57	3	8	6	6	49	2	108	46	10
Vavra, Joseph, Lodi*	.312	110	420	58	131	154	19	2	0	37	0	0	5	1	37	2	26	6	4
Vega, Luis, Bakersfield	.000	4	8	0	0	0	0	0	0	0	0	0	0	0	0	0	3	0	0
Walker, John, Lodi†	.275	69	244	31	67	96	9	4	4	24	1	4	1	0	21	0	30	4	3
Walsh, James, Salinas	.258	76	275	26	71	95	9	6	1	30	2	1	3	4	22	0	70	3	2
Wasinger, Mark, Reno	.331	83	308	46	102	137	13	5	4	53	1	4	5	3	38	0	45	22	8
Watanabe, Curt, Stockton	.252	80	206	22	52	61	7	1	0	25	4	1	1	0	45	1	35	1	3
West, Reginald, Redwood*	.318	35	132	23	42	52	3	2	1	15	1	1	0	3	13	2	19	11	6
Williams, Brian, Lodi*	.301	103	408	58	123	157	16	6	2	42	3	2	3	0	23	5	47	8	2
Williams, Edward, Lodi	.282	108	372	42	105	133	14	4	2	40	1	4	3	14	31	0	57	12	4
Wilson, Ricky, Bakersfield	.249	102	362	46	90	133	16	0	9	44	5	2	3	2	32	2	55	1	4
Worden, William, Redwood	.276	81	294	43	81	138	20	5	9	37	4	0	2	1	18	1	86	1	1
Wright, Paul, Redwood	.167	66	132	18	22	27	0	1	1	8	0	0	0	1	17	0	38	3	1
Wrona, William, Bakersfield	.245	52	163	23	40	47	4	0	1	14	1	6	2	2	26	0	25	3	1
Zacher, Todd, Fresno*	.215	94	326	48	70	89	11	4	0	40	7	6	3	5	45	2	55	24	7
Zambrana, Luis, Redwood	.261	106	357	56	93	126	13	7	2	49	9	2	3	2	66	0	79	4	2

The following pitchers, listed alphabetically by club, with games in parentheses, had no plate appearances, primarily through use of designated hitters:

BAKERSFIELD—Bartley, Gregory (53); Cuellar, Robert (4); Evans, Michael (42); Guetterman, Lee (25); Hayes, Terry (39); Holland, Donald (25); Johnson, Michael (49); McDonald, Jeffrey (27); Meister, Mickey (8); Murray, Jed (3); Pedersen, Mark (40); Ramirez, Randolph (26); Schassler, Jeffrey (22).

FRESNO—Barling, Glenn (13); Blobaum, Jeffrey (27); Bockus, Randy (30); Chue, Jose (13); Crews, Lawrence (19); Gallo, Bernard (22); Lusted, Charles (1); Mathiesen, Marty (32); Morse, Randy (15); Murtha, Brian (29); Robinson, Jeffrey (14); Schafer, Dennis (23); Wilcox, Steven (19); Winters, Mark (25).

LODI—Burns, Ronald (10); Carne, Gregory (28); Cunningham, Michael (25); Eichhorn, David (12); Heuer, Mark (9); Marsden, Stephen (18); Meeks, Timothy (22); Smith, Don (40); Tejeda, Felix (9); Thurman, Richard (11); Walker, Steven (7).

MODESTO—Barry, Eric (26); Beard, David (1); Gorman, Michael (34); Herron, Anthony (13); Hilton, Stan (10); Jarrett, Mark (26); Kobernus, Jeffrey (30); Lambert, Timothy (42); Langford, Rick (1); Myers, Edward (17); Vavrock, Robert (31); Wortham, Richard (14); Zmudosky, Thomas (27).

REDWOOD—Ahern, Jeffrey (16); Angulo, Kenneth (31); Bankowski, Kris (37); Bryden, Thomas (44); Harris, Craig (4); Jones, Lee (13); Kammeyer, Timothy (27); Lugo, Rafael (11); Mack, Tony (27); McCaskill, Kirk (16); Oliver, Scott (26); Price, Kevin (26); Rentschler, Thomas (5); Salazar, Jeffrey (8); Smith, Jeffrey (11).

RENO—Biko, Thomas (36); Crabb, Gregory (31); Jones, James (17); Kutsukos, Peter (50); Macias Robert (24); Mills, Michael (2); Ortiz, Elsis (5); Plesac, Joseph (40); Steffanich, Gregory (35); Towers, Kevin (24); Vosberg, Edward (15); Williams, Mitchell (11).

SALINAS—Adamczak, James (16); Boudreau, James (24); Brahms, Russell (42); Bryant, Neil (16); Buonantony, Richard (22); Carpio, Jorge (28); Clarke, Timothy (25); Housey, Joseph (17); Johnson, Scott (31); Kaufman, Ronald (51); Lockie, Randall (1); Potestio, Douglas (32).

SAN JOSE—Butler, Mark (19); Cook, Kerry (29); DeHart, Gregory (5); Escribano, Eduardo (18); Feeley, James (9); Gilbert, Jeffrey (28); Guinn, Charles (24); Hoke, Leon (10); Jacob, Mark (39); Legumina, Gary (28); Leiter, Kurt (12); Marietta, Louis (17); McCullock, Alec (19); McDonough, Brian (8); O'Connor, Nicholas (1); Summers, Jeffrey (6); Ueda, Sadahito (31); Wilson, Randall (42).

STOCKTON—Antunez, Martin (45); Collins, Donald (12); Derksen, Robert (18); Duquette, Bryan (14); Effrig, Mark (4); Embser, Richard (20); Evans, Gary (24); Kranitz, Richard (6); McCoy, Kevin (18); Moore, Robert (5); Norton, Douglas (20); Puryear, Nathaniel (4); Tatsuno, Derek (25); Teahan, James (12); Torres, Anthony (6); Walker, Cameron (26); Wegman, William (25); Wood, Johnson (3).

VISALIA—Arney, Jeffrey (6); Arrington, Samuel (27); Belanger, Lee (55); Cartwright, Mark (32); Eufemia, Frank (64); Henderson, Craig (8); Kindred, Curtis (26); McMahon, John (27); Sheppard, Philip (17); Wardle, Curtis (49); Wiseman, Timothy (14).

GRAND-SLAM HOME RUNS—Junker 3; Brantley, Ouellette, 2 each; Abe, Bonner, Brown, Cartwright, R. Davis, Dunn, Erdahl, Fields, Harper, Hennell, Howe, Morales, Stanicek, Tettleton, Thoma, J. Walker, 1 each.

AWARDED FIRST BASE ON CATCHER'S INTERFERENCE—Cimo 2 (Cordova, Wilson); Hardgrave 2 (Nokes 2); B. Smith (Holmes, Tettleton); Aragon (Brady); G. Jones (Brady); Sferrazza (Castro); Sowards (Wilson); Sveum (Harper); Tramble (Turner).

CLUB FIELDING

Club	Pct.	G.	PO.	A.	E.	DP.	PB.
Modesto	.967	139	3514	1486	169	123	27
Stockton	.965	138	3593	1483	182	93	32
Visalia	.964	140	3636	1432	190	121	17
Redwood	.963	138	3449	1328	183	91	37
Fresno	.960	140	3544	1510	211	128	22
Salinas	.957	140	3558	1510	225	105	31
Lodi	.957	138	3483	1355	219	127	54
Bakersfield	.956	140	3635	1544	240	112	29
Reno	.954	139	3495	1501	241	104	24
San Jose	.951	140	3513	1455	257	117	31

Triple play—Bakersfield.

INDIVIDUAL FIELDING

*Throws lefthanded.

FIRST BASEMEN

Player and Club	Pct.	G.	PO.	A.	E.	DP.
Abe, San Jose*	.986	68	518	39	8	44
Aldrete, Fresno*	.990	20	189	9	2	20
Bathe, Modesto	1.000	1	6	3	0	0
Bonner, Redwood	.983	110	900	37	16	71
E. Castro, Reno*	.979	36	306	23	7	22
Chinn, Lodi	1.000	1	4	0	0	0
Cimo, Fresno	1.000	3	26	1	0	3
J. Daaugherty, San Jose*	.990	84	670	25	7	63
W. Daugherty, Reno	1.000	3	4	0	0	0
DeCosta, Visalia	.967	9	28	1	1	3
DeFazio, Fresno	.984	16	125	2	2	13
Dunn, Fresno	.982	26	200	17	4	17
EPPARD, Modesto*	.9914	131	1086	74	10	97
Flammang, Bakersfield*	1.000	6	44	3	0	2
F. Gomez, Reno	1.000	2	2	1	0	0
Greer, Reno	.980	17	134	12	3	10
Hanggie, Bakersfield	.993	13	128	7	1	8
Hardgrave, Reno	.963	11	100	4	4	7
Harper, Redwood	.978	31	256	15	6	11
Henderson, Salinas	.979	64	515	55	12	42
Hennell, Stockton*	.986	49	379	34	6	26
T. Johnson, Salinas	.990	74	647	50	7	49
Johnston, Stockton	1.000	8	74	1	0	3
Kubit, Visalia	.983	136	1104	75	21	105
Lucido, Fresno	1.000	1	4	0	0	0
McNair, Reno*	.985	65	557	53	9	39
Miller, Salinas	.970	4	31	1	1	2
Monceratt, Bakersfield*	.833	3	5	0	1	0
Ouellette, Fresno	1.000	15	111	1	0	7
Peterson, Modesto*	.900	2	8	1	1	1
Rosenhahn, Salinas	1.000	1	1	0	0	0
Smelko, Redwood	1.000	6	28	2	0	3
B. Smith, Bakersfield	.990	122	1084	92	11	87
G. Smith, Lodi	.978	138	1076	109	27	114
Sowards, Fresno	1.000	1	1	0	0	0
Stanicek, Fresno	.978	73	596	63	15	50
Strom, Modesto	.981	16	104	2	2	10
Stromer, Redwood	1.000	1	8	0	0	2
J. Thomas, Reno	.980	14	91	6	2	9
Van Burkleo, Stockton*	.981	88	759	57	16	56

Triple play—Flammang.

SECOND BASEMEN

Player and Club	Pct.	G.	PO.	A.	E.	DP.
Amador, Modesto	966	106	235	276	18	63
Aragon, Visalia	.964	116	240	324	21	55
Bates, Fresno	.952	50	93	144	12	30
Benson, Reno	.886	8	28	11	5	3
Carrasco, Redwood	.959	132	287	363	28	58
DeCosta, Visalia	.950	31	63	71	7	13
M. Diaz, Bakersfield	.960	9	24	24	2	7
Dye, San Jose	.625	2	1	4	3	1
Etchebarren, Reno	.941	24	42	70	7	8
Freeman, Reno	.960	4	10	14	1	5
Garza, Redwood	.977	11	21	22	1	4
E. Gomez, Bakersfield	.953	78	163	219	19	37
B. Graham, Modesto	.983	25	54	65	2	18
Gutierrez, Lodi	.969	92	220	220	14	60
Hanggie, Bakersfield	.938	56	140	163	20	37
Hudson, Lodi	.667	2	1	1	1	0
Johnston, Stockton	1.000	3	6	6	0	1
Miranda, San Jose	.886	27	46	55	13	9
Montanari, Salinas	.900	9	15	21	4	4
Morales, Stockton	.978	9	24	20	1	3
Moran, Lodi	1.000	1	1	4	0	2
Murphy, Modesto	.935	12	15	28	3	6
Noce, Reno	.980	25	64	80	3	11
Rodriguez, Bakersfield	1.000	1	0	2	0	0
Rosenhahn, Salinas	.900	4	2	7	1	0
Samuel, Stockton	1.000	2	0	3	0	0
Sferrazza, Stockton	.952	128	285	363	33	54
Shirahata, San Jose	.957	27	34	55	4	10
SPRINGER, San Jose	.984	105	216	279	8	54
Steen, Redwood	1.000	2	2	2	0	0
J. Thomas, Reno	1.000	1	0	3	0	0
Thompson, Fresno	.965	63	118	185	11	41
Thrower, San Jose	1.000	3	3	10	0	2
Varsho, Salinas	.950	130	284	339	33	71
Vavra, Lodi	.963	45	106	127	9	21
Wasinger, Reno	.978	79	164	241	9	35
E. Williams, Lodi	1.000	3	5	4	0	1
Zacher, Fresno	.965	30	61	78	5	6

Triple play—Hanggie.

THIRD BASEMEN

Player and Club	Pct.	G.	PO.	A.	E.	DP.
Akiyama, San Jose	.869	50	27	66	14	4
Bathe, Modesto	.904	110	76	227	32	21
Beard, Lodi	1.000	1	0	1	0	1
Benson, Reno	.941	7	1	15	1	1
Bogart, Bakersfield	.808	11	6	15	5	1
Crabtree, Fresno	.667	1	0	2	1	0
DeCosta, Visalia	.887	30	16	39	7	4
Dunlop, San Jose	.908	30	16	43	6	6
DUNN, Fresno	.907	110	103	230	34	27
Dye, San Jose	.650	6	4	9	7	1
Etchebarren, Reno	.928	45	36	80	9	7
Ferrigno, Visalia	.939	42	22	71	6	4
Franko, Visalia	1.000	6	2	2	0	0
Freeman, Reno	.895	7	5	12	2	1
B. Graham, Modesto	.875	3	2	5	1	0
Granger, San Jose	.900	3	5	4	1	1
Hamilton, Lodi	.833	40	23	62	17	6
Henderson, Salinas	.905	39	20	85	11	4
Holmes, Visalia	1.000	1	0	1	0	0
Junker, Redwood	.913	11	4	17	2	0
Lucido, Fresno	1.000	2	1	3	0	0
Miranda, San Jose	.591	9	7	6	9	1
Montanari, Salinas	.897	27	15	46	7	5
Moran, Lodi	.821	18	12	20	7	2
Murphy, Modesto	.940	31	20	59	5	4
Nichols, San Jose	.727	5	2	6	3	1
Nixon, Bakersfield	.872	132	98	249	51	15
Noce, Reno	.925	16	8	29	3	1
Olson, San Jose	.000	1	0	0	1	0
Perna, Fresno	1.000	2	0	1	0	0
Pott, Reno	1.000	1	0	3	0	0
Ramppen, Visalia	.892	70	66	108	21	10
Rosenhahn, Salinas	.860	53	47	106	25	10
Rutledge, Salinas	1.000	2	1	3	0	0
Shirahata, San Jose	.725	26	10	19	11	1
Smelko, Redwood	.750	3	1	2	1	0
Stromer, Redwood	.934	50	29	99	9	2
Sveum, Stockton	.901	129	94	261	39	24
J. Thomas, Reno	.937	67	52	125	12	11
Thrower, San Jose	.810	6	3	14	4	1
Tiefenthaler, San Jose	.902	28	17	38	6	5
Tramble, Salinas	.944	26	22	46	4	5
Vavra, Lodi	.900	21	10	26	4	4
Watanabe, Stockton	.952	12	13	27	2	3
E. Williams, Lodi	.898	63	48	101	17	12
Worden, Redwood	.926	79	62	127	15	8
Zacher, Fresno	.920	37	25	67	8	4

SHORTSTOPS

Player and Club	Pct.	G.	PO.	A.	E.	DP.
Alvarez, Lodi	.967	7	11	18	1	3
Barragan, San Jose	.864	4	6	13	3	2
Benson, Reno	.882	4	8	7	2	2
Bogart, Bakersfield	.892	26	35	64	12	10
Brassil, Reno	.899	111	149	278	48	47
Chavez, San Jose	.918	107	159	303	41	54
Crabtree, Fresno	.9518	101	121	294	21	51
Davis, Redwood	.907	47	58	127	19	13
DeCosta, Visalia	.500	2	0	1	1	0
M. Diaz, Bakersfield	.905	42	68	122	20	24
Eakes, Redwood	.921	37	39	90	11	15
Espinoza, Visalia	.939	128	256	364	40	76
Flores, Lodi	.925	44	68	118	15	23
Franko, Visalia	.941	20	21	27	3	6
Freeman, Reno	.878	12	14	29	6	4
Garza, Redwood	.945	55	63	110	10	16
E. Gomez, Bakersfield	.909	24	24	76	10	12
B. Graham, Modesto	.750	1	0	3	1	0
Gutierrez, Lodi	1.000	1	2	3	0	1
Hudson, Lodi	.876	22	35	50	12	13
Johnston, Stockton	.833	3	3	7	2	1
Lucido, Fresno	.923	9	6	18	2	2

SHORTSTOPS—Continued

Player and Club	Pct.	G.	PO.	A.	E.	DP.
Montanari, Salinas	.895	5	5	12	2	0
Morales, Stockton	.951	75	94	179	14	16
Murphy, Modesto	.946	12	13	22	2	7
Noce, Reno	.922	21	27	68	8	10
Perna, Fresno	.898	28	34	63	11	11
Rosales, Stockton	1.000	1	0	1	0	0
RUTLEDGE, Salinas	.9522	96	140	279	21	34
Samuel, Stockton	.932	66	88	201	21	34
Shirahata, San Jose	1.000	1	0	1	0	0
Smelko, Redwood	.886	9	15	16	4	1
Springer, San Jose	.944	28	33	86	7	13
Steen, Redwood	1.000	1	0	3	0	0
Sveum, Stockton	.969	7	11	20	1	2
Thoma, Modesto	.946	131	205	395	34	77
Thrower, San Jose	.928	16	21	43	5	8
Tramble, Salinas	.894	41	66	120	22	23
Vavra, Lodi	.867	2	4	9	2	0
J. Walker, Lodi	.938	69	135	198	22	39
Worden, Redwood	1.000	1	1	0	0	0
Wrona, Bakersfield	.921	52	71	161	20	33
Zacher, Fresno	.872	20	17	51	10	9

OUTFIELDERS

Player and Club	Pct.	G.	PO.	A.	E.	DP.
Akiyama, San Jose	.967	38	55	4	2	1
Anderson, Reno	1.000	11	14	1	0	0
Austin, Salinas	.972	80	129	9	4	3
Bertucio, San Jose*	1.000	18	34	2	0	0
Bogart, Bakersfield	.912	29	29	2	3	1
Brantley, Bakersfield	.984	40	59	3	1	1
Brown, Bakersfield	.970	104	186	5	6	0
Cartwright, Stockton*	.987	133	220	9	3	0
Chinn, Lodi	.961	58	97	1	4	0
Cimo, Fresno	1.000	17	25	2	0	0
Copeland, Modesto*	.968	121	264	6	9	1
Coughlon, Modesto	.980	129	183	12	4	2
W. Daugherty, Reno	.964	15	26	1	1	1
R. Davis, Lodi*	.962	96	144	9	6	1
DeCosta, Visalia	.857	9	6	0	1	0
Denman, Reno	.980	38	43	7	1	2
Doggett, Salinas	.981	123	312	6	6	2
Erdahl, Bakersfield	.972	120	203	5	6	1
Fields, San Jose	.972	116	234	6	7	0
Flammang, Bakersfield*	.977	22	40	2	1	0
Freeman, Reno	1.000	1	2	0	0	0
Gibbons, Stockton*	.975	97	188	5	5	0
Gilbert, Redwood	1.000	24	34	2	0	0
Gonzalez, Lodi	.979	74	182	7	4	3
B. Graham, Modesto	1.000	4	6	0	0	0
E. Graham, Fresno*	.966	111	252	7	9	1
Granger, San Jose	.956	117	309	17	15	3
Greer, Reno	.919	38	64	4	6	0
Hamilton, Lodi	1.000	3	3	0	0	0
Hazewood, San Jose	.929	18	38	1	3	1
Hennell, Stockton*	1.000	5	2	1	0	1
Hill, Bakersfield	.977	126	243	10	6	1
Hobbs, Modesto	.948	87	155	9	9	3
Hoskins, Reno	.971	124	289	12	9	3
Howe, Visalia	.967	133	304	16	11	1
Jackson, Salinas	.951	129	237	15	13	3
Johnston, Stockton	1.000	1	4	0	0	0
G. Jones, Fresno	.938	121	180	18	13	4
M. Jones, Fresno*	.938	16	29	1	2	0
Junker, Redwood	.966	49	84	2	3	0
Key, Redwood	.943	90	160	5	10	1
KLIPSTEIN, Stockton	.992	133	238	4	2	0
Komazaki, San Jose*	.976	34	36	4	1	1
Kwiecinski, Reno	.921	90	125	3	11	0
Madril, Redwood	.979	105	221	8	5	3
McInerny, San Jose*	.968	34	54	7	2	0
Miller, Salinas	.956	24	37	6	2	0
Miranda, San Jose	1.000	5	3	0	0	0
Moran, Lodi	.932	44	64	5	5	2
Murphy, Modesto	1.000	1	1	0	0	0
Nichols, San Jose	.875	13	11	3	2	1
Noce, Reno	1.000	1	1	0	0	0
Olson, Reno	.636	3	7	0	4	0
Orejas, Visalia*	.958	8	22	1	1	0
Penigar, Fresno	.964	118	201	11	8	2
Perna, Fresno	1.000	3	8	0	0	0
Peterson, Modesto*	.989	56	80	8	1	1
Puckett, Visalia	.982	137	253	22	5	5
Ramsey, Lodi*	1.000	3	6	0	0	0
Reynolds, Lodi	.986	37	70	2	1	1
Richie, Visalia	.935	104	141	3	10	0
Rojas, Modesto*	1.000	8	5	0	0	0
Rosales, Stockton	.971	63	98	2	3	0
Rupe, Visalia*	.976	50	78	2	2	0
Shirahata, San Jose	.913	25	21	0	2	0
Sowards, Fresno	.969	45	62	1	2	1
Tettleton, Modesto	.900	7	9	0	1	0
Thomas, Modesto-San Jose	.970	85	156	7	5	2
R. Thompson, Reno	.986	113	203	8	3	1
Vanderburg, San Jose*	1.000	2	2	0	0	0
Vavra, Lodi	.976	19	38	2	1	0
Walsh, Salinas	.968	68	118	3	4	1
West, Redwood	.983	35	58	0	1	0
B. Williams, Lodi	.954	99	196	12	10	3
Wright, Redwood	.929	50	63	2	5	1
Zacher, Fresno	1.000	1	2	1	0	0
Zambrana, Redwood	.972	99	160	13	5	2

CATCHERS

Player and Club	Pct.	G.	PO.	A.	E.	DP.	PB.
Beard, Lodi	1.000	1	1	0	0	0	0
BOROWSKY, Visalia	.992	111	640	94	6	7	9
Brady, Redwood	.984	60	272	35	5	2	17
F. Castro, Reno	.943	85	528	72	36	8	16
Cordova, Salinas	.961	63	386	52	18	3	22
Debus, Lodi	.968	61	322	45	12	2	42
DeFazio, Fresno	.970	8	31	1	1	0	2
DeSantis, Salinas	.965	73	400	42	16	5	6
J. Diaz, Modesto	.952	3	19	1	1	0	0
Ferraro, San Jose	.965	57	287	45	12	4	14
Fick, Modesto	.966	29	156	16	6	0	4
Gatewood, Lodi	.988	79	510	60	7	5	12
Gobbo, Stockton	.949	20	101	11	6	0	5
Griggs, Stockton	1.000	5	29	7	0	0	0
Harper, Redwood	.982	37	246	23	5	2	9
Holmes, Visalia	.990	40	265	28	3	2	8
Isherwood, Bakersfield	.986	52	317	40	5	5	6
Loard, Fresno	1.000	4	7	0	0	0	1
McKay, Modesto	.983	19	106	12	2	1	9
Miller, Salinas	1.000	1	2	0	0	0	0
Morris, Stockton	.980	10	47	2	1	1	1
Nago, Stockton	.985	24	174	23	3	4	6
Nichols, San Jose	.948	39	191	30	12	2	8
Noce, Reno	1.000	1	1	0	0	0	0
Nokes, Fresno	.976	101	595	62	16	9	17
Ott, Redwood	.909	2	10	0	1	0	0
Ouellette, Fresno	.996	40	223	17	1	1	2
Pott, Reno	.956	14	76	11	4	2	1
Priessman, San Jose	.939	28	120	19	9	0	5
Soma, San Jose	.980	43	171	22	4	2	4
Stewart, Salinas	1.000	7	35	5	0	0	3
Tanabe, Stockton	.985	96	591	66	10	5	20
Tettleton, Modesto	.984	97	573	46	10	2	14
J. Thomas, Reno	.986	42	238	39	4	2	7
Tryon, Visalia	1.000	6	21	3	0	0	0
Turner, Redwood	.985	59	305	26	5	4	11
Vavra, Lodi	1.000	1	5	1	0	0	0
Vega, Bakersfield	1.000	3	13	2	0	0	1
Ri. Wilson, Bakersfield	.965	89	562	80	23	5	22

Triple play—Wilson.

PITCHERS

Player and Club	Pct.	G.	PO.	A.	E.	DP.
Adamczak, Salinas	.957	16	7	15	1	0
Ahern, Redwood*	.857	16	2	10	2	0
Angulo, Redwood*	1.000	31	2	18	0	0
Antunez, Stockton*	.909	45	2	8	1	0
Arney, Visalia	1.000	6	2	1	0	0
Arrington, Visalia	.929	27	13	26	3	3
Bankowski, Redwood*	1.000	37	1	7	0	1
Barling, Fresno	.875	13	0	7	1	0
Barry, Modesto*	.952	26	9	31	2	3
Bartley, Bakersfield	.971	53	7	26	1	3
C. Beard, Lodi	.900	24	15	12	3	2
Belanger, Visalia*	1.000	55	3	13	0	0
Biko, Reno*	.933	36	4	10	1	0
Blobaum, Fresno	.950	27	6	13	1	2
Bockus, Fresno	.898	30	21	32	6	4
Boudreau, Salinas*	.964	24	5	22	1	1
Brahms, Salinas	.929	42	3	10	1	1
Bryant, Salinas*	.960	16	3	21	1	0

PITCHERS—Continued

Player and Club	Pct.	G.	PO.	A.	E.	DP.
Bryden, Redwood	.947	44	2	16	1	3
Buonantony, Salinas	.975	22	17	22	1	4
Burns, Lodi	1.000	10	5	7	0	0
Butler, San Jose*	.938	19	0	15	1	1
Carne, Lodi*	1.000	28	2	5	0	0
CARPIO, Salinas	1.000	28	9	18	0	0
M. Cartwright, Visalia	.963	32	8	18	1	1
Chue, Fresno	1.000	13	7	5	0	2
Clarke, Salinas	.951	25	22	36	3	2
Collins, Stockton	.923	12	5	7	1	0
Cook, San Jose	.878	29	14	22	5	1
Crabb, Reno	.905	31	11	27	4	2
Crews, Fresno	.886	19	15	16	4	2
Cunningham, Lodi	.889	25	7	9	2	0
DeHart, San Jose	1.000	5	1	1	0	0
Derksen, Stockton	1.000	18	1	3	0	0
Duquette, Stockton*	.818	14	2	7	2	0
Effrig, Stockton	1.000	4	1	0	0	0
Eichhorn, Lodi	.929	12	2	11	1	1
Embser, Stockton*	.833	20	2	18	4	1
Escribano, San Jose	1.000	18	2	5	0	1
Eufemia, Visalia	.971	64	7	27	1	2
G. Evans, Stockton	1.000	24	4	5	0	0
M. Evans, Bakersfield*	.933	42	5	9	1	0
Feeley, San Jose	.800	9	2	2	1	0
Gallo, Fresno*	.857	22	2	4	1	0
Gilbert, San Jose*	1.000	28	3	9	0	0
Gorman, Modesto	.938	34	2	13	1	1
Guetterman, Bakersfield*	.925	25	13	24	3	1
Guinn, San Jose	.917	24	3	19	2	0
Harris, Redwood	1.000	4	0	1	0	0
Hayes, Bakersfield*	.958	39	5	18	1	1
Henderson, Visalia*	.875	8	1	13	2	0
Herron, Modesto*	.889	13	5	19	3	1
Heuer, Lodi	1.000	9	6	6	0	0
Hilton, Modesto	.889	10	3	5	1	1
Hoke, San Jose	1.000	10	1	1	0	0
Holland, Bakersfield	.889	25	4	12	2	0
Housey, Salinas	1.000	17	5	12	0	0
Hummel, Fresno*	.966	19	12	16	1	0
Jacob, San Jose	.968	39	14	16	1	4
Jarrett, Modesto	.974	26	6	31	1	1
M. Johnson, Bakersfield	.933	49	7	7	1	1
S. Johnson, Salinas*	1.000	31	4	12	0	1
J. Jones, Reno	.970	17	11	21	1	1
L. Jones, Redwood	1.000	13	2	2	0	0
Kaiser, Modesto*	.962	25	7	44	2	4
Kammeyer, Redwood	.918	27	14	31	4	1
Kaufman, Salinas	.923	51	2	10	1	1
Kindred, Visalia	.955	26	7	14	1	0
Kobernus, Modesto*	1.000	30	5	11	0	1
Koontz, Stockton	1.000	54	5	7	0	0
Kranitz, Stockton	1.000	6	2	7	0	0
Kutsukos, Reno	.882	50	5	10	2	1
Lambert, Modesto	1.000	42	7	8	0	1
Langford, Modesto	1.000	1	0	1	0	0
Legumina, San Jose*	.857	28	4	14	3	0
Leiter, San Jose	1.000	12	5	10	0	0
Lugo, Redwood	1.000	11	2	11	0	1
Macias, Reno	1.000	24	3	6	0	0
Mack, Redwood	.979	27	16	31	1	2
Marietta, San Jose	.857	17	6	18	4	1
Marsden, Lodi	.880	18	11	11	3	1
Mathiesen, Fresno	1.000	32	8	11	0	0
McCaskill, Redwood	.882	16	3	12	2	1
McCoy, Stockton	1.000	18	3	5	0	0
McCullock, San Jose	.778	19	1	6	2	0
McDonald, Bakersfield	.945	27	14	38	3	2
McDonough, San Jose	1.000	8	1	2	0	0
McMahon, Visalia	.867	27	13	26	6	0
Meeks, Lodi	.886	22	11	20	4	3
Meister, Bakersfield	1.000	8	2	2	0	0
Mills, Reno	.500	2	1	1	2	0
Moore, Stockton	1.000	5	2	2	0	0
Morse, Fresno*	.842	15	2	14	3	0
Murray, Bakersfield	1.000	3	0	4	0	0
Murtha, Fresno*	.900	29	3	6	1	1
Myers, Modesto	1.000	17	1	8	0	2
Nago, Stockton	1.000	1	1	1	0	0
Norton, Stockton	1.000	20	2	8	0	0
Oliver, Redwood	.929	26	0	13	1	1
Parsons, Reno	.949	28	10	27	2	3
Pedersen, Bakersfield	.919	40	13	21	3	0
Piper, Lodi	.033	26	3	11	1	1
Plesac, Reno	.909	40	9	11	2	0
Portugal, Visalia	.806	24	9	16	6	5
Potestio, Salinas	.943	32	12	21	2	2
Price, Redwood	.872	26	12	22	5	1
Ramirez, Bakersfield	.974	26	13	25	1	0
Ramsey, Lodi*	.895	24	11	23	4	2
Reade, Lodi	.933	31	6	8	1	0
Rentschler, Redwood*	1.000	5	3	1	0	0
Robinson, Fresno	.895	14	7	10	2	1
Rosenhahn, Salinas	1.000	5	0	1	0	0
Salazar, Redwood	1.000	8	0	4	0	0
Schafer, Fresno	.889	23	3	5	1	0
Schassler, Bakersfield	.952	22	8	12	1	0
Sheppard, Visalia	1.000	17	2	4	0	1
Shields, Lodi	1.000	6	0	2	0	0
D. Smith, Lodi	1.000	40	4	5	0	1
J. Smith, Redwood	1.000	11	1	3	0	0
Steffanich, Reno*	1.000	35	5	8	0	1
Summers, San Jose	.917	6	5	6	1	1
Tatsuno, Stockton*	.951	23	7	32	2	3
Teahan, Stockton	1.000	11	3	4	0	0
Tejeda, Lodi*	.750	9	0	3	1	0
Thurman, Lodi	1.000	11	1	5	0	0
Torres, Stockton	.833	6	0	5	1	0
Towers, Reno	.882	24	9	21	4	2
Ueda, San Jose	1.000	31	4	5	0	0
Vavrock, Modesto	.947	31	5	13	1	1
Vosberg, Reno*	.972	15	6	29	1	0
S. Walker, Lodi	1.000	7	1	4	0	0
Walker, Stockton	.952	26	13	27	2	2
Wardle, Visalia*	.926	49	8	17	2	2
Wegman, Stockton	.956	24	16	27	2	1
Wilcox, Fresno	.923	19	6	6	1	0
M. Williams, Reno*	.833	11	2	8	2	1
Ra. Wilson, San Jose	.926	42	1	24	2	4
Winters, Frenso*	.955	25	6	15	1	1
Wiseman, Visalia	.875	14	3	4	1	0
Wortham, Modesto*	1.000	14	2	5	0	0
Zmudosky, Modesto	.906	27	8	21	3	1

The following players do not have any recorded accepted chances at the positions indicated and therefore are not listed in the fielding averages for those particular positions: Abe, of; Beard, p; E. Castro, of; Cuellar, p; Franko, of; Gibbons, p; Hanggie, 3b; Holmes, p; Junker, ss; Lockie, p; Lusted, p; Nixon, of; O'Connor, p; Ortiz, p; Puryear, p; Rosales, p; Rutledge, 2b; Shirahata, c; R. Thomas, 3b, ss; Watanabe, p; Wood, p.

CLUB PITCHING

Club	ERA.	G.	CG.	ShO.	Sv.	IP.	H.	R.	ER.	HR.	HB.	BB.	Int. BB.	SO.	WP.	Bk.
Bakersfield	3.21	140	23	8	33	1211.2	1177	585	432	57	27	498	20	856	60	9
Stockton	3.22	138	34	14	29	1197.2	1094	527	429	54	26	512	22	923	67	12
Fresno	3.44	140	31	18	29	1181.1	1141	583	452	61	34	448	12	807	75	4
Redwood	3.53	138	46	6	23	1149.2	1062	573	451	60	44	584	18	788	55	10
Visalia	3.65	140	20	9	40	1212.0	1184	605	491	72	35	561	10	896	61	10
Modesto	3.89	139	39	11	28	1171.1	1242	600	506	67	30	446	14	802	69	13
Salinas	4.07	140	29	6	24	1186.0	1225	678	536	73	45	457	5	765	72	7
Lodi	4.43	138	31	8	21	1161.0	1205	713	572	84	29	629	19	803	66	9
San Jose	4.71	140	18	4	24	1171.0	1259	784	613	63	34	596	42	711	79	15
Reno	4.92	139	32	5	25	1165.0	1324	799	637	67	41	564	25	804	86	14

PITCHERS' RECORDS

(Leading Qualifiers for Earned-Run Average Leadership—112 or More Innings)

*Throws lefthanded.

Pitcher—Club	W.	L.	Pct.	ERA.	G.	GS.	CG.	GF.	ShO.	Sv.	IP.	H.	R.	ER.	HR.	HB.	BB.	Int. BB.	SO.	WP.
Wegman, William, Stockton	16	5	.762	1.30	24	23	15	1	4	0	186.2	149	33	27	1	1	45	1	135	4
Meeks, Timothy, Lodi	14	4	.778	2.35	22	22	11	0	4	0	165.0	135	55	43	12	0	44	0	124	2
Wardle, Curtis, Visalia*	8	6	.571	2.65	49	4	1	17	0	8	146.0	118	52	43	6	3	55	1	134	5
Jones, James, Reno	7	5	.583	2.70	17	17	6	0	1	0	116.2	96	50	35	0	3	49	2	79	3
Pedersen, Mark, Bakersfield	9	9	.500	2.87	40	12	0	4	0	0	141.1	136	62	45	5	7	51	2	85	5

Pitcher—Club	W.	L.	Pct.	ERA.	G.	GS.	CG.	GF.	ShO.	Sv.	IP.	H.	R.	ER.	HR.	HB.	BB.	Int. BB.	SO.	WP.
Ramirez, Randolph, Bakersfield	11	7	.611	2.98	26	26	5	0	2	0	169.0	146	76	56	13	4	43	0	136	13
McDonald, Jeffrey, Bakersfield	12	12	.500	3.03	27	26	8	1	2	0	178.0	181	85	60	8	4	84	4	115	4
Cartwright, Mark, Visalia	12	2	.857	3.04	32	19	7	6	0	0	159.2	164	67	54	7	3	53	0	92	8
Kammeyer, Timothy, Redwood	11	9	.550	3.18	27	27	8	0	3	0	186.2	157	89	66	5	8	103	3	136	8
Guetterman, Lee, Bakersfield*	12	6	.667	3.22	25	25	6	0	1	0	156.1	164	72	56	5	0	45	0	93	4

Departmental Leaders: G—Eufemia, 64; W—Wegman, 16; L—Clarke, 17; Pct.—Cartwright, Crews, .857; GS—Bockus, 30; CG—Mack, Wegman, 15; GF—Eufemia, 53; ShO—Meeks, Wegman, 4; Sv.—Kutsukos, 19; IP—Mack, 196.1; H—Parsons, 241; R—Parsons, 130; ER—Parsons, 107; HR—Crabb, Legumina, 15; HB—Bryden, 13; BB—Ramsey, 116; IBB—Jacob, 8; SO—Bockus, 144; WP—Plesac, 21.

(All Pitchers—Listed Alphabetically)

Pitcher—Club	W.	L.	Pct.	ERA.	G.	GS.	CG.	GF.	ShO.	Sv.	IP.	H.	R.	ER.	HR.	HB.	BB.	Int. BB.	SO.	WP.
Adamczak, Salinas	1	10	.091	6.99	16	12	2	1	0	0	67.0	99	69	52	6	6	36	1	23	3
Ahern, Redwood*	4	6	.400	3.95	16	16	3	0	0	0	93.1	96	56	41	4	2	45	1	27	5
Angulo, Redwood*	6	6	.500	4.06	31	13	1	6	0	2	108.2	88	57	49	5	1	70	1	94	3
Antunez, Stockton*	1	4	.200	5.43	45	4	0	15	0	2	68.0	71	53	41	5	0	36	3	53	8
Arney, Visalia	0	0	.000	3.68	6	0	0	2	0	0	7.1	3	4	3	1	0	10	0	7	0
Arrington, Visalia	12	7	.632	4.22	27	26	5	0	2	0	155.2	157	88	73	8	10	72	0	110	8
Bankowski, Redwood*	0	2	.000	3.68	37	0	0	22	0	3	29.1	25	14	12	2	2	15	0	19	1
Barling, Fresno	2	4	.333	1.36	13	4	0	6	0	2	39.2	27	19	6	1	3	28	0	42	2
Barry, Modesto*	12	9	.571	4.28	26	26	11	0	1	0	174.1	208	102	83	12	9	57	1	104	15
Bartley, Bakersfield	5	8	.385	3.05	53	1	1	29	0	10	97.1	97	39	33	2	0	42	6	61	2
C. Beard, Lodi	3	5	.375	5.40	24	10	3	9	1	0	80.0	99	64	48	4	9	40	2	41	9
D. Beard, Modesto	0	0	.000	0.00	1	0	0	0	0	0	1.0	0	0	0	0	0	0	0	2	0
Belanger, Visalia*	10	7	.588	3.19	55	0	0	31	0	14	98.2	99	43	35	6	1	39	3	92	2
Biko, Reno*	5	5	.500	4.52	36	6	1	14	0	4	71.2	82	44	36	5	0	30	4	46	4
Blobaum, Fresno	0	5	.000	2.03	27	0	0	25	0	11	48.2	39	16	11	0	2	11	2	33	2
Bockus, Fresno	14	6	.700	3.58	30	30	6	0	3	0	196.0	185	89	78	8	8	78	2	144	13
Boudreau, Salinas*	7	12	.368	3.40	24	23	7	0	2	0	156.0	155	77	59	11	4	43	0	101	3
Brahms, Salinas	2	3	.400	3.42	42	0	0	32	0	4	52.2	66	26	20	0	3	22	1	41	3
Bryant, Salinas*	3	10	.231	4.07	16	16	5	0	0	0	97.1	87	64	44	4	2	47	0	67	11
Bryden, Redwood	6	5	.545	3.36	44	1	0	32	0	9	69.2	53	34	26	5	13	55	7	42	6
Buonantony, Salinas	6	7	.462	3.46	22	22	2	0	1	0	138.0	136	73	53	6	3	62	0	97	10
Burns, Lodi	1	4	.200	7.91	10	5	0	1	0	0	38.2	61	41	34	8	1	14	2	17	3
Butler, San Jose*	4	1	.800	1.54	19	0	0	14	0	7	41.0	34	9	7	0	1	12	2	26	3
Carne, Lodi*	1	0	1.000	3.29	28	1	0	18	0	2	65.2	69	30	24	3	1	34	0	43	1
Carpio, Salinas	10	9	.526	4.20	28	16	2	5	0	2	135.0	150	76	63	10	4	52	0	90	9
M. Cartwright, Visalia	12	2	.857	3.04	32	19	7	6	0	0	159.2	164	67	54	7	3	53	0	92	8
Chue, Fresno	2	1	.667	3.98	13	1	0	2	0	0	31.2	37	21	14	1	4	12	1	24	0
Clarke, Salinas	6	17	.261	5.45	25	25	6	0	1	0	155.1	190	110	94	13	8	49	0	62	5
Collins, Stockton	2	2	.500	3.39	12	11	1	1	0	0	66.1	60	30	25	1	1	30	1	52	5
Cook, San Jose	7	13	.350	4.47	29	25	3	1	0	1	151.0	161	102	75	4	2	92	5	64	12
Crabb, Reno	6	13	.316	5.67	31	20	5	5	0	0	146.0	197	106	92	15	6	40	2	81	9
Crews, Fresno	12	2	.857	3.27	19	18	8	1	3	0	135.0	126	54	49	11	6	36	0	84	5
Cuellar, Bakersfield	0	0	.000	11.81	4	0	0	3	0	0	5.1	7	7	7	1	0	3	0	2	1
Cunningham, Lodi	10	8	.556	4.33	25	20	7	4	2	0	143.1	145	75	69	7	1	68	3	83	8
DeHart, San Jose	0	1	.000	6.62	5	3	0	0	0	0	17.2	19	16	13	1	1	15	1	4	4
Derksen, Stockton	3	1	.750	3.42	18	0	0	6	0	2	23.2	28	9	9	1	0	14	1	21	0
Duquette, Stockton*	4	0	1.000	0.78	14	0	0	10	0	2	23.0	11	4	2	0	0	11	2	31	0
Effrig, Stockton	0	1	.000	9.00	4	0	0	2	0	1	4.0	6	4	4	0	0	4	1	1	1
Eichhorn, Lodi	2	5	.286	5.36	12	8	0	0	0	0	48.2	60	38	29	2	0	31	1	16	1
Embser, Stockton*	6	6	.500	3.55	20	18	4	1	2	0	99.0	90	51	39	2	3	60	1	88	5
Escribano, San Jose	1	1	.500	4.34	18	2	0	8	0	2	37.1	35	22	18	1	6	26	1	34	1
Eufemia, Visalia	10	4	.714	2.45	64	0	0	53	0	18	95.2	79	27	26	9	0	29	3	78	0
G. Evans, Stockton	3	3	.500	4.21	24	6	0	6	0	2	62.0	68	33	29	0	2	37	2	37	4
M. Evans, Bakersfield*	2	2	.500	0.51	42	0	0	32	0	14	52.2	31	8	3	1	0	10	3	53	1
Feeley, San Jose	0	1	.000	10.05	9	1	0	7	0	0	14.1	20	18	16	3	6	18	0	2	6
Gallo, Fresno*	2	2	.500	5.75	22	2	0	10	0	0	40.2	47	31	26	3	0	40	0	30	6
Gibbons, Stockton*	0	0	.000	0.00	1	0	0	1	0	0	1.0	1	1	0	0	1	2	0	0	0
Gilbert, San Jose*	6	2	.750	5.16	28	12	2	7	0	0	89.0	94	61	51	5	1	52	2	42	5
Gorman, Modesto	4	2	.667	3.08	34	1	0	16	0	4	79.0	76	28	27	3	0	24	0	84	5
Guetterman, Bakersfield*	12	6	.667	3.22	25	25	6	0	1	0	156.1	164	72	56	5	0	45	0	93	4
Guinn, San Jose	6	11	.353	4.44	24	21	4	2	0	0	123.2	129	76	61	5	0	55	3	54	4
Harris, Redwood	0	1	.000	6.75	4	1	0	1	0	0	4.0	6	5	3	0	0	9	0	2	1
Hayes, Bakersfield*	5	3	.625	2.89	39	7	0	7	0	0	109.0	103	53	35	4	3	54	3	73	7
Henderson, Visalia*	2	5	.286	4.05	8	8	0	0	0	0	46.2	45	28	21	2	0	21	0	40	4
Herron, Modesto*	3	6	.333	3.76	13	13	4	0	3	0	83.2	81	39	35	4	3	37	0	71	2
Heuer, Lodi	2	5	.286	4.84	9	7	2	1	0	0	48.1	51	30	26	5	1	15	0	16	3
Hilton, Modesto	3	4	.429	4.95	10	10	2	0	1	0	56.1	57	35	31	3	2	28	0	36	4
Hoke, San Jose	0	0	.000	11.15	10	0	0	7	0	1	15.1	26	27	19	1	1	13	1	16	6
Holland, Bakersfield	5	11	.313	5.32	25	23	2	1	0	0	115.0	143	87	68	8	1	58	0	62	11
Holmes, Visalia	0	0	.000	0.00	1	0	0	1	0	0	1.0	0	0	0	0	0	0	0	0	0
Housey, Salinas	9	5	.643	3.35	17	17	5	0	2	0	121.0	108	53	45	9	6	36	0	89	6
Hummel, Fresno*	4	12	.250	4.32	19	18	3	0	1	0	98.0	103	59	47	6	1	61	0	52	6
Jacob, San Jose	9	13	.409	4.64	39	15	1	15	0	0	128.0	150	88	66	9	2	67	8	98	5
Jarrett, Modesto	14	10	.583	3.89	26	26	9	0	2	0	187.1	206	97	81	10	3	49	2	110	4
M. Johnson, Bakersfield	2	7	.222	2.54	49	0	0	37	0	9	67.1	49	26	19	3	5	52	2	97	5
S. Johnson, Salinas*	4	4	.500	4.57	31	3	0	12	0	2	82.2	87	53	42	4	1	42	0	65	10
J. Jones, Reno	7	5	.583	2.70	17	17	6	0	1	0	116.2	96	50	35	0	3	49	2	79	3
L. Jones, Redwood	0	1	.000	4.74	13	0	0	6	0	2	19.0	17	15	10	3	1	9	0	13	3
Kaiser, Modesto*	12	9	.571	3.83	25	25	4	0	0	0	164.2	160	84	70	4	5	80	2	102	9
Kammeyer, Redwood	11	9	.550	3.18	27	27	8	0	3	0	186.2	157	89	66	5	8	103	3	136	8
Kaufman, Salinas	3	4	.429	2.73	51	0	0	43	0	13	66.0	55	22	20	5	3	20	2	50	3
Kindred, Visalia	8	6	.571	4.64	26	18	2	2	1	0	106.2	106	67	55	10	1	71	1	61	7
Kobernus, Modesto*	2	3	.400	4.36	30	1	0	18	0	5	43.1	52	23	21	8	2	16	0	27	1
Koontz, Stockton	8	7	.533	2.22	54	1	0	46	0	17	89.0	56	26	22	3	2	46	3	72	7
Kranitz, Stockton	3	1	.750	2.22	6	6	2	0	2	0	44.2	30	16	11	2	0	21	0	44	2
Kutsukos, Reno	4	5	.444	3.17	50	0	0	45	0	19	71.0	61	36	25	4	1	30	4	59	4
Lambert, Modesto	6	4	.600	1.74	42	1	0	33	0	13	77.2	65	20	15	1	0	30	6	64	7
Langford, Modesto	0	0	.000	3.00	1	1	0	0	0	0	6.0	4	2	2	0	0	2	0	2	0
Legumina, San Jose*	6	12	.333	5.94	28	23	3	2	0	1	139.1	173	110	92	15	1	52	3	73	6
Leiter, San Jose	2	9	.182	4.25	12	12	2	0	0	0	72.0	75	45	34	4	0	32	1	37	3

Pitcher—Club	W.	L.	Pct.	ERA.	G.	GS.	CG.	GF.	ShO.	Sv.	IP.	H.	R.	ER.	HR.	HB.	BB.	Int. BB.	SO.	WP.
Lockie, Salinas	0	0	.000	12.00	1	0	0	0	0	0	3.0	5	4	4	1	0	1	0	3	0
Lugo, Redwood	5	5	.500	3.90	11	11	5	0	0	0	64.2	59	36	28	6	1	31	0	58	5
Lusted, Fresno	0	0	.000	0.00	1	0	0	1	0	0	2.0	1	0	0	0	0	1	0	1	0
Macias, Reno	7	4	.636	5.60	24	12	3	5	0	0	88.1	119	69	55	9	1	40	7	40	7
Mack, Redwood	13	9	.591	3.48	27	27	15	0	1	0	196.1	191	92	76	14	4	77	1	133	9
Marietta, San Jose	5	8	.385	4.05	17	15	4	1	2	0	104.1	111	66	47	5	7	42	5	70	4
Marsden, Lodi	7	5	.583	4.83	18	14	3	2	1	0	95.0	106	58	51	10	1	36	0	51	6
Mathiesen, Fresno	5	5	.500	3.52	32	8	1	23	0	8	92.0	91	48	36	6	0	33	3	72	6
McCaskill, Redwood	6	5	.545	2.33	16	15	4	0	2	0	108.1	78	39	28	5	2	60	1	100	3
McCoy, Stockton	4	0	1.000	1.37	18	2	0	4	0	0	39.1	29	10	6	0	0	20	0	32	3
McCullock, San Jose	0	1	.000	3.41	19	0	0	14	0	1	31.2	29	13	12	0	2	17	0	31	6
McDonald, Bakersfield	12	12	.500	3.03	27	26	8	1	2	0	178.0	181	85	60	8	4	84	4	115	4
McDonough, San Jose	1	2	.333	7.56	8	1	0	3	0	1	16.2	25	16	14	1	1	3	1	5	2
McMahon, Visalia	11	7	.611	3.47	27	27	4	0	1	0	163.1	168	85	63	13	5	71	0	90	8
Meeks, Lodi	14	4	.778	2.35	22	22	11	0	4	0	165.0	135	55	43	12	0	44	0	124	2
Meister, Bakersfield	1	2	.333	4.05	8	3	0	3	0	0	20.0	19	13	9	0	0	11	0	14	1
Mills, Reno	2	0	1.000	1.17	2	2	1	0	1	0	15.1	13	3	2	0	0	6	0	11	1
Moore, Stockton	1	2	.333	3.51	5	4	0	0	0	0	25.2	25	13	10	1	1	5	0	15	0
Morse, Fresno*	7	1	.875	2.87	15	12	2	2	2	0	84.2	85	34	27	4	1	17	0	45	3
Murray, Bakersfield	0	0	.000	1.38	3	3	0	0	0	0	13.0	11	6	2	1	0	2	0	7	1
Murtha, Fresno*	5	3	.625	3.67	29	0	0	13	0	4	68.2	68	38	28	3	1	34	1	49	3
Myers, Modesto	3	2	.600	0.70	17	1	1	15	0	6	25.2	11	3	2	0	0	13	0	27	1
Nago, Stockton	0	0	.000	7.36	1	0	0	1	0	0	3.2	5	4	3	1	0	1	0	0	0
Norton, Stockton	3	2	.600	3.70	20	1	0	7	0	3	48.2	48	22	20	2	1	19	1	33	7
O'Connor, San Jose	0	0	.000	4.50	1	0	0	1	0	0	2.0	3	1	1	0	1	0	0	2	0
Oliver, Redwood	4	1	.800	1.30	26	0	0	16	0	6	34.2	42	10	5	0	1	14	2	23	4
Ortiz, Reno	0	0	.000	8.10	5	0	0	4	0	0	3.1	3	6	3	1	3	3	0	3	0
Parsons, Reno	9	14	.391	5.14	28	28	8	0	0	0	187.1	241	130	107	14	5	68	3	118	9
Pedersen, Bakersfield	9	9	.500	2.87	40	12	0	4	0	0	141.1	136	62	45	5	7	51	2	85	5
Piper, Lodi	4	11	.267	4.57	26	7	0	11	0	2	84.2	83	58	43	5	2	66	2	67	8
Plesac, Reno	2	5	.286	9.31	40	4	0	15	0	0	67.2	85	84	70	4	5	79	1	51	21
Portugal, Visalia	10	5	.667	4.18	24	23	2	1	0	0	131.1	142	77	61	6	5	84	1	132	10
Potestio, Salinas	6	1	.857	3.25	32	6	1	15	0	3	102.1	77	47	37	4	5	43	1	61	8
Price, Redwood	15	10	.600	3.76	26	26	10	0	0	0	189.0	191	90	79	10	9	67	0	118	4
Puryear, Stockton	0	1	.000	9.95	4	2	0	0	0	0	6.1	6	8	7	0	1	12	0	6	1
Ramirez, Bakersfield	11	7	.611	2.98	26	26	5	0	2	0	169.0	146	76	56	13	4	43	0	136	13
Ramsey, Lodi*	5	7	.417	5.02	24	23	6	1	0	0	127.1	124	84	71	9	2	116	1	101	5
Reade, Lodi	2	6	.250	4.93	31	1	0	14	0	3	73.0	75	55	40	5	2	55	0	68	8
Rentschler, Redwood*	1	1	.500	7.36	5	1	0	3	0	1	11.0	18	12	9	1	0	5	0	4	1
Robinson, Fresno	7	6	.538	2.28	14	13	7	1	2	0	94.2	88	35	24	3	2	21	1	78	5
Rosales, Stockton	0	0	.000	0.00	1	0	0	1	0	0	1.0	0	0	0	0	0	1	0	0	0
Rosenhahn, Salinas	0	1	.000	2.79	5	0	0	2	0	0	9.2	10	4	3	0	0	4	0	16	1
Salazar, Redwood	1	1	.500	3.80	8	0	0	5	0	0	21.1	20	12	9	0	0	16	0	10	0
Schafer, Fresno	5	2	.714	3.38	23	0	0	18	0	3	32.0	36	22	12	3	2	6	0	18	2
Schassler, Bakersfield	4	5	.444	4.33	22	14	1	0	1	0	87.1	90	51	42	5	3	43	0	58	6
Sheppard, Visalia	1	0	1.000	3.65	17	4	0	4	0	0	44.1	34	29	18	1	4	34	1	28	5
Shields, Lodi	0	1	.000	9.82	6	1	0	3	0	0	11.0	15	18	12	1	1	15	0	7	4
D. Smith, Lodi	5	5	.500	2.69	40	0	0	38	0	14	60.1	52	22	18	2	3	19	5	68	1
J. Smith, Redwood	1	3	.250	7.24	11	0	0	1	0	0	13.2	22	12	11	0	0	8	2	9	2
Steffanich, Reno*	3	1	.750	4.68	35	0	0	18	0	2	73.0	81	51	38	5	3	30	2	64	3
Summers, San Jose	1	3	.250	5.52	6	6	0	0	0	0	29.1	34	24	18	3	0	15	0	15	1
Tatsuno, Stockton*	10	6	.625	3.24	23	22	5	0	2	0	155.2	132	65	56	13	6	47	0	111	4
Teahan, Stockton	1	4	.200	7.56	11	5	0	2	0	0	33.1	47	29	28	9	1	12	0	24	1
Tejeda, Lodi*	0	3	.000	6.37	9	4	0	2	0	0	29.2	40	25	21	2	0	16	1	30	3
Thurman, Lodi	2	6	.250	4.17	11	8	0	1	0	0	49.2	47	32	23	6	3	34	0	43	3
Torres, Stockton	3	2	.600	2.04	6	5	1	0	0	0	35.1	28	12	8	1	0	13	0	26	3
Towers, Reno	11	11	.500	4.42	24	24	6	0	2	0	169.0	176	103	83	4	6	90	1	138	13
Ueda, San Jose	3	2	.600	5.60	31	4	0	11	0	1	70.2	72	52	44	2	2	45	2	74	4
Vavrock, Modesto	5	3	.625	5.15	31	12	2	12	1	0	87.1	126	59	50	12	4	24	0	47	3
Vosberg, Reno*	6	6	.500	3.87	15	15	3	0	0	0	97.2	111	61	42	3	3	39	0	70	3
C. Walker, Stockton	11	11	.500	3.77	26	26	6	0	0	0	174.1	191	91	73	10	2	74	6	138	12
S. Walker, Lodi	2	3	.400	4.43	7	7	1	0	0	0	40.2	41	28	20	3	2	26	2	28	1
Wardle, Visalia*	8	6	.571	2.65	49	4	1	17	0	8	146.0	118	52	43	6	3	55	1	134	5
Watanabe, Stockton	0	0	.000	13.50	1	0	0	0	0	0	2.0	6	5	3	0	0	0	0	0	0
Wegman, Stockton	16	5	.762	1.30	24	23	15	1	4	0	186.2	149	33	27	1	1	45	1	135	4
Wilcox, Fresno	3	4	.429	4.30	19	10	0	7	0	1	60.2	59	34	29	6	1	30	2	51	12
M. Williams, Reno*	1	7	.125	7.14	11	11	0	0	0	0	58.0	58	56	46	1	4	60	0	44	9
Ra. Wilson, San Jose	5	4	.556	2.46	42	0	0	28	0	9	87.2	69	38	24	3	0	40	7	64	7
Winters, Fresno*	10	9	.526	3.67	25	24	4	0	1	0	157.0	150	83	64	6	2	41	0	84	9
Wiseman, Visalia	3	4	.429	5.50	14	11	0	2	0	0	55.2	70	38	34	3	3	22	0	32	4
Wood, Stockton	0	1	.000	12.60	3	2	0	0	0	0	5.0	7	8	7	2	4	2	0	4	1
Wortham, Modesto*	2	3	.400	6.75	14	5	2	3	0	0	44.0	45	41	33	2	0	42	1	44	12
Zmudosky, Modesto	9	9	.500	3.60	27	17	4	3	0	0	140.0	151	67	56	8	2	44	2	82	6

BALKS—Wegman, 5; Kaiser, Ueda, Vosberg, 4 each; Arrington, Guinn, Hayes, Jarrett, McCaskill, Ramirez, Tatsuno, Tejeda, Zmudosky, 3 each; Belanger, Biko, Butler, Henderson, Hummel, J. Jones, Legumina, Macias, Marietta, Price, Towers, C. Walker, 2 each; Adamczak, Ahern, Angulo, Barry, Bartley, C. Beard, Blobaum, Bockus, Bryant, Bryden, Buonantony, Burns, Clarke, DeHart, Eichhorn, Embser, Guetterman, Housey, Kaufman, Kindred, Kobernus, Lambert, Leiter, McDonald, Meeks, Meister, Norton, Oliver, Piper, Plesac, Potestio, Salazar, Schassler, Shields, D. Smith, Wardle, Williams, Wiseman, 1 each.

COMBINATION SHUTOUTS—Murray-McDonald, Ramirez-Evans, Bakersfield; Bockus-Mathiesen, Hummel-Mathiesen, Hummel-Murtha, Mathiesen-Murtha-Schafer, Robinson-Mathiesen, Wilcox-Barling, Fresno; Barry-Lambert-Kobernus, Hilton-Lambert, Zmudosky-Kobernus-Lambert, Modesto; Vosberg-Kutsukos, Reno; Guinn-Butler, Guinn-Escribano, San Jose; Antunez-McCoy, Collins-Moore-Teahan, Embser-Koontz, McCoy-Koontz, Stockton; Arrington-Belanger-Eufemia, Cartwright-Wardle, Cartwright-Eufemia, McMahon-Eufemia, Portugal-Eufemia-Belanger, Visalia.

PERFECT GAME—Ramirez, Bakersfield, defeated Stockton, 1-0, August 3.

NO-HIT GAMES—Meeks, Lodi, defeated Visalia, 3-0, April 26; Marietta, San Jose, defeated Visalia, 5-0, June 28; Cunningham, Lodi, defeated Redwood, 2-0 (seven innings), July 4.

Carolina League

CLASS A

CHAMPIONSHIP WINNERS IN PREVIOUS YEARS

1945—Danville	.681
1946—Greensboro	.599
Raleigh (2nd)†	.563
1947—Burlington	.613
Raleigh (3rd)†	.574
1948—Raleigh	.592
Martinsville (2nd)†	.570
1949—Danville	.601
Burlington (4th)†	.500
1950—Winston-Salem*	.693
1951—Durham	.600
Wins-Salem (2nd)†	.583
1952—Raleigh	.581
Reidsville (4th)†	.536
1953—Raleigh	.593
Danville (2nd)†	.572
1954—Fayetteville*	.628
1955—HP-Thomasville	.580
Danville (2nd)†	.533
1956—HP-Thomasville	.591
Fayetteville (4th)†	.523
1957—Durham	.632
HP-Thomasville	.622
1958—Danville	.576
Burlington (4th)†	.511
1959—Raleigh	.600
Wilson (2nd)†	.550
1960—Greensboro‡	.636
Burlington	.586
1961—Wilson	.594
1962—Durham	.636
Wilson	.600
Kinston (2nd)†	.593
1963—Kinston§	.538
Greensboro§	.590
Wilson (2nd)†	.535
1964—Kinston§	.572
Winston-Salem§†	.590
1965—Peninsula§	.597
Durham§	.580
Tidewater†	.528
1966—Kinston§	.547
Winston-Salem§	.586
Rocky Mount†	.533
1967—Durham x (West.)	.536
Raleigh (East.)	.542
1968—Salem (West.)	.607
Ral-Dur (East.)	.597
HP-Thom. y (W.)	.493
1969—Rocky M (East.)	.569
Salem (West.)	.542
Ral-Dur z (East.)	.560
1970—Winston-Salem‡	.586
Burlington	.597
1971—Peninsula‡	.647
Kinston	.623
1972—Salem‡	.657
Burlington	.632
1973—Lynchburg	.588
Winston-Salem‡	.557
1974—Salem	.671
Salem	.582
1975—Rocky Mount	.667
Rocky Mount	.614
1976—Winston-Salem	.618
Winston-Salem	.551
1977—Lynchburg	.591
Peninsula‡	.556
1978—Peninsula	.696
Lynchburg‡	.614
1979—Winston-Salem a	.607
1980—Peninsula‡	.714
Durham	.600
1981—Peninsula	.522
Hagerstown‡	.507
1982—Alexandria‡	.597
Durham	.588

*Won championship and four-club playoff. †Won four-club playoff. ‡Won split-season playoff. §League was divided into Eastern, Western divisions. xWon eight-club, two-division playoff. yWon eight-club, two-division playoff against Raleigh-Durham. zWon eight-club, two-division playoff against Burlington. aWon both halves of split-season (no playoffs).

STANDING OF CLUBS AT CLOSE OF FIRST HALF, JUNE 21

NORTHERN DIVISION

Club	W.	L.	T.	Pct.	G.B.
Lynchburg (Mets)	49	20	0	.710	....
Hagerstown (Orioles)	41	25	0	.621	6½
Alexandria (Pirates)	35	32	0	.522	13
Salem (Padres)	20	49	0	.290	29

SOUTHERN DIVISION

Club	W.	L.	T.	Pct.	G.B.
Winston-Salem (Red Sox)	36	34	0	.514	....
Durham (Braves)	33	34	0	.493	1½
Kinston (Blue Jays)	32	36	0	.471	3
Peninsula (Phillies)	26	42	0	.382	9

STANDING OF CLUBS AT CLOSE OF SECOND HALF, SEPTEMBER 3

NORTHERN DIVISION

Club	W.	L.	T.	Pct.	G.B.
Lynchburg (Mets)	47	23	0	.671	....
Hagerstown (Orioles)	43	27	0	.614	4
Alexandria (Pirates)	34	36	0	.486	13
Salem (Padres)	30	40	0	.429	17

SOUTHERN DIVISION

Club	W.	L.	T.	Pct.	G.B.
Winston-Salem (Red Sox)	38	32	0	.543	....
Peninsula (Phillies)	32	38	0	.457	6
Kinston (Blue Jays)	30	40	0	.429	8
Durham (Braves)	26	44	0	.371	12

COMPOSITE STANDING OF CLUBS AT CLOSE OF SEASON, SEPTEMBER 3

Club	Lyn.	Hag.	W-S	Alex.	Kin.	Dur.	Pen.	Sal.	W.	L.	T.	Pct.	G.B.
Lynchburg (Mets)	....	12	13	12	15	16	15	13	96	43	0	.691	....
Hagerstown (Orioles)	8	....	14	14	14	11	12	11	84	52	0	.618	10½
Winston-Salem (Red Sox)	7	6	....	14	11	13	10	13	74	66	0	.529	22½
Alexandria (Pirates)	8	4	6	....	11	12	15	13	69	68	0	.504	26
Kinston (Blue Jays)	5	6	9	9	....	11	9	13	62	76	0	.449	33½
Durham (Braves)	4	8	7	8	7	....	11	14	59	78	0	.431	36
Peninsula (Phillies)	5	7	10	4	11	9	....	12	58	80	0	.420	37½
Salem (Padres)	6	9	7	7	7	6	8	....	50	89	0	.360	46

Major league affiliations in parentheses.

Peninsula represented Hampton, Va.

Playoffs—Lynchburg defeated Winston-Salem, three games to none, to win league championship.

Regular-Season Attendance—Alexandria, 41,404; Durham, 142,370; Hagerstown, 153,660; Kinston, 45,125; Lynchburg, 80,104; Peninsula, 34,053; Salem, 56,451; Winston-Salem, 54,803; Total—607,970; Playoffs, 1,911; All-Star Game at Hagerstown, 1,043.

Managers—Alexandria, John Lipon; Durham, Brian Snitker; Hagerstown, John Hart; Kinston, Ron Clark (to August 11) and Doug Ault; Lynchburg, Sam Perlozzo; Peninsula, Tony Taylor; Salem, Steve Smith; Winston-Salem, Bill Slack.

All-Star Team: 1B—Sam Nattile, Winston-Salem; 2B—Fermin Ubri, Lynchburg; 3B—Jim Opie, Alexandria; SS—Mike Mesh, Winston-Salem; OF—Lenny Dykstra, Lynchburg; Ken Gerhart, Hagerstown; Mark Carreon, Lynchburg; C—Danny Sheaffer, Winston-Salem; LHP—Mike Rochford, Winston-Salem; RHP—Dwight Gooden, Lynchburg; Manager-of-the-Year—Sam Perlozzo, Lynchburg.

(Compiled by Howe News Bureau, Boston, Mass.)

CLUB BATTING

Club	Pct.	G.	AB.	R.	OR.	H.	TB.	2B.	3B.	HR.	RBI.	GW.	SH.	SF.	HP.	BB.	Int. BB.	SO.	SB.	CS.	LOB.
Lynchburg	.278	139	4620	786	553	1285	1805	163	48	87	674	87	22	55	34	671	26	791	244	77	1059
Hagerstown	.266	136	4503	789	621	1197	1985	250	32	158	703	73	24	31	46	671	36	871	136	50	1044
Salem	.255	139	4589	675	847	1172	1709	187	25	100	579	42	23	29	43	546	13	975	164	81	953
Peninsula	.255	138	4565	624	710	1164	1655	179	30	84	544	49	49	23	33	524	21	881	148	74	978
Winston-Salem	.253	140	4550	659	654	1149	1719	189	30	107	570	66	46	50	33	554	30	951	159	57	1002
Kinston	.252	138	4660	660	685	1176	1703	176	27	99	588	54	45	31	34	594	12	1075	202	81	1026
Durham	.252	137	4542	633	742	1144	1663	182	20	99	566	49	32	36	26	608	19	886	102	47	1058
Alexandria	.250	137	4532	665	679	1134	1714	186	29	112	584	57	43	38	33	528	15	979	135	84	940

INDIVIDUAL BATTING

(Leading Qualifiers for Batting Championship—378 or More Plate Appearances)

*Bats lefthanded. †Switch-hitter.

Player and Club	Pct.	G.	AB.	R.	H.	TB.	2B.	3B.	HR.	RBI.	GW.	SH.	SF.	HP.	BB.	Int. BB.	SO.	SB.	CS.
Dykstra, Leonard, Lynchburg*	.358	136	525	132	188	264	24	14	8	81	5	1	1	7	107	9	35	105	23
Carreon, Mark, Lynchburg	.334	128	491	94	164	196	13	8	1	67	15	2	11	3	76	2	39	36	8
Seibert, B. Gibson, Peninsula	.305	119	443	83	135	196	21	5	10	54	3	6	3	2	79	2	84	9	11
Wiggins, Kevin, Salem*	.301	115	412	58	124	186	22	5	10	59	5	3	3	0	44	3	99	13	5
Opie, James, Alexandria	.294	125	462	86	136	229	23	5	20	71	8	3	1	4	49	1	115	25	5
Milligan, Randy, Lynchburg	.292	106	349	60	102	140	13	5	5	56	6	1	4	2	85	1	81	41	7
Bundy, Lorenzo, Alexandria*	.291	116	405	72	118	220	25	1	25	88	7	3	3	4	39	2	71	3	2
Salcedo, Ronnie, Hagerstown*	.290	129	504	85	146	252	39	2	21	93	14	2	0	8	77	5	65	6	3
DeLaRosa, Nelson, Alexandria*	.290	109	407	70	118	188	21	2	15	63	7	4	5	0	32	3	81	24	18
Brunenkant, S. Barry, Salem	.287	130	460	81	132	186	23	2	9	61	4	0	6	2	80	0	67	7	3

Departmental Leaders: G—Bonilla, Dykstra, 136; AB—Dykstra, 525; R—Dykstra, 132; H—Dykstra, 188; TB—Gerhart, 275; 2B—Salcedo, 39; 3B—Dykstra, 14; HR—Gerhart, 31; RBI—Cochrane, 102; GWRBI—Cochrane, 18; SH—Escobar, 13; SF—Carreon, 11; HP—Murray, 13; BB—Dykstra, 107; IBB—Nattile, 12; SO—Kinnard, 153; SB—Dykstra, 105; CS—Dykstra, 23.

(All Players—Listed Alphabetically)

Player and Club	Pct.	G.	AB.	R.	H.	TB.	2B.	3B.	HR.	RBI.	GW.	SH.	SF.	HP.	BB.	Int. BB.	SO.	SB.	CS.
Ackley, John, Winston-Salem	.282	90	280	44	79	133	13	1	13	44	8	1	4	1	45	1	65	1	1
Alomar, Victor, Winston-Salem*	.233	55	150	11	35	42	5	1	0	9	1	0	2	0	5	0	23	1	1
Aulenback, James, Alexandria	.206	71	214	31	44	75	8	1	7	36	4	3	4	2	23	1	57	0	0
Bard, Paul, Hagerstown	.205	41	122	15	25	50	4	0	7	17	1	0	0	1	14	0	35	0	0
Bishop, James, Kinston	.267	125	457	79	122	191	30	3	11	66	7	1	2	1	64	1	105	7	4
Bonilla, Roberto, Alexandria†	.256	136	504	88	129	195	19	7	11	59	10	1	1	2	78	5	105	28	14
Brown, Anthony, Peninsula*	.198	23	81	14	16	18	0	1	0	5	1	0	0	0	12	0	15	10	3
Brown, Samuel, Alexandria	.242	81	306	41	74	106	12	1	6	28	4	2	4	3	25	0	56	10	8
Brunenkant, S. Barry, Salem	.287	130	460	81	132	186	23	2	9	61	4	0	6	2	80	0	67	7	3
Buckmier, James, Alexandria	.000	35	1	0	0	0	0	0	0	0	0	0	0	0	0	0	1	0	0
Bundy, Lorenzo, Alexandria*	.291	116	405	72	118	220	25	1	25	88	7	3	3	4	39	2	71	3	2
Burrell, Kevin, Winston-Salem	.240	61	200	28	48	76	10	0	6	29	0	1	1	2	19	0	52	0	0
Burrows, Bryan, Alexandria	.243	13	37	6	9	10	1	0	0	2	0	0	0	1	1	0	4	0	1
Cain, Michael, Hagerstown	.222	27	45	9	10	13	1	1	0	5	0	0	0	0	3	0	8	5	2
Cannon, Joseph J., Kinston*	.196	18	51	5	10	15	3	1	0	4	0	0	0	0	2	0	15	4	0
Carreon, Mark, Lynchburg	.334	128	491	94	164	196	13	8	1	67	15	2	11	3	76	2	39	36	8
Castaneda, Nick, Alexandria*	.279	74	222	24	62	95	9	0	8	29	3	0	2	0	41	2	56	2	0
Childress, Willie John, Durham*	.250	66	256	35	64	75	8	0	1	24	3	1	3	0	29	1	41	4	7
Chmil, Stephen, Durham	.265	85	309	47	82	107	13	0	4	40	5	2	4	3	37	1	43	10	2
Cipolloni, Joseph, Peninsula	.231	98	347	41	80	111	14	1	5	39	4	1	1	3	15	1	63	10	3
Clack, Marvin, Alexandria†	.207	126	449	68	93	118	15	2	2	30	2	9	2	5	90	0	106	17	15
Cochrane, David, Lynchburg†	.263	120	445	73	117	210	16	1	25	102	18	0	2	2	71	11	146	4	2
Coleman, Rickey, Salem	.276	108	409	69	113	151	14	3	6	45	2	1	1	3	29	1	57	16	5
Cormack, Terry, Durham	.232	87	302	35	70	119	14	1	11	31	3	4	1	0	40	1	60	0	0
Corman, David, Hagerstown	.285	110	326	60	93	137	26	3	4	50	5	0	3	4	75	2	72	10	8
Croft, Paul, Hagerstown	.299	23	77	22	23	50	3	0	8	18	1	2	0	1	17	0	20	8	3
Currier, Willard, Peninsula*	.100	10	30	4	3	4	1	0	0	2	0	0	0	0	5	1	12	1	0
Cusack, David, Hagerstown	.248	81	258	41	64	116	16	0	12	49	1	0	3	1	30	2	74	2	1
DeLaRosa, Nelson, Alexandria*	.290	109	407	70	118	188	21	2	15	63	7	4	5	0	32	3	81	24	18
Denby, Darryl, Lynchburg	.278	107	367	57	102	160	16	3	12	53	4	0	2	1	21	1	81	21	6
Denman, John, Hagerstown	.271	31	96	26	26	47	2	2	5	19	3	1	1	0	26	2	35	8	4
Doerr, Jeffrey, Hagerstown	.179	48	151	22	27	55	2	1	8	21	1	1	2	1	19	1	49	1	1
Downs, Dorley, Alexandria	.000	31	1	0	0	0	0	0	0	0	0	0	0	0	0	0	1	0	0
Dumouchelle, Patrick, Hagerstown	.284	89	313	55	89	136	16	2	9	48	5	3	2	1	56	2	38	4	3
Dykstra, Leonard, Lynchburg*	.358	136	525	132	188	264	24	14	8	81	5	1	1	7	107	9	35	105	23
Escobar, Jose, Kinston	.266	125	458	47	122	154	18	4	2	49	2	13	1	0	42	0	71	7	7
Faherty, Sean, Alexandria*	.000	26	1	0	0	0	0	0	0	1	0	0	0	0	0	0	0	0	0
Falcone, David, Hagerstown*	.321	24	78	11	25	42	5	0	4	14	2	1	1	0	15	2	12	1	0
Felt, James, Alexandria	.198	39	111	17	22	31	3	0	2	15	0	0	5	1	25	0	39	5	2
Fisher, Charles, Winston-Salem	.174	27	69	14	12	17	3	1	0	9	2	0	1	0	14	0	23	2	0
Freeman, Donald, Salem	.221	77	271	39	60	85	12	2	3	36	4	0	2	1	38	0	80	12	8
Garcia, Agustin, Lynchburg	.241	44	133	24	32	48	3	2	3	18	3	4	2	1	22	0	39	2	2
Gerhart, H. Kenneth, Hagerstown	.273	130	501	131	137	275	29	8	31	86	6	2	4	7	85	2	129	45	8
Goldthorn, Burk, Alexandria*	.247	27	81	11	20	24	1	0	1	6	0	0	1	1	15	0	19	0	1
Gomez, Jose, Salem*	.260	71	231	40	60	93	7	1	8	38	1	0	1	2	46	3	60	0	1
Gordon, Timothy, Winston-Salem	.210	104	324	41	68	105	14	4	5	35	5	4	2	2	48	1	92	0	1
Granger, L. Randle, Hagerstown†	.246	15	57	13	14	23	6	0	1	4	1	1	0	3	3	0	15	8	1
Greenwell, Michael, Winston-Salem*	.278	48	158	23	44	61	8	0	3	21	2	0	2	4	19	0	23	4	0
Guerrero, Inocencio, Durham	.332	62	217	45	72	120	11	2	11	44	5	0	2	1	50	2	36	2	2
Hagman, Keith, Durham*	.284	67	243	37	69	105	13	1	7	38	6	0	3	3	39	3	23	1	2
Harkins, James, Salem	.000	46	1	0	0	0	0	0	0	0	0	0	0	0	0	0	1	0	0
Hatcher, Johnny, Durham	.221	61	190	26	42	57	6	0	3	21	2	1	3	0	22	1	44	4	3
Hearn, Edward, Lynchburg	.272	91	290	37	79	112	16	1	5	47	6	3	4	3	47	0	40	5	3
Heller, John, Lynchburg*	.274	56	135	26	37	58	7	1	4	15	1	1	1	2	24	1	16	1	1
Hodge, Patrick, Durham*	.263	97	308	49	81	123	16	1	8	31	3	3	0	3	65	2	87	4	4
Hood, Scott, Durham*	.268	54	164	28	44	61	8	0	3	23	2	3	1	1	28	1	28	1	0
Hoppie, Bryan, Peninsula†	.270	62	200	28	54	72	11	2	1	17	4	4	0	0	21	0	33	8	5
Horn, Samuel, Winston-Salem*	.240	68	217	33	52	88	9	0	9	29	4	1	3	1	50	11	78	0	0
Isambert, Sergio, Peninsula	.191	16	47	4	9	13	1	0	1	5	0	0	0	1	3	0	17	1	2
Jacobson, Jeffrey, Hagerstown	.221	39	95	10	21	25	2	1	0	8	0	3	1	1	9	0	14	1	0
Johnson, Larry, Alexandria	.261	58	176	22	46	58	3	0	3	17	1	0	3	1	8	1	37	1	1

Player and Club	Pct.	G.	AB.	R.	H.	TB.	2B.	3B.	HR.	RBI.	GW.	SH.	SF.	HP.	BB.	Int. BB.	SO.	SB.	CS.
Jones, Keith, Salem†	.245	113	445	67	109	115	3	0	1	33	2	6	1	1	41	0	74	67	17
Jones, Kenneth, Peninsula	.262	99	351	38	92	120	10	3	4	43	3	5	3	2	26	1	83	17	8
Jose, Manuel, Winston-Salem†	.271	110	354	53	96	119	13	2	2	27	3	3	0	3	25	0	86	46	14
Keiser, Kent, Peninsula*	.313	67	249	36	78	97	15	2	0	30	1	2	4	1	30	5	25	5	3
Kelly, Ronald, Hagerstown*	.258	42	120	11	31	57	5	0	7	27	3	1	0	3	19	3	18	0	0
Kennard, David, Peninsula	.247	116	380	54	94	110	10	3	0	30	3	8	3	9	37	0	48	26	11
Khalifa, Sam, Alexandria	.270	103	356	42	96	130	19	6	1	49	4	4	3	2	51	0	50	9	6
Kinnard, Kenneth, Kinston†	.242	118	426	62	103	124	14	2	1	35	2	2	1	2	67	0	153	50	16
Knox, Michael, Durham	.250	121	404	54	101	124	13	2	2	36	2	5	1	1	45	1	86	8	5
Langie, Louis, Salem	.204	93	275	42	56	78	6	2	4	18	0	4	1	2	35	0	85	20	11
Latham, Anthony, Winston-Salem	.275	40	131	19	36	46	2	1	2	9	1	1	1	1	10	0	32	2	2
LeBoeuf, Alan, Peninsula*	.265	112	396	54	105	169	15	2	15	68	5	2	2	7	56	4	70	8	3
Lowery, Edward, Peninsula	.208	116	404	52	84	127	15	2	8	34	4	11	2	1	47	0	74	6	4
Luzon, Robert, Durham	.235	91	298	41	70	115	17	5	6	39	3	1	3	4	30	2	81	18	3
Lyons, Barry, Lynchburg	.143	2	7	0	1	1	0	0	0	2	1	0	0	0	0	0	0	0	0
Machin, John, Peninsula*	.200	21	5	0	1	1	0	0	0	1	0	0	0	0	0	0	4	0	0
Malave, Omar, Kinston	.239	14	46	4	11	15	1	0	1	10	0	1	0	0	7	0	8	0	1
Manzanillo, Ravelo, Alexandria*	.333	26	9	1	3	6	0	0	1	1	1	0	0	0	1	0	0	0	0
Marcano, Jose, Lynchburg	.220	58	164	23	36	41	2	0	1	17	2	1	1	1	19	0	22	2	5
Marte, Alexis, Kinston*	.257	116	409	53	105	124	7	3	2	36	3	7	2	1	43	1	56	47	13
Martinez, Z. Tomas, Alexandria	.192	118	369	43	71	90	9	2	2	28	2	11	1	1	31	0	92	9	9
McGriff, Frederick, Kinston*	.243	94	350	53	85	164	14	1	21	57	6	3	2	6	55	2	112	3	2
McNutt, Lawrence, Lynchburg	.277	73	224	30	62	94	9	1	7	40	1	0	3	6	27	0	64	6	6
McPhail, Marlin, Lynchburg	.301	41	143	28	43	63	7	2	3	26	5	1	2	3	27	0	25	1	1
Mejia, Manuel, Alexandria	.000	15	2	3	0	0	0	0	0	0	0	0	0	0	0	0	2	0	0
Mejia, Oscar, Salem	.263	122	457	55	120	167	23	3	6	55	2	0	3	4	39	4	39	5	9
Melillo, Gerry, Hagerstown	.260	88	246	46	64	88	14	2	2	28	6	2	1	2	43	0	41	5	0
Mesh, Michael, Winston-Salem	.268	114	406	78	109	157	15	6	7	52	4	7	7	1	59	1	59	43	15
Milligan, Randy, Lynchburg	.292	106	349	60	102	140	13	5	5	56	6	1	4	2	85	1	81	41	7
Moncada, L. Rafael, Alexandria	.069	9	29	2	2	5	0	0	1	4	0	0	0	0	0	0	4	0	0
Moreno, Jaime, Salem	.263	103	346	48	91	131	17	1	7	48	4	2	5	5	17	1	50	1	1
Morrison, Bruce, Lynchburg	.244	56	201	22	49	57	6	1	0	19	1	0	1	1	18	0	34	0	0
Moscat, Fernando, Lynchburg	.000	1	2	0	0	0	0	0	0	0	0	1	0	0	0	0	1	0	0
Moser, Larry, Durham†	.222	11	18	4	4	8	1	0	1	3	0	1	0	1	1	0	7	0	0
Murray, Steven, Salem	.262	100	328	66	86	178	18	4	22	66	4	1	3	13	63	0	98	14	6
Nattile, Samuel, Winston-Salem*	.285	122	397	60	113	206	26	2	21	80	9	2	4	3	42	12	77	1	3
Neal, Bryan, Durham*	.234	125	441	54	103	171	17	0	17	64	5	1	1	0	62	2	95	3	2
Neuendorff, Tony, Durham	.208	13	24	1	5	6	1	0	0	0	0	1	0	0	4	0	8	0	0
Olander, James, Peninsula	.249	126	503	62	125	197	21	3	15	79	9	3	1	1	43	1	146	12	8
Oliva, David, Winston-Salem	.240	121	412	55	99	134	13	2	6	49	7	3	3	2	25	0	78	24	7
Oliver, Bruce, Salem	.000	49	1	0	0	0	0	0	0	0	0	0	0	0	0	0	1	0	0
Olmedo, Luis, Winston-Salem	.234	75	239	29	56	77	12	3	1	17	2	3	2	3	17	0	43	7	1
Olson, Gregory, Lynchburg	.230	107	318	56	73	80	7	0	0	22	5	3	7	1	54	0	36	0	1
Opie, James, Alexandria	.294	125	462	86	136	229	23	5	20	71	8	3	1	4	49	1	115	25	5
Paula, Julio, Lynchburg†	.222	55	180	27	40	57	3	1	4	17	1	1	3	0	19	0	44	4	2
Pena, Jorge, Salem	.214	25	70	5	15	18	3	0	0	9	1	0	0	1	4	0	19	0	1
Poole, Mark, Kinston	.242	94	339	56	82	137	14	1	13	53	4	5	4	5	46	2	50	3	2
Quade, G. Michael, Alexandria	.194	13	31	5	6	11	0	1	1	4	0	0	0	0	3	0	4	0	1
Redfield, Joseph, Lynchburg	.203	62	192	32	39	69	4	7	4	27	3	2	3	0	25	0	44	5	2
Rembielak, Richard, Hagerstown	.244	113	393	48	96	136	16	3	6	47	5	1	2	2	43	3	63	2	1
Reynolds, Leonardo, Peninsula	.234	13	47	3	11	14	0	0	1	7	0	1	0	0	1	0	13	1	1
Reynolds, Michael, Durham*	.226	21	62	7	14	19	2	0	1	1	0	0	0	0	5	0	10	2	0
Rice, A. Cepedia, Alexandria	.214	34	14	3	3	3	0	0	0	3	0	0	0	1	2	0	6	1	0
Rivas, Rafael, Kinston	.236	96	314	42	74	127	15	1	12	47	4	1	2	3	42	0	81	4	4
Robertson, Gary, Salem*	.170	36	100	12	17	26	1	1	2	10	1	0	0	2	25	1	20	0	2
Rodriguez, D. Ruben, Alexandria	.228	79	254	19	58	86	14	1	4	31	3	2	1	5	6	0	63	0	1
Rodriguez, Rigo, Salem	.250	130	444	52	111	145	20	1	4	48	5	6	3	4	44	0	118	9	11
Rodriguez, Yonis, Peninsula	.000	6	1	0	0	0	0	0	0	0	0	0	0	0	0	0	0	0	0
Romagna, Randolph, Kinston	.200	38	15	2	3	6	0	0	1	3	1	0	0	0	0	0	1	0	1
Rowe, Peter, Alexandria	.289	20	76	10	22	31	3	0	2	17	1	1	2	0	7	0	6	1	0
Salcedo, Ronnie, Hagerstown*	.290	129	504	85	146	252	39	2	21	93	14	2	0	8	77	5	65	6	3
Santos, Edward, Kinston	.262	67	252	27	66	84	12	0	2	29	4	1	3	3	26	2	48	0	3
Scanlon, Kenneth, Durham	.230	50	161	24	37	42	2	0	1	12	2	0	1	0	27	0	24	5	1
Schaefer, Jeffrey, Hagerstown	.266	68	229	32	61	87	15	4	1	16	4	2	3	1	9	0	20	8	2
Schroeder, Jay, Kinston	.206	92	281	30	58	98	9	2	9	43	3	4	5	3	48	0	103	5	1
Schu, Rick, Peninsula	.268	122	444	69	119	189	22	3	14	63	3	1	3	3	48	1	83	29	8
Seibert, B. Gibson, Peninsula	.305	119	443	83	135	196	21	5	10	54	3	6	3	2	79	2	84	9	11
Sharperson, Michael, Kinston	.266	90	361	55	96	121	8	1	5	41	6	0	0	2	39	0	65	20	8
Sheaffer, Danny, Winston-Salem	.276	112	380	48	105	168	14	2	15	63	7	3	8	3	36	1	50	1	1
Siriano, Rick, Durham*	.255	34	110	16	28	36	2	0	2	10	0	2	0	3	20	0	18	6	4
Skripko, J. Scott, Winston-Salem	.196	115	311	53	61	91	7	4	5	27	4	8	2	1	53	0	82	26	8
Soreca, Vincent, Peninsula	.000	46	1	0	0	0	0	0	0	0	0	0	0	0	1	0	1	0	0
Suarez, Brian, Peninsula	.248	114	387	45	96	138	14	2	8	41	8	4	1	0	54	4	73	4	2
Susce, Steven, Alexandria	.333	22	3	0	1	1	0	0	0	0	0	0	0	0	0	0	1	0	0
Sutton, L. Ricardo, Kinston	.265	125	460	73	122	193	17	3	16	76	7	1	4	5	52	3	112	9	3
Tatis, Bernardo, Kinston†	.265	114	441	72	117	150	14	5	3	39	5	6	5	3	61	1	95	43	16
Taylor, Donald, Alexandria	.000	28	1	0	0	0	0	0	0	0	0	0	0	0	0	0	1	0	0
Taylor, Johnny, Alexandria	.100	35	10	1	1	2	1	0	0	2	0	0	0	0	0	0	2	0	0
Thomas, Andres, Durham	.248	70	290	17	72	92	14	0	2	41	3	4	3	0	10	0	48	3	3
Tiburcio, Fredrick, Durham	.262	110	446	62	117	157	12	8	4	51	3	3	4	3	45	2	85	30	8
Timko, Andrew, Hagerstown*	.256	53	207	32	53	70	12	1	1	24	1	1	2	0	22	2	17	0	3
Tipton, Jeffery, Hagerstown	.265	56	162	29	43	76	9	0	8	29	0	0	2	0	13	2	50	1	0
Traber, James, Hagerstown*	.274	128	449	73	123	189	22	1	14	79	10	1	4	7	75	8	81	21	10
Tumpane, Robert, Durham*	.232	82	285	48	66	122	11	0	15	57	2	0	6	3	47	0	61	1	1
Tyner, Matthew, Hagerstown	.371	21	70	18	26	61	6	1	9	21	4	0	0	3	18	0	14	0	0
Ubri, Fermin, Lynchburg	.267	115	454	65	121	155	17	1	5	66	10	1	8	1	29	1	44	11	8
Van Horn, David, Durham	.214	4	14	3	3	4	1	0	0	0	0	0	0	0	2	0	1	0	0
Vanderburg, Michael, Hagerstown*	.000	2	4	0	0	0	0	0	0	0	0	0	0	0	0	0	1	0	0
Walck, Craig, Winston-Salem	.257	132	435	60	112	171	21	1	12	63	7	8	7	5	80	3	83	0	1
Walters, Kevin, Peninsula†	.288	57	160	27	46	53	7	0	0	15	0	1	0	3	36	1	16	1	2
Westmoreland, John, Salem*	.230	101	339	41	78	150	18	0	18	53	7	0	0	3	41	0	107	0	1
Wiggins, Kevin, Salem*	.301	115	412	58	124	186	22	5	10	59	5	3	3	0	44	3	99	13	5
Williams, Billy, Peninsula	.180	25	89	10	16	26	2	1	2	11	1	0	0	0	10	0	21	0	0
Williams, Dana, Winston-Salem	.279	24	86	10	24	28	4	0	0	7	0	0	1	1	7	0	4	1	2
Wilson, James, Winston-Salem	.000	12	1	0	0	0	0	0	0	0	0	0	0	0	0	0	1	0	0

The following pitchers, listed alphabetically by club, with games in parentheses, had no plate appearances, primarily through use of designated hitters:

ALEXANDRIA—Bailes, Scott (53); Borland, Scott (8); Cacciatore, Paul (13); Cooke, John (3); Gonzales, Fernando (9); Johnson, David (46); Lein, Christopher (17); Ray, Arthur (9).

DURHAM—Baker, John (9); Bormann, Michael (44); Clary, Martin (15); Clay, David (19); Cole, Timothy (23); Dooner, Glenn (8); Hatcher, Richard (4); Lamb, Todd (15); Lance, Mark (11); Leggatt, Richard (34); Lubert, Dennis (17); Pettaway, Felix (28); Ruiz, August (19); Sears, Allen (5); Smith, Zane (27); Ward, Duane (28); West, Matthew (12).

HAGERSTOWN—Alexander, Tommy (35); Arias, Juan (1); Butler, Mark (6); Cabassa, Carlos (9); Charley, Tandy (23); Concepcion, Carlos (54); Cratch, Richard (23); Gilbert, Jeffrey (4); Grier, David (9); Guinn, Charles (5); Habyan, John (11); Konopa, Robert (17); Krsnich, Nicholas (6); Leiter, Kurt (4); Leiter, Mark (8); Maples, Timothy (27); McCullock, Alec (15); Mulcahy, Timothy (32); Palmer, James (2); Rowe, Thomas (7); Summers, Jeffrey (20); Willsher, Christopher (13); Wilson, Randall (7).

KINSTON—Alba, Gibson (23); Alexander, Doyle (1); Elam, Scot (18); Gillam, Donald (28); Harper, Devallon (34); Knapp, Christian (6); Layton, Thomas (28); Lychak, Perry (49); Phillips, Christopher (27); Pursell, Joseph (50); Reish, Stephan (20); Rodgers, Timothy (28); Valenzuela, Guillermo (3); Wells, David (25).

LYNCHBURG—Bettendorf, Jeffrey (21); Fultz, William (4); Gardner, Wesley (49); Gooden, Dwight (27); Graves, Joseph (42); Jackson, Reginald (29); Latham, William (13); Pickett, Richard (17); Ray, Arthur (12); Schiraldi, Calvin (6); Sunderlage, Jeffrey (30); Tibbs, Jay (28); Vaughn, DeWayne (13); Wyatt, David (24).

PENINSULA—Arnold, Jerry (30); Bartholow, Foster (22); Bystrom, Martin (1); Childress, Rodney (58); Cole, William (25); Griffin, Frankie (7); Hunter, Brian (1); Maddux, Michael (14); Reilly, James (10); Seiler, David (28); Surhoff, Richard (29), Warner, Harold (26).

SALEM—Brosious, Frank (19); George, William (5); Gerhardt, William (6); Hardwick, Willie (9); Knapp, Richard (7); Leach, Martin (17); Maki, Timothy (24); Murphy, Pat (28); Poston, Mark (25); Raymer, Gregory (11); Schefsky, Steven (19); Smith, Daryl (13); Smith, Wesley (11); Swift, Weldon (9); Taylor, William (7); Teutsch, Mark (13).

WINSTON-SALEM—Araujo, Anazario (4); Bowlin, Allan (16); Dale, Charles (19); Diez, Scott (30); Grubbs, Kevin (31); Johnson, Mitchell (31); McCarthy, Thomas (35); Parkins, Robert (24); Peterson, David (27); Plainte, Brandon (14); Rochford, Michael (29); Weinbrecht, Mark (9); Woodward, Robert (30).

GRAND SLAM HOME RUNS—Cochrane, 3; Gerhart, Murray, Neal, Olander, 2 each; Bundy, Cusack, Denby, Dykstra, Gomez, Hearn, LeBoeuf, McGriff, Poole, Sheaffer, Skripko, Sutton, Timko, Tumpane, 1 each.

AWARDED FIRST BASE ON CATCHER'S INTERFERENCE—Mesh 6 (Schroeder 2, Brunenkant, Cormack, Heller, D. Ruben Rodriguez); Gerhart 2 (Burrell, Walters); Bard (Rivas); Lowery (Poole); Oliva (Brunenkant).

CLUB FIELDING

Club	Pct.	G.	PO.	A.	E.	DP.	PB.
Hagerstown	.964	136	3479	1492	183	124	14
Kinston	.962	138	3658	1657	208	130	50
Lynchburg	.962	139	3624	1359	195	114	19
Winston-Salem	.961	140	3585	1551	210	127	20
Durham	.959	137	3536	1616	222	125	22
Alexandria	.958	137	3580	1499	224	107	31
Peninsula	.956	138	3564	1549	235	127	16
Salem	.954	139	3550	1562	245	123	39

INDIVIDUAL FIELDING

FIRST BASEMEN

*Throws lefthanded.

Player and Club	Pct.	G.	PO.	A.	E.	DP.
Ackley, Winston-Salem	.966	27	210	16	8	23
Aulenback, Alexandria	.940	9	44	3	3	4
Bonilla, Alexandria	.978	12	83	6	2	3
Brunenkant, Salem	.833	2	15	0	3	2
Bundy, Alexandria*	.977	29	210	6	5	14
Burrell, Winston-Salem	.917	5	20	2	2	1
Castaneda, Alexandria	.993	63	511	30	4	36
Chmil, Durham	1.000	3	18	2	0	2
Cusack, Hagerstown	1.000	2	14	0	0	2
DeLaRosa, Alexandria*	1.000	2	22	0	0	0
Doerr, Hagerstown	1.000	2	19	1	0	4
Dumouchelle, Hagerstown	1.000	2	8	1	0	0
Falcone, Hagerstown	.973	8	70	1	2	4
Gomez, Salem*	.978	64	535	37	13	39
Guerrero, Durham	.971	42	370	30	12	31
Hagman, Durham*	.996	55	506	42	2	46
Hearn, Lynchburg	.968	14	116	6	4	12
Horn, Winston-Salem*	.975	39	363	24	10	23
Kelly, Hagerstown*	.965	10	74	8	3	11
LeBoeuf, Peninsula	.990	49	379	25	4	36
Martinez, Alexandria	.973	30	242	13	7	21
McGriff, Kinston*	.988	83	784	57	10	69
McNutt, Lynchburg	.983	15	101	12	2	4
Milligan, Lynchburg	.978	66	495	39	12	43
Moreno, Salem	.963	22	202	8	8	14
Morrison, Lynchburg	.979	45	351	24	8	40
Nattile, Winston-Salem	.984	87	684	47	12	64
Poole, Kinston	1.000	6	62	4	0	4
Redfield, Lynchburg	.966	7	52	5	2	1
Rivas, Kinston	.987	20	142	9	2	12
Robertson, Salem	.990	33	286	13	3	22
Ri. Rodriguez, Salem	.992	13	111	6	1	14
Rowe, Alexandria	.974	15	140	11	4	15
Santos, Kinston	.981	28	243	17	5	25
Schroeder, Kinston	.944	8	65	2	4	9
Sheaffer, Winston-Salem	1.000	6	9	1	0	0
Suarez, Peninsula	.987	92	794	71	11	75
TRABER, Hagerstown*	.991	119	1006	54	10	96
Tumpane, Durham*	.993	39	378	28	3	29
Walters, Peninsula	1.000	4	24	0	0	1
Westmoreland, Salem	.985	17	120	10	2	9

SECOND BASEMEN

Player and Club	Pct.	G.	PO.	A.	E.	DP.
Bishop, Kinston	1.000	4	4	6	0	1
Brunenkant, Salem	.921	20	24	46	6	7
Burrows, Alexandria	.950	13	22	35	3	8
Cain, Hagerstown	.943	7	17	16	2	3
Childress, Durham	.941	5	4	12	1	2
Chmil, Durham	.990	18	46	55	1	15
Clack, Alexandria	.957	107	221	272	22	45
Corman, Hagerstown	.953	57	122	144	13	38
Dumouchelle, Hagerstown	.500	2	1	0	1	0
Escobar, Kinston	.966	49	112	142	9	33
Freeman, Salem	.905	26	55	69	13	13
Gordon, Winston-Salem	.963	78	126	210	13	46
Hoppie, Peninsula	.936	26	53	64	8	12
Jacobson, Hagerstown	.958	31	50	65	5	12
Kennard, Peninsula	.956	113	228	320	25	66
Khalifa, Alexandria	1.000	2	0	1	0	0
Knox, Durham	.952	68	131	184	16	39
Langie, Salem	.944	80	159	244	24	46
Malave, Kinston	1.000	1	4	2	0	0
Marcano, Lynchburg	.985	19	25	41	1	11
Martinez, Alexandria	.912	18	40	53	9	12
Mejia, Salem	.974	6	19	19	1	3
Moreno, Salem	1.000	1	1	1	0	0
Moscat, Lynchburg	1.000	1	4	3	0	1
Olmedo, Winston-Salem	.956	63	112	172	13	31
Paula, Lynchburg	.977	9	15	27	1	5
Pena, Salem	.975	19	30	47	2	11
Poole, Kinston	.857	2	3	3	1	0
Quade, Alexandria	.864	4	8	11	3	1
Redfield, Lynchburg	1.000	1	1	1	0	0
Reynolds, Durham	1.000	4	4	2	0	1
Scanlon, Durham	.941	47	88	103	12	15
Schaefer, Hagerstown	.982	54	115	162	5	39
Schu, Peninsula	1.000	3	5	12	0	2
Sharperson, Kinston	1.000	4	7	6	0	1
Tatis, Kinston	.950	86	196	260	24	55
UBRI, Lynchburg	.970	114	192	301	15	57
Van Horn, Durham	.944	4	7	10	1	1
Williams, Winston-Salem	.886	6	9	22	4	2
Wilson, Winston-Salem	1.000	2	2	0	0	0

THIRD BASEMEN

Player and Club	Pct.	G.	PO.	A.	E.	DP.
Bishop, Kinston	.883	110	72	201	36	15
Cain, Hagerstown	1.000	2	0	1	0	0
Castaneda, Alexandria	.889	3	0	8	1	0
Childress, Durham	.947	5	3	15	1	1
Chmil, Durham	.908	62	39	118	16	13
Cochrane, Lynchburg	.900	114	66	167	26	22
Corman, Hagerstown	.830	23	10	34	9	4
Doerr, Hagerstown	.826	45	27	73	21	8
Dumouchelle, Hagerstown	.911	32	18	54	7	5
Escobar, Kinston	.955	9	5	16	1	1
Freeman, Salem	.903	23	15	41	6	3
Gordon, Winston-Salem	.818	4	1	8	2	2
Hearn, Lynchburg	.933	7	2	12	1	1
Hodge, Durham	.836	65	44	119	32	9
Hoppie, Peninsula	.889	19	11	37	6	2
LeBoeuf, Peninsula	.833	2	1	4	1	0
Lowery, Peninsula	.927	18	13	25	3	2
Malave, Kinston	.933	7	2	12	1	1
Martinez, Alexandria	.909	29	21	59	8	4
McPhail, Lynchburg	.826	15	8	30	8	1
Nattile, Winston-Salem	.786	9	1	10	3	2
OPIE, Alexandria	.934	107	70	243	22	17
Pena, Salem	.833	2	1	4	1	0
Poole, Kinston	1.000	2	3	3	0	0
Redfield, Lynchburg	.941	8	5	11	1	3
Rembielak, Hagerstown	.930	40	21	85	8	5
Reynolds, Durham	.972	9	11	24	1	1
Rivas, Kinston	1.000	1	0	1	0	0
Rodriguez, Salem	.932	118	99	231	24	18
Romagna, Kinston	1.000	5	8	8	0	0
Salcedo, Hagerstown	1.000	1	0	1	0	0
Schu, Peninsula	.929	106	64	211	21	20
Sharperson, Kinston	1.000	11	2	39	0	2
Timko, Hagerstown	1.000	2	1	5	0	1
Walck, Winston-Salem	.933	131	94	266	26	25

SHORTSTOPS

Player and Club	Pct.	G.	PO.	A.	E.	DP.
Childress, Durham	.979	12	13	33	1	7
Clack, Alexandria	.938	16	30	30	4	14
Cusack, Hagerstown	1.000	1	0	2	0	0
Dumouchelle, Hagerstown	.933	3	9	5	1	0
Escobar, Kinston	.949	62	94	224	17	39
Freeman, Salem	.905	31	49	94	15	15
Garcia, Lynchburg	.947	44	56	124	10	19
Gordon, Winston-Salem	.867	22	23	55	12	7
Hoppie, Peninsula	.800	11	23	21	11	4
Jacobson, Hagerstown	1.000	6	1	1	0	0
Khalifa, Alexandria	.929	101	156	278	33	51
Knox, Durham	.896	52	65	159	26	23
Langie, Salem	1.000	1	1	0	0	0
Lowery, Peninsula	.931	95	155	279	32	53
Malave, Kinston	.944	5	9	8	1	2
Marcano, Lynchburg	.896	28	34	61	11	7
Martinez, Alexandria	.884	24	34	50	11	6
MEJIA, Salem	.946	109	165	381	31	69
Mesh, Winston-Salem	.943	113	159	358	31	67
Opie, Alexandria	1.000	2	3	8	0	1
Paula, Lynchburg	.910	40	68	83	15	14
Pena, Salem	.923	2	6	6	1	1
Redfield, Lynchburg	.922	36	56	86	12	21
Rembielak, Hagerstown	.927	75	101	267	29	53
L. Reynolds, Peninsula	.929	12	14	38	4	7
M. Reynolds, Durham	.957	7	4	18	1	2
Schaefer, Hagerstown	.970	14	30	35	2	10
Schu, Peninsula	.824	10	13	29	9	2
Seibert, Peninsula	.892	13	21	45	8	6
Sharperson, Kinston	.952	72	133	241	19	49
Thomas, Durham	.911	70	107	222	32	47
Timko, Hagerstown	.970	50	75	150	7	19
Williams, Winston-Salem	.905	10	12	26	4	5

OUTFIELDERS

Player and Club	Pct.	G.	PO.	A.	E.	DP.
Ackley, Winston-Salem	.917	10	9	2	1	0
Alomar, Winston-Salem	1.000	30	38	3	0	0
Aulenback, Alexandria	1.000	5	8	2	0	0
Bonilla, Alexandria	.933	122	176	6	13	0
A. Brown, Peninsula	.953	22	36	5	2	1
S. Brown, Alexandria	.921	78	136	4	12	1
Brunenkant, Salem	1.000	1	1	0	0	0
Bundy, Alexandria*	.970	18	32	0	1	0
Cain, Hagerstown	1.000	9	10	0	0	0
Cannon, Kinston	.938	12	29	1	2	1
Carreon, Lynchburg*	.928	127	173	8	14	2
Castaneda, Alexandria	1.000	4	4	1	0	1
Childress, Durham	.935	43	70	2	5	0
Clack, Alexandria	1.000	1	3	1	0	1
Coleman, Salem	.916	98	159	5	15	1
Corman, Hagerstown	1.000	2	2	0	0	0
Croft, Hagerstown	.920	13	23	0	2	0
Currier, Peninsula	1.000	6	5	0	0	0
Cusack, Hagerstown	.951	35	39	0	2	0
DeLaRosa, Alexandria*	.972	102	195	13	6	2
Denby, Lynchburg	.960	101	159	10	7	1
Denman, Hagerstown	1.000	29	53	0	0	0
Dumouchelle, Hagerstown	.962	57	74	2	3	1
Dykstra, Lynchburg*	.975	131	268	9	7	2
Felt, Alexandria	.944	25	31	3	2	0
Fisher, Winston-Salem	.926	22	24	1	2	1
Gerhart, Hagerstown	.956	128	274	11	13	3
Granger, Hagerstown	.842	15	16	0	3	0
Greenwell, Winston-Salem	.967	29	28	1	1	0
Hatcher, Durham	1.000	4	6	0	0	0
Heller, Lynchburg	1.000	7	9	0	0	0
Hodge, Durham	.943	19	31	2	2	0
Isambert, Peninsula	1.000	15	27	2	0	1
Johnson, Alexandria	.943	49	60	6	4	2
Kei. Jones, Salem	.955	108	199	12	10	3
Ken Jones, Peninsula	.908	81	123	16	14	3
Jose, Winston-Salem*	.877	98	126	10	19	1
Keiser, Peninsula	.919	51	64	4	6	1
Kennard, Peninsula	1.000	4	11	1	0	1
Kinnard, Kinston	.948	117	212	7	12	0
Langie, Salem	1.000	5	6	2	0	0
Latham, Winston-Salem	.973	38	66	5	2	0
LeBoeuf, Peninsula	1.000	1	2	0	0	0
Luzon, Durham	.971	87	158	11	5	2
Malave, Kinston	.667	1	2	0	1	0
Marte, Kinston*	.960	114	180	13	8	2
Martinez, Alexandria	.969	20	29	2	1	1
McNutt, Lynchburg	.783	14	16	2	5	0
McPhail, Lynchburg	.935	20	27	2	2	0
Melillo, Hagerstown	1.000	1	1	0	0	0
Milligan, Lynchburg	.985	32	63	2	1	2
Moncada, Alexandria	.917	5	10	1	1	0
Moreno, Salem	.950	14	19	0	1	0
Moser, Durham*	1.000	10	11	0	0	0
Murray, Salem	.986	93	201	15	3	4
Nattile, Winston-Salem	.938	12	14	1	1	0
Neal, Durham	.989	110	171	14	2	4
Olander, Peninsula	.960	126	296	19	13	2
Oliva, Winston-Salem	.954	118	216	11	11	3
Quade, Alexandria	1.000	7	6	0	0	0
Redfield, Lynchburg	1.000	1	1	0	0	0
Rivas, Kinston	.936	70	81	7	6	1
Romagna, Kinston	1.000	1	2	0	0	0
Salcedo, Hagerstown	.968	111	144	9	5	1
Schroeder, Kinston	1.000	16	21	1	0	1
Seibert, Peninsula	.956	103	207	10	10	2
Sheaffer, Winston-Salem	1.000	3	1	0	0	0
Siriano, Durham*	.983	34	56	3	1	1
SKRIPKO, Winston-Salem	.995	111	192	8	1	3
Sutton, Kinston	.963	94	152	6	6	2
Tatis, Kinston	.974	16	37	0	1	0
Tiburcio, Durham	.959	106	216	15	10	3
Tipton, Hagerstown	.500	3	1	0	1	0
Traber, Hagerstown*	1.000	6	6	0	0	0
Tumpane, Durham*	1.000	10	11	1	0	1
Tyner, Hagerstown	.920	21	22	1	2	0
Vanderburg, Hagerstown	1.000	2	2	0	0	0
Wiggins, Salem*	.950	103	160	10	9	0
B. Williams, Peninsula	.907	24	36	3	4	0
D. Williams, Winston-Salem	1.000	2	1	0	0	0

CATCHERS

Player and Club	Pct.	G.	PO.	A.	E.	DP.	PB.
Ackley, Winston-Salem	.988	47	313	27	4	3	9
Aulenback, Alexandria	.985	49	300	39	5	1	11
Bard, Hagerstown	.990	39	236	48	3	2	3
Brunenkant, Salem	.969	77	455	42	16	4	25
Burrell, Winston-Salem	.988	38	244	13	3	3	5
Cipolloni, Peninsula	.980	97	625	76	14	10	12
Cormack, Durham	.981	82	553	62	12	7	16
Dumouchelle, Hagerstown	1.000	1	3	0	0	0	0
Goldthorn, Alexandria	1.000	25	142	20	0	2	4
Hearn, Lynchburg	.983	32	215	19	4	3	4

CATCHERS—Continued

Player and Club	Pct.	G.	PO.	A.	E.	DP.	PB.
Heller, Lynchburg	.954	19	58	4	3	0	2
Hood, Durham	.986	54	301	42	5	8	5
Hoppie, Peninsula	1.000	2	5	2	0	0	1
Lyons, Lynchburg	1.000	2	21	4	0	0	0
Martinez, Alexandria	1.000	4	22	2	0	0	0
Melillo, Hagerstown	.986	86	573	55	9	4	6
Moreno, Salem	.988	28	145	16	2	0	4
Neuendorff, Durham	.939	8	28	3	2	0	1
OLSON, Lynchburg	.990	107	881	82	10	5	13
Poole, Kinston	.980	66	438	61	10	7	15
Rivas, Kinston	.960	6	42	6	2	0	1
Rodriguez, Alexandria	.981	75	496	70	11	4	16
Rowe, Alexandria	1.000	3	18	0	0	0	0
Schroeder, Kinston	.968	72	433	50	16	1	33
Sharperson, Kinston	1.000	1	6	0	0	0	1
Sheaffer, Winston-Salem	.987	66	417	43	6	5	6
Tipton, Hagerstown	1.000	28	163	10	0	0	5
Walters, Peninsula	.983	44	268	28	5	3	3
Westmoreland, Salem	.971	41	247	22	8	1	10

PITCHERS

Player and Club	Pct.	G.	PO.	A.	E.	DP.
Alba, Kinston*	1.000	23	1	3	0	0
D. Alexander, Kinston	1.000	1	0	1	0	0
T. Alexander, Hagerstown	1.000	35	2	10	0	0
Araujo, Winston-Salem	1.000	4	1	0	0	0
Arnold, Peninsula*	.944	30	4	30	2	1
Bailes, Alexandria*	1.000	52	3	10	0	0
Baker, Durham*	.846	9	2	9	2	1
Bartholow, Peninsula	1.000	22	2	5	0	0
Bettendorf, Lynchburg	.973	21	13	23	1	1
Borland, Alexandria	1.000	8	1	6	0	0
Bormann, Durham	.978	44	8	36	1	6
Bowlin, Winston-Salem*	.833	16	1	9	2	1
Brosious, Salem	.909	19	6	14	2	0
Buckmier, Alexandria	.932	35	14	27	3	2
Butler, Hagerstown*	.500	6	1	0	1	0
Cabassa, Hagerstown*	1.000	9	2	8	0	1
Cacciatore, Alexandria	1.000	13	0	3	0	1
Castaneda, Alexandria	1.000	3	0	1	0	0
Charley, Hagerstown*	.950	23	5	33	2	1
Childress, Peninsula	.917	58	3	8	1	1
Clary, Durham	.923	15	6	18	2	4
Clay, Durham	.963	19	8	18	1	0
T. Cole, Durham*	1.000	23	4	9	0	0
W. Cole, Peninsula	.843	25	14	29	8	0
Concepcion, Hagerstown	.947	54	2	16	1	2
Cratch, Hagerstown	.947	23	15	21	2	5
Dale, Winston-Salem	.889	19	1	7	1	0
Diez, Winston-Salem*	1.000	30	2	12	0	0
Dooner, Durham	.500	8	0	1	1	0
Downs, Alexandria	.556	31	0	5	4	0
Elam, Kinston	.857	18	5	13	3	1
Faherty, Alexandria*	.933	25	1	27	2	1
Felt, Alexandria	1.000	3	0	1	0	0
Fultz, Lynchburg	.800	4	1	3	1	1
Gardner, Lynchburg	1.000	49	5	15	0	2
George, Salem*	1.000	5	0	3	0	0
Gerhardt, Salem	1.000	6	0	1	0	0
Gilbert, Hagerstown*	1.000	4	1	2	0	0
Gillam, Kinston*	.981	28	10	43	1	2
Gonzales, Alexandria	.909	8	0	10	1	1
Gooden, Lynchburg	.903	27	13	15	3	1
Graves, Lynchburg	1.000	42	4	20	0	1
Grier, Hagerstown	1.000	9	3	9	0	0
Griffin, Peninsula*	1.000	7	5	7	0	1
Grubbs, Winston-Salem	.981	31	15	37	1	0
Guinn, Hagerstown	1.000	5	1	0	0	0
Habyan, Hagerstown	1.000	11	0	7	0	1
Hardwick, Salem	.786	9	3	8	3	1
Harkins, Salem*	.900	46	7	20	3	0
Harper, Kinston	.923	34	6	18	2	2
Hatcher, Durham	1.000	4	1	2	0	0
Jackson, Lynchburg	.939	29	14	17	2	0
D. Johnson, Alexandria	.848	46	4	24	5	0
M. Johnson, Winston-Salem	.976	31	6	34	1	0
C. Knapp, Kinston	1.000	6	1	1	0	0
R. Knapp, Salem	1.000	7	1	1	0	0
Konopa, Hagerstown*	.938	17	3	12	1	1
Krsnich, Hagerstown	1.000	6	0	2	0	0
Lamb, Durham	.923	15	8	16	2	1
Lance, Durham*	.875	11	1	6	1	0
Latham, Lynchburg*	.962	13	6	19	1	0
Layton, Kinston	.944	28	4	13	1	1
Leach, Salem	.960	17	7	17	1	0
Leggatt, Durham	.889	34	6	18	3	1
Lein, Alexandria	1.000	17	3	14	0	1
K. Leiter, Hagerstown	1.000	4	0	7	0	0
M. Leiter, Hagerstown	.727	8	2	6	3	0
Lubert, Durham*	1.000	17	4	13	0	2
Lychak, Kinston*	1.000	49	4	15	0	0
Machin, Peninsula*	1.000	20	2	21	0	1
Maddux, Peninsula	1.000	14	6	16	0	0
Maki, Salem	.778	24	3	4	2	0
Manzanillo, Alexandria*	.943	22	4	29	2	1
Maples, Hagerstown	.941	27	2	14	1	0
McCarthy, Winston-Salem	.912	35	7	24	3	1
McCullock, Hagerstown	1.000	15	2	2	0	0
Mejia, Alexandria	1.000	12	0	1	0	1
Mulcahy, Hagerstown*	1.000	32	1	9	0	0
Murphy, Salem	.933	28	9	5	1	2
Oliver, Salem	.947	49	7	11	1	0
Palmer, Hagerstown	1.000	2	2	4	0	0
Parkins, Winston-Salem	.750	24	4	5	3	0
Peterson, Winston-Salem	.714	27	2	3	2	1
Pettaway, Durham	.889	28	5	11	2	0
Phillips, Kinston	1.000	27	2	11	0	1
Pickett, Lynchburg*	1.000	17	4	2	0	0
Plainte, Winston-Salem*	.818	14	3	6	2	0
Poston, Salem	.842	25	6	26	6	3
Pursell, Kinston	.946	50	7	28	2	2
Ray, 9 Alex.-12 Lynch.	.875	21	3	11	2	1
Raymer, Salem	.929	11	2	11	1	0
Reilly, Peninsula	.818	9	4	5	2	0
Reish, Kinston	1.000	20	3	6	0	0
Rice, Alexandria	.771	25	7	20	8	0
Rochford, Winston-Salem*	.960	29	13	35	2	5
Rodgers, Kinston	.958	28	13	33	2	3
R. Rodriguez, Salem	1.000	2	1	1	0	0
Y. Rodriguez, Peninsula	.714	6	1	4	2	0
Romagna, Kinston	1.000	30	12	28	0	2
Rowe, Hagerstown	.889	7	0	8	1	1
Ruiz, Durham*	1.000	19	1	12	0	0
Schefsky, Salem	.850	19	2	15	3	0
Schiraldi, Lynchburg	1.000	6	1	1	0	0
Seiler, Peninsula*	.917	28	10	34	4	2
D. Smith, Salem	1.000	13	2	19	0	0
W. Smith, Salem	1.000	11	1	6	0	0
Z. SMITH, Durham*	1.000	27	15	54	0	4
Soreca, Peninsula	1.000	46	3	19	0	1
Summers, Hagerstown	.833	20	1	14	3	0
Sunderlage, Lynchburg*	.923	30	5	7	1	1
Surhoff, Peninsula	.938	29	1	14	1	3
Susce, Alexandria	.952	21	6	14	1	1
Swift, Salem	.800	9	3	9	3	1
D. Taylor, Alexandria	1.000	28	6	3	0	0
J. Taylor, Alexandria	1.000	32	3	7	0	1
W. Taylor, Salem	.833	7	2	3	1	0
Teutsch, Salem	1.000	13	3	7	0	1
Tibbs, Lynchburg	.957	28	12	33	2	3
Valenzuela, Kinston	1.000	3	0	1	0	0
Vaughn, Lynchburg	1.000	13	4	18	0	1
Ward, Durham	.952	28	13	46	3	1
Warner, Peninsula*	.810	26	6	11	4	0
Weinbrecht, Winston-Salem*	.750	9	0	3	1	0
Wells, Kinston*	.921	25	5	30	3	0
West, Durham	.909	12	4	16	2	0
Willsher, Hagerstown	1.000	13	2	5	0	1
J. Wilson, Winston-Salem	1.000	10	1	0	0	0
R. Wilson, Hagerstown	1.000	7	1	2	0	0
Woodward, Winston-Salem	.980	30	15	34	1	3
Wyatt, Lynchburg*	.933	24	4	10	1	2

The following players had no recorded accepted chances at the positions indicated and therefore are not listed in the fielding averages for those particlar positions: Arias, p; Bard, of; Bystrom, p; Chmil, ss; Cooke, p; Downs, 1b; Freeman, of; Hearn, of; Hunter, p; Isambert, p; LeBoeuf, 2b; Langie, 3b; Malave, p; Quade, p; Ru. Rodriguez, 1b; Santos, 3b; Scanlon, 3b; Sears, p; Sheaffer, 3b; Skripko, p; Westmoreland, of.

CLUB PITCHING

Club	ERA.	G.	CG.	ShO.	Sv.	IP.	H.	R.	ER.	HR.	HB.	BB.	Int. BB.	SO.	WP.	Bk.
Lynchburg	3.13	139	32	13	40	1208.0	1082	553	420	92	24	528	14	1145	63	11
Hagerstown	3.96	136	35	9	20	1159.2	1142	621	510	92	38	574	13	944	57	4
Winston-Salem	4.07	140	43	10	17	1195.0	1132	654	540	88	36	512	16	933	86	7
Alexandria	4.07	137	10	4	33	1193.1	1104	679	540	99	39	676	14	993	87	21
Kinston	4.20	138	16	10	30	1219.1	1173	685	569	102	30	664	54	912	91	6
Peninsula	4.33	138	22	5	27	1188.0	1306	710	572	96	33	535	25	832	68	10
Durham	4.45	137	25	5	18	1178.2	1188	742	583	138	40	557	19	842	66	7
Salem	5.15	139	22	4	17	1183.1	1294	847	677	139	42	650	17	808	101	13

PITCHERS' RECORDS

(Leading Qualifiers for Earned-Run Average Leadership—112 or More Innings)

*Throws lefthanded.

Pitcher—Club	W.	L.	Pct.	ERA.	G.	GS.	CG.	GF.	ShO.	Sv.	IP.	H.	R.	ER.	HR.	HB.	BB.	Int. BB.	SO.	WP.
Gooden, Lynchburg	19	4	.826	2.50	27	27	10	0	6	0	191.0	121	58	53	11	3	112	0	300	6
Bettendorf, Lynchburg	13	4	.765	2.91	21	21	3	0	0	0	148.1	142	74	48	13	6	62	1	138	7
Tibbs, Lynchburg	14	8	.636	2.92	28	28	10	0	2	0	203.2	172	94	66	8	2	96	1	170	13
Buckmier, Alexandria	10	6	.625	2.94	35	17	3	4	1	1	153.0	120	65	50	6	4	88	0	127	13
Rochford, Winston-Salem*	16	11	.593	3.00	29	29	12	0	1	0	210.1	182	85	70	9	4	57	2	165	10
D. Johnson, Alexandria	7	5	.583	3.01	46	2	1	18	0	8	113.2	100	52	38	6	3	42	3	95	6
M. Johnson, Winston-Salem	15	8	.652	3.11	31	28	14	3	4	1	214.0	197	97	74	13	5	59	4	146	4
Bormann, Durham	10	8	.556	3.30	44	9	2	31	1	5	133.2	131	63	49	16	3	37	5	69	1
Summers, Hagerstown	9	2	.818	3.49	20	18	5	2	1	1	116.0	112	52	45	9	3	50	0	85	2
Cratch, Hagerstown	10	7	.588	3.60	23	21	7	0	3	0	150.0	140	74	60	16	8	62	1	111	6

Departmental Leaders: G—Childress, 58; W—Gooden, 19; L—Brosious, Seiler, Z. Smith, 15; Pct.—Konopa, .857; GS—Rochford, Woodward, 29; CG—M. Johnson, 14; GF—Childress, Concepcion, 50; ShO—Gooden, 6; Sv.—Childress, 16; IP—M. Johnson, 214; H—Seiler, 202; R—Seiler, 121; ER—Seiler, 95; HR—Poston, 22; HB—Cratch, Schefsky, 8; BB—Gooden, 112; IBB—Pursell, 9; SO—Gooden, 300; WP—Seiler, 21.

Pitcher—Club	W.	L.	Pct.	ERA.	G.	GS.	CG.	GF.	ShO.	Sv.	IP.	H.	R.	ER.	HR.	HB.	BB.	Int. BB.	SO.	WP.
Alba, Kinston*	2	3	.400	6.67	23	2	0	14	0	6	29.2	18	25	22	2	3	34	1	51	3
D. Alexander, Kinston	0	0	.000	0.00	1	1	0	0	0	0	6.0	3	0	0	0	0	0	0	4	0
T. Alexander, Hagerstown	3	1	.750	3.78	35	1	0	12	0	0	66.2	68	31	28	7	1	49	2	65	2
Araujo, Winston-Salem	0	0	.000	1.80	4	0	0	4	0	2	5.0	3	1	1	0	0	3	0	5	1
Arias, Hagerstown	0	0	.000	27.00	1	0	0	0	0	0	1.1	5	4	4	2	0	0	0	0	0
Arnold, Peninsula*	3	6	.333	4.95	30	11	0	4	0	0	107.1	126	81	59	9	3	51	1	83	9
Bailes, Alexandria*	5	2	.714	3.36	52	1	0	27	0	7	75.0	67	38	28	7	4	45	2	101	7
Baker, Durham*	1	3	.250	4.53	9	7	2	1	1	0	45.2	40	28	23	6	1	24	0	44	4
Bartholow, Peninsula	3	4	.429	3.40	22	0	0	12	0	2	55.2	60	30	21	3	2	33	6	36	5
Bettendorf, Lynchburg	13	4	.765	2.91	21	21	3	0	0	0	148.1	142	74	48	13	6	62	1	138	7
Borland, Alexandria	1	2	.333	3.77	8	3	1	2	0	0	31.0	31	14	13	3	1	8	0	20	1
Bormann, Durham	10	8	.556	3.30	44	9	2	31	1	5	133.2	131	63	49	16	3	37	5	69	1
Bowlin, Winston-Salem*	2	5	.286	8.35	16	4	0	7	0	0	32.1	41	33	30	7	1	17	1	25	2
Brosious, Salem	2	15	.118	6.41	19	18	4	0	0	0	105.1	134	98	75	21	2	59	0	65	15
Buckmier, Alexandria	10	6	.625	2.94	35	17	3	4	1	1	153.0	120	65	50	6	4	88	0	127	13
Butler, Hagerstown*	0	1	.000	6.14	6	0	0	2	0	0	7.1	10	6	5	2	0	3	2	5	0
Bystrom, Peninsula	1	0	1.000	0.00	1	1	0	0	0	0	6.0	5	1	0	0	0	1	0	9	1
Cabassa, Hagerstown*	5	2	.714	3.35	9	9	0	0	0	0	48.1	43	20	18	4	2	27	0	29	3
Cacciatore, Alexandria	1	1	.500	3.46	13	1	0	5	0	0	26.0	20	13	10	1	0	20	0	22	2
Castaneda, Alexandria	0	0	.000	2.25	3	0	0	3	0	0	4.0	4	4	1	0	0	4	0	2	0
Charley, Hagerstown*	7	3	.700	4.34	23	17	4	2	1	1	120.1	126	74	58	10	3	53	0	92	12
Childress, Peninsula	4	7	.364	4.36	58	0	0	50	0	16	74.1	87	47	36	6	0	31	6	43	2
Clary, Durham	3	8	.273	5.02	15	14	2	0	1	0	89.2	101	65	50	10	2	39	1	58	8
Clay, Durham	5	2	.714	3.40	19	8	2	9	0	2	87.1	83	42	33	11	3	43	1	53	1
T. Cole, Durham*	3	2	.600	5.08	23	4	0	7	0	1	51.1	41	35	29	5	2	47	1	66	4
W. Cole, Peninsula	9	13	4.09	3.87	25	25	7	0	2	0	167.1	173	91	72	12	1	73	1	105	7
Concepcion, Hagerstown	9	5	.643	2.30	54	0	0	50	0	13	74.1	56	25	19	4	3	40	1	64	1
Cooke, Alexandria	0	0	.000	0.00	3	0	0	3	0	0	2.2	1	0	0	0	0	1	0	1	0
Cratch, Hagerstown	10	7	.588	3.60	23	21	7	0	3	0	150.0	140	74	60	16	8	62	1	111	6
Dale, Winston-Salem	3	1	.750	1.96	19	0	0	16	0	4	23.0	19	7	5	1	0	5	2	17	0
Diez, Winston-Salem*	2	4	.333	5.72	30	5	0	9	0	0	61.1	59	45	39	4	7	44	0	56	8
Dooner, Durham	0	0	.000	2.63	8	0	0	3	0	0	13.2	20	10	4	1	0	4	2	11	3
Downs, Alexandria	3	6	.333	2.93	31	0	0	28	0	9	40.0	33	16	13	3	1	17	4	26	1
Elam, Kinston	3	6	.333	5.30	18	15	0	1	0	0	73.0	72	57	43	8	3	59	0	44	17
Faherty, Alexandria*	7	9	.438	4.99	25	25	1	0	0	0	124.1	131	85	69	10	6	81	0	72	10
Felt, Alexandria	0	0	.000	27.00	3	0	0	0	0	0	3.0	5	9	9	2	0	7	0	4	3
Fultz, Lynchburg	1	0	1.000	5.16	4	4	0	0	0	0	22.2	23	15	13	3	0	8	0	18	0
Gardner, Lynchburg	6	3	.667	1.87	49	0	0	41	0	15	62.2	55	16	13	7	0	32	3	67	6
George, Salem*	0	3	.000	15.23	5	4	0	1	0	0	13.0	29	31	22	4	0	13	0	10	1
Gerhardt, Salem	0	1	.000	1.98	6	1	0	1	0	0	13.2	12	5	3	0	0	8	2	12	1
Gilbert, Hagerstown*	2	1	.667	3.16	4	3	1	1	0	0	25.2	24	12	9	3	0	4	0	20	3
Gillam, Kinston*	8	11	.421	4.24	28	28	2	0	1	0	176.0	182	97	83	16	4	72	5	13	12
Gonzales, Alexandria	2	1	.667	4.28	8	7	0	0	0	0	40.0	41	26	19	5	1	12	1	31	3
Gooden, Lynchburg	19	4	.826	2.50	27	27	10	0	6	0	191.0	121	58	53	11	3	112	0	300	6
Graves, Lynchburg	6	4	.600	2.78	42	0	0	24	0	8	77.2	69	37	24	3	5	35	3	69	4
Grier, Hagerstown	2	2	.500	6.63	9	7	0	1	0	0	36.2	54	29	27	4	2	8	0	17	0
Griffin, Peninsula*	3	1	.750	4.28	7	7	0	0	0	0	40.0	41	19	19	3	2	26	0	34	0
Grubbs, Winston-Salem	10	11	.476	3.78	31	22	8	6	2	0	173.2	166	90	73	10	2	48	1	112	5
Guinn, Hagerstown	3	2	.600	5.18	5	5	0	0	0	0	24.1	29	21	14	0	0	12	1	21	3
Habyan, Hagerstown	2	3	.400	5.81	11	11	1	0	0	0	48.0	54	41	31	3	1	29	0	42	5
Hardwick, Salem	4	3	.571	3.59	9	9	4	0	0	0	62.2	53	32	25	7	0	26	1	51	2
Harkins, Salem*	4	6	.400	5.11	46	5	2	17	1	2	135.2	164	92	77	17	7	75	0	71	10
Harper, Kinston	8	6	.571	4.28	34	11	1	8	0	0	109.1	85	58	52	9	1	91	4	103	14
Hatcher, Durham	0	0	.000	24.16	4	0	0	0	0	0	6.1	20	19	17	6	0	2	0	1	2
Hunter, Peninsula	0	0	.000	0.00	1	0	0	0	0	0	1.0	0	0	0	0	0	0	0	0	0
Isambert, Peninsula	0	0	.000	12.00	1	0	0	0	0	0	3.0	5	4	4	0	0	4	0	0	0
Jackson, Lynchburg	9	8	.529	4.32	29	15	1	3	0	1	127.0	131	67	61	15	0	38	3	101	9
D. Johnson, Alexandria	7	5	.583	3.01	46	2	1	18	0	8	113.2	100	52	38	6	3	42	3	95	6
M. Johnson, Winston-Salem	15	8	.652	3.11	31	28	14	3	4	1	214.0	197	97	74	13	5	59	4	146	4

Pitcher—Club	W.	L.	Pct.	ERA.	G.	GS.	CG.	GF.	ShO.	Sv.	IP.	H.	R.	ER.	HR.	HB.	BB.	Int. BB.	SO.	WP.
C. Knapp, Kinston	2	2	.500	4.23	6	6	0	0	0	0	27.2	24	15	13	1	2	16	0	32	1
R. Knapp, Salem	0	0	.000	8.47	7	0	0	3	0	0	17.0	24	21	16	2	2	8	0	12	0
Konopa, Hagerstown*	12	2	.857	2.77	17	14	10	1	3	1	110.1	96	39	34	6	6	37	1	127	5
Krsnich, Hagerstown	1	1	.500	7.11	6	1	0	1	0	0	12.2	16	13	10	0	0	4	1	6	0
Lamb, Durham	4	7	.364	4.83	15	14	0	0	0	0	82.0	88	61	44	8	4	44	3	53	9
Lance, Durham*	2	3	.400	5.65	11	5	2	2	0	0	36.2	39	30	23	6	1	18	0	25	0
Latham, Lynchburg*	8	4	.667	2.13	13	13	4	0	2	0	84.1	81	34	20	2	3	22	0	54	1
Layton, Kinston	3	2	.600	4.55	28	0	0	6	0	1	65.1	72	39	33	6	1	46	7	35	8
Leach, Salem	7	7	.500	4.06	17	16	2	1	0	0	113.0	116	68	51	8	3	53	2	79	4
Leggatt, Durham	4	5	.444	3.19	34	5	1	18	0	4	79.0	71	38	28	5	6	26	3	57	4
Lein, Alexandria	4	1	.800	5.93	17	8	0	1	0	0	60.2	81	47	40	8	3	31	0	47	7
K. Leiter, Hagerstown	1	3	.250	1.87	4	4	4	0	0	0	33.2	28	11	7	1	0	10	1	20	1
M. Leiter, Hagerstown	1	5	.167	7.25	8	8	0	0	0	0	36.0	42	31	29	0	3	28	1	18	3
Lubert, Durham*	1	0	1.000	7.29	17	4	0	6	0	0	42.0	60	37	34	10	1	16	0	21	4
Lychak, Kinston*	4	5	.444	4.79	49	2	0	25	0	5	67.2	65	42	36	3	1	54	5	63	9
Machin, Peninsula*	5	7	.417	3.88	20	20	1	0	0	0	116.0	124	59	50	7	4	48	2	100	3
Maddux, Peninsula	8	4	.667	3.62	14	14	6	0	0	0	99.1	92	46	40	6	0	35	0	78	2
Maki, Salem	2	3	.400	7.16	24	3	0	11	0	0	49.0	59	48	39	4	2	37	1	33	15
Malave, Kinston	0	0	.000	0.00	1	0	0	1	0	0	0.1	0	0	0	0	0	1	0	0	0
Manzanillo, Alexandria*	7	7	.500	4.44	22	20	1	0	0	0	105.1	107	68	52	9	2	79	0	66	6
Maples, Hagerstown	4	2	.667	4.25	27	1	0	6	0	1	65.2	74	34	31	7	2	56	1	63	4
McCarthy, Winston-Salem	8	6	.571	4.13	35	8	2	18	0	8	98.0	91	56	45	9	2	54	2	100	18
McCullock, Hagerstown	2	2	.500	4.50	15	0	0	8	0	2	32.0	27	17	16	2	0	11	1	33	2
Mejia, Alexandria	2	0	1.000	3.66	12	2	0	2	0	0	32.0	27	19	13	2	2	17	3	19	2
Mulcahy, Hagerstown*	4	1	.800	2.59	32	3	1	10	1	1	48.2	37	20	14	5	0	25	0	49	1
Murphy, Salem	1	5	.167	5.50	28	6	0	16	0	2	88.1	107	60	54	7	5	44	1	63	6
Oliver, Salem	5	11	.313	4.23	49	3	0	44	0	10	76.2	79	46	36	7	4	37	8	48	3
Palmer, Hagerstown	2	0	1.000	3.46	2	2	0	0	0	0	13.0	13	6	5	3	0	2	0	11	0
Parkins, Winston-Salem	2	4	.333	5.13	24	12	0	6	0	1	80.2	87	58	46	5	1	60	0	58	11
Peterson, Winston-Salem	2	2	.500	5.48	27	1	0	12	0	1	44.1	41	31	27	6	3	27	0	45	7
Pettaway, Durham	3	4	.429	3.64	28	0	0	20	0	4	64.1	48	32	26	9	5	33	1	70	5
Phillips, Kinston	2	3	.400	3.86	27	0	0	15	0	3	46.2	38	22	20	2	3	33	4	26	2
Pickett, Lynchburg*	1	0	1.000	1.42	17	0	0	13	0	10	19.0	12	5	3	2	0	9	1	21	2
Plainte, Winston-Salem*	0	2	.000	8.00	14	1	0	5	0	0	27.0	34	28	24	4	2	17	1	27	4
Poston, Salem	10	9	.526	4.78	25	22	5	2	1	0	145.0	155	98	77	22	6	54	2	76	9
Pursell, Kinston	4	9	.308	3.09	50	0	0	32	0	9	90.1	87	39	31	8	6	42	9	46	2
Quade, Alexandria	0	0	.000	0.00	1	0	0	1	0	0	1.0	0	0	0	0	0	0	0	0	0
Ray, 9 Alex.-12 Lynch.	5	3	.625	4.78	21	11	0	8	0	0	75.1	59	48	40	10	0	50	1	82	8
Raymer, Salem	2	6	.250	5.31	11	11	0	0	0	0	61.0	64	48	36	6	0	57	0	61	12
Reilly, Peninsula	0	3	.000	5.15	9	5	0	2	0	2	36.2	34	23	21	7	5	21	0	25	3
Reish, Kinston	2	2	.500	3.41	20	0	0	15	0	5	31.2	28	12	12	2	0	12	4	22	3
Rice, Alexandria	6	11	.353	4.37	25	25	0	0	0	0	117.1	108	77	57	8	4	89	0	101	11
Rochford, Winston-Salem*	16	11	.593	3.00	29	29	12	0	1	0	210.1	182	85	70	9	4	57	2	165	10
Rodgers, Kinston	12	13	.480	4.44	28	28	6	0	1	0	184.1	190	113	91	21	4	75	6	146	12
R. Rodriguez, Salem	0	0	.000	6.75	2	0	0	2	0	0	5.1	6	4	4	2	0	3	0	1	0
Y. Rodriguez, Peninsula	1	2	.333	7.98	6	6	0	0	0	0	29.1	44	29	26	6	3	15	0	19	2
Romagna, Kinston	6	8	.429	3.96	30	20	2	3	0	1	147.2	162	82	65	11	1	57	6	85	6
Rowe, Hagerstown	1	4	.200	2.94	7	4	1	1	0	0	33.2	34	17	11	1	3	15	0	20	1
Ruiz, Durham*	1	1	.500	3.29	19	0	0	13	0	2	27.1	26	12	10	2	0	14	1	26	1
Schefsky, Salem	7	9	.438	4.13	19	17	3	0	1	0	100.1	104	62	46	7	8	45	0	70	4
Schiraldi, Lynchburg	4	1	.800	4.45	6	6	0	0	0	0	30.1	28	16	15	4	2	17	0	41	2
Sears, Durham	0	2	.000	11.81	5	0	0	2	0	0	5.1	6	7	7	0	0	4	0	5	0
Seiler, Peninsula*	6	15	.286	4.74	28	28	5	0	1	0	180.1	202	121	95	10	7	95	3	111	21
Skripko, Winston-Salem	0	0	.000	9.00	1	0	0	1	0	0	1.0	1	1	1	0	1	2	0	2	0
D. Smith, Salem	1	2	.333	4.20	13	3	1	2	1	1	55.2	53	30	26	3	1	32	0	35	5
W. Smith, Salem	3	0	1.000	4.95	11	5	0	5	0	0	40.0	32	25	22	7	1	15	0	43	2
Z. Smith, Durham*	9	15	.375	4.90	27	27	7	0	0	0	170.2	183	109	93	19	2	83	0	126	11
Soreca, Peninsula	7	7	.500	5.06	46	2	0	26	0	5	96.0	116	66	54	10	1	30	2	54	6
Summers, Hagerstown	9	2	.818	3.49	20	18	5	2	1	1	116.0	112	52	45	9	3	50	0	85	2
Sunderlage, Lynchburg*	2	1	.667	5.08	30	1	0	9	0	5	51.1	50	36	29	8	3	25	0	26	4
Surhoff, Peninsula	3	2	.600	2.45	29	0	0	22	0	2	51.1	50	16	14	4	1	15	2	35	2
Susce, Alexandria	7	5	.583	3.66	21	12	3	3	0	0	108.1	112	54	44	10	2	22	0	86	4
Swift, Salem	0	6	.000	8.42	9	9	0	0	0	0	36.1	48	39	34	5	0	39	0	28	6
D. Taylor, Alexandria	2	7	.222	7.90	28	1	0	18	0	5	35.1	38	33	31	6	2	30	1	22	5
J. Taylor, Alexandria	1	3	.250	3.47	32	4	0	12	0	3	70.0	39	32	27	6	4	49	0	99	3
W. Taylor, Salem	1	1	.500	6.26	7	7	1	0	0	0	41.2	30	34	29	7	0	42	0	42	5
Teutsch, Salem	1	2	.333	1.90	13	0	0	12	0	2	23.2	25	6	5	3	1	3	0	8	1
Tibbs, Lynchburg	14	8	.636	2.92	28	28	10	0	2	0	203.2	172	94	66	8	2	96	1	170	13
Valenzuela, Kinston	0	1	.000	4.05	3	0	0	2	0	0	6.2	6	3	3	0	0	1	1	8	0
Vaughn, Lynchburg	8	3	.727	3.38	13	13	2	0	0	0	88.0	100	40	33	8	0	20	1	61	4
Ward, Durham	11	13	.458	4.29	28	28	6	0	2	0	178.1	165	103	85	20	6	75	1	115	6
Warner, Peninsula*	5	9	.357	4.42	26	19	3	0	1	0	124.1	147	77	61	13	4	57	2	100	5
Weinbrecht, Winston-Salem*	0	1	.000	6.52	9	0	0	2	0	0	9.2	12	9	7	0	0	13	0	8	1
Wells, Kinston*	6	5	.545	3.73	25	25	5	0	0	0	157.0	141	81	65	13	1	71	2	115	7
West, Durham	2	5	.286	4.27	12	12	1	0	0	0	65.1	66	51	31	4	4	48	0	42	3
Willsher, Hagerstown	3	2	.600	6.18	13	7	1	1	0	0	39.1	35	32	27	2	1	41	0	34	3
J. Wilson, Winston-Salem	1	0	1.000	4.24	10	1	0	7	0	0	17.0	22	10	8	1	1	6	0	10	2
R. Wilson, Hagerstown	1	1	.500	4.60	7	0	0	3	0	0	15.2	19	12	8	1	0	8	0	12	0
Woodward, Winston-Salem	13	11	.542	4.14	30	29	7	1	3	0	197.2	177	103	91	19	7	100	3	157	13
Wyatt, Lynchburg*	4	2	.667	3.49	24	9	2	9	0	1	77.1	78	40	30	5	0	36	0	49	0

BALKS—Rice, 7; Jackson, 5; Buckmier, Faherty, Gooden, Machin, Ward, 3 each; Childress, Manzanillo, Rochford, Rodgers, Schefsky, D. Smith, Soreca, J. Taylor, 2 each; Alba, T. Alexander, Arnold, Bormann, Clary, Concepcion, Cratch, Fultz, George, Gonzales, Grubbs, Hardwick, Harper, M. Johnson, Lamb, Layton, Leach, Leggatt, Lein, M. Leiter, Maddux, Maki, McCarthy, Murphy, Oliver, Parkins, Peterson, Ray, Raymer, Y. Rodriguez, Romagna, Sunderlage, Susce, Swift, W. Taylor, Tibbs, 1 each.

COMBINATION SHUTOUTS—Lein-Buckmeier, Ray-D. Taylor, Buckmier-Downs, Alexandria; Gillam-Reish 2, Elam-Romagna, Knapp-Reish, Knapp-Harper, Wells-Reish, Romagna-Lychak, Rodgers-Lychak, Kinston; Gooden-Gardner, Gooden-Ray, Jackson-Gardner, Lynchburg; Cole-Soreca, Peninsula.

NO-HIT GAME—None.

Florida State League

CLASS A

CHAMPIONSHIP WINNERS IN PREVIOUS YEARS

Year	Club	Pct.
1919	Sanford*	.605
	Orlando*	.703
1920	Tampa	.654
	Tampa	.722
1921	Orlando	.635
1922	St. Petersburg	.503
	St. Petersburg	.618
1923	Orlando	.667
	Orlando	.678
1924	Lakeland	.695
	Lakeland	.683
1925	St. Petersburg	.667
	Tampa†	.696
1926	Sanford	.647
	Sanford	.623
1927	Orlando†	.600
	Miami	.661
1928-35	Did not operate.	
1936	Gainesville	.542
	St. Augustine (4th)†	.492
1937	Gainesville§	.616
1938	Leesburg	.626
	Gainesville (2nd)‡	.615
1939	Sanford§	.787
1940	Daytona Beach	.619
	Orlando (4th)‡	.507
1941	St. Augustine	.659
	Leesburg (4th)‡	.488
1942-45	Did not operate.	
1946	Orlando§	.681
1947	St. Augustine	.625
	Gainesville (2nd)‡	.584
1948	Orlando	.643
	Daytona Beach (2nd)‡	.616
1949	Gainesville	.635
	St. Augustine (3rd)‡	.556
1950	Orlando	.629
	DeLand (3rd)‡	.590
1951	DeLand§	.643
1952	DeLand x	.704
	Palatka (3rd)‡	.569
1953	Daytona Beach†	.657
	DeLand	.703
1954	Jacksonville Beach	.629
	Lakeland†	.594
1955	Orlando	.671
	Orlando	.643
1956	Cocoa	.614
	Cocoa	.671
1957	Palatka	.629
	Tampa†	.681
1958	St. Petersburg	.732
	St. Petersburg	.681
1959	Tampa	.591
	St. Petersburg†	.612
1960	Lakeland	.731
	Palatka†	.614
1961	Tampa†	.710
	Sarasota	.696
1962	Sarasota	.689
	Fort Lauderdale†	.623
1963	Sarasota	.645
	Sarasota	.667
1964	Fort Lauderdale†	.629
	St. Petersburg	.594
1965	Fort Lauderdale	.627
	Fort Lauderdale	.634
1966	Leesburg†	.781
	St. Petersburg	.700
1967	St. Petersburg y	.691
	Orlando	.638
1968	Miami	.613
	Orlando z	.579
1969	Miami a	.606
	Orlando	.606
1970	Miami b	.662
	St. Petersburg	.600
1971	Miami b	.667
	Daytona Beach	.586
1972	Miami c	.562
	Daytona Beach	.606
1973	St. Petersburg d	.575
	West Palm Beach	.580
1974	West Palm Beach d	.598
	Fort Lauderdale	.626
1975	St. Petersburg d	.652
	Miami	.581
1976	Tampa	.559
	Lakeland d	.536
1977	Lakeland d	.616
	West Palm Beach	.583
1978	Lakeland	.565
	Miami§	.539
1979	Fort Lauderdale	.643
	Winter Haven e	.577
1980	Daytona Beach	.628
	Fort Lauderdale d	.606
1981	Fort Myers	.554
	Daytona Beach f	.504
1982	Fort Lauderdale f	.621
	Tampa	.546

*Split-season playoff abandoned after each team won three games. †Won split-season playoff. ‡Won four-club playoff. §Won championship and four-club playoff. xWon both halves of split season. yLeague divided into Eastern and Western divisions with split season. St. Petersburg and Orlando won both halves of split season; St. Petersburg won playoff. zLeague divided into Eastern and Western divisions. Miami won regular-season pennant on basis of highest won-lost percentage. Orlando won four-club playoff involving first two teams in each division. aLeague divided into Southern and Central divisions. Miami won playoff between division leaders. (NOTE—Pennant awarded to playoff winner in 1936.) bLeague divided into Eastern and Western divisions. Miami won regular-season pennant on basis of highest won-loss percentage, and also won four-club playoff involving first two teams in each division. cLeague divided into Eastern and Western divisions. Won four-club playoff involving first two teams in each division. dLeague divided into Northern and Southern divisions. Won four-club playoff involving first two teams in each division. eLeague divided into Northern and Southern divisions. Same two clubs won both halves; won playoffs. fWon split-season playoff.

STANDING OF CLUBS AT CLOSE OF FIRST HALF, JUNE 14

NORTHERN DIVISION

Club	W.	L.	T.	Pct.	G.B.
Daytona Beach (Astros)	43	24	0	.642	....
Lakeland (Tigers)	32	33	0	.492	10
Tampa (Reds)	33	35	0	.485	10½
St. Petersburg (Cardinals)	33	35	0	.485	10½
Winter Haven (Red Sox)	25	44	0	.362	19

SOUTHERN DIVISION

Club	W.	L.	T.	Pct.	G.B.
Fort Myers (Royals)	45	22	0	.672	....
Fort Lauderdale (Yankees)	41	26	0	.612	4
West Palm Beach (Expos)	34	31	0	.523	10
Vero Beach (Dodgers)	28	41	0	.406	18
Miami (Padres)	21	46	0	.313	24

STANDING OF CLUBS AT CLOSE OF SECOND HALF, AUGUST 25

NORTHERN DIVISION

Club	W.	L.	T.	Pct.	G.B.
Daytona Beach (Astros)	42	25	0	.627	....
St. Petersburg (Cardinals)	37	29	0	.561	4½
Lakeland (Tigers)	26	39	0	.400	15
Tampa (Reds)	23	37	0	.383	15½
Winter Haven (Red Sox)	24	40	0	.375	16½

SOUTHERN DIVISION

Club	W.	L.	T.	Pct.	G.B.
Vero Beach (Dodgers)	41	24	0	.631	....
West Palm Beach (Expos)	41	26	0	.612	1
Fort Lauderdale (Yankees)	36	28	0	.563	4½
Fort Myers (Royals)	29	31	0	.483	9½
Miami (Padres)	23	43	0	.348	18½

COMPOSITE STANDING OF CLUBS AT CLOSE OF SEASON, AUGUST 25

Club	Day.	FtL.	FtM	WPB	St.P.	V.B.	Lak.	Tam.	WH	Mia.	W.	L.	T.	Pct.	G.B.
Daytona Beach (Astros)	....	5	4	4	16	9	9	17	16	5	85	49	0	.634	....
Fort Lauderdale (Yankees)	5	....	13	7	4	12	6	4	8	18	77	54	0	.588	6½
Fort Myers (Royals)	6	8	....	12	4	12	5	9	5	13	74	53	0	.583	7½
West Palm Beach (Expos)	6	13	7	....	5	11	5	5	7	16	75	57	0	.568	9
St. Petersburg (Cardinals)	6	5	5	5	....	3	15	8	17	6	70	64	0	.526	15
Vero Beach (Dodgers)	1	9	7	11	7	....	7	6	6	15	69	65	0	.515	16
Lakeland (Tigers)	11	4	5	4	7	3	....	8	11	5	58	72	0	.446	25
Tampa (Reds)	4	4	0	5	13	4	9	....	12	5	56	72	0	.438	26
Winter Haven (Red Sox)	6	2	4	3	4	4	11	9	....	6	49	84	0	.368	35½
Miami (Padres)	4	4	8	6	4	7	5	5	1	....	44	89	0	.336	40½

Major league affiliations in parentheses.

Playoffs—Vero Beach defeated Fort Myers, two games to one; and Vero Beach defeated Daytona Beach, three games to two, to win league championship.

Regular Season Attendance—Daytona Beach, 100,155; Fort Lauderdale, 45,415; Fort Myers, 124,259; Lakeland, 49,220; Miami, 40,652; St. Petersburg, 150,138; Tampa, 64,754; West Palm Beach, 147,805; Winter Haven, 24,585. Total, 824,839. Playoffs, 8,385. All Star Game, 2,371.

Managers—Daytona Beach, Dave Cripe; Fort Lauderdale, Carl Merrill; Fort Myers, Rick Mathews; Lakeland, Ted Brazell; Miami, Jim Breazeale; St. Petersburg, Nick Leyva; Tampa, Jim Hoff; Vero Beach, Stan Wasiak; West Palm Beach, Tommy Thompson; Winter Haven, Tom Kotchman.

All-Star Team—Northern Division—1B—Glen Carpenter, Daytona Beach; 2B—Chris Pittaro, Lakeland; 3B—Dave Hall, Tampa; SS—Brad Luther, St. Petersburg; OF—Crestwell Pratt, Tampa; Tony Walker, Daytona Beach; Curtis Burke, Daytona Beach; C—Tim Wallace, St. Petersburg; Mike Williams, Lakeland; DH—Randy Braun, Daytona Beach; RHP—Mike Hogan, Daytona Beach; Mike Ferguson, Tampa; LHP—John Martin, St. Petersburg; Manny Hernandez, Daytona Beach; Manager—Dave Cripe, Daytona Beach. Southern Division—1B—Orestes Destrade, Fort Lauderdale; 2B—Casey Candaele, West Palm Beach; 3B—Tom Barrett, Fort Lauderdale; SS—Dickie Scott, Fort Lauderdale; OF—Willie Neal, Fort Myers; Reggie Williams, Vero Beach; Tommy Francis, Miami; C—Roger Hansen, Fort Myers; Jim Cecchini, West Palm Beach; DH—Gary Newson, Vero Beach; RHP—Bret Saberhagen, Fort Myers; Jose Rijo, Fort Lauderdale; LHP—Tim Birtsas, Fort Lauderdale; Reggie Wyatt, Fort Myers; Manager—Rick Mathews, Fort Myers.

(Compiled by Howe News Bureau, Boston Mass.)

CLUB BATTING

Club	Pct.	G.	AB.	R.	OR.	H.	TB.	2B.	3B.	HR.	RBI.	GW.	SH.	SF.	HP.	BB.	Int. BB.	SO.	SB.	CS.	LOB.
Daytona Beach	.281	134	4398	782	577	1234	1747	218	68	53	686	73	32	49	43	627	39	747	149	66	1018
West Palm Beach	.266	132	4417	623	575	1173	1561	177	38	45	548	67	38	40	33	508	25	632	98	71	1006
Lakeland	.264	130	4265	591	661	1124	1600	176	39	74	507	49	80	31	41	495	40	783	94	65	985
St. Petersburg	.261	135	4229	529	501	1104	1429	185	28	28	460	59	56	40	32	447	26	708	83	63	954
Fort Myers	.254	127	4067	558	414	1031	1356	139	39	36	475	64	49	36	35	469	31	783	166	52	913
Tampa	.254	128	4060	547	629	1031	1472	165	51	58	477	48	62	33	32	465	37	766	100	44	903
Fort Lauderdale	.252	131	4127	581	409	1041	1495	179	34	69	498	70	51	34	36	513	19	755	143	54	933
Vero Beach	.250	134	4300	590	606	1077	1475	167	63	35	512	62	46	39	46	561	39	825	238	96	970
Miami	.246	134	4248	462	710	1046	1381	178	35	29	405	39	49	29	47	452	25	788	78	65	953
Winter Haven	.245	133	4216	551	732	1033	1420	167	35	50	477	39	39	44	34	529	28	815	89	46	966

INDIVIDUAL BATTING

(Leading Qualifiers for Batting Championship—373 or More Plate Appearances)

*Bats lefthanded. †Switch-hitter.

Player and Club	Pct.	G.	AB.	R.	H.	TB.	2B.	3B.	HR.	RBI.	GW.	SH.	SF.	HP.	BB.	Int. BB.	SO.	SB.	CS.
Barrett, Thomas, Fort Lauderdale†	.327	103	397	80	130	153	21	1	0	32	5	1	1	5	46	2	16	55	17
Walker, Anthony, Daytona Beach†	.326	92	350	84	114	126	8	2	0	41	2	2	2	4	75	0	51	43	11
Francis, Thomas, Miami*	.321	132	489	58	157	196	23	5	2	52	8	6	2	7	50	6	35	6	10
Pratt, Crestwell, Tampa	.320	127	422	72	135	237	27	6	21	102	8	0	7	6	58	9	115	8	3
Braun, Randall, Daytona Beach*	.309	118	427	85	132	206	27	10	9	96	15	0	9	8	60	10	71	14	4
Silverio, Virgilio, Lakeland*	.307	88	335	61	103	138	13	8	2	27	1	13	0	2	34	1	48	18	4
Wallace, Timothy, St. Petersburg	.306	122	405	51	124	158	31	0	1	44	7	5	2	10	32	2	62	2	4
Candaele, Casey, West Palm Beach†	.305	127	511	77	156	200	26	9	0	45	8	8	1	2	51	2	44	22	17
Delgado, Juan, Daytona Beach	.301	122	455	78	137	187	22	5	6	60	2	7	5	5	37	4	92	8	4
Meadows, Michael, Daytona Beach*	.293	112	382	68	112	192	25	14	9	71	7	1	4	5	58	3	80	27	12

Departmental Leaders: G—Luther, 134; AB—Candaele, 511; R—Braun, 85; H—Francis, 157; TB—Pratt, 237; 2B—Burke, 48; 3B—Duncan, 15; HR—Pratt, 21; RBI—Carpenter, 104; GWRBI—Braun, Destrade, 15; SH—Ruiz, 17; SF—Braun, Hansen, James, 9; HP—Wallace, 10; BB—Baker, Destrade, 82; IBB—Kingery, 11; SO—Cataline, 138; SB—Duncan, 56; CS—Simmons, 19.

(All Players—Listed Alphabetically)

Player and Club	Pct.	G.	AB.	R.	H.	TB.	2B.	3B.	HR.	RBI.	GW.	SH.	SF.	HP.	BB.	Int. BB.	SO.	SB.	CS.
Adams, Peter, Fort Lauderdale	.000	9	8	1	0	0	0	0	0	0	0	0	0	0	1	0	1	0	0
Allinger, Robert, Miami	.192	75	208	18	40	54	6	4	0	12	0	2	0	3	20	0	66	1	1
Alvarez, Carmello, Vero Beach†	.214	50	126	20	27	30	1	1	0	8	0	4	0	1	21	0	23	14	5
Arce, Lorenzo, Lakeland	.288	117	431	58	124	179	22	3	9	56	4	6	3	6	36	1	53	6	10
Arfstrom, Joseph, Winter Haven†	.200	94	270	19	54	61	7	0	0	20	3	4	1	1	33	4	51	3	2
Baker, Derrell, West Palm Beach	.292	129	459	80	134	158	16	1	2	51	10	3	4	6	82	1	37	11	7
Baker, Robert, Lakeland*	.241	46	133	12	32	38	4	1	0	6	0	3	1	1	19	1	29	6	2
Barrett, Thomas, Fort Lauderdale†	.327	103	397	80	130	153	21	1	0	32	5	1	1	5	46	2	16	55	17
Bartlett, Charles, Vero Beach	.208	14	48	5	10	10	0	0	0	4	0	0	1	0	4	0	4	0	2
Batista, Francisco, St. Petersburg	.282	101	354	49	100	158	27	11	3	41	3	3	2	4	22	1	70	5	8
Belue, Benjamin, West Palm Beach	.271	94	332	44	90	106	11	1	1	32	5	3	3	2	22	1	43	8	10
Benzinger, Todd, Winter Haven†	.279	125	480	56	134	199	34	5	7	68	5	3	4	3	43	4	75	4	3
Berti, Donald, Daytona Beach	.263	68	175	33	46	67	5	2	4	28	4	1	4	1	44	3	25	6	5
Blair, Michael, Vero Beach	.259	44	147	11	38	49	9	1	0	25	4	4	0	0	5	0	13	0	1
Boddy, William, Tampa	.500	4	2	0	1	2	1	0	0	0	0	0	0	0	0	0	0	0	0
Boncore, Steven, Vero Beach	.226	17	53	4	12	15	3	0	0	6	0	0	0	0	9	1	4	0	0
Bonk, Thomas, Winter Haven*	.234	96	308	35	72	99	7	4	4	35	0	2	5	1	36	4	48	2	2
Botkin, Michael, Daytona Beach*	.286	101	297	60	85	106	8	5	1	42	5	1	1	1	64	4	29	11	3
Braun, Randall, Daytona Beach*	.309	118	427	85	132	206	27	10	9	96	15	0	9	8	60	10	71	14	4
Browning, Thomas, Tampa*	.167	11	24	3	4	4	0	0	0	1	0	5	0	0	5	0	6	0	0
Brumley, A. Michael, Winter Haven†	.314	44	153	25	48	65	6	4	1	18	0	2	3	3	16	0	31	4	3
Bryant, Ralph, Vero Beach*	.264	130	489	74	129	208	27	11	10	65	8	1	5	6	49	3	135	17	7
Burke, Curtis, Daytona Beach	.292	117	456	77	133	222	48	10	7	72	10	1	2	7	40	5	81	12	8
Burley, Anthony, Tampa	.256	65	180	21	46	55	4	1	1	12	1	0	0	3	16	0	23	9	4
Burns, James, St. Petersburg*	.239	99	230	25	55	80	10	3	3	26	2	1	2	0	29	5	49	1	3
Burrell, Kevin, Winter Haven	.221	27	86	10	19	30	5	0	2	6	1	1	0	1	4	0	23	1	0
Butterfield, Brian, Miami†	.238	71	240	34	57	68	9	1	0	24	2	2	2	4	45	2	30	5	1
Cain, Jerald, Vero Beach	.214	27	56	11	12	15	1	1	0	4	0	0	1	0	12	1	11	1	0
Candaele, Casey, West Palm Beach†	.305	127	511	77	156	200	26	9	0	45	8	8	1	2	51	2	44	22	17
Cannizzaro, Chris, Winter Haven†	.241	60	203	35	49	58	6	0	1	24	3	0	3	2	46	0	30	15	4
Cannon, Timothy, Miami†	.177	53	181	19	32	46	6	1	2	12	0	2	0	3	20	1	53	9	5
Carpenter, Glenn, Daytona Beach	.282	129	475	83	134	186	22	3	8	104	12	3	6	5	70	4	101	3	4
Carrasquel, Emilio, Lakeland	.133	11	30	5	4	5	1	0	0	3	1	1	0	1	3	0	2	0	0
Casasnovas, Roberto, Lakeland*	.218	58	179	22	39	45	2	2	0	10	2	2	2	1	32	1	44	6	2
Castiglia, Patrick, Winter Haven*	.261	106	345	39	90	129	14	2	7	48	5	4	5	1	31	6	69	2	2
Castillo, Carlos, Miami	.000	1	1	0	0	0	0	0	0	0	0	0	0	0	0	0	0	0	0
Castro, Edgar, Miami*	.231	71	221	26	51	83	12	1	6	21	2	0	2	5	37	3	37	0	3
Cataline, Daniel, Vero Beach	.219	123	401	62	88	156	12	7	14	59	8	3	4	3	80	1	138	28	12
Cecchini, James, West Palm Beach	.255	85	298	30	76	101	12	2	3	38	6	3	2	1	28	0	63	0	0
Chadwick, George, West Palm Beach	.111	4	9	0	1	1	0	0	0	1	0	0	0	0	1	0	0	0	0

Player and Club	Pct.	G.	AB.	R.	H.	TB.	2B.	3B.	HR.	RBI.	GW.	SH.	SF.	HP.	BB.	Int. BB.	SO.	SB.	CS.
Champion, K. Randall, St. Pete.†	.165	59	91	8	15	15	0	0	0	9	0	0	1	0	20	1	22	3	1
Christianson, David, Lakeland*	.234	110	350	45	82	141	16	2	13	54	5	1	2	3	55	8	97	2	1
Cimorelli, Bruce, Tampa*	.000	11	3	1	0	0	0	0	0	0	0	0	0	0	0	0	3	0	0
Citari, Joseph, Fort Myers	.233	111	361	45	84	104	6	1	4	43	7	2	2	2	65	3	87	7	2
Conley, K. Virgil, Tampa*	.118	26	17	1	2	3	1	0	0	2	0	1	0	0	0	0	7	0	0
Cruz, Marino, Vero Beach	.167	9	18	1	3	3	0	0	0	1	0	0	0	1	2	0	5	0	0
Culver, Lanell, Tampa†	.210	112	310	43	65	98	8	8	3	23	1	3	2	7	36	1	92	11	6
D'Onofrio, Gary, Daytona Beach†	.242	48	178	25	43	60	8	3	1	20	2	0	4	3	16	1	20	1	3
Dalena, Peter, Fort Lauderdale*	.314	49	169	16	53	72	9	2	2	28	4	0	3	1	17	0	16	0	0
Datz, Jeffrey, Daytona Beach	.273	47	143	17	39	54	9	0	2	19	2	0	0	0	13	1	21	0	0
Daugherty, William, Miami	.173	68	214	13	37	45	5	0	1	17	1	4	2	0	19	2	53	2	0
Davis, Ronald, Lakeland*	.309	84	246	38	76	102	14	0	4	35	2	4	2	6	49	6	49	5	2
Delany, Dennis, West Palm Beach	.230	62	196	26	45	54	7	1	0	17	1	3	2	1	25	0	17	2	1
Delgado, Juan, Daytona Beach	.301	122	455	78	137	187	22	5	6	60	2	7	5	5	37	4	92	8	4
DelRosario, Manuel, Miami†	.181	58	160	10	29	33	2	1	0	4	1	4	0	0	22	0	32	6	0
Demeter, Todd, Fort Lauderdale	.215	77	256	28	55	82	8	2	5	30	3	1	1	3	35	1	60	5	0
Dennett, James, Winter Haven	.218	52	156	17	34	64	7	1	7	25	0	0	0	2	15	1	36	0	0
Destrade, Orestes, Fort Lauderdale†	.292	127	425	61	124	212	24	5	18	74	15	1	2	1	82	8	86	3	4
Dodd, Timothy, Tampa	.154	23	26	3	4	4	0	0	0	0	0	5	0	0	4	0	6	0	0
Doerrer, Robert, West Palm Beach	.246	26	61	13	15	19	0	2	0	5	0	1	1	1	6	0	9	2	3
Dotson, Hardy, West Palm Beach*	.261	107	398	58	104	134	12	3	4	43	2	7	3	3	35	1	55	10	9
Duncan, Mariano, Vero Beach†	.266	109	384	73	102	142	10	15	0	42	4	5	2	8	44	4	87	56	13
Ender, Scot, Tampa	.273	17	11	1	3	3	0	0	0	1	0	1	0	0	0	0	3	0	0
Evans, Anthony, Tampa	.188	44	112	13	21	29	2	0	2	12	1	1	0	2	19	2	19	1	2
Felice, J. Jason, Tampa	.273	87	264	28	72	103	13	3	4	33	6	3	1	0	22	4	27	5	3
Feliz, L. Adolfo, Tampa	.231	81	268	29	62	76	7	2	1	25	3	2	2	4	30	2	56	4	1
Ferguson, Michael, Tampa	.059	25	34	3	2	2	0	0	0	0	0	5	0	1	1	0	13	0	0
Fiorillo, Nicholas, Tampa*	.100	9	10	2	1	1	0	0	0	0	0	0	0	0	4	0	0	1	0
Foley, John, Tampa*	.208	61	125	21	26	32	0	3	0	13	1	5	0	1	18	1	20	6	2
Francis, Thomas, Miami*	.321	132	489	58	157	196	23	5	2	52	8	6	2	7	50	6	35	6	10
Freeman, Clements, Tampa*	.000	45	16	1	0	0	0	0	0	0	0	2	0	0	1	0	4	0	0
Frierson, John, Miami	.230	102	318	37	73	106	9	0	8	35	3	3	2	6	33	2	76	5	3
Funk, Gregory, Fort Lauderdale	.204	17	49	6	10	14	4	0	0	2	0	0	0	0	3	0	15	2	1
Galarraga, Andres, West Palm Beach	.289	104	401	55	116	170	18	3	10	66	9	1	1	7	33	6	68	7	5
Garcia, Frank, St. Petersburg	.235	73	226	32	53	70	14	0	1	24	4	0	3	0	25	1	43	0	2
Gaunce, David, Fort Myers	.228	34	92	3	21	25	4	0	0	8	2	1	0	0	3	0	24	0	0
Geels, Rob, Winter Haven*	.312	27	93	12	29	31	2	0	0	12	1	3	0	0	18	0	14	3	1
Gilcrease, Douglas, Fort Myers	.237	121	430	54	102	156	19	4	9	61	5	6	1	4	32	4	80	10	5
Gilles, Robert, Vero Beach	.147	49	116	7	17	22	5	0	0	13	2	2	0	1	17	0	39	2	0
Gjesdal, Brent, Fort Lauderdale	.202	80	188	23	38	52	9	1	1	21	4	1	0	4	29	0	66	7	1
Gleissner, James, Fort Myers	.207	43	135	14	28	38	4	0	2	15	3	0	0	6	8	1	26	0	0
Gomez, Jose, Miami*	.293	51	167	26	49	77	15	2	3	27	2	1	4	1	30	3	32	1	2
Gonzalez, Orlando, Tampa	.272	78	250	20	68	79	9	1	0	7	1	5	1	0	12	1	18	1	1
Gregory, John, Vero Beach*	.219	129	448	45	98	122	16	4	0	52	5	4	8	5	44	7	68	4	6
Guzman, Hector, Vero Beach	.229	77	223	31	51	66	10	1	1	20	5	5	0	2	19	0	41	11	3
Hall, David, Tampa	.286	128	454	77	130	197	25	9	8	64	8	5	7	1	56	2	76	10	5
Hall, Matthew, Fort Myers*	.273	103	377	61	103	125	10	6	0	34	7	6	2	2	40	0	95	28	5
Hansen, Roger, Fort Myers	.282	107	387	51	109	130	13	1	2	62	7	2	9	4	50	3	49	1	1
Hatcher, Harold, Fort Myers	.252	80	310	32	78	112	18	2	4	41	6	2	2	1	26	1	69	1	3
Hawkins, Johnny, Fort Lauderdale†	.221	41	104	17	23	25	2	0	0	15	0	5	0	2	10	1	12	3	2
Helsom, Robert, St. Petersburg*	.295	64	200	24	59	81	11	1	3	28	3	1	2	1	35	2	50	0	1
Hertzler, Paul, West Palm Beach*	.272	129	463	79	126	178	16	6	8	69	8	2	6	3	77	7	51	15	10
Hilgenkamp, Russell, Lakeland	.203	32	79	9	16	22	3	0	1	16	1	4	2	0	5	0	32	0	0
Hocutt, Michael, West Palm Beach*	.206	105	364	41	75	112	15	2	6	49	6	1	7	1	32	4	75	9	1
Hough, Stanley, Daytona Beach	.500	5	4	2	2	5	1	1	0	2	0	0	0	0	0	0	0	0	0
Hubbard, Tyson, Tampa	.048	29	21	1	1	4	0	0	1	1	0	1	0	1	2	0	13	0	0
Hudler, Rex, Fort Lauderdale	.270	91	345	55	93	118	15	2	2	50	4	5	6	5	26	1	44	30	7
Hume, Timothy, Tampa	.081	22	37	4	3	3	0	0	0	0	0	0	0	0	4	0	16	0	0
Hunsinger, Alan, St. Petersburg	.268	36	112	11	30	43	6	2	1	23	3	1	2	0	17	0	13	0	4
Ireland, Billy, Miami	.232	120	401	46	93	113	16	2	0	31	5	5	7	6	45	2	47	2	5
Jabalera, Francisco, Daytona Beach*	.275	28	80	16	22	25	3	0	0	6	1	1	1	0	14	2	7	4	0
James, Richard, St. Petersburg	.282	112	330	37	93	112	11	4	0	47	4	4	9	2	40	2	31	4	4
Jones, Daniel, Miami	.272	74	250	30	68	96	13	6	1	34	2	3	3	2	32	0	32	3	4
Jones, Thomas, Fort Lauderdale*	.244	73	217	31	53	62	5	2	0	12	2	3	0	0	19	0	38	6	2
Jones, Tracy, Tampa	.271	53	118	27	32	46	5	3	1	15	1	4	3	0	10	1	8	3	1
Jongewaard, Steven, Winter Haven	.155	27	71	8	11	14	3	0	0	8	1	0	3	1	15	0	29	3	1
Jordan, Timothy, Fort Lauderdale*	.115	11	26	3	3	6	1	1	0	0	0	0	0	0	0	0	4	0	0
Kempton, Gary, Fort Lauderdale	.233	48	120	14	28	41	6	2	1	13	3	3	0	1	13	0	28	2	1
Kiesling, Larry, Daytona Beach	.357	5	14	4	5	10	2	0	1	4	1	0	0	0	3	0	4	1	0
Kincanon, William, Tampa†	.000	16	2	0	0	0	0	0	0	0	0	0	0	0	1	0	1	0	0
Kingery, Michael, Fort Myers*	.266	123	436	68	116	145	9	7	2	51	4	4	7	3	56	11	70	31	9
Kolotka, Charles, Miami	.500	38	2	1	1	2	1	0	0	0	0	0	0	0	0	0	1	0	0
Lamar, Daniel, Tampa	.275	96	273	36	75	104	16	2	3	33	3	4	4	2	25	2	36	7	2
Langdon, L. Ted, Tampa	.400	27	5	1	2	2	0	0	0	0	0	0	0	0	0	0	1	0	0
Ledbetter, Jeffrey, Winter Haven*	.274	99	347	51	95	147	23	1	9	52	6	3	6	1	41	6	39	0	2
Lesieur, Paul, Fort Lauderdale	.173	38	81	6	14	14	0	0	0	7	0	2	0	0	3	0	6	1	1
Lindeman, James, St. Petersburg	.276	70	232	45	64	103	13	1	8	37	6	3	2	0	27	2	51	9	2
Lindsey, William, Fort Lauderdale	.242	82	260	33	63	93	12	0	6	33	4	4	2	4	20	1	35	2	1
Lombardi, Phillip, Fort Lauderdale	.224	17	49	1	11	13	2	0	0	3	1	0	0	0	7	0	8	1	0
Long, Anthony, Lakeland	.297	70	155	26	46	53	5	1	0	10	2	7	2	2	14	0	17	8	2
Luther, Bradley, St. Petersburg	.262	134	461	59	121	141	16	2	0	42	3	3	2	4	49	2	53	9	8
Maloney, Joseph, Lakeland	.097	21	31	4	3	4	1	0	0	3	1	2	0	1	11	0	4	0	2
McAllister, Steven, Daytona Beach†	.197	79	218	33	43	62	4	3	3	30	4	4	3	0	28	0	36	3	4
McGilvray, James, Daytona Beach	.250	34	108	19	27	39	3	3	1	21	2	3	2	1	13	1	35	0	0
McGriff, Terence, Tampa	.254	87	260	21	66	98	11	3	5	45	4	1	1	1	26	3	62	2	0
Meadows, Michael, Daytona Beach*	.293	112	382	68	112	192	25	14	9	71	7	1	4	5	58	3	80	27	12
Medina, Pedro, Fort Lauderdale†	.240	33	125	14	30	38	2	0	2	17	1	4	1	0	2	0	23	2	0
Meleski, Mark, Winter Haven†	.231	68	186	30	43	50	7	0	0	14	0	4	0	1	32	2	27	6	2
Merulla, Tony, Fort Lauderdale*	.219	48	137	15	30	51	4	1	5	18	3	0	4	1	20	1	19	0	1
Metil, William, Tampa*	.333	20	54	7	18	20	2	0	0	6	1	0	0	0	8	0	3	2	0
Miggins, Mark, Miami*	.455	26	11	1	5	6	1	0	0	0	0	0	0	0	0	0	1	0	0
Molnar, Rick, Fort Lauderdale	.188	29	64	5	12	14	2	0	0	4	2	4	2	1	6	0	10	1	0
Montalvo, Rafael, Vero Beach	.000	43	1	0	0	0	0	0	0	0	0	0	0	0	0	0	1	0	0

Player and Club	Pct.	G.	AB.	R.	H.	TB.	2B.	3B.	HR.	RBI.	GW.	SH.	SF.	HP.	BB.	Int. BB.	SO.	SB.	CS.
Neal, Willie, Fort Myers	.273	115	421	56	115	160	17	5	6	51	5	2	3	5	36	3	94	22	10
Neuzil, Jeffrey, Fort Myers	.236	105	347	54	82	99	12	1	1	20	6	13	2	1	27	0	41	10	6
Newson, Gary, Vero Beach	.274	122	409	52	112	137	13	6	0	52	7	10	4	4	62	4	50	19	14
Noce, Paul, Miami	.268	65	220	26	59	78	11	4	0	23	3	1	1	1	23	0	53	5	2
O'Neill, Paul, Tampa*	.278	121	413	62	115	176	23	7	8	51	3	1	2	0	56	7	70	20	5
Oliver, Warren, Fort Myers	.144	58	160	13	23	24	1	0	0	14	2	3	5	0	15	0	60	2	0
Ortiz, Leopoldo, Lakeland	.222	32	99	15	22	28	6	0	0	9	2	2	1	1	6	0	9	5	0
Oruna, Roland, Fort Myers	.273	38	88	18	24	34	3	2	1	14	3	0	0	5	14	2	18	10	2
Pasqua, Daniel, Fort Lauderdale*	.273	131	451	83	123	225	25	10	19	84	12	0	5	4	80	2	125	12	4
Pate, Brian, Winter Haven	.238	125	420	44	100	138	14	3	6	37	2	2	6	6	37	0	73	3	4
Pecota, William, Fort Myers	.269	65	234	48	63	89	7	2	5	33	4	3	3	1	45	0	31	28	5
Perkins, Harold, Vero Beach†	.252	99	337	50	85	116	15	5	2	31	5	3	4	5	55	6	46	32	9
Pittaro, Christopher, Lakeland†	.270	107	392	43	106	136	19	4	1	39	4	6	5	4	51	2	62	10	10
Pratt, Crestwell, Tampa	.320	127	422	72	135	237	27	6	21	102	8	0	7	6	58	9	115	8	3
Priessman, Kraig, Lakeland	.200	35	120	11	24	33	6	0	1	13	0	3	0	0	8	0	25	0	1
Radloff, Scott, Tampa*	.284	36	88	14	25	28	3	0	0	8	2	0	1	1	23	1	20	1	6
Reddish, Michael, Fort Lauderdale	.263	45	133	21	35	55	9	1	3	15	3	2	1	1	22	0	29	3	2
Reynolds, Mark, Vero Beach*	.258	69	229	25	59	84	16	3	1	35	4	0	3	1	38	5	30	1	3
Richardson, Billy Joe, Winter Haven	.192	73	219	31	42	73	10	3	5	25	2	2	2	0	23	1	66	0	0
Rivas, Pedro, Miami	.133	4	15	1	2	3	1	0	0	0	0	0	0	0	0	0	10	0	0
Rivera, Luis, West Palm Beach	.227	129	419	63	95	138	18	5	5	53	5	3	4	4	58	0	88	6	3
Rivera, Luis, Vero Beach	.221	26	68	5	15	19	1	0	1	12	0	2	0	1	3	0	11	0	0
Rivera, Ricardo, Daytona Beach†	.235	35	81	10	19	23	2	1	0	9	1	0	0	1	10	0	16	1	0
Rizzo, Richard, Fort Myers	.338	37	139	26	47	68	9	6	0	17	2	4	0	1	17	0	19	13	4
Rodriguez, Jose, St. Petersburg	.250	125	348	34	87	100	8	1	1	26	2	8	1	4	16	1	46	6	3
Rollin, Rondal, Lakeland	.293	78	297	52	87	152	15	4	14	63	6	0	4	2	27	5	70	4	3
Roman, Luis, St. Petersburg*	.245	24	49	9	12	15	1	1	0	8	1	0	2	0	6	0	10	2	1
Roth, John, Winter Haven	.310	72	203	41	63	80	6	4	1	25	4	0	1	5	22	0	55	8	4
Ruiz, Benny, Lakeland	.219	130	416	48	91	97	6	0	0	25	1	17	0	0	42	3	58	7	8
Sanchez, Jose, St. Petersburg	.277	22	47	4	13	13	0	0	0	3	0	3	0	1	2	0	8	0	2
Santiago, Benito, Miami	.247	122	429	34	106	152	25	3	5	56	4	7	2	7	11	1	79	3	7
Sayler, Barry, St. Petersburg	.207	64	184	19	38	51	8	1	1	15	2	4	0	3	27	1	30	3	0
Sayles, Stephen, Miami	.257	81	280	29	72	85	9	2	0	22	2	5	1	1	21	0	70	4	3
Schulte, Mark, St. Petersburg*	.282	63	213	31	60	84	9	0	5	28	7	4	1	2	11	4	21	3	2
Scott, Richard, Fort Lauderdale	.217	120	345	40	75	102	11	2	4	32	4	11	3	1	44	0	93	7	7
Silverio, Virgilio, Lakeland*	.307	88	335	61	103	138	13	8	2	27	1	13	0	2	34	1	48	18	4
Simmons, Allison, Miami†	.261	118	441	53	115	138	14	3	1	35	4	4	1	1	44	3	81	26	19
Simons, Neil, Fort Lauderdale*	.213	66	178	28	38	53	8	2	1	8	0	4	3	2	28	2	21	1	3
Smith, Mark, Lakeland	.287	45	171	26	49	79	7	1	7	29	3	0	1	4	8	2	22	1	2
Steinmetz, Kevin, Tampa	.182	68	143	19	26	30	2	1	0	11	2	0	1	1	14	1	14	9	2
Strickland, Terry, West Palm Beach	.317	31	101	11	32	40	5	0	1	21	2	0	2	0	9	1	11	4	1
Swindle, Allen, Tampa*	.000	33	7	2	0	0	0	0	0	0	0	0	0	0	2	0	3	0	0
Terry, Scott, Tampa	.238	66	105	14	25	35	6	2	0	12	2	7	1	1	12	0	28	0	1
Thomas, Deron, St. Petersburg†	.217	88	221	25	48	51	3	0	0	21	5	10	3	1	40	0	61	5	4
Thomas, James, Daytona Beach†	.283	101	368	66	104	132	15	5	1	38	3	4	3	0	44	1	37	12	7
Thomas, Reginald, Lakeland*	.272	121	486	77	132	224	24	10	16	59	5	7	5	1	40	4	106	8	11
Thompson, Richard, Daytona Beach	.161	41	112	16	18	21	3	0	0	7	0	2	1	2	29	0	28	2	1
Threatt, Anthony, Tampa	1.000	1	1	0	1	1	0	0	0	0	0	0	0	0	0	0	0	0	0
Turco, Steve, St. Petersburg*	.254	130	402	50	102	116	14	0	0	23	5	5	3	0	43	2	55	25	13
Turgeon, Stephen, St. Petersburg	.242	56	124	15	30	38	3	1	1	15	2	1	3	0	6	0	33	6	1
Vaughn, Michael, West Palm Beach	.216	15	51	6	11	18	1	0	2	11	1	0	1	0	4	2	9	0	1
Vazquez, Francisco, Winter Haven	.215	80	246	26	53	68	9	3	0	23	3	4	0	1	37	0	53	12	6
Velasquez, I. Javier, Vero Beach	.351	25	74	9	26	29	3	0	0	12	0	1	0	0	9	0	11	0	0
Vitato, Richard, Fort Myers*	.240	48	150	15	36	47	7	2	0	11	1	1	0	0	35	3	20	3	0
Walker, Anthony, Daytona Beach†	.326	92	350	84	114	126	8	2	0	41	2	2	2	4	75	0	51	43	11
Walker, Stephen, Winter Haven†	.256	102	328	61	84	99	5	5	0	28	3	4	3	4	59	0	57	20	8
Wallace, Timothy, St. Petersburg	.306	122	405	51	124	158	31	0	1	44	7	5	2	10	32	2	62	2	4
Watson, K. Steven, Tampa	.000	55	5	0	0	0	0	0	0	0	0	0	0	0	0	0	3	0	0
Weislak, Kenneth, West Palm Beach	.274	101	354	40	97	132	20	3	3	47	4	3	3	2	45	0	62	2	3
White, William, Vero Beach	.289	111	380	52	110	140	14	5	2	39	6	1	4	6	53	6	57	6	7
Williams, Jaime, Daytona	.253	29	75	6	19	24	3	1	0	16	0	2	2	0	9	0	13	1	0
Williams, Michael, Lakeland	.279	107	315	39	88	124	12	3	6	50	9	2	1	6	55	6	56	8	5
Williams, Reginald, Vero Beach	.283	81	293	53	83	112	11	3	4	32	4	1	3	2	35	1	51	47	14
Zell, Brian, Winter Haven*	.127	54	102	11	13	15	2	0	0	9	0	1	2	1	21	0	39	3	2

The following pitchers, listed alphabetically by club, with games in parentheses, had no plate appearances, primarily through use of designated hitters:

DAYTONA BEACH—Bombard, Richard (38); Callahan, Michael (4); Castro, Guillermo (10); Everett, Conrad (10); Hernandez, Manuel (18); Hogan, Michael (25); Kasprzak, Michael (34); Knudson, Mark (12); Moore, Sam (6); Noble, Raymer (14); Paris, Zacarias (8); Regalado, Uvaldo (16); Reilly, Edward (32); Schimpf, Rex (26); Shouppe, Jamey (43); Strasser, Richard (3); Wiedenbauer, Thomas (32).

FORT LAUDERDALE—Andrews, Sheldon (3); Beahan, Scot (7); Bersano, Mark (23); Birtsas, Timothy (23); Brown, Rory (29); Deshaies, James (20); Fedor, Francis (2); Mendez, Mark (4); Plunk, Eric (20); Raftice, Robert (6); Rijo, Jose (21); Silva, Mark (8); Siwiec, Michael (16); Smalley, David (3); Szymczak, David (18); Tewksbury, Robert (2); Tomaselli, Charles (23); Williams, Timothy (10); Woodworth, David (31).

FORT MYERS—Bryant, John (18); Cook, Douglas (12); Drizmala, Thomas (8); Evans, Richard (5); Jones, Michael (18); Martinez, Arthur (16); Miner, James (26); Morales, Edwin (4); Olson, Michael (15); Pone, Vincent (3); Saberhagen, Bret (16); Swanson, Perry (38); Walberg, Mark (28); Ware, Duane (3); Wilder, William (38); Wyatt, Reginald (24), Yowler, John (1).

LAKELAND—Barlow, Ricky (2), Dunn, Allen (11); Edgell, Thor (23); Faber, Walter (7); Furman, Jon (24); Garcia, Alejandro (12); Halley, Michael (15); Harvey, Randall (26); Held, Thomas (8); Hinz, William (11); James, Duane (39); Monteleone, Richard (24); Moya, Ernest (20); O'Connor, Donald (20); O'Connor, Nicholas (6); Perrotte, Joseph (12); Raubolt, Arthur (13); Robinson, Jeffrey (11); Ross, James (32); Tabor, Scott (4); Willis, Carl (4).

MIAMI—Cota, Francisco (24); Dean, Jeffrey (34); DelRosario, Sergio (6); Gardner, Scott (22); George, William (16); Gerhardt, William (5); McClain, Michael (23); McLoughlin, Timothy (6); Nodell, Raymond (14); Raymer, Gregory (15); Rhoads, Kevin (28); Ricci, Frank (3); Walter, Gene (42).

ST. PETERSBURG—Boever, Joseph (53); Carranza, Javier (35); Carson, Henry (31); Coatney, Rickey (4); Cox, Daniel (5); Dozier, Thomas (26); Epple, Thomas (24); Hartley, Michael (10); Hurst, Dale (1); Kish, Robert (19); Martin, John (29); Martinez, Christian (30); Martinez, Randy (1); Riggins, Mark (30); Silva, Freddie (30); Young, Scott (26).

TAMPA—Kurant, Tom (7); Lowrey, Steven (5); Riley, Michael (1).

VERO BEACH—Beuder, Michael (36); Cherry, Michael (11); Duffy, Thomas (11); Felt, Richard (11); Gentle, Michael (11); Hammond, Shayne (12); Innis, Brian (27); Jones, Charles (11); Kenyon, Robert (13); Lovelace, Vance (24); Madden, Morris (16); Scudder, William (46); Slezak, Robert (16); Sonberg, Erik (11); Thomas, Christopher (32).

WEST PALM BEACH—Chapin, Peter (16); Chesser, Brandon (23); Dopson, John (23); Edwards, Derek (3); Flores, David (12); Gause, Ernest (26); Gilbreath, Ronald (42); Groves, Larry (23); Jefferson, James (9); Krzanik, Andrew (13); McKay, Troy (25); Nurthen, John (9); St. Claire, Randy (42); Stoll, Richard (13); Torres, Miguel (6); Valliant, Robert (9); Williams, Mark (10); Yenser, Steven (1).

WINTER HAVEN—Araujo, Anazario (46); Bowlin, Allan (6); Cappadona, Anthony (23); Clemens, Roger (4); Clinton, Kevin (30); Davis, Charles (13); Ellsworth, Steven (20); Gering, Scott (39); Knight, Larry (32); Lockhart, Bruce (41); Minor, Bruster (18); Proodian, Gary (29); Sellers, Jeffrey (21); Weinbrecht, Mark (6); Weppner, Daniel (14).

GRAND SLAM HOME RUNS—Demeter, Rollin, R. Thomas, 2 each; D. Baker, Braun, Burke, Carpenter, Cecchini, Christianson, D. Hall, Lamar, Ledbetter, Pate, Pratt, J. Rodriguez, 1 each.

AWARDED FIRST BASE ON CATCHER'S INTERFERENCE—Hocutt 3 (Hansen, Bartlett, Priessman); Ender 2 (Berti 2); Gjesdel 2 (Lamar, Wallace); Turgeon 2 (Hansen, Frierson); White 2 (Diaz, Sayler); Baker (Bartlett); Berti (Wallace); Burke (Priessman); Culver (M. Williams); Daugherty (Priessman); Duncan (Cecchini); Oruna (Priessman); Vaughn (Berti).

CLUB FIELDING

Club	Pct.	G.	PO.	A.	E.	DP.	PB.
Fort Myers	.973	127	3216	1337	126	94	9
Fort Lauderdale	.968	131	3284	1378	156	120	20
Lakeland	.965	130	3312	1315	170	125	25
Daytona Beach	.964	134	3416	1531	183	141	17
St. Petersburg	.964	135	3340	1404	179	120	18
West Palm Beach	.964	132	3434	1555	184	136	24
Miami	.958	134	3345	1352	204	121	33
Vero Beach	.955	134	3444	1475	231	133	37
Tampa	.954	128	3152	1235	211	110	16
Winter Haven	.953	133	3310	1389	233	109	26

Triple plays—Daytona Beach, Tampa.

INDIVIDUAL FIELDING

*Throws lefthanded.

FIRST BASEMEN

Player and Club	Pct.	G.	PO.	A.	E.	DP.
Benzinger, Winter Haven	1.000	2	10	1	0	1
Berti, Daytona Beach	1.000	1	1	1	0	0
Bonk, Winter Haven	.978	46	375	33	9	28
Botkin, Daytona Beach	1.000	1	4	0	0	0
Braun, Daytona Beach	.976	25	231	17	6	21
Burns, St. Petersburg*	.970	81	489	63	17	38
Carpenter, Daytona Beach*	.988	111	943	97	13	98
Casasnovas, Lakeland	.932	6	41	0	3	4
Castiglia, Winter Haven*	.982	90	713	64	14	63
Castro, Miami*	.976	71	540	34	14	47
Christianson, Lakeland*	.984	91	686	51	12	76
CITARI, Fort Myers	.994	93	756	76	5	52
D'Onofrio, Daytona Beach	1.000	1	2	0	0	0
Dalena, Fort Lauderdale	.974	20	171	17	5	14
Daugherty, Miami	.947	4	18	0	1	0
Davis, Lakeland	.981	26	199	3	4	9
Demeter, Fort Lauderdale	.988	74	588	48	8	61
Destrade, Fort Lauderdale	.991	40	309	21	3	27
Foley, Tampa*	1.000	36	209	15	0	23
Galarraga, West Palm Beach	.988	90	848	77	11	101
Gomez, Miami*	.980	49	437	11	9	38
Gregory, Vero Beach*	.990	129	1149	92	13	109
Hall, Tampa	.975	14	65	12	2	7
Hansen, Fort Myers	1.000	1	8	0	0	1
Hatcher, Fort Myers	.991	36	307	19	3	25
Helsom, St. Petersburg	.988	13	78	7	1	12
Hertzler, West Palm Beach*	1.000	2	3	2	0	0
Hocutt, West Palm Beach	.979	43	396	31	9	28
Hunsinger, St. Petersburg	.989	33	260	19	3	32
Ireland, Miami	.980	11	89	7	2	9
D. Jones, Miami	1.000	11	50	4	0	5
Lamar, Tampa	1.000	1	4	0	0	0
Lindsey, Fort Lauderdale	1.000	3	11	3	0	0
O'Neill, Tampa	1.000	1	1	1	0	0
Pratt, Tampa	.981	69	484	44	10	40
Radloff, Tampa*	.991	32	209	14	2	23
Reddish, Fort Lauderdale	1.000	1	1	0	0	0
Richardson, Winter Haven	.941	6	15	1	1	1
Sayler, St. Petersburg	.990	28	182	16	2	21
Schulte, St. Petersburg	1.000	9	94	5	0	3
White, Vero Beach	1.000	11	83	5	0	3
Williams, Lakeland	1.000	24	143	10	0	12

Triple plays—Carpenter, Radloff.

SECOND BASEMEN

Player and Club	Pct.	G.	PO.	A.	E.	DP.
Baker, West Palm Beach	1.000	2	1	1	0	0
Barrett, Fort Lauderdale	.954	32	45	59	5	15
Botkin, Daytona Beach	.750	2	1	2	1	1
Burley, Tampa	.976	42	73	88	4	19
Butterfield, Miami	.986	13	28	43	1	6
Candaele, West Palm Beach	.956	117	255	391	30	87
Cannizzaro, Winter Haven	.955	60	98	159	12	29
Chadwick, West Palm Beach	1.000	1	1	0	0	0
D'Onofrio, Daytona Beach	1.000	33	86	97	0	27
Doerrer, West Palm Beach	.989	17	33	56	1	10
Duncan, Vero Beach	.914	24	40	66	10	6
Feliz, Tampa	.938	50	112	131	16	29
Funk, Fort Lauderdale	.964	16	23	30	2	7
Gilcrease, Fort Myers	.975	120	235	321	14	55
Gonzalez, Tampa	.917	4	4	7	1	2
Guzman, Vero Beach	.750	1	0	3	1	0
Hudler, Fort Lauderdale	.973	87	188	239	12	57
Hume, Tampa	1.000	4	0	4	0	1
Ireland, Miami	1.000	1	1	1	0	0
Jongewaard, Winter Haven	1.000	1	2	2	0	1
Long, Lakeland	.952	34	57	83	7	13
McAllister, Daytona Beach	1.000	1	0	3	0	0
Medina, Fort Lauderdale	.969	12	29	33	2	5
Meleski, Winter Haven	.940	19	25	38	4	6
Metil, Tampa	.896	15	19	24	5	2
Newson, Vero Beach	1.000	29	60	72	0	13
Noce, Miami	1.000	7	12	11	0	2
Oliver, Fort Myers	.976	7	17	23	1	2
Perkins, Vero Beach	.961	86	187	230	17	65
PITTARO, Lakeland	.978	104	222	306	12	71
Rivera, Daytona Beach	.905	9	15	23	4	4
Sanchez, St. Petersburg	.980	15	19	29	1	8
Scott, Fort Lauderdale	1.000	1	1	2	0	0
Simmons, Miami	.976	116	275	332	15	69
Steinmetz, Tampa	.961	37	68	79	6	19
Strickland, West Palm Beach	1.000	1	1	3	0	1
D. Thomas, St. Petersburg	.955	86	172	214	18	46
J. Thomas, Daytona Beach	.963	100	214	286	19	66
Turco, St. Petersburg	.982	60	91	128	4	27
Vazquez, Winter Haven	1.000	3	5	6	0	2
Walker, Winter Haven	.942	58	124	150	17	28
Weislak, West Palm Beach	1.000	1	1	0	0	0

Triple play—D'Onofrio.

THIRD BASEMEN

Player and Club	Pct.	G.	PO.	A.	E.	DP.
Arce, Lakeland	.925	116	76	194	22	23
Arfstrom, Winter Haven	.750	1	1	2	1	0
Barrett, Fort Lauderdale	.910	84	54	148	20	17
Benzinger, Winter Haven	.000	1	0	0	1	0
Botkin, Daytona Beach	.907	19	16	23	4	4
Burley, Tampa	.895	11	5	12	2	1
Butterfield, Miami	1.000	20	7	29	0	1
Candaele, West Palm Beach	.778	4	2	5	2	0
D'Onofrio, Daytona Beach	.833	4	2	8	2	1
Delgado, Daytona Beach	.863	116	65	212	44	16
Feliz, Tampa	.909	18	15	25	4	1
Garcia, St. Petersburg	.920	63	45	127	15	13
Guzman, Vero Beach	.810	32	10	41	12	5
Hall, Tampa	.891	88	67	137	25	11
Hocutt, West Palm Beach	.857	9	8	10	3	2
Hume, Tampa	1.000	2	0	2	0	0
Ireland, Miami	.898	84	76	153	26	15
D. Jones, Miami	.956	18	8	35	2	2
T. Jones, Tampa	.722	15	14	12	10	3
Lamar, Tampa	.667	1	0	2	1	0
Lesieur, Fort Lauderdale	1.000	24	11	20	0	4
Lindeman, St. Petersburg	.838	70	36	98	26	6

THIRD BASEMEN—Continued

Player and Club	Pct.	G.	PO.	A.	E.	DP.
Long, Lakeland	.727	5	4	4	3	0
Maloney, Lakeland	1.000	6	5	6	0	1
Medina, Fort Lauderdale	.971	15	10	24	1	2
Meleski, Winter Haven	.923	8	2	22	2	1
Merulla, Fort Lauderdale	.923	6	3	9	1	1
Molnar, Fort Lauderdale	.964	27	16	37	2	2
Newson, Vero Beach	.897	14	9	26	4	6
Noce, Miami	.921	20	7	28	3	5
Oliver, Fort Myers	.934	21	16	41	4	4
Pate, Winter Haven	.912	123	124	207	32	12
Pecota, Fort Myers	.958	65	46	114	7	13
Rivera, Daytona Beach	1.000	3	1	3	0	1
Sanchez, St. Petersburg	1.000	1	1	3	0	1
Steinmetz, Tampa	.909	27	15	15	3	3
Strickland, West Palm Beach	.893	23	11	39	6	2
Turco, St. Petersburg	.929	8	8	5	1	1
Turgeon, St. Petersburg	1.000	5	4	7	0	1
Vazquez, Winter Haven	1.000	10	0	10	0	3
Vitato, Fort Myers	.895	44	30	89	14	7
WEISLAK, West Palm Beach	.935	101	63	195	18	15
White, Vero Beach	.893	100	61	198	31	21
Williams, Lakeland	.889	9	4	12	2	1

SHORTSTOPS

Player and Club	Pct.	G.	PO.	A.	E.	DP.
Adams, Fort Lauderdale	.900	9	2	7	1	2
Alvarez, Vero Beach	.926	43	57	142	16	20
Brumley, Winter Haven	.874	38	40	92	19	19
Burley, Tampa	1.000	4	1	4	0	0
Butterfield, Miami	.894	38	61	108	20	14
Candaele, West Palm Beach	1.000	2	1	1	0	0
D'Onofrio, Daytona Beach	.967	15	22	36	2	9
DelRosario, Miami	.900	58	97	128	25	36
Duncan, Vero Beach	.848	29	38	85	22	16
Evans, Tampa	.888	39	70	88	20	18
Feliz, Tampa	.944	16	19	32	3	5
Funk, Fort Lauderdale	1.000	1	1	1	0	0
Gonzalez, Tampa	.921	75	100	181	24	45
Guzman, Vero Beach	.857	6	5	13	3	3
Hudler, Fort Lauderdale	.813	10	7	6	3	1
Hume, Tampa	.805	10	19	14	8	4
D. Jones, Miami	.898	13	23	30	6	4
Jongewaard, Winter Haven	867	3	1	12	2	2
Luther, St. Petersburg	.940	133	188	317	32	73
McAllister, Daytona Beach	.943	79	121	209	20	57
Medina, Fort Lauderdale	.971	8	12	21	1	8
Meleski, Winter Haven	.942	34	58	104	10	17
Molnar, Fort Lauderdale	1.000	2	1	9	0	0
Neuzil, Fort Myers	.959	103	164	283	19	38
Newson, Vero Beach	.945	65	114	198	18	45
Noce, Miami	.925	35	54	107	13	19
Oliver, Fort Myers	.938	30	27	79	7	11
Pate, Winter Haven	.833	1	0	5	1	0
Pittaro, Lakeland	1.000	3	2	4	0	0
L. Rivera, West Palm Beach	.928	129	217	436	51	95
R. Rivera, Daytona Beach	.864	19	16	41	9	7
RUIZ, Lakeland	.963	130	229	346	22	78
Scott, Fort Lauderdale	.939	119	177	350	34	69
Simmons, Miami	1.000	1	0	2	0	0
Strickland, West Palm Beach	.957	3	4	18	1	4
Thompson, Daytona Beach	.959	41	60	102	7	21
Turco, St. Petersburg	.979	18	16	30	1	4
Vazquez, Winter Haven	.918	65	109	203	28	36

Triple play—McCallister, Gonzalez.

OUTFIELDERS

Player and Club	Pct.	G.	PO.	A.	E.	DP.
Allinger, Miami	.950	67	110	3	6	0
Arfstrom, Winter Haven	.967	88	132	13	5	4
D. BAKER, West Palm Beach	.993	95	142	10	1	2
R. Baker, Lakeland*	.988	42	78	4	1	1
Batista, St. Petersburg	.984	102	173	17	3	4
Belue, West Palm Beach	.952	70	116	4	6	1
Benzinger, Winter Haven	.967	91	196	9	7	2
Botkin, Daytona Beach	.971	71	98	4	3	2
Braun, Daytona Beach	.957	23	43	2	2	0
Brumley, Winter Haven	.917	8	11	0	1	0
Bryant, Vero Beach	.960	130	231	12	10	3
Burke, Daytona Beach	.957	111	174	4	8	1
Cain, Vero Beach	.842	16	15	1	3	0
Candaele, West Palm Beach	1.000	7	13	0	0	0
Cannon, Miami	.981	51	153	5	3	1
Casasnovas, Lakeland	.979	33	43	4	1	0
Castillo, Miami	1.000	1	1	0	0	0
Cataline, Vero Beach	.952	119	192	7	10	1
Culver, Tampa*	.957	104	217	5	10	0
Daugherty, Miami	.982	57	106	2	2	1
Destrade, Fort Lauderdale	.952	83	116	3	6	1
Dotson, West Palm Beach*	.991	104	217	7	2	3
Duncan, Vero Beach	.951	54	91	6	5	0
Felice, Tampa	.967	79	115	2	4	0
Foley, Tampa*	1.000	2	1	0	0	0
Francis, Miami*	.983	131	272	11	5	3
Frierson, Miami	.984	30	56	5	1	2
Galarraga, West Palm Beach	.867	8	13	0	2	0
Gjesdal, Fort Lauderdale	.972	57	99	4	3	1
D. Hall, Tampa	1.000	37	51	3	0	0
M. Hall, Fort Myers*	.980	99	191	7	4	0
Hatcher, Fort Myers	1.000	1	1	0	0	0
Helsom, St. Petersburg	.875	5	7	0	1	0
Hertzler, West Palm Beach*	.963	125	194	13	8	2
Jabalera, Daytona Beach*	.955	26	42	0	2	0
James, St. Petersburg	.981	99	143	9	3	2
D. Jones, Miami	1.000	10	14	0	0	0
Th. Jones, Fort Lauderdale	.944	56	66	2	4	0
Tr. Jones, Tampa	.976	24	40	0	1	0
Jongewaard, Winter Haven	.975	19	36	3	1	0
Jordan, Fort Lauderdale*	.933	5	13	1	1	1
Kiesling, Daytona Beach	.857	4	6	0	1	0
Kingery, Fort Myers*	.977	123	200	16	5	4
Lamar, Tampa	1.000	8	6	0	0	0
Ledbetter, Winter Haven*	.971	95	163	4	5	2
Lesieur, Fort Lauderdale	1.000	6	4	0	0	0
Long, Lakeland	1.000	8	12	0	0	0
Maloney, Lakeland	1.000	9	18	0	0	0
Meadows, Daytona Beach*	.978	92	169	5	4	1
Neal, Fort Myers	.951	107	187	9	10	3
Noce, Miami	1.000	7	16	1	0	1
O'Neill, Tampa	.958	120	217	13	10	2
Oruna, Fort Myers	.932	19	41	0	3	0
Pasqua, Fort Lauderdale*	.978	125	213	8	5	4
Perkins, Vero Beach	1.000	1	1	0	0	0
Pratt, Tampa	.916	47	72	4	7	2
Reddish, Fort Lauderdale	1.000	36	37	2	0	1
Reynolds, Vero Beach	.939	25	28	3	2	0
Rivera, Daytona Beach	1.000	1	1	0	0	0
Rizzo, Fort Myers	.987	36	73	2	1	0
Rodriguez, St. Petersburg	.978	122	248	17	6	4
Rollin, Lakeland	.896	69	90	5	11	0
Roman, St. Petersburg*	.909	15	19	1	2	0
Roth, Winter Haven	.980	71	142	2	3	0
Sayler, St. Petersburg	1.000	5	5	0	0	0
Sayles, Miami	.956	74	146	6	7	0
Schulte, St. Petersburg	1.000	14	28	0	0	0
Silverio, Lakeland*	.968	87	200	11	7	2
Simons, Fort Lauderdale*	.990	58	100	4	1	1
Smith, Lakeland	.987	39	72	5	1	0
Terry, Tampa	.952	35	54	6	3	0
Thomas, Lakeland*	.964	114	246	18	10	7
Turco, St. Petersburg	.966	63	82	4	3	0
Turgeon, St. Petersburg	.934	35	52	5	4	0
Vaughn, West Palm Beach	1.000	3	2	0	0	0
A. Walker, Daytona Beach	.985	91	196	4	3	0
S. Walker, Winter Haven	.929	18	25	1	2	0
Wallace, St. Petersburg	.889	13	16	0	2	0
Williams, Vero Beach	.948	70	142	3	8	1
Zell, Winter Haven	.952	48	56	3	3	2

CATCHERS

Player and Club	Pct.	G.	PO.	A.	E.	DP.	PB.
Bartlett, Vero Beach	.981	13	91	12	2	1	3
Berti, Daytona Beach	.982	55	283	50	6	8	6
Blair, Vero Beach	.984	36	215	24	4	4	9
Boddy, Tampa	1.000	4	4	1	0	0	0
Boncore, Vero Beach	.992	14	109	18	1	1	5
Burrell, Winter Haven	.935	26	127	17	10	1	2
Carrasquel, Lakeland	1.000	10	67	6	0	0	0
Cecchini, West Palm Beach	.976	76	462	61	13	9	15
Champion, St. Petersburg	.994	43	144	18	1	1	3
Cruz, Vero Beach	.976	7	40	1	1	0	3
Datz, Daytona Beach	.984	45	215	38	4	4	6
Delany, West Palm Beach	.989	60	329	29	4	1	9
Dennett, Winter Haven	.951	34	183	13	10	1	9
Frierson, Miami	.965	36	149	16	6	2	5
Gaunce, Fort Myers	.994	30	158	21	1	5	4
Geels, Winter Haven	1.000	18	104	12	0	1	2
Gilles, Vero Beach	.987	45	203	29	3	4	7
Gleissner, Fort Myers	.968	26	163	16	6	2	1

CATCHERS— Continued

Player and Club	Pct.	G.	PO.	A.	E.	DP.	PB.
HANSEN, Fort Myers	.993	83	516	33	4	3	4
Hawkins, Fort Lauderdale	.985	31	187	10	3	1	4
Hilgenkamp, Lakeland	.966	27	127	14	5	1	5
Hough, Daytona Beach	1.000	5	12	1	0	0	0
Kempton, Fort Lauderdale	.980	41	269	28	6	4	4
Lamar, Tampa	.989	65	321	39	4	6	4
Lesieur, Fort Lauderdale	1.000	2	13	0	0	0	1
Lindsey, Fort Lauderdale	.995	57	367	51	2	7	11
Lombardi, Fort Lauderdale	.943	10	77	6	5	0	0
McGilvray, Daytona Beach	.994	26	148	13	1	2	4
McGriff, Tampa	.985	83	403	67	7	6	12
Merulla, Fort Lauderdale	1.000	3	14	0	0	0	0
Noce, Miami	1.000	2	5	0	0	0	1
Ortiz, Lakeland	.966	19	127	14	5	4	1
Priessman, Lakeland	.956	32	170	26	9	3	10
Richardson, Winter Haven	.975	65	348	37	10	1	13
Rivas, Miami	1.000	3	16	1	0	0	1
Rivera, Vero Beach	.957	26	121	12	6	2	8
Santiago, Miami	.963	102	471	69	21	12	26
Sayler, St. Petersburg	.960	17	82	14	4	1	2
Velasquez, Vero Beach	.987	14	72	6	1	1	2
Wallace, St. Petersburg	.976	104	548	55	15	6	13
J. Williams, Daytona Beach	.993	26	125	25	1	1	1
M. Williams, Lakeland	.973	59	336	53	11	6	9

PITCHERS

Player and Club	Pct.	G.	PO.	A.	E.	DP.
Araujo, Winter Haven	.920	46	5	18	2	1
Beahan, Fort Lauderdale	.833	7	1	4	1	1
Bersano, Fort Lauderdale	1.000	23	2	3	0	0
Beuder, Vero Beach*	1.000	35	5	5	0	0
Birtsas, Fort Lauderdale*	.857	23	6	24	5	0
Boever, St. Petersburg	1.000	53	7	17	0	2
Bombard, Daytona Beach	1.000	38	3	18	0	0
Bowlin, Winter Haven*	.750	6	3	3	2	0
Brown, Fort Lauderdale*	1.000	29	3	12	0	1
Browning, Tampa*	1.000	11	6	5	0	0
Bryant, Fort Myers	1.000	18	2	3	0	0
Callahan, Daytona Beach	.800	4	0	4	1	0
Cappadona, Winter Haven*	1.000	23	4	16	0	2
Carranza, St. Petersburg*	.889	35	5	11	2	0
Carson, St. Petersburg	.963	31	8	18	1	1
Castro, Daytona Beach*	1.000	10	0	1	0	0
Chapin, West Palm Beach	1.000	16	9	11	0	1
Cherry, Vero Beach	.778	11	3	4	2	1
CHESSER, West Palm Beach	1.000	23	15	16	0	1
Cimorelli, Tampa*	1.000	11	2	10	0	0
Clemens, Winter Haven	1.000	4	2	2	0	0
Clinton, Winter Haven	.935	30	14	15	2	1
Coatney, St. Petersburg	1.000	4	1	1	0	1
Conley, Tampa*	1.000	24	8	17	0	1
Cook, Fort Myers	.947	12	9	9	1	4
Cota, Miami	.923	24	4	20	2	0
Cox, St. Petersburg	.846	5	4	7	2	1
Davis, Winter Haven	.944	13	5	12	1	0
Dean, Miami	.850	34	5	12	3	2
DelRosario, Miami	1.000	6	0	1	0	0
Deshaies, Fort Lauderdale*	.882	20	8	22	4	0
Dodd, Tampa	.879	23	7	22	4	1
Dopson, West Palm Beach	.979	23	21	26	1	3
Dozier, St. Petersburg	.979	26	18	29	1	3
Drizmala, Fort Myers*	.857	8	0	6	1	0
Duffy, Vero Beach	.857	11	2	10	2	1
Dunn, Lakeland	.900	11	1	8	1	0
Edgell, Lakeland	.889	23	3	13	2	0
Edwards, West Palm Beach	1.000	3	2	0	0	0
Ellsworth, Winter Haven	1.000	20	4	7	0	1
Ender, Tampa	1.000	17	3	11	0	0
Epple, St. Petersburg*	1.000	24	1	5	0	0
Evans, Fort Myers*	1.000	5	1	7	0	0
Everett, Daytona Beach	1.000	10	1	2	0	0
Faber, Lakeland	.750	7	0	3	1	0
Felt, Vero Beach*	1.000	11	9	17	0	1
Ferguson, Tampa	.885	25	8	15	3	1
Fiorillo, Tampa*	.600	9	1	2	2	0
Flores, West Palm Beach	.833	12	2	3	1	0
Freeman, Tampa*	.909	45	6	14	2	1
Furman, Lakeland	.793	24	7	16	6	1
Garcia, Lakeland*	.750	12	2	1	1	0
Gardner, Miami	.920	22	5	18	2	1
Gause, West Palm Beach*	1.000	26	3	6	0	0
Gentle, Vero Beach*	.750	11	2	4	2	0
George, Miami*	1.000	16	2	8	0	0
Gering, Winter Haven	.900	39	10	17	3	0
Gilbreath, West Palm Beach	.962	42	6	19	1	0
Groves, West Palm Beach	1.000	23	5	7	0	1
Halley, Lakeland	1.000	15	2	9	0	0
Hammond, Vero Beach*	1.000	12	1	1	0	1
Hartley, St. Petersburg	1.000	9	2	7	0	1
Harvey, Lakeland*	1.000	26	2	5	0	0
Held, Lakeland	1.000	8	2	5	0	0
Hernandez, Daytona Beach	.933	18	11	17	2	2
Hinz, Lakeland	1.000	11	5	5	0	1
Hogan, Daytona Beach	.945	25	18	34	3	4
Hubbard, Tampa	.926	28	9	16	2	2
Innis, Vero Beach	.881	26	14	23	5	1
James, Lakeland	.824	39	2	12	3	0
Jefferson, West Palm Beach	.875	9	2	5	1	0
C. Jones, Vero Beach	.917	11	3	8	1	0
M. Jones, Fort Myers*	.966	18	7	21	1	0
Kasprzak, Daytona Beach	1.000	34	8	15	0	2
Kenyon, Vero Beach	.900	13	4	5	1	1
Kincanon, Tampa	.889	16	2	6	1	1
Kish, St. Petersburg	.920	19	11	12	2	2
Knight, Winter Haven	.917	32	8	14	2	1
Knudson, Daytona Beach	1.000	12	9	18	0	1
Kolotka, Miami	1.000	38	4	7	0	0
Krzanik, West Palm Beach	1.000	13	1	3	0	0
Kurant, Tampa	1.000	7	2	1	0	0
Langdon, Tampa	.875	27	4	3	1	0
Lockhart, Winter Haven*	.810	41	3	14	4	1
Lovelace, Vero Beach*	.872	24	8	26	5	0
Lowrey, Tampa	1.000	5	0	2	0	0
Madden, Vero Beach*	.833	16	2	8	2	1
Martin, St. Petersburg	.953	28	17	24	2	0
A. Martinez, Fort Myers	1.000	16	1	2	0	0
C. Martinez, St. Petersburg	.952	30	9	11	1	1
McClain, Miami	.886	23	11	28	5	2
McKay, West Palm Beach	.857	24	12	18	5	1
McLoughlin, Miami	1.000	6	2	5	0	0
Mendez, Fort Lauderdale	1.000	4	2	2	0	0
Miggins, Miami*	1.000	22	2	16	0	2
Miner, Fort Myers	.938	26	8	22	2	2
Minor, Winter Haven	.929	18	9	17	2	2
Montalvo, Vero Beach	.855	43	6	17	3	1
Monteleone, Lakeland	.913	24	8	13	2	0
Moore, Daytona Beach	.750	6	1	2	1	0
Morales, Fort Myers	1.000	4	1	0	0	0
Moya, Lakeland	.889	20	6	10	2	0
Noble, Daytona Beach*	1.000	14	7	14	0	2
Nodell, Miami	.833	12	1	4	1	0
Nurthen, West Palm Beach	1.000	9	4	5	0	0
D. O'Connor, Lakeland	1.000	20	6	8	0	1
N. O'Connor, Lakeland	1.000	6	1	4	0	0
Olson, Fort Myers	.943	15	11	22	2	2
Paris, Daytona Beach	.857	8	1	11	2	1
Perrotte, Lakeland*	1.000	12	0	7	0	1
Plunk, Fort Lauderdale	.880	20	8	14	3	0
Pone, Fort Myers	1.000	3	1	3	0	0
Proodian, Winter Haven	1.000	29	1	10	0	0
Raftice, Fort Lauderdale*	1.000	6	0	3	0	0
Raubolt, Lakeland	.750	13	2	1	1	0
Raymer, Miami	.800	15	0	4	1	0
Regalado, Daytona Beach	.867	16	2	11	2	1
Reilly, Daytona Beach	.919	32	10	24	3	3
Rhoads, Miami	.970	28	5	27	1	2
Ricci, Miami	1.000	3	0	1	0	0
Riggins, St. Petersburg*	.833	30	1	4	1	0
Rijo, Fort Lauderdale	.970	21	9	23	1	0
Robinson, Lakeland	.625	11	2	3	3	0
Roman, St. Petersburg*	1.000	5	0	2	0	1
Ross, Lakeland	1.000	32	3	8	0	1
Saberhagen, Fort Myers	.889	16	14	10	3	0
Schimpf, Daytona Beach	.938	26	9	21	2	1
Scudder, Vero Beach	.833	46	5	10	3	1
Sellers, Winter Haven	.875	21	13	15	4	1
Shouppe, Daytona Beach*	1.000	43	5	6	0	0
F. Silva, St. Petersburg	.974	29	12	25	1	3
M. Silva, Fort Lauderdale	1.000	8	0	2	0	0
Siwiec, Fort Lauderdale	.600	16	1	2	2	2
Slezak, Vero Beach	1.000	16	6	11	0	0
Sonberg, Vero Beach*	.923	11	2	10	1	1
St. Claire, West Palm Beach	.960	42	4	20	1	0
Stoll, West Palm Beach	.789	13	7	8	4	1
Strasser, Daytona Beach	1.000	3	3	3	0	1
Swanson, Fort Myers	.905	38	7	12	2	1
Swindle, Tampa*	.750	33	1	5	2	0
Szymczak, Fort Lauderdale	.955	18	7	14	1	1
Tabor, Lakeland	1.000	4	3	3	0	0
Terry, Tampa	1.000	30	6	10	0	1
Tewksbury, Fort Lauderdale	1.000	2	0	1	0	0
Thomas, Vero Beach	.950	32	8	11	1	0
Tomaselli, Fort Lauderdale*	1.000	23	1	29	0	1
Torres, West Palm Beach	.857	6	2	4	1	0
Valliant, West Palm Beach*	1.000	9	1	1	0	0
Walberg, Fort Myers	.933	28	10	32	3	1
Walter, Miami*	.962	42	6	19	1	3
Ware, Fort Myers	1.000	3	2	1	0	0
Watson, Tampa	.929	55	13	13	2	1
Weinbrecht, Winter Haven*	1.000	6	2	1	0	0
Weppner, Winter Haven*	.833	14	2	3	1	0

PITCHERS—Continued

Player and Club	Pct.	G.	PO.	A.	E.	DP.
Wiedenbauer, Daytona Beach	.976	32	16	24	1	3
Wilder, Fort Myers	.900	38	5	13	2	0
M. Williams, West Palm Beach	.950	10	5	14	1	1
T. Williams, Fort Lauderdale	.667	10	1	1	1	0
Willis, Lakeland	1.000	4	1	2	0	0
Woodworth, Fort Lauderdale*	.905	31	0	19	2	0
Wyatt, Fort Myers*	.963	24	1	25	1	1
Young, St. Petersburg	.974	26	14	23	1	3

The following players do not have any recorded accepted chances at the positions indicated and therefore are not listed in the fielding averages for those particular positions: Andrews, p; Arce, 2b; Arfstrom, p; Barlow, p; Bonk, c; Burley, of; Cain, c; Champion, of; Evans, 3b; Fedor, p; Francis, 2b; Frierson, 3b; Galarraga, 3b; Geels, of; Gerhardt, p; Hume, of; Hunsinger, of; Hurst, p; D. Jones, p; Tr. Jones, 1b, ss; Lamar, 2b; Maloney, p; R. Martinez, p; Metil, 3b; Ortiz, 3b, of; Pate, of; Riley, p; Sanchez, of; Smalley, p; Steinmetz, p; Threatt, p; Yenser, p; Yowler, p.

CLUB PITCHING

Club	ERA.	G.	CG.	ShO.	Sv.	IP.	H.	R.	ER.	HR.	HB.	BB.	Int. BB.	SO.	WP.	Bk.
Fort Lauderdale	2.67	131	50	20	17	1094.2	905	409	325	30	32	513	24	896	65	5
Fort Myers	2.95	127	31	15	25	1072.0	990	414	351	38	19	351	8	804	27	4
St. Petersburg	3.06	135	22	9	34	1113.1	1040	501	379	52	36	440	59	727	60	9
West Palm Beach	3.51	132	23	5	28	1144.2	1061	575	447	64	46	465	27	760	62	8
Daytona Beach	3.56	134	16	9	32	1138.2	1118	577	451	59	42	485	28	772	78	7
Vero Beach	3.57	134	17	7	41	1148.0	1050	606	456	38	36	642	30	833	100	14
Tampa	4.25	128	14	12	31	1050.2	1108	629	496	49	32	497	31	687	58	10
Miami	4.49	134	35	7	16	1115.0	1249	710	556	54	55	466	18	607	69	17
Lakeland	4.65	130	10	3	23	1104.0	1095	661	571	45	46	705	57	796	91	14
Winter Haven	4.84	133	19	5	25	1103.1	1278	732	593	48	35	502	27	720	69	10

PITCHERS' RECORDS

(Leading Qualifiers for Earned-Run Average Leadership—110 or More Innings)

*Throws lefthanded.

Pitcher—Club	W.	L.	Pct.	ERA.	G.	GS.	CG.	GF.	ShO.	Sv.	IP.	H.	R.	ER.	HR.	HB.	BB.	Int. BB.	SO.	WP.
Rijo, Fort Lauderdale	15	5	.750	1.68	21	21	15	0	4	0	160.1	129	38	30	6	2	43	3	152	4
Birtsas, Fort Lauderdale*	12	8	.600	2.36	23	22	9	0	3	0	167.2	120	57	44	0	10	88	0	160	15
Deshaies, Fort Lauderdale*	11	3	.786	2.52	20	19	5	1	2	0	117.2	105	44	33	5	2	58	1	128	2
Martin, St. Petersburg	14	10	.583	2.68	28	25	6	1	1	0	178.0	145	68	53	6	6	52	7	111	17
Plunk, Fort Lauderdale	8	10	.444	2.74	20	20	5	0	4	0	125.0	115	55	38	1	3	63	4	109	6
Tomaselli, Fort Lauderdale*	12	6	.667	2.77	23	19	6	3	2	0	133.0	110	47	41	7	5	61	2	91	7
Dozier, St. Petersburg	11	7	.611	2.94	26	24	3	2	1	0	153.0	133	63	50	9	3	60	5	109	4
Young, St. Petersburg	12	7	.632	2.98	26	23	4	3	1	1	148.0	136	59	49	11	5	54	6	71	6
Wyatt, Fort Myers*	7	6	.538	3.08	24	23	1	0	0	0	131.2	107	51	45	2	1	63	0	115	2
Walberg, Fort Myers	8	7	.533	3.26	28	17	6	3	1	3	135.1	135	53	49	5	3	39	1	91	1
M. Jones, Fort Myers*	5	8	.385	3.26	18	18	4	0	0	0	116.0	135	47	42	6	1	31	1	68	3

Departmental Leaders: G—Watson, 55; W—Rijo, 15; L—Rhoads, 14; Pct.—Hogan, .824; GS—Hogan, Innis, Martin, 25; CG—Rijo, 15; GF—Boever, 46; ShO—Plunk, Rijo, 4; Sv.—Boever, 26; IP—Martin, 178; H—Rhoads, 185; R—Rhoads, 101; ER—Rhoads, 82; HR—Chesser, Young, 11; HB—Lovelace, 25; BB—Innis, 107; IBB—Boever, 12; SO—Birtsas, 160; WP—Lovelace, 25.

(All Pitchers—Listed Alphabetically)

Pitcher—Club	W.	L.	Pct.	ERA.	G.	GS.	CG.	GF.	ShO.	Sv.	IP.	H.	R.	ER.	HR.	HB.	BB.	Int. BB.	SO.	WP.
Andrews, Fort Lauderdale	0	2	.000	8.31	3	2	0	1	0	0	8.2	11	8	8	0	0	4	0	1	0
Araujo, Winter Haven	2	10	.167	4.36	46	7	1	33	0	11	86.2	104	58	42	2	3	36	4	59	6
Arfstrom, Winter Haven	0	0	.000	18.00	2	0	0	1	0	0	3.0	9	7	6	0	0	3	0	2	3
Barlow, Lakeland	0	1	.000	24.30	2	2	0	0	0	0	3.1	9	9	9	0	0	6	0	2	3
Beahan, Fort Lauderdale	0	2	.000	5.31	7	3	1	2	0	0	20.1	23	13	12	1	0	14	0	16	3
Bersano, Fort Lauderdale	4	0	1.000	2.43	23	0	0	16	0	2	29.2	23	9	8	2	1	7	1	25	1
Beuder, Vero Beach*	1	2	.333	4.32	35	1	1	22	0	3	50.0	43	34	24	2	0	35	1	42	8
Birtsas, Fort Lauderdale*	12	8	.600	2.36	23	22	9	0	3	0	167.2	120	57	44	0	10	88	0	160	15
Boever, St. Petersburg	5	6	.455	3.02	53	0	0	46	0	26	80.1	61	29	27	2	3	37	12	57	1
Bombard, Daytona Beach	3	4	.429	4.35	38	0	0	28	0	6	60.0	65	35	29	8	1	25	2	47	5
Bowlin, Winter Haven*	1	2	.333	4.50	6	5	1	0	0	0	32.0	41	20	16	2	2	16	1	19	2
Brown, Fort Lauderdale*	3	3	.500	2.25	29	4	1	13	0	3	64.0	49	21	16	2	0	39	3	50	6
Browning, Tampa*	8	1	.889	1.49	11	11	4	0	1	0	78.2	53	19	13	3	0	36	1	101	3
Bryant, Fort Myers	2	3	.400	6.48	18	1	0	11	0	4	25.0	30	24	18	2	4	27	0	23	0
Callahan, Daytona Beach	1	1	.500	2.93	4	4	0	0	0	0	15.1	13	8	5	2	0	12	0	12	0
Cappadona, Winter Haven*	9	4	.692	2.85	23	6	1	7	0	1	72.2	65	30	23	1	4	38	2	60	0
Carranza, St. Petersburg*	4	5	.444	2.70	35	5	0	11	0	2	60.0	64	36	18	5	0	27	6	43	5
Carson, St. Petersburg	1	4	.200	4.40	31	8	1	7	0	0	77.2	97	49	38	4	3	27	4	37	5
Castro, Daytona Beach*	0	0	.000	8.49	10	0	0	6	0	1	11.2	12	13	11	2	0	11	1	7	0
Chapin, West Palm Beach	3	7	.300	4.75	16	16	0	0	0	0	72.0	93	50	38	5	6	36	0	43	7
Cherry, Vero Beach	4	4	.500	3.48	11	11	2	0	1	0	72.1	68	33	28	6	0	27	2	57	3
Chesser, West Palm Beach	5	8	.385	3.76	23	18	2	1	0	0	122.0	114	66	51	11	2	49	3	70	7
Cimorelli, Tampa*	2	5	.286	6.00	11	9	2	0	1	0	42.0	54	33	28	1	0	15	0	15	1
Clemens, Winter Haven	3	1	.750	1.24	4	4	3	0	1	0	29.0	22	4	4	0	1	0	0	36	2
Clinton, Winter Haven	3	9	.250	6.34	30	13	1	5	0	1	98.0	105	81	69	6	3	62	1	59	11
Coatney, St. Petersburg	0	1	.000	0.82	4	2	0	0	0	0	11.0	11	3	1	0	1	4	0	9	1
Conley, Tampa*	5	8	.385	5.20	24	15	0	3	0	0	83.0	94	56	48	5	4	32	1	33	2
Cook, Fort Myers	6	4	.600	2.92	12	10	4	1	1	0	71.0	55	25	23	2	1	41	0	66	5
Cota, Miami	6	9	.400	3.29	24	20	4	1	2	0	128.2	126	65	47	8	5	46	0	68	7
Cox, St. Petersburg	2	2	.500	2.53	5	5	2	0	0	0	32.0	26	10	9	0	0	14	2	22	1
Davis, Winter Haven	4	5	.444	3.49	13	13	2	0	1	0	85.0	87	38	33	3	1	24	1	54	1
Dean, Miami	2	8	.200	5.38	34	5	1	16	0	2	88.2	110	65	53	7	4	28	3	37	6
DelRosario, Miami	0	0	.000	6.35	6	0	0	4	0	0	5.2	5	4	4	2	2	7	0	2	2
Deshaies, Fort Lauderdale*	11	3	.786	2.52	20	19	5	1	2	0	117.2	105	44	33	5	2	58	1	128	2
Dodd, Tampa	4	11	.267	3.74	23	23	4	0	2	0	137.0	145	71	57	6	4	53	2	68	8
Dopson, West Palm Beach	13	6	.684	3.44	23	23	5	0	2	0	146.2	141	82	56	10	3	38	2	69	5
Dozier, St. Petersburg	11	7	.611	2.94	26	24	3	2	1	0	153.0	133	63	50	9	3	60	5	109	4
Drizmala, Fort Myers*	2	4	.333	3.64	8	8	0	0	0	0	47.0	42	22	19	3	0	29	0	49	2
Duffy, Vero Beach	1	4	.200	6.19	11	11	0	0	0	0	56.2	63	49	39	3	2	51	0	36	8
Dunn, Lakeland	2	2	.500	4.00	11	5	0	4	0	1	45.0	35	22	20	1	0	28	0	44	3
Edgell, Lakeland	4	5	.444	4.30	23	18	2	2	1	1	106.2	93	64	51	3	7	102	6	52	15
Edwards, West Palm Beach	0	0	.000	7.71	3	1	0	2	0	0	4.2	6	5	4	0	0	7	0	4	0
Ellsworth, Winter Haven	1	11	.083	7.56	20	20	1	0	0	0	83.1	119	81	70	6	1	34	1	47	9

Pitcher—Club	W.	L.	Pct.	ERA.	G.	GS.	CG.	GF.	ShO.	Sv.	IP.	H.	R.	ER.	HR.	HB.	BB.	Int. BB.	SO.	WP.
Ender, Tampa	2	5	.286	4.29	17	5	1	9	0	5	50.1	54	29	24	3	1	25	1	41	2
Epple, St. Petersburg	2	1	.667	2.90	24	0	0	9	0	1	31.0	28	12	10	2	1	11	1	35	2
Evans, Fort Myers*	4	1	.800	0.79	5	5	3	0	2	0	34.1	18	3	3	0	0	4	0	23	0
Everett, Daytona Beach	2	0	1.000	5.96	10	0	0	4	0	0	22.2	23	15	15	2	1	16	4	18	3
Faber, Lakeland*	1	1	.500	5.76	7	6	0	0	0	0	25.0	32	16	16	2	1	10	0	15	2
Fedor, Fort Lauderdale	0	0	.000	3.00	2	0	0	0	0	0	3.0	1	1	1	0	0	6	0	3	5
Felt, Vero Beach*	4	6	.400	3.14	11	11	1	0	0	0	71.2	67	37	25	2	3	35	0	39	6
Ferguson, Tampa	11	8	.579	3.56	25	24	0	0	0	0	129.0	113	68	51	6	2	86	2	68	6
Fiorillo, Tampa*	2	6	.250	4.38	9	8	0	0	0	0	39.0	37	24	19	3	2	18	0	29	6
Flores, West Palm Beach	1	2	.333	5.83	12	7	0	3	0	0	41.2	44	36	27	4	5	28	1	33	6
Freeman, Tampa*	6	6	.500	4.33	45	6	0	15	0	1	87.1	111	61	42	7	2	18	4	48	6
Furman, Lakeland	4	5	.444	4.45	24	7	1	12	0	2	87.0	86	55	43	1	4	38	7	59	5
Garcia, Lakeland*	2	0	1.000	2.28	12	0	0	7	0	3	27.2	19	7	7	1	2	13	2	31	1
Gardner, Miami	5	11	.313	3.62	22	21	9	0	1	0	159.1	179	83	64	5	2	42	3	69	7
Gause, West Palm Beach*	2	0	1.000	5.16	26	2	0	14	0	0	52.1	55	33	30	2	4	30	2	43	4
Gentle, Vero Beach*	0	6	.000	6.49	11	11	0	0	0	0	51.1	64	52	37	2	1	40	1	30	10
George, Miami*	5	7	.417	4.39	16	16	4	0	1	0	92.1	116	62	45	3	1	30	0	34	5
Gerhardt, Miami	0	0	.000	12.08	5	0	0	2	0	1	12.2	27	22	17	1	1	6	1	8	1
Gering, Winter Haven	4	7	.364	4.18	39	9	3	19	0	5	112.0	132	72	52	5	6	38	2	62	8
Gilbreath, West Palm Beach	8	5	.615	1.64	42	1	0	33	0	15	99.0	80	32	18	3	2	33	5	64	5
Groves, West Palm Beach	5	3	.625	2.82	23	1	0	9	0	0	67.0	63	26	21	2	1	18	2	43	1
Halley, Lakeland	1	2	.333	6.99	15	1	0	7	0	1	28.1	22	23	22	0	3	29	2	14	7
Hammond, Vero Beach*	1	0	1.000	0.00	12	0	0	8	0	5	16.1	2	1	0	0	0	10	0	14	0
Hartley, St. Petersburg	1	3	.250	3.34	9	4	1	2	0	0	29.2	25	14	11	2	3	24	1	18	1
Harvey, Lakeland*	5	2	.714	2.28	26	0	0	21	0	2	55.1	44	16	14	2	1	30	5	47	4
Held, Lakeland	2	4	.333	5.88	8	7	2	0	0	0	41.1	53	36	27	4	2	25	3	23	2
Hernandez, Daytona Beach	10	3	.769	2.99	18	17	1	0	0	0	102.1	86	46	34	5	5	27	0	73	6
Hinz, Lakeland	0	5	.000	7.07	11	9	1	1	0	0	42.0	49	35	33	2	4	36	2	18	3
Hogan, Daytona Beach	14	3	.824	3.62	25	25	5	0	2	0	154.0	155	70	62	6	7	71	1	101	7
Hubbard, Tampa	5	8	.385	4.25	28	17	3	6	2	3	112.1	122	64	53	2	4	36	0	81	5
Hume, Tampa	0	0	.000	0.00	1	0	0	0	0	0	1.1	1	0	0	0	0	2	0	2	0
Hurst, St. Petersburg	0	0	.000	36.00	1	0	0	0	0	0	1.0	6	5	4	1	0	1	0	2	0
Innis, Vero Beach	8	10	.444	3.84	26	25	4	0	0	0	175.2	161	92	75	7	3	107	5	104	6
James, Lakeland	8	9	.471	4.12	39	5	0	23	0	5	94.0	72	54	43	4	8	100	8	102	7
Jefferson, West Palm Beach	2	2	.500	4.34	9	9	1	0	0	0	47.2	54	28	23	2	0	27	0	31	4
C. Jones, Vero Beach	6	2	.750	2.96	11	5	1	1	0	0	48.2	46	23	16	1	0	25	3	39	2
D. Jones, Miami	0	0	.000	6.75	1	0	0	1	0	0	4.0	6	3	3	0	1	3	0	4	0
M. Jones, Fort Myers*	5	8	.385	3.26	18	18	4	0	0	0	116.0	135	47	42	6	1	31	1	68	3
Kasprzak, Daytona Beach	3	2	.600	2.92	34	0	0	21	0	6	74.0	73	27	24	2	6	15	2	55	2
Kenyon, Vero Beach	2	4	.333	2.33	13	4	1	3	0	0	46.1	41	18	12	2	1	17	1	20	1
Kincanon, Tampa	1	2	.333	4.85	16	1	0	5	0	0	26.0	29	22	14	0	2	15	2	15	2
Kish, St. Petersburg	5	5	.500	3.69	19	13	3	2	0	0	78.0	84	43	32	2	2	27	3	31	4
Knight, Winter Haven	6	6	.500	4.88	32	14	0	6	0	1	118.0	126	71	64	3	3	63	3	89	3
Knudson, Daytona Beach	5	3	.625	2.40	12	12	2	0	1	0	78.2	80	29	21	3	1	22	2	47	6
Kolotka, Miami	6	2	.750	2.29	38	0	0	28	0	5	55.0	49	20	14	2	3	23	2	23	3
Krzanik, West Palm Beach	3	0	1.000	2.70	13	0	0	7	0	2	23.1	15	7	7	1	0	8	1	21	0
Kurant, Tampa	2	0	1.000	2.57	7	0	0	2	0	0	14.0	15	5	4	2	0	3	1	9	0
Langdon, Tampa	1	3	.250	5.15	27	0	0	14	0	1	43.2	48	33	25	1	2	35	2	43	4
Lockhart, Winter Haven*	2	4	.333	4.73	41	3	0	9	0	3	93.1	111	63	49	4	2	53	5	50	5
Lovelace, Vero Beach*	8	10	.444	4.77	24	20	2	2	0	0	115.0	104	80	61	3	13	93	2	95	25
Lowrey, Tampa	1	1	.500	8.10	5	0	0	2	0	0	6.2	10	10	6	3	0	4	2	4	0
Madden, Vero Beach*	2	4	.333	4.30	16	4	0	5	0	2	46.0	50	33	22	0	2	25	0	44	1
Maloney, Lakeland	0	0	.000	12.00	2	0	0	2	0	0	3.0	6	4	4	2	0	5	0	0	0
Martin, St. Petersburg	14	10	.583	2.68	28	25	6	1	1	0	178.0	145	68	53	6	6	52	7	111	17
A. Martinez, Fort Myers	2	0	1.000	1.45	16	0	0	15	0	4	18.2	14	4	3	0	0	5	0	20	0
C. Martinez, St. Petersburg	5	5	.500	2.27	30	9	1	6	0	0	91.0	63	33	23	3	5	42	5	105	8
R. Martinez, St. Petersburg*	0	0	.000	0.00	1	0	0	0	0	0	0.0	3	7	5	0	0	4	0	0	0
McClain, Miami	5	12	.294	5.17	23	21	5	2	1	0	134.0	169	96	77	8	8	66	1	63	10
McKay, West Palm Beach	10	6	.625	4.34	24	21	4	0	0	0	137.0	123	76	66	8	1	75	0	100	6
McLoughlin, Miami	0	2	.000	2.60	6	3	1	2	0	0	27.2	20	10	8	3	1	5	0	19	0
Mendez, Fort Lauderdale	0	0	.000	2.08	4	0	0	4	0	2	13.0	9	3	3	1	0	9	0	13	1
Miggins, Miami*	3	2	.600	2.09	22	0	0	19	0	4	43.0	30	15	10	0	5	18	1	25	4
Miner, Fort Myers	8	0	1.000	3.16	26	7	5	6	1	1	94.0	87	38	33	3	4	20	0	67	5
Minor, Winter Haven	4	8	.333	5.28	18	13	3	3	1	0	75.0	96	57	44	5	3	32	2	44	1
Montalvo, Vero Beach	5	5	.500	1.55	43	0	0	32	0	16	75.1	61	18	13	2	5	31	8	55	7
Monteleone, Lakeland	9	8	.529	4.11	24	24	1	0	0	0	142.1	146	80	65	6	3	80	4	124	12
Moore, Daytona Beach	0	1	.000	2.63	6	1	0	1	0	1	24 .0	16	11	7	2	0	15	0	15	4
Morales, Fort Myers	0	0	.000	2.19	4	0	0	3	0	0	12.1	13	12	3	0	0	7	0	10	1
Moya, Lakeland	6	8	.429	3.74	20	14	1	2	0	0	98.2	88	51	41	1	4	47	0	87	3
Noble, Daytona Beach*	6	5	.545	3.36	14	13	0	0	0	0	77.2	87	37	29	4	2	20	1	43	2
Nodell, Miami	0	2	.000	8.80	12	3	0	4	0	0	29.2	40	32	29	3	3	25	0	12	6
Nurthen, West Palm Beach	2	5	.286	5.56	9	4	0	3	0	0	34 .0	39	24	21	3	3	11	1	19	3
D. O'Connor, Lakeland	1	2	.333	3.56	20	0	0	11	0	3	48.0	54	19	19	1	0	15	3	28	3
N. O'Connor, Lakeland	0	3	.000	7.24	6	6	0	0	0	0	32.1	44	29	26	2	0	19	1	32	3
Olson, Fort Myers	8	5	.615	3.16	15	15	5	0	1	0	94.0	88	38	33	3	3	16	0	53	0
Paris, Daytona Beach	5	3	.625	4.03	8	8	0	0	0	0	44.2	46	29	20	1	1	18	0	29	4
Perrotte, Lakeland*	4	5	.444	6.02	12	12	0	0	0	0	49.1	54	38	33	4	1	36	2	30	3
Plunk, Fort Lauderdale	8	10	.444	2.74	20	20	5	0	4	0	125.0	115	55	38	1	3	63	4	109	6
Pone, Fort Myers	1	2	.333	5.14	3	3	0	0	0	0	14.0	15	8	8	0	1	10	0	20	0
Proodian, Winter Haven	1	2	.333	5.65	29	0	0	20	0	1	43.0	50	30	27	3	3	24	5	34	4
Raftice, Fort Lauderdale*	2	1	.667	8.31	6	3	1	3	1	0	21.2	27	20	20	0	0	18	0	12	0
Raubolt, Lakeland	0	1	.000	5.13	13	3	0	3	0	0	40.1	43	23	23	2	0	31	4	23	7
Raymer, Miami	0	6	.000	10.07	15	9	0	1	0	0	44.2	62	57	50	2	1	45	0	22	1
Regalado, Daytona Beach	6	2	.750	3.63	16	4	0	5	0	2	62.0	55	27	25	2	2	15	0	40	2
Reilly, Daytona Beach	8	4	.667	2.73	32	12	1	11	0	1	108.2	110	55	33	2	4	41	5	68	7
Rhoads, Miami	7	14	.333	4.84	28	24	7	3	2	0	152.1	185	101	82	8	6	58	3	104	5
Ricci, Miami	0	1	.000	1.13	3	2	0	1	0	1	16.0	11	2	2	0	1	3	0	12	0
Riggins, St. Petersburg*	4	1	.800	1.54	30	1	0	14	0	2	35.0	22	8	6	1	0	16	3	21	3
Rijo, Fort Lauderdale	15	5	.750	1.68	21	21	15	0	4	0	160.1	129	38	30	6	2	43	3	152	4
Riley, Tampa	0	0	.000	13.50	1	0	0	0	0	0	2.0	3	3	3	1	0	1	0	2	0
Robinson, Lakeland	2	5	.286	5.94	11	10	1	0	0	0	50.0	61	38	33	5	1	19	1	23	7
Roman, St. Petersburg	0	0	.000	2.08	5	0	0	4	0	0	4.1	3	1	1	0	0	3	0	2	0
Ross, Lakeland	2	3	.400	5.75	32	0	0	19	0	4	61.0	68	39	39	2	4	28	6	27	1

Pitcher—Club	W.	L.	Pct.	ERA.	G.	GS.	CG.	GF.	ShO.	Sv.	IP.	H.	R.	ER.	HR.	HB.	BB.	Int. BB.	SO.	WP.
Saberhagen, Fort Myers	10	5	.667	2.30	16	16	3	0	1	0	109.2	98	34	28	4	0	19	0	82	4
Schimpf, Daytona Beach	4	5	.444	5.08	26	18	3	4	0	0	102.2	110	75	58	10	4	58	4	71	12
Scudder, Vero Beach	7	0	1.000	3.63	46	1	1	26	0	7	72.0	72	43	29	2	4	27	3	55	7
Sellers, Winter Haven	8	9	.471	4.51	21	20	3	0	0	0	117.2	149	77	59	3	1	47	0	68	7
Shouppe, Daytona Beach*	6	5	.545	2.35	43	0	0	32	0	13	61.1	52	26	16	4	2	33	4	64	1
F. Silva, St. Petersburg	5	7	.417	3.66	29	16	1	6	0	2	103.1	133	61	42	4	4	37	4	54	2
M. Silva, Fort Lauderdale	0	1	.000	2.63	8	1	0	4	0	3	13.2	14	6	4	0	2	7	1	12	1
Siwiec, Fort Lauderdale	0	1	.000	2.70	16	0	0	8	0	2	23.1	18	8	7	1	1	14	0	19	4
Slezak, Vero Beach	9	4	.692	3.09	16	16	1	0	0	0	93.1	71	41	32	3	0	61	0	77	6
Smalley, Fort Lauderdale*	0	0	.000	7.36	3	0	0	1	0	0	3.2	6	3	3	1	0	1	0	7	0
Sonberg, Vero Beach*	6	2	.750	3.32	11	10	2	1	1	1	59.2	58	26	22	1	1	31	1	43	5
St. Claire, West Palm Beach	5	7	.417	2.11	42	0	0	32	0	11	98.0	72	33	23	4	1	31	9	77	7
Steinmetz, Tampa	0	0	.000	0.00	1	0	0	1	0	0	0.2	1	0	0	0	0	0	0	0	0
Stoll, West Palm Beach	8	3	.727	3.01	13	13	6	0	1	0	83.2	71	30	28	1	11	34	0	60	4
Strasser, Daytona Beach	3	0	1.000	1.17	3	3	3	0	1	0	23.0	13	4	3	0	0	7	0	12	2
Swanson, Fort Myers	1	5	.167	2.66	38	0	0	31	0	9	64.1	57	22	19	5	0	18	3	46	4
Swindle, Tampa*	0	0	.000	4.96	33	2	0	11	0	2	52.2	54	36	29	1	2	47	1	37	4
Szymczak, Fort Lauderdale	4	3	.571	3.46	18	7	2	7	0	1	67.2	59	35	26	0	3	27	2	21	3
Tabor, Lakeland	2	1	.667	1.98	4	1	1	3	0	1	13.2	11	3	3	0	1	3	0	8	0
Terry, Tampa	3	3	.500	4.25	30	6	0	16	0	6	59.1	60	34	28	0	1	30	4	52	3
Tewksbury, Fort Lauderdale	2	0	1.000	0.00	2	2	1	0	0	0	16.0	6	1	0	0	0	1	0	5	0
Thomas, Vero Beach	5	2	.714	1.94	32	4	1	17	0	7	97.2	79	26	21	2	1	27	3	83	5
Threatt, Tampa	0	1	.000	9.00	1	1	0	0	0	0	4.0	6	5	4	1	0	1	0	2	0
Tomaselli, Fort Lauderdale*	12	6	.667	2.77	23	19	6	3	2	0	133.0	110	47	41	7	5	61	2	91	7
Torres, West Palm Beach	1	0	1.000	1.52	6	5	0	0	0	0	29.2	19	8	5	2	1	9	0	24	1
Valliant, West Palm Beach*	2	1	.667	6.53	9	2	0	4	0	0	20.2	23	18	15	3	1	20	0	18	2
Walberg, Fort Myers	8	7	.533	3.26	28	17	6	3	1	3	135.1	135	53	49	5	3	39	1	91	1
Walter, Miami*	6	13	.316	3.78	42	10	4	15	0	3	121.1	114	73	51	2	11	61	4	105	12
Ware, Fort Myers	2	1	.667	3.38	3	3	0	0	0	0	16.0	16	7	6	0	0	6	0	11	0
Watson, Tampa	3	4	.429	5.29	55	0	0	30	0	13	81.2	98	56	48	4	6	40	8	37	6
Weinbrecht, Winter Haven*	0	1	.000	4.80	6	1	0	4	0	0	15.0	12	9	8	2	1	12	0	7	3
Weppner, Winter Haven*	1	5	.167	6.13	14	5	0	7	0	2	39.2	50	34	27	3	1	20	0	30	4
Wiedenbauer, Daytona Beach	9	8	.529	4.58	32	17	1	6	1	2	116.0	122	70	59	4	6	79	2	70	15
Wilder, Fort Myers	8	1	.889	1.59	38	0	0	26	0	4	85.0	71	22	15	1	1	13	3	57	0
M. Williams, West Palm Beach	5	2	.714	1.96	10	9	5	1	1	0	64.1	49	21	14	3	5	11	1	39	0
T. Williams, Fort Lauderdale	0	2	.000	1.66	10	1	0	3	0	1	21.2	14	8	4	0	2	20	4	15	1
Willis, Lakeland	3	0	1.000	0.00	4	0	0	3	0	0	9.2	6	0	0	0	0	5	1	7	0
Woodworth, Fort Lauderdale*	4	7	.364	2.87	31	7	4	15	2	3	84.2	66	32	27	3	1	33	3	57	6
Wyatt, Fort Myers*	7	6	.538	3.08	24	23	1	0	0	0	131.2	107	51	45	2	1	63	0	115	2
Yenser, West Palm Beach	0	0	.000	0.00	1	0	0	0	0	0	1.0	0	0	0	0	0	0	0	2	0
Young, St. Petersburg	12	7	.632	2.98	26	23	4	3	1	1	148.0	136	59	49	11	5	54	6	71	6
Yowler, Fort Myers*	0	1	.000	9.82	1	1	0	0	0	0	3.2	9	4	4	2	0	3	0	3	0

BALKS—Lovelace, McClain, 6 each; Hogan, 4; DelRosario, Edgell, Martin, Miner, 3 each; Carson, Cherry, Deshaies, Fiorillo, Groves, Held, James, Langdon, Lockhart, C. Martinez, Moya, Proodian, Saberhagen, Stoll, Walter, Watson, 2 each; Araujo, Boever, Brown, Browning, Chesser, Cimorelli, Conley, Dopson, Duffy, Dunn, Faber, Gardner, Gentle, Gilbreath, Harvey, Jefferson, D. Jones, Kenyon, Knight, Kolotka, Miggins, Montalvo, Noble, Paris, Perrotte, Pone, Raubolt, Rayner, Rhoades, Rijo, Sellers, Shouppe, F. Silva, Slezak, Swindle, Thomas, Tomaselli, Wyatt, 1 each.

COMBINATION SHUTOUTS—Hernandez-Castro, Knudson-Regalado, Hogan-Bombard, Regalado-Bombard, Daytona Beach; Tewksbury-Bersano, Tomaselli-Szymczak, Fort Lauderdale; Evans-Swanson, Wyatt-Swanson, Saberhagen-Wilder, Jones-Wilder, Walberg-Swanson, Miner-Wilder-Martinez, Olson-Swanson, Saberhagen-Martinez, Fort Myers; Edgell-D. O'Connor, Faber-Harvey, Lakeland; Dozier-Kish-Carson, Kish-Young, Dozier-Carranza-Boever, Young-Boever, Silva-Boever, Dozier-Riggins, St. Petersburg; Browning-Watson, Ferguson-Watson, Hubbard-Ender, Ferguson-Terry, Fiorillo-Terry, Ferguson-Freeman-Terry, Tampa; Slezak-Hammond 2, Slezak-Montalvo, Sonberg-Thomas, Lovelace-Montalvo, Vero Beach; Valliant-Groves, West Palm Beach; Ellsworth-Lockhart-Gering, Sellers-Cappadona, Winter Haven.

NO-HIT GAMES—Cota, Miami, defeated Tampa, 1-0 (second game), April 23; Olson, Fort Myers, defeated St. Petersburg, 3-0, May 18.

Midwest League

CLASS A

CHAMPIONSHIP WINNERS IN PREVIOUS YEARS

1947—Belleville	.667
Belleville	.672
1948—West Frankfort*	.708
1949—Centralia	.627
Paducah (4th)†	.454
1950—Centralia‡	.675
1951—Paris§	.700
Danville (4th)†	.432
1952—Danville x	.685
Decatur (3rd)†	.584
1953—Decatur*	.576
1954—Decatur	.587
Danville (2nd)‡	.528
1955—Dubuque*	.587
1956—Paris y	.656
Dubuque	.603
1957—Decatur y	.683
Clinton	.623
1958—Michigan City	.623
Waterloo z	.613
1959—Waterloo	.613
Waterloo	.613
1960—Waterloo	.629
Waterloo	.677
1961—Waterloo	.613
Quincy z	.594
1962—Dubuque z	.667
Waterloo	.625
1963—Clinton	.710
Clinton	.629
1964—Clinton	.667
Fox Cities z	.667
1965—Burlington	.667
Burlington	.677
1966—Fox Cities z	.689
Cedar Rapids	.762
1967—Wisconsin Rapids	.685
Appleton z	.587
1968—Decatur	.656
Quad Cities z	.648
1969—Appleton	.648
Appleton	.690
1970—Quincy z	.691
Quad Cities	.581
1971—Appleton	.642
Quad Cities a	.548
1972—Appleton	.598
Danville a	.584
1973—Wisconsin Rapids a	.562
Danville	.537
1974—Appleton	.593
Danville a	.517
1975—Waterloo a	.727
Quad Cities	.624
1976—Waterloo a	.600
Cedar Rapids	.595
1977—Waterloo	.580
Burlington a	.511
1978—Appleton a	.708
Burlington	.500
1979—Waterloo	.600
Quad Cities a	.579
1980—Waterloo a	.610
Quad Cities	.532
1981—Wausau a	.636
Quad Cities	.570
1982—Madison	.626
Appleton b	.579

*Won championship and four-club playoff. †Won four-club playoff. ‡Playoff finals canceled because of bad weather. §Won both halves of split-season. xWon first half of split-season and tied Paris for second-half title. yWon first-half title and four-team playoff. zWon split-season playoff. aLeague divided into Northern and Southern divisions and played split-season. Playoff winner. bLeague divided into Northern, Central and Southern divisions and played split-season. Playoff winner. (NOTE—Known as Illinois State League in 1947-48 and Mississippi-Ohio Valley League from 1949 through 1955.)

STANDING OF CLUBS AT CLOSE OF SEASON, SEPTEMBER 3

NORTHERN DIVISION

Club	W.	L.	T.	Pct.	G.B.
Appleton (White Sox)	87	50	0	.635	....
Wisconsin Rapids (Twins)	71	67	0	.514	16½
Madison (A's)	71	67	0	.514	16½
Wausau (Mariners)	55	83	0	.399	32½

CENTRAL DIVISION

Club	W.	L.	T.	Pct.	G.B.
Waterloo (Indians)	76	64	0	.543	....
Cedar Rapids (Reds)	76	64	0	.543	....
Beloit (Brewers)	66	71	0	.482	8½
Clinton (Giants)	56	82	0	.406	19

SOUTHERN DIVISION

Club	W.	L.	T.	Pct.	G.B.
Springfield (Cardinals)	80	59	0	.576	....
Burlington (Rangers)	71	68	0	.511	9
Quad Cities (Cubs)	68	71	0	.489	12
Peoria (Angels)	54	85	0	.388	26

COMPOSITE STANDING OF CLUBS AT CLOSE OF SEASON, SEPTEMBER 3

Club	Apl.	Spr.	Wat.	C.R.	W.R.	Mad.	Bur.	QC	Bel.	Cln.	Wau.	Peo.	W.	L.	T.	Pct.	G.B.
Appleton (White Sox)	....	3	8	4	14	10	6	7	7	6	15	7	87	50	0	.635	....
Springfield (Cardinals)	6	....	4	7	3	7	10	10	6	8	8	11	80	59	0	.576	8
Waterloo (Indians)	2	6	....	10	4	6	6	4	12	12	8	6	76	64	0	.543	12½
Cedar Rapids (Reds)	6	3	10	....	5	3	8	4	8	14	8	7	76	64	0	.543	12½
Wisconsin Rapids (Twins)	6	7	6	5	....	11	4	3	4	6	12	7	71	67	0	.514	16½
Madison (A's)	10	3	4	7	9	....	7	6	5	6	10	4	71	67	0	.514	16½
Burlington (Rangers)	4	10	4	2	6	3	....	11	7	7	4	13	71	68	0	.511	17
Quad Cities (Cubs)	3	10	6	6	6	4	9	....	3	5	4	12	68	71	0	.489	20
Beloit (Brewers)	2	4	8	12	5	4	3	7	....	12	4	5	66	71	0	.482	21
Clinton (Giants)	3	2	8	6	4	4	3	5	8	....	7	6	56	82	0	.406	31½
Wausau (Mariners)	5	2	2	2	8	10	5	6	6	2	....	7	55	83	0	.399	32½
Peoria (Angels)	3	9	4	3	3	5	7	8	5	4	3	....	54	85	0	.388	34

Quad Cities represented Davenport and Bettendorf, Ia., and Moline and Rock Island, Ill.

Major league affiliations in parentheses.

Playoffs—Appleton defeated Waterloo, two games to one; Springfield defeated Cedar Rapids, two games to none; and Appleton defeated Springfield, three games to one, to win league championship.

Regular-Season Attendance—Appleton, 68,751; Beloit, 91,448; Burlington, 49,828; Cedar Rapids, 134,328; Clinton, 98,641; Madison, 131,646; Peoria, 84,765; Quad Cities, 185,677; Springfield, 144,844; Waterloo, 89,158; Wausau, 50,147; Wisconsin Rapids, 51,717. Total, 1,180,950. Playoffs, 10,124. All-Star Game, 1,585.

Managers—Appleton, John Boles; Beloit, Tim Nordbrook; Burlington, Orlando Gomez; Cedar Rapids, Bruce Kimm; Clinton, Bill Lachemann; Madison, Brad Fischer; Peoria, Joe Coleman; Quad Cities, Larry Cox; Springfield, Dave Bialas; Waterloo, Gomer Hodge; Wausau, R.J. Harrison; Wisconsin Rapids, Charlie Manuel.

All-Star Team—1B—Patrick Adams, Appleton; 2B—Gary Jones, Quad Cities; 3B—William J. Robidoux, Beloit; SS—Shawon Dunston, Quad Cities; OF—John Cangelosi, Appleton; Curtis Ford, Springfield; Javier Ortiz, Burlington; Randy Washington, Waterloo; C—Ronald Karkovice, Appleton; DH—David McLaughlin, Appleton; RHP—Michael Trujillo, Appleton; LHP—John Young, Springfield; Manager of the Year—Gomer Hodge, Waterloo.

(Compiled by Howe News Bureau, Boston, Mass.)

CLUB BATTING

Club	Pct.	G.	AB.	R.	OR.	H.	TB.	2B.	3B.	HR.	RBI.	GW.	SH.	SF.	HP.	BB.	Int. BB.	SO.	SB.	CS.	LOB.
Springfield	.277	139	4712	745	624	1304	1973	211	37	128	649	71	39	42	40	520	28	832	117	61	1026
Burlington	.264	139	4512	728	669	1191	1800	213	36	108	619	55	54	32	43	468	24	1060	220	76	864
Madison	.261	138	4330	626	534	1129	1594	183	24	78	561	63	74	35	25	584	29	895	188	110	972
Appleton	.260	137	4339	650	449	1126	1641	197	45	76	556	66	49	39	47	510	27	935	204	92	916
Wausau	.254	138	4374	613	784	1109	1683	176	16	122	536	50	50	35	36	489	12	896	173	79	889
Waterloo	.253	140	4324	590	590	1093	1633	188	26	100	514	59	87	37	45	467	33	934	213	80	915
Wisconsin Rapids	.251	138	4334	598	587	1090	1674	184	14	124	513	61	59	28	66	498	19	907	155	73	933
Peoria	.250	139	4497	598	721	1123	1685	211	36	93	534	46	42	29	38	431	20	1009	140	74	886
Quad Cities	.249	139	4386	612	621	1092	1533	165	48	60	505	60	39	48	45	480	25	1088	302	140	815
Beloit	.247	137	4378	576	663	1082	1555	189	19	82	489	59	48	38	46	543	27	956	105	65	1013
Cedar Rapids	.244	140	4448	613	583	1085	1629	191	31	97	506	66	44	31	47	485	22	917	171	79	882
Clinton	.237	138	4469	508	632	1059	1377	162	30	32	428	44	66	18	40	491	22	905	80	63	995

INDIVIDUAL BATTING

(Leading Qualifiers for Batting Championship—378 or More Plate Appearances)

*Bats lefthanded. †Switch-hitter.

Player and Club	Pct.	G.	AB.	R.	H.	TB.	2B.	3B.	HR.	RBI.	GW.	SH.	SF.	HP.	BB.	Int. BB.	SO.	SB.	CS.
Ortiz, Javier, Burlington	.352	101	378	72	133	212	23	4	16	79	9	2	3	2	42	3	94	10	6
Tanner, Edwin, Springfield†	.319	128	511	93	163	204	28	2	3	51	3	10	7	5	43	6	29	15	11
McLaughlin, David, Appleton*	.319	112	385	52	123	142	14	1	1	44	6	2	3	0	35	11	32	9	8
Robidoux, William J., Beloit*	.317	126	435	70	138	200	30	1	10	61	10	0	2	3	79	7	74	2	4
Dunston, Shawon, Quad Cities	.310	117	455	65	141	186	17	8	4	62	10	4	4	10	7	2	51	58	23
Jones, Gary, Quad Cities*	.308	133	428	105	132	179	23	3	6	34	2	2	3	4	126	4	105	58	22
Wilson, Jeffrey, Wisconsin Rapids*	.303	114	330	52	100	128	19	0	3	30	4	6	4	2	67	3	41	17	9
Myers, David, Wausau	.301	123	448	66	135	182	16	2	9	61	7	7	6	3	38	0	51	26	9
Felix, Paul, Wisconsin Rapids†	.298	138	477	61	142	229	22	1	21	76	15	2	3	12	52	2	105	1	2
Reece, Thad, Madison*	.295	118	393	69	116	153	27	2	2	44	6	10	1	1	90	5	49	42	16

Departmental Leaders: G—Felix, 138; AB—Blackwell, 522; R—G. Jones, 105; H—E. Tanner, 163; TB—Ford, 236; 2B—Lee, 31; 3B—Christenson, 10; HR—Heath, 27; RBI—Ford, 91; GWRBI—Felix, 15; SH—Noboa, 18; SF—Allen, 9; HP—Salery, 15; BB—G. Jones, 126; IBB—McLaughlin, 11; SO—Roomes, 167; SB—Cangelosi, 87; CS—Cangelosi, 35.

(All Players—Listed Alphabetically)

Player and Club	Pct.	G.	AB.	R.	H.	TB.	2B.	3B.	HR.	RBI.	GW.	SH.	SF.	HP.	BB.	Int. BB.	SO.	SB.	CS.
Abbott, Ricardo, Beloit	.270	87	319	34	86	110	13	1	3	25	3	8	2	6	30	1	71	2	4
Adams, Patrick, Appleton	.292	120	411	62	120	191	30	1	13	71	8	3	2	14	57	5	105	1	3
Allanson, Andrew, Waterloo	.200	17	50	4	10	10	0	0	0	0	0	0	0	0	7	0	10	1	1
Allen, James, Quad Cities†	.230	110	352	45	81	126	13	4	8	54	7	4	9	1	44	5	57	7	4
Alonzo, Raymond, Madison*	.313	34	112	25	35	66	13	0	6	21	4	0	1	1	18	1	11	4	1
Alpert, George, Waterloo*	.210	19	62	11	13	22	3	0	2	7	1	1	1	2	5	1	15	2	1
Anderson, Steven, Beloit	.176	30	91	9	16	18	2	0	0	9	0	0	1	3	5	0	24	0	1
Andrade, John, Burlington	.159	16	44	6	7	9	2	0	0	4	0	1	1	0	6	0	7	1	1
Antonelli, John, Beloit	.261	122	417	40	109	144	16	2	5	38	5	3	1	2	28	4	94	26	7
Aponte, Edwin, Waterloo	.294	63	218	32	64	108	12	1	10	52	6	0	2	3	19	1	21	17	2
Baez, Jesse, Wausau	.225	24	80	8	18	27	3	0	2	10	0	1	2	1	9	0	20	2	0
Baier, Martin, Clinton*	.270	118	408	43	110	149	25	1	4	50	5	2	3	2	39	8	60	0	2
Bell, Terence, Wausau	.176	17	51	4	9	9	0	0	0	1	0	1	0	1	5	1	8	2	1
Ben, Elijah, Burlington	.233	91	279	56	65	118	13	2	12	41	3	5	2	2	29	1	92	32	7
Benza, Brett, Springfield	.268	104	358	56	96	119	7	5	2	34	5	7	3	1	49	0	58	9	8
Bernstine, Nehames, Waterloo†	.233	130	455	83	106	154	14	8	6	29	3	5	2	4	59	3	104	51	10
Blackwell, Orlando, Clinton†	.249	129	522	71	130	164	19	6	1	39	5	8	1	3	39	3	52	19	10
Blanke, Scott, Clinton	.193	44	140	13	27	50	6	1	5	23	4	0	0	0	14	0	40	0	0
Blume, David, Wausau*	.211	9	19	2	4	4	0	0	0	1	0	0	0	0	5	0	3	1	0
Boddy, William, Cedar Rapids	.288	40	111	19	32	39	2	1	1	10	1	0	2	0	11	0	24	7	0
Boderick, W. Stanley, Quad Cities	.188	128	458	45	86	106	6	4	2	37	6	3	2	3	27	0	124	45	21
Bonham, Wayne, Clinton	.186	47	140	12	26	33	4	0	1	9	1	3	0	2	17	0	56	2	1
Boroski, Stanley, Beloit	.073	31	82	6	6	7	1	0	0	4	0	2	0	0	5	0	35	0	1
Brier, S. Coe, Wisconsin Rapids	.181	57	171	10	31	48	5	0	4	10	1	3	0	0	7	1	48	1	1
Briggs, Kenneth, Wausau	.259	70	220	35	57	97	9	2	9	25	3	1	1	1	22	0	56	9	5
Brito, Bernardo, Waterloo	.202	35	119	13	24	40	4	0	4	17	2	1	1	1	10	1	40	3	2
Brower, Robert, Burlington	.312	43	138	35	43	74	4	6	5	28	1	2	1	0	34	1	43	18	1
Cabell, F. William, Clinton†	.216	50	116	11	25	30	3	1	0	7	0	0	1	0	16	0	41	3	4
Cangelosi, John, Appleton*	.282	128	439	87	124	147	12	4	1	48	2	9	3	8	99	2	81	87	35
Canseco, Jose, Madison	.159	34	88	8	14	27	4	0	3	10	1	0	1	1	10	1	36	2	2
Cardenas, Leo, Wisconsin Rapids†	.230	30	74	11	17	25	3	1	1	5	1	0	0	0	6	0	17	2	3
Carroll, Carson, Wisconsin Rapids	.270	48	178	28	48	63	6	3	1	19	4	3	1	3	25	1	29	24	3
Cawthon, D. Christopher, Waterloo*	.164	27	61	3	10	14	4	0	0	4	0	1	0	0	5	0	27	2	0
Christenson, Kim, Appleton	.261	130	452	79	118	182	23	10	7	64	6	4	5	3	53	1	64	14	13
Christy, Alexander, Peoria	.190	67	200	17	38	60	9	2	3	16	0	0	2	3	13	1	63	4	3
Cimo, Matthew, Clinton	.256	86	320	46	82	124	17	2	7	40	2	5	2	3	40	1	80	7	5
Clark, David, Waterloo*	.277	58	159	20	44	66	8	1	4	20	2	0	1	3	19	3	32	2	2
Clements, David, Springfield	.265	122	468	71	124	208	24	0	20	84	10	1	5	4	34	0	107	15	2
Colton, Bradford, Wausau	.282	42	142	22	40	67	1	1	8	24	1	2	3	2	10	1	33	4	1
Conklin, Graham, Wausau	.239	110	394	48	94	152	11	1	15	46	7	2	2	4	22	1	108	7	7
Cordner, Steven, Quad Cities	.254	120	425	55	108	165	14	5	11	49	6	3	3	3	33	4	108	8	3
Costello, Robert, Wisconsin Rapids	.182	7	22	1	4	4	0	0	0	3	0	0	0	0	3	0	4	0	0
Cottrell, Gregory, Wisconsin Rapids	.189	51	132	10	25	35	4	0	2	13	0	2	0	1	11	0	22	1	1
Crawford, Jack, Peoria	.244	47	172	20	42	57	10	1	1	16	3	2	1	1	7	0	41	9	2
Crum, George, Burlington	.293	113	441	79	129	150	9	6	0	37	2	6	0	3	35	4	65	74	12
Cruz, Juan, Madison	.262	123	446	70	117	155	17	3	5	53	5	15	5	5	37	1	96	34	10
Cruz, Luis, Wisconsin Rapids*	.167	29	60	3	10	13	0	0	1	4	0	1	0	0	1	0	18	1	0
Daniels, Kalvoski, Cedar Rapids*	.251	101	342	51	86	125	14	5	5	28	4	0	1	4	39	2	73	31	9
David, Brian, Wausau	.221	122	425	73	94	130	21	0	5	36	3	12	6	6	78	1	57	30	8
Davidson, Mark, Wisconsin Rapids	.220	111	363	63	80	136	15	1	13	48	5	4	3	4	50	1	84	26	7
Davis, Kevin, Peoria	.281	43	135	17	38	47	7	1	0	17	2	1	0	2	6	0	35	5	1
Dawson, Gary, Madison	.244	119	397	59	97	131	13	6	3	43	2	3	4	6	30	1	112	14	14
DeValk, Brian, Wausau*	.242	44	128	19	31	44	5	1	2	19	3	2	0	3	16	1	40	4	1
Diaz, Eduardo, Waterloo	.000	3	3	0	0	0	0	0	0	0	0	0	0	0	0	0	0	0	0
Diaz, Edgar, Beloit	.208	107	307	29	64	66	2	0	0	15	1	4	1	0	35	0	41	6	4
Diaz, Jorge, Madison	.234	34	107	8	25	31	3	0	1	13	2	1	1	0	7	0	21	0	2

Player and Club	Pct.	G.	AB.	R.	H.	TB.	2B.	3B.	HR.	RBI.	GW.	SH.	SF.	HP.	BB.	Int. BB.	SO.	SB.	CS.
Diaz, Richard, Waterloo	.215	25	79	12	17	27	4	0	2	5	0	1	0	0	4	0	22	1	1
Dillard, Ronald, Burlington	.286	16	42	13	12	15	3	0	0	9	0	1	0	0	9	0	6	7	3
Doran, Mark, Peoria	.222	69	234	25	52	75	7	2	4	22	0	2	1	1	31	1	75	0	5
Dorsett, Brian, Madison	.255	58	204	16	52	68	7	0	3	27	2	0	2	0	17	1	35	2	1
Duggan, Thomas, Wausau	.247	114	393	49	97	140	18	2	7	45	2	3	3	3	34	1	94	8	4
Duncan, John, Wausau	.240	99	308	40	74	83	9	0	0	23	2	3	1	1	26	0	44	13	6
Dunston, Shawon, Quad Cities	.310	117	455	65	141	186	17	8	4	62	10	4	4	10	7	2	51	58	23
Edwards, Glenn, Waterloo	.270	73	244	28	66	110	14	3	8	29	3	3	2	7	14	0	78	3	6
Empting, J. Michael, Clinton	.260	101	308	33	80	102	15	2	1	33	2	6	0	0	31	1	53	1	5
Espinal, Feliz, Clinton	.197	86	304	29	60	78	9	0	3	23	5	6	2	2	19	0	70	9	2
Farmar, Damon, Quad Cities†	.230	126	427	54	98	140	16	4	6	43	3	4	8	5	38	2	122	33	15
Felix, Paul, Wisconsin Rapids†	.298	138	477	61	142	229	22	1	21	76	15	2	3	12	52	2	105	1	2
Feliz, L. Adolfo, Cedar Rapids	.222	3	9	1	2	5	0	0	1	1	0	0	0	0	2	0	2	0	2
Ferro, Robert, Wisconsin Rapids	.233	116	305	37	71	101	10	1	6	25	3	11	1	8	55	1	92	12	7
Ficklin, Winston, Waterloo†	.292	128	425	61	124	170	18	2	8	43	8	9	3	4	46	4	83	35	7
Finley, Brian, Beloit*	.254	131	461	78	117	153	16	4	4	40	7	3	4	9	75	3	87	28	11
Foit, James, Burlington	.216	41	148	29	32	42	3	2	1	15	1	2	2	0	18	4	39	5	1
Ford, Curtis, Springfield*	.290	126	465	80	135	236	27	7	20	91	14	3	4	8	71	7	62	28	12
Francis, Todd, Wausau*	.095	24	42	2	4	4	0	0	0	4	0	0	0	0	8	1	11	0	0
Gambeski, Michael, Springfield	.296	101	314	47	93	143	18	4	8	38	3	0	3	1	31	4	78	1	2
Garrett, Eric, Madison	.217	16	23	6	5	9	1	0	1	4	0	0	0	0	1	0	6	0	1
Geren, Robert, Springfield	.265	124	434	67	115	214	21	3	24	73	3	3	4	3	40	1	127	0	0
Gergen, Robert, Burlington	.280	112	389	53	109	173	27	2	11	50	5	2	4	7	21	0	85	6	8
Gertz, T. Michael, Waterloo*	.233	107	322	54	75	125	16	2	10	49	4	5	3	4	53	5	96	6	2
Gile, Mark, Burlington*	.189	13	37	7	7	10	0	0	1	3	0	3	0	0	7	0	12	2	1
Gill, Shawn, Madison	.213	59	150	15	32	42	1	0	3	16	1	6	1	0	25	1	27	3	3
Gobbo, Michael, Beloit	.000	3	4	0	0	0	0	0	0	0	0	0	0	0	2	0	2	0	1
Gomez, Marcos, Beloit†	.276	52	163	30	45	75	9	0	7	20	1	1	1	2	18	0	23	2	1
Gonzalez, Otto, Burlington	.267	108	389	49	104	168	28	0	12	58	4	2	1	2	35	1	73	2	6
Gordon, William, Clinton	.264	60	201	21	53	61	4	2	0	20	1	4	0	2	17	0	38	0	2
Graham, J. Brian, Madison	.234	74	231	31	54	74	7	2	3	41	5	9	1	2	23	0	26	14	9
Graupmann, Timothy, Wis. Rapids	.148	54	115	16	17	29	4	1	2	7	1	3	1	3	15	0	23	0	0
Gundelfinger, Matthew, Springfield	.283	111	364	71	103	190	15	3	22	65	5	1	0	8	62	5	99	10	4
Guzman, Ruben, Cedar Rapids	.231	92	316	39	73	109	12	3	6	34	5	1	0	5	26	1	69	14	9
Haberle, David, Cedar Rapids*	.179	35	78	13	14	21	1	0	2	5	0	0	0	2	19	2	22	6	0
Halberg, Eric, Clinton	.200	10	30	2	6	6	0	0	0	2	0	1	0	0	5	0	9	0	0
Haley, Samuel, Wausau	.156	17	32	5	5	9	1	0	1	5	0	0	1	0	0	0	9	2	0
Harry, Whitney, Burlington	.257	130	467	84	120	223	23	4	24	78	6	4	4	8	57	2	157	22	6
Hartsock, Brian, Peoria*	.306	100	333	42	102	135	17	2	4	48	5	1	4	0	35	3	44	17	7
Hausladen, Robert, Burlington*	.252	87	274	54	69	104	11	0	8	35	3	4	2	2	48	4	51	1	2
Hawley, G. William, Cedar Rapids*	.048	26	21	1	1	1	0	0	0	0	0	6	0	0	1	0	6	0	0
Hazard, Richard, Beloit*	.194	63	222	28	43	82	10	1	9	34	5	2	3	1	21	2	67	2	2
Heath, David, Peoria	.271	121	417	70	113	228	28	3	27	71	3	4	1	3	21	3	119	2	4
Heatherly, Stephen, Peoria	.194	64	227	26	44	59	5	2	2	18	2	3	1	0	21	0	36	3	3
Henley, Michael, Appleton	.208	46	130	15	27	36	6	0	1	20	4	2	6	0	21	0	39	4	2
Hennessy, Brendan, Burlington	.164	19	55	4	9	13	4	0	0	5	0	0	1	2	4	0	21	1	0
Hill, David, Wausau	.243	23	74	9	18	27	6	0	1	1	0	2	0	0	4	0	19	1	1
Hill, Orsino, Cedar Rapids*	.229	118	375	51	86	144	12	2	14	52	11	2	3	2	48	2	110	17	10
Hoyt, David, Springfield	.245	47	151	21	37	50	4	3	1	15	3	0	1	1	16	0	33	6	2
Huey, John, 7 Mad.-43 Quad C.	.000	50	1	0	0	0	0	0	0	0	0	0	0	0	0	0	1	0	0
Hunt, Damon, Clinton*	.232	45	138	12	32	34	2	0	0	16	1	5	0	2	16	2	17	3	3
Jackson, Larry, Beloit*	.282	47	163	28	46	61	9	0	2	15	2	5	3	4	12	0	27	5	1
James, Dewey, Beloit†	.232	62	198	24	46	72	10	2	4	24	4	8	2	3	22	0	58	5	5
Jimenez, Ramon, Peoria	.231	26	65	5	15	19	4	0	0	5	1	1	0	0	16	0	11	1	1
Johnson, John, Quad Cities	.114	16	35	3	4	4	0	0	0	1	0	0	0	1	5	0	19	1	0
Johnston, J. Mark, Beloit*	.280	90	296	45	83	141	19	0	13	61	4	3	4	9	44	4	36	3	3
Jones, Gary, Quad Cities*	.308	133	428	105	132	179	23	3	6	34	2	2	3	4	126	4	105	58	22
Jones, Scott, Cedar Rapids	.214	15	14	2	3	4	1	0	0	0	0	1	0	1	1	0	5	1	1
Joyner, Wallace, Peoria*	.328	54	192	25	63	92	16	2	3	33	3	0	1	2	19	1	25	1	1
Karkovice, Ronald, Appleton	.239	97	326	54	78	140	17	3	13	48	3	3	2	4	31	1	90	10	1
Keeton, Garry, Appleton	.274	84	288	42	79	117	16	2	6	35	7	4	3	3	25	1	46	8	3
Kent, Wesley, Appleton	.176	23	74	13	13	29	4	0	4	8	0	0	0	1	7	0	42	1	0
King, Kevin, Wausau†	.313	42	144	27	45	101	6	4	14	32	3	0	0	1	21	1	40	2	5
Kinsel, David, Appleton	.217	70	143	22	31	46	6	3	1	21	3	2	3	1	23	0	17	4	1
Kirby, Charles, Beloit	.200	32	90	14	18	22	2	1	0	9	0	2	0	0	8	0	21	2	3
Kline, Kris, Peoria	.244	102	352	52	86	106	16	2	0	25	4	7	2	3	35	0	58	15	8
Klump, Kenneth, Wisconsin Rapids	.000	26	1	0	0	0	0	0	0	0	0	0	0	0	0	0	1	0	0
Knox, Michael, Cedar Rapids	.160	34	25	2	4	8	1	0	1	4	1	3	0	0	0	0	10	0	0
Konderla, Michael, Cedar Rapids	.100	45	10	0	1	2	1	0	0	3	0	0	0	0	0	0	5	0	0
Kunkel, Jeffrey, Burlington	.287	31	122	22	35	62	7	1	6	18	3	1	1	2	1	0	19	6	0
Landers, Harold, Beloit	.228	109	325	38	74	129	20	4	9	45	6	1	8	3	47	4	81	5	4
Lauck, Jeffrey, Springfield†	.273	8	22	4	6	8	2	0	0	4	0	0	1	0	0	0	13	0	0
Lee, Terry, Cedar Rapids	.262	123	405	60	106	196	31	1	19	67	8	2	2	4	40	4	86	11	5
Lewis, Jay, Peoria	.223	97	319	30	71	107	11	5	5	40	1	0	3	1	27	2	89	5	3
Loard, Billy, Clinton	.074	13	27	2	2	3	1	0	0	0	0	0	0	1	4	0	13	0	0
Lochner, David, Cedar Rapids*	.333	26	27	4	9	10	1	0	0	4	2	3	0	0	3	0	6	0	0
Lopez, Juan, Waterloo	.190	47	121	11	23	29	3	0	1	11	2	4	1	0	4	0	24	0	1
Loscalzo, Robert, Madison*	.275	120	353	58	97	139	12	3	8	45	7	5	2	1	65	3	83	23	11
Mace, Jeffrey, Burlington	.248	92	331	48	82	115	18	0	5	34	5	6	1	4	22	1	91	10	6
Malespin, Gustavo, Springfield	.266	130	473	67	126	175	19	0	10	54	9	4	4	4	53	1	35	6	5
Mancuso, Paul, Wisconsin Rapids*	.000	51	1	0	0	0	0	0	0	0	0	0	0	0	0	0	0	0	0
Manfre, Michael, Cedar Rapids	.265	111	339	51	90	149	14	6	11	49	5	0	4	2	34	1	59	8	7
Marquardt, John, Madison	.294	62	211	27	62	79	15	1	0	19	1	7	2	1	23	0	28	3	5
Marr, Alan, Clinton	.233	120	425	49	99	116	13	2	0	23	2	8	2	9	64	0	91	5	13
Martelli, Vincent, Waterloo	.250	24	56	9	14	22	5	0	1	5	1	0	0	0	11	0	7	1	1
Martin, Sam, Springfield†	.244	115	353	41	86	95	5	2	0	25	2	6	3	0	28	1	31	12	5
Martinez, David, Quad Cities*	.244	44	119	17	29	39	6	2	0	10	1	0	2	1	26	0	30	10	8
Martinez, Randy, Springfield*	.000	28	4	0	0	0	0	0	0	0	0	0	0	0	0	0	1	0	0
Martinez, Ray, Waterloo*	.231	17	39	5	9	15	0	0	2	4	0	0	1	0	1	0	9	0	0
McCulla, Henry, Springfield	.256	106	348	55	89	140	17	2	10	51	6	3	3	2	39	1	86	1	3
McLaughlin, David, Appleton*	.319	112	385	52	123	142	14	1	1	44	6	2	3	0	35	11	32	9	8
McLemore, Mark, Peoria†	.240	95	329	42	79	92	7	3	0	18	3	6	3	2	53	0	64	15	11
Meier, H. Randal, Wausau	.271	101	365	39	99	116	11	0	2	44	3	7	1	2	32	1	43	20	9

Player and Club	Pct.	G.	AB.	R.	H.	TB.	2B.	3B.	HR.	RBI.	GW.	SH.	SF.	HP.	BB.	Int. BB.	SO.	SB.	CS.
Merrifield, Billy, Peoria	.249	80	289	38	72	123	19	1	10	40	4	4	4	1	18	1	67	2	2
Michel, John, Madison*	.265	100	317	37	84	112	14	1	4	43	6	4	4	2	31	7	70	0	3
Miles, J. Edward, Appleton	.205	59	219	20	45	69	7	4	3	28	4	1	4	1	14	2	56	5	0
Miller, Scott, Quad Cities*	.261	58	184	30	48	73	10	3	3	35	5	1	1	0	26	2	49	5	1
Mills, Kenneth, Clinton*	.000	14	1	0	0	0	0	0	0	0	0	0	0	0	0	0	0	0	0
Mitchell, Joseph, Beloit	.053	11	19	1	1	1	0	0	0	0	0	0	0	1	1	0	5	0	1
Mitchell, John, Beloit*	.241	40	87	13	21	31	4	0	2	5	2	1	0	0	12	0	18	3	3
Moreno, Michael, Wisconsin Rapids	.262	131	474	68	124	211	24	0	21	88	8	3	4	2	40	3	112	11	8
Moseley, Lester, Clinton*	.077	9	26	1	2	2	0	0	0	3	1	0	0	1	6	0	16	2	0
Munson, Jay, Cedar Rapids	.211	31	90	8	19	22	3	0	0	4	1	1	0	0	6	0	22	3	1
Murphy, Robert, Cedar Rapids*	.200	36	20	1	4	5	1	0	0	2	0	1	0	0	1	0	7	0	1
Myers, David, Wausau	.301	123	448	66	135	182	16	2	9	61	7	7	6	3	38	0	51	26	9
Naber, Robert, Clinton	.259	108	374	54	97	131	15	5	3	43	7	3	3	2	29	3	72	6	3
Nalley, Jerry, Waterloo	.281	10	32	3	9	10	1	0	0	1	0	1	0	1	2	1	5	1	1
Nieves, Juan, Beloit*	.000	13	4	0	0	0	0	0	0	0	0	0	0	0	0	0	2	0	0
Noboa, Milciades, Waterloo	.256	132	449	64	115	146	22	3	1	29	3	18	2	5	48	1	71	47	20
Ortiz, Javier, Burlington	.352	101	378	72	133	212	23	4	16	79	9	2	3	2	42	3	94	10	6
Padia, Steven, Cedar Rapids*	.255	97	275	43	70	100	18	0	4	31	5	2	3	8	44	2	48	6	5
Pedraza, Nelson, Waterloo	.233	135	417	39	97	141	16	2	8	43	6	12	5	1	33	1	82	11	4
Pellant, Gary, Wausau†	.297	28	64	9	19	27	2	0	2	7	3	0	0	0	7	0	21	1	1
Pino, Rolando, Appleton	.262	101	290	53	76	119	14	4	7	33	7	6	3	3	47	0	80	14	7
Piwnica, William, Beloit	.203	24	69	6	14	16	2	0	0	3	1	0	0	0	10	0	12	2	1
Powell, Alonzo, Clinton	.195	36	113	14	22	29	5	1	0	9	0	2	0	2	15	1	27	2	1
Pryor, Depew, Cedar Rapids	.302	74	192	41	58	88	9	0	7	26	4	0	1	0	32	1	29	2	2
Quinones, Hector, Beloit	.208	27	72	9	15	19	1	0	1	6	0	3	1	0	5	0	25	4	0
Quinones, Rene, Waterloo†	.309	72	246	30	76	102	9	1	5	33	4	10	3	2	19	5	35	12	7
Radloff, Scott, Cedar Rapids*	.206	42	107	14	22	28	2	2	0	11	2	0	1	0	20	1	32	0	2
Rainey, Scott, Clinton	.218	66	197	15	43	59	5	1	3	21	1	3	2	2	18	1	37	1	1
Ransom, H. Eugene, Madison†	.251	118	363	50	91	119	8	1	6	40	4	10	2	2	49	1	79	37	18
Reece, Thad, Madison*	.295	118	393	69	116	153	27	2	2	44	6	10	1	1	90	5	49	42	16
Remo, Jeffrey, Quad Cities	.222	9	27	4	6	10	4	0	0	3	2	0	0	0	2	0	12	0	0
Reuschel, Ricky, Quad Cities	.500	13	2	1	1	1	0	0	0	1	0	0	0	0	0	0	1	0	0
Reynolds, C. Timothy, Cedar Rapids†	.167	24	18	2	3	4	1	0	0	0	0	1	0	0	1	0	6	0	0
Rhodes, Jeffrey, Cedar Rapids	.186	106	311	32	58	101	12	2	9	39	8	0	3	4	17	2	85	6	7
Riley, Thomas, Cedar Rapids	.229	116	345	37	79	87	6	1	0	26	1	5	2	4	36	1	51	7	2
Rivera, Jose, Quad Cities*	.246	26	69	8	17	20	3	0	0	9	0	2	1	1	9	0	10	6	2
Rizzo, Michael, Peoria	.230	65	204	29	47	66	10	0	3	15	2	2	0	3	14	0	33	3	3
Roadcap, Steve, Quad Cities†	.257	80	206	28	53	65	9	0	1	25	4	3	1	0	40	0	61	3	6
Robidoux, William J., Beloit*	.317	126	435	70	138	200	30	1	10	61	10	0	2	3	79	7	74	2	4
Robles, Gregory, Madison*	.289	125	429	57	124	195	23	0	16	78	10	1	4	1	43	2	47	3	6
Roebuck, Scott, Wausau	.231	63	225	24	52	82	15	0	5	23	3	2	1	2	25	0	46	7	4
Roman, Miguel, Waterloo	.167	9	30	2	5	5	0	0	0	1	0	2	0	0	3	1	7	2	0
Roomes, Rolando, Quad Cities	.214	122	416	47	89	130	6	4	9	40	2	3	0	6	18	1	167	26	12
Rover, Vincent, Cedar Rapids†	.257	119	369	53	95	127	24	1	2	38	2	7	6	9	38	0	52	7	2
Sabo, Christopher, Cedar Rapids	.274	77	274	43	75	134	11	6	12	37	3	1	2	2	26	3	39	15	4
Salery, Johnny, Wisconsin Rapids	.263	135	475	89	125	190	21	1	14	52	4	3	4	15	65	0	90	46	14
Sandry, William, Appleton	.290	13	31	4	9	16	1	0	2	8	0	1	0	1	2	0	6	1	0
Saverino, Michael, Peoria	.286	13	35	9	10	13	1	1	0	6	0	0	1	0	6	0	9	1	0
Scarpace, Kenneth, Cedar Rapids*	.269	9	26	2	7	9	2	0	0	5	0	1	0	0	6	0	2	2	1
Scheer, Ronald, Wisconsin Rapids	.262	130	386	53	101	170	15	3	16	47	2	5	1	11	28	1	86	3	7
Sciacca, Christopher, Quad Cities†	.200	15	45	4	9	11	2	0	0	1	0	1	0	0	3	0	11	1	0
Scott, Timothy, Cedar Rapids	.000	46	4	0	0	0	0	0	0	0	0	1	0	0	0	0	0	0	0
Sedar, Edward, Appleton	.251	108	251	30	63	96	11	5	4	34	3	1	1	1	35	3	55	7	7
Segura, Americo, Peoria	.250	11	32	5	8	9	1	0	0	3	0	1	0	1	3	0	9	0	0
Skoglund, Brad, Wisconsin Rapids*	.215	27	65	5	14	17	3	0	0	6	0	1	0	1	6	0	11	0	0
Slavin, Timothy, Wausau	.252	101	301	41	76	131	11	1	14	42	2	3	4	4	36	0	92	7	6
Smajstrla, Craig, Appleton†	.276	93	330	42	91	115	16	4	0	24	4	4	0	2	26	1	38	10	4
Smith, David, Wausau*	.274	131	423	77	116	227	29	2	26	80	6	1	4	2	71	3	87	20	8
Smith, Kelvin, Clinton	.183	31	109	12	20	29	0	3	1	12	0	0	0	1	15	0	29	6	3
Smith, Shaun, Wisconsin Rapids	.225	54	129	8	29	38	6	0	1	15	2	3	3	0	6	2	22	1	2
Smith, Thomas, Peoria	.251	118	402	54	101	164	18	3	13	61	5	2	2	1	36	3	87	22	4
Sorce, Samuel, Burlington	.244	87	266	36	65	99	17	1	5	43	7	3	3	3	33	2	42	1	2
Sowards, Van, Clinton	.301	56	193	29	58	71	9	2	0	20	3	4	1	4	31	0	21	5	2
Spagnola, Glenn, Cedar Rapids*	.167	21	12	1	2	5	0	0	1	2	0	0	0	0	2	0	7	0	0
Stalp, R. Joseph, Cedar Rapids	.000	32	9	1	0	0	0	0	0	0	0	0	0	0	0	0	4	0	0
Steinmetz, Kevin, Cedar Rapids	.500	3	4	1	2	2	0	0	0	0	0	0	0	0	2	0	0	0	0
Stewart, Charles, Quad Cities	.222	57	153	19	34	59	8	1	5	23	3	3	3	0	19	2	51	3	4
Stewart, Edward, Clinton†	.225	119	377	39	85	106	10	1	3	35	4	6	1	2	56	2	83	9	6
Stock, Kevin, Burlington	.245	74	245	26	60	77	9	1	2	30	2	2	3	2	27	0	61	11	6
Strom, Phillip, Madison	.262	52	141	18	37	70	5	2	8	25	3	1	1	0	27	1	50	0	0
Stromer, Richard, Peoria	.254	41	130	23	33	56	8	0	5	14	1	0	0	2	34	0	20	3	1
Stryffeler, Daniel, Springfield*	.293	127	447	72	131	191	24	6	8	64	8	1	4	3	54	2	73	14	7
Sutton, Mark, Burlington	.213	84	272	28	58	72	8	3	0	30	2	4	2	3	19	1	69	3	4
Tanner, Edwin, Springfield†	.319	128	511	93	163	204	28	2	3	51	3	10	7	5	43	6	29	15	11
Tarnow, Greg, Appleton	.176	13	17	3	3	3	0	0	0	2	0	0	0	0	2	0	7	0	0
Taylor, Johnny, Appleton	.217	49	138	12	30	39	2	2	1	15	1	2	1	1	7	0	29	2	0
Thoma, Raymond, Madison	.111	3	9	1	1	1	0	0	0	0	0	0	0	0	0	0	3	1	0
Tramble, Otis, Quad Cities†	.278	28	108	18	30	42	6	3	0	12	2	0	1	0	9	0	19	10	5
Triplett, Antonio, Burlington	.267	67	195	27	52	64	4	4	0	22	2	4	1	1	21	0	33	8	4
Trout, Jeffrey, Wisconsin Rapids*	.341	64	229	30	78	117	15	0	8	31	3	3	1	1	22	2	26	5	8
Trujillo, Louie, Cedar Rapids	.000	52	3	0	0	0	0	0	0	0	0	1	0	0	1	0	2	0	0
Tryon, Michael, Wisconsin Rapids	.225	26	80	7	18	28	4	0	2	9	1	2	0	1	5	0	12	1	0
Utecht, Timothy, Beloit	.269	125	432	61	116	181	20	3	13	67	7	2	5	0	61	1	126	7	4
Valera, Alcadio, Waterloo†	.083	12	12	3	1	1	0	0	0	0	0	1	0	0	2	0	6	1	0
Velazquez, Juan, Quad Cities	.157	19	51	5	8	10	2	0	0	3	1	0	2	1	5	0	13	4	0
Verkuilen, D. Michael, Wis. Rapids*	.223	76	215	34	48	83	7	2	8	21	5	2	1	1	29	2	43	2	1
Vollmer, W. Robert, Wausau*	.229	37	96	14	22	24	2	0	0	7	2	1	0	0	20	0	14	7	3
Washington, Randy, Waterloo	.291	127	413	66	120	207	24	3	19	89	11	8	4	4	62	5	108	9	5
Weatherford, Joel, Beloit*	.197	41	122	13	24	27	3	0	0	8	1	0	0	0	23	1	27	1	4
Weiss, James, Wisconsin Rapids	.154	31	52	10	8	9	1	0	0	4	2	2	1	1	5	0	21	1	0
White, Devon, Peoria†	.253	117	430	69	109	177	17	6	13	66	7	6	3	12	36	5	124	32	15
Wilder, David, Madison	.242	115	356	71	86	123	13	3	6	39	4	2	3	2	88	4	116	6	8
Williams, Kenneth, Appleton	.231	124	415	60	96	154	18	2	12	53	8	5	3	4	26	0	148	27	8

Player and Club	Pct.	G.	AB.	R.	H.	TB.	2B.	3B.	HR.	RBI.	GW.	SH.	SF.	HP.	BB.	Int. BB.	SO.	SB.	CS.
Wilson, Jeffrey, Wisconsin Rapids*	.303	114	330	52	100	128	19	0	3	30	4	6	4	2	67	3	41	17	9
Wilson, Phillip, Waterloo	.247	82	239	32	59	96	10	0	9	41	3	4	6	2	35	1	34	6	5
Woods, Tony, Quad Cities	.278	122	425	59	118	167	20	7	5	63	6	6	8	9	43	3	77	24	14
Wooster, Robert, Waterloo	.164	36	73	5	12	13	1	0	0	2	0	1	0	2	6	0	18	0	2
Young, Delwyn, Cedar Rapids†	.265	94	317	40	84	104	12	1	2	28	3	5	1	0	29	0	54	28	9

The following pitchers, listed alphabetically by club, with games in parentheses, had no plate appearances, primarily through use of designated hitters:

APPLETON—Atkinson, William (20); Babcock, William (12); Correa, Edwin (19); DeVincenzo, Richard (27); Heath, Allan (5); Hernandez, Carlo (15); Jones, Alfornia (55); McKeon, Joel (19); Moses, John (51); Noworyta, Steven (34); Ruzek, Donald (8); Tanner, Bruce (4); Trujillo, Michael (29).

BELOIT—Aldrich, Jay (28); Birkbeck, Michael (7); Bosio, Christopher (17); Crim, Charles (26); Diaz, Derek (23); Fedor, Francis (24); Gyarmati, Jeffrey (1); Murphy, Daniel (8); Norton, Douglas (13); Parrett, Jeffrey (10); Pena, Hipolito (1); Rice, Woolsey (27); Scarpetta, Daniel (19); Shamblin, Archie (32); Teahan, James (13); Torres, Anthony (11); Williams, Bruce (41).

BURLINGTON—Bass, Barry (19); Buckley, John (17); Cook, Glenn (9); Dewechter, Pat (18); Gerhardt, William (6); Guzman, Jose (25); Hartman, Albert (7); Hopkins, David (42); Hudson, Anthony (23); Johnson, Terrance (22); Joslin, Christopher (15); Kordish, Steve (4); Kramer, Randall (26); Maki, Timothy (12); Schulte, Todd (41); Smith, Mark (10); Soper, Michael (30); Waldron, Jose (10).

CLINTON—Bargerhuff, Brian (44); Bautista, Ramon (28); Corbell, Charles (6); Gladden, Jeffrey (29); Hughes, John (10); Lambert, Gene (23); Mattson, Kurt (42); Norman, Scott (20); Oakes, Todd (15); Raithel, Kirk (8); Taft, Dennie (27); Tavarez, David (1); Weibel, Randy (11); Weir, James (16).

MADISON—Call, Keith (25); Conquest, Thomas (23); Escribano, Eduardo (4); Fischer, Todd (49); Godwin, Glenn (36); Gonzalves, Dennis (28); Hallas, Robert (26); Jackson, Milton (11); Kendrick, Peter (52); Kobernus, Jeffrey (8); Leiper, David (16); Myers, Edward (31); Retzer, Edwin (23); Wex, Gary (17).

PEORIA—Clements, Patrick (15); Glanz, Scott (9); Gonzales, Julian (44); Groh, Donald (47); Kemmerling, Byron (17); King, Joseph (46); Kipper, Robert (22); Lugo, Rafael (15); McKenzie, Douglas (23); Migliore, Brian (16); Rentschler, Thomas (29); Salazar, Jeffrey (14); Suehr, Scott (42); Timberlake, Donald (23); Valdez, Jose (6).

QUAD CITIES—Adamczak, James (9); Baker, Mark (40); Balmer, J. Stephen (17); Blevins, Bradley (47); Capel, Michael (18); Chestnut, Troy (20); Cook, Mitchell (11); Cox, John (10); Fruge, Jeffrey (29); German, Rene (18); Grachen, Timothy (12); Lockie, Randall (13); Noles, Dickie (3); Parmenter, Gary (11); Serafini, Rudolph (42); Tuller, Brian (8).

SPRINGFIELD—Arigoni, Scott (27); Blunt, Bradley (1); Cherry, Paul (28); Dozier, Thomas (1); Droschak, David (25); Dunn, Gregory (29); Mason, Martin (54); Morlock, Allen (23); Perry, Patrick (6); Pittman, Michael (24); Shade, Michael (47); Silkwood, Joe (24); Thurberg, Thomas (6); Young, John (23).

WATERLOO—Anthony, Dane (28); Barkley, Jeffrey (24); Browne, Richard (5); Keeler, Jay (36); McDonald, Rodney (13); Miglio, John (50); Ortiz, Andrew (23); Pierorazio, Wesley (33); Piphus, Benjamin (18); Poindexter, Michael (26); Ritter, Reggie (31); Roman, Jose (34); Street, Michael (1).

WAUSAU—Baldrick, Robert (28); Barnhouse, Scott (50); Bergendahl, Wray (13); Burns, Thomas (46); Dixon, Ronn (30); Enriquez, Martin (15); Hinson, Robert (9); McDonald, Rodney (13); Meister, Mickey (3); Newman, Randall (38); Parent, Eric (16); Poloni, John (5); Roy, Kevin (13); Schneider, Paul (49); Sismondo, Ronald (2); Taylor, Terry (24).

WISCONSIN RAPIDS—Anderson, Allen (8); Arney, Jeffrey (7); Baehr, David (1); Burnos, James (15); Clay, Danny (7); Gibson, Scott (15); Henderson, Craig (13); Higgins, Kiel (6); Hobaugh, Brian (25); Kearns, John (11); Klawitter, Thomas (23); Klingbeil, Scott (22); Larcom, Mark (2); Maack, Michael (30); Parham, Terrill (9); Sain, Joseph (10); Steinberg, David (4); Thompson, Timothy (7).

GRAND SLAM HOME RUNS—Johnston, White, 2 each; Alonzo, Briggs, Colton, Cordner, Davidson, Ford, Geren, O. Gonzalez, Morenko, Myers, J. Ortiz, Pedraza, Sandry, Scheer, Slavin, T. Smith, Utecht, 1 each.

AWARDED FIRST BASE ON CATCHER'S INTERFERENCE—Gundelfinger 8 (Velazquez 2, Sorce, Lopez, Blume, Gill, Roadcap, Duncan); Loscalzo 2 (Roadcap, Lopez); Ben (Lopez); J. Cruz (Sorce); Empting (P. Wilson); Ford (Sorce); Utecht (P. Wilson).

CLUB FIELDING

Club	Pct.	G.	PO.	A.	E.	DP.	PB.
Appleton	.968	137	3462	1379	158	84	29
Cedar Rapids	.967	140	3577	1420	170	99	30
Springfield	.966	139	3625	1407	177	92	26
Madison	.965	138	3458	1467	177	123	14
Wisconsin Rapids	.963	138	3467	1439	190	111	24
Wausau	.961	138	3435	1533	203	108	37
Beloit	.959	137	3457	1309	205	120	35
Clinton	.957	138	3543	1480	225	94	14
Waterloo	.957	140	3472	1481	223	128	33
Burlington	.954	139	3517	1492	240	113	21
Peoria	.954	139	3516	1466	242	95	30
Quad Cities	.954	139	3573	1576	246	108	19

INDIVIDUAL FIELDING

*Throws lefthanded.

FIRST BASEMEN

Player and Club	Pct.	G.	PO.	A.	E.	DP.
Adams, Appleton	.986	118	897	107	14	56
Allen, Quad Cities	.989	51	413	36	5	36
Baier, Clinton*	.986	104	867	65	13	45
Blanke, Clinton	.975	23	149	9	4	19
Brier, Wisconsin Rapids	.000	1	0	0	0	0
Cawthon, Waterloo	.985	21	127	7	2	8
Cimo, Clinton	.995	28	172	29	1	16
Conklin, Wausau	1.000	5	36	4	0	2
Cordner, Quad Cities	.984	93	859	59	15	57
L. Cruz, Wisconsin Rapids*	1.000	5	13	1	0	1
R. Diaz, Waterloo	1.000	1	5	0	0	0
Felix, Wisconsin Rapids	.986	138	1153	70	17	86
Francis, Wausau*	1.000	10	46	4	0	7
Gambeski, Springfield	.991	72	533	38	5	31
Geren, Springfield	1.000	1	3	2	0	0
Gertz, Waterloo*	.983	96	761	55	14	67
Gonzalez, Burlington	1.000	2	12	1	0	2
Gundelfinger, Springfield	.983	67	510	26	9	44
Harry, Burlington	.982	119	1017	59	20	85
Hartsock, Peoria	1.000	4	26	0	0	3
Hausladen, Burlington	.995	23	178	13	1	17
Hazard, Beloit*	1.000	13	85	5	0	10
Heath, Peoria	1.000	1	6	0	0	0
Hennessy, Burlington	1.000	1	1	0	0	0
Johnston, Beloit	1.000	2	12	1	0	1
Joyner, Peoria*	.989	54	480	45	6	28
Kent, Appleton	.982	7	49	7	1	3
Landers, Beloit	1.000	2	5	0	0	0
LEE, Cedar Rapids	.992	115	946	64	8	67
Loard, Clinton	.889	1	8	0	1	0
Manfre, Cedar Rapids	1.000	4	8	0	0	0
R. Martinez, Waterloo*	.990	15	90	9	1	10
McCulla, Springfield	.948	16	83	8	5	9
McLaughlin, Appleton	1.000	1	3	0	0	0
Meier, Wausau	1.000	1	3	0	0	1
Michel, Madison	.969	4	30	1	1	5
Miller, Quad Cities	1.000	3	20	0	0	0
Mitchell, Beloit	1.000	1	4	0	0	0
D. Myers, Wausau	1.000	5	40	2	0	4
Nalley, Waterloo	1.000	10	66	7	0	7
Pellant, Wausau	1.000	2	2	0	0	0
Radloff, Cedar Rapids*	.976	36	227	22	6	14
Rivera, Quad Cities*	1.000	1	1	1	0	0
Rizzo, Peoria	.975	14	111	6	3	8
Robidoux, Beloit	.953	5	39	2	2	3
Robles, Madison*	.987	122	967	70	14	96
Sandry, Appleton	1.000	1	2	0	0	0
Sedar, Appleton	.982	19	108	4	2	12
Skoglund, Wisconsin Rapids*	.000	1	0	0	0	0
D. Smith, Wausau*	.986	126	1108	70	17	83
T. Smith, Peoria	.974	51	384	29	11	36
Strom, Madison	.994	25	162	11	1	6
Stromer, Peoria	.965	25	206	13	8	9
Trout, Wisconsin Rapids	.000	1	0	0	0	0
Utecht, Beloit	.989	120	957	62	11	94
P. Wilson, Waterloo	.867	2	12	1	2	0
Wooster, Waterloo	.976	18	112	9	3	11

SECOND BASEMEN

Player and Club	Pct.	G.	PO.	A.	E.	DP.
Abbott, Beloit	.977	80	154	193	8	47
Allen, Quad Cities	1.000	2	3	3	0	1
Andrade, Burlington	.988	14	29	51	1	11
Bernstine, Waterloo	.800	3	3	5	2	1
Boddy, Cedar Rapids	1.000	1	1	4	0	0
Cabell, Clinton	.947	12	10	8	1	2
Carroll, Wisconsin Rapids	.967	46	89	116	7	23
J. Cruz, Madison	.973	43	104	116	6	23
David, Wausau	.964	121	227	310	20	54
R. Diaz, Waterloo	.947	9	12	24	2	3
Dillard, Burlington	.981	13	28	23	1	5
Espinal, Clinton	.932	51	98	147	18	20
Ferro, Wisconsin Rapids	.800	2	2	6	2	1
Ford, Springfield	1.000	7	3	3	0	0
Gergen, Burlington	.953	11	24	17	2	3
Gile, Burlington	.897	13	26	26	6	7
Graham, Madison	.973	58	132	125	7	37
Heatherly, Peoria	.957	62	132	154	13	32
D. Hill, Wausau	1.000	9	26	23	0	4
Johnston, Beloit	.965	37	53	83	5	14
G. Jones, Quad Cities	.953	130	251	364	30	63
Keeton, Appleton	.962	70	139	140	11	35
Kinsel, Appleton	1.000	3	1	3	0	0
Kirby, Beloit	.953	26	34	48	4	12
Marr, Clinton	.942	16	29	36	4	8
Martin, Springfield	.982	29	52	55	2	12
McLemore, Peoria	.953	60	118	146	13	20
Meier, Wausau	.500	1	0	1	1	1
Moreno, Wisconsin Rapids	1.000	7	10	16	0	4
D. Myers, Wausau	1.000	7	15	19	0	1
Noboa, Waterloo	.962	130	257	354	24	81
Pellant, Wausau	.800	2	0	4	1	0
Piwnica, Beloit	.973	9	18	18	1	7
H. Quinones, Beloit	.846	3	5	6	2	2
R. Quinones, Waterloo	1.000	5	14	14	0	2
Reece, Madison	.951	47	82	92	9	24
Riley, Cedar Rapids	1.000	1	1	0	0	0
Rizzo, Peoria	.978	24	39	50	2	8
Robidoux, Beloit	.000	1	0	0	0	0
Rover, Cedar Rapids	.972	73	142	176	9	31
Saverino, Peoria	.000	1	0	0	0	0
Smajstrla, Appleton	.982	76	159	166	6	29
Smith, Wisconsin Rapids	1.000	9	5	20	0	4
Steinmetz, Cedar Rapids	1.000	1	1	2	0	0
E. Stewart, Clinton	.946	68	136	159	17	28
Stock, Burlington	.941	11	18	14	2	1
Sutton, Burlington	.952	84	174	221	20	38
TANNER, Springfield	.970	122	234	307	17	56
Tramble, Quad Cities	.982	9	24	32	1	6
Triplett, Burlington	1.000	1	1	6	0	1
Trout, Wisconsin Rapids	.973	59	97	121	6	26
Valera, Waterloo	1.000	3	0	2	0	0
J. Wilson, Wisconsin Rapids	.962	22	34	41	3	10
Wooster, Waterloo	.000	1	0	0	0	0
D. Young, Cedar Rapids	.924	71	105	149	21	22

THIRD BASEMEN

Player and Club	Pct.	G.	PO.	A.	E.	DP.
Allen, Quad Cities	.943	35	22	60	5	2
Andrade, Burlington	.000	1	0	0	0	0
Aponte, Waterloo	.932	61	43	121	12	7
Blackwell, Clinton	.956	21	20	45	3	5
Boddy, Cedar Rapids	1.000	1	0	1	0	0
Cardenas, Wisconsin Rapids	.833	4	4	6	2	1
Carroll, Wisconsin Rapids	.818	2	4	5	2	1
CHRISTENSON, Appleton	.943	130	86	275	22	24
Clements, Springfield	.932	68	37	113	11	8
Conklin, Wausau	.867	32	23	62	13	4
R. Diaz, Waterloo	1.000	8	3	15	0	1
Duggan, Wausau	.937	106	92	204	20	13
Edwards, Waterloo	.714	3	1	4	2	0
Empting, Clinton	.000	1	0	0	0	0
Felix, Wisconsin Rapids	1.000	2	2	4	0	0
Ferro, Wisconsin Rapids	.895	90	58	138	23	8
Gambeski, Springfield	.000	4	0	0	1	0
Gergen, Burlington	.938	36	27	79	7	9
Graham, Madison	.857	4	1	5	1	0
Haberle, Cedar Rapids	.889	24	15	25	5	1
Harry, Burlington	1.000	1	0	1	0	0
Johnston, Beloit	.909	14	8	22	3	1
Keeton, Appleton	1.000	1	1	3	0	2
Kinsel, Appleton	.905	12	5	14	2	1
Kline, Peoria	.887	39	25	77	13	4
Landers, Beloit	.714	8	2	3	2	0
Lee, Cedar Rapids	.000	1	0	0	0	0
Malespin, Springfield	.933	82	60	122	13	7
Manfre, Cedar Rapids	.953	48	35	86	6	3
Marr, Clinton	.930	104	88	191	21	13
Meier, Wausau	1.000	1	0	1	0	0
Merrifield, Peoria	.896	75	47	168	25	17
Mitchell, Beloit	.714	3	0	5	2	1
Moreno, Wisconsin Rapids	1.000	10	3	21	0	3
Pellant, Wausau	.857	2	2	4	1	0
Piwnica, Beloit	.944	16	5	29	2	4
H. Quinones, Beloit	.000	1	0	0	0	0
R. Quinones, Waterloo	.948	64	44	119	9	18
Ransom, Madison	.923	115	95	251	29	27
Reece, Madison	.896	24	16	44	7	5
Rizzo, Peoria	.883	20	18	35	7	0
Robidoux, Beloit	.908	110	65	161	23	12
Roman, Waterloo	1.000	1	2	1	0	0
Rover, Cedar Rapids	1.000	2	0	3	0	0
Sabo, Cedar Rapids	.951	74	43	130	9	12
Saverino, Peoria	.813	8	4	9	3	2
Sciacca, Quad Cities	1.000	1	1	2	0	1
Smith, Peoria	.000	1	0	0	0	0
Sorce, Burlington	1.000	10	0	10	0	0
Steinmetz, Cedar Rapids	1.000	1	0	1	0	0
E. Stewart, Clinton	.949	15	9	28	2	3
Stock, Burlington	.937	63	37	142	12	5
Strom, Madison	.000	1	0	0	0	0
Thoma, Madison	1.000	1	1	0	0	0
Tramble, Quad Cities	1.000	1	0	2	0	0
Triplett, Burlington	.903	37	19	65	9	4
Utecht, Beloit	.000	1	0	0	0	0
J. Wilson, Wisconsin Rapids	.899	53	39	94	15	6
Woods, Quad Cities	.915	115	81	232	29	20
Wooster, Waterloo	1.000	14	5	21	0	3
D. Young, Cedar Rapids	1.000	1	2	1	0	0

SHORTSTOPS

Player and Club	Pct.	G.	PO.	A.	E.	DP.
Abbott, Beloit	.947	13	12	24	2	4
Anderson, Beloit	.000	1	0	0	0	0
Blackwell, Clinton	.934	110	169	327	35	50
Cardenas, Wisconsin Rapids	.868	11	13	20	5	3
Clements, Springfield	.905	65	46	126	18	18
Conklin, Wausau	.898	39	44	97	16	17
J. Cruz, Madison	.939	77	142	213	23	40
Davis, Peoria	.903	43	63	105	18	13
E. Diaz, Beloit	.911	106	173	258	42	57
R. Diaz, Waterloo	.833	1	0	5	1	1
Dillard, Burlington	.000	1	0	0	1	0
Dunston, Quad Cities	.914	114	172	326	47	48
Espinal, Clinton	.940	33	49	77	8	9
Feliz, Cedar Rapids	1.000	3	4	6	0	1
Ferro, Wisconsin Rapids	.783	5	4	14	5	0
Foit, Burlington	.911	40	61	134	19	26
Gergen, Burlington	.947	51	81	116	11	19
Johnston, Beloit	.917	5	7	4	1	3
Kinsel, Appleton	.944	53	58	112	10	15
Kirby, Beloit	.923	5	10	14	2	3
Kline, Peoria	.938	64	88	168	17	25
Kunkel, Burlington	.906	30	38	88	13	17
Manfre, Cedar Rapids	.889	5	6	10	2	2
Marquardt, Madison	.938	60	84	173	17	30
Martin, Springfield	.913	86	110	226	32	42
McLemore, Peoria	.934	37	52	104	11	17
Moreno, Wisconsin Rapids	.9475	106	181	343	29	59
Myers, Wausau	.941	99	149	330	30	48
Noboa, Waterloo	1.000	2	3	1	0	0
Pedraza, Waterloo	.910	135	188	346	53	68
Pellant, Wausau	1.000	1	0	3	0	0
Pino, Appleton	.897	99	135	187	37	29
Piwnica, Beloit	.000	2	0	0	0	0
H. Quinones, Beloit	.835	23	27	54	16	11
R. Quinones, Waterloo	1.000	5	3	10	0	2
Reece, Madison	1.000	2	2	6	0	0
RILEY, Cedar Rapids	.9476	114	162	327	27	51
Rover, Cedar Rapids	.883	30	25	43	9	6
Saverino, Peoria	1.000	3	7	7	0	2
Sciacca, Quad Cities	.932	12	21	34	4	12
S. Smith, Wisconsin Rapids	.989	28	28	65	1	13
E. Stewart, Clinton	.889	2	5	3	1	1
Tanner, Springfield	.818	8	8	10	4	2
Thoma, Madison	1.000	1	2	5	0	0
Tramble, Quad Cities	.907	9	19	30	5	6
Triplett, Burlington	.909	22	31	69	10	11
Valera, Waterloo	.889	6	3	5	1	2
Woods, Quad Cities	.931	10	7	20	2	3
Wooster, Waterloo	1.000	1	2	2	0	0
D. Young, Cedar Rapids	.000	1	0	0	0	0

OUTFIELDERS

Player and Club	Pct.	G.	PO.	A.	E.	DP.
Alonzo, Madison*	.905	13	18	1	2	0
Alpert, Waterloo*	1.000	19	27	1	0	0
Ben, Burlington	.911	81	123	0	12	0
Benza, Springfield	.959	100	198	14	9	2
Bernstine, Waterloo	.952	38	57	2	3	1
Blanke, Clinton	1.000	3	3	0	0	0
Boddy, Cedar Rapids	.000	1	0	0	0	0
Boderick, Quad Cities	.917	119	158	7	15	0
Bonham, Clinton	.968	35	58	3	2	0
Boroski, Beloit	.000	1	0	0	0	0
Briggs, Wausau	.930	66	101	5	8	1
Brito, Waterloo	.935	35	41	2	3	1
Brower, Burlington	.941	41	60	4	4	1
Cabell, Clinton	.923	17	23	1	2	0
Cangelosi, Appleton*	.978	128	262	10	6	2
Canseco, Madison	.962	25	23	2	1	0
Cardenas, Wisconsin Rapids	.600	3	3	0	2	0
Christy, Peoria	.976	57	78	2	2	0
Cimo, Clinton	.956	65	126	3	6	0
Clark, Waterloo	.976	21	37	4	1	2
Colton, Wausau	.952	40	52	7	3	1
Conklin, Wausau	1.000	2	4	0	0	0
Cordner, Quad Cities	.000	2	0	0	0	0
Cottrell, Wisconsin Rapids	1.000	2	4	0	0	0
Crawford, Peoria	.923	35	46	2	4	0
Crum, Burlington	.922	104	115	3	10	1
L. Cruz, Wisconsin Rapids*	1.000	6	4	0	0	0
Daniels, Cedar Rapids	.985	81	130	5	2	1
Davidson, Wisconsin Rapids	.969	107	181	6	6	3
Dawson, Madison	.974	115	222	5	6	1
DeValk, Wausau	.941	25	29	3	2	2
J. Diaz, Madison	.000	1	0	0	0	0
Doran, Peoria	.939	65	121	2	8	0
Edwards, Waterloo	.937	69	125	8	9	4
Farmar, Quad Cities	.972	123	269	8	8	2
Ferro, Wisconsin Rapids	1.000	12	9	0	0	0
Ficklin, Waterloo	.957	118	187	11	9	2
Finley, Beloit*	.970	129	217	9	7	2
Ford, Springfield	.958	113	178	4	8	0
Francis, Wausau*	1.000	2	1	0	0	0
Garrett, Madison	.000	1	0	0	0	0
Gergen, Burlington	1.000	11	18	1	0	0
Gertz, Waterloo*	.944	12	14	3	1	1
Gill, Madison	.000	1	0	0	0	0
Gomez, Beloit	.968	50	85	7	3	4
Gordon, Clinton	.979	49	89	3	2	0
Graham, Madison	1.000	10	14	2	0	0
Groh, Peoria*	.000	1	0	0	0	0
Gundelfinger, Springfield	1.000	6	6	0	0	0
R. Guzman, Cedar Rapids	.977	88	125	4	3	0
Haley, Wausau	.800	6	4	0	1	0
Hartsock, Peoria	.857	13	12	0	2	0
Hazard, Beloit*	.985	38	64	2	1	1
Henley, Appleton	.963	39	25	1	1	0
Hennessy, Burlington	.938	11	14	1	1	0
D. Hill, Wausau	.900	10	9	0	1	0
O. Hill, Cedar Rapids	.959	114	180	6	8	1
Hoyt, Springfield	.970	39	61	3	2	0
Hunt, Clinton*	.958	40	67	1	3	0
Jackson, Beloit*	.920	20	22	1	2	0
James, Beloit	.922	58	89	6	8	1
Karkovice, Appleton	.000	1	0	0	1	0
Keeton, Appleton	.000	1	0	0	0	0
King, Wausau*	.953	21	36	5	2	1
Knox, Cedar Rapids	.000	1	0	0	0	0
Landers, Beloit	.947	85	121	5	7	0
Lauck, Springfield*	1.000	7	11	0	0	0
Lee, Cedar Rapids	.000	4	0	0	0	0
Lewis, Peoria	.945	94	173	15	11	2
Lochner, Cedar Rapids*	1.000	1	1	0	0	0
Loscalzo, Madison*	.961	110	167	7	7	1
Mace, Burlington	.947	92	132	12	8	2
Malespin, Springfield	.986	47	65	6	1	0
Manfre, Cedar Rapids	.937	39	56	3	4	2
D. Martinez, Quad Cities*	.982	34	47	8	1	2
R. Martinez, Waterloo*	.000	1	0	0	0	0
McCulla, Springfield	1.000	18	10	0	0	0
McLaughlin, Appleton	1.000	24	20	2	0	0
Meier, Wausau	.945	82	99	4	6	1
Michel, Madison	.914	51	50	3	5	0
Miles, Appleton	.989	53	81	7	1	1
Miller, Quad Cities	.964	36	48	6	2	0
Mitchell, Beloit*	.931	27	27	0	2	0
Moreno, Wisconsin Rapids	1.000	13	31	1	0	1
Moseley, Clinton	1.000	9	10	1	0	0
Munson, Cedar Rapids	.965	30	54	1	2	1
Naber, Clinton	.961	96	143	3	6	1
Ortiz, Burlington	.930	90	126	7	10	1
Powell, Clinton	.932	34	66	2	5	1
Reece, Madison	1.000	3	6	0	0	0
Rhodes, Cedar Rapids	.900	94	110	7	13	1
Rivera, Quad Cities*	.944	8	14	3	1	0
Roebuck, Wausau	.924	52	54	7	5	1
Roman, Waterloo	1.000	6	6	0	0	0
Roomes, Quad Cities	.944	116	216	22	14	7
Salery, Wisconsin Rapids	.956	115	187	10	9	0
Sandry, Appleton	1.000	4	3	0	0	0
Scarpace, Cedar Rapids*	1.000	9	13	0	0	0
SCHEER, Wisconsin Rapids	.980	128	233	18	5	9
Sedar, Appleton	.961	83	97	2	4	1
Skoglund, Wisconsin Rapids*	.938	9	15	0	1	0
Slavin, Wausau	.963	101	139	15	6	3
K. Smith, Clinton	.947	31	68	4	4	0
T. Smith, Peoria	.968	54	85	5	3	0
Sorce, Burlington	1.000	1	1	0	0	0
Sowards, Clinton	.950	56	106	8	6	2
Stryffeler, Springfield	.977	120	205	8	5	2
Triplett, Burlington	.750	6	3	0	1	0
Tryon, Wisconsin Rapids	.833	10	5	0	1	0
Verkuilen, Wisconsin Rapids*	.918	39	45	0	4	0
Vollmer, Wausau	.933	33	52	4	4	0
Washington, Waterloo	.975	118	147	12	4	1
Weatherford, Beloit*	.976	30	38	2	1	0
White, Peoria	.962	115	267	8	11	2
Wilder, Madison	.953	115	189	16	10	0
Williams, Appleton	.958	123	218	10	10	1
J. Wilson, Wisconsin Rapids	.889	14	16	0	2	0
P. Wilson, Waterloo	1.000	3	4	0	0	0
D. Young, Cedar Rapids	1.000	7	12	2	0	1

CATCHERS

Player and Club	Pct.	G.	PO.	A.	E.	DP.	PB.
Allanson, Waterloo	.973	16	99	8	3	3	3
Anderson, Beloit	.991	28	193	25	2	3	9
Antonelli, Beloit	.980	87	640	82	15	9	11
Baez, Wausau	.979	23	160	26	4	1	2
Bell, Wausau	.991	15	93	12	1	2	1
Blume, Wausau	.962	9	47	4	2	0	2
Boddy, Cedar Rapids	.985	35	230	32	4	1	6
Boroski, Beloit	.959	30	192	19	9	2	12
Brier, Wisconsin Rapids	.972	36	211	32	7	3	6
Costello, Wisconsin Rapids	1.000	4	20	1	0	1	0
Cottrell, Wisconsin Rapids	.980	44	225	23	5	5	2
E. Diaz, Waterloo	1.000	2	5	0	0	0	0
J. Diaz, Madison	.991	33	191	30	2	4	2
Dorsett, Madison	.985	56	337	51	6	4	9
Duncan, Wausau	.980	95	637	82	15	5	28
Empting, Clinton	.976	78	427	54	12	7	7
Felix, Wisconsin Rapids	1.000	1	2	1	0	0	0
Garrett, Madison	.963	6	23	3	1	0	1
Geren, Springfield	.988	104	826	102	11	3	17
Gill, Madison	.989	56	338	38	4	5	2
Gobbo, Beloit	1.000	3	10	1	0	0	1
Gonzalez, Burlington	.983	56	413	62	8	7	4
Graupmann, Wisconsin Rapids	.993	41	250	16	2	3	11
Halberg, Clinton	.980	8	45	4	1	0	0
Harry, Burlington	1.000	1	1	0	0	0	0
Hausladen, Burlington	.977	28	198	16	5	1	3
Heath, Peoria	.971	109	637	97	22	10	21
Jimenez, Peoria	.981	23	140	13	3	1	6
Johnson, Quad Cities	.959	16	103	14	5	1	2
KARKOVICE, Appleton	.996	95	682	91	3	3	18
Loard, Clinton	1.000	9	43	3	0	1	1
Lopez, Waterloo	.977	47	300	36	8	3	12
Martelli, Waterloo	.984	22	115	12	2	3	2
McCulla, Springfield	.978	44	322	27	8	2	9
Miller, Quad Cities	.857	1	6	0	1	0	2
Mitchell, Beloit	1.000	4	11	2	0	0	2
Padia, Cedar Rapids	.979	73	517	51	12	9	16
Pellant, Wausau	.971	6	30	3	1	0	4
Pryor, Cedar Rapids	.983	56	351	42	7	4	8
Rainey, Clinton	.977	61	370	50	10	2	6
Remo, Quad Cities	.909	2	10	0	1	0	0
Roadcap, Quad Cities	.979	72	381	48	9	4	4
Roebuck, Wausau	.857	3	6	0	1	0	0
Segura, Peoria	.942	11	63	2	4	0	3
Sorce, Burlington	.971	65	442	54	15	1	14
C. Stewart, Quad Cities	.971	49	234	31	8	1	6
Tarnow, Appleton	1.000	13	57	6	0	0	1
Taylor, Appleton	.982	48	281	49	6	7	10
Tryon, Wisconsin Rapids	.982	19	134	27	3	3	3
Velazquez, Quad Cities	.937	17	96	8	7	2	5
Weiss, Wisconsin Rapids	.983	28	104	11	2	1	2
P. Wilson, Waterloo	.973	74	483	56	15	5	16

PITCHERS

Player and Club	Pct.	G.	PO.	A.	E.	DP.
Adamczak, Quad Cities	.846	9	12	10	4	1
Aldrich, Beloit	.880	28	7	15	3	2
Anderson, Wisconsin Rapids*	1.000	7	0	4	0	0
Anthony, Waterloo	.930	28	18	35	4	3
Arigoni, Springfield*	.789	27	3	12	4	2
Arney, Wisconsin Rapids	1.000	7	3	2	0	0
Atkinson, Appleton	.900	20	11	16	3	2
Babcock, Appleton*	.900	12	3	6	1	0
Baehr, Wisconsin Rapids	.000	1	0	0	0	0
Baker, Quad Cities	.841	40	14	23	7	1
Baldrick, Wausau*	.935	28	5	24	2	0
Balmer, Quad Cities	.875	17	2	5	1	1
Bargerhuff, Clinton	1.000	44	4	6	0	0
Barkley, Waterloo	1.000	24	0	5	0	0
Barnhouse, Wausau	.857	50	5	7	2	1
Bass, Burlington	.946	19	10	25	2	5
Bautista, Clinton	.854	26	10	25	6	0
Bergendahl, Wausau	.909	13	5	15	2	1
Birkbeck, Beloit	.909	7	4	6	1	0
Blevins, Quad Cities	.974	47	9	29	1	3
Blunt, Springfield	1.000	1	0	1	0	0
Bosio, Beloit	.914	17	13	19	3	3
Browne, Waterloo*	1.000	5	2	5	0	0
Buckley, Burlington	.875	17	6	8	2	0
Burnos, Wisconsin Rapids	.800	15	1	7	2	1
Burns, Wausau	.943	46	10	23	2	3
Call, Madison	.885	25	6	17	3	1
Capel, Quad Cities	1.000	8	1	7	0	0
Cherry, Springfield*	1.000	28	3	35	0	1
Chestnut, Quad Cities	.947	20	9	27	2	1
Clay, Wisconsin Rapids	.286	4	2	0	5	0
Clements, Peoria*	.905	15	3	16	2	1
Conquest, Madison	.919	23	8	26	3	1
G. Cook, Burlington	.900	9	4	14	2	3
M. Cook, Quad Cities	.935	11	6	23	2	1
Corbell, Clinton	.889	6	6	10	2	1
Correa, Appleton	.931	19	15	12	2	0
Cox, Quad Cities*	.864	10	5	14	3	1
Crim, Beloit	.963	25	8	18	1	4
DeVincenzo, Appleton*	.972	27	6	29	1	2
Dewechter, Burlington	1.000	18	0	4	0	0
Diaz, Beloit	1.000	23	2	5	0	1
Dixon, Wausau*	.881	30	8	29	5	4
Dozier, Springfield	.667	1	1	1	1	1
Droschak, Springfield	1.000	24	7	9	0	3
Dunn, Springfield	.962	27	7	18	1	0
Enriquez, Wausau	1.000	15	0	5	0	0
Escribano, Madison	.000	4	0	0	0	0
Fedor, Beloit	1.000	24	2	3	0	1
Fischer, Madison	.920	49	4	19	2	1
Fruge, Quad Cities	.947	29	12	24	2	3
Gambeski, Springfield	.000	1	0	0	0	0
Gerhardt, Burlington	1.000	6	0	3	0	0
German, Quad Cities	1.000	18	2	1	0	0
Gibson, Wisconsin Rapids	.800	15	1	3	1	0
Gladden, Clinton	.857	29	10	20	5	0
Glanz, Peoria	.778	9	1	6	2	0
Godwin, Madison*	.917	36	4	7	1	0
Gonzales, Peoria	.875	44	10	18	4	0
Gonzalves, Madison	.750	28	1	2	1	0
Grachen, Quad Cities*	.857	12	1	11	2	0
Groh, Peoria*	.917	46	7	15	2	1
Guzman, Burlington	.938	25	15	30	3	4
Gyarmati, Beloit	.000	1	0	0	0	0
Hallas, Madison	.897	25	7	28	4	2
Hartman, Burlington	.773	7	5	12	5	2
Hawley, Cedar Rapids	.964	26	8	19	1	1
Heath, Appleton*	.400	5	0	2	3	0
Henderson, Wisconsin Rapids*	1.000	11	0	8	0	0
Hernandez, Appleton*	1.000	15	2	11	0	0
Higgins, Wisconsin Rapids	1.000	6	2	4	0	0
Hinson, Wausau	1.000	9	5	7	0	0
Hobaugh, Wisconsin Rapids	.889	25	3	13	2	0
Hopkins, Burlington	.882	42	4	11	2	1
Hudson, Burlington	.714	23	0	5	2	0
Huey, 7 Mad.-43 Quad.	.875	50	4	10	2	2
Hughes, Clinton*	.850	10	2	15	3	0
Jackson, Madison	.750	10	1	2	1	0
Johnson, Burlington*	.840	22	3	18	4	1
A. Jones, Appleton	.960	55	7	17	1	0
S. Jones, Cedar Rapids*	1.000	12	1	7	0	0
Joslin, Burlington*	1.000	15	4	10	0	1
Kearns, Wisconsin	1.000	11	2	4	0	0
Keeler, Waterloo	.864	36	3	16	3	0
Kemmerling, Peoria	1.000	17	3	4	0	0
Kendrick, Madison*	.970	52	5	27	1	1
King, Peoria	.952	46	6	14	1	0
Kipper, Peoria*	.966	22	5	23	1	0
Klawitter, Wisconsin Rapids*	.882	23	3	42	6	2
Klingbeil, Wisconsin Rapids	.875	22	1	6	1	0
Klump, Wisconsin Rapids	.919	25	7	27	3	1
Knox, Cedar Rapids	.983	32	18	40	1	3
Kobernus, Madison*	1.000	8	0	2	0	0
Konderla, Cedar Rapids	.944	45	5	12	1	0
Kordish, Burlington	1.000	4	1	2	0	0
Kramer, Burlington	.880	26	3	19	3	1
Lambert, Clinton*	.889	23	5	19	3	1
Larcom, Wisconsin Rapids*	1.000	2	0	1	0	0
Leiper, Madison*	1.000	16	1	26	0	1
Lewis, Peoria	.000	1	0	0	0	0
Lochner, Cedar Rapids*	.946	23	6	29	2	1
Lockie, Quad Cities	1.000	13	1	2	0	1
Lugo, Peoria	.969	15	13	18	1	2
Maack, Wisconsin Rapids*	.943	30	12	38	3	2
Maki, Burlington	.875	12	2	5	1	0
Mancuso, Wisconsin Rapids*	.944	51	3	14	1	1
Manfre, Cedar Rapids	.000	1	0	0	0	0
Martinez, Springfield*	.929	27	6	7	1	0
Mason, Springfield	.933	54	4	10	1	0
Mattson, Clinton	1.000	42	9	17	0	1
McDonald, Waterloo	.800	13	4	4	2	0
McKenzie, Peoria	.967	23	8	21	1	2
McKeon, Appleton*	.909	19	2	18	2	0
Meister, Wausau	.000	3	0	0	0	0
Miglio, Waterloo*	.880	50	7	15	3	0
Migliore, Peoria	.955	16	6	15	1	1
Miller, Quad Cities	.000	1	0	0	0	0
Mills, Clinton*	1.000	14	4	15	0	0
Morlock, Springfield	.967	23	5	24	1	3
Moses, Appleton*	.889	51	4	12	2	0
D. Murphy, Beloit	1.000	8	1	2	0	0
R. Murphy, Cedar Rapids*	.938	36	7	23	2	2
D. Myers, Wausau	.000	2	0	0	0	0
E. Myers, Madison	1.000	31	1	2	0	0
Newman, Wausau*	.884	38	11	27	5	1
Nieves, Beloit*	1.000	12	4	5	0	0
Noles, Quad Cities	.500	3	0	2	2	0
Norman, Clinton	.914	20	8	24	3	0
Norton, Beloit	.944	13	4	13	1	0
Noworyta, Appleton	.913	34	11	10	2	0
Oakes, Clinton	1.000	15	4	12	0	0
Ortiz, Waterloo*	.889	23	1	15	2	0
Parent, Wausau	.963	16	6	20	1	2
Parham, Wisconsin Rapids*	1.000	9	4	9	0	1
Parmenter, Quad Cities	1.000	11	4	1	0	0
Parrett, Beloit	.500	10	1	3	4	0
Pena, Beloit*	.000	1	0	0	0	0
Perry, Springfield*	1.000	6	1	6	0	0
Pierorazio, Waterloo*	.889	33	4	20	3	0
Piphus, Waterloo	.920	18	6	17	2	0
Pittman, Springfield*	1.000	24	5	21	0	1
Poindexter, Waterloo	.813	26	7	19	6	0
Poloni, Wausau*	1.000	5	0	1	0	0
Raithel, Clinton	1.000	8	7	3	0	0
Rentschler, Peoria*	.941	29	5	11	1	0
Retzer, Madison	.955	23	16	26	2	2
Reuschel, Quad Cities	.933	13	9	19	2	3
Reynolds, Cedar Rapids	.870	24	4	16	3	4
Rice, Beloit	.923	27	4	8	1	1
Ritter, Waterloo	.875	31	6	22	4	1
Roman, Waterloo	.771	34	11	16	8	1
Roy, Wausau	1.000	13	4	12	0	0
Ruzek, Appleton	1.000	8	5	5	0	0
Sain, Wisconsin Rapids	1.000	10	0	1	0	0
Salazar, Peoria	.957	14	9	13	1	1
Scarpetta, Beloit*	.947	19	1	17	1	0
Scheer, Wisconsin Rapids	1.000	1	1	0	0	0
Schneider, Wausau	1.000	49	4	20	0	2
Schulte, Burlington*	.944	41	4	13	1	3
Scott, Cedar Rapids	.950	46	4	15	1	4
Serafini, Quad Cities*	.938	42	4	11	1	0
Shade, Springfield	1.000	47	7	11	0	0
Shamblin, Beloit	1.000	32	1	8	0	1
Silkwood, Springfield	.957	24	3	19	1	1
Sismondo, Wausau*	.000	2	0	0	0	0
Smith, Burlington	1.000	10	2	1	0	0
Soper, Burlington*	.800	30	3	13	4	1
Sorce, Burlington	1.000	8	3	3	0	0
Spagnola, Cedar Rapids	.960	21	6	18	1	2
STALP, Cedar Rapids	1.000	32	12	27	0	0
Steinberg, Wisconsin Rapids	1.000	4	0	1	0	0
Steinmetz, Cedar Rapids	.000	1	0	0	0	0
Street, Waterloo	.000	1	0	0	0	0
Suehr, Peoria	1.000	42	6	14	0	1
Taft, Clinton*	.795	27	8	23	8	1
Tanner, Appleton	1.000	4	0	2	0	0
Tavarez, Clinton	.000	1	0	0	0	0
J. Taylor, Appleton	.000	1	0	0	0	0
T. Taylor, Wausau	.919	24	6	28	3	0
Teahan, Beloit	.939	13	14	17	2	1
Thompson, Wisconsin Rapids	1.000	7	4	8	0	0
Thurberg, Springfield	.769	6	2	8	3	0
Timberlake, Peoria	.808	23	6	15	5	2
Torres, Beloit	.867	11	2	11	2	1
L. Trujillo, Cedar Rapids	.938	52	4	11	1	2
M. Trujillo, Appleton	.946	29	27	43	4	3

PITCHERS—Continued

Player and Club	Pct.	G.	PO.	A.	E.	DP.
Tuller, Quad Cities	1.000	8	2	2	0	0
Valdez, Peoria	1.000	6	0	1	0	0
Waldron, Burlington	1.000	10	0	1	0	0
Weibel, Clinton	.846	11	2	9	2	1
Weir, Clinton	.853	16	11	18	5	0
Wex, Madison	1.000	16	6	12	0	1
Williams, Beloit	.917	41	5	6	1	1
J. Young, Springfield*	.921	23	10	25	3	2

The following players do not have any recorded accepted chances at the positions indicated and therefore are not listed in the fielding averages for those particular positions: S. Anderson, ss; Andrade, 3b; Baehr, p; Boddy, of; Boroski, of; Brier, 1b; Cordner, of; J. Diaz, of; Empting, 3b; Escribano, p; Gambeski, p; Garrett, of; Gill, of; Groh, of; Gyarmati, p; Keeton, of; Knox, of; Lee, 3b, of; Lewis, p; Manfre, p; R. Martinez, of; Meister, p; Miller, p; D. Myers, p; Pena, p; Piwnica, ss; H. Quinones, 3b; Robidoux, 2b; Saverino, 2b; Sismondo, p; Skoglund, 1b; T. Smith, 3b; Steinmetz, p; Street, p; Strom, 3b; Tavarez, p; J. Taylor, p; Trout, 1b; Utecht, 3b; Wooster, 2b; D. Young, ss.

CLUB PITCHING

Club	ERA.	G.	CG.	ShO.	Sv.	IP.	H.	R.	ER.	HR.	HB.	BB.	Int. BB.	SO.	WP.	Bk.
Appleton	2.83	137	27	7	33	1154.0	955	449	363	66	23	466	16	997	58	11
Waterloo	3.44	140	34	11	29	1157.1	1077	590	442	72	61	523	21	976	100	13
Quad Cities	3.50	139	19	6	41	1191.0	1194	621	463	83	41	399	32	776	62	16
Madison	3.52	138	21	13	25	1152.2	1151	534	451	96	45	381	22	848	56	15
Springfield	3.67	139	21	12	27	1208.1	1098	624	493	103	38	525	30	1128	88	9
Cedar Rapids	3.68	140	22	13	35	1192.1	1091	583	488	88	31	496	25	1089	71	9
Wisconsin Rapids	3.75	138	38	6	27	1155.2	1071	587	481	116	40	507	21	914	70	17
Clinton	3.86	138	29	7	25	1181.0	1210	632	506	82	32	475	40	843	73	18
Beloit	4.08	137	29	9	25	1152.1	1107	663	523	80	53	548	8	1022	86	10
Burlington	4.10	139	17	10	28	1172.1	1106	669	534	92	50	573	31	1007	85	15
Peoria	4.34	139	23	4	23	1172.0	1221	721	565	90	42	445	11	802	90	17
Wausau	5.04	138	21	5	21	1145.0	1202	784	641	132	62	628	31	932	105	12

PITCHERS' RECORDS

(Leading Qualifiers for Earned-Run Average Leadership—112 or More Innings)

*Throws lefthanded.

Pitcher—Club	W.	L.	Pct.	ERA.	G.	GS.	CG.	GF.	ShO.	Sv.	IP.	H.	R.	ER.	HR.	HB.	BB.	Int. BB.	SO.	WP.
Bass, Burlington	9	5	.643	1.68	19	18	5	1	1	0	118.0	81	39	22	3	2	42	1	105	7
Fischer, Madison	13	9	.591	2.28	49	7	3	31	1	8	114.1	100	35	29	9	4	35	5	110	7
Morlock, Springfield	10	4	.714	2.37	23	14	6	3	4	1	140.2	99	44	37	15	1	20	0	143	8
M. Trujillo, Appleton	15	8	.652	2.40	29	29	11	0	1	0	198.2	146	75	53	7	6	63	3	148	14
DeVincenzo, Appleton*	18	6	.750	2.50	27	26	8	0	2	0	179.2	141	56	50	10	1	74	1	193	6
Roman, Waterloo	6	7	.462	2.56	34	12	1	12	0	5	126.1	103	49	36	8	5	56	5	132	13
J. Young, Springfield*	15	4	.789	2.70	23	23	3	0	2	0	133.1	87	56	40	4	0	104	4	162	12
Knox, Cedar Rapids	16	5	.762	2.72	32	18	8	5	3	0	158.2	152	58	48	12	5	31	3	94	7
Guzman, Burlington	12	8	.600	2.97	25	24	2	1	1	0	154.2	135	68	51	8	4	52	1	146	3
Klawitter, Wisconsin Rapids*	10	5	.667	2.99	23	21	10	1	2	0	156.1	146	64	52	10	5	71	4	90	2

Departmental Leaders: G—A. Jones, 55; W—DeVincenzo, 18; L—Taft, 16; Pct.—A. Jones, .917; GS—M. Trujillo, 29; CG—Anthony, Crim, M. Trujillo, 11; GF—A. Jones, 50; ShO—Morlock, 4; Sv.—Huey, 27; IP—M. Trujillo, 198.2; H—Taft, 182; R—Dixon, 102; ER—Dixon, 97; HR—Dixon, Hobaugh, 20; HB—Burns, 19; BB—J. Young, 104; IBB—Bargarhuff, 12; SO—DeVincenzo, 193; WP—Pierorazio, 19.

(All Pitchers—Listed Alphabetically)

Pitcher—Club	W.	L.	Pct.	ERA.	G.	GS.	CG.	GF.	ShO.	Sv.	IP.	H.	R.	ER.	HR.	HB.	BB.	Int. BB.	SO.	WP.
Adamczak, Quad Cities	3	3	.500	3.15	9	9	2	0	1	0	60.0	51	24	21	3	1	15	0	29	3
Aldrich, Beloit	7	4	.636	4.17	28	11	0	8	0	5	103.2	114	59	48	5	4	35	0	96	7
Anderson, Wisconsin Rapids*	0	4	.000	6.82	7	6	0	1	0	0	30.1	36	28	23	4	2	17	0	46	3
Anthony, Waterloo	9	12	.429	3.36	28	26	11	0	1	0	166.0	163	89	62	12	9	66	3	133	5
Arigoni, Springfield*	1	6	.143	4.86	27	7	0	10	0	0	70.1	76	46	38	10	2	27	1	58	13
Arney, Wisconsin Rapids	4	2	.667	2.04	7	5	1	1	0	0	39.2	33	17	9	3	2	18	1	28	0
Atkinson, Appleton	6	2	.750	3.60	20	5	2	11	0	2	80.0	86	37	32	6	0	13	1	50	4
Babcock, Appleton*	2	5	.286	2.44	12	10	1	2	0	0	44.1	42	15	12	2	1	7	0	38	0
Baehr, Wisconsin Rapids	0	0	.000	18.00	1	0	0	0	0	0	2.0	2	4	4	0	0	4	0	2	5
Baker, Quad Cities	11	7	.611	3.06	40	12	2	16	0	1	150.0	125	63	51	13	9	58	3	98	2
Baldrick, Wausau*	10	6	.625	3.40	28	24	9	2	2	0	164.0	168	70	62	16	5	54	1	125	4
Balmer, Quad Cities	3	3	.500	3.36	17	8	0	5	0	1	59.0	59	27	22	3	1	24	1	30	2
Bargerhuff, Clinton	5	1	.833	1.00	44	0	0	37	0	10	71.2	62	15	8	1	6	27	12	81	2
Barkley, Waterloo	5	2	.714	2.68	24	0	0	21	0	9	37.0	27	11	11	1	1	14	1	65	4
Barnhouse, Wausau	7	5	.583	3.14	50	0	0	41	0	14	66.0	41	34	23	3	4	46	6	105	7
Bass, Burlington	9	5	.643	1.68	19	18	5	1	1	0	118.0	81	39	22	3	2	42	1	105	7
Bautista, Clinton	8	12	.400	4.27	26	26	6	0	3	0	151.2	154	95	72	7	8	68	5	113	12
Bergendahl, Wausau	1	8	.111	6.20	13	11	0	1	0	0	65.1	61	57	45	5	3	55	1	47	14
Birkbeck, Beloit	2	4	.333	3.43	7	7	0	0	0	0	42.0	35	22	16	2	2	17	1	38	3
Blevins, Quad Cities	7	6	.538	3.39	47	4	1	24	0	5	93.0	105	40	35	2	1	36	9	42	5
Blunt, Springfield	0	0	.000	3.00	1	0	0	0	0	0	3.0	4	5	1	1	0	3	0	2	0
Bosio, Beloit	3	10	.231	5.60	17	17	3	0	0	0	107.2	125	82	67	9	4	41	0	71	8
Browne, Waterloo*	2	1	.667	4.18	5	5	1	0	0	0	28.0	21	16	13	6	2	11	0	23	5
Buckley, Burlington	3	2	.600	1.73	17	0	0	13	0	2	41.2	28	16	8	1	2	18	1	42	4
Burnos, Wisconsin Rapids	0	0	.000	3.96	15	1	0	7	0	0	36.1	34	22	16	3	1	17	3	21	4
Burns, Wausau	6	9	.400	4.43	46	6	3	16	0	1	134.0	124	88	66	12	19	72	7	91	18
Call, Madison	9	6	.600	3.48	25	25	3	0	2	0	150.0	152	72	58	10	13	35	0	93	5
Capel, Quad Cities	3	2	.600	2.42	8	6	1	1	0	1	44.2	32	15	12	6	6	14	0	35	5
Cherry, Springfield*	10	6	.625	3.58	28	27	3	0	0	0	166.0	166	80	66	14	2	56	2	132	6
Chestnut, Quad Cities	9	8	.529	3.85	20	20	1	0	0	0	121.2	127	83	52	13	1	34	2	89	9
Clay, Wisconsin Rapids	0	4	.000	6.00	4	4	0	0	0	0	21.0	18	17	14	3	0	12	0	15	3
Clements, Peoria*	4	7	.364	4.48	15	14	4	0	0	0	92.1	113	56	46	5	3	24	1	67	8
Conquest, Madison	11	9	.550	3.81	23	23	3	0	0	0	137.0	167	68	58	13	8	32	0	71	3
G. Cook, Burlington	4	2	.667	4.10	9	9	0	0	0	0	52.2	50	28	24	4	2	24	0	59	1
M. Cook, Quad Cities	5	5	.500	3.34	11	11	0	0	0	0	70.0	69	38	26	4	4	19	0	40	2
Corbell, Clinton	0	2	.000	4.88	6	5	0	1	0	0	31.1	38	22	17	3	1	11	1	23	2
Correa, Appleton	3	9	.250	4.45	19	18	0	0	0	0	95.0	81	59	47	7	3	61	1	87	11
Cox, Quad Cities*	5	2	.714	2.95	10	10	3	0	1	0	64.0	60	31	21	2	1	27	1	35	5
Crim, Beloit	11	10	.524	3.47	25	23	11	2	2	0	163.1	150	83	63	14	12	50	1	154	8
DeVincenzo, Appleton*	18	6	.750	2.50	27	26	8	0	2	0	179.2	141	56	50	10	1	74	1	193	6
Dewechter, Burlington	1	2	.333	3.78	18	1	0	14	0	3	33.1	39	17	14	4	2	11	5	21	0

Pitcher—Club	W.	L.	Pct.	ERA.	G.	GS.	CG.	GF.	ShO.	Sv.	IP.	H.	R.	ER.	HR.	HB.	BB.	Int. BB.	SO.	WP.
Diaz, Beloit	3	3	.500	3.24	23	0	0	20	0	4	33.1	25	14	12	2	1	16	0	39	2
Dixon, Wausau*	2	11	.154	8.31	30	19	1	6	0	0	105.0	123	102	97	20	5	100	1	76	13
Dozier, Springfield	0	0	.000	1.35	1	1	0	0	0	0	6.2	3	2	1	0	0	5	0	9	1
Droschak, Springfield	1	5	.167	8.48	24	6	0	3	0	0	63.2	91	76	60	8	6	46	7	51	9
Dunn, Springfield	2	7	.222	4.45	27	15	1	3	1	1	95.0	86	66	47	12	6	52	1	84	6
Enriquez, Wausau	0	1	.000	8.10	15	0	0	7	0	0	23.1	40	28	21	11	2	10	0	15	3
Escribano, Madison	0	0	.000	2.89	4	0	0	2	0	1	9.1	6	4	3	2	0	1	0	4	0
Fedor, Beloit	1	1	.500	4.72	24	0	0	19	0	5	34.1	34	23	18	2	1	34	0	46	10
Fischer, Madison	13	9	.591	2.28	49	7	3	31	1	8	114.1	100	35	29	9	4	35	5	110	7
Fruge, Quad Cities	8	11	.421	3.70	29	23	8	4	1	3	163.0	177	83	67	8	4	48	11	111	4
Gambeski, Springfield	0	0	.000	0.00	1	0	0	1	0	0	1.0	1	0	0	0	0	0	0	0	0
Gerhardt, Burlington	0	0	.000	5.68	6	0	0	1	0	0	12.2	18	10	8	1	1	9	1	8	2
German, Quad Cities	1	3	.250	4.83	18	2	0	7	0	2	31.2	40	23	17	2	5	11	0	22	1
Gibson, Wisconsin Rapids	3	0	1.000	2.95	15	2	0	7	0	2	42.2	38	20	14	4	1	25	1	34	5
Gladden, Clinton	7	3	.700	2.77	29	2	1	10	0	1	94.1	71	35	29	6	3	29	3	83	4
Glanz, Peoria	1	5	.167	10.03	9	9	0	0	0	0	35.0	43	44	39	3	5	28	0	19	3
Godwin, Madison*	3	2	.600	2.27	36	4	1	6	0	0	79.1	69	28	20	3	2	31	4	68	8
Gonzales, Peoria	2	4	.333	5.00	44	2	0	16	0	2	86.1	85	72	48	6	5	42	0	67	15
Gonzalves, Madison	1	3	.250	4.19	28	1	0	12	0	1	43.0	42	21	20	8	0	19	1	36	4
Grachen, Quad Cities*	4	3	.571	4.38	12	7	1	1	0	0	51.1	67	32	25	5	1	13	0	27	3
Groh, Peoria*	5	3	.625	2.31	46	0	0	31	0	10	62.1	44	21	16	4	2	29	1	45	2
Guzman, Burlington	12	8	.600	2.97	25	24	2	1	1	0	154.2	135	68	51	8	4	52	1	146	3
Gyarmati, Beloit	0	0	.000	45.00	1	0	0	0	0	0	1.0	5	5	5	0	1	3	0	0	0
Hallas, Madison	9	10	.474	4.09	25	25	5	0	1	0	151.2	160	81	69	15	4	35	2	92	5
Hartman, Burlington	3	4	.429	4.25	7	7	2	0	1	0	48.2	43	24	23	6	5	19	0	25	3
Hawley, Cedar Rapids	11	9	.550	3.89	26	26	3	0	0	0	152.2	173	83	66	10	7	31	1	99	5
Heath, Appleton*	1	0	1.000	4.91	5	5	0	0	0	0	22.0	16	15	12	3	0	19	0	20	1
Henderson, Wisconsin Rapids*	4	4	.500	4.66	11	11	3	0	1	0	56.0	52	34	29	7	2	18	0	49	4
Hernandez, Appleton*	6	5	.545	4.41	15	15	1	0	0	0	83.2	79	45	41	7	2	47	2	73	4
Higgins, Wisconsin Rapids	0	3	.000	10.61	6	4	0	0	0	0	18.2	27	23	22	6	2	8	0	10	1
Hinson, Wausau	2	4	.333	4.62	9	9	2	0	0	0	48.2	48	29	25	7	3	25	1	32	6
Hobaugh, Wisconsin Rapids	11	8	.579	3.35	25	24	7	1	1	0	147.2	116	71	55	20	3	68	0	120	6
Hopkins, Burlington	3	9	.250	4.18	42	2	1	29	0	12	79.2	66	42	37	8	2	66	7	67	10
Hudson, Burlington	5	4	.556	4.91	23	1	1	13	0	4	40.1	48	24	22	4	2	16	3	28	1
Huey, 7 Mad.-43 Quad Cities	2	4	.333	3.28	50	1	0	39	0	27	68.2	57	31	25	4	3	29	5	53	6
Hughes, Clinton*	1	5	.167	4.29	10	10	1	0	0	0	50.1	55	29	24	5	1	32	0	39	6
Jackson, Madison	0	2	.000	7.90	10	1	0	3	0	0	13.2	18	14	12	0	2	17	0	12	3
Johnson, Burlington*	7	5	.583	3.87	22	21	1	1	1	1	118.2	97	68	51	10	8	61	0	127	10
A. Jones, Appleton	11	1	.917	0.97	55	0	0	50	0	22	102.0	54	13	11	1	3	39	2	124	4
S. Jones, Cedar Rapids*	3	2	.600	4.99	12	8	0	2	0	0	39.2	39	26	22	4	1	41	0	36	4
Joslin, Burlington*	2	2	.500	5.10	15	8	0	4	0	0	47.2	41	34	27	4	1	25	2	48	7
Kearns, Wisconsin Rapids	1	3	.250	4.19	11	4	0	4	0	0	34.1	42	21	16	3	1	9	1	15	3
Keeler, Waterloo	6	6	.500	3.46	36	5	1	20	1	8	83.1	85	49	32	3	5	35	4	66	9
Kemmerling, Peoria	2	1	.667	3.00	17	0	0	8	0	0	36.0	39	14	12	0	0	12	2	19	3
Kendrick, Madison*	9	7	.563	3.87	52	3	1	29	0	4	83.2	90	42	36	5	2	27	3	65	3
King, Peoria	3	8	.273	3.15	46	0	0	29	0	10	68.2	68	33	24	3	2	20	3	41	5
Kipper, Peoria*	5	8	.385	4.65	22	21	2	0	0	0	127.2	112	77	66	17	1	52	1	105	3
Klawitter, Wisconsin Rapids*	10	5	.667	2.99	23	21	10	1	2	0	156.1	146	64	52	10	5	71	4	90	2
Klingbeil, Wisconsin Rapids	4	1	.800	2.32	22	0	0	15	0	4	54.1	46	15	14	3	2	14	0	39	3
Klump, Wisconsin Rapids	13	7	.650	3.40	25	20	8	0	0	0	161.2	150	77	61	16	8	77	3	116	10
Knox, Cedar Rapids	16	5	.762	2.72	32	18	8	5	3	0	158.2	152	58	48	12	5	31	3	94	7
Kobernus, Madison*	0	0	.000	6.94	8	0	0	3	0	0	11.2	19	10	9	3	0	5	0	12	2
Konderla, Cedar Rapids	1	4	.200	5.05	45	3	2	18	0	4	101.2	101	62	57	14	3	44	1	91	5
Kordish, Burlington	1	2	.333	7.52	4	4	0	0	0	0	20.1	36	20	17	6	0	4	0	16	0
Kramer, Burlington	6	8	.429	5.16	26	26	4	0	1	0	132.2	131	97	76	9	4	92	1	113	14
Lambert, Clinton*	3	4	.429	3.34	23	5	1	12	0	0	97.0	100	45	36	8	1	38	3	67	2
Larcom, Wisconsin Rapids*	0	1	.000	14.73	2	1	0	0	0	0	3.2	9	7	6	3	0	1	0	2	0
Leiper, Madison*	5	4	.556	3.74	16	15	0	0	0	0	79.1	89	43	33	4	2	37	0	60	4
Lewis, Peoria	0	0	.000	3.00	1	0	0	0	0	0	3.0	2	1	1	0	0	3	0	2	0
Lochner, Cedar Rapids*	7	11	.389	4.56	23	22	3	1	0	0	124.1	102	67	63	10	3	72	3	131	6
Lockie, Quad Cities	0	1	.000	5.19	13	0	0	9	0	0	17.1	22	12	10	4	0	1	0	11	1
Lugo, Peoria	8	5	.615	2.52	15	15	7	0	0	0	107.0	82	39	30	10	6	28	0	96	6
Maack, Wisconsin Rapids*	11	9	.550	3.66	30	23	8	4	0	1	164.2	155	77	67	13	4	43	3	153	8
Maki, Burlington	0	1	.000	8.10	12	3	0	3	0	0	30.0	38	33	27	1	1	27	2	21	5
Mancuso, Wisconsin Rapids*	6	10	.375	3.39	51	0	0	48	0	20	82.1	78	37	31	6	0	39	3	98	6
Manfre, Cedar Rapids	0	0	.000	36.00	1	0	0	1	0	0	1.0	3	4	4	1	0	0	0	1	0
Martinez, Springfield*	5	2	.714	3.05	27	3	1	13	0	1	76.2	56	32	26	10	1	44	0	62	5
Mason, Springfield	9	3	.750	2.65	54	0	0	46	0	13	74.2	63	26	22	3	1	16	4	79	3
Mattson, Clinton	8	5	.615	0.97	42	0	0	40	0	14	74.1	40	10	8	2	0	25	5	85	7
McDonald, Waterloo	2	7	.222	4.88	13	8	1	3	0	0	51.2	61	36	28	4	2	22	5	33	3
McKenzie, Peoria	4	4	.500	3.92	23	16	2	1	0	0	96.1	102	56	42	10	2	35	0	62	11
McKeon, Appleton*	5	5	.500	2.62	19	19	1	0	1	0	99.2	74	34	29	5	1	58	2	110	3
Meister, Wausau	0	1	.000	7.71	3	1	0	1	0	0	9.1	14	8	8	0	0	5	0	11	0
Miglio, Waterloo*	6	4	.600	3.84	50	0	0	31	0	6	79.2	69	40	34	4	9	38	1	81	7
Migliore, Peoria	3	8	.273	6.53	16	12	3	3	0	0	71.2	88	61	52	2	8	39	0	37	12
Miller, Quad Cities	0	0	.000	0.00	1	0	0	1	0	0	2.0	4	0	0	0	0	1	0	0	0
Mills, Clinton*	2	3	.400	5.05	14	5	1	3	0	0	51.2	59	32	29	5	1	40	2	30	6
Morlock, Springfield	10	4	.714	2.37	23	14	6	3	4	1	140.2	99	44	37	15	1	20	0	143	8
Moses, Appleton*	6	5	.545	3.10	51	1	0	28	0	7	107.1	100	47	37	8	3	38	3	66	7
D. Murphy, Beloit	0	0	.000	4.01	8	0	0	4	0	1	24.2	21	14	11	1	0	14	0	22	1
R. Murphy, Cedar Rapids*	6	10	.375	3.33	36	18	2	6	1	2	140.2	120	66	52	7	3	69	3	137	8
D. Myers, Wausau	0	0	.000	10.80	2	0	0	2	0	0	1.2	2	2	2	0	0	0	0	2	0
E. Myers, Madison	2	2	.500	1.95	31	0	0	27	0	9	37.0	18	9	8	2	1	18	2	52	4
Newman, Wausau*	6	9	.400	4.13	38	14	3	13	0	2	130.2	134	77	60	17	5	57	6	132	9
Nieves, Beloit*	7	1	.875	1.30	12	10	2	2	2	0	69.1	43	11	10	5	2	15	0	89	0
Noles, Quad Cities	0	1	.000	5.25	3	3	0	0	0	0	12.0	19	11	7	1	0	5	0	12	0
Norman, Clinton	9	7	.563	3.52	20	20	8	0	3	0	135.1	133	65	53	5	2	43	4	75	4
Norton, Beloit	4	3	.571	3.28	13	12	3	0	0	0	74.0	76	39	27	3	5	27	1	60	6
Noworyta, Appleton	8	3	.727	2.80	34	5	0	13	0	1	93.1	93	38	29	9	3	29	1	39	2
Oakes, Clinton	2	7	.222	4.41	15	13	2	1	0	0	81.2	92	47	40	10	1	19	1	45	2
Ortiz, Waterloo*	11	2	.846	3.35	23	22	4	1	2	0	137.0	133	67	51	11	3	46	0	137	3
Parent, Wausau	6	9	.400	5.59	16	16	1	0	0	0	85.1	108	67	53	12	2	30	2	38	5

Pitcher—Club	W.	L.	Pct.	ERA.	G.	GS.	CG.	GF.	ShO.	Sv.	IP.	H.	R.	ER.	HR.	HB.	BB.	Int. BB.	SO.	WP.
Parham, Wisconsin Rapids*	2	4	.333	3.79	9	6	1	2	1	0	38.0	28	17	16	3	2	29	2	25	3
Parmenter, Quad Cities	1	2	.333	4.54	11	6	0	4	0	0	39.2	43	29	20	1	3	9	0	32	2
Parrett, Beloit	2	2	.500	4.02	10	8	0	1	0	0	47.0	40	26	21	3	0	29	0	34	12
Pena, Beloit*	0	0	.000	0.00	1	0	0	0	0	0	1.0	0	0	0	0	0	2	0	0	0
Perry, Springfield*	1	1	.500	2.22	6	2	0	2	0	1	24.1	17	6	6	2	0	5	0	31	0
Pierorazio, Waterloo*	7	8	.467	3.95	33	17	3	7	1	0	123.0	125	81	54	4	8	72	1	60	19
Piphus, Waterloo	10	2	.833	2.25	18	17	4	0	2	0	100.0	63	27	25	4	5	46	0	89	9
Pittman, Springfield*	7	8	.467	4.38	24	23	2	1	1	0	125.1	132	70	61	11	3	57	3	90	5
Poindexter, Waterloo	8	6	.571	4.13	26	18	6	4	1	0	113.1	115	64	52	5	9	59	0	71	12
Poloni, Wausau*	0	0	.000	0.00	5	0	0	5	0	0	6.0	4	0	0	0	0	1	0	5	0
Raithel, Clinton	0	1	.000	5.70	8	0	0	3	0	0	23.2	32	17	15	3	1	12	0	12	1
Rentschler, Peoria*	1	6	.143	4.30	29	5	0	8	0	0	73.1	74	46	35	10	1	30	0	66	7
Retzer, Madison	5	8	.385	3.43	23	21	3	0	2	0	144.1	130	59	55	15	3	57	2	111	5
Reuschel, Quad Cities	3	4	.429	2.42	13	13	0	0	0	0	70.2	73	29	19	3	1	9	0	56	0
Reynolds, Cedar Rapids	6	4	.600	3.99	24	10	0	7	0	2	76.2	74	39	34	6	0	18	2	74	4
Rice, Beloit	2	4	.333	4.46	27	2	0	8	0	1	74.2	79	49	37	9	5	34	1	52	8
Ritter, Waterloo	4	7	.364	3.68	31	10	2	7	0	1	110.0	111	61	45	10	3	55	1	85	10
Roman, Waterloo	6	7	.462	2.56	34	12	1	12	0	5	126.1	103	49	36	8	5	56	5	132	13
Roy, Wausau	3	4	.429	7.69	13	13	0	0	0	0	59.2	82	60	51	8	2	40	2	37	6
Ruzek, Appleton	6	0	1.000	1.66	8	4	3	2	0	0	43.1	38	13	8	0	0	13	0	47	2
Sain, Wisconsin Rapids	0	0	.000	5.59	10	1	0	3	0	0	19.1	23	15	12	4	1	16	0	15	0
Salazar, Peoria	3	8	.273	5.16	14	12	2	0	0	0	82.0	100	61	47	4	2	23	1	43	3
Scarpetta, Beloit*	6	6	.500	3.89	19	18	3	0	1	0	106.1	113	61	46	7	1	38	0	77	3
Scheer, Wisconsin Rapids	0	0	.000	0.00	1	0	0	1	0	0	1.0	0	0	0	0	0	0	0	0	0
Schneider, Wausau	3	7	.300	4.54	49	0	0	22	0	4	107.0	118	68	54	8	4	52	4	90	9
Schulte, Burlington*	8	3	.727	5.77	41	2	1	18	0	5	73.1	84	52	47	8	4	36	2	49	6
Scott, Cedar Rapids	6	6	.500	3.04	46	6	2	30	2	10	106.2	84	39	36	6	0	41	3	127	10
Serafini, Quad Cities*	1	3	.250	3.34	42	1	0	10	0	2	59.1	48	35	22	4	0	42	2	42	8
Shade, Springfield	9	5	.643	2.86	47	0	0	33	0	10	78.2	69	39	25	2	5	32	4	85	7
Shamblin, Beloit	3	3	.500	4.17	32	0	0	19	0	5	58.1	69	36	27	4	3	14	0	40	2
Silkwood, Springfield	9	3	.750	3.17	24	12	4	3	0	0	113.2	102	47	40	7	10	39	4	114	9
Sismondo, Wausau*	0	0	.000	0.00	2	1	0	1	0	0	8.1	4	0	0	0	1	2	0	8	0
Smith, Burlington	0	0	.000	9.98	10	0	0	3	0	0	15.1	31	18	17	5	2	5	1	15	2
Soper, Burlington*	4	10	.286	4.38	30	13	0	8	0	0	115.0	111	69	56	9	4	55	4	94	9
Sorce, Burlington	1	0	1.000	1.23	8	0	0	6	0	0	14.2	6	2	2	1	1	5	0	11	0
Spagnola, Cedar Rapids	5	5	.500	4.00	21	21	1	0	1	0	99.0	100	59	44	10	4	56	1	92	9
Stalp, Cedar Rapids	8	3	.727	3.09	32	8	1	10	0	1	105.0	87	46	36	6	0	39	3	92	4
Steinberg, Wisconsin Rapids	0	0	.000	12.60	4	0	0	4	0	0	5.0	8	7	7	3	2	0	0	5	0
Steinmetz, Cedar Rapids	0	1	.000	27.00	1	0	0	1	0	0	0.1	1	1	1	0	0	1	0	1	1
Street, Waterloo	0	0	.000	0.00	1	0	0	0	0	0	2.0	1	0	0	0	0	3	0	1	1
Suehr, Peoria	6	7	.462	3.45	42	7	1	18	0	1	88.2	96	43	34	5	4	23	2	54	4
Taft, Clinton*	6	16	.273	4.71	27	25	3	2	1	0	153.0	182	101	80	11	1	71	3	84	10
Tanner, Appleton	0	1	.000	3.00	4	0	0	3	0	1	3.0	3	1	1	0	0	3	0	1	0
Tavarez, Clinton	0	0	.000	27.00	1	0	0	0	0	0	0.2	2	3	2	1	0	0	0	0	0
J. Taylor, Appleton	0	0	.000	4.50	1	0	0	1	0	0	2.0	2	1	1	1	0	2	0	1	0
T. Taylor, Wausau	9	9	.500	5.44	24	24	2	0	0	0	130.2	131	94	79	13	7	79	0	118	11
Teahan, Beloit	4	7	.364	5.97	13	13	1	0	0	0	72.1	83	58	48	5	4	36	0	43	4
Thompson, Wisconsin Rapids	2	2	.500	2.88	7	5	0	1	0	0	40.2	30	14	13	2	2	21	0	31	4
Thurberg, Springfield	1	5	.167	5.86	6	6	1	0	0	0	35.1	46	29	23	4	1	19	0	26	4
Timberlake, Peoria	7	10	.412	4.75	23	23	2	0	1	0	127.0	156	86	67	11	1	44	0	68	5
Torres, Beloit	2	8	.200	4.04	11	11	4	0	1	0	64.2	62	37	29	6	0	43	0	60	0
L. Trujillo, Cedar Rapids	7	4	.636	2.62	52	0	0	37	0	16	86.0	55	33	25	2	5	53	5	114	8
M. Trujillo, Appleton	15	8	.652	2.40	29	29	11	0	1	0	198.2	146	75	53	7	6	63	3	148	14
Tuller, Quad Cities	2	3	.400	7.18	8	4	0	0	0	0	26.1	34	25	21	5	1	12	0	21	4
Valdez, Peoria	0	1	.000	4.30	6	3	0	2	0	0	14.2	17	11	7	0	0	13	0	11	3
Waldron, Burlington	2	1	.667	1.96	10	0	0	7	0	1	23.0	23	8	5	0	3	6	0	12	1
Weibel, Clinton	2	6	.250	4.54	11	11	3	0	0	0	69.1	82	43	35	5	0	26	0	61	4
Weir, Clinton	3	10	.231	5.78	16	16	3	0	0	0	95.0	108	73	61	10	6	34	1	45	11
Wex, Madison	4	5	.444	3.28	16	12	2	3	1	1	85.0	73	38	31	7	3	24	1	53	3
Williams, Beloit	9	5	.643	4.58	41	5	2	25	1	4	74.2	33	44	38	3	8	100	4	101	12
J. Young, Springfield*	15	4	.789	2.70	23	23	3	0	2	0	133.1	87	56	40	4	0	104	4	162	12

BALKS—Maack, 7; Conquest, Kipper, Ritter, 4 each; Baker, DeVincenzo, Dixon, Dunn, Gonzales, Norman, Parmenter, Roman, Salazar, Scarpetta, Taft, M. Trujillo, 3 each; Bass, Bautista, Burns, Call, Cherry, M. Cook, Fischer, Fruge, Guzman, Hernandez, Hopkins, Hughes, Joslin, Kearns, Kramer, Lochner, Moses, Newman, Nieves, Oakes, Ortiz, Pierorazio, Pittman, Retzer, Sain, Spagnola, Timberlake, 2 each; Baldrick, Balmer, Blevins, Bosio, Capel, G. Cook, Correa, Crim, Droschak, Enriquez, Gibson, Gladden, Godwin, Grachen, Hawley, Hobaugh, Huey, Johnson, Keeler, Kendrick, Klawitter, Klingbeil, Klump, Knox, Koberus, Leiper, Lugo, Maki, McDonald, McKenzie, Meister, Morlock, E. Myers, Noles, Norton, Parent, Rentschler, Reynolds, Rice, Schulte, Scott, Shamblin, Suehr, T. Taylor, Thompson, L. Trujillo, Valdez, Waldron, Weibel, Weir, 1 each.

COMBINATION SHUTOUTS—DeVincenzo-Jones, Noworyta-Jones, Hernandez-Jones, Appleton; Nieves-Williams, Parrett-Aldrich, Beloit; Cook-Joslin, Johnson-Joslin, Kramer-Dewechter, Kramer-Hudson, Johnson-Hopkins, Burlington; Murphy-Knox-Scott, Hawley-Knox-L. Trujillo, Murphy-Stalp, Lochner-Knox, Hawley-L. Trujillo, Knox-Murphy, Cedar Rapids; Godwin-Kendrick, Conquest-Kendrick, Godwin-Gonsalves, Wex-Godwin-Kendrick, Hallas-Gonsalves, Conquest-Leiper-Kendrick, Madison; Kipper-Rentschler, Kipper-Suehr, McKenzie-Groh, Peoria; Chestnut-Fruge, Fruge-Grachen-Huey, Cook-Serafini-Baker, Quad Cities; Cherry-Martinez-Mason, Young-Dunn-Martinez, Young-Mason, Perry-Shade, Springfield; Piphus-Barkley, Poindexter-Barkley-Roman, Piphus-Poindexter-Keeler, Waterloo; Bergendahl-Newman, Baldrick-Barnhouse, Dixon-Barnhouse, Wausau; Hobaugh-Mancuso, Wisconsin Rapids.

NO-HIT GAME—Bautista, Clinton, defeated Appleton, 2-0 (seven innings), May 9.

NY-Pennsylvania League

CLASS A

CHAMPIONSHIP WINNERS IN PREVIOUS YEARS

Year	Club	Pct.
1939	Olean*	.631
1940	Olean*	.625
1941	Jamestown	.618
	Bradford (2nd)†	.549
1942	Jamestown*	.672
1943	Lockport	.591
	Wellsville (3rd)†	.532
1944	Lockport	.608
	Jamestown (2nd)†	.565
1945	Batavia*	.677
1946	Jamestown‡	.672
	Batavia‡	.672
1947	Jamestown*	.690
1948	Lockport*	.603
1949	Bradford*	.635
1950	Hornell	.653
	Olean (2nd)†	.568
1951	Olean	.622
	Hornell (3rd)†	.568
1952	Hamilton	.659
	Jamestown (2nd)†	.643
1953	Jamestown*	.704
1954	Corning*	.621
1955	Hamilton*	.656
1956	Wellsville*	.617
1957	Wellsville	.632
	Erie (2nd)†	.598
1958	Wellsville	.556
	Geneva (2nd)†	.548
1959	Wellsville†	.635
1960	Erie	.643
	Wellsville (2nd)†	.535
1961	Geneva	.616
	Olean (4th)†	.512
1962	Jamestown	.580
	Auburn (3rd)†	.521
1963	Auburn	.585
	Batavia (3rd)†	.485
1964	Auburn§	.622
1965	Binghamton	.677
	Binghamton	.607
1966	Auburn x	.620
	Binghamton	.646
1967	Auburn	.667
1968	Auburn	.645
	Oneonta (2nd)*	.558
1969	Oneonta	.662
1970	Auburn	.623
1971	Oneonta	.662
1972	Niagara Falls	.686
1973	Auburn	.667
1974	Oneonta	.768
1975	Newark	.688
	Newark	.714
1976	Elmira	.727
	Elmira	.703
1977	Oneonta y	.671
	Batavia	.600
1978	Oneonta	.729
	Geneva z	.718
1979	Geneva	.725
	Oneonta z	.618
1980	Oneonta y	.662
	Geneva	.649
1981	Oneonta y	.658
	Jamestown	.649
1982	Oneonta	.566
	Niagara Falls y	.553

*Won championship and four-club playoff. †Won four-club playoff. ‡Jamestown and Batavia declared co-champions; Batavia defeated Jamestown in final of four-club playoff. §Won championship and two-club playoff. xWon split-season playoff. yLeague divided into Eastern and Western Divisions; won playoff. zLeague divided into Wrigley and Yawkey Divisions; won playoff. (NOTE—Known as Pennsylvania-Ontario-New York League from 1939 through 1956.)

STANDING OF CLUBS AT CLOSE OF SEASON, SEPTEMBER 2

EASTERN DIVISION

Club	W.	L.	T.	Pct.	G.B.
Utica (Independent)	48	26	0	.649	....
Little Falls (Mets)	48	27	0	.640	½
Auburn (Astros)	43	31	0	.581	5
Elmira (Red Sox)	38	36	0	.514	10
Oneonta (Yankees)	32	44	0	.421	17
Watertown (Pirates)	21	55	0	.276	28

WESTERN DIVISION

Club	W.	L.	T.	Pct.	G.B.
Newark (Orioles)	48	26	0	.649	....
Jamestown (Expos)	38	36	0	.514	10
Erie (Cardinals)	37	38	0	.493	11½
Geneva (Cubs)	33	40	0	.452	14½
Batavia (Indians)	32	43	0	.427	16½
Niagara Falls (White Sox)	29	45	0	.392	19

COMPOSITE STANDING OF CLUBS AT CLOSE OF SEASON, SEPTEMBER 2

Club	Uti.	New.	L.F.	Aub.	Jam.	Elm.	Eri.	Gen.	Bat.	Ont.	N.F.	Wat.	W.	L.	T.	Pct.	G.B.
Utica (Independent)	....	2	4	5	3	6	3	4	4	5	1	11	48	26	0	.649	....
Newark (Orioles)	2	....	2	3	5	2	6	11	5	3	5	4	48	26	0	.649	....
Little Falls (Mets)	5	2	....	4	4	7	3	3	1	11	2	6	48	27	0	.640	½
Auburn (Astros)	3	5	4	...	2	4	2	2	3	7	2	9	43	31	0	.581	5
Jamestown (Expos)	1	1	0	2	....	2	6	7	7	2	6	4	38	36	0	.514	10
Elmira (Red Sox)	4	2	2	8	2	....	0	2	2	8	3	5	38	36	0	.514	10
Erie (Cardinals)	1	2	1	2	8	4	....	3	5	1	6	4	37	38	0	.493	12
Geneva (Cubs)	0	2	1	0	2	1	7	....	8	2	7	3	33	40	0	.452	14½
Batavia (Indians)	0	4	3	1	3	2	5	3	....	2	7	2	32	43	0	.427	16½
Oneonta (Yankees)	4	1	4	3	2	2	3	2	2	....	2	7	32	44	0	.421	17
Niagara Falls (White Sox)	3	5	2	2	5	1	3	2	4	2	....	0	29	45	0	.392	19
Watertown (Pirates)	3	0	4	1	0	5	0	1	2	1	4	....	21	55	0	.276	28

Major league affiliations in parentheses.

Playoffs—Utica defeated Newark, two games to one, to win league championship.

Regular-Season Attendance—Auburn, 55,328; Batavia, 27,766; Elmira, 63,382; Erie, 47,111; Geneva, 29,542; Jamestown, 36,109; Little Falls, 29,867; Newark, 25,001; Niagara Falls, 28,301; Oneonta, 37,384; Utica, 42,779; Watertown, 78,460. Total, 501,030. Playoffs, 2,780.

Managers—Auburn, Bob Hartsfield; Batavia, Brian Doyle; Elmira, Dick Berardino; Erie, Joe Rigoli; Geneva, Tony Franklin; Jamestown, Moby Benedict; Little Falls, Mike Cubbage; Newark, Art Mazmanian; Niagara Falls, Fred Nelson; Oneonta, Bill Livesey; Utica, Jim Gattis; Watertown, Bill Bryk.

All-Star Team—1B—Rey Martinez, Batavia; 2B—Rich Mattocks, Oneonta; 3B—Vic Madden, Batavia; SS—Rey Quinones, Elmira; OF—George Chadwick, Jamestown; Stanley Jefferson, Little Falls; John Rigos, Erie; and Paul Thoutsis, Elmira; C—Carl Nichols, Newark, (tie) Tom Pagnozzi, Erie; and Robbie Wine, Auburn; RHP—John Boyles, Little Falls; Jeff Innis, Little Falls; LHP—Rich Sauveur, Watertown; Hector Stewart, Elmira; DH-Don Jacoby, Utica; Manager-of-the-Year—Mike Cubbage, Little Falls.

(Compiled by Howe News Bureau, Boston, Mass.)

CLUB BATTING

Club	Pct.	G.	AB.	R.	OR.	H.	TB.	2B.	3B.	HR.	RBI.	GW.	SH.	SF.	HP.	BB.	Int. BB.	SO.	SB.	CS.	LOB.
Utica	.313	74	2530	526	336	793	1229	122	13	96	473	42	39	16	20	314	7	362	86	26	546
Newark	.281	74	2515	481	387	706	1137	144	19	83	423	38	14	33	33	365	15	542	75	40	589
Jamestown	.268	74	2473	369	366	664	959	108	29	43	316	33	20	23	22	281	10	405	40	26	538
Little Falls	.267	75	2584	432	335	690	1010	98	18	62	374	43	11	19	22	304	12	472	90	30	566
Erie	.266	74	2515	409	444	668	1008	109	9	71	349	30	23	20	11	288	9	527	67	27	542
Elmira	.261	73	2482	408	406	648	961	107	16	58	349	32	32	23	29	285	10	559	65	13	568
Geneva	.258	73	2451	376	379	632	878	116	14	34	308	27	22	18	29	285	10	563	97	44	521

CLUB BATTING

Club	Pct.	G.	AB.	R.	OR.	H.	TB.	2B.	3B.	HR.	RBI.	GW.	SH.	SF.	HP.	BB.	Int. BB.	SO.	SB.	CS.	LOB.
Auburn	.257	74	2526	415	366	650	977	122	26	51	355	33	11	20	19	286	10	503	101	17	532
Niagara Falls	.250	74	2405	356	423	602	895	108	19	49	310	28	28	26	22	283	7	589	39	18	532
Batavia	.242	75	2429	351	419	587	940	74	12	85	299	26	23	13	23	299	11	488	50	40	508
Watertown	.236	76	2551	332	481	603	881	99	13	51	275	18	24	19	30	241	6	604	69	25	513
Oneonta	.234	76	2450	329	442	573	814	80	19	41	285	27	23	24	21	315	7	610	98	15	560

INDIVIDUAL BATTING

(Leading Qualifiers for Batting Championship—205 or More Plate Appearances)

*Bats lefthanded. †Switch-hitter.

Player and Club	Pct.	G.	AB.	R.	H.	TB.	2B.	3B.	HR.	RBI.	GW.	SH.	SF.	HP.	BB.	Int. BB.	SO.	SB.	CS.
Chadwick, George, Jamestown	.387	44	181	41	70	99	7	2	6	28	5	4	4	0	18	2	14	7	3
Jacoby, Donald, Utica*	.386	70	272	67	105	185	12	1	22	74	7	0	2	1	28	0	36	2	1
Coyle, Rock, Utica	.381	71	260	66	99	165	16	1	16	59	6	5	3	1	21	0	27	18	3
Moss, Barry, Utica†	.359	74	281	67	101	169	19	2	15	66	2	0	2	5	48	3	32	7	1
Birriel, Jose, Elmira*	.351	59	194	39	68	119	19	1	10	56	7	2	0	3	21	5	35	1	1
Mucha, Keith, Newark	.344	54	183	42	63	106	14	4	7	38	3	1	0	5	30	1	38	5	1
Wolfe, Edward, Utica	.338	72	281	55	95	144	17	1	10	65	4	0	2	2	26	1	34	2	1
Thielker, Dave, Newark*	.330	62	218	51	72	139	18	2	15	55	3	0	5	6	26	3	26	2	3
Smith, Timothy, Newark	.329	68	219	43	72	106	13	3	5	37	2	1	2	2	26	0	48	2	5
Jelks, Patrick, Elmira	.324	62	207	35	67	112	7	1	12	35	3	1	0	1	19	0	51	10	3

Departmental Leaders: G—Mattocks, Roman, 75; AB—Caraballo, 308; R—Jacoby, Moss, 67; H—Jacoby, 105; TB—Jacoby, 185; 2B—Caraballo, 21; 3B—Mitchell, 7; HR—Jacoby, 22; RBI—Jacoby, 74; GWRBI—Caraballo, 9; SH—Gourlay, 8; SF—Freytes, Lockwood, 6; HP—Kramer, 9; BB—Saccocia, 58; IBB—Englehart, 6; SO—Kent, 91; SB—Jefferson, 35; CS—Kramer, Lockwood, 10.

(All Players—Listed Alphabetically)

Player and Club	Pct.	G.	AB.	R.	H.	TB.	2B.	3B.	HR.	RBI.	GW.	SH.	SF.	HP.	BB.	Int. BB.	SO.	SB.	CS.
Abone, Anthony, Jamestown	.000	1	3	0	0	0	0	0	0	0	0	0	0	0	0	0	0	0	0
Afenir, M. Troy, Auburn	.115	7	26	2	3	3	0	0	0	0	0	0	0	0	0	0	15	0	0
Agostinelli, Salvatore, Erie	.260	21	73	13	19	31	5	2	1	16	2	0	1	0	9	0	4	3	0
Allanson, Andrew, Batavia	.262	51	145	27	38	41	3	0	0	6	0	4	0	0	25	0	16	3	0
Amaral, Richard, Geneva	.253	67	269	63	68	94	17	3	1	24	1	1	1	2	45	2	47	22	7
Anderson, J. David, Jamestown*	.333	27	84	14	28	37	6	0	1	12	0	1	0	0	7	1	13	0	0
Angelo, Mark, Erie*	.310	48	187	34	58	100	10	1	10	37	4	0	3	0	21	3	32	4	3
Antone, Ralph, Jamestown	.329	42	140	31	46	61	7	1	2	25	3	0	1	1	33	0	13	2	1
Barragan, Gerardo, Newark†	.203	58	148	19	30	35	5	0	0	10	1	3	1	1	14	0	28	4	2
Barton, Shawn, Utica	.273	46	132	27	36	41	2	0	1	15	2	6	0	0	25	0	15	2	0
Baumgartner, Thomas, N. Falls*	.282	23	78	15	22	29	4	0	1	13	0	0	0	2	10	0	18	0	0
Belcik, Keith, Little Falls	.222	23	72	6	16	26	4	0	2	12	2	0	0	0	3	0	19	0	0
Berger, Michael, Watertown	.258	74	260	44	67	128	19	3	12	45	3	1	3	6	40	1	85	5	1
Birkofer, Kevin, Jamestown*	.247	73	239	33	59	84	10	0	5	31	6	2	5	1	33	2	31	0	0
Birriel, Jose, Elmira*	.351	59	194	39	68	119	19	1	10	56	7	2	0	3	21	5	35	1	1
Blair, Fred, Jamestown	.310	63	216	29	67	107	13	3	7	40	1	0	4	3	33	1	33	2	3
Breslin, Michael, Erie	.190	31	79	12	15	27	3	0	3	11	0	0	0	0	19	0	30	1	2
Brito, Bernardo, Batavia	.243	60	206	18	50	87	10	3	7	34	2	2	1	5	15	1	65	5	1
Brown, Kenneth, Watertown	.197	48	132	23	26	40	2	0	4	15	1	3	1	0	14	0	49	5	2
Bruno, Angelo, Newark	.313	19	48	12	15	28	7	0	2	13	0	0	0	1	4	0	8	2	0
Burks, Ellis, Elmira	.241	53	174	30	42	57	9	0	2	23	3	2	0	1	17	0	43	9	0
Burton, Steven, Geneva*	.226	52	164	25	37	72	5	3	8	30	2	1	0	2	17	0	54	12	4
Caianiello, John, Niagara Falls*	.278	27	79	8	22	24	2	0	0	5	0	1	0	1	10	0	19	1	1
Cain, Michael, Newark	.179	9	28	5	5	6	1	0	0	1	1	1	0	0	7	0	5	3	0
Canning, Paul, Niagara Falls	.000	4	10	0	0	0	0	0	0	1	0	0	0	0	0	0	3	0	0
Caraballo, Wilmer, Little Falls	.299	74	308	50	92	152	21	0	13	66	9	1	3	2	11	0	55	6	2
Carpenter, Douglas, Oneonta	.250	7	8	4	2	6	1	0	1	3	0	0	0	1	8	0	3	1	0
Carrasco, Claudio, Batavia†	.174	24	46	6	8	11	0	0	1	1	0	0	0	0	7	0	15	0	2
Cawthon, D. Christopher, Batavia*	.268	43	149	24	40	80	7	0	11	26	4	2	3	1	23	2	26	2	1
Chadwick, George, Jamestown	.387	44	181	41	70	99	7	2	6	28	5	4	4	0	18	2	14	7	3
Chestna, Mark, Oneonta	.000	16	15	0	0	0	0	0	0	0	0	0	0	0	2	0	9	1	0
Cobb, Robert, Jamestown*	.285	68	246	37	70	110	10	6	6	34	2	2	1	5	28	0	21	0	3
Connerty, Kenneth, Batavia	.229	51	118	12	27	31	4	0	0	6	2	2	1	0	15	0	25	1	3
Cortez, Johnny, Watertown	.281	71	235	33	66	85	7	0	4	26	2	1	1	2	33	2	41	17	3
Coyle, Rock, Utica	.381	71	260	66	99	165	16	1	16	59	6	5	3	1	21	0	27	18	3
Cunningham, Herman, Oneonta	.192	32	78	11	15	19	1	0	1	8	0	0	0	3	10	0	31	0	0
Cusack, David, Newark	.236	31	110	22	26	49	6	1	5	17	2	0	1	1	15	0	27	3	0
Dahse, David, Newark	.210	30	62	12	13	15	0	1	0	6	1	3	0	1	4	0	18	3	3
Davidson, Todd, Watertown*	.202	63	208	33	42	78	13	4	5	24	1	1	1	2	17	2	48	7	2
Davila, Peter, Watertown	.125	13	24	3	3	7	1	0	1	3	0	2	0	0	2	0	11	0	0
DeJesus, Jorge, Batavia*	.196	17	46	4	9	12	0	0	1	2	0	1	0	0	8	1	3	0	2
Delucci, Ronald, Watertown	.255	73	278	33	71	103	10	2	6	30	3	2	5	3	15	0	72	7	4
Denis, Orlando, Auburn	.239	15	46	7	11	21	2	1	2	11	1	0	1	0	6	0	15	1	0
Depiano, Jeffrey, Jamestown	.233	54	180	23	42	69	11	2	4	27	1	1	0	2	12	0	49	0	0
Diaz, Eduardo, Batavia	.125	10	16	2	2	2	0	0	0	0	0	0	0	0	3	0	1	0	0
Dichiaro, Louis, Newark*	.283	50	159	34	45	59	8	3	0	28	3	2	4	1	28	0	36	9	1
Dickerson, James, Geneva	.290	38	124	26	36	54	9	0	3	18	0	3	0	7	22	1	29	3	1
Dinkel, Jeffrey, Little Falls	.249	69	241	49	60	96	11	2	7	30	8	0	1	3	41	1	58	4	2
Ditto, Bradley, Geneva†	.328	40	122	16	40	49	6	0	1	11	2	4	0	0	15	0	20	7	4
Doerr, Jeffrey, Newark	.264	55	193	41	51	92	9	1	10	43	3	0	4	4	28	0	58	4	3
Dougherty, Mark, Erie	.252	57	234	40	59	82	14	0	3	23	0	3	1	1	19	2	45	10	1
Dreizler, Robin, Utica	.138	20	29	3	4	8	1	0	1	3	0	1	0	0	4	0	5	0	0
Dyrek, David, Auburn*	.260	45	150	32	39	52	10	0	1	25	2	0	2	0	32	0	24	8	3
Edwards, David, Auburn	.240	69	258	36	62	90	14	4	2	39	1	0	5	3	15	0	60	5	0
Englehart, William, Oneonta*	.258	57	163	18	42	65	9	1	4	19	1	0	2	1	32	6	37	2	1
Estrada, Asdrubal, Elmira	.254	50	173	25	44	59	4	4	1	15	2	5	0	2	7	0	33	6	0
Eurton, James, Watertown	.211	55	171	16	36	47	6	1	1	13	0	3	1	2	10	0	53	2	1
Fairbanks, Shane, Auburn*	.190	6	21	3	4	10	3	0	1	4	2	0	0	0	0	0	0	0	0
Fermin, Felix, Watertown	.197	67	234	27	46	54	6	1	0	14	0	3	1	3	16	0	30	5	1
Fernandez, Carlos, Batavia	.100	7	10	1	1	1	0	0	0	0	0	0	0	0	1	0	6	0	0
Fortaleza, Raymond, Jamestown	.222	20	63	6	14	16	2	0	0	3	0	0	0	0	3	0	21	1	0
Frederick, David, Oneonta*	.217	44	143	15	31	54	3	1	6	17	1	0	0	2	17	0	51	2	0
Freytes, Hector, Geneva	.246	62	232	33	57	102	15	0	10	44	3	2	6	0	12	1	59	1	0

Player and Club	Pct.	G.	AB.	R.	H.	TB.	2B.	3B.	HR.	RBI.	GW.	SH.	SF.	HP.	BB.	Int. BB.	SO.	SB.	CS.
Funk, Gregory, Oneonta	.265	9	34	5	9	12	3	0	0	7	1	2	0	0	9	0	4	0	1
Gattis, James, Utica	.000	3	5	0	0	0	0	0	0	0	0	0	0	0	0	0	1	0	0
Glynn, Dennis, Little Falls	.192	15	52	11	10	16	3	0	1	5	1	0	0	0	6	0	7	1	0
Gonzalez, Robinson, Jamestown	.213	53	183	18	39	42	2	1	1	11	1	2	1	3	6	0	26	4	3
Goodman, Adolph, Geneva	.262	33	122	7	32	37	5	0	0	9	1	0	1	1	4	0	29	2	5
Gordon, Kevin, Watertown	.000	19	1	0	0	0	0	0	0	0	0	0	0	0	0	0	0	0	0
Gourlay, Timothy, Niagara Falls†	.210	74	233	34	49	68	10	0	3	20	2	8	2	0	24	0	58	10	5
Graham, Michael, Elmira*	.146	24	41	5	6	11	3	1	0	2	1	1	0	1	5	0	15	0	0
Hale, Demarlo, Elmira	.286	61	220	33	63	80	7	2	2	42	6	0	3	2	15	0	32	10	3
Hall, R. David, Elmira	.177	34	79	15	14	18	1	0	1	6	0	1	1	2	14	1	31	0	0
Hall, Mark, Jamestown	.182	30	55	10	10	13	1	1	0	5	1	0	1	1	8	0	12	1	0
Hamilton, Alvin, Elmira	.193	41	114	17	22	31	4	1	1	12	1	1	1	0	20	0	36	4	0
Hawkins, Eugene, Little Falls	.198	56	131	27	26	29	3	0	0	9	1	2	0	1	17	1	37	9	3
Hendershot, Robert, Utica	.298	60	215	51	64	116	6	2	14	49	6	2	0	1	37	0	42	7	3
Hernandez, Felipe, Geneva	.289	32	90	17	26	42	7	0	3	14	1	2	0	2	13	0	31	0	0
Hickey, James, Niagara Falls	.300	21	10	2	3	4	1	0	0	1	0	0	0	0	4	0	6	0	0
Hodge, Simon, Auburn	.235	32	98	16	23	32	3	0	2	13	1	0	1	1	12	0	22	5	1
Holecek, Joseph, Niagara	.229	18	48	3	11	13	2	0	0	5	0	0	0	0	0	0	13	0	0
Houp, Scott, Auburn	.228	49	171	31	39	67	8	1	6	22	2	0	0	2	27	1	40	5	0
Howard, Brian, Watertown	.304	5	23	3	7	9	2	0	0	5	0	0	0	0	2	0	4	0	0
Jackson, Lavern, Elmira	.130	39	69	7	9	15	1	1	1	6	0	0	0	1	8	0	16	2	1
Jacoby, Donald, Utica*	.386	70	272	67	105	185	12	1	22	74	7	0	2	1	28	0	36	2	1
Jefferson, Stanley, Little Falls	.320	71	281	57	90	124	5	1	9	36	2	0	2	0	40	1	55	35	8
Jelks, Patrick, Elmira	.324	62	207	35	67	112	7	1	12	35	3	1	0	1	19	0	51	10	3
Jenson, Roger, Niagara Falls	.297	68	239	41	71	125	19	4	9	53	6	1	2	3	26	2	55	4	1
Jimenez, Luis, Oneonta	.000	2	3	0	0	0	0	0	0	0	0	0	0	0	0	0	2	0	0
Jiminez, Francisco, Watertown*	.375	3	8	0	3	3	0	0	0	1	1	0	0	0	1	0	1	1	0
Johnson, John, Geneva	.211	34	109	25	23	27	4	0	0	9	0	0	0	5	21	0	46	4	1
Johnson, Stanley, Oneonta	.238	13	21	3	5	7	0	1	0	1	0	1	0	1	3	0	7	1	0
Jones, Alan, Oneonta	.234	72	239	24	56	83	11	2	4	32	1	1	3	2	32	0	41	3	0
Jongewaard, Steven, Elmira	.234	34	94	9	22	26	2	1	0	11	1	0	2	1	10	0	30	0	1
Kane, Michael, Elmira*	.317	53	142	28	45	63	8	2	2	19	2	2	2	3	34	1	20	2	0
Karr, Jeff, Little Falls	.197	29	71	10	14	20	1	1	1	9	0	0	0	0	5	0	13	0	0
Kaull, Kurtis, Erie	.261	72	276	41	72	89	9	1	2	25	4	5	3	0	34	0	33	8	2
Kavanaugh, Tim, Erie	.195	44	123	11	24	33	4	1	1	11	3	0	0	0	11	0	36	4	1
Kelly, Roberto, Oneonta	.216	48	167	17	36	47	1	2	2	17	5	1	0	0	12	0	20	12	2
Kelly, Ronald, Newark*	.283	63	226	46	64	121	10	1	15	54	3	0	3	1	39	4	33	1	1
Kent, Wesley, Niagara Falls	.239	61	226	29	54	103	11	1	12	48	3	0	4	1	15	1	91	0	0
Killings, Jeffrey, Batavia*	.111	5	9	0	1	1	0	0	0	0	0	0	0	0	1	0	5	0	0
Knapp, Timothy, Newark*	.150	16	20	5	3	3	0	0	0	1	0	1	0	0	11	0	4	3	1
Kordeck, David, Watertown	.059	8	17	2	1	1	0	0	0	0	0	0	0	1	4	0	11	0	0
Kramer, Joseph, Batavia	.274	73	252	47	69	135	7	4	17	55	6	0	2	9	38	0	58	12	10
Krsnich, Nicholas, Newark	.500	26	2	0	1	1	0	0	0	0	0	0	0	0	0	0	0	0	0
Krynitsky, Mark, Utica	.229	66	179	28	41	63	9	2	3	31	3	5	1	1	26	1	46	3	1
Lauck, Jeffrey, Erie†	.200	13	15	6	3	4	1	0	0	1	0	0	0	0	3	0	5	0	0
Lawrence, Andy, Little Falls	.280	68	261	39	73	110	9	2	8	40	5	1	1	4	13	0	48	3	2
Lee, Lawrence, Utica†	.316	67	234	29	74	96	9	2	3	36	6	4	3	1	14	2	23	3	6
Lee, Manuel, Little Falls*	.289	17	45	10	13	13	0	0	0	5	0	2	0	0	9	0	11	2	1
Lewallen, Richard, Oneonta	.282	69	259	37	73	96	13	2	2	37	4	3	5	1	22	0	38	7	0
Lipinski, Steven, Auburn	.128	17	39	5	5	12	4	0	1	5	0	0	0	0	8	0	13	1	0
Lockwood, Richard, Newark†	.293	74	280	51	82	138	18	1	12	44	4	1	6	1	47	1	61	18	10
Lopez, John, Oneonta	.000	4	2	0	0	0	0	0	0	0	0	0	0	0	0	0	2	0	0
Lopez, Juan, Batavia	.176	11	34	0	6	6	0	0	0	1	1	0	0	0	1	0	7	0	0
Lopez, Michael, Newark*	.296	49	169	27	50	72	8	1	4	19	1	0	1	1	15	1	29	8	4
Lyden, Mitchell, Oneonta	.148	47	128	14	19	20	1	0	0	7	0	2	2	2	12	0	36	3	0
Lynn, Charles, Newark	.240	49	146	23	35	52	8	0	3	22	5	0	3	2	17	0	32	2	2
Lyon, Bruce, Little Falls*	.000	2	3	1	0	0	0	0	0	0	0	0	0	0	1	0	0	0	0
Machuca, Freddy, Oneonta	.209	20	43	6	9	14	3	1	0	5	1	0	2	1	7	0	9	3	0
Mackin, Brian, Auburn	.287	36	115	13	33	47	8	0	2	16	1	0	1	0	3	0	22	2	1
Madden, Victor, Batavia*	.266	72	244	44	65	121	8	0	16	44	4	0	3	0	57	3	36	1	3
Mahler, Gary, Jamestown*	.226	66	261	23	59	84	9	5	2	36	4	1	3	1	13	3	45	1	2
Maloney, Chris, Little Falls*	.297	59	192	26	57	81	11	2	3	26	3	0	3	0	34	3	31	3	1
Martelli, Vincent, Batavia	.208	12	24	4	5	9	1	0	1	5	1	0	0	0	8	0	6	0	1
Martin, Rodney, Auburn	.238	12	42	8	10	13	1	1	0	5	0	0	0	0	6	0	10	1	1
Martinez, David, Geneva*	.261	64	241	35	63	97	15	2	5	33	6	1	2	0	40	1	52	16	6
Martinez, Modesto, Watertown	.281	65	242	38	68	81	5	1	2	23	2	0	4	4	23	0	34	7	3
Martinez, Rey, Batavia*	.281	57	203	36	57	102	4	1	13	44	3	1	0	2	41	3	36	1	5
Martinez, Wilfredo, Erie	.000	2	2	0	0	0	0	0	0	0	0	0	0	0	0	0	1	0	0
Mattocks, Richard, Oneonta	.271	75	258	49	70	89	7	3	2	26	3	3	5	1	42	0	46	34	4
McGilvray, James, Auburn	1.000	1	1	1	1	4	0	0	1	1	0	0	0	0	0	0	0	0	0
McKnight, Jeff, Little Falls*	.217	39	115	10	25	30	3	1	0	9	0	1	0	0	15	1	18	1	1
Merenda, Robert, Utica*	.172	19	29	6	5	7	2	0	0	1	0	1	0	0	4	0	13	1	0
Mitchell, Thomas, Auburn	.264	70	292	59	77	118	9	7	6	26	4	4	1	2	34	0	67	16	4
Molnar, Richard, Oneonta	.208	7	24	7	5	8	0	0	1	1	0	0	0	0	4	0	5	1	0
Moncada, L. Rafael, Watertown	.196	26	56	8	11	15	1	0	1	3	0	4	0	1	7	0	15	1	1
Montgomery, Donald, Jamestown*	.286	45	154	19	44	67	8	3	3	18	1	0	0	1	12	0	31	1	1
Moore, Charles, Niagara Falls	.221	60	199	38	44	66	7	3	3	18	1	4	3	3	33	1	59	3	1
Morena, Russell, Little Falls*	.183	27	60	14	11	20	1	1	2	10	3	1	1	1	9	0	4	3	0
Mosley, Michael, Newark	.182	18	33	2	6	9	3	0	0	2	0	0	0	1	5	0	12	0	0
Moss, Barry, Utica†	.359	74	281	67	101	169	19	2	15	66	2	0	2	5	48	3	32	7	1
Mucha, Keith, Newark	.344	54	183	42	63	106	14	4	7	38	3	1	0	5	30	1	38	5	1
Nichols, Carl, Newark	.290	66	217	40	63	92	14	0	5	26	5	1	3	4	36	1	59	4	3
O'Dell, James, Auburn*	.318	50	151	30	48	85	8	1	9	46	6	1	4	1	27	5	17	8	1
O'Dell, Jeffrey, Niagara Falls	.241	58	170	24	41	67	7	2	5	20	2	5	1	1	20	0	38	4	0
O'Donnell, Steven, Oneonta†	.385	4	13	3	5	5	0	0	0	0	0	0	0	0	2	0	1	2	0
Packer, William, Erie	.248	66	214	46	53	94	8	0	11	31	2	1	1	2	42	1	63	5	1
Pagnozzi, Thomas, Erie	.310	45	168	28	52	81	9	1	6	22	2	2	2	0	14	0	34	3	0
Parker, Marvin, Little Falls*	.272	71	265	49	72	117	11	5	8	44	2	2	4	2	49	4	33	8	3
Pasquale, Jeffrey, Erie	.210	59	195	28	41	60	8	1	3	17	0	3	2	1	23	0	42	2	2
Perez, Edgar, Niagara Falls	.261	71	253	32	66	87	12	3	1	27	4	4	5	2	29	0	62	5	3
Peruso, Steven, Oneonta	.269	31	104	11	28	48	3	1	5	22	2	0	0	2	11	0	22	0	0
Picchioni, Joseph, Utica	.176	18	17	5	3	3	0	0	0	3	0	0	0	1	4	0	10	1	0
Pitts, Daryl, Utica*	.307	53	163	34	50	80	11	2	5	29	3	0	1	1	22	0	8	9	2

Player and Club	Pct.	G.	AB.	R.	H.	TB.	2B.	3B.	HR.	RBI.	GW.	SH.	SF.	HP.	BB.	Int. BB.	SO.	SB.	CS.
Pitty, Marcelino, Oneonta	.150	22	40	2	6	8	0	1	0	2	0	2	0	1	1	0	14	2	1
Pleis, W. Scott, Erie	.321	60	209	27	67	81	8	0	2	32	3	3	1	0	14	1	48	3	6
Pomeranz, Patrick, Niagara Falls	.242	58	190	28	46	79	10	1	7	27	5	0	2	3	23	0	62	1	2
Quade, G. Michael, Watertown	.100	3	10	0	1	1	0	0	0	0	0	0	0	0	0	0	3	0	1
Quinonez, Rey, Elmira	.295	67	234	38	69	116	11	0	12	55	2	0	4	1	22	1	33	1	1
Ramos, Alfonso, Batavia	.000	6	11	0	0	0	0	0	0	0	0	0	0	0	0	0	10	0	0
Reboulet, James, Erie	.235	12	34	6	8	11	0	0	1	2	0	0	0	0	5	0	1	2	1
Remo, Jeffrey, Geneva	.229	49	144	18	33	44	8	0	1	15	0	0	1	1	22	1	48	5	0
Richmond, Seth, Auburn*	.296	65	223	39	66	91	14	1	3	30	5	0	0	1	28	1	19	16	4
Rigos, John, Erie	.319	73	279	60	89	153	10	0	18	54	7	1	2	3	35	1	48	10	4
Rivera, Jose, Oneonta	.254	55	185	30	47	81	8	1	8	26	2	3	2	0	14	0	54	4	1
Rivera, Jose, Geneva*	.300	67	230	31	69	76	5	1	0	24	5	2	2	0	26	2	17	8	4
Roberts, John, Elmira	.237	43	139	26	33	42	4	1	1	8	1	6	0	2	10	0	20	9	0
Robinette, D. Kelly, Batavia	.154	45	104	16	16	16	0	0	0	5	0	5	0	1	9	0	9	2	2
Robinson, Brian, Utica	.265	58	170	37	45	62	8	0	3	17	1	7	2	2	23	0	31	10	2
Robinson, S. Michael, Erie	.284	72	264	38	75	118	15	2	8	51	2	3	1	2	20	1	71	10	1
Rodriguez, Ramon, Auburn	.273	54	183	28	50	74	4	4	4	28	4	3	0	2	11	0	31	5	1
Rojas, Octavio, Newark*	.185	28	54	5	10	14	2	1	0	7	1	0	0	1	13	4	20	2	1
Roman, Miguel, Batavia	.251	75	283	34	71	112	14	0	9	27	0	3	1	0	10	0	57	2	3
Rood, Nelson, Auburn	.233	73	292	46	68	86	11	2	1	26	2	1	1	1	30	0	39	16	0
Rosado, Manuel, Jamestown	.143	17	49	5	7	12	1	2	0	7	2	2	0	1	7	0	11	2	0
Rossi, Thomas, Erie	.202	56	163	19	33	44	5	0	2	16	1	2	3	2	19	0	34	2	3
Ruffner, William, Oneonta	.189	39	106	11	20	28	2	0	2	9	0	1	0	1	14	0	51	1	2
Saccocia, Michael, Jamestown	.286	73	273	65	78	109	15	2	4	21	4	5	2	3	58	1	45	18	9
Sandry, William, Niagara Falls	.308	62	224	42	69	93	12	0	4	32	1	0	2	4	36	0	27	2	0
Sciacca, Christopher, Geneva†	.246	68	280	35	69	84	10	1	1	33	1	5	1	5	9	0	64	4	4
Sheffield, Ralph, Utica*	.298	54	181	39	54	66	6	0	2	16	0	8	0	1	26	0	18	20	3
Sherlock, Glenn, Auburn*	.328	35	125	15	41	51	5	1	1	18	0	1	1	1	9	2	17	2	0
Sickles, Joseph, Niagara Falls	.207	32	92	18	19	24	2	0	1	7	0	2	0	1	19	2	15	1	0
Simmons, Michael, Oneonta	.226	35	84	13	19	20	1	0	0	8	0	3	0	0	12	0	17	5	2
Simon, Kelly, Watertown	.000	20	1	0	0	0	0	0	0	0	0	0	0	0	0	0	0	0	0
Smith, Dan, Watertown	.255	53	164	22	42	58	7	0	3	17	1	0	0	1	9	0	20	5	2
Smith, Jeffrey, Oneonta	.257	27	74	13	19	24	2	0	1	11	1	0	0	1	14	0	33	7	1
Smith, Rick, Jamestown	.214	45	145	15	31	45	6	1	2	18	2	0	1	0	10	0	39	1	1
Smith, Steven, Batavia	.254	73	252	38	64	102	12	1	8	33	2	1	2	3	20	1	53	17	2
Smith, Timothy, Newark	.329	68	219	43	72	106	13	3	5	37	2	1	2	2	26	0	48	2	5
Sproesser, Steve, Utica	.207	31	82	12	17	24	4	0	1	9	2	0	0	3	6	0	21	1	3
Spurlin, Robert, Watertown	.256	27	86	7	22	26	4	0	0	8	1	3	0	2	14	1	17	0	0
Starnes, Vance, Oneonta	.194	17	36	6	7	9	2	0	0	6	1	0	1	0	7	0	13	2	0
Swindell, Daniel, Little Falls*	.329	49	149	23	49	53	4	0	0	24	3	1	2	1	16	0	11	4	2
Talotta, Frank, Auburn	.232	33	95	12	22	37	3	0	4	18	1	1	3	3	9	0	24	4	0
Tarnow, Greg, Niagara Falls	.188	10	32	3	6	7	1	0	0	2	1	0	2	0	2	0	16	0	0
Thielker, Dave, Newark*	.330	62	218	51	72	139	18	2	15	55	3	0	5	6	26	3	26	2	3
Thomas, Troy, Niagara Falls*	.270	50	152	26	41	56	4	4	1	11	1	2	2	0	22	1	27	2	3
Thompson, Randolph, Watertown	.183	36	104	12	19	35	5	1	3	12	1	0	1	1	10	0	44	1	0
Thoutsis, Paul, Elmira*	.262	61	187	36	49	80	13	0	6	28	2	1	4	5	34	1	38	0	0
Tindall, Mark, Jamestown*	.000	15	1	0	0	0	0	0	0	0	0	0	0	0	0	0	1	0	0
Toale, John, Elmira*	.223	36	94	14	21	26	5	0	0	5	0	0	2	0	10	0	25	0	0
Todd, Scott, Oneonta	.156	15	32	6	5	7	0	1	0	4	1	0	0	0	5	0	13	2	0
Todman, Jens, Geneva*	.267	48	165	24	44	55	3	4	0	29	4	1	4	1	15	2	25	8	3
Tremblay, Gary, Elmira	.162	54	142	18	23	47	3	0	7	16	1	6	2	0	15	0	55	0	0
Valera, Alcadio, Batavia	.214	50	140	18	30	39	2	2	1	4	1	1	0	1	12	0	42	3	3
Vasquez, Jesse, Niagara Falls*	.224	59	170	13	38	50	4	1	2	20	2	1	1	1	10	0	20	6	2
Velazquez, Juan, Geneva	.220	53	159	21	35	45	7	0	1	15	1	0	0	3	24	0	42	5	5
Wainwright, John, Watertown	.236	26	89	11	21	24	3	0	0	6	0	1	0	2	3	0	20	6	3
Washington, Issac, Oneonta	.156	18	32	6	5	5	0	0	0	1	0	0	0	0	2	0	10	0	0
Watson, Michael, Little Falls	.216	53	148	19	32	45	5	1	2	21	1	0	2	2	16	0	31	8	4
Wiley, Jeffrey, Oneonta	.250	3	4	1	1	1	0	0	0	0	0	0	0	0	0	0	1	0	0
Williams, Dana, Elmira	.384	29	99	24	38	46	6	1	0	2	0	1	0	3	12	1	8	11	3
Williams, Edward, Little Falls	.263	50	190	30	50	78	6	2	6	28	3	0	0	6	19	1	41	3	1
Williams, Rafael, Batavia	.203	36	133	20	27	31	2	1	0	6	0	1	0	1	5	0	12	1	2
Wine, Robert, Auburn	.242	53	198	32	48	84	15	3	5	22	1	0	0	2	29	1	68	6	1
Winfield, Richard, Elmira	.163	31	80	9	13	13	0	0	0	8	0	3	2	1	12	0	38	0	0
Winkler, Brad, Oneonta*	.252	47	155	17	39	58	9	2	2	16	3	1	2	1	21	1	40	2	0
Wolfe, Edward, Utica	.338	72	281	55	95	144	17	1	10	65	4	0	2	2	26	1	34	2	1
Wooster, Robert, Batavia	.250	1	4	0	1	1	0	0	0	0	0	0	0	0	0	0	0	0	0
Yoder, Frederick, Watertown*	.246	59	207	17	51	86	8	0	9	30	2	0	1	0	21	0	46	0	1

The following pitchers, listed alphabetically by club, with games in parentheses, had no plate appearances, primarily through use of designated hitters:

AUBURN—Coughlin, Richard (15); Dube, Gregory (13); Friedrich, Michael (9); Funk, Thomas (25); Hammond, Randy (21); Kelley, Anthony (14); Mathews, Charles (13); Moore, Sam (14); Samuels, Roger (6); Shaab, Douglas (17); Smith, Scott (9); Verrone, Stephen (11).

BATAVIA—Arbogast, Steve (14); Browne, Richard (10); Cisco, Shawn (15); Clark, Edward (14); Greer, Michael (13); Holmes, Andre (1); Murphy, Michael (17); Pagani, Michael (6); Perry, Paul (25); Reynolds, Thomas (26); Street, Michael (20); Tamarez, Manuel (18); Ventura, Juan (3); Whitmyer, Stephen (11).

ELMIRA—Bencomo, Omar (19); Corder, Timothy (14); Dalton, Michael (21); Hines, James (16); Johnson, Roger (13); Kiecker, Dana (16); Manzanillo, Josiah (12); Mitchell, John (16); Silva, Jesus (7); Stewart, Hector (14).

ERIE—Behrend, Michael (20); Brisco, Jamie (13); Burwell, Phil (20); Carrasco, Ernest (19); Caulfield, Thomas (14); Costello, John (15); Farley, Brian (14); Gass, Jeffrey (22); Hartley, Michael (7); Herzog, Hans (26); McGrath, Charles (14); Turnbull, Keith (2).

GENEVA—Ballard, James (6); Brewer, Jeffrey (14); Doyle, James (29); Engle, Stephen (11); German, Rene (12); Grachen, Timothy (16); Kopf, David (13); Slowik, Thaddeus (21); Tuller, Brian (14); Volkman, John (23); Walck, Harold (7).

JAMESTOWN—Bargo, Gregory (2); Brahs, Gary (12); Hess, James (26); Holman, Brian (2); Miller, Richard (16); Norton, Randy (14); Ratliff, Daniel (16); Richards, Gregory (29); Soma, Charles (8); Stanton, Bernard (6); Traen, Thomas (14); Volquez, Alejandro (2); Zucco, Curtis (2).

LITTLE FALLS—Adams, Ralph (15); Adams, Scott (2); Aguilera, Richard (17); Bardwell, Scott (14); Boyles, John (17); Friedel, Charles (22); Gay, Steven (11); Hartshorn, Ronald (15); Innis, Jeffrey (28); Lundgren, Kurt (14); Moody, Anthony (21); Reed, Kenneth (19).

NEWARK—Adams, Gerald (3); Bell, Eric (19); Bianchi, Ben (19); Caldwell, Richard (19); Habyan, John (11); Heise, Larry (17); Lackie, Jeffrey (13); Ledbetter, David (2); Mason, Victor (14); Medina, Richard (15); Rice, Richard (13); Wilson, Randall (1).

NIAGARA FALLS—Barber, Ronald (21); Drabek, Douglas (16); Guzman, Pedro (17); Heath, Allan (17); Imig, Paul (18); Jordan, Herbert (24); Sunde, Bjerne (21); Tanner, Bruce (16); Varner, Robert (8).

ONEONTA—Byron, Timothy (8); Corsi, James (11); Davis, Fernando (5); Devlin, Robert (12); Fingerlow, Steven (19); Fletcher, Joseph (13); Frey, Steven (28); Fulton, William (14); Gammage Terry (4); Hall, James (3); Hudson, John (2); Humphrey, Daryl (6); Lewis, Larry (8); Morgan, Stacy (4); Niemiec, David (1); Rebiejo, Kenneth (13); Sarno, Anthony (13); Smalley, David (2); Stidham, Clayton (9); Westgard, Charles (1); Williams, Timothy (3); York, Michael (9).

UTICA—Finnegan, William (11); Gyarmati, Jeffrey (3); Hurst, Scott (20); Mehalko, Andrew (4); Moore, Jerry (12); Moretti, Roy (41); Oatman, Bryan (13); Perrino, Dominic (6); Roma, Daniel (17); Seitz, John (17); Tompkins, Jimmy Don (23); Wright, James (6); Zamba, Michael (16).

WATERTOWN—Blasucci, Anthony (14); Catlett, Justin (13); Cunningham, Charles (26); Fansler, Stanley (14); Felt, James (2); Giron, Tomas (21); Gonzalez, Jose (11); Kiernan, Michael (6); Lind, Orlando (10); Lopez, Saul (13); Oberbruner, James (22); Sauver, Richard (16); Simmons, Scott (5); Toffey, John (4).

GRAND SLAM HOME RUNS—Kelly, Moss, 2 each; Brito, Burton, Cusack, Dipiano, Jefferson, Jelks, Kent, Krynitsky, R. Martinez, Richmond, M. Robinson, Sheffield, Thielker, Thoutsis, 1 each.

AWARDED FIRST BASE ON CATCHER'S INTERFERENCE—K. Brown (J. Johnson); Cortez (F. Hernandez); Dyrek (Nichols); Parker (Nichols); Tolotta (J. Johnson).

CLUB FIELDING

Club	Pct.	G.	PO.	A.	E.	DP.	PB.
Jamestown	.965	74	1914	844	101	74	10
Newark	.960	74	1923	822	113	70	26
Auburn	.959	74	1935	813	116	66	15
Little Falls	.958	75	1968	709	118	61	17
Elmira	.957	73	1885	815	120	56	23
Geneva	.953	73	1895	818	135	79	18
Batavia	.948	75	1905	793	148	53	31
Utica	.948	74	1875	803	146	67	16
Erie	.946	74	1908	773	153	56	23
Niagara Falls	.945	74	1858	742	151	66	18
Oneonta	.944	76	1926	723	156	44	35
Watertown	.936	76	1976	805	189	65	30

INDIVIDUAL FIELDING

*Throws lefthanded.

FIRST BASEMEN

Player and Club	Pct.	G.	PO.	A.	E.	DP.
Angelo, Erie	.978	48	428	19	10	36
Baumgartner, Niagara Falls	1.000	1	2	0	0	0
Berger, Watertown	.985	45	364	25	6	27
Birriel, Elmira*	.976	42	333	26	9	23
Blair, Jamestown	1.000	13	109	6	0	15
Breslin, Erie	1.000	9	56	6	0	1
Caraballo, Little Falls	1.000	2	2	0	0	0
Cawthon, Batavia	.978	25	204	18	5	21
Connerty, Batavia	1.000	1	4	0	0	0
Denis, Auburn	1.000	1	12	0	0	0
Dinkel, Little Falls	1.000	1	4	1	0	0
Doerr, Newark	.968	10	88	3	3	5
Edwards, Auburn	.987	8	73	5	1	5
Englehart, Oneonta*	.978	49	383	22	9	26
Frederick, Oneonta	.935	3	26	3	2	2
Hale, Elmira	.983	36	328	16	6	23
Jacoby, Utica	1.000	2	11	1	0	3
Jones, Oneonta	.949	19	124	5	7	9
Kelly, Newark*	.992	53	441	27	5	36
Kent, Niagara Falls	.970	12	91	6	3	8
Kordeck, Watertown	1.000	1	5	0	0	0
Lawrence, Little Falls	.964	50	377	23	15	33
Mackin, Auburn	.988	31	217	20	3	22
Madden, Batavia	1.000	1	10	0	0	2
MAHLER, Jamestown	.997	63	582	31	2	52
Maloney, Little Falls*	.996	30	207	15	1	17
M. Martinez, Watertown	1.000	1	3	0	0	0
R. Martinez, Batavia*	.976	50	413	29	11	23
Moss, Utica	.895	5	32	2	4	4
Mucha, Newark	1.000	2	7	0	0	2
O'Dell, Auburn*	.990	47	378	18	4	36
Packer, Erie	.982	19	153	8	3	11
Pasquale, Erie	1.000	1	3	0	0	1
Pomeranz, Niagara Falls	.961	29	156	15	7	14
Remo, Geneva	.984	34	296	16	5	32
Rivera, Geneva*	.981	7	48	3	1	5
Ruffner, Oneonta	1.000	7	22	1	0	1
Sandry, Niagara Falls	.991	43	303	26	3	32
Sickles, Niagara Falls	.966	3	28	0	1	1
Smith, Oneonta	.952	11	54	5	3	0
Sproesser, Utica	1.000	2	12	1	0	2
Thielker, Newark	.993	26	138	7	1	9
Thompson, Watertown	.981	34	244	12	5	29
Todman, Geneva*	.986	42	336	24	5	30
Wolfe, Utica	.984	66	568	39	10	52
Yoder, Watertown	.983	9	54	4	1	3

SECOND BASEMEN

Player and Club	Pct.	G.	PO.	A.	E.	DP.
Amaral, Geneva	.959	59	123	178	13	39
Barragan, Newark	1.000	2	2	1	0	0
Bruno, Newark	.920	10	8	15	2	3
Caraballo, Little Falls	.979	14	13	33	1	5
Carrasco, Batavia	.957	9	8	14	1	3
Cobb, Jamestown	.955	59	123	154	13	39
Cortez, Watertown	1.000	2	3	5	0	2
Dichiaro, Newark	.946	44	93	118	12	34
Ditto, Geneva	.986	15	31	40	1	5
Dougherty, Erie	.949	57	124	172	16	26
Estrada, Elmira	.933	49	87	135	16	25
Funk, Oneonta	.920	5	10	13	2	1
Glynn, Little Falls	.882	5	7	8	2	0
Gourlay, Niagara Falls	.921	9	15	20	3	6
D. Hall, Elmira	.961	16	22	27	2	5
M. Hall, Jamestown	.947	21	46	44	5	12
Hamilton, Elmira	1.000	1	4	5	0	0
Howard, Watertown	.933	5	8	20	2	3
Jacoby, Utica	.938	15	21	40	4	8
Kaull, Erie	.903	11	24	32	6	8
Kramer, Batavia	.857	2	3	3	1	1
L. LEE, Utica	.965	58	108	141	9	37
M. Lee, Little Falls	.961	15	34	40	3	16
Lockwood, Newark	.952	30	49	71	6	10
Maloney, Little Falls*	1.000	1	1	0	0	0
M. Martinez, Watertown	.909	49	109	131	24	30
Mattocks, Oneonta	.952	67	131	149	14	25
Moore, Niagara Falls	.929	48	94	129	17	27
Morena, Little Falls	.884	8	12	26	5	5
Mucha, Newark	1.000	1	3	2	0	1
O'Dell, Niagara Falls	.667	1	1	1	1	1
Perez, Niagara Falls	.931	22	24	30	4	9
Picchioni, Utica	.800	7	1	3	1	1
Quade, Watertown	1.000	3	4	6	0	1
Reboulet, Erie	.939	10	22	24	3	5
Robinette, Batavia	.960	4	9	15	1	5
Robinson, Utica	.800	4	6	6	3	0
Rodriguez, Auburn	.952	52	110	129	12	33
Sandry, Niagara Falls	.667	2	1	5	3	0
D. Smith, Watertown	.856	27	43	58	17	11
S. Smith, Batavia	.952	68	129	191	16	28
Swindell, Little Falls	.947	46	66	113	10	21
Talotta, Auburn	.950	28	63	69	7	12
Washington, Oneonta	.906	8	12	17	3	2
Wiley, Oneonta	.800	1	4	0	1	0
Williams, Elmira	.933	15	30	40	5	9

THIRD BASEMEN

Player and Club	Pct.	G.	PO.	A.	E.	DP.
Abone, Jamestown	1.000	1	0	2	0	0
Amaral, Geneva	1.000	7	8	17	0	1
Berger, Watertown	.864	9	13	6	3	0
BIRKOFER, Jamestown	.917	73	58	164	20	23
Caraballo, Little Falls	.927	26	20	31	4	1
Cobb, Jamestown	.917	3	1	10	1	0
Cortez, Watertown	.859	66	39	95	22	10
Cusack, Newark	1.000	2	2	5	0	0
Denis, Auburn	.000	1	0	0	1	0
Ditto, Geneva	.868	19	25	34	9	6
Doerr, Newark	.924	38	29	68	8	5
Edwards, Auburn	.903	57	50	126	19	10
Eurton, Watertown	.667	2	0	2	1	0
Freytes, Geneva	.829	39	31	71	21	7
Glynn, Little Falls	1.000	1	0	1	0	0
D. Hall, Elmira	.900	6	4	5	1	1

THIRD BASEMEN—Continued

Player and Club	Pct.	G.	PO.	A.	E.	DP.
Hamilton, Elmira	.895	32	12	39	6	2
Jacoby, Utica	.887	39	20	82	13	5
Jenson, Niagara Falls	.714	4	2	3	2	0
Johnson, Oneonta	1.000	2	0	1	0	0
Kane, Elmira	.943	37	17	65	5	6
Kaull, Erie	.867	62	61	115	27	12
Kelly, Oneonta	.833	3	3	2	1	1
Lee, Utica	1.000	9	4	14	0	0
Lockwood, Newark	.917	20	14	30	4	3
Madden, Batavia	.853	49	25	85	19	5
M. Martinez, Watertown	.714	5	1	9	4	0
Mitchell, Auburn	.895	16	6	28	4	1
Molnar, Oneonta	.870	7	5	15	3	2
Mucha, Newark	.887	28	17	46	8	6
Nichols, Newark	.727	3	2	6	3	0
O'Dell, Niagara Falls	1.000	1	1	0	0	0
Pasquale, Erie	.854	16	11	30	7	6
Perez, Niagara Falls	.882	54	53	81	18	11
Pitty, Oneonta	.846	11	5	17	4	2
Robinette, Batavia	.600	3	0	3	2	0
Robinson, Utica	.895	14	9	25	4	0
Rodriguez, Auburn	.667	3	0	4	2	0
Ruffner, Oneonta	.814	30	21	36	13	2
Sandry, Niagara Falls	.782	25	16	27	12	0
Simmons, Oneonta	.870	27	26	34	9	1
Smith, Watertown	1.000	3	1	2	0	0
Sproesser, Utica	.886	14	8	23	4	4
Starnes, Oneonta	1.000	4	1	3	0	0
Thompson, Watertown	1.000	2	0	1	0	0
Toale, Elmira	.794	13	6	21	7	0
Todd, Oneonta	.833	11	6	14	4	0
Velazquez, Geneva	.780	10	8	24	9	5
E. Williams, Little Falls	.888	50	50	53	13	4
R. Williams, Batavia	.847	26	17	33	9	1
Wolfe, Utica	.923	6	3	9	1	1

SHORTSTOPS

Player and Club	Pct.	G.	PO.	A.	E.	DP.
Amaral, Geneva	.933	2	4	10	1	1
BARRAGAN, Newark	.954	53	65	144	10	23
Barton, Utica	.901	46	77	142	24	34
Caraballo, Little Falls	.920	38	54	106	14	21
Carrasco, Batavia	.733	8	4	7	4	0
Cobb, Jamestown	.903	9	13	15	3	5
Ditto, Geneva	.842	4	6	10	3	4
Fermin, Watertown	.914	66	94	223	30	38
Funk, Oneonta	.875	2	2	12	2	1
Glynn, Little Falls	.921	9	10	25	3	10
Gonzalez, Jamestown	.907	53	68	156	23	24
Gourlay, Niagara Falls	.916	65	103	171	25	38
Hall, Elmira	.889	8	13	19	4	3
Hamilton, Elmira	.923	4	5	19	2	2
Johnson, Oneonta	.778	11	7	14	6	1
Kaull, Erie	.000	1	0	0	1	0
Kavanaugh, Erie	.813	44	52	105	36	20
Lockwood, Newark	.904	40	36	105	15	22
Mattocks, Oneonta	.000	1	0	0	1	0
McKnight, Little Falls	.878	38	43	72	16	15
Mitchell, Auburn	1.000	1	1	6	0	2
Moore, Niagara Falls	.951	15	23	35	3	8
Nichols, Newark	.667	1	4	2	3	1
O'Donnell, Oneonta	.667	3	1	3	2	0
Pasquale, Erie	.935	44	42	102	10	9
Pitty, Oneonta	.906	10	10	19	3	4
Quinonez, Elmira	.925	63	107	226	27	32
Rivera, Oneonta	.941	55	85	155	15	19
Robinette, Batavia	.944	38	38	80	7	12
Robinson, Utica	.920	39	53	96	13	17
Rood, Auburn	.923	73	121	228	29	46
Rosado, Jamestown	.951	16	22	36	3	8
Rossi, Erie	1.000	1	0	1	0	0
Sciacca, Geneva	.933	68	96	210	22	42
Simmons, Oneonta	1.000	6	2	11	0	0
Smith, Watertown	.957	12	16	28	2	5
Valera, Batavia	.907	49	65	130	20	22
Williams, Elmira	.917	5	5	6	1	2
Wooster, Batavia	.800	1	1	3	1	0

OUTFIELDERS

Player and Club	Pct.	G.	PO.	A.	E.	DP.
Anderson, Jamestown	1.000	6	10	0	0	0
Berger, Watertown	.906	17	23	6	3	0
Blair, Jamestown	.950	17	16	3	1	0
Breslin, Erie	.966	21	28	0	1	0
Brito, Batavia	.884	52	54	7	8	0
Brown, Watertown	.897	44	62	8	8	0
Bruno, Newark	1.000	4	1	0	0	0
Burks, Elmira	.979	52	89	5	2	1
Burton, Geneva*	.882	23	28	2	4	1
Cain, Newark	.889	9	7	1	1	0
Carpenter, Oneonta	1.000	6	7	1	0	0
Catlett, Watertown	.000	1	0	0	1	0
Cawthon, Batavia	1.000	9	6	0	0	0
Chadwick, Jamestown	1.000	44	71	3	0	1
Chestna, Oneonta	.857	9	6	0	1	0
Connerty, Batavia	1.000	29	16	3	0	0
Coyle, Utica	.963	68	94	9	4	3
Cunningham, Oneonta	.857	14	18	0	3	0
Cusack, Newark	.906	27	28	1	3	0
Dahse, Newark	.976	28	36	4	1	2
Davidson, Watertown	.934	56	83	2	6	0
Davila, Watertown	.882	11	15	0	2	0
Delucci, Watertown	.906	73	110	6	12	2
Depiano, Jamestown	.969	52	85	8	3	3
Dickerson, Geneva	1.000	37	50	6	0	1
Dinkel, Little Falls	.957	47	82	6	4	0
Doerr, Newark	1.000	14	18	1	0	0
Dyrek, Auburn	.976	29	39	2	1	0
Fairbanks, Auburn*	1.000	3	6	1	0	0
Fernandez, Batavia	.750	5	3	0	1	0
Frederick, Oneonta	.912	24	30	1	3	0
Goodman, Geneva	.978	24	39	5	1	0
Graham, Elmira	.857	9	5	1	1	0
Hendershot, Utica	.957	59	64	3	3	1
Hodge, Auburn	1.000	24	30	4	0	0
Houp, Auburn	.967	48	84	5	3	0
Jackson, Elmira	1.000	30	26	4	0	1
Jefferson, Little Falls	.976	68	153	7	4	1
Jelks, Elmira	.979	62	89	5	2	1
Jenson, Niagara Falls	.940	62	119	6	8	0
Jiminez, Watertown*	1.000	3	5	0	0	0
Jongewaard, Elmira	.929	27	37	2	3	0
Kelly, Oneonta	.944	39	67	1	4	0
Knapp, Newark	1.000	15	17	1	0	0
Kramer, Batavia	.952	73	149	9	8	1
Lauck, Erie*	1.000	8	5	0	0	0
Lewallen, Oneonta	.971	65	125	8	4	1
Lipinski, Auburn	1.000	11	16	0	0	0
Lopez, Newark*	1.000	19	36	1	0	1
Lynn, Newark	1.000	3	2	0	0	0
Machuca, Oneonta	.909	16	27	3	3	0
Martin, Auburn	1.000	6	6	0	0	0
D. Martinez, Geneva*	.945	63	132	6	8	0
R. Martinez, Batavia*	1.000	4	3	0	0	0
Merenda, Utica*	.900	10	8	1	1	0
Mitchell, Auburn	.976	55	112	8	3	1
Moncada, Watertown	.914	24	32	0	3	0
Montgomery, Jamestown	.865	40	43	2	7	0
Moore, Niagara Falls	1.000	1	2	0	0	0
Morena, Little Falls	1.000	7	12	1	0	1
Moss, Utica	.947	15	16	2	1	0
Mucha, Newark	1.000	19	15	1	0	1
Nichols, Newark	1.000	10	12	1	0	0
O'Dell, Niagara Falls	.902	47	51	4	6	1
Parker, Little Falls	.953	71	107	14	6	1
Peruso, Oneonta	.979	27	44	2	1	0
Pitts, Utica*	.973	44	63	8	2	1
Pleis, Erie	1.000	19	33	4	0	0
Pomeranz, Niagara Falls	.892	32	30	3	4	0
Ramos, Batavia	.500	4	0	1	1	0
Richmond, Auburn	.895	58	77	8	10	0
Rigos, Erie	.938	73	127	10	9	4
Rivera, Geneva*	.913	60	78	6	8	2
Roberts, Elmira	.975	39	77	1	2	0
Robinson, Erie	.969	68	152	4	5	1
Rojas, Newark*	1.000	25	34	3	0	1
Roman, Batavia	.947	74	135	9	8	2
ROSSI, Erie	.986	51	71	2	1	1
Saccocia, Jamestown	.967	73	138	9	5	2
Sheffield, Utica	.952	48	89	10	5	1
Sickles, Niagara Falls	.941	27	46	2	3	0
D. Smith, Watertown	1.000	1	1	0	0	0
J. Smith, Oneonta	1.000	9	10	1	0	0
S. Smith, Batavia	1.000	3	1	0	0	0
T. Smith, Newark*	.943	66	96	4	6	0
Starnes, Oneonta	1.000	1	1	0	0	0
Thielker, Newark	.935	48	70	2	5	0
Thomas, Niagara Falls	.955	49	62	1	3	0
Thoutsis, Elmira*	.957	51	83	5	4	1
Vasquez, Niagara Falls*	.943	37	49	1	3	0
Velazquez, Geneva	.824	28	26	2	6	1
Wainwright, Watertown	.976	26	41	0	1	0
Watson, Little Falls	.962	44	70	5	3	1
Winkler, Oneonta	.875	40	48	1	7	0

CATCHERS

Player and Club	Pct.	G.	PO.	A.	E.	DP.	PB.
Afenir, Auburn	1.000	7	48	2	0	0	2
Agostinelli, Erie	1.000	18	117	7	0	0	6
Allanson, Batavia	.988	51	372	27	5	4	18
Antone, Jamestown	.993	21	136	13	1	0	2
Baumgartner, Niagara Falls	.981	23	139	13	3	0	3
Belcik, Little Falls	.982	23	158	9	3	0	8
Berger, Watertown	1.000	1	8	1	0	0	0
Blair, Jamestown	1.000	1	6	0	0	0	0
Caianiello, Niagara Falls	.995	27	179	23	1	3	4
Canning, Niagara Falls	.960	4	21	3	1	0	1
Connerty, Batavia	.967	5	27	2	1	0	7
Denis, Auburn	1.000	5	30	2	0	0	1
Diaz, Batavia	1.000	8	36	5	0	0	1
Dreizler, Utica	.960	18	66	6	3	1	5
Eurton, Watertown	.969	51	362	17	12	1	25
Fortaleza, Jamestown	.990	19	86	16	1	0	2
Graham, Elmira	.923	8	9	3	1	0	3
Hawkins, Little Falls	.983	52	321	36	6	6	7
Hernandez, Geneva	.983	27	156	18	3	6	9
Holecek, Niagara	.988	13	82	3	1	1	3
Johnson, Geneva	.980	32	209	30	5	3	6
Jones, Oneonta	.972	41	250	32	8	2	18
Karr, Little Falls	.971	21	126	10	4	1	2
Kordeck, Watertown	.895	3	14	3	2	0	0
Krynitsky, Utica	.988	66	452	35	6	2	9
Jo. Lopez, Oneonta	1.000	2	1	0	0	0	0
Ju. Lopez, Batavia	.989	11	84	10	1	1	4
LYDEN, Oneonta	.991	47	310	28	3	0	17
Lynn, Newark	.977	23	150	17	4	2	2
Martelli, Batavia	.980	10	45	3	1	1	1
Martinez, Erie	1.000	1	1	0	0	0	0
McGilvray, Auburn	1.000	1	1	0	0	0	0
Mosley, Newark	.983	13	50	8	1	0	8
Nichols, Newark	.990	49	330	47	4	6	16
O'Dell, Niagara	1.000	8	40	5	0	1	4
Packer, Erie	.974	30	169	20	5	1	10
Pagnozzi, Erie	.985	30	183	20	3	5	7
Pleis, Erie	1.000	3	4	0	0	0	0
Remo, Geneva	.990	13	88	8	1	1	1
Sherlock, Auburn	.991	14	95	11	1	1	2
Smith, Jamestown	.980	39	273	19	6	4	6
Sproesser, Utica	.968	11	55	6	2	2	2
Spurlin, Watertown	.985	27	181	20	3	3	5
Tarnow, Niagara	.988	10	69	13	1	1	3
Tremblay, Elmira	.976	54	296	31	8	5	6
Velazquez, Geneva	.933	8	35	7	3	0	2
Wine, Auburn	.984	51	327	35	6	2	10
Winfield, Elmira	1.000	31	168	17	0	2	14

PITCHERS

Player and Club	Pct.	G.	PO.	A.	E.	DP.
G. Adams, Newark	1.000	3	1	2	0	1
R. Adams, Little Falls	1.000	15	5	7	0	0
S. Adams, Little Falls	1.000	2	1	0	0	0
Aguilera, Little Falls	1.000	17	5	8	0	1
Arbogast, Batavia	.889	14	4	12	2	1
Ballard, Geneva	1.000	6	1	4	0	0
Barber, Niagara Falls	1.000	21	1	5	0	0
Bardwell, Little Falls	1.000	14	1	1	0	0
Behrend, Erie	1.000	20	2	6	0	0
Bell, Newark*	.846	18	1	10	2	0
Bencomo, Elmira	.929	19	3	10	1	0
Bianchi, Newark	.938	19	3	12	1	0
Blasucci, Watertown*	.882	14	4	11	2	0
Boyles, Little Falls	1.000	17	7	4	0	0
Brahs, Jamestown*	1.000	12	2	11	0	0
Brewer, Geneva	.938	14	6	9	1	1
Brisco, Erie	.944	13	4	13	1	0
Browne, Batavia*	.889	10	3	5	1	0
Burwell, Erie	.857	20	0	6	1	0
Byron, Oneonta	.818	8	3	6	2	0
Caldwell, Newark	.875	19	0	7	1	1
Carrasco, Erie	1.000	19	4	9	0	0
Catlett, Watertown	1.000	12	3	3	0	0
Caulfield, Erie*	.900	14	6	12	2	0
Cisco, Batavia	.958	15	5	18	1	0
Clark, Batavia*	1.000	14	0	2	0	0
Corder, Elmira	.923	14	1	11	1	1
Corsi, Oneonta	1.000	11	2	10	0	0
Costello, Erie	1.000	15	5	7	0	0
Coughlin, Auburn	.889	15	2	6	1	1
Cunningham, Watertown	.783	26	4	14	5	2
Dalton, Elmira*	1.000	21	1	8	0	0
Davis, Oneonta*	1.000	5	0	1	0	0
Devlin, Oneonta	.900	12	3	6	1	0
Doyle, Geneva	1.000	29	1	4	0	2
Drabek, Niagara Falls	.840	16	8	13	4	2
Dube, Auburn	.900	13	2	7	1	0
Engle, Geneva*	1.000	11	3	6	0	0
Fansler, Watertown	.667	14	0	4	2	0
Farley, Erie	.923	14	6	6	1	0
Fingerlow, Oneonta	.667	19	1	3	2	0
Finnegan, Utica	.571	11	0	4	3	0
Fletcher, Oneonta	1.000	13	2	9	0	0
Frey, Oneonta*	.889	28	8	8	2	0
Friedel, Little Falls	1.000	21	2	5	0	2
Friedrich, Auburn	1.000	9	4	6	0	1
Fulton, Oneonta	.867	14	3	10	2	0
Funk, Auburn*	.889	25	0	8	1	0
Gammage, Oneonta	1.000	4	1	1	0	0
Gass, Erie	.889	22	5	11	2	1
Gay, Little Falls	1.000	11	4	11	0	0
German, Geneva	1.000	12	2	5	0	0
Giron, Watertown	.889	21	4	12	2	1
Gonzalez, Watertown	1.000	11	3	3	0	1
Gordon, Watertown	.875	18	1	6	1	0
Grachen, Geneva*	.966	16	10	18	1	2
Greer, Batavia	.688	13	3	8	5	1
Guzman, Niagara Falls	.867	17	13	13	4	1
Habyan, Newark	.889	11	3	5	1	0
J. Hall, Oneonta	1.000	3	0	1	0	0
Hammond, Auburn	1.000	21	5	4	0	0
Hartley, Erie	.889	7	1	7	1	0
Hartshorn, Little Falls	.929	15	2	11	1	0
Heath, Niagara Falls*	.875	17	5	16	3	1
Heise, Newark*	1.000	17	4	6	0	0
Herzog, Erie*	1.000	26	2	5	0	0
Hess, Jamestown	1.000	26	1	18	0	0
Hickey, Niagara Falls	.960	16	7	17	1	0
Hines, Elmira	.933	16	4	10	1	0
Holman, Jamestown	1.000	2	0	4	0	0
Humphrey, Oneonta	1.000	6	5	10	0	1
Hurst, Utica	.857	20	8	16	4	0
Imig, Niagara Falls	.929	18	5	8	1	0
Innis, Little Falls	1.000	28	3	12	0	0
Jackson, Elmira	1.000	2	0	1	0	0
Johnson, Elmira	.875	13	4	3	1	0
Jongewaard, Elmira	1.000	3	1	1	0	0
Jordan, Niagara Falls	.917	24	5	17	2	0
Kelley, Auburn	1.000	14	2	17	0	2
Kiecker, Elmira	1.000	16	8	18	0	2
Kiernan, Watertown	.667	6	0	2	1	0
Kopf, Geneva	.947	13	8	10	1	1
Krsnich, Newark	1.000	26	1	3	0	0
Lackie, Newark*	.917	13	4	7	1	1
Ledbetter, Newark	1.000	2	0	1	0	0
Lewis, Oneonta	1.000	8	1	3	0	0
Lind, Watertown	.667	10	2	2	2	0
Lopez, Watertown	.957	13	6	16	1	0
Lundgren, Little Falls	1.000	14	2	2	0	0
Manzanillo, Elmira	1.000	12	2	4	0	0
Mason, Newark	.875	14	1	6	1	0
Mathews, Auburn	.968	13	8	22	1	0
McGrath, Erie	.895	14	7	10	2	0
Medina, Newark*	1.000	15	3	10	0	0
Mehalko, Utica*	.333	4	0	1	2	0
Miller, Jamestown	.913	16	7	14	2	1
Mitchell, Elmira	1.000	16	6	10	0	1
Moody, Little Falls	1.000	21	4	4	0	0
J. Moore, Utica*	1.000	12	1	5	0	0
S. Moore, Auburn	.941	14	5	11	1	2
Moretti, Utica	.909	41	5	15	2	1
Morgan, Oneonta	1.000	4	2	6	0	0
Murphy, Batavia	.895	17	3	14	2	0
Niemiec, Oneonta	1.000	1	1	0	0	1
Norton, Jamestown	.938	14	1	14	1	0
Oatman, Utica*	.667	13	1	3	2	0
Oberbruner, Watertown	.889	22	0	8	1	1
Pagani, Batavia	1.000	6	3	0	0	0
Perrino, Utica*	.600	6	1	2	2	0
Perry, Batavia	1.000	25	4	8	0	0
Ratliff, Jamestown	.946	16	7	28	2	2
Rebiejo, Oneonta	.929	13	4	9	1	0
Reed, Little Falls	1.000	19	3	9	0	0
Reynolds, Batavia	.931	26	6	21	2	1
Rice, Newark	.857	13	2	10	2	0
Richards, Jamestown	.938	29	4	11	1	1
Roma, Utica	.767	17	5	18	7	2
Samuels, Auburn*	1.000	6	1	9	0	0
Sarno, Oneonta	.636	13	2	5	4	1
Sauver, Watertown*	1.000	16	3	23	0	0
Seitz, Utica	.929	17	9	17	2	3
Shaab, Auburn*	.667	17	2	6	4	0
Silva, Elmira	.750	7	1	2	1	0
S. Simmons, Watertown*	1.000	5	0	1	0	0
Simon, Watertown	.889	19	8	8	2	1
Slowik, Geneva	1.000	21	3	6	0	0
Smith, Auburn	1.000	9	0	2	0	0
Soma, Jamestown	1.000	8	1	12	0	0
Stanton, Jamestown	1.000	6	0	4	0	0
Stewart, Elmira*	.941	14	2	14	1	0

PITCHERS—Continued

Player and Club	Pct.	G.	PO.	A.	E.	DP.
Stidham, Oneonta	1.000	9	2	2	0	0
Street, Batavia	1.000	20	1	1	0	1
SUNDE, Niagara Falls	1.000	21	11	17	0	1
Tamarez, Batavia*	.813	18	6	7	3	0
Tanner, Niagara Falls	1.000	16	1	6	0	1
Tindall, Jamestown*	1.000	15	2	20	0	0
Toffey, Watertown*	1.000	4	0	2	0	1
Tompkins, Utica	1.000	23	3	4	0	0
Traen, Jamestown*	.950	14	3	16	1	0
Tuller, Geneva	.875	14	5	9	2	0
Varner, Niagara Falls*	1.000	8	0	3	0	0
Vasquez, Niagara Falls*	1.000	3	0	1	0	0
Verrone, Auburn	.857	11	2	4	1	0
Volkman, Geneva	.933	23	3	11	1	0
Volquez, Jamestown	1.000	2	0	1	0	0
Walck, Geneva	1.000	7	0	9	0	0
Whitmyer, Batavia	.941	11	6	10	1	1
Williams, Oneonta	1.000	3	0	1	0	0
Wilson, Newark	1.000	1	0	1	0	0
Wright, Utica	.500	6	1	1	2	0
York, Oneonta	1.000	9	2	3	0	0
Zamba, Utica	.824	16	1	13	3	0

The following players had no recorded accepted chances at the positions indicated and therefore are not listed in the fielding averages for those particular positions: Bargo, p; Caraballo, of; Carrasco, 3b; Davila, 3b; DeJesus, c; Diaz, p; Edwards, of; Felt, p; Goodman, 3b; Graham, p; Gyarmati, p; Hale, of; Hudson, p; Jimenez, of; Kent, p; Killings, of; Maloney, 3b, of; O'Donnell, 2b; Perez, ss; Picchioni, of; Pitty, 2b; Pleis, 3b, p; Pomeranz, 2b; Ruffner, p; Sandry, of; Sickles, 3b; M. Simmons, of, p; Simon, of; Smalley, p; Thielker, p; Thomas, p; Turnbull, p; Ventura, p; Westgard, p; Zucco, p.

CLUB PITCHING

Club	ERA.	G.	CG.	ShO.	Sv.	IP.	H.	R.	ER.	HR.	HB.	BB.	Int. BB.	SO.	WP.	Bk.
Utica	3.63	74	8	2	20	625.0	598	336	252	71	31	282	4	571	47	11
Little Falls	3.69	75	6	6	20	656.0	598	335	269	53	19	330	8	578	49	3
Auburn	3.93	74	12	3	17	645.0	644	366	282	71	20	247	11	490	55	3
Newark	4.16	74	17	5	18	641.0	684	387	296	42	19	309	4	528	53	3
Jamestown	4.23	74	17	2	11	638.0	650	366	300	44	16	258	7	490	45	4
Geneva	4.39	73	7	4	13	631.2	629	379	308	71	21	300	19	486	63	4
Niagara Falls	4.52	74	10	3	11	619.1	685	423	311	47	22	298	13	528	66	4
Watertown	4.58	76	2	1	11	658.2	671	481	335	67	37	337	9	549	42	12
Elmira	4.64	73	10	4	14	628.1	637	406	324	60	8	263	17	464	54	4
Erie	4.68	74	8	1	15	636.0	691	444	331	86	40	289	11	452	57	2
Oneonta	4.72	76	14	3	13	642.0	656	442	337	35	26	336	1	548	70	8
Batavia	4.72	75	13	2	11	635.0	673	419	333	77	22	297	10	540	56	7

PITCHERS' RECORDS

(Leading Qualifiers for Earned-Run Average Leadership—61 or More Innings)

*Throws lefthanded.

Pitcher—Club	W.	L.	Pct.	ERA.	G.	GS.	CG.	GF.	ShO.	Sv.	IP.	H.	R.	ER.	HR.	HB.	BB.	Int. BB.	SO.	WP.
Friedrich, Auburn	6	2	.750	1.79	9	9	4	0	1	0	70.1	58	20	14	6	1	12	0	75	5
Moretti, Utica	7	2	.778	2.18	41	2	2	36	0	10	82.2	58	25	20	8	4	32	0	116	5
Sauver, Watertown*	7	5	.583	2.31	16	12	1	0	0	0	93.2	80	41	24	6	1	31	0	73	2
Zamba, Utica	12	2	.857	2.32	16	15	2	0	0	0	97.0	100	36	25	13	5	22	0	69	3
Boyles, Little Falls	12	1	.923	2.41	17	13	0	2	0	0	89.2	71	30	24	5	0	33	0	68	10
Seitz, Utica	12	4	.750	2.61	17	17	3	0	0	0	107.0	100	40	31	8	3	27	1	83	5
Kiecker, Elmira	11	5	.688	2.74	16	15	4	1	1	0	111.2	92	50	34	7	1	44	4	78	5
Frey, Oneonta*	4	6	.400	2.74	28	1	0	24	0	9	72.1	47	27	22	2	0	35	1	86	5
Lopez, Watertown	4	5	.444	2.79	13	13	1	0	1	0	61.1	61	33	19	6	3	24	0	53	1
Caulfield, Erie*	6	3	.667	2.81	14	12	3	1	0	0	83.1	70	32	26	8	1	34	1	82	7
Mathews, Auburn	7	3	.700	2.82	13	13	6	0	1	0	95.2	76	41	30	13	3	15	0	60	6

Departmental Leaders: G—Moretti, 41; W—Boyles, Seitz, Zamba, 12; L—Fansler, 10; Pct.—Boyles, .923; GS—Seitz, 17; CG—Mathews, Rice, 6; GF—Moretti, 36; ShO—Aguilera, Imig, Rice, Traen, 2; Sv.—Moretti, 10; IP—Kiecker, 111.2; H—Aguilera, 109; R—Fansler, McGrath, 69; ER—Guzman, 52; HR—Roma, 14; HB—Burwell, 9; BB—Tuller, 62; IBB—Tanner, 6; SO—Moretti, 116; WP—Tuller, 23.

(All Pitchers—Listed Alphabetically)

Pitcher—Club	W.	L.	Pct.	ERA.	G.	GS.	CG.	GF.	ShO.	Sv.	IP.	H.	R.	ER.	HR.	HB.	BB.	Int. BB.	SO.	WP.
G. Adams, Newark	1	0	1.000	2.63	3	1	1	1	0	0	13.2	8	4	4	1	0	8	0	15	1
R. Adams, Little Falls	5	6	.455	3.81	15	12	0	0	0	0	82.2	76	40	35	10	2	55	0	55	2
S. Adams, Little Falls	0	0	.000	7.71	2	0	0	2	0	0	2.1	3	4	2	1	0	1	0	2	0
Aguilera, Little Falls	5	6	.455	3.72	16	15	4	0	2	0	104.0	109	55	43	5	3	26	1	84	3
Arbogast, Batavia	3	4	.429	4.89	14	14	2	0	0	0	81.0	95	57	44	12	2	29	2	62	3
Ballard, Geneva	3	0	1.000	3.52	6	0	0	4	0	1	15.1	14	6	6	2	1	1	0	8	0
Barber, Niagara Falls	0	1	.000	5.40	21	0	0	9	0	0	28.1	28	26	17	5	2	14	0	27	6
Bardwell, Little Falls	1	0	1.000	9.24	14	2	0	2	0	0	25.1	33	33	26	3	2	22	1	24	3
Bargo, Jamestown*	0	0	.000	11.74	2	1	0	0	0	0	7.2	16	13	10	1	0	4	0	4	3
Behrend, Erie	1	1	.500	4.54	20	0	0	7	0	2	41.2	53	35	21	8	4	15	1	33	2
Bell, Newark*	3	2	.600	4.95	18	5	2	8	0	6	60.0	71	44	33	5	1	30	0	56	4
Bencomo, Elmira	3	2	.600	3.61	19	4	0	11	0	5	57.1	48	27	23	4	0	24	1	53	2
Bianchi, Newark	3	2	.600	5.02	19	2	0	10	0	0	43.0	59	32	24	1	1	20	0	35	3
Blasucci, Watertown*	1	7	.125	3.84	14	14	0	0	0	0	65.2	54	50	28	6	1	40	0	67	8
Boyles, Little Falls	12	1	.923	2.41	17	13	0	2	0	0	89.2	71	30	24	5	0	33	0	68	10
Brahs, Jamestown*	2	5	.286	4.44	12	6	2	3	0	0	50.2	60	33	25	3	0	19	0	31	6
Brewer, Geneva	2	7	.222	5.73	14	14	0	0	0	0	75.1	81	58	48	10	6	31	1	51	5
Brisco, Erie	5	5	.500	3.69	13	12	2	0	0	0	83.0	76	49	34	12	3	25	2	31	0
Browne, Batavia*	5	3	.625	4.15	10	10	2	0	0	0	65.0	64	38	30	6	1	24	0	66	4
Burwell, Erie	1	1	.500	6.75	20	0	0	7	0	1	24.0	26	33	18	2	9	24	0	12	9
Byron, Oneonta	1	2	.333	5.29	8	5	0	0	0	0	32.1	40	22	19	2	2	18	0	24	4
Caldwell, Newark	6	2	.750	3.14	19	5	0	5	0	0	66.0	69	34	23	1	1	20	1	68	4
Carrasco, Erie	1	3	.250	5.11	19	3	0	13	0	1	37.0	31	24	21	3	1	20	1	24	3
Catlett, Watertown	0	5	.000	7.67	12	7	0	2	0	0	31.2	44	37	27	6	0	24	0	23	2
Caulfield, Erie*	6	3	.667	2.81	14	12	3	1	0	0	83.1	70	32	26	8	1	34	1	82	7
Cisco, Batavia	5	4	.556	3.22	15	10	4	2	1	0	81.0	83	39	29	9	3	22	1	64	7
Clark, Batavia*	0	2	.000	5.47	14	2	0	6	0	0	24.2	24	20	15	5	3	19	0	32	1
Corder, Elmira	3	3	.500	3.00	14	4	2	10	0	4	54.0	42	21	18	2	0	22	3	47	8
Corsi, Oneonta	3	6	.333	4.25	11	10	2	1	0	0	59.1	76	38	28	1	1	21	0	47	2
Costello, Erie	2	5	.286	6.64	15	9	2	3	0	2	63.2	79	51	47	9	6	21	0	41	4
Coughlin, Auburn	2	3	.400	3.93	15	4	0	9	0	2	50.1	53	35	22	6	0	24	2	49	7
Cunningham, Watertown	2	3	.400	4.29	26	1	0	13	0	2	71.1	56	44	34	6	2	47	2	60	4
Dalton, Elmira*	3	1	.750	2.65	21	1	0	17	0	5	51.0	48	19	15	1	0	15	1	49	6

Pitcher—Club	W.	L.	Pct.	ERA.	G.	GS.	CG.	GF.	ShO.	Sv.	IP.	H.	R.	ER.	HR.	HB.	BB.	Int. BB.	SO.	WP.
Davis, Oneonta*	2	0	1.000	5.57	5	5	0	0	0	0	21.0	22	20	13	2	0	9	0	11	1
Devlin, Oneonta	2	2	.500	2.38	12	3	2	5	0	1	41.2	28	20	11	1	2	18	0	40	5
Diaz, Batavia	0	0	.000	0.00	2	0	0	2	0	0	2.2	1	0	0	0	1	1	0	2	0
Doyle, Geneva	3	3	.500	4.42	29	0	0	28	0	7	38.2	34	19	19	2	1	25	5	22	7
Drabek, Niagara Falls	6	7	.462	3.65	16	13	3	2	0	0	103.2	99	52	42	10	2	48	0	103	7
Dube, Auburn	3	4	.429	6.64	13	11	0	2	0	0	61.0	71	58	45	7	4	52	0	38	3
Engle, Geneva*	7	2	.778	3.63	11	11	1	0	0	0	72.0	61	31	29	10	1	21	1	77	3
Fansler, Watertown	0	10	.000	8.05	14	14	0	0	0	0	57.0	79	69	51	8	6	28	0	49	9
Farley, Erie	5	2	.714	4.83	14	13	1	0	0	0	78.1	82	58	42	13	4	40	0	70	10
Felt, Watertown	0	0	.000	3.86	2	0	0	1	0	0	2.1	1	1	1	0	0	1	0	3	0
Fingerlow, Oneonta	0	0	.000	6.10	19	0	0	7	0	0	38.1	49	35	26	3	3	17	0	45	2
Finnegan, Utica	0	1	.000	7.85	11	3	0	4	0	0	18.1	16	18	16	1	3	21	0	15	5
Fletcher, Oneonta	2	2	.500	5.57	13	4	0	4	0	0	32.1	32	25	20	3	2	26	0	8	5
Frey, Oneonta*	4	6	.400	2.74	28	1	0	24	0	9	72.1	47	27	22	2	0	35	1	86	5
Friedel, Little Falls	5	0	1.000	2.61	22	1	0	4	0	1	51.2	40	19	15	5	3	26	0	60	3
Friedrich, Auburn	6	2	.750	1.79	9	9	4	0	1	0	70.1	58	20	14	6	1	12	0	75	5
Fulton, Oneonta	4	7	.364	3.74	14	13	4	0	1	0	84.1	73	49	35	2	3	35	0	77	9
Funk, Auburn*	5	4	.556	2.03	25	3	1	12	0	4	53.1	42	20	12	4	0	18	0	46	2
Gammage, Oneonta	0	0	.000	4.05	4	0	0	1	0	0	6.2	7	6	3	0	0	8	0	1	0
Gass, Erie	4	3	.571	5.13	22	2	0	15	0	4	66.2	79	43	38	9	2	26	1	54	6
Gay, Little Falls	3	6	.333	3.06	11	11	2	0	0	0	70.2	65	36	24	7	0	24	0	45	3
German, Geneva	2	3	.400	7.36	12	3	0	3	0	0	33.0	39	30	27	7	4	19	0	24	4
Giron, Watertown	2	6	.250	4.86	21	6	0	11	0	1	66.2	74	47	36	11	2	26	0	49	3
Gonzalez, Watertown	0	0	.000	4.15	11	0	0	5	0	0	17.1	17	13	8	0	2	9	0	15	0
Gordon, Watertown	0	3	.000	3.70	18	2	0	10	0	5	48.2	39	30	20	5	5	32	1	56	3
Grachen, Geneva*	5	5	.500	2.95	16	11	2	4	0	0	94.2	107	51	31	6	1	22	1	78	5
Graham, Elmira	0	0	.000	9.00	1	0	0	1	0	0	1.0	2	1	1	0	1	0	0	0	0
Greer, Batavia	2	7	.222	6.67	13	13	0	0	0	0	58.0	67	52	43	10	1	36	0	35	8
Guzman, Niagara Falls	2	7	.222	6.53	17	13	0	2	0	0	71.2	85	63	52	10	7	45	0	55	13
Gyarmati, Utica	0	0	.000	1.23	3	0	0	1	0	0	7.1	7	3	1	0	1	3	0	4	3
Habyan, Newark	5	3	.625	3.39	11	11	1	0	1	0	71.2	68	34	27	6	2	29	2	64	4
Hall, Oneonta	0	1	.000	8.22	3	2	0	0	0	0	7.2	8	7	7	0	1	14	0	5	4
Hammond, Auburn	3	0	1.000	6.44	21	0	0	12	0	4	29.1	42	24	21	3	1	15	3	16	2
Hartley, Erie	1	3	.250	6.75	7	7	0	0	0	0	32.0	36	27	24	6	3	31	0	25	3
Hartshorn, Little Falls	4	7	.364	4.48	15	15	0	0	0	0	80.1	83	53	40	9	5	36	0	63	4
Heath, Niagara Falls*	1	6	.143	4.37	17	11	1	2	0	1	68.0	65	52	33	4	0	47	0	61	4
Heise, Newark*	7	3	.700	5.45	17	13	2	2	0	0	77.2	102	61	47	7	1	27	0	60	4
Herzog, Erie*	6	2	.750	1.85	26	0	0	19	0	5	39.0	44	16	8	3	1	17	5	27	2
Hess, Jamestown	5	3	.625	2.80	26	0	0	23	0	7	45.0	46	16	14	1	1	14	2	54	4
Hickey, Niagara Falls	7	4	.636	3.91	16	15	2	0	0	0	94.1	102	50	41	3	3	39	1	76	9
Hines, Elmira	3	3	.500	5.68	16	12	0	3	0	0	69.2	74	49	44	6	1	34	0	31	7
Holman, Jamestown	0	0	.000	11.81	2	2	0	0	0	0	5.1	7	7	7	1	1	4	0	5	0
Hudson, Oneonta	0	0	.000	27.00	2	0	0	0	0	0	2.2	8	8	8	0	1	3	0	0	2
Humphrey, Oneonta	0	2	.000	7.65	6	3	0	3	0	0	20.0	29	18	17	1	1	13	0	11	4
Hurst, Utica	4	3	.571	5.37	20	6	0	7	0	2	67.0	65	45	40	5	3	52	0	51	5
Imig, Niagara Falls	5	5	.500	4.80	18	11	3	4	2	1	75.0	89	48	40	7	0	33	0	67	9
Innis, Little Falls	8	0	1.000	1.37	28	0	0	25	0	8	46.0	29	8	7	0	0	28	3	68	4
Jackson, Elmira	0	0	.000	9.00	2	0	0	2	0	0	5.0	4	7	5	0	1	10	0	2	0
Johnson, Elmira	2	4	.333	9.69	13	4	0	6	0	0	39.0	59	49	42	6	0	20	2	11	5
Jongewaard, Elmira	0	0	.000	12.86	3	0	0	2	0	0	7.0	10	10	10	1	1	4	0	3	4
Jordan, Niagara Falls	3	5	.375	3.21	24	1	0	19	0	7	56.0	66	34	20	2	3	19	4	53	4
Kelley, Auburn	5	2	.714	3.83	14	11	0	1	0	0	82.1	88	40	35	7	3	17	1	49	2
Kent, Niagara Falls	0	0	.000	0.00	2	0	0	0	0	0	1.0	0	0	0	0	0	2	0	0	0
Kiecker, Elmira	11	5	.688	2.74	16	15	4	1	1	0	111.2	92	50	34	7	1	44	4	78	5
Kiernan, Watertown	0	0	.000	9.82	6	0	0	3	0	0	11.0	19	14	12	1	0	4	0	9	1
Kopf, Geneva	4	6	.400	4.80	13	13	3	0	1	0	69.1	66	44	37	11	1	42	2	59	3
Krsnich, Newark	5	3	.625	2.79	26	0	0	21	0	7	38.2	36	20	12	5	2	12	0	39	2
Lackie, Newark*	5	4	.556	5.64	13	10	1	2	0	0	60.2	56	42	38	4	2	61	0	41	13
Ledbetter, Newark	0	0	.000	0.00	2	0	0	1	0	0	1.2	0	0	0	0	0	3	0	2	1
Lewis, Oneonta	1	0	1.000	5.40	8	0	0	2	0	0	15.0	16	12	9	1	0	12	0	13	3
Lind, Watertown	1	4	.200	7.75	10	7	0	2	0	0	33.2	40	33	29	6	4	22	0	24	1
Lopez, Watertown	4	5	.444	2.79	13	13	1	0	1	0	61.1	61	33	19	6	3	24	0	53	1
Lundgren, Little Falls	2	1	.667	1.48	14	0	0	11	0	3	30.1	18	5	5	3	0	8	2	33	2
Manzanillo, Elmira	1	5	.167	7.98	12	4	0	5	0	0	38.1	52	44	34	7	2	20	1	19	5
Mason, Newark	0	2	.000	2.16	14	1	0	4	0	3	33.1	33	15	8	3	1	16	0	18	3
Mathews, Auburn	7	3	.700	2.82	13	13	6	0	1	0	95.2	76	41	30	13	3	15	0	60	6
McGrath, Erie	3	9	.250	5.49	14	14	0	0	0	0	77.0	104	69	47	12	5	28	0	43	8
Medina, Newark*	7	3	.700	4.73	15	14	4	1	0	1	80.0	89	51	42	5	3	44	0	67	11
Mehalko, Utica*	1	0	1.000	5.68	4	1	0	0	0	1	6.1	6	6	4	2	0	3	0	4	1
Miller, Jamestown	5	3	.625	5.67	16	10	2	1	0	0	73.0	80	54	46	5	3	33	0	52	5
Mitchell, Elmira	5	6	.455	4.90	16	10	2	5	1	0	75.1	78	57	41	11	0	41	4	72	3
Moody, Little Falls	3	0	1.000	5.67	21	3	0	13	0	3	33.1	31	24	21	3	2	40	1	32	8
J. Moore, Utica*	3	1	.750	5.18	12	6	1	1	0	0	41.2	36	30	24	7	1	32	1	38	9
S. Moore, Auburn	3	6	.333	4.71	14	14	1	0	0	0	86.0	77	55	45	12	2	46	1	55	10
Moretti, Utica	7	2	.778	2.18	41	2	2	36	0	10	82.2	58	25	20	8	4	32	0	116	5
Morgan, Oneonta	3	0	1.000	3.57	4	3	1	1	1	1	22.2	19	12	9	0	1	6	0	22	2
Murphy, Batavia	2	2	.500	4.70	17	2	0	2	0	0	46.0	46	32	24	3	4	38	1	36	6
Niemiec, Oneonta	1	0	1.000	4.50	1	0	0	0	0	0	2.0	0	1	1	0	0	5	0	1	1
Norton, Jamestown	2	6	.250	4.62	14	7	2	3	0	1	62.1	69	38	32	3	3	28	1	49	7
Oatman, Utica*	0	1	.000	4.12	13	1	0	7	0	1	19.2	14	12	9	1	2	16	1	27	0
Oberbruner, Watertown	2	3	.400	3.67	22	0	0	17	0	1	41.2	43	29	17	1	6	21	3	24	1
Pagani, Batavia	0	3	.000	7.24	6	3	0	0	0	0	13.2	16	15	11	3	2	5	0	17	4
Perrino, Utica*	1	1	.500	9.17	6	5	0	0	0	0	17.2	25	21	18	6	0	13	0	19	4
Perry, Batavia	6	3	.667	4.22	25	4	0	15	0	4	59.2	62	32	28	8	1	25	1	58	5
Pleis, Erie	0	0	.000	0.00	1	0	0	1	0	0	1.1	1	0	0	0	0	1	0	2	1
Ratliff, Jamestown	4	6	.400	3.78	16	13	4	1	0	0	104.2	102	51	44	10	3	35	2	80	3
Rebiejo, Oneonta	4	4	.500	3.59	13	11	1	2	0	0	67.2	76	41	27	4	4	31	0	67	8
Reed, Little Falls	0	0	.000	6.13	19	3	0	10	0	5	39.2	40	28	27	2	2	31	0	44	7
Reynolds, Batavia	1	2	.333	3.98	26	0	0	17	0	3	52.0	62	31	23	6	2	23	1	32	2
Rice, Newark	6	1	.857	3.97	13	12	6	1	2	1	90.2	89	47	40	3	4	38	1	59	2
Richards, Jamestown	7	3	.700	2.98	29	2	0	22	0	3	63.1	40	26	21	5	0	16	1	43	4
Roma, Utica	5	7	.417	3.60	17	16	0	1	0	1	95.0	103	61	38	14	4	38	1	80	4
Ruffner, Oneonta	0	0	.000	13.50	2	0	0	1	0	0	1.1	0	2	2	0	0	4	0	1	0

Pitcher—Club	W.	L.	Pct.	ERA.	G.	GS.	CG.	GF.	ShO.	Sv.	IP.	H.	R.	ER.	HR.	HB.	BB.	Int. BB.	SO.	WP.
Samuels, Auburn*	3	2	.600	3.48	6	5	0	1	0	0	33.2	33	19	13	1	3	19	0	21	3
Sarno, Oneonta	4	8	.333	5.71	13	13	4	0	0	0	69.1	66	56	44	9	3	35	0	61	9
Sauver, Watertown*	7	5	.583	2.31	16	12	1	0	0	0	93.2	80	41	24	6	1	31	0	73	2
Seitz, Utica	12	4	.750	2.61	17	17	3	0	0	0	107.0	100	40	31	8	3	27	1	83	5
Shaab, Auburn*	1	2	.333	4.75	17	0	0	11	0	1	36.0	50	25	19	7	1	12	2	40	5
Silva, Elmira	1	1	.500	5.16	7	6	0	0	0	0	29.2	32	20	17	3	1	13	1	23	3
M. Simmons, Oneonta	0	0	.000	9.00	1	0	0	1	0	0	1.0	2	1	1	1	0	0	0	0	0
S. Simmons, Watertown*	0	0	.000	1.93	5	0	0	2	0	0	4.2	6	2	1	0	0	3	0	2	1
Simon, Watertown	2	4	.333	4.44	19	0	0	7	0	2	48.2	54	30	24	5	5	17	3	39	5
Slowik, Geneva	3	4	.429	5.23	21	1	0	13	0	2	62.0	64	42	36	8	0	33	5	51	8
Smalley, Oneonta*	0	1	.000	6.23	2	1	0	1	0	1	8.2	8	6	6	1	0	5	0	10	0
Smith, Auburn	3	1	.750	6.52	9	0	0	7	0	3	9.2	13	8	7	1	2	6	2	7	2
Soma, Jamestown	6	1	.857	2.41	8	7	1	0	0	0	52.1	46	21	14	3	0	16	0	46	1
Stanton, Jamestown	0	0	.000	5.63	6	0	0	3	0	0	8.0	13	10	5	1	0	7	0	5	2
Stewart, Elmira*	6	5	.545	4.03	14	13	2	0	1	0	89.1	96	52	40	12	0	16	0	76	6
Stidham, Oneonta	1	2	.333	7.27	9	1	0	3	0	0	17.1	24	18	14	1	0	11	0	13	1
Street, Batavia	3	3	.500	5.95	20	3	0	12	0	4	39.1	39	31	26	6	0	27	3	50	5
Sunde, Niagara Falls	2	5	.286	6.79	21	5	0	6	0	0	58.1	74	60	44	5	2	25	2	28	5
Tamarez, Batavia*	4	4	.500	3.39	18	6	2	4	1	0	71.2	70	33	27	6	1	17	0	53	4
Tanner, Niagara Falls	2	3	.400	3.60	16	0	0	15	0	2	25.0	30	16	10	0	1	17	6	31	6
Thielker, Newark	0	0	.000	18.00	1	0	0	1	0	0	1.0	2	2	2	0	1	0	0	0	1
Thomas, Niagara Falls	0	0	.000	0.00	1	0	0	1	0	0	2.0	2	1	0	0	0	0	0	2	0
Tindall, Jamestown*	3	5	.375	4.38	15	13	3	1	0	0	78.0	85	44	38	4	4	33	1	48	5
Toffey, Watertown*	0	0	.000	10.80	4	0	0	1	0	0	3.1	4	8	4	0	0	8	0	3	1
Tompkins, Utica	2	2	.500	3.33	23	0	0	6	0	5	48.2	51	26	18	4	4	18	0	53	2
Traen, Jamestown*	4	4	.500	3.83	14	13	3	0	2	0	84.2	79	41	36	7	1	42	0	71	4
Tuller, Geneva	3	4	.429	3.63	14	14	1	0	0	0	89.1	76	48	36	5	3	62	0	59	23
Turnbull, Erie	1	1	.500	5.00	2	2	0	0	0	0	9.0	10	7	5	1	1	7	0	8	2
Varner, Niagara Falls*	1	2	.333	2.70	8	5	1	1	0	0	30.0	38	14	9	1	1	5	0	21	2
Vasquez, Niagara Falls*	0	0	.000	4.50	3	0	0	3	0	0	6.0	7	7	3	0	1	4	0	4	1
Ventura, Batavia	0	0	.000	0.00	3	0	0	2	0	0	3.0	2	1	0	0	0	2	0	1	0
Verrone, Auburn	2	2	.500	4.58	11	4	0	7	0	3	37.1	41	21	19	4	0	11	0	34	8
Volkman, Geneva	1	2	.333	2.57	23	1	0	14	0	3	56.0	44	25	16	5	2	31	2	42	4
Volquez, Jamestown	0	0	.000	54.00	2	0	0	0	0	0	1.0	4	7	6	0	0	4	0	0	0
Walck, Geneva	0	4	.000	7.96	7	5	0	0	0	0	26.0	43	25	23	5	1	13	2	15	1
Westgard, Oneonta	0	1	.000	12.00	1	1	0	0	0	0	3.0	4	4	4	0	0	1	0	0	0
Whitmyer, Batavia	1	6	.143	7.96	11	8	3	0	0	0	37.1	42	38	33	3	1	29	1	32	7
Williams, Oneonta	0	0	.000	2.08	3	0	0	2	0	1	4.1	3	1	1	1	0	1	0	2	0
Wilson, Newark	0	1	.000	3.00	1	0	0	0	0	0	3.0	2	1	1	1	0	1	0	4	0
Wright, Utica	1	2	.333	4.32	6	3	0	2	0	0	16.2	17	13	8	2	1	5	0	12	1
York, Oneonta	0	0	.000	8.18	9	0	0	4	0	0	11.0	19	13	10	0	2	8	0	3	3
Zamba, Utica	12	2	.857	2.32	16	15	2	0	0	0	97.0	100	36	25	13	5	22	0	69	3
Zucco, Jamestown*	0	0	.000	9.00	2	0	0	0	0	0	2.0	3	5	2	0	0	3	0	2	1

BALKS—Davis, Hurst, Sauver, 4 each; Browne, 3; Bencomo, Blasucci, Coughlin, Kiecker, Lackie, Tamarez, Walck, 2 each; Bardwell, Brahs, Corsi, Costello, Devlin, Engle, Fansler, Finnegan, Fulton, German, Giron, Gonzalez, Gordon, Hartshorn, Hickey, Imig, Innis, Lind, McGrath, Medina, J. Moore, S. Moore, Moretti, Morgan, Murphy, Oatman, Oberbruner, Reynolds, Roma, Seitz, Soma, Sunde, Tanner, Tompkins, Traen, Volquez, 1 each.

COMBINATION SHUTOUTS—Samuels-Hammond, Auburn; Mitchell-Dalton, Elmira; Brisco-Gass, Erie; Tuller-Volkman, Brewer-Doyle, Tuller-Ballard, Geneva; Gay-Aguilera, Boyles-Innis, Moody-Lundgren-Reed-Innis, Boyles-Reed, Little Falls; Habyan-Bell, Caldwell-Krsnich, Newark; Jordan-Tanner, Niagara Falls; Rebiejo-Devlin, Oneonta; Seitz-Moretti 2, Utica.

NO-HIT GAME—Fulton, Oneonta, defeated Geneva, 1-0, July 25.

Northwest League

CLASS A

CHAMPIONSHIP WINNERS IN PREVIOUS YEARS

1901—Portland	.675
1902—Butte	.608
1903—Butte	.578
1904—Boise	.625
1905—Vancouver	.586
Everett*	.667
1906—Tacoma	.600
1907—Aberdeen	.625
1908—Vancouver	.578
1909—Seattle	.653
1910—Spokane	.596
1911—Vancouver	.628
1912—Seattle	.600
1913—Vancouver	.600
1914—Vancouver	.632
1915—Seattle	.564
1916—Spokane	.622
1917—Great Falls	.592
1918—Seattle	.588
1919—Seattle	.590
1920—Victoria	.600
1921—Yakima	.710
Yakima	.660
1922—Calgary†	.600
1923-36—Did not operate.	
1937—Wenatchee	.603
Tacoma*	.627
1938—Yakima	.583
Bellingham (2nd)†	.511
1939—Wenatchee	.601
Tacoma (2nd)†	.533
1940—Spokane	.587
Tacoma (4th)†	.500
1941—Spokane	.669
1942—Vancouver	.594
1943-45—Did not operate.	
1946—Wenatchee	.622
1947—Vancouver	.566
1948—Spokane	.614
1949—Yakima	.660
Vancouver (2nd)†	.615
1950—Yakima	.613
1951—Spokane	.655
1952—Victoria	.631
1953—Salem	.635
Spokane*	.590
1954—Vancouver*	.636
Lewiston	.629
1955—Salem	.646
Eugene*	.639
1956—Yakima	.691
Yakima	.619
1957—Eugene	.576
Wenatchee*	.647
1958—Lewiston	.621
Yakima*	.594
1959—Salem	.623
Yakima*	.563
1960—Yakima	.638
Yakima	.562
1961—Lewiston*	.621
Yakima	.600
1962—Wenatchee*	.574
Tri-City	.580
1963—Lewiston	.594
Yakima*	.613
1964—Eugene	.636
Yakima*	.611
1965—Lewiston	.667
Tri-City*	.681
1966—Tri-City	.679
1967—Medford	.607
1968—Tri-City	.600
1969—Rogue Valley	.633
1970—Lewiston a	.538
Coos Bay-No. Bend	.563
1971—Tri-City a	.625
Bend	.538
1972—Lewiston a	.675
Walla Walla	.513
1973—Walla Walla b	.638
Portland	.563
1974—Bellingham	.619
Eugene c	.571
1975—Portland	.545
Eugene d	.684
1976—Portland	.556
Walla Walla d	.639
1977—Bellingham e	.618
Portland	.667
1978—Grays Harbor f	.671
Eugene	.514
1979—Central Oregon d	.606
Walla Walla	.571
1980—Bellingham g	.643
Eugene g	.529
1981—Medford d	.600
Bellingham	.557
1982—Medford	.757
Salem d	.486

*Won split-season playoff. †Won four-club playoff. §League disbanded June 18. aLeague divided into Northern and Southern divisions, declared champion under league rules. bLeague divided into Eastern and Western divisions, declared champion under league rules. cLeague divided into Eastern and Western divisions; won two-team playoff. dLeague divided into Northern and Southern divisions; won two-team playoff. eLeague divided into Affiliate and Independent divisions; won two-team playoff. fDeclared league champion after winning one-game playoff. Balance of playoff canceled due to rain and wet grounds. g Declared co-champion after winning one game. Balance of playoff canceled due to rain and wet grounds. (NOTE—Known as Pacific Northwest League 1901-02, Pacific National League 1903-04, Northwestern League 1905-18, Pacific Coast International League 1919-22 and Western International League 1937-54.)

STANDING OF CLUBS AT CLOSE OF SEASON, SEPTEMBER 1

Club	Bell	WW	TC	Spo	Med	Eug	Bend	Sal	W.	L.	T.	Pct.	G.B.
WASHINGTON DIVISION													
Bellingham (Mariners)	....	11	6	8	3	5	4	3	40	28	1	.588	....
Walla Walla (Co-op)	2	....	8	8	2	3	6	4	33	36	1	.478	7½
Tri-Cities (Rangers)	8	6	....	9	0	3	4	3	33	37	0	.471	8
Spokane (Padres)	5	6	5	....	2	2	2	1	23	46	0	.333	17½
OREGON DIVISION													
Medford (A's)	4	5	7	5	....	9	10	10	50	18	0	.735	....
Eugene (Reds)	2	4	4	5	3	....	7	8	33	34	0	.493	16½
Bend (Phillies)	3	1	3	5	4	6	....	10	32	37	0	.464	18½
Salem (Angels)	4	3	4	6	4	6	4	....	31	39	0	.443	20

Tri-Cities represented Richland, Pasco and Kennewick, Wash.

Major league affiliations in parentheses.

Playoff—Medford defeated Bellingham, two games to none.

Regular-Season Attendance—Bellingham, 12,944; Bend, 29,063; Eugene, 85,021; Medford, 73,278; Salem, 31,458; Spokane, 40,137; Tri-Cities, 48,896; Walla Walla, 9,019. Total, 329,816. Playoffs, 2,287, All-Star Game, 1,260.

Managers—Bellingham, Jeff Scott; Bend, Jay Ward; Eugene, Sam Mejias; Medford, Dennis Rogers; Salem, Joe Maddon; Spokane, Ed Olsen; Tri-Cities, Dave Oliver; Walla Walla, Ron Mihal.

All-Star Team: 1B—Jose Tolentino, Medford; 2B—Keith Thrower, Medford; 3B—Robert Martinez, Tri-Cities; SS—Tony Evans, Eugene; OF—Oriol Perez, Bellingham; Larry Beardman, Medford; Mike O'Hara, Salem; C—(tie) Bill Hance, Tri-Cities, and Greg Toler, Eugene; LHP—Mike Fulmer, Medford; RHP—Mark Bauer, Medford; DH—Jose Canseco, Medford; Manager—Dennis Rogers, Medford.

(Compiled by William J. Weiss, League Statistician, San Mateo, Calif.)

CLUB BATTING

Club	Pct.	G.	AB.	R.	OR.	H.	TB.	2B.	3B.	HR.	RBI.	GW.	SH.	SF.	HP.	BB.	Int. BB.	SO.	SB.	CS.	LOB.
Eugene	.275	67	2327	415	394	641	905	117	24	33	332	24	25	27	29	285	7	411	66	25	557
Medford	.275	68	2284	431	277	629	951	109	24	55	350	38	21	16	30	306	5	461	153	45	498
Tri-Cities	.253	70	2329	367	354	590	876	105	11	53	319	30	18	20	39	333	8	528	75	34	554
Bend	.250	69	2370	362	392	592	800	89	25	23	291	28	8	21	26	299	8	572	127	47	525
Salem	.250	70	2331	326	387	584	786	62	37	22	270	25	21	21	18	268	10	502	106	45	510
Bellingham	.239	69	2298	375	289	549	851	104	14	57	319	31	20	29	24	360	3	588	59	32	545
Walla Walla	.234	70	2348	320	331	549	740	79	17	26	262	27	39	15	25	299	11	592	102	29	552
Spokane	.230	69	2285	252	424	526	684	75	19	15	200	16	28	14	22	261	10	465	86	46	532

INDIVIDUAL BATTING

(Leading Qualifiers for Batting Championship—189 or More Plate Appearances)

*Bats lefthanded. †Switch-hitter.

Player and Club	Pct.	G.	AB.	R.	H.	TB.	2B.	3B.	HR.	RBI.	GW.	SH.	SF.	HP.	BB.	Int. BB.	SO.	SB.	CS.
Hance, William, Tri-Cities*	.340	45	159	24	54	75	14	1	5	30	1	0	2	1	33	1	13	0	0
Thrower, Keith, Medford†	.333	58	213	50	71	102	11	4	4	31	2	3	2	2	31	2	24	63	10
Tolentino, Jose, Medford*	.331	49	181	33	60	94	11	1	7	39	4	0	2	3	15	2	17	1	1
Berge, Jordan, Eugene*	.326	58	215	32	70	101	7	6	4	37	2	1	4	0	18	0	25	3	1
Martinez, Robert, Tri-Cities	.324	61	219	55	71	121	14	3	10	39	2	0	2	8	40	3	44	13	5
Moses, Steven, Bend*	.319	53	204	36	65	79	12	1	0	22	2	0	1	0	22	1	19	15	4
Steinbach, Terry, Medford	.315	62	219	42	69	103	16	0	6	38	4	0	1	5	28	0	22	8	4
Ward, Kevin, Bend	.307	55	199	33	61	83	12	2	2	29	1	0	0	4	31	2	35	18	8
Montgomery, Reginald, Salem	.306	68	265	39	81	114	10	4	5	47	4	1	4	4	16	1	44	7	4
Reibel, Douglas, Salem*	.303	68	211	46	64	99	9	4	6	34	1	0	2	4	62	2	44	12	8

Departmental Leaders: G—O'Hara, 69; AB—O'Hara, 295; R—Guinn, 61; H—O'Hara, 86; TB—O. Perez, 122; 2B—Machado, 17; 3B—Buchanon, Mota, 8; HR—O. Perez, 15; RBI—Montgomery, 47; GWRBI—Beardman, 9; SH—Paulson, 8; SF—Beardman, 6; HP—R. Martinez, 8; BB—Reibel, 62; IBB—Dillard, R. Martinez, Munson, Spellmon, 3; SO—Canseco, 78; SB—Thrower, 62; CS—Guinn, 12.

(All Players—Listed Alphabetically)

Player and Club	Pct.	G.	AB.	R.	H.	TB.	2B.	3B.	HR.	RBI.	GW.	SH.	SF.	HP.	BB.	Int. BB.	SO.	SB.	CS.
Adams, Bert, Salem	.184	44	103	8	19	26	7	0	0	7	0	0	1	0	5	0	33	3	3
Alfredson, Thomas, Salem	.178	52	163	13	29	34	2	0	1	17	1	0	3	0	14	0	56	5	2
Amaya, Benjamin, Bellingham	.267	57	180	30	48	76	11	1	5	35	3	2	3	1	39	0	38	1	5
Anderson, Willie, Spokane	.230	67	243	26	56	78	12	2	2	22	1	3	1	1	30	1	58	12	7
Artiles, Orlando, Medford	.244	25	78	10	19	25	3	0	1	12	0	0	0	0	10	0	17	4	1
Bailey, Gregory, Tri-Cities	.171	50	164	26	28	36	2	0	2	16	2	1	1	1	25	1	48	6	2
Balmer, Gary, Bellingham	.225	36	89	21	20	28	5	0	1	16	1	1	3	1	28	0	19	4	0
Barba, Douglas, Eugene	.000	12	1	0	0	0	0	0	0	0	0	0	0	0	0	0	1	0	0
Beardman, Lawrence, Medford	.301	60	229	51	69	107	10	2	8	42	9	2	6	4	21	0	40	19	5
Berge, Jordan, Eugene*	.326	58	215	32	70	101	7	6	4	37	2	1	4	0	18	0	25	3	1
Bowden, Mark, Eugene*	.000	3	1	0	0	0	0	0	0	0	0	0	0	0	0	0	0	0	0
Bradley, Paul, Medford	.221	52	136	25	30	47	6	1	3	16	0	4	1	4	33	0	42	1	0
Bruzik, Robert, Bellingham	.291	49	158	29	46	69	7	2	4	18	0	2	1	1	17	0	31	7	5
Buchanon, Bobby, Salem*	.290	63	221	35	64	90	4	8	2	24	3	1	1	0	35	1	43	17	3
Cain, Marty, Salem	.000	5	8	0	0	0	0	0	0	0	0	0	0	0	0	0	7	0	0
Canseco, Jose, Medford	.269	59	197	34	53	105	15	2	11	40	6	0	1	5	30	0	78	6	2
Carlucci, Anthony, Tri-Cities	.188	37	101	18	19	29	4	0	2	17	1	2	0	5	35	2	35	0	0
Cesario, James, Tri-Cities	.259	50	186	29	48	77	11	0	6	31	2	0	2	1	20	0	43	7	5
Clawson, Kenneth, Spokane	.237	55	186	19	44	49	3	1	0	14	1	4	2	2	16	0	39	2	2
Cloninger, Darrin, Spokane	.000	7	0	1	0	0	0	0	0	0	0	0	0	0	0	0	0	0	0
Colpitt, Michael, Bend	.217	18	46	7	10	16	1	1	1	4	0	0	0	1	11	0	26	2	2
Colton, Bradford, Bellingham	.400	10	30	9	12	15	3	0	0	3	1	0	0	0	6	0	3	2	0
Curry, Clinton, Tri-Cities	.226	52	190	20	43	62	8	1	3	30	2	0	5	3	19	0	42	3	0
Dannenberg, Wayne, Bend*	.250	50	176	24	44	63	12	2	1	16	3	0	1	3	22	0	51	4	0
Davis, James, Eugene	.250	25	68	12	17	19	2	0	0	8	1	4	2	1	5	0	16	0	1
Davis, Lee, Bend	.163	28	80	8	13	23	1	3	1	10	0	0	0	0	7	0	28	3	3
Day, Randall, Bend	.276	49	163	24	45	79	16	0	6	40	4	0	3	2	23	1	47	5	3
del Rosario, Manuel, Spokane†	.218	49	179	18	39	50	7	2	0	8	0	2	0	1	20	0	43	5	5
Diaz, Jorge, Medford	.184	15	38	3	7	11	1	0	1	5	1	0	0	0	3	0	9	0	0
Dillard, David, Spokane*	.255	53	161	20	41	57	6	2	2	21	2	3	2	3	25	3	37	9	5
Dorsett, Brian, Medford	.271	14	48	11	13	20	2	1	1	10	1	0	0	0	5	0	5	0	0
Duncan, Lindon, Tri-Cities	.311	17	61	10	19	26	4	0	1	7	1	0	0	0	7	0	20	4	1
Engram, Gralyn, Bend	.270	25	89	15	24	30	3	0	1	8	1	2	1	2	16	0	12	7	1
Evans, Anthony, Eugene	.294	60	204	43	60	87	12	3	3	32	4	2	2	5	33	0	35	8	4
Ferguson, James, Walla Walla	.295	14	44	4	13	16	1	1	0	4	0	0	1	1	4	0	5	2	0
Ferrin, Trent, Eugene	.000	22	2	0	0	0	0	0	0	0	0	2	0	0	0	0	1	0	0
Floyd, Joe Max, Bend	.148	21	61	6	9	9	0	0	0	4	0	0	0	2	4	0	14	1	0
Francis, Todd, Bellingham*	.246	40	134	22	33	54	3	0	6	21	3	1	3	0	23	0	31	2	0
Fulgencio, Elvin, Eugene	.274	52	190	29	52	71	10	3	1	21	2	2	3	2	8	0	35	3	2
Gile, Mark, Tri-Cities*	.266	51	207	32	55	72	9	1	2	22	4	3	2	1	13	0	43	9	5
Gomez, Freddy, Spokane	.100	18	40	4	4	4	0	0	0	2	0	0	0	0	5	0	16	0	1
Gomez, Nelson, Salem	.133	8	15	0	2	2	0	0	0	1	0	0	0	0	1	0	8	0	0
Grant, Kenneth, Salem	.234	44	145	13	34	50	1	3	3	30	3	2	1	3	9	0	39	7	4
Guinn, Brian, Medford†	.251	66	247	61	62	99	9	5	6	32	3	3	1	1	40	0	45	26	12
Haberle, David, Eugene*	.273	27	88	11	24	37	2	1	3	15	2	0	1	0	12	0	17	1	0
Haley, Samuel, Bellingham	.312	50	157	37	49	76	5	2	6	25	3	0	2	2	15	0	35	9	3
Hallow, John, Spokane*	.187	52	187	11	35	41	6	0	0	17	2	1	2	1	11	2	18	2	2
Hamb, Andre, Walla Walla*	.270	50	148	19	40	51	2	3	1	15	3	0	2	3	20	0	41	10	3
Hance, William, Tri-Cities*	.340	45	159	24	54	85	14	1	5	30	1	0	2	1	33	1	13	0	0
Hansen, Ronald, Tri-Cities	.244	40	131	20	32	47	6	0	3	14	0	2	0	4	23	1	36	0	1
Hardgrave, Eric, Spokane	.296	37	125	25	37	60	7	2	4	17	0	0	1	6	21	1	29	6	1
Harms, Duane, Eugene	.083	13	12	0	1	2	1	0	0	0	0	1	0	0	0	0	4	0	0
Hengel, David, Bellingham	.333	9	27	4	9	13	4	0	0	6	1	0	0	1	5	0	6	2	1
Hennessy, Brendan, Tri-Cities	.221	47	163	21	36	59	4	2	5	23	2	0	1	4	12	0	37	1	1
Houston, Barry, Walla Walla*	.295	42	129	24	38	70	4	5	6	19	1	0	0	1	14	1	46	5	2
Howell, Jack, Salem*	.395	21	76	23	30	51	2	5	3	12	1	0	0	0	17	0	11	2	1
Howell, Toney, Walla Walla	.222	8	9	0	2	2	0	0	0	2	1	0	0	1	1	0	1	0	1
Hubbard, Henry, Spokane	.231	66	238	21	55	62	5	1	0	21	2	5	2	0	24	0	52	17	11
Hudson, Lance, Walla Walla†	.236	59	203	25	48	60	5	2	1	21	1	3	1	1	18	0	40	16	2
Jackson, James, Medford*	.065	26	62	4	4	4	0	0	0	3	0	0	0	2	8	0	32	0	1
Jimenez, Ramon, Salem	.297	39	128	21	38	45	5	1	0	25	2	3	0	1	25	0	15	2	1
Johnson, Aubrey, Medford	.286	9	21	1	6	6	0	0	0	1	0	1	0	0	1	0	4	0	0
Johnson, Todd, Bend	.233	29	103	16	24	34	2	1	2	10	1	0	1	2	6	0	29	7	1
Jones, Scott, Eugene	.000	1	1	1	0	0	0	0	0	0	0	0	0	1	0	0	0	0	0
Jones, Tracy, Eugene	.266	55	203	42	54	69	12	0	1	26	0	1	3	6	26	0	24	14	3
Kane, Mark, Walla Walla	.247	54	154	25	38	61	12	1	3	21	1	1	2	3	26	0	58	2	3
Keehn, Michael, Tri-Cities	.161	42	137	12	22	28	1	1	1	13	1	4	3	1	21	0	38	4	3
Keller, David, Eugene	.280	65	236	50	66	110	12	1	10	44	4	0	2	2	55	1	63	2	0
Komeiji, Keith, Bellingham	.133	6	15	2	2	2	0	0	0	2	0	0	0	1	4	0	9	1	0
Kraft, Kenneth, Bend	.233	44	159	26	37	41	4	0	0	16	3	1	2	3	20	0	30	7	1

Player and Club	Pct.	G.	AB.	R.	H.	TB.	2B.	3B.	HR.	RBI.	GW.	SH.	SF.	HP.	BB.	Int. BB.	SO.	SB.	CS.
Lantigua, Wilfredo, Salem	.091	5	11	1	1	1	0	0	0	0	0	0	0	0	1	0	7	0	0
Lawson, Jeffrey, Bellingham	.268	34	112	16	30	52	6	2	4	17	0	0	0	1	19	1	24	1	0
Lee, Steve, Salem 18-WW 20*	.214	38	126	12	27	32	3	1	0	11	0	0	0	0	16	2	42	4	1
Lora, Jose, Spokane	.164	41	110	9	18	22	1	0	1	5	1	2	0	2	13	1	34	6	3
Lynds, Mark, Salem	.071	19	42	3	3	3	0	0	0	3	0	0	0	0	9	0	23	1	1
Machado, Ruben, Eugene	.276	64	275	47	76	119	17	4	6	40	2	3	1	1	11	1	25	3	1
Maples, Randall, Bend	.178	30	90	10	16	20	1	0	1	12	1	0	1	0	22	0	31	2	0
Marquez, Edwin, Salem	.091	14	33	3	3	4	1	0	0	1	0	1	0	0	3	0	7	0	1
Martinez, David, Walla Walla	.233	32	103	19	24	30	1	1	1	8	1	4	0	1	13	0	13	5	1
Martinez, Edgar, Bellingham	.173	32	104	14	18	21	1	1	0	5	2	1	1	2	18	0	24	1	3
Martinez, Robert, Tri-Cities	.324	61	219	55	71	121	14	3	10	39	2	0	2	8	40	3	44	13	5
Matos, Rafael, Bellingham	.128	19	47	7	6	11	0	1	1	5	0	1	0	0	9	1	23	3	0
McLean, Malcolm, Medford†	.301	57	176	34	53	67	7	2	1	21	1	3	2	1	26	0	29	10	6
McLemore, Kevin, Salem	.154	7	13	3	2	2	0	0	0	2	0	0	0	0	2	0	6	0	0
Mendoza, Raymond, Medford*	.261	59	203	38	53	82	9	4	4	35	6	0	0	2	28	1	44	8	3
Meyer, Michael, Walla Walla	.242	66	211	33	51	58	7	0	0	28	5	7	3	0	36	1	47	13	3
Mills, Michael, Spokane	.000	11	1	0	0	0	0	0	0	0	0	0	0	0	0	0	1	0	0
Minyard, John, Eugene	.111	17	9	2	1	4	0	0	1	1	0	1	0	0	1	0	4	0	0
Mitchell, Donald, Eugene	.200	6	5	0	1	1	0	0	0	1	0	1	0	0	1	0	2	0	0
Mitchell, William, Salem	.074	21	54	3	4	5	1	0	0	2	1	0	1	0	1	0	24	0	0
Moncerratt, Pablo, Bellingham*	.185	25	81	12	15	26	5	0	2	9	2	0	0	1	11	0	33	0	2
Monda, Gregory, Eugene*	.243	61	210	29	51	67	8	1	2	26	3	0	5	5	22	1	29	5	2
Montgomery, Reginald, Salem	.306	68	265	39	81	114	10	4	5	47	4	1	4	4	16	1	44	7	4
Moriarty, James, Walla Walla	.260	68	258	33	67	84	9	1	2	20	1	2	0	1	24	1	47	13	5
Morris, Manuel, Bellingham	.202	29	114	12	23	34	5	0	2	17	0	1	0	0	3	0	24	1	1
Moses, Steven, Bend*	.319	53	204	36	65	79	12	1	0	22	2	0	1	0	22	1	19	15	4
Mosley, Reginald, Tri-Cities	.226	52	168	35	38	69	7	0	8	31	6	0	0	3	50	0	57	19	5
Mota, Luis, Bend*	.293	58	229	35	67	102	7	8	4	39	7	1	2	3	12	2	46	4	5
Munson, Jay, Eugene	.254	56	185	29	47	59	8	2	0	16	0	1	2	2	23	3	36	8	5
Neel, Steven, Walla Walla*	.077	15	39	4	3	11	0	1	2	7	0	1	1	1	8	1	10	1	0
Nichols, Howard, Bend	.198	28	91	10	18	23	2	0	1	13	0	0	2	2	8	0	26	2	0
Odgers, Daniel, Bend	.259	54	205	32	53	66	7	3	0	28	1	1	1	1	19	1	38	14	5
O'Hara, Michael, Salem*	.295	69	292	38	86	113	7	7	2	25	2	3	3	1	11	1	27	27	8
Olson, Randy, Spokane	.262	57	202	24	53	69	6	2	2	21	1	1	1	2	17	0	38	4	0
Oquendo, Jorge, Medford*	.290	41	124	17	36	45	5	2	0	14	0	0	0	1	13	0	30	6	0
Paulson, Kenneth, Walla Walla	.224	48	152	12	34	41	4	0	1	16	1	8	0	1	11	1	34	3	2
Peel, Allen, Walla Walla	.214	15	42	3	9	11	2	0	0	5	0	3	0	0	4	0	10	1	0
Peltola, William, Walla Walla	.000	20	1	0	0	0	0	0	0	0	0	0	0	0	0	0	1	0	0
Pereira, Reinaldo, Bellingham	.500	2	2	0	1	1	0	0	0	0	0	0	0	1	0	0	1	0	0
Perez, Oriol, Bellingham	.281	63	221	46	62	122	11	2	15	42	6	3	3	0	42	1	66	7	4
Perez, Sergio, Bend	.147	28	95	11	14	16	2	0	0	10	0	1	1	0	7	0	20	3	2
Phaup, Robert, Walla Walla	.000	25	1	0	0	0	0	0	0	0	0	0	0	0	0	0	1	0	0
Phillips, Robert, Eugene*	.212	15	33	7	7	9	2	0	0	4	1	2	0	0	2	0	4	1	0
Porter, Jason, Spokane	.231	66	242	29	56	83	14	2	3	25	1	4	2	4	32	1	52	2	1
Posillico, James, Walla Walla	.196	54	153	19	30	39	5	2	0	14	1	3	0	0	18	1	40	8	0
Priftis, George, Bellingham*	.256	41	117	11	30	37	2	1	1	14	1	1	3	1	26	0	29	2	1
Psaltis, Spiro, Walla Walla*	.000	14	0	1	0	0	0	0	0	0	0	0	0	0	0	0	0	0	0
Rantz, Michael, Medford	.071	13	28	3	2	2	0	0	0	2	0	4	0	0	9	0	6	1	0
Reibel, Douglas, Salem*	.303	68	211	46	64	99	9	4	6	34	1	0	2	4	62	2	44	12	8
Reid, Craig, Spokane	.233	23	73	8	17	23	1	1	1	7	0	0	0	0	8	0	12	9	4
Rhoades, David, Walla Walla	.224	61	210	35	47	59	9	0	1	19	2	4	1	3	33	1	43	11	0
Riley, Mickey, Walla Walla†	.269	21	67	10	18	19	1	0	0	7	0	0	1	1	14	1	7	1	3
Rivera, Angel, Spokane	.111	14	36	3	4	4	0	0	0	0	0	1	0	0	5	1	10	1	0
Roberts, Jay, Walla Walla	.208	62	231	30	48	69	6	0	5	28	4	2	2	5	18	0	75	9	3
Rodriguez, David, Bellingham	.088	25	68	6	6	7	1	0	0	5	0	1	0	0	14	0	42	0	1
Roebuck, Scott, Bellingham	.297	35	111	20	33	55	8	1	4	21	1	0	1	1	19	0	19	2	0
Ross, Keith, Bend*	.237	40	118	21	28	39	2	3	1	9	0	2	2	1	28	0	49	11	5
Sakowski, Vincent, Tri-Cities	.280	57	246	35	69	81	12	0	0	23	4	5	0	2	15	0	20	7	5
Sambo, Ramon, Bend†	.262	49	164	33	43	50	2	1	1	9	1	0	1	0	27	0	53	20	6
Sciacca, Steven, Salem	.113	25	62	3	7	10	1	1	0	5	0	0	0	0	2	0	18	1	0
Segura, Americo, Salem	.153	18	59	7	9	11	2	0	0	7	0	2	1	0	3	0	9	0	1
Simpson, Danny, Tri-Cities	.283	54	198	30	56	84	9	2	5	23	2	1	2	5	20	0	52	2	1
Smith, Kenneth, Walla Walla*	.500	15	2	1	1	1	0	0	0	2	0	0	0	0	0	0	1	0	0
Smith, Paul, Bellingham	.248	43	145	25	36	50	11	0	1	17	1	1	3	4	16	0	29	4	1
Snediker, James, Eugene	.167	14	6	2	1	2	1	0	0	0	0	1	0	0	0	0	2	0	0
Souza, Gilbert, Walla Walla†	.200	38	120	18	24	43	10	0	3	19	5	1	1	2	29	2	48	1	1
Spector, Douglas, Eugene	.000	16	5	0	0	0	0	0	0	0	0	1	0	0	1	0	2	0	0
Spellmon, Terrence, Salem†	.213	48	141	16	30	36	2	2	0	11	2	5	1	0	18	3	38	3	5
Spisok, Jeffrey, Eugene	.301	29	103	22	31	41	7	0	1	12	0	2	1	2	22	0	31	11	3
Steen, Gregory, Salem	.272	61	239	44	65	73	6	1	0	13	5	3	3	5	26	1	24	16	2
Steinbach, Terry, Medford	.315	62	219	42	69	103	16	0	6	38	4	0	1	5	28	0	22	8	4
Steinbach, Thomas, Bellingham	.166	48	163	23	27	47	9	1	3	21	5	0	3	0	25	0	38	1	0
Stewart, Jeffery, Spokane	.000	15	1	0	0	0	0	0	0	0	0	0	0	0	0	0	1	0	0
Stis, Douglas, Eugene	.250	18	4	1	1	1	0	0	0	1	0	0	0	0	1	0	1	1	0
Stout, Steven, Eugene	.000	25	3	0	0	0	0	0	0	0	0	0	0	0	0	0	1	0	0
Stowe, Kelly, Bend	.214	35	98	15	21	27	3	0	1	12	3	0	2	0	14	1	18	2	1
Thrower, Keith, Medford†	.333	58	213	50	71	102	11	4	4	31	2	3	2	2	31	2	24	63	10
Tolentino, Jose, Medford*	.331	49	181	33	60	94	11	1	7	39	4	0	2	3	15	2	17	1	1
Toler, Gregory, Eugene	.289	53	187	39	54	72	13	1	1	33	3	0	1	2	28	0	36	5	0
Tunnell, Frank, Bellingham	.214	36	117	16	25	29	4	0	0	10	0	5	0	3	12	0	36	5	4
Uribe, Jorge, Bellingham	.205	22	73	13	15	22	1	0	2	8	1	0	3	2	4	0	23	3	1
Vega, Luis, Bellingham	.091	16	33	0	3	5	2	0	0	2	0	0	0	1	5	0	5	1	0
Walsh, Thomas, Medford	.284	23	67	10	19	25	3	0	1	6	1	1	0	0	2	0	11	0	0
Ward, Kevin, Bend	.307	55	199	33	61	83	12	2	2	29	1	0	0	4	31	2	35	18	8
Wesley, Joseph, Medford*	.176	11	17	4	3	7	1	0	1	3	0	0	0	0	3	0	6	0	0
Wilburn, Fred, Salem	.000	13	3	0	0	0	0	0	0	0	0	0	0	0	0	0	1	0	0
Wilks, Darryl, Eugene	.333	31	81	17	27	34	3	2	0	15	0	0	0	0	16	1	17	1	3
Williams, Mitchell, Spokane*	.000	15	1	0	0	0	0	0	0	0	0	0	0	0	0	0	0	0	0
Wolff, Steven, Spokane	.258	67	260	34	67	82	7	4	0	20	5	2	1	0	34	0	25	11	4

The following pitchers, listed alphabetically by club, with games in parentheses, had no plate appearances, primarily through use of designated hitters:

BELLINGHAM—Akerfelds, Darrel (12); Bergendahl, Wray (11); Bryant, James (19); Gunnarson, Robert (25); Hinson, Robert (3); Luecken, Richard (14); Meister, Mickey (3); Nielsen, Scott (2); Roy, Kevin (11); Salazar, Edward (20); Smith, David (19); Swearingen, Douglas (18); Wilkinson, William (13).

BEND—Abrego, Johnny (14); Baccala, Aldo (1); Beal, Bron (1); Caraballo, Ramon (21); Collier, Randy (13); Evetts, Anthony (16); Johnson, Kyle (19); McLarnan, John (15); Menard, Darryl (14); Morton, William (13); Powell, John (13); Rasnick, James (15); Stewart, Wayne (9); Weatherford, Brant (14).

EUGENE—Dibble, Robert (7); Johns, Richard (2); Mitchell, Darryl (4); Salgueiro, Miguel (11).

MEDFORD—Bailey, James (13); Bauer, Mark (15); Cadaret, Gregory (12); Fulmer, Michael (14); Gomez, Steven (21); Hanna, David (5); Hilton, Stan (2); Odom, Joe (11); Scherer, Douglas (28); Wanzer, Scott (15); Whaley, Scott (16).

SALEM—Cannon, Scott (22); Carter, Richard (25); Cedeno, Vinicio (14); Chadwick, Ray (16); Glanz, Scott (9); Gonzales, James (21); Hernandez, Carlos (3); Kemmerling, Byron (9); Ojeda, Jorge (8); Stanfield, Donald (9); Tinkey, James (13); Valdez, Jose (10).

SPOKANE—Childers, Jeffrey (15); Hubbard, Marlon (16); James, Mark (15); McLoughlin, Timothy (4); Ortiz, Elsis (10); Parks, Jeffrey (17); Sierra, Ulises (23); Valdez, Efrain (13).

TRI-CITIES—Allison, James (13); Bass, Regan (8); Burns, Kerry (14); Cipres, Mark (16); Esposito, Nick (17); Fryhoff, John (16); Keathley, Robin (10); Kipper, Bruce (14); Knight, Dennis (14); Kordish, Steven (10); Lindquist, Dan (18); Munley, John (15); Sebra, Robert (12).

WALLA WALLA—Allen, Robert (17); Armitage, Dean (14); Blas, William (15); Diez, Mark (3); Glanz, Scott (6); Miquel, George (13); Saylor, Allen (8); Spini, Michael (13).

GRAND SLAM HOME RUNS—Bradley, Grant, Kane, Keehn, Lawson, Machado, O. Perez, Roebuck, Thrower, Tolentino, 1 each.

AWARDED FIRST BASE ON CATCHER'S INTERFERENCE—Day 2 (Dorsett, Toler); Monda 2 (Amaya, Bradley); Dorsett (Haberle); Hudson (Porter); Mendoza (Marquez); Paulson (Amaya); Posillico (Haberle).

CLUB FIELDING

Club	Pct.	G.	PO.	A.	E.	DP.	PB.
Medford	.959	68	1779	750	108	57	13
Bellingham	.952	69	1831	668	125	47	18
Eugene	.948	67	1720	694	132	47	18
Tri-Cities	.947	70	1810	709	140	54	12
Spokane	.944	69	1798	745	150	51	27
Walla Walla	.939	70	1850	704	166	48	19
Bend	.937	69	1833	722	168	61	27
Salem	.928	70	1810	674	192	32	35

Triple play—Salem.

INDIVIDUAL FIELDING

*Throws lefthanded.

FIRST BASEMEN

Player and Club	Pct.	G.	PO.	A.	E.	DP.
Buchanon, Salem	.963	10	72	6	3	0
Cesario, Tri-Cities	1.000	1	1	1	0	0
Clawson, Spokane	1.000	2	5	1	0	0
Day, Bend	.970	6	31	1	1	2
Dillard, Spokane*	.986	33	271	16	4	16
Francis, Bellingham*	.973	19	134	9	4	11
Gile, Tri-Cities	1.000	1	1	0	0	0
Gomez, Spokane	.976	7	40	1	1	3
Hansen, Tri-Cities	.972	29	195	15	6	19
Hardgrave, Spokane	.976	23	187	16	5	12
Houston, Walla Walla*	.961	18	138	11	6	8
Howell, Walla Walla	1.000	1	5	1	0	0
Jackson, Medford	.941	18	123	4	8	12
Kane, Walla Walla	.961	19	143	3	6	11
Keller, Eugene	.979	39	305	24	7	22
Lee, Walla Walla*	.889	1	8	0	1	0
D. Martinez, Walla Walla	1.000	2	21	0	0	0
R. Martinez, Tri-Cities	1.000	1	8	1	0	0
Mendoza, Medford*	.990	11	90	8	1	4
Monceratt, Bellingham*	.984	17	120	6	2	7
Monda, Eugene*	.991	28	208	21	2	14
Montgomery, Salem	.966	11	69	15	3	4
Mosley, Tri-Cities	.986	45	395	17	6	27
Mota, Bend*	.972	52	459	36	14	40
Neel, Walla Walla*	.991	13	104	4	1	5
Nichols, Bend	.959	19	132	10	6	12
Olson, Spokane	.962	8	72	3	3	5
Reibel, Salem*	.957	52	400	28	19	26
Roberts, Walla Walla	1.000	1	5	0	0	1
P. Smith, Bellingham	.985	41	303	25	5	18
Souza, Walla Walla	.980	22	189	11	4	15
Steinbach, Medford	1.000	1	3	0	0	0
TOLENTINO, Medford	.983	49	425	27	8	37

Triple play—Reibel.

SECOND BASEMEN

Player and Club	Pct.	G.	PO.	A.	E.	DP.
Alfredson, Salem	.818	3	3	6	2	0
Clawson, Spokane	.914	7	13	19	3	4
Davis, Eugene	.731	10	8	11	7	1
Duncan, Tri-Cities	.900	12	12	33	5	4
Engram, Bend	.930	25	55	65	9	17
Gile, Tri-Cities	.955	21	52	53	5	17
Grant, Salem	1.000	1	2	1	0	1
Howell, Salem	.900	7	13	14	3	1
Hudson, Walla Walla	1.000	2	3	2	0	0
T. Jones, Eugene	.935	23	47	39	6	13
Keehn, Tri-Cities	.907	32	56	80	14	13
Kraft, Bend	.919	13	20	37	5	8
Machado, Eugene	.942	12	19	30	3	3
D. Martinez, Walla Walla	1.000	4	7	11	0	3
R. Martinez, Tri-Cities	1.000	1	4	1	0	0
Matos, Bellingham	.905	16	23	34	6	6
McLean, Medford	1.000	1	3	2	0	0
Meyer, Walla Walla	.952	63	125	154	14	28
Priftis, Bellingham	.980	39	63	86	3	8
Rantz, Medford	.957	13	18	26	2	5
Reid, Spokane	1.000	1	0	2	0	0
Riley, Walla Walla	1.000	4	7	7	0	0
Rodriguez, Bellingham	.931	23	34	47	6	6
Sakowski, Tri-Cities	.927	11	16	22	3	2
Sambo, Bend	.870	37	62	99	24	13
Spellmon, Salem	.929	28	53	51	8	6
Spisok, Eugene	.978	28	87	87	4	20
Steen, Salem	.958	41	105	99	9	12
Thrower, Medford	.958	44	73	109	8	21
Walsh, Medford	.951	18	26	51	4	8
Wesley, Medford	1.000	3	8	7	0	1
WOLFF, Spokane	.966	62	119	168	10	25

THIRD BASEMEN

Player and Club	Pct.	G.	PO.	A.	E.	DP.
Amaya, Bellingham	.667	2	0	2	1	0
Balmer, Bellingham	.905	27	18	49	7	6
Buchanon, Salem	.767	15	18	15	10	1
Cain, Salem	.600	3	0	3	2	0
Clawson, Spokane	.892	25	20	46	8	3
Day, Bend	.850	19	16	35	9	2
Duncan, Tri-Cities	.800	1	1	3	1	0
Gomez, Spokane	.833	2	1	4	1	0
Grant, Salem	.899	33	24	65	10	6
Haberle, Eugene	1.000	2	1	0	0	0
Hallow, Spokane	.895	16	8	9	2	1
Hennessy, Tri-Cities	1.000	3	1	9	0	0
Howell, Salem	.750	11	6	18	8	2
T. Jones, Eugene	.889	16	20	28	6	1
Kane, Walla Walla	.852	14	8	15	4	2
Kraft, Bend	.667	2	1	1	1	0
Lawson, Bellingham	.917	16	2	20	2	0
MACHADO, Eugene	.926	53	43	95	11	9
D. Martinez, Walla Walla	.816	10	10	21	7	3
E. Martinez, Bellingham	.930	31	22	58	6	6
R. Martinez, Tri-Cities	.918	56	49	119	15	15
Odgers, Bend	.920	51	50	99	13	5
Olson, Spokane	.875	22	12	30	6	2
Perez, Bend	1.000	1	1	0	0	0
Reid, Spokane	.830	14	13	26	8	2
Rhoades, Walla Walla	.855	37	31	69	17	2
Riley, Walla Walla	.935	15	8	21	2	2
Sakowski, Tri-Cities	.758	12	9	16	8	3
Spellmon, Salem	.892	17	9	24	4	0
Steinbach, Medford	.906	62	41	122	17	13
Thrower, Medford	.850	10	7	10	3	2
Wesley, Medford	.800	3	4	0	1	0

SHORTSTOPS

Player and Club	Pct.	G.	PO.	A.	E.	DP.
Alfredson, Salem	.814	46	53	87	32	11
Bruzik, Bellingham	.872	44	64	86	22	18
Clawson, Spokane	.851	21	29	51	14	8
Colpitt, Bend	.829	18	29	29	12	13
Davis, Eugene	.944	14	14	20	2	5
del Rosario, Spokane	898	48	73	138	24	20
Evans, Eugene	.913	57	97	143	23	25
Gile, Tri-Cities	.866	28	40	63	16	12
Grant, Salem	.846	3	5	6	2	0
GUINN, Medford	.934	65	103	208	22	30
Hudson, Walla Walla	.878	55	99	139	33	28
T. Jones, Eugene	1.000	1	2	2	0	0
Keehn, Tri-Cities	.871	8	6	21	4	1
Kraft, Bend	.882	32	42	85	17	16
Meyer, Walla Walla	1.000	1	1	0	0	0
Perez, Bend	.926	28	38	75	9	15
Rhoades, Walla Walla	.880	24	30	65	13	4
Ross, Bend	1.000	1	0	2	0	0
Sakowski, Tri-Cities	.868	35	42	89	20	18
Spellmon, Salem	.750	2	2	4	2	0
Spisok, Eugene	1.000	1	0	1	0	0
Steen, Salem	.895	25	32	70	12	6
Thrower, Medford	.850	7	4	13	3	2
Tunnell, Bellingham	.860	34	51	53	17	8
Wolff, Spokane	.850	3	8	9	3	3

Triple play—Steen.

OUTFIELDERS

Player and Club	Pct.	G.	PO.	A.	E.	DP.
Adams, Salem	.949	40	54	2	3	0
Anderson, Spokane	.945	67	108	13	7	3
Artiles, Medford*	1.000	15	11	1	0	0
Bailey, Tri-Cities	.971	41	61	6	2	2
BEARDMAN, Medford	.979	58	89	4	2	1
Berge, Eugene	.972	56	96	7	3	0
Buchanon, Salem	1.000	16	22	1	0	1
Canseco, Medford	.911	48	46	5	5	1
Cesario, Tri-Cities	1.000	46	82	2	0	1
Colton, Bellingham	1.000	7	8	0	0	0
Curry, Tri-Cities	1.000	43	57	3	0	1
Dannenberg, Bend*	.902	35	37	0	4	0
David, Bend	1.000	28	45	3	0	0
Day, Bend	1.000	11	15	2	0	1
Dillard, Spokane	1.000	2	3	0	0	0
Evans, Eugene	1.000	1	4	0	0	0
Ferguson, Walla Walla	1.000	13	21	0	0	0
Fulgencio, Eugene	.927	50	104	11	9	2
F. Gomez, Spokane	1.000	1	2	0	0	0
N. Gomez, Salem	.857	8	6	0	1	0
Haley, Bellingham	.894	34	40	2	5	0
Hallow, Spokane	.957	31	41	4	2	0
Hamb, Walla Walla*	.897	25	30	5	4	1
Hardgrave, Spokane	.929	8	11	2	1	0
Hengel, Bellingham	1.000	5	10	0	0	0
Hennessy, Tri-Cities	.939	33	56	6	4	1
Houston, Walla Walla*	.000	5	0	0	2	0
Howell, Walla Walla	1.000	2	2	0	0	0
H. Hubbard, Spokane	.948	66	141	5	8	1
T. Johnson, Bend	.957	26	44	1	2	0
T. Jones, Eugene	1.000	16	14	1	0	0
Kane, Walla Walla	1.000	5	4	0	0	0
Lantigua, Salem	1.000	4	5	0	0	0
Lee, Salem-Walla Walla*	.947	36	53	1	3	1
Lora, Spokane	.937	40	56	3	4	1
Lynds, Salem	.842	16	15	1	3	0
Machado, Eugene	1.000	1	1	0	0	0
Martinez, Walla Walla	1.000	3	3	0	0	0
McLean, Medford	.964	54	74	6	3	0
Mendoza, Medford*	.974	37	36	2	1	0
Mitchell, Salem	.867	20	26	0	4	0
Monda, Eugene*	.923	10	24	0	2	0
Montgomery, Salem	.949	46	71	3	4	0
Moriarty, Walla Walla	.959	63	85	8	4	1
Morris, Bellingham	.926	22	25	0	2	0
Moses, Bend*	.950	44	84	7	5	1
Munson, Eugene	.962	56	123	3	5	1
O'Hara, Salem*	.972	69	133	6	4	0
Olson, Spokane	1.000	2	4	0	0	0
Oquendo, Medford*	1.000	11	13	0	0	0
Perez, Bellingham*	.957	61	106	6	5	0
Phillips, Eugene*	1.000	8	14	0	0	0
Posillico, Walla Walla	.978	44	86	2	2	1
Reibel, Salem*	1.000	5	12	0	0	0
Roberts, Walla Walla	.955	55	105	1	5	2
Roebuck, Bellingham	.911	30	41	0	4	0
Ross, Bend	.956	29	40	3	2	0
Simpson, Tri-Cities	.932	52	103	6	8	1
Steinbach, Bellingham	.940	46	61	2	4	1
Thrower, Medford	.667	2	2	0	1	0
Uribe, Bellingham	.893	21	24	1	3	1
Ward, Bend	.890	48	70	3	9	1
Wilks, Eugene*	.907	25	35	4	4	1

CATCHERS

Player and Club	Pct.	G.	PO.	A.	E.	DP.	PB.
Adams, Salem	.955	4	21	0	1	0	0
Amaya, Bellingham	.982	55	499	61	10	9	14
BRADLEY, Medford	.988	52	374	29	5	3	5
Carlucci, Tri-Cities	.985	32	239	23	4	1	3
Diaz, Medford	.986	12	61	7	1	1	1
Dorsett, Medford	.979	12	85	8	2	0	4
Floyd, Bend	.952	20	107	11	6	0	5
Gomez, Spokane	.917	6	11	0	1	0	1
Haberle, Eugene	.955	22	126	22	7	2	9
Hallow, Spokane	.970	4	30	2	1	0	1
Hance, Tri-Cities	.980	32	258	31	6	1	5
Hansen, Tri-Cities	.927	6	35	5	3	1	4
Jimenez, Salem	.984	39	272	32	5	1	15
Johnson, Medford	1.000	7	24	2	0	0	3
Komeiji, Bellingham	.983	6	47	11	1	0	0
Maples, Bend	.990	26	108	8	2	0	13
Marquez, Salem	.951	14	92	5	5	0	7
Martinez, Walla Walla	.955	11	76	8	4	0	2
Do. Mitchell, Eugene	1.000	3	2	0	0	0	0
Moriarty, Walla Walla	1.000	3	17	0	0	0	0
Paulson, Walla Walla	.965	42	301	30	12	5	8
Peel, Walla Walla	1.000	14	105	13	0	0	4
Porter Spokane	.962	61	437	68	20	5	20
Rivera, Spokane	.982	6	49	6	1	2	5
Sciacca, Salem	.957	3	17	1	3	0	2
Segura, Salem	.972	18	129	12	4	1	7
Souza, Walla Walla	1.000	4	21	3	0	0	5
Stowe, Bend	.983	35	223	10	4	0	9
Toler, Eugene	.960	46	271	44	13	5	9
Vega, Bellingham	.991	13	97	11	1	0	4

PITCHERS

Player and Club	Pct.	G.	PO.	A.	E.	DP.
Abrego, Bend	.933	14	5	23	2	3
Akerfelds, Bellingham	.938	12	4	11	1	2
Allen, Walla Walla*	1.000	17	2	9	0	1
Allison, Tri-Cities	.800	13	2	6	2	0
Armitage, Walla Walla	1.000	14	2	5	0	0
Baccala, Bend	1.000	1	0	1	0	0
Bailey, Medford	.583	13	0	7	5	1
Barba, Eugene	1.000	12	0	2	0	0
Bass, Tri-Cities	1.000	8	1	2	0	0
Bauer, Medford	.952	15	9	11	1	0
Bergendahl, Bellingham	.857	11	11	4	8	2
Blas, Walla Walla	.829	15	3	26	6	1
Bowden, Eugene*	.667	3	0	2	1	0
Bryant, Bellingham	1.000	19	1	9	0	1
Burns, Tri-Cities	.909	14	4	6	1	0
Cadaret, Medford*	1.000	12	3	10	0	1
Cannon, Salem	.778	22	4	10	4	0
Caraballo, Bend	.846	21	0	11	2	1
Carter, Salem	1.000	25	0	7	0	0
Cedeno, Salem	.750	14	3	6	3	0
Chadwick, Salem	.808	16	9	12	5	1
Childers, Spokane	.727	15	0	8	3	0
Cipres, Tri-Cities	.900	16	2	7	1	0
Cloninger, Spokane	1.000	5	3	6	0	0
Collier, Bend*	1.000	13	2	3	0	0
Dibble, Eugene	.818	7	3	6	2	0
Diez, Walla Walla	.000	3	0	0	1	0
Esposito, Tri-Cities	.800	17	1	3	1	0
Evetts, Bend	.850	16	4	13	3	0
Ferrin, Eugene	.846	22	1	10	2	1
Fryhoff, Tri-Cities*	1.000	16	1	6	0	0
Fulmer, Medford*	.977	14	11	31	1	2
Glanz, Salem-Walla Walla	.667	14	3	9	6	0
Gomez, Medford	.909	21	0	10	1	0
Gonzales, Salem	.867	21	5	8	2	1
Gunnarson, Bellingham*	1.000	25	2	3	0	0

PITCHERS—Continued

Player and Club	Pct.	G.	PO.	A.	E.	DP.
Hanna, Medford	.800	5	2	2	1	1
Harms, Eugene	.889	13	6	18	3	0
Hernandez, Salem	1.000	3	0	2	0	0
Hilton, Medford	1.000	2	2	1	0	0
Hinson, Bellingham	1.000	3	1	3	0	0
M. Hubbard, Spokane	1.000	16	2	10	0	0
James, Spokane	.824	15	7	7	3	1
Johns, Eugene	1.000	2	0	1	0	0
K. Johnson, Bend	1.000	19	2	8	0	0
Keathley, Tri-Cities	1.000	10	2	6	0	0
Kemmerling, Salem	1.000	9	1	2	0	0
Kipper, Tri-Cities*	.882	14	5	10	2	1
Knight, Tri-Cities	1.000	14	4	9	0	0
Kordish, Tri-Cities	1.000	10	3	10	0	1
Lindquist, Tri-Cities*	.923	18	3	9	1	0
Luecken, Bellingham	.947	14	6	12	1	0
McLarnan, Bend	.933	15	5	9	1	0
McLoughlin, Spokane	1.000	4	2	5	0	0
Meister, Bellingham	1.000	3	1	1	0	0
Menard, Eugene	.938	14	3	12	1	0
Mills, Spokane	.955	11	4	17	1	0
Minyard, Eugene	.870	17	6	14	3	0
Miquel, Walla Walla*	.643	13	1	8	5	1
Da. Mitchell, Eugene	1.000	4	1	1	0	0
Do. Mitchell, Eugene	.500	2	0	1	1	0
Morton, Bend*	1.000	13	2	0	0	0
Munley, Tri-Cities	.833	15	3	2	1	0
Nielsen, Bellingham	1.000	2	2	3	0	0
Odom, Medford	1.000	11	3	1	0	0
Ojeda, Salem	1.000	8	1	2	0	0
Parks, Spokane	.833	17	2	13	3	0
Peltola, Walla Walla	.778	20	2	5	2	0

Player and Club	Pct.	G.	PO.	A.	E.	DP.
Phaup, Walla Walla	.875	24	2	5	1	0
Powell, Bend	.938	13	7	8	1	0
Psaltis, Walla Walla*	.880	13	1	21	3	0
Rasnick, Bend	.750	15	3	3	2	1
Roy, Bellingham	.875	11	4	10	2	0
Salazar, Bellingham*	.889	20	0	8	1	1
Salgueiro, Eugene	.857	11	2	4	1	0
Saylor, Walla Walla	.500	8	1	1	2	0
Scherer, Medford	.900	28	1	8	1	0
Sebra, Tri-Cities	.889	12	2	6	1	0
Sierra, Spokane	.917	23	1	10	1	1
D. Smith, Bellingham	.944	19	5	12	1	1
K. Smith, Walla Walla*	1.000	13	3	10	0	0
Snediker, Eugene	.903	14	9	19	3	1
Spector, Eugene	.889	16	4	4	1	0
Spini, Walla Walla	.800	13	3	9	3	0
Stanfield, Salem	1.000	9	3	2	0	0
J. Stewart, Spokane	1.000	15	0	4	0	1
W. Stewart, Bend	.917	9	5	6	1	0
STIS, Eugene	1.000	18	8	8	0	0
Stout, Eugene	.941	25	3	13	1	1
Swearingen, Bellingham*	1.000	18	4	7	0	0
Tinkey, Salem	.905	13	8	11	2	0
E. Valdez, Spokane*	1.000	13	0	5	0	0
J. Valdez, Salem	.800	10	1	3	1	0
Wanzer, Medford	.900	15	4	5	1	2
Weatherford, Bend	.889	14	3	5	1	1
Whaley, Medford	1.000	16	1	11	0	0
Wilburn, Salem	.943	12	7	26	2	0
Wilkinson, Bellingham*	.923	13	4	8	1	1
Williams, Spokane*	.969	14	10	21	1	3

Triple play—Wilburn.

The following players do not have any recorded accepted chances at the positions indicated and therefore are not listed in the fielding averages for those particular positions: Beal, p; Grant, of; Haberle, of; S. Jones, p; Matos, of; Odgers, ss; Olson, 2b; Ortiz, p; Phillips, ss; Psaltis, of; Rhoades, 2b; Wesley, of.

CLUB PITCHING

Club	ERA.	G.	CG.	ShO.	Sv.	IP.	H.	R.	ER.	HR.	HB.	BB.	Int. BB.	SO.	WP.	Bk.
Medford	3.23	68	11	8	17	593.0	536	277	213	23	14	262	2	543	42	8
Walla Walla	3.31	70	19	4	10	616.2	571	331	227	34	30	276	14	497	36	3
Bellingham	3.33	69	5	9	15	610.1	531	289	226	33	20	316	10	640	56	5
Salem	3.79	70	11	0	11	603.1	587	387	254	23	26	301	4	508	58	5
Tri-Cities	4.09	70	3	6	17	603.1	580	354	274	43	26	312	2	544	60	3
Bend	4.20	69	7	1	13	611.0	617	392	285	50	41	273	12	505	47	3
Eugene	4.65	67	5	3	11	573.1	597	394	296	47	21	339	16	376	53	4
Spokane	4.88	69	8	3	9	599.1	641	424	325	31	35	332	2	508	59	5

PITCHERS' RECORDS

(Leading Qualifiers for Earned-Run Average Leadership—56 or More Innings)

*Throws lefthanded.

Pitcher—Club	W.	L.	Pct.	ERA.	G.	GS.	CG.	GF.	ShO.	Sv.	IP.	H.	R.	ER.	HR.	HB.	BB.	Int. BB.	SO.	WP.
Spini, Walla Walla	8	1	.889	1.34	13	13	7	0	1	0	94.1	100	28	14	3	6	23	0	41	0
Swearingen, Bellingham*	2	2	.500	1.81	18	2	0	5	0	2	74.2	53	23	15	2	2	30	0	78	5
Bauer, Medford	12	0	1.000	1.96	15	14	6	1	4	0	105.2	82	30	23	7	2	33	0	93	6
Blas, Walla Walla	3	4	.429	2.19	15	14	5	1	1	0	102.2	85	39	25	7	3	14	0	70	1
Kordish, Tri-Cities	5	4	.556	2.37	10	10	1	0	0	0	57.0	62	25	15	4	1	5	0	34	2
Fulmer, Medford*	11	1	.917	2.69	14	14	2	0	0	0	97.0	83	37	29	4	2	33	1	57	5
Spector, Eugene	8	2	.800	2.75	16	6	1	3	0	1	68.2	76	33	21	5	0	19	3	45	2
Bergendahl, Bellingham	5	1	.833	2.93	11	11	0	0	0	0	58.1	43	21	19	4	1	36	0	60	9
Tinkey, Salem	4	5	.444	3.10	13	13	3	0	0	0	93.0	103	48	32	1	5	30	1	64	5
Roy, Bellingham	2	4	.333	3.23	11	11	2	0	0	0	61.1	60	33	22	5	4	35	1	52	4

Departmental Leaders: G—Scherer, 28; W—Bauer, 12; L—Cannon, Mills, 8; Pct.—Bauer, 1.000; GS—Seven pitchers had 14; CG—Spini, 7; GF—Scherer, 26; ShO—Bauer, 4; Sv.—Scherer, 8; IP—Bauer, 105.2; H—Tinkey, 103; R—Chadwick, 63; ER—Chadwick, Williams, 46; HR—Allison, Stis, 9; HB—Abrego, 14; BB—Allison, 71; IBB—Phaup, 7; SO—Whaley, 111; WP—Williams, 14.

(All Pitchers—Listed Alphabetically)

Pitcher—Club	W.	L.	Pct.	ERA.	G.	GS.	CG.	GF.	ShO.	Sv.	IP.	H.	R.	ER.	HR.	HB.	BB.	Int. BB.	SO.	WP.
Abrego, Bend	7	5	.583	3.97	14	14	4	0	1	0	88.1	81	58	39	6	14	40	0	59	6
Akerfelds, Bellingham	5	3	.625	4.48	12	11	0	1	0	1	68.1	62	36	34	5	3	36	0	85	7
Allen, Walla Walla	0	1	.000	4.29	17	0	0	9	0	2	35.2	34	26	17	5	2	18	2	25	4
Allison, Tri-Cities	3	7	.300	7.18	13	13	0	0	0	0	52.2	37	47	42	9	2	71	0	59	6
Armitage, Walla Walla	1	2	.333	4.78	14	3	0	6	0	2	26.1	25	16	14	3	3	18	1	26	7
Baccala, Bend	0	0	.000	9.00	1	0	0	0	0	0	3.0	2	3	3	0	0	3	0	6	1
Bailey, Medford	1	1	.500	4.02	13	5	0	0	0	0	47.0	49	29	21	1	0	32	0	41	5
Barba, Eugene	1	2	.333	4.11	12	0	0	8	0	1	15.1	8	7	7	0	2	20	1	22	2
Bass, Tri-Cities	0	2	.000	5.11	8	4	0	4	0	1	12.1	15	9	7	2	0	5	0	9	0
Bauer, Medford	12	0	1.000	1.96	15	14	6	1	4	0	105.2	82	30	23	7	2	33	0	93	6
Beal, Bend	0	0	.000	0.00	1	0	0	0	0	0	1.1	0	0	0	0	0	0	0	1	0
Bergendahl, Bellingham	5	1	.833	2.93	11	11	0	0	0	0	58.1	43	21	19	4	1	36	0	60	9
Blas, Walla Walla	3	4	.429	2.19	15	14	5	1	1	0	102.2	85	39	25	7	3	14	0	70	1
Bowden, Eugene*	0	0	.000	14.73	3	2	0	0	0	0	3.2	4	10	6	0	1	9	0	6	1
Bryant, Bellingham	5	0	1.000	5.14	19	0	0	13	0	2	28.0	37	17	16	3	2	11	2	19	0
Burns, Tri-Cities	0	5	.000	4.58	14	1	0	9	0	3	39.1	41	27	20	3	0	16	1	48	8
Cadaret, Medford*	7	3	.700	4.36	12	11	1	0	1	0	64.0	73	36	31	2	1	36	0	51	3
Cannon, Salem	1	8	.111	3.62	22	8	2	13	0	3	69.2	73	45	28	3	2	38	0	66	11
Carabello, Bend	2	3	.400	3.53	21	0	0	13	0	7	35.2	29	19	14	2	2	19	4	24	2

Pitcher—Club	W.	L.	Pct.	ERA.	G.	GS.	CG.	GF.	ShO.	Sv.	IP.	H.	R.	ER.	HR.	HB.	BB.	Int. BB.	SO.	WP.
Carter, Salem	5	3	.625	1.38	25	0	0	17	0	5	39.0	30	17	6	3	2	18	0	44	2
Cedeno, Salem	1	2	.333	4.05	14	6	0	4	0	0	40.0	39	31	18	0	2	29	1	32	7
Chadwick, Salem	3	5	.375	4.97	16	10	1	0	0	0	83.1	72	63	46	3	2	51	0	82	8
Childers, Spokane	3	5	.375	6.36	15	7	0	5	0	1	52.1	66	43	37	3	7	24	0	40	4
Cipres, Tri-Cities	2	1	.667	1.51	16	0	0	10	0	6	47.2	34	13	8	2	4	17	0	45	5
Cloninger, Spokane	0	3	.000	3.54	5	4	1	1	0	1	28.0	24	15	11	2	1	13	0	32	1
Collier, Bend*	0	0	.000	4.78	13	0	0	8	0	0	26.1	27	14	14	3	0	19	0	21	2
Dibble, Eugene	3	2	.600	5.73	7	7	1	0	0	0	37.2	38	28	24	5	0	18	0	17	2
Diez, Walla Walla	0	3	.000	14.40	3	2	0	0	0	0	5.0	5	9	8	0	0	8	0	3	0
Esposito, Tri-Cities	4	1	.800	2.35	17	0	0	14	0	3	30.2	19	11	8	1	0	15	0	34	3
Evetts, Bend	4	5	.444	4.52	16	10	1	1	0	1	65.2	69	46	33	7	4	27	0	49	5
Ferrin, Eugene	2	4	.333	3.57	22	2	0	17	0	5	45.1	42	24	18	3	1	15	3	26	0
Fryhoff, Tri-Cities	0	1	.000	2.98	16	1	0	4	0	0	51.1	48	27	17	3	2	35	0	52	5
Fulmer, Medford*	11	1	.917	2.69	14	14	2	0	0	0	97.0	83	37	29	4	2	33	1	57	5
Glanz, Salem 9-WW 5	3	4	.429	3.78	14	11	1	0	0	0	78.2	74	46	33	2	7	32	0	79	7
Gomez, Medford	3	2	.600	3.16	21	1	0	13	0	7	42.2	33	16	15	1	1	20	0	34	6
Gonzales, Salem	4	3	.571	4.12	21	2	0	10	0	2	45.2	37	28	20	3	4	22	0	33	1
Gunnarson, Bellingham*	3	2	.600	2.95	25	0	0	22	0	4	36.2	25	13	12	3	0	11	2	43	2
Hanna, Medford	1	0	1.000	1.59	5	0	0	4	0	0	11.1	12	7	2	1	0	4	0	9	0
Harms, Eugene	5	4	.556	4.30	13	13	1	0	0	0	81.2	92	46	39	6	1	34	0	40	10
Hernandez, Salem	0	1	.000	5.40	3	1	0	1	0	0	8.1	7	7	5	1	0	7	0	6	1
Hilton, Medford	0	0	.000	2.79	2	2	0	0	0	0	9.2	9	4	3	1	1	7	0	9	0
Hinson, Bellingham	1	0	1.000	0.60	3	1	0	1	0	1	15.0	3	1	1	0	0	9	0	12	1
Hubbard, Spokane	3	3	.500	4.22	16	6	0	8	0	2	53.1	68	35	25	1	2	32	0	41	2
James, Spokane	2	5	.286	5.10	15	10	1	3	0	1	77.2	96	53	44	6	0	28	0	39	7
Johns, Eugene	0	0	.000	7.50	2	1	0	0	0	0	6.0	9	6	5	1	1	7	0	5	1
Johnson, Bend	3	2	.600	3.86	19	0	0	11	0	0	39.2	47	29	17	5	2	14	4	25	3
Jones, Eugene*	0	0	.000	4.50	1	1	0	0	0	0	4.0	3	2	2	0	0	5	0	4	1
Keathley, Tri-Cities	2	2	.500	6.68	10	5	0	2	0	0	32.1	45	27	24	5	1	16	1	14	5
Kemmerling, Salem	2	1	.667	1.13	9	0	0	8	0	1	16.0	11	7	2	0	0	13	2	13	5
Kipper, Tri-Cities*	5	3	.625	4.40	14	14	0	0	0	0	71.2	73	41	35	4	6	39	0	64	13
Knight, Tri-Cities	2	4	.333	5.57	14	5	1	5	1	1	51.2	66	36	32	3	4	19	0	37	7
Kordish, Tri-Cities	5	4	.556	2.37	10	10	1	0	0	0	57.0	62	25	15	4	1	5	0	34	2
Lindquist, Tri-Cities*	5	2	.714	3.20	18	4	0	9	0	0	50.2	49	28	18	1	2	30	0	53	1
Luecken, Bellingham	5	4	.556	3.56	14	12	2	1	0	0	78.1	70	39	31	4	4	37	0	83	5
McLarnan, Bend	3	5	.375	4.02	15	6	0	7	0	1	56.0	63	39	25	5	2	11	0	57	2
McLoughlin, Spokane	1	1	.500	4.05	4	1	0	3	0	0	13.1	12	8	6	1	1	7	0	15	0
Meister, Bellingham	1	2	.333	2.87	3	3	0	0	0	0	15.2	15	8	5	0	1	8	0	17	4
Menard, Bend	3	7	.300	3.96	14	14	1	0	0	0	84.0	91	51	37	5	4	27	0	65	4
Mills, Spokane	1	8	.111	4.09	11	11	2	0	0	0	70.1	71	47	32	1	6	29	0	51	9
Minyard, Eugene	2	4	.333	5.91	17	8	0	4	0	0	64.0	67	59	42	3	7	56	4	59	10
Miquel, Walla Walla*	1	6	.143	7.40	13	9	0	0	0	0	41.1	50	48	34	2	4	42	1	30	4
Da. Mitchell, Eugene	0	0	.000	0.00	4	3	0	0	0	0	7.1	3	0	0	0	0	4	0	5	1
Do. Mitchell, Eugene	0	0	.000	5.19	2	0	0	1	0	0	8.2	10	5	5	2	1	2	1	4	1
Morton, Bend*	0	2	.000	2.50	13	0	0	8	0	2	18.0	18	7	5	0	2	11	2	21	0
Munley, Tri-Cities	1	2	.333	4.15	15	1	1	10	0	3	47.2	43	27	22	4	2	15	0	25	1
Nielsen, Bellingham	2	0	1.000	2.08	2	2	0	0	0	0	13.0	11	4	3	0	1	2	0	13	2
Odom, Medford	0	1	.000	5.22	11	4	0	5	0	0	29.1	32	29	17	3	1	20	0	38	5
Ojeda, Salem	2	2	.500	3.58	8	4	1	4	0	0	32.2	31	14	13	2	2	9	0	17	1
Ortiz, Spokane	1	0	1.000	9.45	10	1	0	3	0	0	26.2	35	36	28	4	2	27	0	12	4
Parks, Spokane	3	5	.375	5.01	17	6	1	8	1	1	64.2	64	47	36	4	5	32	0	65	8
Peltola, Walla Walla	3	4	.429	1.35	20	0	0	18	0	6	33.1	20	7	5	2	2	17	1	23	0
Phaup, Walla Walla	3	5	.375	4.86	24	0	0	14	0	0	50.0	49	38	27	2	2	34	7	48	2
Powell, Bend	4	4	.500	4.07	13	11	1	1	0	1	66.1	67	39	30	7	7	27	1	45	6
Psaltis, Walla Walla*	8	2	.800	3.29	13	13	4	0	1	0	93.0	88	49	34	5	3	41	0	91	6
Rasnick, Bend	2	1	.667	1.59	15	2	0	7	0	0	39.2	27	17	7	1	1	30	1	42	9
Roy, Bellingham	2	4	.333	3.23	11	11	2	0	0	0	61.1	60	33	22	5	4	35	1	52	4
Salazar, Bellingham*	2	3	.400	4.03	20	2	0	13	0	3	44.2	39	22	20	1	1	32	3	56	6
Salgueiro, Eugene	1	3	.250	7.57	11	6	0	5	0	0	27.1	26	34	23	4	1	41	0	29	11
Saylor, Walla Walla	1	0	1.000	1.66	8	0	0	3	0	0	21.2	17	14	4	0	1	18	2	21	5
Scherer, Medford	5	1	.833	2.70	28	0	0	26	0	8	53.1	49	20	16	1	1	17	0	68	3
Sebra, Tri-Cities	4	3	.571	4.01	12	12	0	0	0	0	58.1	48	36	26	2	2	29	0	70	4
Sierra, Spokane	1	5	.167	5.35	23	0	0	20	0	3	37.0	44	33	22	1	4	21	1	31	5
D. Smith, Bellingham	3	2	.600	4.10	19	1	0	7	0	2	52.2	59	31	24	4	0	15	2	35	4
K. Smith, Walla Walla*	3	7	.300	3.87	13	13	2	0	0	0	81.1	77	46	35	4	0	32	0	77	5
Snediker, Eugene	6	2	.750	4.95	14	12	1	1	0	0	72.2	77	58	40	4	4	50	0	35	9
Spector, Eugene	8	2	.800	2.75	16	6	1	3	0	1	68.2	76	33	21	5	0	19	3	45	2
Spini, Walla Walla	8	1	.889	1.34	13	13	7	0	1	0	94.1	100	28	14	3	6	23	0	41	0
Stanfield, Salem	1	0	1.000	4.91	9	3	0	2	0	0	25.2	28	18	14	1	1	11	0	24	4
J. Stewart, Spokane	1	5	.167	3.00	15	8	0	4	0	0	54.0	37	24	18	1	1	47	1	68	2
W. Stewart, Bend	2	2	.500	6.69	9	5	0	2	0	0	36.1	46	30	27	4	0	12	0	32	4
Stis, Eugene	3	5	.375	4.05	18	6	1	9	1	2	73.1	77	40	33	9	0	30	2	35	1
Stout, Eugene	2	6	.250	4.84	25	1	0	14	0	2	57.2	65	42	31	5	2	29	2	44	1
Swearingen, Bellingham*	2	2	.500	1.81	18	2	0	5	0	2	74.2	53	23	15	2	2	30	0	78	5
Tinkey, Salem	4	5	.444	3.10	13	13	3	0	0	0	93.0	103	48	32	1	5	30	1	64	5
E. Valdez, Spokane*	0	0	.000	6.98	13	1	0	6	0	0	29.2	40	32	23	3	2	17	0	27	3
J. Valdez, Salem	1	2	.333	6.52	10	3	0	1	0	0	19.1	20	19	14	2	1	15	0	14	6
Wanzer, Medford	2	4	.333	4.72	15	4	0	6	0	1	47.2	49	28	25	1	1	14	0	32	5
Weatherford, Bend	2	1	.667	6.04	14	7	0	4	0	1	50.2	50	40	34	5	3	33	0	58	3
Whaley, Medford	8	5	.615	3.59	16	13	2	2	1	1	85.1	65	41	34	1	4	46	1	111	4
Wilburn, Salem	6	4	.600	3.53	12	12	4	0	0	0	84.0	83	55	33	3	2	37	0	76	2
Wilkinson, Bellingham*	4	5	.444	3.39	13	13	1	0	1	0	63.2	54	41	24	2	1	54	0	87	7
Williams, Spokane*	7	6	.538	4.48	14	14	3	0	1	0	92.1	84	51	46	4	4	55	0	87	14

BALKS—Fulmer, Odom, Salazar, Scherer, Spini, Swearingen, E. Valdez, Williams, 2 each; Bailey, Bowden, Burns, Cadaret, Dibble, Fryhoff, Glanz, Gonzales, Harms, Hernandez, Menard, Miguel, Da. Mitchell, Morton, Ortiz, Sebra, W. Stewart, Tinkey, Wilburn, Wilkinson, 1 each.

COMBINATION SHUTOUTS—Akerfelds-Bryant, Akerfelds-Swearingen-Gunnarson, Bergendahl-Salazar, Hinson-Gunnarson, Luecken-Gunnarson, Meister-Smith-Gunnarson, Salazar-Bryant, Smith-Luecken-Gunnarson, Bellingham; Da. Mitchell-Spector-Salgueiro, Salgueiro-Spector, Eugene; Bauer-Hanna, Odom-Hanna, Medford; Mills-Hubbard, Spokane; Allison-Lindquist, Kipper-Esposito, Kordish-Lindquist, Lindquist-Knight, Sebra-Munley, Tri-Cities; Spini-Peltola, Walla Walla.

NO-HIT GAMES—Allison-Lindquist, Tri-Cities, defeated Spokane, 4-0 (seven innings, second game), June 28; Allison-Esposito, Tri-Cities, defeated Salem, 2-1, July 8.

South Atlantic League

CLASS A

CHAMPIONSHIP WINNERS IN PREVIOUS YEARS

Year	Club	Pct.
1948	Lincolnton*	.627
1949	Newton-Conover	.667
	Ruth'ford Co. (2nd)†	.627
1950	Newton-Conover	.627
	Lenoir (2nd)†	.626
1951	Morganton	.645
	Shelby (2nd)†	.604
1952	Lincolnton	.649
	Shelby (2nd)†	.645
1953-59	League inactive.	
1960	Lexington	.707
	Salisbury (2nd)†	.650
1961	Salisbury	.627
	Shelby (4th)†	.481
1962	Statesville	.563
	Statesville	.700
1963	Greenville†	.576
	Salisbury	.631
1964	Rock Hill	.672
	Salisbury‡	.631
1965	Salisbury	.641
	Rock Hill‡	.603
1966	Spartanburg	.682
	Spartanburg	.767
1967	Spartanburg	.730
	Spartanburg	.567
1968	Spartanburg	.597
	Greenwood‡	.597
1969	Greenwood‡	.587
	Shelby	.565
1970	Greenville	.576
	Greenville	.619
1971	Greenwood	.631
	Greenwood	.759
1972	Spartanburg‡	.788
	Greenville	.652
1973	Spartanburg‡	.646
	Gastonia	.619
1974	Gastonia	.606
	Gastonia	.672
1975	Spartanburg	.543
	Spartanburg	.614
1976	Asheville	.544
	Greenwood‡	.600
1977	Greenwood	.557
	Gastonia‡	.590
1978	Greenwood	.614
	Greenwood	.565
1979	Greenwood‡	.565
	Spartanburg	.525
1980	Greensboro	.590
	Charleston	.561
1981	Greensboro‡	.695
	Greenwood	.549
1982	Greensboro‡	.681
	Florence	.546

*Won championship and four-club playoff. †Won four-club playoff. ‡Won split-season playoff. (NOTE—Known as Western Carolina League from 1948 through 1962 and known as Western Carolinas League through 1979.)

STANDING OF CLUBS AT CLOSE OF FIRST HALF, JUNE 19

NORTHERN DIVISION

Club	W.	L.	T.	Pct.	G.B.
Gastonia (Expos)	41	30	0	.577	....
Greensboro (Yankees)	39	33	0	.542	2½
Anderson (Braves)	37	34	0	.521	4
Asheville (Astros)	35	37	0	.486	6½
Spartanburg (Phillies)	32	39	0	.451	9

SOUTHERN DIVISION

Club	W.	L.	T.	Pct.	G.B.
Columbia (Mets)	43	27	0	.614	....
Florence (Blue Jays)	36	35	0	.507	7½
Macon (Cardinals)	33	39	0	.458	11
Greenwood (Pirates)	32	40	0	.444	12
Charleston (Royals)	29	43	0	.403	15

STANDING OF CLUBS AT CLOSE OF SECOND HALF, AUGUST 31

NORTHERN DIVISION

Club	W.	L.	T.	Pct.	G.B.
Gastonia (Expos)	43	29	0	.597	....
Spartanburg (Phillies)	40	32	0	.556	3
Greensboro (Yankees)	34	38	0	.472	9
Asheville (Astros)	29	43	0	.403	14
Anderson (Braves)	27	45	0	.375	16

SOUTHERN DIVISION

Club	W.	L.	T.	Pct.	G.B.
Columbia (Mets)	45	27	0	.625	....
Macon (Cardinals)	38	34	0	.528	7
Florence (Blue Jays)	35	37	0	.486	10
Charleston (Royals)	35	37	0	.486	10
Greenwood (Pirates)	34	38	0	.472	11

COMPOSITE STANDING OF CLUBS AT CLOSE OF SEASON, AUGUST 31

Club	Col.	Gas.	Gbr.	Spar.	Flo.	Mac.	Gwd.	And.	Char.	Ash.	W.	L.	T.	Pct.	G.B.
Columbia (Mets)	....	7	7	5	11	14	14	7	15	8	88	54	0	.620	....
Gastonia (Expos)	5	....	13	11	11	9	7	10	6	12	84	59	0	.587	4½
Greensboro (Yankees)	5	8	....	15	6	4	6	8	9	12	73	71	0	.507	16
Spartanburg (Phillies)	6	13	6	....	4	7	6	16	6	8	72	71	0	.503	16½
Florence (Blue Jays)	6	1	6	8	....	15	12	7	11	5	71	72	0	.497	17½
Macon (Cardinals)	7	3	8	5	6	....	13	8	11	10	71	73	0	.493	18
Greenwood (Pirates)	10	5	6	6	9	8	....	8	7	7	66	78	0	.458	23
Anderson (Braves)	5	7	13	5	5	4	4	....	6	15	64	79	0	.488	24½
Charleston (Royals)	6	6	3	6	13	10	11	6	....	3	64	80	0	.444	25
Asheville (Astros)	4	9	9	10	7	2	5	9	9	....	64	80	0	.444	25

Major league affiliations in parentheses.

Playoffs—Gastonia defeated Columbia, three games to two, to capture league championship.

Regular-Season Attendance—Anderson, 34,193; Asheville, 70,985; Charleston, 100,318; Columbia, 107,113; Florence, 54,779; Gastonia, 65,094; Greensboro, 159,064; Greenwood, 8,345; Macon, 37,992; Spartanburg, 57,331. Total, 695,214. Playoffs, 4,771. All-Star Game, 1,471.

Managers—Anderson, Rick Albert; Asheville, Tom Spencer; Charleston, Roy Tanner; Columbia, John Tamargo; Florence, Dennis Holmberg; Gastonia, Junior Miner; Greensboro, Carlos Tosca; Greenwood, Joe Frisina; Macon, Lloyd Merritt; Spartanburg, Roly Dearmas.

All-Star Team—1B—Cecil Fielder, Florence; 2B—Armando Moreno, Gastonia; 3B—Christopher James, Spartanburg; SS—Timothy Thiessen, Gastonia; OF—Vincent Coleman, Macon; Paul Hollins, Columbia; Van Snider, Charleston; C—David Stenhouse, Florence; DH—Keith Hughes, Spartanburg; RHP—Charles Kerfeld, Asheville; LHP—Randall Myers, Columbia; RH Reliever—Johnny Baldwin, Greensboro; LH Reliever—John Mortillaro, Anderson; Manager of the Year—John Tamargo, Columbia.

(Compiled by Howe News Bureau, Boston, Mass.)

CLUB BATTING

Club	Pct.	G.	AB.	R.	OR.	H.	TB.	2B.	3B.	HR.	RBI.	GW.	SH.	SF.	HP.	BB.	Int. BB.	SO.	SB.	CS.	LOB.
Columbia	.284	142	4756	819	614	1351	1924	211	52	86	704	83	25	51	33	536	18	842	174	62	1015
Gastonia	.276	143	4680	810	640	1290	1821	215	20	92	662	70	38	45	30	659	26	689	187	67	1037
Spartanburg	.268	143	4726	797	797	1268	1909	221	42	112	679	52	21	58	63	584	15	956	229	55	1030
Macon	.267	144	4779	767	835	1276	1741	170	53	63	642	59	42	50	40	657	16	913	259	78	1084
Florence	.265	143	4654	770	742	1234	1811	222	35	95	644	61	28	39	47	599	18	985	144	55	1009
Asheville	.262	144	4684	735	802	1225	1944	232	35	139	631	53	39	43	38	597	11	920	159	57	1015
Greensboro	.261	144	4715	787	753	1230	1815	220	37	97	687	66	30	35	32	715	17	1102	147	69	1078
Charleston	.249	144	4672	713	783	1164	1670	168	34	90	596	56	18	39	33	567	15	966	181	67	934
Greenwood	.247	144	4741	645	764	1170	1584	170	59	42	520	52	25	33	52	567	12	1044	208	71	1072
Anderson	.238	143	4575	578	691	1089	1584	181	31	84	488	52	44	22	42	506	15	1081	91	55	965

INDIVIDUAL BATTING

(Leading Qualifiers for Batting Championship—389 or More Plate Appearances)

*Bats lefthanded. †Switch-hitter.

Player and Club	Pct.	G.	AB.	R.	H.	TB.	2B.	3B.	HR.	RBI.	GW.	SH.	SF.	HP.	BB.	Int. BB.	SO.	SB.	CS.
Coleman, Vincent, Macon	.350	113	446	99	156	178	8	7	0	53	5	0	2	9	56	3	85	145	31
Springer, Steven, Columbus	.338	130	488	99	165	243	24	9	12	88	18	1	7	2	35	2	50	22	4
Hughes, Keith, Spartanburg*	.329	131	484	80	159	243	31	4	15	90	5	2	5	4	67	5	83	16	1
Moreno, Armando, Gastonia	.327	115	367	89	120	165	19	1	8	63	7	4	1	6	86	2	52	17	7
Roberts, Leon, Greenwood†	.320	122	438	78	140	188	20	5	6	63	10	2	6	10	69	1	43	27	16
Fielder, Cecil, Florence	.312	140	500	81	156	236	28	2	16	94	8	1	3	5	58	2	90	2	2
Stellern, Michael, Asheville	.312	119	449	94	140	229	27	10	14	57	7	4	3	5	55	0	89	23	4
Pevey, Marty, Macon*	.312	122	436	74	136	184	23	2	7	77	9	2	4	2	45	2	70	8	5
Javier, Stanley, Greensboro†	.311	129	489	109	152	234	34	6	12	77	10	2	2	2	75	2	95	33	7
Thiessen, Timothy, Gastonia	.302	143	513	95	155	199	21	4	5	55	7	2	2	4	77	0	73	34	18

Departmental Leaders: G—Thiessen, 143; AB—Szekely, 521; R—Leiva, 128; H—Springer, 165; TB—James, 257; 2B—Javier, 34; 3B—Stellern, 10; HR—Dophied, 27; RBI—James, 121; GWRBI—Springer, 18; SH—Van Horn, 9; SF—Dearth, 10; HP—James, Tejeda, 12; BB—Jackson, 114; IBB—Camelo, Hughes, 5; SO—Wagner, 159; SB—V. Coleman, 145; CS—V. Coleman, 31.

(All Players—Listed Alphabetically)

Player and Club	Pct.	G.	AB.	R.	H.	TB.	2B.	3B.	HR.	RBI.	GW.	SH.	SF.	HP.	BB.	Int. BB.	SO.	SB.	CS.
Abone, Anthony, Gastonia	.355	15	31	6	11	11	0	0	0	4	0	1	1	0	2	1	4	0	0
Alcala, Jesus, Greensboro	.167	9	30	3	5	5	0	0	0	0	0	1	0	0	2	0	7	0	0
Allen, Edward, Charleston†	.137	53	153	18	21	23	2	0	0	10	1	3	0	1	48	0	73	16	2
Anglin, Russell, Anderson	.229	83	280	37	64	111	8	0	13	49	8	0	2	1	24	3	71	0	0
Antone, Ralph, Gastonia	.231	6	13	2	3	3	0	0	0	1	0	0	0	1	4	0	3	0	0
Aruca, Daniel, Asheville*	.219	9	32	3	7	9	2	0	0	2	0	0	0	0	1	0	4	1	0
Aubin, D. Gerard, Greensboro	.167	9	24	4	4	8	1	0	1	2	0	0	0	3	2	0	9	1	0
Aulenback, James, Greenwood	.175	12	40	2	7	9	0	1	0	3	1	0	1	0	5	0	13	0	0
Bagnall, James, Charleston	.253	66	249	33	63	86	10	2	3	19	2	0	3	1	21	1	54	1	1
Bailey, J. Mark, Asheville†	.263	122	410	68	108	190	23	1	19	62	2	0	7	5	84	3	87	5	1
Baker, Kerry, Greenwood	.211	113	336	53	71	107	13	4	5	30	1	0	0	2	60	1	114	9	1
Barbosa, Rafael, Anderson	.156	29	90	11	14	26	2	2	2	8	1	0	1	0	15	0	25	0	0
Beauchamp, J. Kash, Florence	.269	133	468	80	126	190	19	6	11	69	5	2	4	4	58	1	100	22	6
Blaser, Mark, Greensboro	.289	76	242	44	70	107	14	1	7	48	2	2	1	1	24	0	44	4	3
Bocock, Thomas, Macon	.240	137	458	71	110	163	22	5	7	61	9	4	9	4	77	1	87	10	2
Bolivar, Esteban, Florence	.175	50	154	19	27	39	6	0	2	20	0	2	0	1	21	0	38	3	2
Borders, Patrick, Florence	.274	131	457	62	125	179	31	4	5	54	8	1	1	1	46	2	116	4	1
Bragg, D. Keith, Greensboro*	.307	25	75	14	23	33	1	0	3	18	0	0	1	0	20	0	11	1	0
Brill, Clint, Anderson	.206	50	155	13	32	46	8	0	2	19	3	5	1	3	18	0	31	0	0
Brown, Anthony, Spartanburg*	.292	83	298	42	87	130	14	4	7	46	3	1	3	0	15	1	47	9	4
Bryeans, Christian, Charleston*	.219	55	169	18	37	49	3	0	3	15	2	0	3	1	20	0	29	5	7
Burrows, Bryan, Greenwood	.225	13	40	4	9	10	1	0	0	2	0	0	0	1	2	0	10	4	1
Butters, David, Greenwood	.100	6	10	0	1	2	1	0	0	0	0	0	0	0	1	0	4	0	0
Calloway, Vaughn, Spartanburg	.194	32	62	6	12	14	2	0	0	6	1	0	1	2	17	0	22	1	0
Camelo, Peter, Gastonia*	.243	114	371	70	90	160	15	2	17	66	3	6	4	3	74	5	71	7	1
Carpenter, Douglas, Greensboro	.143	24	35	10	5	10	3	1	0	4	0	0	0	0	7	0	18	1	1
Chadwick, George, Gastonia	.269	9	26	4	7	9	2	0	0	4	1	0	0	1	2	0	2	0	0
Chapman, Ronald, Florence†	.261	99	253	51	66	81	4	4	1	23	1	1	1	9	55	1	33	17	8
Ching, Mauricio, Greensboro*	.269	118	402	61	108	163	20	1	11	59	7	0	1	2	84	4	123	9	4
Clark, Henry, Asheville	.265	126	453	62	120	201	31	1	16	66	3	1	3	3	46	2	59	9	6
Clark, T. Kennedy, Anderson	.208	72	212	25	44	55	6	1	1	16	1	0	1	1	36	0	62	3	7
Coleman, Jerome, Gastonia*	.258	115	376	59	97	104	7	0	0	23	4	4	4	3	52	3	25	27	14
Coleman, Vincent, Macon	.350	113	446	99	156	178	8	7	0	53	5	0	2	9	56	3	85	145	31
Cooley, Willie, Gastonia†	.000	7	15	1	0	0	0	0	0	0	0	0	0	0	1	0	7	0	1
Coss, David, Greenwood	.252	85	290	41	73	91	10	4	0	18	1	1	1	1	31	1	66	20	5
Dearth, Ronald, Gastonia	.251	116	343	56	86	123	15	2	6	56	6	0	10	0	57	2	88	5	5
Denis, Orlando, Asheville	.264	20	53	6	14	22	5	0	1	5	1	0	0	0	4	0	14	0	0
Diaz, Angel, Florence	.269	27	67	9	18	25	2	1	1	10	1	0	0	2	4	0	18	0	1
Digioia, John, Macon	.250	110	360	63	90	167	11	3	20	65	3	2	6	2	58	1	117	3	1
Dophied, W. Tracy, Asheville*	.258	120	387	86	100	200	13	3	27	79	7	7	3	4	65	2	96	11	4
Espinal, Nelson, Asheville	.280	20	50	6	14	21	4	0	1	4	1	0	0	0	5	0	12	0	0
Fairbanks, Shane, Asheville*	.270	54	174	16	47	57	10	0	0	5	1	1	0	2	9	0	15	1	0
Falls, Robert, Asheville†	.250	111	348	52	87	128	12	4	7	35	3	3	4	3	33	0	75	12	7
Fennell, Michael, Greensboro*	.231	101	294	56	68	118	14	0	12	52	3	1	3	0	91	3	98	1	1
Fernandez, Jose, Florence†	.272	100	324	50	88	105	15	1	0	24	1	1	5	4	21	2	47	14	5
Fettig, Thomas, Gastonia	.274	104	365	45	100	164	17	1	15	60	7	2	4	3	45	0	70	0	2
Fielder, Cecil, Florence	.312	140	500	81	156	236	28	2	16	94	8	1	3	5	58	2	90	2	2
Frishman, Mark, Spartanburg	.213	78	249	34	53	75	13	0	3	28	5	0	1	1	29	1	56	8	3
Garcia, Agustin, Columbia	.253	80	281	37	71	90	8	4	1	25	3	3	2	0	32	0	78	7	0
Garcia, Ramon, Asheville	.200	74	200	24	40	56	7	0	3	30	2	3	2	0	17	0	28	8	1
Gayden, Huey, Macon*	.286	106	350	63	100	120	8	3	2	47	3	4	1	1	41	2	25	26	5
Giansanti, Ralph, Anderson	.215	80	260	29	56	69	7	3	0	28	2	2	2	6	33	0	45	8	2
Gill, Gary, Macon	.268	128	444	76	119	174	19	6	8	70	9	3	4	2	82	2	105	10	2
Glynn, Dennis, Columbia	.308	10	26	4	8	9	1	0	0	4	0	0	0	0	7	0	5	0	0
Gonzalez, Felipe, Spartanburg	.246	51	171	11	42	51	6	0	1	18	1	1	0	1	3	0	30	2	2
Gonzalez, Fredi, Greensboro	.192	56	151	25	29	53	6	0	6	23	1	0	1	2	37	0	62	2	0
Goodin, Craig, Charleston	.223	56	193	27	43	61	7	4	1	26	1	2	0	1	30	0	30	9	3
Griffin, D. Alan, Anderson	.275	139	499	63	137	219	31	3	15	71	7	2	1	3	56	3	93	0	0
Gutierrez, Isidro, Macon†	.209	97	282	28	59	72	5	4	0	19	1	5	3	2	25	1	38	8	6
Haas, Stanley, Macon	.233	87	266	40	62	82	15	1	1	27	1	4	4	5	28	0	60	6	2
Haro, Samuel, Greenwood†	.248	137	495	72	123	155	13	5	3	53	2	3	3	4	63	1	92	30	14
Harris, Kenneth, Columbia	.301	88	282	63	85	126	18	1	7	57	7	1	5	2	58	1	24	9	1
Hawkins, Johnny, Greensboro†	.185	33	92	12	17	21	1	0	1	10	1	0	0	0	14	0	15	3	1
Hearron, Jeffrey, Florence	.285	47	144	19	41	67	11	0	5	20	3	0	3	2	22	0	35	1	2
Hempfield, Vaughn, Charleston	.198	50	111	21	22	30	3	1	1	10	1	2	0	2	9	1	44	2	1
Henderson, Ramon, Spartanburg	.298	65	198	36	59	78	11	1	2	21	0	1	3	1	23	1	40	7	4
Hinson, Bobby Joe, Asheville	.286	87	262	35	75	91	12	2	0	30	0	5	6	1	50	1	16	9	5
Hollins, Paul, Columbia*	.301	130	458	81	138	226	21	2	21	97	6	0	7	1	66	4	74	5	4
Hoppie, Bryan, Spartanburg†	.301	25	93	17	28	34	4	1	0	7	1	0	1	1	12	0	9	15	3
Hughes, Keith, Spartanburg*	.329	131	484	80	159	243	31	4	15	90	5	2	5	4	67	5	83	16	1
Infante, Alexis, Florence	.279	128	480	88	134	177	25	3	4	56	10	7	5	6	44	0	77	37	9

Player and Club	Pct.	G.	AB.	R.	H.	TB.	2B.	3B.	HR.	RBI.	GW.	SH.	SF.	HP.	BB.	Int. BB.	SO.	SB.	CS.
Ingle, Randy, Anderson	.400	7	20	3	8	11	0	0	1	4	0	0	0	0	2	0	2	0	0
Isaac, Johnny, Asheville†	.247	105	348	53	86	127	15	4	6	36	3	6	2	3	14	1	114	15	2
Isambert, Sergio, Spartanburg	.237	39	139	17	33	44	8	0	1	18	4	0	3	1	10	0	36	8	1
Jackson, Kenneth, Spartanburg	.236	131	449	95	106	148	21	3	5	49	4	5	8	7	114	2	104	27	7
Jacobson, Jeffrey, Asheville	.190	24	58	11	11	16	2	0	1	5	1	0	1	0	9	0	10	1	2
James, D. Christopher, Spartanburg	.297	129	499	94	148	257	23	4	26	121	12	1	9	12	41	1	93	11	3
Jarrell, Joseph, Charleston	.226	71	274	38	62	87	5	1	6	40	3	0	1	1	9	1	53	10	5
Javier, Stanley, Greensboro†	.311	129	489	109	152	234	34	6	12	77	10	2	2	2	75	2	95	33	7
Jelks, Gregory, Spartanburg	.261	123	418	81	109	209	24	2	24	75	5	2	8	3	61	0	110	16	2
Jiminez, Francisco, Greenwood*	.268	41	142	26	38	45	1	3	0	12	1	1	1	4	30	1	33	9	6
Job, Ryan, Asheville	.275	92	313	38	86	108	14	1	2	33	1	0	3	2	38	1	45	10	7
Kanter, John, Spartanburg†	.201	78	239	34	48	90	7	1	11	33	1	2	3	5	25	0	80	14	3
Kelly, Roberto, Greensboro	.265	20	49	6	13	13	0	0	0	3	1	0	0	2	3	0	5	3	4
Kiesling, Larry, Asheville	.257	100	300	60	77	169	15	7	21	53	7	1	3	5	48	0	88	20	5
Kimball, D. Scott, Florence	.169	26	77	14	13	16	3	0	0	6	1	0	1	1	9	1	29	0	0
Lacava, Tony, Greenwood	.000	5	11	1	0	0	0	0	0	0	0	0	0	0	2	0	1	0	0
Latorre, Pedro, Macon	.213	122	399	57	85	103	13	1	1	38	3	6	4	4	79	1	70	23	10
Lauck, Jeffrey, Macon†	.143	10	28	2	4	6	2	0	0	2	0	1	0	1	9	0	10	3	1
Lawrence, Andy, Columbia	.257	54	202	32	52	77	9	2	4	26	2	0	2	1	14	1	54	4	2
Leiva, Jose, Spartanburg	.272	138	519	128	141	189	21	9	3	43	2	5	3	8	108	1	99	78	13
Lemon, Ricky, Gastonia*	.294	105	357	67	105	157	19	3	9	60	1	0	3	1	26	2	58	30	3
Lewis, Herman, Columbia†	.249	92	177	34	44	49	5	0	0	14	1	3	2	1	17	1	23	26	3
Liriano, Nelson, Florence†	.259	129	478	87	124	176	24	5	6	57	3	4	3	3	70	2	81	27	9
Llewellyn, Paul, Anderson	.188	108	378	40	71	124	15	1	12	41	3	0	2	2	30	1	149	14	5
Lombardi, Phillip, Greensboro	.300	94	330	63	99	135	15	0	7	43	5	1	6	5	49	0	44	5	6
Lyon, Bruce, Columbia*	.000	2	1	0	0	0	0	0	0	0	0	0	0	0	0	0	1	0	0
Lyons, Barry, Columbia	.297	92	316	55	94	122	9	2	5	45	7	1	5	2	42	0	32	3	0
Mackay, Joey, Greensboro	.250	128	420	61	105	153	25	4	5	57	4	6	3	3	42	2	105	8	7
Magadan, David, Columbia*	.336	64	220	41	74	98	13	1	3	32	4	1	1	1	51	2	29	2	2
Malave, Omar, Florence	.250	88	232	41	58	83	8	4	3	27	1	3	1	1	35	1	34	2	5
Marchand, Rene, Gastonia	.269	118	435	57	117	185	24	1	14	58	10	2	3	2	53	2	58	8	0
Massiah, Omar, Greenwood	.205	98	332	34	68	97	15	1	4	28	3	2	1	2	23	1	96	14	5
McGriff, Frederick, Florence*	.311	33	119	26	37	63	3	1	7	26	2	1	0	1	20	4	35	3	0
McPhail, Marlin, Columbia	.303	42	132	17	40	54	8	0	2	24	2	0	3	1	11	0	22	1	2
Medina, Pedro, Greensboro†	.256	92	347	34	89	116	17	5	0	38	5	4	1	1	29	0	72	9	7
Mena, Cesar, Greenwood	.238	88	281	35	67	92	9	5	2	25	0	1	1	4	25	3	59	11	4
Miller, John, Asheville	.000	4	15	2	0	0	0	0	0	1	0	0	1	0	1	0	2	0	0
Moore, Bryant, Greenwood	.296	77	274	44	81	111	12	6	2	41	1	1	2	9	38	0	61	6	2
Moreno, Armando, Gastonia	.327	115	367	89	120	165	19	1	8	63	7	4	1	6	86	2	52	17	7
Morgan, Stacy, Greensboro	.000	22	1	0	0	0	0	0	0	0	0	0	0	0	0	0	0	0	0
Morris, David, Anderson	.193	77	228	28	44	74	6	0	8	24	2	8	1	2	18	1	74	6	3
Moscat, Fernando, Columbia	.274	127	514	89	141	179	16	5	4	55	4	2	3	2	43	1	81	20	11
Moser, Larry, Anderson†	.218	69	252	38	55	68	6	2	1	27	3	3	2	1	58	1	43	8	9
Moyer, Todd, Greenwood	.198	119	384	60	76	116	19	0	7	49	12	4	5	5	63	0	116	9	4
Nieves, Tito, Gastonia	.213	38	61	16	13	16	3	0	0	5	2	0	0	0	10	0	20	3	0
O'Donnell, Steven, Greensboro†	.253	34	91	13	23	27	2	1	0	8	0	0	0	2	9	0	18	1	4
Oruna, Roland, Charleston	.212	19	52	5	11	17	3	0	1	15	0	1	4	0	4	0	11	3	0
Packer, William, Macon	.069	13	29	2	2	2	0	0	0	2	0	1	0	0	11	0	8	1	1
Pagnozzi, Thomas, Macon	.246	18	57	7	14	18	2	1	0	6	0	0	1	1	6	0	13	0	0
Palma, G. Jay, Anderson	.258	125	450	68	116	167	17	5	8	50	7	8	6	0	30	1	76	10	5
Paredes, Johnny, Spartanburg	.238	46	130	14	31	37	0	3	0	11	0	0	0	1	12	0	22	10	4
Paula, Julio, Columbia†	.306	48	160	28	49	72	10	2	3	27	1	1	2	1	21	2	30	3	5
Perdomo, Felix, 15 Col.-112 Gboro.	.253	127	438	63	111	168	18	6	9	69	9	3	5	3	32	1	123	14	6
Pettis, Stacey, Greenwood*	.247	103	388	49	96	135	5	8	6	54	5	1	5	1	35	1	105	35	4
Pevey, Marty, Macon*	.312	122	436	74	136	184	23	2	7	77	9	2	4	2	45	2	70	8	5
Phillips, W. Joseph, Charleston	.207	130	483	68	100	117	13	2	0	41	4	1	5	2	71	2	49	27	7
Phillips, Steven, Columbia*	.277	58	148	21	41	59	8	2	2	24	4	3	1	2	29	1	40	4	4
Pirruccello, Mark, Charleston*	.262	114	386	72	101	195	15	2	25	73	6	1	0	8	76	3	94	1	1
Piskol, Peter, Greenwood	.260	107	354	40	92	117	9	5	2	48	7	5	2	3	59	1	76	14	3
Pleis, W. Scott, Macon	.232	55	155	21	36	45	3	3	0	14	1	1	1	0	23	0	40	1	0
Post, E. Peter, Greensboro*	.077	7	13	2	1	1	0	0	0	1	0	0	0	0	2	0	5	0	0
Ragsdale, Jerry, Anderson	.234	79	244	25	57	88	11	4	4	21	1	2	1	1	23	1	70	2	0
Ramler, Steven, Gastonia	.195	46	133	20	26	34	6	1	0	23	3	1	2	2	20	2	21	0	0
Ramos, Luis, Greenwood	.249	105	382	47	95	126	16	6	1	39	4	2	2	0	19	0	89	13	5
Richards, Nicky, Charleston	.236	21	55	9	13	15	2	0	0	4	2	0	0	2	5	0	19	1	1
Richardson, Timothy, Charleston	.335	74	278	55	93	118	7	6	2	31	3	0	4	2	30	0	26	13	3
Riggs, James, Greensboro*	.262	133	481	77	126	196	23	4	13	95	12	3	6	1	68	3	53	5	3
Rivera, Hector, Gastonia	.266	108	383	53	102	140	20	0	6	54	6	2	2	0	34	3	42	6	0
Rivera, Jose, Greensboro	.210	43	143	18	30	50	3	1	5	21	1	0	2	0	19	1	58	3	1
Rivera, Ricardo, Asheville†	.286	21	84	11	24	30	3	0	1	12	1	1	0	0	10	0	9	18	3
Roarke, Thomas, Asheville	.257	102	338	42	87	134	20	0	9	61	6	0	2	2	38	1	69	1	2
Roberts, R. Jay, Anderson	.103	21	58	7	6	10	1	0	1	6	1	1	0	1	13	1	22	1	1
Roberts, Leon, Greenwood†	.320	122	438	78	140	188	20	5	6	63	10	2	6	10	69	1	43	27	16
Roman, Luis, Macon*	.375	47	8	1	3	3	0	0	0	3	0	0	0	0	4	1	0	1	0
Ross, Carey, Charleston	.229	73	253	30	58	69	11	0	0	29	6	1	3	2	30	0	39	16	2
Rossi, Thomas, Macon	.204	19	49	4	10	10	0	0	0	3	0	0	0	0	5	0	12	0	0
Ruffner, William, Greensboro	.183	29	60	10	11	17	3	0	1	4	0	1	0	0	7	0	27	2	1
Russell, Anthony, Greensboro	.285	129	471	97	134	178	18	7	4	56	5	4	4	6	97	1	103	43	13
Sanchez, Jose, Macon	.302	48	139	23	42	49	4	0	1	11	0	1	2	2	14	0	12	2	1
Sarmiento, Ramon, Florence	.190	97	294	46	56	100	12	1	10	47	3	1	4	3	34	0	133	10	4
Schexnayder, Wade, Columbia	.259	102	316	44	82	137	19	6	8	49	2	0	2	7	34	0	68	4	4
Schulte, Mark, Macon*	.305	61	236	37	72	113	17	3	6	52	7	0	3	1	19	0	35	1	0
Seoane, Mitchell, Greensboro*	.228	27	92	13	21	26	3	1	0	8	1	2	0	0	5	0	19	3	1
Sherman, James, Asheville	.314	44	159	29	50	92	10	1	10	28	3	0	3	0	22	0	23	2	3
Shuffield, Jack, Charleston*	.271	132	501	76	136	186	20	9	4	50	3	5	3	3	23	0	63	15	10
Simons, Neil, Asheville*	.186	19	43	5	8	11	1	1	0	6	2	0	0	0	9	0	10	1	0
Sliwinski, Kevin, Florence	.238	86	277	48	66	118	15	2	11	56	5	2	4	2	54	0	68	1	0
Smith, Rick, Gastonia	.200	3	5	1	1	2	1	0	0	1	0	0	0	0	1	0	2	0	0
Snider, Van, Charleston*	.291	123	467	86	136	226	26	2	20	94	10	0	2	2	45	2	111	26	8
Soriano, Hilario, Florence	.083	6	12	0	1	1	0	0	0	0	0	0	0	0	1	0	4	0	0
Springer, Steven, Columbia	.338	130	488	99	165	243	24	9	12	88	18	1	7	2	35	2	50	22	4
Spurlin, Robert, Greenwood	.286	7	14	1	4	4	0	0	0	1	0	0	0	0	7	1	2	0	0
Steele, Paul, Macon	.163	23	49	4	8	12	2	1	0	3	0	1	0	0	8	0	10	0	1

Player and Club	Pct.	G.	AB.	R.	H.	TB.	2B.	3B.	HR.	RBI.	GW.	SH.	SF.	HP.	BB.	Int. BB.	SO.	SB.	CS.
Stellern, Michael, Asheville	.312	119	449	94	140	229	27	10	14	57	7	4	3	5	55	0	89	23	4
Stenhouse, David, Florence	.308	95	318	48	98	155	16	1	13	55	9	2	4	2	47	2	47	1	1
Stinnett, James, Greenwood	.500	25	2	0	1	1	0	0	0	0	0	0	0	0	0	0	1	0	0
Strickland, Terry, Gastonia	.240	51	171	25	41	53	9	0	1	23	3	3	1	2	13	1	26	7	2
Szajko, Daniel, Gastonia	.299	106	394	81	118	153	11	3	6	62	4	7	4	1	59	0	34	22	7
Szekely, Joseph, Charleston*	.276	142	521	83	144	216	17	5	15	87	10	1	8	2	55	2	122	12	5
Tejada, Wilfredo, Spartanburg	.249	90	273	33	68	92	14	2	2	29	4	0	5	12	10	0	47	0	4
Then, Hediberto, Greenwood	.130	21	77	8	10	15	2	0	1	9	0	0	2	3	9	0	33	1	0
Thiessen, Timothy, Gastonia	.302	143	513	95	155	199	21	4	5	55	7	2	2	4	77	0	73	34	18
Thomas, Andres, Anderson	.315	61	251	33	79	98	8	4	1	20	0	3	0	2	14	1	44	10	4
Thompson, Richard, Anderson	.266	117	413	64	110	152	16	1	8	43	6	1	1	9	41	0	80	20	7
Thompson, Richard, Asheville	.209	63	196	30	41	49	5	0	1	21	2	6	0	3	39	0	50	12	5
Thornton, Louis, Columbia*	.268	119	448	80	120	189	24	6	11	73	16	2	4	6	32	0	90	22	8
Tiamo, Jesus, Greenwood	.261	114	440	49	115	160	24	6	3	43	4	2	1	3	26	0	30	6	0
Turgeon, Stephen, Macon	.296	74	270	51	80	132	8	7	10	54	6	5	5	2	41	1	59	9	5
Van Horn, David, Anderson	.270	105	392	46	106	131	19	3	0	26	2	9	0	5	35	2	35	5	5
Vaughn, Michael, Macon*	.277	94	318	43	88	108	8	6	0	35	2	1	1	2	26	1	57	2	5
Velez, David, Charleston	.164	24	73	5	12	19	1	0	2	5	0	0	1	1	6	0	22	0	0
Vest, James, Spartanburg	.285	132	505	75	144	218	22	8	12	84	4	1	5	4	37	3	78	7	1
Vitato, Richard, Charleston*	.296	51	169	38	50	66	10	0	2	17	1	1	0	0	42	3	21	2	0
Wagner, Jeffrey, Anderson†	.229	117	393	48	90	135	20	2	7	35	5	0	1	5	60	0	159	4	7
Wallace, Thomas, Charleston	.222	71	230	25	51	79	13	0	5	26	1	0	0	2	35	0	92	16	4
Weinberger, Gary, Gastonia*	.305	102	321	63	98	143	26	2	5	44	6	4	4	1	43	3	33	21	7
Welch, Billy, Columbia	.179	43	106	14	19	20	1	0	0	11	1	1	2	1	8	0	26	2	0
Williams, Jaime, Asheville	.250	3	12	2	3	4	1	0	0	0	0	1	0	0	0	0	5	0	0
Williamson, Keith, Charleston†	.200	16	55	6	11	11	0	0	0	4	0	0	2	0	8	0	14	6	7
Wilson, John, Columbia*	.268	124	426	71	114	157	16	9	3	44	4	6	2	2	33	3	103	36	11
Yoder, Frederick, Greenwood*	.273	3	11	1	3	3	0	0	0	2	0	0	0	0	0	0	0	0	1

The following pitchers, listed alphabetically by club, with games in parentheses, had no plate appearances, primarily through use of designated hitters:

ANDERSON—Aviles, Brian (9); Baker, John (16); Candelaria, Albert (17); Cano, Jose (20); Eldridge, Jeffrey (12); Lance, Mark (13); Leggatt, Richard (3); Lynn, Kenneth (15); Mehalko, Andrew (9); Morelock, Charles (5); Mortillaro, John (24); Rivera, James (44); Rogers, Randy (36); Rosario, Maximo (21); Smith, Mark (8); Torres, Rudy (20); Valdez, Silverio (20); Vargas, Ramon (14).

ASHEVILLE—Acker, Larry (17); Alburquerque, Claudio (4); Bailey, Kirk (19); Castro, Guillermo (26); Cerefin, Michael (15); Coughlin, Richard (4); Kasprzak, Michael (11); Kerfeld, Charles (28); Koenig, Kalvin (48); Lucas, Arbrey (32); Mize, Gregory (20); Perkins, Ray (51); Polemir, Miguel (18); Robertson, Charles (35); Samuels, Roger (10); Smith, Scott (9); Strasser, Richard (30); Troncoso, Martin (6).

CHARLESTON—Aube, Brian (29); Bass, Edward (13); Bryant, John (19); Cook, Douglas (9); Davis, Bradley (20); Davis, John (20); Debord, Robert (38); Drizmala, Thomas (15); Goodin, Richard (32); Marrero, Frank (22); McCormack, Ronald (12); Perez, Valerio (6); Pone, Vincent (10); Sanchez, Israel (30); Serritella, John (12); Steinberg, Scott (20).

COLUMBIA—Brown, Kevin (29); Foulks, Stuart (31); Gay, Steven (5); Hartshorn, Ronald (9); Jensen, David (26); Klink, Joseph (12); Lockenmeyer, Mark (18); Murray, Scott (57); Myers, Randall (28); Pruitt, Edwin (37); Ray, Steven (2); Weissman, Craig (18); Weston, Michael (37); Youmans, Floyd (23).

FLORENCE—Aquino, Luis (29); Carter, Tyson (26); Castro, Eddy (29); Cullen, Michael (25); Davis, Steven (23); Gallagher, Glenn (32); Gorden, Daniel (28); Johnson, Ronald (6); McKay, Alan (17); Mesa, Jose (28); Moore, Gregory (53); Phillips, Christopher (5); Ruetter, Derrick (10); Walsh, David (41).

GASTONIA—Branam, Barry (33); Edwards, Derek (11); Flores, David (18); Gause, Ernest (9); Glidewell, John (27); Hess, James (12); Huber, Randolph (22); Johnson, Gregory (30); Kinns, Glenn (28); Mielke, Shawn (26); Moran, Steven (26); Nicometi, Anthony (26); Richards, Gregory (13); Scott, Charles (5); Valliant, Robert (15); Waymire, Ronald (9).

GREENSBORO—Bailey, Kirk (3); Baldwin, Johnny (43); Beahan, Scot (18); Byron, Timothy (10); Canseco, Osvaldo (27); Corsi, James (12); Doty, Paul (5); Easley, Logan (29); Fedor, Francis (14); Gaston, John (8); George, Stephen (37); Graham, Randle (30); Gumbert, Richard (12); Humphrey, Daryl (8); Mathison, Charles (10); Raftice, Robert (3); Ray, Steven (3); Seidel, Richard (22); Smalley, David (10); Teegarden, Robert (12); White, Randall (18).

GREENWOOD—Borland, Scott (21); Catlett, Justin (2); Cooke, John (34); Cunningham, Charles (10); Downs, Dorley (20); Felt, James (1); Grudzinski, Gary (26); Holman, Shawn (22); Marty, Charles (18); McKelvey, Mitch (28); Mejia, Manuel (21); Pol, Frank (17); Sanchez, Leopoldo (19); Simmons, Scott (11); Stanton, Bernard (5); Stone, Shawn (28); Taylor, Donald (12).

MACON—Bear, David (53); Blunt, Bradley (3); Brown, Brian (26); Donathan, William (9); Dunn, Bruce (25); Farley, Brian (9); Fincher, Steve (24); Hartley, Michael (7); Meadows, Geoffrey (28); Mitchell, William (45); North, Jay (31); Ortega, Jose (44); Strichek, James (27); Turnbull, Keith (5).

SPARTANBURG—Brewer, Stanley (48); Bulls, David (12); Coker, Kevin (27); Ferguson, Billy (14); Hill, John (38); Maddux, Michael (14); McCullers, Lance (22); Miller, Todd (7); Morel, Nelson (25); Olson, James (25); Rodriguez, Yonis (21); Scarpetta, Dennis (11); Segura, Jose (40); Witt, Stephen (14).

GRAND SLAM HOME RUNS—Bocock, Harris, Javier, Snider, 2 each; Blaser, Camelo, Ching, F. Gonzalez, Infante, James, Jarrell, Kiesling, Lattore, Liriano, Moreno, Moscat, Perdomo, Pettis, Pevey, Riggs, Roarke, J. Roberts, Vest, Weinberger, 1 each.

AWARDED FIRST BASE ON CATCHER'S INTERFERENCE—Vaughn 4 (Bailey, Hearron, Rivera, Schexnayder); Bocock 3 (Kimball, Szekely, Welch); Ching (M. Bailey); K. Clark (F. Gonzalez); Kanter (Brill); Pleis (Welch); Riggs (Stenhouse).

CLUB FIELDING

Club	Pct.	G.	PO.	A.	E.	DP.	PB.
Gastonia	.966	143	3647	1497	180	130	30
Anderson	.957	143	3626	1561	232	117	39
Asheville	.954	144	3628	1673	257	152	39
Greenwood	.954	144	3671	1654	255	137	34
Columbia	.953	142	3623	1376	245	107	32
Macon	.953	144	3713	1451	256	138	50
Spartanburg	.952	143	3630	1511	260	122	28
Greensboro	.951	144	3669	1446	263	116	23
Charleston	.950	144	3654	1550	276	140	27
Florence	.948	143	3595	1535	280	120	41

Triple play—Anderson.

INDIVIDUAL FIELDING

*Throws lefthanded.

FIRST BASEMEN

Player and Club	Pct.	G.	PO.	A.	E.	DP.
Anglin, Anderson	1.000	13	106	7	0	7
Bagnall, Charleston	.987	66	568	32	8	53
Bailey, Asheville	.997	36	299	23	1	25
Bryeans, Charleston	1.000	4	31	4	0	4
Ching, Greensboro*	.973	74	566	38	17	59
Clark, Asheville	.988	47	370	42	5	43
Coleman, Gastonia*	.991	30	222	9	2	15
Denis, Asheville	1.000	13	101	4	0	6
Espinal, Asheville	1.000	6	46	2	0	4
Fairbanks, Asheville*	1.000	6	36	2	0	6
Fennell, Greensboro	.985	73	549	43	9	45
Fernandez, Florence*	.986	9	64	8	1	4
Fettig, Gastonia	1.000	3	18	3	0	3
Fielder, Florence	.985	108	957	64	16	88

FIRST BASEMEN—Continued

Player and Club	Pct.	G.	PO.	A.	E.	DP.
GILL, Macon	.992	114	948	54	8	97
Gonzalez, Greensboro	.833	1	3	2	1	0
Griffin, Anderson	.986	131	1197	76	18	96
Haas, Macon	.983	8	53	4	1	6
Hughes, Spartanburg*	.948	12	106	3	6	6
Jelks, Spartanburg	.982	121	1078	59	21	100
Lacava, Greenwood	.857	2	12	0	2	0
Lawrence, Columbia	.983	54	434	23	8	40
Lyons, Columbia	.882	8	28	2	4	1
Magadan, Columbia	.988	64	520	37	7	36
Malave, Florence	1.000	1	1	0	0	0
Marchand, Gastonia	.991	118	969	71	9	94
McGriff, Florence*	.978	30	250	14	6	16
McPhail, Columbia	.984	25	174	9	3	12
Moyer, Greenwood	.980	112	952	65	21	89
Palma, Anderson	.909	1	9	1	1	0
Paredes, Spartanburg	.972	12	65	4	2	2
Pirruccello, Charleston	.983	15	109	10	2	15
Richardson, Charleston	.991	61	557	25	5	47
Riggs, Greensboro	.500	1	1	0	1	0
Rivera, Gastonia	.938	2	15	0	1	1
Roarke, Asheville	.972	53	460	22	14	45
Ruffner, Greensboro	1.000	1	8	0	0	1
Schulte, Macon	.996	26	213	9	1	19
Simons, Asheville*	1.000	8	52	0	0	3
Steele, Macon	1.000	1	3	0	0	1
Tiamo, Greenwood	.989	35	333	29	4	34
Van Horn, Anderson	1.000	1	3	0	0	0
Vest, Spartanburg	.966	9	53	4	2	3

Triple play—Griffin.

SECOND BASEMEN

Player and Club	Pct.	G.	PO.	A.	E.	DP.
Alcala, Greensboro	.917	9	19	14	3	3
Bocock, Macon	.917	8	10	12	2	1
Bryeans, Charleston	.945	12	20	32	3	10
Chapman, Florence	.921	34	64	88	13	16
Espinal, Asheville	.955	5	8	13	1	1
Falls, Asheville	.939	77	144	210	23	52
Giansanti, Anderson	.951	69	153	177	17	42
Glynn, Columbia	.946	10	16	19	2	6
Gutierrez, Macon	.967	17	33	26	2	13
Hempfield, Charleston	.977	9	18	24	1	8
Henderson, Spartanburg	.939	52	121	125	16	27
Hinson, Asheville	.964	67	116	176	11	35
Hoppie, Spartanburg	.915	15	36	39	7	9
Ingle, Anderson	1.000	1	4	2	0	0
Job, Asheville	.923	19	36	60	8	11
Kanter, Spartanburg	.939	78	166	221	25	52
Latorre, Macon	.949	118	241	330	31	74
Liriano, Florence	.940	114	214	323	34	63
McPhail, Columbia	1.000	1	1	3	0	0
Medina, Greensboro	.903	22	39	54	10	11
Mena, Greenwood	.940	38	78	109	12	23
Moreno, Gastonia	.941	108	218	262	30	72
Moscat, Columbia	1.000	7	4	9	0	0
Nieves, Gastonia	1.000	7	10	15	0	1
O'Donnell, Greensboro	.969	18	27	35	2	9
Paredes, Spartanburg	.976	9	17	24	1	4
Perdomo, 15 Col.-80 Gboro	.949	95	196	211	22	46
J. Phillips, Charleston	.949	129	310	342	35	76
S. Phillips, Columbia	.930	47	88	86	13	18
ROBERTS, Greenwood	.962	113	267	309	23	76
Sanchez, Macon	.967	15	28	31	2	8
Seoane, Greensboro	.981	27	71	85	3	25
Springer, Columbia	.957	77	179	202	17	45
Strickland, Gastonia	.975	10	17	22	1	7
Szajko, Gastonia	.968	22	42	50	3	11
Turgeon, Macon	1.000	1	2	0	0	0
Van Horn, Anderson	.976	75	160	201	9	46
Vaughn, Macon	1.000	1	0	1	0	0

THIRD BASEMEN

Player and Club	Pct.	G.	PO.	A.	E.	DP.
Abone, Gastonia	.957	11	7	15	1	0
Barbosa, Anderson	.907	15	23	26	5	4
Blaser, Greensboro	.867	22	11	41	8	1
Bocock, Macon	.827	17	15	28	9	3
Borders, Florence	.881	125	70	233	41	14
Brown, Spartanburg	1.000	1	0	1	0	0
Bryeans, Charleston	.896	15	6	37	5	3
Burrows, Greenwood	1.000	12	12	21	0	3
Chapman, Florence	.829	19	7	22	6	2
Clark, Asheville	.920	49	36	102	12	11
Dearth, Gastonia	.941	103	76	227	19	21
Denis, Asheville	1.000	1	0	2	0	0
Dophied, Asheville	.931	13	5	22	2	0
Espinal, Asheville	.895	11	3	14	2	0
Falls, Asheville	.944	18	10	24	2	2
Fennell, Greensboro	.900	8	6	21	3	0
Frishman, Spartanburg	.871	68	54	121	26	6
Haas, Macon	.647	7	2	9	6	1
HARO, Greenwood	.946	112	85	245	19	27
Harris, Columbia	.884	27	26	35	8	6
Hempfield, Charleston	.897	12	7	28	4	3
Hinson, Asheville	1.000	10	3	14	0	0
Hoppie, Spartanburg	.889	6	4	4	1	0
Ingle, Anderson	.867	3	3	10	2	0
James, Spartanburg	.935	55	32	84	8	11
Job, Asheville	.857	10	11	19	5	3
Malave, Florence	.950	8	3	16	1	1
McPhail, Columbia	.692	6	3	6	4	0
Medina, Greensboro	1.000	1	1	0	0	0
Mena, Greenwood	.667	1	0	2	1	0
Miller, Asheville	.625	4	1	4	3	1
Moscat, Columbia	.931	111	67	215	21	11
Moyer, Greenwood	.895	5	7	10	2	0
Palma, Anderson	.905	107	97	238	35	19
Paredes, Spartanburg	.855	24	16	31	8	3
Pleis, Macon	.888	53	24	71	12	8
Riggs, Greensboro	.914	120	103	228	31	13
Ross, Charleston	.916	71	56	129	17	20
Schexnayder, Columbia	.857	2	4	2	1	1
Sherman, Asheville	.866	41	37	79	18	9
Springer, Columbia	.833	5	2	13	3	2
Steele, Macon	.667	7	1	7	4	0
Strickland, Gastonia	.958	34	27	64	4	9
Szajko, Gastonia	.962	7	10	15	1	1
Then, Greenwood	.807	18	12	34	11	1
Turgeon, Macon	.871	71	63	106	25	14
Van Horn, Anderson	.929	20	12	53	5	4
Vaughn, Macon	.667	2	1	1	1	0
Vitato, Charleston	.933	51	33	93	9	9

Triple play—Palma.

SHORTSTOPS

Player and Club	Pct.	G.	PO.	A.	E.	DP.
Bocock, Macon	.948	77	102	210	17	50
Bryeans, Charleston	.932	24	30	66	7	14
Clark, Anderson	.904	70	65	228	31	34
Dearth, Gastonia	1.000	2	3	2	0	0
Falls, Asheville	.932	11	6	35	3	6
Garcia, Columbia	.922	80	105	236	29	39
Giansanti, Anderson	.909	7	8	12	2	3
Goodin, Charleston	.892	56	73	158	28	27
Gutierrez, Macon	.906	80	106	232	35	46
Haro, Greenwood	.905	22	19	67	9	4
Hempfield, Charleston	.846	5	5	6	2	2
Henderson, Spartanburg	.875	13	14	21	5	6
Hoppie, Spartanburg	.765	3	4	9	4	1
Infante, Florence	.913	127	197	393	56	76
Ingle, Anderson	.667	1	1	1	1	0
Jackson, Spartanburg	.931	131	167	430	44	80
Jarrell, Charleston	.916	63	70	215	26	32
Job, Asheville	.922	53	62	187	21	42
Latorre, Macon	1.000	2	1	1	0	0
Malave, Florence	.872	18	16	52	10	8
Medina, Greensboro	.920	71	88	187	24	41
Mena, Greenwood	.885	20	22	47	9	5
Moscat, Columbia	.911	13	18	23	4	1
O'Donnell, Greensboro	.875	10	9	19	4	4
Palma, Anderson	.786	2	1	10	3	0
Paula, Columbia	.925	48	63	135	16	17
Perdomo, Greensboro	.935	31	54	91	10	24
Phillips, Columbia	.800	7	5	11	4	2
Piskol, Greenwood	.939	107	158	369	34	67
J. Rivera, Greensboro	.890	38	44	101	18	17
R. Rivera, Asheville	.971	21	28	73	3	11
Roberts, Greenwood	.889	1	6	2	1	2
Szajko, Gastonia	1.000	2	1	3	0	1
THIESSEN, Gastonia	.942	142	186	410	37	81
Thomas, Anderson	.915	61	61	197	24	28
Thompson, Asheville	.937	62	93	191	19	44
Van Horn, Anderson	.813	3	3	10	3	1

OUTFIELDERS

Player and Club	Pct.	G.	PO.	A.	E.	DP.
Allen, Charleston	.961	52	97	2	4	1
Aruca, Asheville*	.938	9	15	0	1	0
Aubin, Greensboro	.875	6	7	0	1	0
Beauchamp, Florence	.955	128	239	13	12	1
Blaser, Greensboro	.946	27	34	1	2	0
Bocock, Macon	.977	45	78	6	2	2
Bolivar, Florence	.908	50	53	6	6	1
Bragg, Greensboro*	1.000	2	1	0	0	0
Brown, Spartanburg	.945	65	97	6	6	2
CAMELO, Gastonia*	.976	113	189	15	5	3
Carpenter, Greensboro	.905	14	19	0	2	0
Chadwick, Gastonia	1.000	8	7	0	0	0
Clark, Asheville	1.000	16	19	1	0	1
J. Coleman, Gastonia*	.947	80	119	7	7	2
V. Coleman, Macon	.968	111	225	18	8	4
Cooley, Gastonia	1.000	7	6	0	0	0
Coss, Greenwood	.968	76	115	5	4	3
Digioia, Macon	.909	53	58	2	6	0
Dophied, Asheville	.937	101	140	9	10	2
Fairbanks, Asheville*	.986	45	67	4	1	1
Fernandez, Florence*	.946	82	103	2	6	0
Garcia, Asheville	1.000	12	15	1	0	0
Gayden, Macon*	.913	99	148	9	15	1
Haas, Macon	.977	33	39	3	1	1
Harris, Columbia	1.000	1	1	0	0	0
Hempfield, Charleston	.913	14	20	1	2	1
Hollins, Columbia	.919	104	108	5	10	2
Hughes, Spartanburg*	.985	44	65	2	1	0
Isaac, Asheville	.905	74	98	7	11	1
Isambert, Spartanburg	.940	34	47	0	3	0
James, Spartanburg	.938	71	118	4	8	0
Jarrell, Charleston	.909	7	10	0	1	0
Javier, Greensboro	.945	127	250	10	15	2
Jiminez, Greenwood*	.941	39	75	5	5	1
Kelly, Greensboro	1.000	16	30	2	0	0
Kiesling, Asheville	.946	94	126	14	8	3
Lauck, Macon*	.929	10	11	2	1	1
Leiva, Spartanburg	.950	136	284	17	16	3
Lemon, Gastonia*	.923	84	102	6	9	1
Lewis, Columbia	.960	83	116	5	5	2
Llewellyn, Anderson	.968	106	199	13	7	1
Lombardi, Greensboro	1.000	6	4	0	0	0
MacKay, Greensboro	.963	125	171	11	7	1
Malave, Florence	.967	57	86	3	3	0
Massiah, Greenwood	.906	70	109	6	12	2
McPhail, Columbia	1.000	8	12	0	0	0
Moore, Greenwood	.935	70	83	4	6	0
Morris, Anderson	.939	74	118	6	8	2
Moser, Anderson*	.981	69	151	5	3	2
Nieves, Gastonia	1.000	7	3	1	0	0
Oruna, Charleston	.962	12	23	2	1	0
Pettis, Greenwood	.929	93	198	10	16	2
Pevey, Macon	.941	21	31	1	2	0
Post, Greensboro	1.000	5	5	1	0	0
Ramos, Greenwood	.960	96	161	9	7	1
Roberts, Anderson	.844	12	24	3	5	0
Rossi, Macon	.960	19	22	2	1	0
Ruffner, Greensboro	.969	20	29	2	1	0
Russell, Greensboro	.961	114	239	6	10	0
Sanchez, Macon	1.000	5	6	2	0	0
Sarmiento, Florence	.810	64	61	3	15	0
Schulte, Macon	1.000	19	21	1	0	0
Shuffield, Charleston*	.949	131	227	13	13	1
Simons, Asheville*	.857	9	5	1	1	0
Sliwinski, Florence	.946	82	120	2	7	0
Snider, Charleston	.911	121	207	17	22	7
Springer, Columbia	.959	51	69	2	3	0
Stellern, Asheville	.945	112	171	19	11	6
Szajko, Gastonia	.971	75	121	15	4	4
Thompson, Anderson	.944	95	125	10	8	0
Thornton, Columbia	.950	116	193	18	11	1
Vaughn, Macon	.938	65	100	6	7	0
Velez, Charleston	.973	23	35	1	1	0
Vest, Spartanburg	.949	90	141	7	8	1
Wagner, Anderson	.945	85	132	6	8	2
Wallace, Charleston	.929	69	113	5	9	2
Weinberger, Gastonia*	.989	90	173	10	2	0
Williamson, Charleston	.947	15	18	0	1	0
Wilson, Columbia	.928	120	197	10	16	3

CATCHERS

Player and Club	Pct.	G.	PO.	A.	E.	DP.	PB.
Anglin, Anderson	.975	28	184	13	5	1	10
Antone, Gastonia	.972	5	33	2	1	0	1
Aulenback, Greenwood	.946	10	83	5	5	0	0
BAILEY, Asheville	.989	74	468	54	6	7	17
Baker, Greenwood	.975	113	653	115	20	8	26
Brill, Anderson	.980	50	310	39	7	4	8
Butters, Greenwood	.778	6	14	0	4	0	1
Calloway, Spartanburg	.985	29	116	15	2	0	6
Denis, Asheville	1.000	4	21	1	0	0	1
Diaz, Florence	.963	20	94	10	4	1	6
Digioia, Macon	1.000	2	13	0	0	0	2
Garcia, Asheville	.959	55	288	36	14	2	18
Fe. Gonzalez, Spartanburg	.976	51	293	36	8	1	10
Fr. Gonzalez, Greensboro	.973	52	328	38	10	2	9
Haas, Macon	.974	37	270	34	8	8	15
Hawkins, Greensboro	.958	24	165	18	8	1	1
Hearron, Florence	.975	42	235	40	7	2	6
Jacobson, Asheville	.993	24	126	18	1	2	3
Kimball, Florence	.979	23	132	8	3	1	17
Lombardi, Greensboro	.978	80	560	52	14	5	13
Lyon, Columbia	1.000	2	3	0	0	0	0
Lyons, Columbia	.968	51	359	31	13	4	7
Nieves, Gastonia	.988	11	70	9	1	0	1
Packer, Macon	1.000	5	41	4	0	1	3
Pagnozzi, Macon	.947	17	125	18	8	1	2
Pevey, Macon	.984	76	500	50	9	4	22
Pirruccello, Charleston	.953	39	232	31	13	3	7
Ragsdale, Anderson	.974	73	406	36	12	2	21
Ramler, Gastonia	.988	43	292	25	4	6	15
Richards, Charleston	.965	20	103	8	4	0	3
Rivera, Gastonia	.980	95	628	54	14	4	13
Schexnayder, Columbia	.976	73	484	56	13	6	22
Smith, Gastonia	1.000	3	16	1	0	0	0
Soriano, Florence	1.000	6	29	6	0	0	0
Spurlin, Greenwood	1.000	7	42	6	0	2	4
Stenhouse, Florence	.986	69	517	45	8	2	12
Szekely, Charleston	.973	92	624	69	19	9	17
Tejada, Spartanburg	.977	90	483	63	13	3	12
Tiamo, Greenwood	.957	18	97	13	5	1	3
Vaughn, Macon	.957	16	117	16	6	3	6
Welch, Columbia	.970	42	267	25	9	2	3
Williams, Asheville	1.000	3	25	2	0	0	0

PITCHERS

Player and Club	Pct.	G.	PO.	A.	E.	DP.
Acker, Asheville*	1.000	17	1	6	0	1
Aquino, Florence	.923	29	12	24	3	3
Aube, Charleston	.917	29	9	13	2	1
Aviles, Anderson	.750	9	1	2	1	0
Bailey, 3 Gboro-19 Ashe	.909	22	5	5	1	0
Baker, Anderson*	.914	16	10	22	3	3
Baldwin, Greensboro	.909	43	4	6	1	1
Bass, Charleston	.842	13	2	14	3	2
Beahan, Greensboro	.833	18	5	5	2	0
Bear, Macon	.950	53	4	15	1	5
Blunt, Macon	1.000	3	0	1	0	0
BORLAND, Greenwood	1.000	21	11	24	0	1
Branam, Gastonia	.938	33	2	13	1	1
Brewer, Spartanburg	1.000	48	6	14	0	0
B. Brown, Macon	.778	26	4	17	6	0
K. Brown, Columbia*	.939	29	3	28	2	4
Bryant, Charleston	.800	19	1	11	3	1
Bulls, Spartanburg	1.000	12	2	8	0	1
Byron, Greensboro	.909	10	3	7	1	0
Candelaria, Anderson*	.952	17	2	18	1	1
Cano, Anderson	.966	20	8	20	1	0
Canseco, Greensboro	.810	27	2	15	4	0
Carter, Florence	.893	26	15	10	3	2
E. Castro, Florence	.953	29	13	28	2	3
G. Castro, Asheville*	.828	26	7	17	5	1
Cerefin, Asheville	.700	15	3	4	3	1
Coker, Spartanburg	.938	27	6	9	1	1
Cook, Charleston	.750	9	2	7	3	0
Cooke, Greenwood	.952	34	5	15	1	0
Corsi, Greensboro	1.000	12	3	8	0	1
Coughlin, Asheville	.800	4	0	4	1	0
Cullen, Florence	.600	25	1	2	2	0
Cunningham, Greenwood	.857	10	3	3	1	0
B. Davis, Charleston	1.000	20	3	5	0	0
J. Davis, Charleston	.778	20	3	11	4	0
S. Davis, Florence*	1.000	23	1	21	0	2
Debord, Charleston	1.000	38	4	10	0	1
Donathan, Macon	1.000	9	1	1	0	0
Doty, Greensboro	1.000	5	0	4	0	1
Downs, Greenwood	.929	20	2	11	1	0
Drizmala, Charleston*	.871	15	5	22	4	1
Dunn, Macon	.947	25	6	12	1	2
Easley, Greensboro	.933	29	7	21	2	1
Edwards, Gastonia	1.000	11	0	4	0	0
Eldridge, Anderson	1.000	12	2	2	0	0
Farley, Macon	.833	9	3	2	1	0
Fedor, Greensboro	1.000	14	3	7	0	0
Felt, Greenwood	1.000	1	0	1	0	0

PITCHERS—Continued

Player and Club	Pct.	G.	PO.	A.	E.	DP.
Ferguson, Spartanburg	1.000	14	6	12	0	0
Fincher, Macon*	.882	24	5	10	2	1
Flores, Gastonia	.826	18	6	13	4	0
Foulks, Columbia	.800	31	0	8	2	0
Gallagher, Florence	.885	29	6	17	3	2
Gaston, Greensboro	.889	8	2	6	1	0
Gause, Gastonia*	1.000	9	2	7	0	0
Gay, Columbia	1.000	5	1	2	0	0
George, Greensboro*	.857	35	5	13	3	0
Glidewell, Gastonia	.750	27	10	17	9	0
Goodin, Charleston*	1.000	32	3	22	0	0
Gorden, Florence	1.000	28	0	9	0	0
Graham, Greensboro	1.000	30	6	16	0	0
Grudzinski, Greenwood	.818	26	4	14	4	1
Gumbert, Greensboro	.750	12	1	8	3	0
Hartley, Macon	.800	7	2	6	2	1
Hartshorn, Columbia	.800	9	0	4	1	0
Hill, Spartanburg	1.000	38	3	12	0	2
Holman, Greenwood	.944	22	6	11	1	0
Huber, Gastonia	.700	22	5	2	3	0
Humphrey, Greensboro	.900	8	1	8	1	0
Ingle, Anderson	1.000	2	1	1	0	0
Jensen, Columbia*	1.000	26	6	14	0	1
G. Johnson, Gastonia	1.000	30	2	10	0	0
R. Johnson, Florence	.667	6	1	1	1	0
Kasprzak, Asheville	.750	11	0	3	1	1
Kerfeld, Asheville	.875	28	14	21	5	1
Kinns, Gastonia	.939	28	10	21	2	1
Klink, Columbia*	1.000	12	3	4	0	1
Koenig, Asheville*	1.000	48	3	8	0	1
Lance, Anderson*	1.000	13	6	11	0	1
Leggatt, Anderson	1.000	3	0	3	0	0
Lockenmeyer, Columbia	1.000	18	6	7	0	0
Lucas, Asheville	.923	32	11	13	2	2
Lynn, Anderson	.842	15	6	10	3	1
Maddux, Spartanburg	1.000	13	4	12	0	0
Malave, Florence	1.000	4	2	1	0	1
Marrero, Charleston	.808	22	4	17	5	1
Marty, Greenwood	.857	18	7	17	4	1
Mathison, Greensboro	.857	10	4	2	1	0
McCormack, Charleston	.875	12	0	7	1	1
McCullers, Spartanburg	.884	22	10	28	5	3
McKay, Florence*	.857	17	4	8	2	0
McKelvey, Greenwood	.957	28	7	15	1	1
Meadows, Macon	.957	28	6	16	1	1
Mehalko, Anderson*	1.000	9	1	7	0	0
Mejia, Greenwood	1.000	21	4	8	0	0
Mesa, Florence	.895	28	7	27	4	3
Mielke, Gastonia	1.000	26	7	10	0	2
Miller, Spartanburg	.833	7	0	5	1	0
Mitchell, Macon	.895	45	5	12	2	1
Mize, Asheville	.688	28	3	8	5	1
Moore, Florence	.905	53	8	11	2	1
Moran, Gastonia*	.844	26	5	22	5	2
Morel, Spartanburg*	.900	25	0	9	1	0
Morelock, Anderson	1.000	5	0	2	0	0
Morgan, Greensboro	1.000	22	4	7	0	1
Mortillaro, Anderson*	.935	24	7	22	2	4
Murray, Columbia	.857	57	1	11	2	0
Myers, Columbia*	.826	28	4	15	4	0
Nicometi, Gastonia*	.983	26	9	48	1	3
North, Macon	.900	30	11	25	4	2
Olson, Spartanburg	.880	25	5	17	3	1
Ortega, Macon	.875	44	1	6	1	0
Perez, Charleston	1.000	6	0	6	0	0
Perkins, Asheville	.885	51	4	19	3	2
Phillips, Florence	1.000	5	3	5	0	0
Pol, Greenwood	1.000	17	2	3	0	0
Polemir, Asheville	.947	18	4	14	1	0
Pone, Charleston	.667	10	1	5	3	0
Pruitt, Columbia*	.867	37	3	10	2	0
Raftice, Greensboro*	1.000	3	0	1	0	0
Ray, 2 Col-3 Gboro*	.857	5	2	4	1	1
Richards, Gastonia	1.000	13	1	1	0	0
Rivera, Anderson	.938	44	3	2	1	1
Robertson, Asheville	.947	35	7	11	1	2
Rodriguez, Spartanburg	.920	21	2	21	2	1
Rogers, Anderson*	1.000	36	4	11	0	0
Roman, Macon*	.818	35	3	6	2	0
Rosario, Anderson*	1.000	21	7	11	0	1
Ruetter, Florence*	1.000	10	4	4	0	0
Samuels, Asheville*	.947	10	4	14	1	0
I. Sanchez, Charleston*	.919	30	7	27	3	0
L. Sanchez, Greenwood*	.900	19	6	3	1	0
Scarpetta, Spartanburg	.750	11	0	3	1	0
Scott, Gastonia	1.000	5	2	1	0	0
Segura, Spartanburg	.842	40	3	13	3	1
Seidel, Greensboro	.778	22	5	9	4	0
Serritella, Charleston	.833	12	3	2	1	0
Simmons, Greenwood*	.857	11	2	4	1	0
Smalley, Greensboro*	1.000	10	0	9	0	0
M. Smith, Anderson	1.000	8	1	7	0	2
Stanton, Greenwood	1.000	5	1	1	0	0
Steinberg, Charleston	.929	20	5	21	2	2
Stinnett, Greenwood	.923	25	4	8	1	2
Stone, Greenwood	.846	28	10	23	6	0
Strasser, Asheville	.831	30	14	35	10	1
Strichek, Macon	.900	27	11	16	3	0
Taylor, Greenwood	.909	12	4	6	1	0
Teegarden, Greensboro	.818	11	2	7	2	0
Torres, Anderson	.941	20	6	10	1	1
Troncoso, Asheville	.875	6	2	5	1	0
Valdez, Anderson	1.000	20	3	5	0	0
Valliant, Gastonia*	1.000	15	4	12	0	0
Vargas, Anderson	1.000	14	3	5	0	0
Walsh, Florence*	.880	41	6	16	3	0
Waymire, Gastonia	1.000	9	2	3	0	1
Weissman, Columbia	.875	18	5	2	1	0
Weston, Columbia	1.000	37	2	12	0	1
White, Greensboro*	.375	18	1	2	5	0
Witt, Spartanburg	.923	14	6	18	2	0
Youmans, Columbia	.889	23	14	10	3	2

The following players do not have any recorded accepted chances at the positions indicated and therefore are not listed in the fielding averages for those particular positions: Alburquerque, p; Anglin, p; Bocock, p; Borders, of; Catlett, p; Espinal, ss; Haro, of; Hawkins, of; Hess, p; Hinson, p; Kelly, ss; Lyons, of; O'Donnell, 3b; Phillips, of; Pleis, p; Ragsdale, of; Riggs, 2b; Ruffner, p; S. Smith, p; Springer, p; Strickland, ss; Turnbull, p; Wilson, p.

CLUB PITCHING

Club	ERA.	G.	CG.	ShO.	Sv.	IP.	H.	R.	ER.	HR.	HB.	BB.	Int. BB.	SO.	WP.	Bk.
Columbia	3.41	142	22	5	41	1207.2	1077	614	457	99	33	528	18	1090	85	3
Anderson	3.97	143	30	3	25	1208.2	1126	691	533	85	45	563	11	875	132	10
Gastonia	4.03	143	38	10	22	1215.2	1158	640	545	96	42	606	14	1011	117	6
Florence	4.03	143	24	9	23	1198.1	1156	742	536	88	41	537	4	990	92	8
Greensboro	4.28	144	19	6	30	1223.0	1256	753	582	93	39	639	16	987	110	19
Charleston	4.43	144	28	6	23	1218.0	1375	783	599	69	32	553	9	926	102	10
Greenwood	4.48	144	27	9	20	1223.2	1246	764	609	103	30	651	25	852	109	15
Spartanburg	4.79	143	31	7	27	1210.0	1300	797	644	83	43	589	20	863	128	11
Macon	4.88	144	29	10	24	1237.2	1315	835	671	69	57	680	13	1008	99	13
Asheville	4.91	144	26	7	21	1209.1	1288	802	660	115	48	641	33	896	112	4

PITCHERS' RECORDS

*Throws lefthanded.

(Leading Qualifiers for Earned-Run Average Leadership—115 or More Innings)

Pitcher—Club	W.	L.	Pct.	ERA.	G.	GS.	CG.	GF.	ShO.	Sv.	IP.	H.	R.	ER.	HR.	HB.	BB.	Int. BB.	SO.	WP.
K. Brown, Columbia*	15	7	.682	2.74	29	25	6	3	2	2	170.2	110	69	52	11	4	85	1	221	6
E. Castro, Florence	9	9	.500	2.76	29	19	7	6	0	0	153.0	127	77	47	12	6	48	1	118	9
Kerfeld, Asheville	16	10	.615	2.91	28	28	12	0	2	0	192.0	171	84	62	18	5	85	1	189	14
Jensen, Columbia*	11	6	.647	2.99	26	26	3	0	0	0	171.2	158	72	57	20	1	30	0	152	3
Mortillaro, Anderson*	11	9	.550	3.16	24	20	8	1	0	0	153.2	131	67	54	6	1	40	2	124	17
S. Davis, Florence*	10	7	.588	3.22	23	23	7	0	2	0	153.2	129	66	55	7	1	52	0	167	9
Nicometi, Gastonia*	10	7	.588	3.39	26	25	7	1	2	0	185.2	180	78	70	11	6	71	2	118	12
Youmans, Columbia	12	3	.800	3.42	23	23	6	0	1	0	134.1	112	77	51	5	9	73	0	117	12
Moran, Gastonia*	9	11	.450	3.47	26	26	9	0	1	0	161.0	123	79	62	16	6	117	0	156	14
I. Sanchez, Charleston*	10	6	.625	3.59	30	19	3	9	1	2	163.0	172	92	65	11	6	70	2	130	18

Departmental Leaders: G—Murray, 57; W—Kerfeld, 16; L—Stone, 13; Pct.—Walsh, .833; GS—Kerfeld, Myers, Stone, 28; CG—Kerfeld, 12; GF—Murray, 46; ShO—Easley, 4; Sv.—Murray, 21; IP—Kerfeld, 192; H—Nicometi, 180; R—Mesa, 116; ER—B. Brown, 89; HR—Jensen, 20; HB—Meadows, 15; BB—Moran, 117; IBB—Perkins, 10; SO—K. Brown, 221; WP—Grudzinski, Kinns, Olson, 21.

(All Pitchers—Listed Alphabetically)

Pitcher—Club	W.	L.	Pct.	ERA.	G.	GS.	CG.	GF.	ShO.	Sv.	IP.	H.	R.	ER.	HR.	HB.	BB.	Int. BB.	SO.	WP.
Acker, Asheville*	4	1	.800	2.84	17	5	1	4	0	1	57.0	58	22	18	4	2	12	0	38	3
Alburquerque, Asheville	0	0	.000	17.18	4	0	0	2	0	0	3.2	8	8	7	2	0	5	0	1	1
Anglin, Anderson	0	0	.000	4.50	1	0	0	1	0	0	2.0	2	1	1	0	0	1	0	0	2
Aquino, Florence	7	9	.438	5.25	29	21	5	2	1	0	133.2	128	91	78	10	12	61	0	104	2
Aube, Charleston	2	11	.154	4.78	29	13	5	8	0	1	122.1	149	85	65	12	4	55	0	90	7
Aviles, Anderson	2	4	.333	4.86	9	9	1	0	0	0	53.2	57	32	29	5	1	21	0	45	3
Bailey, 3 Gboro-19 Ashe.	1	1	.500	8.94	22	2	0	4	0	2	49.1	69	50	49	5	3	36	1	34	2
Baker, Anderson*	8	4	.667	3.03	16	16	1	0	0	0	101.0	87	49	34	8	6	45	1	69	9
Baldwin, Greensboro	7	5	.583	1.63	43	1	0	40	0	19	83.0	51	19	15	4	3	31	1	104	0
Bass, Charleston	7	5	.583	3.21	13	13	3	0	0	0	81.1	92	47	29	2	0	28	0	54	6
Beahan, Greensboro	6	3	.667	3.03	18	9	1	3	0	1	74.1	71	40	25	2	1	36	0	53	14
Bear, Macon	4	3	.571	3.24	53	0	0	32	0	6	72.1	80	42	26	3	0	30	5	45	5
Blunt, Macon	1	0	1.000	5.40	3	3	1	0	0	0	13.1	8	9	8	2	0	11	0	14	3
Bocock, Macon	0	0	.000	1.35	3	0	0	2	0	0	6.2	4	1	1	0	1	2	0	6	0
Borland, Greenwood	8	11	.421	3.97	21	20	7	1	1	0	140.2	144	80	62	11	1	44	3	71	2
Branam, Gastonia	6	1	.857	4.90	33	0	0	16	0	2	75.1	75	47	41	10	4	45	4	65	19
Brewer, Spartanburg	7	9	.438	4.56	48	0	0	44	0	12	73.0	88	42	37	6	5	37	5	68	10
B. Brown, Macon	11	9	.550	4.84	26	26	5	0	3	0	165.1	176	105	89	7	3	110	0	148	9
K. Brown, Columbia*	15	7	.682	2.74	29	25	6	3	2	2	170.2	110	69	52	11	4	85	1	221	6
Bryant, Charleston	3	5	.375	3.04	19	8	1	11	0	5	68.0	60	26	23	2	3	31	0	82	9
Bulls, Spartanburg	5	2	.714	4.29	12	10	2	1	0	0	71.1	68	39	34	3	3	28	0	67	5
Byron, Greensboro	2	4	.333	4.59	10	6	2	1	0	0	49.0	49	28	25	4	0	23	0	34	3
Candelaria, Anderson*	5	3	.625	4.50	17	14	1	2	1	0	76.0	64	46	38	4	4	68	1	68	8
Cano, Anderson	5	8	.385	4.11	20	16	6	1	0	1	111.2	112	70	51	9	5	33	1	59	11
Canseco, Greensboro	3	6	.333	5.05	27	13	1	5	1	0	87.1	98	62	49	14	3	49	1	59	5
Carter, Florence	5	8	.385	5.28	26	19	0	2	0	0	116.0	124	88	68	13	1	53	0	78	10
E. Castro, Florence	9	9	.500	2.76	29	19	7	6	0	0	153.0	127	77	47	12	6	48	1	118	9
G. Castro, Asheville*	6	9	.400	4.58	26	21	2	1	0	0	131.2	147	87	67	19	0	64	1	76	8
Catlett, Greenwood	0	0	.000	2.25	2	0	0	2	0	0	4.0	4	1	1	0	0	3	1	5	1
Cerefin, Asheville	0	7	.000	10.09	15	14	0	0	0	0	58.0	84	77	65	5	2	67	0	41	12
Coker, Spartanburg	10	12	.455	5.33	27	26	6	0	1	0	148.2	155	106	88	14	2	79	0	81	6
Cook, Charleston	2	2	.500	3.44	9	9	1	0	0	0	52.1	50	27	20	0	0	29	0	55	4
Cooke, Greenwood	7	4	.636	3.94	34	2	1	21	0	4	82.1	89	51	36	5	0	34	8	48	7
Corsi, Greensboro	2	2	.500	4.09	12	7	1	2	0	1	50.2	59	37	23	0	5	33	1	37	8
Coughlin, Asheville	0	2	.000	6.08	4	1	0	0	0	0	13.1	15	10	9	1	1	8	0	9	3
Cullen, Florence	0	4	.000	4.81	25	5	0	18	0	8	33.2	18	24	18	0	2	50	0	54	13
Cunningham, Greenwood	1	4	.200	6.46	10	4	0	3	0	0	30.2	45	27	22	4	1	15	1	19	4
B. Davis, Charleston	2	1	.667	4.30	20	0	0	16	0	6	29.1	28	19	14	2	0	10	0	23	1
J. Davis, Charleston	5	6	.455	6.58	20	11	4	6	1	0	78.0	104	64	57	5	1	40	0	48	7
S. Davis, Florence*	10	7	.588	3.22	23	23	7	0	2	0	153.2	129	66	55	7	1	52	0	167	9
Debord, Charleston	4	5	.444	4.40	38	0	0	34	0	6	61.1	70	42	30	4	4	39	3	43	2
Donathan, Macon	0	1	.000	8.90	9	2	0	3	0	0	29.1	47	36	29	5	1	13	0	30	2
Doty, Greensboro	0	1	.000	5.70	5	4	0	0	0	0	23.2	30	18	15	0	2	6	1	14	0
Downs, Greenwood	8	1	.889	2.67	20	4	2	13	0	1	64.0	49	25	19	4	1	22	2	54	5
Drizmala, Charleston*	7	5	.583	2.60	15	15	3	0	0	0	100.1	91	44	29	8	1	40	0	82	7
Dunn, Macon	7	7	.500	5.00	25	10	3	0	0	0	104.1	109	72	58	7	3	59	0	68	9
Easley, Greensboro	14	8	.636	4.04	29	22	7	3	4	1	158.1	157	82	71	12	4	62	1	116	5
Edwards, Gastonia	0	0	.000	3.42	11	1	0	8	0	2	23.2	25	9	9	0	0	8	0	16	2
Eldridge, Anderson	0	1	.000	5.04	12	1	0	5	0	0	25.0	24	20	14	3	3	14	1	14	7
Farley, Macon	1	3	.250	8.64	9	6	0	0	0	0	33.1	52	40	32	5	1	18	0	25	3
Fedor, Greensboro	1	0	1.000	3.24	14	3	0	6	0	0	41.2	27	17	15	2	1	36	1	41	17
Felt, Greenwood	0	0	.000	6.75	1	0	0	0	0	0	1.1	1	1	1	0	0	1	0	0	0
Ferguson, Spartanburg	5	6	.455	3.67	14	14	2	0	0	0	88.1	95	49	36	3	2	35	1	48	14
Fincher, Macon*	2	7	.222	5.87	24	10	0	3	0	2	79.2	97	66	52	4	3	42	0	60	5
Flores, Gastonia	6	1	.857	3.53	18	7	3	4	0	0	79.0	79	32	31	8	2	30	1	66	2
Foulks, Columbia	5	4	.556	3.97	31	5	0	12	0	2	77.0	68	49	34	6	2	51	1	69	7
Gallagher, Florence	7	7	.500	3.17	29	12	1	9	1	1	108.0	122	66	38	7	4	29	0	71	7
Gaston, Greensboro	1	2	.333	3.77	8	4	0	2	0	0	28.2	35	16	12	1	0	11	0	17	0
Gause, Gastonia*	2	3	.400	4.67	9	0	0	8	0	2	17.1	16	11	9	2	0	7	0	15	0
Gay, Columbia	1	2	.333	6.65	5	3	1	1	0	0	21.2	29	17	16	7	0	3	1	9	3
George, Greensboro*	5	4	.556	5.04	35	9	0	16	0	4	84.0	93	65	47	7	0	64	3	78	13
Glidewell, Gastonia	14	7	.667	3.79	27	26	9	1	2	0	185.0	162	92	78	9	3	87	2	151	17
Goodin, Charleston*	9	7	.563	4.27	32	10	5	13	1	0	128.2	132	76	61	2	3	58	1	104	6
Gorden, Florence	5	1	.833	3.86	28	1	0	16	0	1	56.0	50	33	24	3	1	22	0	49	5
Graham, Greensboro	6	11	.353	4.90	30	10	2	10	0	0	97.1	125	63	53	9	1	18	3	51	10
Grudzinski, Greenwood	4	8	.333	6.81	26	20	1	5	1	2	105.2	128	98	80	11	4	83	1	63	21
Gumbert, Greensboro	6	2	.750	4.45	12	10	1	1	0	1	64.2	67	41	32	4	1	43	0	54	1
Hartley, Macon	2	3	.400	10.24	7	7	1	0	0	0	29.0	36	36	33	2	8	30	0	12	12
Hartshorn, Columbia	1	3	.250	6.89	9	7	0	0	0	0	32.2	46	32	25	4	0	22	0	20	2
Hess, Gastonia	0	2	.000	1.93	12	0	0	10	0	3	9.1	11	6	2	1	0	4	0	15	1
Hill, Spartanburg	2	4	.333	4.84	38	0	0	22	0	6	80.0	75	51	43	3	6	53	4	60	5
Hinson, Asheville	0	0	.000	9.00	1	0	0	1	0	0	1.0	3	1	1	0	0	0	0	0	0
Holman, Greenwood	5	9	.357	5.79	22	20	1	2	0	1	102.2	126	80	66	15	2	49	0	60	6
Huber, Gastonia	7	0	1.000	3.48	22	1	0	13	0	2	31.0	29	16	12	2	1	15	2	27	2
Humphrey, Greensboro	1	2	.333	5.23	8	6	0	0	0	0	31.0	34	23	18	6	2	20	0	19	1
Ingle, Anderson	0	0	.000	10.80	2	0	0	2	0	0	5.0	5	6	6	0	1	3	0	2	0
Jensen, Columbia*	11	6	.647	2.99	26	26	3	0	0	0	171.2	158	72	57	20	1	30	0	152	3
G. Johnson, Gastonia	2	3	.400	3.86	30	0	0	22	0	9	46.2	49	25	20	5	3	17	0	37	4
R. Johnson, Florence	1	0	1.000	1.80	6	0	0	3	0	0	10.0	12	2	2	0	0	4	0	5	0
Kasprzak, Asheville	1	2	.333	4.50	11	0	0	6	0	0	22.0	28	14	11	1	0	10	1	14	3
Kerfeld, Asheville	16	10	.615	2.91	28	28	12	0	2	0	192.0	171	84	62	18	5	85	1	189	14
Kinns, Gastonia	11	9	.550	4.28	28	27	5	1	3	1	160.0	128	82	76	9	9	97	0	167	21
Klink, Columbia*	2	2	.500	4.62	12	1	0	5	0	0	25.1	24	16	13	6	0	14	0	14	3
Koenig, Asheville*	4	1	.800	3.60	48	0	0	20	0	2	45.0	43	23	18	1	1	26	4	44	4
Lance, Anderson*	3	5	.375	3.94	13	11	4	1	0	0	77.2	78	41	34	4	3	30	1	43	5
Leggatt, Anderson	1	0	1.000	2.57	3	0	0	3	0	1	7.0	6	2	2	0	0	4	0	2	1
Lockenmeyer, Columbia	6	1	.857	2.10	18	6	1	7	1	2	77.0	73	24	18	3	2	17	0	74	5
Lucas, Asheville	4	8	.333	4.93	32	18	3	8	1	2	133.1	145	85	73	9	7	63	5	105	8
Lynn, Anderson	4	5	.444	5.01	15	9	2	2	0	1	79.0	85	56	44	7	2	35	0	59	4
Maddux, Spartanburg	4	6	.400	5.44	13	13	3	0	0	0	84.1	98	62	51	6	0	47	3	85	10
Malave, Florence	0	0	.000	5.40	4	0	0	3	0	0	3.1	5	2	2	0	0	4	0	3	0

Pitcher—Club	W.	L.	Pct.	ERA.	G.	GS.	CG.	GF.	ShO.	Sv.	IP.	H.	R.	ER.	HR.	HB.	BB.	Int. BB.	SO.	WP.
Marrero, Charleston	5	7	.417	4.10	22	17	1	3	0	1	101.0	112	63	46	6	1	46	0	62	14
Marty, Greenwood	2	4	.333	4.48	18	10	2	3	0	0	82.1	88	65	41	7	0	48	0	31	7
Mathison, Greensboro	1	2	.333	5.18	10	6	0	0	0	0	41.2	39	25	24	5	2	31	0	28	2
McCormack, Charleston	0	3	.000	6.75	12	3	0	3	0	1	32.0	47	29	24	2	0	26	0	23	9
McCullers, Spartanburg	9	6	.600	4.03	22	21	6	1	2	0	136.1	139	79	61	12	2	57	0	87	12
McKay, Florence*	2	4	.333	6.98	17	6	0	6	0	0	40.0	54	40	31	5	3	14	0	24	7
McKelvey, Greenwood	5	8	.385	3.64	28	16	1	8	0	2	116.1	96	68	47	3	7	86	0	117	12
Meadows, Macon	8	9	.471	4.28	28	27	6	0	1	0	155.2	148	96	74	11	15	98	0	133	12
Mehalko, Anderson*	3	0	1.000	1.74	9	3	0	2	0	0	31.0	30	7	6	1	0	18	0	18	5
Mejia, Greenwood	4	5	.444	3.84	21	6	4	13	1	3	75.0	77	37	32	10	2	27	3	45	2
Mesa, Florence	6	12	.333	5.48	28	27	1	1	0	0	141.1	153	116	86	14	6	93	0	91	14
Mielke, Gastonia	8	6	.571	4.59	26	16	4	6	1	0	115.2	126	71	59	5	3	42	1	80	6
Miller, Spartanburg	1	0	1.000	11.37	7	0	0	0	0	0	12.2	25	26	16	0	1	11	2	5	3
Mitchell, Macon	8	6	.571	3.86	45	0	0	31	0	11	88.2	84	51	38	3	4	45	3	105	4
Mize, Asheville	3	5	.375	4.43	28	6	0	7	0	0	65.0	53	34	32	5	5	46	2	51	5
Moore, Florence	6	5	.545	2.04	53	0	0	38	0	10	92.2	76	43	21	2	0	50	2	97	10
Moran, Gastonia*	9	11	.450	3.47	26	26	9	0	1	0	161.0	123	79	62	16	6	117	0	156	14
Morel, Spartanburg*	1	3	.250	6.18	25	3	0	6	0	2	67.0	78	51	46	8	2	29	0	49	6
Morelock, Anderson	2	1	.667	2.70	5	2	0	1	0	0	16.2	13	7	5	0	1	13	0	13	6
Morgan, Greensboro	1	2	.333	4.90	22	1	0	12	0	1	60.2	65	38	33	6	2	18	0	52	8
Mortillaro, Anderson*	11	9	.550	3.16	24	20	8	1	0	0	153.2	131	67	54	6	1	40	2	124	17
Murray, Columbia	5	4	.556	1.73	57	0	0	46	0	21	83.0	68	30	16	3	3	24	8	64	6
Myers, Columbia*	14	10	.583	3.63	28	28	3	0	0	0	173.1	146	94	70	15	4	108	0	164	19
Nicometi, Gastonia*	10	7	.588	3.39	26	25	7	1	2	0	185.2	180	78	70	11	6	71	2	118	12
North, Macon	11	5	.688	4.50	30	26	5	3	2	0	162.0	163	103	81	4	6	71	0	100	6
Olson, Spartanburg	15	4	.789	3.92	25	22	4	2	2	1	144.2	125	78	63	9	6	87	0	140	21
Ortega, Macon	3	4	.429	5.53	44	0	0	22	0	4	68.1	80	49	42	4	4	37	1	49	8
Perez, Charleston	2	0	1.000	2.93	6	0	0	5	0	1	15.1	17	6	5	1	0	4	0	7	0
Perkins, Asheville	7	9	.438	4.41	51	0	0	42	0	13	67.1	73	45	33	2	7	30	10	47	6
Phillips, Florence	2	2	.500	3.48	5	4	1	1	0	0	31.0	31	15	12	1	0	8	0	20	1
Pleis, Macon	0	0	.000	2.25	2	0	0	0	0	0	4.0	3	1	1	0	0	2	0	6	0
Pol, Greenwood	0	2	.000	7.33	17	0	0	12	0	5	23.1	32	23	19	6	2	13	1	13	0
Polemir, Asheville	4	9	.308	7.67	18	17	0	0	0	0	85.2	98	88	73	13	6	67	0	59	11
Pone, Charleston	2	5	.286	6.80	10	9	0	0	0	0	42.1	46	37	32	3	6	32	2	37	6
Pruitt, Columbia*	5	5	.500	3.95	37	1	0	24	0	8	54.2	50	30	24	6	1	21	6	48	4
Raftice, Greensboro*	0	1	.000	11.37	3	2	0	0	0	0	6.1	9	10	8	0	1	8	0	11	1
Ray, 2 Col.-3 Greensboro*	0	2	.000	3.47	5	4	0	1	0	0	23.1	24	21	9	2	3	16	0	18	2
Richards, Gastonia	1	3	.250	5.32	13	0	0	8	0	1	22.0	30	13	13	6	1	4	0	16	1
Rivera, Anderson	4	8	.333	3.61	44	0	0	36	0	12	84.2	85	54	34	3	6	28	2	79	7
Robertson, Asheville	1	4	.200	5.26	35	2	1	16	0	1	63.1	67	42	37	4	3	39	2	45	7
Rodriguez, Spartanburg	7	5	.583	3.89	21	12	6	4	1	1	106.1	116	60	46	7	2	31	1	65	8
Rogers, Anderson*	3	6	.333	3.04	36	2	0	27	0	6	71.0	65	37	24	8	3	22	0	59	10
Roman, Macon*	2	5	.286	3.70	35	1	0	16	0	1	41.1	47	25	17	2	2	36	4	37	3
Rosario, Anderson*	3	6	.333	3.99	21	15	4	5	0	0	103.2	89	54	46	8	6	61	1	73	14
Ruetter, Florence*	1	2	.333	5.81	10	3	1	0	0	0	26.1	32	26	17	5	0	15	0	19	3
Ruffner, Greensboro	0	0	.000	15.75	2	0	0	1	0	0	4.0	7	7	7	1	0	4	0	3	2
Samuels, Asheville*	3	4	.429	4.05	10	9	1	0	0	0	60.0	60	33	27	12	0	30	2	47	10
I. Sanchez, Charleston*	10	6	.625	3.59	30	19	3	9	1	2	163.0	172	92	65	11	6	70	2	130	18
L. Sanchez, Greenwood*	2	0	1.000	4.11	19	1	0	10	0	0	50.1	53	26	23	3	0	26	0	24	6
Scarpetta, Spartanburg	1	2	.333	7.36	11	7	0	2	0	0	40.1	54	36	33	3	1	17	0	30	5
Scott, Gastonia	1	3	.250	8.71	5	5	0	0	0	0	20.2	31	22	20	4	1	16	0	22	3
Segura, Spartanburg	1	6	.143	6.44	40	1	0	30	0	5	65.2	77	59	47	4	2	42	4	54	15
Seidel, Greensboro	7	5	.583	4.01	22	15	3	2	1	0	94.1	94	60	42	7	5	59	2	92	3
Serritella, Charleston	0	7	.000	9.97	12	9	0	1	0	0	43.1	74	62	48	5	1	18	0	28	4
Simmons, Greenwood*	0	1	.000	5.57	11	1	0	5	0	0	21.0	20	15	13	1	0	16	2	14	0
Smalley, Greensboro*	3	1	.750	2.63	10	4	0	3	0	1	41.0	34	17	12	3	1	25	0	42	0
M. Smith, Anderson	2	5	.286	6.80	8	8	0	0	0	0	41.0	38	35	31	1	1	22	0	21	7
S. Smith, Asheville	0	1	.000	8.00	9	0	0	5	0	0	9.0	11	9	8	3	0	5	0	12	2
Springer, Columbia	0	0	.000	9.00	1	0	0	1	0	0	2.0	4	2	2	1	0	1	0	2	0
Stanton, Greenwood	0	1	.000	4.97	5	0	0	5	0	0	12.2	16	8	7	1	0	12	0	9	3
Steinberg, Charleston	4	5	.444	4.80	20	8	2	7	0	0	99.1	131	64	53	4	2	27	1	58	2
Stinnett, Greenwood	4	4	.500	5.88	25	0	0	14	0	2	49.0	47	36	32	6	3	36	3	44	5
Stone, Greenwood	10	13	.435	3.79	28	28	5	0	2	0	180.2	158	88	76	12	2	96	0	156	17
Strasser, Asheville	11	5	.688	3.73	30	15	6	2	2	0	128.0	129	73	53	7	4	42	4	75	9
Strichek, Macon	11	9	.550	3.98	27	23	8	2	3	0	169.2	163	87	75	9	5	65	0	158	10
Taylor, Greenwood	6	3	.667	3.53	12	12	3	0	0	0	81.2	73	35	32	4	5	40	0	79	11
Teegarden, Greensboro	2	6	.250	6.86	11	8	1	1	0	0	40.2	55	38	31	1	2	25	0	36	11
Torres, Anderson	4	8	.333	3.48	20	15	3	2	0	1	88.0	72	52	34	6	2	68	0	71	12
Troncoso, Asheville	0	2	.000	5.72	6	6	0	0	0	0	28.1	29	18	18	3	2	13	0	11	4
Turnbull, Macon	0	2	.000	9.20	5	3	0	1	0	0	14.2	18	16	15	1	1	11	0	12	8
Valdez, Anderson	3	4	.429	5.76	20	1	0	13	0	1	45.1	43	35	29	9	0	21	0	32	2
Valliant, Gastonia*	6	3	.667	4.76	15	8	1	4	0	0	58.2	67	37	31	5	1	34	0	43	11
Vargas, Anderson	1	2	.333	4.29	14	1	0	9	0	2	35.2	40	20	17	3	0	16	1	24	2
Walsh, Florence*	10	2	.833	3.34	41	3	1	14	1	3	99.2	95	53	37	9	5	34	1	90	2
Waymire, Gastonia	1	0	1.000	4.74	9	1	0	3	0	0	24.2	27	20	13	3	2	12	2	17	2
Weissman, Columbia	8	4	.667	3.57	18	14	2	1	0	0	93.1	84	45	37	5	4	47	0	77	4
Weston, Columbia	2	2	.500	4.34	37	1	0	20	0	6	74.2	87	48	36	5	1	22	1	46	8
White, Greensboro*	4	3	.571	4.25	18	2	0	15	0	1	42.1	38	31	20	5	2	20	2	33	6
Wilson, Columbia	1	0	1.000	1.69	1	0	0	0	0	0	5.1	8	2	1	0	0	4	0	6	1
Witt, Spartanburg	4	6	.400	4.24	14	14	2	0	0	0	91.1	107	59	43	5	9	36	0	24	8
Youmans, Columbia	12	3	.800	3.42	23	23	6	0	1	0	134.1	112	77	51	5	9	73	0	117	12

BALKS—Holman, McKelvey, 5 each; George, Roman, I. Sanchez, 4 each; Corsi, Glidewell, Meadows, Mortillaro, Olson, Pone, Rodriguez, Seidel, 3 each; Canseco, Carter, Cooke, Coughlin, Dunn, Morel, Myers, Rosario, L. Sanchez, Teegarden, White, 2 each; Aquino, Aviles, Baldwin, Beahan, Bear, Borland, B. Brown, K. Brown, Cano, E. Castro, B. Davis, Drizmala, Farley, Flores, Gallagher, Hill, Lynn, Maddux, McCormack, McCullers, Mesa, Moore, Moran, Morgan, Nicometi, North, Perkins, Rogers, Strasser, Torres, Walsh, 1 each.

COMBINATION SHUTOUTS—Smith-Valdez, Baker-Rivera, Anderson; Polemir-Koenig, Samuels-Koenig, Asheville; Drizmala-Aube, Cook-Goodin-Debord, Marrero-Perez, Charleston; Foulks-Murray, Columbia; Carter-Moore, Castro-Moore, Davis-Moore, Aquino-Moore, Florence; Kinns-Huber, Gastonia; Stone-Sanchez-Downs, Holman-Stinnett, Stone-Grudzinski-Simmons, Taylor-Borland, Greenwood; Meadows-Ortega, Macon; Coker-Segura, Spartanburg.

NO-HIT GAMES—Brown-Strichek, Macon, defeated Florence, 10-5, April 12; Glidewell, Gastonia, defeated Greensboro, 3-0 (seven innings), May 21; Lucas, Asheville, defeated Columbia, 1-0, June 13; Strasser, Asheville, defeated Anderson, 1-0, July 16.

Appalachian League

SUMMER CLASS A CLASSIFICATION

CHAMPIONSHIP WINNERS IN PREVIOUS YEARS

Year	Club	Pct.
1921	Greenville	.608
	Johnson City*	.627
1922	Bristol	.557
1923	Knoxville	.635
1924	Knoxville*	.642
	Bristol	.607
1925	Greenville	.667
1926-36	Did not operate.	
1937	Elizabethton	.559
	Pennington Gap*	.580
1938	Elizabethton	.664
	Greenville (3rd)†	.571
1939	Elizabethton‡	.597
1940	Johnson City§	.726
	Elizabethton	.750
1941	Johnson City	.614
	Elizabethton*	.661
1942	Bristol	.667
	Bristol x	.660
1943	Bristol	.755
	Bristol y	.617
1944	Kingsport‡	.575
1945	Kingsport‡	.670
1946	New River‡	.675
1947	Pulaski	.648
	New River (3rd)†	.516
1948	Pulaski‡	.680
1949	Bluefield‡	.721
1950	Bluefield	.600
	Bluefield z	.745
1951	Kingsport‡	.659
1952	Johnson City	.595
	Welch (3rd)†	.509
1953	Welch*	.705
	Johnson City	.672
1954	Bluefield‡	.619
1955	Salem**	.689
1956	Did not operate.	
1957	Bluefield	.701
1958	Johnson City	.662
1959	Morristown	.603
1960	Wytheville	.614
1961	Middlesboro	.591
1962	Bluefield	.671
1963	Bluefield	.652
1964	Johnson City	.662
1965	Salem	.614
1966	Marion	.623
1967	Bluefield	.627
1968	Marion	.583
1969	Pulaski a	.576
	Johnson City	.544
1970	Bluefield	.638
1971	Bluefield a	.609
	Kingsport	.559
1972	Bristol a	.588
	Covington	.586
1973	Kingsport	.757
1974	Bristol a	.754
	Bluefield	.536
1975	Marion	.515
	Johnson City a	.603
1976	Johnson City a	.714
	Bluefield	.600
1977	Kingsport	.623
1978	Elizabethton	.594
1979	Paintsville	.800
1980	Paintsville	.657
1981	Paintsville	.657
1982	Bluefield a	.681
	Johnson City	.478

*Won split-season playoff. †Won four-team playoff. ‡Won championship and four-team playoff. §Johnson City, first-half winner, won playoff involving six clubs. xWon both halves and defeated second-place Elizabethton in playoff. yWon both halves, but Erwin won four-team playoff. zWon both halves, but Bristol won two-club playoff. **Salem and Johnson City declared playoff co-champions when weather forced cancellation of final series. aLeague was divided into Northern, Southern divisions; declared league champion, based on highest won-lost percentage.

COMPOSITE STANDING OF CLUBS AT CLOSE OF SEASON, AUGUST 31

Club	Pvl.	Pul.	Bri.	Pike.	Blu.	J.C.	Eliz.	W.	L.	T.	Pct.	G.B.
Paintsville (Brewers)	....	6	5	10	8	7	10	46	24	1	.653	....
Pulaski (Braves)	6	....	8	9	6	8	8	45	26	0	.639	½
Bristol (Tigers)	7	4	....	4	6	7	6	34	38	1	.472	13
Pikeville (Cubs)	2	2	8	....	4	7	10	33	37	0	.471	13
Bluefield (Orioles)	3	6	6	7	....	6	4	32	38	0	.457	14
Johnson City (Cardinals)	5	4	5	5	6	....	5	30	42	0	.417	17
Elizabethton (Twins)	1	4	6	2	8	7	....	28	42	0	.389	18

Major league affiliations in parentheses.

Playoffs—None.

Regular-Season Attendance—Bluefield, 25,767; Bristol, 8,217; Elizabethton, 9,983; Johnson City, 18,420; Paintsville, 8,023; Pikeville, 4,998; Pulaski, 15,470. Total, 90,878.

Managers—Bluefield, Greg Biagini; Bristol, Boots Day; Elizabethton, Fred Waters; Johnson City, Rich Hacker; Paintsville, Tom Gamboa; Pikeville, Jim Fairey; Pulaski, Buddy Bailey.

All-Star Team—1B—Glenn Harris, Johnson City; 2B—Jim Walewander, Bristol; 3B—Kerry Evertt, Paintsville; SS—Hector Quinones, Paintsville; OF—Glenn Braggs, Paintsville; Lavel Freeman, Paintsville; Chris Baird, Pulaski; C—Sal D'Allesandro, Pulaski; DH—George Page, Bluefield; RHP—Mark Ciardi, Paintsville; LHP—Dan Plesac, Paintsville; Manager of Year—Buddy Bailey, Pulaski.

(Compiled by Howe News Bureau, Boston, Mass.)

CLUB BATTING

Club	Pct.	G.	AB.	R.	OR.	H.	TB.	2B.	3B.	HR.	RBI.	GW.	SH.	SF.	HP.	BB.	Int. BB.	SO.	SB.	CS.	LOB.
Paintsville	.295	73	2351	482	342	693	1021	132	8	60	423	39	21	14	28	347	12	464	77	52	567
Pulaski	.274	72	2254	465	344	618	986	101	12	81	389	38	18	23	33	394	8	547	83	24	560
Bristol	.261	73	2250	408	438	587	842	83	17	46	330	31	19	17	9	325	17	451	115	28	487
Elizabethton	.256	72	2282	379	439	584	833	106	7	43	310	21	6	15	23	358	6	446	57	14	595
Pikeville	.256	70	2165	394	413	555	803	91	8	47	333	30	16	19	22	346	4	445	113	63	472
Bluefield	.254	70	2200	377	444	558	848	121	8	51	304	25	15	23	23	283	5	442	115	25	478
Johnson City	.241	72	2172	327	412	524	762	79	15	43	272	26	9	18	18	285	2	467	90	27	482

INDIVIDUAL BATTING

(Leading Qualifiers for Batting Championship—194 or More Plate Appearances)

*Bats lefthanded. †Switch-hitter.

Player and Club	Pct.	G.	AB.	R.	H.	TB.	2B.	3B.	HR.	RBI.	GW.	SH.	SF.	HP.	BB.	Int. BB.	SO.	SB.	CS.
Braggs, Glenn, Paintsville	.390	73	241	65	94	164	20	1	16	74	7	0	0	4	54	6	52	22	6
McClure, David, Bristol	.329	54	170	31	56	80	8	2	4	35	1	0	0	1	21	3	35	4	1
Walewander, James, Bristol†	.319	73	285	56	91	121	14	2	4	28	3	2	3	1	34	2	29	35	4
Lebeau, David, Pulaski	.314	66	226	62	71	119	9	3	11	41	8	3	2	2	35	0	33	12	6
Scime, Joseph, Pulaski	.309	66	191	48	59	87	16	0	4	44	6	4	4	6	42	1	31	5	3
Schugel, Jeffrey, Elizabethton	.308	68	247	40	76	104	10	0	6	46	4	1	4	3	28	0	39	9	1
Freeman, Lavel, Paintsville*	.307	71	264	64	81	119	17	0	7	50	9	1	1	4	42	1	47	13	8
Appino, Kevin, Paintsville	.306	64	222	48	68	90	11	1	3	28	1	3	0	1	33	2	41	7	4
Millis, Joseph, Bristol	.305	57	200	44	61	79	8	2	2	24	0	0	1	0	30	1	53	18	2
Page, George, Bluefield	.303	50	178	39	54	77	10	2	3	26	2	1	3	4	22	1	37	25	5

Departmental Leaders: G—Braggs, Walewander, 73; AB—Walewander, 285; R—Braggs, 65; H—Braggs, 94; TB—Braggs, 164; 2B—Braggs, 20; 3B—Turner, 4; HR—Baird, Braggs, 16; RBI—Braggs, 74; GWRBI—Freeman, 9; SH—Washington, 5; SF—Baird, 9; HP—Milner, Scime, 6; BB—Braggs, 54; IBB—Braggs, 6; SO—Baird, 74; SB—Walewander, 35; CS—Richardson, 10.

(All Players—Listed Alphabetically)

Player and Club	Pct.	G.	AB.	R.	H.	TB.	2B.	3B.	HR.	RBI.	GW.	SH.	SF.	HP.	BB.	Int. BB.	SO.	SB.	CS.
Agostinelli, Salvatore, Johnson City	.236	35	89	18	21	28	3	2	0	11	1	0	0	1	18	0	1	4	3
Amante, Thomas, Johnson City	.261	51	161	24	42	83	8	0	11	33	2	0	1	2	19	1	33	1	1
Anderson, Steven, Paintsville	.258	23	62	9	16	23	4	0	1	10	1	0	1	1	5	0	9	0	1
Appino, Kevin, Paintsville	.306	64	222	48	68	90	11	1	3	28	1	3	0	1	33	2	41	7	4
Baez, Juan, Pikeville	.216	24	51	8	11	16	5	0	0	4	0	0	0	0	15	0	14	2	2
Bailey, Timothy, Bristol	.250	1	4	0	1	1	0	0	0	0	0	0	0	0	0	0	0	0	0
Baird, Christopher, Pulaski*	.275	67	218	44	60	115	5	1	16	58	2	0	9	1	48	1	74	16	3
Baker, Jonathan, Pikeville	.200	36	115	11	23	34	5	0	2	15	2	1	0	1	5	0	21	1	1
Baker, Robert, Bristol*	.190	7	21	7	4	9	2	0	1	6	0	0	0	0	6	2	6	3	0
Ballou, Gary, Pulaski	.268	59	179	29	48	64	5	1	3	22	1	0	1	4	35	1	54	6	5
Barreto, Jose, Bristol	.260	51	146	22	38	50	3	0	3	27	2	3	2	1	15	0	24	3	2
Bayron, Angel, Elizabethton*	.324	29	68	13	22	27	5	0	0	9	0	0	1	0	14	0	11	0	2
Beattie, Brad, Bluefield	.234	29	107	14	25	34	6	0	1	11	1	0	0	2	8	0	14	3	0
Beuerlein, John, Paintsville	.325	52	154	35	50	65	9	0	2	21	2	1	0	2	24	0	34	1	1
Black, Jonathan, Bluefield	.325	37	123	25	40	79	10	1	9	32	2	0	0	3	13	0	38	1	0
Braggs, Glenn, Paintsville	.390	73	241	65	94	164	20	1	16	74	7	0	0	4	54	6	52	22	6
Brumfield, Jacob, Pikeville	.257	42	113	17	29	40	0	1	3	15	2	1	2	0	25	1	34	8	5
Bruno, Angelo, Bluefield	.183	28	104	12	19	30	8	0	1	6	0	0	0	1	7	0	17	5	0
Bunnell, Ronald, Pulaski	.213	36	94	10	20	21	1	0	0	7	0	0	1	3	13	0	14	1	0
Butcher, Matt, Elizabethton	.239	58	197	21	47	62	12	0	1	23	0	1	0	1	16	2	43	1	0
Calley, Robert, Elizabethton	.314	50	156	18	49	66	12	1	1	23	3	0	3	2	22	1	19	0	0
Camara, David, Pulaski*	.336	46	143	39	48	57	4	1	1	11	0	1	0	0	18	0	14	8	1
Carden, Allen, Pulaski*	.000	6	6	2	0	0	0	0	0	1	0	0	0	1	1	0	3	0	0
Cardenas, Leo, Elizabethton†	.219	25	64	13	14	21	2	1	1	8	0	2	0	1	11	0	15	3	0
Carvajal, Luis, Johnson City	.105	20	38	5	4	8	1	0	1	2	0	1	0	0	7	0	9	0	0
Castillo, Julio, Paintsville	.143	14	14	3	2	3	1	0	0	0	0	0	0	0	1	0	6	0	0
Castro, Victor, Johnson City	.200	24	50	7	10	13	3	0	0	8	1	0	1	0	4	0	21	0	0
Cijntje, Sherwin, Bluefield*	.248	49	161	21	40	47	4	0	1	19	3	2	1	1	16	0	24	12	2
Codinach, Rafael, Elizabethton	.258	67	233	41	60	115	17	1	12	54	5	0	2	3	40	0	53	1	0
Coppola, Craig, Elizabethton*	.227	61	203	27	46	69	14	0	3	30	1	0	1	0	30	0	46	0	0
Cruz, Luis, Pikeville	.233	65	232	49	54	72	10	1	2	23	1	1	3	0	47	0	45	26	5
Cunningham, Anthony, Bristol	.030	19	33	3	1	1	0	0	0	2	0	0	0	0	3	0	13	2	0
D'Alessandro, Salvatore, Pulaski	.314	49	140	20	44	74	6	0	8	28	2	4	0	0	18	0	31	4	1
Daddario, Paul, Pulaski	.300	11	30	2	9	9	0	0	0	1	0	0	0	0	6	0	11	1	0
Dahse, David, Bluefield	.261	15	46	9	12	15	0	0	1	6	0	2	1	2	7	0	8	4	1
Davis, Daryl, Johnson City†	.169	40	77	5	13	14	1	0	0	8	1	0	2	0	4	0	24	1	2
Derby, Terrence, Paintsville†	.329	36	73	16	24	28	1	0	1	9	0	3	0	2	22	0	20	9	9
Diaz, Serafin, Elizabethton*	.250	13	32	6	8	12	2	1	0	3	0	0	0	0	5	0	4	0	0
Dickerson, James, Pikeville	.300	28	100	15	30	50	5	0	5	26	0	0	1	4	11	1	28	5	5
Ditto, Bradley, Pikeville†	.176	12	34	2	6	7	1	0	0	1	0	1	0	1	5	0	7	7	1
Edwards, Terrence, Pikeville	.255	63	188	50	48	83	5	0	10	35	2	0	1	3	45	0	56	11	5
Edwards, Tracy, Pulaski†	.245	37	106	15	26	51	5	1	6	22	1	0	0	3	17	1	33	0	0
Embry, Paul, Bristol	.120	12	25	3	3	3	0	0	0	2	0	0	1	0	3	0	12	0	0
Everett, Kerry, Paintsville	.297	69	263	56	78	135	12	3	13	59	4	1	0	0	22	0	52	2	3
Fitzgerald, Francis, Bluefield	.240	54	192	31	46	73	12	0	5	26	4	0	2	1	13	1	34	7	3
Fitzpatrick, Danny, Bluefield	.175	18	40	4	7	14	1	0	2	3	1	1	0	1	2	0	12	0	0
Forgione, Christopher, Elizabethton*	.289	70	256	49	74	88	9	1	1	22	1	0	1	2	31	1	56	10	5
Freeman, Lavel, Paintsville*	.307	71	264	64	81	119	17	0	7	50	9	1	1	4	42	1	47	13	8
Garcia, Angel, Elizabethton	.158	20	38	9	6	7	1	0	0	4	0	0	0	1	3	0	11	0	1
Giron, Ysidro, Bristol	.000	6	7	0	0	0	0	0	0	0	0	0	0	0	1	0	3	0	0
Glendening, Robert, Pikeville	.301	59	183	31	55	90	8	0	9	41	4	0	2	1	34	0	38	0	7
Gomez, Sixto, Elizabethton	.158	14	38	2	6	9	0	0	1	3	0	0	0	0	3	0	11	0	0
Goodwin, Larry, Bristol	.184	13	38	6	7	7	0	0	0	3	1	0	0	1	6	0	7	1	0
Graupmann, Timothy, Elizabethton	.077	10	26	4	2	2	0	0	0	1	0	0	0	1	3	0	5	0	0
Gutierrez, Roberto, Bluefield†	.280	56	182	28	51	72	11	2	2	32	2	2	2	0	34	1	24	4	4
Hall, Gary, Pulaski	.217	64	244	40	53	79	10	2	4	20	5	1	0	3	21	0	71	10	3
Hardamon, Derrick, Pikesville	.149	39	101	16	15	15	0	0	0	7	2	1	0	3	13	0	22	2	3
Harris, Glenn, Johnson City*	.273	67	198	30	54	80	14	3	2	29	3	1	1	1	29	1	31	1	1
Harrison, Wayne, Pulaski	.291	61	175	46	51	103	11	1	13	52	4	1	2	3	47	0	54	8	0
Hatley, L.Todd, Elizabethton*	.277	19	65	6	18	21	3	0	0	6	0	1	0	0	7	0	11	1	1
Hazard, Richard, Paintsville*	.296	9	27	6	8	16	2	0	2	5	0	0	0	0	5	0	6	1	0
Hernandez, Felipe, Pikeville	.000	7	15	3	0	0	0	0	0	2	0	0	2	0	3	0	7	0	0
Hernandez, Juan B., Bristol	.219	14	32	6	7	11	1	0	1	3	0	0	1	0	3	0	14	0	0
Hernandez, Juan M., Bristol	.181	41	116	16	21	32	5	0	2	11	3	2	2	1	10	0	28	4	1
Heyison, Mark, Bluefield	.240	30	100	23	24	50	5	0	7	16	0	1	1	3	8	0	36	3	1
Jackson, Larry, Paintsville*	.341	15	41	3	14	17	3	0	0	7	2	1	1	0	5	0	3	0	1
Kinard, Charles, Johnson City	.248	43	109	18	27	34	5	1	0	9	2	1	0	1	11	0	32	3	2
Kingsley, Ross, Pulaski*	.256	66	227	47	58	74	11	1	1	24	4	2	3	2	35	0	43	9	1
Kumiega, Peter, Pikeville	.293	52	191	40	56	98	7	1	11	57	7	0	1	3	19	0	35	1	1
Lebeau, David, Pulaski	.314	66	226	62	71	119	9	3	11	41	8	3	2	2	35	0	33	12	6
Leriger, Jeffrey, Bluefield	.237	54	173	30	41	59	7	1	3	20	3	3	2	2	40	0	31	15	4
Linares, Carlos, Elizabethton	.000	4	9	2	0	0	0	0	0	0	0	0	0	1	4	0	3	0	0
Lopez, Frank, Bluefield	.271	45	133	22	36	58	8	1	4	23	1	1	3	0	15	1	30	2	1
Martinez, Wilfredo, Johnson City	.280	36	93	10	26	38	3	0	3	13	0	1	1	0	10	0	29	1	0
Martinez, Zoilo, Johnson City	.000	3	4	0	0	0	0	0	0	0	0	0	0	0	0	0	3	0	0
McClure, David, Bristol	.329	54	170	31	56	80	8	2	4	35	1	0	0	1	21	3	35	4	1
McDermott, Gerald, Paintsville	.261	72	238	34	62	88	12	1	4	38	4	0	2	5	31	1	46	2	1
McManus, Robert, Bristol	.277	72	235	51	65	114	9	2	12	53	6	0	1	0	50	2	65	10	3
Meyer, Urban, Pulaski	.250	15	32	8	8	13	2	0	1	4	0	1	0	0	8	0	9	0	0
Millis, Joseph, Bristol	.305	57	200	44	61	79	8	2	2	24	0	0	1	0	30	1	53	18	2
Mills, R. Craig, Bristol	.238	58	181	34	43	55	7	1	1	24	1	1	2	3	35	2	19	6	1
Milner, Theodore, Johnson City*	.265	62	155	30	41	60	3	2	4	19	1	1	2	6	23	0	32	14	3
Mirabito, Thomas, Bristol*	.231	8	13	0	3	4	1	0	0	1	0	0	0	0	2	0	2	0	0
Mitchell, John, Paintsville*	.189	33	74	11	14	19	2	0	1	13	2	2	1	0	18	1	16	3	0
Morris, Steve, Bluefield*	.273	54	165	37	45	84	12	0	9	29	1	1	2	1	34	1	37	3	1
Nipper, R. Michael, Pulaski	.259	72	243	53	63	120	16	1	13	54	5	1	1	5	50	4	72	3	1
Nunez, Mauricio, Johnson City	.260	65	227	38	59	95	8	2	8	34	5	1	3	0	25	0	43	11	2

Player and Club	Pct.	G.	AB.	R.	H.	TB.	2B.	3B.	HR.	RBI.	GW.	SH.	SF.	HP.	BB.	Int. BB.	SO.	SB.	CS.
Nunley, Angelo, Johnson City	.107	42	56	10	6	10	1	0	1	9	1	2	1	0	13	0	17	3	0
O'Connor, James, Johnson City	.137	31	73	8	10	18	2	0	2	12	3	0	0	0	7	0	27	0	0
Orman, Nelson, Bluefield†	.288	17	66	15	19	29	7	0	1	9	0	0	1	0	7	0	9	3	0
Page, George, Bluefield	.303	50	178	39	54	77	10	2	3	26	2	1	3	4	22	1	37	25	5
Palacios, R. Rey, Bristol	.302	47	139	28	42	72	7	1	7	28	0	1	2	0	19	1	26	2	4
Palmer, Doug, Elizabethton	.295	69	254	59	75	91	7	0	3	31	3	0	3	4	51	0	18	25	1
Pancake, James, Elizabethton	.126	37	87	16	11	21	2	1	2	4	1	1	0	0	20	0	32	2	0
Paulino, Victor, Johnson City†	.253	53	146	18	37	42	3	1	0	14	2	0	1	4	16	0	11	7	6
Pena, Nelson, Johnson City	.231	32	78	11	18	22	2	1	0	13	0	0	1	2	6	0	19	2	0
Perez, Pedro, Johnson City†	.200	4	5	0	1	2	1	0	0	2	0	0	0	0	1	0	1	0	0
Piazza, Nicholas, Bluefield	.222	40	99	18	22	29	7	0	0	10	0	1	1	0	17	0	38	13	1
Quinones, Hector, Paintsville	.269	63	197	32	53	64	8	0	1	29	2	4	2	3	14	0	35	3	4
Reboulet, James, Johnson City	.246	47	142	17	35	49	5	0	3	7	1	0	0	0	29	0	15	11	2
Richardson, Donald, Pikesville	.297	62	232	49	69	92	14	0	3	26	4	2	2	1	22	0	46	21	10
Ripken, William, Bluefield	.217	48	152	24	33	39	6	0	0	13	1	0	2	1	12	0	13	7	2
Rojas, Octavio, Bluefield	.323	22	65	10	21	35	6	1	2	8	3	0	0	1	11	0	19	1	0
Sanders, Archie, Elizabethton	.000	19	4	1	0	0	0	0	0	0	0	0	0	0	0	0	1	0	0
Santana, Radhames, Bristol	.143	7	7	2	1	2	1	0	0	1	0	0	0	0	5	0	3	0	0
Schugel, Jeffrey, Elizabethton	.308	68	247	40	76	104	10	0	6	46	4	1	4	3	28	0	39	9	1
Scime, Joseph, Pulaski	.309	66	191	48	59	87	16	0	4	44	6	4	4	6	42	1	31	5	3
Shannon, Timothy, Johnson City†	.171	32	76	6	13	15	2	0	0	6	1	0	1	0	3	0	25	0	0
Smith, Michael, Paintsville	.301	54	146	33	44	76	17	0	5	34	3	1	2	1	23	0	28	4	5
Smith, Raymond, Elizabethton*	.274	26	62	13	17	24	5	1	0	9	0	0	0	1	18	0	12	1	1
Soto, Miguel, Johnson City	.257	60	148	17	38	41	3	0	0	14	1	1	1	0	7	0	20	5	3
Spalt, Steven, Bluefield	.202	46	114	15	23	24	1	0	0	15	1	0	2	0	17	0	21	7	0
Todman, Jens, Pikeville*	.111	9	27	1	3	3	0	0	0	0	0	0	0	0	2	0	6	1	0
Traylor, Keith, Bristol	.220	60	173	28	38	54	4	3	2	23	4	5	0	0	24	1	24	6	3
Turner, John, Pikeville*	.280	64	218	49	61	86	14	4	1	30	3	3	1	0	35	1	20	14	7
Tyson, Marty, Pikeville	.288	62	191	26	55	66	9	1	0	24	1	4	1	2	22	0	39	4	5
Vargas, Jose, Paintsville	.220	35	91	15	20	22	2	0	0	11	0	1	3	2	4	1	18	4	3
Vaughn, Ron, Bristol	.000	5	4	0	0	0	0	0	0	0	0	0	0	0	0	0	3	0	0
Vetsch, Dave, Elizabethton*	.218	70	243	39	53	94	5	0	12	34	3	0	0	3	52	2	56	4	2
Vogel, George, Johnson City	.278	67	216	50	60	97	9	2	8	24	1	0	2	0	45	0	64	26	2
Walewander, James, Bristol†	.319	73	285	56	91	121	14	2	4	28	3	2	3	1	34	2	29	35	4
Ward, Michael, Bristol*	.271	64	203	42	55	87	7	2	7	36	7	0	2	1	42	2	43	4	1
Washington, Marc, Bristol	.229	62	218	29	50	60	6	2	0	23	3	5	0	0	16	1	42	17	6
White, Brian, Pikeville	.230	64	174	27	40	51	8	0	1	27	2	2	3	3	43	1	27	10	6
Williams, Fred, Paintsville	.266	69	244	52	65	92	11	2	4	35	2	3	1	3	44	0	51	6	6
Willman, Timothy, Johnson City	.290	15	31	5	9	13	2	1	0	5	0	0	0	1	8	0	10	0	0

The following pitchers, listed alphabetically by club, with games in parentheses, had no plate appearances, primarily through use of designated hitters:

BLUEFIELD—Adams, Gerald (11); Burroughs, Anthony (2); Cobe, William (17); Conley, Michael (14); Crumley, Hubert (1); Gilbert, Jeffrey (1); King, Randy (13); Kline, Robert (6); Leiter, Mark (6); Mason, Victor (3); Ninneman, Scott (20); Pobur, Hugh (5); Rohan, Edward (13); Skinner, Michael (7); Wilp, Kenneth (16); Wilson, Roger (15); Wilson, Wayne (3).

BRISTOL—Baker, Scott (10); Barnes, Tyrone (13); Bauldry, John (20); Cooper, William (11); Dotson, Wayne (12); Garcia, Alejandro (3); Halley, Michael (11); Held, Thomas (5); Patterson, Michael (11); Perrotte, Joseph (13); Poissant, Rodney (11); Raubold, Arthur (10); Scudero, James (16); Simmons, Glenn (11); Wheeler, Bradley (19); Whitmore, Ronnie (13); Willis, Carl (2).

ELIZABETHTON—Anderson, Allen (6); Burnos, James (18); Clay, Danny (15); Cloninger, Michael (11); Galloway, Kenneth (9); Gonzalez, Henry (14); Hammond, Kevin (9); Iasparro, Donnie (16); Ortega, Luis (9); Perez, Yorkis (3); Thompson, Timothy (8); Tolentino, Renaldo (16).

JOHNSON CITY—Blunt, Bradley (9); Ellis, Richard (14); Grossman, James (9); Hein, Jack (19); Maldonado, Luis (4); Monett, Ruben (17); Moon, Kevin (18); Oates, Paul (13); Perry, Jeff (15); Sinclair, Kenneth (18); Turnbull, Keith (13); Waddill, Dale (11); Whitaker, Kevin (8).

PAINTSVILLE—Birkbeck, Michael (7); Bosio, Christopher (7); Ciardi, Mark (13); Diaz, Derek (2); Fingers, Robert (11); Gilbert, Jeff (17); Kleean, Thomas (19); Morris, James (13); Murphy, Daniel (11); Parrett, Jeffrey (3); Plesac, Daniel (14); Reece, Jeffrey (13); Selden, Kyle (2); Serviente, Michael (14); Simmons, Gregory (12); Thompson, John (1); Watkins, Troy (17); Williams, Scott (13).

PIKEVILLE—Balmer, Stephen (8); Bell, Gregory (14); Cox, John (4); Davidson, Jackie (2); Filippo, Richard (16); Hamilton, Carlton (6); Holmes, Dean (5); Lenderman, David (9); Louis, Joseph (11); Phillips, James (14); Pobur, Hugh (10); Reid, Timothy (13); Schwarz, Jeffrey (13); Toll, Timothy (23).

PULASKI—Aviles, Brian (6); Bates, Douglas (11); Candelaria, Albert (10); Castellano, Anthony (18); Cotter, Steven (14); Green, Jeffrey (15); Layne, Richard (4); Lynn, Kenneth (3); Mehalko, Andrew (4); Morelock, Charles (14); Nagle, Michael (17); Rodgers, Mac (15); Schreiber, Martin (12); Shirley, Eric (21); Ziem, Stephen (20).

GRAND SLAM HOME RUNS—Harrison, 3; Baird, Codinach, Schugel, 2 each; Beuerlein, Braggs, Butcher, Dickerson, Tr. Edwards, Everett, Freeman, Kumiega, McManus, Vogel, Walewander, 1 each.

AWARDED FIRST BASE ON CATCHER'S INTERFERENCE—Braggs 2 (J. Baker, Palacios); Ripken 2 (Glendening, F. Hernandez); Bunnell (J. Baker); Butcher (F. Hernandez); Codinach (Fitzgerald); Fitzgerald (Gomez); An. Garcia (Fitzgerald); McClure (Amante); Page (Gomez); Turner (O'Connor).

CLUB FIELDING

Club	Pct.	G.	PO.	A.	E.	DP.	PB.
Pulaski	.952	72	1729	700	122	41	16
Paintsville	.951	73	1753	675	124	43	16
Bristol	.948	73	1713	736	134	50	26
Bluefield	.942	70	1688	765	152	46	17
Johnson City	.941	72	1674	750	152	58	24
Elizabethton	.938	72	1693	714	160	46	18
Pikeville	.927	70	1690	718	190	50	23

INDIVIDUAL FIELDING

*Throws lefthanded.

FIRST BASEMEN

Player and Club	Pct.	G.	PO.	A.	E.	DP.
Agostinelli, Johnson City	1.000	1	1	0	0	0
Amante, Johnson City	1.000	9	58	0	0	3
Beattie, Bluefield	.983	29	222	9	4	16
Castro, Johnson City	.917	6	11	0	1	2
Codinach, Elizabethton	.987	8	74	2	1	5
COPPOLA, Elizabethton*	.992	59	474	24	4	31
D'Alessandro, Pulaski	1.000	1	1	0	0	0
Edwards, Pulaski	.975	6	35	4	1	4
Fitzgerald, Bluefield	.800	2	11	1	3	2
Giron, Bristol	1.000	6	20	1	0	2
Gutierrez, Bluefield*	.989	20	162	12	2	13
Harris, Johnson City*	.989	64	503	28	6	42
Harrison, Pulaski	.974	23	139	11	4	7
Jackson, Paintsville*	1.000	1	5	0	0	0
Kinard, Johnson City	1.000	1	4	1	0	0
Kumiega, Pikeville	.980	51	415	29	9	32
Lopez, Bluefield	1.000	3	22	0	0	0
McDermott, Paintsville	.978	64	418	24	10	34

FIRST BASEMEN—Continued

Player and Club	Pct.	G.	PO.	A.	E.	DP.
McManus, Bristol	.990	22	182	9	2	13
Pena, Johnson City	1.000	1	1	0	0	0
Rojas, Bluefield	.994	20	159	11	1	12
Schugel, Elizabethton	.933	6	40	2	3	4
Scime, Pulaski	.985	53	382	23	6	25
Shannon, Johnson City	.929	4	13	0	1	1
Smith, Paintsville	1.000	10	75	8	0	5
Todman, Pikeville*	.905	2	18	1	2	3
Turner, Pikeville*	.967	18	139	6	5	9
Ward, Bristol*	.982	50	415	27	8	29
Williams, Paintsville	1.000	3	32	3	0	2
Willman, Johnson City	.963	4	24	2	1	3

SECOND BASEMEN

Player and Club	Pct.	G.	PO.	A.	E.	DP.
Agostinelli, Johnson City	1.000	2	3	2	0	2
Bruno, Bluefield	.969	12	27	35	2	6
Carden, Pulaski	1.000	2	1	4	0	0
Cijntje, Bluefield*	1.000	1	0	1	0	0
Cruz, Pikeville	.929	27	59	58	9	21
Daddario, Pulaski	.929	9	26	13	3	2
Derby, Paintsville	.915	16	20	23	4	5
Kinard, Johnson City	.500	1	1	0	1	0
Lebeau, Pulaski	.958	62	140	157	13	30
Leriger, Bluefield	.952	44	72	108	9	19
Meyer, Pulaski	.818	2	6	3	2	1
Millis, Bristol	.911	11	20	21	4	6
Mills, Bristol	1.000	2	3	4	0	0
Nunley, Johnson City	.897	20	32	29	7	5
Orman, Bluefield	.918	16	42	47	8	7
Palmer, Elizabethton	.965	65	127	147	10	27
Paulino, Johnson City	.900	6	8	10	2	2
Perez, Johnson City	.750	4	0	3	1	0
REBOULET, Johnson City	.977	47	89	119	5	24
Smith, Elizabethton	.973	9	11	25	1	4
Soto, Johnson City	.837	14	9	27	7	4
Spalt, Bluefield	1.000	1	2	1	0	0
Tyson, Pikeville	1.000	1	2	1	0	0
Vargas, Paintsville	.944	11	13	21	2	1
Walewander, Bristol	.969	62	125	188	10	33
White, Pikeville	.950	46	90	119	11	17
Williams, Paintsville	.928	59	116	115	18	23

THIRD BASEMEN

Player and Club	Pct.	G.	PO.	A.	E.	DP.
Agostinelli, Johnson City	.872	13	11	23	5	2
Bruno, Bluefield	.966	10	7	21	1	3
Carden, Pulaski	.667	4	1	1	1	1
Cardenas, Elizabethton	.000	1	0	0	1	0
Davis, Johnson City	.000	1	0	0	1	0
Dickerson, Pikeville	.500	1	1	1	2	0
Everett, Paintsville	.901	69	47	108	17	5
Fitzgerald, Bluefield	.000	1	0	0	1	0
Heyison, Bluefield	.843	30	25	50	14	2
Kinard, Johnson City	.783	29	14	40	15	2
Leriger, Bluefield	.727	4	5	3	3	1
Lopez, Bluefield	.833	14	14	16	6	0
Martinez, Johnson City	.750	2	1	2	1	1
McManus, Bristol	.889	29	15	49	8	3
Meyer, Pulaski	.750	2	2	4	2	0
Millis, Bristol	1.000	1	0	1	0	1
Mills, Bristol	.932	44	21	75	7	7
NIPPER, Pulaski	.935	70	51	108	11	9
Nunley, Johnson City	.840	12	3	18	4	2
O'Connor, Johnson City	.000	1	0	0	1	0
Paulino, Johnson City	.821	16	4	19	5	2
Ripken, Bluefield	.889	6	6	10	2	2
Schugel, Elizabethton	.866	57	46	109	24	5
Shannon, Johnson City	.864	18	8	30	6	4
Smith, Elizabethton	.756	15	7	24	10	1
Spalt, Bluefield	.909	10	8	22	3	0
Tyson, Pikeville	.827	56	30	104	28	8
Vargas, Paintsville	.833	3	0	5	1	0
Vogel, Johnson City	.000	1	0	0	1	0
White, Pikeville	.942	15	14	35	3	5
Williams, Paintsville	.857	5	1	5	1	0

SHORTSTOPS

Player and Club	Pct.	G.	PO.	A.	E.	DP.
Baez, Pikeville	.767	17	20	36	17	8
Barreto, Bristol	.854	51	57	119	30	13
Butcher, Elizabethton	.883	53	79	156	31	18
Cardenas, Elizabethton	.811	21	23	50	17	14
Cruz, Pikeville	.874	41	52	114	24	12
Ditto, Pikeville	.873	12	15	40	8	7
Embry, Bristol	.765	4	2	11	4	1
Hardamon, Pikeville	.778	8	8	13	6	4
Hernandez, Bristol	.500	2	0	2	2	1
Kinard, Johnson City	.929	6	8	18	2	3
Kingsley, Pulaski	.886	66	81	183	34	16
Lebeau, Pulaski	.857	4	3	9	2	1
Leriger, Bluefield	.938	3	6	9	1	1
Meyer, Pulaski	.706	8	4	8	5	2
Millis, Bristol	.852	6	8	15	4	2
Mills, Bristol	.938	5	6	9	1	2
Paulino, Johnson City	.924	30	32	77	9	8
QUINONES, Paintsville	.890	63	80	146	28	26
Ripken, Bluefield	.909	42	76	135	21	20
Shannon, Johnson City	1.000	2	3	5	0	0
Soto, Johnson City	.923	45	51	129	15	21
Spalt, Bluefield	.928	34	39	90	10	13
Vargas, Paintsville	.902	22	12	34	5	5
Walewander, Bristol	.891	11	15	34	6	5
White, Pikeville	.800	3	3	9	3	2

OUTFIELDERS

Player and Club	Pct.	G.	PO.	A.	E.	DP.
Appino, Paintsville	.962	60	48	2	2	0
Baird, Pulaski	.937	65	80	9	6	0
Baker, Bristol*	.923	7	12	0	1	0
Ballou, Pulaski	.861	58	61	7	11	0
Bayron, Elizabethton*	.875	19	13	1	2	0
Black, Bluefield	.932	29	40	1	3	0
Braggs, Paintsville	.953	72	115	8	6	1
Brumfield, Pikeville	.881	25	34	3	5	1
Bruno, Bluefield	1.000	6	11	0	0	0
Camara, Pulaski*	1.000	24	29	0	0	0
Castro, Johnson City	.875	13	7	0	1	0
Cijntje, Bluefield*	.926	47	106	7	9	1
Codinach, Elizabethton	.891	34	37	4	5	1
Cunningham, Bristol	.857	13	5	1	1	0
Dahse, Bluefield	.962	15	22	3	1	0
Davis, Johnson City	.958	26	21	2	1	1
Derby, Paintsville	.750	8	3	0	1	0
Diaz, Elizabethton	.500	4	1	0	1	0
Dickerson, Pikeville	.933	26	39	3	3	0
Te. Edwards, Pikeville	.876	50	82	3	12	0
Tr. Edwards, Pulaski	.931	18	25	2	2	0
Embry, Bristol	1.000	4	4	0	0	0
FORGIONE, Elizabethton*	1.000	70	121	6	0	1
Freeman, Paintsville*	.944	68	96	5	6	0
Garcia, Elizabethton*	.933	12	11	3	1	0
Goodwin, Bristol	.909	12	19	1	2	0
Graupmann, Elizabethton	1.000	1	3	0	0	0
Gutierrez, Bluefield*	.887	30	41	6	6	1
Hall, Pulaski	.957	64	102	8	5	2
Hardamon, Pikeville	.907	24	34	5	4	0
Harris, Johnson City*	1.000	3	2	0	0	0
Hatley, Elizabethton*	.926	19	24	1	2	0
J.B. Hernandez, Bristol	.750	8	8	1	3	0
J.M. Hernandez, Bristol	.930	38	37	3	3	0
Jackson, Paintsville*	1.000	11	6	0	0	0
Linares, Elizabethton*	.333	2	1	0	2	0
Lopez, Bluefield	1.000	2	5	0	0	0
Millis, Bristol	.985	35	65	1	1	0
Milner, Johnson City*	.859	58	54	1	9	1
Mitchell, Paintsville*	.941	16	16	0	1	0
Morris, Bluefield	.942	49	62	3	4	1
Nunez, Johnson City	.916	60	68	8	7	0
Page, Bluefield	1.000	7	4	0	0	0
Pena, Johnson City	.871	24	27	0	4	0
Piazza, Bluefield	.919	34	52	5	5	1
Richardson, Pikeville	.971	62	131	5	4	2
Todman, Pikeville*	1.000	4	6	0	0	0
Traylor, Bristol	.942	59	106	8	7	4
Turner, Pikeville*	.955	25	41	1	2	0
Vetsch, Elizabethton	.962	69	131	6	11	2
Vogel, Johnson City	.966	63	108	7	4	2
Washington, Bristol	.921	61	68	2	6	1
Williams, Paintsville	1.000	3	2	0	0	0

CATCHERS

Player and Club	Pct.	G.	PO.	A.	E.	DP.	PB.
Agostinelli, Johnson City	1.000	7	20	4	0	2	1
Amante, Johnson City	.974	20	99	14	3	1	6
Anderson, Paintsville	.982	22	145	19	3	2	8
Baker, Pikeville	.961	32	186	11	8	1	9
Beuerlein, Paintsville	.991	51	414	34	4	1	6
Bunnell, Pulaski	.987	32	204	29	3	1	5
Calley, Elizabethton	.981	24	138	13	3	1	4
Carvajal, Johnson City	.987	16	68	8	1	1	5
Castillo, Paintsville	1.000	2	5	0	0	0	0
D'ALESSANDRO, Pulaski	.994	43	280	32	2	0	7
Edwards, Pulaski	1.000	6	40	6	0	1	4
Fitzgerald, Bluefield	.971	47	251	54	9	2	10
Fitzpatrick, Bluefield	1.000	8	45	3	0	0	1
Glendening, Pikeville	.967	40	212	25	8	0	10
Gomez, Elizabethton	.940	14	57	6	4	0	4
Graupmann, Elizabethton	.949	7	33	4	2	0	1
Harrison, Pulaski	1.000	3	10	0	0	0	0
Hernandez, Pikeville	.923	5	19	5	2	1	3
Lopez, Bluefield	.962	21	114	12	5	0	6
Martinez, Johnson City	.957	12	58	8	3	0	5
McClure, Bristol	.987	44	268	28	4	2	13
McDermott, Paintsville	1.000	9	47	9	0	0	2
O'Connor, Johnson City	.963	30	167	16	7	2	7
Palacios, Bristol	.968	33	187	22	7	2	12
Pancake, Elizabethton	.962	36	203	23	9	2	9
Paulino, Johnson City	1.000	1	2	0	0	0	0
Piazza, Bluefield	.500	1	1	0	1	0	0
Santana, Bristol	.750	2	3	0	1	0	1
Smith, Paintsville	1.000	3	5	0	0	0	0
Vaughn, Bristol	.889	5	7	1	1	0	0
Willman, Johnson City	.956	9	42	1	2	0	0

PITCHERS

Player and Club	Pct.	G.	PO.	A	E.	DP
Adams, Bluefield	.909	11	2	8	1	1
Anderson, Elizabethton*	1.000	6	0	4	0	0
Baker, Bristol	.857	10	1	5	1	1
Balmer, Pikeville	.800	8	1	3	1	0
Barnes, Bristol	1.000	13	1	3	0	0
Bates, Pulaski*	.750	11	0	3	1	0
Bauldry, Bristol	1.000	20	0	8	0	0
Bell, Pikeville*	1.000	14	3	11	0	0
Birkbeck, Paintsville	1.000	7	3	10	0	1
Blunt, Johnson City	.875	9	2	5	1	1
Bosio, Paintsville	.800	7	4	12	4	3
Burnos, Elizabethton	.800	18	4	4	2	1
Candelaria, Pulaski*	.917	10	4	7	1	1
Castellano, Pulaski	1.000	18	2	8	0	1
Ciardi, Paintsville	.769	13	2	8	3	0
Clay, Elizabethton	.912	15	4	27	3	1
Cloninger, Elizabethton	.826	11	3	16	4	0
Cobe, Bluefield	1.000	17	2	7	0	1
Conley, Bluefield*	.750	14	1	2	1	0
Cooper, Bristol	1.000	11	5	8	0	1
Cotter, Pulaski	.750	14	1	2	1	0
Cox, Pikeville*	.909	4	1	9	1	0
Crumley, Bluefield	.500	1	0	1	1	0
Davidson, Pikeville	.500	2	1	0	1	0
Diaz, Paintsville	1.000	2	0	1	0	0
Dotson, Bristol	.778	12	2	5	2	0
Ellis, Johnson City*	.833	14	3	2	1	0
Filippo, Pikeville*	.857	16	5	7	2	0
Fingers, Paintsville	1.000	11	1	3	0	0
Fitzpatrick, Bluefield	1.000	5	0	2	0	0
Galloway, Elizabethton*	1.000	9	0	2	0	0
Garcia, Bristol*	1.000	3	0	4	0	0
E.J. Gilbert, Bluefield*	1.000	1	1	2	0	0
J. Gilbert, Paintsville	.800	17	3	1	1	0
Gonzalez, Elizabethton	1.000	14	5	9	0	0
GREEN, Pulaski	1.000	15	3	22	0	2
Grossman, Johnson City	.875	9	1	6	1	1
Halley, Bristol	.875	11	3	11	2	0
Hamilton, Pikeville*	1.000	5	0	3	0	0
Hammond, Elizabethton	1.000	9	2	3	0	0
Hein, Johnson City	.962	19	9	16	1	0
Held, Bristol	1.000	5	1	3	0	1
Holmes, Pikeville	.500	5	1	0	1	0
Iasparro, Elizabethton	.852	16	4	19	4	1
King, Bluefield	.857	13	5	7	2	0
Kleean, Paintsville*	1.000	19	1	3	0	0
Kline, Bluefield	1.000	6	1	5	0	0
Leiter, Bluefield	.600	6	2	4	4	0
Lenderman, Pikeville	.909	9	4	6	1	1
Louis, Pikeville*	.750	11	2	1	1	0
Lynn, Pulaski	1.000	3	3	1	0	0
Mason, Bluefield	1.000	3	2	0	0	0
Mehalko, Pulaski*	1.000	4	0	1	0	0
Monett, Johnson City	1.000	17	4	9	0	0
Moon, Johnson City	.933	17	4	10	1	0
Morelock, Pulaski	.813	14	6	7	3	0
Morris, Paintsville*	.923	13	2	10	1	1
Murphy, Paintsville	.667	11	1	5	3	0
Nagle, Pulaski	1.000	17	1	0	0	1
Ninneman, Bluefield	.786	20	1	10	3	1
Oates, Johnson City*	.941	13	0	16	1	0
Ortega, Elizabethton	.500	9	0	1	1	0
Parrett, Paintsville	1.000	3	2	3	0	0
Patterson, Bristol	.923	11	2	10	1	0
Perrotte, Bristol*	.917	13	1	10	1	2
Perry, Johnson City	.800	15	5	11	4	1
Phillips, Pikeville	.935	14	9	20	2	3
Plesac, Paintsville*	.944	14	0	17	1	0
Pobur, 5 Blue-10 Pikeville	.714	15	3	2	2	0
Poissant, Bristol	.889	11	2	6	1	0
Raubolt, Bristol	.833	10	2	3	1	0
Reece, Paintsville*	.926	13	10	15	2	2
Reid, Pikeville	1.000	13	2	8	0	0
Rodgers, Pulaski	1.000	15	0	8	0	1
Rohan, Bluefield	.846	13	2	9	2	1
Sanders, Elizabethton	1.000	19	5	16	0	1
Schreiber, Pulaski*	.917	12	3	8	1	0
Schwarz, Pikeville	.864	13	5	14	3	0
Scudero, Bristol*	.933	16	3	11	1	1
Serviente, Paintsville	1.000	14	0	2	0	0
Shirley, Pulaski	.800	21	0	4	1	0
Gl. Simmons, Bristol	1.000	11	7	6	0	0
Gr. Simmons, Paintsville	1.000	12	2	3	0	0
Sinclair, Johnson City	.875	18	2	5	1	0
Skinner, Bluefield	.750	7	0	3	1	0
T. Thompson, Elizabethton	.867	8	7	6	2	0
Tolentino, Elizabethton	1.000	16	5	1	0	0
Toll, Pikeville	.917	23	3	8	1	0
Turnbull, Johnson City	.882	13	3	12	2	1
Waddill, Johnson City*	1.000	11	1	2	0	0
Watkins, Paintsville	1.000	17	0	10	0	0
Wheeler, Bristol*	1.000	19	5	7	0	0
Whitaker, Johnson City*	1.000	8	5	5	0	1
Whitmore, Bristol	.750	13	0	3	1	0
Williams, Paintsville	1.000	13	1	3	0	0
Wilp, Bluefield*	1.000	16	2	12	0	2
R. Wilson, Bluefield*	.926	15	8	17	2	0
Ziem, Pulaski	.917	20	3	8	1	0

The following players do not have any recorded accepted chances at the positions indicated and therefore are not listed in the fielding averages for those particular positions: Agostinelli, of; Aviles, p; Baez, of; Bunnell, 1b; Burroughs, p; Daddario, ss; D'Alessandro, 3b; Derby, 3b; Tr. Edwards, p; Glendening, 3b; J.B. Hernandez, 3b; Kinard, of; Layne, p; Lopez, p; Maldonado, p; Morris, 2b; Nunley, ss; Perez, p; Ripken, p; Selden, p; Spalt, p; J. Thompson, p; Willis, p; W. Wilson, p.

CLUB PITCHING

Club	ERA.	G.	CG.	ShO.	Sv.	IP.	H.	R.	ER.	HR.	HB.	BB.	Int. BB.	SO.	WP.	Bk.
Paintsville	4.00	73	13	4	13	584.1	529	342	260	42	18	348	8	600	70	7
Pulaski	4.33	72	6	4	20	576.1	535	344	277	39	19	385	4	517	67	1
Pikeville	4.87	70	15	3	12	563.1	629	413	305	49	17	266	12	408	42	3
Johnson City	5.15	72	15	2	9	558.0	570	412	319	66	32	343	9	455	81	2
Bristol	5.47	73	11	2	11	571.0	589	438	347	62	35	352	8	448	58	10
Elizabethton	5.50	72	23	3	5	564.1	586	439	345	63	17	302	8	435	68	3
Bluefield	5.97	70	10	3	11	562.2	681	444	373	50	18	342	5	399	66	7

PITCHERS' RECORDS

(Leading Qualifiers for Earned-Run Average Leadership—58 or More Innings)

*Throws lefthanded.

Pitcher—Club	W.	L.	Pct.	ERA.	G.	GS.	CG.	GF.	ShO.	Sv.	IP.	H.	R.	ER.	HR.	HB.	BB.	Int. BB.	SO.	WP.
Hein, Johnson City	8	3	.727	2.53	19	8	3	8	0	1	74.2	57	32	21	3	3	39	1	68	12
Clay, Elizabethton	6	7	.462	3.13	15	14	6	1	2	0	97.2	82	47	34	3	0	42	1	80	3
Ciardi, Paintsville	7	2	.778	3.23	13	10	6	0	1	0	69.2	62	33	25	4	1	17	0	80	3
Bell, Pikeville*	5	2	.714	3.36	14	9	3	4	2	1	75.0	73	38	28	5	2	25	0	54	1
Green, Pulaski	8	4	.667	3.49	15	12	3	0	0	0	80.0	68	43	31	6	3	46	0	42	6
Plesac, Paintsville*	9	1	.900	3.50	14	14	2	0	0	0	82.1	76	44	32	6	1	57	1	85	11
Candelaria, Pulaski*	4	2	.667	3.57	10	9	1	1	1	1	58.0	52	27	23	5	2	36	0	66	3
Reece, Paintsville*	7	2	.778	3.58	13	13	1	0	0	0	78.0	73	39	31	2	0	42	0	78	12
Perry, Johnson City	3	6	.333	3.62	15	10	2	2	0	0	69.2	56	39	28	6	6	37	1	37	9
Phillips, Pikeville	6	5	.545	3.66	14	12	8	1	1	1	86.0	86	49	35	11	0	16	1	47	2

Departmental Leaders: G—Toll, 23; W—Plesac, 9; L—Sanders, 9; Pct.—Plesac, .900; GS—Clay, Plesac, 14; CG—Phillips, 8; GF—Toll, 22; ShO—Bell, Clay, 2; Sv.—Gilbert, Toll, 7; IP—Clay, 97.2; H—Sanders, 94; R—Oates, 63; ER—Sanders, 52; HR—Sanders, 15; HB—Morelock, Perry, Poissant, 6; BB—R. Wilson, 65; IBB—Toll, 7; SO—Plesac, 85; WP—Cloninger, 17.

(All Pitchers—Listed Alphabetically)

Pitcher—Club	W.	L.	Pct.	ERA.	G.	GS.	CG.	GF.	ShO.	Sv.	IP.	H.	R.	ER.	HR.	HB.	BB.	Int. BB.	SO.	WP.
Adams, Bluefield	1	6	.143	7.17	11	5	0	3	0	2	37.2	46	39	30	6	2	27	0	21	6
Anderson, Elizabethton*	1	3	.250	8.53	6	6	0	0	0	0	12.2	17	12	12	1	0	7	0	12	1
Aviles, Pulaski	1	0	1.000	2.08	6	1	0	4	0	2	13.0	13	3	3	0	0	6	0	19	1
Baker, Bristol	1	0	1.000	7.06	10	2	0	6	0	1	21.2	20	17	17	1	1	22	0	12	5
Balmer, Pikeville	2	1	.667	6.08	8	8	1	0	0	0	37.0	51	29	25	2	1	17	0	21	4
Barnes, Bristol	1	1	.500	4.76	13	3	0	4	0	0	22.2	16	18	12	1	2	23	0	26	4
Bates, Pulaski*	1	3	.250	7.61	11	11	0	0	0	0	36.2	47	35	31	5	0	37	0	27	6
Bauldry, Bristol	1	1	.500	2.79	20	0	0	12	0	4	38.2	44	26	12	5	2	12	2	28	0
Bell, Pikeville*	5	2	.714	3.36	14	9	3	4	2	1	75.0	73	38	28	5	2	25	0	54	1
Birkbeck, Paintsville	3	1	.750	1.88	7	5	0	0	0	0	28.2	17	12	6	1	2	17	1	38	3
Blunt, Johnson City	4	2	.667	4.15	9	9	2	0	1	0	56.1	47	26	26	2	3	30	0	63	15
Bosio, Paintsville	2	2	.500	2.84	7	7	2	0	1	0	44.1	30	18	14	3	4	18	0	43	0
Burnos, Elizabethton	2	3	.400	5.02	18	0	0	15	0	2	28.2	30	24	16	3	3	18	2	20	3
Burroughs, Bluefield	1	0	1.000	11.88	2	2	0	0	0	0	8.1	8	11	11	2	4	8	0	4	5
Candelaria, Pulaski*	4	2	.667	3.57	10	9	1	1	1	1	58.0	52	27	23	5	2	36	0	66	3
Castellano, Pulaski	6	4	.600	3.52	18	3	0	4	0	1	46.0	49	24	18	5	0	23	0	35	6
Ciardi, Paintsville	7	2	.778	3.23	13	10	6	0	1	0	69.2	62	33	25	4	1	17	0	80	3
Clay, Elizabethton	6	7	.462	3.13	15	14	6	1	2	0	97.2	82	47	34	3	0	42	1	80	3
Cloninger, Elizabethton	4	6	.400	5.72	11	10	3	0	0	0	61.1	64	55	39	6	2	33	0	21	17
Cobe, Bluefield	3	3	.500	7.87	17	1	0	10	0	1	42.1	67	40	37	4	0	17	1	23	0
Conley, Bluefield*	3	5	.375	7.11	14	9	0	2	0	1	50.2	52	45	40	6	1	58	1	34	6
Cooper, Bristol	0	2	.000	6.18	11	2	0	3	0	0	27.2	33	22	19	2	1	14	1	17	2
Cotter, Pulaski	2	2	.500	5.70	14	3	0	11	0	3	23.2	26	22	15	3	1	13	1	25	4
Cox, Pikeville*	1	3	.250	1.67	4	4	2	0	0	0	27.0	23	10	5	2	1	4	0	25	0
Crumley, Bluefield	0	0	.000	3.86	1	1	0	0	0	0	2.1	3	1	1	0	0	2	0	0	1
Davidson, Pikeville	0	1	.000	14.85	2	2	0	0	0	0	6.2	10	14	11	1	1	7	0	5	0
Diaz, Paintsville	0	0	.000	0.00	2	0	0	1	0	1	4.2	1	0	0	0	0	2	0	3	2
Dotson, Bristol	4	2	.667	7.62	12	12	1	0	0	0	54.1	63	54	46	9	3	39	0	49	7
Edwards, Pulaski	0	0	.000	6.75	2	0	0	2	0	0	1.1	1	1	1	0	0	1	0	0	0
Ellis, Johnson City*	0	2	.000	7.30	14	3	0	4	0	0	24.2	35	32	20	9	1	20	1	21	1
Filippo, Pikeville*	4	2	.667	3.71	16	3	0	10	0	1	53.1	55	27	22	1	0	24	1	35	7
Fingers, Paintsville	1	2	.333	3.52	11	0	0	8	0	3	15.1	18	7	6	2	2	1	1	10	1
Fitzpatrick, Bluefield	0	0	.000	4.09	5	0	0	3	0	1	11.0	13	5	5	0	0	2	0	12	1
Galloway, Elizabethton*	0	0	.000	7.04	9	0	0	5	0	0	15.1	20	22	12	2	3	10	0	15	2
Garcia, Bristol*	2	0	1.000	1.86	3	0	0	1	0	0	9.2	9	2	2	0	0	2	0	14	0
E.J. Gilbert, Bluefield*	1	0	1.000	1.29	1	1	1	0	0	0	7.0	6	1	1	0	0	2	0	2	0
J. Gilbert, Paintsville	1	1	.500	1.66	17	0	0	13	0	7	21.2	13	6	4	1	1	11	1	22	3
Gonzalez, Elizabethton	5	5	.500	5.67	14	13	5	0	0	0	79.1	74	62	50	13	0	34	1	57	9
Green, Pulaski	8	4	.667	3.49	15	12	3	0	0	0	80.0	68	43	31	6	3	46	0	42	6
Grossman, Johnson City	0	1	.000	6.08	9	2	0	5	0	0	23.2	32	24	16	3	3	21	0	12	1
Halley, Bristol	1	4	.200	6.36	11	11	1	0	0	0	52.1	49	49	37	4	4	45	1	27	9
Hamilton, Pikeville*	0	2	.000	6.23	5	4	0	1	0	1	13.0	12	11	9	2	0	18	1	16	2
Hammond, Elizabethton	0	0	.000	7.36	9	0	0	6	0	0	14.2	15	17	12	3	0	14	0	16	2
Hein, Johnson City	8	3	.727	2.53	19	8	3	8	0	1	74.2	57	32	21	3	3	39	1	68	12
Held, Bristol	4	0	1.000	1.93	5	3	0	0	0	0	18.2	11	6	4	1	1	11	0	15	2
Holmes, Pikeville	0	3	.000	7.11	5	0	0	3	0	0	12.2	18	17	10	0	0	6	1	6	0
Iasparro, Elizabethton	4	4	.500	4.86	16	9	2	4	0	0	76.0	83	48	41	6	2	47	2	60	6
King, Bluefield	4	5	.444	5.84	13	12	1	1	1	0	69.1	93	60	45	10	2	33	0	38	4
Kleean, Paintsville*	1	2	.333	5.23	19	0	0	9	0	1	20.2	29	18	12	2	0	13	2	25	2
Kline, Bluefield	0	3	.000	6.60	6	6	0	0	0	0	30.0	38	24	22	3	2	17	0	28	5
Layne, Pulaski	0	2	.000	8.76	4	2	0	0	0	0	12.1	13	13	12	2	2	17	0	8	5
Leiter, Bluefield	2	1	.667	2.70	6	6	2	0	0	0	36.2	33	17	11	0	3	13	0	35	2
Lenderman, Pikeville	2	1	.667	6.82	9	3	0	3	0	0	34.1	46	28	26	5	1	14	0	20	0
Lopez, Bluefield	0	0	.000	9.00	2	0	0	1	0	0	4.0	8	7	4	1	0	7	0	1	0
Louis, Pikeville*	2	0	1.000	4.28	11	2	0	6	0	0	33.2	40	24	16	4	2	16	0	33	3
Lynn, Pulaski	2	0	1.000	4.50	3	2	0	1	0	0	12.0	12	6	6	1	0	4	0	10	3
Maldonado, Johnson City*	0	0	.000	11.57	4	0	0	3	0	0	7.0	10	11	9	1	0	6	0	4	2
Mason, Bluefield	0	0	.000	14.21	3	0	0	1	0	1	6.1	11	11	10	2	0	3	0	5	3
Mehalko, Pulaski*	1	0	1.000	2.08	4	0	0	2	0	0	4.1	4	1	1	1	0	3	1	4	1
Monett, Johnson City	2	3	.400	6.35	17	3	0	5	0	2	39.2	50	35	28	8	1	11	0	27	2
Moon, Johnson City	1	5	.167	7.80	17	6	0	6	0	1	45.0	60	45	39	10	4	42	2	38	7
Morelock, Pulaski	3	3	.500	5.74	14	13	0	0	0	0	62.2	63	54	40	2	6	56	0	33	16
Morris, Paintsville*	3	6	.333	5.10	13	13	0	0	0	0	67.0	58	50	38	11	0	42	0	75	13
Murphy, Paintsville	3	1	.750	3.72	11	4	2	1	1	0	38.2	43	22	16	2	0	26	1	29	3
Nagle, Pulaski	0	0	.000	8.47	17	1	0	8	0	1	34.0	29	36	32	2	1	43	0	38	4
Ninneman, Bluefield	2	1	.667	6.10	20	1	0	15	0	4	41.1	62	29	28	2	1	11	0	20	2
Oates, Johnson City*	3	8	.273	6.86	13	12	3	1	0	0	60.1	65	63	46	11	3	40	0	41	14
Ortega, Elizabethton	0	0	.000	11.49	9	0	0	6	0	0	15.2	30	20	20	3	1	19	0	11	3
Parrett, Paintsville	2	0	1.000	2.12	3	3	0	0	0	0	17.0	12	6	4	1	0	8	0	21	3
Patterson, Bristol	1	4	.200	8.25	11	2	0	3	0	0	24.0	34	28	22	5	1	15	0	17	4
Perez, Elizabeththon*	0	1	.000	20.25	3	1	0	0	0	0	4.0	5	9	9	1	0	9	0	6	0

Pitcher—Club	W.	L.	Pct.	ERA.	G.	GS.	CG.	GF.	ShO.	Sv.	IP.	H.	R.	ER.	HR.	HB.	BB.	Int. BB.	SO.	WP.
Perrotte, Bristol*	4	4	.500	4.44	13	13	3	0	0	0	77.0	74	47	38	8	3	40	0	69	4
Perry, Johnson City	3	6	.333	3.62	15	10	2	2	0	0	69.2	56	39	28	6	6	37	1	37	9
Phillips, Pikeville	6	5	.545	3.66	14	12	8	1	1	1	86.0	86	49	35	11	0	16	1	47	2
Plesac, Paintsville*	9	1	.900	3.50	14	14	2	0	0	0	82.1	76	44	32	6	1	57	1	85	11
Pobur, 5 Blue-10 Pike	3	0	1.000	6.97	15	1	0	7	0	1	41.1	62	41	32	4	0	25	1	27	4
Poissant, Bristol	1	7	.125	6.04	11	9	3	0	0	0	44.2	48	38	30	6	6	28	0	24	5
Raubolt, Bristol	0	5	.000	11.74	10	3	0	2	0	1	23.0	27	36	30	4	2	23	0	24	3
Reece, Paintsville*	7	2	.778	3.58	13	13	1	0	0	0	78.0	73	39	31	2	0	42	0	78	12
Reid, Pikeville	4	4	.500	7.92	13	10	0	0	0	0	44.1	50	50	39	5	4	41	0	28	7
Ripken, Bluefield	0	0	.000	0.00	1	0	0	1	0	0	0.2	1	0	0	0	0	1	0	2	0
Rodgers, Pulaski	3	1	.750	3.48	15	4	1	5	0	1	41.1	37	21	16	2	1	26	1	45	2
Rohan, Bluefield	3	2	.600	4.76	13	8	2	1	1	0	51.0	65	39	27	3	1	22	0	28	7
Sanders, Elizabethton	3	9	.250	5.42	19	11	4	7	1	3	86.1	94	59	52	15	2	22	1	68	9
Schreiber, Pulaski*	5	0	1.000	2.20	12	5	1	5	1	2	49.0	35	14	12	0	2	27	0	59	5
Schwarz, Pikeville	3	8	.273	5.19	13	13	1	0	0	0	69.1	73	61	40	7	4	45	0	61	10
Scudero, Bristol*	5	1	.833	3.13	16	1	0	9	0	1	37.1	27	14	13	3	2	21	0	39	5
Selden, Paintsville*	0	0	.000	36.00	2	0	0	1	0	0	1.0	1	4	4	0	1	5	0	2	1
Serviente, Paintsville	2	3	.400	6.75	14	1	0	8	0	0	24.0	23	19	18	0	0	20	1	24	2
Shirley, Pulaski	4	1	.800	3.00	21	1	0	12	0	3	48.0	43	17	16	1	1	25	0	54	2
Gl. Simmons, Bristol	4	3	.571	5.22	11	11	2	0	0	0	58.2	64	40	34	9	3	24	1	38	2
Gr. Simmons, Paintsville	1	1	.500	7.06	12	2	0	5	0	0	21.2	26	21	17	3	2	18	0	23	4
Sinclair, Johnson City	3	1	.750	3.89	18	1	0	14	0	5	37.0	36	22	16	1	0	21	0	47	6
Skinner, Bluefield	2	1	.667	3.57	7	1	0	5	0	0	22.2	13	9	9	1	0	14	1	30	3
Spalt, Bluefield	0	0	.000	60.75	2	0	0	1	0	0	1.1	8	9	9	1	0	3	0	2	1
J. Thompson, Paintsville	0	0	.000	9.00	1	0	0	1	0	0	2.0	4	4	2	0	0	2	0	2	1
T. Thompson, Elizabethton	1	3	.250	4.64	8	7	3	1	0	0	42.2	46	35	22	6	4	22	0	40	1
Tolentino, Elizabethton	2	3	.400	7.80	16	1	0	4	0	0	30.0	26	29	26	1	0	25	1	29	12
Toll, Pikeville	1	5	.167	4.35	23	0	0	22	0	7	41.1	49	30	20	1	1	17	7	37	4
Turnbull, Johnson City	4	5	.444	4.27	13	11	4	1	0	0	71.2	74	41	34	9	3	39	0	52	5
Waddill, Johnson City*	0	2	.000	4.86	11	0	0	7	0	0	16.2	10	13	9	0	1	17	3	17	3
Watkins, Paintsville	3	1	.750	5.75	17	0	0	10	0	1	20.1	20	17	13	2	2	16	0	13	2
Wheeler, Bristol*	5	2	.714	4.25	19	0	0	12	0	3	36.0	38	20	17	3	3	16	2	26	0
Whitaker, Johnson City*	2	4	.333	7.67	8	7	1	1	0	0	31.2	38	29	27	3	4	20	1	28	4
Whitmore, Bristol	0	1	.000	5.32	13	1	1	8	0	1	22.0	32	20	13	1	1	13	0	20	6
Williams, Paintsville	2	0	1.000	6.08	13	1	0	3	0	0	26.2	23	22	18	2	2	33	0	27	4
Willis, Bristol	0	1	.000	3.38	2	0	0	2	0	0	2.2	0	1	1	0	0	4	1	3	0
Wilp, Bluefield*	5	4	.556	4.84	16	1	1	14	1	1	44.2	43	26	24	3	2	22	1	43	3
R. Wilson, Bluefield*	5	6	.455	4.83	15	13	3	0	0	0	78.1	84	50	42	3	0	65	0	62	15
W. Wilson, Bluefield	0	1	.000	6.75	3	2	0	0	0	0	5.1	8	5	4	2	0	6	1	2	0
Ziem, Pulaski	6	4	.600	3.33	20	5	0	11	0	6	54.0	43	27	20	4	0	22	1	52	3

BALKS—Plesac, 3; Dotson, Ellis, King, Poissant, Reece, Scudero, Skinner, 2 each; Adams, Balmer, Barnes, Bates, Burnos, Burroughs, Conley, Halley, Held, Iasparro, Louis, Morris, Perez, Schwarz, Serviente, G. Simmons, 1 each.

COMBINATION SHUTOUTS—Simmons-Bauldry, Simmons-Bauldry-Wheeler, Bristol; Hein-Sinclair, Johnson City; Bosio-Kleean, Paintsville; Candelaria-Nagle, Castellano-Shirley-Ziem, Pulaski.

NO-HIT GAMES—Green-Cotter, Pulaski, defeated Paintsville, 3-1, July 15; Schreiber, Pulaski, defeated Elizabethton, 5-0, August 17.

Gulf Coast League

SUMMER CLASS A CLASSIFICATION

CHAMPIONSHIP WINNERS IN PREVIOUS YEARS

1964—Sarasota Braves	.610	1971—Kansas City	.755	1977—Chicago-A.L	.731
1965—Bradenton Astros	.632	1972—Chicago N.L. a	.651	1978—Texas	.600
1966—New York A.L.	.667	Kansas City a	.651	1979—Houston	.635
1967—Kansas City	.614	1973—Texas	.732	1980—Kansas City-Blue	.635
1968—Oakland	.650	1974—Chicago N.L.	.702	1981—Kansas City-Gold	.688
1969—Montreal	.585	1975—Texas	.774	1982—New York-A.L.	.667
1970—Chicago A.L.	.600	1976—Texas	.704		

(Note—Known as Sarasota Rookie League in 1964 and Florida Rookie League in 1965.) aDeclared co-champions; no playoff.

STANDING OF CLUBS AT CLOSE OF SEASON, AUGUST 30

NORTHERN DIVISION

Club	W.	L.	T.	Pct.	G.B.
Los Angeles (Dodgers)	37	23	0	.617	....
Atlanta (Braves)	32	28	0	.533	5
Pittsburgh (Pirates)	28	32	0	.467	9
Toronto (Blue Jays)	15	46	0	.246	22½

SOUTHERN DIVISION

Club	W.	L.	T.	Pct.	G.B.
Texas (Rangers)	40	22	0	.645	....
Chicago-AL (White Sox)	38	24	0	.613	2
Kansas City (Royals)	30	31	0	.492	9½
Houston (Astros)	29	32	0	.475	10½
New York-NL (Mets)	24	35	0	.407	14½

COMPOSITE STANDING OF CLUBS AT CLOSE OF SEASON, AUGUST 30

Club	Tex.	L.A.	Chi-AL	Atl.	K.C.	Hou.	Pitt.	N.Y.-NL	Tor.	W.	L.	T.	Pct.	G.B.
Texas (Rangers)	....	4	5	3	6	6	6	5	5	40	22	0	.645	....
Los Angeles (Dodgers)	4	....	5	5	4	6	3	5	5	37	23	0	.617	2
Chicago-AL (White Sox)	3	3	....	5	4	6	4	6	7	38	24	0	.613	2
Atlanta (Braves)	5	3	2	....	7	2	4	4	5	32	28	0	.533	7
Kansas City (Royals)	1	3	4	1	....	4	6	6	5	30	31	0	.492	9½
Houston (Astros)	2	1	2	5	3	....	4	4	8	29	32	0	.475	10½
Pittsburgh (Pirates)	2	4	4	3	2	4	....	2	7	28	32	0	.467	11
New York-NL (Mets)	3	2	1	3	3	4	4	....	4	24	35	0	.407	14½
Toronto (Blue Jays)	2	3	1	3	2	0	1	3	....	15	46	0	.246	24½

Games played at Bradenton and Saratoga, Fla.

Major league affiliations in parentheses.

Playoffs—Los Angeles defeated Texas, one game to none, to win league championship.

Regular-season attendance—2,460. Playoff—700.

Managers—Atlanta, Pedro Gonzalez; Chicago-AL, Steve Dillard; Houston, Jose Tartabull; Kansas City, Joe Jones; Los Angeles, Gary Laroque; New York-NL, Vern Hoscheit; Pittsburgh, Elwood Huyke; Texas, Andy Hancock; Toronto, Eppy Guerrero.

All-Star Team—1B—Peter Mueller, Houston; 2B—Juan Picart, Los Angeles; 3B—Dimas Gutierrez, Pittsburgh; SS—Martin Blair, Texas; OF—Michael Taylor, Chicago-AL; Gary Thurman, Kansas City; Fausto Aquino, Texas; C—Andrew Hall, Pittsburgh; Pitcher—Dennis Powell, Los Angeles; Relief Pitcher—David Harmon, Texas; Manager of Year—Gary Laroque, Los Angeles.

(Compiled by Howe News Bureau, Boston, Mass.)

CLUB BATTING

Club	Pct.	G.	AB.	R.	OR.	H.	TB.	2B.	3B.	HR.	RBI.	GW.	SH.	SF.	HP.	BB.	Int. BB.	SO.	SB.	CS.	LOB.
Texas	.265	62	2079	340	246	551	711	83	22	11	284	29	19	23	21	278	8	350	59	32	495
Pittsburgh	.263	60	1999	279	270	525	679	74	16	16	220	25	16	14	15	220	10	424	71	33	444
Houston	.256	61	1964	331	263	503	675	76	24	16	272	21	19	24	27	281	9	376	62	37	440
Chicago-AL	.255	62	1998	323	268	510	673	79	21	14	260	24	28	23	31	272	15	376	114	43	482
Atlanta	.239	60	1961	290	294	468	625	56	22	19	248	29	23	14	13	318	8	382	63	35	473
Los Angeles	.238	60	1888	279	229	449	560	68	5	11	213	27	31	15	13	289	12	277	88	37	446
Kansas City	.233	61	1964	283	281	458	589	68	15	11	223	20	20	15	18	326	13	434	183	53	481
New York-NL	.226	59	1879	242	321	424	518	62	13	2	184	16	18	26	21	251	9	375	75	34	433
Toronto	.210	61	1928	204	399	404	498	61	3	9	154	12	11	14	20	197	8	386	77	40	362

INDIVIDUAL BATTING

(Leading Qualifiers for Batting Championship—170 or More Plate Appearances)

*Bats lefthanded. †Switch-hitter.

Player and Club	Pct.	G.	AB.	R.	H.	TB.	2B.	3B.	HR.	RBI.	GW.	SH.	SF.	HP.	BB.	Int. BB.	SO.	SB.	CS.
Mueller, Peter, Houston*	.376	60	210	52	79	102	12	4	1	44	1	0	1	1	40	5	33	3	2
Devlin, Donald, Chicago-AL	.354	59	206	49	73	96	9	7	0	26	5	3	2	4	40	0	27	25	6
Picart, Juan, Los Angeles	.339	41	168	27	57	65	8	0	0	20	3	2	0	1	13	0	15	7	4
Taylor, Michael, Chicago-AL	.333	56	192	55	64	113	15	5	8	34	5	1	2	6	33	4	34	11	4
Aquino, Fausto, Texas*	.321	55	218	32	70	91	8	2	3	41	6	4	5	4	10	0	25	5	2
Lacava, Tony, Pittsburgh	.302	43	149	22	45	61	6	2	2	28	1	0	1	0	21	2	24	3	1
Lind, Jose, Pittsburgh	.301	45	163	26	49	60	3	4	0	18	0	4	0	2	13	0	18	12	1
Pacheco, Jose, Pittsburgh*	.297	46	165	32	49	55	6	0	0	16	2	1	0	2	22	0	23	12	5
Bachmann, Warren, Atlanta*	.296	60	213	46	63	95	13	2	5	47	4	0	0	1	51	1	22	1	1
Kirby, Wayne, Los Angeles*	.292	60	216	43	63	72	7	1	0	13	1	4	1	1	34	0	19	23	8

Departmental Leaders: G—Bachmann, Kirby, Lora, Mejia, Mueller, 60; AB—Aquino, 218; R—Taylor, 55; H—Mueller, 79; TB—Taylor, 113; 2B—Taylor, 15; 3B—Aruca, 8; HR—Gutierrez, Taylor, 8; RBI—Bachmann, 47; GWRBI—Gutierrez, Price, 8; SH—Koch, 6; SF—Aruca, 7; HP—Soper, 7; BB—Bachmann, 51; IBB—Mejia, Mueller, 5; SO—Thurman, 58; SB—Escobar, 35; CS—Garcia, 11.

(All Players—Listed Alphabetically)

Player and Club	Pct.	G.	AB.	R.	H.	TB.	2B.	3B.	HR.	RBI.	GW.	SH.	SF.	HP.	BB.	Int. BB.	SO.	SB.	CS.
Acevedo, Ernesto, Los Angeles	.333	12	21	4	7	7	0	0	0	2	0	0	0	0	3	0	5	0	1
Afenir, M. Troy, Houston	.292	27	89	16	26	48	5	1	5	24	3	1	2	2	17	0	34	2	3
Alcantara, Agapito, Texas	.315	26	73	9	23	27	4	0	0	11	0	0	1	0	15	0	18	7	3
Andrade, John, Texas	.224	18	58	19	13	15	0	1	0	6	2	1	0	1	15	0	8	1	0
Antonio, Ramon, Los Angeles†	.105	7	19	6	2	2	0	0	0	0	0	2	0	0	2	0	1	2	0
Aquino, Fausto, Texas*	.321	55	218	32	70	91	8	2	3	41	6	4	5	4	10	0	25	5	2
Aruca, Daniel, Houston*	.278	48	180	32	50	83	8	8	3	43	5	2	7	0	16	0	18	3	3
Bachmann, Warren, Atlanta*	.296	60	213	46	63	95	13	2	5	47	4	0	0	1	51	1	22	1	1
Baez, Juan, Los Angeles	.188	31	85	10	16	23	4	0	1	9	3	3	0	0	9	0	14	0	0
Balcomb, Alan, Los Angeles†	.260	15	50	3	13	14	1	0	0	5	0	1	0	0	4	0	5	1	1
Barrios, Johnny, Houston*	.133	28	60	6	8	9	1	0	0	3	0	1	0	2	9	2	10	2	0
Berry, Robert, Atlanta	.293	37	133	18	39	52	4	3	1	21	4	0	2	0	20	0	16	8	3
Beucher, Gregory, Los Angeles	.148	41	122	15	18	24	6	0	0	3	0	3	1	1	10	0	23	3	1
Blackwell, Rex, Chicago-AL	.239	46	155	27	37	50	9	2	0	19	1	2	2	1	13	0	40	3	1
Blair, Martin, Texas†	.283	53	187	44	53	66	7	3	0	20	2	4	2	5	42	3	26	10	3
Bolivar, Esteban, Toronto	.200	6	15	4	3	4	1	0	0	1	0	0	1	1	2	0	3	0	0
Borras, Juan, Pittsburgh	.130	22	54	4	7	11	1	0	1	4	0	1	1	2	5	0	18	0	0
Brooks, Desmond, New York-NL	.272	40	92	14	25	32	5	1	0	10	0	0	1	1	19	0	22	3	2
Brooks, Samuel, New York-NL	.000	17	1	1	0	0	0	0	0	1	0	0	1	0	1	0	0	0	0
Brown, Pat, Pittsburgh	.256	33	90	13	23	30	3	2	0	8	2	2	3	1	12	0	25	7	3
Browne, Jerome, Texas†	.282	48	181	34	51	57	2	2	0	20	2	4	0	1	31	0	16	8	2
Burrows, Bryan, Pittsburgh	.321	12	53	5	17	19	2	0	0	3	0	0	0	0	1	0	2	0	2
Butters, David, Pittsburgh	.200	13	35	4	7	8	1	0	0	2	0	0	0	0	3	0	12	0	0
Cain, Jerald, Los Angeles	.284	57	211	32	60	65	3	1	0	15	2	1	0	1	26	2	18	18	6
Campbell, Scott, Kansas City*	.269	49	160	19	43	54	8	0	1	28	3	0	1	1	18	2	42	7	0
Carden, Allen, Atlanta*	.186	38	113	13	21	29	0	1	2	10	1	2	0	1	19	0	13	1	4
Carmichael, Alan, New York-NL	.220	39	82	16	18	18	0	0	0	8	0	3	4	1	13	0	9	3	0
Carr, Charles, Pittsburgh	.269	27	78	4	21	29	8	0	0	6	1	0	0	0	10	0	30	0	1
Carrion, Jesus, Houston	.231	18	52	7	12	15	1	1	0	5	0	0	3	0	6	0	10	1	0
Chance, R. Anthony, Pittsburgh	.293	13	41	6	12	15	3	0	0	6	3	1	0	0	5	0	12	0	0
Chappell, Enrico, New York-NL	.225	45	129	16	29	30	1	0	0	9	0	2	1	3	11	0	25	3	2
Ciamaichelo, Karl, Los Angeles†	.267	54	172	26	46	58	9	0	1	27	4	1	3	0	30	1	20	5	2
Clay, Kenneth, Texas	.189	35	74	16	14	19	2	0	1	6	2	1	0	0	9	0	31	2	2
Clifton, Charles, New York-NL*	.250	5	4	0	1	1	0	0	0	1	0	0	1	0	0	0	0	0	1
Colon, Jose, Chicago-AL†	.143	18	21	1	3	4	1	0	0	1	0	1	0	1	2	0	6	1	2
Constanzo, Fernando, Atlanta	.200	15	25	4	5	9	1	0	1	4	1	1	0	0	3	0	6	0	1
Conte, Michael, Kansas City	.231	40	104	17	24	45	5	2	4	15	1	0	1	0	26	3	31	3	1
Cruz, Marino, Los Angeles	.186	33	70	10	13	16	3	0	0	8	1	1	0	1	8	0	11	1	1
Cuevas, Johni, Atlanta	.227	22	66	4	15	17	2	0	0	8	0	0	2	0	7	0	20	0	1
Daddario, Paul, Atlanta	.179	34	106	15	19	24	5	0	0	10	1	1	1	2	20	0	26	2	1
Daniel, Federico, Los Angeles*	.129	16	31	2	4	5	1	0	0	2	0	0	1	1	4	0	10	2	1
Davis, Glenn, Texas*	.297	34	128	26	38	59	12	0	3	29	2	0	0	1	17	1	30	4	0
Davis, Robert, Kansas City	.240	35	104	11	25	29	4	0	0	14	0	1	1	1	14	0	17	2	2
Devlin, Donald, Chicago-AL	.354	59	206	49	73	96	9	7	0	26	5	3	2	4	40	0	27	25	6
Devoy, Charles, Houston†	.248	34	109	21	27	37	3	2	1	15	0	0	0	6	12	0	24	4	0
Diaz, Angel, Toronto	.255	17	51	5	13	18	3	1	0	2	0	0	0	1	2	0	7	2	1
Diaz, Jose, Toronto	.187	22	75	6	14	14	0	0	0	6	1	1	1	0	11	0	12	1	2
Diaz, Miguel, Pittsburgh	.276	37	87	18	24	27	3	0	0	5	0	2	0	0	7	0	12	8	2
Dicesare, Joseph, Texas	.258	35	132	17	34	44	6	2	0	18	2	0	1	2	6	0	15	2	1
Diehl, John, Los Angeles*	.195	44	113	20	22	33	8	0	1	13	1	5	2	1	24	1	26	6	1
Duncan, Alan, Pittsburgh*	.148	10	27	3	4	4	0	0	0	1	0	0	0	1	5	0	14	1	1
Dye, Mark, Houston	.220	38	118	17	26	33	7	0	0	7	0	5	1	0	14	0	20	9	3
Elbin, Bret, Texas†	.209	30	91	16	19	27	5	0	1	13	1	1	1	1	22	0	11	0	1
Escobar, Santiago, Toronto	.197	51	188	23	37	40	3	0	0	10	1	0	0	2	16	1	36	35	3
Fermin, Felix, Pittsburgh	.250	1	4	1	1	1	0	0	0	1	0	0	0	0	0	0	0	0	0
Fich, Miguel, Atlanta	.288	24	59	10	17	21	4	0	0	9	0	0	0	1	7	0	16	2	2
Fitzpatrick, David, Atlanta	.203	48	158	16	32	45	3	2	2	21	3	4	1	1	14	0	48	5	2
Frazier, Andre, Kansas City	.188	28	96	15	18	24	3	0	1	8	0	1	1	1	11	0	23	9	6
Fredymond, Juan, Atlanta	.198	38	96	15	19	23	0	2	0	7	1	4	0	1	13	0	25	0	2
Fulgencio, Jose, Toronto	.172	58	186	18	32	37	5	0	0	12	0	0	1	1	20	0	32	3	1
Gant, Ronnie, Atlanta	.233	56	193	32	45	54	2	2	1	14	2	0	1	0	41	2	34	4	6
Garcia, Carlos, Toronto	.242	57	194	17	47	56	6	0	1	16	2	3	0	0	18	0	38	6	11
Gillermo, Carlos, Toronto	.229	60	205	16	47	56	6	0	1	17	3	0	4	0	18	3	34	7	3
Gilmore, Kirk, Chicago-AL	.302	15	53	10	16	21	5	0	0	8	0	1	0	2	5	0	13	2	2
Green, Charles, Kansas City	.277	46	112	19	31	34	3	0	0	9	0	2	0	2	16	0	22	25	10
Guance, Johnny, Toronto†	.286	8	7	2	2	2	0	0	0	0	0	0	0	0	0	0	2	0	0
Guerrero, Jonas, Houston	.232	20	69	8	16	21	2	0	1	11	3	0	0	1	4	0	28	1	1
Gutierrez, Dimas, Pittsburgh	.251	49	191	27	48	87	9	3	8	33	8	1	5	2	12	1	25	0	2
Hall, D. Andrew, Pittsburgh	.287	40	129	16	37	43	4	1	0	15	2	0	2	0	10	0	30	3	3
Hendricks, Kenneth, Chicago-AL	.217	27	69	8	15	16	1	0	0	9	0	1	1	0	6	1	26	1	0
Hernandez, Efrain, Kansas City	.224	36	107	9	24	34	7	0	1	12	0	1	1	1	9	0	14	3	0
Hodge, Simon, Houston	.526	6	19	6	10	11	1	0	0	6	1	0	0	0	2	0	2	1	0
Houston, Michael, New York-NL	.216	47	102	8	22	25	3	0	0	7	1	2	2	1	11	0	26	5	4
Howard, Michael, New York-NL	.316	15	38	3	12	15	3	0	0	4	0	0	0	0	4	0	6	4	0
Huggins, Charles, New York-NL	.238	41	101	16	24	29	3	1	0	17	2	0	2	0	8	0	23	2	2
Hunsucker, Mikel, Chicago-AL	.207	51	174	21	36	46	4	0	2	24	1	2	2	0	20	1	31	3	3
Hupp, Mark, Texas	.185	23	65	6	12	15	1	1	0	6	0	0	2	0	10	0	8	1	0
Jabalera, Guadalupe, Houston	.176	49	170	32	30	35	3	1	0	7	0	1	1	6	20	0	24	6	4
Jackson, Todd, Texas	.303	27	89	11	27	31	4	0	0	15	2	0	1	0	4	0	17	7	3
Jarman, David, New York-NL	.151	30	53	2	8	11	0	0	1	7	0	0	2	1	9	1	18	2	1
Jimenez, Victor, Atlanta	.283	43	92	21	26	38	4	4	0	10	0	0	0	0	16	2	28	8	1
Jiminez, Francisco, Pittsburgh*	.231	10	26	6	6	6	0	0	0	2	0	0	0	0	7	1	8	0	1
Johnson, Everton, New York-NL	.225	44	89	15	20	25	3	1	0	5	0	0	1	0	12	1	28	1	0
Johnson, Richard, Chicago-AL	.168	52	161	21	27	30	3	0	0	12	2	3	4	1	23	0	41	12	2
Jones, J. Bradley, Texas	.333	25	78	11	26	31	5	0	0	8	1	0	2	0	6	0	8	0	1
Jones, Kevin, Chicago-AL*	.265	17	49	12	13	15	2	0	0	4	0	0	0	0	7	0	12	12	3
Kimball, D. Scott, Toronto	.000	15	10	0	0	0	0	0	0	0	0	0	0	0	1	0	4	0	0
King, Boris, Pittsburgh†	.208	32	96	10	20	21	1	0	0	11	0	0	0	0	20	0	30	9	4
King, Wayne, Texas*	.278	28	97	13	27	34	5	1	0	19	2	2	1	1	14	2	4	1	2
Kirby, Wayne, Los Angeles*	.292	60	216	43	63	72	7	1	0	13	1	4	1	1	34	0	19	23	8
Koch, Bryan, Chicago-AL*	.231	50	143	16	33	37	4	0	0	17	1	6	1	2	24	0	25	1	2

Player and Club	Pct.	G.	AB.	R.	H.	TB.	2B.	3B.	HR.	RBI.	GW.	SH.	SF.	HP.	BB.	Int. BB.	SO.	SB.	CS.
Krol, John, Houston	.211	18	38	3	8	8	0	0	0	1	0	3	0	0	2	0	7	1	0
Lacava, Tony, Pittsburgh	.302	43	149	22	45	61	6	2	2	28	1	0	1	0	21	2	24	3	1
Lawrence, R. Mark, Texas*	.221	22	68	9	15	25	3	2	1	11	2	0	1	2	12	1	15	0	0
Lawton, Marcus, New York-NL	.257	51	187	25	48	53	3	1	0	16	1	2	1	0	26	1	18	19	3
Ledezma, C. Julio, Atlanta	.203	25	69	6	14	20	3	0	1	11	1	0	0	1	8	0	12	0	1
Lee, Manuel, New York-NL*	.247	32	97	8	24	28	2	1	0	12	0	1	0	1	13	1	14	2	3
Lemke, Mark, Atlanta†	.263	53	209	37	55	61	6	0	0	19	5	3	2	0	30	0	19	10	4
Leverette, Michael, Atlanta	.000	2	4	1	0	0	0	0	0	0	0	0	0	0	3	0	1	0	0
Limon, Salvatore, New York-NL	.202	31	84	5	17	20	3	0	0	5	1	2	0	0	4	1	19	4	0
Lind, Jose, Pittsburgh	.301	45	163	26	49	60	3	4	0	18	0	4	0	2	13	0	18	12	1
Lora, Cesar, Atlanta	.263	60	217	30	57	88	5	4	6	39	4	4	3	2	32	2	39	15	3
Lora, Jesus, Houston	.232	32	95	11	22	26	4	0	0	6	1	1	0	1	7	0	20	8	2
Lovely, Frederick, Texas	.185	17	54	5	10	17	4	0	1	5	0	1	1	0	5	0	17	0	0
Lutz, John, Kansas City*	.202	39	99	9	20	25	3	1	0	10	1	1	1	1	14	2	31	3	1
Lyon, Bruce, New York-NL*	.065	21	46	3	3	3	0	0	0	1	0	0	0	0	5	0	12	0	0
Mabe, Todd, Kansas City†	.242	47	149	27	36	42	4	1	0	15	1	3	2	1	35	0	37	24	5
Marin, Julio, Los Angeles	.232	49	142	29	33	48	4	1	3	21	0	4	2	4	29	2	30	2	2
Mart, James, Texas	.171	27	82	7	14	14	0	0	0	8	0	0	0	0	6	0	14	0	0
Martin, Rodney, Houston	.298	38	141	29	42	62	9	1	3	18	0	1	0	1	21	0	25	3	2
Martinez, Jose, Houston	.273	14	33	2	9	12	1	1	0	4	0	1	0	2	6	0	10	0	3
Martinez, Juan, Toronto	.224	55	165	20	37	42	2	0	1	13	1	1	0	5	10	0	18	8	5
Mateo, Jose, Toronto	.204	59	186	19	38	47	4	1	1	24	2	2	0	1	35	1	51	5	2
Mejia, Manuel, Toronto	.192	55	177	17	34	43	7	1	0	14	1	1	2	5	10	0	39	4	7
Mejia, Simon, Chicago-AL†	.258	60	198	35	51	71	5	3	3	37	3	1	3	3	29	5	42	13	6
Mercedes, Luis, Atlanta	.254	46	130	15	33	40	3	2	0	14	1	1	1	1	21	1	35	6	2
Meyer, Urban, Atlanta	.120	9	25	5	3	3	0	0	0	2	0	2	1	0	8	0	6	1	1
Miller, John, Houston	.308	40	146	23	45	60	8	2	1	31	4	0	4	1	18	1	12	4	2
Miyar, Jorge, Los Angeles	.114	21	44	5	5	6	1	0	0	5	1	0	1	0	5	0	13	1	1
Morena, Russell, New York-NL*	.271	17	48	9	13	17	4	0	0	9	4	3	2	2	9	0	6	2	1
Mueller, Peter, Houston*	.376	60	210	52	79	102	12	4	1	44	1	0	1	1	40	5	33	3	2
Newsome, Louis, Atlanta*	.000	15	1	0	0	0	0	0	0	0	0	0	0	0	0	0	0	0	0
O'Brien, Christopher, Pittsburgh*	.259	27	81	12	21	39	7	1	3	11	2	0	0	1	25	4	21	1	0
Oquendo, Randall, Chicago-AL	.171	18	41	3	7	7	0	0	0	4	0	1	0	0	2	0	6	0	0
Pacheco, Jose, Pittsburgh*	.297	46	165	32	49	55	6	0	0	16	2	1	0	2	22	0	23	12	5
Perdomo, Cristobal, Kansas City	.156	11	32	3	5	6	1	0	0	2	0	0	2	0	4	0	6	1	0
Perez, Hector, New York-NL*	.235	55	162	19	38	52	8	3	0	12	4	0	1	4	25	2	31	6	5
Petersen, Geoff, Kansas City	.283	59	205	40	58	88	11	5	3	29	5	1	2	3	49	1	47	13	3
Picart, Juan, Los Angeles	.339	41	168	27	57	65	8	0	0	20	3	2	0	1	13	0	15	7	4
Price, David, Los Angeles†	.284	45	148	24	42	63	5	2	4	39	8	0	3	1	41	2	20	15	7
Quintero, Daniel, Kansas City	.232	40	125	6	29	32	3	0	0	14	3	2	0	0	13	0	25	2	2
Ramon, Ernesto, New York-NL	.143	35	77	8	11	16	3	1	0	6	0	1	1	0	13	0	20	0	1
Rector, Darryl, Chicago-AL*	.158	15	38	3	6	6	0	0	0	5	0	1	0	0	3	0	7	0	0
Reese, R. Kyle, Atlanta	.093	15	43	1	4	5	1	0	0	2	1	1	0	2	3	0	11	0	0
Ricketts, P. Erick, New York-NL	.205	46	146	18	30	39	9	0	0	16	2	0	3	1	12	1	31	3	2
Rivera, Luis, Los Angeles	.114	30	79	5	9	10	1	0	0	5	0	1	1	1	12	0	11	0	0
Roberts, James, Los Angeles†	.213	47	150	16	32	41	6	0	1	23	3	2	0	0	28	3	21	2	1
Robles, Jesus, Los Angeles	.042	10	24	0	1	1	0	0	0	0	0	0	0	0	3	0	12	0	0
Rodriguez, Aristides, Houston	.149	29	94	5	14	17	3	0	0	11	1	0	2	1	9	0	16	2	2
Roman, Cesar, Toronto	.198	56	192	18	38	51	10	0	1	20	1	0	2	3	14	1	38	1	1
Roque, Gustavo, Pittsburgh	.246	50	199	28	49	60	4	2	1	25	3	2	1	0	10	0	45	2	0
Russell, Ronald, Houston	.236	26	72	12	17	17	0	0	0	6	0	1	0	0	11	0	17	2	1
Samuel, Fernando, Toronto	.189	30	53	6	10	11	1	0	0	2	0	2	0	1	2	0	14	1	0
Sanchez, Cito, Toronto	.256	13	43	8	11	19	2	0	2	5	0	0	1	0	5	1	11	1	1
Sanchez, Eduardo, Toronto	.227	58	172	25	39	56	11	0	2	12	0	1	2	0	32	0	47	3	3
Sanchez, Zoilo, New York-NL	.238	57	164	21	39	48	5	2	0	24	1	1	1	3	20	0	38	5	2
Satzinger, Jeffrey, Pittsburgh	.000	9	3	0	0	0	0	0	0	0	0	0	0	0	1	0	3	0	0
Shaheed, Daraka, Houston*	.191	32	89	16	17	20	3	0	0	11	0	1	1	0	21	0	16	1	3
Sierra, Ruben, Texas	.242	48	182	26	44	60	7	3	1	26	3	0	4	1	16	1	38	3	4
Snyder, Doug, Houston*	.250	56	180	33	45	59	5	3	1	19	2	1	2	3	46	1	50	9	6
Soper, Michael, Chicago-AL	.276	53	199	22	55	66	11	0	0	26	5	3	5	7	16	1	28	2	2
Soriano, Hilario, Toronto	.222	3	9	0	2	2	0	0	0	0	0	0	0	0	1	1	0	0	0
Steele, Thad, Pittsburgh	.223	30	94	11	21	21	0	0	0	3	0	2	0	1	13	1	26	5	2
Sturdivant, Darren, Kansas City	.114	16	35	3	4	8	1	0	1	2	0	0	0	0	6	0	13	0	0
Taylor, Michael, Chicago-AL	.333	56	192	55	64	113	15	5	8	34	5	1	2	6	33	4	34	11	4
Thompson, James, Atlanta	.111	3	9	1	1	1	0	0	0	0	0	0	0	0	2	0	5	0	0
Threadgill, George, Texas	.264	49	163	30	43	55	6	3	0	11	0	1	0	1	30	0	31	7	7
Thurman, Gary, Kansas City	.256	59	203	32	52	64	8	2	0	19	3	6	2	0	34	0	58	31	8
Thurston, Curtis, Pittsburgh	.214	4	14	2	3	3	0	0	0	1	0	0	0	0	2	0	2	0	1
Trevathan, James, Chicago-AL*	.231	49	147	12	34	43	7	1	0	25	1	1	0	4	21	2	12	1	0
Vasquez, Alberto, Kansas City†	.167	16	12	6	2	3	1	0	0	0	0	0	0	0	3	0	5	1	0
Vasquez, R. Angelo, Texas*	.305	23	59	9	18	24	2	2	0	11	0	0	1	1	8	0	18	1	1
Velasquez, I. Javier, Los Angeles	.261	9	23	2	6	7	1	0	0	3	0	1	0	0	4	1	3	0	0
Vilella, Lazaro, Kansas City*	.079	23	38	4	3	5	0	1	0	2	0	1	0	0	7	0	8	1	0
Wainwright, John, Pittsburgh	.239	20	71	10	17	24	4	0	1	8	0	0	0	2	6	1	14	6	2
Walker, Scott, Pittsburgh*	.290	42	145	18	42	53	9	1	0	13	1	0	1	1	10	0	30	2	2
Whitehurst, Willis, Kansas City	.174	39	109	11	19	23	4	0	0	10	0	1	1	2	7	0	29	8	3
Williamson, Keith, Kansas City†	.252	37	127	31	32	36	2	1	0	12	0	0	0	1	33	4	19	34	7
Woods, Vincent, Chicago-AL	.263	41	152	28	40	52	3	3	1	9	0	1	1	0	28	1	26	27	10
Yoder, Frederick, Pittsburgh*	.500	1	4	1	2	2	0	0	0	0	0	0	0	0	0	0	0	0	0
Young, Gerald, New York-NL†	.237	56	177	34	42	56	7	2	1	14	0	1	2	3	35	1	29	11	5
Zelenka, John, Kansas City	.224	46	147	21	33	37	0	2	0	22	3	0	0	4	27	1	7	16	5

The following pitchers, listed alphabetically by club, with games in parentheses, had no plate appearances, primarily through use of designated hitters:

ATLANTA—Assenmacher, Paul (10); Bartlett, James (9); Castellano, Anthony (1); Coffman, Kevin (6); DelRosario, Maximo (12); Jimenez, Cesar (14); Jones, David (15); Jones, Keith (12); Layne, Richard (9); Parker, Darren (1); Perez, Otilio (17); Reeves, Jay (2); Roth, Michael (8); Tomsick, Troy (8); Winters, Joseph (7).

CHICAGO-AL—D'Agostino, Robert (16); Davis, Joel (12); Diaz, Maximiano (11); Gonzales, Gary (18); Hardy, John (4); Johnson, John (14); Kristan, Kevin (14); Ruckebeil, Mark (11); Stacey, Shawn (12); Walker, Kurt (28).

HOUSTON—Alburquerque, Claudio (9); Baez, Joaquin (9); Bailey, Kirk (10); Cerefin, Michael (12); Friedrich, Michael (3); Hale, Michael (9); Heredia, Geysi (11); Jimenez, Diogenes (2); Paradez, Juan (11); Polemir, Miguel (8); Retz, Robert (6); Richard, James Rodney (9); Santos, Rolando (5); Severino, Leandro (8); Sloan, Barry (4); Vargas, Jose (3); Verrone, Stephen (4); Vizcaino, Jorge (10); Welborn, Sammye (1); Wilmore, Orlando (2).

KANSAS CITY—Burke, Richard (12); Cuevas, Miguel (8); Devan, Edward (22); Hull, Jeffrey (13); Koller, David (14); McCormack, Ronald (8); Morales, Edwin (3); Perez, Valerio (11); Powers, Russell (15); Smith, Floyd (12); Tuck, Kevin (22); Velazquez, Jose (10); Yowler, John (10).

LOS ANGELES—Baird, Theodore (20); Cuba, Angel (20); Duffy, Thomas (13); Galvez, Balvino (13); Hernandez, Pedro (11); Kakabar, Thomas (11); Mena, Andres (14); Mesa, Narciso (10); Phillips, William (16); Powell, Dennis (11); Stehling, Brian (7); Veliz, Francisco (7).

NEW YORK-NL—Bautista, Jose (13); Belen, Rolando (12); Ciszkowski, Jeffrey (10); Dobie, Reginald (12); Elie, Andre (14); Faria, Kenneth (13); Gomez, Carlos (19); Page, Kelvin (14); Pimentel, Jose (20); Reed, Kenneth (1); Stiles, William (20); West, David (12).

PITTSBURGH—Adkins, Terry (6); Azcona, Manuel (6); Blaylock, Russell (21); Carlie, Aaron (11); Cepeda, Octavio (10); Clark, Dino (3); Colina, Edgar (1); Drummond, Timothy (14); Felt, James (6); Gordon, Kevin (1); Jones Frederick (8); Kiernan, Michael (16); Machiz, Engles (2); Mercedes, Guillermo (19); Morban, Domingo (8); Perez, Selcio (8); Simon, Kelly (1); Smiley, John (12); Welch, Jack (5).

TEXAS—Daniel, Stephen (14); Dersin, Eric (7); Dewechter, Pat (5); Harman, David (24); Harrington, John (11); Henry, Dwayne (3); Hester, Ricky (12); Hicks, Robert (7); Knapp, Richard (9); Linton, David (9); McLin, Larry (7); Novak, Mark (13); Patton, John (16); Rogers, Kenneth (15); Ubri, Ramon (11); Waldron, Jose (6).

TORONTO—Alexander, Arsenio (21); Bautista, Camilo (21); Burgos, Enrique (13); Castillo, Antonio (1); Diaz, Victor (18); Peraza, Oswald (3); Reyes, Pablo (23); Santana, Fernando (19); Tejada, Henry (16); Valenzuela, Victor (12).

GRAND SLAM HOME RUNS—Affenir, Bachmann, Miller, Taylor, 1 each.

AWARDED FIRST BASE ON CATCHER'S INTERFERENCE—Ciamaichelo 3 (Carmichael 2, Ledezma); Lawrence 3 (Borras 2, Travathan); R. Martin 2 (B. Jones, Cuevas); Alcantara (Kimball); G. Davis (J. Martinez); Devoy (Carmichael); K. Jones (Borras); S. Mejia (Borras); Z. Sanchez (Carrion); Woods (A. Rodriguez).

CLUB FIELDING

Club	Pct.	G.	PO.	A.	E.	DP.	PB.
Chicago-AL	.952	62	1569	672	114	38	17
Pittsburgh	.950	60	1534	688	118	45	20
Texas	.950	62	1625	723	124	46	10
Houston	.949	61	1540	708	120	48	19
Atlanta	.946	60	1569	672	127	46	11
Kansas City	.946	61	1575	705	129	56	18
Los Angeles	.944	60	1538	714	133	56	11
New York-NL	.936	59	1508	642	147	48	16
Toronto	.928	61	1554	661	172	58	6

Triple play—Los Angeles.

INDIVIDUAL FIELDING

*Throws lefthanded.

FIRST BASEMEN

Player and Club	Pct.	G.	PO.	A.	E.	DP.
BACHMANN, Atlanta*	.995	60	532	29	3	34
Barrios, Houston	1.000	4	14	2	0	1
Berry, Atlanta	1.000	1	1	0	0	0
Carden, Atlanta	1.000	4	2	1	0	0
Carr, Pittsburgh	.988	23	162	7	2	9
G. Davis, Texas	.990	19	184	14	2	11
A. Diaz, Toronto	.956	12	82	5	4	4
Fulgencio, Toronto	.903	16	98	4	11	9
Hunsucker, Chicago-AL	.984	51	452	25	8	26
Jarman, New York-NL	.973	26	102	6	3	9
B. King, Pittsburgh	.958	4	22	1	1	0
W. King, Texas*	.986	22	194	14	3	14
Koch, Chicago-AL	1.000	3	2	1	0	0
Krol, Houston	1.000	1	2	0	0	0
Lacava, Pittsburgh	1.000	3	16	2	0	1
Lawrence, Texas*	.977	22	203	12	5	12
Marin, Los Angeles	.987	21	151	4	2	13
Mercedes, Atlanta	.889	5	8	0	1	1
Morena, New York-NL	1.000	1	3	0	0	0
Mueller, Houston*	.987	60	559	27	8	37
Oquendo, Chicago-AL	1.000	4	23	2	0	1
H. Perez, New York-NL*	.963	55	409	29	17	29
Petersen, Kansas City	.974	16	141	9	4	15
Quintero, Kansas City	.981	38	287	24	6	20
Rector, Chicago-AL*	.929	1	11	2	1	1
Roberts, Los Angeles	.990	44	356	23	4	30
Robles, Los Angeles	1.000	7	38	7	0	5
Roman, Toronto	.973	14	132	11	4	18
Sanchez, Toronto	.962	30	216	11	9	17
Trevathan, Chicago-AL	.938	9	56	4	4	4
Vilella, Kansas City*	.978	23	123	9	3	12
Walker, Pittsburgh*	.969	40	351	19	12	26

SECOND BASEMEN

Player and Club	Pct.	G.	PO.	A.	E.	DP.
Andrade, Texas	.958	13	32	37	3	11
Balcomb, Los Angeles	.857	2	2	4	1	2
Browne, Texas	.939	47	92	123	14	20
Burrows, Pittsburgh	.969	5	14	17	1	1
Ciamaichelo, Los Angeles	.943	20	28	54	5	10
Devlin, Chicago-AL	.915	14	30	35	6	4
Devoy, Houston	.935	17	27	45	5	10
J. Diaz, Toronto	1.000	1	6	3	0	0
Mi. Diaz, Pittsburgh	.932	15	34	34	5	6
Elbin, Texas	.893	5	11	14	3	3
ESCOBAR, Toronto	.963	43	117	117	9	28
Fich, Atlanta	.500	2	1	0	1	0
Fredymond, Atlanta	.963	25	62	69	5	9
Green, Kansas City	.943	35	80	70	9	10
Huggins, New York-NL	.905	34	34	52	9	5
Jabalera, Houston	.961	39	60	113	7	15
R. Johnson, Chicago-AL	.929	51	87	137	17	17
Lee, New York-NL	.937	24	35	54	6	12
Lemke, Atlanta	.943	37	81	101	11	20
Limon, New York-NL	1.000	8	12	14	0	3
Lind, Pittsburgh	.959	40	97	115	9	18
Meyer, Atlanta	.875	1	5	2	1	0
Morena, New York-NL	.949	11	24	32	3	10
Picart, Los Angeles	.871	39	78	105	27	24
Roman, Toronto	.969	17	36	27	2	8
Roque, Pittsburgh	.933	4	6	8	1	1
Samuel, Toronto	.714	3	3	2	2	1
Shaheed, Houston	.968	13	33	28	2	10
Steele, Pittsburgh	1.000	1	2	0	0	0
Vasquez, Kansas City	.857	9	4	8	2	1
Zelenka, Kansas City	.978	28	63	73	3	18

THIRD BASEMEN

Player and Club	Pct.	G.	PO.	A.	E.	DP.
Ju. Baez, Los Angeles	.946	31	8	62	4	3
Berry, Atlanta	.730	12	9	18	10	1
Burrows, Pittsburgh	.923	6	8	16	2	3
Carden, Atlanta	.854	12	18	17	6	2
Chance, Pittsburgh	.667	2	0	2	1	0
Ciamaichelo, Los Angeles	.857	11	5	19	4	2
Conte, Kansas City	.917	14	14	19	3	1
Daddario, Atlanta	.919	33	21	81	9	3
Devlin, Chicago-AL	.903	36	19	74	10	1
Devoy, Houston	1.000	3	0	2	0	0
Mi. Diaz, Pittsburgh	.963	7	4	22	1	5
Dicesare, Texas	.882	32	16	66	11	2
Dye, Houston	1.000	1	0	1	0	0
Elbin, Texas	.946	23	14	39	3	2
Fulgencio, Toronto	.874	44	36	89	18	8
Garcia, Toronto	.800	5	4	4	2	0
Gilmore, Chicago-AL	.861	14	8	23	5	1
Guance, Toronto	1.000	1	0	1	0	0
GUTIERREZ, Pittsburgh	.897	44	39	83	14	4
Hendricks, Chicago-AL	.781	21	8	17	7	0
Hernandez, Kansas City	.919	28	36	43	7	7
Huggins, New York-NL	.750	1	2	1	1	1
Hunsucker, Chicago-AL	1.000	1	1	0	0	0
Krol, Houston	1.000	16	8	22	0	0
Lacava, Pittsburgh	.667	3	2	2	2	0
Lawton, New York-NL	.500	1	0	1	1	0
Limon, New York-NL	.875	17	17	18	5	2
J. Lora, Houston	.926	12	10	15	2	3
Lovely, Texas	.857	11	7	23	5	0
Lutz, Kansas City	.929	34	32	73	8	6
Marin, Los Angeles	.881	28	26	63	12	8
Mercedes, Atlanta	.667	1	1	1	1	0
Meyer, Atlanta	.929	6	0	13	1	0
Miller, Houston	.857	38	31	83	19	4
Morena, New York-NL	1.000	2	1	1	0	0
Roman, Toronto	.800	9	8	16	6	2
Samuel, Toronto	1.000	5	7	2	0	0
E. Sanchez, Toronto	.800	7	7	9	4	2
Z. Sanchez, New York-NL	.877	54	50	85	19	9
Shaheed, Houston	1.000	2	1	5	0	0

SHORTSTOPS

Player and Club	Pct.	G.	PO.	A.	E.	DP.
Antonio, Los Angeles	829	7	10	19	6	0
Beucher, Los Angeles	.877	41	73	106	25	22
Blair, Texas	.927	49	87	155	19	23
Ciamaichelo, Los Angeles	.904	19	34	51	9	11
Devlin, Chicago-AL	.959	11	15	32	2	9
Devoy, Houston	.949	15	20	36	3	5
J. Diaz, Toronto	.931	21	48	74	9	16
M. Diaz, Pittsburgh	.849	8	20	25	8	2
Escobar, Toronto	1.000	2	2	5	0	0
Fermin, Pittsburgh	1.000	1	1	4	0	0
Fich, Atlanta	.860	16	18	31	8	9
Fredymond, Atlanta	.929	5	3	10	1	0
Gant, Atlanta	.902	49	68	134	22	15
Garcia, Toronto	.815	32	48	75	28	9
Gutierrez, Pittsburgh	1.000	4	3	13	0	1
Jackson, Texas	.820	13	14	27	9	2

Triple play—Beucher.

Player and Club	Pct.	G.	PO.	A.	E.	DP.
Lawton, New York-NL	.898	50	75	127	23	19
Lee, New York-NL	.944	7	9	25	2	2
Lind, Pittsburgh	1.000	4	5	10	0	0
Lora, Houston	.906	18	27	50	8	9
Lovely, Texas	.667	1	1	3	2	2
Mabe, Kansas City	.893	34	51	99	18	18
Meyer, Atlanta	.875	2	3	4	1	1
ROQUE, Pittsburgh	.932	46	77	144	16	20
Russell, Houston	.856	21	33	56	15	13
Samuel, Toronto	.762	11	13	19	10	1
Sanchez, New York-NL	.500	1	1	0	1	0
Shaheed, Houston	.922	13	14	33	4	3
Soper, Chicago-AL	.927	53	65	150	17	19
Whitehurst, Kansas City	.867	31	42	82	19	13
Young, New York-NL	.706	4	7	5	5	2

OUTFIELDERS

Player and Club	Pct.	G.	PO.	A.	E.	DP.
Alcantara, Texas	.946	23	33	2	2	1
Aquino, Texas*	.961	55	68	6	3	1
Aruca, Houston*	.985	48	67	0	1	0
Barrios, Houston	.889	10	6	2	1	0
Blackwell, Chicago-AL	.937	41	59	0	4	0
Bolivar, Toronto	1.000	5	8	1	0	0
Brown, Pittsburgh	1.000	30	43	3	0	0
Cain, Los Angeles	.987	57	72	2	1	0
Campbell, Kansas City	.956	24	40	3	2	1
Carden, Atlanta	.947	21	33	3	2	0
Chance, Pittsburgh	.955	10	19	2	1	1
Chappell, New York-NL	.958	42	44	2	2	0
Clay, Texas	1.000	24	30	2	0	0
Clifton, New York-NL	.000	1	0	0	0	0
Colon, Chicago-AL*	1.000	13	11	0	0	0
Daniel, Los Angeles*	.889	6	8	0	1	0
Diehl, Los Angeles	.947	15	18	0	1	0
Duncan, Pittsburgh	.895	8	16	1	2	1
Dye, Houston	.933	36	40	2	3	0
Fich, Atlanta	1.000	2	2	0	0	0
Fitzpatrick, Atlanta	.964	48	102	5	4	2
Frazier, Kansas City	.947	26	33	3	2	1
Fredymond, Atlanta	1.000	5	2	0	0	0
Garcia, Toronto	.900	24	34	2	4	0
Guerrero, Houston	.962	19	24	1	1	0
Hodge, Houston	1.000	5	4	0	0	0
Houston, New York-NL	.962	40	49	2	2	0
C. Jimenez, Atlanta	.906	39	47	1	5	0
Jiminez, Pittsburgh*	1.000	8	10	0	0	0
Johnson, New York-NL	.900	36	32	4	4	0
K. Jones, Chicago-AL*	.947	15	17	1	1	0
B. King, Pittsburgh	.955	25	40	2	2	1
Kirby, Los Angeles	.990	60	89	9	1	2
C. Lora, Atlanta	.975	59	113	6	3	2

Player and Club	Pct.	G.	PO.	A.	E.	DP.
J. Lora, Houston	1.000	2	1	0	0	0
Martin, Houston	1.000	21	29	2	0	0
Ju. Martinez, Toronto	.924	38	60	1	5	0
Mateo, Toronto	.975	57	105	12	3	5
M. Mejia, Toronto	.887	45	84	2	11	0
S. Mejia, Chicago-AL	.946	56	75	12	5	3
Mercedes, Atlanta	.922	35	45	2	4	1
Miyar, Los Angeles	1.000	11	8	0	0	0
O'Brien, Pittsburgh	.973	23	31	5	1	1
Oquendo, Chicago-AL	1.000	1	1	0	0	0
Pacheco, Pittsburgh*	.979	45	88	7	2	3
Perdomo, Kansas City	.875	9	17	4	3	1
Petersen, Kansas City	.934	37	67	4	5	0
PRICE, Los Angeles	1.000	45	68	6	0	1
Ramon, New York-NL	.960	21	22	2	1	0
Rector, Chicago-AL*	.923	11	11	1	1	0
Ricketts, New York-NL	.942	42	42	7	3	2
Roque, Pittsburgh	1.000	1	1	0	0	0
C. Sanchez, Toronto	1.000	13	27	1	0	0
E. Sanchez, Toronto	.929	20	24	2	2	1
Sierra, Texas	.948	48	67	6	4	2
Snyder, Houston	.973	56	97	11	3	1
Steele, Pittsburgh	.955	27	39	3	2	0
Taylor, Chicago-AL	.976	33	38	2	1	0
Thompson, Atlanta	1.000	3	4	0	0	0
Threadgill, Texas	.940	46	75	3	5	0
Thurman, Kansas City	.979	58	127	13	3	3
Thurston, Pittsburgh	1.000	4	10	0	0	0
Vasquez, Texas*	1.000	9	8	2	0	0
Wainwright, Pittsburgh	1.000	17	36	0	0	0
Whitehurst, Kansas City	1.000	1	1	0	0	0
Williamson, Kansas City	.951	33	57	1	3	0
Woods, Chicago-AL	.963	39	77	2	3	0
Young, New York-NL	.977	48	81	4	2	2

CATCHERS

Player and Club	Pct.	G.	PO.	A.	E.	DP.	PB.
Acevedo, Los Angeles	.952	12	33	7	2	1	0
Afenir, Houston	.976	17	101	19	3	2	4
Blair, Texas	.500	1	0	1	1	0	0
Borras, Pittsburgh	.895	20	78	7	10	1	3
Brooks, New York-NL	.975	28	107	10	3	2	6
Burrows, Pittsburgh	1.000	1	2	0	0	0	0
Butters, Pittsburgh	.963	13	70	9	3	1	4
Carmichael, New York-NL	.946	39	215	32	14	1	7
Carrion, Houston	.950	14	87	8	5	0	1
Constanzo, Atlanta	.965	15	50	5	2	0	1
Conte, Kansas City	.972	26	114	23	4	0	5
Cruz, Los Angeles	.989	31	155	19	2	2	3
Cuevas, Atlanta	.956	22	115	16	6	1	7
R. Davis, Kansas City	.966	35	155	45	7	5	12
A. Diaz, Toronto	1.000	2	4	1	0	0	0
Mi. Diaz, Pittsburgh	.667	1	1	1	1	0	0
Gillermo, Toronto	.958	57	295	66	16	4	6
Hall, Pittsburgh	.979	37	159	27	4	1	13

Player and Club	Pct.	G.	PO.	A.	E.	DP.	PB.
Howard, New York-NL	.976	14	67	13	2	1	1
Hupp, Texas	.987	23	130	23	2	2	2
C. Jimenez, Atlanta	1.000	1	3	0	0	0	0
B. Jones, Texas	.973	23	166	15	5	1	4
Kimball, Toronto	.933	4	10	4	1	1	0
KOCH, Chicago-AL	.995	50	342	39	2	5	10
Ledezma, Atlanta	.969	24	107	20	4	0	2
Lyon, New York-NL	1.000	7	36	8	0	0	2
Mart, Texas	.968	27	157	25	6	3	4
Jo. Martinez, Houston	.947	14	65	7	4	0	7
Oquendo, Chicago-AL	.979	13	42	4	1	0	5
Reese, Atlanta	.966	14	78	7	3	3	1
Rivera, Los Angeles	.972	29	174	37	6	1	7
Rodriguez, Houston	.965	24	161	34	7	1	7
Soriano, Toronto	.909	3	17	3	2	4	0
Sturdivant, Kansas City	.959	16	56	14	3	0	1
Trevathan, Chicago-AL	.988	15	76	7	1	0	2
Velasquez, Los Angeles	.944	9	61	7	4	2	1

PITCHERS

Player and Club	Pct.	G.	PO.	A.	E.	DP.
Adkins, Pittsburgh	.833	7	3	2	1	0
Alburquerque, Houston	.714	9	1	4	2	0
Alexander, Toronto	.857	21	1	5	1	0
Assenmacher, Atlanta*	1.000	10	3	5	0	0
Azcona, Pittsburgh	.000	6	0	0	1	0
Jo. Baez, Houston	.909	9	1	9	1	0
Bailey, Houston	1.000	10	2	5	0	0
Baird, Los Angeles	1.000	20	0	5	0	0
Bartlett, Atlanta	1.000	9	2	6	0	0
C. Bautista, Toronto	.933	21	3	11	1	0
J. Bautista, New York-NL	.885	13	5	18	3	2
Belen, New York-NL	.958	12	7	16	1	2

Player and Club	Pct.	G.	PO.	A.	E.	DP.
Blaylock, Pittsburgh	1.000	21	2	9	0	1
Brooks, New York-NL	1.000	16	1	2	0	0
Burgos, Toronto*	1.000	13	3	7	0	0
Burke, Kansas City*	.889	12	1	7	1	0
Carlie, Pittsburgh*	.882	11	0	15	2	0
Castillo, Toronto*	1.000	1	0	1	0	0
Cepeda, Pittsburgh	.750	10	2	4	2	0
Cerefin, Houston	.786	12	1	10	3	0
Ciszkowski, New York-NL	.917	9	4	7	1	0
Clark, Pittsburgh	1.000	3	1	0	0	0
Coffman, Atlanta	1.000	6	4	6	0	0
Cuba, Los Angeles	1.000	20	2	7	0	0

PITCHERS—Continued

Player and Club	Pct.	G.	PO.	A.	E.	DP.
Cuevas, Kansas City	1.000	8	0	1	0	0
D'Agostino, Chicago-AL	.923	16	3	9	1	1
S. Daniel, Texas	.786	14	3	8	3	1
J. Davis, Chicago-AL	.929	12	4	9	1	0
DelRosario, Atlanta	.880	12	8	14	3	3
Dersin, Texas	1.000	7	0	2	0	0
Devan, Kansas City	.833	22	4	11	3	0
Dewechter, Texas	1.000	5	2	8	0	0
M. Diaz, Chicago-AL	.857	11	4	2	1	0
V. Diaz, Toronto*	.800	18	2	6	2	0
Dobie, New York-NL	.818	12	3	6	2	0
Drummond, Pittsburgh	.957	14	9	13	1	0
Duffy, Los Angeles	.905	13	7	12	2	1
Elie, New York-NL	.875	14	3	18	3	1
Faria, New York-NL	1.000	13	1	6	0	0
Felt, Pittsburgh	1.000	6	1	4	0	0
Friedrich, Houston	1.000	3	0	6	0	0
Galvez, Los Angeles	.962	13	11	14	1	1
Gomez, New York-NL	.800	19	2	10	3	2
Gonzales, Chicago-AL	1.000	18	2	11	0	0
Gordon, Pittsburgh	1.000	1	1	0	0	0
Hale, Houston*	1.000	9	2	2	0	0
Hardy, Chicago-AL	1.000	4	1	2	0	0
Harman, Texas	.913	24	5	16	2	0
Harrington, Texas	.923	11	4	8	1	1
Henry, Texas	1.000	3	1	0	0	0
Heredia, Houston	.824	11	3	11	3	0
Hernandez, Los Angeles	1.000	11	1	6	0	1
Hester, Texas	.938	12	3	12	1	0
Hicks, Texas	.833	7	0	5	1	1
Hull, Kansas City	.941	13	4	12	1	1
C. Jimenez, Atlanta	1.000	14	1	12	0	0
D. Jimenez, Houston	1.000	2	1	0	0	0
J. Johnson, Chicago-AL	.810	14	3	14	4	1
D. Jones, Atlanta	.938	14	4	11	1	0
F. Jones, Pittsburgh	1.000	8	0	3	0	0
K. Jones, Atlanta	.818	12	3	6	2	1
Kakabar, Los Angeles	.833	11	3	7	2	0
Kiernan, Pittsburgh	1.000	16	3	5	0	2
Kimball, Toronto	.800	11	0	4	1	0
Knapp, Texas	.875	9	2	5	1	0
Koller, Kansas City	.824	14	1	13	3	0
Kristan, Chicago-AL	.886	14	9	22	4	1
Layne, Atlanta	.600	9	2	1	2	0
Linton, Texas*	1.000	9	1	3	0	0
Machiz, Pittsburgh	1.000	2	0	1	0	1
McCormack, Kansas City	.875	8	5	2	1	0
McLin, Texas*	.833	7	1	4	1	1
Mena, Los Angeles	.857	14	3	3	1	0
Mercedes, Pittsburgh	.857	19	2	10	2	0
Mesa, Los Angeles	.750	10	0	6	2	0
Morales, Kansas City	1.000	3	1	4	0	0
Morban, Pittsburgh	.846	8	1	10	2	0
Newsome, Atlanta*	.857	15	2	4	1	1
Novak, Texas	.944	13	8	9	1	1
Page, New York-NL	.000	14	0	0	2	0
Paradez, Houston	1.000	11	1	5	0	1
Parker, Atlanta	.667	1	0	2	1	0
Patton, Texas	1.000	16	4	5	0	0
Peraza, Toronto	1.000	3	0	2	0	0
O. Perez, Atlanta	.909	17	2	8	1	0
S. Perez, Pittsburgh	1.000	8	0	2	0	0
V. Perez, Kansas City	1.000	11	1	4	0	1
Phillips, Los Angeles	.939	16	9	22	2	4
Pimentel, New York-NL	.867	20	2	11	2	0
Polemir, Houston	.846	8	3	8	2	0
Powell, Los Angeles*	.800	11	4	8	3	1
Powers, Kansas City	.833	15	4	6	2	0
Reed, New York-NL	1.000	1	0	2	0	0
Reeves, Atlanta	1.000	2	1	3	0	0
Retz, Houston*	1.000	6	1	4	0	0
Reyes, Toronto*	.893	23	2	23	3	1
Richard, Houston	.769	9	0	10	3	0
Rogers, Texas*	.895	15	0	17	2	0
Roth, Atlanta	1.000	8	1	6	0	0
Ruckebeil, Chicago-AL	.846	11	4	7	2	3
C. Sanchez, Toronto	1.000	2	0	1	0	1
SANTANA, Toronto	1.000	19	8	18	0	2
Santos, Houston	1.000	5	0	4	0	1
Satzinger, Pittsburgh	.750	8	1	2	1	0
Severino, Houston	1.000	8	0	3	0	0
Sloan, Houston	.714	4	0	5	2	0
Smiley, Pittsburgh*	.813	12	2	11	3	0
F. Smith, Kansas City	1.000	12	4	4	0	0
Stacey, Chicago-AL	.867	12	10	16	4	2
Stehling, Los Angeles	.714	7	2	3	2	0
Stiles, New York-NL	.750	20	1	2	1	0
Tejada, Toronto	.933	16	3	11	1	0
Tomsick, Atlanta	.889	8	2	6	1	0
Tuck, Kansas City	.875	22	3	4	1	2
Ubri, Texas*	.500	11	0	4	4	0
Valenzuela, Toronto	.800	12	1	3	1	0
Vargas, Houston	.750	3	0	3	1	0
Velazquez, Kansas City	.778	10	3	4	2	1
Veliz, Los Angeles*	.947	7	1	17	1	1
Verrone, Houston	.778	4	1	6	2	0
Vizcaino, Houston*	1.000	10	2	9	0	0
Waldron, Texas	1.000	6	2	5	0	0
Walker, Chicago-AL	.929	28	3	10	1	1
Welch, Pittsburgh	1.000	5	0	6	0	0
West, New York-NL*	.929	12	3	10	1	1
Winters, Atlanta*	.857	7	0	6	1	0
Yowler, Kansas City*	.947	10	4	14	1	1

The following players do not have any recorded accepted chances at the positions indicated and therefore are not listed in the fielding averages for those particular positions: Barrios, 3b, ss; Blair, of; Castellano, p; Chance, 1b; Clay, 1b, c; Clifton, of; Colina, p; Daddario, 2b; Devoy, of; Ma. Diaz, 1b; Mi. Diaz, 1b; Fich, 3b; Frazier, 1b; Fredymond, 1b; Fulgencio, p; Garcia, p; Green, 3b, c; Guance, 1b, of; Hendricks, p; E. Hernandez, of; Jackson, c; E. Johnson, c; B. Jones, of; D. Jones, c; Lacava, of; Mabe, c; Marin, ss; Miyar, 1b; Rodriguez, of; Russell, of; Samuel, 1b, p; E. Sanchez, 2b; Simon, p; Al. Vasquez, c; Welborn, p; Wilmore, p; Zelenka, of.

CLUB PITCHING

Club	ERA.	G.	CG.	ShO.	Sv.	IP.	H.	R.	ER.	HR.	HB.	BB.	Int. BB.	SO.	WP.	Bk.
Los Angeles	2.48	60	8	8	8	512.2	438	229	141	6	18	266	19	425	54	6
Texas	2.92	62	3	9	17	541.2	446	246	176	4	19	244	1	441	35	7
Chicago-AL	3.18	62	15	5	10	523.0	492	268	185	8	17	220	4	446	29	5
Kansas City	3.29	61	7	3	8	525.0	461	281	192	13	25	278	5	311	53	9
Houston	3.44	61	16	1	4	513.1	464	263	196	5	23	260	2	408	64	5
Atlanta	3.49	60	5	3	9	523.0	478	294	203	12	20	273	16	345	57	9
Pittsburgh	3.49	60	3	3	9	511.1	451	270	198	18	17	271	13	297	38	8
New York-NL	4.19	59	4	1	8	502.2	470	321	234	22	28	349	14	399	52	10
Toronto	4.71	61	9	1	7	518.0	592	399	271	21	12	271	18	308	52	10

PITCHERS' RECORDS

(Leading Qualifiers for Earned-Run Average Leadership—50 or More Innings)

*Throws lefthanded.

Pitcher—Club	W.	L.	Pct.	ERA.	G.	GS.	CG.	GF.	ShO.	Sv.	IP.	H.	R.	ER.	HR.	HB.	BB.	Int. BB.	SO.	WP.
Hester, Texas	7	0	1.000	1.17	12	8	1	1	1	0	61.1	32	17	8	0	1	19	0	48	3
Drummond, Pittsburgh	7	2	.778	1.43	14	13	3	1	1	0	88.0	73	20	14	3	3	21	1	40	3
Powell, Los Angeles*	8	2	.800	1.46	11	11	3	0	2	0	74.0	52	22	12	0	2	23	0	103	8
Kristan, Chicago-AL	9	3	.750	1.71	14	12	6	1	1	1	89.1	72	28	17	1	2	13	0	69	0
Phillips, Los Angeles	5	4	.556	1.82	16	5	2	8	0	0	54.1	50	23	11	1	1	17	5	31	3
Burke, Kansas City*	6	1	.857	1.88	12	8	2	2	1	0	71.2	40	20	15	1	1	34	0	57	5
J. Davis, Chicago-AL	6	2	.750	1.91	12	12	3	0	1	0	75.1	51	23	16	1	2	26	0	95	2
Duffy, Los Angeles	5	2	.714	2.15	13	13	3	0	1	0	79.2	59	29	19	0	4	55	1	47	4
Yowler, Kansas City*	4	1	.800	2.18	10	7	2	0	0	0	57.2	51	20	14	3	1	16	0	37	2
Johnson, Chicago-AL	6	4	.600	2.23	14	13	5	0	0	0	80.2	80	34	20	0	1	23	0	62	4

Departmental Leaders: G—Walker, 28; W—Kristan, 9; L—Burgos, Tejada, 9; Pct.—Burke, .857; GS—Tejada, 15; CG—Kristan, 6; GF—Walker, 25; ShO—Powell, 2; Sv.—Harman, 9; IP—Santana, 102; H—Santana, 110; R—Santana, 65; ER—Smiley, 43; HR—Faria, Santana, Smiley, Tejada, 5; HB—Elie, 12; BB—Koller, 64; IBB—Alexander, DelRosario, Phillips, 5; SO—Powell, 103; WP—Faria, 14.

(All Pitchers—Listed Alphabetically)

Pitcher—Club	W.	L.	Pct.	ERA.	G.	GS.	CG.	GF.	ShO.	Sv.	IP.	H.	R.	ER.	HR.	HB.	BB.	Int. BB.	SO.	WP.
Adkins, Pittsburgh	2	0	1.000	2.57	6	3	0	1	0	0	21.0	21	11	6	0	0	9	1	17	1
Alburquerque, Houston	2	1	.667	1.93	9	0	0	8	0	2	14.0	10	6	3	0	1	7	1	13	3
Alexanderi, Toronto	0	3	.000	8.71	21	1	0	12	0	0	31.0	56	42	30	4	0	26	5	13	1
Assenmacher, Atlanta*	1	0	1.000	2.21	10	3	1	5	1	2	36.2	35	14	9	0	1	4	0	44	2
Azcona, Pittsburgh	0	0	.000	9.28	6	0	0	3	0	0	10.2	15	12	11	0	1	9	0	3	1
Jo. Baez, Houston	2	2	.500	6.08	9	7	1	1	0	0	40.0	54	31	27	2	1	16	0	28	6
Bailey, Houston	2	3	.400	2.63	10	2	1	7	0	0	27.1	24	10	8	0	1	19	0	24	4
Baird, Los Angeles	5	2	.714	1.91	20	0	0	17	0	5	28.1	13	7	6	0	0	20	3	35	4
Bartlett, Atlanta	0	0	.000	3.90	9	1	0	4	0	1	27.2	22	15	12	0	3	27	0	26	4
C. Bautista, Toronto	2	5	.286	4.01	21	6	0	7	0	3	67.1	73	44	30	1	0	14	3	44	7
J. Bautista, New York-NL	4	3	.571	2.31	13	13	2	0	0	0	81.2	66	31	21	2	0	32	1	44	5
Belen, New York-NL	4	1	.800	2.79	12	4	0	2	0	1	42.0	42	23	13	2	1	14	2	18	1
Blaylock, Pittsburgh	4	4	.500	1.34	21	0	0	18	0	4	33.2	25	13	5	0	1	15	2	11	6
S. Brooks, New York-NL	0	0	.000	5.33	16	0	0	7	0	2	25.1	26	21	15	1	2	20	1	20	1
Burgos, Toronto*	0	9	.000	4.78	13	8	1	1	0	0	49.0	52	37	26	1	2	32	2	19	4
Burke, Kansas City*	6	1	.857	1.88	12	8	2	2	1	0	71.2	40	20	15	1	1	34	0	57	5
Carlie, Pittsburgh*	4	2	.667	2.27	11	4	0	1	0	0	39.2	26	21	10	0	0	33	2	32	4
Castellano, Atlanta	0	0	.000	0.00	1	0	0	1	0	0	2.0	1	0	0	0	0	0	0	1	0
Castillo, Toronto*	0	0	.000	3.00	1	0	0	1	0	1	3.0	3	1	1	0	0	0	0	4	0
Cepeda, Pittsburgh	2	5	.286	4.59	10	9	0	0	0	0	49.0	45	27	25	4	1	25	0	17	4
Cerefin, Houston	3	6	.333	5.02	12	11	2	0	0	0	66.1	60	42	37	0	7	60	0	61	13
Ciszkowski, New York-NL	3	4	.429	2.37	9	6	0	2	0	0	38.0	29	17	10	2	1	18	1	23	5
Clark, Pittsburgh	0	0	.000	5.68	3	1	0	0	0	0	6.1	5	5	4	0	0	11	1	0	0
Coffman, Atlanta	2	4	.333	6.59	6	6	1	0	0	0	28.2	27	29	21	0	0	39	0	25	11
Colina, Pittsburgh	0	0	.000	4.50	1	0	0	0	0	0	2.0	0	1	1	0	0	1	0	2	0
Cuba, Los Angeles	4	3	.571	2.11	20	0	0	13	0	1	38.1	37	11	9	1	1	10	2	18	4
Cuevas, Kansas City	0	1	.000	3.86	8	0	0	5	0	0	14.0	17	9	6	1	0	6	1	10	2
D'Agostino, Chicago-AL	0	5	.000	8.37	16	6	0	2	0	0	33.1	42	42	31	1	2	39	0	29	3
S. Daniel, Texas	1	3	.250	3.83	14	4	0	6	0	0	40.0	43	27	17	0	2	20	0	23	3
J. Davis, Chicago-AL	6	2	.750	1.91	12	12	3	0	1	0	75.1	51	23	16	1	2	26	0	95	2
DelRosario, Atlanta	5	3	.625	3.16	12	12	3	0	0	0	77.0	70	36	27	2	2	29	5	36	7
Dersin, Texas	1	2	.333	2.75	7	4	0	0	0	0	19.2	19	9	6	0	0	7	0	21	0
Devan, Kansas City	4	2	.667	2.66	22	1	0	13	0	1	50.2	51	23	15	0	2	12	1	22	0
Dewechter, Texas	3	1	.750	2.13	5	2	0	3	0	1	25.1	26	6	6	0	1	3	0	21	0
M. Diaz, Chicago-AL	1	0	1.000	7.43	11	0	0	8	0	0	23.0	24	23	19	1	2	22	1	17	5
V. Diaz, Toronto*	3	4	.429	5.63	18	6	0	5	0	0	48.0	57	34	30	1	1	39	1	34	3
Dobie, New York-NL	0	4	.000	3.27	12	6	2	2	0	1	44.0	47	21	16	2	0	31	1	44	3
Drummond, Pittsburgh	7	2	.778	1.43	14	13	3	1	1	0	88.0	73	20	14	3	3	21	1	40	3
Duffy, Los Angeles	5	2	.714	2.15	13	13	3	0	1	0	79.2	59	29	19	0	4	55	1	47	4
Elie, New York-NL	0	8	.000	5.96	14	8	0	1	0	0	45.1	50	45	30	1	12	39	0	38	4
Faria, New York-NL	5	7	.417	7.52	13	11	0	1	0	0	46.2	52	45	39	5	4	44	0	29	14
Felt, Pittsburgh	0	1	.000	3.48	6	4	0	1	0	0	20.2	9	10	8	0	0	18	0	17	3
Friedrich, Houston	3	0	1.000	1.71	3	3	2	0	0	0	21.0	11	4	4	0	0	3	0	20	1
Fulgencio, Toronto	0	0	.000	0.00	1	0	0	1	0	0	0.2	0	0	0	0	0	0	0	0	0
Galvez, Los Angeles	4	3	.571	2.98	13	9	0	2	0	1	66.1	62	33	22	2	1	19	2	51	4
Garcia, Toronto	0	0	.000	13.50	1	0	0	0	0	0	1.1	2	2	2	0	0	2	0	0	0
Gomez, New York-NL	2	0	1.000	5.45	19	0	0	9	0	0	33.0	40	23	20	4	2	16	0	16	1
Gonzales, Chicago-AL	1	0	1.000	3.64	18	2	0	4	0	1	47.0	47	28	19	2	0	36	1	27	6
Gordon, Pittsburgh	0	0	.000	0.00	1	0	0	0	0	0	4.0	1	0	0	0	0	2	0	3	0
Hale, Houston*	0	2	.000	5.06	9	0	0	6	0	0	10.2	13	7	6	0	0	3	0	13	2
Hardy, Chicago-AL	1	1	.500	1.83	4	3	1	1	0	1	19.2	19	7	4	0	0	2	0	10	0
Harman, Texas	5	4	.556	2.77	24	0	0	22	0	9	52.0	49	20	16	0	1	9	0	33	1
Harrington, Texas	5	1	.833	2.62	11	11	1	0	1	0	55.0	30	18	16	0	3	30	0	63	0
Hendricks, Chicago-AL	0	0	.000	0.00	1	0	0	1	0	0	0.1	1	0	0	0	1	1	0	0	0
Henry, Texas	0	0	.000	4.00	3	2	0	0	0	0	9.0	10	6	4	0	1	1	0	11	0
Heredia, Houston	4	4	.500	2.56	11	8	3	1	1	0	59.2	44	24	17	0	2	20	0	45	3
Hernandez, Los Angeles	1	0	1.000	1.90	11	0	0	4	0	1	23.2	27	11	5	1	1	10	0	15	2
Hester, Texas	7	0	1.000	1.17	12	8	1	1	1	0	61.1	32	17	8	0	1	19	0	48	3
Hicks, Texas	1	2	.333	7.36	7	2	0	1	0	0	22.0	26	19	18	1	2	17	0	14	2
Hull, Kansas City	2	4	.333	3.14	13	12	1	1	0	0	66.0	59	40	23	2	6	30	0	32	13
C. Jimenez, Atlanta	3	4	.429	3.18	14	10	0	3	0	0	56.2	50	33	20	0	0	16	2	32	2
D. Jimenez, Houston	0	0	.000	0.00	2	0	0	0	0	0	2.0	1	0	0	0	0	2	0	1	0
J. Johnson, Chicago-AL	6	4	.600	2.23	14	13	5	0	0	0	80.2	80	34	20	0	1	23	0	62	4
D. Jones, Atlanta	6	3	.667	2.34	14	9	0	2	0	0	69.1	61	30	18	2	3	32	4	36	1
F. Jones, Pittsburgh	0	0	.000	1.10	8	0	0	3	0	0	16.1	12	5	2	1	1	6	0	6	0
K. Jones, Atlanta	2	2	.500	3.42	12	0	0	8	0	2	26.1	25	13	10	0	2	16	1	21	2
Kakabar, Los Angeles	1	3	.250	4.37	11	9	0	0	0	0	47.1	51	36	23	0	4	31	3	44	4
Kiernan, Pittsburgh	3	4	.429	2.59	16	0	0	15	0	2	31.1	28	11	9	1	2	11	2	26	2
Kimball, Toronto	0	0	.000	9.17	11	0	0	7	0	0	17.2	18	24	18	1	2	31	1	14	9
Knapp, Texas	3	1	.750	1.29	9	8	0	0	0	0	42.0	31	12	6	0	0	6	0	36	3
Koller, Kansas City	0	7	.000	6.92	14	14	1	0	0	0	53.1	47	54	41	2	3	64	0	46	5
Kristan, Chicago-AL	9	3	.750	1.71	14	12	6	1	1	1	89.1	72	28	17	1	2	13	0	69	0
Layne, Atlanta	2	2	.500	5.63	9	0	0	6	0	1	24.0	25	20	15	2	0	20	2	19	4
Linton, Texas*	0	2	.000	6.75	9	4	1	3	0	0	21.1	19	16	16	0	0	28	0	20	4
Machiz, Pittsburgh	0	1	.000	4.05	2	2	0	0	0	0	6.2	6	3	3	1	0	2	0	4	0
McCormack, Kansas City	1	4	.200	6.93	8	6	0	1	0	0	24.2	35	25	19	0	0	11	0	16	3
McLin, Texas	2	2	.500	4.19	7	3	0	1	0	1	19.1	16	11	9	0	1	22	0	16	1
Mena, Los Angeles	1	1	.500	2.10	14	1	0	4	0	0	25.2	25	7	6	0	0	15	3	20	2
Mercedes, Pittsburgh	0	3	.000	4.32	19	0	0	10	0	2	33.1	39	29	16	3	2	15	2	16	1
Mesa, Los Angeles	0	0	.000	3.60	10	0	0	3	0	0	20.0	20	14	8	0	2	14	0	14	3
Morales, Kansas City	2	0	1.000	0.87	3	1	0	1	0	0	10.1	11	2	1	0	1	3	0	3	0
Morban, Pittsburgh	0	2	.000	5.34	8	4	0	0	0	0	30.1	27	25	18	0	3	26	1	19	2
Newsome, Atlanta*	2	1	.667	3.51	15	0	0	9	0	0	25.2	21	19	10	0	3	22	1	12	5
Novak, Texas	5	2	.714	3.72	13	6	0	2	0	1	46.0	43	26	19	2	2	20	0	28	2
Page, New York-NL	1	0	1.000	8.85	14	0	0	3	0	0	20.1	14	25	20	0	2	32	1	32	2
Paradez, Houston	0	0	.000	4.63	11	0	0	5	0	1	23.1	23	12	12	2	1	7	0	10	1
Parker, Atlanta	0	0	.000	3.38	1	0	0	0	0	0	2.2	0	1	1	0	0	3	0	2	1
Patton, Texas	2	1	.667	2.08	16	0	0	9	0	1	34.2	24	17	8	1	0	10	0	37	2
Peraza, Toronto	0	1	.000	5.93	3	3	0	0	0	0	13.2	16	16	9	1	2	11	0	11	2
O. Perez, Atlanta	3	4	.429	3.75	17	2	0	11	0	3	48.0	53	23	20	2	2	15	0	28	5
S. Perez, Pittsburgh	0	0	.000	3.68	8	0	0	3	0	1	14.2	13	7	6	0	0	7	0	5	1

Pitcher—Club	W.	L.	Pct.	ERA.	G.	GS.	CG.	GF.	ShO.	Sv.	IP.	H.	R.	ER.	HR.	HB.	BB.	Int. BB.	SO.	WP.
V. Perez, Kansas City	4	1	.800	3.20	11	0	0	7	0	2	19.2	18	9	7	0	2	8	2	6	4
Phillips, Los Angeles	5	4	.556	1.82	16	5	2	8	0	0	54.1	50	23	11	1	1	17	5	31	3
Pimentel, New York-NL	1	3	.250	4.98	20	0	0	13	0	0	34.1	37	27	19	1	2	25	3	28	2
Polemir, Houston	4	4	.500	3.12	8	8	2	0	0	0	52.0	49	26	18	0	3	23	0	41	2
Powell, Los Angeles*	8	2	.800	1.46	11	11	3	0	2	0	74.0	52	22	12	0	2	23	0	103	8
Powers, Kansas City	2	4	.333	2.32	15	7	0	1	0	0	50.1	54	23	13	2	0	21	0	18	4
Reed, New York-NL	0	0	.000	1.50	1	1	0	0	0	0	6.0	6	1	1	0	0	3	1	7	0
Reeves, Atlanta	0	1	.000	2.00	2	2	0	0	0	0	9.0	10	7	2	1	0	2	0	7	0
Retz, Houston*	1	0	1.000	3.07	6	0	0	4	0	0	14.2	9	6	5	0	1	11	0	7	2
Reyes, Toronto*	4	7	.364	4.15	23	10	2	3	0	2	84.2	105	55	39	1	0	27	0	42	5
Richard, Houston	2	3	.400	3.18	9	9	1	0	0	0	51.0	44	23	18	0	1	31	0	46	8
Rogers, Texas	4	1	.800	2.36	15	6	0	2	0	1	53.1	40	21	14	0	4	20	0	36	7
Roth, Atlanta	4	0	1.000	1.97	8	4	0	3	0	0	32.0	21	10	7	1	0	9	1	26	4
Ruckebeil, Chicago-AL	1	2	.333	3.31	11	3	0	5	0	1	32.2	40	22	12	1	2	15	0	24	4
Samuel, Toronto	0	0	.000	9.00	1	0	0	1	0	0	2.0	3	2	2	1	0	1	0	0	0
C. Sanchez, Toronto	0	0	.000	12.60	2	0	0	0	0	0	5.0	10	11	7	0	1	7	1	6	1
Santana, Toronto	3	8	.273	3.35	19	12	5	5	1	1	102.0	110	65	38	5	2	21	4	60	6
Santos, Houston	0	0	.000	4.32	5	0	0	3	0	0	8.1	11	6	4	0	0	2	0	4	2
Satzinger, Pittsburgh	1	2	.333	5.03	8	7	0	0	0	0	19.2	19	16	11	0	1	23	0	23	1
Severino, Houston	2	1	.667	1.88	8	0	0	4	0	0	24.0	18	8	5	0	1	9	1	18	1
Simon, Pittsburgh	0	1	.000	3.60	1	1	0	0	0	0	5.0	6	3	2	0	0	2	0	3	0
Sloan, Houston	0	1	.000	2.25	4	0	0	3	0	1	8.0	10	5	2	0	1	1	0	6	0
Smiley, Pittsburgh*	3	4	.429	5.92	12	12	0	0	0	0	65.1	69	45	43	5	1	27	0	42	7
F. Smith, Kansas City	2	1	.667	4.64	12	3	1	4	0	1	33.0	31	19	17	2	1	26	0	23	7
Stacey, Chicago-AL	6	2	.750	3.86	12	11	0	0	0	0	72.1	73	39	31	0	4	29	0	56	4
Stehling, Los Angeles	1	2	.333	4.84	7	5	0	1	0	0	22.1	18	20	12	0	1	26	0	19	9
Stiles, New York-NL	2	1	.667	3.62	20	0	0	13	0	4	32.1	20	14	13	1	1	23	2	44	4
Tejada, Toronto	3	9	.250	3.40	16	15	1	1	0	0	76.2	65	45	29	5	2	42	0	54	11
Tomsick, Atlanta	1	2	.333	4.13	8	5	0	2	0	0	32.2	35	20	15	2	3	13	0	19	7
Tuck, Kansas City	2	3	.400	1.81	22	0	0	15	0	4	49.2	30	19	10	0	5	30	1	31	4
Ubri, Texas*	0	0	.000	4.50	11	2	0	5	0	0	20.0	21	16	10	0	1	21	0	21	6
Valenzuela, Toronto	0	0	.000	5.63	12	0	0	8	0	0	16.0	22	21	10	0	0	18	1	7	3
Vargas, Houston	0	1	.000	0.00	3	1	1	1	0	0	13.2	10	2	0	0	0	1	0	6	1
Velazquez, Kansas City	1	2	.333	4.13	10	2	0	4	0	0	24.0	17	18	11	0	3	17	0	10	4
Veliz, Los Angeles*	2	1	.667	2.20	7	7	0	0	0	0	32.2	24	16	8	1	1	26	0	28	7
Verrone, Houston	2	1	.667	2.51	4	4	3	0	0	0	28.2	19	11	8	1	0	12	0	25	2
Vizcaino, Houston*	2	3	.400	4.00	10	8	0	0	0	0	45.0	49	34	20	0	1	27	0	37	10
Waldron, Texas	1	0	1.000	1.31	6	0	0	4	0	3	20.2	17	5	3	0	0	11	1	13	1
Walker, Chicago-AL	7	5	.583	2.92	28	0	0	25	0	6	49.1	43	22	16	1	1	14	2	57	1
Welborn, Houston	0	0	.000	5.40	1	0	0	0	0	0	1.2	3	5	1	0	1	3	0	1	2
Welch, Pittsburgh	2	1	.667	2.63	5	0	0	1	0	0	13.2	12	6	4	0	1	8	1	11	2
West, New York-NL*	2	4	.333	2.85	12	10	0	2	0	0	53.2	41	28	17	1	1	52	1	56	10
Wilmore, Houston	0	0	.000	4.50	2	0	0	2	0	0	2.0	2	1	1	0	1	3	0	2	1
Winters, Atlanta*	1	2	.333	5.84	7	6	0	1	0	0	24.2	22	24	16	0	1	26	0	11	2
Yowler, Kansas City*	4	1	.800	2.18	10	7	2	0	0	0	57.2	51	20	14	3	1	16	0	37	2

BALKS—DelRosario, Dobie, Koller, Mercedes, Tejada, 3 each; Burgos, V. Diaz, Duffy, Elie, Newsome, Pimentel, Smiley, Velazquez, 2 each; Alburquerque, Assenmacher, Azcona, C. Bautista, J. Bautista, Brooks, Carlie, Cepeda, Cuba, Daniel, J. Davis, Devan, Galvez, Gonzales, Harrington, Heredia, Hester, Hicks, Hull, C. Jimenez, Knapp, Linton, Mesa, Novak, O. Perez, V. Perez, Retz, Reyes, Richard, Ruckebeil, C. Sanchez, Stacey, Stehling, Tomsick, Vizcaino, Walker, West, Yowler, 1 each.

COMBINATION SHUTOUTS—Winters-Roth, C. Jimenez-O. Perez, Atlanta; Davis-Hardy, Davis-Walker, Ruckebeil-Walker, Chicago-AL; Powers-Morales-V. Perez, F. Smith-Tuck, Kansas City; Duffy-Cuba, Phillips-Baird, Galvez-Baird, Galvez-Mana, Veliz-Cuba, Los Angeles; West-Brooks-Stiles, New York-NL; Drummond-Mercedes-Blaylock, Satzinger-Mercedes, Pittsburgh; Hester-Harman 2, Dewechter-Daniel, Knapp-Novak-Patton, Harrington-Rogers, Hester-McLin, Novak-Dersin-Harman, Texas.

NO-HIT GAME—Burke, Kansas City, defeated Los Angeles, 13-0, August 24.

Pioneer League

SUMMER CLASS A CLASSIFICATION

CHAMPIONSHIP WINNERS IN PREVIOUS YEARS

1939—Twin Falls* .581
1940—Salt Lake City .608
Ogden (4th)* .492
1941—Boise .623
Ogden (2nd)* .598
1942—Pocatello† .690
Boise .683
1943-44-45—Did not operate.
1946—Twin Falls‡ .585
Salt Lake City† .585
1947—Salt Lake City .618
Twin Falls† .600
1948—Pocatello .611
Twin Falls (2nd)* .595
1949—Twin Falls .624
Pocatello (3rd)* .595
1950—Pocatello .635
Billings (3rd)* .571
1951—Salt Lake City .618
Great Falls (3rd)* .559
1952—Pocatello .595
Idaho Falls (2nd)* .573
1953—Ogden .679
Salt Lake C. (4th)* .527
1954—Salt Lake City .595
Great Falls (4th)* .530
1955—Boise .588
Magic Valley (4th)* .489
1956—Boise .561
1957—Salt Lake City .650
Billings† .582
1958—Great Falls .582
Boise† .615
1959—Boise .633
Billings (2nd)* .523
1960—Boise† .686
Idaho Falls .650
1961—Boise .638
Great Falls* .571
1962—Boise§ .565
Billings† .706
1963—Idaho Falls .702
Magic Valley† .643
1964—Treasure Valley .615
1965—Treasure Valley .530
1966—Ogden .591
1967—Ogden .621
1968—Ogden .609
1969—Ogden .620
1970—Idaho Falls .629
1971—Great Falls .643
1972—Billings .694
1973—Billings .629
1974—Idaho Falls .569
1975—Great Falls .577
1976—Great Falls .577
1977—Lethbridge .629
1978—Billings x .735
1979—Helena .623
Lethbridge y .559
1980—Lethbridge y .743
Billings .629
1981—Calgary .657
Butte y .557
1982—Medicine Hat y .629
Idaho Falls .600

*Won four-club playoff. †Won split-season playoff. ‡Ended first half in tie with Salt Lake City and won one-game playoff. §Ended first half in tie with Billings and Great Falls and won playoff. xBillings (first place) defeated Idaho Falls (second place) in First Place-Second Place playoff. yLeague divided in Northern and Southern divisions; won two-club playoff.

STANDING OF CLUBS AT CLOSE OF SEASON, AUGUST 31

NORTHERN DIVISION

Club	Cal.	Leth.	G.F.	M.H.	Bil.	But.	I.F.	Hel.	W.	L.	T.	Pct.	G.B.
Calgary (Expos)	....	5	5	7	6	4	8	7	42	28	1	.600	....
Lethbridge (Dodgers)	5	....	7	6	1	7	6	7	39	31	0	.557	3
Great Falls (Giants)	5	3	....	6	4	4	5	9	36	34	0	.514	6
Medicine Hat (Blue Jays)	3	4	4	....	4	5	4	9	33	34	1	.493	7½

SOUTHERN DIVISION

Club	Cal.	Leth.	G.F.	M.H.	Bil.	But.	I.F.	Hel.	W.	L.	T.	Pct.	G.B.
Billings (Reds)	4	9	6	6	....	7	5	6	43	27	0	.614	....
Butte (Royals)	6	3	6	5	3	....	9	9	41	29	0	.586	2
Idaho Falls (A's)	2	4	5	3	5	1	....	7	27	40	0	.403	14½
Helena (Phillies)	3	3	1	1	4	1	3	....	16	54	0	.229	27

Major league affiliations in parentheses.

Playoff—Billings defeated Calgary, three games to one, to win league championship.

Regular-Season Attendance—Billings, 88,534; Butte, 28,623; Calgary, 41,333; Great Falls, 57,684; Helena, 10,694; Idaho Falls, 21,261; Lethbridge, 24,051; Medicine Hat, 49,811. Playoffs—9,548.

Managers—Billings, Marc Bombard; Butte, Thomas Jones; Calgary, Talcott Creech; Great Falls, Terry Christman; Helena, Paul Carey; Idaho Falls, Keith Lieppman, James Nettles; Lethbridge, Gail Henley; Medicine Hat, Duane Larson.

All-Star Team—1B—Thomas Krupa, Calgary; 2B— Kenneth Harvey, Lethbridge; 3B—Mark Van Blaricom, Butte; SS—Jeffrey Hamilton, Lethbridge; OF—Scott Loseke, Billings; William Moore, Calgary; Otis Green, Medicine Hat; C—Michael Rupp, Calgary; P—Hubert Kemp, Billings; Jeffrey Montgomery, Billings; Joaquin Torres, Medicine Hat; Manager—Thomas Jones, Butte.

(Compiled by William J. Weiss, League Statistician, San Mateo, Calif.)

CLUB BATTING

Club	Pct.	G.	AB.	R.	OR.	H.	TB.	2B.	3B.	HR.	RBI.	GW.	SH.	SF.	HP.	BB.	Int. BB.	SO.	SB.	CS.	LOB.
Butte	.294	70	2371	503	383	696	984	112	28	40	404	31	24	19	23	333	15	485	111	18	533
Calgary	.289	71	2370	457	438	684	1032	127	19	61	398	39	20	25	19	337	21	428	68	25	555
Lethbridge	.285	70	2407	451	366	686	996	125	10	55	403	37	15	21	22	332	22	475	58	23	585
Great Falls	.274	70	2299	366	376	631	894	106	23	37	297	29	24	26	22	283	20	500	91	34	526
Billings	.274	70	2400	418	350	658	905	108	11	39	360	37	21	30	19	328	18	474	38	13	576
Medicine Hat	.259	68	2258	385	423	584	856	67	14	59	337	31	19	15	35	341	16	598	62	14	544
Idaho Falls	.253	67	2242	361	395	568	818	87	17	43	303	25	17	21	19	309	15	594	64	26	506
Helena	.233	70	2357	336	546	550	799	84	18	43	279	14	6	15	19	277	8	646	97	34	499

INDIVIDUAL BATTING

(Leading Qualifiers for Batting Championship—189 or More Plate Appearances)

*Bats lefthanded. †Switch-hitter.

Player and Club	Pct.	G.	AB.	R.	H.	TB.	2B.	3B.	HR.	RBI.	GW.	SH.	SF.	HP.	BB.	Int. BB.	SO.	SB.	CS.
Davila, Victor, Butte†	.391	55	169	42	66	80	8	3	0	25	2	1	1	3	27	1	22	2	2
Moore, William, Calgary	.362	59	199	63	72	132	19	1	13	51	6	0	1	5	52	1	31	5	1
Henika, Ronald, Billings*	.350	70	266	56	93	142	16	0	11	55	6	2	4	4	40	4	17	3	0
Seitzer, Kevin, Butte	.345	68	238	60	82	104	14	1	2	45	3	4	2	3	46	0	36	11	6
Loseke, Scott, Billings*	.340	68	253	64	86	128	17	2	7	41	6	1	4	0	53	4	42	5	3
Lowe, Dion, Helena*	.340	50	194	31	66	88	13	3	1	23	0	1	1	2	28	0	39	16	9
Beringhele, Vincent, Lethbridge	.338	70	278	64	94	128	14	4	4	46	6	1	4	0	34	2	39	11	4
Hamilton, Jeffrey, Lethbridge	.335	68	281	48	94	130	23	2	3	61	2	1	2	2	21	0	47	3	0
Krupa, Thomas, Calgary*	.335	69	233	63	78	156	16	1	20	70	7	1	3	0	49	5	53	3	2
Schulz, Jeffrey, Butte*	.327	61	211	44	69	106	12	2	7	55	3	1	3	1	26	4	25	8	1

Departmental Leaders: G—Beringhele, Gerard, Henika, 70; AB—Hamilton, 281; R—Harvey, 70; H—Beringhele, Hamilton, 94; TB—Krupa, 156; 2B—Hamilton, 23; 3B—Rooker, 7; HR—Krupa, 20; RBI—Krupa, 70; GWRBI—Gerard, 8; SH—Lucas, 6; SF—McCue, 6; HP—Nasser, 8; BB—Loseke, 53; IBB—Chapman, 8; SO—Howard, 96; SB—M. Miller, 24; CS—Lowe, 9.

(All Players—Listed Alphabetically)

Player and Club	Pct.	G.	AB.	R.	H.	TB.	2B.	3B.	HR.	RBI.	GW.	SH.	SF.	HP.	BB.	Int. BB.	SO.	SB.	CS.
Adkins, Todd, Helena	.158	22	63	5	10	10	0	0	0	4	0	1	0	0	5	0	12	2	5
Akers, Howard, Medicine Hat*	.238	62	206	46	49	70	10	1	3	20	2	1	0	7	28	1	63	15	1
Aldrete, Michael, Great Falls*	.417	38	132	30	55	82	11	2	4	31	6	0	3	1	31	3	22	7	2
Allen, Edward, Butte	.247	62	227	41	56	69	1	3	2	28	2	2	3	2	29	0	65	22	2
Allen, David, Great Falls	.321	58	224	44	72	112	15	5	5	33	2	1	2	2	16	0	44	5	8
Arp, Phillip, Great Falls	.326	25	95	11	31	42	6	1	1	11	0	1	0	0	6	0	16	1	0
Bagnall, James, Butte	.206	29	63	9	13	15	2	0	0	6	2	0	0	0	7	0	14	1	0
Belaguer, Roberto, Billings	.174	35	69	18	12	20	1	2	1	8	1	0	2	0	24	0	30	1	0
Bartlett, Charles, Lethbridge	.254	40	138	23	35	60	4	0	7	23	1	1	2	2	9	0	25	1	0
Batista, Juan, Calgary†	.216	18	37	4	8	9	1	0	0	2	0	0	0	0	4	0	9	0	0
Beringhele, Vincent, Lethbridge	.338	70	278	64	94	128	14	4	4	46	6	1	4	0	34	2	39	11	4
Boever, Daniel, Billings	.294	22	85	24	25	44	8	1	3	20	2	1	3	1	14	1	11	3	1
Borowski, Richard, Idaho Falls	.246	53	175	32	43	57	5	0	3	20	2	3	1	5	30	1	37	3	4
Brock, Eric, Lethbridge*	.354	45	144	27	51	66	7	1	2	26	5	2	1	1	19	0	13	1	2
Calvert, Mark, Billings	.273	14	11	3	3	3	0	0	0	2	0	0	0	0	0	0	5	0	0
Campbell, Curtis, Lethbridge	.185	14	27	7	5	6	1	0	0	6	0	0	0	0	5	0	12	2	1
Castain, Maurice, Idaho Falls	.268	46	138	20	37	45	3	1	1	18	0	3	1	1	14	1	23	7	0
Chapman, Christopher, Lethbridge	.281	67	235	42	66	122	17	0	13	57	7	1	4	3	52	8	35	3	0
Chumas, Steven, Idaho Falls*	.273	58	209	30	57	100	15	2	8	42	3	1	3	0	36	2	54	3	1
Claxton, Keith, Calgary	.229	49	175	29	40	58	10	1	2	20	3	4	0	2	16	2	30	12	3
Collins, Allan, Medicine Hat*	.000	16	1	0	0	0	0	0	0	0	0	0	0	0	0	0	1	0	0
Colpitt, Michael, Helena	.151	32	106	14	16	28	3	0	3	7	1	0	0	0	17	2	46	1	2
Correa, Manuel, Billings	.074	19	27	1	2	2	0	0	0	0	0	0	0	0	3	0	13	0	0
Cousinard, Prince, Helena	.188	25	80	14	15	20	0	1	1	5	1	0	0	1	3	0	23	8	2
Criswell, Timothy, Lethbridge	.333	20	9	2	3	4	1	0	0	0	0	0	0	0	0	0	3	0	0
Davila, Victor, Butte†	.391	55	169	42	66	80	8	3	0	25	2	1	1	3	27	1	22	2	2
de la Rosa, Marino, Helena	.237	30	97	13	23	30	0	2	1	13	1	0	0	0	9	0	30	4	1
DeLaune, Gregory, Helena*	.259	57	197	40	51	91	6	5	8	30	3	0	0	0	38	1	35	10	4
Denbo, Gary, Billings	.230	41	100	12	23	23	0	0	0	9	1	5	1	0	13	0	21	2	1
DeVall, Alan, Calgary†	.178	29	45	8	8	8	0	0	0	3	0	0	0	1	9	1	12	1	1
Devich, John, Butte*	.224	36	76	11	17	30	4	0	3	13	2	1	0	1	6	0	19	2	0
DeWillis, Jeffrey, Medicine Hat	.242	56	190	34	46	69	8	0	5	21	2	1	1	3	32	1	54	2	2
Dibble, Robert, Billings*	.000	5	1	0	0	0	0	0	0	0	0	0	0	0	1	0	1	0	0
Dotson, Kevin, Lethbridge	.229	41	140	27	32	46	6	1	2	9	0	0	1	2	29	1	28	0	1
Dull, Darrell, Idaho Falls	.200	32	95	10	19	29	5	1	1	13	2	0	0	1	9	0	37	3	0
Engram, Gralyn, Helena	.233	23	73	13	17	25	8	0	0	5	0	1	0	1	13	1	13	2	1
Ergle, Robert, Billings*	.000	13	7	0	0	0	0	0	0	1	0	0	0	0	4	0	4	0	0
Escobar, Angel, Great Falls†	.211	44	109	15	23	28	3	1	0	6	1	5	1	3	8	0	27	5	0
Estes, Dean, Helena	.182	30	88	17	16	24	6	1	0	6	0	1	1	0	10	0	34	3	0
Fabun, Brian, Great Falls	.077	4	13	0	1	1	0	0	0	0	0	0	0	0	2	0	2	0	0
Flores, Norberto, Lethbridge*	.268	56	205	40	55	67	12	0	0	31	4	1	0	0	43	4	50	5	3
Flores, Richard, Lethbridge†	.255	43	137	22	35	41	6	0	0	12	0	2	1	2	17	0	30	6	2
Garrett, Eric, Idaho Falls	.255	19	51	11	13	15	2	0	0	4	0	0	0	0	7	0	11	3	0
Gerard, Mark, Medicine Hat*	.275	68	247	36	68	121	9	1	14	63	8	1	4	4	42	5	54	0	0
Giddens, Ronnie, Billings	.290	65	221	33	64	80	10	0	2	39	1	1	4	2	27	0	44	4	2
Giddings, Wayne, Idaho Falls	.000	20	0	0	0	0	0	0	0	0	0	0	0	0	1	0	0	0	0
Gomez, Jose, Great Falls	.222	6	9	0	2	2	0	0	0	0	0	0	0	0	0	0	2	0	0
Gordon, William, Great Falls	.000	2	6	0	0	0	0	0	0	0	0	0	0	0	1	0	2	0	0
Graf, Steven, Calgary	.219	39	96	12	21	28	7	0	0	8	0	1	1	0	6	1	35	2	2
Green, Otis, Medicine Hat*	.315	59	241	44	76	118	8	2	10	37	4	0	1	1	19	4	40	10	1
Griffin, Danny, Helena	.128	16	39	3	5	9	1	0	1	7	0	0	1	1	6	0	22	2	0
Grimm, Peter, Billings	.250	13	8	2	2	2	0	0	0	2	0	0	0	1	1	0	3	0	0
Halberg, Eric, Great Falls	.271	40	118	19	32	43	6	1	1	13	3	1	0	1	11	0	20	0	1
Hamilton, Jeffrey, Lethbridge	.335	68	281	48	94	130	23	2	3	61	2	1	2	2	21	0	47	3	0
Hammond, Mark, Billings	1.000	10	1	0	1	1	0	0	0	0	0	0	0	0	0	0	0	0	0
Hansen, Darel, Idaho Falls	.200	16	5	2	1	1	0	0	0	1	0	0	0	0	3	0	1	0	0
Harris, Leonard, Billings*	.281	56	224	37	63	76	8	1	1	26	5	4	1	1	13	0	35	7	1
Harris, Twayne, Idaho Falls	.183	39	126	17	23	25	2	0	0	7	0	1	0	0	14	0	36	1	2
Harvey, Kenneth, Lethbridge	.274	66	263	70	72	104	10	2	6	36	2	4	1	6	45	2	41	16	5
Hayes, Charles, Great Falls	.261	34	111	9	29	37	4	2	0	9	0	0	0	1	7	1	26	1	2
Held, Matthew, Idaho Falls	.265	54	200	24	53	70	8	0	3	27	2	1	3	0	12	1	33	4	1
Henika, Ronald, Billings*	.350	70	266	56	93	142	16	0	11	55	6	2	4	4	40	4	17	3	0
Hill, Glenallen, Medicine Hat	.256	46	133	26	34	63	3	4	6	27	0	2	0	1	17	0	49	4	4
Hill, Timothy, Lethbridge	.244	67	270	29	66	99	12	0	7	43	4	0	2	1	10	1	70	1	2
Houp, Kenneth, Billings	.250	3	8	0	2	2	0	0	0	1	1	0	0	0	2	0	3	0	0
Howard, Steven, Idaho Falls	.222	61	203	40	45	75	4	4	6	33	1	0	4	4	37	1	96	9	1
Hudson, James, Medicine Hat	.289	48	149	30	43	68	5	1	6	27	3	1	0	2	18	0	47	5	1
Humphrey, Sylvester, Idaho Falls*	.261	50	161	21	42	60	6	3	2	19	1	0	3	1	11	2	43	3	2
Jones, Anthony, Great Falls	.272	57	184	33	50	69	8	1	3	19	1	4	2	7	27	0	41	11	6
Jordan, Paul, Helena	.296	60	247	32	73	97	7	1	5	33	3	0	1	0	12	0	35	3	0
Karmeris, Joseph, Lethbridge	.222	10	36	6	8	9	1	0	0	5	0	1	0	0	2	0	11	0	0
Katich, Blaze, Calgary	.231	14	26	5	6	6	0	0	0	5	0	0	1	0	8	0	9	2	0
Kemp, Hubert, Billings*	.400	14	10	3	4	4	0	0	0	0	0	1	0	0	3	0	4	0	0
Krupa, Thomas, Calgary*	.335	69	233	63	78	156	16	1	20	70	7	1	3	0	49	5	53	3	2
Kuziomko, Timothy, Medicine Hat	.229	47	96	10	22	23	1	0	0	8	0	0	1	2	18	0	23	0	0
Landrith, David, Butte	.282	43	131	19	37	47	7	0	1	21	1	3	2	1	6	0	23	0	0
Lane, Eric, Great Falls	.260	55	169	33	44	83	10	1	9	41	5	2	5	1	30	2	34	0	1
LaPierre, Michael, Calgary*	.053	12	19	3	1	1	0	0	0	1	0	0	0	0	3	0	9	0	0
Leonette, Mark, Idaho Falls	.000	14	3	0	0	0	0	0	0	0	0	1	0	0	0	0	2	0	0
Lewis, Kenneth, Helena	.181	36	116	12	21	29	1	2	1	10	0	0	1	1	10	0	35	8	2
Linkmeyer, Thomas, Medicine Hat	.204	47	108	16	22	32	2	1	2	17	2	1	0	4	25	2	57	7	0
Loard, Billy, Great Falls	.000	3	1	0	0	0	0	0	0	0	0	0	0	1	1	0	1	0	0
Long, Donald, Great Falls†	.284	65	225	38	64	102	15	1	7	40	4	0	0	2	38	6	63	6	1
Longenecker, Jere, Butte	.308	53	169	37	52	68	8	1	2	28	2	0	3	3	17	0	30	4	1
Lopes, Howard, Calgary	.316	68	247	55	78	127	13	3	10	44	7	1	3	0	34	1	34	6	4
Loseke, Scott, Billings*	.340	68	253	64	86	128	17	2	7	41	6	1	4	0	53	4	42	5	3
Lowe, Dion, Helena*	.340	50	194	31	66	88	13	3	1	23	0	1	1	2	28	0	39	16	9
Lucas, David, Calgary	.264	67	242	53	64	77	7	3	0	25	1	6	2	1	28	1	21	12	1
Lukes, Louis, Helena	.226	45	159	22	36	58	5	1	5	22	0	0	2	0	15	1	39	9	4

Player and Club	Pct.	G.	AB.	R.	H.	TB.	2B.	3B.	HR.	RBI.	GW.	SH.	SF.	HP.	BB.	Int. BB.	SO.	SB.	CS.
Lumpe, James, Calgary*	.283	58	180	25	51	70	6	2	3	26	3	3	2	1	32	5	22	2	4
Magrann, Thomas, Helena	.220	43	127	17	28	38	4	0	2	15	0	0	0	0	16	1	29	1	0
Mason, John, Medicine Hat	.174	13	23	4	4	4	0	0	0	1	0	0	1	0	4	0	7	2	0
Mattern, Michael, Billings	.200	47	105	18	21	28	2	1	1	12	1	2	1	1	13	0	26	2	1
McCue, Deron, Great Falls*	.216	55	176	32	38	53	6	3	1	17	1	1	6	0	24	1	55	15	2
Meert, Timothy, Helena	.192	26	78	9	15	16	1	0	0	7	1	0	0	1	14	0	26	0	0
Middleton, Scott, Billings	.333	15	3	0	1	1	0	0	0	0	0	1	0	0	0	0	0	0	0
Miller, Michael, Butte	.315	56	216	65	68	99	12	2	5	33	0	3	0	4	42	2	32	24	2
Miller, Stephen, Great Falls*	.313	45	131	14	41	46	2	0	1	13	1	3	0	0	13	3	29	3	1
Mitchell, Donald, Billings	.214	18	56	10	12	24	7	1	1	10	2	1	0	0	3	0	11	1	0
Mohr, Tom, Butte*	.217	35	60	11	13	19	1	1	1	13	0	0	0	0	13	1	24	0	0
Moncrief, Anthony, Idaho Falls	.323	53	186	35	60	90	12	3	4	41	4	2	4	0	21	0	36	10	3
Monson, Steven, Helena	.094	21	64	4	6	9	0	0	1	4	0	0	1	2	7	0	33	0	0
Montgomery, Jeffrey, Billings	.200	20	5	1	1	1	0	0	0	0	0	0	0	0	0	0	1	0	0
Moore, William, Calgary	.362	59	199	63	72	132	19	1	13	51	6	0	1	5	52	1	31	5	1
Moseley, Lester, Great Falls*	.250	10	16	4	4	4	0	0	0	0	0	0	0	0	2	0	1	4	1
Nasser, David, Medicine Hat	.254	57	177	45	45	50	3	1	0	18	2	8	1	8	39	2	27	9	1
Nelson, Robert, Idaho Falls*	.291	54	196	42	57	109	12	2	12	38	5	0	1	2	37	3	65	2	1
Newell, Thomas, Helena	.274	34	113	17	31	46	6	0	3	13	1	0	1	1	15	0	30	4	1
Niemann, Thomas, Butte	.205	25	44	5	9	9	0	0	0	3	0	1	0	0	5	0	6	0	0
Oliver, Joseph, Billings	.215	56	186	21	40	56	4	0	4	28	1	0	1	4	15	0	47	1	0
Oliveros, Romulo, Billings	.182	15	22	2	4	4	0	0	0	2	0	0	0	1	4	0	7	0	0
Oxner, Stanley, Butte	.141	35	64	20	9	12	1	1	0	2	1	2	0	0	13	0	13	6	0
Padilla, Juan, Billings	.364	8	11	2	4	5	1	0	0	2	0	0	0	0	4	1	5	0	0
Pagan, Felix, Idaho Falls*	.306	24	72	8	22	25	3	0	0	10	1	0	0	2	15	1	13	0	0
Polanco, Carlos, Helena	.222	11	27	5	6	8	0	1	0	4	0	0	0	0	4	0	9	1	0
Pascual, Camilo, Idaho Falls	.000	20	1	0	0	0	0	0	0	0	0	0	0	0	0	0	0	0	0
Pena, Jose, Great Falls	.235	30	81	7	19	19	0	0	0	8	1	0	1	0	3	0	27	2	0
Perez, Sergio, Helena	.222	25	90	10	20	22	2	0	0	9	1	1	1	0	5	0	13	4	1
Powell, Alonzo, Great Falls	.221	51	149	13	33	42	2	2	1	16	1	2	0	1	12	1	34	10	4
Pratt, Andrew, Lethbridge	.276	42	123	17	34	52	6	0	4	20	6	0	1	3	23	3	44	1	0
Price, David, Lethbridge*	.424	16	59	18	25	50	4	0	7	20	0	0	1	0	11	0	7	7	1
Ramirez, Danilo, Calgary	.000	8	11	1	0	0	0	0	0	0	0	0	0	0	3	0	5	0	0
Rantz, Michael, Idaho Falls	.186	33	86	16	16	17	1	0	0	7	0	5	0	0	19	1	17	6	2
Ray, Randy, Calgary	.198	29	81	11	16	28	2	2	2	12	2	2	2	0	14	1	21	5	0
Reilly, John, Calgary	.286	16	42	4	12	14	2	0	0	11	0	0	1	0	2	0	7	1	1
Riley, Darren, Billings*	.175	39	114	13	20	27	7	0	0	8	0	2	0	1	11	0	34	2	1
Ritter, Kenneth, Great Falls	.133	16	30	4	4	4	0	0	0	2	0	0	1	0	2	0	9	2	0
Rojas, Miguel, Idaho Falls	.163	28	92	12	15	22	1	0	2	5	0	0	0	0	4	1	34	1	1
Rooker, David, Butte	.292	57	212	37	62	95	10	7	3	41	4	2	1	1	18	3	48	10	1
Rossi, Domingo, Medicine Hat†	.282	46	131	18	37	40	1	1	0	8	0	1	0	1	10	0	41	6	2
Rubel, John, Butte*	.314	49	137	29	43	72	11	3	4	26	1	2	1	2	18	3	24	7	0
Rupp, Michael, Calgary	.326	56	190	38	62	90	15	2	3	39	2	2	4	3	36	1	20	1	2
Salmen, David, Billings†	.242	52	157	20	38	55	7	2	2	13	1	0	1	1	10	2	32	2	2
Samples, Van, Calgary	.299	43	127	17	38	56	5	2	3	17	1	0	1	2	6	0	41	5	1
Schulz, Jeffrey, Butte*	.327	61	211	44	69	106	12	2	7	55	3	1	3	1	26	4	25	8	1
Seitzer, Kevin, Butte	.345	68	238	60	82	104	14	1	2	45	3	4	2	3	46	0	36	11	6
Serrano, Luis, Billings†	.284	60	197	30	56	78	10	0	4	37	6	0	4	1	28	3	50	0	0
Smith, Daniel, Billings	.000	28	3	1	0	0	0	0	0	0	0	0	0	0	0	0	0	0	0
Smith, Henry, Helena	.255	66	220	36	56	86	15	0	5	32	1	1	1	5	39	2	84	14	2
Spring, James, Great Falls*	.296	46	159	27	47	67	11	0	3	18	2	0	4	1	19	2	14	9	1
Stanley, Kevin, Butte*	.242	42	132	21	32	39	4	0	1	14	1	0	3	0	20	1	49	2	0
Stark, Matthew, Medicine Hat	.282	60	206	29	58	88	6	0	8	49	4	0	4	0	31	0	33	0	1
Stillwell, Kurt, Billings†	.324	65	250	47	81	99	10	1	2	44	3	0	4	1	42	3	28	5	1
Tenacen, Francisco, Helena	.218	50	179	22	39	65	6	1	6	30	1	0	4	4	11	0	59	5	0
Thomas, Todd, Great Falls*	.281	43	128	30	36	51	6	3	1	15	1	2	1	0	22	0	13	9	2
Thompson, Jeffrey, Medicine Hat	.245	66	229	35	56	79	9	1	4	29	3	1	2	2	39	1	56	0	1
Torres, Joaquin, Medicine Hat	.263	28	38	5	10	13	1	1	0	3	0	2	0	0	10	0	5	2	0
Tostenson, Ronald, Calgary*	.298	61	228	39	68	89	14	2	1	33	4	0	3	2	21	0	28	9	2
Van Blaricom, Mark, Butte	.306	65	222	52	68	120	17	4	9	51	7	2	0	2	40	0	55	12	3
Wadley, Anthony, Idaho Falls	.000	13	5	0	0	0	0	0	0	0	0	0	0	0	0	0	1	0	0
Walker, Darcy, Calgary*	.352	46	162	25	57	79	10	0	4	29	2	0	1	2	11	2	26	2	1
Washington, Keith, Calgary	.133	14	30	2	4	4	0	0	0	2	1	0	0	0	3	0	15	0	0
Webb, Sherman, Great Falls†	.182	27	33	3	6	7	1	0	0	5	0	2	0	1	8	1	18	1	2
Wesley, Joseph, Idaho Falls*	.237	14	38	4	9	13	1	0	1	4	1	0	0	0	5	0	11	0	1
Whitfield, Kenneth, Medicine Hat	.169	35	83	7	14	18	1	0	1	9	1	0	0	0	9	0	41	0	0
Wilder, Michael, Idaho Falls	.280	54	200	37	56	65	7	1	0	14	3	0	1	3	34	1	44	9	7
Zapolski, Timothy, Lethbridge	.177	25	62	9	11	12	1	0	0	8	0	1	1	0	12	1	20	1	2

The following pitchers, listed alphabetically by club, with games in parentheses, had no plate appearances, primarily through use of designated hitters:

BILLINGS—Goedde, Michael (8); Kurant, Thomas (2); Petties, James (9).

BUTTE—Boatright, Dennis (15); Chelini, Daniel (20); Davis, Bradley (20); Digirolamo, David (18); Edens, Thomas (13); George, Phillip (14); Klein, Gary (29); Lipson, Stefan (20); Luman, Charles (9); Robinson, Randolph (15); Serritella, John (13); Snell, David (21); Torres, Jose (13); Vodvarka, Robert (9).

CALGARY—Andujar, Ramon (21); Bargo, Gregory (6); Collins, Allen (15); Dodd, John (13); Fisher, Michael (14); Hilton, Charles (11); Impagliazzo, Joseph (28); Litano, Christopher (11); Maldonado, Ovidio (3); Page, Gary (16); Pascho, David (13); Traen, Thomas (2); Valdez, Sergio (13); Young, Clifford (13).

GREAT FALLS—Burkett, John (13); Corbell, Charles (8); Dressler, Kenneth (9); Ferran, George (7); Gehrke, Steven (5); Henning, Richard (14); Kenney, Joey (2); King, Eric (20); Lee, Kurt (15); Smith, Stephen (13); Tavarez, Davis (14); Villa, Michael (16); Wood, Brian (20); Yokubaitis, Dan (23).

HELENA—Barton, Jeffrey (8); Cram, David (22); Dombek, Damon (9); Hisey, Glen (15); Householder, Brian (13); Jackson, Terrence (5); Lloyd, Raymond (8); Long, Bruce (12); Longman, Kenneth (12); McDevitt, Stephen (10); Norwood, Jeffrey (13); Shepard, Royce (7); Siblerud, Daniel (6); Strutz, Stanley (16); Valdez, Julio (6); Vargas, Miguel (16).

IDAHO FALLS—Bowens, Stevie (13); Chasteen, Stephen (11); de Chavez, Oscar (13); Hanna, David (10); Johnson, Perry (8); Law, Joseph (14); Mangum, Wade (12); Smith, Lawrence (15); Vantrease, Roberts (12).

LETHBRIDGE—Burns, Ronald (12); Cobbs, Todd (11); Gentle, Michael (14); Hamilton, Robert (13); Hamrick, Randy (16); Kolb, Michael (24); Lee, Derek (13); May, Scott (13); Meagher, Adrian (8); Rexrode, John (23); Rowen, Robert (18).

MEDICINE HAT—Bajus, Mark (8); Clemons, Mark (14); Dickman, Mark (14); Emerson, Robin (4); Ferlenda, Gregory (16); Holbrook, Robert (12); Mader, Perry (11); Miller, Duane (3); Murray, Dennis (13); Phillips, Timothy (5); Robbins, Ronnie (28); Ruetter, Derrick (11); Werner, Michael (8).

GRAND SLAM HOME RUNS—Chapman, Howard, Schulz, 2 each; Beringhele, Boever, Borowski, Chumas, DeWillis, Giddens, Harvey, Hudson, Long, Lumpe, M. Miller, Nelson, Pratt, Price, Thompson, 1 each.

AWARDED FIRST BASE ON CATCHER'S INTERFERENCE—Krupa 3 (Landrith, Lane, Stark); Loseke 2 (Stark 2); Jones (Meert); Pratt (Halberg); Rubel (Stark); H. Smith (Halberg).

CLUB FIELDING

Club	Pct.	G.	PO.	A.	E.	DP.	PB.
Lethbridge	.952	70	1783	753	128	66	30
Billings	.951	70	1822	649	126	43	22
Calgary	.950	71	1781	787	136	76	14
Idaho Falls	.947	67	1721	713	136	52	27
Butte	.947	70	1753	748	140	60	15
Medicine Hat	.945	68	1744	678	141	72	22
Great Falls	.944	70	1758	697	145	60	20
Helena	.924	70	1786	728	208	53	36

Triple play—Medicine Hat.

INDIVIDUAL FIELDING

*Throws lefthanded.

FIRST BASEMEN

Player and Club	Pct.	G.	PO.	A.	E.	DP.
Aldrete, Great Falls*	.985	31	247	16	4	20
Arp, Great Falls	.990	13	90	13	1	12
Bagnall, Butte	.994	26	148	7	1	19
Borowski, Idaho Falls	.962	12	96	5	4	6
Brock, Lethbridge	1.000	1	5	0	0	1
Chapman, Lethbridge	.979	67	566	36	13	61
DeLaune, Helena*	1.000	1	8	1	0	0
DeWillis, Medicine Hat	1.000	1	2	0	0	0
Gerard, Medicine Hat*	.980	68	547	30	12	66
Halberg, Great Falls	1.000	1	9	0	0	1
Held, Idaho Falls	1.000	1	8	0	0	0
Henika, Billings	.983	70	533	39	10	40
Jordan, Helena	.986	60	486	35	7	37
KRUPA, Calgary	.987	49	423	38	6	46
Lane, Great Falls	.900	1	9	0	1	0
Long, Great Falls	1.000	1	8	0	0	0
Longenecker, Butte	.987	22	148	9	2	11
Meert, Helena	.945	9	76	10	5	7
Moore, Calgary*	.979	8	42	4	1	5
Nelson, Idaho Falls*	.986	49	418	32	6	36
Oliver, Billings	1.000	2	1	1	0	0
Pagan, Idaho Falls*	.983	7	53	4	1	3
Powell, Great Falls	.939	17	97	11	7	14
Pratt, Lethbridge	.913	2	20	1	2	0
Reilly, Calgary	1.000	4	17	2	0	2
Rojas, Idaho Falls	1.000	2	11	1	0	1
Serrano, Billings	1.000	4	5	0	0	1
Stanley, Butte*	.981	41	289	18	6	25
Thomas, Great Falls	1.000	16	97	6	0	8
Walker, Calgary*	.993	15	125	9	1	15

SECOND BASEMEN

Player and Club	Pct.	G.	PO.	A.	E.	DP.
Brock, Lethbridge	1.000	5	7	14	0	1
Davila, Butte	.848	21	22	34	10	6
Denbo, Billings	.962	13	8	17	1	1
DeVall, Calgary	.900	12	7	11	2	1
Dull, Idaho Falls	.818	2	3	6	2	1
Engram, Helena	.962	23	51	77	5	14
Escobar, Great Falls	.861	16	15	16	5	2
Estes, Helena	.932	29	46	64	8	11
Giddens, Billings	.962	63	134	167	12	31
Gomez, Great Falls	1.000	6	2	6	0	1
Harris, Idaho Falls	.833	2	2	3	1	0
Harvey, Lethbridge	.957	66	156	198	16	49
Lewis, Helena	.853	25	33	60	16	8
Linkmeyer, Medicine Hat	.908	19	27	42	7	7
Longenecker, Butte	1.000	3	0	5	0	0
Lopes, Calgary	.954	67	145	205	17	57
MILLER, Butte	.969	55	112	169	9	40
Nasser, Medicine Hat	.951	54	114	139	13	40
Perez, Helena	1.000	3	5	5	0	1
Rantz, Idaho Falls	.966	16	27	29	2	5
Rojas, Idaho Falls	1.000	1	1	1	0	0
Rossi, Medicine Hat	.889	6	9	7	2	1
Spring, Great Falls	.938	45	75	123	13	25
Thomas, Great Falls	.950	9	15	23	2	7
Webb, Great Falls	.930	16	19	21	3	7
Wesley, Idaho Falls	.926	9	9	16	2	3
Wilder, Idaho Falls	.963	48	106	128	9	27

Triple play—Nasser.

THIRD BASEMEN

Player and Club	Pct.	G.	PO.	A.	E.	DP.
Batista, Calgary	1.000	4	3	5	0	1
Borowski, Idaho Falls	.921	14	6	29	3	3
CHUMAS, Idaho Falls	.912	53	36	119	15	8
Denbo, Billings	.947	20	9	27	2	1
Dull, Idaho Falls	.000	1	0	0	1	0
Fabun, Great Falls	1.000	1	0	3	0	0
J. Hamilton, Lethbridge	.902	68	38	118	17	16
Harris, Billings	.854	56	34	95	22	6
Hayes, Great Falls	.840	23	10	32	8	1
Hudson, Medicine Hat	.900	17	10	17	3	1
Humphrey, Idaho Falls	1.000	1	1	0	0	0
Kuziomko, Medicine Hat	.902	44	24	68	10	10
Linkmeyer, Medicine Hat	.854	19	8	33	7	2
Long, Great Falls	.874	55	31	87	17	12
Longenecker, Butte	1.000	3	0	5	0	0
Lumpe, Calgary	.891	56	33	114	18	12
Mattern, Billings	.857	4	2	4	1	0
Mitchell, Billings	1.000	1	1	2	0	0
Polanco, Helena	.727	10	10	6	6	2
Rooker, Butte	.333	3	0	1	2	0
Rossi, Medicine Hat	.800	13	2	14	4	1
Rupp, Calgary	.917	7	6	16	2	2
Seitzer, Butte	.896	66	50	122	20	12
Smith, Helena	.807	66	53	110	39	5
Washington, Calgary	.857	11	9	15	4	4
Wesley, Idaho Falls	.667	3	1	7	4	0
Zapolski, Lethbridge	.800	4	0	4	1	0

Triple play—Hudson.

SHORTSTOPS

Player and Club	Pct.	G.	PO.	A.	E.	DP.
Adkins, Helena	.830	21	28	55	17	8
Batista, Calgary	.878	13	11	25	5	5
Brock, Lethbridge	.897	31	30	66	11	10
Colpitt, Helena	.866	31	49	74	19	14
Davila, Butte	.727	10	7	17	9	2
Denbo, Billings	.862	9	9	16	4	1
Dull, Idaho Falls	.841	26	48	58	20	14
Escobar, Great Falls	.874	30	35	48	12	11
Fabun, Great Falls	.895	3	5	12	2	2
R. Flores, Lethbridge	.886	43	62	140	26	32
Garrett, Idaho Falls	1.000	1	1	1	0	0
Harris, Idaho Falls	.912	38	34	90	12	11
Long, Great Falls	.917	10	15	29	4	8
Longenecker, Butte	1.000	2	0	1	0	1
LUCAS, Calgary	.950	67	81	202	15	40
Miller, Great Falls	.899	43	54	106	18	17
Nasser, Medicine Hat	.950	7	8	11	1	3
Perez, Helena	.907	24	34	64	10	14
Rantz, Idaho Falls	.923	8	10	14	2	5
Seitzer, Butte	.800	2	2	2	1	0
Stillwell, Billings	.875	65	73	137	30	24
Thompson, Medicine Hat	.909	66	106	182	29	48
Van Blaricom, Butte	.908	65	89	187	28	33
Webb, Great Falls	1.000	3	1	0	0	0
Wilder, Idaho Falls	1.000	3	3	6	0	2

Triple play—Thompson.

OUTFIELDERS

Player and Club	Pct.	G.	PO.	A.	E.	DP.
Akers, Medicine Hat	.937	61	99	5	7	0
Aldrete, Great Falls*	1.000	6	10	1	0	0
D. Allen, Great Falls	.958	58	108	6	5	2
E. Allen, Butte	.963	62	98	7	4	1
Balaguer, Billings	.964	31	27	0	1	0
Beringhele, Lethbridge	.975	70	116	2	3	2
Boever, Billings	.875	22	34	1	5	1
Borowski, Idaho Falls	.978	25	43	2	1	0
Brock, Lethbridge	1.000	1	2	0	0	0
Campbell, Lethbridge	.667	3	2	0	1	0
Castain, Idaho Falls	.885	38	46	0	6	0
Claxton, Calgary	.941	49	94	2	6	0
Correa, Billings	.900	17	9	0	1	0
Cousinard, Helena	.909	21	29	1	3	1
de la Rosa, Helena	.927	25	34	4	3	0
DeLaune, Helena*	.930	30	52	1	4	0
DeVall, Calgary	1.000	4	4	2	0	0
Devich, Butte	1.000	8	5	0	0	0
DeWillis, Medicine Hat	.900	7	7	2	1	0
N. FLORES, Lethbridge*	1.000	54	46	6	0	0
Garrett, Idaho Falls	1.000	1	1	0	0	0
Graf, Calgary	.930	38	38	2	3	0
Green, Medicine Hat*	.936	58	102	1	7	0
Griffin, Helena	.941	11	16	0	1	0
Hansen, Idaho Falls	1.000	2	2	0	0	0
Hayes, Great Falls	.750	7	3	0	1	0
G. Hill, Medicine Hat	.917	42	63	3	6	0
T. Hill, Lethbridge	.942	67	93	4	6	0
Howard, Idaho Falls	.929	54	77	2	6	0
Hudson, Medicine Hat	1.000	11	5	0	0	0
Humphrey, Idaho Falls*	.934	45	61	10	5	0
Jones, Great Falls	.951	52	53	5	3	0
Karmeris, Lethbridge	1.000	4	4	0	0	0
Katich, Calgary	.833	8	5	0	1	0

Player and Club	Pct.	G.	PO.	A.	E.	DP.
LaPierre, Calgary	.833	6	4	1	1	0
Linkmeyer, Medicine Hat	1.000	4	3	0	0	0
Loseke, Billings*	.953	68	134	8	7	2
Lowe, Helena	.983	32	57	2	1	0
Lukes, Helena	.942	38	78	3	5	1
Mason, Medicine Hat	1.000	12	13	2	0	0
Mattern, Billings	.980	41	43	5	1	0
McCue, Great Falls	.973	54	68	4	2	1
Mohr, Butte*	.964	30	22	5	1	0
Moncrief, Idaho Falls	.959	52	112	5	5	2
Moore, Calgary	.948	53	83	8	5	3
Moseley, Great Falls	1.000	7	5	0	0	0
Newell, Helena	.923	29	40	8	4	1
Oxner, Butte	1.000	1	1	0	0	0
Padilla, Billings	.750	5	3	0	1	0
Powell, Great Falls	.971	28	30	4	1	0
Price, Lethbridge	1.000	16	30	1	0	0
Ramirez, Calgary	1.000	7	3	1	0	0
Reilly, Calgary	.000	1	0	0	1	0
Riley, Billings	.936	33	42	2	3	0
Ritter, Great Falls	1.000	15	10	1	0	0
Rooker, Butte	.886	56	85	8	12	1
Rubel, Butte*	.948	42	52	3	3	0
Salmen, Billings	.932	43	54	1	4	0
Samples, Calgary	.898	34	42	2	5	0
Schulz, Butte	.942	47	59	6	4	0
Tenacen, Helena	.863	40	59	4	10	2
Thomas, Great Falls	1.000	6	8	0	0	0
Torres, Medicine Hat	.824	24	13	1	3	0
Tostenson, Calgary	.968	51	51	9	2	0
Wadley, Idaho Falls	.000	1	0	0	2	0
Whitfield, Medicine Hat	.971	31	33	1	1	0
Zapolski, Lethbridge	.000	4	0	0	1	0

CATCHERS

Player and Club	Pct.	G.	PO.	A.	E.	DP.	PB.
Bartlett, Lethbridge	.983	39	329	25	6	1	15
Campbell, Lethbridge	1.000	1	9	0	0	0	3
DeWillis, Medicine Hat	.979	42	308	24	7	3	11
Dotson, Lethbridge	.977	32	232	28	6	1	12
Garrett, Idaho Falls	.958	11	62	6	3	0	4
Halberg, Great Falls	.974	24	174	11	5	2	10
Held, Idaho Falls	.976	46	296	31	8	2	12
Houp, Billings	1.000	3	17	1	0	0	0
Landrith, Butte	.966	41	262	26	10	2	4
Lane, Great Falls	.965	38	276	29	11	2	6
Loard, Great Falls	1.000	1	3	0	0	0	0
Magrann, Helena	.944	42	268	33	18	4	16
Meert, Helena	.961	17	110	14	5	1	13

Player and Club	Pct.	G.	PO.	A.	E.	DP.	PB.
Mitchell, Billings	.986	17	134	10	2	0	6
Monson, Helena	.971	19	124	12	4	0	7
Niemann, Butte	.991	23	104	4	1	2	4
OLIVER, Billings	.989	52	425	38	5	1	15
Oliveros, Billings	1.000	15	57	6	0	0	1
Oxner, Butte	.978	27	165	16	4	0	7
Pena, Great Falls	.973	23	132	10	4	0	4
Ray, Calgary	.961	25	181	17	8	2	6
Rojas, Idaho Falls	.962	19	114	12	5	1	11
Rupp, Calgary	.983	48	326	25	6	2	8
Samples, Calgary	1.000	1	1	0	0	0	0
Stark, Medicine Hat	.959	32	215	19	10	1	11

PITCHERS

Player and Club	Pct.	G.	PO.	A.	E.	DP.
Andujar, Calgary*	.857	21	2	4	1	0
Bargo, Calgary	.600	6	1	2	2	0
Barton, Helena	.846	8	4	7	2	0
Boatright, Butte	1.000	15	1	0	0	0
Bowens, Idaho Falls*	.917	13	2	9	1	1
Burkett, Great Falls	.917	13	4	7	1	0
Burns, Lethbridge	.913	12	7	14	2	0
Calvert, Billings	.944	14	4	13	1	0
Chasteen, Idaho Falls	1.000	11	4	10	0	0
Chelini, Butte	1.000	20	0	5	0	0
Clemons, Medicine Hat	.920	14	6	17	2	3
Cobbs, Lethbridge	1.000	11	1	8	0	1
A. Collins, Calgary	1.000	15	4	8	0	0
A.C. Collins, Medicine Hat*	.833	16	1	4	1	0
Corbell, Great Falls	.933	8	5	9	1	0
Cram, Helena	.895	22	5	12	2	1
Criswell, Lethbridge	.800	18	3	5	2	1
de Chavez, Idaho Falls	.955	13	5	16	1	0
Dibble, Billings	1.000	5	3	2	0	0
Dickman, Medicine Hat	.750	14	1	2	1	0
Digirolamo, Butte*	.800	18	0	4	1	0
Dodd, Calgary*	.818	13	3	6	2	1
Dombek, Helena*	.909	9	1	9	1	1
Dressler, Great Falls	.500	9	0	1	1	0
Edens, Butte	1.000	13	6	8	0	0
Emerson, Medicine Hat	1.000	4	1	3	0	0
Ergle, Billings	.909	13	6	4	1	1
Ferlenda, Medicine Hat	.714	16	2	3	2	0
Ferran, Great Falls	.889	7	3	5	1	1
Fisher, Calgary	.857	14	5	7	2	2
Gehrke, Great Falls	.800	5	2	2	1	0
Gentle, Lethbridge*	.857	13	3	9	2	0
GEORGE, Butte*	1.000	14	6	15	0	2
Giddings, Idaho Falls	1.000	20	3	10	0	0
Goedde, Billings	1.000	8	0	2	0	0
Grimm, Billings	.857	13	6	6	2	0
R. Hamilton, Lethbridge	1.000	13	5	15	0	3

Player and Club	Pct.	G.	PO.	A.	E.	DP.
Hammond, Billings	.667	10	2	2	2	0
Hamrick, Lethbridge*	.778	16	1	6	2	0
Hanna, Idaho Falls	.800	10	1	3	1	0
Hansen, Idaho Falls	.909	13	1	9	1	1
Henning, Great Falls	1.000	14	3	8	0	3
Hilton, Calgary	.667	11	0	2	1	0
Hisey, Helena	.667	15	2	2	2	0
Holbrook, Medicine Hat	.889	12	1	7	1	0
Householder, Helena*	.727	13	6	2	3	0
Impagliazzo, Calgary	1.000	28	2	3	0	0
Kemp, Billings	.960	14	4	20	1	1
King, Great Falls	.545	20	4	2	5	0
Klein, Butte	.875	29	1	6	1	1
Kolb, Lethbridge	.800	24	3	5	2	1
Law, Idaho Falls	1.000	14	2	1	0	0
D. Lee, Lethbridge	.840	13	5	16	4	0
K. Lee, Great Falls*	.917	15	3	8	1	0
Leonette, Idaho Falls	.875	13	2	12	2	0
Lipson, Butte	1.000	20	2	6	0	0
)itano, Calgary	.571	11	3	1	3	0
Lloyd, Helena*	1.000	8	2	6	0	0
Long, Helena	.929	12	4	9	1	2
Longman, Helena	.875	12	1	6	1	1
Luman, Butte	1.000	9	0	4	0	0
Mader, Medicine Hat	.917	11	1	10	1	2
Mangum, Idaho Falls	.750	12	1	2	1	0
May, Lethbridge	.929	13	5	8	1	0
McDevitt, Helena	1.000	10	2	3	0	0
Meagher, Lethbridge	.833	8	0	5	1	0
Middleton, Billings	.923	15	4	8	1	1
Montgomery, Billings	.600	20	1	5	4	0
Murray, Medicine Hat	.909	13	4	16	2	1
Norwood, Helena*	.947	13	5	13	1	0
Page, Calgary	.667	16	3	5	4	1
Pascho, Calgary	.750	13	11	10	7	0
Pascual, Idaho Falls	1.000	19	1	3	0	0
Petties, Billings	.667	9	1	1	1	0

PITCHERS—Continued

Player and Club	Pct.	G.	PO.	A.	E.	DP.
Phillips, Medicine Hat	1.000	5	3	4	0	0
Rexrode, Lethbridge	.842	23	2	14	3	1
Robbins, Medicine Hat	1.000	28	5	6	0	3
Robinson, Butte	1.000	15	3	3	0	0
Rowen, Lethbridge*	1.000	18	1	5	0	0
Ruetter, Medicine Hat*	1.000	11	1	3	0	0
Serritella, Butte	.900	13	3	15	2	2
Shepard, Helena	.750	7	2	1	1	0
Siblerud, Helena	1.000	6	1	2	0	0
D. Smith, Billings*	.923	28	3	9	1	0
L. Smith, Idaho Falls*	1.000	15	4	6	0	0
S. Smith, Great Falls	.923	13	12	12	2	0
Snell, Butte	.818	21	2	7	2	1
Strutz, Helena	.800	16	2	6	2	1
Tavarez, Great Falls	1.000	13	0	3	0	0
Torres, Butte	.789	13	6	9	4	1
Traen, Calgary*	1.000	2	1	3	0	0
J. Valdez, Helena*	.500	6	0	1	1	0
S. Valdez, Calgary	.870	13	7	13	3	2
Vantrease, Idaho Falls*	.864	12	6	13	3	0
Vargas, Helena	.900	16	3	6	1	0
Villa, Great Falls	.800	16	2	2	1	0
Vodvarka, Butte*	.900	9	0	9	1	1
Wadley, Idaho Falls	.750	12	1	2	1	0
Werner, Medicine Hat*	.667	8	0	2	1	1
Wood, Great Falls*	1.000	20	2	5	0	1
Yokubaitis, Great Falls*	.933	23	4	10	1	1
Young, Calgary*	.867	13	5	8	2	0

The following players do not have any recorded accepted chances at the positions indicated and therefore are not listed in the fielding averages for those particular positions: Adkins, 2b; Bajus, p; Borowski, p; Brock, 3b; B. Davis, p; Gordon, of; Jackson, p; Johnson, p; Kenney, p; Kuralt, p; LaPierre, p; Lumpe, 1b; Maldonado, p; Mattern, p; D. Miller, p; Mohr, p; Nasser, 3b; Powell, 3b; Salmen, p; Serrano, of; Washington, 1b, ss.

CLUB PITCHING

Club	ERA.	G.	CG.	ShO.	Sv.	IP.	H.	R.	ER.	HR.	HB.	BB.	Int. BB.	SO.	WP.	Bk.
Billings	4.08	70	14	5	14	607.1	611	350	275	42	13	271	14	618	50	4
Lethbridge	4.27	70	8	2	17	594.1	574	366	282	41	31	335	20	559	54	1
Butte	4.33	70	4	4	10	584.1	597	383	281	35	27	328	38	517	42	3
Great Falls	4.45	70	12	3	6	586.0	626	376	290	45	23	276	21	570	64	5
Medicine Hat	4.80	68	12	2	14	581.1	611	423	310	53	19	349	13	500	46	2
Idaho Falls	4.94	67	11	2	9	573.2	660	395	315	38	24	262	5	463	47	5
Calgary	5.25	71	10	1	17	593.2	709	438	346	62	13	293	4	486	32	5
Helena	6.21	70	10	1	2	595.1	669	546	411	61	28	426	20	487	99	7

PITCHERS' RECORDS

(Leading Qualifiers for Earned-Run Average Leadership—56 or More Innings)

*Throws lefthanded.

Pitcher—Club	W.	L.	Pct.	ERA.	G.	GS.	CG.	GF.	ShO.	Sv.	IP.	H.	R.	ER.	HR.	HB.	BB.	Int. BB.	SO.	WP.
Kemp, Billings	9	3	.750	2.21	14	14	8	0	3	0	110.0	82	39	27	3	2	46	2	138	11
Henning, Great Falls	5	3	.625	2.63	14	9	1	2	0	1	61.2	51	26	18	2	1	41	3	58	6
Clemons, Medicine Hat	6	6	.500	2.69	14	14	5	0	1	0	107.0	106	51	32	4	2	31	3	73	5
Robbins, Medicine Hat	5	4	.556	2.83	28	0	0	24	0	9	60.1	48	25	19	4	3	39	5	64	4
S. Smith, Great Falls	8	3	.727	2.87	13	13	5	0	2	0	94.0	95	38	30	6	4	16	0	107	1
Torres, Butte	8	3	.727	3.00	13	13	1	0	0	0	69.0	55	31	23	2	4	37	1	75	8
George, Butte*	5	3	.625	3.11	14	14	1	0	1	0	75.1	73	35	26	3	1	28	2	66	2
Grimm, Billings	9	2	.818	3.16	13	13	4	0	0	0	88.1	94	39	31	6	2	30	2	71	4
Serritella, Butte	7	3	.700	3.52	13	13	1	0	1	0	69.0	69	42	27	2	3	23	2	58	1
Vantrease, Idaho Falls*	2	4	.333	3.69	12	11	2	1	0	0	68.1	77	35	28	6	4	17	0	51	2

Departmental Leaders: G—Klein, 29; W—Grimm, Kemp, D. Lee, 9; L—Long, 9; Pct.—D. Lee, .900; GS—Calvert, Clemons, George, Kemp, 14; CG—Kemp, 8; GF—Impagliazzo, 26; ShO—Kemp, 3; Sv.—Impagliazzo, 12; IP—Kemp, 110; H—Pascho, 108; R—Long, 70; ER—Long, 59; HR—Middleton, 12; HB—Burns, de Chavez, D. Lee, 5; BB—Hamrick, 57; IBB—Klein, 9; SO—Kemp, 138; WP—Long, 18.

(All Pitchers—Listed Alphabetically)

Pitcher—Club	W.	L.	Pct.	ERA.	G.	GS.	CG.	GF.	ShO.	Sv.	IP.	H.	R.	ER.	HR.	HB.	BB.	Int. BB.	SO.	WP.
Andujar, Calgary*	1	0	1.000	4.72	21	1	0	13	0	2	34.1	31	23	18	2	0	22	1	38	1
Bajus, Medicine Hat*	0	0	.000	3.24	8	1	0	2	0	0	16.2	8	10	6	2	0	17	0	24	3
Bargo, Calgary*	0	0	.000	9.22	6	0	0	1	0	0	13.2	20	21	14	2	3	13	0	9	8
Barton, Helena	1	5	.167	6.88	8	7	1	1	0	0	35.1	35	32	27	4	1	32	0	22	5
Boatright, Butte	4	1	.800	4.95	15	4	0	4	0	0	36.1	32	26	20	3	1	27	0	26	5
Borowski, Idaho Falls	0	0	.000	0.00	1	0	0	0	0	0	1.0	1	0	0	0	0	1	0	1	0
Bowens, Idaho Falls*	6	6	.500	5.45	13	13	4	0	1	0	76.0	78	57	46	4	2	50	0	51	3
Burkett, Great Falls	2	6	.250	6.26	13	9	0	1	0	0	50.1	73	44	35	1	2	30	2	38	8
Burns, Lethbridge	4	5	.444	4.31	12	10	2	2	0	0	62.2	72	42	30	4	5	14	2	35	7
Calvert, Billings	6	5	.545	5.31	14	14	1	0	0	0	81.1	98	64	48	6	2	35	2	77	4
Chasteen, Idaho Falls	2	6	.250	4.76	11	10	1	0	0	0	58.2	69	39	31	4	2	22	0	41	6
Chelini, Butte	1	1	.500	3.77	20	0	0	11	0	0	28.2	29	15	12	2	2	15	2	18	3
Clemons, Medicine Hat	6	6	.500	2.69	14	14	5	0	1	0	107.0	106	51	32	4	2	31	3	73	5
Cobbs, Lethbridge	0	2	.000	6.29	11	1	0	4	0	0	24.1	34	24	17	2	4	11	0	22	3
A.C. Collins, Medicine Hat*	2	3	.400	5.18	16	1	0	8	0	1	40.0	38	30	23	6	0	17	0	42	3
A. Collins, Calgary	5	3	.625	4.36	15	7	0	3	0	2	64.0	74	39	31	4	1	41	0	43	4
Corbell, Great Falls	3	3	.500	2.98	8	8	1	0	0	0	54.1	47	23	18	6	4	14	3	43	5
Cram, Helena	1	7	.125	5.37	22	5	1	13	0	1	67.0	82	56	40	7	2	33	5	45	4
Criswell, Lethbridge	2	1	.667	3.00	18	0	0	11	0	2	30.0	34	20	10	1	1	11	0	27	1
Davis, Butte	0	0	.000	2.25	2	0	0	2	0	1	4.0	3	1	1	0	0	4	0	8	1
de Chavez, Idaho Falls	6	4	.600	4.09	13	13	3	0	1	0	83.2	95	48	38	4	5	25	1	74	7
Dibble, Billings	0	1	.000	7.82	5	2	0	2	0	0	12.2	18	13	11	1	0	11	0	7	2
Dickman, Medicine Hat	0	0	.000	7.66	14	0	0	9	0	1	22.1	32	27	19	1	3	23	0	18	10
Digirolamo, Butte*	2	2	.500	7.34	18	2	0	5	0	0	34.1	42	36	28	5	4	21	5	18	0
Dodd, Calgary*	1	5	.167	6.68	13	6	1	2	0	0	33.2	47	33	25	6	0	17	0	19	0
Dombek, Helena*	2	4	.333	4.59	9	8	1	0	0	0	33.1	29	25	17	0	1	39	0	25	7
Dressler, Great Falls	1	1	.500	6.37	9	2	1	5	1	0	29.2	36	24	21	4	0	22	3	38	4
Edens, Butte	2	3	.400	4.32	13	12	1	0	0	0	58.1	65	47	28	3	3	33	0	44	4
Emerson, Medicine Hat	0	2	.000	6.06	4	3	1	1	0	0	16.1	18	13	11	4	0	10	0	9	1
Ergle, Billings	3	5	.375	4.62	13	13	0	0	0	0	87.2	96	55	45	12	3	38	1	66	4
Ferlenda, Medicine Hat	4	6	.400	6.01	16	11	2	2	1	1	70.1	76	58	47	9	2	41	4	83	4
Ferran, Great Falls	0	1	.000	4.32	7	2	0	1	0	0	16.2	19	11	8	1	0	10	0	10	1
Fisher, Calgary	5	3	.625	6.27	14	9	0	1	0	0	56.0	79	47	39	8	0	30	0	48	3
Gehrke, Great Falls	0	0	.000	7.88	5	0	0	1	0	0	8.0	8	9	7	2	0	4	0	10	0
Gentle, Lethbridge*	3	7	.300	3.81	13	13	2	0	0	0	80.1	80	51	34	3	4	43	0	70	5
George, Butte*	5	3	.625	3.11	14	14	1	0	1	0	75.1	73	35	26	3	1	28	2	66	2

Pitcher—Club	W.	L.	Pct.	ERA.	G.	GS.	CG.	GF.	ShO.	Sv.	IP.	H.	R.	ER.	HR.	HB.	BB.	Int. BB.	SO.	WP.
Giddings, Idaho Falls	2	1	.667	3.23	20	2	0	10	0	3	39.0	42	17	14	0	0	13	0	37	6
Goedde, Billings	1	2	.333	9.31	8	2	0	4	0	0	9.2	9	11	10	1	1	11	0	9	2
Grimm, Billings	9	2	.818	3.16	13	13	4	0	0	0	88.1	94	39	31	6	2	30	2	71	4
Hamilton, Lethbridge	6	3	.667	4.60	13	13	1	0	0	0	76.1	75	48	39	8	2	41	3	62	9
Hammond, Billings	0	0	.000	5.02	10	0	0	5	0	1	28.2	28	22	16	1	1	13	0	18	4
Hamrick, Lethbridge*	4	4	.500	4.48	16	10	1	3	0	1	68.0	59	43	34	6	4	57	1	104	12
Hanna, Idaho Falls	0	1	.000	23.76	10	1	0	6	0	1	8.1	30	25	22	1	0	8	1	7	0
Hansen, Idaho Falls	1	5	.167	3.08	13	2	0	4	0	0	38.0	36	21	13	2	0	25	2	41	0
Henning, Great Falls	5	3	.625	2.63	14	9	1	2	0	1	61.2	51	26	18	2	1	41	3	58	6
Hilton, Calgary	0	3	.000	10.23	11	3	0	3	0	1	22.0	37	29	25	3	2	21	0	17	1
Hisey, Helena	0	4	.000	4.79	15	3	1	3	0	0	47.0	59	38	25	4	1	24	3	43	8
Holbrook, Medicine Hat	4	4	.500	7.06	12	10	1	0	0	0	57.1	74	57	45	8	1	44	1	27	3
Householder, Helena*	0	1	.000	6.32	13	3	0	4	0	0	37.0	42	36	26	5	4	29	1	34	9
Impagliazzo, Calgary	6	1	.857	1.83	28	0	0	26	0	12	39.1	22	10	8	2	0	23	0	62	3
Jackson, Helena*	0	1	.000	21.86	5	1	0	0	0	0	7.0	11	21	17	0	1	20	2	11	4
Johnson, Idaho Falls	1	2	.333	7.07	8	1	0	2	0	0	14.0	21	20	11	3	1	8	1	7	1
Kemp, Billings	9	3	.750	2.21	14	14	8	0	3	0	110.0	82	39	27	3	2	46	2	138	11
Kenney, Great Falls	0	0	.000	27.00	2	0	0	1	0	0	1.1	4	4	4	0	0	3	1	1	0
King, Great Falls	3	4	.429	4.31	20	7	1	9	0	2	56.1	58	31	27	6	2	14	1	61	2
Klein, Butte	2	5	.286	4.15	29	1	0	21	0	8	47.2	45	28	22	1	1	29	9	58	4
Kolb, Lethbridge	4	4	.500	5.74	24	1	0	12	0	2	31.1	34	21	20	1	2	28	8	39	3
Kurant, Billings	2	0	1.000	1.80	2	0	0	0	0	0	5.0	4	1	1	0	0	0	0	8	1
LaPierre, Calgary	0	0	.000	0.00	1	0	0	1	0	0	2.1	1	2	0	0	0	6	0	1	2
Law, Idaho Falls	0	3	.000	3.45	14	0	0	10	0	2	15.2	17	12	6	1	3	7	0	20	5
D. Lee, Lethbridge	9	1	.900	4.35	13	13	1	0	1	0	82.2	69	50	40	10	5	42	1	75	4
K. Lee, Great Falls*	1	3	.250	6.95	15	8	1	4	0	0	55.2	67	47	43	6	1	31	2	58	16
Leonette, Idaho Falls	5	2	.714	4.76	13	10	1	0	0	0	68.0	77	44	36	6	0	32	0	49	4
Lipson, Butte	4	1	.800	3.42	20	3	0	4	0	0	50.0	46	28	19	5	2	37	8	57	3
Litano, Calgary	1	0	1.000	4.94	11	2	0	4	0	0	23.2	26	19	13	2	1	12	0	27	2
Lloyd, Helena*	0	3	.000	4.59	8	4	1	2	0	0	33.1	35	23	17	5	2	20	0	37	5
Long, Helena	1	9	.100	10.41	12	11	1	1	0	0	51.0	77	70	59	5	3	56	0	31	18
Longman, Helena	1	2	.333	4.88	12	0	0	12	0	1	24.0	28	14	13	3	2	8	1	19	1
Luman, Butte	1	0	1.000	13.09	9	0	0	2	0	0	11.0	22	16	16	0	1	12	1	9	4
Mader, Medicine Hat	2	2	.500	7.90	11	5	0	0	0	0	27.1	40	29	24	4	4	29	0	21	3
Maldonado, Calgary	0	0	.000	19.64	3	0	0	1	0	0	3.2	6	8	8	2	2	4	0	4	0
Mangum, Idaho Falls	0	1	.000	6.75	12	0	0	2	0	0	18.2	24	17	14	0	3	7	0	11	1
Mattern, Billings	0	0	.000	36.00	1	0	0	1	0	0	1.0	4	4	4	0	0	1	0	1	0
May, Lethbridge	2	1	.667	5.01	13	6	1	3	1	1	46.2	46	29	26	3	2	30	0	36	2
McDevitt, Helena	2	3	.400	5.01	10	9	2	1	0	0	46.2	37	33	26	8	1	34	0	50	10
Meagher, Lethbridge	1	1	.500	4.67	8	3	0	3	0	1	27.0	27	17	14	3	1	21	4	24	4
Middleton, Billings	1	4	.200	5.55	15	8	1	1	0	0	61.2	79	52	38	9	0	30	4	42	7
Miller, Medicine Hat	0	0	.000	6.35	3	1	0	2	0	0	5.2	8	7	4	1	1	1	0	3	0
Mohr, Butte*	0	0	.000	0.00	1	0	0	1	0	0	2.0	1	0	0	0	0	0	0	2	0
Montgomery, Billings	6	2	.750	2.42	20	0	0	16	0	5	44.2	31	13	12	1	0	13	0	90	2
Murray, Medicine Hat	6	4	.600	4.01	13	13	2	0	0	0	76.1	77	47	34	4	3	38	0	46	1
Norwood, Helena*	2	6	.250	4.99	13	13	2	0	0	0	79.1	77	59	44	3	4	54	1	90	10
Page, Calgary	3	2	.600	4.50	16	2	0	6	0	0	52.0	62	38	26	6	0	20	3	27	0
Pascho, Calgary	7	5	.583	4.32	13	13	3	0	1	0	85.1	108	50	41	9	2	15	0	62	3
Pascual, Idaho Falls	1	0	1.000	5.61	19	0	0	15	0	3	25.2	24	16	16	1	3	17	0	21	7
Petties, Billings	1	1	.500	7.40	9	4	0	1	0	0	24.1	24	24	20	0	1	26	0	21	5
Phillips, Medicine Hat	1	2	.333	3.95	5	5	1	0	0	0	27.1	27	20	12	2	0	11	0	30	4
Rexrode, Lethbridge	3	1	.750	2.01	23	0	0	16	0	6	44.2	30	10	10	0	0	22	1	44	2
Robbins, Medicine Hat	5	4	.556	2.83	28	0	0	24	0	9	60.1	48	25	19	4	3	39	5	64	4
Robinson, Butte	1	1	.500	7.71	15	1	0	4	0	0	23.1	28	26	20	1	0	19	2	15	1
Rowen, Lethbridge*	1	1	.500	3.60	18	0	0	8	0	4	20.0	14	11	8	0	1	15	0	21	2
Ruetter, Medicine Hat*	2	1	.667	6.46	11	4	0	4	0	1	39.0	46	38	28	3	0	32	0	37	2
Salmen, Billings	0	0	.000	13.50	2	0	0	1	0	0	2.0	4	3	3	0	0	0	0	2	0
Serritella, Butte	7	3	.700	3.52	13	13	1	0	1	0	69.0	69	42	27	2	3	23	2	58	1
Shepard, Helena	0	1	.000	7.43	7	2	0	0	0	0	23.0	23	23	19	4	1	18	0	13	5
Siblerud, Helena	0	0	.000	9.17	6	1	0	3	0	0	17.2	23	25	18	1	2	13	1	11	8
D. Smith, Billings*	5	2	.714	1.61	28	0	0	25	0	8	50.1	40	10	9	2	1	17	3	68	4
L. Smith, Idaho Falls*	1	4	.200	6.55	15	3	0	4	0	0	34.1	44	28	25	4	0	16	0	33	3
S. Smith, Great Falls	8	3	.727	2.87	13	13	5	0	2	0	94.0	95	38	30	6	4	16	0	107	1
Snell, Butte	3	3	.500	3.65	21	1	0	11	0	1	44.1	43	25	18	4	4	22	4	42	5
Strutz, Helena	1	2	.333	6.96	16	0	0	9	0	0	32.1	39	33	25	4	2	21	3	17	3
Tavarez, Great Falls	2	0	1.000	2.60	13	1	1	8	0	0	27.2	28	20	8	3	1	10	1	16	0
Torres, Butte	8	3	.727	3.00	13	13	1	0	0	0	69.0	55	31	23	2	4	37	1	75	8
Traen, Calgary*	0	2	.000	6.17	2	2	1	0	0	0	11.2	10	9	8	1	0	6	0	16	0
J. Valdez, Helena*	0	0	.000	2.25	6	0	0	5	0	0	8.0	5	4	2	1	1	9	0	6	0
S. Valdez, Calgary	6	3	.667	5.57	13	13	1	0	0	0	72.2	88	55	45	7	2	31	0	41	3
Vantrease, Idaho Falls*	2	4	.333	3.69	12	11	2	1	0	0	68.1	77	35	28	6	4	17	0	51	2
Vargas, Helena	5	6	.455	6.08	16	3	0	6	0	0	53.1	67	54	36	7	0	16	3	33	1
Villa, Great Falls	1	1	.500	7.22	16	1	0	11	0	1	28.2	36	27	23	3	1	21	1	23	10
Vodvarka, Butte*	1	3	.250	6.10	9	6	0	1	0	0	31.0	44	27	21	4	1	21	2	21	1
Wadley, Idaho Falls	0	1	.000	5.55	12	1	0	2	0	0	24.1	25	16	15	2	1	14	0	19	2
Werner, Medicine Hat*	1	0	1.000	3.52	8	0	0	4	0	1	15.1	13	11	6	1	0	16	0	23	3
Wood, Great Falls*	2	3	.400	5.00	20	3	0	7	0	0	36.0	34	29	20	4	4	23	3	30	3
Yokubaitis, Great Falls*	8	6	.571	3.84	23	7	1	8	0	2	65.2	70	43	28	1	3	37	1	77	8
Young, Calgary*	7	1	.875	5.11	13	13	4	0	0	0	79.1	98	55	45	8	0	32	0	72	2

BALKS—Norwood, 3; Burkett, Chasteen, Henning, McDevitt, 2 each; Andujar, Bargo, Corbell, Ergle, Fisher, George, Grimm, Hamrick, Householder, Leonette, Long, Montgomery, Murray, Pascual, Robbins, D. Smith, L. Smith, Torres, Traen, Vodvarka, Young, 1 each.

COMBINATION SHUTOUTS—Middleton-Smith-Goedde, Grimm-Goedde, Billings; Torres-Chelini-Luman-Robinson, George-Robinson-Klein, Butte; McDevitt-Vargas, Helena.

NO-HIT GAMES—Edens, Butte, defeated Helena, 6-1 (second game, seven innings), August 22; Grimm, Billings, defeated Calgary, 5-0 (first game of playoffs), September 1.

WADE BOGGS
• RED SOX •
BATTING CHAMPION (.361)
ON-BASE PCT. (.449)

JIM RICE
• RED SOX •
HOME RUNS (39)
RBIs (126—tie)

CAL RIPKEN
• ORIOLES •
RUNS (121)
HITS (211)
DOUBLES (47)

1983 A.L. LEADERS

LaMARR HOYT
• WHITE SOX •
WINS (24)

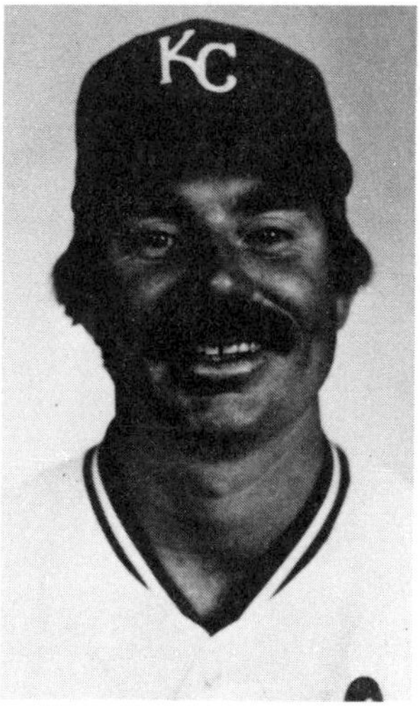

DAN QUISENBERRY
• ROYALS •
SAVES (45)
GAMES (69)

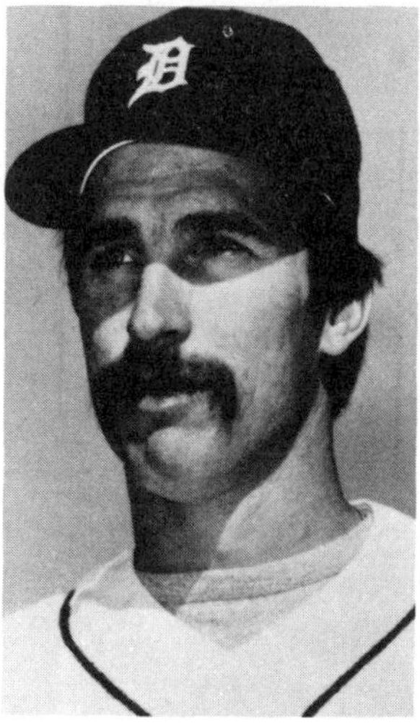

JACK MORRIS
• TIGERS •
INNINGS (293.2)
STRIKEOUTS (232)

1984 A.L. EAST DIVISION SLATE . . .

1984	EAST AT MILWAUKEE	AT DETROIT	AT CLEVELAND	AT TORONTO	AT BALTIMORE	AT NEW YORK	AT BOSTON
MILWAUKEE...		June 21*,22*,23,**24** Sept. 17*,18*,19*	May 28*,29*,30* Aug. 17*,18*,**19**	June 19*,20 Sept. 20*,21*,22,**23**	June 4*,5*,6* Sept. 7*,8*,**9**	April 27*,28*,**29** July 30*,31* Aug. 1*,2*	June 7*,8*,9,**10** Sept. 10*,11*,12*
DETROIT.........	June 15*,16*,**17** Sept. 24*,25*,26*		May 4*,5,**6** July 23*,24*,25*,26*	June 11*,12*,13* Sept. 7*,8,**9**	June 8*,9-9,**10** Sept. 10*,11*,12*	June 25*,26*,27* Sept. 27*,28*,29,**30**	April 13,**15**,16 Aug. 6*,7*,8*
CLEVELAND ...	May 18*,19*,**20** Aug. 27*,28*,29*,30	April 27*,28,**29** July 31* Aug. 1*,2		May 25*,26,**27-27** Aug. 21*,22*,23	April 30* May 1*,2 July 27*,28*,**29**	May 7*,8*,9*,10* Aug. 3*,4*,**5**	May 21*,22*,23* Aug. 24*,25,**26**
TORONTO	June 25(Tn),26*,27 Sept. 28*,29,**30**	June 4*,5*,6*,7 Sept. 14*,15,**16**	May 11*,12,**13** Aug. 14*,15*,16*		May 7*,8*,9* Aug. 3*,4*,**5**	June 8*,9*,**10** Sept. 3,4*,5*	June 21*,22*,23,**24** Sept. 24*,25*,26*
BALTIMORE....	June 11*,12*,13*,14 Sept. 14*,15,**16**	June 1*,2,**3** Sept. 3*,4*,5*	April 14,**15,**16 Aug. 6*,7*,8*,9*	April 17, 18, 19 Aug. 10*,11,**12**,13*		June 15*,16,**17** Sept. 17*,18*,19*	June 19*,20* Sept. 27*,28*,29,**30**
NEW YORK	May 4*,5*,**6** July 23*,24*,25*	June 18*,19*,20* Sept. 21*,22,**23**	April 17*,18* Aug. 10*,11*,**12,**13*	June 1*,2,**3** Sept. 10*,11*,12*,13*	June 21*,22*,23*,**24** Sept. 24*,25*,26*		June 11*,12*,13*,14* Sept. 7*,8,**9**
BOSTON	June 1*,2,**3** Sept, 3,4*,5*	May 1*,2*,3 July 27 (Tn),28*,**29**	May 14*,15*,16*,17* Aug. 31* Sept. 1,**2**	June 15*,16,**17** Sept. 17*,18*,19*	June 25*,26*,27* Sept. 20*,21*,22*,**23**	June 4*,5*,6* Sept. 14*,15*,**16**	
SEATTLE........	April 20*,21,**22** July 2*,3*,4	May 14*,15*,16* Aug. 17*,18*,**19**	June 8*,9,**10-10** Sept. 25*,26*	April 23,24* July 5*,6*,7,**8**	May 18*,19*,**20** Aug. 20*,21*,22*	May 11*,12*,**13** Aug. 14*,15,16*	April 25*,26* June 28*,29*,30 July **1**
OAKLAND	April 23*,24* July 5*,6*,7*,**8**	May 18*,19*,**20** Aug. 20*,21*,22*	June 4*,5*,6* Sept. 7*,8,**9**	April 25*,26 June 28*,29*,30 July **1**	May 11*,12*,**13** Aug. 14*,15*,16*	May 14*,15*,16* Aug. 17*,18*,**19**	April 20*,21,**22** July 2*,3*,4
CALIFORNIA...	April 25*,26 June 28*,29*,30* July **1**	May 11*,12,**13** Aug. 14*,15*,16	June 1*,2*,**3** Sept. 3*,4*,5*	April 20,21,**22** July 2,3*,4*	May 14*,15*,16* Aug. 17*, 18,**19**	May 18*,19,**20** Aug. 20*,21*,22*	April 23*,24* July 5*,6*,7,**8**
TEXAS	May 15*,16*,17 Aug. 24*,25,**26**	April 10,12 July 19*,20*,21*,**22**	April 23,24 June 28*,29*,30* July **1**	April 30* May 1*,2* July 27*,28*,**29**	April 27*,28*,**29** July 30*,31* Aug. 1*	April 20*,21,**22** July 16*,17*,18	April 17*,18*,19 Aug. 3*,4,**5**
KANSAS CITY	May 1*,2*,3 July 27,28*,**29**	April 17*,18* Aug. 3*,4,**5-5**	April 20,21,**22** July 2*,3*,4	May 4*,5,**6** July 30*,31* Aug. 1*	April 10*,11* July 5*,6*,7*,**8**	April 23*,24 July 12*,13*,14,**15**	May 25*,26,**27** Aug. 20*,21*,22*
MINNESOTA...	May 11*,12,**13** Aug. 21*,22*,23	April 23*,24* June 29 (Tn),30* July **1**	June 26*,27* Sept.27*,28*,29,**30**	May 21,22*,23* Aug. 31* Sept. 1,**2**	April 20*,21*,**22** July 16*,17*,18*	April 10,12* July 19*,20*,21,**22**	May 28,29*,30* Aug. 17*,18,**19**
CHICAGO........	April 17,19 Aug.3*,4,**5**,6*	April 20*,21,**22** July 16*,17*,18*	April 25,26 July 19*,20*,21,**22**	May 17*,18*,19,**20** Aug. 28*,29*	April 2,4 July 12*,13*,14*,**15**	April 13*,14,**15** Aug. 7*,8,9*	May 4*,5,**6** July 24*,25*,26*
1984	80 HOME DATES 49 NIGHTS	78 HOME DATES 51 NIGHTS	80 HOME DATES 49 NIGHTS	80 HOME DATES 45 NIGHTS	80 HOME DATES 61 NIGHTS	81 HOME DATES 55 NIGHTS	81 HOME DATES 53 NIGHTS

***NIGHT GAME**
NIGHT GAME: Any game starting after 6:00 p.m.
HEAVY BLACK FIGURES DENOTE SUNDAY

AND COMPLETE WEST SCHEDULES

1984	WEST						
	AT SEATTLE	AT OAKLAND	AT CALIFORNIA	AT TEXAS	AT KANSAS CITY	AT MINNESOTA	AT CHICAGO
MILWAUKEE...	April 6*,7*,**8** July 16*,17*,18	April 3*,4* July 19*,20*,21,**22**	April 10*,11* July 12*,13*,14*,**15**	May 22*,23*,24* Aug. 31* Sept. 1*,**2**	April 13*,14*,**15** Aug. 7*,8*,9*	May 25*,26,**27** Aug. 13*,14*,15*	May 7*,8*,9* Aug. 10*,11*,**12**
DETROIT.........	May 25*,26*,**27** Aug. 28*,29*,30*	May 28*,29*,30 Aug. 31* Sept. 1,**2**	May 22*,23*,24* Aug. 24*,25*,**26**	April 25*,26* July 5*,6*,7*,**8***	May 7*,8*,9* Aug. 10*,11*,**12**	April 3,5 July 12,13*,14*,**15**	April 6,7,**8** July 2*,3*,4*
CLEVELAND ...	June 22*,23*,**24** Sept. 17*,18*,19*	June 12*,13,14 Sept. 14*,15,**16**	June 15*,16*,**17** Sept. 11*,12*,13*	April 3*,5* July 12*,13*,14*,**15***	April 6*,7*,**8** July 16*,17*,18*	June 19*,20*,21 Sept. 21*,22,**23**	April 10*,11 July 5,6*,7,**8**
TORONTO	April 4*,5* July 19*,20*,21*,**22**	April 9*,10* July 12,13*,14,**15**	April 6*,7,**8** July 16*,17*,18*	April 13*,14,**15** Aug. 6*,7*,8*	April 27*,28*,**29** July 23*,24*,25*	May 15*,16 Aug. 24*,25,**26,** 27*	May 28*,29*,30* Aug. 17*,18*,**19**
BALTIMORE....	May 28*,29*,30 Aug. 31* Sept. 1*,**2**	May 22*,23,24 Aug. 24*,25,**26**	May 25*,26,**27** Aug. 27*,28*,29	May 4*,5*,**6** July 23*,24*,25*	April 25*,26* July 19*,20*,21,**22**	April 6*,7,**8** July 2*,3*,4*	April 23*,24* June 28*,29*,30* July **1**
NEW YORK	May 22*,23*,24* Aug. 24*,25*,**26**	May 25*,26,**27** Aug. 27*,28*,29*	May 28,29*,30* Aug. 31* Sept. 1*,**2**	April *6,7,**8** July 2*,3*,4*	April 2,4*,5* June 29*,30 July **1**	April 25*,26 July 5*,6*,7*,**8**	April 30* May 1*,2* July 27*,28,**29**
BOSTON.........	April 10*,11* July 12*,13*,14*,**15**	April 6*,7,**8** July 16*,17*,18	April 2*,4*,5* July 20*,21,**22**	May 8*,9* Aug. 9*,10*,11*,**12***	May 11*,12*,**13** Aug. 13*,14*,15*	May 18*,19*,**20** Aug. 28*,29*,30*	April 27*,28,**29** July 30*,31* Aug. 1*
SEATTLE........		May 7*,8,9 Aug. 3(Tn),4,**5**	April 27*,28,**29,**30* July 23*,24*,25*	June 1*,2*,**3*** Sept. 3*,4*,5*	June 4*,5*,6*,7* Sept. 7*,8*,**9**	April 13*,14,**15** July 30*,31* Aug. 1	June 25*,26*,27* Sept. 21*,22,**23**
OAKLAND	April 16*,17*,18 July 27*,28*,**29**		May 1*,2* Aug. 9*,10*,11*,**12**	June 8*,9*,**10***,11* Sept. 24*,25*,26*	June 25*,26(Tn),27* Sept. 21*,22*,**23**	May 4*,5,**6** July 23*,24*,25*	May 31* June 1*,2*,**3** Sept. 3,4*,5*
CALIFORNIA...	May 4*,5*,**6** Aug. 6*,7*,8	April 12,13*,14,**15** July 30*,31* Aug. 1		June 25*,26*,27* Sept. 27*,28*,29*,**30**	June 8*,9*,**10** Sept. 24*,25*,26*	April 16*,17*,18* July 27*,28*,**29**	June 4*,5*,6* Sept. 6*,7*,8,**9**
TEXAS	June 15*,16*,**17** Sept. 10*,11*,12*,13*	June 22*,23,**24** Sept. 17*,18*,19	June 18*,19*,20* Sept. 21*,22,**23**		May 18*,19*,**20** Aug. 28*,29*,30*	June 4*,5*,6*,7 Sept. 7*,8,**9**	May 10*,11*,12,**13** Aug. 13*,14*,15*
KANSAS CITY	June 12*,13*,14 Sept. 14*,15*,**16**	June 18*,19*,20 Sept. 28*,29,**30**	June 22*,23*,**24** Sept. 17*,18*,19*,20*	May 28*,29*,30* Aug. 16*,17*,18*,**19***		May 31* June 1*,2*,**3** Sept. 10*,11*,12*	May 14*,15*,16* Aug. 31* Sept. 1*,**2**
MINNESOTA...	May 1*,2*,3* Aug. 9*,10*,11*,**12**	April 27*,28,**29-29** Aug. 6*,7*,8	May 7*,8*,9* Aug. 2*,3*,4*,**5**	June 12*,13*,14* Sept. 14*,15*,**16**	June 15*,16*,**17** Sept. 3*,4*,5*		June 8*,9,**10** Sept. 24*,25*,26*
CHICAGO........	June 18*,19*,20 Sept. 27*,28*,29*,**30**	June 15*,16,**17** Sept. 10*,11*,12	June 12*,13*,14* Sept. 14*,15*,**16**	May 25*,26*,**27** Aug. 20*,21*,22*	May 21*,22*,23* Aug. 24*,25*,**26**,27*	June 22*,23*,**24** Sept. 17*,18*,19*,20	
1984	81 HOME DATES 62 NIGHTS	79 HOME DATES 38 NIGHTS	81 HOME DATES 61 NIGHTS	81 HOME DATES 72 NIGHTS	80 HOME DATES 64 NIGHTS	81 HOME DATES 52 NIGHTS	81 HOME DATES 54 NIGHTS

JULY 10—ALL STAR GAME AT SAN FRANCISCO
AUGUST 13—HALL OF FAME GAME AT COOPERSTOWN, N.Y. (Detroit Tigers vs. Atlanta Braves)

1984 N.L. EAST DIVISION SLATE . . .

1984	EAST					
	AT CHICAGO	AT MONTREAL	AT NEW YORK	AT PHILADELPHIA	AT PITTSBURGH	AT ST. LOUIS
CHICAGO........		June 5*,6*,7* Aug. 9*,10*,11,**12** Sept. 5*,6*	May 1*,2* July 27*,28,**29-29** Sept. 7*,8*,**9**	May 31* June 1*,2,**3** July 23*,24*,25 Sept. 3*,4*	April 27*,28*,**29** June 19*,20*,21* Sept. 24*,25*,26*	April 23*,24*,25 June 8*,9*,**10** Sept. 21*,22,**23**
MONTREAL	June 11,12,13 Aug. 2,3,4,**5** Sept. 12,13		April 17,18,19 June 22*,23,**24** Sept. 21*,22,**23**	April 30* May 1*,2* July 27*,28*,**29** Sept. 14*,15*,**16**	May 31* June 1*,2*,**3** July 30*,31* Aug. 1* Sept. 10*,11*	April 20*,21*,**22** June 25*,26*,27* Sept. 18*,19*,20*
NEW YORK	April, 13,14,**15** Aug. 6,7,8 Sept. 14,15,**16**	April 23,24,25 June 8*,9*,**10** Sept. 28*,29*,**30**		April 20*,21,**22** June 25*,26*,27* Sept. 17*,18*,19*	June 4*,5*,6* Aug. 2*,3*,4*,**5** Sept. 5*,6*	June 14*,15*,16*,**17** July 30*,31* Aug. 1 Sept. 3*,4*
PHILADELPHIA	June 14,15,16,**17** July 30,31 Aug. 1 Sept. 10,11	April 13,14,**15** Aug. 6*,7*,8* Sept. 7*,8*,**9**	April 27*,28,**29** June 19*,20*,21 Sept. 24*,25*,26		April 17,18,19 June 22*,23*,**24** Sept. 21*,22*,**23**	June 4*,5*,6* Aug. 2*,3*,4*,**5** Sept. 5*,6*
PITTSBURGH..	April 20,21,**22** June 25,26,27 Sept. 18,19,20	June 14*,15*,16,**17** July 24*,25*,26* Sept. 3,4*	June 11*,12*,13* Aug. 9*,10*,11*,**12** Sept. 12*,13	April 24*,25* June 8 (Tn),9*,**10** Sept. 28*,29*,**30**		April 13*,14*,**15** Aug. 6*,7*,8* Sept. 14*,15,**16**
ST. LOUIS	April 17,18,19 June 22,23,**24** Sept. 28,29,**30**	April 27,28,**29** June 18*,19*,20* Sept. 24*,25*,26*	May 31* June 1*,2*,**3** July 23*,24*,25 Sept. 10*,11*	June 11*,12*,13* Aug. 9*,10*,11*,**12** Sept. 12*,13*	April 30* May 1*,2* July 27*,28,**29** Sept. 7*,8*,**9**	
ATLANTA.......	May 22,23,24 Aug. 24,25,**26**	May 4*,5,**6** July 16*,17*,18*	May 9*,10 June 28*,29*,30* July **1**	May 7*,8* July 5*,6*,7,**8**	May 18*,19*,**20** Aug. 20*,21*,22*	May 15*,16*,17 Aug. 17*,18,**19**
CINCINNATI ...	May 25,26,**27**,28 Aug. 28,29	May 9*,10 July 12*,13*,14*,**15**	May 7*,8* July 5*,6*,7*,**8**	May 4*,5*,**6** July 2*,3*,4*	May 22*,23*,24* Aug. 24*,25*,**26**	May 18*,19*,**20** Aug. 13*,14*,15*
HOUSTON.......	May 18,19,**20** Aug. 20,21,22	May 7*,8 July 5,6*,7*,**8**	May 4*,5*,**6** July 2*,3*,4*	April 10,11* June 28*,29*,30* July **1**	May 14*,15*,16* Aug. 17*,18*,**19**	May 21*,22*,23 Aug. 31* Sept. 1*,**2**
LOS ANGELES	May 9,10 July 12,13,14,**15**	May 28*,29*,30* Aug. 31* Sept. 1,**2**	May 25*,26,**27** Aug. 27*,28*,29*	May 22*,23*,24* Aug. 24*,25,**26**	May 4*,5,**6** July 16*,17*,18*	May 7*,8* July 19*,20*,21,**22**
SAN DIEGO.....	May 4,5,**6** July 16,17,18	May 22*,23* Aug. 24 (Tn),25*,**26**	May 28,29*,30* Aug. 31* Sept. 1*,**2**	May 25*,26*,**27** Aug. 27*,28*,29*	May 7*,8* July 19*,20*,21*,**22**	May 9*,10 July 12*,13*,14*,**15**
SAN FRAN......	May 7,8 July 19,20,21,**22**	May 25*,26*,**27** Aug. 27*,28*,29*	May 22*,23*,24* Aug. 24*,25*,**26**	May 28*,29*,30* Aug. 31* Sept. 1*,**2**	May 9*,10 July 12*,13*,14,**15**	May 4*,5*,**6** July 16*,17*,18*
1984	81 HOME DATES 0 NIGHTS	80 HOME DATES 54 NIGHTS	80 HOME DATES 53 NIGHTS	80 HOME DATES 62 NIGHTS	81 HOME DATES 61 NIGHTS	81 HOME DATES 59 NIGHTS

*NIGHT GAME
NIGHT GAME: Any game starting after 5:00 p.m.
HEAVY BLACK FIGURES DENOTE SUNDAY

AND COMPLETE WEST SCHEDULES

1984	WEST					
	AT ATLANTA	AT CINCINNATI	AT HOUSTON	AT LOS ANGELES	AT SAN DIEGO	AT SAN FRANCISCO
CHICAGO........	May 29*,30* Aug. 30*,31* Sept. 1,**2**	May 15*,16*,17 Aug. 17*,18*,**19**	May 11*,12,**13*** Aug. 13*,14*,15*	April 9*,11* June 28*,29*,30* July **1**	April 6*,7*,**8** July 2*,3*,4*	April 3,5* July 5*,6*,7,**8**
MONTREAL	April 6*,7*,**8** July 2,3*,4*	April 9*,10*,11 June 29*,30* July **1**	April 3*,4* July 19*,20*,21*,**22***	May 18*,19*,**20** Aug. 20*,21*,22	May 14*,15*,16*,17 Aug. 17*,**19**	May 11*,12,**13** Aug. 14*,15,16*
NEW YORK	April 10*,11* July 12*,13*,14*,**15**	April 2,4* July 19*,20*,21*,**22**	April 6*,7*,**8*** July 16*,17*,18*	May 11*,12,**13** Aug. 13*,14*,15*	May 18*,19*,**20** Aug. 20*,21*,22*	May 15*,16 Aug. 17*,18,**19-19**
PHILADELPHIA	April 3*,4* July 19*,20*,21,**22**	April 6*,7,**8** July 16*,17*,18*	May 9*,10* July 12*,13*,14*,**15***	May 14*,15*,16* Aug. 17*,18*,**19**	May 11*,12*,**13** Aug. 14*,15*,16	May 18*,19,**20** Aug. 20*,21*,22
PITTSBURGH..	May 11*,12*,**13** Aug. 14*,15*,16*	May 29*,30* Aug. 30*,31* Sept. 1*,**2**	May 25*,26*,**27***,28* Aug. 28*,29*	April 6*,7,**8** July 2*,3*,4*	April 3*,5 July 5,6*,7*,**8**	April 10*,11 June 28*,29*,30 July **1**
ST. LOUIS	May 25*,26,**27**,28* Aug. 28*,29*	May 11*,12,**13** Aug. 20*,21*,22*	May 29*,30* Aug. 23*,24*,25*,**26***	April 3,5* July 5*,6*,7*,**8**	April 10*,11* June 28*,29*,30* July **1**	April 6*,7,**8** July 3,4-4
ATLANTA.......		April 17*,18 June 1 (Tn),2*,**3** Sept. 25*,26*,27*	April 27*,28,**29*** July 30*,31* Aug. 1* Sept. 10*,11*,12*	June 7*,8*,9,**10** July 24*,25*,26* Sept. 5*,6*	April 12*,13*,14*,**15** June 11*,12* Sept. 21*,22*,**23**	June 4*,5*,6 July 27*,28,**29** Sept. 7*,8,**9**
CINCINNATI ...	April 24*,25*,26* June 14*,15*,16*,**17** Sept. 19*,20*		April 13*,14*,**15*** June 11*,12*,13* Sept. 21*,22*,**23***	June 4*,5*,6* July 27*,28,**29** Sept. 7*,8*,**9**	June 7,8*,9*,**10** July 24*,25*,26 Sept. 5*,6	April 19*,20*,21,**22** June 25*,26*,27 Sept. 3,4*
HOUSTON.......	April 20*,21*,**22** June 25 (Tn),26*,27* Sept. 3*,4*	May 1*,2*,3 Aug. 10*,11*,**12** Sept. 28*,29,**30**		April 23*,24*,25* June 1*,2*,**3** Sept. 24*,25*,26*	June 4*,5*,6* July 27*,28 (Tn),**29** Sept. 7*,**9**	June 7*,8*,9,**10** July 24*,25,26* Sept. 5*,6
LOS ANGELES	June 22*,23,**24** Aug. 6*,7*,8*,9* Sept. 17*,18*	June 19*,20*,21* Aug. 3*,4,**5** Sept. 14*,15*,**16**	April 16*,17*,18* June 14*,15*,16*,**17*** Sept. 19*,20*		April 26,27*,28*,**29** July 30*,31* Aug. 1* Sept. 11*,12*	April 30* May 1*,2 Aug. 10*,11,**12** Sept. 21*,22,**23**
SAN DIEGO.....	May 1*,2*,3* Aug. 10*,11*,**12** Sept. 28*,29*,**30**	June 22*,23*,**24** Aug. 6*,7*,8*,9* Sept. 17*,18	June 19*,20*,21* Aug. 3*,4*,**5*** Sept. 14*,15,**16***	April 19*,20*,21,**22** June 25*,26*,27* Sept. 3*,4*		April 17*,18 June 1*,2,**3-3** Sept. 24*,25*,26
SAN FRAN......	June 19*,20*,21* Aug. 3*,4*,**5** Sept. 14*,15*,**16**	April 27*,28,**29-29** July 31* Aug. 1*,2* Sept. 11*,12*	June 22*,23*,**24*** Aug. 6*,7*,8*,9* Sept. 17*,18*	April 13*,14,**15** June 11*,12*,13 Sept. 28*,29,**30**	April 23*,24*,25* June 14,15*,16*,**17** Sept. 19*,20	
1984	80 HOME DATES 63 NIGHTS	79 HOME DATES 56 NIGHTS	81 HOME DATES 78 NIGHTS	81 HOME DATES 58 NIGHTS	80 HOME DATES 58 NIGHTS	78 HOME DATES 37 NIGHTS

JULY 10—ALL STAR GAME AT SAN FRANCISCO
AUGUST 13—HALL OF FAME GAME AT COOPERSTOWN, N.Y. (Detroit Tigers vs. Atlanta Braves)

BILL MADLOCK
• PIRATES •
BATTING CHAMPION (.323)

MIKE SCHMIDT
• PHILLIES •
HOME RUNS (40)
ON-BASE PCT. (.399)

DALE MURPHY
• BRAVES •
RBIs (121)
SLUGGING PCT. (.540)

1983 N.L. LEADERS

JOHN DENNY
• PHILLIES •
WINS (19)

ATLEE HAMMAKER
• GIANTS •
ERA (2.25)

LEE SMITH
• CUBS •
SAVES (29)

Index to Contents

Index to Minor League Clubs, Cities

NOTES

NOTES